Preface

Unlike other subjects in the law school curriculum, International Law is a whole legal system. In no other field of law is such a broad sweep of ideas, concepts, institutions, principles and rules expected to be digested within the limited span of a single course, now typically three hours per week for one semester. As teachers familiar with this daunting prospect, we offer this volume of materials for just such an introduction to international law. Inevitably we have had to make a severe selection not only of legal materials but also of subject matter, leaving out whole branches of international law of interest and importance. What we have tried to do is to present the fundamental principles and processes of the international legal system as it has so far evolved, exploring these ideas through as many different areas of its operation as the size of the volume allows.

The book is primarily designed for our students, and others like them, who experience the world from a Canadian perspective. Although international law applies globally, it is subject to many different interpretations. Accordingly, we have prepared a volume of materials which, while they include all the principal documents and decisions of whatever origin, they also draw extensively on the practice of international law chiefly as interpreted and applied in Canada.* For this approach, much gratitude is owed to one of our number, Jean-Gabriel Castel, who pioneered three previous editions under the same title. We often had cause to refer to his work in the course of preparing this new volume.

An additional purpose of this book is to provide a reference of first resort for anyone who has need of international legal sources. These users, we imagine, might be members of the legal profession confronted with a legal problem containing international elements, or other persons wishing to discover Canadian practice in a particular area of international

---

* A comprehensive bibliography is provided by C.L. Wiktor, *Canadian Bibliography of International Law* (1984).

law. As fully as the confines of the book permit, we have included comments and citations which we hope will assist our readers to direct their research along the most appropriate lines of enquiry.

June 1987   Hugh M. Kindred
                                       General Editor

Summary Table of Contents

Detailed Table of Contents

Table of Cases

This table includes cases referred to by the authors. It does not include cases cited within the reproduced texts and reports. A bold face page number indicates that a (partial) report of the case is reproduced in the text. An ''n'' after a page number indicates that the case is to be found in footnotes.

Dalhousie Law Journal — Maps of Canadian coastal baselines from (1982-83), vol. 7, at 32-36.

International Bar Association — Excerpts from S.A. Williams, "Public International Law Governing Transboundary Pollution" [1984] *Int. Bus. Lawyer*, at 243 fwd.

International Law Association — Excerpts from the Helsinki Rules on the Uses of the Waters of International Rivers, Report of the 52nd Conference (1966), at 486-89, 491, 496-97, and 501.

Excerpts from the Montreal Rules on Water Pollution in an International Drainage Basin, Report of the 60th Conference (1982), at 535 and 538-545.

International Law Reports — Excerpt from the *Eichmann Case* (1961), vol. 36, at 310.

Excerpts from the *Lake Lanoux Arbitration* (1963), vol. 24, at 123, 127-30, 139, and 140-41.

McGill Law Journal — Excerpts from I. Head, "Canadian Claims to Territorial Sovereignty in the Arctic Regions" (1963), vol. 9, at 202-3, 208-10, and 216.

Manchester University Press — Two diagrams concerning maritime boundaries from R.P. Churchill and A.V. Lowe, *The Law of the Sea* (1983), at 24 and 39.

Dr. F.E. Moseley — Excerpts from *The United States – Canadian Great Lakes Pollution Agreement: A Study in International Water Pollution Control* (1980), at 205-07.

Martinus Nijhoff — Excerpts from D. Pharand, "The Legal Status of the Arctic Regions" (1979), 163 *Hague Recueil des Cours* at 59-61.

Excerpts from M. Lachs, "The Development and General Trends of International Law in Our Time" (1980), 169 *Hague Recueil des Cours*, at 220-21.

Oxford University Press — Excerpts from J.L. Brierley, *The Law of Nations* (6ed., Waldock, 1963), at 49-56, and 68-78.

Stevens & Sons — Excerpts from W. Friedmann, *The Changing Structure of International Law* (1964), at 60-66.

Stevens & Sons, and Professor B. Cheng	Diagram of the sources of international law from G. Schwarzenberger, *A Manual of International Law* (5ed., 1967), at 27.
Supply and Services, Canada	Excerpts from Department of External Affairs, *Federalism and International Relations* (1968), at 11, 16, 26, 28, 30, and 33.
	Portions of a memorandum on the Canadian practice of recognition, Department of External Affairs (July 18, 1974).
	Excerpt from a memorandum on the Canadian position with respect to U.N. Resolutions, Department of External Affairs (August 28, 1974).
	Comments by the Canadian Delegation on the U.N. Definition of Aggression, from Department of External Affairs, Press Release No. 14 (October 14, 1974).
	Two fisheries zones maps from Department of External Affairs, Communiqué no. 16 (November 2, 1976).
	Excerpts concerning Canada's claim in respect of Cosmos 954, from Department of External Affairs, Note no. FLA-268 (January 23, 1979).
	Excerpt from a memorandum on the use of force by states, Department of External Affairs (November 27, 1981).
	Map of the Canadian Arctic, from Statement in the House of Commons by the Secretary of State for External Affairs, Statement 85/49 (September 10, 1985).
	Extract from a memorandum on "Current Issues of International Law of Particular Importance to Canada", Department of External Affairs (October 1986), at 15-16.
Sweet & Maxwell Ltd.	Excerpts from J.G. Merills, *International Dispute Settlement* (1984), at 6-9, 20-21, 23, 30-32, 52, and 60-64.
University of Toronto Law Journal	Excerpts from D.C. Vanek, "Is International Law a Part of the Law of Canada?" (1949-50), vol. 8, at 266-67, 274-76, and 292.
University of Toronto Press	Excerpts from R. St. J. Macdonald, G.L. Morris and D.M. Johnston (eds.), *Canadian Perspectives on International Law and Organization* (1974), being M. Cohen, "Canada and the International Legal Order: An Inside Perspective", at 3-4 and 6-8; and R. St. J. Macdonald, "The Relationship between International Law and Domestic Law in Canada", at 111-13, 119, and 127.

U.S. Government
Printing Office

Excerpts from G.H. Hackworth, *Digest of International Law* (1943), vol. 5, at 471-72 and 526-27.

CHAPTER ONE

Introduction to International Law

Public international law has traditionally been regarded as a system of principles and rules designed to govern relations between sovereign states. As a point of departure for a study of international law, this description has the merit of emphasizing the central and still dominant position of states in international affairs. However, in recent times the scope of international law has been steadily expanding so that, in the words of Wilfred Jenks "it represents the common law of mankind in an early state of development, of which the law governing the relations between states is one, but only one, major division."[1] Perhaps the most significant development is the status newly accorded to individuals in the international legal process. In the field of human rights, for example, the individual now possesses international legal rights independently of, and even against, his national state.

While states remain the dominant actors in the international legal order, modern international law also reflects the new realities of international life, such as the interdependence of states, the growth of global organizations, the scientific and technological revolutions, the influence of giant multinational corporations, and the massive transnational movements of individuals and ideas. As this volume will demonstrate, international law is a dynamic system of norms which is capable of evolving to meet the regulatory needs of a rapidly changing international society.

The beginnings of international law as it is known today are usually traced to the sixteenth and seventeenth centuries, and coincide with the rise of the nation state.[2] Hugo Grotius, a Dutch jurist and diplomat, is widely regarded as the father of international law on account of his classic treatise *De Jure Belli Ac Pacis* written in 1625. The treaties of Westphalia, which in 1648 ended the Thirty Years' War, are often credited with the establishment of the system of sovereign states at the core of international law. History[3]

---

[1] C.W. Jenks, *The Common Law of Mankind* (1958), at 58.

[2] And hence, until comparatively recently, it was known as the "law of nations."

[3] See A. Nussbaum, *A Concise History of the Law of Nations* (Rev. ed., 1954). See also F.L. Ganshof, *The Middle Ages, A History of International Relations* (trans. by R.I. Hall, 1970); and C. de Visscher, *Theory and Reality in Public International Law* (trans. by P.E. Corbett, rev. ed., 1968), Book 1.

records also the existence of ancient systems of rules which governed relations between Greek states and between Roman citizens and foreigners but these were not carried forward as a body of law during medieval times. Their influence has been felt mainly as an inspiration for the political philosophers of later centuries who sought to impose some rational order in inter-state relations following the break up of the Holy Roman Empire into many independent, warring political units.

Since international law originated in Europe, it has been infused with European social and political cultures and values. Politically speaking, international law was nourished by then new ideas about the sovereignty of independent states. It met the limited needs for diplomatic relations in the conduct of war and peace. Philosophically, international law was rooted in the law of nature as expounded by the classical textwriters. Some of these authors, reflecting a Christian heritage, based their theses on the Divine Order while others, in the rationalist tradition, derived their ideas from universal reason. In the face of a confused mass of local customs and bilateral treaties, natural law provided the textwriters with the basis for ordering the conduct of foreign affairs into a system of rules and for subjecting states and their leaders to the authority of the law. Later, the rise of positivism in political and legal philosophy exerted a powerful influence on international law. Positivist thought[4] enhanced the concept of the sovereignty of states and imbued international law with the notion that legal obligations are based on consent.

In the course of colonial expansion, the ideas and values embodied in international law were carried by the European powers to other parts of the world. While the process of colonization and subjugation of foreign lands was not governed by international law, when some of the conquered territories, notably in North and South America, acquired independence the European practice of international law was extended to them. Only in the latter part of the nineteenth century were non-Christian countries, like Turkey, China and Japan, admitted as subjects of the international legal system. Not until the adoption of the Covenant of the League of Nations, following World War I, was international law formally applied to all states without discrimination. Even so, only through the process of decolonization after World War II, under the auspices of the United Nations, did the reach of international law become truly global.

Entry into the international legal system during this century, and particularly since 1945, of many new states with varied political, cultural, social and legal backgrounds has had, and is still having, a profound and lasting effect on international law. The original "Concert of Europe" has now been expanded to more than one hundred and sixty states on six continents. The number and diversity of the actors in the world arena have increased exponentially the difficulties of administering the decentralized system of nation states. More importantly, the new participants entered the community of states with very different perspectives and soon began to challenge the enduring validity of some of the Eurocentric concepts and principles of international law.

The first major challenge to the simple belief in the universal acceptance of classical international law was posed after the Russian Revolution by the emergence of Soviet

---

[4] The extreme positivist doctrine holds that international law consists exclusively of rules to which states have given their consent.

views[5] on the role of the state, the sources of the law and the contents of many of its principles. More recently, the developing countries of Latin America, Africa and Asia have been urging a reformulation of international law, especially those parts governing foreign investment, development and other incidents of their former colonial circumstances.[6] As a result, some of the traditional principles of international law have been either altogether abandoned (e.g., principles governing the acquisition of territory by force), or materially altered (e.g., rules relating to the amount of compensation payable upon the expropriation of foreign property), or, in other instances, wholly new concepts have been introduced (e.g., the right of self-determination of peoples, and the principle of a state's permanent sovereignty over its natural resources).

Phenomenal advances in science and technology have also profoundly affected international law. Thus the advent of nuclear energy, mass air travel, space flight, seabed mining and satellite telecommunications, to mention only a few major new activities, have prompted the creation of wholly new branches of international law, such as space law and environmental law, and great expansion of some traditional ones, most notably the law of the sea. In addition, the revolution in transportation and communications has enormously increased the movement and interaction of people all over the world, resulting in the need for international law to harmonize and accommodate many diverse and competing human interests. One conspicuous consequence has been the emergence of a great number of international organisations covering a wide variety of human activities. These organisations have become associated since 1945 with the United Nations, which has filled the role of a global coordinating organ, and they have been supported by the growth of a whole new body of law regarding international institutions. Second, the unprecedented growth of world trade, fueled by the huge energy of the modern multinational enterprise, has given rise to a growing corpus of international economic law to govern transnational commercial transactions. Third, much greater awareness of the plight of millions of human beings, who suffer from poverty, hunger, disease, illiteracy and the effects of tyranny and war, has brought about organized efforts to improve human well-being everywhere and, particularly, to promote economic and social advancement in the less developed countries. These concerns have found their legal expression in such new developments as humanitarian laws, the protection of human rights and international development law. In sum, international law in the United Nations era has had to adapt to a much transformed, multinational and increasingly interdependent world.[7]

---

[5] See H.W. Baade, ed., *The Soviet Impact on International Law* (1965); K. Grzybowski, *Soviet Public International Law: Doctrines and Diplomatic Practice* (1970); G.I. Tunkin, ed., *Contemporary International Law* (1969); and G.I. Tunkin, *Theory of International Law* (trans. by W.E. Butler, 1974).

[6] See R.P. Anand, ed., *Asian States and the Development of Universal Law* (1972); R.P. Anand, *New States and International Law* (1972); T.O. Elias, *Africa and the Development of International Law* (1972); F.C. Okoye, *International Law and the New African States* (1972); and J.J. Syatauw, *Some Newly Established Asian States and the Development of International Law* (1961). The particular contribution of communist China is considered in J.A. Cohen, ed., *China's Practice of International Law: Some Case Studies* (1972); J.A. Cohen and H. Chiu, *People's China and International Law: A Documentary Study* (2 vols., 1974); J.C. Hsiung, *Law and Policy in China's Foreign Relations* (1972); and S.C. Leng and H. Chiu, *Law in Chinese Foreign Policy* (1972).

[7] See P.E. Corbett, *The Growth of World Law* (1971); R. Falk, *The Status of Law in International Society*

In addition to this brief outline of the development of the international legal system, it is also necessary to examine the nature of the law itself. In one way or another, the questions raised in such an examination invariably focus on the basis of obligation and the means of enforcement in international law. Many writers have addressed these problems, including Professor Brierly who has provided the following lucid commentary:[8]

Traditionally there are two rival doctrines which attempt to answer the question why states should be bound to observe the rules of international law.

The doctrine of "fundamental rights" is a corollary of the doctrine of "state of nature," in which men are supposed to have lived before they formed themselves into political communities or states; for states, not having formed themselves into a super-state, are still supposed by the adherents of this doctrine to be living in such a condition. It teaches that the principles of international law, or the primary principles upon which the others rest, can be deduced from the essential nature of the state. Every state, by the very fact that it is a state, is endowed with certain fundamental, or inherent, or natural, rights. Writers differ in enumerating what these rights are, but generally five rights are claimed, namely self-preservation, independence, equality, respect, and intercourse. It is obvious that the doctrine of fundamental rights is merely the old doctrine of the natural rights of man transferred to states. That doctrine has played a great part in history; Locke justified the English Revolution by it and from Locke it passed to the leaders of the American Revolution and became the philosophical basis of the Declaration of Independence. But hardly any political scientist today would regard it as a true philosophy of political relations and all the objections to it apply with even greater force when it is applied to the relations of states. It implies that men or states, as the case may be, bring with them into society certain primordial rights not derived from their membership of society, but inherent in their personality as individuals and that out of these rights a legal system is formed, whereas the truth is that a legal right is a meaningless phrase unless we first assume the existence of a legal system from which it gets its validity. Further, the doctrine implies that the social bond between man and man, or between state and state, is somehow less natural, or less a part of the whole personality, than is the individuality of the man or the state and that is not true; the only individuals we know are individuals-in-society. It is especially misleading to apply this atomistic view of the nature of the social bond to states. In its application to individual men it has a certain plausibility because

---

(1970); W. Friedmann, *The Changing Structure of International Law* (1964); L. Henkin, *How Nations Behave* (2 ed., 1979); W. Jenks, *The Common Law of Mankind* (1958), and *A New World of Law?* (1969); P.C. Jessup, *Transnational Law* (1956); O. Lissitzyn, *International Law Today and Tomorrow* (1965); R. St. J. Macdonald and D.M. Johnston, eds., *The Structure and Process of International Law* (1983); G. Schwarzenberger, *The Frontiers of International Law* (1962); and J. Stone, *Visions of World Order* (1984). For Canadian opinions, see L.C. Green, *International Law: A Canadian Perspective* (1984); and R. St. J. Macdonald, G.L. Morris, D.M. Johnston, eds., *Canadian Perspectives on International Law and Organisation* (1974).

[8] J.L. Brierly, *The Law of Nations* (6 ed., Waldock, 1963), at 49–56, 68–78. See also J.L. Brierly, *The Basis of Obligation in International Law* (1958), c. 1; E.K. Nantwi, *The Enforcement of International Judicial Decisions and Arbitral Awards in Public International Law* (1966); L. Oppenheim, *International Law* (8 ed., H. Lauterpacht, 1955), at 4–14; G. Schwarzenberger, International Law and Order (1958); S.M. Schwebel, ed., *The Effectiveness of International Decisions* (1971); and C.W. Jenks, *Law, Freedom and Welfare* (1963), c. 5, in which he refers to a wide range of other opinions.

it seems to give a philosophical justification to the common feeling that human personality has certain claims on society; and in that way it has played its part in the development of human liberty. But in the society of states the need is not for greater liberty for the individual states, but for a strengthening of the social bond between them, not for the claimant assertion of their rights, but for a more insistent reminder of their obligations towards one another. Finally, the doctrine is really a denial of the possibility of development in international relations; when it asserts that such qualities as independence and equality are inherent in the very nature of states, it overlooks the fact that their attribution to states is merely a stage in an historical process; we know that until modern times states were not regarded either as independent or equal and we have no right to assume that the process of development has stopped. On the contrary it is not improbable and it is certainly desirable, that there should be a movement towards the closer interdependence of states and therefore away from the state of things which this doctrine would stabilize as though it were part of the fixed order of nature.

The doctrine of positivism, on the other hand, teaches that international law is the sum of the rules by which states have *consented* to be bound, and that nothing can be law to which they have not consented. This consent may be given expressly, as in a treaty, or it may be implied by a state acquiescing in a customary rule. But the assumption that international law consists of nothing save what states have consented to is an inadequate account of the system as it can be seen in actual operation and even if it were a complete account of the contents of the law, it would fail to explain why the law is binding. It is in the first place quite impossible to fit the facts into a consistently consensual theory of the nature of international law. *Implied* consent is not a philosophically sound explanation of customary law, international or domestic; a customary rule is observed, not because it has been consented to, but because it is believed to be binding and whatever may be the explanation or the justification for that belief, its binding force does not depend, and is not felt by those who follow it to depend, on the approval of the individual or the state to which it is addressed. Further, in the practical administration of international law, states are continually treated as bound by principles which they cannot, except by the most strained construction of the facts, be said to have consented to and it is unreasonable, when we are seeking the true nature of international rules, to force the facts into a preconceived theory instead of finding a theory which will explain the facts as we have them. For example, a state which has newly come into existence does not in any intelligible sense *consent* to accept international law; it does not regard itself and it is not regarded by others, as having any option in the matter. The truth is that states do not regard their international legal relations as resulting from consent, except when the consent is express, and that the theory of implied consent is a fiction invented by the theorist; only a certain plausibility is given to a consensual explanation of the nature of their obligations by the fact, important indeed to any consideration of the methods by which the system develops, that, in the absence of any international machinery for legislation by majority vote, a *new* rule of law cannot be imposed upon states merely by the will of other states.

But in the second place, even if the theory did not involve a distortion of the facts, it would fail as an explanation. For consent cannot of itself create an obligation; it can do so only within a system of law which declares that consent duly given, as in a treaty or a contract, shall be binding on the party consenting. To say that the rule *pacta servanda sunt* is itself founded on consent is to argue in a circle. A consistently consensual theory again would have to admit that if consent is withdrawn, the obligation created by it comes to an end. Most positivist writers would not admit this, but to deny it is in effect to fall back on an unacknowledged source of obligation, which, whatever it may be, is not the consent of the state, for that has ceased to exist. Some modern German writers, however, do not shrink from facing the full consequences of the theory of a purely consensual basis for the law; they have inherited from Hegel a doctrine known as the "auto-limitation of sovereignty," which teaches that states are sovereign persons, possessed of wills which reject all external limitation and that if we find, as we appear to do in international law, something which limits their wills, this limiting something can only proceed from themselves. Most of these writers admit that a self-imposed limitation is no limitation at all; they conclude, therefore, that so-called international law is nothing, but "external public law" (*äusseres Staatsrecht*), binding the state only because and only so long as, it consents to be bound. There is no flaw in this argument; the flaw lies in the premisses, because these are not derived, as all positivist theory professes to be, from an observation of international facts. The real contribution of positivist theory to international law has been its insistence that the rules of the system are to be ascertained from observation of the practice of states and not from *a priori* deductions, but positivist writers have not always been true to their own teaching; and they have been too ready to treat a method of legal reasoning as though it were an explanation of the nature of the law.

There need be no mystery about the source of the obligation to obey international law. The same problem arises in any system of law and it can never be solved by a merely *juridical* explanation. The answer must be sought outside the law and it is for legal philosophy to provide it. The notion that the validity of international law raises some peculiar problem arises from the confusion which the doctrine of sovereignty has introduced into international legal theory. Even when we do not believe in the absoluteness of state sovereignty we have allowed ourselves to be persuaded that the fact of their sovereignty makes it necessary to look for some specific quality, not to be found in other kinds of law, in the law to which states are subject. We have accepted a false idea of the state as a personality with a life and a will of its own, still living in a "state of nature", and we contrast this with the "political" state in which individual men have come to live. But this assumed condition of states is the very negation of law and no ingenuity can explain how the two can exist together. It is a notion as false analytically as it admittedly is historically. The truth is that states are not persons, however convenient it may often be to personify them; they are merely *institutions*, that is to say, organizations which men establish among themselves for securing certain objects, of which the most fundamental is a system of order within which the activities of their common life can be carried on. They have no wills except the wills of the individual human beings who direct their affairs; and they exist not in a political vacuum, but in continuous political relations with one another. Their subjection to law is as yet imperfect, though it is real as far as it goes; the problem of extending it is one of great practical difficulty, but it is not one of intrinsic impossibility. There are important differences between international law and the law under which individuals live in a state, but those differences do not lie in metaphysics or in any mystical qualities of the entity called state sovereignty.

The international lawyer then is under no special obligation to explain why the law with which he is concerned should be binding upon its subjects. If it were true that the essence of all law is a command and that what makes the law of the state binding is that for some reason, for which no satisfactory explanation can ever be given, the will of the person issuing a command is superior to that of the person receiving it, then indeed it would be necessary to look for some special explanation of the binding force of international law. But that view of the nature of law has been long discredited. If we are to explain why any kind of law is binding, we cannot avoid some such assumption as that which the Middle Ages made and which Greece and Rome had made before them, when they spoke of natural law. The ultimate explanation of the binding force of all law is that man, whether he is a single individual or whether he is associated with other men in a state, is constrained, in so far as he is a reasonable being, to believe that order and not chaos is the governing principle of the world in which he has to live ... .

It has often been said that international law ought to be classified as a branch of ethics rather than of law. The question is partly one of words, because its solution will clearly depend on the definition of law which we choose to adopt; in any case it does not affect the value of the subject one way or the other, though those who deny the legal character of international law often speak as though "ethical" were a depreciatory epithet, but in fact it is both practically inconvenient and also contrary to the best juristic thought to deny its legal character. It is inconvenient because if international law is nothing but international morality, it is certainly not the whole of international morality, and it is difficult to see how we are to distinguish it from those other admittedly moral standards which we apply in forming our judgments on the conduct of states. Ordinary usage certainly uses two tests in judging the "rightness" of a state's act, a moral test and one which is somehow felt to be independent of morality. Every state habitually commits acts of selfishness which are often gravely injurious to other states, and yet are not contrary to international law; but we do not on that account necessarily judge them to have been "right." It is confusing and pedantic to say that both these tests are moral. Moreover, it is the pendantry of the theorist and not of the practical man; for questions of international law are invariably treated as legal questions by the foreign offices which conduct our international business, and in the courts, national or international, before which they are brought; legal forms and methods are used in diplomatic controversies and in judicial and arbitral proceedings, and authorities and precedents are cited in argument as a matter of course. It is significant too that when a breach of international law is alleged by one party to a controversy, the act impugned is practically never defended by claiming the right of private judgment, which would be the natural defence if the issue concerned the morality of the act, but always by attempting to prove that no rule has been violated. ...

But if international law is not the same thing as international morality, and if in some important respects at least it certainly resembles law, why should we hesitate to accept its definitely legal character? The objection comes in the main from the followers of writers such as Hobbes and Austin, who regard nothing as law which is not the will of a political superior. But this is a misleading and inadequate analysis even of the law of a modern state; it cannot, for instance, unless we distort the facts so as to fit them into the definition, account for the existence of the English Common Law. ...

If, as Sir Frederick Pollock [*First Book of Jurisprudence*, at 28.] writes, and as probably most competent jurists would today agree, the only essential conditions for the existence of law are the existence of a political community, and the recognition by its members of settled rules binding upon them in that capacity, international law seems on the whole to satisfy these conditions.

But it is more important to understand the nature of the system than to argue whether it ought to be called law or something else. The best view is that international law is in fact just a system of customary law, upon which has been erected, almost entirely within the last two generations, a superstructure of 'conventional' or treaty-made law, and some of its chief defects are precisely those that the history of law teaches us to expect in a customary system. It is a common mistake to suppose that of these the most conspicuous is the frequency of its violation.

Violations of law are rare in all customary systems, and they are so in international law. The explanation of that fact is simple, and so too is the explanation of the common belief to the contrary. For the law is normally observed because, as we shall see, the demands that it makes on states are generally not exacting, and on the whole states find it convenient to observe it; but this fact receives little notice because the interest of most people in international law is not in the ordinary routine of international legal business, but in the occasions, rare but generally sensational, on which it is flagrantly broken. Such breaches generally occur either when some great political issue has arisen between states, or in that part of the system which professes to regulate the conduct of war. But our diagnosis of what is wrong with the system will be mistaken if we fail to realize that the laws of peace and the great majority of treaties are on the whole regularly observed in the daily intercourse of states. And this is no small service to international life, however far it may fall short of the ideal by which we rightly judge the achievements of the system. If we fail to understand this, we are likely to assume, as many people do, that all would be well with international law if we could devise a better system for enforcing it; but the weakness of international law lies deeper than any mere question of sanctions. It is not the existence of a police force that makes a system of law strong and respected, but the strength of the law that makes it possible for a police force to be effectively organized. The imperative character of law is felt so strongly and obedience to it has become so much a matter of habit within a highly civilized state that national law has developed a machinery of enforcement which generally works smoothly, though never so smoothly as to make breaches impossible. If the imperative character of international law were equally strongly felt, the institution of definite international sanctions would easily follow.

A customary system of law can never be adequate to the needs of any but a primitive society, and the paradox of the international society is that, whilst on the material side it is far from primitive, and therefore needs a strong and fairly elaborate system of law for the regulation of the clashes to which the material interdependence of different states is constantly giving rise, its spiritual cohesion is ... weak, and as long as that is so the weakness will inevitably be reflected in a weak and primitive system of law. ...

Whether ... we ought to conclude that international law is a failure depends upon what we assume to be its aim. It has not failed to serve the purposes for which states have chosen to use it; in fact it serves these purposes reasonably well. The layman hears little of international law as a working system, for most of its practice goes on within the walls of foreign offices, which on principle are secretive; and even if the foreign offices were inclined to be more communicative the layman would not find what they could tell him very interesting, any more than he would normally be interested in the working of a solicitor's office. For in fact the practice of international law proceeds on much the same lines as that of any other kind of law, with the foreign offices taking the place of the private legal adviser and exchanging arguments about the facts and the law, and later, more often than is sometimes supposed, with a hearing before some form of international tribunal. The volume of this work is considerable, but most of it is not sensational, and it only occasionally relates to matters of high political interest. That does not mean that the matters to which it does relate are unimportant in themselves; often they are very important to particular interests or individuals. But it means that international law is performing a useful and indeed a necessary function in international life in enabling states to carry on their day-to-day intercourse along orderly and predictable lines. That is the role for which states have chosen to use it and for that it has proved a serviceable instrument.

Brierly's well-recognized book does not express the only acceptable view on these matters. It is best to form one's own opinion – not in advance but on the basis of the evidence to be found amongst the materials of international law collected in the rest of this volume. Chapters 2, 3 and 4 provide the basis for an assessment of the international legal system. These three chapters present the available evidence of the legal organisation of international society and the means to create and to apply international law. Successive chapters deal with the substantive rights and obligations assumed by states as the principle subjects of international law. Chapter 5 canvasses one of the most longstanding aspects of international law, namely the rules governing the conduct of diplomatic relations. Chapters 6 to 9 discuss the existence of international controls on the exercise of state power and authority under the legal rubrics of jurisdiction and responsibility. Chapters 10 and 11 add evidence of the growing domain of international law through the recent development of two particular subject areas, the protection of human rights and the law of the sea. In the context of some other new fields of international concern, the final Chapter 12 invites concluding reflections on the scope, the force and the character of international law.

CHAPTER TWO

International Legal Persons

SUBJECTS OF INTERNATIONAL LAW

International law applies to certain entities as "subjects" of international law. These entities have a legal personality, that is, a capacity similar to that of an individual person in domestic law, to enter into legal relations and to create the consequent rights and duties attached to that capacity. Without this capacity an entity will be unable to maintain any claims. International law itself determines who shall have legal personality and not all entities possess the same personality.

Until the twentieth century the prevailing view was that only states could possess international legal personality. This was due mainly to the fact that the concept of the state had predominated in the international system and the question of personality had been regarded as belonging exclusively to this domain. Thus, entities other than states could have no standing on the international scene.

As a result of changes in this century, international organizations and even individuals have attained some measure of international legal personality. It must be stressed, however, that they do not possess the same rights and duties as states. Rather, international law has recognized that there are entities other than states which have the capacity to maintain legal relations, to enjoy rights and possibly to assume obligations in certain given situations set down and regulated by law. These legal relations are severely limited in comparison to that of states. Political realities of the international scene lead to the logical conclusion that states, not individuals, are the dominant and vital feature of international relations.[1]

---

[1] From S.A. Williams and A.L.C. de Mestral, *An Introduction to International Law* (2ed. 1987), at 43. See also I. Brownlie, *Principles of Public International Law* (3ed. 1979), cc. 3 and 4; J. Crawford, *The Creation of States in International Law* (1979); L.C. Green, *International Law: A Canadian Perspective* (1984) at 73-103; J.G. Starke, *Introduction to International Law* (9ed. 1984), cc. 3, 5, 11, and 12; P. Vellas, *Droit international public* (2ed. 1970), at 219ff.; and B. Broms "Subjects: Entitlement in the International System" in R. St. J. Macdonald, D.M. Johnston eds., *The Structure and Process of International Law* (1983), at 383.

The purpose of this chapter is to look at the candidates for legal personality. A number of pertinent questions arise: first, does a particular entity fulfill the prerequisites for "subject" status? Second, what does this capacity for legal personality entail? Third, in new candidates, such as peoples seeking self-determination, individuals, international organizations and multinational corporations, is there or must there be demonstrable legal capacity and, if so, what are its parameters? These questions go to the criteria for becoming a subject of international law. Even so, it is only when recognition has been accorded by the international community that an entity will acquire the status of "personality" and the exact extent of its rights and duties laid down.

STATES AND STATEHOOD

States are the principal subjects of the international legal system. The question that confronts us as international lawyers is how to characterize statehood. What are the relevant criteria to look for? What relevance does recognition of the new candidate for statehood by other states members of the international community play in the establishment of full international personality? The mechanism of recognition will be considered in detail in Chapter 5 but its vital role must not be overlooked at this juncture as even if the view is taken that recognition does not constitute a new state it is still of immeasurable importance.

Montevideo Convention on Rights and Duties of States
(1936), 165 *L.N.T.S.* 19; (1934), 28 *Am. J. Int. L. Supp.* 75

The Montevideo Convention, 1933 is the best known formula for setting out the basic characteristics of statehood. The United States and fifteen Latin American states are parties to it. Despite the small number, it is seen as reflecting the classical conditions under customary international law which a prospective state must satisfy.

Article I

The state as a person of international law should possess the following qualifications: (a) a permanent population; (b) a defined territory; (c) government; and (d) capacity to enter into relations with other states.

NOTES

1) It has been suggested that these characteristics outlined in the Montevideo Convention are based on the principle of effectiveness but consideration should also be given to developments in modern international law that suggest that in exceptional cases other

criteria either supplement or go against this principle.[2] For example, see the later discussions of statehood and self-determination.

2) Population. A permanent population is necessary although there is no minimum requirement. Canada recognized Nauru, which in 1982 had a population of 8,421, and the Seychelles, which in 1983 had a population of 69,000. It is not necessary that the population possesses the nationality of the new state. This stems from the fact that nationality is dependent on statehood and not vice versa.[3]

3) Territory. There is no requirement as to the minimum amount of territory necessary for a prospective state to acquire power over. It may, therefore, be a small area such as Nauru (21 square kms.). Likewise, there is no requirement that a state have territorial unity. For example, Pakistan was in two parts prior to 1971. A state may also come into being and continue to exist despite border disputes, as was the case with Israel.

4) Government. This requirement can be regarded as central to the candidature for statehood. It is a concomitant of independence, the other main criteria, as both indicate a state that is in separate effective control of itself. It is the governmental capacity to exercise power over an area of territory and population that is the key feature. *Quaere* whether the Congo (today Zaire) in 1960 had an effective government. However, its application for membership to the U.N. was approved without a dissenting vote being cast.[4] Perhaps this was a case of premature recognition based on the state gaining independence from a previous sovereign, Belgium. Can it be so justified? Is the pre-condition of effective government relative to other considerations?

Civil strife can act to obscure an entity's transformation into a state. This was the case in Finland. When the Soviet government decreed that all its peoples had the right of self-determination in 1917, Finland (then part of the Russian empire) declared itself independent. Yet large numbers within Finland opposed independence and, for a time, no organized authority existed. The date of Finland's emergence as a state was an important preliminary matter in the *Aaland Islands' Case*. There, the Commission appointed by the League of Nations stated:[5]

> ... for a considerable time the conditions required for the formation of a sovereign state did not exist. In the midst of revolution and anarchy, certain elements essential to the existence of a state, even some elements of fact, were lacking for a fairly considerable period. Political and social life was disorganised: the authorities were not strong enough to assert themselves; civil war was rife; further, the Diet, the legality of which had been disputed by a large section of the people had been dispersed by the revolutionary party, and the Government had been chased from the capital and forcibly prevented from carrying out its duties: the armed camps and the police were divided into two opposing forces, and Russian troops, and after a time Germans also, took part in the civil war between the inhabitants and between the Red and White Finnish

---

[2] See J. Crawford, *supra* n.1, at 77-84; and R. Higgins, *The Development of International Law through the Political Organs of the United Nations* (1963), at 11-57.

[3] J. Crawford, *supra*, n.1, at 40-42.

[4] U.N.S.C. Res. 142, July 7, 1960; U.N.G.A. Res. 1480 (XV) Sept. 20, 1960, 1 U.N.GAOR, Supp. (No. 16); U.N. Doc. A/4684 (1960).

[5] (1920), L.N.O.J., Special Supp. (No. 3) 3.

out these obligations.''[8] Article 8(1) provides that each member of the General Assembly of the United Nations shall have one vote. The General Assembly is comprised of all member states. Does this legal equality in the General Assembly produce political equality? Of what significance is the veto power on all nonprocedural matters in the Security Council of the five permanent members (China, France, United Kingdom, USSR and the United States): see article 27(3) of the United Nations Charter.

3) Article 6 of the Charter of the Organization of American States, 1948,[9] provides that: ''States are juridically equal, enjoy equal rights and equal capacity to exercise these rights, and have equal duties. The rights of each State depend not upon its power to ensure the exercise thereof, but upon the mere fact of its existence as a person under international law.''

Declaration on Principles of International Law Concerning Friendly Relations and Co-operation among States in Accordance with the Charter of the United Nations[10]
October 24th, 1970, U.N.G.A. Res. 2625 (XXV), 25 U.N. GAOR, Supp. (No. 28) 121; U.N. Doc. A/8028 (1971); reprinted in (1970), 9 *Int. Leg. Mat.* 1292

The General Assembly

Reaffirming in the terms of the Charter that the maintenance of international peace and security and the development of friendly relations and co-operation between nations are among the fundamental purposes of the United Nations,

Recalling that the peoples of the United Nations are determined to practice tolerance and live together in peace with one another as good neighbours,

Bearing in mind the importance of maintaining and strengthening international peace founded upon freedom, equality, justice and respect for fundamental human rights and of developing friendly relations among nations irrespective of their political, economic and social systems or the levels of their development,

Bearing in mind also the paramount importance of the Charter of the United Nations in the promotion of the rule of law among nations,

Considering that the faithful observance of the principles of international law concerning friendly relations and co-operation among States, and fulfillment in good faith of the obligations assumed by States, in accordance with the Charter, is of the greatest

---

[8] For an authoritative discussion of this Article, see the International Court's advisory opinion in *Conditions of Admission to the United Nations* [1948] I.C.J. Rep. 57.

[9] 119 U.N.T.S. 3; U.S.T. 2394; Protocol of Amendment, 1967, 21 U.S.T. 607.

[10] See G. Arangio-Ruiz, *The U.N. Declaration on Friendly Relations and the System of Sources of International Law* (1979); and R. Rosenstock, ''The Declaration of Principles of International Law Concerning Friendly Relations; A Survey'' (1971), 65 *Am. J. Int. L.* 713.

importance for the maintenance of international peace and security, and for the implementation of the other purposes of the United Nations,

Noting that the great political, economic and social changes and scientific progress which have taken place in the world since the adoption of the Charter of the United Nations give increased importance to these principles and to the need for their more effective application in the conduct of States wherever carried on,

Recalling the established principle that outer space, including the Moon and other celestial bodies, is not subject to national appropriation by claim of sovereignty by means of use or occupation or by any other means, and mindful of the fact that consideration is being given in the United Nations to the question of establishing other appropriate provisions similarly inspired,

Convinced that the strict observance by States of the obligation not to intervene in the affairs of any other State is an essential condition to ensure that nations live together in peace with one another since the practice of any form of intervention not only violates the spirit and letter of the Charter of the United Nations but also leads to the creation of situations which threaten international peace and security,

Recalling the duty of States to refrain in their international relations from military, political, economic or any other form of coercion aimed against the political independence or territorial integrity of any State,

Considering it essential that all States shall refrain in their international relations from the threat or use of force against the territorial integrity or political independence of any State, or in any other manner inconsistent with the purposes of the United Nations,

Considering it equally essential that all States shall settle their international disputes by peaceful means in accordance with the Charter,

Reaffirming, in accordance with the Charter, the basic importance of sovereign equality and stressing that the purposes of the United Nations can be implemented only if States enjoy sovereign equality and comply fully with the requirements of this principle in their international relations,

Convinced that the subjection of peoples to alien subjugation, domination and exploitation constitutes a major obstacle to the promotion of international peace and security,

Convinced that the principle of equal rights and self-determination of peoples constitutes a significant contribution to contemporary international law, and that its effective application is of paramount importance for the promotion of friendly relations among States, based on respect for the principle of sovereign equality,

Convinced in consequence that any attempt aimed at the partial or total disruption of the national unity and territorial integrity of a State or country or at its political independence is incompatible with the purposes and principles of the Charter,

Considering the provisions of the Charter as a whole and taking into account the role of relevant resolutions adopted by the competent organs of the United Nations relating to the content of the principles,

Considering the progressive development and codification of the following principles:

   (a) The principle that States shall refrain in their international relations from the threat or use of force against the territorial integrity or political independence of any State, or in any other manner inconsistent with the purposes of the United Nations.

   (b) The principle that States shall settle their international disputes by peaceful means in such a manner that international peace and security and justice are not endangered.

(c) The duty not to intervene in matters within the domestic jurisdiction of any State, in accordance with the Charter.

(d) The duty of States to co-operate with one another in accordance with the Charter.

(e) The principle of equal rights and self-determination of peoples.

(f) The principle of sovereign equality of States.

(g) The principle that States shall fulfil in good faith the obligations assumed by them in accordance with the Charter,

so as to secure their more effective application within the international community, would promote the realization of the purposes of the United Nations,

Having considered the principles of international law relating to friendly relations and co-operation among States,

1. *Solemnly proclaims* the following principles:

The principle that States shall refrain in their international relations from the threat or use of force against the territorial integrity or political independence of any State, or in any manner inconsistent with the purposes of the United Nations

Every State has the duty to refrain in its international relations from the threat or use of force against the territorial integrity or political independence of any State, or in any other manner inconsistent with the purposes of the United Nations. Such a threat or use of force constitutes a violation of international law and the Charter of the United Nations and shall never be employed as a means of settling international issues.

A war of aggression constitutes a crime against the peace, for which there is responsibility under international law.

In accordance with the purposes and principles of the United Nations, States have the duty to refrain from propaganda for wars of aggression.

Every State has the duty to refrain from the threat or use of force to violate the existing international boundaries of another State or as a means of solving international disputes, including territorial disputes and problems concerning frontiers of States.

Every State likewise has the duty to refrain from the threat or use of force to violate international lines of demarcation, such as armistice lines, established by or pursuant to an international agreement to which it is a party or which it is otherwise bound to respect. Nothing in the foregoing shall be construed as prejudicing the positions of the parties concerned with regard to the status and effects of such lines under their special régimes or as affecting their temporary character.

States have a duty to refrain from acts of reprisal involving the use of force.

Every State has the duty to refrain from any forcible action which deprives peoples referred to in the elaboration of the principle of equal rights and self-determination of their right to self-determination and freedom and independence.

Every State has the duty to refrain from organizing or encouraging the organization of irregular forces or armed bands, including mercenaries, for incursion into the territory of another State.

Every State has the duty to refrain from organizing, instigating, assisting or participating in acts of civil strife or terrorist acts in another State or acquiescing in organized activities within its territory directed towards the commission of such acts, when the acts referred to in the present paragraph involve a threat or use of force.

The territory of a State shall not be the object of military occupation resulting from the use of force in contravention of the provisions of the Charter. The territory of a State shall not be the object of acquisition by another State resulting from the threat or use of force. No territorial acquisition resulting from the threat or use of force shall be recognized as legal. Nothing in the foregoing shall be construed as affecting:

(a) Provisions of the Charter or any international agreement prior to the Charter régime and valid under international law, or

(b) The powers of the Security Council under the Charter.

All States shall pursue in good faith negotiations for the early conclusion of a universal treaty on general and complete disarmament under effective international control and strive to adopt appropriate measures to reduce international tensions and strengthen confidence among States.

All States shall comply in good faith with their obligations under the generally recognized principles and rules of international law with respect to the maintenance of international peace and security, and shall endeavour to make the United Nations security system based upon the Charter more effective.

Nothing in the foregoing paragraphs shall be construed as enlarging or diminishing in any way the scope of the provisions of the Charter concerning cases in which the use of force is lawful.

The principle that States shall settle their international disputes by peaceful means in such a manner that international peace and security and justice are not endangered

Every State shall settle its international disputes with other States by peaceful means, in such a manner that international peace and security, and justice, are not endangered.

States shall accordingly seek early and just settlement of their international disputes by negotiation, inquiry, mediation, conciliation, arbitration, judicial settlement, resort to regional agencies or arrangements or other peaceful means of their choice. In seeking such a settlement, the parties shall agree upon such peaceful means as may be appropriate to the circumstances and nature of the dispute.

The parties to a dispute have the duty, in the event of failure to reach a solution by any one of the above peaceful means, to continue to seek a settlement of the dispute by other peaceful means agreed upon by them.

States parties to an international dispute, as well as other States, shall refrain from any action which may aggravate the situation so as to endanger the maintenance of international peace and security, and shall act in accordance with the purposes and principles of the United Nations.

International disputes shall be settled on the basis of the sovereign equality of States and in accordance with the principle of free choice of means. Recourse to, or acceptance of, a settlement procedure freely agreed to by States with regard to existing or future disputes to which they are parties shall not be regarded as incompatible with sovereign equality.

Nothing in the foregoing paragraphs prejudices or derogates from the applicable provisions of the Charter, in particular those relating to the pacific settlement of international disputes.

The principle concerning the duty not to intervene in matters within the
domestic jurisdiction of any State, in accordance with the Charter

No State or group of States has the right to intervene, directly or indirectly, for any reason whatever, in the internal or external affairs of any other State. Consequently, armed intervention and all other forms of interference or attempted threats against the personality of the State or against its political, economic and cultural elements, are in violation of international law.

No State may use or encourage the use of economic, political, or any other type of measures to coerce another State in order to obtain from it the subordination of the exercise of its sovereign rights and to secure from it advantages of any kind. Also, no State shall organize, assist, foment, finance, incite or tolerate subversive terrorist or armed activities directed towards the violent overthrow of the régime of another State, or interfere in civil strife in another State.

The use of force to deprive peoples of their national identity constitutes a violation of their inalienable rights and of the principle of non-intervention.

Every State has an inalienable right to choose its political, economic, social and cultural systems, without interference in any form by another State.

Nothing in the foregoing paragraphs shall be construed as affecting the relevant provisions of the Charter relating to the maintenance of international peace and security.

The duty of States to co-operate with one another in accordance with
the Charter

States have the duty to co-operate with one another, irrespective of the differences in their political, economic and social systems, in the various spheres of international relations, in order to maintain international peace and security and to promote international economic stability and progress, the general welfare of nations and international co-operation free from discrimination based on such differences.

To this end:

(a) States shall co-operate with other States in the maintenance of international peace and security;

(b) States shall co-operate in the promotion of universal respect for and observance of human rights and fundamental freedoms for all, and in the elimination of all forms of racial discrimination and all forms of religious intolerance;

(c) States shall conduct their international relations in the economic, social, cultural, technical and trade fields in accordance with the principles of sovereign equality and non-intervention;

(d) States Members of the United Nations have the duty to take joint and separate action in co-operation with the United Nations in accordance with the relevant provisions of the Charter.

States shall co-operate in the economic, social and cultural fields as well as in the field of science and technology and for the promotion of international cultural and educational progress. States should co-operate in the promotion of economic growth throughout the world, especially that of the developing countries.

The principle of equal rights and self-determination of peoples

By virtue of the principle of equal rights and self-determination of peoples enshrined in the Charter, all peoples have the right freely to determine, without external interference, their political status and to pursue their economic, social and cultural development, and every State has the duty to respect this right in accordance with the provisions of the Charter.

Every State has the duty to promote, through joint and separate action, the realization of the principle of equal rights and self-determination of peoples, in accordance with the provisions of the Charter, and to render assistance to the United Nations in carrying out the responsibilities entrusted to it by the Charter regarding the implementation of the principle in order:

(a) To promote friendly relations and co-operation among States; and

(b) To bring a speedy end to colonialism, having due regard to the freely expressed will of the peoples concerned;

and bearing in mind that subjection of peoples to alien subjugation, domination and exploitation constitutes a violation of the principle, as well as a denial of fundamental human rights, and is contrary to the Charter of the United Nations.

Every State has the duty to promote through joint and separate action universal respect for and observance of human rights and fundamental freedoms in accordance with the Charter.

The establishment of a sovereign and independent State, the free association or integration with an independent State or the emergence into any other political status freely determined by a people constitute modes of implementing the right of self-determination by that people.

Every State has the duty to refrain from any forcible action which deprives peoples referred to above in the elaboration of the present principle of their right to self-determination and freedom and independence. In their actions against the resistance to such forcible action in pursuit of the exercise of their right to self-determination, such peoples are entitled to seek and to receive support in accordance with the purposes and principles of the Charter of the United Nations.

The territory of a colony or other non-self-governing territory has, under the Charter of the United Nations, a status separate and distinct from the territory of the State administering it; and such separate and distinct status under the Charter shall exist until the people of the colony or non-self-governing territory have exercised their right of self-determination in accordance with the Charter, and particularly its purposes and principles.

Nothing in the foregoing paragraphs shall be construed as authorizing or encouraging any action which would dismember or impair, totally or in part, the territorial integrity or political unity of sovereign and independent States conducting themselves in compliance with the principle of equal rights and self-determination of peoples as described above and thus possessed of a government representing the whole people belonging to the territory without distinction as to race, creed or colour.

Every state shall refrain from any action aimed at the partial or total disruption of the national unity and territorial integrity of any other State or country.

The principle of sovereign equality of States

All States enjoy sovereign equality. They have equal rights and duties and are equal members of the international community, notwithstanding differences of an economic, social, political or other nature.

In particular, sovereign equality includes the following elements:
(a) States are juridically equal;
(b) Each State enjoys the rights inherent in full sovereignty;
(c) Each State has the duty to respect the personality of other States;
(d) The territorial integrity and political independence of the State are inviolable;
(e) Each State has the right freely to choose and develop its political, social, economic and cultural systems;
(f) Each State has the duty to comply fully and in good faith with its international obligations and to live in peace with other States.

The principle that States shall fulfil in good faith the obligations assumed by them in accordance with the Charter

Every State has the duty to fulfil in good faith the obligations assumed by it in accordance with the Charter of the United Nations.

Every State has the duty to fulfil in good faith its obligations under the generally recognized principles and rules of international law.

Every State has the duty to fulfil in good faith its obligations under international agreements valid under the generally recognized principles and rules of international law.

Where obligations arising under international agreements are in conflict with the obligations of Members of the United Nations under the Charter of the United Nations, the obligations under the Charter shall prevail.

General Part

2. *Declares* that:

In their interpretation and application the above principles are interrelated and each principle should be construed in the context of the other principles.

Nothing in this Declaration shall be construed as prejudicing in any manner the provisions of the Charter or the rights and duties of Member States under the Charter or the rights of peoples under the Charter taking into account the elaboration of these rights in this Declaration.

3. *Declares further* that:

The principles of the Charter which are embodied in this Declaration constitute basic principles of international law, and consequently appeals to all States to be guided by these principles in their international conduct and to develop their mutual relations on the basis of their strict observance.

NOTES

1) In acccordance with these principles, once a state has an irrefutable title to territory it is able to claim exclusive control over it, subject only to international law. A state alone can perform acts of sovereignty on its territory. Thus, if state A were to authorize its agents to enter state B for the purpose of arresting individuals located there who had violated the criminal law of state A, this would be a breach of international law. On the question of state responsibility for illegal arrest see the Jaffe case in Chapter 9, which relates to the violation of the exclusive jurisdiction of Canada by two United States bounty-hunters acting under colour of authority of the State of Florida.[11]

2) In the *Corfu Channel Case (Merits)*,[12] between the United Kingdom and Albania, the International Court of Justice held that the British act of mine sweeping in Albanian territorial waters in the Corfu Channel was a violation of the sovereignty of Albania. This was so notwithstanding Albania's earlier responsibility for damage done to two British destroyers by allowing mines to be placed in those waters through negligence. The Albanians had done nothing to prevent the disaster. See Chapter 9 section 2 on state responsibility for injuries done to aliens and their property.

3) According to the first of these Principles, States have a duty to prevent their territory being used as a base for the training of terrorist or armed activities against another state. See also section VI of Final Act of the Conference on Security and Cooperation in Europe 1975 (The "Helsinki Accords").[13]

4) In the decision of the International Court of Justice in *Military Activities In and Against Nicaragua*[14] the Court held that the adoption of the Declaration by states "affords an indication of their *opinio juris* as to customary international law on the question" of the less grave forms of the use of force. The Court would appear to distinguish grave forms of the use of force (those constituting an armed attack) from other less grave forms.

5) The Declaration originated in 1961 as an initiative by the Soviet Union to codify the "principles of peaceful co-existence" in international law. Many newly independent, developing countries took the opportunity to call for a wholesale rewriting of the principles of international law. Western states resisted these pressures steadfastly. The debate continued for 10 years before the Declaration, in its final form, was adopted. In what respects does it reinforce, elaborate, modify, change or revolutionize the principles of the U.N. Charter? What legal force and effect does it have?

---

[11] See also the *Eichmann* case (1961-62), 36 I.L.R. 5; and Sharon Williams and J.G. Castel, *Canadian Criminal Law: International and Transnational Aspects* (1981), at 144-48.
[12] [1949] I.C.J. Rep. 4, reported *infra* in Chapter 11.
[13] (1975), 14 *Int. Leg. Mat.* 1292.
[14] [1986] I.C.J. Rep. 14, at 101.

Non-Intervention

The principle of non-intervention is one of great importance.[15] It relates not only to the basic rights and duties of individual states but is of paramount importance to international peace and security. Intervention by one state or states in another state's affairs without legal justification can trigger off untold repercussions. This section analyzes the basic right of a state not to be interfered with. The next section considers the right of a state to defend itself against intervention.

One of the most flagrant forms of infringement of the independence of States is intervention. A definition of intervention might be an act of interference of a coercive nature, whether the act in question involves the use of force or merely economic or political pressure. Interference may manifest itself by action or inaction or by a threat of a nature that is hostile, or deemed to be hostile, if the state in question does not yield to it. This does not mean that to constitute intervention the act of interference must in fact force the victim State into compliance. Even if the State refused to be coerced or intimidated by threats, there might be an intention on the part of the intervening State to coerce the sovereign will of the other State. In the opinion of some jurists, the form which the intervention takes does not in any way change its nature. Intervention could be practised by processes of diplomacy. It could be more or less direct, more or less overt. It could be directed against the internal or external affairs of the State.

According to other authorities, intervention means exclusively intervention in a state's internal affairs. However, this position fails to take account of the fact that external independence is just as much an attribute of sovereignty as internal independence. Furthermore, intervention presupposes the existence of a state of peace between the states concerned.

Intervention could also be characterized as the dictatorial exercise of influence over the internal affairs or foreign policy of a State, aimed at destroying its markets, violating its laws, damaging its prestige and reputation, controlling its policy, or subverting its government. It includes such activities as propaganda, espionage, infiltration, bribery, assassination, assistance to guerrillas, and peremptory diplomatic demands. However, it is only when such activities are carried out by agents of a government with a view to controlling or subverting the government of another state that they contravene international law. Short of military expeditions, any propaganda or subversive activity undertaken by private individuals or enterprises is not usually regarded as intervention unless there is government complicity.

In the world of today, subversion is perhaps the most common and most dangerous form of intervention, whether it consists of hostile propaganda or of incitement to revolt or violently overthrow the established order. Such forms of subversion, which are themselves ancient, have come to characterize the ideological struggle which divides the world. The goal is no longer to overthrow a rival or hostile government, but to change completely the political, economic, and social structure of another State in the name of supposedly

---

[15] See generally W. Friedmann, *supra*, n. 7, at 253-74; J.N. Moore, ed., *Law and Civil War in the Modern World* (1974); and J.F. Murphy, *The United Nations and the Control of International Violence* (1982).

superior ideological principles. The ideological struggle is now assuming so violent a character that it presents, in the atomic age, enormous risks.

Forms of subversive or terrorist acts supported from outside are the most typical cases of violation of the independence of states and not only include the organization, training, and preparation on the territory of one State of groups of individuals who may then infiltrate into another State for purposes of subversion and terrorism, but also involve encouragement, material aid, provocation and any support whatsoever given by a state to minority groups operating in another State against the established regime.

Today it is generally agreed that there exists a duty not to intervene in the affairs of other states. This concept of non-intervention has evolved from a political principle to a principle of general international law. It was given expression in article 15(8) of the League of Nations Covenant, embodied in the Montevideo Convention on Rights and Duties of States in 1933 and further affirmed in the Additional Protocol Relative to Non-Intervention adopted at the Inter-American Conference for the Maintenance of Peace held in 1956 and in other international instruments.

While the Charter of the United Nations contains no provision dealing explicitly with the principle of non-intervention by States, this principle must be regarded as implicit in it. The principle is clearly embodied in article 2(1), which proclaims the sovereign equality of states and thus prohibits one state from interfering in the affairs of another state and protects the second state against such interference. In customary law, sovereign equality was the foundation of the duty of non-intervention, and sovereign equality would be meaningless if states were entitled to intervene in the domestic affairs of other states. Thus, the legal concept of non-intervention as between member states of the United Nations, could be regarded as springing from the concepts of respect for the personality and political independence of the state, concepts which constituted elements of sovereign equality, as well as from the principle of juridical equality.

In addition, since article 2(7) of the U.N. Charter prohibits intervention by the organization in the domestic affairs of member states, that prohibition should extend *a fortiori* to member states in their relations with each other. The principle of non-intervention could then be considered as a corollary of the principle of respect for the territorial integrity and political independence of states protected by article 2(4) of the Charter, which postulates implicitly the free and unhampered development of states as an aspect of their national independence.

In 1965, the General Assembly adopted an eight-point Declaration on the Inadmissibility of Intervention in the Domestic Affairs of States and the Protection of Their Independence and Sovereignty.[16] In 1966, in examining the status of the implementation of the Declaration, the Assembly expressed deep concern at the evidence of unceasing armed intervention and other forms of interference by certain states in the domestic affairs of others in different parts of the world, resulting in increased international tension. It reaffirmed all the principles and rules embodied in the Declaration, it urged the immediate

---

[16] Adopted by 109 votes in favour to 0 against with 1 abstention, G.A. Res. 2131 (XX), 20 U.N. GAOR, U.N. Doc. A/6014 (1966); 60 *Am. J. Int. L.* 662.

cessation of intervention, in any form whatever and it called upon all States to carry out faithfully their obligations under the Charter and the provisions of the Declaration.

The duties to avoid the use of force and to refrain from intervention in another state are reiterated again in the first and third Principles of International Law reported in the previous section.

NOTES

1) Refer to articles 2(3), (4) of the U.N. Charter and to the 1970 Declaration on Principles of International Law reported in the last section. What does "the threat or use of force" in article 2(4) mean? Does it prohibit economic measures or political pressure? Goodrich, Hambro and Simons[17] argue that it is directed against armed force alone. Do you agree? Does the 1970 Declaration clarify article 2(4) of the Charter? Article 2(4) stipulates that the threat or use of force must be "against the territorial integrity or political independence of any state ... ." What justifications does this allow for?

2) In the case concerning *Military Activities In and Against Nicaragua*[18] the International Court of Justice stated that the principle of non-intervention, despite examples of not infrequent violation, is part of customary international law. The Court found numerous examples of expressions of *opinio juris* to support this view. This *opinio juris* on the part of states is backed up by established practice. This is so not withstanding the lack of specific reference to the principle of non-intervention in the United Nations Charter. The Court was of the opinion that "... it was never intended that the Charter should embody written confirmation of every essential principle of international law in force". The principle has been reflected in numerous resolutions and declarations by international organizations and conferences, such as for example the 1970 Declaration on Principles of International Law, reported in the previous section.

Definition of Aggression[19]
December 14, 1974, U.N.G.A. Res. 3314 (XXIX), 29 U.N. GAOR, Supp.
(No. 31) 142; U.N. Doc. A/9631 (1974); reprinted in (1974), 13 *Int. Leg. Mat.* 710

The General Assembly

Basing itself on the fact that one of the fundamental purposes of the United Nations is to maintain international peace and security and to take effective collective measures

---

[17] L.M. Goodrich *et al.*, *Charter of the United Nations* (3 ed., 1969), at 49. See also R. Higgins, *The Development of International Law through the Political Organs of the United Nations* (1963), at 167-239.

[18] [1986] I.C.J. Rep. 14, at 106.

[19] See B. Ferencz, *Defining International Aggression* (2 vols., 1975); and J. Stone, *Conflict Through Consensus: U.N. Approaches to Aggression* (1977).

for the prevention and removal of threats to the peace, and for the suppression of acts of aggression or other breaches of the peace,

Recalling that the Security Council, in accordance with Article 39 of the Charter of the United Nations, shall determine the existence of any threat to the peace, breach of the peace or act of aggression and shall make recommendations, or decide what measures shall be taken in accordance with Articles 41 and 42, to maintain or restore international peace and security,

Recalling also the duty of States under the Charter to settle their international disputes by peaceful means in order not to endanger international peace, security and justice,

Bearing in mind that nothing in this definition shall be interpreted as in any way affecting the scope of the provisions of the Charter with respect to the functions and powers of the organs of the United Nations,

Considering also that, since aggression is the most serious and dangerous form of the illegal use of force, being fraught, in the conditions created by the existence of all types of weapons of mass destruction, with the possible threat of a world conflict and all its catastrophic consequences, aggression should be defined at the present stage,

Reaffirming the duty of States not to use armed force to deprive peoples of their right to self-determination, freedom and independence, or to disrupt territorial integrity,

Reaffirming also that the territory of a State shall not be violated by being the object, even temporarily, of military occupation or of other measures of force taken by another State in contravention of the Charter, and that it shall not be the object of acquisition by another State resulting from such measures or the threat thereof,

Reaffirming also the provisions of the Declaration on Principles of International Law concerning Friendly Relations and Co-operation among States in accordance with the Charter of the United Nations,

Convinced that the adoption of a definition of aggression ought to have the effect of deterring a potential aggressor, would simplify the determination of acts of aggression and the implementation of measures to suppress them and would also facilitate the protection of the rights and lawful interests of, and the rendering of assistance to, the victim,

Believing that, although the question whether an act of aggression has been committed must be considered in the light of all the circumstances of each particular case, it is nevertheless desirable to formulate basic principles as guidance for such determination,

Adopts the following Definition:

Article 1

Aggression is the use of armed force by a State against the sovereignty, territorial integrity or political independence of another State, or in any other manner inconsistent with the Charter of the United Nations, as set out in this Definition.

Explanatory note: In this Definition the term "State"

(a) Is used without prejudice to questions of recognition or to whether a State is a Member of the United Nations, and

(b) Includes the concept of a "group of States" where appropriate.

Article 2

The first use of armed force by a State in contravention of the Charter shall constitute prima facie evidence of an act of aggression although the Security Council may, in conformity with the Charter, conclude that a determination that an act of aggression has been committed would not be justified in the light of other relevant circumstances including the fact that the acts concerned or their consequences are not of sufficient gravity.

Article 3

Any of the following acts, regardless of a declaration of war, shall, subject to and in accordance with the provisions of article 2, qualify as an act of aggression:

(a) The invasion or attack by the armed forces of a State of the territory of another State, or any military occupation, however temporary, resulting from such invasion or attack, or any annexation by the use of force of the territory of another State or part thereof;

(b) Bombardment by the armed forces of a State against the territory of another State or the use of any weapons by a State against the territory of another State;

(c) The blockade of the ports or coasts of a State by the armed forces of another State;

(d) An attack by the armed forces of a State on the land, sea or air forces, or marine and air fleets of another State;

(e) The use of armed forces of one State which are within the territory of another State with the agreement of the receiving State, in contravention of the conditions provided for in the agreement or any extension of their presence in such territory beyond the termination of the agreement;

(f) The action of a State in allowing its territory, which it has placed at the disposal of another State, to be used by that other State for perpetrating an act of aggression against a third State;

(g) The sending by or on behalf of a State of armed bands, groups, irregulars or mercenaries, which carry out acts of armed force against another State of such gravity as to amount to the acts listed above, or its substantial involvement therein.

Article 4

The acts enumerated above are not exhaustive and the Security Council may determine that other acts constitute aggression under the provisions of the Charter.

Article 5

No consideration of whatever nature, whether political, economic, military or otherwise, may serve as a justification for aggression.

A war of aggression is a crime against international peace. Aggression gives rise to international responsibility.

No territorial acquisition or special advantage resulting from aggression are or shall be recognized as lawful.

Article 6

Nothing in this Definition shall be construed as in any way enlarging or diminishing the scope of the Charter including its provisions concerning cases in which the use of force is lawful.

Article 7

Nothing in this Definition, and in particular article 3, could in any way prejudice the right to self-determination, freedom and independence, as derived from the Charter, of peoples forcibly deprived of that right and referred to in the Declaration on Principles of International Law concerning Friendly Relations and Co-operation among States in accordance with the Charter of the United Nations, particularly peoples under colonial and racist régimes or other forms of alien domination; nor the right of these peoples to struggle to that end and to seek and receive support, in accordance with the principles of the Charter and in conformity with the above-mentioned Declaration.

Article 8

In their interpretation and application the above provisions are interrelated and each provision should be construed in the context of the other provisions.

Comments by Canadian Delegation
Oct. 10, 1974, *Press Release* No. 14

Article 1

The Canadian Government is satisfied with the basic definition of aggression as contained in Article 1. Although cases of indirect aggression are not specifically referred to in the article, this aspect of the problem is adequately dealt with elsewhere in the declaration.

The explanatory note to Article 1 makes it clear that the concept of statehood, however defined, is not an essential element of the definition of aggression, thereby recognizing one of the realities of international life and, at the same time, avoiding a restriction on the scope of the definition so as not to unduly hamper its applicability.

Article 2

The wording of Article 2 represents a carefully worked out compromise following considerable difficulties regarding the inclusion of the concept of aggressive intent. This compromise is a workable one. It retains the notion of the use of armed force as the essential element to be considered by the Security Council in its determination as to the fact of aggression. At the same time, by constituting armed force as *prima facie* evidence of aggression it leaves the field of inquiry open to the other aspects of each particular case. This is further emphasized by the use of the term "other relevant circumstances." This approach reflects the realities of international conflict. In a great number of cases the simple act of armed force cannot be the only criterion to be identified. Aggressive intent is one of the other criteria which should be taken into consideration. The Canadian Government attaches considerable importance to intent as one of the necessary elements which, in combination, constitute the wrongful act. This is the *mens rea* of the criminal law. Admittedly, it is difficult to establish and prove this element, more so in the area of international conflict. Nonetheless, it is of central importance and in many cases could be one of the most important factors to be considered by the Security Council.

As understood by Canada, the use of armed force raises a rebuttable presumption that an act of aggression has been committed. It is an important, but not an exclusive determinant. The existence of an aggressive intent may be significant as one of the other ''relevant factors'' that can either rebut or support this presumption.

Article 3

The list of acts of aggression on paras. (a) to (h) of Article 3 is intended to be illustrative rather than exhaustive. It would be unnecessary, impractical and perhaps impossible to have it otherwise.

Moreover, it is clear that Article 3 is made subject to the previous article. It is important to read the two articles in conjunction for it then becomes obvious that this is a two-stage process, governed by Article 2 and supplemented by Article 3.

The Council will of course weigh all the circumstances of a particular act or use of armed force as it sees fit. The process of determination would be as follows: first, with the aid of this non-exhaustive list as a guideline, the Council would examine the particular act in question. If the act fell within one of the five categories the Council's deliberations would be substantially simplified. Whether it did or not, however, by virtue of Article 2, the act would still constitute only *prima facie* evidence of aggression. The Council would then broaden the scope of its inquiry into the other relevant circumstances in order to arrive at a final determination. The conclusion to be drawn then is that this list is intended to be an aid, albeit an important one. It is not necessary that one of the five categories be automatically applied to any situation which arises without further inquiry. It may well be, of course, that the Council could decide upon a course other than a determination of an act of aggression, for example, with a view to encouraging the parties to seek a peaceful settlement of their differences.

The wording of Article 3(d) might possibly be interpreted sufficiently widely to include enforcement measures taken by a coastal state, perhaps even within its territorial sea, but certainly within an economic or fishing zone, even if these measures related to fisheries or pollution control. The Canadian Delegation placed on record its understanding that nothing in this definition, and in particular Article 3(d) shall be construed as in any way prejudicing or diminishing the authority of a coastal state to exercise its rights in maritime zones within the limits of its national jurisdiction.

Paragraphs (f) and (g) describe situations which have long been a source of international tension and conflict yet which fall short of what has traditionally been thought of as acts of aggression, at least when we equate this concept with acts of war.

Paragraph (f) addresses itself to the situation wherein one state allows its territory to be used to further the aggressive purposes of another state against a third. This is an important aspect of the problem of aggression and one which should be recognized.

Nevertheless, this criterion should be applied with caution. It should be remembered that the knowledge or control which states may have regarding the improper use of their territory may vary considerably. Such a state may be more offended against than offending, a variable which will have to be carefully examined in every case.

Paragraph (g) provides further elaboration on the idea of indirect aggression. The inclusion of this paragraph is an indication of the acceptance of the thesis that the distinction between direct and indirect aggression is artificial. The determining factor should be the degree of force used and the degree of responsibility which can be attributed to the state rather than the means or modalities by which that force is used. This paragraph represents a recognition of the fact that aggression which is perpetrated under the guise of a third or intermediary agent is just as much an act of aggression as an outright attack by one state on another. It attempts to outlaw one aspect of the serious problem of terrorism which starkly confronts the international community. It is true that terroristic acts may be of a relatively limited nature. It is equally true that they may be of such magnitude as to leave no doubt of their intent and purpose and thereby constitute an act of aggression as harmful and offensive as any other.

The acquiescence in or indeed encouragement by one state of attacks of armed bands against a second state is rejected by the world community in this paragraph. State complicity in acts of international terrorism is a problem with which the world community has yet to come to grips. This paragraph is an encouraging sign of movement in the right direction.

Article 5

While the first paragraph of this article is perhaps a truism, the second is of value in that it makes reference to international law and in particular affirms the continuing validity of the principles of the Nuremberg Charter and the Declaration on Friendly Relations.

The last paragraph is a necessary corollary to the fact of the illegality of aggression in that it stipulates the fruits of aggression will not be recognized. While this paragraph singles out territorial acquisition as a harmful effect of aggression, there are many others including loss of life and destruction of property and institutions which are equally opprobrious.

Article 7

The seventh article was the subject of considerable controversy in the Special Committee. As it provides that the right of self-determination, freedom and independence will not be prejudiced by the definition, equal emphasis must be given to the proposition that Article 7 be interpreted subject to the Charter of the U.N.

Canada supports peoples engaged in the struggle for self-determination and human dignity. However, the settlement of such political conflicts need not be accomplished by violent means. The reference to struggle must mean struggle by peaceful means and not one which condones the use of force contrary to the provisions of the Charter. Furthermore, the article must not be interpreted as endorsing assault on the territorial integrity of any state or condoning the dismemberment of any state by violent means.

Recent events may serve to make us hopeful that this article will be of limited appli-

in 1956, Jordan and Lebanon in 1958, the Congo in 1960, Afghanistan in 1980 and Namibia in 1981.

5) What is the effect of the General Assembly "making appropriate recommendations to Members for collective measures"? Are member states bound to undertake the measures if they disagree with them? What authority does the General Assembly have in regard to collective measures? Consider the U.N. Charter Article 10-17, reprinted in the Appendix. Does this Resolution enlarge the Assembly's powers? Can it?

Security Council Resolutions on Korea

Resolution of June 25, 1950[22]
5 U.N. SCOR, Resols. and Decs. 4-5; U.N. Doc.S/INF/5/Rev.1(1965)

The Security Council ...

Recalling the finding of the General Assembly in its resolution 293(IV) of 21st October 1949 that the Government of the Republic of Korea is a lawfully established government having effective control and jurisdiction over that part of Korea where the United Nations Temporary Commission on Korea was able to observe and consult and in which the great majority of the people of Korea reside: that this Government is based on elections which were a valid expression of the free will of the electorate of that part of Korea and which were observed by the Temporary Commission; and that this is the only such Government in Korea;

Mindful of the concern expressed by the General Assembly in its resolutions 195(III) of 12 December 1948 and 293 (IV) of 21 October 1949 about the consequences which might follow unless Member States refrained from acts derogatory to the results sought to be achieved by the United Nations in bringing about the complete independence and unity of Korea; and the concern expressed that the situation described by the United Nations Commission on Korea in its report menaces the safety and well-being of the Republic of Korea and of the people of Korea and might lead to open military conflict there;

Noting with grave concern the armed attack on the Republic of Korea by forces from North Korea.

Determines that this action constitutes a breach of the peace; and

I. *Calls for* the immediate cessation of hostilities; *Calls upon* the authorities in North Korea to withdraw forthwith their armed forces to the 38th parallel; ...

III. *Calls upon* all Member States to render every assistance to the United Nations in the execution of this resolution and to refrain from giving assistance to the North Korean authorities.

---

[22] Adopted by 9 votes in favour to 0 against with 1 abstention (Yugoslavia). The U.S.S.R. was not present.

Resolution of June 27, 1950[23]
5 U.N. SCOR, Resols. and Decs. 5; U.N. Doc. S/INF/5/Rev. 1 (1965)

The Security Council ...

Having noted from the report of the United Nations Commission on Korea that the authorities in North Korea have neither ceased hostilities nor withdrawn their armed forces to the 38th parallel, and that urgent military measures are required to restore international peace and security;

Having noted the appeal from the Republic of Korea to the United Nations for immediate and effective steps to secure peace and security;

Recommends that the Members of the United Nations furnish such assistance to the Republic of Korea as may be necessary to repel the armed attack and to restore international peace and security in the area.

Resolution of July 7, 1950[24]
5 U.N. SCOR, Resols. and Decs. 5; U.N. Doc. S/INF/5/Rev. 1 (1965)

The Security Council ...

1. *Welcomes* the prompt and vigorous support which Governments and peoples of the United Nations have given to its Resolutions ... of 25 and 27 June 1950 to assist the Republic of Korea in defending itself against armed attack and thus to restore international peace and security in the area;

2. *Notes* that Members of the United Nations have transmitted to the United Nations offers of assistance for the Republic of Korea;

3. *Recommends* that all Members providing military forces and other assistance pursuant to the aforesaid Security Council resolutions make such forces and other assistance available to a unified command under the United States of America;

4. *Requests* the United States to designate the commander of such forces;

5. *Authorizes* the unified command at its discretion to use the United Nations flag in the course of operations against North Korean forces concurrently with flags of the various nations participating;

6. *Requests* the United States to provide the Security Council with reports as appropriate on the course of action taken under the unified command.

NOTES

Was the action by the Security Council in adopting the above resolutions constitutional? Refer to the powers of the Security Council contained in the U.N. Charter Articles

---

[23] Adopted by 7 votes in favour to 1 against (Yugoslavia) with 2 abstentions. The U.S.S.R. was not present.
[24] Adopted by 7 votes in favour to 0 against with 3 abstentions. The U.S.S.R. was not present.

24-28, reprinted in the Appendix. Note that neither South or North Korea is yet a member of the United Nations. What relevance was the absence of the U.S.S.R.? Does absence like an abstention not constitute a veto or does it have a blocking effect?[25] Was the U.S.S.R. in violation itself of article 28 of the Charter by being absent? Can article 27 be read so as to mean the permanent members present and voting? What if all the permanent members were absent?

Humanitarian Intervention and Invitation

In creating the United Nations Charter, the world community evidenced a distrust for unilateral action on the part of states. While article 51 allows for self-defense in certain defined circumstances, including, arguably the defense of a state's own nationals (see the next section), a general right to intervene forcibly for humanitarian reasons is acutely controversial. If self-defense of citizens abroad is open to abuse, general humanitarian intervention would clearly be more susceptible to aspersions being cast on its altruistic and genuine nature.[26] Some governments could use this concept as an excuse for meddling in the affairs of another state. Would such an action only be taken against less-powerful states by the more-powerful? Would there be one rule for the strong and another for the weak? Would such action encourage counter-action by other states?

This is not to say that action under the auspices of the United Nations could not be called for, especially if the matter was a threat to international peace and security.

When an invitation is issued by one government to another to participate in its domestic or external affairs, such involvement would not be classed as intervention or aggression. But the requesting government must be in control of the country and must be its lawful government and the invitation must be genuine and voluntary. Such a request may be seen as a legitimate response to acts of aggression by a third state in contravention of article 2(4) of the Charter. Thus, there is nothing wrong in state A giving help to state B which is being threatened or made the subject of attacks by state C. More problematic, however, is whether state A should give assistance to the government of state B when state B is suffering civil unrest. The proper response may be for state A to stay out. However, if the insurgents in state B are receiving outside support, can state A argue that it is merely countering that illegal intervention? Would it make a difference if the insurgents have the majority of the population supporting them? What if they have not yet established control over any part of the country? See the 1970 Declaration on Principles of International Law reported previously at the beginning of this section.

Examples of asserted intervention and claimed invitation abound: Hungary (1956), Dominican Republic (1965), Afghanistan (1979) and Grenada (1983) are but a few. In the case of the Soviet entry into Czechoslovakia in 1968, it was first argued by the Soviet Union that its government had been invited there. At a later stage, it was explained as an extraordinary measure dictated by necessity, on the basis that the actions of enemies

---

[25] On the question of abstention see the *Namibia Case*, [1971] I.C.J. Rep. 16, at 22.

[26] See I. Brownlie, "Humanitarian Intervention" in J.N. Moore ed., *Law and Civil War in the Modern World* (1974), at 217-28. Note also in support of the concept R.B. Lillich, "Intervention to Protect Human Rights" (1969), 15 *McGill L.J.* 205.

of socialism created a threat to the common socialist interest. This claim to excuse the intervention is known as the "Brezhnev Doctrine."[27]

In this context it is worthwhile to note the justification used by the United States for its entry into the Vietnamese War. It argued that it was defending the South from subversion from the North. Could the North Vietnamese have argued that before they helped the insurgents the United States had been providing the South Vietnamese government with economic and military aid? The same arguments are being made today by the United States to support its assistance to government or contra-government forces in Central America.[28]

In statements to the Senate Foreign Relations Committee, both U.S. Secretary of State George Schultz and Defence Secretary Casper Weinberger have indicated that the right to use force is legitimate where democracy is at stake.[29] The United States would appear to take the view that it is in its interest to stand by its "friends" in their struggle for freedom. Its actions are justified, it is argued, because other forces are aiding and abetting the opposing sides in the name of "proletarian internationalism."[30]

Self-defense[31]

Charter of the United Nations

See Article 51 in the Appendix.

This Article is more limited in its extent than the right granted under customary international law, and it raises a number of significant questions. Must it be interpreted literally and the right of self-defence restricted to cases of "armed attack"? Must this article be read to mean if *and only if* an armed attack occurs? What has happened to the customary law rule of preemptive self-defense?

The Caroline
United Kingdom v. United States
(1837), 2 Moore 409

[The 1837 Canadian Rebellion found active support from volunteers in the United States. These volunteers joined with the rebels and encamped on Navy Island in the Chippewa Channel in Canadian waters. From there this force raided the Canadian riverside and British ships. The United States authorities knew of these activities but did not stop them.

---

[27] See (1968), 20 *Curr. Dig. Soviet Press*, No. 46, at 3-4.

[28] And see the dissenting opinion of Judge Schwebel in *Military Activities In and Against Nicaragua*, [1986] I.C.J. Rep. 14, at 259.

[29] *The Globe and Mail*, February 1, 1985, at A1.

[30] See S.A. Williams and A.L.C. de Mestral, *supra*, n. 1, at 51.

[31] See I. Brownlie, *International Law and the Use of Force by States* (1963), cc. 12-14; and D. Bowett, *Self-Defence in International Law* (1958).

The ship *Caroline* was involved in supplying men and materials to Navy Island. On December 29-30, 1837 the British seized the *Caroline* which was docked at Fort Schlosser on the United States side. They set her alight and sent her over Niagara Falls. Two United States citizens were killed. This action was discussed in correspondence between the British and United States governments, when the British sought to obtain the release of one McLeod, a British subject who had been arrested on charges of murder and arson.]

MR. WEBSTER to Mr. Fox (April 24, 1841): ... It will be for ... [Her Majesty's] Government to show a necessity of self-defence, instant, over-whelming, leaving no choice of means, and no moment for deliberation. It will be for it to show, also, that the local authorities of Canada, even supposing the necessity of the moment authorized them to enter the territories of The United States at all, did nothing unreasonable or excessive; since the act, justified by the necessity of self-defence, must be limited by that necessity, and kept clearly within it. It must be shown that admonition or remonstrance to the persons on board the Caroline was impracticable, or would have been unavailing; it must be shown that day-light could not be waited for; that there could be no attempt at discrimination between the innocent and the guilty; that it would not have been enough to seize and detain the vessel; but that there was a necessity, present and inevitable, for attacking her in the darkness of the night, while moored to the shore, and while unarmed men were asleep on board, killing some and wounding others, and then drawing her into the current, above the cataract, setting her on fire, and, careless to know whether there might not be in her the innocent with the guilty, or the living with the dead, committing her to a fate which fills the imagination with horror. A necessity for all this, the Government of The United States cannot believe to have existed.

LORD ASHBURTON to Mr. Webster (July 28, 1842): ... It is so far satisfactory to perceive that we are perfectly agreed as to the general principles of international law applicable to this unfortunate case. Respect for the inviolable character of the territory of independent nations is the most essential foundation of civilization ... .

NOTES

1) Clearly, the United States Government accepted the justification of self-defense. The British argued that what had been done was out of the necessity of self-preservation. There was, it was stated, a danger of future threats. However, on the facts as it saw them, the United States rejected the plea. This incident was the first apparent recognition internationally of pre-emptive or preventive self-defense. To be legitimate, self-defense must not only be born out of necessity, it must also be proportionate to the harm to be countered.

2) Although article 2 of the Definition of Aggression, reproduced in the previous section, states that: "The first use of armed force by a state in contravention of the Charter shall constitute *prima facie* evidence of an act of aggression", it qualifies this presumption in the face of "other relevant circumstances."[32]

---

[32] See also the Comments by the Canadian Delegation on Article 2, *supra* in the previous section.

Military Activities In and Against Nicaragua Case
Nicaragua v. United States of America
[1986] I.C.J. Rep. 14, at 102-3

[The following few paragraphs are taken from the judgment on the merits in the case between Nicaragua and the United States. Nicaragua claimed, *inter alia*, that the United States had acted in violation of Article 2(4) of the United Nations Charter and of the customary international law obligation to refrain from the threat or use of force; that its conduct amounted to intervention in the internal affairs of Nicaragua. The United States did not file any pleadings on the merits of the case and was not represented at the hearings before the International Court of Justice. However, in its counter-memorial on the earlier adjudicated questions of jurisdiction and admissibility[33] the United States had claimed that by providing, upon request, proportionate and appropriate assistance to third states not before the Court it was acting in reliance on the inherent right to collective self-defence in Article 51 of the Charter.]

THE COURT: ... [With] regard to the existence of this right [of self-defence and in particular collective self-defence, the Court] ... notes that in the language of Article 51 of the United Nations Charter, the inherent right (or "droit naturel") which any State possesses in the event of armed attack, covers both collective and individual self-defence. Thus, the Charter itself testifies to the existence of the right in customary international law. Moreover, just as the wording of certain General Assembly declarations adopted by States demonstrates their recognition of the principle of prohibition of force as definitely a matter of customary international law, some of the wording in those declarations operates similarly in respect of the right of self-defence (both collective and individual). Thus, ... the declaration ... on the Principles of International Law concerning Friendly Relations and Cooperation among States ... demonstrates that the States represented in the General Assembly regard the exception to the prohibition of force constituted by the right of individual or collective self-defence as already a matter of customary international law ... .

Nürnberg War Crimes Trials
(1947), 1 *Trial of the Major War Criminals* 171, at 206-9.

[The following extract is taken from the Final Judgment of the International Military Tribunal at Nürnberg. The 22 defendants, the major war criminals whose crimes had no exact geographical location, were indicted with crimes against peace, war crimes and crimes against humanity. They were also charged with participating in the formulation or execution of a common plan or conspiring to commit all these crimes. The Tribunal held that to initiate a war of aggression is the supreme international crime. It further held that under article 6 of the Charter of the International Military Tribunal that there was individual responsibility for such offences.[34]]

---

[33] [1984] I.C.J. Rep. 392.
[34] See *infra* under "Other Legal Persons: Individuals" for this portion of the case.

THE TRIBUNAL: On the 1st March, Hitler issued a directive regarding the Weser Exercise which contained the words:

The development of the situation in Scandinavia requires the making of all preparations for the occupation of Denmark and Norway by a part of the German Armed Forces. This operation should prevent British encroachment on Scandinavia and the Baltic; further, it should guarantee our ore base in Sweden and give our Navy and Air Force a wider start line against Britain. ... The crossing of the Danish border and the landings in Norway must take place simultaneously ... . It is most important that the Scandinavian States as well as the Western opponents should be taken by surprise by our measures.

On the 24th March the naval operation orders for the Weser Exercise were issued, and on the 30th March the defendant Doenitz as Commander in Chief of U-boats issued his operational order for the occupation of Denmark and Norway. On the 9th April 1940, the German forces invaded Norway and Denmark.

... it is clear that as early as October 1939 the question of invading Norway was under consideration. The defense that has been made here is that Germany was compelled to attack Norway to forestall an Allied invasion, and her action was therefore preventive.

It must be remembered that preventive action in foreign territory is justified only in case of "an instant and overwhelming necessity for self-defense, leaving no choice of means and no moment of deliberation." ("The Caroline Case," *Moore's Digest of International Law,* Vol. II, at 412.) How widely the view was held in influential German circles that the Allies intended to occupy Norway cannot be determined with exactitude. Quisling asserted that the Allies would intervene in Norway with the tacit consent of the Norwegian Government. The German Legation at Oslo disagreed with this view, although the Naval Attaché at that Legation shared it.

... it is clear that when the plans for an attack on Norway were being made, they were not made for the purpose of forestalling an imminent Allied landing, but, at the most, that they might prevent an Allied occupation at some future date.

When the final orders for the German invasion of Norway were given, the diary of the Naval Operations Staff for 23 March, 1940 records:

A mass encroachment by the English into Norwegian territorial waters ... is not to be expected at the present time.

And Admiral Assmann's entry 26 March says:

British landing in Norway not considered serious.

It was further argued that Germany alone could decide, in accordance with the reservations made by many of the Signatory Powers at the time of the conclusion of the Kellogg-Briand Pact, whether preventive action was a necessity, and that in making her decision her judgment was conclusive. But whether action taken under the claim of self-defence was in fact aggressive or defensive must ultimately be subject to investigation and adjudication if international law is ever to be enforced.

In the light of all the available evidence it is impossible to accept the contention that the invasions of Denmark and Norway were defensive, and in the opinion of the Tribunal they were acts of aggressive war.

NOTES

1) In the context of responsiblity for crimes against peace[35] see article 227 of the Versailles Treaty[36] which provided for the arraignment of Kaiser Wilhelm II, the former German Emperor for "a supreme offence against international morality and the sanctity of treaties";[37] and the Pact of Paris of August 27, 1928[38] (otherwise known as the Kellogg-Briand Pact) which stated in article I that the contracting parties condemned "recourse to war for the solution of international controversies and renounced it as an instrument of national policy in their relations with one another".[39]

2) The International Law Commission has been preparing a Draft Code of Offences Against the Peace and Security of Mankind.[40] The Draft presented in 1954,[41] which comprised thirteen criminal acts was concerned primarily with aggression and intervention. It failed to be of value on account of the necessity at that time to define aggression. Even though the Definition of Aggression[42] was adopted by consensus in 1974, it was not until 1982 that the draft code was actively being considered again. Since 1981, a special rapporteur and working group has been appointed by the Commission. The special rapporteur has produced four reports.[43] Three basic questions are being addressed: (1) Scope of the Draft; (2) Methodology and (3) Implementation.

---

[35] See M.R. Garcia-Mora, "Crimes Against Peace in International Law: From Nürnberg to the Present" (1964), 53 *Ky. L.J.* 35; M.R. Garcia-Mora, "Crimes Against Peace" (1965), 34 *Fordham L. Rev.* 1; F.B. Schick, "Crimes Against Peace" (1948), 38 *J. Crim. L. and Criminol* 445.

[36] 2 Bevans 43.

[37] The Dutch Government refused to surrender the Kaiser on the ground that it had no duty "to associate itself with this high act of policy of the powers," and the trial was not proceeded with. See J.W. Garner, *International Law and the World War* (1920), Vol. 2, at 488-95.

[38] 1929 Can. T.S. No. 7; 4 Malloy 5130; 94 L.N.T.S. 57.

[39] See C.J. Colombos, "The Paris Pact, Otherwise Called the Kellogg Pact" (1928), 14 *Grotius* 87. See also Convention II respecting the limitation of employment of force for the recovery of contract debts, signed at the Hague October 18, 1907, 2 Malloy 2248. Canada is a party to the 1907 Convention.

[40] The U.N. General Assembly directed the Commission to: (a) formulate the principles of international law recognized by the Nürnberg Charter and Judgment and (b) prepare a draft code of offences: see U.N.G.A. Res. 177 (II), 2 U.N. GAOR, Supp. (No. 1) III; U.N. Doc. A/519 (1947).

[41] Adopted at Paris, 28 July 1954, 9 U.N. GAOR, Supp. (No. 9) 9; U.N. Doc. A/2693 (1954).

[42] Reproduced in the previous section.

[43] See U.N. Doc. A/CN. 4/364; U.N. Doc. A/CN. 4/377 and Corr. 1; A/CN.4/378 and Corr. 1 and 2 and A/CN.4/398 and Corr. 1-3.

3) The assertion of self-defense to justify the Cuban Quarantine[44] raises a number of interesting issues. On October 22nd, 1962, an announcement was made by President Kennedy that the United States intended to carry out a strictly imposed quarantine on all offensive military weapons and materials being shipped to Cuba. The Security Council of the United Nations took no action. The Council of the Organization of American States adopted a resolution[45] which recommended that its member states in accordance with articles 6 and 8 of the Rio Treaty[46] should take all individual and collective measures, including the armed force deemed necessary, to prevent Cuba from continuing to receive military material from the Sino-Soviet powers. The resolution states that such supplies would threaten the peace and security of the continent. By such a quarantine, the Cuban missiles were prevented from becoming an active threat.

Was this quarantine and the resulting interceptions of two ships (one a USSR tanker and one a foreign ship under charter to the USSR) on the high seas justifiable, or were they acts of aggression? Was the quarantine in breach of article 2(4) of the U.N. Charter? Was it justifiable under Chapter VIII of the U.N. Charter?[47]

4) Self-defense must be distinguished from reprisals, which constitute retaliation not defence, whether actual or anticipatory. Reprisals by means of armed force are clearly illegal. The controversial question is whether economic reprisals which are not taken pursuant to United Nations authorization are justifiable. Are such acts illegal under the United Nations Charter? What prerequisites would be necessary to put forward a case for their justification?[48]

5) In 1981 the United States sent U.S. Navy jet fighters across the line proclaimed by Libya as marking the baseline from which the territorial waters of Libya would be measured. Waters behind the line would be internal. The United States stated that they were asserting internationally accepted rights as the line drawn across the Gulf of Sidra some 130 miles from the Libyan coast was in violation of international law. See Chapter 11 on the Law of the Sea. The U.S. fighters shot down two Libyan planes after one attacked them. Was this a case of self-defence by the United States? Was it provocation? Again in March 1986 the United States crossed the "line of death" as proclaimed by Muammar Gaddafi. It sent across part of the U.S. 6th Fleet and responded to a missile attack by Libya by sinking at least three Libyan boats, and hitting a shore battery. Do you consider that the United States was acting in an acceptable way? Further, was the subsequent U.S. action in bombing certain targets in Libya justifiable on account of Libya's alleged part in encouraging international terrorism? Was this action in the Gulf of Sidra self-defence, pre-emptive self-defence or a reprisal in your estimation?

---

[44] As to the Cuban Quarantine see, L.C. Meeker, "Defensive Quarantine and the Law" (1963), 57 *Am. J. Int. L.* 515; Q. Wright, "The Cuban Quarantine" (1963), 57 *Am. J. Int. L.* 546.

[45] (1962), 47 *U.S. Dept. of State Bull.* 734.

[46] The Inter-American Treaty of Reciprocal Assistance (1947), 21 U.N.T.S. 93.

[47] See D. Acheson, "Comments" (1963), 57 *Proc. Am. Soc. Int. L.* 13.

[48] See D.W. Bowett, "Economic Coercion and Reprisals by States" (1972), 13 *Va J. Int. L.* 1; and R.B. Lillich, "Economic Coercion and the International Legal Order", in R.B. Lillich, ed., *Economic Coercion and the New International Economic Order* (1976), at 73.

The Israeli Attack on Iraqi Nuclear Research Centre

Security Council Debate
June 12, 1981, U.N. DOC., S/PV. 2280, reprinted in (1981),
20 *Int. Leg. Mat.* 965

[On Sunday June 7th, 1981, at 6:37 p.m. local time in Iraq, Israeli military aircraft flew over Iraq and bombed the nuclear installation situated near Baghdad. Iraq asserted this was an act of aggression, while Israel claimed that it was an act of self-preservation. Here is an excerpt from the Security Council's debate,[49] followed by other materials from its reports:]

MR. HAMMADI (Iraq): Mr. President, allow me first to express to you, and through you to the members of the Security Council, my gratitude for convening this meeting and for giving me the opportunity to address the Council on the question of the flagrant act of aggression committed by Israel against Iraq.

On Sunday, 7 June 1981, at 1837 hours Baghdad local time, Israeli war-planes raided the nuclear installations situated near Baghdad, causing many civilian casualties and much material damage. The Zionist aggressors announced on the following day their responsibility for the attack, brazenly claiming the total destruction of the installations ... .

MR. BLUM (Israel): ... On Sunday, 7 June 1981, the Israel Air Force carried out an operation against the Iraqi reactor called "Osiraq". That reactor was in its final stages of construction near Baghdad. The pilots' mission was to destroy it. They executed their mission successfully.

In destroying Osiraq, Israel performed an elementary act of self-preservation, both morally and legally. In so doing, Israel was exercising its inherent right of self-defence as understood in general international law and as preserved in Article 51 of the United Nations Charter.

A threat of nuclear obliteration was being developed against Israel by Iraq, one of Israel's most implacable enemies. Israel tried to have that threat halted by diplomatic means. Our efforts bore no fruit. Ultimately we were left with no choice. We were obliged to remove that mortal danger. We did it cleanly and effectively. The Middle East has become a safer place. We trust that the international community has also been given pause to make the world a safer place ... .

[Meanwhile the International Atomic Energy Agency (IAEA) passed a resolution[50] in

---

[49] From U.N. Doc., S/PV. 2280 of June 12th, 1981, reprinted in (1981), 20 *Int. Leg. Mat.* 965. Also note R.A. Friedlander, "Might can also be Right: the Israeli Nuclear Reactor Bombing and International Law" (1980), 28 *Chitty's L.J.* 352.

[50] 36 U.N. SCOR, Supp. (Jan.-March/81) 64; U.N. Doc. S/14532 of June 15th, 1981. The Board of Governors adopted the Resolution by a vote of 29 in favour to 2 against (Canada, United States) with 3 abstentions (Australia, Sweden, Switzerland).

which it condemned Israel for ''this premeditated and unjustified attack'' on the Iraqi nuclear research centre and recommended the suspension of technical assistance to Israel by the Agency. It also recommended that the U.N. General Assembly should consider suspending Israel's membership of the United Nations and it reminded states of the U.N. resolution calling for an end to the transfer of nuclear materials and technology to Israel. This IAEA resolution was communicated to the Security Council, which noted it in the preamble to the following resolution of its own.]

Security Council Resolution 487 (1981)[51]
36 U.N. SCOR, Res. and Decs. 10; U.N. DOC.S/INF/37 (1982)

The Security Council ...

Fully aware of the fact that Iraq has been a party to the Treaty on the Non-Proliferation of Nuclear Weapons since it came into force in 1970, that in accordance with that Treaty Iraq has accepted Agency safeguards on all its nuclear activities, and that the Agency has testified that these safeguards have been satisfactorily applied to date,

Noting furthermore that Israel has not adhered to the non-proliferation Treaty on Non-Proliferation of Nuclear Weapons,

Deeply concerned about the danger to international peace and security created by the premeditated Israeli air attack on Iraqi nuclear installations on 7 June 1981, which could at any time explode the situation in the area, with grave consequences for the vital interests of all States,

Considering that, under the terms of Article 2, paragraph 4, of the Charter of the United Nations: ''All Members shall refrain in their international relations from the threat or use of force against the territorial integrity or political independence of any State, or in any other manner inconsistent with the purposes of the United Nations''.

1. *Strongly condemns* the military attack by Israel in clear violation of the Charter of the United Nations and the norms of international conduct;

2. *Calls upon* Israel to refrain in the future from any such acts or threats thereof;

3. *Further considers* that the said attack constitutes a serious threat to the entire safeguards régime of the International Atomic Energy Agency, which is the foundation of the Treaty on the Non-Proliferation of Nuclear Weapons;

4. *Fully recognizes* the inalienable sovereign right of Iraq, and all other States, especially the developing countries, to establish programmes of technological and nuclear development to develop their economy and industry for peaceful purposes in accordance with their present and future needs and consistent with the internationally accepted objectives of preventing nuclear-weapons proliferation;

5. *Calls upon* Israel urgently to place its nuclear facilities under the safeguards of the International Atomic Energy Agency;

---

[51] Adopted unanimously, June 19, 1981.

6. *Considers* that Iraq is entitled to appropriate redress for the destruction it has suffered, responsibility for which has been acknowledged by Israel.

7. *Requests* the Secretary-General to keep the Security Council regularly informed of the implementation of the present resolution.

NOTES

1) What was the relevance to this incident of the fact that Iraq, according to Mr. Blum, had been in a state of war with Israel since 1948?

2) In the Security Council debate,[52] Mr. Blum argued that the Israeli government had the right to protect the lives of Israeli citizens. In doing so it was exercising its inherent right under article 51 of the Charter. Note the following details provided by Mr. Blum: the strike was on a Sunday, late in the day and the loss in life was minimal. What is their relevance?

3) Why do you think the Security Council voted *unanimously* against Israel? Note that Iraq was a party to the Nuclear Non-Proliferation Treaty[53] and had accepted IAEA Safeguards. Israel had not. The United States through its ambassador, Mrs. Kirkpatrick, stated after the vote that the United States was of the view that the Israelis only violated the United Nations Charter because Israel had not exhausted peaceful means for the resolution of the dispute.[54] Note that the United States and Canada had voted against the IAEA Resolution.

4) The Canadian view on the legality of the "first strike" was presented in a memorandum of November 27th, 1981 from the Legal Bureau of the Department of External Affairs:[55]

The basic rules pertaining to the use of force by States are laid down in Art. 2(4) and Art. 51 of the United Nations Charter. The first one prohibits the use of force, including the threat of such use, against any State, whereas the second rule, as an exception to the first one, declares that every State has an "inherent right" to use force "if an armed attack occurs against" it. The use of armed force would thus appear confined to situations where it is necessary to repel actual aggression as defined by examples in Art. 3 of the U.N.G.A. resolution No. 2625 XXV of December 14, 1974. In all other circumstances States would have an obligation to resort to pacific means of settlement of international disputes according to Art. 2(3) and Chapter VI of the U.N. Charter, unless the U.N. Security Council decides otherwise.

It is, however, well known that modern weapons in possession of some States, much more powerful than others, as well as the exercise of the veto power within the U.N. Security Council, have both significantly modified the conditions in which resort could be made to the right of self-defence

---

[52] U.N. Doc. S/PV. 2280, June 12th, 1981, at 37-60.
[53] 729 U.N.T.S. 161.
[54] See U.N. Doc. S/PV. 2288, June 19th, 1981, at 58-73.
[55] (1982), 20 *Can. Y. B. Int. L.* 303.

based on Art. 51 of the Charter. In practical terms, no help would be expected by some States from the United Nations, while the use of rapid and all-destructive weapons leaves no room for awaiting of an attack, if the concept of self-defence is to serve its original purpose.

Some States and some writers are therefore favourable to that traditional concept (which fell from respect) that anticipatory self-defence is permissible under international law, although this view is vigorously disputed by others. In the opinion of the former, Art. 51 of the Charter cannot be interpreted so as to prevent a State from acting in its own defence. It would therefore be permitted to engage in an anticipatory "attack in self-defence" if:

– an armed aggression is imminent according to clear evidence based on the facts
– this armed aggression, if allowed to happen, might put in jeopardy the existence of the victim-State (as opposed to inflicting even serious damages).

The proof of the necessity of such self-preservation falls on the State that accomplishes the "first-strike" action. Such an occurrence would only be conceivable in the case of the small State, from the point of view of which no effective self-defence is possible after the moment of a massive armed attack by a more powerful neighbour or an over-whelming coalition of other States. This conclusion appears at least indirectly supported by the terms of Art. 2 of the aforementioned U.N.G.A. resolution on Definition of Aggression: "The first use of armed force by a State in contravention of the Charter shall constitute *prima facie* evidence of an act of aggression although the Security Council may, in conformity with the Charter, conclude that a determination that an act of aggression has been committed would not be justified in the light of other relevant circumstances ... .

5) Judge Schwebel, the United States judge on the International Court of Justice, stated in his dissenting opinion in the case concerning *Military Activities In and Against Nicaragua*[56] that he did not agree with construing Article 51 of the United Nations Charter as if it were worded: "Nothing in the present Charter shall impair the inherent right of individual or collective self-defence, if and only if, an armed attack occurs ...". He was of the view that the wording and intent of Article 51 do not eliminate the right of self-defence under customary international law or confine its overall scope to the expression of Article 51.

The Falklands/Malvinas Crisis[57]

The armed forces of Argentina invaded the Falkland Islands/Malvinas on April 2nd, 1982. On April 3rd, 1982, Argentina likewise took by armed force the island of South Georgia. The small British military contingents in both places surrendered after some fighting had taken place. Argentina claimed that it had sovereignty over these islands. See Chapter 6 on State Jurisdiction over Territory for a full discussion of title to territory. The President

---

[56] [1986] I.C.J. Rep. 14, at 347.
[57] See Fawcett in A. Pearce, ed., *The Falkland Islands Dispute: International Diversions* (1982), at 5; R. Perl, *The Falkland Islands Dispute in International Law and Politics* (1983); T.M. Franck, "Comments" (1983), 77 *Am. J. Int. L.* 109.

of the Security Council had called upon Argentina and the United Kingdom on April 1st to refrain from the use of force or threat of force in the region.[58] On April 3rd, after the actions of Argentina, the Security Council adopted Resolution 502 (1982)[59], by which it determined a breach of the peace existed and demanded the immediate cessation of hostilities followed by the immediate withdrawal of all Argentine forces. The resolution also called on the two governments to settle their differences diplomatically and to respect the principles of the U.N. Charter. A British Task Force sailed for the Falklands/Malvinas on April 25th, 1982. It landed in the Falklands/Malvinas on May 21st, 1982 after diplomatic efforts had failed to achieve results. On June 14th, 1982 the Argentine forces surrendered.

NOTES

1) In the debates in the Security Council[60] Mr. Roca, on behalf of Argentina, claimed that his government had proclaimed the recovery of its national sovereignty over the islands and was acting in self-defense to acts of aggression by the United Kingdom. It is difficult to establish what their acts of aggression were. The only two possibilities are:
- (a) The British action in 1833 when Britain decided to reassert their claims to the Falklands and sent a warship "Clio" there. The Argentine garrison of 50 men was ordered to leave and the Union Jack hoisted.
- (b) An incident on south Georgia island in March 1982 in which employees of an Argentine scrap metal company landed on the island and having hoisted the Argentine flag were asked to obtain landing permission by the British Government. The Argentine Government refused. This question was not resolved before April 2nd, 1982.

2) On what basis could the United Kingdom claim to be acting in self-defense? If the Argentine taking of the islands was illegal, was its occupation illegal? See the 1970 Declaration on Principles of International Law,[61] which states that "the territory of a State shall not be the object of military occupation resulting from the use of force in contravention of the Charter." Was the Argentine occupation contrary to Resolution 502? Sir Anthony Parsons, the U.K. Ambassador to the United Nations argued that the United Kingdom was fully entitled to take measures pursuant to article 51 of the Charter as Argentina had not complied with Resolution 502 by withdrawing its forces. On account of this non-compliance, was a breach of the peace therefore still subsisting? Argentina argued, *inter alia*, that the adoption of Resolution 502 amounted to the Security Council taking "measures necessary to maintain international peace and security" and therefore,

---

[58] UN. Doc. S/PV. 2345, at 33.
[59] Reprinted in (1982), 21 *Int. Leg. Mat.* 679. This resolution was adopted by 10 votes in favour (France, Guyana, Ireland, Japan, Jordan, Togo, Uganda, U.K., U.S.A., Zaire) to 1 against (Panama) with 4 abstentions (China, Poland, Spain and U.S.S.R.).
[60] U.N. Doc. S/PV. 2346, at 6-7.
[61] *Supra*.

there is an obligation under article 51 to suspend any self-defence action. Would this be an aggressor's licence?

3) Resolution 502 was adopted under article 40 of the United Nations Charter. This is important as, had the resolution been adopted under Chapter VI or under article 52(3), the United Kingdom would have been obligated by article 27(3) of the United Nations Charter to abstain from voting.

4) Was it an act of self-defense by the United Kingdom when, on May 2nd, 1982, a British Submarine sank the Argentine Cruiser, the General Belgrano, just beyond the 200 mile exclusion zone around the islands which had been declared by the British Government?

Self-Defense of Nationals

As with pre-emptive self-defense, this excuse for intervention raises questions as to the interpretation of article 51 of the United Nations Charter. Is a state justified in taking self-help measures to protect its nationals if they are in imminent danger? Must all peaceful avenues first have been exhausted?

The Entebbe Raid[62]

[On June 28, 1976, after a stop-over in Athens, an Air France airplane, with over 250 passengers and 12 crew en route from Israel to France was hijacked by terrorists. The airplane was forced to land at Benghazi, Libya and then finally at Entebbe Airport, Uganda. The hijackers, acting on behalf of the Popular Front for the Liberation of Palestine, demanded the release of about 153 terrorists imprisoned in France, Israel, Kenya, Switzerland and West Germany. On June 30, 1976, they set free 47 passengers who were not Israeli citizens. The next day they freed an additional one hundred. The other 104 passengers and crew remained at Entebbe until rescued by an Israeli military commando unit on July 3, 1976, which then flew them to Israel. The reports following the rescue indicated that 3 hostages, 1 Israeli soldier, 7 of the hijackers and a number of Ugandan soldiers were killed. Opinions conflicted at the time as to whether the Ugandan government had tried to protect the hostages and negotiate their release or whether it had been collaborating with the hijackers.

The Security Council debated the incident without reaching any definite conclusion. The following excerpts from the Security Council's debate exposes the contending characterizations of the Israeli action:]

MR. HERZOG (Israel):[63] ... Uganda violated a basic tenet of international law in failing to protect foreign nationals on its territory. Furthermore, it behaved in a manner which constituted a gross violation of the 1970 Hague Convention on the Suppression of

---

[62] See L.C. Green, "Rescue at Entebbe – Legal Aspects" (1976), 6 *Israel Yearbook on Human Rights* 312; L.M. Salter, "Commando Coup at Entebbe: Humanitarian Intervention or Barbaric Aggression?" (1977), 11 *Int. Law.* 331.

[63] U.N. Doc. S/PV. 1939, July 9, 1976, at 51-59, reprinted in (1976), 15 *Int. Leg. Mat.* at 1228.

Unlawful Seizure of Aircraft. This Convention had been ratified by both Israel and Uganda. [See Chapter 8 for this Convention.]

... The right of a State to take military action to protect its nationals in mortal danger is recognized by all legal authorities in international law. In Self-Defence in International Law, Professor Bowett states, on page 87, that "The right of the State to intervene by the use or threat of force for the protection of its nationals suffering injuries within the territory of another State is generally admitted, both in the writings of jurists and in the practice of States. In the arbitration between Great Britain and Spain in 1925, one of the series known as the Spanish Moroccan claims, Judge Huber, as Rapporteur of the Commission, stated:

However, it cannot be denied that at a certain point the interest of a State in exercising protection over its nationals and their property can take precedence over territorial sovereignty, despite the absence of any conventional provisions. This right of intervention has been claimed by all States. Only its limits are disputed. We now envisage action by the protecting State which involves a *prima facie* violation of the independence and territorial inviolability of the territorial State. In so far as this action takes effect in derogation of the sovereignty of the territorial States, it must necessarily be exceptional in character and limited to those cases in which no other means of protection are available. It presupposes the inadequacy of any other means of protection against some injury, actual or imminent, to the persons or property of nations and, moreover, an injury which results either from the acts of the territorial State and its authorities or from the acts of individuals or groups of individuals which the territorial State is unable, or unwilling, to prevent.

In the *Law of Nations*, Sixth Edition, page 627, Brierly states as follows:

Whether the landing of detachments of troops to save the lives of nationals under imminent threat of death or serious injury owing to the breakdown of law and order may be justifiable is a delicate question. Cases of this form of intervention have been not infrequent in the past and, when not attended by suspicion of being a pretext for political pressure, have generally been regarded as justified by the sheer necessity of instant action to save the lives of innocent nationals whom the local government is unable or unwilling to protect.

He goes on to observe that:

Every effort must be made to get the United Nations to act. But, if the United Nations is not in a position to move in time and the need for instant action is manifest it would be difficult to deny the legitimacy of action in defence of nationals which every responsible Government would feel bound to take if it had the means to do so. This is, of course, on the basis that the action was strictly limited to securing the safe removal of the threatened national.

In support of this contention, O'Connell states in *International Law*, Second Edition, at 303:

... Article 2(4) of the United Nations Charter should be interpreted as prohibiting acts of force against the territorial integrity and political independence of nations, and not to prohibit a use of force which is limited in intention and effect to the protection of a State's own integrity and its nationals' vital interests, when the machinery envisaged by the United Nations Charter is ineffective in the situation.

The act of hijacking can well be regarded as one of piracy. Pirates have been *hostis humani generis* – enemies of the human race – since the early days of international law in the Middle Ages. During the war against the slave trade and piracy, certain norms were established in international law which permitted intervention in case of ships engaged in slave trade between Africa and America and against the centres of piracy in North Africa. The principle of national sovereignty was overruled by the higher principles of man's liberty

... The right of self-defence is enshrined in international law and in the Charter of the United Nations and can be applied on the basis of the classic formulation, as was done in the well-known Caroline Case ... . That was exactly the situation which faced the Government of Israel.

... What mattered to the Government of Israel in this instance was the lives of the hostages, in danger of their very lives. No consideration other than this humanitarian consideration motivated the Government of Israel. Israel's rescue operation was not directed against Uganda. Israeli forces were not attacking Uganda – and they were certainly not attacking Africa. They were rescuing their nationals from a band of terrorists and kidnappers who were being aided and abetted by the Ugandan authorities. The means used were the minimum necessary to fulfil that purpose, as is laid down in international law.

Some parallels could be drawn with the right of an individual to use appropriate means to defend himself if he kills someone who is trying to kill him. He is not liable to be found guilty of murder. Judgment takes into account the context and the purpose of the act. The same applies to the use of force in international affairs.

MR. OYONO (United Republic of Cameroon):[64] ... Israel took the initiative of attacking the territory of Uganda – a sovereign State separated from Israel by more than 3,000 kilometers – with commandos from its regular army, airlifted by three military planes. In so doing, Israel deliberately initiated hostilities against Uganda and for that reason is the aggressor in this affair, as defined by international law.

The Security Council, which is responsible for international peace and security, must vigorously condemn this barbaric act which constitutes a flagrant violation of the norms of international law and flouts the spirit and letter of the United Nations Charter, Article 2, paragraph 4 ... .

In the spirit of the Charter, that prohibition means that Member States have an obligation to settle their international disputes by peaceful means in order to maintain international peace and security. I need hardly remind you that our Organization is not dedicated to anarchy or to the notion that might makes right, but is an organized community whose

---

[64] *Supra*, n. 48, at 92.

mutually accepted principles and rules must be scrupulously respected, and their violation adequately punished.

It is the corner-stone of our Organization that there can be no justification for the use of force against the sovereignty, independence or territorial integrity of a State, unless we wish to imperil international co-operation in its present form and indeed the very existence of States that do not yet possess modern, sophisticated systems of detection and deterrence.

MR. SCRANTON (United States):[65] ... Israel's action in rescuing the hostages necessarily involved a temporary breach of the territorial integrity of Uganda. Normally, such a breach would be impermissible under the Charter of the United Nations. However, there is a well established right to use limited force for the protection of one's own nationals from an imminent threat of injury or death in a situation where the State in whose territory they are located is either unwilling or unable to protect them. The right, flowing from the right of self-defence, is limited to such use of force as is necessary and appropriate to protect threatened nationals from injury.

The requirements of this right to protect nationals were clearly met in the Entebbe case. Israel had good reason to believe that at the time it acted Israeli nationals were in imminent danger of execution by the hijackers. Moreover, the actions necessary to release the Israel nationals or to prevent substantial loss of Israeli lives had not been taken by the Government of Uganda, nor was there a reasonable expectation such actions would be taken. In fact, there is substantial evidence that the Government of Uganda co-operated with and aided the hijackers. A number of the released hostages have publicly related how the Ugandan authorities allowed several additional terrorists to reinforce the original group after the plane landed, permitted them to receive additional arms and additional explosives, participated in guarding the hostages and, according to some accounts, even took over sole custody of some or all of the passengers to allow the hijackers to rest. The ease and success of the Israeli effort to free the hostages further suggests that the Ugandan authorities could have overpowered the hijackers and released the hostages if they had really had the desire to do so.

The apparent support given to the hijackers by the Ugandan authorities causes us to question whether Uganda lived up to its international legal obligations under the Hague Convention. The rights of a State carry with them important responsibilities which were not met by Uganda in this case. The Israeli military action was limited to the sole objective of extricating the passengers and crew and terminated when that objective was accomplished. The force employed was limited to what was necessary for the rescue of the passengers and crew.

That Israel might have secured the release of its nationals by complying with the terrorists' demands does not alter these conclusions. No State is required to yield control over persons in lawful custody in its territory under criminal charges. Moreover, it would be a self-defeating and dangerous policy to release prisoners, convicted in some cases of earlier acts of terrorism, in order to accede to the demands of terrorists.

---

[65] U.N. Doc. S/PV. 1941, July 12, 1976, reprinted in (1976), 15 *Int. Leg. Mat.* 1232.

It should be emphasized that this assessment of the legality of Israeli actions depends heavily on the unusual circumstances of this specific case. In particular, the evidence is strong that, given the attitude of the Ugandan authorities, co-operation with or reliance on them in rescuing the passengers and crew was impracticable. It is to be hoped that these unique circumstances will not arise in the future.

NOTES

1) This excuse for intervention is open to abuse unless safeguarded by certain pre-requisite conditions. What should they be? Is there any basis for this excuse in the U.N. Charter? What arguments can be made to support the view that such action is not contrary to article 2(4) of the Charter? Could a state exercise the justification to protect its nationals' property abroad, rather than their lives?

2) The *U.S. Diplomatic and Consular Staff in Tehran Case*[66] concerned Iran's responsibility to the United States for certain American hostages. In addition to the case, the United States also made an unsuccessful attempt to rescue the hostages. The World Court did not rule on this action. Could the United States claim that its intervention was a legitimate act of self-defense of its nationals?

TYPES OF STATES

The internal organizational arrangements of states are many and varied. They include unitary and confederal states as well as less than sovereign units, such as protectorates, dependencies and colonies. Apart from the stereotype unitary state, the two most important configurations in international affairs today are the federal state and the mandated or trust territory, specifically Namibia.

Federal States[67]
from S.A. Williams and A.L.C. de Mestral, *An Introduction to International Law* (2ed., 1987), at 53-54

The most important composite state today is the federation. This is a union of two or more units comprising a federal political unit and numerous internal political units. No doubt exists that a federal state enjoys international personality in the same manner as a unitary state. Important federal states of the world such as Australia, Brazil, Canada, the Federal Republic of Germany and the United States have always been accorded full international personality despite the fact that the central authorities do not necessarily exercise all the sovereign legislative powers within their respective territories. The problem

---

[66] [1979] I.C.J. Rep. 23, reproduced in Chapter 5 in the section on Diplomatic Immunities.
[67] See I. Bernier, *International Legal Aspects of Federalism* (1973).

lies with standing and powers of the constituent units of a federal state on the international level. Some federations such as Australia and the United States vest exclusive authority over the conduct of external affairs in the federal authority and hence appear to preclude any role to the constituent unit. Some others such as the Federal Republic of Germany and the Swiss Confederation grant limited treaty making powers to their constituent units. The U.S.S.R., upon entry to the United Nations insisted upon separate seats for the Byelorussian and the Ukrainian Socialist Republics. Does this imply that the constituent units of a federation can also be subjects of international law?

The leading authorities on international law are almost equally divided on this issue[68] and leading textbooks in many countries take different positions. This divergence of views was particularly evident in the debates of the International Law Commission during preparation of the draft on the law of treaties. Powerful arguments exist against according any capacity under international law to the constituent units of federal states. Divergent policies on such questions as recognition of foreign states would lead to insuperable, political and legal deadlock, and divergent policies on matters such as cultural or economic relations would create great strains upon any federation. The greatest fear is that direct relations between the constituent units and foreign states could herald the disintegration of the federation itself. On the other hand, if constituent units are to have full exercise of their powers, it appears arbitrary and impractical to deny them any international dimensions. Since today there are few governmental legislative and executive acts that have no international impact in an increasingly interdependent world, any local government which is active in cultural, social and economic issues will resent being forced to go through the central authority for all contacts with foreign governments.

The Vienna Conference meeting to adopt a multilateral Convention on the Law of Treaties failed to resolve this issue. At the behest of many federations, including Canada, the conference rejected a clause which would have granted explicit recognition to the treaty-making capacity of constituent units of federal states. In the absence of a clear treaty rule customary law governs. At present customary international law does not accept that constituent units can be treated fully as states but does allow them some limited treaty-making capacity.

[For a discussion of the conduct of external affairs in Canada, in particular the power to conclude treaties, see Chapter 3. The evolution of Canada into an independent federal state is described in the following essay by Professor Max Cohen.]

Canada and the International Legal Order: An Inside Perspective
by M. Cohen in R. St. J. Macdonald, G.L. Morris and D.M. Johnston eds., *Canadian Perspectives on International Law and Organization* (1974), at 3-8

In a sense Canadian experience with the international legal order is part of the very beginnings of Canada itself. Conquest, war-making, treaty law, and the rights of a new

---

[68] See P. Painchaud, ed., *Le Canada et le Quebec sur la scène internationale* (1977), at 520-24.

subject people related to a grand imperial-colonial design marked the beginnings of the experiment that was to become Canada. In a curious way the 'victories' of 1759 and 1760, the proclamations establishing the new imperial government, and the Treaty of Paris of 1763 all laid the foundations for what was then in fact a united, continental British North America, except for Spanish claims largely in the southern and southwestern territories and the Russian presence on the Alaska mainland for another century. But within less than two decades, in 1783, another Treaty of Paris climaxed the revolution of 1776, and British North America's ambitions now were split between a 'loyal' north and the rebellious south – the independent Thirteen, now the United States of America. Revolution, war, and new boundaries had reshaped the British North American remnant, infusing it with a deep and lasting imprint so that, in a sense, the creation of the components that one day were to become an independent Canada had first to be defined by an international legal settlement, itself the product of revolt, war, and dissolution of the first British Empire to be quickly replaced by the second.

Hence it may be said that Canada was sired in warfare, mothered in treaties, and nurtured in the delicate crèche of both imperial constitutional relations and international law as they were in the latter eighteenth century. To this day the most urgent and powerful concerns of Canadian policy, for its growth and identity, are an evolutionary reflection of these fractured imperial beginnings. Canada's boundaries were not made final until as late as the Alaska Panhandle dispute of 1903, and a continuing anxiety exists for the management of a society and an economy where the pull of continental integration was always to parallel the stress of searching for national self-definition and political autonomy. No one could have foreseen in 1776 or 1783 that the new, independent English-speaking United States would grow so rapidly as to overshadow quickly the imperial remnant to the north and create by these geopolitical facts the permanent crisis in Canadian life; namely, its development beside an immense neighbour who would outstrip Canada in everything, perhaps, but the determination to achieve an integrity of its own. It is no surprise, therefore, that the long-term Canadian international experience *par excellence*, and the concomitant political – legal preoccupation, should have been the form and substance for managing Canadian relations with the United States; and this remains true to the present day.

Yet side by side with these continental parameters, imposed by geography, politics, and law on an emerging Canada, there was an almost equally important school for that 'emergence' in the shift from Empire to Commonwealth. The dominant role played by the position of Canada in the evolution of the second British Empire, and its transformation in the latter half of the nineteenth century and the first quarter of the twentieth into the Commonwealth, proved to be a double training ground of paramount significance. For at one and the same time the movement from "colony to nation" required a search for political and "constitutional" solutions within the imperial system which slowly transformed dependence to independence for those British North American communites that remained outside the United States solution of 1783. That process trained Canadians to obtain in peace what their revolutionary cousins in the United States sought and only realized with war: responsible government, representative and essentially independent in the management of local life from a centralized, distant imperial control ...

If the Commonwealth was the "original" school for Canadian nationhood and for evolving international personality, it was the United States that gave Canada its first taste of learning to live in the severe world of realpolitik where bilateral dealings with an immensely powerful neighbour were the basic geopolitical facts of life for Canada. It is no surprise, therefore, that some of the most important and creative international legal experiences for Canada have emerged from its almost two centuries of dealings with the sometime imperial brothers who went their own national way. Tariffs (and reciprocity agreements), boundaries, boundary waters, fisheries, immigration, and joint obligations to native peoples were all a product of the nineteenth-century process of Canada learning to live successfully with the United States. "Continentalism," no popular word today, was nevertheless destiny for both, and many legal arrangements were mirrors of that shared reality.

The twentieth century multiplied the interpenetration of the two societies, accentuated by two world wars and the military-economic-political co-operation to which these led. And so a complex regulatory network evidenced by instruments ranging from a simple exchange of notes to formal treaties marked the era of expanding involvement – in defence production, west coast fisheries, post-World War II military policy for the continent, resource development with the emphasis on mineral, petroleum, forest products, the energy demands from the United States (from the Columbia River Treaty to natural gas exports), and the St. Lawrence Seaway. More recently contradictory trends have emerged such as the new limits on immigration and restrictive economic policies side by side with an immense common obligation to refresh the Great Lakes system from joint pollution over many years. Some interesting case law, through the arbitral process in one form or another, has come out of these relations, albeit infrequently. "Hot pursuit" in the *I'm Alone*, poisonous fumes from the *Trail Smelter*, and the flooding of recreational shorelines by *Gut Dam* have resulted in doctrines and footnotes uniquely North American in their origin but perhaps universal in their significance. This is certainly true for the *Trail Smelter* case, the first transnational air pollution dispute to invite arbitration and become a precedent … .

Hence, while it is true that responsible government and essential autonomy were *de facto* true by the third or fourth quarter of the nineteenth century, there were a number of imperial threads still tying the robust Canadian image to the "Mother Country." Good illustrations of this mixture of the imperial-Commonwealth procedures, and their effect on clear international personality as such, may be seen in the powers of the governor general, perhaps until 1947; the pre-World War I appointment of the commander in chief of the Canadian forces from among imperial officers, particularly the royal family; the disputes over the Canadian contribution to and management of its forces in the Boer War; the controversy over Canadian naval policy in the first years of the twentieth century; and the crucial role for image and fact of sovereignty or independence played by military issues in World War I, since the independence of the Canadian Corps and the determination to have a separate identity for that corps had important psychological and political consequences. They probably influenced the legal-political decision for Canada to be a separate 'signatory' (through initials at least) to the Treaty of Versailles. And when to these events are added the Commonwealth conferences of 1926 and 1930 and the Balfour Resolution in 1926, climaxed by the Statute of Westminster in 1931, and the abolition of criminal appeals to the Judicial Committee in the same year – to which should be added the establishment of the Department of External Affairs as a working organism in 1928 (although the department itself was created in 1909), along with the Canadian treaty series – it is obvious how intermixed were the growth lines of a sovereign independent Canada with the evolutionary patterns of the Commonwealth itself.

World War II virtually destroyed any pretensions of "automatic" political or military response to the policies of the United Kingdom or any juridical theories of "subordination." The insistence on a separate Canadian declaration of war on 9 September 1939, the determined position of the government with respect to status and command of Canadian troops, and the special case of the Royal Canadian Air Force, and even the insistent claims to independence for the Royal Canadian Navy were all part of the final erosion of umbilical links to London – as if the reality had not already been forecast by World War I, the Chanak incident over Turkey, and Canadian behaviour generally in the League of Nations and in the multilateral world of the interwar years. What became clear, however, was that the political, military, and legal fading of authority from United Kingdom, imperial-Commonwealth sources was being replaced by the voluntary alliances of the NATO-NORAD system and this, in effect, provided the primary focus of the new struggle for independence *de facto* if not *de jure*, together with economic questions to be turned now towards the American neighbour and away from the imperial "mother." But unlike the Commonwealth story, there were no historical-juridical anomalies to be resolved. United States-Canadian relations have been a case of bilateral dealings between sovereign equals on a plane of majestic inequality.

Mandated and Trust Territories
from S.A. Williams and A.L.C. de Mestral, *An Introduction to International Law* (2 ed., 1987), at 55

In 1919-1920 under the League of Nations (the predecessor of the United Nations) the Mandate System was instituted. This system (or experiment as it was called) was supposed to deal with the problem of former enemy territories which were unable to govern themselves. These former colonies were therefore given under a mandate to allied states which were to administer them under the guidance of the League of Nations. The terms of each mandate were worked out between the League and the mandatory state.

After the Second World War and the birth of the United Nations in 1945, a new system was introduced to deal with "trust territories". These included the old mandated territories, territories taken from the enemy in the Second World War and territories surrendered voluntarily by those states responsible for them. The League territories were never formally transferred to the new system after the League mandate system ended in 1946, and many, such as Israel, Jordan, Lebanon, Syria and Iraq had or were on the point of independence, and it was thought that the others would be voluntarily placed under the trust system. South Africa did not, however, place South West Africa (Namibia) under the authority of the United Nations.

The supervision of the trust territories has been carried out by the Trusteeship Council of the United Nations. Today, with the exception of the Pacific Islands which have a special title of a "strategic trust" area and are administered by the United States under the supervision of the Security Council there is no trust territory left. The last one to gain independence was New Guinea in 1976. The states which administered the mandated and trust territories did not have sovereignty over them. Where the sovereignty did lie is a question of only academic interest since all but the two special cases of the Pacific Islands and Namibia have been settled. As one writer puts it, "there is much to be said for the view that sovereignty resided latently in the peoples themselves."[69]

Covenant of the League of Nations

Article 22

To those colonies and territories which as a consequence of the late war have ceased to be under the sovereignty of the States which formerly governed them and which are inhabited by peoples not yet able to stand by themselves under the strenuous conditions of the modern world, there should be applied the principle that the well-being and development of such peoples form a sacred trust of civilization and that securities for the performance of this trust should be embodied in this Covenant.

The best method of giving practical effect to this principle is that the tutelage of such peoples should be entrusted to advanced nations who by reason of their resources, their experience or their geographical position can best undertake this responsibility, and who are willing to accept it, and that this tutelage should be exercised by them as Mandatories on behalf of the League.

Charter of the United Nations

Read Articles 73-91 in the Appendix.

General Assembly Resolution 2145 on South West Africa
October 27, 1966, 21 U.N. GAOR, Supp. (No. 16) 2

The General Assembly

1. *Reaffirms* that the provisions of General Assembly resolution 1514 (XV) are fully applicable to the people of the Mandated Territory of South West Africa and that, therefore, the people of South West Africa have the inalienable right to self-determination, freedom and independence in accordance with the Charter of the United Nations;

2. *Reaffirms* further that South West Africa is a territory having international status and that it shall maintain this status until it achieves independence;

3. *Declares* that South Africa has failed to fulfil its obligations in respect of the administration of the Mandated Territory and to ensure the moral and material well-being

---

[69] J.G. Starke, *Introduction to International Law*, (9 ed. 1984), at 116.

and security of the indigenous inhabitants of South West Africa and has, in fact, disavowed the Mandate;

4. *Decides* that the Mandate conferred upon His Britannic Majesty to be exercised on his behalf by the Government of the Union of South Africa is therefore terminated, that South Africa has no other right to administer the Territory and that henceforth South West Africa comes under the direct responsibility of the United Nations;

5. *Resolves* that in these circumstances the United Nations must discharge those responsibilities with respect to South West Africa; ...

Namibia Case[70]
Adv. Op. [1971] I.C.J. Rep. 16

[Following Resolution 2145 (XXI) *supra*, in which the General Assembly terminated South Africa's mandate, the Security Council called upon South Africa to withdraw from Namibia.[71] South Africa failed to do this and so the Security Council passed resolution 276(1970) in which it declared South Africa's presence in Namibia was illegal and its actions there were invalid. The Security Council further requested an advisory opinion from the International Court on the question: "What are the legal consequences for states of the continued presence of South Africa in Namibia, notwithstanding Security Council Resolution 276 (1970)?" The Court first confirmed its earlier opinions that the mandate had survived the collapse of the League of Nations and had been brought into the United Nations system. It then proceeded to discuss the effects of the United Nations' actions, beginning with General Assembly resolution 2145.]

THE COURT: ...

94. In examining this action of the General Assembly it is appropriate to have regard to the general principles of international law regulating termination of a treaty relationship on account of breach. For even if the mandate is viewed as having the character of an institution, as is maintained, it depends on those international agreements which created the system and regulated its application. As the Court indicated in 1962 "this Mandate, like practically all other similar Mandates" was "a special type of instrument composite in nature and instituting a novel international régime. It incorporates a definite agreement ..." (I.C.J. Reports 1962, at 331). The Court stated conclusively in that Judgment that the Mandate "... in fact and in law, is an international agreement having the character of a treaty or convention" (I.C.J. Reports 1952 at 330). The rules laid down by the Vienna Convention on the Law of Treaties concerning termination of a treaty relationship on account of breach (adopted without a dissenting vote) may in many respects be considered as a codification of existing customary law on the subject. In the light of these

---

[70] See I. Sagay, *The Legal Aspects of the Namibian Dispute* (1975); and Lejeune, *The Case for South West Africa* (1971).

[71] South West Africa was renamed Namibia by G.A. Res. 2372 (XXII), 22 U.N. GAOR, Supp. (No. 16A) (1968).

rules, only a material breach of a treaty justifies termination, such breach being defined as:

    (a) a repudiation of the treaty not sanctioned by the present Convention; or

    (b) the violation of a provision essential to the accomplishment of the object or purpose of the treaty (Art. 60, para. 3).

95. General Assembly resolution 2145 (XXI) determines that both forms of material breach had occurred in this case. By stressing that South Africa "has in fact, disavowed the Mandate", the General Assembly declared in fact that it had repudiated it. The resolution in question is therefore to be viewed as the exercise of the right to terminate a relationship in case of a deliberate and persistent violation of obligations which destroys the very object and purpose of that relationship.

96. It has been contended that the Covenant of the League of Nations did not confer on the Council of the League power to terminate a mandate for misconduct of the mandatory and that no such power could therefore be exercised by the United Nations, since it could not derive from the League greater powers that the latter itself had. For this objection to prevail it would be necessary to show that the mandates system, as established under the League, excluded the application of the general principle of law that a right of termination on account of breach must be presumed to exist in respect of all treaties, except as regards provisions relating to the protection of the human person contained in treaties of a humanitarian character (as indicated in Art. 60, para. 5, of the Vienna Convention). The silence of a treaty as to the existence of such a right cannot be interpreted as implying the exclusion of a right which has its source outside of the treaty, in general international law, and is dependent on the occurrence of circumstances which are not normally envisaged when a treaty is concluded. ...

102. In a further objection to General Assembly resolution 2145 (XXI) it is contended that it made pronouncements which the Assembly, not being a judicial organ, and not having previously referred the matter to any such organ, was not competent to make. Without dwelling on the conclusions reached in the 1966 Judgment in the South West Africa contentious cases, it is worth recalling that in those cases the applicant States, which complained of material breaches of substantive provisions of the Mandate, were held not to "possess any separate self-contained right which they could assert ... to require the due performance of the Mandate in discharge of the 'sacred trust'" (I.C.J. Reports 1966, at 29 and 51). On the other hand, the Court declared that: " ... any divergences of view concerning the conduct of a mandate were regarded as being matters that had their place in the political field, the settlement of which lay between the mandatory and the competent organs of the League" (ibid., at 45). To deny to a political organ of the United Nations which is a successor of the League in this respect the right to act, on the argument that it lacks competence to render what is described as a judicial decision, would not only be inconsistent but would amount to a complete denial of the remedies available against fundamental breaches of an international undertaking.

103. The Court is unable to appreciate the view that the General Assembly acted unilaterally as party and judge in its own cause. In the 1966 Judgment in the South West Africa Cases, referred to above, it was found that the function to call for the due execution of the relevant provisions of the mandate instruments appertained to the League acting as an entity through its appropriate organs. The right of the League "in the pursuit of its collective, institutional activity, to require the due performance of the Mandate in discharge of the 'sacred trust','' was specifically recognized (ibid., at 29). Having regard to this finding, the United Nations as a successor to the League, acting through its competent organs, must be seen above all as the supervisory institution, competent to pronounce, in that capacity, on the conduct of the mandatory with respect to its international obligations, and competent to act accordingly ... .

105. General Assembly resolution 2145 (XXI), after declaring the termination of the Mandate, added in operative paragraph 4 ''that South Africa has no other right to administer the Territory''. This part of the resolution has been objected to as deciding a transfer of territory. That in fact is not so. The pronouncement made by the General Assembly is based on a conclusion, referred to earlier, reached by the Court in 1950:

The authority which the Union Government exercises over the Territory is based on the Mandate. If the Mandate lapsed, as the Union Government contends, the latter's authority would equally have lapsed. (I.C.J. Reports 1950, at 133.)

This was confirmed by the Court in its Judgment of 21 December 1962 in the South West Africa Cases (Ethiopia v. South Africa; Liberia v. South Africa) (I.C.J. Reports 1962, at 333). Relying on these decisions of the Court, the General Assembly declared that the Mandate having been terminated ''South Africa has no other right to administer the Territory''. This is not a finding on facts, but the formulation of a legal situation. For it would not be correct to assume that, because the General Assembly is in principle vested with recommendatory powers, it is debarred from adopting, in specific cases within the framework of its competence, resolutions which make determinations or have operative design.

106. By resolution 2145 (XXI) the General Assembly terminated the Mandate. However, lacking the necessary powers to ensure the withdrawal of South Africa from the Territory, it enlisted the co-operation of the Security Council by calling the latter's attention to the resolution, thus acting in accordance with Article 11, paragraph 2, of the Charter. ...

108. Resolution 264 (1969) [of the Security Council], in paragraph 3 of its operative part, calls upon South Africa to withdraw its administration from Namibia immediately. Resolution 269 (1969), in view of South Africa's lack of compliance, after recalling the obligations of Members under Article 25 of the Charter, calls upon the Government of South Africa, in paragraph 5 of its operative part, ''to withdraw its administration from the territory immediately and in any case before 4 October 1969.'' The preamble of resolution 276 (1970) reaffirms General Assembly resolution 2145 (XXI) and espouses it, by referring to the decision, not merely of the General Assembly, but of the United Nations ''that the Mandate of South-West Africa was terminated.'' In the operative part, after condemning the non-compliance by South Africa with General Assembly and Security Council resolutions pertaining to Namibia, the Security Council declares, in paragraph 2, that ''the continued presence of the South African authorities in Namibia is illegal'' and that consequently all acts taken by the Government of South Africa ''on behalf of or concerning Namibia after the termination of the Mandate are illegal and invalid.'' In paragraph 5 the Security Council ''Calls upon all States, particularly those which have economic and other interests in Namibia, to refrain from any dealings with the Government of South Africa which are inconsistent with operative paragraph 2 of this resolution.''

109. ... The Security Council, when it adopted these resolutions, was acting in the exercise of what it deemed to be its primary responsibility, the maintenance of peace and security, which, under the Charter, embraces situations which might lead to a breach of the peace. (Art. 1, para. 1.) In the preamble of resolution 264 (1969) the Security Council was ''Mindful of the grave consequences of South Africa's continued occupation of Namibia'' and in paragraph 4 of that resolution it declared ''that the actions of the Government of South Africa designed to destroy the national unity and territorial integrity of Namibia through the establishment of Bantustans are contrary to the provisions of the United Nations Charter.'' In operative paragraph 3 of resolution 269 (1969) the Security Council decided ''that the continued occupation of the territory of Namibia by the South African authorities constitutes an aggressive encroachment on the authority of the United Nations, ...'' In operative paragraph 3 of resolution 276 (1970) the Security Council declared further ''that the defiant attitude of the Government of South Africa towards the Council's decisions undermines the authority of the United Nations.''

110. As to the legal basis of the resolution, Article 24 of the Charter vests in the Security Council the necessary authority to take action such as that taken in the present case. The reference in paragraph 2 of this Article to specific powers of the Security Council under certain chapters of the Charter does not exclude the existence of general powers to discharge the responsibilities conferred in paragraph 1. Reference may be made in this respect to the Secretary-General's Statement, presented to the Security Council on 10 January, 1947, to the effect that ''the powers of the Council under Article 24 are not restricted to the specific grants of authority contained in Chapters VI, VII, VIII and XI ... the Members of the United Nations have conferred upon the Security Council powers commensurate with its responsibility for the maintenance of peace and security. The only limitations are the fundamental principles and purposes found in Chapter I of the Charter.''

111. As to the effect to be attributed to the declaration contained in paragraph 2 of resolution 276 (1970), the Court considers that the qualification of a situation as illegal does not by itself put an end to it. It can only be the first, necessary step in an endeavour to bring the illegal situation to an end.

112. It would be an untenable interpretation to maintain that, once such a declaration had been made by the Security Council under Article 24 of the Charter, on behalf of all member States, those Members would be free to act in disregard of such illegality or even to recognize violations of law resulting from it. When confronted with such an internationally unlawful situation, Members of the United Nations would be expected to act in consequence of the declaration made on their behalf. The question therefore arises as to the effect of this decision of the Security Council for States Members of the United Nations in accordance with Article 25 of the Charter.

113. It has been contended that Article 25 of the Charter applies only to enforcement measures adopted under Chapter VII of the Charter. It is not possible to find in the Charter any support for this view. Article 25 is not confined to decisions in regard to enforcement action but applies to ''the decisions of the Security Council'' adopted in accordance with

3) Refer also to the fifth principle of the Declaration on Principles of International Law, reported in the section above, and to Article 7 of the Definition of Aggression, reported above. In the light of all these materials, can it be said that the principle of self-determination is now opposable to all states? Does it refer only to peoples in colonial or neo-colonial situations or under regimes of apartheid? Do the newly independent states wish to keep the old colonial boundaries intact? Does Resolution 1514 (1960) seek to do this?

4) What is meant by "self-determination"? Refer to all the U.N. resolutions and the *Western Sahara Case*, reported below. What forms may self-determination take? For instance, does it include the possibility of independence for a people, apart from colonial situations?

5) In 1980 the possibility of inserting the right of self-determination into the Canadian constitution was debated but not maintained. The 1985 *Draft Agreement on the Constitution* proposal by the Quebec government does not propose self-determination but rather explicit recognition of the existence of a people of Quebec. It also specifies that the division of powers in Canada under the Constitution needs amendment to take into proper consideration the needs of Quebec. The Inuit and the Indians of Canada have also made various claims for distinctive status and autonomy. What support can they find for their claims in the principle of self-determination?

6) Has the idea of self-determination yet attained the status of a rule of international law? The answer largely depends on the law-making capacity of the General Assembly. What impact do these General Assembly Resolutions have? Are they interpretations of the Charter, or do they go beyond it? See Chapter 3 on Creation of International Law, and the opinion of the International Court of Justice in the *Namibia Case*[76] and in the *Western Sahara Case*, as follows.

Western Sahara Case
Adv. Op. [1975] I.C.J. Rep. 12

[In 1884, Spain colonized the Western Sahara and it remained until very recently a colony. Its population was mostly nomads. Its assets lie in phosphates. In 1966, the General Assembly of the United Nations invited Spain to decolonize on the basis of Resolution 1514 and asked Spain in Resolution 2229[77] to consult with neighbouring Mauritania and Morocco to determine procedures for holding a referendum under the auspices of the United Nations. Spain agreed to hold a referendum in 1975. At that time, Morocco under King Hassan, claimed the territory based on a "historic title" that predated Spain's acquisition. Mauritania did the same. At the behest of Morocco and Mauritania, the General Assembly sought an advisory opinion in 1974 as to the status of the territory. In the course of doing this, the Court addressed the issue of self-determination.]

---

[76] [1971], I.C.J. Rep. 16, at 31.
[77] 21 U.N. GAOR, Supp. (No. 16) 72; U.N. Doc. A/6316 (1967).

THE COURT: ...

54. The Charter of the United Nations, in Article 1, paragraph 2, indicates, as one of the purposes of the United Nations: ''To develop friendly relations among nations based on respect for the principle of equal rights and self-determination of peoples ... '' This purpose is further developed in Articles 55 and 56 of the Charter. Those provisions have direct and particular relevance for non-self-governing territories, which are dealt with in Chapter XI of the Charter. As the Court stated in its Advisory Opinion of 21 June 1971 on *The Legal Consequences for States of the Continued Presence of South Africa in Namibia (South West Africa) notwithstanding Security Council Resolutions 276* (1970):

... the subsequent development of international law in regard to non-self-governing territories, as enshrined in the Charter of the United Nations, made the principle of self-determination applicable to all of them (I.C.J. Reports 1971, at 31).

55. The principle of self-determination as a right of peoples, and its application for the purpose of bringing all colonial situations to a speedy end, were enunciated in the Declaration on the Granting of Independence to Colonial Countries and Peoples, General Assembly resolution 1514 (XV) ... . The above provisions, in particular paragraph 2, thus confirm and emphasize that the application of the right of self-determination requires a free and genuine expression of the will of the peoples concerned.

56. The Court had occasion to refer to this resolution in the above-mentioned Advisory Opinion of 21 June 1971. Speaking of the development of international law in regard to non-self-governing territories, the Court there stated:

A further important stage in this development was the Declaration on the Granting of Independence to Colonial Countries and Peoples (General Assembly resolution 1514 (XV) of 14 December 1960), which embraces all peoples and territories which ''have not yet attained independence.'' (I.C.J. Reports 1971, at 31).

It went on to state:

... the Court must take into consideration the changes which have occurred in the supervening half-century, and its interpretation cannot remain unaffected by the subsequent development of law, through the Charter of the United Nations and by way of customary law (ibid.).

The Court concluded:

In the domain to which the present proceedings relate, the last fifty years, as indicated above, have brought important developments. These developments leave little doubt that the ultimate objective of the sacred trust was the self-determination and independence of the peoples concerned. In this domain, as elsewhere, the corpus iuris gentium has been considerably enriched, and this the Court, if it is faithfully to discharge its functions, may not ignore. (Ibid. at 31 et seq.).

57. General Assembly resolution 1514 (XV) provided the basis for the process of decolonization which has resulted since 1960 in the creation of many States which are today Members of the United Nations. It is complemented in certain of its aspects by

General Assembly resolution 1541 (XV), which has been invoked in the present proceedings. The latter resolution contemplates for non-self-governing territories more than one possibility, namely:

(a) emergence as a sovereign independent State;
(b) free association with an independent State; or
(c) integration with an independent State.

At the same time, certain of its provisions give effect to the essential feature of the right of self-determination as established in resolution 1514 (XV). Thus principle VII of resolution 1541 (XV) declares that: "Free association should be the result of a free and voluntary choice by the Peoples of the territory concerned expressed through informed and democratic processes." Again, principle IX of resolution 1541 declares that:

Integration should have come about in the following circumstances:
(b) The integration should be the result of the freely expressed wishes of the territory's peoples acting with the full knowledge of the change in their status, their wishes having been expressed through informed and democratic processes, impartially conducted and based on universal adult suffrage. The United Nations could, when it deems it necessary, supervise these processes.

58. General Assembly resolution 2625 (XXV), "Declaration on Principles of International Law concerning Friendly Relations and Co-operation among States in accordance with the Charter of the United Nations" ... mentions other possibilities besides independence, association or integration. But in doing so it reiterates the basic need to take account of the wishes of the people concerned ...

59. The validity of the principle of self-determination, defined as the need to pay regard to the freely expressed will of peoples, is not affected by the fact that in certain cases the General Assembly has dispensed with the requirement of consulting the inhabitants of a given territory. Those instances were based either on the consideration that a certain population did not constitute a "people" entitled to self-determination or on the conviction that a consultation was totally unnecessary, in view of special circumstances.

Separate opinion of JUDGE DILLARD: At the broadest level there is the problem of determining whether the right of self-determination in the context of non-self-governing territories can qualify as a norm of contemporary international law ... .

As is well known [this] ... problem has elicited conflicting views which, in terms of opposing poles, may be described as follows. At one extreme is the contention that even if a particular resolution of the General Assembly is not binding, the cumulative impact of many resolutions when similar in content, voted for by overwhelming majorities and frequently repeated over a period of time may give rise to a general *opinio juris* and thus constitute a norm of customary international law. According to this view, this is the precise situation manifested by the long list of resolutions which, following in the wake of resolution 1514 (XV), have proclaimed the principle of self-determination to be an operative right in the decolonization of non-self-governing territories.

At the opposite pole are those who, resisting generally the law-creating powers of the General Assembly, deny that the principle has developed into a "right" with correspond-

ing obligations or that the practice of decolonization has been more than an example of
a usage dictated by political expediency or convenience and one which, in addition, has
been neither constant nor uniform.

I need not dwell on the theoretical aspects of this broad problem which, as everyone
knows, commands an immense literature. Suffice it to call attention to the fact that the
present opinion is forthright in proclaiming the existence of the "right" in so far as the
present proceedings are concerned.

This is made explicit in paragraph 56 and is fortified by calling into play two dicta in
the *Namibia* case (I.C.J. Reports 1971, at 31) to which are added an analysis of the
numerous resolutions of the General Assembly dealing in general with its decolonization
policy ... .

The pronouncements of the Court thus indicate, in my view, that a norm of international
law has emerged applicable to the decolonization of those non-self-governing territories
which are under the aegis of the United Nations.

It seemed hardly necessary to make more explicit the cardinal restraint which the legal
right of self-determination imposes. That restraint may be captured in a single sentence.
It is for the people to determine the destiny of the territory and not the territory the destiny
of the people. Viewed in this perspective it becomes almost self-evident that the existence
of ancient "legal ties" of the kind described in the Opinion, while they may influence
some of the projected procedures for decolonization, can have only a tangential effect in
the ultimate choices available to the people.

Economic Self-Determination

The right of all states and hence peoples to exercise full permanent sovereignty over their
natural resources and all economic activity carried on within its boundaries, can be
considered from a number of perspectives. First, it can be viewed as an attribute of
statehood, based on the sovereign equality and territorial integrity of states. Second, it
can centre on the assertion that all peoples freed from foreign occupation or alien or
colonial domination or apartheid have a right to restitution and full compensation for the
exploitation, depletion of and damage to their natural and other resources. Third, it can
be viewed from the general perspective of the development of a new international economic order and lastly it can be seen specifically to refer to the question of nationalization
and compensation discussed in Chapter 9 on State Responsibility. The most inclusive
document is the Declaration on the Establishment of a New International Economic Order.
As you read it, consider what principles it seeks to add to the U.N. Charter and the
Declaration on Principles of International Law, reported above, and what effect it may
have as a matter of law. Do this in conjunction with the other documents, concerning
permanent sovereignty over natural resources and the economic rights and duties of states,
reported in Chapter 9.

Declaration on the Establishment of a New International Economic Order
U.N.G.A. Spec. Sess. A/RES/3201 (S-VI); (1974), 13 *Int. Leg. Mat.* 715

4. The new international economic order should be founded on full respect for the
following principles:

(a) Sovereign equality of States, self-determination of all peoples, inadmissibility of the acquisition of territories by force, territorial integrity and non-interference in the internal affairs of other States;

(b) The broadest co-operation of all the States members of the international community, based on equity, whereby the prevailing disparities in the world may be banished and prosperity secured for all;

(c) Full and effective participation on the basis of equality of all countries in the solving of world economic problems in the common interest of all countries, bearing in mind the necessity to ensure the accelerated development of all the developing countries, while devoting particular attention to the adoption of special measures in favour of the least developed, land-locked and island developing countries as well as those developing countries most seriously affected by economic crises and natural calamities, without losing sight of the interests of other developing countries;

(d) The right to every country to adopt the economic and social system that it deems to be the most appropriate for its own development and not to be subjected to discrimination of any kind as a result;

(e) Full permanent sovereignty of every State over its natural resources and all economic activities. In order to safeguard these resources, each State is entitled to exercise effective control over them and their exploitation with means suitable to its own situation, including the right to nationalization or transfer of ownership to its nationals, this right being an expression of the full permanent sovereignty of the State. No State may be subjected to economic, political or any other type of coercion to prevent the free and full exercise of this inalienable right;

(f) The right of all States, territories and peoples under foreign occupation, alien and colonial domination or apartheid to restitution and full compensation for the exploitation and depletion of, and damages to, the natural resources and all other resources of those States, territories and peoples;

(g) Regulation and supervision of the activities of transnational corporations by taking measures in the interest of the national economies of the countries where such transnational corporations operate on the basis of the full sovereignty of those countries;

(h) The right of the developing countries and the peoples of territories under colonial and racial domination and foreign occupation to achieve their liberation and to regain effective control over their natural resources and economic activities;

(i) The extending of assistance to developing countries, peoples and territories which are under colonial and alien domination, foreign occupation, racial discrimination or apartheid or are subjected to economic, political or any other type of coercive measures to obtain from them the subordination of the exercise of their sovereign rights and to secure from them advantages of any kind, and to neo-colonialism in all its forms, and which have established or are endeavouring to establish effective control over their natural resources and economic activities that have been or are still under foreign control;

(j) Just and equitable relationship between the prices of raw materials, primary prod-
     ucts, manufactured and semi-manufactured goods exported by developing coun-
     tries and the prices of raw materials, primary commodities, manufactures, capital
     goods and equipment imported by them with the aim of bringing about sustained
     improvement in their unsatisfactory terms of trade and the expansion of the world
     economy;

(k) Extension of active assistance to developing countries by the whole international
     community, free of any political or military conditions;

(l) Ensuring that one of the main aims of the reformed international monetary system
     shall be the promotion of the development of the developing countries and the
     adequate flow of real resources to them;

(m) Improving the competitiveness of natural materials facing competition from syn-
     thetic substitutes;

(n) Preferential and non-reciprocal treatment for developing countries, wherever fea-
     sible, in all fields of international economic co-operation whenever possible;

(o) Securing favourable conditions for the transfer of financial resources to developing
     countries;

(p) Giving to the developing countries access to the achievements of modern science
     and technology, and promoting the transfer of technology and the creation of
     indigenous technology for the benefit of the developing countries in forms and in
     accordance with procedures which are suited to their economies;

(q) The need for all States to put an end to the waste of natural resources, including
     food products;

(r) The need for developing countries to concentrate all their resources for the cause
     of development;

(s) The strengthening, through individual and collective actions, of mutual economic,
     trade, financial and technical co-operation among the developing countries, mainly
     on a preferential basis;

(t) Facilitating the role which producers' associations may play within the framework
     of international co-operation and, in pursuance of their aims, inter alia assisting
     in the promotion of sustained growth of world economy and accelerating the
     development of developing countries.

International Organizations[78]

Intergovernmental Organizations
from S.A. Williams and A.L.C. de Mestral, *An Introduction to International
Law* (2 ed., 1987), at 61

International governmental organizations must be differentiated at the outset from non-
governmental organizations. International governmental organizations or institutions are

---

[78] See generally D. Bowett, *The Law of International Institutions* (4 ed., 1982); H.G. Schermer, *International*

set up by agreement between states. Non-governmental organizations, as the title suggests, are set up by individuals.

The number of both types has multiplied to the extent that their scope encompasses almost every type of activity and interest of humanity. The underlying reason for the development is a realization of the need for international dialogue. Bilateral association was felt to be inadequate, as today's needs necessitate dealings at the international level. The organizations vary from the global such as the United Nations, to the regional, such as the European Communities.

What type of legal personality do these subjects of international law enjoy? The answer depends upon the circumstances of the particular arrangement. Thus, it is necessary to look at the institution's constitution to determine its standing. For example article 104 of the U.N. Charter provides that "the organization shall enjoy in the territory of each of its members such legal capacity as may be necessary for the exercise of its functions and the fulfillment of its purposes." This article means that the United Nations has personality under the domestic laws of all its members.

International personality in the context of international organizations is a relative concept. One organization may have certain rights that others do not. Each particular organization has to be examined in detail to determine such factors.

The United Nations[79]

The United Nations is the preeminent example amongst international organizations. Before considering its legal personality, it is appropriate to survey, very briefly, its structure, functions and powers.

Charter of the United Nations

Read Articles 1, 2, 7-32, 55-105 in the Appendix.
 Consider carefully:
 The organization of the United Nations displayed in the chart on the next page.
 The purposes of the United Nations, in Article 1.
 The principles of the United Nations, in Article 2, discussed previously.
 The composition, powers and voting procedures of the General Assembly compared
   to the Security Council, in Articles 9, 10, 18, 23, 24, 27.
 The responsibilities of member states regarding disputes in Article 33.
 The powers of the Security Council over disputes; compare Articles 36 and 39.

Institutional Law (2 ed., 1980); M. Rama-Montaldo, "International Legal Personality and Implied Powers of International Organizations" (1970), 44 *Br. Y.B. Int. L.* 111; and D. Vignes, "The Impact of International Organization on the Development and Application of Public International Law," in R. St. J. Macdonald, D.M. Johnston, eds., *The Structure and Process of International Law* (1983), at 809.

[79] L.M. Goodrich, E. Hambro, A.P. Simons, *Charter of the United Nations* (3 ed., 1969); L.B. Sohn, *Cases on United Nations Law* (2 ed., 1967); A. Vandenbosch, W.N. Hogan, *United Nations: Background, Organization, Functions, Activities* (1970); Q. Wright, *International Law and the United Nations* (1960). Annual surveys of U.N. activities are published in the *Yearbooks of the United Nations*.

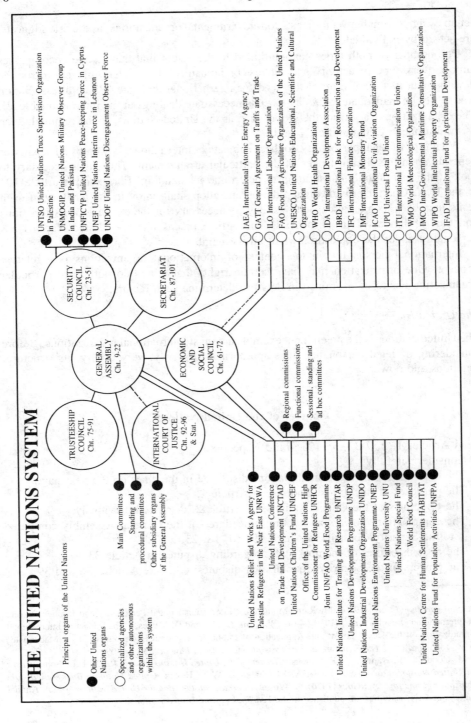

THE UNITED NATIONS SYSTEM

○ Principal organs of the United Nations

● Other United Nations organs

○ Specialized agencies and other autonomous organizations within the system

Main Committees
Standing and procedural committees
Other subsidiary organs of the General Assembly

TRUSTEESHIP COUNCIL
Cht. 75-91

INTERNATIONAL COURT OF JUSTICE
Cht. 92-96 & Stat.

GENERAL ASSEMBLY
Cht. 9-22

SECURITY COUNCIL
Cht. 23-51

SECRETARIAT
Cht. 87-101

ECONOMIC AND SOCIAL COUNCIL
Cht. 61-72

Regional commissions
Functional commissions
Sessional, standing and ad hoc committees

UNTSO United Nations Truce Supervision Organization in Palestine
UNMOGIP United Nations Military Observer Group in India and Pakistan
UNFICYP United Nations Peace-keeping Force in Cyprus
UNEF United Nations Interim Force in Lebanon
UNDOF United Nations Disengagement Observer Force

IAEA International Atomic Energy Agency
GATT General Agreement on Tariffs and Trade
ILO International Labour Organization
FAO Food and Agriculture Organization of the United Nations
UNESCO United Nations Educational, Scientific and Cultural Organization
WHO World Health Organization
IDA International Development Association
IBRD International Bank for Reconstruction and Development
IFC International Finance Corporation
IMF International Monetary Fund
ICAO International Civil Aviation Organization
UPU Universal Postal Union
ITU International Telecommunication Union
WMO World Meteorological Organization
IMCO Inter-Governmental Maritime Consultative Organization
WIPO World Intellectual Property Organization
IFAD International Fund for Agricultural Development

United Nations Relief and Works Agency for Palestine Refugees in the Near East UNRWA
United Nations Conference on Trade and Development UNCTAD
United Nations Children's Fund UNICEF
Office of the United Nations High Commissioner for Refugees UNHCR
Joint UN/FAO World Food Programme
United Nations Institute for Training and Research UNITAR
United Nations Development Programme UNDP
United Nations Industrial Development Organization UNIDO
United Nations Environment Programme UNEP
United Nations University UNU
United Nations Special Fund
World Food Council
United Nations Centre for Human Settlements HABITAT
United Nations Fund for Population Activities UNFPA

Adapted from *Basic Facts about the United Nations*
Cht. = U.N. Charter
Stat. = Statute of the International Court of Justice

The purposes and powers of the Economic and Social Council, in Articles 55, 62.
The trusteeship system has been discussed previously.
The International Court is considered in Chapter 4.

United Nations' Powers and Processes

The high-minded objectives of the Charter have created equally high expectations of the United Nations which have not always been fulfilled. In practice, the United Nations' ability to cope with the world's crises is only as great as the institutional machinery provided to the organization. This machinery maintains a particular balance of authority and powers between the General Assembly and the Security Council as the organs most directly responsible for the maintenance of international peace.

The experience of the General Assembly and the Security Council in trying to deal simultaneously with Iran's taking of American diplomats as hostages and the Soviet Union's invasion of Afghanistan is a good demonstration of U.N. powers and processes in operation. Both these crises arose late in 1979 and, while the Iranian incident has since been resolved, the Afghan situation has not. But the uppermost questions at the time were what the United Nations could and should do in the circumstances. The diary of events set out below provides a brief outline of what the United Nations proceeded to do. It is followed by a series of questions to elucidate the authority that was exercised under the Charter.

Diary of Events:

November 4, 1979	Iranians seized U.S. embassy and staff.
November 9, 27 and December 4, 1979	Security Council resolved unanimously that Iran had to free the American hostages.
December 17, 1979	General Assembly by resolution declared unanimously that the hostage taking was "an offence of grave concern to the international community."
December 24, 1979	Soviet invasion of Afghanistan began.
December 31, 1979	Secretary General Waldheim flew to Tehran for talks with the Iranian authorities.
December 31, 1979	Security Council called on Iran to release the hostages by January 7, 1980 or it would "adopt effective measures." The vote was 11 for to 0 against, with 4 abstentions including U.S.S.R.
January 7, 1980	Security Council met to handle the Afghan crisis. A resolution protesting Soviet military intervention was defeated by a vote of 13 for to 2 against, including U.S.S.R.
January 9, 1980	Security Council resolved to call General Assembly into emergency session regarding the Afghan situation. The vote was 12 for to 2 against, including U.S.S.R.
January 10, 1980	General Assembly met under the Uniting for Peace formula to discuss the Afghan crisis.

January 13, 1980   Security Council returned to unfinished Iranian business. A
                                    resolution to authorize collective sanctions was defeated by
                                    a vote of 10 for to 2 against, including U.S.S.R.

QUESTIONS

1) By what authority could the Security Council become seized of the Iranian crisis
on November 9? See Articles 33-38.

2) By what authority could the General Assembly become seized of the same matter
on December 17? At the same time as the Security Council? See Articles 11(2), 12, 14.

3) What powers did the General Assembly then have in the matter? How much further
could it have gone beyond its declaration of "an offence of grave concern"? See Articles
2(7), 10-18.

4) On what authority could the Secretary General take the initiative to intervene
personally in the Iranian crisis on December 31? See Articles 97-101.

5) Also on December 31, the Security Council directed Iran to comply with its earlier
resolutions or face effective measures. What was the Council's authority to order a member
state such as Iran to do anything? See Articles 24, 25 and the *Namibia* case reported
previously.

6) As to the threat of enforcement, what kind of measures might the Security Council
have taken? What steps were prerequisite to any Security Council action? See Articles
39-51.

7) How come the voting patterns on the three Security Council resolutions of December
31 (on Iran), January 7 and 9 (on Afghanistan) were so consistent but the results were
quite different? See Article 27 and the Security Council resolutions on Korea reported,
previously.

8) By what authority could the General Assembly become seized of the Afghan crisis
on January 10 when it was no longer in session? See Article 20.

9) What powers were available to the General Assembly to deal with the Afghan
situation, compared to the Iranian crisis? See Articles 2(7), 10-18 and the Uniting for
Peace Resolution, reported previously.

10) The discussions in the General Assembly and the Security Council came to nought.
Was the failure of the United Nations to resolve either crisis due more to the lack of
legal capacity in the Organization or the absence of political capability in the member
states?

Following this brief survey of the organs and powers of the United Nations, it is
necessary to consider its status, (and by analogy the legal personality of other international
organizations) at international law. This important question was authoritatively determined
by the International Court in the following case.

Reparations Case
Adv. Op. [1949] I.C.J. Rep. 174

[In 1948, Count Bernadotte, a Swedish national and the United Nations mediator in
Palestine was killed in Jerusalem which was in Israeli possession. At that time Israel was

not yet a member of the United Nations. Before commencing an action for compensation against Israel, the General Assembly asked the International Court for an opinion as to the legal capacity of the organization to bring the claim.]

THE COURT:

The first question asked of the Court is as follows:

In the event of an agent of the United Nations in the performance of his duties suffering injury in circumstances involving the responsibility of a State, has the United Nations, as an Organization, the capacity to bring an international claim against the responsible *de jure* or *de facto* government with a view to obtaining the reparation due in respect of the damage caused (a) to the United Nations, (b) to the victim or to persons entitled through him? ...

The subjects of law in any legal system are not necessarily identical in their nature or in the extent of their rights, and their nature depends upon the needs of the Community. Throughout its history, the development of international law has been influenced by the requirements of international life, and the progressive increase in the collective action of States has already given rise to instances of action upon the international plane by certain entities which are not States. This development culminated in the establishment in June 1945 of an international organization whose purposes and principles are specified in the Charter of the United Nations. But to achieve these ends the attribution of international personality is indispensable.

The Charter has not been content to make the Organization created by it merely a centre "for harmonizing the actions of nations in the attainment of these common ends" (Article 1, para. 4). It has equipped that centre with organs, and has given it special tasks. It has defined the position of the Members in relation to the Organization by requiring them to give it every assistance in any action undertaken by it (Article 2, para. 5), and to accept and carry out the decisions of the Security Council; by authorizing the General Assembly to make recommendations to the Members; by giving the Organization legal capacity and privileges and immunities in the territory of each of its Members; and by providing for the conclusion of agreements between the Organization and its Members. Practice – in particular the conclusions of conventions to which the Organization is a party – has confirmed the character of the Organization, which occupies a position in certain respects in detachment from its Members, and which is under a duty to remind them, if need be, of certain obligations. It must be added that the Organization is a political body, charged with political tasks of an important character, and covering a wide field namely the maintenance of international peace and security, the development of friendly relations among nations, and the achievement of international co-operation in the solution of problems of an economic, social, cultural or humanitarian character (Article 1); and in dealing with its Members it employs political means. The "Convention on the Privileges and Immunities of the United Nations" of 1946 creates rights and duties between each of the signatories and the Organization (see in particular, Section 35). It is difficult to see how such a convention could operate except upon the international plane and as between parties possessing international personality.

In the opinion of the Court, the Organization was intended to exercise and enjoy, and is in fact exercising and enjoying, functions and rights which can only be explained on the basis of the possession of a large measure of international personality and the capacity to operate upon an international plane. It is at present the supreme type of international organization, and it could not carry out the intentions of its founders if it was devoid of international personality. It must be acknowledged that its Members, by entrusting certain functions to it, with the attendant duties and responsibilities, have clothed it with the competence required to enable those functions to be effectively discharged.

Accordingly, the Court has come to the conclusion that the Organization is an international person. That is not the same thing as saying that it is a State, which it certainly is not, or that its legal personality and rights and duties are the same as those of a State. Still less is it the same thing as saying that it is ''a super-State,'' whatever that expression may mean. It does not even imply that all its rights and duties must be upon the international plane, any more than all the rights and duties of a State must be upon that plane. What it does mean is that it is a subject of international law and capable of possessing international rights and duties, and that it has capacity to maintain its rights by bringing international claims.

The next question is whether the sum of the international rights of the Organization comprises the right to bring the kind of international claim described in the Request for this Opinion. That is a claim against a State to obtain reparation in respect of the damage caused by the injury of an agent of the Organization in the course of the performance of his duties. Whereas a State possesses the totality of international rights and duties recognized by international law, the rights and duties of an entity such as the Organization must depend upon its purposes and functions as specified or implied in its constituent documents and developed in practice. The functions of the Organization are of such a character that they could not be effectively discharged if they involved the concurrent action, on the international plane, of fifty-eight or more Foreign Offices, and the Court concludes that the Members have endowed the Organization with capacity to bring international claims when necessitated by the discharge of its functions. ...

It cannot be doubted that the Organization has the capacity to bring an international claim against one of its Members which has caused injury to it by a breach of its international obligations towards it. The damage specified in Question I(a) means exclusively damage caused to the interests of the Organization itself, to its administrative machine, to its property and assets, and to the interests of which it is the guardian. It is clear that the Organization has the capacity to bring a claim for this damage. As the claim is based on the breach of an international obligation on the part of the Member held responsible by the Organization, the Member cannot contend that this obligation is governed by municipal law, and the Organization is justified in giving its claim the character of an international claim.

When the Organization has sustained damage resulting from a breach by a Member of its international obligations, it is impossible to see how it can obtain reparation unless it possesses capacity to bring an international claim. It cannot be supposed that in such an event all the Members of the Organization, save the defendant State must combine to bring a claim against the defendant for the damage suffered by the Organization.

In dealing with the question of law which arises out of Question I(b) ... [t]he only legal question which remains to be considered is whether, in the course of bringing an international claim of this kind, the Organization can recover "the reparation due in respect of the damage caused ... to the victim ... ."

The traditional rule that diplomatic protection is exercised by the national State does not involve the giving of a negative answer to Question I(b).

In the first place, this rule applies to claims brought by a State. But here we have the different and new case of a claim that would be brought by the Organization.

In the second place, even in inter-State relations, there are important exceptions to the rule, for there are cases in which protection may be exercised by a State on behalf of persons not having its nationality.

In the third place, the rule rests on two bases. The first is that the defendant State has broken an obligation towards the national State in respect of its nationals. The second is that only the party to whom an international obligation is due can bring claim in respect of its breach. This is precisely what happens when the Organization, in bringing a claim for damage suffered by its agent, does so by invoking the breach of an obligation towards itself. Thus, the rule of the nationality of claims affords no reason against recognizing that the Organization has the right to bring a claim for the damage referred to in Question I(b). On the contrary, the principle underlying this rule leads to the recognition of this capacity as belonging to the Organization, when the Organization invokes, as the ground of its claim, a breach of an obligation towards itself.

Nor does the analogy of the traditional rule of diplomatic protection of nations abroad justify in itself an affirmative reply. It is not possible, by a strained use of the concept of allegiance, to assimilate the legal bond which exists, under Article 100 of the Charter, between the Organization on the one hand, and the Secretary-General and the staff on the other, to the bond of nationality existing between a State and its nationals.

The Court is here faced with a new situation. The questions to which it gives rise can only be solved by realizing that the situation is dominated by the provisions of the Charter considered in the light of the principles of international law ... .

The question ... presupposes that the injury for which the reparation is demanded arises from a breach of an obligation designed to help an agent of the Organizaton in the performance of his duties. It is not a case in which the wrongful act or omission would merely constitute a breach of the general obligations of a State concerning the position of aliens; claims made under this head would be within the competence of the national State and not, as a general rule, within that of the Organization.

The Charter does not expressly confer upon the Organization the capacity to include, in its claim for reparation, damage caused to the victim or to persons entitled through him. The Court must therefore begin by enquiring whether the provisions of the Charter concerning the functions of the Organization, and the part played by its agents in the performance of those functions, imply for the Organization power to afford its agents the limited protection that would consist in the bringing of a claim on their behalf for reparation for damage suffered in such circumstances. Under international law, the Organization must be deemed to have those powers which, though not expressly provided in the Charter, are conferred upon it by necessary implication as being essential to the performance of its duties. This principle of law was applied by the Permanent Court of International Justice to the International Labour Organization in its Advisory Opinion

No. 13 of July 23rd, 1926 (Series B., No. 13, at 18) and must be applied to the United Nations.

Having regard to its purposes and functions already referred to, the Organization may find it necessary, and has in fact found it necessary, to entrust its agents with important missions to be performed in disturbed parts of the world. Many missions, from their very nature, involve the agents in unusual dangers to which ordinary persons are not exposed. For the same reason, the injuries suffered by its agents in these circumstances will sometimes have occurred in such a manner that their national State would not be justified in bringing a claim for reparation on the ground of diplomatic protection, or, at any rate, would not feel disposed to do so. Both to ensure the efficient and independent performance of these missions and to afford effective support to its agents, the Organization must provide them with adequate protection ... .

In order that the agent may perform his duties satisfactorily, he must feel that this protection is assured to him by the Organization, and that he may count on it. To ensure the independence of the agent, and, consequently, the independent action of the Organization itself, it is essential that in performing his duties he need not have to rely on any other protection than that of the Organization (save of course for the direct and immediate protection due from the State in whose territory he may be). In particular, he should not have to rely on the protection of his own State. If he had to rely on that State, his independence might well be compromised, contrary to the principle applied by Article 100 of the Charter. And lastly, it is essential that – whether the agent belongs to a powerful or to a weak State; to one more affected or less affected by the complications of international life; to one in sympathy or not in sympathy with the mission of the agent – he should know that in the performance of his duties he is under the protection of the Organization. This assurance is even more necessary when the agent is stateless ...

The obligations entered into by States to enable the agents of the Organization to perform their duties are undertaken not in the interest of the agents, but in that of the Organization. When it claims redress for a breach of these obligations, the Organization is invoking its own right, the right that the obligations due to it should be respected. On this ground, it asks for reparation of the injury suffered, for "it is a principle of international law that the breach of an engagement involves an obligation to make reparation in an adequate form;" as was stated by the Permanent Court in its Judgment No. 8 of July 26th, 1927 (Series A., No. 9, at 21). In claiming reparation based on the injury suffered by its agent, the Organization does not represent the agent, but is asserting its own right, the right to secure respect for undertakings entered into towards the Organization.

Having regard to the foregoing considerations, and to the undeniable right of the Organization to demand that its Members shall fulfil the obligations entered into by them in the interest of the good working of the Organization, the Court is of the opinion that in the case of a breach of these obligations, the Organization has the capacity to claim adequate reparation, and that in assessing this reparation it is authorized to include the damage suffered by the victim or by persons entitled through him.

The question remains whether the Organization has "the capacity to bring an international claim against the responsible *de jure* or *de facto* government with a view to obtaining the reparation due in respect of the damage caused (a) to the United Nations,

(b) to the victim or to persons entitled through him'' when the defendant State is not a member of the Organization.

In considering this aspect of Question I (a) and (b), it is necessary to keep in mind the reasons which have led the Court to give an affirmative answer to it when the defendant State is a Member of the Organization. It has now been established that the Organization has capacity to bring claims on the international plane, and that it possessed a right of functional protection in respect of its agents. Here again the Court is authorized to assume that the damage suffered involves the responsibility of a State, and it is not called upon to express an opinion upon the various ways in which that responsibility might be engaged. Accordingly, the question is whether the Organization has capacity to bring a claim against the defendant State to recover reparation in respect of that damage or whether, on the contrary, the defendant State, not being a member, is justified in raising the objection that the Organization lacks the capacity to bring an international claim. On this point, the Court's opinion is that fifty States, representing the vast majority of the members of the international community, had the power, in conformity with international law, to bring into being an entity possessing objective international personality and not merely personality recognized by them alone, together with capacity to bring international claims ...

Accordingly, the Court arrives at the conclusion that an affirmative answer should be given to Question I(a) and (b) whether or not the dependant state is a Member of the United Nations.

Question II is as follows:

In the event of an affirmative reply on point I(b), how is action by the United Nations to be reconciled with such rights as may be possessed by the State of which the victim is a national?

The affirmative reply given by the Court on point I(b) obliges it now to examine Question II. When the victim has a nationality, cases can clearly occur in which the injury suffered by him may engage the interest both of his national State and of the Organization. In such an event, competition between the State's right of diplomatic protection and the Organization's right of functional protection might arise, and this is the only case with which the Court is invited to deal.

In such a case, there is no rule of law which assigns priority to the one or to the other, or which compels either the State or the Organization to refrain from bringing an international claim. The Court sees no reason why the parties concerned should not find solutions inspired by goodwill and common sense, and as between the Organization and its Members it draws attention to their duty to render ''every assistance'' provided by Article 2, paragraph 5, of the Charter.

Although the bases of the two claims are different, that does not mean that the defendant State can be compelled to pay the reparation due in respect of the damage twice over. International tribunals are already familiar with the problem of a claim in which two or more national States are interested, and they know how to protect the defendant State in such a case.

NOTES

1) In 1950, Israel paid to the United Nations the sum requested by the Secretary-General for the injuries done on account of Israeli negligence.

2) This case was not only important for the United Nations. It is a landmark decision for all international organizations. It shows that the powers possessed by an organization do not have to be expressly incorporated in its charter or the treaty creating it but can be implied so far as is necessary for the organization to be able to fulfil the functions for which it was set up. But how far may this functional approach to the interpretation of the Charter be extended? For instance, what are the implications of the Court's opinion for (a) a claim by the United Nations to acquire territory; or (b) a claim against the United Nations by a state in respect of the breach of a treaty between them?

3) Is it possible for a few states to establish by treaty an international organization for a specialized purpose, say to operate a system of telecommunications satellites, and then to demand that other states respect its independent existence and responsibility? For instance, should the organization or the founding states be responsible for an accident, such as the crash landing of a satellite, which causes injuries in a foreign territory? What features of the United Nations did the International Court stress in recognizing its objective personality?

4) The European Community is a regional economic organization but has the potential for a political organization.[80] To be precise, there are three communities, the European Coal and Steel Community, the European Economic Community and the European Atomic Energy Community. Since 1986 the "Community" is comprised of twelve member states: Belgium, Denmark, France, the Federal Republic of Germany, Greece, Ireland, Italy, Luxembourg, the Netherlands, Portugal, Spain and the United Kingdom.

Non-Governmental Organizations[81]

Although references to international organizations are commonly to intergovernmental bodies, there are very many more organizations of a truly international character that are non-governmental. These NGO's tend to be overlooked by lawyers as participants in the international system because they do not even have the limited legal personality of their intergovernmental cousins. In fact, this shortsightedness excludes a host of actors who exert a major influence on the creation and application of international law.

The foremost example of this activity must be the International Red Cross, whose contribution has been assessed by Lador-Lederer in these words:[82]

Charity, and not legislation, is emphasized as the essential feature of the Red Cross, and yet the Red Cross – initiated international law is the main part of that branch of the law. In other words,

---

[80] See A. Kerr, *The Common Market and How it Works* (1977); J. Megret, J.V. Louis, D. Vignes and M. Waelbroek, *Le Droit de la Communauté économique éuropéenne* (14 vols., 1973-   ); D. Lasok and J. Bridge, *An Introduction to the Law and Institutions of the Common Market* (3 ed., 1982).

[81] See J.J. Lador-Lederer, *International Non-Governmental Organizations* (1963); and L.C. White, *International Non-Governmental Organizations: Their Purposes, Methods and Accomplishments* (1951).

[82] J.J. Lador-Lederer, *supra*, at 84.

the main part of the humanization of war, of the *iura in bello*, was imposed upon the technicians of warfare by a movement of bourgeois revolt against the management of international politics, including war, by a group of aristocratic professionals whether in the military or in the diplomatic branch. After the horrible experience of, and the magnificent work done by Florence Nightingale in the Crimea in 1856, the human aspect of warfare could hardly be said to have remained a secret, and still the slaughter at Solferino, 1859, took place as if it were an unpredictable and unavoidable mishap. Is it a complete coincidence that the Red Cross and the great legislative movements of experts in International Law were born at a time when Bismarck put his policy of continuous warfare into effect? There was no international organization of the legal profession up to 1872 ... . But in the following 25 years, thirteen legal NGO's, covering the main branches of law, were established. This number included the Institut de Droit International, the International Law Association, the Inter-Parliamentary Union and the Pan-American Union, the International associations for the protection of intellectual property and the Comité Maritime International. Having succeeded in inspiring several international conventions, the Red Cross can be said to have become the initiator of a treble legislative movement: of a codification of the law of warfare, of priority of humanitarian considerations in hostilities, and of the granting of a status in international law to NGO's.

The status of NGO's at international law to a degree has been formally recognized by the U.N. Charter Article 71. It provides that the Economic and Social Council may grant consultative status to NGO's, and several hundred of them have accepted it. Similar arrangements exist in other organizations in the U.N. family. Consultative status typically permits the NGO to send representatives to meetings as observers, to submit written materials for circulation as U.N. documents and to use the services provided by the Secretariat. In other words, they have access to participate and influence the work of the body to which they are accredited but they cannot participate in its decision by voting, though even this deficiency is less significant now that many matters are concluded by consensus.

NGO's exist in every field of human activity. They include scientific, medical, professional, sporting, and humanitarian organizations. A few well known examples are the Roman Catholic Church, Amnesty International, the International Olympic Committee, and the International Bar Association. To these world-wide bodies must be added all the federations and international unions of national associations representing business, labour, sports, sciences and art and so on. A couple of conspicuous examples are the International Chamber of Commerce and the World Council of Churches.

Although they have not been accorded any official authority by governments, many NGO's make and apply rules and standards for their fields of concern which are accepted generally as the international norms of conduct in those areas of endeavour. While traditional legal theory minimizes the formal place of NGO's in the international system, their exclusion must not blind us to their bustling reality.

Corporations[83]

The colossal expansion of international trade and commerce in recent decades has brought with it a wide variety of corporate organizational structures. With governments themselves

---

[83] See W. Friedmann, *The Changing Structure of International Law* (1964) 213-231; and D. Wallace Jr., *International Regulation of Multinational Corporations* (1976).

now so greatly involved one way or another in much of this business activity, it is no longer possible to confine the corporation to the status of a juridical person under national law. A great many corporations have acquired an international dimension but their diversity presents difficulties for the international legal system. Holder and Brennan have offered this threefold classification:[84]

1. *Government corporations.* Both Communist and capitalist governments have pursued their national interests through corporations wholly or largely government owned and with greater or lesser freedom from direct governmental control. Most Communist trade is carried on by such entities; Western governments increasingly foster airlines and trading bodies; and developing countries engage in the exploitation of their resources by the government corporation.

When the Australian Wheat Board negotiates sales of wheat with sovereign governments, does it act as an autonomous national or as an organ representing the Australian government? When Quantas claims certain rights or other benefits, does it do so as the corporation (the shares of which are owned by the Australian government) or as spokesman for the Australian government? The hybrid legal status of such corporations results from the mixing of private national law and international law. In organization, legal form, and objective, such government corporations are private. Yet they engage in international transactions at the behest of government policy. They enjoy diplomatic assistance and they directly invoke certain rights explicable only in terms of a developing public commercial law.

2. *Intergovernmental corporations.* The corporation may bring together a number of governments, and possibly private enterprise also, for functions such as the creation or servicing of public utilities – for example, the building of a tunnel under the English Channel, or the organization of an airline, or for the development of natural resources. Again such corporations fall somewhere between the public and private domain. By linking governments international law seems to apply to the joint enterprise. By the form of the participation and the relatively independent corporate nature of the enterprise – perhaps registered as a national company – national law controls the operation.

State co-operation for satellite communications provides a topical example of the intergovernmental corporation. The state agreement in 1964, establishing the International Telecommunications Satellite Consortium (INTELSAT), contemplated a world satellite communication system run as a commercial enterprise. It purports to be open to all nations without discrimination, with signatory states participating through designed communication entities. In fact the United States representative, the private corporation COMSAT (registered in Washington, D.C.), occupies a controlling position. Not only does COMSAT by Article VIII, ''act as the manager in the design, development, construction, establishment, operation and maintenance of the space segment,'' but in addition the United States participation of 61 per cent gives it a virtual veto over decisions.

3. *Non-governmental corporations.* The obvious importance of private corporate activities to the international legal system is yet to be accommodated in legal theory, which still equates them with the individual. As participants certain multinational enterprises control resources more extensive than many states, and their decisions contribute to the shaping of the political structure of national and international régimes. As put by one observer, ''the international combine has

---

[84] W.E. Holder and G.A. Brennan, *The International Legal System* (1972), at 296, footnotes omitted.

wrested the substance of sovereignty from the so-called sovereign state.'' Their effective power permits them to negotiate and agree as equals with governments.

The multinational involvement of private corporations has now become the focus of much international attention. Since their activities carry them across state frontiers yet they are not international in the traditional sense of being intergovernmental, their in-between status has been aptly described by Judge Jessup as ''transnational.'' But as yet there is no certain body of transnational law by which to regulate these corporations. As a result a large number of legal uncertainties surround transnational corporations concerning, for instance, their nationality,[85] the law governing their agreements with foreign governments,[86] and their amenability to the jurisdiction of national authorities extraterritorially.[87] These matters touch issues that are fundamental to the international legal system and generate deeply held opposing views.

In recent years several international initiatives have been taken to create a suitable body of rules.[88] Their objectives are to regulate the conduct of transnational corporations and to define the rights and duties of states commercially connected to them. The principal thrust of United Nations efforts in this regard has been to develop a comprehensive U.N. Code of Conduct on Transnational Corporations.[89] This Code is based on the earlier statements of principle by the General Assembly to be found in the Charter of Economic Rights and Duties of States.[90] The Code elaborates standards for the conduct of transnational corporations regarding respect for the sovereignty, the economic and social policies and the laws of the host state, and concerning their ownership, control, financing, taxation, transfer of technology, consumer and environmental protection and disclosure of corporate information within the foreign state. The Code also spells out the treatment to be accorded to transnational corporations by the host state, including provisions on nationalization, compensation and jurisdiction. The U.N. Code of Conduct is at present only in draft form. Many matters have yet to be agreed, including the question of its ultimate legal force as a voluntary or obligatory regime.

The United Nations has also worked on three other sets of principles which complement and buttress the more general U.N. Code of Conduct. Their titles explain their subject matter. They are the non-binding Set of Multilaterally Agreed, Equitable Principles and Rules for the Control of Restrictive Business Practices,[91] the draft International Code of Conduct on the Transfer of Technology,[92] and the draft International Agreement on Illicit

---

[85] Discussed *infra* in Chapter 7.

[86] Discussed *infra* in Chapter 9.

[87] Discussed *infra* in Chapter 8.

[88] In addition to the efforts of the United Nations described here, see also International Labour Organization, Tripartite Declaration of Principles Concerning Multinational Enterprises and Social Policy, reprinted in (1978), 17 *Int. Leg. Mat.* 423; OECD Guidelines for Multinational Enterprises, reprinted in (1976), 15 *Int. Leg. Mat.* 967, as revised (1979), 18 *Int. Leg. Mat.* 986 and 1171; and generally see J.G. Castel, A.L.C. de Mestral, and W.C. Graham, *International Business Transactions and Economic Relations* (1986), c. 9.

[89] Reprinted in (1984), 23 *Int. Leg. Mat.* 626.

[90] U.N.G.A. Res. 3281 (XXIX), reprinted in (1975) 14 *Int. Leg. Mat.* 251, reported *infra*.

[91] Reprinted in (1980), 19 *Int. Leg. Mat.* 813.

[92] U.N. Doc. TD/Code TOT/47 (1985).

Payments.[93] Since 1966 there has also been an International Centre for the Settlement of Investment Disputes.[94] The significance of this growing body of transnational business standards and procedures in the context of questions about legal personality is that they join states and corporations in mixed arrangements that trample the traditional boundaries of subject and object status at international law.

Individuals

Until the twentieth century the prevailing view was that states alone possessed true international legal personality.[95] Still today, states alone have standing in contentious proceedings before the International Court of Justice. However, especially in the area of Protection of Human Rights considered in Chapter 10, the individual has attained standing before different international bodies.

In other instruments too the procedural capacity of the individual has been recognized.[96] For example under the Polish-German Convention of 1922, which dealt with Upper Silesia, the procedural standing of individuals as claimants was recognized even as against their own state.[97]

Further in the *Danzig Railway Officials' Case*[98] the Permanent Court of International Justice held that if by a treaty states parties agree to confer rights on individuals, then an international court should recognize and give effect to them at international law.

In the area of obligations individuals have had status for a longer period of time. Especially since the second World War, it is without controversy that individuals can be prosecuted for criminal violations of international customary or conventional law. The following extracts demonstrate the direct applicability of international law to individuals.

Nürnberg War Crimes Trials[99]
(1947), 1 *Trial of the Major War Criminals* 171

[Twenty-two defendants, the major war criminals whose crimes had no exact geographical location, were indicted before the International Military Tribunal established at Nürnberg

---

[93] U.N. Doc. E/AC. 67/L.3/Add.1 (1979).

[94] 575 U.N.T.S. 159. See A. Broches, "The Convention on the Settlement of Investment Disputes; Some Observations on Jurisdiction" (1966), 5 *Colum. J. Transnat. L.* 263.

[95] A.A. Norgaard, *The Position of the Individual in International Law* (1962); P.P. Remec, *The Position of the Individual in International Law according to Grotius and Vattel* (1960); H. Lauterpacht, "The Subjects of the Law of Nations" (1947), 63 *L.Q.R.* 438 and (1948), 64 *L.Q.R.* 97.

[96] H. Lauterpacht, *Survey of International Law in Relation to the Work of Codification of the International Law Commission*, U.N. Doc. A/CN. 4/1/Rev. 1, Feb. 10, 1949, at 19-20, reprinted in E. Lauterpacht, ed., *International Law being the Collected Papers of Hersch Lauterpacht* (1970), vol. 1, at 469-71. See also W.P. Gormley, *The Procedural Status of the Individual before International and Supranational Tribunals* (1966).

[97] See, before the Upper Silesia Mixed Tribunal, *Steiner and Gross v. Polish State* (1927-28), 4 Ann. Dig. 291.

[98] *Jurisdiction of the Courts of Danzig*, Adv. Op. (1928), C.I.J. Rep., Ser. B. No. 15.

[99] See Woetzel, *The Nürnberg Trials in International Law* (1960). The portion of the judgment concerning acts of aggression is also reported *supra*. On war crimes generally, see L.C. Green, *International Law: A Canadian Perspective* (1984), at 288-303.

pursuant to an agreement between France, the United Kingdom, the United States and the U.S.S.R. and 19 other adherents. The defendants were charged with crimes against peace, war crimes and crimes against humanity. They were also charged with participating in the formulation or execution of a common plan or conspiring to commit all these crimes. At the conclusion of the trial, the Tribunal held all but three of the accused guilty, twelve of whom it sentenced to death, three to life imprisonment and the remainder to prison for lengthy terms.]

THE TRIBUNAL: ... The individual defendants are indicted under article 6 of the Charter, which is as follows:

The Tribunal established by the Agreement referred to in Article 1 hereof for the trial and punishment of the major war criminals of the European Axis countries shall have the power to try and punish persons who, acting in the interests of the European Axis countries, whether as individuals or as members of organizations, committed any of the following crimes.

The following acts, or any of them, are crimes coming within the jurisdiction of the Tribunal for which there shall be individual responsibility: –

(a) Crimes against peace: namely, planning, preparation, initiation or waging of a war of aggression, or a war in violation of international treaties, agreements or assurances, or participation in a common plan or conspiracy for the accomplishment of any of the foregoing;

(b) War crimes: namely, violations of the laws or customs of war. Such violations shall include, but not be limited to, murder, ill-treatment or deportation to slave labour or for any other purpose of the civilian population of or in occupied territory, murder or ill-treatment of prisoners of war or persons on the seas, killing of hostages, plunder of public or private property, wanton destruction of cities, towns or villages, or devastation not justified by military necessity;

(c) Crimes against humanity: namely, murder, extermination, enslavement, deportation, and other inhumane acts committed against any civilian population, before or during the war, or persecutions on political, racial or religious grounds in execution of or in connection with any crime within the jurisdiction of the Tribunal, whether or not in violation of the domestic law of the country where perpetrated.

Leaders, organizers, instigators and accomplices participating in the formulation or execution of a common plan or conspiracy to commit any of the foregoing crimes are responsible for all acts performed by any persons in execution of such plan ...

The making of the Charter was the exercise of the sovereign legislative power by the countries to which the German Reich unconditionally surrendered; and the undoubted right of these countries to legislate for the occupied territories has been recognized by the civilized world. The Charter is not an arbitrary exercise of power on the part of the victorious nations, but in the view of the Tribunal, as will be shown, it is the expression of international law existing at the time of its creation; and to that extent is itself a contribution to international law. ...

It was submitted that international law is concerned with the actions of sovereign States, and provides no punishment for individuals; and further, that where the act in question is an act of State, those who carry it out are not personally responsible, but are protected by the doctrine of the sovereignty of the State. In the opinion of the Tribunal, both these submissions must be rejected. That international law imposes duties and liabilities upon individuals as well as upon states has long been recognized. ... Crimes against international law are committed by men, not by abstract entities, and only by punishing individuals who commit such crimes can the provisions of international law be enforced. ...

The principle of international law, which under certain circumstances, protects the representatives of a State, cannot be applied to acts which are condemned as criminal by international law. The authors of these acts cannot shelter themselves behind their official position in order to be freed from punishment in appropriate proceedings. Article 7 of the Charter expressly declares: "The official position of defendants, whether as heads of State, or responsible officials in government departments, shall not be considered as freeing them from responsibility, or mitigating punishment."

On the other hand the very essence of the Charter is that individuals have international duties which transcend the national obligations of obedience imposed by the individual State. He who violates the laws of war cannot obtain immunity while acting in pursuance of the authority of the State if the State in authorizing action moves outside its competence under international law.

It was also submitted on behalf of these defendants that in doing what they did they were acting under the orders of Hitler, and therefore cannot be held responsible for the acts committed by them in carrying out these orders. The Charter specifically provides in Article 8: "The fact that the defendant acted pursuant to orders of his Government or of a superior shall not free him from responsibility, but may be considered in mitigation of punishment."

The provisions of this Article are in conformity with the law of all nations. That a soldier was ordered to kill or torture in violation of the international law of war has never been recognized as a defense to such acts of brutality, though, as the Charter here provides, the order may be urged in mitigation of the punishment. The true test, which is found in varying degrees in the criminal law of most nations, is not the existence of the order, but whether moral choice was in fact possible.

NOTES

1) The United Nations General Assembly affirmed the principles of international law recognized in the Nürnberg Charter and the judgment of the International Military Tribunal on December 11th 1946.[100] The International Law Commission at the behest of the General Assembly formulated the Nürnberg Principles.[101]

2) After World War I, under articles 228-230 of the Versailles Treaty 1919, the German government recognized the right of the Allied and Associated Powers to bring persons accused of committing acts in violation of the laws and customs of war to trial before military tribunals. A demand was submitted to Germany for the trial of 901 persons under

---

[100] U.N.G.A. Res. 95 (I), GAOR, Res. First Sess., Pt. 11, at 188;
[101] U.N.G.A. Res. 174 (II), U.N. Doc. A/519, at 105-10 (1947).

the aforementioned articles. Germany refused and as a compromise the Allies accepted that Germany should prosecute a selected number of individuals. Of 45 names that were selected only 13 actually were tried. Of these, 6 were acquitted. The heaviest sentence imposed was 4 years imprisonment.[102]

3) Many other trials, too numerous to mention, have considered the applicability of international criminal law to individuals. Of special note are the Tokyo War Trials, by the International Military Tribunal for the Far East, of the major war criminals of that arena;[103] *In Re Flick and Others*[104] where the United States Military Tribunal held that: " ... International law binds every citizen as does ordinary municipal law ... . The application of international law to individuals is no novelty''; and *In Re Ohlendorf and Others*[105] where the United States Military Tribunal held again that ''[i]t is a fallacy of no small proportion that international obligations can apply only to the abstract entities called States.''

4) The International Convention on the Suppression and Punishment of Apartheid[106] provides that apartheid is a crime against humanity. It relies upon states parties to adopt legislative, judicial and administrative measures to prosecute and punish those persons responsible for such offenses. It is stated that this should be done regardless of territorial jurisdiction or national status of the offender. Article 5 provides that jurisdiction may be exercised by domestic or international tribunals. To date it has not proved an effective mechanism.

5) The 1948 Convention on the prevention and punishment of the Crime of Genocide[107] provides that genocide whether committed in time of war or peace is an international crime. Article IV states that ''persons committing genocide [or other acts mentioned in the Convention] shall be punished, whether they are constitutionally responsible rulers, public officials or private individuals.'' However, Article VI on enforcement is weak. It provides that persons charged with crimes under the Convention ''shall be tried by a competent tribunal of the State in the territory of which the act was committed, or by such international penal tribunal as may have jurisdiction ... .'' Would former President for Life Idi Amin of Uganda or Prime Minister Botha of South Africa present themselves before a domestic or international tribunal while still in authority? Who is likely to be prosecuted under this Convention? Why did the United Nations not provide for universal jurisdiction here?

Eichmann Case[108]
(1961), 36 I.L.R. 277, at 310 (Israel Supreme Court)

[The Israel Supreme Court, sitting as a court of criminal appeal on May 29th, 1962, dismissed an appeal by Adolf Eichmann from the judgment and sentence of the District

---

[102] See The *Dover Castle Case* and *The Llandovery Castle Case* (1923-24), 2 Ann Dig. 429 and 436.

[103] International Military Tribunal, Tokyo (1948), 15 Ann. Dig. 356.

[104] (1947), 14 Ann. Dig. 266.

[105] Otherwise known as the Einsatzgruppen Trial (1948), 15 *Int. L.R.* 656.

[106] (1974), 13 *Int. Leg. Mat.* 50. Canada is not a party.

[107] 78 U.N.T.S. 277. Canada ratified this convention on September 3, 1952. See *Criminal Code* s. 281.1.

[108] See H. Arendt, *Eichmann in Jerusalem* (1964); P. Papadatos, *The Eichmann Trial* (1964); L.C. Green, ''The Eichmann Case'' (1962), 38 *Br.Y.B.Int.L.* 181.

Court. Eichmann had been abducted in 1960 from Argentina where he had lived since 1950 under an assumed name. He signed a paper purporting to consent to trial in Israel. He was charged with offences under the Nazi and Nazi Collaborators (Punishment) Law 1950, *inter alia*, for his part in the "Final Solution of the Jewish Problem with the intent to exterminate the Jewish people."]

THE SUPREME COURT: ... It is impossible for a state to sanction an act that violates its severe prohibitions, and from this follows the idea ... that a person who was a party to such a crime must bear individual responsibility for it.

STATE SUCCESSION[109]

There is a definite distinction to be made between state succession and state continuity. State continuity means that a state continues to exist regardless of changes of government, until it is extinguished by absorption into another state or by dissolution. Changes in government, as well as in types of government either by legal or by unconstitutional means, do not affect the continuity of the state in terms of its international legal personality. By the same token, a state is bound by any acts or engagements of governments that may have become extinct.

State succession, on the other hand concerns the legal consequences that follow when one state replaces another. Succession can occur in a variety of ways, for example, total absorption of one state by another; partial absorption; independence of one state from another; merger of two existing states or dismemberment of one state into distinct parts.

In such a circumstance certain questions of international law must be considered. They can be summed up as follows: to what extent are the existing rights and obligations of the predecessor state extinguished and to what extent does the successor state take up those rights and obligations? As between the two states concerned, the answers are frequently to be found in their Pact of Union or other treaty of succession. In the absence of an agreed solution and vis-à-vis third parties the international rules are by no means settled. The Legal Division of the Department of External Affairs advised in 1968 that:[110]

... the question of state succession is highly complex and is one in which the State practice of newly (i.e. post-World War II) independent States has departed from the general principles of pre-War international law with the result that present practice is confused and contradictory and the present state of the law highly uncertain.

An event of state succession affects a long list of subject matter. *Ratione materiae* succession usually involves treaty rights and obligations, territorial rights, membership

---

[109] See D.P. O'Connell, *State Succession in Municipal and International Law*, 2 vols. (1967); I. Brownlie, *supra*, n. 1, c. 28; J. Crawford, *supra*, n. 1, c. 16; L.C. Green, *International Law: A Canadian Perspective* (1984) 131-41; A.D. McNair, *The Law of Treaties* (1961), c. 37.

[110] See J.G. Castel, *International Law* (3 ed., 1976), at 126.

in international organizations, and contractual rights and obligations including concessionary contracts, public debts, claims in tort, public funds and public property, nationality, private and municipal law rights, and the like. *Ratione personae* succession includes rights and obligations (i) between the new State and the predecessor State; (ii) between the new State and third States; (iii) of the new State with respect to individuals (including legal persons). It is a subject not governed by settled rules.

In the sections that follow brief consideration will be given to continuity; the rights and duties acquired; state responsibility for the legal interests of private individuals and changes of their nationality.

Changes of Government and State Continuity

Matters concerning the recognition of a new government are discussed in Chapter 5 on Inter-State Relations. But quite apart from its acceptability internationally, the new government inherits the rights and obligations of the persisting state and its acts bind the state:

Tinoco Arbitration
Great Britian v. Costa Rica
(1923), 1 R.I.A.A. 375

[In 1914 Tinoco overthrew the Government of Costa Rica. He assumed power, called an election and established a new constitution. In 1919 Tinoco retired on account of ill health and went to Europe. After his government fell a month later, the old constitution was restored and new elections held under it. The new government subsequently passed a law nullifying many of the obligations assumed by the Tinoco régime towards foreigners, including the Royal Bank of Canada and other British nationals. Britain brought this claim on account of the alleged mistreatment of her nationals and, in the course of deciding it, the sole arbitrator, Taft, C.J.U.S., considered the status of the Tinoco government.]

TAFT, Arbitrator: ... Great Britain contends, first, that the Tinoco government was the only government of Costa Rica *de facto* and *de jure* for two years and nine months; that during that time there was no other government disputing its sovereignty, that it was in peaceful administration of the whole country, with the acquiescence of its people.

Second, that the succeeding government could not by legislative decree avoid responsibility for acts of that government affecting British subjects, or appropriate or confiscate rights and property by that government except in violation of international law; that the Act of Nullities is as to British interests, therefore itself a nullity, and is to be disregarded, with the consequence that the contracts validly made with the Tinoco government must be performed by the present Costa Rica Government, and that the property which has been invaded or the rights nullified must be restored.

To these contentions the Costa Rican Government answers: First, that the Tinoco government was not a *de facto* or *de jure* government according to the rules of international law. This raises an issue of fact.

   Second, that the contracts and obligations of the Tinoco government, set up by Great Britain on behalf of its subjects, are void, and do not create a legal obligation, because the government of Tinoco and its acts were in violation of the constitution of Costa Rica of 1871.

   Third, that Great Britain is stopped by the fact that it did not recognize the Tinoco government during its incumbency, to claim on behalf of its subjects that Tinoco's was a government which could confer rights binding on its successor.

   Fourth, that the subjects of Great Britain, whose claims are here in controversy, were either by contract or the law of Costa Rica bound to pursue their remedies before the courts of Costa Rica and not to seek diplomatic interference on the part of their home government.

   Dr. John Bassett Moore ... in his *Digest of International Law* ... announces the general principle which has had such universal acquiescence as to become well-settled international law:

Changes in the government or in the internal policy of a State do not as a rule affect its position in international law. A monarchy may be transformed into a republic or a republic into a monarchy; absolute principles may be substituted for constitutional, or the reverse; but, though the government changes, the nation remains, with rights and obligations unimpaired ... .
The principle of the continuity of States has important results. The State is bound by engagements entered into by governments that have ceased to exist; the restored government is generally liable for the acts of the usurper ... .

Again Dr. Moore says:

The origin and organization of government are questions generally of internal discussion and decision. Foreign Powers deal with the existing *de facto* government, when sufficiently established to give reasonable assurance of its permanence, and of the acquiescence of those who constitute the State in its ability to maintain itself, and discharge its internal duties and its external obligations.

   The same principle is announced in Professor Borchard's new work on *The Diplomatic Protection of Citizens Abroad*:

... [A] general government *de facto* having completely taken the place of the regularly constituted authorities in the State binds the nation. So far as its international obligations are concerned, it represents the State. It succeeds to the debts of the regular government it has displaced and transmits its own obligations to succeeding titular governments. Its loans and contracts bind the State and the State is responsible for the governmental acts of the *de facto* authorities. In general its treaties are valid obligations of the State. It may alienate the national territory and the judgments of its courts are admitted to be effective after its authority has ceased. An exception to these rules has occasionally been noted in the practice of some of the States of Latin America, which declare null and void the acts of an usurping *de facto* intermediary government, when the regular government it has displaced succeeds in restoring its control. Nevertheless, acts validly undertaken in the name of the State and having an international character cannot lightly be repudiated and foreign governments generally insist on their binding force. The legality or constitutional legitimacy of a *de facto* government is without importance internationally so far as the matter of representing the State is concerned. ...

First, what are the facts to be gathered from the documents and evidence submitted by the two parties as to the de facto character of the Tinoco government?

In January, 1917, Frederico A. Tinoco was Secretary of War under Alfredo Gonzalez, the then President of Costa Rica. On the ground that Gonzalez was seeking reelection as President in violation of a constitutional limitation, Tinoco used the army and navy to seize the government, assume the provisional headship of the Republic and become Commander-in-Chief of the army. Gonzalez took refuge in the American Legation, thence escaping to the United States. Tinoco constituted a provisional government at once and summoned the people to an election for deputies to a constituent assembly on the first of May, 1917. At the same time he directed an election to take place for the Presidency and himself became a candidate. An election was held. Some 61,000 votes were cast for Tinoco and 259 for another candidate. Tinoco then was inaugurated as the President to administer his powers under the former constitution until the creation of a new one. A new constitution was adopted June 8, 1917, supplanting the constitution of 1871. For a full two years Tinoco and the legislative assembly under him peaceably administered the affairs of the Government of Costa Rica, and there was no disorder of a revolutionary character during that interval. No other government of any kind asserted power in the country. The courts sat, Congress legislated, and the government was duly administered. Its power was fully established and peaceably exercised. The people seemed to have accepted Tinoco's government with great good will when it came in, and to have welcomed the change. ...

Though Tinoco came in with popular approval, the result of his two years administration of the law was to rouse opposition to him. Conspiracies outside of the country were projected to organize a force to attack him. But this did not result in any substantial conflict or even a nominal provisional government on the soil until considerably more than two years after the inauguration of his government, and did not result in the establishment of any other real government until September of that year, he having renounced his Presidency in August preceding, on the score of his ill health, and withdrawn to Europe. The truth is that throughout the record as made by the case and counter case, there is no substantial evidence that Tinoco was not in actual peaceable administration without resistance or conflict or contest by anyone until a few months before the time when he retired and resigned. ...

It is not important, however, what were the causes that enabled Tinoco to carry on his government effectively and peaceably. The question is, must his government be considered a link in the continuity of the Government of Costa Rica? I must hold that from the evidence that the Tinoco government was an actual sovereign government.

But it is urged that many leading Powers refused to recognize the Tinoco government, and that recognition by other nations is the chief and best evidence of the birth, existence and continuity of succession of a government. Undoubtedly recognition by other Powers is an important evidential factor in establishing proof of the existence of a government in the society of nations. What are the facts as to this? The Tinoco government was recognized by ... 20 states excluding United States, Great Britain, France and Italy.

The non-recognition by other nations of a government claiming to be a national personality, is usually appropriate evidence that it has not attained the independence and control entitling it by international law to be classed as such. But when recognition *vel non* of a government is by such nations determined by inquiry, not into its *de facto* sovereignty and complete governmental control, but into its illegitimacy or irregularity of origin, their non-recognition loses something of evidential weight on the issue with which those applying the rules of international law are alone concerned. What is true of the non-recognition of the United States in its bearing upon the existence of a *de facto* government under Tinoco for thirty months is probably in a measure true of the non-recognition by her Allies in the European War. Such non-recognition for any reason, however, cannot outweigh the evidence disclosed by this record before me as to the *de facto* character of Tinoco's government, according to the standard set by international law.

Second. It is ably and earnestly argued on behalf of Costa Rica that the Tinoco government cannot be considered a *de facto* government, because it was not established and maintained in accord with the constitution of Costa Rica of 1871. To hold that a government which establishes itself and maintains a peaceful administration, with the acquiescence of the people for a substantial period of time, does not become a *de facto* government unless it conforms to a previous constitution would be to hold that within the rules of international law a revolution contrary to the fundamental law of the existing government cannot establish a new government. This cannot be, and is not, true. The change by revolution upsets the rule of the authorities in power under the then existing fundamental law, and sets aside the fundamental law in so far as the change of rule makes it necessary. To speak of a revolution creating a *de facto* government, which conforms to the limitations of the old constitution is to use a contradiction in terms. The same government continues internationally, but not the internal law of its being. The issue is not whether the new government assumes power or conducts its administration under constitutional limitations established by the people during the incumbency of the government it has overthrown. The question is, has it really established itself in such a way that all within its influence recognize its control, and that there is no opposing force assuming to be a government in its place? Is it discharging its functions as a government usually does, respected within its own jurisdiction? ...

Third. It is further objected by Costa Rica that Great Britain by her failure to recognize the Tinoco government is estopped now to urge claims of her subjects dependent upon the acts and contracts of the Tinoco government. The evidential weight of such non-recognition against the claim of its *de facto* character I have already considered and admitted. The contention here goes further and precludes a government which did not recognize a *de facto* government from appearing in an international tribunal on behalf of its nationals to claim any rights based on the acts of such government.

To sustain this view a great number of decisions in English and American courts are cited to the point that a municipal court cannot, in litigation before it, recognize or assume the *de facto* character of a foreign government which the executive department of foreign affairs of the government of which the court is a branch has not recognized. This is clearly true ... .

But such cases have no bearing on the point before us. Here the executive of Great Britain takes the position that the Tinoco government which it did not recognize, was nevertheless a *de facto* government that could create rights in British subjects which it now seeks to protect. Of course, as already emphasized, its failure to recognize the *de facto* government can be used against it as evidence to disprove the character it now attributes to that government, but this does not bar it from changing its position. ...

I do not understand the arguments on which an equitable estoppel in such case can rest. The failure to recognize the *de facto* government did not lead the succeeding government to change its position in any way upon the faith of it. Non-recognition may have aided the succeeding government to come into power; but subsequent presentation of claims based on the *de facto* existence of the previous government and its dealings does not work an injury to the succeeding government in the nature of a fraud or breach of faith. An equitable estoppel to prove the truth must rest on previous conduct of the person to be estopped, which has led the person claiming the estoppel into a position in which the truth will injure him. There is no such case here.

There are other estoppels recognized in municipal law than those which rest on equitable considerations. They are based on public policy. It may be urged that it would be in the interest of the stability of governments and the orderly adjustment of international relations, and so a proper rule of international law, that a government in recognizing or refusing to recognize a government claiming admission to the society of nations should thereafter be held to an attitude consistent with its deliberate conclusion on this issue. Arguments for and against such a rule occur to me; but it suffices to say that I have not been cited to text writers of authority or to decisions of significance indicating a general acquiescence of nations in such a rule. Without this, it cannot be applied here as a principle of international law ... .

The fourth point made on behalf of Costa Rica against the claims here pressed is that both claimants are bound either by their own contractual obligation entered into with the Government of Costa Rica, to which they subscribed, not to present their claims by way of diplomatic intervention of their home government, but to submit their claims to the Courts of Costa Rica. This is in effect a plea in abatement to the jurisdiction of the arbitrator, which under the terms of the arbitration, Costa Rica has the right to advance ... .

It has been held in a number of important arbitrations, and by several foreign secretaries, that such restrictions are not binding upon a home government and will not prevent it from exercising its diplomatic functions to protect its nationals against the annulment of the rights secured to them by the laws of the country in force when the obligations arose ... .

However this may be, these restrictions upon each claimant would seem to be inapplicable to a case like the present where is involved the obligation of a restored government for the acts or contracts of an usurping government. The courts of the restored government are bound to administer the law of the restored government under its constitution and their decisions are necessarily affected by the limitations of that instrument. This may prevent the courts from giving full effect to international law that may be at variance with the municipal law which under the restored constitution the national courts have to administer. It is obvious that the obligations of a restored government for the acts of the usurping *de facto* government it succeeds cannot, from the international standpoint, be prejudiced by a constitution which, though restored to life, is for purposes of this discussion, exactly as if it were new legislation which was not in force when the obligations arose. ...

This is not an exceptional instance of an essential difference between the scope and effect of a decision by the highest tribunal of a country and of an international tribunal. The Constitution of the United States makes the Constitution, laws passed in pursuance thereof, and treaties of the United States the supreme law of the land. Under that provision, a treaty may repeal a statute, and a statute may repeal a treaty. The Supreme Court cannot under the Constitution recognize and enforce rights accruing to aliens under a treaty which Congress has repealed by statute. In an international tribunal, however, the unilateral repeal of a treaty by a statute would not affect the rights arising under it and its judgment would necessarily give effect to the treaty and hold the statute repealing it of no effect ... .

A consideration of the issues before us, therefore, recurs to the merits of the two claims. The decision on them must be governed by the answer to the question whether the claims would have been good against the Tinoco government as a government, unaffected by the Law of Nullities, and unaffected by the Costa Rican Constitution of 1871 ... .

NOTES

1) The British claim was ultimately rejected because the obligations undertaken by the Tinoco Government towards the Royal Bank and the other foreigners were held to be invalid under the law in existence at the time, i.e., the constitution and laws of Costa Rica under the Tinoco regime.

2) It is clear from this decision that changes in government do not affect the personality or identity of the state. Thus, the rights and obligations of a state survive such changes in government, whether they be legal or revolutionary.[111] It can even be said that the state continues to exist though there may be a period when there is no effective government, or when the government is in exile because of belligerent occupation of the territory.

Succession to Rights and Obligations[112]

Various views have been expressed as to succession by a new state to the rights and obligations of its predecessor. It has been argued that the new state starts off with a clean slate (a *tabula rasa*) and succeeds to no pre-existing rights and obligations. The opposing view is complete succession to all rights and obligations. The middle approach is that it

---

[111] J. Crawford, *supra*, n. 1, at 28.

[112] See I. Sinclair, "Some Reflections on the Vienna Convention on Succession of States in Respect of Treaties," in *Essays in Honour of Erik Castren* (1979), at 149; Note (1975), 16 *Harv. Int. L.J.* 638; and G. Caggiano, "The ILC Draft on the Succession of States in Respect of Treaties: A Critical Appraisal" (1975), 1 *Ital. Y.B. Int. L.* 69. See also L.-F. Chen, *State Succession Relating to Unequal Treaties* (1974).

is necessary to distinguish between the different circumstances of succession and approach the question of rights and obligations not as a package but individually. The law is most unsettled: one area in which certainty has been sought by agreement is succession to treaty obligations.

Vienna Convention on Succession of States in Respect of Treaties
(1978), 17 *Int. Leg. Mat.* 1488

Article 2

1. For the purposes of the present Convention: ...
(b) "succession of States" means the replacement of one State by another in the responsibility for the international relations of territory; ...

Article 8

1. The obligations or rights of a predecessor State under treaties in force in respect of a territory at the date of a succession of States do not become the obligations or rights of the successor State towards other States parties to those treaties by reason only of the fact that the predecessor State and the successor State have concluded an agreement providing that such obligations or rights shall devolve upon the successor State.

2. Notwithstanding the conclusion of such an agreement, the effects of a succession of States on treaties which, at the date of that succession of States, were in force in respect of the territory in question are governed by the present Convention.

Article 9

1. Obligations or rights under treaties in force in respect of a territory at the date of a succession of States do not become the obligations or rights of the successor State or of other States parties to those treaties by reason only of the fact that the successor State has made a unilateral declaration providing for the continuance in force of the treaties in respect of its territory.

2. In such a case, the effects of the succession of States on treaties which, at the date of that succession of States, were in force in respect of the territory in question are governed by the present Convention.

Article 10

1. When a treaty provides that, on the occurrence of a succession of States, a successor State shall have the option to consider itself a party to the treaty, it may notify its succession in respect of the treaty in conformity with the provisions of the treaty or, failing any such provisions, in conformity with the provisions of the present Convention.

2. If a treaty provides that, on the occurrence of a succession of States, a successor State shall be considered as a party to the treaty, that provision takes effect as such only if the successor State expressly accepts in writing to be so considered.

3. In cases falling under paragraph 1 or 2, a successor State which establishes its consent to be a party to the treaty is considered as a party from the date of the succession of States unless the treaty otherwise provides or it is otherwise agreed.

Article 11

A succession of States does not as such affect:
  (a) a boundary established by a treaty; or
  (b) obligations and rights established by a treaty and relating to the régime of a boundary.

Article 12

1. A succession of States does not as such affect:
  (a) obligations relating to the use of any territory, or to restrictions upon its use established by a treaty for the benefit of any territory of a foreign State and considered as attaching to the territories in question;
  (b) rights established by a treaty for the benefit of any territory and relating to the use, or to restrictions upon the use, of any territory of a foreign State and considered as attaching to the territories in question.

2. A succession of States does not as such affect:
  (a) obligations relating to the use of any territory, or to restrictions upon its use, established by a treaty for the benefit of a group of States or of all States and considered as attaching to that territory;
  (b) rights established by a treaty for the benefit of a group of States or of all States and relating to the use of any territory, or to restrictions upon its use, and considered as attaching to that territory.

3. The provisions of the present article do not apply to treaty obligations of the predecessor State providing for the establishment of foreign military bases on the territory to which the succession of States relates.

Article 15

When part of the territory of a State, or when any territory for the international relations of which a State is responsible, not being part of the territory of that State, becomes part of the territory of another State:
  (a) treaties of the predecessor State cease to be in force in respect of the territory to which the succession of States relates from the date of the succession of States; and
  (b) treaties of the successor State are in force in respect of the territory to which the succession of States relates from the date of the succession of States, unless it appears from the treaty or is otherwise established that the application of the treaty to that territory would be incompatible with the object and purpose of the treaty or would radically change the conditions for its operation.

Article 16

A newly independent State is not bound to maintain in force, or to become a party to, any treaty by reason only of the fact that at the date of the succession of States the treaty was in force in respect of the territory to which the succession of States relates.

Article 17

1. Subject to paragraphs 2 and 3, a newly independent State may, by a notification of succession, establish its status as a party to any multilateral treaty which at the date of the succession of States was in force in respect of the territory to which the succession of States relates.

2. Paragraph 1 does not apply if it appears from the treaty or is otherwise established that the application of the treaty in respect of the newly independent State would be incompatible with the object and purpose of the treaty or would radically change the conditions for its operation.

3. When, under the terms of the treaty or by reason of the limited number of the negotiating States and the object and purpose of the treaty, the participation of any other State in the treaty must be considered as requiring the consent of all the parties, the newly independent State may establish its status as a party to the treaty only with such consent.

Article 24

1. A bilateral treaty which at the date of a succession of States was in force in respect of the territory to which the succession of States relates is considered as being in force between a newly independent State and the other State party when:

(a) they expressly so agree; or

(b) by reason of their conduct they are to be considered as having so agreed.

2. A treaty considered as being in force under paragraph 1 applies in the relations between the newly independent State and the other State party from the date of the succession of States, unless a different intention appears from their agreement or is otherwise established.

NOTES

1) Fifteen states' parties are needed to bring this Convention into force. The Convention was based upon a draft prepared by the International Law Commission. The Convention purports to codify customary international law.

2) Where territorial changes have occurred a treaty will likely be terminated either by way of provisions therein concerning denunciation or by the doctrine of fundamental change of circumstances (*rebus sic stantibus*).[113] After the Russian Revolution the U.S.S.R. made the claim that a new state had come into being, not simply a new government. It was argued that the new government should not be responsible for the obligations, including debts, of the previous Czarist regime. The doctrine of *rebus sic stantibus* was called in aid of release from such obligations. This argument was rejected by many states. The new government also adopted inconsistent positions with regard to retention of rights belonging to Czarist Russia.[114]

---

[113] Discussed *infra* under the "Operation of Treaties" in Chapter 3.

[114] See K. Grzybowski, *Soviet Public International Law: Doctrines and Diplomatic Practice* (1970), at 92-95.

3) There have to be exceptions to the *tabula rasa* approach. First, treaties that evidence
or codify customary international law are binding on the successor state. Secondly,
dispositive or localized treaties that, for example, concern rights of transit over territory,
navigation, fishing rights or port facilities as well as boundary treaties have to endure.[115]
The traditional view of state succession has proceeded from a division of treaties into
personal and real. The former category comprised treaties properly personal to the contracting parties in the sense that they presupposed the continued existence of the same
parties as the very basis of the agreement. Treaties of alliance, mutual defence, guarantee,
arbitration and other treaties of a political character fell into this class and were held to
be the kind which did not survive a change of sovereignty. The category of real or
dispositive treaties was said to include those which imposed more on the land and less
on the particular personality of the parties. Boundary treaties and treaties granting rights
of transit, water, grazing, etc., were the sort held to be in this class and to be the kind
which generally survived a change in sovereignty.

4) Within the Commonwealth, it certainly was the traditional view, prior to World
War II, that the older British dominions had inherited all the treaty rights and obligations
of general application to the United Kingdom at the time they gained separate international
status. However, since World War II this approach has been generally discarded and is
regarded as having been too broad. The other extreme, advocated by certain former
colonies, is that the doctrine of sovereign equality of states requires that new states, upon
attaining independence, have absolute freedom to accept or reject the treaty obligations
incurred on their behalf by the former metropolitan power.[116] So far as Canada is concerned, both the Department of External Affairs and the courts[117] adhere to the older view
that Canada continues to be bound by the treaties made by the United Kingdom affecting
her.

5) State succession problems in practice are dealt with by devolution agreements, by
unilateral declarations and by original accession to treaties by new states. What is the
effect of devolution agreements and unilateral declarations in light of Articles 8 and 9 of
the 1978 Vienna Convention?[118]

6) In 1983 the *Convention on the Succession of States in Respect to State Property,*

---

[115] Article 12 above respects this reality, but cp. I. Brownlie, *Principles of Public International Law* (3 ed.,
1979), at 666-67.

[116] For cases arising out of the independence of former British or French colonies see, for instance, *Re Westerling,*
[1951] Malayan L.R. 288; *Dabrai v. Air India Ltd.,* [1954] Bombay L.R. 944; *Yangtse (London) Ltd. v.
Barlas Bros.,* [1961] Pakistani L. Dec. 573; *Trésor Public v. Air Laos et C.A.M.A.T.* (1961), Rev. Fr. Droit
Aérien 276; See also A.P. Lister, "State Succession to Treaties in the Commonwealth" (1963), 12 *Int. &
Comp. L.Q.* 475.

[117] See *Ex parte O'Dell and Griffen,* [1953] O.R. 190 (H.C.), reported in Chapter 3 below; and D.P. O'Connell,
"State Succession and Problems of Treaty Interpretation" (1964), 58 *Am. J. Int. L.* 41.

[118] See the Commentary of the I.L.C. to the Draft Articles of the 1978 Treaty, [1974] Y.B.I.L.C. II, 174ff.
I. Brownlie, *supra,* n. 115, at 669, lists those states that have made unilateral declarations following the
example set by Tanganyika (Tanzania) in 1961. See *Molefi v. Principal Legal Adviser,* [1971] A.C. 182
(P.C.), in which such a declaration by Lesotho was held to be an accession to the *Convention Relating to
the Status of Refugees* (1951), 189 U.N.T.S. 137.

Archives and Debts was adopted in Vienna but is not yet in force.[119] This Convention seeks to deal systematically with the other aspects of state succession. Clearly, under the rules of customary international law, a successor state acquiring the entire territory of a predecessor state succeeds to all the public property, movable or immovable wherever it is located.[120] Where a state is not extinguished but merely loses some of its territory then the state that acquires that territory succeeds to the public property located there in the absence of an agreement by both parties to the contrary. Any property located in the predecessor state or in a third state would remain with the predecessor absent an agreement.

7) There is little uniform practice as to state debts. It has been suggested[121] that if the debt was incurred to improve the territory of the state then the successor is responsible. Where, however, the debt was incurred for some purpose hostile to the successor then it is argued there is no obligation to repay it.[122] If a state is dissolved, the problem is even more complex. Theoretically, the public debt should be apportioned between the successor states based upon agreement between them. The 1983 Convention provides for succession to financial obligations chargeable to a state. It seeks to provide bases on which apportionment should take place. Distinctions are drawn here, as elsewhere, in the 1983 Convention between succession resulting from transfer of territory by one state to another, newly independent states, uniting of states, and succession and dissolution.

Respect for Private Rights

Private vested or acquired rights should be respected by the successor state. A change in states of itself does not affect rights, including contracts and concessions made by the former state which were acquired under its laws. But the continuance of those laws is subject to the sovereign authority of the successor state. Yet, even though the successor may change the domestic legal system it is still under a duty to observe a certain minimum standard of treatment for aliens.[123]

The Lighthouses Arbitration
France v. Greece
(1956), 12 R.I.A.A. 155; 23 I.L.R. 659

[This case concerned, *inter alia*, claims by France that Greece was responsible for breach of state concessions to its citizens by the autonomous state of Crete. The breaches were committed prior to the extension of Greek sovereignty over Crete.]

---

[119] U.N. Doc. A/CONF.117/14 (1983); reprinted in (1983), 22 *Int. Leg. Mat.* 306.

[120] See *Haile Selassie v. Cable and Wireless Ltd. (No. 2)*, [1939] Ch. 182 (C.A.), reported *infra*, Chapter 5. The problems there concerned the recognition of a government and its right to public property located abroad.

[121] M. Shaw, *International Law* (1977), at 338.

[122] S.A. Williams and A.L.C. de Mestral, *supra*, n. 1, at 101-2.

[123] The existence and content of this standard of treatment of aliens is discussed in Chapter 9 on "State Responsibility." See the *German Settlers Case* (1923), P.C.I.J., Ser. B, No. 6; *German Interests in Polish Upper Silesia* (1926), P.C.I.J., Ser. A, No. 7, at 21-22; *Chorzow Factory Case* (1928), P.C.I.J., Ser. A, No. 17, at 46-48, reported *infra*, in Chapter 9.

THE TRIBUNAL: ... the Tribunal can only come to the conclusion that Greece, having adopted the illegal conduct of Crete in its recent past as an autonomous State, is bound, as successor State, to take upon its charge the financial consequences of the breach of the concession contract. Otherwise, the avowed violation of a contract committed by one of the two States ... with the assent of the other, would, in the event of their merger, have the thoroughly unjust consequence of cancelling a definite financial responsibility and of sacrificing the undoubted rights of a private firm holding a concession to a so-called principle of non-transmission of debts in cases of territorial succession, which in reality does not exist as a general and absolute principle. In this case, the Greek government with good reason commenced by recognizing its own responsibility.

NOTES

1) Questions as to the obligation to pay compensation in cases of nationalization by a predecessor government are discussed in Chapter 9 on State Responsibility. Should different considerations apply to investments made before the independence of a state as opposed to afterwards? Should economic self-determination, considered earlier, be one of those considerations?

2) Disregard of these acquired or vested rights must be distinguished from international claims for other personal injuries, which do not devolve upon the successor state. See the following case:

Robert E. Brown Claim
United States-Great Britain Claims Arbitration Tribunal
(1923), 6 R.I.A.A. 120; (1925), 19 *Am. J. Int. L.* 193

[The United States sought damages from Great Britain for the denial of rights claimed by Brown, an American citizen, in South Africa prior to its conquest by Great Britain. Brown had staked a large number of gold mining claims at Witfontein even though he had been refused any prospecting licences. The circumstances of this refusal were confused by the actions of the government in Pretoria which had at first proclaimed the area open to prospecting but had then postponed it. When Brown brought a suit demanding the licences or damages for their denial, the High Court held that since the notice of post-ponement was not proclaimed in the Official Gazette until the day after the opening of prospecting, it was ineffectual and consequently no grounds existed to refuse Brown's application on that day. Brown was issued licences valid for one month but, their renewal being denied, he was forced to return to court on his alternative claim for damages. By the time the case was heard the Chief Justice had been dismissed and the High Court had been reorganized with new justices partial to the government. The decision of this court effectively non-suited Brown.

On these facts, the Claims Tribunal first held Brown had suffered a denial of justice according to the standards of international law at the hands of the government of South

Africa. It then turned to the question whether the British Government succeeded to that liability.]

THE TRIBUNAL: ... Passing to the second main question involved, we are equally clear that this liability never passed to or was assumed by the British Government. Neither in the terms of peace granted at the time of the surrender of the Boer forces, nor in the Proclamation of Annexation, can there be found any provision referring to the assumption of liabilities of this nature. It should be borne in mind that this was simply a pending claim for damages against certain officials and had never become a liquidated debt of the former State. Nor is there, properly speaking, any question of State succession here involved. The United States plants itself squarely on two propositions: first, that the British Government, by the acts of its own officials with respect to Brown's case, has become liable to him; and, secondly, that in some way a liability was imposed upon the British Government by reason of the peculiar relation of suzerainty which is maintained with respect to the South African Republic.

The first of these contentions is set forth in the Reply as follows:

The United States reaffirms that Brown suffered a denial of justice at the hands of authorities of the South African Republic. Had it not been for this denial of justice, it may be assumed that a diplomatic claim would not have arisen. But it does not follow that, as is contended in His Majesty's Government's Answer, it is incumbent on the United States to show that there is a rule of international law imposing liability on His Majesty's Government for the tortious acts of the South African Republic. Occurrences which took place during the existence of the South African Republic are obviously relevant and important in connection with the case before the Tribunal, but the United States contends that acts of the British Government and of British officials and the general position taken by them with respect to Brown's case have fixed liability on His Majesty's Government.

Again on page 8 of the Reply it is said:

The succeeding British authorities to whom Brown applied for the licenses to which he had been declared entitled by the Court also refused to grant the licenses, and therefore refused to carry out the decree of the Court which the United States contends was binding on them. And they have steadfastly refused to make compensation to Brown in lieu of the licenses to which the Court declared Brown to be entitled, failing the granting of the licenses.

The American Agent quoted these passages in his oral argument, and disclaimed any intention of maintaining ''that there is any general liability for torts of a defunct State.'' We have searched the record for any indication that the British authorities did more than leave this matter exactly where it stood when annexation took place. They did not redress the wrong which had been committed, nor did they place any obstacles in Brown's path; they took no action one way or the other. No British official nor any British court undertook to deny Brown justice or to perpetuate the wrong. The Attorney General of the Colony, in his opinion, declared that the courts were still open to the claimant. The contention of the American Agent amounts to an assertion that a succeeding State acquiring a territory by conquest without any undertaking to assume such liabilities is bound to take affirmative steps to right the wrongs done by the former State. We cannot indorse this doctrine ... .

We may grant that a special relation between Great Britain and the South African State, varying considerably in its scope and significance from time to time, existed from the beginning. No doubt Great Britain's position in South Africa imposed upon her a peculiar status and responsibility. She repeatedly declared and asserted her authority as the so-called paramount Power in the region; but the authority which she exerted over the South African Republic certainly at the time of the occurrences here under consideration, in our judgment fell far short of which would be required to make her responsible for the wrong inflicted upon Brown ... . Nowhere is there any clause indicating that Great Britain had any right to interest herself in the internal administration of the country, legislative, executive or judicial; nor is there any evidence that Great Britain ever did undertake to interfere in this way. Indeed the only remedy which Great Britain ever had for maladministration affecting British subjects and those of other Powers, residing in the South African Republic was, as the event proved, to resort to war. If there had been no South African war, we hold that the United States Government would have been obliged to take up Brown's claim with the Government of the Republic and that there would have been no ground for bringing it to the attention of Great Britain. The relation of suzerain did not operate to render Great Britain liable for the acts complained of.

Now therefore: The decision of the Tribunal is that the claim of the United States Government be disallowed.

Change of Nationality[124]

When a predecessor state becomes extinct the population takes the nationality of the successor state. However, in other cases leading to succession precision is lacking. There are no uniform rules to apply. It is necessary to look at the treaty between the predecessor and successor state, and their domestic legislation pertaining to nationality in order to determine whether the inhabitants of the territory have taken a new nationality, retained the old or have both.

The Providence
(1810), Stewart 186 (N.S. V-Adm.)

[At issue was the effect of the independence of the United States of America upon the allegiance of natural-born subjects to the British Crown.[125]]

DR. CROKE: ... [G]enerally speaking, it is an indisputable maxim of law, that natural allegiance with its duties and the privileges derived from it, is perpetual, unalienable, and indefeasible. But Sir Michael Foster, one of the first authorities in the British law,

---

[124] Acquisition of nationality in the absence of state succession is discussed in Chapter 7.
[125] See also *Salter v. Hughes* (1864), 5 N.S.R. 409 (C.A.); and *Montgomery v. Graham* (1871), 31 U.C.Q.B. 57 (C.A.).

justly observes, "that though this doctrine of allegiance, founded in birth, may be considered as a good general rule, yet it is not universally true. Cases may be put which will be considered as exceptions to it." It must be admitted to be one of those exceptions, where the tie between the sovereign and the subject is broken; and the connection dissolved by the concurrent acts of the sovereign, to whom it is due, and of the party himself. For all compacts, and the duties and obligations of allegiance are in the nature of a compact, may be dissolved by the mutual consent of all parties interested. A dissolution of this nature took place between the king of Great Britain, and his subjects in the United States, when their independence was acknowledged by the treaty of peace, in the years 1782 and 1783. By the first article of that treaty, His Majesty acknowledged the thirteen States to be free, sovereign, and independent States, and for himself, his heirs, and successors, relinquished all claims to the government, propriety, and territorial rights of the same. This is a complete renunciation of the rights of allegiance, on the part of His Majesty, and a perfect discharge of the inhabitants of that country, from all their obligations as subjects. This treaty was directly authorized by a preceding act of Parliament, 22 Geo. III. c. 46, by which it was enacted, that it should be lawful for His Majesty to conclude a peace with the colonies, any law to the contrary notwithstanding, and was subsequently, though indirectly, confirmed by other acts. There was the sanction therefore of the legislature as well as of the sovereign. On the other hand there was the assent of all the inhabitants of the thirteen colonies, represented and expressed by the ratification of their government, which had been established by their own free choice. From this concurrence of all parties concerned, no act could be more valid, or unexceptionable. The inhabitants of that country, from that time, became aliens to every purpose, and liable to all the disabilities of aliens. As they were no longer bound to any allegiance, so neither were they entitled to any of the privileges of British born subjects ... .

NOTES

1) In some devolution agreements between former colonial regimes and newly independent states, provision has been made for the inhabitants to choose between the nationalities of the predecessor and successor states. Of specific Canadian interest is *The Treaty of Paris*, 1763 by which France ceded Canada to Great Britain and made arrangements for French nationals to withdraw or to change their allegiance to the British Crown. The treaty is reported in Chapter 6 on "State Jurisdiction over Territory."

2) In *Donegani v. Donegani*,[126] it was held that "the cession [of Canada] to Britain involved a change of sovereignty as a result of which the law of England, and not the law of France, would determine the question who were aliens; ... " Note that there was a distinction in English public law between a settled colony and one conquered or ceded. The common law did not automatically apply to the latter. The private law of the former sovereign continued in force until the Crown ordered otherwise.[127] The question as to the

---

[126] (1834), 3 Knapp 62; 12 E.R. 571.
[127] *Campbell v. Hall* (1774), 1 Cowp. 204; 98 E.R. 1045.

extent to which the law of England applied in Canada arose many times until it was settled by the Quebec Act of 1774.[128]

3) In the face of the growing number of persons dispossessed of their nationality, and thus of the right of access to any country, as a result of so many changes to the states of the world, a Convention on the Reduction of Statelessness was adopted in 1961.[129] It came into force in 1975, and has applied to Canada since her accession in 1978.

Convention on the Reduction of Statelessness
U.N. Doc. A/CONF. 9/15 (1961)

Article 10

1. Every treaty between Contracting States providing for the transfer of territory shall include provisions designed to secure that no person shall become stateless as a result of the transfer. A Contracting State shall use its best endeavours to secure that any such treaty made by it with a State which is not a party to this Convention includes such provisions.

2. In the absence of such provisions a Contracting State to which territory is transferred or which otherwise acquires territory shall confer its nationality on such persons as would otherwise become stateless as a result of the transfer or acquisition.

---

[128] 14 Geo. III, c. 83, s. 8; R.S.C. 1952, vol. VI, at 6133. In general, see J.G. Castel, *The Civil Law System of the Province of Quebec* (1962), at 5-35, especially at 22; also T. Hodgins, "The Law of Allegiance in Canada" (1881), 1 *Can. L.T.* 1, and *Perlman v. Lieut. Col. Piché* (1918), 54 S.C. 170 (Que.).

[129] See P. Weis, *Nationality and Statelessness in International Law* (2 ed., 1979), at 135-60; D.P. O'Connell, *International Law* (2 ed., 1970), at 391-93.

CHAPTER THREE

Creation and Ascertainment of International Law

SOURCES OF LAW[1]

International law governs relations between independent States. The rules of law binding upon States therefore emanate from their own free will as expressed in conventions or by usages generally accepted as expressing principles of law and established in order to regulate the relations between these coexisting independent communities or with a view to the achievement of common aims.[2]

Statute of the International Court of Justice
Article 38

1. The Court, whose function is to decide in accordance with international law such disputes as are submitted to it, shall apply:

   a)   international conventions, whether general or particular, establishing rules expressly recognized by the contesting states;

   b)   international custom, as evidence of a general practice accepted as law;

   c)   the general principles of law recognized by civilized nations;

   d)   subject to the provisions of Art. 59, judicial decisions and the teachings of the most highly qualified publicists of the various nations, as subsidiary means for the determination of rules of law.

   2. This provision shall not prejudice the power of the Court to decide a case *ex aequo et bono*, if the parties agree thereto.

---

[1] In general, see G.A. Finch, *The Sources of Modern International Law* (1937); A.M. Jacomy-Millette, *Treaty Law in Canada* (1975); A.E. Gotlieb, *Canadian Treaty Making* (1968); Lord McNair, *The Law of Treaties: British Practice and Opinions* (1938); C. Parry, *The Sources and Evidence of International Law* (1965); M. Sorensen, *Les sources du droit international* (1946); G.J.H. van Hoof, *Rethinking the Sources of International Law* (1983).

[2] From *The Steamship Lotus* (1927), P.C.I.J., Ser. A, No. 10, at 18.

NOTES

1) Article 59 provides that "The decision of the Court has no binding force except between the parties and in respect of that particular case."

2) Article 38(1) is considered as the authoritative statement of the law-creating processes of international law. In order for the court to apply any asserted rule of positive international law, it must be shown that the rule is the product of one, or more, of the three law-creating processes mentioned in sub-paragraphs, a, b or c. These law-creating processes are exclusive for the court. However, when the court decides a case *ex aequo et bono* in accordance with article 38(2), it is not so limited.

3) Article 38(1)(d), when it refers to "subsidiary means for the determination of rules of law," indicates that decisions of judicial institutions and the teachings of the most highly qualified publicists of the various nations are subsidiary law-determining agencies and not law-creating processes. As Schwarzenberger has pointed out, "Whereas, in the case of the law-creating processes, the emphasis lies on the forms by which any particular rule of international law is created, in the case of the law-determining agencies it is on how an alleged rule is to be verified."[3] In other words, they are evidence by reference to which the existence and contents of the rules of positive international law are determined. The diplomatic practice of individual states and national courts are also law-determining agencies. These distinctions are well represented in the diagram on the next page.[4]

4) Does article 38(1) contain an exhaustive enumeration of the law-creating processes or are there others? For instance, are decisions of international bodies, such as the United Nations, a new law-creating process or manifestations of existing law-creating processes? See *infra*, "Other Sources of Law?"

5) Does the exclusiveness of the law-creating process help to understand the distinction between rules on which the generality of states has expressed agreement (*de lege lata*) and rules introducing new principles which are rejected by certain representative groups of states and have nothing more than a *de lege ferenda* value (would-be law) in the eyes of the states that have adopted them?

6) Article 38(1) makes no hierarchical distinction among the three law-creating processes. They are all of equal authority. The potential exists, therefore, for a conflict of rules from different sources to occur. As between the parties, a treaty could possibly override pre-existing custom and a subsequent custom might overreach a treaty. Quite often a conflict between a treaty and a custom is more apparent than real; it may be resolved by interpreting the rules so as to avoid conflict. Frequently, the treaty provision is so much more specific than the customary rule that it may be applied without doing harm to the integrity of the more general principle. International tribunals have had few occasions to express themselves on conflicts of applicable rules. A recent exception is the *English Channel Arbitration*[5] concerning the delimitation of the continental shelf

---

[3] G. Schwarzenberger, *International Law* (3 ed., 1957), Vol. 1, at 27.
[4] From G. Schwarzenberger, *A Manual of International Law* (5 ed., 1967), at 27.
[5] (1977), 18 R.I.A.A.3, at 36-37. And see M. Akehurst, "The Hierarchy of the Sources of International Law" (1974-75), 47 *Br. Y.B. Int. L.* 273.

		Subjects of International Law	
Law-creating Agents			
Law-creating Processes	Consensual Understandings	International Customary Law	The General Principles of Law Recognized by Civilized Nations
Scope	*inter partes*	universal, general or particular	near-universal
Constituent Elements	agreement (*consensus ad idem*)	general practice (*consuetudo*) / accepted as law (*opinio juris sive necessitatis*)	principles of law / generality in character / recognition by civilised nations
Bases of Obligation	Consent, Acquiescence, Recognition and Good Faith		
CREATION OF RULES OF INTERNATIONAL LAW			

ASCERTAINMENT OF RULES OF INTERNATIONAL LAW	**Law-determining Agencies** (means for determining the existence of individual rules of international law, and their meaning and scope)	Acts of the contracting parties; treaty text; preparatory work; subsequent practice	Practice of the Subjects of International Law / Doctrine of International Law

Practice of the Subjects of International Law:

- collective
  - international institutions
    - international judicial or arbitral practice
    - practice of other international institutions
- individual
  - external
    - diplomatic and treaty practice
  - internal
    - legis-lative
    - exe-cutive
    - judi-cial

between the United Kingdom and France. It took place in 1977 while the U.N. Conference on the Law of the Sea was still in progress. The award states:

47. The Court is directed by Article 2 of the Arbitration Agreement to decide the course of the boundary ''in accordance with the rules of international law applicable in the matter as between the Parties''; and, as the Parties agree, the rules of international law to be applied by the Court under this rubric are unquestionably the rules in force today. At the same time, the Court recognises both the importance of the evolution of the law of the sea which is now in progress and the possibility that a development in customary law may, under certain conditions, evidence the assent of the States concerned to the modification, or even termination, of previously existing treaty rights and obligations. But the Continental Shelf Convention of 1958 entered into force as between the Parties little more than a decade ago. Moreover, the information before the Court contains references by the French Republic and the United Kingdom, as well as by other States, to the Convention as an existing treaty in force which are of quite recent date. Consequently, only the most conclusive indications of the intention of the parties to the 1958 Convention to regard it as terminated could warrant this Court in treating it as obsolete and inapplicable as between the French Republic and the United Kingdom in the present matter. In the opinion of the Court, however, neither the records of the Third United Nations Conference on the Law of the Sea nor the practice of States outside the Conference provide any such conclusive indication that the Continental Shelf Convention of 1958 is today considered by its parties to be already obsolete and no longer applicable as a treaty in force.

48. The Court accordingly finds that the Geneva Convention of 1958 on the Continental Shelf is a treaty in force, the provisions of which are applicable as between the Parties to the present proceedings under Article 2 of the Arbitration Agreement. This finding, the Court wishes at the same time to emphasise, does not mean that it regards itself as debarred from taking any account in these proceedings of recent developments in customary law. On the contrary, the Court has no doubt that it should take due account of the evolution of the law of the sea in so far as this may be relevant in the context of the present case.

7) It is possible that the same rule may be derived from more than one of the law-creating processes. For example, law-making treaties often include provisions that are codifications of custom. In such instances, does treaty law supervene over customary law? In *Military Activities In and Against Nicaragua*[6] the International Court rejected the view put forward by the United States that the existence of certain principles in the United Nations Charter or other multilateral treaties precluded the possibility that similar rules might exist independently in customary international law either because existing customary rules had been incorporated into the Charter or because the Charter influenced the later adoption of customary rules with a corresponding content. '' ... [E]ven if a treaty norm and a customary norm relevant to the ... dispute were to have exactly the same content, this would not be a reason for the Court to take the view that the operation of the treaty

---

[6] [1986] I.C.J. Rep. 14: In this case it was decided that the United States had violated its customary international law obligations a) not to intervene in the affairs of Nicaragua and b) not to use force against it.

process must necessarily deprive the customary norm of its separate applicability."[7]
Customary international law continues to exist alongside treaty law. The Court elaborated
on this point, giving the following example:[8]

> There are a number of reasons for considering that, even if two norms belonging to two sources
> of international law appear identical in content, and even if the States in question are bound
> by these rules both on the level of treaty-law and on that of customary international law, these norms
> retain a separate existence. This is so from the standpoint of their applicability. In a legal dispute
> affecting two States, one of them may argue that the applicability of a treaty rule to its own conduct
> depends on the other State's conduct in respect of the application of other rules, on other subjects,
> also included in the same treaty. For example, if a State exercises its right to terminate or
> suspend the operation of a treaty on the ground of the violation by the other party of a "provision
> essential to the accomplishment of the object or purpose of the treaty" (in the words of Art. 60,
> para. 3(b), of the Vienna Convention on the Law of Treaties), it is exempted, vis-à-vis the other
> State, from a rule of treaty-law because of the breach by that other State of a different rule of
> treaty law. But if the two rules in question also exist as rules of customary international law, the
> failure of the one State to apply the one rule does not justify the other State in declining to apply
> the other rule. Rules which are identical in treaty law and in customary international law are also
> distinguishable by reference to the methods of interpretation and application. A State may accept
> a rule contained in a treaty not simply because it favours the application of the rule itself, but
> also because the treaty establishes what that State regards as desirable institutions or mechanisms
> to ensure implementation of the rule. Thus, if that rule parallels a rule of customary international
> law, two rules of the same content are subject to separate treatment as regards the organs competent
> to verify their implementation, depending on whether they are customary rules or treaty rules.
> The present dispute illustrates this point.

It will therefore be clear that customary international law continues to exist and to
apply, separately from international treaty law, even where the two categories of law
have an identical content.

8) A distinction is often made between formal sources, (from which rules of law derive
their force, such as in Canada an act of Parliament or a regulation promulgated in the
Official Gazette), and material sources of law, (those which supply the substance of the
rules of law, for instance the speeches, committee hearings and government reports during
the passage of a bill through Parliament or the departmental materials and Cabinet minutes
in the preparation of new regulations). While law-making treaties may resemble a formal
source of law, in the opinion of some writers it is difficult to maintain the distinction in
the field of international law, as there is no constitutional machinery, like a legislature,
for the creation of rules of international law.[9]

---

[7] Para. 175, at 94. And see para. 177, at 94-95.
[8] Paras. 178-179, at 95-96.
[9] See I. Brownlie, *Principles of Public International Law* (3 ed., 1979), at 1-4.

TREATIES

Generally

Although it is generally stated that treaties are a major law-creating process or source of international law, a distinction must be made between law-making treaties and treaty-contracts. Only law-making treaties can be regarded as a law-creating process because they are treaties in which a substantial number of states have declared what the law is or should be on a particular topic, provided, of course, that such treaties have actually entered into force. A good example of law-making treaties is the 1961 Vienna Convention on Diplomatic Relations.[10]

Law-making treaties may codify, define, interpret, or abolish existing customary or conventional rules of international law or create new rules for future international conduct. They may also create international institutions. Treaty-contracts, whether bilateral or multilateral, do not create general rules of international law. They create special rights and obligations like private law contracts by virtue of the principle *pacta sunt servanda*, which is a general principle of law (see discussion, *infra*). However, in some cases treaty-contracts may lead to the formation of rules of customary international law or be evidence of the existence of such rules (See "Custom," *infra*). The distinction between law-making treaties and treaty-contracts could be questioned on the ground that both types are of a purely contractual character since they are based on mutual consent.

The basic principles of the law of treaties are nowadays set down in the 1969 Vienna Convention on the Law of Treaties which came into force in 1980.[11] A memorandum prepared by the Department of External Affairs dated June 4, 1970, expressed this opinion of the Vienna Convention:

This Convention constitutes a law-making treaty laying down the fundamental principles of contemporary treaty law. Because of the paramount importance of treaties as a source of the international legal obligations binding upon states and the diversity and comprehensiveness of the interlocking network of treaties which today regulate the major part of transactions between states and serve to establish the relationships among them, the Convention must be viewed as virtually the constitutional basis, second in importance only to the U.N. Charter, of the international community of states.

Vienna Convention on the Law of Treaties
(1969), *Int. Leg. Mat.* 679

Article 1

The present Convention applies to treaties between states.

---

[10] 500 U.N.T.S. 95, reported *infra* in Chapter 5.

[11] (1969), 8 *Int. Leg. Mat.* 679. Canada deposited an instrument of ratification to the Convention on October 14, 1970. It entered into force for Canada on January 27, 1980. In general, see T. Elias, *The Modern Law of Treaties* (1974); A. Gotlieb, *Canadian Treaty-Making* (1968); J. Hendry, *Treaties and Federal Constitutions* (1955); P. Hogg, *Constitutional Law of Canada* (2 ed., 1984), c. 11; A. McNair, *The Law of Treaties: British Practice and Opinions* (1938); A. Jacomy-Millette, *Treaty Law in Canada* (1975); I. Sinclair, *The Vienna Convention on the Law of Treaties* (2 ed., 1984).

certain patterns for particular agreements. In Canada, apart perhaps from the Extradition Act which defines extradition arrangements with foreign states as those made by Her Majesty, there is no provision in Canadian law relating to the form or type of agreement, which is therefore largely a matter of convenience to the Canadian Government. In fact, Canadian practice over the years has largely adopted the following types:

    a)   International agreements between heads of states;

    b)   Intergovernmental agreements;

    c)   Exchanges of notes.

Gotlieb[17] indicates that between 1907 and 1967 Canada has used the following types:

act	financial agreement
additional protocol	general act
administrative agreement	instrument
agreed minute	joint statement
agreement	long-term agreement
arrangement	long-term arrangement
articles of agreement	memorandum of agreement
charter	memorandum of understanding
commercial agreement	*modus vivendi*
constitution	payments agreement
convention	*procès-verbal*
decision	protocol
declaration	provisional arrangement
declaration of understanding	special protocol
exchange of letters	statute
exchange of notes	supplementary exchange of notes
executive agreement	supplementary protocol
final act	treaty
trust agreement	

He also points out that "over seventy per cent of all Canadian bilateral treaties have, since the last war, been in exchange-of-notes form."[18]

    The term treaty is seldom used by Canada except in relation to peace, neutrality, arms-control and United States-Canada water problems. Canada prefers the word convention. Canadian international agreements employing the term treaty or convention almost invariably require ratification.

    A Voluntary Restraint, Memorandum of Understanding or Assurances, must be distinguished from a Treaty. Thus, the letter from the Japanese Ambassador describing the voluntary restraints that the Japanese government was applying on the export of certain products to Canada in 1965 or the memorandum of understanding between the governments of Canada and Hong Kong respecting the restriction of certain cotton textiles exports to Canada did not create binding obligations at international law. In the case of

---

[17] A. Gotlieb, *supra*, n. 1, at 21.

[18] A. Gotlieb, *supra*, n. 1, at 84.

China, the Chinese Communist State Trading Corporation agreed as part of the terms of a long-term wheat agreement, to limit annual exports to Canada of sensitive items. This voluntary restraint was not a treaty obligation.

The distinction between treaties and intergovernmental Memoranda of Understanding is observed by the Canadian government thus:[19]

In Canadian practice, arrangements or understandings between the governments of two or more States, no matter what form they take (e.g., a Memorandum of Understanding or an Exchange of Notes or Letters) create commitments of a political and moral character and are not binding in, or governed by, international law. Obviously the mere fact that the instrument is called a Memorandum of Understanding is not decisive in itself, but a conscious effort is made in every instance to ensure that instruments of this kind do not embody clauses of legal obligation. "Will" is used in place of "shall" and the form of the instrument is kept as simple as possible. It is our practice to register these instruments in a Register of Understandings and Arrangements separate from the Treaty Register. They are not published in the Canada Treaty Series but copies are available on request.

Cooperative arrangements at the technical level are frequently concluded between Canadian Government departments or agencies and their counterparts in other countries. Such arrangements, which have multiplied in recent years, constitute an important means of enabling Canadian Government departments and agencies to function more effectively by developing close working-level links with departments and agencies of foreign Governments in fields of common interest.

On occasion, when department-to-department or agency-to-agency arrangements are under negotiation, a need will arise to provide for the settlement of disputes or the handling of claims for personal injury or property damage. Our practice is to embody such clauses in a covering exchange of notes which constitutes an international agreement.

We understand "implementing agreements" as meaning subsidiary arrangements concluded under an umbrella agreement which constitutes a treaty. A typical example would be a development aid or economic cooperation agreement which envisages the need for project agreements. Such subsidiary arrangements are not regarded as treaties and wording is customarily inserted to specify that they shall be considered as administrative arrangements.

The number of government-to-government, department-to-department and agency-to-agency arrangements has increased greatly in recent years. Because of this trend, Canada would welcome the development of some basic ground rules regarding such instruments as Memoranda of Understanding, in particular an understanding that normally they cannot be regarded as creating legal obligations governed by international law.

Treaty Making

The conclusion of a treaty is attended by a number of formalities. In the first place, the representative of a state must have "full powers" to give the consent of his state (see Article 7 of the Vienna Convention below) and if he does not his agreement is without legal effect unless afterwards confirmed by that state (Article 8). Second, the mode of

---

[19] (1980), 18 *Can. Y.B. Int. L.* at 312-15.

adoption of the treaty, whether by consensus or voting, has to be agreed upon (Article 9). Third, the means to authenticate the definitive text, or texts if the original is in several languages, must be settled (Article 10). Finally the particular steps to express consent to the treaty need to be set down (Articles 11-16). Signature is the usual choice, although an exchange of instruments may constitute a bilateral treaty. Multilateral treaties frequently require more than the signature of a representative at the negotiations, demanding the subsequent confirmation by ratification, acceptance or approval of his state. A multilateral treaty typically will also permit a state, which did not sign the agreement, subsequently to accede to it. Nowadays the process of giving consent is extended even further by separating the negotiations from the act of signature. A multilateral treaty frequently states that it will be open for signature at a particular place from a certain future date for a stated time. At the end of the negotiating conference, there will be a signing ceremony but these signatures will only adopt the final act of the conference which will include the authentic text of the treaty. A signature to adopt the text is not a substitute for a signature to express consent to be bound by the treaty.

Vienna Convention on the Law of Treaties

Article 7
FULL POWERS

1. A person is considered as representing a state for the purpose of adopting or authenticating the text of a treaty or for the purpose of expressing the consent of the state to be bound by a treaty if:
   a)   he produces appropriate full powers; or
   b)   it appears from the practice of the states concerned or from other circumstances that their intention was to consider that person as representing the state for such purposes and to dispense with full powers.

2. In virtue of their functions and without having to produce full powers, the following are considered as representing their state:
   a)   Heads of State, Heads of Government and Ministers for Foreign Affairs, for the purpose of performing all acts relating to the conclusion of a treaty;
   b)   heads of diplomatic missions, for the purpose of adopting the text of a treaty between the accrediting state and the state to which they are accredited;
   c)   representatives accredited by states to an international conference or to an international organization or one of its organs, for the purpose of adopting the text of a treaty in that conference, organization or organ.

Article 16
EXCHANGE OR DEPOSIT OF INSTRUMENTS OF RATIFICATION,
ACCEPTANCE, APPROVAL OR ACCESSION

Unless the treaty otherwise provides, instruments of ratification, acceptance, approval or accession establish the consent of a state to be bound by a treaty upon:
   a)   their exchange between the contracting states;

b)   their deposit with the depositary; or

c)   their notification to the contracting states or to the depositary, if so agreed.

Article 18
OBLIGATION NOT TO DEFEAT THE OBJECT AND PURPOSE OF A TREATY
PRIOR TO ITS ENTRY INTO FORCE

A state is obliged to refrain from acts which would defeat the object and purpose of a treaty when:

a)   it has signed the treaty or has exchanged instruments constituting the treaty subject to ratification, acceptance or approval, until it shall have made its intention clear not to become a party to the treaty; or

b)   it has expressed its consent to be bound by the treaty, pending the entry into force of the treaty and provided that such entry into force is not unduly delayed.

Treaty-Making Powers in Canada
from Canada, Department of External Affairs
Federalism and International Relations (1968), at 11-16, 26-28, 30-33.

(A) The Treaty-Making Power
The exclusive responsibility of the Federal Government in the field of treaty-making rests upon three considerations: the principles of international law relating to the power of component parts of federal states to make treaties; the constitutions and constitutional practices of federal states; and, finally, the Canadian Constitution and constitutional practice. These three aspects are examined below.

(i) The Principles of International Law
The question whether the members of a federal union can make treaties or international agreements has been studied at length by the International Law Commission, a subsidiary organ of the United Nations General Assembly, and by various experts on the law of treaties who have prepared reports for the Commission. The Commission has taken the view that the question whether a member of a federal union can have a treaty-making capacity depends upon the constitution of the country concerned. In other words, the Commission is of the view that international law cannot by itself decide whether or not a member of a federal union can make a treaty. International law looks, in the first instance, to the constitution of the state in question to determine the treaty-making capacity ... .

(ii) The Constitutions of Federal States
The constitutions of the great majority of states reserve to the federal government the responsibility for the conclusion of international agreements and make it clear that the constituent parts do not possess this right. There are, however, some federal states (Switzerland, the United States, the Federal Republic of Germany and the U.S.S.R.) whose constitutional practice apparently allows the constituent parts to enter into certain

b) Education *Entente*: In June 1964 the Province of Quebec expressed an interest in entering into arrangements with France covering the exchange of professors and students between Quebec and France. The Federal Government stated that it had no objection to applying the procedure followed in the case of ASTEF to the proposed programme in the field of education. The procedure eventually used consisted of a *procès verbal* recording the results of discussions between Quebec and French officials which was signed by the Ministers of Education of Quebec and France and the Director-General of Cultural and Technical Affairs in the French Foreign Ministry. It was agreed that the signing of the *procès verbal* would be accompanied by an exchange of letters between the French Ambassador and the Secretary of State for External Affairs, requesting and granting the Canadian Government's assent in the proposed exchange programme. In January 1965, the title *procès verbal* was changed to *entente*, and the *entente* was signed in Paris on February 27, 1965, with the exchange of letters mentioned above taking place in Ottawa on the same day.

c) Proposed International Bridge Across St. Croix: The proposal of the State of Maine and the Province of New Brunswick to construct an international bridge at Milltown on the St. Croix River requires an agreement between the state and the province. New Brunswick requested the authorization of the Federal Government and the Government agreed in 1965 to a procedure whereby Canada and the United States would enter into an agreement authorizing provincial participation. Under United States constitutional law, however, the State of Maine required authorization from the United States Congress to conclude such an agreement. A bill was proposed in Congress to authorize the State of Maine to enter into the agreement with New Brunswick. When it asked for an expression of Canadian views, the State Department was informed that the proposed agreement was welcomed by the Canadian Government, but that it should be accompanied by an exchange of notes between the two governments recording the fact that the agreement was being concluded with their assent. ...

It may be noted that occasionally agreements of this nature have been authorized by Act of Parliament, for example an Act of Parliament of 1958 authorizing an agreement between New Brunswick and Maine for the construction of the Campobello-Lubec Bridge.

d) Quebec Cultural Entente with France: On November 24, 1965, Quebec entered into a cultural *entente* with France. This arrangement was similar in its legal form to the education *entente* and was signed by the French Ambassador on behalf of France and by the Quebec Minister of Culture for the province. On November 17, 1965, a cultural agreement and exchange of letters between Canada and France had been signed by the French Ambassador in Ottawa and the Secretary of State for External Affairs. This agreement established a general framework (*accord cadre*) designed to facilitate arrangements between provincial governments and the French Government, and provided that such arrangements could be entered into by the provinces either by reference to the *accord cadre* and exchange of notes or by specific authorization on the part of the Federal Government through a further exchange of letters. The latter procedure was employed in the case of the France-Quebec Cultural *Entente* which was authorized by an exchange of letters, dated November 24, 1965, between the Secretary of State for External Affairs and the French Ambassador.

Contracts Subject to Private Law

It appears that the Canadian provinces have entered into and continue to enter into a variety of contracts of a private law character. For example, many Canadian provinces maintain offices in the United States or Europe and it may be assumed that they have entered into contracts with governmental agencies in the jurisdictions within which their offices are located relating to leases, fuel and power supply, telephones and a variety of other matters. These contracts, it should be noted, are exclusively of a private or commercial nature. ...

(B) Co-operation in Treaty-Making and Implementation

For some time the Federal Government has followed the practice of consulting with the provinces on various questions related to treaty-making and treaty-implementation. This procedure provides a means for harmonizing the interests of the federal and provincial governments and, in addition, offers an opportunity to give effect to the wishes of the provinces with respect to treaties in areas in which they have legislative responsibility. In the latter field, it is also a necessary component of the process leading to the implementation of international agreements.

Consultation may take a number of forms, including direct discussions between the federal and provincial authorities, and may be initiated prior to or during negotiations on a proposed treaty, as well as in the stages subsequent to signature when questions regarding implementation may require federal-provincial co-operation. Although they have not followed a fixed pattern, the procedures which have been devised thus far have proved successful in many cases, and have resulted in a substantial Canadian achievement in respect of ratification and implementation. ... Nevertheless, it is a record which the Government recognizes could be improved through more effective means of consultation.

As suggested [above], the provinces may enter into a variety of administrative arrangements which are not binding in international law. In addition, various means for giving international validity to agreements involving the provinces have been employed or contemplated. Certain of these techniques are instructive as an indication of the means which are open for more extensive co-operation. Most prominent among them are indemnity agreements, *ad hoc* covering agreements and general framework agreements (*accords cadres*).

Indemnity Agreements

According to this procedure the Federal Government, after consultation with a province or provinces, enters into an agreement with the government of a foreign state on a matter of interest to a province. The agreement is supplemented, on the Canadian side, by an agreement between the Federal Government and the province concerned, under which the province undertakes to provide such legislative authority as might be necessary to enable the discharge within its territory of its obligations under the agreement. The province also indemnifies the Federal Government in respect of any liability that might arise by reason of the default of the province in implementing the obligations of Canada under its international agreement with the foreign state. An example of this technique is the Columbia River Treaty and Protocol. The procedure adopted was that, after extensive consultations with the British Columbia government, a federal delegation including representatives from the province negotiated a bilateral agreement with the United States. An arrangement was worked out with the Province of British Columbia whereby the province undertook to execute the terms of the treaty and to indemnify the Federal Government in the event of its failure to do so. Another example is the procedure worked out in the case of the St. Lawrence Seaway, involving the Province of Ontario.

As the examples cited above suggest, this technique may have particular merit in cases in which a province wishes to conclude an agreement with a U.S. state on a local matter of joint concern. An added advantage of this type of arrangement is that a province can be directly involved in the consultations leading to the bilateral agreement which forms the basis of Canada's international obligation.

Ad hoc Covering Agreements

This technique allows the provincial authorities a direct way of achieving international arrangements in matters affecting their interests. It would normally take the form of an exchange of notes between the Federal Government and the foreign state concerned, which gives assent to arrangements between the provincial authorities and a foreign governmental agency. The exchange of notes gives international legal effect to the arrangements between the province and the foreign entity, but does not involve the province itself acquiring international rights or accepting international obligations. Only the Canadian Government is bound internationally by the agreement, but the province participates fully in treaty making through co-operation with the federal authorities.

An example of this procedure is the "education *entente*" discussed [above] in which an understanding in the field of education between Quebec and France was given international status by an exchange of notes between the French Ambassador in Ottawa and the Secretary of State for External Affairs.

General Framework Agreements or *Accords Cadres*

This technique is similar to the *ad hoc* procedure described above except that it is not intended to be restricted in its application to a specific agreement between a province and a foreign entity, but rather to allow for future agreements in a given field by any province which may be interested. As in the case of the *ad hoc* procedure, the Federal Government remains responsible in international law for such arrangements. At the same time, the provinces are provided with an open-ended opportunity to provide for their interests in a given field, for example, educational or cultural exchanges, whenever they wish to take advantage of the framework agreement to conclude appropriate arrangements with the foreign government in question.

The best known example of this type is the cultural agreement and accompanying exchange of letters signed by the Canadian and French Governments on November 17, 1965. As noted above, this agreement provides for the possibility of collaboration in the cultural field between France and any of the Canadian provinces, and was accompanied by an exchange of letters which specified that the authority for the provinces to enter into *ententes* with France could be derived in future, if they so wished, from the cultural agreement and exchange of letters or through a further exchange of notes by the Governments of Canada and France.

The above methods provide a broad and flexible range of techniques which, when employed in conjunction with close consultation and co-operation between the federal and provincial authorities, are capable of allowing for the full expression of provincial interests in treaty-making. At the same time, they give validity in international law to provincial arrangements with foreign jurisdictions, thereby avoiding confusion as to the rights and responsibilities of the members of the Canadian federation on the international plane. Put in other words, they are fully as capable of taking account of substantive provincial interests as any arrangement which a province might wish to conclude itself without reference to the federal authorities, and at the same time they engage the Canadian Government on behalf of the interests of the province. Thus, they appear to the Government to provide adequate means of allowing within the existing constitutional framework for arrangements with foreign entities which the provinces may wish to conclude, and where there is an evident need for such arrangements which could not otherwise be met. They depend for their full success, however, upon effective consultative procedures between the provinces and the Federal Government. ... [25]

Treaty Implementation in Canada

In Canada, legislative jurisdiction to adopt laws for the purpose of implementing, i.e., giving effect to, international treaties that require such action is determined by the ordinary rules governing the division of legislative power under the Constitution Act. Apart from the powers vested by section 132 of this Act for "performing the Obligations of Canada or of any Province thereof as part of the British Empire towards Foreign Countries, arising under Treaties between the Empire and such Foreign Countries," the federal Parliament has no special jurisdiction under the residuary clause of section 91 of the Constitution Act to implement international treaties concerning matters within provincial legislative jurisdiction. When Canada achieved independent status, section 132 became a vestige of the past.

Labour Conventions Case
Attorney General for Canada v. Attorney General for Ontario
[1937] A.C. 326; [1937] 1 D.L.R. 673 (J.C.P.C.)

[In 1935 Canada ratified three conventions prepared by the International Labour Conference. The Parliament then proceeded to pass legislation in accordance with the provisions of the conventions. On appeal from the Supreme Court of Canada, the Judicial Committee advised that the legislation was *ultra vires* the federal Parliament; that legislative competence on the subject concerned was vested in the legislatures of the Provinces.]

---

[25] See also T.A. Levy, "Provincial International Status Revisited" (1976-77), 3 *Dal. L.J.* 70; R. St. J. Macdonald, "International Treaty Law and the Domestic Law of Canada" (1975), 2 *Dal. L.J.* 307; E. McWhinney, "The Constitutional Competence Within Federal Systems as to International Agreements" (1964-68), 1 *Can. Legal Studies* 145. For consideration of the Quebec viewpoint see A. Jacomy-Millette, *supra*, n.11, at 78; and J.-Y. Morin, "La conclusion d'accords internationaux par les provinces canadiennes à la lumière du droit comparé" (1965), 3 *Can. Y.B. Int. L.* 127.

LORD ATKIN: ... It will be essential to keep in mind the distinction between the formation and the performance, of the obligations constituted by a treaty, using that word as comprising any agreement between two or more sovereign States. Within the British Empire there is a well-established rule that the making of a treaty is an executive act, while the performance of its obligations, if they entail alteration of the existing domestic law, requires legislative action. Unlike some other countries, the stipulations of a treaty duly ratified do not within the Empire, by virtue of the treaty alone, have the force of law. If the national executive, the government of the day, decide to incur the obligations of a treaty which involved alteration of law they have to run the risk of obtaining the assent of Parliament to the necessary statute or statutes. To make themselves as secure as possible they will often in such cases before final ratification seek to obtain from Parliament an expression of approval. But it has never been suggested, and it is not the law, that such an expression of approval operates as law, or that in law it precludes the assenting Parliament, or any subsequent Parliament, from refusing to give its sanction to any legislative proposals that may subsequently be brought before it. Parliament, no doubt, as the Chief Justice points out, has a constitutional control over the executive: but it cannot be disputed that the creation of the obligations undertaken in treaties and the assent to their form and quality are the function of the executive alone. Once they are created, while they bind the State as against the other contracting parties, Parliament may refuse to perform them and so leave the State in default. In a unitary State whose Legislature possesses unlimited powers the problem is simple. Parliament will either fulfil or not treaty obligations imposed upon the State by its executive. The nature of the obligations does not affect the complete authority of the Legislature to make them law if it so chooses. But in a State where the Legislature does not possess absolute authority, in a federal State where legislative authority is limited by a constitutional document, or is divided up between different Legislatures in accordance with the classes of subject-matter submitted for legislation, the problem is complex. The obligations imposed by treaty may have to be performed, if at all, by several Legislatures; and the executive have the task of obtaining the legislative assent not of the one Parliament to whom they may be responsible, but possibly of several Parliaments to whom they stand in no direct relation. The question is not how is the obligation formed, that is the function of the executive; but how is the obligation to be performed, and that depends upon the authority of the competent Legislature or Legislatures. ...

For the purposes of ss. 91 and 92, *i.e.*, the distribution of legislative powers between the Dominion and the Provinces, there is no such thing as treaty legislation as such. The distribution is based on classes of subjects; and as a treaty deals with a particular class of subjects so will the legislative power of performing it be ascertained. No one can doubt that this distribution is one of the most essential conditions, probably the most essential condition, in the inter-provincial compact to which The British North America Act gives effect.

NOTES

1) Lord Atkin refused to decide whether the federal executive has independent authority to enter into a treaty or convention relating to a matter which, apart from the

treaty or convention, is within the provincial legislative authority. Duff, C.J. at the Supreme Court level stated that it did.[26]

2) Should the Federal Parliament have the power to implement treaties, even when they touch on areas of domestic competence of the Provinces? Would this ensure that Canada carries out her international obligations under a treaty? The courts have given a few indefinite hints that the *Labour Conventions* case might be reconsidered. See *MacDonald and Railquip Enterprises Ltd. v. Vapor Canada Ltd.* where the late Chief Justice Laskin in an *obiter dictum* said:[27]

Although the foregoing references would support a reconsideration of the *Labour Conventions* case, I find it unnecessary to do so here. ...

If the *Labour Conventions* case were to be reconsidered, would it be destructive of federalism as we know it? What type of checks and balances in the federal legislative process would be necessary?[28]

3) Is the rule of implementation illustrated and laid down in the *Labour Conventions* case an intolerable restraint on the federal treaty-making power and hence upon the conduct of Canada's foreign relations?

4) Article 46 of the Vienna Convention on the Law of Treaties deals with the rules of international law regarding competence to conclude treaties:

1. A State may not invoke the fact that its consent to be bound by a treaty has been expressed in violation of a provision of its internal law regarding competence to conclude treaties as invalidating its consent unless that violation was manifest and concerned a rule of its internal law of fundamental importance.

2. A violation is manifest if it would be objectively evident to any State conducting itself in the matter in accordance with normal practice and in good faith.

To avoid the consequences of this provision, Canada uses a federal state clause when signing a treaty that requires implementation by the provinces. See below.

5) There is judicial authority for the proposition that in the event of an apparent conflict

---

[26] [1936] S.C.R. 461, at 488. Generally on the case, see C.C. Hyde, "Canada's 'Water-Tight Compartments' " (1937), 31 *Am. J. Int. L.* 466; G. LaForest, "The Labour Conventions Case Revisited" (1974), 12 *Can. Y.B. Int. L.* 137; W. Lederman, "Legislative Power to Implement Treaty Obligations in Canada," in J.H. Aitchison, ed., *The Political Process in Canada* (1963), at 171; N. MacKenzie, "Canada and the Treaty-Making Power" (1937), 15 *Can. Bar Rev.* 436; W.G. Rice, "Can Canada Ratify International Labour Conventions?" (1937), 12 *Wis. L. Rev.* 185; F.R. Scott, "The Consequences of the Privy Council Decisions" (1937), 15 *Can. Bar Rev.* 485; R. Stewart, "Canada and International Labour Conventions" (1938), 32 *Am. J. Int. L.* 36.

[27] [1977] 2 S.C.R. 134, at 169. See *Schneider v. The Queen*, [1982] 2 S.C.R. 112, (1983), 139 D.L.R. (3d) 417, for other *obiter* dicta concerning the treaty-power. Note A.L.C. de Mestral, Comment, (1983), 61 *Can. Bar. Rev.* 856; and P. Hogg, *Constitutional Law of Canada* (2 ed., 1984), at 251.

[28] See G.L. Morris, "Canadian Federalism and International Law," and A. Dufour, "Fédéralisme Canadien et droit international," in R. St. J. Macdonald, G.L. Morris and D.M. Johnston, eds., *Canadian Perspectives on International Law and Organisation* (1974), at 55 and 72 respectively.

between a treaty and a provincial statute, the courts will favor a construction to resolve the conflict.[29] However, if resolution is not possible, *intra vires* provincial laws prevail as the constitutional autonomy of the Province in its own fields means that very likely it may legislate in violation of international law.[30]

Protection of the Canadian Constitutional Position

One method by which the federal government may facilitate implementation of a treaty in areas requiring provincial legislation is by inserting a federal state clause in the treaty.[31] Such a clause enables the treaty to be brought into effect on a phased basis as individual provinces agree to be bound. The clause permits Canada to ratify with respect to one or more of the provinces that signify their agreement. This practice is increasingly common in treaties which have been concluded at the Hague Conference on Private International Law, UNCITRAL, UNIDROIT and OAS. Here is an example taken from the UN Convention on Recovery Abroad of Maintenance, Article 11:[32]

> In the case of a Federal or non-unitary State, the following provisions shall apply:
> (a) With respect to those articles of this Convention that come within the legislative jurisdiction of the federal legislative authority, the obligations of the Federal Government shall to this extent be the same as those of Parties which are not Federal States;
> (b) With respect to those articles of this Convention that come within the legislative jurisdiction of constituent States, provinces or cantons which are not, under the constitutional system of the Federation, bound to take legislative action, the Federal Government shall bring such articles with a favourable recommendation to the notice of the appropriate authorities of States, provinces or cantons at the earliest possible moment;
> (c) A Federal State Party of this Convention shall, at the request of any other Contracting Party transmitted through the Secretary-General, supply a statement of the law and practice of the Federation and its constituent units in regard to any particular provision of the Convention, showing the extent to which effect has been given to that provision by legislative or other action.

When no federal state clause is included in the text of a treaty, Canada may deposit a reservation with its signature. For instance, in connection with the UN Convention on the Political Rights of Women,[33] Canada stated:

> Inasmuch as under the Canadian constitutional system legislative jurisdiction in respect of political rights is divided between the provinces and the Federal Government, the Government

---

[29] See *Re Arrow River and Tributaries Slide and Boom Co. Ltd.*, [1932] 2 D.L.R. 250 (S.C.C.); *R. v. Syliboy*, [1929] 1 D.L.R. 307 (N.S. Co. Ct.).

[30] See the discussion on Power to Legislate Contrary to International Law, *infra* in Chapter 4.

[31] H.A. Leal, "Federal State Clauses and the Conventions of the Hague Conference on Private International Law" (1984), 8 *Dal. L.J.* 257.

[32] (1957), 268 U.N.T.S. 32.

[33] 1957 Can. T.S. No. 3.

of Canada is obliged, in acceding to this Convention, to make a reservation in respect of rights within the legislative jurisdiction of the provinces.

Special arrangements are now in place to deal with the difficulties created by the *Labour Conventions* case as follows:

CONSTITUTION OF INTERNATIONAL LABOUR ORGANIZATION[34]
Article 19, paragraph 7

7. In the case of a federal State, the following provisions shall apply:

(a)   in respect of Conventions and Recommendations which the federal Government regards as appropriate under its constitutional system, in federal action, the obligations of the federal State shall be the same as those of Members which are not federal States:

(b)   in respect of Conventions and Recommendations which the federal Government regards as appropriate under its constitutional system, in whole or in part, for action by the constituent States, provinces, or cantons rather than for federal action, the federal Government shall:

     (i)   make, in accordance with its Constitution and the Constitutions of the States, provinces or cantons concerned, effective arrangements for the reference of such Conventions and recommendations not later than eighteen months from the closing of the session of the Conference to the appropriate federal State, provincial or cantonal authorities for the enactment of legislation or other action;

     (ii)   arrange, subject to the concurrence of the State, provincial or cantonal Governments concerned, for periodical consultations between the federal and the State, provincial or cantonal authorities with a view to promoting within the federal State co-ordinated action to give effect to the provisions of such Conventions and Recommendations;

     (iii)   inform the Director-General of the International Labour Office of the measures taken in accordance with this Article to bring such Conventions and recommendations before the appropriate federal State, Provincial or cantonal authorities regarded as appropriate and of the action taken by them;

     (iv)   in respect of each such Convention which it has not ratified, report to the Director-General of the International Labour Office, at appropriate intervals as requested by the Governing Body, the position of the law and practice of the federation and its constituent States, provinces or cantons in regard to the Convention, showing the extent to which effect has been given, or is proposed to be given, to any of the provisions of the Convention, by legislation, administrative action, collective agreement, or otherwise;

---

[34] 1946 Can. T.S. No. 48.

agreements which Canada signs or to which she adheres, or by periodic listing of Orders-in-Council including those authorizing signature of an agreement or its ratification. The bulletin *External Affairs*, replaced in 1972 by *International Perspectives*, also contains a current report on international agreements developments. A new publication, *Treaties in Force for Canada* as of January 1, 1982, is now available. The text of international agreements that require implementation is often found as an appendix to the federal or provincial implementing statute (e.g., tax treaties, international convention on child abduction). The text of international agreements dealing with taxation may also be found in the C.C.H. Canadian Tax Reporter.

International agreements concluded by the United Kingdom that are binding on Canada may be found in the British Treaty Series 1892. Canadian international agreements and instruments of ratification for the period 1875-1939 may also be found in the "Prefix to Statutes" included in the federal statutes for that period. For international agreements concluded with the United States of America, it is also convenient to consult the annual edition of *Treaties in Force* published by the United States Government.

As to the proof of treaties in Canadian courts, the *Canada Evidence Act*[46] section 21 states that:

21. ... evidence of a treaty to which Canada is a party, may be given in all of any of the modes following, that is to say:

a) by the production of a copy of the Canada Gazette, or a volume of the Acts of the Parliament of Canada purporting to contain a copy of such treaty ... or a notice thereof;

b) by the production of a copy of such treaty, ... purporting to be printed by the Queen's Printer for Canada; ...

Once an international agreement has come into force, it is also registered with the Secretariat of the United Nations, as required by the Charter, Article 102 (See Appendix). International agreements thus registered with the Secretariat are published in the United Nations Treaty Series (formerly League of Nations Treaty Series 1920-1945).

Vienna Convention on the Law of Treaties

Article 80
REGISTRATION AND PUBLICATION OF TREATIES

1. Treaties shall, after their entry into force, be transmitted to the Secretariat of the United Nations for registration or filing and recording, as the case may be, and for publication.

2. The designation of a depositary shall constitute authorization for it to perform the acts specified in the preceding paragraph.

---

[46] R.S.C. 1970, c. E-10. Treaties may be located by reference to C.L. Wiktor, *Canadian Treaty Calendar 1928-1978* (2 Vols., 1983).

Entry Into Force

The date an agreement enters into force varies according to the intention of the parties and may be:

1) On ratification or a given period after that event,[47] or

2) If ratification is unnecessary, a treaty may come into force immediately or in a given period after signature, or

3) In the case of Exchange of Notes, normally the date of the second note, or

4) In the case of a multilateral treaty, it is usually upon ratification by a given number of states as stated in the text of the treaty. For instance, although the U.N. Convention on the Law of the Sea has been signed by over 150 states, by virtue of Article 308 it will not come into force until twelve months after the sixtieth ratification.

The Vienna Convention Article 24 reiterates that the mode and moment a treaty enters into force depends upon the intentions of the parties, but, failing any explicit arrangements, it will take effect as soon as consent to be bound has been given by all the parties. Articles 25 and 28 recognize that exceptionally, if the parties so indicate, a treaty may be applied provisionally pending its entry into force, or it may be made to operate retroactively. By contrast, an early Canadian case took a wider view of treaty application. See *In Re Cannon*,[48] where a treaty of extradition was construed to operate retroactively as it did not contain a provision expressly declaring that its stipulations should not apply to crimes committed prior to its conclusion.

Reservations

The Department of External Affairs has commented:[49]

A state which has previously signed a convention may be unwilling to ratify it as it stands, and may accordingly make a reservation against the operation of one or more of its provisions. The practice of opening conventions for accession by states which have not participated at the drafting stage is conducive to the deposit by such states of instruments of accession which include reservations.

If other states object to such reservations, confusion results – particularly if many states are involved. If the date of entry into force depends on the number of states ratifying or acceding, the confusion is even worse. The problem was considered in the League of Nations, where it was generally agreed that a state could not become a party subject to a reservation unless all other contracting states accepted the reservation. This 'classical theory' was based on the view that no state could alter the text of a contract as applied to itself by its own unilateral act unless all other interested states agreed.

Conventions are an important source of international law, and those drafted by international organizations such as the United Nations and its Specialized Agencies are particularly important in this regard. In the past, differences of opinion have arisen as to whether the integrity of the

---

[47] *Spitz v. Secretary of State of Canada*, [1939] Ex. C.R. 162; [1939] 2 D.L.R. 546.

[48] (1908), 17 O.L.R. 352 (S.C.).

[49] Reported in (1952), 4 External Affairs 111; (1960), 12 External Affairs 510.

text of such law-making conventions was more or less important than participation of a large number of states.

After World War II, the controversial question of reservations to multilateral conventions was the subject of long debate at the sixth and seventh sessions of the United Nations General Assembly. The question was also considered in 1951 by the International Court of Justice in relation to the Genocide Convention and, in a more general context, by the International Law Commission.

Reservations to the Convention on Genocide Case
Adv. Op. [1951] I.C.J. Rep. 15

[In 1950 the General Assembly of the United Nations asked the International Court of Justice for an advisory opinion on the following questions:

In so far as concerns the Convention on the Prevention and Punishment of the Crime of Genocide in the event of a State ratifying or acceding to the Convention subject to a reservation made either on ratification or on accession, or on signature followed by ratification:

I. Can the reserving State be regarded as being a party to the Convention while still maintaining its reservation if the reservation is objected to by one or more of the parties to the Convention but not by others?

II. If the answer to Question I is in the affirmative, what is the effect of the reservation as between the reserving State and:
(a) The parties which object to the reservation?
(b) Those which accept it?

III. What would be the legal effect as regards the answer to Question I if an objection to a reservation is made:
(a) By a signatory which has not yet ratified?
(b) By a State entitled to sign or accede but which has not yet done so?]

THE COURT: All three questions are expressly limited by the terms of the Resolution of the General Assembly to the Convention on the Prevention and Punishment of the Crime of Genocide, and the same Resolution invites the International Law Commission to study the general question of reservations to multilateral conventions both from the point of view of codification and from that of the progressive development of international law. The questions thus having a clearly defined object, the replies which the Court is called upon to give to them are necessarily and strictly limited to that Convention. ...

It is well established that in its treaty relations a State cannot be bound without its consent, and that consequently no reservation can be effective against any State without its agreement thereto. It is also a generally recognized principle that a multilateral convention is the result of an agreement freely concluded upon its clauses and that consequently none of the contracting parties is entitled to frustrate or impair, by means of unilateral decisions or particular agreements, the purpose and *raison d'être* of the convention. To this principle was linked the notion of the integrity of the convention as adopted, a notion which in its traditional concept involved the proposition that no reservation was valid unless it was accepted by all the contracting parties without exception, as would have been the case if it had been stated during the negotiations.

This concept, which is directly inspired by the notion of contract is of undisputed value as a principle. However, as regards the Genocide Convention, it is proper to refer to a variety of circumstances which would lead to a more flexible application of this principle. Among these circumstances may be noted the clearly universal character of the United Nations under whose auspices the Convention was concluded, and the very wide degree of participation envisaged by Article XI of the Convention. Extensive participation in conventions of this type has already given rise to greater flexibility in the international practice concerning multilateral conventions. More general resort to reservations, very great allowance made for tacit assent to reservations, the existence of practices which go so far as to admit that the author of reservations which have been rejected by certain contracting parties is nevertheless to be regarded as a party to the convention, in relation to those contracting parties that have accepted the reservations – all these factors are manifestations of a new need for flexibility in the operation of multilateral conventions.

It must also be pointed out that although the Genocide Convention was finally approved unanimously, it is nevertheless the result of a series of majority votes. The majority principle, while facilitating the conclusion of multilateral conventions, may also make it necessary for certain States to make reservations. This observation is confirmed by the great number of reservations which have been made of recent years to multilateral conventions. ...

The objects of such a convention must also be considered. The Convention was manifestly adopted for a purely humanitarian and civilizing purpose. It is indeed difficult to imagine a convention that might have this dual character to a greater degree, since its object on the one hand is to safeguard the very existence of certain human groups and on the other to confirm and endorse the most elementary principles of morality. In such a convention the contracting States do not have any interests of their own; they merely have, one and all, a common interest, namely, the accomplishment of those high purposes which are the *raison d'être* of the convention. Consequently, in a convention of this type one cannot speak of individual advantages or disadvantages to States, or of the maintenance of a perfect contractual balance between rights and duties. The high ideals which inspired the Convention provide, by virtue of the common will of the parties, the foundation and measure of all its provisions. ...

The object and purpose of the Genocide Convention imply that it was the intention of the General Assembly and of the States which adopted it that as many States as possible should participate. The complete exclusion from the Convention of one or more States would not only restrict the scope of its application, but would detract from the authority of the moral and humanitarian principles which are its basis. It is inconceivable that the contracting parties readily contemplated that an objection to a minor reservation should produce such a result. But even less could the contracting parties have intended to sacrifice the very object of the Convention in favour of a vain desire to secure as many participants as possible. The object and purpose of the Convention thus limit both the freedom of making reservations and that of objecting to them. It follows that it is the compatibility of a reservation with the object and purpose of the Convention that must furnish the criterion for the attitude of a State in making the reservation on accession as well as for the appraisal by a State in objecting to the reservation. ...

On the other hand, it has been argued that there exists a rule of international law subjecting the effect of a reservation to the express or tacit assent of all the contracting parties. This theory rests essentially on a contractual conception of the absolute integrity of the convention as adopted. This view, however, cannot prevail if, having regard to the character of the convention, its purpose and its mode of adoption, it can be established that the parties intended to derogate from that rule by admitting the faculty to make reservations thereto.

It does not appear, moreover, that the conception of the absolute integrity of a convention has been transformed into a rule of international law. The considerable part which tacit assent has always played in estimating the effect which is to be given to reservations scarcely permits one to state that such a rule exists, determining with sufficient precision the effect of objections made to reservations. In fact, the examples of objections made to reservations appear to be too rare in international practice to have given rise to such a rule. It cannot be recognized that the report which was adopted on the subject by the Council of the League of Nations on June 17, 1927, has had this effect. ...

It is inconceivable that a State, even if it has participated in the preparation of the Convention, could, before taking one or the other of the two courses of action provided for becoming a party to the Convention, exclude another State. Possessing no rights which derive from the Convention, that State cannot claim such a right from its status as a Member of the United Nations or from the invitation to sign which has been addressed to it by the General Assembly.

The case of a signatory State is different. Without going into the question of the legal effect of signing an international convention, which necessarily varies in individual cases, the Court considers that signature constitutes a first step to participation in the Convention.

It is evident that without ratification, signature does not make the signatory State a party to the Convention; nevertheless, it establishes a provisional status in favour of that State. This status may decrease in value and importance after the Convention enters into force. But, both before and after the entry into force, this status would justify more favourable treatment being meted out to signatory States in respect of objections than to States which have neither signed nor acceded.

As distinct from the latter States, signatory States have taken certain of the steps necessary for the exercise of the right of being a party. Pending ratification, the provisional status created by signature confers upon the signatory a right to formulate as a precautionary measure objections which have themselves a provisional character. These would disappear if the signature were not followed by ratification, or they would become effective on ratification.

Until this ratification is made, the objection of a signatory State can therefore not have an immediate legal effect in regard to the reserving State. It would merely express and proclaim the eventual attitude of the signatory State when it becomes a party to the Convention.

The legal interest of a signatory State in objecting to a reservation would thus be amply safeguarded. The reserving State would be given notice that as soon as the constitutional or other processes which cause the lapse of time before ratification, have been completed, it would be confronted with a valid objection which carries full legal effect and consequently, it would have to decide, when the objection is stated, whether it wishes to maintain or withdraw its reservation. ...

For these reasons the Court is of opinion,

On Question I, by seven votes to five, that a State which has made and maintained a reservation which has been objected to by one or more of the parties to the Convention but not by others, can be regarded as being a party to the Convention if the reservation is compatible with the object and purpose of the Convention; otherwise, that State cannot be regarded as being a party to the Convention.

On Question II, by seven votes to five, (a) that if a party to the Convention objects to a reservation which it considers to be incompatible with the object and purpose of the Convention, it can in fact consider that the reserving State is not a party to the Convention; (b) that if, on the other hand, a party accepts the reservation as being compatible with the object and purpose of the Convention, it can in fact consider that the reserving State is a party to the Convention.

On Question III, by seven votes to five, (a) that an objection to a reservation made by a signatory State which has not yet ratified the Convention can have the legal effect indicated in the reply to Question I only on ratification. Until that moment it merely serves as a notice to the other State of the eventual attitude of the signatory State; (b) that an objection to a reservation made by a State which is entitled to sign or accede but which has not yet done so, is without legal effect.

NOTES

1) No solution to the fundamental question of the admission of reservations having been reached, and, all attempts to achieve a compromise having failed, the 1952 General Assembly adopted resolution 598 (VI), requesting the Secretary-General to continue to act as depositary of documents containing reservations or objections without passing upon their legal effect. The Secretary-General was asked to communicate the text of such documents to all states concerned, leaving it to each state to draw legal consequences from them. Obviously this practice could not be considered entirely satisfactory because it meant that the status of the reservations (and, in consequence, the status of the convention itself) must remain uncertain.

In 1959 the General Assembly of the United Nations requested the Secretary-General to obtain information from all depositary states and international organizations with respect to depositary practice in relation to reservations, and to prepare a summary of such practices including his own for use by the International Law Commission in preparing its reports on the law of treaties and by the General Assembly in considering these reports.

The debate in the United Nations revealed once again a profound divergence of views among delegations on the substantive aspect of reservations. On the other hand, it was noticeable that the idea of the absolute integrity of conventions, requiring unanimity of acceptance before a state making a reservation could be admitted as a contracting party, is losing ground, the majority of UN members favouring greater flexibility in the obligations of treaties by permitting the contracting parties to enter reservations necessary to make the agreement acceptable, thus making it possible for a larger number of countries to participate.

2) Although the difficulties have not been laid to rest, specific rules curtailing the divergence of views and constraining the practice of making reservations have now been set out in the Vienna Convention:

Vienna Convention on the Law of Treaties

Article 2

(d) ''reservation'' means a unilateral statement, however phrased or named, made by a state, when signing, ratifying, accepting, approving or acceding to a treaty, whereby it purports to exclude or to modify the legal effect of certain provisions of the treaty in their application to that state.

Article 19
FORMULATION OF RESERVATIONS

A state may, when signing, ratifying, accepting, approving or acceding to a treaty, formulate a reservation unless:
(a) the reservation is prohibited by the treaty;
(b) the treaty provides that only specified reservations, which do not include the reservation in question, may be made; or
(c) in cases not falling under sub-paragraphs (a) and (b), the reservation is incompatible with the object and purpose of the treaty.

Article 20
ACCEPTANCE OF AND OBJECTION TO RESERVATIONS

1. A reservation expressly authorized by a treaty does not require any subsequent acceptance by the other contracting states unless the treaty so provides.

2. When it appears from the limited number of the negotiating states and the object and purpose of a treaty that the application of the treaty in its entirety between all the parties is an essential condition of the consent of each one to be bound by the treaty, a reservation requires acceptance by all the parties.

3. When a treaty is a constituent instrument of an international organization and unless it otherwise provides, a reservation requires the acceptance of the competent organ of that organization.

4. In cases not falling under the preceding paragraphs and unless the treaty otherwise provides:
(a) acceptance by another contracting state of a reservation constitutes the reserving state a party to the treaty in relation to that other state if or when the treaty is in force for those states;

(b) an objection by another contracting state to a reservation does not preclude the entry into force of the treaty as between the objecting and reserving states unless a contrary intention is definitely expressed by the objecting state;

(c) an act expressing a state's consent to be bound by the treaty and containing a reservation is effective as soon as at least one other contracting state has accepted the reservation.

5. For the purposes of paragraphs 2 and 4 and unless the treaty otherwise provides, a reservation is considered to have been accepted by a state if it shall have raised no objection to the reservation by the end of a period of twelve months after it was notified of the reservation or by the date on which it expressed its consent to be bound by the treaty, whichever is later.

Article 21
LEGAL EFFECTS OF RESERVATIONS AND OF OBJECTIONS TO RESERVATIONS

1. A reservation established with regard to another party in accordance with Articles 19, 20 and 23:

(a) modifies for the reserving state in its relations with that other party the provisions of the treaty to which the reservation relates to the extent of the reservation; and

(b) modifies those provisions to the same extent for that other party in its relations with the reserving state.

2. The reservation does not modify the provisions of the treaty for the other parties to the treaty *inter se*.

3. When a state objecting to a reservation has not opposed the entry into force of the treaty between itself and the reserving state, the provisions to which the reservation relates do not apply as between the two states to the extent of the reservation.

Article 22
WITHDRAWAL OF RESERVATIONS AND OF OBJECTIONS TO RESERVATIONS

1. Unless the treaty otherwise provides, a reservation may be withdrawn at any time and the consent of a state which has accepted the reservation is not required for its withdrawal.

2. Unless the treaty otherwise provides, an objection to a reservation may be withdrawn at any time.

3. Unless the treaty otherwise provides, or it is otherwise agreed:

(a) the withdrawal of a reservation becomes operative in relation to another contracting state only when notice of it has been received by that state;

(b) the withdrawal of an objection to a reservation becomes operative only when notice of it has been received by the state which formulated the reservation.

NOTES

1) In recent years the trend in multilateral treaty making has been to control the difficulties that can arise by specifying in the treaty itself which articles may and which

may not be the subject of reservations. This practice adds the question of reservations to the negotiations of the substantive matters in the treaty-making process. An example is the Hague Convention on the Civil Aspects of International Child Abduction which was signed by Canada on October 25, 1980, and allows the signatory states to enter reservations with respect to the use of the French or the English language and costs.[50]

2) Reservations are important for Canada with regard to the implementation of treaties. Canada frequently strives to have a *federal-state clause* inserted in a multilateral convention or she may enter a reservation, both of which have the effect of reserving Canada's obligations at international law with regard to matters within the legislative jurisdiction of the Provinces. See the discussion in the previous section on ''Protection of the Canadian Constitutional Position.''

Legal Effects of Treaties

Vienna Convention on the Law of Treaties

Article 26
PACTA SUNT SERVANDA

Every treaty in force is binding upon the parties to it and must be performed by them in good faith.

Article 27
INTERNAL LAW AND OBSERVANCE OF TREATIES

A party may not invoke the provisions of its internal law as justification for its failure to perform a treaty. This rule is without prejudice to Article 46. [Provisions of internal law regarding competence to conclude treaties, reported later in this chapter.]

Article 30 provides for successive treaties on the same subject matter. When they are concluded between the same parties, the later treaty will prevail in the event of incompatible provisions, unless it was clearly made subject to the earlier treaty. If the later treaty does not include all the parties to the earlier one, it will take effect amongst states who are parties to both agreements, but they are still bound by the earlier treaty vis-à-vis the other states parties to it alone.

Third Parties: Free Zones Case
France v. Switzerland
(1932), P.C.I.J., Ser. A/B, No. 46, at 96

[Article 435 of the Treaty of Versailles, 1919 provided that France and Switzerland (the latter not a party to this treaty) should settle between themselves the status of certain

---

[50] See Arts. 42, 24 and 26, Hague Conference on Private International Law, *Actes et documents* 1980, Vol. 3, at 413.

territories on their common border. A proposed agreement having been rejected by the Swiss people, France abolished the former status of these territories. The Permanent Court of International Justice was asked whether article 435 had abrogated such status or had created an obligation for Switzerland to abrogate it.]

THE COURT: ... It follows from the foregoing that Article 435, paragraph 2, as such, does not involve the abolition of the free zones. But, even were it otherwise, it is certain that, in any case, Article 435 of the Treaty of Versailles is not binding upon Switzerland, who is not a Party to that Treaty, except to the extent to which that country accepted it. ...

With particular regard to the zone of Gex, the following is to be noted:

Pursuant to Article 6 of the Treaty of Paris of May 30th, 1814, the Powers assembled at the Congress of Vienna addressed to Switzerland, on March 20th, 1815, a "Declaration" to the effect that "as soon as the Helvetic Diet shall have duly and formally acceded to the stipulations in the present instrument, an act shall be prepared containing the acknowledgment and the guarantee, on the part of all the Powers, of the perpetual neutrality of Switzerland, in her new frontiers." The "instrument" which forms part of this Declaration, amongst other territorial clauses, provides that the line of the French customs is to be so placed "that the road which leads from Geneva into Switzerland by Versoy, shall at all times be free."

The proposal thus made to Switzerland by the Powers was accepted by the Federal Diet by means of the "act of acceptance" of May 27th, 1815. ...

On receipt of Switzerland's formal declaration of acceptance, the Powers drew up the instrument promised in their Declaration of March 20th: this instrument is the Declaration of November 20th, 1815.

By this Declaration, signed *inter alios* by France, "the Powers who signed the Declaration of the 20th of March declare ... their formal and authentic acknowledgment of the perpetual neutrality of Switzerland; and they guarantee to that country the integrity and inviolability of its territory in its new limits, such as they are fixed, as well by the Act of the Congress of Vienna as by the Treaty of Paris of this day, and such as they will be hereafter, conformably to the arrangement of the Protocol of November 3rd, extract of which is hereto annexed, which stipulates in favour of the Helvetic Body a new increase of territory, to be taken from Savoy in order to disengage from enclaves, and complete the circle of the Canton of Geneva. ..."

It follows from all the foregoing that the creation of the Gex zone forms part of a territorial arrangement in favour of Switzerland, made as a result of an agreement between that country and the Powers, including France, which agreement confers on this zone the character of a contract to which Switzerland is a Party.

It also follows that no accession by Switzerland to the Declaration of November 20th was necessary and, in fact, no such accession was sought: it has never been contended that this Declaration is not binding owing to the absence of any accession by Switzerland.

The Court, having reached this conclusion simply on the basis of an examination of the situation of fact in regard to this case, need not consider the legal nature of the Gex zone from the point of view of whether it constitutes a stipulation in favour of a third Party.

But were the matter also to be envisaged from this aspect, the following observations should be made:

It cannot be lightly presumed that stipulations favourable to a third State have been adopted with the object of creating an actual right in its favour. There is however nothing to prevent the will of sovereign states from having this object and this effect. The question of the existence of a right acquired under an instrument drawn between other states is therefore one to be decided in each particular case: it must be ascertained whether the states which have stipulated in favour of a third state meant to create for that state an actual right which the latter has accepted as such.

All the instruments above mentioned and the circumstances in which they were drawn up establish, in the Court's opinion, that the intention of the Powers was, beside "rounding out" the territory of Geneva and ensuring direct communication between the Canton of Geneva and the rest of Switzerland, to create in favour of Switzerland a right, on which that country could rely, to the withdrawal of the French customs barrier behind the political frontier of the District of Gex, that is to say, of the Gex free zone.

Vienna Convention on the Law of Treaties

Article 34
GENERAL RULE REGARDING THIRD STATES

A treaty does not create either obligations or rights for a third state without its consent.

Article 35
TREATIES PROVIDING FOR OBLIGATIONS FOR THIRD STATES

An obligation arises for a third state from a provision of a treaty if the parties to the treaty intend the provision to be the means of establishing the obligation and the third state expressly accepts that obligation in writing.

Article 36
TREATIES PROVIDING FOR RIGHTS FOR THIRD STATES

1. A right arises for a third state from a provision of a treaty if the parties to the treaty intend the provision to accord that right either to the third state, or to a group of states to which it belongs, or to all states, and the third state assents thereto. Its assent shall be presumed so long as the contrary is not indicated, unless the treaty otherwise provides.

2. A state exercising a right in accordance with paragraph 1 shall comply with the conditions for its exercise provided for in the treaty or established in conformity with the treaty.

Article 37
REVOCATION OR MODIFICATION OF OBLIGATIONS
OR RIGHTS OF THIRD STATES

1. When an obligation has arisen for a third state in conformity with Article 35, the obligation may be revoked or modified only with the consent of the parties to the treaty and of the third state, unless it is established that they had otherwise agreed.

2. When a right has arisen for a third state in conformity with Article 36, the right may not be revoked or modified by the parties if it is established that the right was intended not to be revocable or subject to modification without the consent of the third state.

Article 38

RULES IN A TREATY BECOMING BINDING ON THIRD STATES
THROUGH INTERNATIONAL CUSTOM

Nothing in Articles 34 to 37 precludes a rule set forth in a treaty from becoming binding upon a third state as a customary rule of international law, recognized as such.

NOTES

1) What is the effect of U.N. Charter Art. 2(6) for non-members?

2) What is the status of a bilateral boundary treaty vis-à-vis a third state?

3) Some of the most common examples of third state rights are most favoured nation clauses. These clauses are often included in bilateral treaties governing trade and commerce in order to ensure that each party will automatically acquire all the benefits that may be agreed in any subsequent treaty by the other party with another state. In this way the first state will become the third party beneficiary of the treatment accorded to the most favoured treaty partners of the other state. The best known instance of MFN clauses is the multilateral example found in the General Agreement on Tariffs and Trade Art. 1, which reads:

With respect to customs duties and charges of any kind ... in connection with importation or exportation ... , any advantage, favour, privilege or immunity granted by any contracting party [to GATT] to any product originating in or destined for any other country shall be accorded immediately and unconditionally to the like product originating in or destined for the territories of all other contracting parties.

The application of MFN clauses was considered in the *Rights of U.S. Nationals in Morocco Case*.[51]

Interpretation of Treaties

Interpretation of Peace Treaties Case
(Second Phase) Adv. Op. [1950] I.C.J. Rep. 221, at 226

[The 1947 Peace Treaties with Bulgaria, Hungary and Romania provided for a system of commissions to resolve any disputes concerning their interpretation and execution.

---

[51] [1952] I.C.J. Rep. 176.

When charges were made about the suppression of human rights contrary to the treaties, Bulgaria, Hungary and Romania refused to participate in the formation of a commission. In an effort to settle the growing dispute, the U.N. General Assembly asked the Court to interpret the treaty provisions about constituting commissions.]

THE COURT: ... Having stated, in its Opinion of March 30th, 1950, that the Governments of Bulgaria, Hungary and Romania are obligated to carry out the provisions of those articles of the Peace Treaties which relate to the settlement of disputes, including the provisions for the appointment of their representatives to the Treaty Commissions, and having received information from the Secretary-General of the United Nations that none of those Governments had notified him, within thirty days from the date of the delivery of the Court's Advisory Opinion, of the appointment of its representative to the Treaty Commissions, the Court is now called upon to answer Question III in the Resolution of the General Assembly of October 22nd, 1949, which reads as follows:

III. If one party fails to appoint a representative to a Treaty Commission under the Treaties of Peace with Bulgaria, Hungary and Romania where that party is obligated to appoint a representative to the Treaty Commission, is the Secretary-General of the United Nations authorized to appoint the third member of the Commission upon the request of the other party to a dispute according to the provisions of the respective Treaties?

Articles 36, 40 and 38, respectively, of the Peace Treaties with Bulgaria, Hungary and Romania, after providing that disputes concerning the interpretation or execution of the Treaties which had not been settled by direct negotiation should be referred to the Three Heads of Mission, continue:

Any such dispute not resolved by them within a period of two months shall, unless the parties to the dispute mutually agree upon another means of settlement, be referred at the request of either party to the dispute to a Commission composed of one representative of each party and a third member selected by mutual agreement of the two parties from nationals of a third country. Should the two parties fail to agree within a period of one month upon the appointment of the third member, the Secretary-General of the United Nations may be requested by either party to make the appointment.

2. The decision of the majority of the members of the Commission shall be the decision of the Commission, and shall be accepted by the parties as definitive and binding.

The question at issue is whether the provision empowering the Secretary-General to appoint the third member of the Commission applies to the present case, in which one of the parties refuses to appoint its own representative to the Commission.

It has been contended that the term "third member" is used here simply to distinguish the neutral member from the two Commissioners appointed by the parties without implying that the third member can be appointed only when the two national Commissioners have already been appointed, and that therefore the mere fact of the failure of the parties, within the stipulated period, to select the third member by mutual agreement satisfies the condition required for the appointment of the latter by the Secretary-General.

The Court considers that the text of the Treaties does not admit of this interpretation. While the text in its literal sense does not completely exclude the possibility of the appointment of the third member before the appointment of both national Commissioners, it is nevertheless true that according to the natural and ordinary meaning of the terms it was intended that the appointment of both the national Commissioners should precede that of the third member. This clearly results from the sequence of the events contemplated by the article: appointment of a national Commissioner by each party; selection of a third member by mutual agreement of the parties; failing such agreement within a month, his appointment by the Secretary-General. Moreover, this is the normal order followed in the practice of arbitration, and in the absence of any express provision to the contrary there is no reason to suppose that the parties wished to depart from it.

The Secretary-General's power to appoint a third member is derived solely from the agreement of the parties as expressed in the disputes clause of the Treaties; by its very nature such a clause must be strictly construed and can be applied only in the case expressly provided for therein. The case envisaged in the Treaties is exclusively that of the failure of the parties to agree upon the selection of a third member and by no means the much more serious case of a complete refusal of co-operation by one of them, taking the form of refusing to appoint its own Commissioner. The power conferred upon the Secretary-General to help the parties out of the difficulty of agreeing upon a third member cannot be extended to the situation which now exists. ...

In these circumstances, the appointment of a third member by the Secretary-General, instead of bringing about the constitution of a three-member Commission such as the Treaties provide for, would result only in the constitution of a two-member Commission. A Commission consisting of two members is not the kind of commission for which the Treaties have provided. The opposition of the Commissioner of the only party represented could prevent a Commission so constituted from reaching any decision whatever. Such a Commission could only decide by unanimity, whereas the dispute clause provides that "the decision of the majority of the members of the Commission shall be the decision of the Commission and shall be accepted by the parties as definitive and binding." Nor would the decisions of a Commission of two members, one of whom is appointed by one party only, have the same degree of moral authority as those of a three-member Commission. In every respect, the result would be contrary to the letter as well as the spirit of the Treaties. ...

As the Court has declared in its Opinion of March 30th, 1950, the Governments of Bulgaria, Hungary and Romania are under an obligation to appoint their representatives to the Treaty Commissions, and it is clear that refusal to fulfil a treaty obligation involves international responsibility. Nevertheless, such a refusal cannot alter the conditions contemplated in the Treaties for the exercise by the Secretary-General of his power of appointment. These conditions are not present in this case, and their absence is not made good by the fact that it is due to the breach of a treaty obligation. The failure of machinery for settling disputes by reason of the practical impossibility of creating the Commission provided for in the Treaties is one thing; international responsibility is another. The breach of a treaty obligation cannot be remedied by creating a Commission which is not the kind of Commission contemplated by the Treaties. It is the duty of the Court to interpret the Treaties, not to revise them.

The principle of interpretation expressed in the maxim: *Ut res magis valeat quam pereat*, often referred to as the rule of effectiveness, (see H. Lauterpacht, in 26 British Year Book (1949), at 48) cannot justify the Court in attributing to the provisions for the settlement of disputes in the Peace Treaties a meaning which, as stated above, would be contrary to their letter and spirit. ...

For these reasons, The Court is of opinion, by eleven votes to two, that, if one party fails to appoint a representative to a Treaty Commission under the Peace Treaties with Bulgaria, Hungary and Romania where that party is obligated to appoint a representative to the Treaty Commission, the Secretary-General of the United Nations is not authorized to appoint the third member of the Commission upon the request of the other party to a dispute.

NOTES

1) The World Court has not always been consistent in its approach to treaty interpretation, although the International Law Commission has commented that its jurisprudence "contains many pronouncements from which it is permissible to conclude that the textual [i.e. ordinary meaning] approach ... is regarded by it as established."[52] Fitzmaurice has ably summed up the difference in approaches in these words:[53]

There are today three main schools of thought on the subject, which could conveniently be called the "intentions of the parties" or "founding fathers" school; the "textual" or "ordinary meaning of the words" school; and the "teleological" or "aims and objects" school. The ideas of these three schools are not necessarily exclusive of one another, and theories of treaty interpretation can be constructed (and are indeed normally held) compounded of all three. However, each tends to confer the primacy on one particular aspect of treaty interpretation, if not to the exclusion, certainly to the subordination of the others. Each, in any case, employs a different approach. For the "intentions" school, the prime, indeed the only legitimate, object is to ascertain and give effect to the intentions, or presumed intentions, of the parties: the approach is therefore to discover what these were, or must be taken to have been. For the "meaning of the text" school, the prime object is to establish what the text means according to the ordinary or apparent signification of its terms: the approach is therefore through the study and analysis of the text. For the "aims and objects" school, it is the general purpose of the treaty itself that counts, considered to some extent as having, or as having come to have, an existence of its own, independent of the original intentions of the framers. The main object is to establish this general purpose, and construe the particular clauses in the light of it: hence it is such matters as the general tenor and atmosphere of the treaty, the circumstances in which it was made, the place it has come to

---

[52] [1966] Y.B.I.L.C. II, 220. And see *Competence of the I.L.O.* (1922), P.C.I.J., Ser. B., Nos. 2 and 3, at 23; *Polish Postal Services in Danzig* (1925), P.C.I.J., Ser. B., No. 11, at 39; *The Steamship Lotus* (1927), P.C.I.J., Ser. A., No. 10, at 16; *Conditions of Admission to the United Nations*, [1948] I.C.J. Rep. 57, at 63 (Adv. Op.); and *Competence of the General Assembly*, [1950] I.C.J. Rep. 4, at 8 (Adv. Op.).

[53] G.G. Fitzmaurice, "The Law and Procedure of the International Court of Justice: Treaty Interpretation and Certain Other Treaty Points" (1951), 28 *Br. Y.B. Int. L.* 1.

have in international life, which for this school indicate the approach to interpretation. It should be added that this last, the teleological, approach has its sphere of operation almost entirely in the field of general multilateral conventions, particularly those of the social, humanitarian, and law-making type. All three approaches are capable, in a given case, of producing the same result in practice; but equally (even though the differences may, on analysis, prove to be more of emphasis and methodology than principle) they are capable of leading to radically divergent results.

He also added in a footnote:

It may be useful to state briefly the main drawback of each method, if employed in isolation or pushed to an extreme. In the case of the "intentions" method, it is the element of unreality or fictitiousness frequently involved. There are so many cases in which the dispute has arisen precisely because the parties had no intentions on the point, or none that were genuinely common. To make the issue dependent on them involves either an abortive search or an artificial construction that does *not* in fact represent their intentions. The "textual" method suffers from the subjective elements involved in the notions of "clear" or "ordinary" meaning, which may be differently understood and applied according to the point of view of the individual judge. There may also be cases where the parties intended a term to be understood in a specialized sense, different from its ordinary one, but failed to make this clear on the face of the text. The teleological method, finally, is always in danger of "spilling over" into judicial legislation:
it may amount, not to interpreting but, in effect, to amending an instrument in order to make it conform better with what the judge regards as its true purposes.

Which school of thought did the World Court follow in the *Interpretation of Peace Treaties Case*?[54] Now review the *Reparations Case*, reported in Chapter 2. What approach to treaty interpretation was employed there? Does it make any difference that the treaty there in question was the constitutional document of an international organization?

Vienna Convention on the Law of Treaties

Article 31
GENERAL RULE OF INTERPRETATION

1. A treaty shall be interpreted in good faith in accordance with the ordinary meaning to be given to the terms of the treaty in their context and in the light of its object and purpose.
2. The context for the purpose of the interpretation of a treaty shall comprise, in addition to the text, including its preamble and annexes:
    (a) any agreement relating to the treaty which was made between all the parties in connexion with the conclusion of the treaty;

---

[54] Compare the strong dissent of Judge Read, [1950] I.C.J. Rep. 221, at 231, who made a large interpretation in order to give effect to the general purposes and objects of the Peace Treaties.

(b) any instrument which was made by one or more parties in connexion with the conclusion of the treaty and accepted by the other parties as an instrument related to the treaty.

3. There shall be taken into account, together with the context:

(a) any subsequent agreement between the parties regarding the interpretation of the treaty or the application of its provisions;

(b) any subsequent practice in the application of the treaty which establishes the agreement of the parties regarding its interpretation;

(c) any relevant rules of international law applicable in the relations between the parties.

4. A special meaning shall be given to a term if it is established that the parties so intended.

Article 32
SUPPLEMENTARY MEANS OF INTERPRETATION

Recourse may be had to supplementary means of interpretation, including the preparatory work of the treaty and the circumstances of its conclusion, in order to confirm the meaning resulting from the application of Article 31, or to determine the meaning when the interpretation according to Article 31:

(a) leaves the meaning ambiguous or obscure; or

(b) leads to a result which is manifestly absurd or unreasonable.

NOTES

1) These articles appear at first glance now to provide an orderly approach to treaty interpretation, but which of Fitzmaurice's schools of thought do they endorse? On a close reading of Article 31, in what circumstances are "the intentions of the parties" relevant? When may preparatory work (*travaux préparatoires*) to the treaty be resorted to? See Article 32. What if it reveals an intended meaning of the parties that differs from the ordinary meaning of the text, or from a subsequent agreement regarding interpretation?

2) When a treaty is implemented by national legislation the act will be regarded as the authoritative application of its provisions for internal legal purposes. But the legislation is not a definitive interpretation of the treaty for international purposes. Indeed, it may amount to a breach of the treaty. The process of determination is explained in the following case.

The David J. Adams
American and British Claims Arbitration (1926), Nielsen's Report, 524

THE TRIBUNAL (Fromageot, Anderson, Fitzpatrick): The United States Government claims from His Britannic Majesty's Government the sum of $8,037.96 with interest thereon from May 7, 1886, for loss resulting from the seizure of the schooner David J.

Adams by the Canadian authorities in Digby Basin, Nova Scotia, on May 7, 1886, and the subsequent condemnation of the vessel by the Vice-Admiralty Court at Halifax on October 20, 1889. ... On May 6, 1886, the American schooner David J. Adams had entered Canadian waters for purposes other than shelter, repairing damages, purchasing wood, or obtaining water, namely, for the purpose of purchasing fresh bait.

... Now this case is presented before this Tribunal under the following conditions:

By reason of certain conditions of fact and for various other considerations, while by the Treaty of London of October 20, 1818, the United States renounced the liberty of fishing in Canadian waters, except on certain specified coasts, the access of American fishermen to the British territorial waters of Canada was conventionally regulated between the American and British Governments as follows:

> The United States hereby renounce forever, any liberty, heretofore enjoyed or claimed by the inhabitants thereof, to take, dry or cure fish on, or within three marine miles of any of the coasts, bays, creeks, or harbors of His Britannic Majesty's Dominions in America not included within the above-mentioned limits: Provided, however, that the American fishermen shall be admitted to enter such bays or harbors for the purpose of shelter and of repairing damages therein, of purchasing wood, and of obtaining water, and for no other purpose whatever.

Great Britain and Canada, acting in the full exercise of their sovereignty and by such proper legislative authority as was established by their municipal public law, had enacted and were entitled to enact such legislative provisions as they considered necessary or expedient to secure observance of the said Treaty; and, so far as they are not inconsistent with the said Treaty, those provisions are binding as municipal public law of the country on any person within the limits of British jurisdiction. At the time of the seizure of the David J. Adams such legislation was embodied in the British Act of 1819 (59 George III, C. 38), and the Canadian Acts of 1868 (31 Vict. 61), 1871 (34 Vict., C. 23).

Great Britain and Canada, acting by such proper judicial authority as was established by their municipal law, were fully entitled to interpret and apply such legislation and to pronounce and impose such penalty as was provided by the same, but such judicial action had the same limits as the aforesaid legislative action, that is to say so far as it was not inconsistent with the said Treaty.

In this case the question is not and cannot be to ascertain whether or not British law has been justly applied by said judicial authorities, nor to consider, revise, reverse, or affirm a decision given in that respect by British Courts. On the contrary, any such decision must be taken as the authorized expression of the position assumed by Great Britain in the subject matter, and, so far as such decision implies an interpretation of said treaty, it must be taken as the authorized expression of British interpretation.

The fundamental principle of the juridical equality of States is opposed to placing one State under the jurisdiction of another State. It is opposed to the subjection of one State to an interpretation of a Treaty asserted by another State. There is no reason why one more than the other should impose such an unilateral interpretation of a contract which is essentially bilateral. The fact that this interpretation is given by the legislative or judicial or any other authority of one of the Parties does not make that interpretation binding upon the other Party. Far from contesting that principle, the British Government did not fail to recognize it.

For that reason the mere fact that a British Court, whatever be the respect and high authority it carries, interpreted the treaty in such a way as to declare the David J. Adams had contravened it, cannot be accepted by this Tribunal as a conclusive interpretation binding upon the United States Government. Such a decision is conclusive from the national British point of view; it is not from the national United States point of view. On the other hand, the way in which the Canadian Acts, enacted to enforce the Treaty, had been applied by the Canadian Courts, and penalties have been imposed, is a municipal question, and this Tribunal has no jurisdiction to deal with them. The only exception would be the case of a denial of justice. But a denial of justice may not be invoked, unless the claimant has exhausted the legal remedies to obtain justice. As has been shown, the claimant in this case renounced his right to appeal against the decision concerning his vessel. Then the duty of this international Tribunal is to determine, from the international point of view, how the provisions of the treaty are to be interpreted and applied to the facts, and consequently whether the loss resulting from the forfeiture of the vessel gives rise to an indemnity.

According to the British view, the stipulation of the Treaty of 1818 according to which the American fishermen shall be admitted to enter the Canadian bays and harbors for shelter, repairing damages, purchasing wood, and obtaining water, "and for no other purpose whatever," means that the American fishermen have no access to the said bays and harbors for purchasing bait.

On the other hand, the United States Government contends that the right of access as such is not prohibited to the American fishermen by the Treaty, except so far as it is inconsistent with the prohibition of taking, drying or curing fish within the three mile limit, accepted by the United States in that Treaty. The four cases (shelter, repairs, wood and water) of admittance, are cases where admittance is secured by the Treaty, and cannot be refused or prohibited by local legislation.

In other words, according to the American view, the United States Government had renounced by the Treaty their former liberty to fish in Canadian territorial waters. That renunciation has as a counterpart the obligation of the Canadian Government to admit American fishermen for shelter, repairs, wood, and water and for no other purpose. That is to say, that Canada has no obligation to admit the said fishermen for any other purpose than these four – that Canada may very well prohibit the entrance for any other purposes; but, so long as entrance for the purpose of purchasing bait is not prohibited by Canadian legislation, it must be considered as the legal exercise of the right of access belonging to any American ship.

In this Tribunal's opinion, a stipulation which says that fishermen "shall be admitted" for certain enumerated purposes and "for no other purpose whatever," seems to be perfectly clear and to mean that for the specified purposes the fishermen shall be admitted and for any other purposes they had no right to be admitted, and it is difficult to contend that by such plain words the right to entrance for purchasing bait is not denied.

No sufficient evidence of contrary intention of the High Contracting Parties is produced to contradict such a clear wording.

It has been said in support of the United States contention that "if the language of the Treaty of 1818 is to be interpreted literally, rather than according to its spirit and plain intent, a vessel engaged in fishing would be prohibited from entering a Canadian port 'for any purpose whatever, except to obtain wood or water, to repair damages, or to seek shelter.' '' And also that ''the literal meaning of an isolated clause is often shown not to be the meaning really understood or intended.''

Such an intention of the negotiators to contradict the literal meaning of the Treaty does not appear in the evidence presented in this case. It appears from the report dated October 20, 1818, from Gallatin and Rush, the two American Plenipotentiaries, that they had in view to procure for the American fishermen fishing on the fishing grounds outside the three-mile limit off Nova Scotia coasts, the privilege (that is to say, the exceptional right) of entering the ports for shelter.

But, assuming the construction contended for by the United States Government, it must be considered that as early as 1819, that is to say, immediately after the Treaty, the British Act of 1819 (59 Geo. III, c. 36, section III) expressly enacted that the entrance into the Canadian bays and harbors should not be lawful. This act says

Be it enacted that it shall be lawful for any fishermen of the said United States to enter into such bays or harbors of His Britannic Majesty's Dominions in America as are last mentioned for the purpose of shelter, and repairing damages therein, and of purchasing wood, and of obtaining water, and for no other purposes whatever.

If the entrance for the other purposes is not lawful, it is difficult to say that such entrance is not prohibited. ...

Treaty Interpretation by Canadian Courts

When a treaty fails to be applied by a national court, should it be interpreted according to the ordinary rules of statutory interpretation or according to international principles? In Canada, this question is particularly pertinent because a treaty is typically given internal effect by legislation. Furthermore Canadian common law principles of statutory interpretation are clearly more restrictive than their international counterparts, especially the firm rule that extrinsic evidence, such as legislative history, is not admissible.

In *R. v. Sikyea* the court stated:[55]

We were invited by counsel for the respondent to apply to the Migratory Birds Convention Act those rules which have been laid down for the interpretation of treaties in international law and we have been referred to many authorities on how these treaties should be interpreted. We are not, however, concerned with interpreting the Convention, but only the legislation by which it is implemented. To that statute the ordinary rules of interpretation are applicable and the authorities referred to have no application.

Estey J., speaking for the Supreme Court in *Schavernoch v. Foreign Claims Com-*

---

[55] (1964), 46 W.W.R. 65, at 79 (N.W.T.C.A.) aff'd. (1964), 49 W.W.R. 306 (S.C.C.).

mission,[56] was hardly less adamant. The case concerned the meaning of regulations passed to distribute the proceeds of a lump sum settlement of Canadian claims against Czechoslovakia. He said:

Extensive references were laid before the court concerning the negotiation of rights by countries for compensation of their nationals by reason of expropriations or confiscation by other countries. These conventions or customs may find some validity in proceedings in specified international tribunals or perhaps even in domestic tribunals where specific legislative authority has made them operative. Here the regulations fail to be interpreted according to the maxims of interpretation applicable to Canadian law generally. The only rule of interpretation which seems to have any bearing in these proceedings is the plain meaning rule because no ambiguity can be found either in the Order in Council or indeed in the agreement therein referred to if the latter step may be validly taken.

Other courts at other times have used treaties as aids to interpreting Canadian law. For instance, in *Albany Packing Co. Inc. v. The Registrar of Trade Marks* Maclean J. said of the 1925 Hague Convention for the Protection of Industrial Property:[57]

... I think, it is correct to say that the terms of the Convention of The Hague may be referred to by the Court as a matter of history, in order to understand the scope and intent of the terms of that Convention, and under what circumstances any of the provisions of the Unfair Competition Act were enacted, in order to give legislative effect to the same. But the terms of the Convention cannot, I think, be employed as a guide in construing any of such provisions so enacted, for the reason that in Canada a treaty or convention with a foreign state binds the subject of the Crown only in so far as it has been embodied in legislation passed into law in the ordinary way.

R. v. Wedge[58] and *Spitz v. Secretary of State of Canada*[59] are two cases in which extensive reference was had to the treaties involved in the course of determining how to apply the regulations made pursuant to them.

The recent tendency of Canadian courts is to apply international principles of interpretation to statutes which implement treaties and not the common law rules of statutory interpretation. This approach is strongly confirmed in *Re Regina and Palacios*, reported below. It seems the only wise practice in view of the purpose of the statute, which is to give internal effect to the treaty.

Even so, when treaties are used for this purpose the courts may follow different approaches to their interpretation. In some cases the inquiry has stopped short at the plain

---

[56] (1982), 136 D.L.R. (3d) 447, reported *infra* in Chapter 4. Strictly speaking, this case did not involve an implementing statute. However, the difficult question concerning the effects of unimplemented treaties also raises similar problems of interpretation; see ''Application of Unimplemented Treaties,'' *infra* in Chapter 4.

[57] [1940] Ex. C.R. 256, at 265.

[58] [1939] 4 D.L.R. 323 (B.C.S.C.).

[59] [1939] 2 D.L.R. 546 (Ex. C.).

meaning of the words of the treaty text,[60] but today this literal approach is more likely to be modified to include a broader teleological investigation. The courts may still look to the intention of the parties as manifested by the words they used but often they will go on to examine the history and purpose of the treaty as evidenced by its preamble, its *travaux préparatoires* and surrounding customary international law. This practice is also demonstrated in *Re Regina and Palacios*. Furthermore, the intertemporal principle of interpretation, often applied by international tribunals, has been accepted so that a treaty is read and construed as applying to the situation at the time it was concluded.[61]

Re Regina and Palacios
(1984), 45 O.R. (2d) 269 (Ont. C.A.)

[The Crown brought charges concerning the possession of drugs and offensive weapons against Palacios, a Nicaraguan diplomat, after his government had informed Canada that he had ended his duties at his mission. Palacios made a short visit to the United States at the end of his diplomatic posting but had returned to Canada to prepare for his final departure when his residence was searched and he was charged with the alleged offences. The issue before the court was whether Palacios had lost his diplomatic status entitling him to immunity from prosecution. Its resolution depended on the meaning of the phrase "when he leaves the country" in Article 39(2) of the Vienna Convention on Diplomatic Relations, which has been given the force of law in Canada by the *Diplomatic and Consular Privileges and Immunities Act*.[62]]

BLAIR J.A.: ... The decision in this case turns on the interpretation of the Convention. Treaties, unlike customary international law, only become part of municipal law if they are expressly implemented by statute: *The "Parlement Belge"* (1879), 4 P.D. 129. The provisions of the Convention applicable to this case have been expressly incorporated in Canadian law by the Act and prevail over the customary international law relating to diplomatic immunities wherever they differ from it. ...

The principles of public international law and not domestic law govern the interpretation of treaties. I adopt the statement of this rule by O'Connell, *International Law*, 2nd ed. (1970), vol. 1, at 257, as follows:

The rules of municipal law for interpretation are not to be utilised unless they can be regarded as "general principles of law recognised by civilised nations." Hence the restrictive rule of common law relating to literal interpretation has no place in international law. The dictionary meaning

---

[60] E.g., *Smith v. Ontario and Minnesota Power Co.* (1918), 45 D.L.R. 266, at 268-69 (Ont. S.C.); *Re Arrow River and Tributaries Slide and Boom Co. Ltd.*, [1932] S.C.R. 494, per Lamont J., at 506, reported *infra* in Chapter 4; *R. v. Wedge*, [1939] 4 D.L.R. 323, at 333-38 (B.C.S.C.); and *Stickel v. Minister of National Revenue*, [1972] F.C. 672, at 679.

[61] See *Re Arrow River and Tributaries Slide and Boom Co. Ltd.* (1929-30), 65 O.L.R. 575, at 583 (Ont. H.C.); and *Samson v. The Queen*, [1957] S.C.R. 832, at 837.

[62] Stats. Can. (1976-77), c. 31, s. 2(1).

of words, and the rules of syntax, may be departed from to produce an "effective" result, but only when this is necessary.

These rules of interpretation apply even where, as in this case, a treaty has been incorporated in a statute, as Lord Macmillan stated in *Stag Line, Ltd. v. Foscolo, Mango & Co., Ltd. et al.,* [1932] A.C. 328, at 350:

It is important to remember that the Act of 1924 was the outcome of an International Conference and that the rules in the Schedule have an international currency. As these rules must come under the consideration of foreign Courts it is desirable in the interests of uniformity that their interpretation should not be rigidly controlled by domestic precedents of antecedent date, but rather that the language of the rules should be construed on broad principles of general acceptance.

(See O'Connell, *op. cit.,* vol 1, at 265).

The basic rule of international law governing the interpretation of treaties is stated by O'Connell, *International Law, op. cit.,* at 251, as follows: "The primary end of treaty interpretation is to give effect to the intentions of the parties, and not frustrate them." This is sometimes called the effectiveness principle which requires courts to read a treaty as a whole to ascertain its purpose and intent and to give effect thereto rather than to rely on a literal interpretation of some articles which might produce results "contrary to the manifest aim of the treaty": O'Connell, *op.cit.,* at 255.

The rules of treaty interpretation make it clear that the court is not bound by the common law canon of literal construction of statutes upon which it appears Osborne J. may have relied. ...

The Convention must be interpreted so as to give effect to its purpose which is to affirm and secure diplomatic privileges and immunities. It cannot be construed as being intended to derogate from any diplomatic immunities previously recognized under customary international law [which the court had reviewed earlier]. I cannot, with respect, accept the argument that there is any doubt as to the meaning of the words "leaves the country" under the customary rules. They refer to permanent departure from the host country. It would require the clearest possible language in the Convention to compel the conclusion that a diplomat would have any lesser protection under it and could lose his immunity by a temporary visit outside the country before he was ready or required to leave the country permanently. I can find no such intention expressed in art. 39(2). On the contrary, that article, read sensibly and realistically, dictates the opposite conclusion.

The critical words in art. 39(2) state that immunities "shall normally cease at the moment when he leaves the country, or on expiry of a reasonable period to do so." The key words in the clause are ambiguous. The word "leaves" could refer to a permanent or temporary departure. The words "reasonable period" cannot be understood without reference to the purpose for which the period is provided. It is, therefore, necessary to resort to the rules of customary international law to ascertain the meaning of these words in the Convention. That meaning, as I have already indicated, is clear and precise. The "leaving" to which the "reasonable period" refers is a permanent departure from the country.

Operation of Treaties

Amendment and Modification

In 1967 the Department of External Affairs sent the following comments in reply to a request for advice on how a multilateral agreement could be amended:[63]

Although it is always open to the parties to a multilateral agreement to amend it, international law is not yet fixed with respect to how and under what conditions such amendment may take place. A great deal depends on whether or not the parties are all in agreement on what they wish to do. If there is a consensus that an agreement is to be amended, then negotiations can take place to determine the precise nature of the amendments required. Once the definitive form of these amendments has been agreed upon by all the parties, they can be embodied in an amending agreement. ... (a "Protocol of Amendment").

If it were decided that instead of concluding a Protocol of Amendment it would be preferable to terminate the main agreement and replace it with an entirely new agreement, that could be achieved in one of two ways. Firstly, the old agreement could be terminated in accordance with [its] provisions, [or], provided that there was unanimity among all the parties, such notice of termination could be dispensed with and a provision in the new agreement to be concluded would only need to state that it was intended to terminate the previous agreement. The form of the new agreement could be whatever the parties wished.

In this analysis it has also been assumed so far that all parties to the present agreement will in fact be agreed upon the desirability either of amending it or of concluding a new one. If, however, one or more of the parties were unwilling to go along with either of these proposals, the situation would become more complicated. Briefly, in such a case it is generally accepted in international law that those among the parties to an earlier agreement who might wish either to amend that agreement or to conclude a further agreement *inter se* are free to do so. However, the effects of such amendment or new agreement are restricted only to the parties directly concerned, and they continue to be bound by the old agreement in their relations with the other parties who have not agreed to the changes.

The Vienna Convention Article 39 confirms that a treaty may be amended by agreement between the parties. Thus, as concerns a multilateral treaty, a proposal for its amendment may be negotiated and concluded by all or some of the parties, but the amending agreement does not bind parties to the original treaty who do not accept it (Article 40(4)), and the amendments may not prejudice their existing treaty rights and obligations (Article 41). A state which becomes a party to the treaty after its amendment will be considered a party to the amended treaty, except in relation to a party which has not accepted the amendment (Article 40(5)).

---

[63] (1967), 5 *Can. Y.B. Int. L.* 277.

Invalidity

Vienna Convention on the Law of Treaties

Article 42
VALIDITY AND CONTINUANCE IN FORCE OF TREATIES

1. The validity of a treaty or of the consent of a state to be bound by a treaty may be impeached only through the application of the present Convention.

2. The termination of a treaty, its denunciation or the withdrawal of a party, may take place only as a result of the application of the provisions of the treaty or of the present Convention. The same rule applies to suspension of the operation of a treaty.

Article 43
OBLIGATIONS IMPOSED BY INTERNATIONAL LAW INDEPENDENTLY OF A TREATY

The invalidity, termination or denunciation of a treaty, the withdrawal of a party from it, or the suspension of its operation, as a result of the application of the present Convention or of the provisions of the treaty, shall not in any way impair the duty of any state to fulfil any obligation embodied in the treaty to which it would be subject under international law independently of the treaty.

Article 46
PROVISIONS OF INTERNAL LAW REGARDING COMPETENCE TO CONCLUDE TREATIES

1. A state may not invoke the fact that its consent to be bound by a treaty has been expressed in violation of a provision of its internal law regarding competence to conclude treaties as invalidating its consent unless that violation was manifest and concerned a rule of its internal law of fundamental importance.

2. A violation is manifest if it would be objectively evident to any state conducting itself in the matter in accordance with normal practice and in good faith.

Article 47
SPECIFIC RESTRICTIONS ON AUTHORITY TO EXPRESS THE CONSENT OF A STATE

If the authority of a representative to express the consent of a state to be bound by a particular treaty has been made subject to a specific restriction, his omission to observe that restriction may not be invoked as invalidating the consent expressed by him unless the restriction was notified to the other negotiating states prior to his expressing such consent.

Article 52
COERCION OF A STATE BY THE THREAT OR USE OF FORCE

A treaty is void if its conclusion has been procured by the threat or use of force in violation of the principles of international law embodied in the Charter of the United Nations.

Article 53
TREATIES CONFLICTING WITH A PEREMPTORY NORM OF GENERAL
INTERNATIONAL LAW (JUS COGENS)

A treaty is void if, at the time of its conclusion, it conflicts with a peremptory norm of general international law. For the purposes of the present Convention, a peremptory norm of general international law is a norm accepted and recognized by the international community of states as a whole as a norm from which no derogation is permitted and which can be modified only by a subsequent norm of general international law having the same character.

Article 64
EMERGENCE OF A NEW PEREMPTORY NORM OF
GENERAL INTERNATIONAL LAW (JUS COGENS)

If a new peremptory norm of general international law emerges, any existing treaty which is in conflict with that norm becomes void and terminates.

Article 69
CONSEQUENCES OF THE INVALIDITY OF A TREATY

1. A treaty the invalidity of which is established under the present Convention is void. The provisions of a void treaty have no legal force.

2. If acts have nevertheless been performed in reliance on such a treaty:

(a) each party may require any other party to establish as far as possible in their mutual relations the position that would have existed if the acts had not been performed;

(b) acts performed in good faith before the invalidity was invoked are not rendered unlawful by reason only of the invalidity of the treaty.

3. In cases falling under Articles 49, 50, 51 or 52, paragraph 2 does not apply with respect to the party to which the fraud, the act of corruption or the coercion is imputable.

4. In the case of invalidity of a particular state's consent to be bound by a multilateral treaty, the foregoing rules apply in the relations between that state and the parties to the treaty.

Article 71
CONSEQUENCES OF THE INVALIDITY OF A TREATY WHICH CONFLICTS WITH
A PEREMPTORY NORM OF GENERAL INTERNATIONAL LAW

1. In the case of a treaty which is void under Article 53 the parties shall:

(a) eliminate as far as possible the consequences of any act performed in reliance on any provision which conflicts with the peremptory norm of general international law; and

(b) bring their mutual relations into conformity with the peremptory norm of general international law.

2. In the case of a treaty which becomes void and terminates under Article 64, the termination of the treaty:

(a) releases the parties from any obligation further to perform the treaty;

(b) does not affect any right, obligation or legal situation of the parties created through the execution of the treaty prior to its termination; provided that those rights, obligations or situations may thereafter be maintained only to the extent that their maintenance is not in itself in conflict with the new peremptory norm of general international law.

[The Vienna Convention Articles 48-51 also include error, fraud, and corruption or coercion of a state's representative by another negotiating state as grounds for invalidity of a treaty.]

Jus Cogens

The phrase *jus cogens* refers to an open set of peremptory norms of international law which cannot be set aside by treaty or acquiescence, but only by the formation of a subsequent peremptory norm of contrary effect. Some principles of international law that have the status of *jus cogens* can be found in treaties, others in custom. They are obligations owed by a state to the international community as a whole.

The provisions on *jus cogens* are some of the most controversial articles in the Convention.[64] The controversy surrounds the concept as well as its contents. Socialist and developing countries seem to attach great importance to the idea that there are some imperatives in international law which will override any treaty made in violation of them. Western states are much more skeptical about *jus cogens*, fearing, perhaps, how such an ill-defined concept may invalidate carefully negotiated agreements and jeopardise the stability of the treaty system. There is also concern that the concept conflicts with the principle of state sovereignty and the consensual character of international law which it implies.

These misgivings would be less if there was more certainty about the contents of *jus cogens*. The main characteristic of these peremptory norms is their fundamental importance to social order. On this ground, the pre-eminent example must be the prohibition against the use of force reiterated in Article 2 of the U.N. Charter. Others, such as the principle *pacta sunt servanda*, reflect what may be regarded as necessary elements for the existence and operation of the international legal system. Yet others can only be described as norms that have become so widely and deeply imbedded in international law that they are inviolable. For instance, it is unimaginable nowadays that any two states could validly agree to divide control of the oceans in violation of the principle of freedom of navigation on the high seas. Peremptory norms can also derive from elementary considerations of human dignity.[65] On this basis, many of the laws for the protection of

---

[64] See I. Sinclair, *supra*, n.11, at 203-26; J. Sztucki, *Jus Cogens and the Vienna Convention on the Law of Treaties* (1974); C. Rozakis, *The Concept of Jus Cogens in the Law of Treaties* (1976); G. Schwarzenberger, "International Jus Cogens?" (1964-65), 43 *Tex. L.R.* 455; and A. Verdross, "Jus Dispositivum and Jus Cogens in International Law" (1966), 60 *Am. J. Int. L.* 55.

[65] In general, see *Barcelona Traction Case (Second Phase)*, [1970] I.C.J. Rep. 3, at 32; and *Reservations to the Convention on Genocide*, [1951] I.C.J. Rep. 23, reported above.

human rights are arguably a part of *jus cogens*. What other rules and principles may also be advanced for inclusion?

Given the uncertainties surrounding *jus cogens* it is fortunate that the Vienna Convention makes particular provision for disputes about peremptory norms. According to Article 66, any one of the parties to a dispute concerning the application or the interpretation of Article 53 or 64 may, by a written application, submit it to the International Court of Justice for a decision, unless the parties by common consent agree to go to arbitration.

Termination and Suspension

Vienna Convention on the Law of Treaties

Article 54
TERMINATION OF OR WITHDRAWAL FROM A TREATY UNDER ITS PROVISIONS OR BY CONSENT OF THE PARTIES

The termination of a treaty or the withdrawal of a party may take place:
(a) in conformity with the provisions of the treaty; or
(b) at any time by consent of all the parties after consultation with the other contracting states.

Article 55
REDUCTION OF THE PARTIES TO A MULTILATERAL TREATY BELOW THE NUMBER NECESSARY FOR ITS ENTRY INTO FORCE

Unless the treaty otherwise provides, a multilateral treaty does not terminate by reason only of the fact that the number of the parties falls below the number necessary for its entry into force.

Article 63
SEVERANCE OF DIPLOMATIC OR CONSULAR RELATIONS

The severance of diplomatic or consular relations between parties to a treaty does not affect the legal relations established between them by the treaty except in so far as the existence of diplomatic or consular relations is indispensable for the application of the treaty.

Ex Parte O'Dell and Griffen
[1953] O.R. 190 (H.C.)

SCHROEDER J.: This is an application for the issue of a writ of *habeas corpus* and a writ of *certiorari* in aid thereof and for the discharge from custody of Maurice O'Dell and Walter Griffen, now lodged in the county gaol in the county of Wentworth, pursuant to an order of Mr. Justice Treleaven made on the 24th January 1953, committing the applicants to prison until surrendered to the State of New York or discharged according to law.

The applicants were arrested under a warrant issued by Mr. Justice Treleaven on 12th December 1952, on which date they were brought before him. They were remanded until 16th January 1953 for final hearing. The fugitives are under indictment in the State of New York on a charge of murder and evidence relating to the charge was presented at the hearing. Counsel for the fugitives conceded that there was sufficient evidence adduced before the learned Judge to justify the order of committal and they base their claim to the relief which is now sought on two grounds, namely, (1) that there was no subsisting extradition treaty or convention between Canada and the United States of America on the date of the issue of the warrant of apprehension: ...

In support of the first ground, it is contended that the only treaty or convention in existence within the meaning of the Extradition Act of Canada, R.S.C. 1927, c. 37, is the Ashburton treaty of 1842, which was entered into between Her Britannic Majesty and the United States of America. This treaty not only provided for the delivery up to justice of persons charged with certain enumerated crimes committed within the jurisdiction of the signing powers, but was also entered into "to settle and define the boundaries between the possessions of Her Britannic Majesty in North America, and the territories of the United States; [and] for the final suppression of the African slave trade."

It is urged by counsel for the fugitives that since the enactment in 1931 of The Statute of Westminster, 22 Geo. V. (Imp.), c.4, the Ashburton treaty ceased to have any validity in Canada; that Canada had only colonial status when that treaty was made, but that since the enactment of The Statute of Westminster Canada has been an independent and self-governing nation. It is argued that while Her Majesty Queen Elizabeth II, the lawful successor of Her Majesty Queen Victoria, is the Queen of Canada as well as the Queen of Great Britain and other realms of the Commonwealth, the present relationship between the Crown and this country is completely different from the relationship which existed in 1842 when Canada was only a possession of Her Britannic Majesty in America and that consequently the Ashburton treaty, not being a treaty made by Her Britannic Majesty on behalf of Canada as a self-governing and independent nation, no longer has any force and effect.

It is undoubtedly true that since 1931 Canada has been independently represented in the United States and in other foreign nations by her own diplomatic representatives and has entered into treaties with foreign countries through her own ministers of state without reference to the Government of the United Kingdom, but I am quite unable to apprehend how it can be said that the enactment of The Statute of Westminster can possibly have the effect ascribed to it by counsel. The true relationship of the Crown to the various countries composing the British Commonwealth is set forth in the preamble of the statute which reads:

And whereas it is meet and proper to set out by way of preamble to this Act that, inasmuch as the Crown is the symbol of the free association of the members of the British Commonwealth of Nations, and as they are united by a common allegiance to the Crown, it would be in accord with the established constitutional position of all the members of the Commonwealth in relation to one another that any alteration in the law touching the Succession to the Throne or the Royal Style and Titles shall hereafter require the assent as well of the Parliaments of all the Dominions as of the Parliament of the United Kingdom:

Another purpose of the statute is set forth in the third clause of the preamble, which reads:

And whereas it is in accord with the established constitutional position that no law hereafter made by the Parliament of the United Kingdom shall extend to any of the said Dominions as part of the law of that Dominion otherwise than at the request and with the consent of that Dominion:

The statute then goes on to provide that The Colonial Laws Validity Act, 1865 shall not apply to any law made after the commencement of The Statute of Westminster by the Parliament of a Dominion. It is declared and enacted that the Parliament of a Dominion has full power to make laws having extraterritorial operation. It is further provided that no Act of the Parliament of the United Kingdom thereafter passed shall extend or be deemed to extend to a Dominion unless it is expressly declared in that Act that the Dominion has requested and consented to the enactment thereof. These and other sections of the Act convey some idea of the purpose for which the statute was passed. Had it been intended that the Ashburton treaty or any other convention which had been entered into or any other statute which had been enacted by the Imperial Government or Parliament prior to this time, affecting Canada or any of its Provinces, should cease to have validity, one would expect to find express provision for it in The Statute of Westminster or in some other statute. There is nothing to prevent Canada from entering into a new treaty with the United States or substituting some other extradition arrangement for the one which is now embraced within the terms of the Ashburton treaty, but until that is done that treaty remains in full force and effect and is binding upon the signatories thereto, including Canada. Indeed it would be a startling and extraordinary thing if Canada and the United States had been without an extradition arrangement for a period of approximately twenty-two years. Many extradition proceedings have taken place during that period and it is rather astonishing, if this point has any merit in it, that it was not at least raised before this date. It would be rather surprising if it escaped the attention of the members of the Court of Appeal in *Re Insull*, [1934] O.W.N. 194; 61 C.C.C. 336; [1934] 2 D.L.R.696, and of the eminent and learned counsel who were before the Court in that case. The application on this branch of the argument must fail. ...

NOTES

1) In *Smith v. Ontario and Minnesota Power Co.*[66] the Court expressed the opinion that the Parliament of Canada and the Government of the United States of America, acting together, have power to abrogate a treaty between His Majesty and the United

---

[66] (1918), 44 O.L.R. 43; 45 D.L.R. 266 (Ont. S.C.), reversing in part 42 O.L.R. 167.

States so far, at least, as it affects the citizens of Canada and the United States. The treaty in question was the Ashburton Treaty of 1842, an Imperial treaty.

2) In *Regina v. Sikyea*[67] the Court of Appeal for the Northwest Territories stated that federal statutes that implement treaties made in accordance with s. 132 of *The B.N.A. Act* (now the Constitution Act), and before the Statute of Westminster (1931) remain valid legislation even when their subject matter falls exclusively under s. 92 of that Act, so long, of course, as the treaties have not been denounced. It would also appear that such statutes can still be amended by the federal Parliament, if that be necessary properly to carry out the terms of the treaties.

Vienna Convention on the Law of Treaties

Article 56
DENUNCIATION OF OR WITHDRAWAL FROM A TREATY CONTAINING NO PROVISION REGARDING TERMINATION, DENUNCIATION OR WITHDRAWAL

1. A treaty which contains no provision regarding its termination and which does not provide for denunciation or withdrawal is not subject to denunciation or withdrawal unless:
  (a) it is established that the parties intended to admit the possibility of denunciation or withdrawal; or
  (b) a right of denunciation or withdrawal may be implied by the nature of the treaty.

2. A party shall give not less than twelve months' notice of its intention to denounce or withdraw from a treaty under paragraph 1.

Article 60[68]
TERMINATION OR SUSPENSION OF THE OPERATION OF A TREATY AS A CONSEQUENCE OF ITS BREACH

1. A material breach of a bilateral treaty by one of the parties entitles the other to invoke the breach as a ground for terminating the treaty or suspending its operation in whole or in part.

2. A material breach of a multilateral treaty by one of the parties entitles:
  (a) the other parties by unanimous agreement to suspend the operation of the treaty in whole or in part or to terminate it either:
     (i) in the relations between themselves and the defaulting state; or
     (ii) as between all the parties;
  (b) a party specially affected by the breach to invoke it as a ground for suspending the operation of the treaty in whole or in part in the relations between itself and the defaulting state;

---

[67] (1964), 46 W.W.R. 65, aff'd. [1964] S.C.R. 642.
[68] Applied by the International Court in the *Namibia Case*, [1971] I.C.J. Rep. 16, reported *supra* in Chapter 2.

(c) any party other than the defaulting state to invoke the breach as a ground for suspending the operation of the treaty in whole or in part with respect to itself if the treaty is of such a character that a material breach of its provisions by one party radically changes the position of every party with respect to the further performance of its obligations under the treaty.

3. A material breach of a treaty, for the purposes of this Article, consists in:

(a) a repudiation of the treaty not sanctioned by the present Convention; or

(b) the violation of a provision essential to the accomplishment of the object or purpose of the treaty.

4. The foregoing paragraphs are without prejudice to any provision in the treaty applicable in the event of a breach.

5. Paragraphs 1 to 3 do not apply to provisions relating to the protection of the human person contained in treaties of a humanitarian character, in particular to provisions prohibiting any form of reprisals against persons protected by such treaties.

Article 61
SUPERVENING IMPOSSIBILITY OF PERFORMANCE

1. A party may invoke the impossibility of performing a treaty as a ground for terminating or withdrawing from it if the impossibility results from the permanent disappearance or destruction of an object indispensable for the execution of the treaty. If the impossibility is temporary, it may be invoked only as a ground for suspending the operation of the treaty.

2. Impossibility of performance may not be invoked by a party as a ground for terminating, withdrawing from or suspending the operation of a treaty if the impossibility is the result of a breach by that party either of an obligation under the treaty or of any other international obligation owed to any other party to the treaty.

Article 62
FUNDAMENTAL CHANGE OF CIRCUMSTANCES

1. A fundamental change of circumstances which has occurred with regard to those existing at the time of the conclusion of a treaty, and which was not foreseen by the parties, may not be invoked as a ground for terminating or withdrawing from the treaty unless:

(a) the existence of those circumstances constituted an essential basis of the parties to be bound by the treaty; and

(b) the effect of the change is radically to transform the extent of obligations still to be performed under the treaty.

2. A fundamental change of circumstances may not be invoked as a ground for terminating or withdrawing from a treaty:

(a) if the treaty establishes a boundary; or

(b) if the fundamental change is the result of a breach by the party invoking it either of an obligation under the treaty or of any other international obligation owed to any other party to the treaty.

3. If, under the foregoing paragraphs, a party may invoke a fundamental change of

circumstances as a ground for terminating or withdrawing from a treaty it may also invoke the change as a ground for suspending the operation of the treaty.

Article 70
CONSEQUENCES OF THE TERMINATION OF A TREATY

1. Unless the treaty otherwise provides or the parties otherwise agree, the termination of a treaty under its provisions or in accordance with the present Convention:

(a) releases the parties from any obligation further to perform the treaty;

(b) does not affect any right, obligation or legal situation of the parties created through the execution of the treaty prior to its termination.

2. If a state denounces or withdraws from a multilateral treaty, paragraph 1 applies in the relations between that state and each of the other parties to the treaty from the date when such denunciation or withdrawal takes effect.

Clausula Rebus Sic Stantibus[69]
International Law Commission, "Commentary," [1966] *Y.B.I.L.C.* II, at 257-58

1) Almost all modern jurists, however reluctantly, admit the existence in international law of the principle with which this article is concerned and which is commonly spoken of as the doctrine of *rebus sic stantibus*. Just as many systems of municipal law recognize that, quite apart from any actual *impossibility* of performance, contracts may become inapplicable through a fundamental change of circumstances, so also treaties may become inapplicable for the same reason. Most jurists, however, at the same time enter a strong *caveat* as to the need to confine the scope of the doctrine within narrow limits and to regulate strictly the conditions under which it may be invoked; for the risks to the security of treaties which this doctrine presents in the absence of any general system of compulsory jurisdiction are obvious. The circumstances of international life are always changing and it is easy to allege that the changes render the treaty inapplicable. ...

4) The principle of *rebus sic stantibus* has not infrequently been invoked in State practice either *eo nomine* or in the form of a reference to a general principle claimed to justify the termination or modification of treaty obligations by reason of changed circumstances. ...

Broadly speaking, it shows a wide acceptance of the view that a fundamental change of circumstances may justify a démand for the termination or revision of a treaty, but also shows a strong disposition to question the right of a party to denounce a treaty unilaterally on this ground. The most illuminating indications as to the attitude of States regarding the principle are perhaps statements submitted to the Court in the cases where the doctrine has been invoked. In the *Nationality Decrees* case[70] the French Government

---

[69] See also K. Sastry, "Clausula rebus sic stantibus in International Law" (1935), 13 *Can. Bar Rev.* 227; and A. Vamvoukos, *Termination of Treaties in International Law* (1985).

[70] *Nationality Decrees in Tunis and Morocco Case* (1923), P.C.I.J. Ser. B, No. 4, at 187-88, and 208-9.

contended that "perpetual" treaties are always subject to termination in virtue of the *rebus sic stantibus* clause and claimed that the establishment of the French protectorate over Morocco had for that reason had the effect of extinguishing certain Anglo-French treaties. The British Government, while contesting the French Government's view of the facts, observed that the most forceful argument advanced by France was that of *rebus sic stantibus*. ...

In the *Free Zones* case[71] the French Government, the Government invoking the *rebus sic stantibus* principle, itself emphasized that the principle does not allow unilateral denunciation of a treaty claimed to be out of date. It argued that the doctrine would cause a treaty to lapse only "*lorsque le changement de circonstances aura été reconnu par un acte faisant droit entre les deux Etats intéressés*"; and it further said: "*cet acte faisant droit entre les deux Etats intéressés peut être soit un accord, lequel accord sera une reconnaissance du changement des circonstances et de son effet sur le traité, soit une sentence du juge international compétent s'il y en a un.*" Switzerland, emphasizing the differences of opinion amongst jurists in regard to the principle, disputed the existence in international law of any such *right* to the termination of a treaty because of changed circumstances enforceable through the decision of a competent tribunal. But she rested her case primarily on three contentions: (a) the circumstances alleged to have changed were not circumstances on the basis of whose continuance the parties could be said to have entered into the treaty; (b) in any event, the doctrine does not apply to treaties creating *territorial* rights; and (c) France had delayed unreasonably long after the alleged changes of circumstances had manifested themselves. France does not appear to have disputed that the doctrine is inapplicable to territorial rights; instead, she drew a distinction between territorial rights and "personal" rights created on the occasion of a territorial settlement. The Court upheld the Swiss Government's contentions on points (a) and (c), but did not pronounce on the application of the *rebus sic stantibus* principle to treaties creating territorial rights.

Fisheries Jurisdiction Case (Jurisdiction)
United Kingdom v. Iceland
[1973] I.C.J. Rep. 3

THE COURT: ...

35. In his letter of 29 May 1972 to the Registrar, the Minister of Foreign Affairs of Iceland refers to "the changed circumstances resulting from the ever-increasing exploitation of the fishery resources in the seas surrounding Iceland."

36. ... the Government of Iceland is basing itself on the principle of termination of a treaty by reason of change of circumstances. International law admits that a fundamental change in the circumstances which determined the parties to accept a treaty, if it has resulted in a radical transformation of the extent of the obligations imposed by it, may,

---

[71] (1932), P.C.I.J. Ser. A/B, No. 46, at 156-58, reported *supra* in Chapter 3.

under certain conditions, afford the party affected a ground for invoking the termination or suspension of the treaty. This principle, and the conditions and exceptions to which it is subject, have been embodied in Article 62 of the Vienna Convention on the Law of Treaties, which may in many respects be considered as a codification of existing customary law on the subject of the termination of a treaty relationship on account of change of circumstances.

37. One of the basic requirements embodied in that Article is that the change of circumstances must have been a fundamental one. In this respect the Government of Iceland has, with regard to developments in fishing techniques, referred ... to the increased exploitation of the fishery resources in the seas surrounding Iceland and to the danger of still further exploitation because of an increase in the catching capacity of fishing fleets. The Icelandic statements recall the exceptional dependence of that country on its fishing for its existence and economic development. ...

44. In the United Kingdom Memorial it is asserted that there is a flaw in the Icelandic contention of change of circumstances: that the doctrine never operates so as to extinguish a treaty automatically or to allow an unchallengeable unilateral denunciation by one party; it only operates to confer a right to call for termination and, if that call is disputed, to submit the dispute to some organ or body with power to determine whether the conditions for the operation of the doctrine are present. In this connection the Applicant alludes to Articles 65 and 66 of the Vienna Convention on the Law of Treaties.

45. In the present case, the procedural complement to the doctrine of changed circumstances is already provided for in the 1961 Exchange of Notes, which specifically calls upon the parties to have recourse to the Court in the event of a dispute relating to Iceland's extension of fisheries jurisdiction. ...

Separate Opinion of JUDGE SIR GERALD FITZMAURICE: ... **17.** With regard to the question of "changed circumstances" I have nothing to add to what is stated in paragraphs 35-43 of the Court's Judgment, except to emphasize that in my opinion the only change that could possibly be relevant (if at all) would be some change relating directly to the, so to speak, operability of the jurisdictional clause itself — not to such things as developments in fishery techniques or in Iceland's situation relative to fisheries. These would indeed be matters that would militate for, not against, adjudication. But as regards the jurisdictional clause itself, the only "change" that has occurred is the purported extension of Icelandic fishery limits. This however is the absolute *reverse* of the type of change to which the doctrine of "changed circumstances" relates, namely one never contemplated by the Parties: it is in fact the actual change they did contemplate, and specified as the one that would give rise to the obligation to have recourse to adjudication.

NOTES

1) Suspension of the operation of a treaty is a possible alternative to denunciation of or withdrawal from it. A treaty may be suspended by consent of all the parties (Article 57), or by agreement amongst some parties only provided their action does not prejudice the rights and obligations of the other parties or the purposes of the treaty (Article 58). A treaty that is incompatible with an earlier agreement on the same subject-matter will

impliedly terminate or suspend that agreement in accordance with the apparent intentions of the parties (Article 59). Suspension releases the parties from further performance of the treaty but it does not otherwise affect their continuing legal relations. The parties are also bound to refrain from actions which might obstruct resumption of the treaty's operation (Article 72).

2) The continuance of a treaty may be affected in two other situations, namely the *post facto* assertion that the agreement was unequal and imposed, and the outbreak of war.[72] Does Article 62 on fundamental change of circumstances cover these situations?

3) It is increasingly common for treaties to contain revision clauses which provide for review after the expiration of a prescribed period of time. Such a clause obliges the signatories to consider amendments requested by one party on account of changed circumstances or for any other reason.

Succession to Treaties

The Vienna Convention on the Law of Treaties does "not prejudge any question that may arise in regard to a treaty from a succession of states ... " (Article 73). The principles of international law that do govern this matter are discussed in Chapter 2 in the section on "State Succession."

CUSTOM

General Customary Law[73]

Customary international law is comprised of two elements: 1) there must be a consistent and general international practice amongst states, and 2) the practice must be accepted as law by the international community. This subjective element of acceptance as law is often known as *opinio juris*.

Three concepts have been advanced to explain why "international custom, as evidence of a general practice accepted as law"[74] is binding on states: consent, estoppel and reasonableness. Reliance on each of these concepts may lead to different opinions about the existence and contents of an alleged customary rule.

---

[72] As to unequal treaties, see S.S. Malawer, *Imposed Treaties and International Law* (1977); C.H. Alexandrowicz, "Treaty and Diplomatic Relations between European and South Asian Powers in the Seventeenth and Eighteenth Centuries" (1960), 100 *Hague Recueil* 203, at 278. As to the effects of war, see *Francis v. The Queen*, [1956] S.C.R. 618. Cp. *Karnuth, Director of Immigration et al. v. United States ex rel. Albro* (1929), 279 U.S. 231; also C. Hurst, "The Effect of War on Treaties" (1921-22), 2 *Br.Y.B.Int.L.*37. Hunting rights: *R. v. Syliboy*, [1929] 1 D.L.R. 307 (N.S. Co. Ct.); mutual naturalization: *Re Cimonian* (1915), 23 D.L.R. 363, at 372-73 (O.S.C.); and copyright: *Louvigny de Montigny v. Cousineau*, [1950] S.C.R. 297, at 311, which were dealt with by international agreement, were held in abeyance during the war at least until the cessation of hostilities and perhaps even until the state of war was formally terminated by a Treaty of Peace: *Spitz v. Secretary of State*, [1939] 2 D.L.R. 546 (Ex. C.).

[73] See A.D'Amato, *The Concept of Custom in International Law* (1971); H.W.A.Thirlway, *International Customary Law and Codification* (1972).

[74] I.C.J. Statute Art. 38(1)(b), reprinted in the Appendix.

It is easy to make these general propositions about the process of creating customary international law and about the basis for determining its application, but in practice these two different operations are complex and controversial. Part of the controversy stems from the apparent paradox that customary rules binding on all are founded in the unilateral acts of individual states. Here is a statement on this dilemma made in the context of the developing law of the sea. It was delivered in 1970 by the Canadian Representative, Mr. J.A. Beesley, to the First Committee of the U.N. General Assembly:

Mr. Chairman, there have been a number of references during our debate to the relative merits of unilateralism as compared to multilateralism as methods of developing the Law of the Sea.

The Canadian position on this issue is well-known. In brief, we do not consider multilateral action and unilateral action as mutually exclusive courses; they should not, in our view, be looked on as clear-cut alternatives. The contemporary international law of the sea comprises both conventional and customary law. Conventional or multilateral treaty law must, of course, be developed primarily by multilateral action, drawing as necessary upon principles of customary international law. Thus multilateral conventions often consist of both a codification of existing principles of international law and progressive development of new principles. Customary international law is, of course, derived primarily from state practice, that is to say, unilateral action by various states, although it frequently draws in turn upon the principles embodied in bilateral and limited multilateral treaties. Law-making treaties often become accepted as such not by virtue of their status as treaties, but through a gradual acceptance by states of the principles they lay down. The complex process of the development of customary international law is still relevant and indeed, in our view, essential to the building of a world order. For these reasons we find it very difficult to be doctrinaire on such questions. The regime of the territorial sea, for example, derives in part from conventional law, including in particular the Geneva Convention on the Territorial Sea (which itself was based in large part upon customary principles) and in part from the very process of the development of customary international law. During the period when it was possible to say, if ever there was such a time, that there existed a rule of law that the breadth of the territorial sea extended to three nautical miles and no further, that principle was created by state practice, and can be altered by state practice, that is to say, by unilateral action on the part of various states, accepted by other states and thus developed into customary international law. How then can we be dogmatic about the merits of either approach to the exclusion of the other? Unilateralism carried to an extreme and based upon differing or conflicting principles could produce complete chaos.

Unilateral action when taken along parallel lines and based upon similar principles can lead to a new regional and perhaps even universal rule of law. Similarly, agreement by the international community reached through a multilateral approach can produce effective rules of law, while doctrinaire insistence upon the multilateral approach as the only legitimate means of developing the law can lead to the situation which has prevailed since the failure of the two Geneva Law of the Sea Conferences to reach agreement upon the breadth of the territorial sea and fishing zones. ... What is required, in our view, is a judicious mix of the two approaches taking into account the complex set of interrelated and sometimes conflicting political, economic and legal considerations, both national and international, and based upon the imperatives of time itself. The seriousness of the problem can determine the urgency of action, which in turn can sometimes dictate the means chosen.

This thesis appears to permit states to act outside the law. Is it acceptable? For instance, in 1970 Canada claimed a large area of jurisdiction over Arctic waters contrary to the principle of the freedom of the high seas. At the time it was a unique unilateral assertion of authority which, however it might have been justified as morally necessary to prevent pollution or politically urgent to protect Canadian sovereignty, was not based on deference to any *opinio juris* in the matter.

One of the best descriptions of the creation of customary international law was provided by Professor Myres McDougal also in the context of discussing the law of the sea. He wrote:[75]

... the international law of the sea is not a mere static body of rules but is rather a whole decision-making process, a public order which includes a structure of authorized decision-makers as well as a body of highly flexible, inherited prescriptions. It is, in other words, a process of continuous interaction, of continuous demand and response, in which the decision-makers of particular nation states unilaterally put forward claims of the most diverse and conflicting character to the use of the world's seas, and in which other decision-makers, external to the demanding state and including both national and international officials, weigh and appraise these competing claims in terms of the interests of the world community and of the rival claimants, and ultimately accept or reject them. As such a process, it is a living, growing law, grounded in the practices and sanctioning expectations of nation-state officials, and changing as their demands and expectations are changed by the exigencies of new interests and technology and by other continually evolving conditions in the world arena. ...

The authoritative decision-makers put forward by the public order of the high seas to resolve all these competing claims include, of course, not merely judges of international courts and other international officials, but also those same nation-state officials who on other occasions are themselves claimants. This duality in function (''*dédoublement fonctionnel*''), or fact that the same nation-state officials are alternately, in a process of reciprocal interaction, both claimants and external decision-makers passing upon the claims of others, need not, however, cause confusion: it merely reflects the present lack of specialization and centralization of policy functions in international law generally. Similarly, it may be further observed, without deprecating the authority of international law, that these authoritative decision-makers projected by nation states for creating and applying a common public order, honor each other's unilateral claims to the use of the world's seas not merely by explicit agreements but also by mutual tolerances – expressed in countless decisions in foreign offices, national courts, and national legislatures – which create expectations that effective power will be restrained and exercised in certain uniformities of pattern. This process of reciprocal tolerance of unilateral claim is, too, but that by which in the present state of world organization most decisions about jurisdiction in public and private international law are, and must be, taken. (It is not of course the unilateral claims but rather the reciprocal tolerances of the external decision-makers which create the expectations of pattern and uniformity in decision, of practice in accord with rule, commonly regarded as law.)

---

[75] M.S. McDougal, ''The Hydrogen Bomb Tests and the International Law of the Sea'' (1955), 49 *Am. J. Int. L.* 356-58.

While Professor MacDougal gives here a lucid depiction of the interactive process of creating customary law, he only hints, in his parenthesis, at how to determine when state practice has passed into law. It is especially difficult to establish whether the general behaviour of states on some particular matter reflects a common practice merely out of convenience or from a sense of legal obligation. Proof of the necessary *opinio juris* is rarely displayed in explicit acceptance of one state's claims by others, rather it is shown by their tolerance of that state's conduct. Professor MacGibbon has analyzed the part played by tolerance and by objection in the creation of customary law:[76]

To determine whether a given practice is being pursued as a matter of right or merely as a matter of convenience may be a task of some difficulty which, however, evidence of either protest or absence of protest may to some extent resolve. In so far as protests are made against refusal to submit to the practice or against aberrations in which the practice takes a substantially different form, they tend strongly if not conclusively to show the conviction on the part of the protesting States that they were acting in defence of their rights, or, in other words, that the practice was being asserted on the basis of a claim of right. On the other hand, acquiescence in refusals to submit to a given practice, or acquiescence in a contrary practice on the part of other States, affords cogent evidence that the practice is not followed on the basis of a claim of right and that submission to its exercise is not regarded as obligatory — in short, that it is not an international custom. ...

The process of action and reaction which Professor McDougal observed as characteristic of the development of a particular set of customary rules is common to the formation of all rules of customary international law. The fact that claims may conflict to a greater or less degree lends complication to the process of determining what part, if any, of differing claims and practices in respect of a particular matter have crystallized into customary practices with legal sanction. It is probable that only by reference to protest and acquiescence can this question be resolved. Those parts of conflicting claims and practices in respect of a particular matter which are common to all of the claimant States and have encountered no protests are, it is submitted, the acceptable *residuum* of the practice or claim which is apt to attain the status of custom; by contrast, protests maintained against certain parts of the claim suffice to prevent those objectionable features from achieving legal sanction. Finally, it is submitted that the extent to which a general uniform practice has been 'accepted as law' may most readily and objectively be gauged by estimating the degree of general consent, or, failing express consent, the degree of general acquiescence which the practice has encountered.

How to weigh the evidence of state practice so as to determine the advent and content of a customary rule of law is considered in the following cases and questions.

---

[76] I.C. MacGibbon, "Customary International Law and Acquiescence" (1957), 33 *Br. Y.B. Int. L.* 115, at 118-19.

The Steamship Lotus
France v. Turkey
(1927), P.C.I.J., Ser. A, No. 10, reported *infra* in Chapter 8

North Sea Continental Shelf Cases
Federal Republic of Germany v. Denmark and v. Netherlands
[1969] I.C.J. Rep. 3

[In 1964 and 1965 the Federal Republic of Germany entered into an agreement with the Netherlands and one with Denmark for the purpose of delimiting the boundaries of their North Sea continental shelves. These agreements only established a partial dividing line for a short distance from the coast beginning at the point at which the land boundary between the states is located. In order to determine the lateral or median lines with more precision, a matter which proved to be impossible to settle by agreement, the Federal Republic of Germany, the Netherlands and Denmark agreed to refer the problem to the International Court of Justice.

The question put to the court was as follows: What principles and rules of international law are applicable to the delimitation as between the Parties of the areas of the continental shelf in the North Sea which appertain to each of them beyond the partial boundary [already] determined ... ?

The Netherlands and Denmark argued that the "equidistance-special circumstances principles" in Art. 6(2) of the 1958 Geneva Convention on the Continental Shelf applied whereas the Federal Republic of Germany relied on the doctrine of the just and equitable share. Article 6 of the Convention reads:

1. Where the same continental shelf is adjacent to the territories of two or more States whose coasts are opposite each other, the boundary of the continental shelf appertaining to such States shall be determined by agreement between them. In the absence of agreement, and unless another boundary line is justified by special circumstances, the boundary is the median line, every point of which is equidistant from the nearest points of the baselines from which the breadth of the territorial sea of each State is measured.

2. Where the same continental shelf is adjacent to the territories of two adjacent States, the boundary of the continental shelf shall be determined by agreement between them. In the absence of agreement, and unless another boundary line is justified by special circumstances, the boundary shall be determined by application of the principle of equidistance from the nearest points of the baselines from which the breadth of the territorial sea of each State is measured.

The Court held that the Federal Republic, which had not ratified the Convention, was not bound by the provisions of Art. 6. Therefore, the question became what customary international law existed to delimit the continental shelf between the parties.]

THE COURT: ...

37. It is maintained by Denmark and the Netherlands that the Federal Republic, whatever its position may be in relation to the Geneva Convention, considered as such, is in any event bound to accept delimitation on an equidistance-special circumstances basis, because the use of this method is not in the nature of a merely conventional obligation, but is, or must now be regarded as involving, a rule that is part of the *corpus* of general international law. ... This contention has both a positive law and a more fundamentalist aspect. ... In its fundamentalist aspect, the view put forward derives from what might be called the natural law of the continental shelf, in the sense that the equidistance principle is seen as a necessary expression in the field of delimitation of the accepted doctrine of the exclusive appurtenance of the continental shelf to the nearby coastal State, and therefore as having an *a priori* character of so to speak juristic inevitability. ...

46. The conclusion drawn by the Court is that the notion of equidistance as being logically necessary, in the sense of being an inescapable *a priori* accompaniment of basic continental shelf doctrine, is incorrect. It is said not to be possible to maintain that there is a rule of law ascribing certain areas to a State as a matter of inherent and original right ... without also admitting the existence of some rule by which those areas can be obligatorily delimited. The Court cannot accept the logic of this view. The problem arises only where there is a dispute and only in respect of the marginal areas involved. The appurtenance of a given area, considered as an entity, in no way governs the precise delimitation of its boundaries, any more than uncertainty as to boundaries can affect territorial rights. ...

60. The conclusions so far reached leave open and still to be considered, the question whether on some basis other than that of an *a priori* logical necessity, i.e. through positive law processes, the equidistance principle has come to be regarded as a rule of customary international law, so that it would be obligatory for the Federal Republic in that way, even though Art. 6 of the Geneva Convention is not, as such, opposable to it. For this purpose it is necessary to examine the status of the principle as it stood when the Convention was drawn up, as it resulted from the effect of the Convention, and in the light of State practice subsequent to the Convention; but it should be clearly understood that in the pronouncements the Court makes on these matters it has in view solely the delimitation provisions (Art. 6) of the Convention, not other parts of it, nor the Convention as such.

61. The first of these questions can conveniently be considered in the form suggested on behalf of Denmark and the Netherlands themselves in the course of the oral hearing, when it was stated that they had not in fact contended that the delimitation article (Art. 6) of the Convention ''embodied already received rules of customary law in the sense that the Convention was merely declatory of existing rules.'' Their contention was, rather, that although prior to the Conference, continental shelf law was only in the formative stage and State practice lacked uniformity, yet ''the process of the definition and consolidation of the emerging customary law took place through the work of the International Law Commission, the reaction of governments to that work and the proceedings of the Geneva Conference''; and this emerging customary law became ''crystallized in the adoption of the Continental Shelf Convention by the Conference.''

62. Whatever validity this contention may have in respect of at least certain parts of the Convention, the Court cannot accept it as regards the delimitation provision (Art. 6), the relevant parts of which were adopted almost unchanged from the draft of the International Law Commission that formed the basis of discussion at the Conference. The status of the rule in the Convention therefore depends mainly on the processes that led the Commission to propose it. These processes ... [indicate] that the principle of equidistance, as it now figures in Art. 6 of the Convention, was proposed by the Commission with considerable hesitation, somewhat on an experimental basis, at most *de lege ferenda*, and not at all *de lege lata* or as an emerging rule of customary international law. This is clearly not the sort of foundation on which Art. 6 of the Convention could be said to have reflected or crystallized such a rule.

63. The foregoing conclusion receives significant confirmation from the fact that Art. 6 is one of those in respect of which, under the reservations article of the Convention (Art. 12) reservations may be made by any State on signing, ratifying or acceding, for, speaking generally, it is a characteristic of purely conventional rules and obligations that, in regard to them, some faculty of making unilateral reservations may, within certain limits, be admitted, whereas this cannot be so in the case of general or customary law rules and obligations which, by their very nature, must have equal force for all members of the international community and cannot therefore be the subject of any right of unilateral exclusion exercisable at will by any one of them in its own favour. Consequently, it is to be expected that when, for whatever reason, rules or obligations of this order are embodied, or are intended to be reflected in certain provisions of a convention, such provisions will figure amongst those in respect of which a right of unilateral reservation is not conferred, or is excluded. This expectation is, in principle, fulfilled by Art. 12 of the Geneva Continental Shelf Convention, which permits reservations to be made to all the articles of the Convention ''other than to Arts. 1 to 3 inclusive'': these three articles being the ones which, it is clear, were then regarded as reflecting, or as crystallizing, or at least as emerging as rules of customary international law relative to the continental shelf, amongst them the question of the seaward extent of the shelf; the juridical character of the coastal State's entitlement; the nature of the rights exercisable; the kind of natural resources to which these relate; and the preservation intact of the legal status as high seas of the waters over the shelf and the legal status of the superjacent air-space.

64. The normal inference would therefore be that any articles that do not figure among those excluded from the faculty of reservation under Article 12, were not regarded as declaratory of previously existing or emergent rules of law; and this is the inference the Court in fact draws in respect of Article 6 (delimitation), having regard also to the attitude of the International Law Commission to this provision, as already described in general terms. Naturally this would not of itself prevent this provision from eventually passing into the general *corpus* of customary international law by one of the processes considered in paragraphs 70-81 below. But that is not here the issue. What is now under consideration is whether it originally figured in the Convention as such a rule.

70. The Court must now proceed to the last stage in the argument put forward on behalf of Denmark and the Netherlands. This is to the effect that even if there was at the date of the Geneva Convention no rule of customary international law in favour of the equidistance principle and no such rule was crystallized in Art. 6 of the Convention, nevertheless such a rule has come into being since the Convention, partly because of its own impact, partly on the basis of subsequent State practice and that this rule, being now a rule of customary international law binding on all States, including therefore the Federal

Republic, should be declared applicable to the delimitation of the boundaries between the Parties' respective continental shelf areas in the North Sea.

71. In so far as this contention is based on the view that Art. 6 of the Convention has had the influence and has produced the effect described, it clearly involves treating that Article as a norm-creating provision which has constituted the foundation of, or has generated a rule which, while only conventional or contractual in its origin, has since passed into the general *corpus* of international law, and is now accepted as such by the *opinio juris*, so as to have become binding even for countries which have never and do not, become parties to the Convention. There is no doubt that this process is a perfectly possible one and does from time to time occur: it constitutes indeed one of the recognized methods by which new rules of customary international law may be formed. At the same time this result is not lightly to be regarded as having been attained.

72. It would in the first place be necessary that the provision concerned should, at all events potentially, be of a fundamentally norm-creating character such as could be regarded as forming the basis of a general rule of law. Considered *in abstracto* the equidistance principle might be said to fulfill this requirement. Yet in the particular form in which it is embodied in Art. 6 of the Geneva Convention and having regard to the relationship of that Article to other provisions of the Convention, this must be open to some doubt. In the first place, Art. 6 is so framed as to put second the obligation to make use of the equidistance method, causing it to come after a primary obligation to effect delimitation by agreement. Such a primary obligation constitutes an unusual preface to what is claimed to be a potential general rule of law. Without attempting to enter into, still less pronounce upon any question of *jus cogens*, it is well understood that, in practice, rules of international law can, by agreement, be derogated from in particular cases, or as between particular parties, but this is not normally the subject of any express provision, as it is in Art. 6 of the Geneva Convention. Secondly the part played by the notion of special circumstances relative to the principle of equidistance as embodied in Art. 6 and the very considerable, still unresolved, controversies as to the exact meaning and scope of this notion, must raise further doubts as to the potentially norm-creating character of the rule. Finally, the faculty of making reservations to Art. 6, while it might not of itself prevent the equidistance principle being eventually received as general law, does add considerably to the difficulty of regarding this result as having been brought about (or being potentially possible) on the basis of the Convention: for so long as this faculty continues to exist and is not the subject of any revision brought about in consequence of a request made under Art. 13 of the Convention, of which there is at present no official indication, it is the Convention itself which would, for the reasons already indicated, seem to deny to the provisions of Art. 6 the same norm-creating character as, for instance, Arts. 1 and 2 possess.

73. With respect to the other elements usually regarded as necessary before a conventional rule can be considered to have become a general rule of international law, it might be that, even without the passage of any considerable period of time, a very widespread and representative participation in the Convention might suffice of itself, provided it included that of States whose interests were specially affected. In the present case however, the Court notes that, even if allowance is made for the existence of a number of States to whom participation in the Geneva Convention is not open, or which, by reason for instance of being land-locked States, would have no interest in becoming parties to it, the number of ratifications and accessions so far secured is, though respectable, hardly sufficient. That non-ratification may sometimes be due to factors other than active disapproval of the convention concerned can hardly constitute a basis on which positive acceptance of its principles can be implied. The reasons are speculative, but the facts remain.

74. As regards the time element, the Court notes that it is over ten years since the Convention was signed, but that it is even now less than five since it came into force in June 1964 and that when the present proceedings were brought it was less than three years, while less than one had elapsed at the time when the respective negotiations between the Federal Republic and the other two Parties for a complete delimitation broke down on the question of the application of the equidistance principle. Although the passage of only a short period of time is not necessarily, or of itself, a bar to the formation of a new rule of customary international law on the basis of what was originally a purely conventional rule, an indispensable requirement would be that within the period in question, short though it might be, State practice, including that of States whose interests are specially affected, would have been both extensive and virtually uniform in the sense of the provision invoked; moreover it should have occurred in such a way as to show a general recognition that a rule of law or legal obligation is involved.

75. The Court must now consider whether State practice in the matter of continental shelf delimitation has, subsequent to the Geneva Convention, been of such a kind as to satisfy this requirement. Leaving aside cases which, for various reasons, the Court does not consider to be reliable guides as precedents, such as delimitations effected between the present Parties themselves, or not relating to international boundaries, some fifteen cases have been cited in the course of the present proceedings, occurring mostly since the signature of the 1958 Geneva Convention, in which continental shelf boundaries have been delimited according to the equidistance principle, in the majority of the cases by agreement, in a few others unilaterally, or else the delimitation was foreshadowed but has not yet been carried out. Amongst these fifteen are the four North Sea delimitations United Kingdom/Norway-Denmark-Netherlands, and Norway/Denmark. ... But even if these various cases constituted more than a very small proportion of those potentially calling for delimitation in the world as a whole, the Court would not think it necessary to enumerate or evaluate them separately, since there are, *a priori*, several grounds which deprive them of weight as precedents in the present context.

76. To begin with, over half the States concerned, whether acting unilaterally or conjointly, were or shortly became parties to the Geneva Convention, and were therefore presumably, so far as they were concerned, acting actually or potentially in the application of the Convention. From their action no inference could legitimately be drawn as to the existence of a rule of customary international law in favour of the equidistance principle. As regards those States, on the other hand, which were not, and have not become parties to the Convention, the basis of their action can only be problematical and must remain entirely speculative. Clearly, they were not applying the Convention. But from that no inference could justifiably be drawn that they believed themselves to be applying a mandatory rule of customary international law. There is not a shred of evidence that they did and ... there is no lack of other reasons for using the equidistance method, so that acting, or agreeing to act in a certain way, does not of itself demonstrate anything of a juridical nature.

77. The essential point in this connection and it seems necessary to stress it, is that even if these instances of action by non-parties to the Convention were much more numerous than they in fact are, they would not, even in the aggregate, suffice in themselves to constitute the *opinio juris*; for, in order to achieve this result, two conditions must be fulfilled. Not only must the acts concerned amount to a settled practice, but they must also be such, or be carried out in such a way, as to be evidence of a belief that this practice is rendered obligatory by the existence of a rule of law requiring it. The need for such a belief, *i.e.*, the existence of a subjective element, is implicit in the very notion of the *opinio juris sive necessitatis*. The States concerned must therefore feel that they are conforming to what amounts to a legal obligation. The frequency, or even habitual character of the acts is not in itself enough. There are many international acts, *e.g.*, in the field of ceremonial and protocol, which are performed almost invariably, but which are motivated only by considerations of courtesy, convenience or tradition, and not by any sense of legal duty.

78. In this respect the Court follows the view adopted by the Permanent Court of International Justice in the *Lotus* case, as stated in the following passage, the principle of which is, by analogy, applicable almost word for word, *mutatis mutandis*, to the present case (P.C.I.J., Series A, No. 10, 1927, at 28):

Even if the rarity of the judicial decisions to be found ... were sufficient to prove ... the circumstance alleged ... it would merely show that States had often, in practice, abstained from instituting criminal proceedings, and not that they recognized themselves as being obliged to do so; for only if such abstention were based on their being conscious of having a duty to abstain would it be possible to speak of an international custom. The alleged fact does not allow one to infer that States have been conscious of having such a duty; on the other hand ... there are other circumstances calculated to show that the contrary is true.

Applying this *dictum* to the present case, the position is simply that in certain cases, not a great number, the States concerned agreed to draw or did draw the boundaries concerned according to the principle of equidistance. There is no evidence that they so acted because they felt legally compelled to draw them in this way by reason of a rule of customary law obliging them to do so, especially considering that they might have been motivated by other obvious factors.

79. Finally, it appears that in almost all of the cases cited, the delimitations concerned were median-line delimitations between opposite States, not lateral delimitations between adjacent States. ... [T]he Court regards the case of median-line delimitations between opposite States as different in various respects and as being sufficiently distinct not to constitute a precedent for the delimitation of lateral boundaries. In only one situation discussed by the parties does there appear to have been a geographical configuration which to some extent resembles the present one, in the sense that a number of States on the same coastline are grouped around a sharp curve or bend of it. No complete delimitation in this area has however yet been carried out. But the Court is not concerned to deny to this case, or any other of those cited, all evidential value in favour of the thesis of

Denmark and the Netherlands. It simply considers that they are inconclusive, and insufficient to bear the weight sought to be put upon them as evidence of such a settled practice, manifested in such circumstances, as would justify the inference that delimitation according to the principle of equidistance amounts to a mandatory rule of customary international law, more particularly where lateral delimitations are concerned. ...

81. The Court accordingly concludes that if the Geneva Convention was not in its origins or inception declaratory of a mandatory rule of customary international law enjoining the use of the equidistance principle for the delimitation of continental shelf areas between adjacent States neither has its subsequent effect been constitutive of such a rule; and that State practice up-to-date has equally been insufficient for the purpose. ...

[Having thus found that neither of the approaches argued for by the parties was a part of international law, the Court then proceeded to spell out the principles and rules that did apply.]

85. It emerges from the history of the development of the legal régime of the continental shelf ... that the essential reason why the equidistance method is not to be regarded as a rule of law is that, if it were to be compulsorily applied in all situations, this would not be consonant with certain basic legal notions which ... have from the beginning reflected the *opinio juris* in the matter of delimitation; those principles being that delimitation must be the object of agreement between the States concerned, and that such agreement must be arrived at in accordance with equitable principles. ...

88. The Court comes next to the rule of equity. The legal basis of that rule in the particular case of the delimitation of the continental shelf as between adjoining States has already been stated. It must however be noted that the rule rests also on a broader basis. [Whatever the legal reasoning of a court of justice, its decisions must by definition be just, and therefore in that sense equitable. Nevertheless, when mention is made of a court dispensing justice or declaring the law, what is meant is that the decision finds its objective justification in considerations lying not outside but within the rules, and in this field it is precisely a rule of law that calls for the application of equitable principles.] There is consequently no question in this case of any decision *ex aequo et bono*, such as would only be possible under the conditions prescribed by Article 38, paragraph 2, of the Court's Statute. ...

89. It must next be observed that, in certain geographical circumstances which are quite frequently met with, the equidistance method, despite its known advantages, leads unquestionably to inequity, ...

91. Equity does not necessarily imply equality. There can never be any question of completely refashioning nature, and equity does not require that a State without access to the sea should be allotted an area of continental shelf, any more than there could be a question of rendering the situation of a State with an extensive coastline similar to that of a State with a restricted coastline. Equality is to be reckoned within the same plane, and it is not such natural inequalities as these that equity could remedy. But in the present case there are three States whose North Sea coastlines are in fact comparable in length and which, therefore, have been given broadly equal treatment by nature except that the configuration of one of the coastlines would, if the equidistance method is used, deny to one of these States treatment equal or comparable to that given the other two. Here indeed is a case where, in a theoretical situation of equality within the same order, an inequity is created. What is unacceptable in this instance is that a State should enjoy continental shelf rights considerably different from those of its neighbours merely because in the one case the coastline is roughly convex in form and in the other it is markedly concave, although those coastlines are comparable in length. It is therefore not a question of totally refashioning geography whatever the facts of the situation but, given a geographical situation of quasi-equality as between a number of States, of abating the effects of an incidental special feature from which an unjustifiable difference of treatment could result.

98. A final factor to be taken account of is the element of a reasonable degree of proportionality which a delimitation effected according to equitable principles ought to bring about between the extent of the continental shelf appertaining to the States concerned and the lengths of their respective coastlines, – these being measured according to their general direction in order to establish the necessary balance between States with straight, and those with markedly concave or convex coasts, or to reduce very irregular coastlines to their truer proportions. The choice and application of the appropriate technical methods would be a matter for the parties. ...

101. For these reasons, THE COURT, by eleven votes to six, finds that, in each case,
   (a) the use of the equidistance method of delimitation not being obligatory as between the Parties; and
   (b) there being no other single method of delimitation the use of which is in all circumstances obligatory;
   (c) the principles and rules of international law applicable to the delimitation as between the Parties ... are as follows:
      1) delimitation is to be effected by agreement in accordance with equitable principles, and taking account of all the relevant circumstances, in such a way as to leave as much as possible to each Party all those parts of the continental shelf that constitute a natural prolongation of its land territory into and under the sea, without encroachment on the natural prolongation of the land territory of the other;
      2) if, in the application of the preceding sub-paragraph, the delimitation leaves to the Parties areas that overlap, these are to be divided between them in agreed proportions or, failing agreement, equally, unless they decide on a régime of joint jurisdiction, user, or exploitation for the zones of overlap or any part of them;
   (d) in the course of the negotiations, the factors to be taken into account are to include:
      1) the general configuration of the coasts of the Parties, as well as the presence of any special or unusual features;
      2) so far as known or readily ascertainable, the physical and geological structure, and natural resources, of the continental shelf areas involved;
      3) the element of a reasonable degree of proportionality, which a delimitation carried out in accordance with equitable principles ought to bring about between the extent of the continental shelf areas appertaining to the coastal State and the length of its coast measured in the general direction of the coastline, account being taken for this purpose of the effects, actual or prospective, of any other continental shelf delimitations between adjacent States in the same region.

JUDGE TANAKA dissenting: ... To decide whether these two factors [usage and *opinio juris*] in the formative process of a customary law exist or not, is a delicate and difficult matter. The repetition, the number of examples of State practice, the duration of time required for the generation of customary law cannot be mathematically and uniformly decided. Each fact requires to be evaluated relatively according to the different occasions and circumstances. ... what is important in the matter at issue is not the number or figure of ratifications of and accessions to the Convention or of examples of subsequent State practice, but the meaning which they would imply in the particular circumstances. We cannot evaluate the ratification of the Convention by a large maritime country or the State practice represented by its concluding an agreement on the basis of the equidistance principle, as having exactly the same importance as similar acts by a land-locked country which possessed no particular interest in the delimitation of the continental shelf.

Next, so far as ... *opinio juris sive necessitatis* is concerned, it is extremely difficult to get evidence of its existence in concrete cases. This factor, relating to international motivation and being of a psychological nature, cannot be ascertained very easily, particularly when diverse legislative and executive organs of a government participate in an internal process of decision-making in respect of ratification or other State acts. There is no other way than to ascertain the existence of *opinio juris* from the fact of the external existence of a certain custom and its necessity felt in the international community, rather than to seek evidence as to the subjective motives for each example of State practice, which is something which is impossible of achievement. ...

JUDGE LACHS dissenting: ... Delay in the ratification of and accession to multilateral treaties is a well-known phenomenon in contemporary treaty practice ... experience indicates that in most cases [it is] caused by factors extraneous to the substance and objective of the instrument in question. ... [This] indicates that the number of ratifications and accessions cannot, in itself, be considered conclusive with regard to the general acceptance of a given instrument.

In the case of the Convention on the Continental Shelf, there are other elements that must be given their due weight. In particular, 31 States came into existence during the period between its signature (28 June, 1958) and its entry into force (10 June, 1964) while 13 other nations have since acceded to independence. Thus the time during which these 44 States could have completed the necessary procedure enabling them to become parties to the Convention has been rather limited, in some cases very limited. Taking into account the great and urgent problems each of them had to face, one cannot be surprised that many of them did not consider it a matter of priority. This notwithstanding, nine of those States have acceded to the Convention. Twenty-six of the total number of States in existence are moreover land-locked and cannot be considered as having a special and immediate interest in speedy accession to the Convention (only five of them in fact acceded).

Finally, it is noteworthy that about 70 States are at present engaged in the exploration and exploitation of continental shelf areas.

It is the above analysis which is relevant, not the straight comparison between the total number of States in existence and the number of parties to the Convention. It reveals in fact that the number of parties to the Convention on the Continental Shelf is very impressive, including as it does the majority of States actively engaged in the exploration of continental shelves.

... in the world today an essential factor in the formation of a new rule of general international law is to be taken into account: namely that States with different political, economic and legal systems, States of all continents, participate in the process. No more can a general rule of international law be established by the *fiat* of one or of a few or, as it was once claimed, by the consensus of European States only. ...

All this leads to the conclusion that the principles and rules enshrined in the Convention and in particular the equidistance rule, have been accepted not only by those States which are parties to the Convention on the Continental Shelf, but also by those which have subsequently followed it in agreements, or in their legislation, or have acquiesced in it when faced with legislative acts of other States affecting them. This can be viewed as evidence of a practice widespread enough to satisfy the criteria for a general rule of law.

For to become binding, a rule or principle of international law need not pass the test of universal acceptance. This is reflected in several statements of the Court, *e.g.*: ''generally ... adopted in the practice of States'' (*Fisheries* Judgment, I.C.J.R. 1951, at 128). Not all States have ... an opportunity or possibility of applying a given rule. The evidence should be sought in the behaviour of a great number of States, possibly the majority of States, in any case the great majority of the interested States. ...

JUDGE AD HOC SORENSEN dissenting: ... I agree, of course, that one should not lightly reach the conclusion that a convention is binding upon a non-contracting State. But I find it necessary to take account of the fact, to which the Court does not give specific weight, that the Geneva Convention belongs to a particular category of multilateral conventions, namely those which result from the work of the United Nations in the field of codification and progressive development of international law, under Art. 13 of the Charter. ...

According to classic doctrine ... [the] practice [necessary to establish a rule of customary international law] must have been pursued over a certain length of time. There have even been those who have maintained the necessity of ''immemorial usage.'' In its previous jurisprudence, however, the Court does not seem to have laid down strict requirements as to the duration of the usage or practice which may be accepted as law. In particular, it does not seem to have drawn any conclusion in this respect from the ordinary meaning of the word ''custom'' when used in other contexts. ... The possibility has thus been reserved for recognizing the rapid emergence of a new rule of customary law based on the recent practice of States. This is particularly important in view of the extremely dynamic process of evolution in which the international community is engaged at the present stage of history. Whether the mainspring of this evolution is to be found in the development of ideas, in social and economic factors, or in new technology, it is characteristic of our time that new problems and circumstances incessantly arise and imperatively call for legal regulation. In situations of this nature, a convention adopted as part of the combined process of codification and progressive development of international law may well constitute, or come to constitute, the decisive evidence of generally accepted new rules of international law. The fact that it does not purport simply to be declaratory of existing customary law is immaterial in this context. The convention may serve as an authoritative guide for the practice of States faced with the relevant new legal problems and its provisions thus become the nucleus around which a new set of generally recognized legal rules may crystallize. The word "custom," with its traditional time connotation, may not even be an adequate expression for the purpose of describing this particular source of law.

... The adoption of the Geneva Convention on the Continental Shelf was a very significant element in the process of creating new rules of international law in a field which urgently required legal regulation. The Convention has been ratified or acceded to by a quite considerable number of States and there is no reason to believe that the flow of ratifications has ceased. It is significant that the States which have become parties to the Convention are fairly representative of all geographical regions of the world and of different economic and social systems. Not only the contracting parties, but also other States, have adapted their action and attitudes so as to conform to the Convention. No State which has exercised sovereign rights over its continental shelf in conformity with the provisions of the Convention has been met with protests by other States. ...

I do not find it necessary to go into the question of the *opinio juris*. This is a problem of legal doctrine which may cause great difficulties in international adjudication. In view of the manner in which international relations are conducted, there may be numerous cases in which it is practically impossible for one government to produce conclusive evidence of the motives which have prompted the action and policy of other governments. Without going into all aspects of the doctrinal debate on this issue, I wish only to cite the following passage by one of the most qualified commentators on the jurisprudence of the Court. Examining the conditions of the *opinio necessitatis juris* Sir Hersch Lauterpacht writes:

Unless judicial activity is to result in reducing the legal significance of the most potent source of rules of international law, namely, the conduct of States, it would appear that the accurate principle on the subject consists in regarding all uniform conduct of Governments (or in appropriate cases, abstention therefrom) as evidencing the *opinio necessitatis juris* except when it is shown that the conduct in question was not accompanied by any such intention. (Sir Hersch Lauterpacht: *The Development of International Law by the International Court* (London 1958), at 380.)

Applying these considerations to the circumstances of the present cases, I think that the practice of States referred to above may be taken as sufficient evidence of the existence of any necessary *opinio juris*.

In my opinion, the conclusion may therefore safely be drawn that as a result of a continuous process over a quarter of a century, the rules embodied in the Geneva Convention on the Continental Shelf have now attained the status of generally accepted rules of international law.

That being so, it is nevertheless necessary to examine in particular the attitude of the Federal Republic of Germany with regard to the Convention. In the *Fisheries* case, the Court said that the ten-mile rule would in any event "appear to be inapplicable as against Norway inasmuch as she has always opposed any attempt to apply it to the Norwegian coast" (I.C.J.R. 1951, at 131). Similarly, it might be argued in the present cases that the Convention on the Continental Shelf would be inapplicable as against the Federal Republic, if she had consistently refused to recognize it as an expression of generally accepted rules of international law and had objected to its applicability as against her. But far from adopting such an attitude, the Federal Republic has gone quite a long way towards recognizing the Convention. It is part of the whole picture, though not decisive in itself, that the Federal Republic signed the Convention in 1958, immediately before the time-limit for signature under Art. 8. More significant is the fact that the Federal Republic has relied on the Convention for the purpose of asserting her own rights in the continental shelf. ... This attitude is relevant, not so much in the context of the traditional legal concepts of recognition, acquiescence or estoppel, as in the context of the general process of creating international legal rules of universal applicability. At a decisive stage of this formative process, an interested State, which was not a party to the Convention, formally recorded its view that the Convention was an expression of generally applicable international law. This view being perfectly well founded, that State is not now in a position to escape the authority of the Convention.

It has been asserted that the possibility, made available by Art. 12, of entering reservations to certain articles of the Convention, makes it difficult to understand the articles in question as embodying generally accepted rules of international law. ... [I]n my view, the faculty of making reservations to a treaty provision has no necessary connection with the question whether or not the provision can be considered as expressing a generally recognized rule of law. To substantiate this opinion it may be sufficient to point out that a number of reservations have been made to provisions of the Convention on the High Seas, although this Convention, according to its preamble, is "generally declaratory of established principles of international law." Some of these reservations have been objected to by other contracting States, while other reservations have been tacitly accepted. The acceptance, whether tacit or express, of a reservation made by a contracting party does not have the effect of depriving the Convention as a whole, or the relevant article in particular, of its declaratory character. It only has the effect of establishing a special contractual relationship between the parties concerned within the general framework of the customary law embodied in the Convention. Provided the customary rule does not belong to the category of *jus cogens*, a special contractual relationship of this nature is not invalid as such. Consequently, there is no incompatibility between the faculty of making reservations to certain articles of the Convention on the Continental Shelf and the recognition of that Convention or the particular articles as an expression of generally accepted rules of international law.

NOTES

Use these opinions to answer the following questions:[77]

1) What constitutes state practice? For instance, do the judgments of municipal courts constitute state practice?[78]

---

[77] For a critique of this decision, see W. Friedmann, "The North Sea Continental Shelf Cases – A Critique" (1970), 64 *Am. J. Int. L.* 229.

[78] See also International Law Commission, [1950] *Y.B.I.L.C.* II, at 368-72 and *Anglo-Norwegian Fisheries Case* (U.K. v. Norway), [1951] I.C.J. Rep. 116, at 191, reported *infra* in Chapter 11.

2) How much state practice is required? Is a single act sufficient to constitute general practice or must there be several acts over a certain period of time? How many states are needed? For instance, would Chad, a land-locked state, have to concur with the practice of the states having a continental shelf?

3) How much consistency in state practice is required? In the recent case of *Military Activities In and Against Nicaragua*, the International Court observed:[79]

It is not to be expected that in the practice of States the application of the rules in question should have been perfect, in the sense that States should have refrained, with complete consistency, from the use of force or from intervention in each other's internal affairs. The Court does not consider that, for a rule to be established as customary, the corresponding practice must be in absolutely rigorous conformity with the rule. In order to deduce the existence of customary rules, the Court deems it sufficient that the conduct of States should, in general, be consistent with such rules, and that instances of State conduct inconsistent with a given rule, should generally have been treated as breaches of that rule, not as indications of the recognition of a new rule. If a State acts in a way prima facie incompatible with a recognized rule, but defends its conduct by appealing to exceptions or justifications contained within the rule itself, then whether or not the State's conduct is in fact justifiable on that basis, the significance of that attitude is to confirm rather than to weaken the rule.

4) Are dissenting and non-participating states bound by custom? This is a very important question with respect to new states.[80] Does the absence of protest mean acquiescence?[81]

5) How do states change a custom? Can the dissent of one state bring down a custom or is that state still bound by it?

6) How do you prove *opinio juris*? Can it be presumed from consistent practice in regard to matters normally treated as involving rights and obligations or is it necessary that the practice be accompanied by assertions of legal duty or right?

7) Can treaties which contain provisions that are declaratory of customary law be invoked as evidence of such law? Should it make a difference that reservations are allowed to a particular treaty rule? Note that in the *Continental Shelf (Libya v. Malta) Case* the International Court stated:[82]

It is of course axiomatic that the material of customary international law is to be looked for primarily in the actual practice and *opinio juris* of States, even though multilateral conventions may have an important role to play in recording and defining rules deriving from custom, or indeed in developing them.

---

[79] Nicaragua v. United States, [1986] I.C.J. Rep. 14, at 98.

[80] See H. Bokor-Szego, *New States and International Law* (1970).

[81] See also *Fisheries Jurisdiction Case (Merits)* (U.K. v. Iceland), [1974] I.C.J. Rep. 3 (Read separate opinion of Judge Dillard, at 58); *Anglo-Norwegian Fisheries Case* (U.K. v. Norway) [1951] I.C.J. Rep. 116, reported *infra* in Chapter 11; *South West Africa Case (Second Phase)* [1966] I.C.J. Rep. 6 (Read Tanaka, J. dissenting, at 291).

[82] [1985] I.C.J. Rep. 13, at 29-30.

Thus, where two states agree to incorporate a particular rule derived from custom in a treaty, their agreement suffices to make that rule binding upon them. But in the field of customary international law, the shared view of the parties as to the content of what they regard as the rule is not enough. The Court must satisfy itself that the existence of the rule is confirmed by state practice.[83]

8) Note how the formation of customary rules is concerned with unilateral acts of states, rather than their multilateral agreement as in law-making treaties. What is the significance of this difference? Consider the commentary by Beesley in the introduction to this section.

Regional or Special Customary Law

Asylum Case
Columbia v. Peru
[1950] I.C.J. Rep 266, at 276-78

[In this case, the Columbian government in claiming that it had the right to give asylum to the Peruvian Haya de la Torre, who had sought refuge in the Columbian Embassy in Peru, relied not only on the rules arising from agreements, but on an alleged regional or local custom peculiar to Latin-American States.]

THE COURT: ... The Party which relies on a custom of this kind must prove that this custom is established in such a manner that it has become binding on the other Party. The Columbian Government must prove that the rule invoked by it is in accordance with a constant and uniform usage practised by the States in question, and that this usage is the expression of a right appertaining to the State granting asylum and a duty incumbent on the territorial State. This follows from Art. 38 of the Statute of the Court, which refers to international custom 'as evidence of a general practice accepted as law.'

In support of its contention concerning the existence of such a custom, the Columbian Government has referred to a large number of extradition treaties which, as already explained, can have no bearing on the question now under consideration. It has cited conventions and agreements which do not contain any provision concerning the alleged rule of unilateral and definitive qualification such as the Montevideo Convention of 1889 on international penal law, the Bolivian Agreement of 1911 and the Havana Convention of 1928. It has invoked conventions which have not been ratified by Peru, such as the Montevideo Conventions of 1933 and 1939. The Convention of 1933 has, in fact, been ratified by not more than eleven States and the Convention of 1939 by two States only. ...

It is particularly the Montevideo Convention of 1933 which Counsel for the Colombian Government has also relied on in this connexion. It is contended that this Convention has merely codified principles which were already recognized by Latin-American custom and that it is valid against Peru as a proof of customary law. The limited number of

---

[83] See *Military Activities In and Against Nicaragua*, [1986] I.C.J. Rep. 14, at 97-98.

States which have ratified this Convention reveals the weakness of this argument and furthermore, it is invalidated by the preamble which states that this Convention modifies the Havana Convention.

Finally, the Colombian Government has referred to a large number of particular cases in which diplomatic asylum was in fact granted and respected. But it has not shown that the alleged rule of unilateral and definitive qualification was invoked or if in some cases it was in fact invoked – that it was, apart from conventional stipulations, exercised by the States granting asylum as a right appertaining to them and respected by the territorial States as a duty incumbent on them and not merely for reasons of political expediency. The facts brought to the knowledge of the Court disclose so much uncertainty and contradiction, so much fluctuation and discrepancy in the exercise of diplomatic asylum and in the official views expressed on various occasions, there has been so much inconsistency in the rapid succession of conventions on asylum, ratified by some States and rejected by others and the practice has been so much influenced by considerations of political expediency in the various cases, that it is not possible to discern in all this any constant and uniform usage, accepted as law, with regard to the alleged rule of unilateral and definitive qualification of the offence.

The Court cannot therefore find that the Columbian Government has proved the existence of such custom. But even if it could be supposed that such a custom existed between certain Latin-American States only, it could not be invoked against Peru which, far from having by its attitude adhered to it, has on the contrary, repudiated it by refraining from ratifying the Montevideo Convention of 1933 and 1939, which were the first to include a rule concerning the qualification of the offence in matters of diplomatic asylum.

NOTES

1) Regional or local customs which supplement or derogate from general customary international law are essentially tacit international agreements which must not violate existing rules of *jus cogens*.

2) Socialist international law is asserted as a special or particular custom applicable to socialist states in their relations *inter se*.[84]

3) Does a special or particular custom require a higher degree of proof than a general custom?[85]

GENERAL PRINCIPLES OF LAW

There is no agreement upon the meaning of ''the general principles of law recognized by civilized nations'' found in Article 38(1)(c) of the Statute of the International Court.

---

[84] See G. Tunkin, *Theory of International Law* (1974), at 444; also M. Akehurst, ''Custom as a Source of International Law'' (1974-75), 47 *Br. Y.B.I.L.* 1.

[85] See *Right of Passage over Indian Territory Case* (Portugal v. India), [1960] I.C.J. Rep. 6; and *Rights of U.S. Nationals in Morocco Case* (U.S. v. France), [1952] I.C.J. Rep. 176.

In the West, these general principles are those which exist in all municipal systems of law that have reached a comparable stage of development. They are primarily principles of private law or procedure. On the other hand, socialist states are of the opinion that general principles of law can mean only general principles of *international* law. In other words, general principles of municipal law are part of international law to the extent that they have been adopted by states as a custom or in a treaty. Therefore, where a principle originally borrowed from municipal law has acquired the status of a custom, there is no need to resort to paragraph (c) of Article 38(1).[86] But what about general principles that are not already part of international customary or conventional law? (For Judge Tanaka certain general principles of law are a primary source of international law because they have the character of *jus rationale* and are "valid through all kinds of human societies."[87])

On several occasions the International Court of Justice has applied principles of municipal law which are generally recognized. These principles constitute a reservoir of law which the court is authorized to apply. For instance, in the *Chorzow Factory Case*[88] the Permanent Court said: "it is ... a general conception of law that any breach of an engagement involves an obligation to make reparation" and in the *Temple of Preah Vihear Case*,[89] the International Court stated: "It is an established rule of law that the plea of error cannot be allowed as an element vitiating consent if the party advancing it contributed by its own conduct to the error." See also the *Effect of Awards of U.N. Administrative Tribunal Case*[90] where the Court said: According to a well-established and generally recognized principle of law, a judgment rendered by a judicial body is *res judicata* and has binding force between the parties to the dispute." As to whether the doctrine of estoppel is a general principle of law, see *Gulf of Maine Case*,[91] where the Chamber observed " ... that in any case the concepts of acquiescence and estoppel, irrespective of the status accorded to them by international law, both follow from the fundamental principles of good faith and equity," and therefore took both concepts into its consideration.

The process by which general principles of law are found and applied by the International Court is demonstrated in the following case.

International Status of South West Africa Case
Adv. Op. (1950) I.C.J. Rep. 128

[In 1949, the U.N. General Assembly asked the International Court to advise on the international status of South West Africa (now Namibia). This request caused the Court to interpret the terms of the Mandate of that territory to South Africa. In the course of his separate opinion, Sir Arnold McNair drew upon general principles of law in order to

---

[86] See C. Tunkin, *Das Volkerrect der Gegenwart* (Wolf trans. 1963), at 125-27.
[87] Dissenting opinion, *South West Africa case (Second Phase)*, [1966] I.C.J. Rep. 6, at 296.
[88] (1928), P.C.I.J. Ser. A, No. 17, at 29.
[89] [1962] I.C.J. Rep. 6, at 26.
[90] [1954] I.C.J. Rep. 47, at 53.
[91] Canada v. U.S. [1984] I.C.J. Rep. 246, para. 129-148.

determine the meaning of the "sacred trust of civilization" accepted by South Africa under the Mandate.]

JUDGE McNAIR: ... What is the duty of an international tribunal when confronted with a new legal institution the object and terminology of which are reminiscent of the rules and institutions of private law? To what extent is it useful or necessary to examine what may at first sight appear to be relevant analogies in private law systems and draw help and inspiration from them? International law has recruited and continues to recruit many of its rules and institutions from private systems of law. Article 38(I)(c) of the Statute of the Court bears witness that this process is still active, and it will be noted that this article authorizes the Court to "apply ... (c) the general principles of law recognized by civilized nations." The way in which international law borrows from this source is not by means of importing private law institutions "lock, stock and barrel," ready-made and fully equipped with a set of rules. It would be difficult to reconcile such a process with the application of "the general principles of law." In my opinion, the true view of the duty of international tribunals in this matter is to regard any features or terminology which are reminiscent of the rules and institutions of private law as an indication of policy and principles rather than as directly importing these rules and institutions. ...

Let us then seek to discover the underlying policy and principles of Article 22 and of the Mandate. No technical significance can be attached to the words "sacred trust of civilization," but they are an apt description of the policy of the authors of the Mandates System, and the words "sacred trust" were not used here for the first time in relation to dependent peoples (see Duncan Hall, *Mandates, Dependencies and Trusteeships*, at 97-100). Any English lawyer who was instructed to prepare the legal instruments required to give effect to the policy of Article 22 would inevitably be reminded of, and influenced by, the trust of English and American law, though he would soon realize the need of much adaptation for the purposes of the new international institution. Professor Brierly's opinion, stated in the *British Year Book of International Law*, 1929, at 217-19, that the governing principle of the Mandates System is to be found in the trust, and his quotation from an article by M. Lepaulle, are here very much in point, and it is worth noting that the historical basis of the legal enforcement of the English trust is that it was something which was binding upon the conscience of the trustee; that is why it was legally enforced. It also seems probable that the conception of the Mandates System owes something to the French *tutelle*.

Nearly every legal system possesses some institution whereby the property (and sometimes the persons) of those who are not *sui juris*, such as a minor or a lunatic, can be entrusted to some responsible person as a trustee or *tuteur* or *curateur*. The Anglo-American trust serves this purpose, and another purpose even more closely akin to the Mandates System, namely, the vesting of property in trustees, and its management by them in order that the public or some class of the public may derive benefit or that some public purpose may be served. The trust has frequently been used to protect the weak and the dependent, in cases where there is "great might on the one side and unmight on the other," and the English courts have for many centuries pursued a vigorous policy in the administration and enforcement of trusts.

There are three general principles which are common to all these institutions:

(a) that the control of the trustee, *tuteur* or *curateur* over the property is limited in one way or another; he is not in the position of the normal complete owner, who can do what he likes with his own, because he is precluded from administering the property for his own personal benefit;

(b) that the trustee, *tuteur* or *curateur* is under some kind of legal obligation, based on confidence and conscience, to carry out the trust or mission confided to him for the benefit of some other person or for some public purpose;

(c) that any attempt by one of these persons to absorb the property entrusted to him into his own patrimony would be illegal and would be prevented by the law.

These are some of the general principles of private law which throw light upon this new institution, and I am convinced that in its future development the law governing the trust is a source from which much can be derived.

Equity

The expression "equity" has at least three different legal senses. Equity may be used to adapt the law to the facts of individual cases (equity *intra legem*); it may be used to fill gaps in the law (equity *praeter legem*); and it may be used as a reason for refusing to apply unjust laws (equity *contra legem*). International tribunals can apply equity *intra legem*. It is more doubtful whether they can apply equity *praeter legem* although, on occasion, they have claimed such power. They cannot apply equity *contra legem* in the absence of an express authorization.[92]

In the *Norwegian Shipowners Claims*[93] the tribunal expressed the view that "law and equity" are to be understood to mean "general principles of justice as distinguished from any particular system of jurisprudence or the municipal law of any State." Be careful to distinguish equity in this international sense from the technical use of the same term in common law jurisdictions. Note too that the World Court's power under its Statute Article 38(2), in the Appendix, to decide a case "ex aequo et bono" is not to be equated to equity in this legal sense either. The following case explains the difference.

Diverson of Water from the Meuse Case
Netherlands v. Belgium
(1937), P.C.I.J., Ser. A/B, No. 70, at 76-77

Separate opinion of JUDGE HUDSON: ...

What are widely known as principles of equity have long been considered to constitute a part of international law, and as such they have often been applied by international tribunals. ... A sharp division between law and equity, such as prevails in the administration of justice in some States, should find no place in international jurisprudence;

---

[92] See M. Akehurst, "Equity and General Principles of Law" (1976), 25 *Int. & Comp. L.Q.* 801.

[93] (1922), 17 *Am. J. Int. L.* 362, at 384. See also the *Cayuga Indians Claim* (1926), Nielsen Rep. 203, at 307 *et seq.*

even in some national legal systems, there has been a strong tendency towards the fusion of law and equity. Some international tribunals are expressly directed by the *compromis* which control them to apply "law and equity." See the *Cayuga Indians Case*, Nielsen's Report of the United States – British Claims Arbitration (1926), at 307. Of such a provision, a special tribunal of the Permanent Court of Arbitration said in 1922 that "the majority of international lawyers seem to agree that these words are to be understood to mean general principles of justice as distinguished from any particular systems of jurisprudence." Proceedings of the United States – Norwegian Tribunal (1922), at 141. Numerous arbitration treaties have been concluded in recent years which apply to differences "which are justiciable in their nature by reason of being susceptible of decision by the application of the principles of law or equity." Whether the reference in an arbitration treaty is to the application of "law and equity," or to justiciability dependent on the possibility of applying "law or equity," it would seem to envisage equity as a part of law.

The Court has not been expressly authorised by its Statute to apply equity as distinguished from law. ... Article 38 of the Statute expressly directs the application of "general principles of law recognised by civilised nations," and in more than one nation principles of equity have an established place in the legal system. The Court's recognition of equity as a part of international law is in no way restricted by the special power conferred upon it "to decide a case *ex aequo et bono*, if the parties agree thereto." ... It must be concluded, therefore, that under Article 38 of the Statute, if not independently of that Article, the Court has some freedom to consider principles of equity as part of the international law which it must apply.

It would seem to be an important principle of equity that where two parties have assumed an identical or a reciprocal obligation, one party which is engaged in a continuing non-performance of that obligation should not be permitted to take advantage of a similar non-performance of that obligation by the other party. The principle finds expression in the so-called maxims of equity which exercised great influence in the creative period of the development of the Anglo-American law. Some of these maxims are, "Equality is equity"; "He who seeks equity must do equity." It is in line with such maxims that "a court of equity refuses relief to a plaintiff whose conduct in regard to the subject-matter of the litigation has been improper." ... A very similar principle was received into Roman Law. ... This conception was the basis of Articles 320 and 322 of the German Civil Code, and even where a code is silent on the point Planiol states the general principle that "*dans tout rapport synallagmatique, chacune des deux parties ne peut exiger la prestation qui lui est due que si elle offre elle-même d'exécuter son obligation.*" ...

North Sea Continental Shelf Cases
Federal Republic of Germany v. Denmark and v. Netherlands
[1969] I.C.J. Rep. 3, reported *supra*.

Read particularly paragraphs 88, 89, 91 and 98.

NOTES

1) In the award made in the *English Channel Arbitration* in 1977, the tribunal applied principles of equity as part of the relevant international law.[94] In the *Continental Shelf (Tunisia v. Libya) Case*[95] the International Court also applied principles of equity to reach an equitable solution. The majority of the Court stated:

71. Equity as a legal concept is a direct emanation of the idea of justice. The Court whose task is by definition to administer justice is bound to apply it. In the course of the history of legal systems the term "equity" has been used to define various legal concepts. It was often contrasted with the rigid rules of positive law, the severity of which had to be mitigated in order to do justice. In general, this contrast has no parallel in the development of international law; the legal concept of equity is a general principle directly applicable as law. Moreover, when applying positive international law, a court may choose among several possible interpretations of the law the one which appears, in the light of the circumstances of the case, to be closest to the requirements of justice. Application of equitable principles is to be distinguished from a decision *ex aequo et bono*. The Court can take such a decision only on condition that the Parties agree (Art. 38, para. 2, of the Statute), and the Court is then freed from the strict application of legal rules in order to bring about an appropriate settlement. The task of the Court in the present case is quite different: it is bound to apply equitable principles as part of international law, and to balance up the various considerations which it regards as relevant in order to produce an equitable result. While it is clear that no rigid rules exist as to the exact weight to be attached to each element in the case, this is very far from being an exercise of discretion or conciliation; nor is it an operation of distributive justice.

Compare the dissenting opinion of Judge Gros:

19. Much more is here involved than a difference of opinion as to how equity should be conceived: what is at issue is the decision dividing a continental shelf between two States which requested that it be delivered in accordance with the law. If a State claiming a right to an area of continental shelf really possesses that right such as it describes it, it is not equity to deprive it of it but an error of law, and therein lies a far-reaching complaint since the judgments of the Court are irreversible as between the Parties. Equity is not a sort of independent and subjective vision that takes the place of law. The Judgment states that there can be no question in the instant case of applying *ex aequo et bono*. Statements are one thing, the effective pronouncements of the Judgment are another. For the foregoing reasons, and those I give below, it is not equity which has struck me as presiding over the construction of the Judgment.

2) See also the arbitral award concerning the *Gulf of Maine Case*.[96] The Chamber of

---

[94] (1979), 18 *Int. Leg. Mat.* 397, at paras. 70, 103, 195-99, reproduced *infra* in Chapter 11. And see M. Blecher, "Equitable Delimitation of the Continental Shelf" (1979), 73 *Am. J. Int. L.* 60.

[95] [1982] I.C.J. Rep. 18.

[96] Canada v. U.S., [1984] I.C.J. Rep. 246, reported *infra* in Chapter 11.

the International Court of Justice was of the opinion that customary international law cannot be expected to specify the equitable criteria to be applied (see paras. 79, 81, 111-112, 157-158). Having drawn the delimitation line requested by the parties, the Chamber then verified whether the result obtained could be considered as intrinsically equitable in the light of all circumstances (para. 230-241).

4) Equity in the sense of humanitarian considerations and principles of morality also has a role to play in the creation of rules of international law.[97]

OTHER SOURCES OF LAW?

Subsidiary Means for the Determination of Rules of Law

Refer to the Statute of the International Court of Justice Article 38(1)(d) and the distinction between law-creating and law-determining means at the very beginning of this chapter.

Judicial Decisions

Although Art. 59 of the Statute of the International Court of Justice provides that "The decision of the Court has no binding force except between the parties and in respect of that particular case," the Court uses legal precedents for guidance as to the law.[98]

Legal Commentaries

Many years before the Statute of the World Court referred inelegantly to the "teachings of the most highly qualified publicists"[99] as a means of determining international law, the status of legal commentaries was fully explained in *R. v. Keyn* by Cockburn C.J. when he said:[100]

For writers on international law, however valuable their labours may be in elucidating and ascertaining the principles and rules of law, cannot make the law. To be binding, the law must have received the assent of the nations who are to be bound by it. This assent may be express, as by treaty or the acknowledged concurrence of governments, or may be implied from established usage, – an instance of which is to be found in the fact that merchant vessels on the high seas are held to be subject only to the law of the nation under whose flag they sail, while in the ports of a foreign state they are subject to the local law as well as to that of their own

---

[97] See I. Lukashuk, "Morality and International Law" (1974), 14 *Indian J. Int. L.* 321; and *Corfu Channel Case (U.K. v. Albania)*, [1949] I.C.J. Rep. 4, at 22.

[98] See, for instance, *Rights of U.S. Nationals in Morocco Case* [1952] I.C.J. Rep. 176, at 200; *Effect of Awards of U.N. Administrative Tribunal* (Adv. Op.), [1954] I.C.J. Rep. 47, at 53, 56; and H. Lauterpacht, *The Development of International Law by the International Court* (1958).

[99] An historical survey of the role and influence of teachings in the development of international law is provided by M. Lachs, a former President of the Court, in *The Teacher in International Law, Teachings and Teaching* (1982).

[100] (1876), 2 Exch. 63, at 202-3.

country. In the absence of proof of assent, as derived from one or other of these sources, no unanimity on the part of theoretical writers would warrant the judicial application of the law on the sole authority of their views or statements. ... It is said that we are to take the statements of the publicists as conclusive proof of the assent in question and much has been said to impress on us the respect which is due to their authority and that they are to be looked upon as witnesses of the facts to which they speak, witnesses whose statements, or the foundation on which those statements rest, we are scarcely at liberty to question. I demur altogether to this position. I entertain a profound respect for the opinion of jurists when dealing with the matters of juridical principle and opinion, but we are here dealing with a question not of opinion but of fact and I must assert my entire liberty to examine the evidence and see upon what foundation these statements are based. The question is not one of theoretical opinion, but of fact, and fortunately, the writers upon whose statements we are called upon to act have afforded us the means of testing those statements by reference to facts. They refer us to two things, and to these alone – treaties and usage.

Law-Making Through International Organizations

Codification and Progressive Development

Codification is one of the methods used for clarifying and developing international law although it is more likely to succeed when law and practice are already reasonably clear, extensive and accepted. The attempts at codification are the result of efforts by private organizations such as the Institut de Droit International and the International Law Association or by international organizations such as the United Nations and its subsidiary organs.

In 1967, the General Assembly of the United Nations, pursuant to the Charter Article 13(1), established the International Law Commission. Composed of thirty-four members elected by the General Assembly for at least a five-year term, who sit as individuals and not as representatives of their governments, it has for objects the promotion of the progressive development of international law and its codification. Article 15 of the Statute of the International Law Commission makes a distinction for convenience between progressive development, meaning ''the preparation of draft conventions on subjects which have not yet been regulated by international law or in regard to which the law has not yet been sufficiently developed in the practice of States,'' and codification, meaning ''the more precise formulation and systematization of rules of international law in fields where there already has been extensive State practice, precedent and doctrine.'' According to the United Nations' own commentary:[101]

The drafters of the Statute conceived progressive development as a conscious effort towards the creation of new rules of international law, whether by means of the regulation of a new topic or by means of the comprehensive revision of existing rules. Accordingly, they considered that

---

[101] U.N. Office of Public Information, *The Work of the International Law Commission* (1967) at 6, 9, and 12.

when the Commission is engaged in the progressive development of any branch of law, the consummation of the work could be achieved only by means of an international convention. Thus the Statute contemplates that the Commission prepares a draft convention, and the General Assembly then decides whether steps should be taken to bring about the conclusion of an international convention.

On the other hand, when the Commission's task is one of codification (namely, the more precise formulation and systematization of existing customary law), the Statute envisages two other possible conclusions to its work: (a) simple publication of its report; and (b) a resolution of the General Assembly, taking note of or adopting the report (article 23, paragraph 1). The Statute also lays down the specific steps to be taken by the Commission in the course of its work on progressive development (articles 16 and 17) and on codification (articles 18 to 23).

The Commission follows essentially the same method for both types of work. A Special Rapporteur is appointed for each topic; an appropriate plan of work is formulated; where desirable, Governments are requested to furnish the texts of relevant laws, decrees, judicial decisions, treaties and diplomatic correspondence; the Special Rapporteur submits a report, on the basis of which a provisional draft is approved by the Commission, normally in the form of articles, with a commentary setting forth precedents, any divergencies of views expressed in the Commission, and alternative solutions considered. ... Governments under current procedure are normally given more than one year in which to study these provisional drafts and present their written observations. The Special Rapporteur studies the replies received, together with any comments made in the debates of the Sixth Committee, and submits a further report, recommending the changes in the provisional draft that seem appropriate. The Commission then, on the basis of that report and the comments, adopts a final draft, which it submits to the General Assembly with a recommendation regarding further action. ...

In practice, codification and progressive development of the law become intermingled. In his dissenting opinion in the *North Sea Continental Shelf Cases*, Judge *ad hoc* Sorenson[102] had this to say:

It has come to be generally recognised, however, that this distinction between codification and progressive development may be difficult to apply rigorously to the facts of international legal relations. Although theoretically clear and distinguishable, the two notions tend in practice to overlap or to leave between them an intermediate area in which it is not possible to indicate precisely where codification ends and progressive development begins. The very act of formulating or restating an existing customary rule may have the effect of defining its contents more precisely and removing such doubts as may have existed as to its exact scope or the modalities of its application. The opportunity may also be taken of adapting the rule to contemporary conditions, whether factual or legal, in the international community. On the other hand, a treaty purporting to create new law may be based on a certain amount of State practice and doctrinal opinion which has not yet crystallised into customary law.

The reports, documents and summary records of discussions of the Commission are

---

[102] [1969] I.C.J. Rep. 4, at 242-43.

published by the United Nations in *Yearbooks of the International Law Commission*. The Commission has been responsible for the preparation of a number of multilateral conventions which are now in force. Two examples included in this book are the 1961 "Vienna Convention on Diplomatic Relations" reported in Chapter 5 and the 1969 "Vienna Convention on the Law of Treaties" reported in this chapter throughout the section on "Treaties."

Resolutions of the United Nations

The legal effects of General Assembly resolutions have proved a fertile subject of continuing discussion.[103] Under the Charter, the General Assembly has clear authority to make binding decisions only with respect to budgetary and administrative matters of the United Nations. (See Article 17 in the Appendix.) For all its other work, the General Assembly is empowered to make "recommendations" (Articles 10-16), which are not considered binding *per se* but can have value as means for the determination of international law.

In the *South West Africa, Voting Procedure Case*, Judge Lauterpacht observed:[104]

A Resolution recommending to an Administering State a specific course of action creates some legal obligation which, however rudimentary, elastic and imperfect, is nevertheless a legal obligation and constitutes a measure of supervision. The State in question, while not bound to accept the recommendation, is bound to give it due consideration in good faith.

In truth, General Assembly resolutions are so varied in purposes, contents and support that their legal value is very individual, depending upon the circumstances under which they are adopted and the principles which they state. The *Western Sahara Case*, reported in Chapter 2, is an example where the International Court made extensive use of General Assembly resolutions in the course of establishing and applying the principle of self-determination of peoples.

Security Council resolutions are more straight-forward in light of the mandatory language of the Charter Article 25, which has been authoritatively interpreted by the Court in the *Namibia Case*.[105]

---

[103] See O.Y. Asamoah, *The Legal Significance of the Declarations of the General Assembly of the United Nations* (1966); H. Boker-Szego, *The Role of the United Nations in International Legislation* (1978); B. Cheng, "United Nations Resolutions on Outer Space: 'Instant' International Customary Law?" (1965), 5 *Ind. J. Int. L.* 23; D. Johnson, "The Effect of Resolutions of the General Assembly of the United Nations" (1955-56), 32 *Br. Y.B. Int. L.* 97; M. Mendelson, "The Legal Character of General Assembly Resolutions: Some Considerations of Principle," in K. Hossain, *Legal Aspects of the New International Economic Order* (1980), at 95; S.M. Schwebel, "The Effect of Resolutions of the U.N. General Assembly on Customary International Law" (1979), 3 *Proc. Am. Soc. Int. L.* 301; and F. Sloan, "The Binding Force of a 'Recommendation' of the General Assembly of the United Nations" (1948), 25 *Br. Y. B. Int. L.* 1.

[104] [1955] I.C.J. Rep. 67, at 118-19.

[105] R. Higgins, "The Advisory Opinion on Namibia: Which U.N. Resolutions Are Binding under Article 25 of the Charter?" (1972), 21 *Int. Comp. L. Q.* 270.

Namibia Case

(1971) I.C.J. Rep. 16, reported *supra* in Chapter 2

Read paras. 111-116.

Texaco v. Libya

(1978), 17 *Int. Leg. Mat.* 1, reported *infra* in Chapter 9

Read paragraphs 80-91 concerning the status of U.N. resolutions on permanent sovereignty over natural resources.

NOTES

1) In *Libyan American Oil Company v. Libya*[106] the arbitrator commented about the same resolutions that "the said Resolutions, if not a unanimous source of law, are evidence of the recent dominant trend of international opinion concerning the sovereign right of states over their natural resources." What is the legal significance of a "dominant trend of international opinion"?

2) In a memorandum dated August 28, 1974, the Legal Bureau of the Department of External Affairs stated the Canadian position with respect to declarations and resolutions of the U.N. General Assembly:[107]

Declarations and resolutions of the General Assembly, while they may contribute to the evolution of norms of international law, do not create legal rights or obligations for any state. A vote for a resolution, or acquiescence in its adoption without a vote (which need not be, and in the case of the 6th UNGA Special Session was not in fact, the same as adoption by "consensus," which implies the full support of virtually all participants), simply expresses a government's policy and intentions on the subject matter. Statements made in explanation of vote serve to clarify this expression of policy. This is particularly true of statements of interpretation and of reservations. If the government in question wishes to change its policy and announce this fact, it will do so in an appropriate way. Until it has done so the earlier statement of policy, including any inter-pretations and reservations, remains valid.

Some developed countries have proposed that, wherever one resolution is referred to in a later resolution, the latter should refer to the former resolution "as adopted." The intention is that the words "as adopted" would incorporate by inference interpretations, reservations and objections expressed to the former resolution at the time it was adopted. The developing countries, because they consider such reservations, etc., of no significance, oppose the "as adopted" formulation. Canada takes the position that such reservations, etc. remain valid whether or not

---

[106] (1981), 20 *Int. Leg. Mat.* 1, at 53.
[107] Reprinted in (1975), 13 *Can. Y.B. Int. L.* 372.

the "as adopted" formula is used; and that they need not be repeated every time the resolution in question is referred to in a subsequent resolution.

3) From the evidence of these cases and comments, what matters should be taken into account in weighing the legal consequences of a particular U.N. resolution?

4) Although General Assembly resolutions rarely establish binding obligations, in what ways do they contribute to the creation and ascertainment of international law? Consider this question in the light of such other important resolutions as the Declaration on Principles of International Law, the Definition of Aggression, the Universal Declaration of Human Rights, and the Seabed Declaration.[108] The latest comment of the World Court on the use that may be made of General Assembly resolutions appears in *Military Activities In and Against Nicaragua*. It was said there:[109]

The Court has however to be satisfied that there exists in customary international law an *opinio juris* as to the binding character of such abstention [from the use of force]. This *opinio juris* may, though with all due caution, be deduced from, *inter alia*, the attitude of the Parties and the attitude of States towards certain General Assembly resolutions, and particularly resolution 2625 (XXV) entitled "Declaration on Principles of International Law concerning Friendly Relations and Co-operation among States in accordance with the Charter of the United Nations." The effect of consent to the text of such resolutions cannot be understood as merely that of a "reiteration or elucidation" of the treaty commitment undertaken in the Charter. On the contrary, it may be understood as an acceptance of the validity of the rule or set of rules declared by the resolution by themselves. The principle of non-use of force, for example, may thus be regarded as a principle of customary international law, ...

---

[108] Reported in chapters 2, 10 and 11, respectively.
[109] [1986] I.C.J. Rep. 14, at 99-100.

CHAPTER FOUR

Application of International Law

NATIONAL APPLICATION IN CANADA[1]

International law has internal as well as intergovernmental applications. The degree of its integration and execution within the national legal system depends on the nature of the relationship between domestic law and international law. The ultimate question to be answered is, to what extent may international legal principles be relied upon as imposing legally enforceable obligations, or conferring legally enforceable rights, on individuals which they may use in their domestic system? This question is, in some contexts, referred to as the "direct applicability" or "direct effect" of international law in the domestic legal system. Different states are more or less receptive to international law as a part of their domestic legal structure.

One's approach to this issue will be influenced by one's theoretical departure point, whether one is "adoptionist" or "transformationist" in outlook. Unfortunately there is little agreement in doctrine on these issues and the cases, which reflect different approaches in different jurisdictions (and are sometimes decided by judges unfamiliar with the international legal process), often do not articulate the theory which underlies the result arrived at by the bench. From a comparative law point of view the matter is further complicated by the diversity of approaches to this issue in different states which have different legal traditions. Ultimately it is the constitutional framework of a state which determines the degree to which international law is applied in any given circumstance. The importance of an understanding of this relationship in any given legal system cannot be overemphasized for it is the degree to which international law is a part of the domestic

---

[1] On international law as applied in domestic systems, generally see I. Brownlie, *Principles of Public International Law* (3 ed., 1979), c. 2; M. Cohen and A.F. Bayefsky, "The Canadian Charter of Rights and Freedoms and Public International Law" (1983), 61 *Can. Bar Rev.* 265; R. St.J. Macdonald, in Macdonald, Morris and Johnston (eds.), *Canadian Perspectives on International Law and Organization* (1974), at 88; M.S. McDougal in *Studies in World Public Order* (1960), at 157; C. Vanek, "Is International Law a Part of the Law of Canada?" (1949–50), 8 *U.T.L.J.* 251.

legal system which determines to what extent international legal principles will be relevant for individual citizens as well as for nation states and their governments.

In Canada certain trends may be observed. A good argument may be made from the cases that follow that Canada is adoptionist in respect of customary international law and transformationist in respect of conventional law, the latter clearly springing from following the British legal tradition that treaties must be enacted into law by Parliament before they will affect private rights.

This in turn gives rise to important constitutional law considerations in the Canadian context as it becomes important to determine which level of government has legislative competence in respect of Canada's international obligations. The federal government has exclusive international personality in the sense that only it may bind Canada to an international agreement. To what extent, however, may it enact legislation giving internal effect to such an agreement?[2] This issue is currently one of considerable practical significance as international undertakings become increasingly important as a source of domestic law (tax treaties, ILO Conventions, the law of the sea, international commercial arbitration, and so forth).

Another issue which often arises is the question of the consequence of a conflict between international law, either customary or conventional, and domestic law. In Canada this matter also has a constitutional dimension; a different approach may be taken depending on whether one is concerned with federal or provincial statutes.[3] There may be a question as to what extent the division of legislative powers contained in sections 91 & 92 of the Constitution Act is influenced by Canada's expanding international obligations, particularly in the commercial field.[4]

Finally there is the question of the role of the *Charter*.[5] To what extent is international law in general applicable both in interpreting the terms contained in the *Charter* and in ascertaining the scope of its provisions? In this respect internationally accepted human rights norms are of particular importance[6] and interpretations of similar language contained in other international human rights instruments, the Covenant on Civil and Political Rights[7] or the European Convention for the Protection of Rights[8] for example, may be of considerable value to a court in applying the *Charter*.

Recent developments lead one to conclude that this is an area of growing concern to lawyers in many areas of practice. An understanding of the relationship between international legal norms and the domestic legal system becomes increasingly important in an interdependent world characterized by complex transnational transactions.

---

[2] See the discussion on treaty-making by Canada *supra* in Chapter 3.

[3] See G.V. La Forest, ''May the Provinces Legislate in Violation of International Law?'' (1961), 39 *Can. Bar Rev.* 78.

[4] S.M. Beck and I. Bernier (eds.), *Canada and the New Constitution: The Unfinished Agenda* (1983).

[5] *Constitution Act, 1982*, Schedule B of the *Canada Act*, Stats. U.K. 1982, c. 11.

[6] See, e.g., *Singh et al. v. Minister of Employment and Immigration*, [1985] 1 S.C.R. 177; and *Re Service Employees' International Union, Local 204 and Broadway Manor Nursing Home* (1984), 44 O.R. (2d) 392 (Div. Ct.).

[7] (1966), 21 U.N. GAOR, Supp. (No. 16) 52, reported *infra* in Chapter 10.

[8] (1969), O.A.S. Treaty Series No. 36, reported *infra* in Chapter 10.

Customary Law

The way the courts approach international law affects the scope and force of its application internally in Canada. Following British ideas, Canadian courts in varying degrees have entertained two approaches, the doctrines of adoption and of transformation. Lord Denning has described, with characteristic pungency, the attributes and the significance of these two doctrines, (where he writes "incorporation" read "adoption" in Canadian parlance):[9]

One school of thought holds to the doctrine of incorporation. It says that the rules of international law are incorporated into English law automatically and considered to be part of English law unless they are in conflict with an Act of Parliament. The other school of thought holds to the doctrine of transformation. It says that the rules of international law are not to be considered as part of English law except in so far as they have been already adopted and made part of our law by the decisions of the judges, or by Act of Parliament, or long established custom. The difference is vital when you are faced with a change in the rules of international law. Under the doctrine of incorporation, when the rules of international law change, our English law changes with them. But, under the doctrine of transformation, the English law does not change. It is bound by precedent. It is bound down to those rules of international law which have been accepted and adopted in the past. It cannot develop as international law develops.

(i) The doctrine of incorporation. The doctrine of incorporation goes back to 1737 in *Buvot v. Barbut* (1736) 3 Burr. 1481; 4 Burr. 2016; sub nom. *Barbuit's Case in Chancery* (1737) Forr. 280, in which Lord Talbot L.C. (who was highly esteemed) made a declaration which was taken down by young William Murray (who was of counsel in the case) and adopted by him in 1764 when he was Lord Mansfield C.J. in *Triquet v. Bath* (1764) 3 Burr. 1478:

Lord Talbot declared a clear opinion – That the law of nations in its full extent was part of the law of England, ... That the law of nations was to be collected from the practice of different nations and the authority of writers. Accordingly, he argued and determined from such instances, and the authorities of Grotius, Barbeyrac, Binkershoek, Wiquefort, etc., there being no English writer of eminence on the subject.

That doctrine was accepted, not only by Lord Mansfield himself, but also by Sir William Blackstone, and other great names, too numerous to mention. In 1853 Lord Lyndhurst in the House of Lords, with the concurrence of all his colleagues there, declared that ... "the law of nations, according to the decision of our greatest judges, is part of the law of England": see Sir George Cornewall Lewis' book, Lewis on Foreign Jurisdiction (1859), at 66–67.

(ii) The doctrine of transformation. The doctrine of transformation only goes back to 1876 in the judgment of Cockburn C.J. in *Reg. v. Keyn* (1876) 2 Ex. D. 63, at 202–3:

For writers on international law, however valuable their labours may be in elucidating and ascertaining the principles and rules of law, cannot make the law. To be binding, the law must have received the assent of the nations who are to be bound by it ... Nor, in my opinion, would the clearest proof of unanimous assent on the part of other nations be sufficient to authorize the tribunals of this country to apply, without an Act of Parliament, what would

---

[9] *Trendtex Trading Corp. Ltd. v. Central Bank of Nigeria*, [1977] Q.B. 529, at 553–554 (C.A.), reported in full, Chapter 5, *infra*.

practically amount to a new law. In so doing, we should be unjustifiably usurping the province of the legislature.

To this I may add the saying of Lord Atkin in *Chung Chi Cheung v. The King* [1939] A.C. 160, at 167–68:

So far, at any rate, as the courts of this country are concerned, international law has no validity save in so far as its principles are accepted and adopted by our own domestic law.

Lord Denning left no doubt that he thought the doctrine of incorporation (adoption) was the correct one for English law. The question is whether the same can be said for Canada. After a careful review of the Canadian cases, Professor Macdonald reached the guarded conclusion "there is room for the view that the law on the relationship of customary international law to domestic law in Canada is the same as it is in England."[10] Consider the following selection of cases as means to elaborate upon this general expression of opinion.

Foreign Legations Case
In the Matter Of A Reference As To The Powers Of The Corporation Of The City of Ottawa And The Corporation Of The Village Of Rockcliffe Park To Levy Rates On Foreign Legations And High Commissioners' Residences, [1943] S.C.R. 208

[In this reference, the Court was asked to advise whether the Ontario Assessment Act, which declared in section 4 that "All real property in Ontario ... shall be liable to taxation," rendered the property of foreign states assessable and exigible to municipal taxation. The basic question was whether Ottawa city council had the power to levy rates on a number of foreign legations.]

DUFF C.J.: ... There are some general principles touching the position of the property of a foreign state and the minister of a foreign state that have been accepted and adopted by the law of England (which, except as modified by statute, is the law of Ontario) as part of the law of nations. It should, however, be observed at the outset that we are only concerned here with such rules as applied in normal times and in normal circumstances. We are not in any way concerned with the qualifications of these rules that may be necessary in order to meet special circumstances in which the interest of the state in relation to public safety, or public order, may be affected. What I have to say as to general principles must, therefore, be taken to be subject to that observation. ...

It is probable that the privileges attributed to foreign representatives by the law in England, as part of the law of nations, are at least as liberal as those recognized by the law of any other country. In *Heathfield v. Chilton* [(1767) 4 Burrow 2015], Lord Mansfield said; –

---

[10] R. St.J. Macdonald, *supra*, n. 1, at 111; and see there at 94 as to the authority of *R. v. Keyn* and *Chung Chi Cheung v. The King* as establishing the doctrine of transformation.

The law of nations will be carried as far in England, as anywhere.

[The Chief Justice then proceeded to ascertain the existence and scope of a foreign state's immunities, including immunity from taxation of its property, under international law. These immunities are discussed in detail in Chapter 5.]

The principles governing the immunities of a foreign sovereign and his diplomatic agents and his property do not, of course, limit the legislative authority of the legislature having jurisdiction in the particular matter affected by any immunity claimed, or alleged. It is not necessary, in the view I take, to consider the respective jurisdictions of the Parliament of Canada and the local legislatures in this matter of taxation in respect of real estate owned, or occupied, by a foreign state, or a diplomatic agent in his character of representative of a foreign state. The general language of the enactments imposing the taxation in question must be construed as saving to the privileges of foreign states. The general principle is put with great clearness and force in the judgment of Marshall C.J., from which I have quoted so freely. These are the words [*Schooner Exchange v. Mc-Faddon*, (1812) 7 Cranch 116, at 146 (U.S.S.C.)]:

Without doubt, the sovereign of the place is capable of destroying this implication. He may claim and exercise jurisdiction either by employing force, or by subjecting such vessels to the ordinary tribunals ... Those general statutory provisions ... which are descriptive of the ordinary jurisdiction ... ought not, in the opinion of this Court, to be so construed as to give them jurisdiction in a case, in which the sovereign power has impliedly consented to waive its jurisdiction.

The questions referred should all be answered in the negative.

RINFRET J. [having accepted the right to immunity of foreign state property as established by Duff C.J., continued:]

The problem is not one which raises questions with regard to the respective competence of the Dominion Parliament and of the Provincial Parliament. It is limited to the ascertainment of the legislative competence of a Provincial Parliament to levy rates or taxes on property of foreign governments owned and occupied as legations.

The solution, it seems to me, must, therefore, be found in the remedies which the municipal corporations are empowered to adopt in order to collect their taxes, including, of course, the powers which the Provincial Legislature is competent to delegate, in that respect, to the municipal corporations. ...

It seems ... a necessary consequence of the legal impossibility of collecting the taxes against foreign states or diplomats that such taxes or rates may not be assessed and levied on the properties owned and occupied by them and used for diplomatic purposes.

Nor do I think that, consistently with principle, the municipal corporation can create any effective charge upon the property under consideration, because obviously the charge would affect the price for which the property could be sold later, if a sale was effected by the foreign State to an ordinary purchaser. This would only mean an indirect way of coercing the foreign State.

For these reasons, in my view, the questions referred should all be answered in the negative.

KERWIN J.: ... On this Reference, I take it that the questions submitted refer to the powers of the councils to impose assessments, taxes and charges and not to their powers, or those of the corporations acting through their officers and agents, to compel payment of these taxes; and I so treat the matter, and my answers are given upon that basis.

I see nothing to prevent the ordinary procedure being adopted with reference to these properties, that is, for the assessors to enter them on the assessment roll and the countries concerned as owners thereof; and for the collector's roll to be prepared and for the proper municipal authorities to enter in that roll that amount of taxes either for general or special rates or assessments; and for the tax collector to send a notice in the usual form showing the amount of taxes. The foreign states may choose to pay all or part of these sums or "as a matter of international courtesy" the Government of Canada may continue to pay them or may decide to pay part. A member of a Minister's staff may presumably enter into a lease of premises and agree to pay rent, although, if disputes arise, the landlord may find himself in difficulties ... This problem does not, of course, arise here, but neither, in my view, does the question as to whether the tax collector might, in the event of non-payment of any part of the taxes, seize goods under section 114 of The Assessment Act or as to whether the foreign states could be sued for the taxes or as to whether the lands themselves could be sold for taxes. When these questions arise they must be decided under those rules of international law that have become part of the domestic law of this country. ...

In my opinion, therefore, it is within the powers of the Council of the Corporation of the City of Ottawa to levy rates on properties in Ottawa owned and occupied as Legations by the Governments of the French State, the United States of America and Brazil, respectively, and it is within the powers of the Council of the Corporation of the Village of Rockcliffe Park to levy rates on property owned and occupied by the Government of the United States of America as the Legation of the United States in Rockcliffe Park; ...

HUDSON J.: ... We next come to the larger and more difficult question as to whether or not the municipalities have the power to impose taxes for municipal purposes on properties owned and occupied as legations of governments of foreign countries and, if so, whether there are any limitations thereto.

It should first be stated that there is no legislation of Canada or of Ontario granting any privileges or immunities in respect of such legations, so that, if any exist, it must be by virtue of some general principle of international law or of Imperial legislation having the force of law in Ontario.

Separate diplomatic representation for and to Canada was not contemplated when the British North America Act was passed and there is no provision therein which allots to the Dominion as against the provinces any special powers applicable thereto. ...

I think that the province would be bound to recognize the status of diplomats, but not necessarily bound to accord them any privileges in matters falling within provincial legislative jurisdiction under section 92 of the British North America Act.

We must then consider the extent of immunities to which diplomatic representatives and legations are entitled under the general principles of international law or the statute law of England and which, if any, such immunities form part of the law of the Province of Ontario. ...

It must, then, be concluded that a court would be bound to hold that in Ontario no action could be proceeded with against any foreign sovereign or state or its diplomatic representatives who pleaded immunity, in respect of taxes imposed by municipal corporations, and the same rule would apply to any proceedings in court calculated to disturb their occupation of the land. ...

But there is another side to the matter. The immunity or privilege is a privilege from action or molestation. It does not destroy liability. ...

A diplomatic representative often incurs liability under contracts. If he pleads immunity, these cannot be enforced as long as the privilege continues, but he still owes the debt.

The tax here in question is imposed on the land for the purpose of maintaining the community life and amenities shared by the inhabitants of the municipality, including the occupants of these particular properties, with all citizens. It is in no way a tax enuring for the benefit of Canada as a state.

The Legislature of Ontario, which is supreme in the matter of municipal institutions and property and civil rights in the province, has not seen fit to exempt the land used for legations from municipal taxes.

The Dominion has the right to give a status to diplomatic representatives, but I cannot see that the granting of such status carries with it immunities from provincial laws beyond those which are recognized by the Provincial Legislature, as has been done, in my view, to the extent of immunity from personal liability. ...

The tax when imposed creates a lien and charge on the land. There are many difficulties in the way of enforcement as long as the privilege continues but, as we have reason to know, diplomatic relations may be severed, or the foreign state or person representing such state may desire to dispose of the land; then the lien might well become effective. Again, a substantial part of municipal taxation is imposed to pay for the services rendered by the municipality, such as water, sewerage, etc., which the municipality would have a right to withhold until taxes are paid.

If I am correct in these views, this leaves the matter in an unsatisfactory position. It arises because Canada's advance to international status was not foreseen when the British North America Act was passed. I take it that the purpose of this Reference is to clarify the legal situation so that the proper authorities may make the necessary adjustments between themselves in such a way as to comply with the necessities of international comity. What I have said perhaps does not clarify the situation but does show the legal difficulties involved in defining the functions of the Dominion as against the province. ...

To question (i) my answer is "Yes," meaning thereby that the council of the municipality can impose such taxes, but this is qualified by the fact that assistance of the courts would not be given to enforce payment so long as the diplomatic immunity continued.

TASCHEREAU J.: ... Of course, the rapid expansion of international relations between Canada and the other countries of the world, could not be foreseen in 1867, but it is common ground that external affairs is a matter which is exclusively under Federal control, and it is in pursuance of these rights that the Canadian Government have exchanged ministers with foreign countries.

I quite agree, that if the Federal authorities contract obligations with foreign countries, their competence does not "become enlarged to keep pace with enlarged functions", and as Lord Atkin said in *Attorney General for Canada v. Attorney General for Ontario* ([1937] A.C. 326, at 352):

In other words, the Dominion cannot, merely by making promises to foreign countries, clothe itself with legislative authority inconsistent with the constitution which gave it birth. ...

The question is whether under International Law, a property belonging to a foreign State may be assessed for municipal purposes. A negative answer would in no way clothe the Dominion with any "enlarged competence", and the denial to the Province and the Municipal authorities of the right to levy such rates, would not extend the field of federal legislative powers.

I have come to the conclusion that practically in all the leading countries of the world, it is a settled and accepted rule of International Law, that property belonging to a foreign Government, occupied by its accredited representative, cannot be assessed and taxed for state or municipal purposes.

The Minister himself, is not, as a rule, subject to the authority of a foreign power, and cannot be impleaded in the courts of the country where he is sent. His immunity from legal process extends to the property of the State, which is exempt from all forms of taxation. It is with this in mind that must be read the *Assessment Act* of Ontario.

I had the advantage of reading the reasons for judgment of the Chief Justice. He has made a thorough review of the jurisprudence and of the opinions of the text-writers on the subject, and with what he has said, I entirely concur.

I would answer ... [the basic question] in the negative.

NOTES

1) Are the judges in this case adoptionist or transformationist in their approach?[11]

2) As a general maxim, a statute will be interpreted in such a way that it will not isolate principles of public international law unless its clear meaning will admit of no other interpretation.[12] Does this case apply the maxim or does it go further?

3) Do any of the judges (in particular, Taschereau J.) suggest that a province lacks constitutional capacity to enact legislation contrary to international law?

4) To what extent are Hudson, Rinfret and Kerwin JJ.'s decisions based upon a view that the *Assessment Act* applies the tax but that any tax would not be collectable because the property of the foreign sovereign would be immune from execution?[13] Is such a distinction sensible?

---

[11] See also *Reference re Exemption of U.S. Forces from Canadian Criminal Law*, [1943] S.C.R. 483; [1943] 4 D.L.R. 11.

[12] See *Re Arrow River and Tributaries Slide and Boom Co. Ltd.*, [1932] 2 D.L.R. 250 (S.C.C.), reported *infra*. Cf. *Gordon v. R. in Right of Canada*, [1980] 5 W.W.R. 668 (B.C.S.C.), reported *infra*.

[13] See the *State Immunity Act*, S.C. 1980–81, c. 95, s. 11, reported *infra* in Chapter 5; and *Re Royal Bank of Canada and Corriveau* (1980), 117 D.L.R. (3d) 199 (O.H.C.).

Saint John v. Fraser-Brace Overseas Corp.
[1958] S.C.R. 263

[Pursuant to an agreement between the governments of Canada and the United States for the construction of a radar defence system, certain contractors in Saint John carried out work on sites located in that city. The materials used in the work were either the property of the United States government or held by the contractors on its behalf. Saint John imposed municipal taxes both on certain leasehold interests in the lands and on personal property situated there. The contractors paid the taxes "under protest" and brought an action to recover them.]

RAND J.: This appeal raises a question of liability to taxation by the appellants of property used by the respondents as contractors with the Government of the United States in the construction of what is described as the "extension and co-ordination of a continental radar defence system within Canada," to serve as an agency of defence for both countries against possible air attacks. ...

Enough has been said to indicate the precise obligation of the contractors to the United States Government. It was essentially one to furnish services, with all property, materials, tools, equipment and other means used or employed in or for the work of construction, supplied by the United States. The fact that this field station was at some distance from the scene of the permanent works does not affect its relation to them or its derivative character. If the works would be exempt, then all property used in or for their construction, including that in field operations, regardless of situs, is necessarily identified with the ultimate purpose. All that was done within the municipality is to be taken as one with the final accomplishment, and the purpose of that accomplishment will determine that of the property used by these subsidiary agencies.

The general principle of immunity from legal processes in the broadest sense in what may be called the host country of public property of a foreign state has been given its authoritative statement for Canada by Duff C.J. in the *Foreign Legations Reference*, [*supra*]. There, as here, he was dealing with taxation under general language in which only the interpretation of the statute was in question. The significant aspect of the matter examined by him was that of the theory on which the immunity is to be placed. ...

It is obvious that the life of every state is, under the swift transformation of these days, becoming deeply implicated with that of the others in a *de facto* society of nations. If in 1767 Lord Mansfield, as in *Heathfield v. Chilton*, could say, "The law of nations will be carried as far in England, as any where," in this country, in the 20th century, in the presence of the United Nations and the multiplicity of impacts with which technical developments have entwined the entire globe, we cannot say anything less.

In the language of Sir Alexander Cockburn quoted by Lord Atkin in *Chung Chi Cheung*, ... in the absence of precise precedent we must seek the rule which "reason and good sense ... would prescribe." In this we are not to disregard the practical consideration, if not the necessity, of that "general assent and reciprocity," of which Lord Macmillan speaks in *Compania Naviera Vascongardo v. The "Cristina" et al.*, cited in the reasons of McNair C.J. But to say that precedent is now required for every proposed application to matter which differs only in accidentals, that new concrete instances must be left to legislation or convention, would be a virtual repudiation of the concept of inherent adaptability which has maintained the life of the common law, and a retrograde step in evolving the rules of international intercourse. However slowly and meticulously they are to be fashioned they must be permitted to meet the necessities of increasing international involvements. It is the essence of the principle of precedent that new applications are to be determined according to their total elements including assumptions and attitudes, and in the international sphere the whole field of the behaviour of states, whether exhibited in actual conduct, conventions, arbitrations or adjudications, is pertinent to the determination of each issue. ...

Public works of this sort are not ordinarily considered subjects of taxation. Their object is to preserve the agencies that produce national wealth, the source of taxes. So to tax Government is simply to remit locally what has been exacted nationally. The work carried on by either Government in its own land would be untaxable, and that principle must carry over to the territory of the joint work.

I am unable, then, to infer that with an identity of purpose, status and rule in each country, either the invitation or its acceptance proceeded upon any other basis than that of the rule of exemption from taxation. Why should we deny to property designed for common national preservation a sovereign character and purpose equal at least to that of an ambassador's furniture? Works of this sort are not to be looked upon, in principle, as furnishing a source of taxation for municipalities nor state necessities an object of revenue; any other view would be a strange commentary upon our conception of the role of Government in these days. Public works may, at times, impose upon local resources burdens of municipal responsibility; but the exemption here does not touch services for which payment is ordinarily made, as water, electricity, etc. These the foreign invitees must, as their food-supply and property generally, acquire as purchasers. If strictly general municipal services providing fire-protection, repair of streets, etc., are excessively affected, the appeal must be to the domestic Government as participant in the work; and adjustment between the two countries becomes a political matter.

Gordon v. R. in Right of Canada
[1980] 5 W.W.R. 668 (B.C.S.C.), aff'd [1980] 6 W.W.R. 519 (B.C.C.A.)

[Petitioner was charged with unlawfully entering and fishing in Canadian waters when he was fishing within the 200 mile fishing zone but outside of the territorial sea.]

MEREDITH J.: ... The petitioner says that it is beyond the competence of the Federal Parliament to pass legislation which contravenes the "customary international law." He says that there is a category of law that can be described as "entrenched" such that: "When this entrenched category of customary international law and the criminal law of Canada come into conflict, the former prevails"; and that: "the customary international law regarding the freedom of the High Seas properly belongs in this entrenched category of customary international law which is beyond the reach of Parliament."

By "High Seas" I understand counsel to mean seas beyond the territorial sea of Canada. The fishing zones extend well beyond the territorial sea. The latter, under the

Territorial Sea and Fishing Zones Act, extends generally only 12 nautical miles seaward
from the coastline. Counsel points to the Geneva Convention on the High Seas (1958),
which suggests that no state may hinder the freedom of navigation or freedom of fishing
on the "High Seas." The convention defines the term "High Seas" as "all parts of the
sea that are not included in the territorial sea or in the internal waters of the state." I
believe that Canada is a signatory to the convention, but the convention itself has not
been made part of the law of Canada.

The petitioner has used the term "High Seas" to invoke the notion of free and unlimited
access. However, where Canada asserts jurisdiction over an area of the sea and purports
to limit access thereto, from the standpoint of domestic law the access is in fact limited
for a special purpose, and even if the law of Canada contravenes "customary international
law," if Parliament, as here, has acted unambiguously, the courts of this country are
bound to apply the domestic law. This is made clear from the following passage from
the judgment of Lord Atkin in *Chung Chi Cheung v. R.*, [1939] A.C. 160, at 167–68,
[1938] 4 All E.R. 786:

It must always be remembered that, so far, at any rate, as the Courts of this country are
concerned, international law has no validity save in so far as its principles are accepted and
adopted by our own domestic law. There is no external power that imposes its rules upon our
own code of substantive law or procedure. The Courts acknowledge the existence of a body of
rules which nations accept amongst themselves. On any judicial issue they seek to ascertain what
the relevant rule is, and, having found it, they will treat it as incorporated into domestic law,
so far as it is not inconsistent with rules enacted by statutes or finally declared by their tribunals. ...

The foregoing passage has been cited with approval time and again and approved by
our highest court in, for instance, *Reference re Powers of Ottawa and Rockcliffe Park
to Levy Rates on Foreign Legations and High Commrs' Residences*, [reported *supra*]. ...

I conclude that the statutory provisions in question here are *intra vires* the government
of Canada and that the Provincial Judge properly took jurisdiction over this matter. The
application must accordingly be refused.

NOTES

1) Is Rand J.'s approach in the *Saint John* case adoptionist or transformationist?

2) Is there any suggestion in the case that there is a hierarchical relationship between
public international law and domestic law and which would prevail in the event of a
conflict?

3) What status did Meredith J. accord to international law in the *Gordon* case? Did
he follow the judgments in the *Foreign Legations Case*, which he referred to; did he
adopt the approach of Rand J. in the *Saint John* case? Today the new U.N. Convention
on the Law of the Sea permits an exclusive 200 mile fishing zone: see Chapter 11 on
"Fisheries."

4) In *Re Newfoundland Continental Shelf*[14] the Supreme Court impliedly confirmed the doctrine of adoption. Both Canada and Newfoundland claimed the rights of the coastal state recognized by international law. The Supreme Court did not pause to consider whether or how international principles might resolve national legal problems, but instead it went straight to the usual sources of international law expressed in the Statute of the International Court, Article 38. Having dismissed treaty sources and general principles as having no application, it framed the question thus:[15]

The critical issue then is whether the sovereign right, arising *ipso jure*, to explore and exploit in the continental shelf was a matter of customary international law by 1949.

The Court immediately made an extensive survey of state claims to the continental shelf beginning in 1942. It took note of the International Law Commission's work, in particular that the matter involved the progressive development of international law, and it discussed such subsidiary caselaw and scholarly commentary as was made available on the subject. It was then stated:[16]

We conclude that international law had not sufficiently developed by 1949 to confer, *ipso jure*, the right of the coastal state to explore and exploit the continental shelf. We think that in 1949 state practice was neither sufficiently widespread to constitute a general practice nor sufficiently consistent to constitute settled law. Furthermore, several of the early state claims exceeded that which international law subsequently recognized in the 1958 Geneva Convention. International Law on the continental shelf developed relatively quickly, but it had not attained concrete form by 1949.

Thus the Supreme Court provided an unusual but admirable demonstration of how a court should canvas the existence of customary international law. Furthermore, it acted on the customary international development of law as if it were automatically a source of law in Canada.

5) In *Mortensen v. Peters*[17] the defendant, a Danish captain of a Norwegian ship was convicted of fishing in a prohibited manner in the Moray Firth, a body of water in Scotland, contrary to the *Herring Fishery (Scotland) Act 1889* which made such type of fishing an offence. He argued that, as he was more than 3 miles from land he was in international waters and beyond the scope of the legislation in question. His appeal was dismissed.

Lord Kyllachy said:

...This Court is of course not entitled to canvass the power of the Legislature to make the enactment. The only question open is as to its just construction. ...

---

[14] [1984] 1 S.C.R. 86, reported *infra* in Chapter 11.
[15] *Supra*, n. 14, at 117.
[16] *Supra*, n. 14, at 124.
[17] (1906), 14 Scot. L.T. 227.

Now dealing, first, with the point of construction – the question as to what the statutory enactment means – it may probably be conceded that there is always a certain presumption against the Legislature of a country asserting or assuming the existence of a territorial jurisdiction going clearly beyond limits established by the common consent of nations – that is to say, by international law. ... But then it is only a presumption, and as such it must always give way to the language used if it is clear, and also to all counter presumptions which may legitimately be had in view in determining, on ordinary principles, the true meaning and intent of the legislation. Express words will of course be conclusive, and so also will plain implication.

After various other convictions and protests from Norway a Foreign Office spokesman stated in the House of Commons that the Act, as interpreted in these cases, was "in conflict with international law."[18] It was therefore amended to prohibit only the landing in the U.K. of fish caught by means prohibited by the legislation. What do these events indicate about the efficacy of international law as a check on assertions of jurisdiction by nation states?

Power to Legislate Contrary to International Law?

Is it true for Canada as Lord Kyllachy declared in *Mortensen v. Peters*[19] for Scotland that the courts are "not entitled to canvass the power of the Legislature to make the enactment" which allegedly contravenes international law? May the Parliament of Canada or the Legislature of a province validly legislate in breach of international law or should the courts strike down such enactments as *ultra vires*?

Vanek has contended that in Canada there is no power to legislate contrary to international law:[20]

Is International Law a Part of the Law of Canada?
by C. Vanek (1949–50), 8 *U.T.L.J.* 251, at 266–67, 274–76 and 292

(iii) We have already observed that the legislature of the United Kingdom, having unlimited competence under English constitutional law, may even enact a statute in contravention of rules of international law, although this theoretical supremacy is considerably modified by a rule of statutory construction which requires the courts, if at all possible, to interpret the statute so that it conforms with the requirements of international law. It does not follow, however, that in Canadian law a similar supremacy, even theoretical, is enjoyed by the Dominion or provincial legislatures. It may well be that under the British North America Act, legislation enacted either by the Dominion or, *a fortiori*, by the provincial legislatures, in contravention of international law, is *ultra vires* and void. This proposition is perhaps somewhat startling to constitutional lawyers mindful

---

[18] (1907) *U.K. Hansard*, H.C. Vol. 170, Col. 472.

[19] *Supra*, at n. 17.

[20] *Supra*, n. 1, at 266–67 and 274–76. See also G.V. LaForest, "May the Provinces Legislate in Violation of International Law?" (1961), 39 *Can. Bar Rev.* 79.

of repeated observations in the decided cases concerning the plenary nature of the legislative powers bestowed upon the federal and provincial legislatures. It is very doubtful, however, whether in those cases the judges had present to mind the specific limitation here suggested, or the principle on which it is based. The consequence of such incapacity would be to emphasize the unity of the systems of international and Canadian law in two important respects:

(a) There would be no reason in principle why the incapacity should not operate in relation to conventional international law as well as to customary international law. Thus, although the provincial legislatures may have exclusive competence to enact legislation in performance of a treaty concluded by the Dominion executive in relation to certain classes of subjects, so that, for failure of such legislatures to act, the Dominion may be left in default internationally, the provincial legislatures, on the other hand, may not have the power to enact legislation contrary to the terms of such treaty. In other words, it may be competent to the provinces to refrain from performing obligations of the Dominion incurred by a treaty, but they cannot enact legislation in contravention of such obligations.

(b) Little occasion would remain for a Canadian court to reject an established rule of international law for repugnancy to an existing statute, within the first branch of the qualification stated by Lord Atkin in the *Cheung Case* – "so far as it is not inconsistent with rules enacted by statutes or finally declared by their tribunals"[21] – because any such Dominion or provincial statute would itself be *ultra vires* and void.

... The second branch of Lord Atkin's qualification – "or finally declared by their tribunals"[22] – can likewise have little, if any, application, either in English or Canadian law. Since international law is part of the common law, it is highly unlikely that the ordinary rules of the common law, as developed by the courts, have been or are today inconsistent with international law. The common law must surely have been developed in the light of the general doctrine of adoption. To assume that a rule of international law falls outside the application of the doctrine of adoption because in its modern form it is contrary to a "well-established" rule of the common law, itself, *ex hypothesi*, developed in conformity with the doctrine, is illogical and defeats the spirit and object of the doctrine. Moreover, international law is not a static system of law, but admits of change and development. It follows that the strict operation of the common law doctrine of *stare decisis* cannot extend to international rules applied in the national courts. ...

The incapacity of Canadian legislatures to enact laws contrary to international law is clearly suggested in a passage of the decision of the Judicial Committee of the Privy Council in *Croft v. Dunphy*. Speaking for the Board, Lord Macmillan observed:[23]

Legislation of the Imperial Parliament, even in contravention of international law, is binding

---

[21] Quoted in full in *Gordon v. R. in Right of Canada, supra.*
[22] *Supra*, n. 21.
[23] [1933] A.C. 156, at 164.

and must be enforced by the Courts of this country, for in these Courts the legislation of the Imperial Parliament cannot be challenged as *ultra vires*: per Lord Justice-General Dunedin in *Mortensen v. Peters*. It may be that legislation of the Dominion Parliament may be challenged as *ultra vires* on the ground that it is contrary to the principles of international law, but that must be because it must be assumed that the British North America Act has not conferred power on the Dominion Parliament to legislate contrary to these principles.

This statement, although purely *obiter*, has probably escaped general notice only because, in the past, attention has been concentrated upon the main ground of decision, which has been much discussed and commented upon, despite the fact that the case has commonly been regarded as merely of academic interest even on this point. By this decision it was recognized that the federal legislature possessed full power to enact legislation having an extraterritorial operation, independently of section 3 of the Statute of Westminster, 1931, under which such power was expressly granted; for although the case was decided after the passing of the Statute of Westminster, it was decided on facts arising prior to the statute, and therefore, apart from the statute. The legislation in question[24] authorized the seizure and forfeiture of vessels containing dutiable goods, with their cargoes, if found hovering within three marine miles of the Canadian shore in the case of any vessel and within twelve marine miles in the case of any vessel registered in Canada.

Although this statute was held *intra vires*, the Judicial Committee were very careful to observe, on the basis of an examination of international authorities, that such legislation was not contrary to international law. They remarked that, under international law, states may exercise a qualified permissive jurisdiction in revenue matters beyond the generally accepted limits of territorial waters; and the passage above-quoted is accordingly followed by the statement: "In the present case, however, there is no question of international law involved, for legislation of the kind here challenged is recognized as legitimate by international law, and in any event the provision impugned has no application to foreign vessels." ... It is noteworthy, then, that the Judicial Committee felt it necessary to enter a *caveat* in a form which, though not conclusive and merely *obiter*, nevertheless carries with it more than a suggestion of approval for the assertion that legislation enacted either by the Dominion or provincial legislatures in contravention of international law is *ultra vires*.

On what reasoning is this assertion founded? The argument may be stated as a simple syllogism.

i) By a well-established rule of statutory construction applicable even to legislation of the Parliament of the United Kingdom, it is presumed that the legislature does not intend to enact a law contrary to international law. It is not lightly to be supposed that the legislature intends to contravene the provisions of international law. It follows, also, that it is not lightly to be assumed that the legislature intends, or intended, to confer such a power on any other authority. This rule is itself intended to implement a basic principle

---

[24] *The Customs Act of Canada*, R.S.C. 1927, c. 42, as amended.

of international law, which requires each state to ensure that its domestic law is in conformity with the rules, doctrines, and principles of international law.

ii) The British North America Act is a statute of the United Kingdom. It does not by express terms confer upon Canadian legislative authorities the power to legislate in contravention of international law.

iii) Therefore, neither the Dominion legislature nor, *a fortiori*, the legislatures of the several provinces (which do not even enjoy ordinary extraterritorial powers) possess the power to enact such legislation.

Indeed, on the basis of the interpretation of the British North America Act by the Judicial Committee, it is difficult to understand how that tribunal could have entertained any other opinion on this point; for they would seem to have been in this dilemma: either the British North America Act is a statute or it is not a statute. The Judicial Committee have often enough asserted that it is a statute, in which event the rule of statutory construction applies with the result indicated. If, however, it is not a statute, then obviously the courts must reconsider the several cases decided on the contrary supposition. It may, however, be observed that the rule of construction is probably not limited merely to the construction of statutes. Even if the British North America Act is a charter, for example, and not merely a statute, it is not lightly to be assumed that it was intended to confer a power to legislate contrary to international law.

[Vanek discusses other Canadian cases before concluding that]

...[A]lthough Canadian legislative authorities may refrain from enacting legislation for the purpose of implementing treaties binding upon Canada, at all events they have not the power, affirmatively, to enact legislation in contravention of the obligations of Canada under such treaties. Neither have Canadian legislative authorities the power to enact legislation in contravention of customary international law, for the same constitutional restriction on the legislative power applies to both with regard to customary and conventional international law.

NOTES

1) By contrast, Professor Macdonald disagrees with Vanek's conclusion:[25]

The *Arrow River*[26] case also touched on the interesting question of the ability of a province to legislate in violation of international law. Vanek has argued that neither the federal nor the provincial legislatures may so legislate; and La Forest has argued that the provinces are under that restriction. It is submitted, with respect, that both these positions are incorrect, at least under present law. First, the dominion and provincial governments enjoy equal and plenary powers within their individual spheres of competence; thus if one may violate international law, so may the other. Second, it is clear that if the English parliament legislates in unambiguous terms contrary to customary international law that legislation is valid. Third, there is no reason to believe that the English rule of the supremacy of parliament does not apply in Canada. Indeed

---

[25] Supra, n. 1, at 119.
[26] [1932] 2 D.L.R. 250 (S.C.C.), reported *infra*.

the passage from *Chung* which sets out the English rule has been cited with approval several times by the Supreme Court of Canada. ... Fourth, the English parliament can override treaty obligations with clear legislation. Fifth, the supremacy of Canadian federal statutes over treaties, that is, conventional international law, was recognized in the *Swait* case where Hyde J. of the Quebec Court of Queen's Bench, in rejecting an argument that the Trustee Act violated Canada's international obligations, said that "whatever may have been the case before the Statute of Westminster, 1931–32 (U.K.), c 4, the laws of Canada are supreme within the framework of the B.N.A. Act and where Parliament has clearly legislated on some matter within its jurisdiction, the validity of that legislation cannot be affected by external treaties."[27] Sixth, the only two judges on the Supreme Court who decided the point held that the province of Ontario could legislate in violation of the Webster-Ashburton Treaty in the *Arrow River* case itself. Thus, it follows that both federal and provincial legislatures, in exercise of their supremacy, may legislate in violation of any form of international law.

2) Do the Canadian cases previously reported in this section provide any indication that a statute which is contrary to international law may be *ultra vires* of Parliament or a provincial legislature? Would such an interpretation of the Canadian constitution be advantageous?

Treaties

The application of a treaty within Canadian law depends upon its implementation[28] by statute. The practice with regard to treaties consistently follows the doctrine of transformation, whereas the cases in the last sub-section show a greater readiness to accept the doctrine of adoption in connection with customary international law. This divergence of approach raises two fundamental issues: (1) Why should international law be treated differently according to the means of its creation? (2) Is an unimplemented treaty wholly without effect within the domestic legal system? While the following cases affirm the practice concerning treaties, they also shed some light on these basic questions.

R. v. Canada Labour Relations Board

(1964), 44 D.L.R. (2d) 440 (Man. Q.B.)

[The Respondent Board certified a trade union as a bargaining agent for certain employees working in defence installations in Canada which were the subject of an agreement between Canada and the United States.]

SMITH J.: ... The applicant attacks the Board's order of certification on six grounds. The first of these is:

(a) The Canada Labour Relations Board had no jurisdiction to hear the application for certification as, by virtue of a Treaty between Canada and the United States of America, dated May 5, 1955, rates of pay and working conditions were to be set after consultation

---

[27] *Swait v. Board of Trustees of Maritime Transportation Unions* (1967), 61 D.L.R. (2d) 317, (Que. C.A.), at 322.

[28] As to the division of the power to make and to implement treaties see the discussion on "Treaty Making," *supra* in Chapter 2.

with the Canadian Department of Labour and not through the ordinary bargaining processes. I note here that the provision respecting rates of pay and working conditions applied to construction contracts only; but counsel, at the hearing before the Board, agreed that subsequently there was an agreement that the United States would operate the Distant Early Warning System, and that in the operation thereof the same terms and conditions would apply as provided in the Treaty for construction contracts. ...

In international law, though some treaties go further and purport to declare law, it is true to say that in general a treaty is a contract between States creating rights and obligations that enure to, and are binding on, the executive Governments which are parties to it. The common law recognizes this rule, but it has long been settled law that a treaty binding the Government does not, *ipso facto*, become part of our law and enforceable in the Courts. Many instances of judicial expressions to this effect might be cited, but it will be sufficient to refer to two.

In *A.-G. Can. v. A.-G. Ont.*, ... [the *Labour Conventions Case*], [1937] 1 D.L.R. 673, [1937] A.C. 326, [1937] 1 W.W.R. 299, Lord Atkin, delivering the judgment of the Judicial Committee, said at 678–79 D.L.R., 347–48 A.C., 306–7 W.W.R.:

Within the British Empire there is a well-established rule that the making of a treaty is an executive act, while the performance of its obligations, if they entail alteration of the existing domestic law, requires legislative action. Unlike some other countries the stipulations of a treaty duly ratified do not within the Empire, by virtue of the treaty alone, have the force of law. If the national executive, the government of the day, decide to incur the obligations of a treaty which involve alteration of law they have to run the risk of obtaining the assent of Parliament to the necessary statute or statutes. To make themselves as secure as possible they will often in such cases before final ratification seek to obtain from Parliament an expression of approval. But it has never been suggested, and it is not the law, that such an expression of approval operates as law, or that in law it precludes the assenting Parliament, or any subsequent Parliament from refusing to give its sanction to any legislative proposals that may subsequently be brought before it.

These words clearly mean that not every treaty requires legislative sanction, but that a treaty which involves a change in existing law does require it and that in such a case a mere expression of approval by Parliament is not sufficient.

In *Francis v. The Queen*, 3 D.L.R. (2d) 641, [1956] S.C.R. 618, an Indian who had paid duties of customs and sales and sales taxes demanded by the Crown on a washing machine, a refrigerator and an oil heater, brought by him into Canada from the United States, claimed by petition of right the return of this money and a declaration that no duties or taxes were payable by him in respect of these goods. The appellant Indian resided on a Quebec Indian Reserve adjoining an Indian Reserve in the State of New York. His claim was based in part on the Jay Treaty, signed in 1794, between His Britannic Majesty and the United States, Article III, of which read:

No duty on entry shall ever be levied by either part on peltries brought by land, or inland navigation into the said territories respectively, nor shall the Indians passing or repassing with their own proper goods and effects of whatever nature, pay for the same any impost or duty whatever. But goods in bales or other large packages, unusual among Indians, shall not be considered as goods belonging *bona fide* to Indians.

In effect this Treaty purported to give to Indians a partial right of exemption from the general law imposing customs duties, which Kerwin, C.J.C., said at 643 D.L.R., 621 S.C.R.:

The Jay Treaty was not a treaty of peace and it is clear that in Canada such rights and privileges as are here advanced of subjects of a contracting party to a treaty are enforceable by the Courts only where the treaty has been implemented or sanctioned by legislation.

Rand, J., at 647 D.L.R., 626 S.C.R., spelled out the law with more particularity:

Except as to diplomatic status and certain immunities and to belligerent rights, treaty provisions affecting matters within the scope of municipal law, that is, which purport to change existing law or restrict the future action of the Legislature, including, under our Constitution, the participation of the Crown, and in the absence of a constitutional provision declaring the treaty itself to be law of the state, as in the United States, must be supplemented by statutory action.

In the case before the Court there is no question but that, under s. 53 thereof, the *Industrial Relations and Disputes Investigation Act*, applies in the Northwest Territories of Canada. By that Act certain rights and obligations are established for employers and for their employees and their bargaining agents. For our purposes the rights we are concerned with are rights and obligations in connection with collective bargaining. If the Agreement of May 5, 1955, between Canada and the United States has the effect of taking away these rights and removing these obligations, it necessarily involves a change in the law of the Territories in so far as these parties are concerned. In my view of the authorities, this would require legislative action by the Parliament of Canada. It has not been suggested that any Act of Parliament has been passed embodying the terms of this Agreement or giving them statutory authority. Though the Agreement was tabled in the House of Commons, as today appears to be the practice with almost all international agreements, such action cannot have the effect of changing the law affecting these parties, or of making such change, if any were intended, enforceable in the Courts.

Apart from the general legal principal, it is noted that s. 6 of the Agreement expressly provides:

6. Nothing in this Agreement shall derogate from the application of Canadian law in Canada, provided that, if in unusual circumstances its application may lead to unreasonable delay or difficulty in construction or operation, the United States authorities concerned may request the assistance of Canadian authorities in seeking appropriate alleviation. In order to facilitate the rapid and efficient construction of the D.E.W. System, Canadian authorities will give sympathetic consideration to any such request submitted by United States Government authorities.

There is no evidence before the Court that the proviso in the above section has ever been invoked.

In the face of the express provision in the opening words of the section concerning Canadian law, I cannot think there was any intention that the Agreement should take away the rights or obligations created by the *Industrial Relations and Disputes Investigation Act* for employees and employers.

In my view, for the foregoing reasons, the Treaty or Agreement has no effect on the Board's jurisdiction and is not a bar to the granting of certification by the respondent Board.

Re Arrow River and Tributaries Slide and Boom Co. Ltd.
(1931), 66 O.L.R. 577 (O.C.A.); rev'd. [1932] 2 D.L.R. 250 (S.C.C.)

[Pursuant to a provincial statute, the *Lakes and Rivers Improvements Act*,[29] the Arrow River Co. was incorporated to construct facilities for the movement of timber down the Arrow river and its tributaries, including the Pigeon river which serves as a part of the border between Canada (Ontario) and the United States. After completion of the work, the Arrow River Co. applied under the Act to the court to fix the tolls to which it was entitled. The appellant, the Pigeon Timber Co., objected to paying any tolls when floating their logs down the Pigeon river, claiming an exemption under the Webster-Ashburton Treaty of 1842, which provided "that all the water communications and all the usual portages along the line ... [including] the Pigeon River, as now actually used, shall be free and open to the use of the subjects and citizens of both countries."]

For the Ontario Court of Appeal, RIDDELL J.A.: ... The objection of the appellant is substantially that, owing to the Ashburton Treaty of 1842, this river was to be "free and open" for the nationals of the two contracting parties, Britain and the United States.

The real argument based upon this Treaty has been misapprehended, the learned Judge disposing of the matter on the proposition, which is undoubted law, namely, that, in British countries, treaties to which Britain is a party are not as such binding upon the individual subjects, but are only contracts binding in honour upon the contracting States. He consequently held that the Arrow company need not pay any attention to the Treaty.

The real argument is that the Treaty was made with her Majesty, and is binding in honour upon her Majesty's successor, his present Majesty, as it was upon his predecessor. Consequently, the Sovereign will not be considered as enacting anything that will conflict with his plain duty, unless the language employed in the statute is perfectly clear and explicit, admitting of no other interpretation. I speak of his Majesty enacting, because, although, by reason of our system of Responsible Government, statutes are approved by the representatives of the people, nevertheless every Ontario Act begins, "*His Majesty*, by and with the advice and consent of the Legislative Assembly of the Province of Ontario, enacts ... " The statutes are all enacted by his Majesty, though the advice and consent of the Legislature is necessary under our Constitution.

The King cannot be thought of as violating his agreement with the other contracting

---

[29] R.S.O. 1927, c. 43.

Power; and, if the legislation can fairly be read in such a way as to reject any imputation of breaking faith, it must be so read.

That the works placed on the bed of the Pigeon river must necessarily interfere with the free navigation of the Pigeon river on the Ontario side is not disputed; consequently, the terms of the Treaty are set at naught.

The company to be incorporated under the Act in question was to be so incorporated for the purpose of "acquiring or constructing and maintaining and operating works upon any lake or river *in Ontario*": sec. 32. This may well be read as meaning what I think it says, i.e., the lake or river is to be "in Ontario," not "partly in Ontario." That it cannot be interpreted as intended to cover such a river as the Pigeon river, is, I think, indicated by sec. 42, giving the company the right to expropriate any land requisite for the undertaking.

To put it simply, placing his Majesty in the position of an honourable man, who had agreed that another should have the right to pass over his land under the water, could it be even imagined that he would either himself build such structures as are in question here or authorise another to do so? To my mind, to ask this question is to answer it.

I think that the statute was not intended to and does not confer upon this company the right to build upon the bed of the Pigeon river anything which may interfere with the enjoyment of free and open use of it by the citizens of the United States. That what the Arrow company has done has such effect is perfectly obvious from the evidence.

I would ... prohibit the fixing of tolls for any part of the Pigeon river.

In the Supreme Court of Canada, SMITH J.: ... It seems to me, ... that looking at the statute as a whole, s. 32 has not the restricted application assigned to it by the Appellate Division. So interpreted, the section would also have no application to boundary streams between Provinces, such as the Ottawa River, and all works in that and other boundary rivers and streams, unless otherwise authorized, would, in consequence, be without legal sanction.

Moreover, s. 14 of the Act has special provisions in relation to works in international streams, and the works there referred to are, I think, unquestionably works authorized by the Act itself, that is by s. 32.

I am, therefore, of opinion that s. 32 has application to the Pigeon River and ... am further of opinion that it is not in conflict with the terms of the treaty. ...

The part of the Pigeon River, in which the works in question are situated, is not stated in the affidavit, filed by respondent, to have been in actual use at the time of the treaty for water communication and the map filed as an exhibit to the affidavit indicates, as the terms of the treaty also indicate, that what was in actual use at that time was the Grand Portage which carried traffic round and past the obstruction of the high falls and rapids that rendered the part of the Pigeon River in question non-navigable for traffic then carried on.

It appears that some of these falls are 120 ft. in height, and that the total drop in this part of the river is 620 ft. All the waters of these streams that were navigable were in use for transportation at the time of the treaty, and at the parts of the river not navigable the portages were used. In my opinion the right preserved by the passage of the treaty quoted was the right to continue to use the water communication and portages then in use. ... What was being dealt with, and what was in the contemplation of the parties, was travel and transportation over the water communications and portages as then used, and there was in my opinion no thought or intention of dealing with the use of these non-navigable rapids and falls that were not in use and could not be used, the passing of which was provided for by the portages. ...

In my opinion the passage of the Ashburton Treaty quoted above does not apply to the non-navigable part of Pigeon River in which the works in question are situated.

The appeal should be allowed ... .

LAMONT J.: ... The first question requiring consideration is: Does the imposition of tolls by the appellants, under s. 52 ... [of the Act] for the use of improvements made by them on Pigeon River, conflict with the provisions of ... the Ashburton-Webster Treaty. ...

1. ... what is the meaning to be given to "water communications" in ... [the Treaty]? These are to be kept "free and open" for the use of the subjects of both countries, as are also the usual portages "along the line," ...

In construing the treaty we have to determine the intentions of the framers thereof as expressed in the words used. Did they intend that the whole river should come within the term "water communications," or only those parts of it between portages over which boats could pass at the date of the treaty? In order to understand these words it is material to inquire what was the subject-matter with respect to which they were used, and the object the framers of the treaty had in view? The subject-matter to which they were applied was the waters of the Pigeon River, and other rivers, streams and lakes up which the boundary line from Lake Superior to the Lake of the Woods was being run. The object of the provision was to secure to the subjects of both countries the free and untrammeled right to use these water stretches irrespective of whether they were on one side of the boundary line or the other.

Although at the date of the treaty the chief purpose for which these water communications were being used was the transportation by boat or canoe of persons and goods, the clause in question places no limit on the purposes for which they might be used. They are to be "free and open" to the people of both countries for whatever purpose they may desire to use them as a water communication. If, therefore, they could be used for any purpose which did not necessitate the making of a portage to get past a point of danger, I see nothing in the clause, or in any other part of the treaty, which would compel the use of the portage in order to have a free passage. To hold that water communications should be limited to those portions of the river navigable by boats at the time the treaty was signed, would, in my opinion, be to give too narrow a construction to the language used, and to impute a want of vision to the framers of the treaty.

Furthermore such a construction would lead to the result that certain portions of the river around which portages had to be made at the date of the treaty owing to low water, would not constitute a water communication at another season when boats could pass over them with ease and safety. ...

If a river may properly be called navigable notwithstanding that it is necessary to make use of portages at certain points, it would seem equally appropriate to designate it as a "water communication ... ."

2. I cannot agree with the appellants' contention that the words "free and open" in the last clause of art. 2, are consistent with the imposition of tolls for the use of improvements erected in the river. In my opinion the meaning of these words in the clause is that the citizens of both countries are to be at liberty, as a matter of right, to travel these waters on both sides of the fixed boundary line without let or hindrance from anyone, or having to pay anything for so doing. This seems to me to be the natural and ordinary meaning of the words and the meaning which, at the time of the treaty, the subjects of both countries would place upon them. That this is the meaning the words were intended to bear seems to me to be indicated also by art. 7 of the treaty, which reads: –

VII. It is further agreed that the channels in the River St. Lawrence on both sides of the Long Sault Island and of Barnhart Island, the channels in the River Detroit, on both sides of the Island Bois Blanc, and between that island and both the Canadian and American shores, and all the several channels and passages between the various islands lying near the junction of the River St. Clair with the lake of that name, shall be equally free and open to the ships, vessels, and boats of both Parties.

If we give effect to the appellants' interpretation of the words "free and open" it would entitle either of the contracting parties who improved the navigation of any of the channels on its own side of these waters to levy a toll on every vessel making use of such channel. I cannot believe such to have been the intention of the parties. As Riddell, J.A. pointed out in his judgment below, ... at 578–79, the appellants here by building upon the bed of the river have interfered with the enjoyment of the free and open use of it by the citizens of the United States. This, as I read it, is contrary to the treaty. The result, therefore is, that in my opinion, s. 52 of the Lakes and Rivers Improvement Act, insofar as it authorizes the imposition of tolls for the use of improvements erected in the Pigeon River, is at variance with the provisions of the treaty.

The next question is: Does the fact that s. 52 is repugnant to the provisions of the treaty make the section invalid as a legislative enactment?

The Second Divisional Court thought that because a former Sovereign had been a party to the treaty and His Majesty was in honour bound to uphold it, and, as the Act in question was passed in His Majesty's name, it should not be given a construction inconsistent with the terms of the treaty if it could fairly be otherwise interpreted. The Court referred to s. 32 of the Act for the purpose of showing that the company was incorporated only for the "acquiring or constructing and maintaining and operating works upon any lake or river in Ontario," and held that as Pigeon River was only partly in Ontario the Act was not intended to apply to that river.

That Pigeon River is only in part in the Province of Ontario, does not, in my opinion, render the Act inapplicable to that part, for provincial legislative enactments, unless restricted as to the area to which they shall apply, effectively operate throughout the whole Province.

Had the Legislature intended to exclude international boundary rivers from the operation of the Act, I think it would have said so in express terms and not have left the matter to inference, particularly when the inference can only be drawn by giving an unusual construction to the language used. The view that the Act was intended to apply to international boundary waters in so far as they were in Ontario is, I think, supported by the reference to such waters in s. 14. The Act, being applicable to boundary waters, was it, in other respects, within the competence of the Legislature to enact.

It has long been well settled by the Privy Council that within the provincial area and the ambit of the classes of subjects enumerated in s. 92 of the B.N.A. Act, 1867, the legislative competence of a provincial Legislature is as plenary and as ample as the Imperial Parliament in the plenitude of its power possessed, and could bestow. That the subject-matter of the Act in question falls within the enumerated heads of s. 92 is not disputed nor indeed could it well be. ... The Act must, therefore, be held to be valid unless the existence of the treaty of itself imposes a limitation upon the provincial legislative power. In my opinion the treaty alone cannot be considered as having that effect. The treaty in itself is not equivalent to an Imperial Act and, without the sanction of Parliament, the Crown cannot alter the existing law by entering into a contract with a foreign power. For a breach of a treaty a nation is responsible only to the other contracting nation and its own sense of right and justice. Where, as here, a treaty provides that certain rights or privileges are to be enjoyed by the subjects of both contracting parties, these rights and privileges are, under our law, enforceable by the Courts only where the treaty has been implemented or sanctioned by legislation rendering it binding upon the subject. Upon this point I agree with the view expressed by both Courts below, ''that in British countries treaties to which Great Britain is a party are not as such binding upon the individual subject but are only contracts binding in honour upon the contracting states.'' ...

In the case before us it is not suggested that any legislation, Imperial or Canadian, was ever passed implementing or sanctioning the provision of the treaty that the water communications above referred to should be free and open to the subjects of both countries. That provision, therefore, has only the force of a contract between Great Britain and the United States which is ineffectual to impose any limitation upon the legislative power exclusively bestowed by the Imperial Parliament upon the Legislature of a Province. In the absence of affirming legislation this provision of the treaty cannot be enforced by any of our Courts whose authority is derived from municipal law. ...

I am, therefore, of opinion that s. 52, in question in this appeal, must be considered to be a valid enactment until the treaty is implemented by Imperial or Dominion legislation.

The appeal should be allowed. ...

ANGLIN C.J.C.: ... I agree in the allowance of this appeal largely for the reasons stated by my brothers Lamont and Smith. I should, however, have preferred it had the majority of the Court seen its way clear to base its decision upon a holding that, upon the true construction of the clause of the Ashburton Treaty ... , it was merely meant to ensure to the citizens of both countries equality of rights in regard to the water communications, portages, etc., and that it never was intended thereby to provide that in no event should either party to the treaty be at liberty, as regards citizens of its own nationality, to impose tolls for the use of improvements lawfully to be made thereon.

In other words, where either party to the treaty saw fit to impose tolls upon its own citizens, in regard to such improvements, it should be at liberty to impose like tolls (but none greater) on citizens of the other country for the use of the improvements so made. Otherwise, it would follow that neither country could impose any tolls whatsoever upon its own citizens, because that would interfere with the water communications, portages, etc., being "free and open" to the use of the subjects and citizens of both countries.

[Rinfret J. concurred with Smith J., while Cannon J. concurred with Lamont J.]

NOTES

1) Riddell J.A., in the Ontario Court of Appeal, in the face of a conflict between the Ashburton Treaty and the Ontario Act construed it away in favour of the treaty. Smith J. in the Supreme Court reached the opposite solution. How could they do so? What principles of Canadian or international law would support which decision?

2) Although Anglin C.J.C. said he agreed largely with the reasons of Lamont and Smith JJ., what approach to treaty application did he seem to take?

3) Since the Ashburton Treaty is unimplemented, Lamont J., who acknowledged the conflict of the statutory and treaty provisions, was able to resolve the dispute in favour of the Ontario Act according to traditional transformationist theory. What would be the effect of implementation today? Who should implement this treaty?[30] Can Parliament legislate in conflict with provincial law so as to override it? Always? In this case? May a province pass legislation contrary to a treaty *after* its implementation, either by Parliament or the provincial Legislature?[31]

4) Was Lamont J.'s resort to traditional theory adequate for this case? This was a boundary treaty: does it have any distinctive effect? The treaty was made in 1842: do its provisions have any legal force other than as part of a treaty?

Application of Unimplemented Treaties

Although the courts have said often enough that a treaty must be transformed by legislation in order to change Canadian law, they have not wholly excluded the influence of unimplemented conventions. As the *Arrow River* case itself shows, the courts will do their best to avoid interpretations of internal law which would violate Canada's treaty obligations. But how far may these best efforts be taken? Here are two recent opinions of the Supreme Court on the impact of treaties in Canadian law.

Capital Cities Communications Inc. v. Canadian Radio-Television Commission
(1978), 81 D.L.R. (3d) 609 (S.C.C.)

[Under authorization of the C.R.T.C., the Rogers group of cablevision companies in Southern Ontario deleted commercial messages from television signals they received from

---

[30] Consider the materials *supra* in Chapter 3 on "Treaty Implementation in Canada" and note the comment of Professor Macdonald that the Ashburton Treaty "was not made 'as part of the British Empire' ... it was made to apply to Canada and the United States only and thus section 132 [of the *Constitution Act, 1867*] would not have applied," *supra*, n. 1, at 135, n. 138.

[31] See the discussion on "Power to Legislate Contrary to International Law?" *supra*.

the United States and substituted local public service announcements before transmitting the programmes to their subscribers. Capital Cities Communications, one of the American programme suppliers, challenged the C.R.T.C.'s decision in part on the ground that it had been made contrary to the Inter-American Radio Communications Convention. Three arguments concerning the application of this Convention were advanced:]

LASKIN C.J.C. for the majority: ... Counsel for the appellants made a number of submissions connected with Canada's adherence as a party to the Inter-American Radio Communications Convention of 1937 to which the United States was also a party. The submissions, which were put forward in challenge of the validity of the decision of the Commission to permit deletion of the commercial messages emanating from the appellants as part of their programmes, were as follows: (1) The Commission was an agent of the Canadian Government and as such bound by the terms of the Convention; (2) the *Broadcasting Act* should be interpreted in the light of the Convention, or in such a way as not to violate Canada's international obligations thereunder; and (3), the most important submission, the implementation of the Convention to have domestic effect was prescribed by s. 3(1)(c) of the *Radio Act*, 1938 (Can.), c. 50, and such implementation is presently in place pursuant to s. 7(1)(d) and s. 8 of the *Radio Act*, R.S.C. 1970, c. R-1, and under s. 11 of the *General Radio Regulations, Part II*, SOR/63–297, which makes effective as part of federal law arts. 11 and 21 of the Convention.

The Convention under discussion was signed by Canada and other parties thereto on December 13, 1937, and ratified by Canada on December 22, 1938, on which date Parts I, III and IV thereof became effective. Part III which consists of arts. 11 to 22 inclusive is the relevant part of the Convention for present purposes. Section 3(1)(c) of the *Radio Act, 1938* reads as follows:

3.(1) The Governor in Council may ...

    (c) accede to any international convention in connection with radio, and make such regulations as may be necessary to carry out and make effective the terms of such convention ...

The present *Radio Act*, by s. 7(1)(d), confers upon the responsible Minister the power to make regulations

    (d) to carry out and make effective the terms of any international agreement, convention or treaty respecting telecommunications to which Canada is a party;

Section 8(1) [rep. & sub. 1974–75, c. 49, s. 18] is in these terms:

8.(1) The Minister shall take such action as may be necessary to secure, by international regulation or otherwise, the rights of Her Majesty in right of Canada in telecommunications matters and shall consult the Canadian Radio-television and Telecommunications Commission with respect to all such matters, that, in his opinion, affect or concern broadcasting.

Turning to the appellant's submission in the order in which they were made, I am unable to appreciate how it can be said that the Commission is an agent or arm of the Canadian Government and as such bound by the Convention provisions in the same way as the Government. There is nothing in the *Broadcasting Act*, nor was our attention directed to any other legislation which would give the Commission any other status than that of a federal regulatory agency established with defined statutory powers. There is nothing to show that it derives any authority from the Convention or that the Convention, *per se*, qualifies the regulatory authority conferred upon the Commission by the *Broadcasting Act*. Indeed, if the contention of the appellants has any force under its first submission it can only relate to the obligations of Canada under the Convention towards other ratifying signatories. There would be no domestic, internal consequences unless they arose from implementing legislation giving the Convention a legal effect within Canada.

The second submission asks this Court to say that the provisions of the *Broadcasting Act* are ambiguous in so far as they relate to the powers of the Commission, and that as an aid to their construction resort would be had to the terms of the Convention. I do not find any ambiguity that would require resort to the Convention, which is, in any event, nowhere mentioned in the *Broadcasting Act*; and certainly the Convention *per se* cannot prevail against the express stipulations of the Act: *cf. R. v. Chief Immigration Officer, Heathrow Airport et al., Ex p. Salamat Bibi*, [1976] 3 All E.R. 843 at 850.

This brings me to the final submission as to the effect, if any, of an alleged implementation of the Convention so as to restrict the powers of the Commission.

I do not see how s. 8(1) of the *Radio Act* has any bearing on the point advanced by the appellants, but s. 7(1)(d) and existing Regulations under the *Radio Act* must be considered. "Telecommunications" referred to in s. 7(1)(d) is defined in s. 2 of the *Radio Act* as follows:

"telecommunication" means any transmission, emission or reception of signs, signals, writing, images or sounds or intelligence of any nature by wire, radio, visual or other electromagnetic system.

This is a definition which in its mention of "radio" embraces, of course, the meaning given to "radio" in s. 2 of the Act, and that meaning is a description of Hertzian waves. The appellants point to s. 11 of the *General Radio Regulations, Part II* as applicable to the present case and to the Rogers companies. It is in these terms:

11. The licensee shall observe the provisions of the International Telecommunication Convention and any bilateral or multi-lateral telecommunication agreements for the time being in force and those regulations pertaining to the operation of radio that are made under the said convention and agreements.

The contention is that the Convention relied upon here was in force pursuant to the *Radio Act, 1938* and is now covered by s. 11 aforementioned. The particular terms of the Convention invoked by the appellants are arts. 11 and 21. Article 11 is a provision entitled "General Principles" and reads as follows:

Article 11
GENERAL PRINCIPLES

(a) The contracting Governments recognize the sovereign right of all nations to the use of every radio broadcasting channel.

(b) The American Governments, upon the sole condition that no interference will be caused to the services of another country, may assign any frequency and any type of wave to any radio station under their authority.

(c) Nevertheless, the Governments recognize that, until technical development reaches a state that permits the elimination of radio interference of international character, regional arrangements are essential in order to promote standardization and to minimize such interference.

(d) For the solution of those problems which, because of special propagation characteristics and interference conditions of radio transmission in the various geographical zones require special provisions, the contracting Governments agree to divide the American continent into three regions, designated as the northern zone, the central zone, and the southern zone (Annex 3).

Assuming that this article has any application to television, I do not see how it assists the appellants' contention that the powers of the Commission, so far as they were used to authorize the deletion of commercial messages from the programmes of the appellants, are restricted thereby. Article 11 merely confirms national claims to the use of radio channels and to the right of the signatories to the Convention to assign radio frequencies provided this will not cause interference to the services of another signatory. It is concerned with the elimination of radio interference, as for example through overlapping frequencies, and not with programming.

There is, moreover, another answer to this third submission of the appellants. Section 11 of the *General Radio Regulations, Part II* concerns licensees under the *Radio Act*, and it is the fact that the Rogers companies hold only technical construction and operating certificates under the *Radio Act*; their programming licences are held under the *Broadcasting Act* which is not a statute in implementation of the Convention.

Article 21 of the Convention, under the heading "Retransmissions," reads:

Article 21
RETRANSMISSIONS

The contracting Governments shall take appropriate measures to ensure that no program transmitted by a broadcasting station may be retransmitted or rebroadcast, in whole or in part, by any other station without the previous authorization of the station of origin.

The rebroadcasting station shall announce at suitable periods during the retransmission the nature of the broadcast, the location and the official call letters or other identification of the station of origin.

One answer to the arguments of the appellants under this article was provided by Ryan, J., in the Federal Court of Appeal, noting in his reasons that "any other station" refers to any other broadcasting station, and the Rogers companies are not of that class but are rather broadcasting receiving undertakings. Further, as pointed out by the respondent, art. 21 itself contemplates particular implementation of its provisions by the contracting Governments, and only if there has been such implementation and to the extent thereof can domestic force be given to the article. In the present case, although licences issued to cable distribution systems prior to 1970 included a provision against the alteration of any signals received from a broadcasting station without the consent of that station, the regulation which authorized this condition was revoked in 1970, and there is no longer any prohibition against authorizing alterations of signals received from a broadcasting station. I should add that it is by no means clear that art. 21 of the Convention has any application to cable distribution systems but I need not decide that here.

In the result, I would dismiss the appeal ... .

PIGEON J. for the dissenting minority: ... The next question is whether the appellants can rely on the International Convention on an appeal to the Courts from the decision of the Commission. The *Radio Act*, R.S.C. 1970, c. R-1, s. 7, includes the following provision:

7.(1) The Minister may make regulations ...
    (d) to carry out and make effective the terms of any international agreement, convention or treaty respecting telecommunications to which Canada is a party;

Pursuant to the predecessor of this enactment, the *General Radio Regulations, Part II*, established by SOR/63–297, included the following provision which is still in force:

11. The licensee shall observe the provisions of the International Telecommunication Convention and any bilateral or multi-lateral telecommunication agreements for the time being in force and those regulations pertaining to the operation of radio that are made under the said convention and agreements.

When this Regulation was enacted, all radio licences including those of TV stations and CATV networks were issued under the *Radio Act*. However, when the *Broadcasting Act* was enacted in 1968 (1967–68 (Can.), c. 25), it was provided that licences to broadcasting undertakings, an expression which includes CATV as well as TV stations, would be issued by the Commission with the Department of Transport issuing a ''technical construction and operating certificate.'' Rogers' submission is that, as a result of this change, they are not licensees within the meaning of s. 11 of the Regulations. In my view, such technical construction of the section is unjustified. The word ''licensee'' is not defined in the *General Radio Regulations, Part II*, or in the *Radio Act*. Under ordinary circumstances it would apply only to licensees under that Act. However, this is a very special situation. The licensing function has been divided between two governmental authorities. Although Rogers are not licensees under the *Radio Act*, they are licensees in respect of their broadcasting undertaking. Nothing in the legislation enacted in 1968 or in the amendments to the Regulations indicates any intention to free broadcasting undertakings from the obligation of complying with Convention provisions. Section 11 of the Regulations was merely left unchanged. Under such circumstances this should mean that its scope and meaning remain unchanged.

Even on the assumption that s. 11 of the Regulations is now applicable to broadcasting undertakings, I cannot agree that the Commission may properly issue authorizations in violation of Canada's treaty obligations. Its duty is to implement the policy established by Parliament. While this policy makes no reference to Canada's treaty obligations, it is an integral part of the national structure that external affairs are the responsibility of the federal Government. It is an over-simplification to say that treaties are of no legal effect unless implemented by legislation. ...

Applying those principles, I would say that, on the appeal from the decision of the Commission, judicial notice ought to be taken that, by virtue of the Convention the appellants had a legal interest entitled to protection in the use of their assigned channels, for broadcasts in an area extending into Canada. Therefore the Commission could not validly authorize an interference with this interest in violation of the convention signed by Canada. ...

For these reasons I would allow the appeal. ...

Schavernoch v. Foreign Claims Commission
(1982), 136 D.L.R. (3d) 447 (S.C.C.)

[Under an agreement made in 1973, Czechoslovakia paid to Canada $3,250,000 as a lump sum settlement of all claims by Canadians for property which had been expropriated by Czechoslovakia. The Canadian government subsequently issued regulations for the distribution of this money to Canadian claimants. The appellant applied to the respondent Commission for payment of her claim but it was denied on the grounds that she was ineligible because her dominant nationality was Czechoslovakian, not Canadian, at the appropriate times.]

ESTEY J. for the Court: ... The narrow problem which arises is whether or not the Commission or a court reviewing the decision of the Commission may interpret the provisions of the *Foreign Claims (Czechoslovakia) Settlement Regulations* by reference to the agreement of 1973 or such clearly extraneous matters as the report from negotiators of the agreement, including the Canadian Ambassador. For example, the reference to dominant or primary citizenship is nowhere to be found in the regulations under which the appellant makes her claim. The entitlement is defined rather in terms only of a Canadian citizen who is defined as being a person who is a Canadian citizen according to the Canadian *Citizenship Act*. I emphasize that we here assume the appellant so qualifies.

If one could assert an ambiguity, either patent or latent, in the regulations it might be that a court could find support for making reference to matters external to the regulations in order to interpret its terms. Because, however, there is in my view no ambiguity arising from the above-quoted excerpt from these regulations, there is no authority and none was drawn to our attention in argument entitling a court to take recourse either to an underlying international agreement or to textbooks on international law with reference to the negotiation of agreements or to take recourse to reports made to the Government of Canada by persons engaged in the negotiation referred to in the regulations.

We are confined entirely to the definition of Canadian citizen drawn from the *Citizenship Act* and for the purposes of this appeal it has been assumed, as I have said, that the appellant so qualifies.

Even if it were accepted that reference could be made to the agreement the further difficulty arises: should a tribunal seek support from the negotiators' report? Nowhere in the agreement is any reference made to the limitation of Canadian claims to those holding *only* Canadian citizenship. Duality of citizenship is not mentioned, nor is there any reference to primary or dominant citizenship. Indeed the agreement reveals no reliance by the Government of Czechoslovakia on any entitlement to release of claims by persons holding Canadian citizenship only, or of freedom from claims by persons who hold whatever a dominant Czechoslovakian citizenship may be found to be. ...

Extensive references were laid before the court concerning the negotiation of rights by countries for compensation of their nationals by reason of expropriations or confiscation by other countries. These conventions or customs may find some validity in proceedings in specified international tribunals or perhaps even in domestic tribunals where specific legislative authority has made them operative. Here the regulations fall to be interpreted according to the maxims of interpretation applicable to Canadian domestic law generally. The only rule of interpretation which seems to have any bearing in these proceedings is the plain meaning rule because no ambiguity can be found either in the Order in Council or indeed in the agreement therein referred to if the latter step may be validly taken. ...

I therefore would allow the appeal ... and ... would remit these proceedings to the Commission for determination of the appellant's claim in accordance with the *Foreign Claims (Czechoslovakia) Settlement Regulations* as interpreted.

NOTES

1) In *Capital Cities Communications v. C.R.T.C.* Laskin C.J. and Pigeon J. differed radically over the status and authority of the C.R.T.C. to apply international law. Which is the preferable approach towards administrative agencies?

2) Laskin C.J. in the *Capital Cities* case and Estey J. in the *Schavernoch* case were both adamant that, unless some ambiguity can be shown to exist in a statute or in regulations, there is no reason to consider the treaty in the background. How does this attitude compare with the approach of the Supreme Court justices in *Re Arrow River?*[32] Does it make a difference whether the court is asked to refer to the treaty in order 1) to determine the outcome of the case directly by using it as the relevant decisional law, 2) to remedy gaps and ambiguities in domestic rules, or 3) to overturn a rule otherwise enforceable by a domestic court?[33]

---

[32] And see *Re Mitchell and The Queen* (1983), 42 O.R. (2d) 481 (H.C.), at 482; and M. Cohen and A.F. Bayefsky *supra*, n. 1, at 298.

[33] See J. Claydon, "The Application of Human Rights Law by Canadian Courts" (1981), 30 *Buff. L. Rev.* 727.

3) As these cases also show incidentally, the influence of a treaty depends upon its interpretation. This is another topic of fertile discussion. The chief question in a domestic context is whether Canadian courts should approach treaties in the same way as statutes or whether they should take the broader approach practised in international law. The issue is particularly acute when the treaty is implemented, i.e., when the court is called upon to interpret a treaty incorporated into a statute. These matters of treaty interpretation are taken up under ''Legal Effects of Treaties'' in Chapter 3.

4) The situation regarding unimplemented treaty obligations is obviously not satisfactory so some attention should be given to ways to improve it. Professor Macdonald has made the following suggestion:[34]

> We must ask again, what domestic status should be accorded a signed and ratified treaty which has no legislative implementation? At present, according to the *Arrow River* rule, it has none if it affects a change in domestic law. The reasons for this were seen to be the problems pertaining to the separation and division of powers. It is submitted that, on the basis of the foregoing discussion, the division of powers difficulty should and could be done away with either by an overruling of the *Labour Conventions* case or by dominion-provincial negotiation. As to the separation of powers between the crown and parliament, it is submitted that this could be preserved while still enabling (and forcing) Canada to fulfil her international obligations by according ratified but unimplemented treaties a status superior to common law but inferior to statute. Thus, if a ratified treaty changed domestic law which was not covered by statute, the treaty would be effective even without legislation. If the treaty changed domestic law governed by statute, the statute and the treaty would be interpreted to avoid conflict, but if that were impossible then the statute would rule until and unless the treaty were implemented by legislation. Thus parliament would still have the final word, yet Canada's solemn international commitments would have some meaning.

How could this change be brought about? Would it be worth making?

Influence on Canadian Law

There are two aspects to the influence of international law on Canadian law. The formal one concerns the process of applying international law, which is bound up with the domestic law concepts of judicial notice and *stare decisis*. The substantive aspect reflects the impact of international legal principles on the content of Canadian law.

As to the procedural interaction of international and Canadian law, Professor Macdonald has commented:[35]

> Throughout our discussion of both the English and Canadian courts' handling of customary international rules, the concept of judicial notice has played a silent but fundamental role; for without it, the entry of these customary rules into our domestic law would be much more complicated. ...
> According to *Black's Law Dictionary*, judicial notice is

---

[34] *Supra*, n. 1, at 127.
[35] *Supra*, n. 1 at 111.

... the act by which a court, in conducting a trial, or framing its decision, will, of its own motion, and without the production of evidence, recognize the existence and truth of certain facts, having a bearing on the controversy at bar, which, from their nature, are not properly the subject of testimony, or which are universally regarded as established by common notoriety, e.g. the laws of the state, international law, historical events, the constitution and course of nature, main geographical features, etc. ...

Fortunately, it is true, as Lauterpacht pointed out, that "international law need not be proved in the same way as foreign law or any other fact must be proved – apparently for the reason that it is not foreign law." He continued: "Judicial notice is taken of it as of Acts of Parliament or of any branch of the unwritten law, although having regard to the frequent absence of direct authority the range of judicial inquiry is wider and, on occasions, more laborious than in the case of ordinary rules of municipal law." ...

In Canada, also, the standard practice has been to notice judicially international law, although, as in England, the Canadian courts have not usually seen fit to comment on this point directly. There have, however, been several judicial comments which make clear that international law is judicially noticed in the same way that domestic law is. In *The North*,[36] Davies J., in upholding the lower court finding, said that the hot pursuit doctrine "being part of the law of nations was properly judicially taken notice of and acted upon." This statement can only mean that customary rules which are part of international law are to be judicially noticed. In the *Armed Forces* reference,[37] Taschereau J. saw his task as, first, "to seek if there exists" the customary rule in question. The implication in this statement is that it is the judge who must do the seeking, just as he does in domestic law; in fact, in domestic law, the task could be described using exactly the same words: to seek if there exists the domestic rule in question. The conclusion that international law is being treated as part of domestic law in this regard is inescapable.

The most explicit statement about the use of international law by Canadian courts was made by Rand J. in *Saint John v. Fraser-Brace Overseas Corp.*, previously reported.[38] Notice how he admonished the courts to "seek the rule which reason and good sense would prescribe." This directive, he interpreted, required courts to take judicial notice of contemporary international rules without too much regard for previous domestic precedents. How could Rand J. override the doctrine of *stare decisis*?

More recently, Pigeon J. also resorted expressly to judicial notice. In his dissent in the *Capital Cities* case, previously reported,[39] he spoke about the implications for the C.R.T.C. of an unimplemented treaty whose provisions would restrain its powers. Did he invoke judicial notice in the same way as Rand J. – as the means to apply an international rule – or was he indicating some other influence for international law, perhaps as part of the public policy of Canadian law?

---

[36] *The King v. The Ship North* (1906), 36 S.C.R. 385.

[37] *Reference re Exemption of U.S. Forces from Canadian Criminal Law*, [1943] S.C.R. 483.

[38] *Supra*. And see Rand J.'s opinion in *Reference re Exemption of U.S. Forces, supra*, n. 37, at 524. In *Pan American World Airways Inc. v. The Queen* (1979), 96 D.L.R. (3d) 267 (F.C.T.D.), Mahoney J. confirmed that international need not be proved like foreign law, and therefore expert opinion as to the construction of a treaty is inadmissible as evidence but may be adopted as argument.

[39] *Supra*.

Regarding the substantive influence of international law, Canadian jurisprudence has many examples of cases which have reviewed international instruments as a means of analyzing Canadian law. The influence is most pronounced in the area of human rights, which is explored fully in Chapter 10. In *Re Drummond Wren*,[40] MacKay J. referred to the U.N. Charter, the Atlantic Charter and the statements of various world leaders condemning racial discrimination as a means of defining "public policy" for the purpose of striking out a restrictive covenant which prohibited the sale of land "to Jews or persons of objectionable nationality" as void as against public policy. In *Re Alberta Provincial Employees and the Crown*,[41] Sinclair, C.J.Q.B., extensively reviewed I.L.O. Conventions in order to consider the question of whether an Alberta Statute prohibiting the right to strike in certain public services violated Canada's international obligations. (He concluded that there was no such customary rule established in international law and therefore did not have to deal with the question of what effect this would have had on the statute in question.) In *Bhadauria v. Board of Governors of Seneca College*[42] the Ontario Court of Appeal referred to international instruments as a way of defining a tort of racial discrimination, a view which was rejected by the Supreme Court of Canada on the grounds that an unimplemented international agreement could not create independent rights at common law.[43]

It has sometimes been suggested that the international law of human rights might be considered in a different light than international law in general insofar as its application in the domestic legal system is concerned.[44] In this respect it is somewhat disappointing that the *Canadian Charter of Rights and Freedoms* makes no express reference to Canada's international obligations.[45] That is not to say however that decisions involving the Charter, its interpretation and application, do not refer to international law. Quite the contrary, the references are numerous.[46] In *Re Service Employees' International Union, Local 204 and Broadway Manor Nursing Home*,[47] for example, the Court extensively reviewed United Nations instruments and I.L.O. Conventions. In *Re Singh and Minister of Employment and Immigration*[48] the Supreme Court had to consider the application of *Charter* rights to a person claiming status as a "convention refugee." In so doing the Court was clearly conscious of the role which international law played in that process. In a recent article one commentator listed some 41 cases where international law or international

---

[40] [1945] 4 D.L.R. 674 (Ont. H.C.).
[41] (1980), 120 D.L.R. (3d) 590 (Alta. Q.B.).
[42] (1979), 105 D.L.R. (3d) 707 (Ont. C.A.).
[43] (1981), 124 D.L.R. (3d) 193 (S.C.C.).
[44] B. Schluter, "The Domestic Status of the Human Rights Clauses of the United Nations Charter" (1973), 61 *Cal. L. Rev.* 110. And see the remarkable American case, *Filartiga v. Pena Irala* (1980), 630 F. 2d 876 (U.S.C.A. 2d Circ.) reported *infra* in Chapter 10.
[45] I. Cotler, in Tarnapolsky and Beaudoin, *Canadian Charter of Rights and Freedoms* (1982), at 136, citing J. Humphrey, "Canada's International Obligations Under the International Covenant on Civil and Political Rights," unpub., 1982, at 1.
[46] See Cohen and Bayefsky, *supra*, n. 1; D. Turp, "Le Recours au Droit International aux Fins de L'Interpretation de la Charte Canadienne des Droits et Libertes: Un Bilan Jurisprudentiel" (1984), 18 *R.J.T.* 353.
[47] (1984), 44 O.R. (2d) 392 (Ont. Div. Ct.).
[48] [1985] 1 S.C.R. 177.

instruments were cited as a means of interpreting the *Charter*.[49] Considering the similarity of language contained in the *Charter* to that found in such basic texts as the Covenant on Civil and Political Rights and the European Convention on Human Rights, to name but two, and considering also that the *Charter* represents a fusion of classic liberties and human rights which may be found also in these other systems, such a result is quite understandable. Indeed its application may well lead to a "Multi-national-transcultural-international approach to patterns of interpretation"[50] thus linking the development of this important part of the Canadian legal system to its international and foreign counterparts. It could well lead to a revision of how we view the way in which international norms are to be applied in the domestic legal system generally.

Meanwhile legislation continues to apply internationally developed norms in order to bring Canadian law and practice into conformity with developments in the international sphere. One very recent example is the passing, by various provinces, and the federal government of legislation to implement the New York Convention on the Recognition and Enforcement of Foreign Arbitral awards.[51] Another is the adoption, by several jurisdictions, of the UNCITRAL Model Law on International Commercial Arbitration which introduces notions quite different from those which have prevailed in arbitration law in Canada up until this time.[52]

A striking example of the influence which the evolution of international law has had on Canadian law may be found in recent revisions to the *Criminal Code*. They represent a radical departure from its previous territorial scope in order to respond to transnational events. Thus in cases of aircraft hijacking, terrorism and crimes directed towards internationally protected persons the Code will now apply extraterritorially, even going so far as to apply the protective personality principle in favour of Canadian citizens taken hostage abroad.[53] These developments are clearly in response to, and are predicated upon, international agreements which have created a new international legal climate favoring the extension of national jurisdiction in order to ensure the suppression of these evils.[54] Similar trends may be observed in respect of the Law of the Sea, where extensions of Canadian jurisdiction have sometimes preceded and contributed to, and sometimes followed, the evolution of new international concepts of jurisdiction in what was formerly the high seas.[55]

---

[49] D. Turp, *supra*, n. 46.

[50] Cohen and Bayefsky, *supra*, n. 1, at 310.

[51] (1959), 330 U.N.T.S. 3, implemented by Canada in the *United Nations Foreign Arbitral Awards Convention Act*, S.C. 1986, c. 21. See also S.B.C. 1985, c. 74; S.A. 1986, c. I-66; S.S. 1986, c. E-9.11; Man. Bill 35 (1986); S.O. 1986, c. 25; S.N.B. 1986, c. I-12.2; S.P.E.I. 1986, c. 14; S.N.S. 1986, c. 12; and S.N. 1986, c. 45.

[52] Adopted in Vienna, June 1985 and implemented in Canada by the *Commercial Arbitration Act*, S.C. 1986, c. 22, and provincially in S.B.C. 1986, c. 14; S.A. 1986; c. I-6.6; Man. Bill 35 (1986); Que. Bill 91 (1986); S.N.B. 1986, c. I-12.2; S.P.E.I. 1986, c. 14; S.N.S. 1986, c. 12; and S.N. 1986, c. 45.

[53] Criminal Code of Canada, ss. 6(1.3) to (1.8), and 247.1, enacted by the *Criminal Law Amendment Act, 1985*, Stats. Can. 1985, c. 19, ss. 5(3) and 41(1).

[54] See the treaty texts and discussion concerning "Hijacking and Other Terrorist Acts," *infra* in Chapter 8.

[55] See A. Gotlieb and C. Dalfen, "National Jurisdiction and International Responsibility: New Canadian Approaches to International Law" (1973), 67 *Am. J. Int. L.* 229.

Rousseau Metal Inc. v. The Queen
unreported, F.C.T.D. no. T-8194-82, Oct. 4, 1985, rev'd F.C.A.
no. A–816–85, Jan. 23, 1987

[Rousseau Metal, a Canadian company, was one of three bidders on a request for proposals from the Department of Supply and Services for tool cabinets to be used in Canadian army trucks. The contract was awarded to Stanley-Vidmar Inc., a U.S. company, as the lowest bidder. Rousseau Metal was classified as the second lowest bidder but claimed damages for loss of the contract on the grounds that the bids had been wrongly evaluated. Initially the Department had indicated that the Canadian content of the product and customs duties would be taken into account, but, after Canada acceded to the GATT Agreement on Government Procurement, the request for proposals was modified to reflect the new Agreement. Although Rousseau Metal was informed about the changes, it alleged that it had been misled by government officials into incurring heavy expenses and that the contract had been awarded contrary to the Department's own terms and conditions.]

DENAULT J. at trial: ... It can be noted, ... government officials took some time to understand and apply the provisions of the Agreement on Government Procurement, which came into force on January 1, 1981. Thus the plaintiff was for a long time given to understand that the Canadian content of its product would be taken into account and that customs duty would be imposed. Since there was no formal request for tenders or proposals at the time, however, this cannot be held against the defendant.

From the time the product qualified, however, the plaintiff's representative established that he was most concerned with the tendering procedure and in particular the way in which the proposals were to be evaluated. Although there were beginning to be clear indications that Canadian content would not be a factor favouring a Canadian bidder, this was not at all the case with customs duty. Not only were customs duties mentioned when the plaintiff sought information in this regard, but Mr. Tremblay, the DSS officer, for greater certainty obtained a ruling (P-30) which confirmed his interpretation of the Agreement on Government Procurement (GATT) and the Defence Supplies Remission Order (DSRO).

It is worth considering these documents briefly. As mentioned earlier, Canada acceded to the Agreement on Government Procurement signed pursuant to the General Agreement on Tariffs and Trade (GATT) on January 1, 1981. Article II deals with national treatment and non-discrimination. It reads as follows:

Article II
NATIONAL TREATMENT AND NON-DISCRIMINATION

1. With respect to all laws, regulations, procedures and practices regarding government procurement covered by this Agreement, parties to this Agreement shall provide immediately and unconditionally to the products and suppliers of other parties offering products originating within the customs territories (including free zones) of the parties to this Agreement treatment no less favourable than:

    (a)   that accorded to domestic products and suppliers; and

(b) that accorded to products and suppliers of any other party.

2. The provisions of paragraph 1 shall not apply to customs duties and charges of any kind imposed on or in connection with importation, the method of levying such duties and charges, and other import regulations and formalities.

3. Parties to this Agreement shall not apply rules of origin to products imported for purposes of government procurement covered by this Agreement from other parties to this Agreement, which are different from the rules of origin applied in the normal course of trade and at the time of importation to imports of the same products from the same parties to this Agreement.

Paragraph V.12 reads in part as follows:

Article V
TENDERING PROCEDURES

12. Tender documentation provided to suppliers shall contain all information necessary to permit them to submit responsive tenders, including: ...

(h) the criteria for awarding the contract, including any factors other than price that are to be considered *in the evaluation of tenders* and the cost elements to be included in evaluating tender prices, such as transport, insurance and inspection cost, and in the case of foreign products, *customs duties* and other import charges, taxes and currency of payment. (emphasis added)

In short, by acceding to this Agreement, Canada has recognized that for contracts covered by it, the Canadian content of the product should no longer be taken into account but customs duties will continue to apply. The DSRO for its part is an order made under the *Financial Administration Act* which provides, as its name indicates, for a remission of customs duty on defence supplies purchased by the Defence Production Department where the contract meets the requirements of Article 3. By its very nature, this document does not contravene the Agreement on Government Procurement but is applicable only when the contract is concluded and not when a tender is being evaluated. ...

The request for proposals (P-6) deserves special attention. According to this document it is clear that the proposals were to be made in accordance with the GATT Agreement on Government procurement and the document expressly states: "including customs duties if applicable." As we have just seen, customs duties are taken into account in a contract under this Agreement. ... Therefore no special terms and conditions, except those under GATT, are imposed.

It is true that the Minister was not required to accept the proposals or even to conclude a contract "as a result of your proposal." But if the Department accepts the proposal, it must follow the rules which it itself established and which were set out in Mr. Petersen's ruling on January 22, 1982 (Exhibit 30). This ruling provides in substance that: (a) the GATT rules have priority over any other considerations; (b) when tenders or proposals from foreign suppliers are being evaluated, customs duties must be taken into account; (c) if this results in a foreign supplier being the lowest bidder, there will be a remission of the duty when the contract is awarded, under the DSRO.

The evidence shows that when Stanley-Vidmar Inc.'s proposal was being evaluated, the customs duty was excluded. This was an error since under GATT it should have been included. In fact, when the proposals were being evaluated, factors that were not part of the terms and conditions of the request for proposals were considered. If the customs duty, being 15.6 per cent *ad valorem*, is added to Stanley-Vidmar Inc.'s proposal at the evaluation stage, the plaintiff becomes the lowest bidder and should have obtained the contract.

It is not easy in this case to specify the individual errors on the part of the various officials who handled this matter. However, there are instances of errors and negligence by the officials both individually and collectively. ...

In short, not only were representations made to the plaintiff to the effect that customs duties would be applied to a foreign bidder, but the defendant, through its employees, itself established clear and precise rules in its request for proposals of May 1, 1982 by referring to GATT, and then ignored it at the time of evaluation. Apart from this fact, the considerable hesitation shown by the defendant's employees in this case created an atmosphere of uncertainty such that the plaintiff was not aware and was not in a position to know at the time of the request for proposals and from reading the latter whether the clear GATT rules, which were subsequently ignored, should apply. The defendant is therefore liable for the actions of its employees which gave rise to this situation, and the plaintiff's action should succeed.

NOTES

Both the procedural acceptance and the substantive influence of international law are exhibited together in this case.[56] Notice how first the government adopted the GATT Agreement into its procurement practices and then the court took judicial notice of it to decide the case. Thus the substance of Canadian rules and policies was altered to conform to international standards. But how was all this possible without legislative implementation of the GATT Agreement? How does this case differ from the *Capital Cities* case, in which Laskin C.J.C. refused to refer to the unimplemented treaty involved there?

THE WORLD COURT[57]

The "World Court" is a phrase that is regularly used to refer collectively to the Permanent Court of International Justice (PCIJ) and its successor, the present International Court of

---

[56] Held on appeal, the trial judge erred in his interpretation of the GATT Agreement and his finding of negligence.

[57] See R. Bernhardt and H. Mosler (eds.), *Judicial Settlement of International Disputes* (1974); T.O. Elias, *The International Court of Justice and Some Contemporary Problems* (1983); L. Gross (ed.), *The Future of the International Court of Justice* (1976), 2 vols.; C.W. Jenks, *The Prospects of International Adjudication* (1964); S. Rosenne, *The Law and Practice of the International Court* (2 ed., 1985); *Procedure in the International Court* (1983); *The World Court: What It Is and How It Works* (3 ed., 1973). The former title by Rosenne is regarded as the leading treatise on the ICJ. A record of the Court's organization and activities may be found in its *Yearbooks*.

Justice (ICJ). The PCIJ was created in 1921 by treaty, known generally as the Statute of the Court. It was not part of the League of Nations strictly speaking and so its continued existence was not affected by the failure of the League. When the United Nations was set up, however, a fresh start was preferred. Thus the International Court of Justice replaced the PCIJ. However, the Statute of the ICJ is practically identical with the old Statute of the PCIJ. The ICJ also absorbed the jurisdiction of the PCIJ. The materials that follow dwell upon the experience of the current court.

The International Court of Justice is one of the six principal organs of the United Nations (Charter Art. 7), and the principal judicial organ (Charter Art. 92). It functions according to the UN Charter Arts. 92–96 and its own Statute, which is annexed to the Charter.

The following notes and questions are designed to introduce the salient features of the ICJ, emphasizing those characteristics of the World Court that differ from the usual arrangements and procedures of national courts. The Statute should be read as directed in these notes: it is reprinted in the Appendix after the UN Charter.

Judges of the Court

1) There are 15 members of the Court (Statute Art. 3). What are their qualifications? Statute Art 2. How are they elected?[58] Statute Arts. 4–8, 10–12. How do you react to the elective process? For instance, where do you suppose the main influence lies? Consider point 3 below. Nationality is mentioned in several places (Statute Arts. 2, 5(2), 10(3)). Do you consider the nationality of the judges is relevant to an impartial and independent court?

2) Individual qualification is not enough. The Bench is expected to represent "the main forms of civilization and … the principal legal systems of the world." Statute Art. 9. What relevance has "civilization" to judicial adjudication? Why should it matter what national legal background a judge possesses if his task is to apply international law? Would political background be relevant?[59]

3) The work of the Court, its reputation and prestige depend entirely on the quality of the bench. It is of utmost significance, therefore, what kind of people are appointed as judges. In your opinion, do the procedures of the Statute produce the right ones? The composition of the Court has changed over the years and currently mirrors the Security Council. By informal understanding, the permanent members of the Security Council each have a national as a judge on the Court. The understood distribution of seats on the Court is usually 5 from Western Europe and North America, 2 from Eastern Europe, 4 from Africa and the Middle East, 2 from Asia and 2 from Latin America. Some say this equitable geographical distribution outside the Statute has politicized elections to the Court. Do you think it is damaging to the Court? In its best interests?

4) Judges serve for 9 years and are eligible for re-election. Five seats come up for

---

[58] For a review of the elections of 1978 and Canadian involvement in them, see M.D. Copithorne, "The Permanent Court of Arbitration and the Election of Members of the International Court of Justice" (1978), 16 *Can. Y.B. Int. L.* 315.

[59] See L.V. Prott, *The Latent Power of Culture and the International Judge* (1979).

election every 3 years. Statute Art. 13. The judges may not engage in any other political, administrative or professional occupation. Statute Art. 16. When engaged on the Court's business, they enjoy diplomatic immunity. Statute Art. 19. A President and Vice-President are elected for 3 years by the Court from amongst its membership. Statute Art. 21. One Canadian has been elected a regular member of the Court. He was Judge John E. Read, who served from 1946–58.

5) Parties to a case may appoint a Judge Ad Hoc if no member of the Court has their nationality. Statute Art. 31. This right exists whether one or neither side has a national on the Court, so the provision is not a matter of evening out the balance between the opposing parties. Compared to national courts, which operate on the principle that none shall judge his own cause, the practice is contrary, particularly in light of the predictable experience that almost invariably the ad hoc judges side with the party appointing them. Why is nationality of the judges so significant? If it is, why should a member of the court, who is the national of a party, be allowed to sit on the case at all? The heterogeneous and plural character of international society is said to falsify the analogy to national courts. Do you agree?

Although it is usual for a state to appoint a national as judge ad hoc, it is not necessary. It seems, too, that only one judge ad hoc per side may be appointed even if there are more than two states, parties. Thus in the 1966 *South West Africa Case*[60] a Nigerian judge ad hoc was appointed by Liberia and Ethiopia.

6) Notionally the Court is permanently in session, but in practice it does not have enough work to keep it so. Its seat is in the Peace Palace at The Hague, Holland. Statute Arts. 22, 23.

Parties Before the Court

1) Only states may be parties in contentious cases before the Court. Statute Art. 34. Is this class too limiting? Who else would you wish had standing before the Court?

2) The Court is not open to every state automatically. A state must become a party to the Statute and may qualify in any one of three ways. Statute Art. 35 and Charter Art. 93. (1) States, members of the United Nations are *ipso facto* parties to the Statute. This class includes the great majority of states. (2) Non-members of the United Nations may become parties to the Statute by accepting the conditions laid down by the General Assembly. Liechtenstein, San Marino, Switzerland, and Japan prior to UN membership, have taken this route. The General Assembly required each of them to accept the provisions of the ICJ Statute, to accept the obligations of compliance with a decision of the Court in Charter Art. 94, and to pay an equitable proportion of the expenses of the Court. (3) Any other state may appear before the Court in a particular case provided it accepts the conditions laid down by the Security Council in 1946 which provide in part:

...such state shall previously have deposited with the Registrar of the Court a declaration by which it accepts the jurisdiction of the Court, in accordance with the Charter of the United Nations

---

[60] *South West Africa Case (Second Phase)*, [1966] I.C.J. Rep. 6.

and with the terms and subject to the conditions of the Statute and Rules of the Court, and undertakes to comply in good faith with the decision or decisions of the Court and to accept all the obligations of a Member of the United Nations under Article 94 of the Charter.

This process has been resorted to on occasion by several states including Albania, Cambodia, Ceylon, Finland, West Germany, Italy, Japan, Laos and Vietnam. All, except Cambodia and Laos, are now members of the United Nations and thus automatically parties to the Statute.

Jurisdiction of the Court

1) The ICJ is distinctively different from national courts in that it does not automatically have jurisdiction over all disputes between parties with standing. While its jurisdiction as to subject matter is universal, its jurisdiction over the parties is not. It cannot hear a contentious case, even though the litigant states are parties to the Statute, unless they all consent. Statute Art. 36(1). This restriction severely limits the number of cases that can be brought before the Court. What do you suppose is the reason for it?

Note that the jurisdiction of the PCIJ is carried over without interruption by Statute Art. 37, at least amongst parties to the present Statute.

2) In an attempt to create a compulsory jurisdiction for the Court, machinery has been provided by Statute Art. 36(2). It is known as the "Optional Clause" as it provides the option or opportunity for a state, party to the Statute, to declare its acceptance of the Court's jurisdiction generally and in advance, subject to certain conditions. Statute Art. 36(2)–(6). As of July 31, 1984, 47 declarations had been made by the following states:[61] Australia, Austria, Barbados, Belgium, Botswana, Canada, Colombia, Costa Rica, Democratic Kampuchea, Denmark, Dominican Republic, Egypt, El Salvador, Finland, Gambia, Haiti, Honduras, India, Israel, Japan, Kenya, Liberia, Liechtenstein, Luxembourg, Nicaragua, Nigeria, Norway, Pakistan, Panama, Philippines, Portugal, Somalia, Sudan, Swaziland, Sweden, Switzerland, Togo, Uganda, United Kingdom, United States, Uruguay. On the same date there were 158 members of the United Nations. Since then, Canada has amended its declaration to remove an exclusion of disputes concerning its jurisdiction in the seas surrounding its coasts, while the United States has withdrawn its declaration completely.[62]

Declarations Recognizing Jurisdiction

Canada

On behalf of the Government of Canada,

1) I give notice that I hereby terminate the acceptance by Canada of the compulsory jurisdiction

---

[61] See I.C.J. *Yearbook 1983–84*, 57 fwd.

[62] For the reasons, see U.S. Department of State's statement reprinted in (1985), 24 *Int. Leg. Mat.*, at 1743. For commentary, see the editorial remarks of T.M. Franck (1985), 79 *Am. J. Int. L.* 379, and W.M. Reisman (1986), 80 *Am. J. Int. L.* 128.

of the International Court of Justice hitherto effective by virtue of the declaration made on 7 April 1970 in conformity with paragraph 2 of Article 36 of the Statute of that Court.

2) I declare that the Government of Canada accepts as compulsory *ipso facto* and without special convention, on condition of reciprocity, the jurisdiction of the International Court of Justice, in conformity with paragraph 2 of Article 36 of the Statute of the Court, until such time as notice may be given to terminate the acceptance, over all disputes arising after the present declaration with regard to situations or facts subsequent to this declaration, other than:

    (a)   disputes in regard to which parties have agreed or shall agree to have recourse to some other method of peaceful settlement;

    (b)   disputes with the Government of any other country which is a member of the Commonwealth of Nations, all of which disputes shall be settled in such manner as the parties have agreed or shall agree;

    (c)   disputes with regard to questions which by international law fall exclusively within the jurisdiction of Canada.

3) The Government of Canada also reserves the right at any time, by means of a notification addressed to the Secretary-General of the United Nations, and with effect as from the moment of such notification, either to add to, amend or withdraw any of the foregoing reservations, or any that may hereafter be added.

It is requested that this notification may be communicated to the governments of all the States that have accepted the Optional Clause and to the Registrar of the International Court of Justice.

New York, September 10, 1985

(Signed) STEPHEN LEWIS,
Ambassador and
Permanent Representative

India

I have the honour to declare, on behalf of the Government of the Republic of India, that they accept, in conformity with paragraph 2 of Article 36 of the Statute of the Court, until such time as notice may be given to terminate such acceptance, as compulsory *ipso facto* and without special agreement, and on the basis and condition of reciprocity, the jurisdiction of the International Court of Justice over all disputes other than:

1) disputes in regard to which the parties to the dispute have agreed or shall agree to have recourse to some other method or methods of settlement;

2) disputes with the government of any State which is or has been a Member of the Commonwealth of Nations;

3) disputes in regard to matters which are essentially within the domestic jurisdiction of the Republic of India;

4) disputes relating to or connected with facts or situations of hostilities, armed conflicts, individual or collective actions taken in self-defence, resistance to aggression, fulfilment of obligations imposed by international bodies, and other similar or related acts, measures or situations in which India is, has been or may in future be involved;

5) disputes with regard to which any other party to a dispute has accepted the compulsory jurisdiction of the International Court of Justice exclusively for or in relation to the purposes of such dispute; or where the acceptance of the Court's compulsory jurisdiction on behalf of a

party to the dispute was deposited or ratified less than 12 months prior to the filing of the application bringing the dispute before the Court;

6) disputes where the jurisdiction of the Court is or may be founded on the basis of a treaty concluded under the auspices of the League of Nations, unless the Government of India specially agree to jurisdiction in each case;

7) disputes concerning the interpretation or application of a multilateral treaty unless all the parties to the treaty are also parties to the case before the Court or Government of India specially agree to jurisdiction;

8) disputes with the Government of any State with which, on the date of an application to bring a dispute before the Court, the Government of India has no diplomatic relations or which has not been recognized by the Government of India;

9) disputes with non-sovereign States or territories;

10) disputes with India concerning or relating to:

(a) the status of its territory or the modification or delimitation of its frontiers or any other matter concerning boundaries;

(b) the territorial sea, the continental shelf and the margins, the exclusive fishery zone, the exclusive economic zone, and other zones of national maritime jurisdiction including for the regulation and control of marine pollution and the conduct of scientific research by foreign vessels;

(c) the condition and status of its islands, bays and gulf and that of the bays and gulfs that for historical reasons belong to it;

(d) the airspace superjacent to its land and maritime territory; and

(e) the determination and delimitation of its maritime boundaries.

11) disputes prior to the date of this declaration, including any dispute the foundations, reasons, facts, causes, origins, definitions, allegations or bases of which existed prior to this date, even if they are submitted or brought to the knowledge of the Court hereafter.

2. This declaration revokes and replaces the previous declaration made by the Government of India on 14 September 1959.

New Delhi, 15 September 1974.

(Signed) SWARAN SINGH,
Minister for External
Affairs

Nicaragua

[*Translation from the French*]

On behalf of the Republic of Nicaragua I recognize as compulsory unconditionally the jurisdiction of the Permanent Court of International Justice.

Geneva, 24 September 1929

(Signed) T.F. MEDINA

United States of America

I, Harry S. Truman, President of the United States of America, declare on behalf of the United States of America, under Article 36, paragraph 2, of the Statute of the International Court of

Justice, and in accordance with the Resolution of 2 August 1946 of the Senate of the United States of America (two-thirds of the Senators present concurring therein), that the United States of America recognizes as compulsory *ipso facto* and without special agreement, in relation to any other State accepting the same obligation, the jurisdiction of the International Court of Justice in all legal disputes hereafter arising concerning

(a) the interpretation of a treaty;

(b) any question of international law;

(c) the existence of any fact which, if established, would constitute a breach of an international obligation;

(d) the nature or extent of the reparation to be made for the breach of an international obligation;

Provided, that this declaration shall not apply to

(a) disputes the solution of which the parties shall entrust to other tribunals by virtue of agreements already in existence or which may be concluded in the future; or

(b) disputes with regard to matters which are essentially within the domestic jurisdiction of the United States of America as determined by the United States of America; or

(c) disputes arising under a multilateral treaty, unless (1) all parties to the treaty affected by the decision are also parties to the case before the Court, or (2) the United States of America specially agrees to jurisdiction; and

Provided further, that this declaration shall remain in force for a period of five years and thereafter until the expiration of six months after notice may be given to terminate this declaration.

Done at Washington this fourteenth day of August 1946.

(Signed) HARRY S. TRUMAN

6 April 1984

I have the honor on behalf of the Government of the United States of America to refer to the Declaration of my Government of August 26, 1946, concerning the acceptance by the United States of America of the compulsory jurisdiction of the International Court of Justice, and to state that the aforesaid Declaration shall not apply to disputes with any Central American state or arising out of or related to events in Central America, any of which disputes shall be settled in such manner as the parties to them may agree.

Notwithstanding the terms of the aforesaid Declaration, this *proviso* shall take effect immediately and shall remain in force for two years, so as to foster the continuing regional dispute settlement process which seeks a negotiated solution to the interrelated political, economic and security problems of Central America.

(Signed) GEORGE P. SHULTZ

Secretary of State of the
United States of America

October 7, 1985

I have the honor on behalf of the Government of the United States of America to refer to the declaration of my Government of 26 August 1946, as modified by my note of 6 April 1984, concerning the acceptance by the United States of America of the compulsory jurisdiction of the

International Court of Justice, and to state that the aforesaid declaration is hereby terminated, with effect six months from the date hereof.

(Signed) GEORGE P. SHULTZ
Secretary of State of the
United States of America

3) The Optional Clause can no longer be described as successful when less than one third of the members of the United Nations have made declarations.[63] Most of the newly independent countries in Africa and Asia have shown a reluctance to adhere to the Court's compulsory jurisdiction and no socialist states appear on the above list. The absence now of four out of five of the permanent members of the Security Council is noticeable. Moreover, many declarations contain extensive reservations and thus fall far short of the general, compulsory jurisdiction intended. These reservations take many forms. They provide time limits, such as making the declaration terminable instantaneously upon notice, and they limit the subject matter and the states towards which the acceptance of jurisdiction is extended.[64] Consider the variety of matters excluded by the declarations reprinted above. Are these kinds of reservations permissible? Statute Art. 36(3).

Reservations may also rebound on the maker. By Statute Art. 36(3), a state may expressly make its declaration subject to a condition of reciprocity, but it already is in some sense by reason of the language of Art. 36(2). It takes the unilateral declaration of each of the opposing states to establish the Court's jurisdiction to hear their case. Thus the Court only has jurisdiction over matters that are common ground between them. By the introduction of an express condition of reciprocity, the Court's jurisdiction is narrowed still further because a state may assert the reservations in its own declaration and those in its opponents'. The *Norwegian Loans Case*[65] displayed the ultimate irony. The claimant state, France, reserved all matters within its domestic jurisdiction as it understood that phrase. This reservation was successfully invoked against France by the defendant state, Norway, on the basis of its condition of reciprocity. The Court was without jurisdiction to hear the case.

4) The Court recently had occasion to consider the effects of time limits in optional declarations in the case of *Military Activities In and Against Nicaragua*.[66] Shortly before Nicaragua commenced the action, the United States deposited the amendment of 6 April 1984, reproduced previously, by which it expected to forestall the jurisdiction of the

---

[63] A careful survey of the state practice surrounding the Optional Clause is provided in the dissenting judgment of Judge Oda in *Military Activities In and Against Nicaragua* (Jurisdiction), [1984] I.C.J. Rep. 392, at 471. See also C.H.M. Waldock, "Decline of the Optional Clause" (1955–56), 32 *Br. Y.B. Int. L.* 244; and B. Cheng, "Flight from Justiciable to Auto-Interpretative International Law: from the Jay Treaty to the Schultz Letter," in *Liber Amicorum Elie van Bogaert* (1985).

[64] See J.G. Merrills, "The Optional Clause Today" (1979), 50 *Br. Y.B. Int. L.* 87. For contrasting opinions on the Canadian declaration as it was prior to 1985, see L. Henkin, "Arctic Anti-Pollution: Does Canada Make or Break International Law?" (1971), 65 *Am. J. Int. L.* 131; and R. St. J. Macdonald, "The New Canadian Declaration of Acceptance of the Compulsory Jurisdiction of the International Court of Justice" (1970), *Can. Y.B. Int. L.* 3.

[65] [1957] I.C.J. Rep. 9.

[66] Jurisdiction and Admissability, [1984] I.C.J. Rep. 392.

Court. It declared it was to take effect immediately even though the then standing U.S. declaration provided for six months notice of termination. Should the United States have been allowed to rely on its amendment or should Nicaragua have been permitted to depend upon the standing declaration? The critical date for establishing commonality of obligations between two declarant states was held in the *Right of Passage Over Indian Territory Case*[67] to be the moment of the filing of an application to commence a case. The United States contended it had a right to amend its unilateral declaration in any event and could take advantage reciprocally of the lack of any provision for notice of termination in the Nicaraguan declaration, reproduced previously. Over several forceful dissents, the Court firmly rejected these arguments, saying:[68]

The notion of reciprocity is concerned with the scope and substance of the commitments entered into, including reservations, and not with the formal conditions of their creation, duration or extinction. It appears clearly that reciprocity cannot be invoked in order to excuse departure from the terms of a State's own declaration, whatever its scope, limitations or conditions.

By 15 votes to 1 (Judge Schwebel from the United States) the Court decided it had jurisdiction in the case. The United States thereafter withdrew from further participation.[69]

5) One form of reservation to a declaration under the Optional Clause is particularly destructive. It was invented by the United States and sometimes bears the name of the author, Connally, or is called the automatic reservation. The reservation excludes from the Court's jurisdiction all matters within the domestic jurisdiction of the declarant *as determined by it*. See the U.S. declaration above. This was the form of France's declaration in the *Norwegian Loans Case* too. What is the scope of the jurisdiction granted to the Court by a declaration that includes such a reservation?

Is the automatic reservation valid?[70] Statute Art. 36(6). In a separate opinion in the *Norwegian Loans Case*,[71] Judge Lauterpacht said that it was contrary to the Statute and, since the declarant government retained control, it had not effected a legal obligation. The majority of the Court declined to rule on the automatic reservation since neither side had questioned its validity.[72]

6) A case is submitted to the Court either by a special agreement or by a "written application." A special agreement is typically used where both states are in agreement that they want the Court to decide their dispute. It has the advantage that it clothes the Court with jurisdiction over their case without question, and therefore it is often used even though each state may have made a declaration under the Optional Clause. A written application is made when a state commences a case unilaterally. Since one party cannot

---

[67] Preliminary Objections, [1957] I.C.J. Rep. 125.

[68] *Supra*, n. 67, at 419. The Court relied on its previous decision in the *Interhandel Case*, [1959] I.C.J. Rep. 6. For a discussion of the case, see Editorial Comments (1985), 79 *Am. J. Int. L.* 373.

[69] See the statements of the United States, reprinted in (1985) 24 *Int. Leg. Mat.* at 246, 249.

[70] J. Crawford, "The Legal Effect of Automatic Reservations to the Jurisdiction of the International Court" (1979), 50 *Br. Y.B. Int. L.* 63.

[71] *Supra*, n. 65, at 44.

[72] *Supra*, n. 65, at 27.

seize the Court with jurisdiction without the consent of the other, it must have good reason to believe that the other party is obliged to submit to the Court. The procedure is used, therefore, when two states, in the heat of dispute, cannot agree even to submit their differences to the Court and one of them takes the other there on the basis of its declaration under the Optional Clause or pursuant to a compromissory clause in a treaty already existing between them, such as occurred in the *U.S. Diplomatic Staff in Tehran Case*.[73]

7) In recent years states, made respondent in the Court by an unilateral application, have increasingly failed to appear to answer the case.[74] The Statute Art. 53 makes plain that the Court may give default judgment provided it is satisfied that it has jurisdiction over the case and that the claim is well founded in fact and in law. Non-appearance of the respondent, however, is a clear indication that it will also ignore any decision. This regrettable practice has been used to the advantage of the errant state. In refusing to appear, the respondent often makes, sometimes lengthy, communications to the Court from the wings.[75] These statements, which typically outline the case the state would make were it to appear, cannot be ignored by the Court. So the respondent state has the advantage of having its arguments aired and considered even while it refrains from appearing.

8) In addition to the original parties to a case, other states may intervene. Statute Articles 62 & 63. What is the difference between these two articles? Previous experience with these articles was slight but positive[76] until three recent cases in each of which the Court refused the would-be intervenor.[77] As a result it is unclear what "interest of a legal nature" of the intervenor must be at stake, whether a jurisdictional link with one or all of the parties is necessary, and even if there is much scope left for interventions at all.[78]

Decisions of the Court

1) The Court decides cases according to international law as found in the sources listed in the Statute Art. 38.[79] It has control over its own procedure, and it has established Rules of Court, the current set dating from 1978.[80]

---

[73] [1979] I.C.J. Rep. 7 & 23; [1980] I.C.J. Rep. 3, reported *infra* Chapter 5.

[74] The United States' withdrawal from the *Military Activities In and Against Nicaragua Case* is only the most recent example. See generally, J.B. Elkind, *Non-Appearance Before the International Court of Justice* (1984); H.W.A. Thirlway, *Non-Appearance Before the International Court of Justice* (1985); and G. Fitzmaurice, "The Problem of the 'Non-Appearing' Defendant Government" (1980), 51 *Br. Y.B. Int. L.* 89.

[75] See e.g., Iran's communications in the *U.S. Diplomatic Staff in Tehran Case, supra,* n. 73.

[76] See *The Steamship Wimbledon* (1923), P.C.I.J., Ser. A, No. 1, at 11 (Poland intervening); *Haya de la Torre Case*, [1951] I.C.J. Rep. 71, at 76 (Cuba intervening); and *Nuclear Tests Cases*, [1974] I.C.J. Rep. 530 and 535 (Fiji's request lapsed with the cases).

[77] *Continental Shelf (Tunisia v. Libya) Case*, [1981] I.C.J. Rep. 3 (Malta refused); *Continental Shelf (Libya v. Malta) Case*, [1984] I.C.J. Rep. 3 (Italy refused); and *Military Activities In and Against Nicaragua*, [1984] I.C.J. Rep. 215 (El Salvador refused).

[78] See the conclusions of C.M. Chinkin, "Third Party Intervention before the International Court of Justice" (1986), 80 *Am. J. Int. L.* 495, at 531. See also G.P. McGinley, "Intervention in the International Court: The Libya/Malta Continental Shelf Case" (1985), 34 *Int. Comp. L.Q.* 671; and J. Sztucki, "Intervention under Article 63 of the I.C.J. Statute in Preliminary Proceedings: The 'Salvadorean Incident' " (1985), 79 *Am. J. Int. L.* 1004.

[79] Discussed *supra* in Chapter 3.

[80] See S. Rosenne, *Procedure in the International Court* (1983).

2) Normally the full court of 15 judges will sit to hear a case, although the quorum is only 9. Statute Art. 25. The Court may also form chambers of as few as three judges. Statute Arts. 26–29. The revision of the Rules of Court in 1978 also granted prospective parties an element of influence over the composition of a chamber as well as its size. Canada and the United States exercised this new procedure for the first time[81] and insisted upon a chamber of 5 judges, all from Western countries. They thereby demonstrated how important it is to states who decides their case. Do you consider this precedent, if followed, will enhance or diminish the work and standing of the Court or the judicial development of international law?[82]

3) A case is decided by a majority of the judges. In the event of a tie, the President has a casting vote, as he was required to exercise in the *Steamship Lotus*.[83] The judgment must contain the reasons of the majority, but there are frequently separate opinions by concurring judges as well as dissenting opinions.[84] Statute Arts. 55–58.

4) What is the force of a decision of the Court? Statute Art. 59. The judgment is final and without appeal, and is subject to revision only in limited circumstances. Statute Arts. 60, 61. In the light of these articles, what impact do you think a judgment has subsequently on international law? Refer to Statute Art. 38(1)(d).

5) All the decisions of the PCIJ were complied with, but the record of the ICJ is not complete. The judgments in the *Corfu Channel Case*,[85] the *Fisheries Jurisdiction Case*,[86] the *U.S. Diplomatic Staff in Tehran Case*[87] and the *Military Activities In and Against Nicaragua Case*[88] were not observed. How may a decision be enforced? Charter Art. 94. Involvement of the Security Council is bound to politicize the judicial resolution of the dispute in question. Why is it necessary to turn to the Security Council for enforcement? Is the process likely to be used?

6) "Provisional measures"[89] may be taken by the Court in the course of a case when necessary "to preserve the respective rights of either party." Statute Art. 41. What is the force of such interim measures? Compare the language of Statute Arts. 41 and 59. Interim measures were pronounced in 5 cases, the *Anglo-Iranian Oil Case*,[90] the *Fisheries Jurisdiction Case*,[91] the *Nuclear Tests Cases*,[92] the *U.S. Diplomatic Staff in Tehran Case*[93]

---

[81] In the *Gulf of Maine Case*, [1982] I.C.J. Rep. 3. A second instance of the use of a Chamber of 5 judges is the *Frontier Dispute Case* between Burkina Faso and Mali, [1985] I.C.J. Rep. 6.

[82] See E. McWhinney, *Supreme Courts and Judicial Law-Making: Constitutional Tribunals and Constitutional Review* (1986), at 30–34; and D.M. McRae, "Adjudication of the Maritime Boundary in the Gulf of Maine" (1979), 17 *Can. Y.B. Int. L.* 292.

[83] *The Steamship Lotus* (1927), P.C.I.J., Ser. A., No. 10, reported *infra* in Chapter 8.

[84] See I. Hussain, *Dissenting and Separate Opinions at the World Court* (1984).

[85] [1949] I.C.J. Rep. 4, reported *infra* in Chapter 11.

[86] [1974] I.C.J. Rep. 3, 175.

[87] *Supra*, n. 73.

[88] [1986] I.C.J. Rep. 14.

[89] See T.O. Elias *supra*, n. 57, at c. 3; J.B. Elkind, *Interim Protection, A Functional Approach* (1981); and J. Sztucki, *Interim Measures in the Hague Court* (1983).

[90] [1951] I.C.J. Rep. 89.

[91] [1972] I.C.J. Rep. 12, 30.

[92] [1973] I.C.J. Rep. 99, 135.

[93] [1979] I.C.J. Rep. 23.

and the *Military Activities In and Against Nicaragua Case*,[94] but they were not honoured in any of them.

What should be the criteria to determine whether the circumstances warrant provisional measures? In the *Aegean Sea Continental Shelf Case*,[95] the Court required proof of "irreparable prejudice to the rights in issue," which, in that situation, it did not find. This is a stiff standard but it is unclear whether it excludes all situations that are compensable by money. The Court applied the same standard in the *U.S. Diplomatic Staff in Tehran Case*[96] and held in favour of the United States, ordering Iran to release the hostages and restore the U.S. embassy. This was clearly an appropriate case for provisional measures, notwithstanding Iran's assertion that the Court would in effect judge the merits. Although the Court had refused to indicate provisional measures in the *Chorzow Factory (Indemnity) Case*[97] because the request was "designed to obtain an interim judgment in favour of a part of the claim" for a sum of money, the U.S. request regarding the hostages was to protect the lives of its nationals and its property pending adjudication of Iran's responsibility for its actions towards them.

7) May the Court indicate provisional measures under Statute Art. 41 at the request of one party, if the other party has not yet consented to the Court's jurisdiction to entertain the merits of the case under Statute Art. 36? In the *Aegean Sea Continental Shelf Case*,[98] the majority of 12 did not consider it necessary to decide the question, however 7 concurring judges wrote separate opinions expressing views that a finding of jurisdiction, with varying degrees of certainty, was an essential prerequisite to pronouncing interim measures. Judge Arechaga considered Art. 41 to be an autonomous grant of jurisdiction, but jurisdiction over the merits was a relevant circumstance in the determination of provisional measures. Three other judges thought the Court must reach a provisional conviction that it has jurisdiction under Art. 36. Judges Morozov and Tarazi said a full finding on jurisdiction is necessary. What would be the practical effect if the views of Judges Morozov and Tarazi prevail? What would be the effect of indicating provisional measures without enquiring into jurisdiction? Consider your opinion on the earlier question as to the legal force of interim measures.

Advisory Opinions[99]

1) The Court is empowered to give advisory opinions on legal questions put to it by the General Assembly, the Security Council and such other organs and specialized agencies

---

[94] [1984] I.C.J. Rep. 169.

[95] [1976] I.C.J. Rep. 3, at 11.

[96] [1979] I.C.J. Rep. 7, at 19 and 16.

[97] (1927), P.C.I.J., Ser. A., No. 12, at 10.

[98] See J.P.A. Bernhardt, "The Provisional Measures Procedure of the International Court of Justice through *U.S. Staff in Tehran: Fiat Iustitia, Pereat Curia?*" (1980), 20 *Va. J. Int. L.* 557; J.B. Elkind, *supra*, n. 89, at c. 7; D.M. McRae, Note (1973), 8 *U.B.C.L.R.* 375; and J. Sztucki; *supra*, n. 89, at c. 5.

[99] See K.J. Keith, *The Extent of the Advisory Jurisdiction of the International Court of Justice* (1971); M. Pomerance, *The Advisory Function of the International Court in the League and U.N. Eras* (1973); D. Pratap, *The Advisory Jurisdiction of the International Court*; and P.C. Szabz, "Enhancing the Advisory Competence of the World Court," in L. Gross, *supra*, n. 57, at 499.

of the United Nations as are authorized by the General Assembly. Charter Art. 96 and Statute Art. 65. Some of the authorized authorities are ECOSOC, ILO, FAO, UNESCO, WHO, World Bank, IFC, IDA, IMF, ICAO, ITU, IMO and WIPO. Why are states denied the right to ask for advisory opinions? Are there other kinds of authorities or organizations who might usefully be given the right to ask for advisory opinions?[100] UN organs and agencies do not ordinarily have standing before the Court. Can they use the process of an advisory opinion to litigate their own disputes? Consider the *Reparations Case*.[101] Advisory opinions are very useful for resolving uncertain legal issues of general concern, such as points of interpretation of the UN Charter of the kind raised in the *Reparations Case*.[102] Eighteen advisory opinions had been requested by the ICJ up to 1985,[103] but on several occasions states involved in the situation subject of the request objected on the basis that they had not consented to the Court's jurisdiction. Is this a valid objection? In the *Interpretation of Peace Treaties Case*,[104] the Court said:

The consent of States, parties to a dispute, is the basis of the Court's jurisdiction in contentious cases. The situation is different in regard to advisory proceedings even when the Request for an Opinion relates to a legal question actually pending between States. The Court's reply is only of an advisory character: as such, it has no binding force. It follows that no State, ... can prevent the giving of an Advisory Opinion which the United Nations considers to be desirable ... . The Court's opinion is given not to the States, but to the organ which is entitled to request it; the reply of the Court, ... in principle should not be refused.

But the Court is alert to the possible judicial impropriety of giving opinions. In the *Western Sahara Case*[105] the Court observed that lack of consent of an interested state "may render the giving of an advisory opinion incompatible with the Court's judicial character." In what circumstances might that be enough to deny the United Nations' request?

Significance of the Court

In the 39 years of the ICJ's existence up to July 1984 it dealt with a total of 70 cases.[106] In those cases it gave 43 judgments and 18 advisory opinions. The others did not go to a decision for a variety of reasons, such as withdrawal or lack of jurisdiction. That is a rate, roughly, of just over one contentious case each year. Not a heavy docket! The political reality is that the World Court is a marginal institution in inter-state relations. This assessment has been confirmed by the United States' recent retraction of its accep-

---

[100] L.B. Sohn, "Broadening the Advisory Jurisdiction of the International Court of Justice" (1983), 77 *Am. J. Int. L.* 124.

[101] [1949] I.C.J. Rep. 174, reported *supra* in Chapter 2.

[102] *Ibid.*

[103] See the list of cases and their requesting agencies in I.C.J. *Yearbook 1983–84*, at 48–49.

[104] [1950] I.C.J. Rep. 65, at 71.

[105] [1975] I.C.J. Rep. 12, at 25.

[106] For the complete list of cases, see I.C.J. *Yearbook 1983–84*, at 3.

tance of the compulsory jurisdiction of the Court. To the question why states do not take more of their many conflicts to the World Court the usual reply raises three considerations.[107]

First, governments are reluctant to surrender control over their affairs. There is a risk of loss in court both of face and merits. The unwillingness to take those risks might suggest that many states are too unsure of their own sovereignty. A more cynical explanation is that too many states are uninterested in an international rule of law. But in counterbalance, Brierly[108] has pointed out that "[i]nternational law at its present stage of development gives a far less effective protection to the reasonable interests of states than does the law of a constitutional state to those of individuals, both because the substance of the law is defective relatively to the interests which it ought to be able to protect, and because the circumstances in which it has to be administered are more difficult." In particular, so many matters of difference between states are beyond the purview of the Court because they are essentially within the domestic jurisdiction of one or other of them.[109]

The main reason why states are unwilling to turn their disputes over to the Court, Akehurst has suggested,[110] is because they believe that judicial decisions are unpredictable. The fact that a dispute cannot be settled by negotiation often indicates that the relevant law or the facts of the case are uncertain. Yet it is these uncertain cases which are ripe for adjudication, and present the most unpredictable results. The risks associated with unpredictability are the greater according as a government regards its vital national interests are at stake. When high matters of state are involved, the desire for straight-forward settlement may not be as great as the risk of losing in court, or risks associated with no settlement, at least for the time being.

Second, many states do not seem to have much confidence in judicial settlement in general and the ICJ in particular. It takes an act of faith for states to remove their dispute from its natural arena of diplomacy into a judicial forum, and that move is not encouraged by a dislike of the Court. One centre of concern has been the composition of the Court – not so much the personal qualifications of individual judges as the aggregate balance of their backgrounds and viewpoints. As Anand has noted,[111] African and Asian nations in particular did not think the make up of the Court kept pace with the increasingly universal composition of the international community. Changes have been wrought, however, so that the geographical distribution of judges now reflects the Security Council.[112] Yet these changes are not enough for some states.

Third, one party to a dispute often considers the international law inadequate to meet its situation. It essentially demands a change in the law, yet it anticipates the Court would only condemn it by existing law. The Canadian declaration accepting the compulsory jurisdiction of the Court is a striking example. In 1970, the day before introduction into

---

[107] See also R.B. Bilder, "Some Limitations of Adjudication as an International Dispute Settlement Technique" (1982–83), 23 *Va. J. Int. L.* 1.

[108] J.L. Brierly, *The Law of Nations* (6 ed., Waldock, 1963), at 369.

[109] UN Charter Art. 2(7), see Appendix.

[110] M.B. Akehurst, *A Modern Introduction to International Law* (3 ed., 1977), at 232.

[111] R.P. Anand, "Role of International Adjudication," in L. Gross, *supra*, n. 57, 1, at 9.

[112] As explained *supra* under "Judges of the Court."

Parliament of the *Arctic Waters Pollution Prevention Act*, making what was then a unique unilateral claim to Arctic jurisdiction, the federal government lodged a new reservation from the ICJ's jurisdiction covering Canada's rights in marine areas adjacent to its coasts.[113] The federal government considered Canada had these legal rights but was not so sure, if challenged, that the Court would think so. If Canada, a participant in the Western culture that has nurtured international law, feels this way how much stronger are the doubts and demands of African and Asian countries who are only recently independent of Western dominance and so different and diverse in cultures and values. Although courts do develop the law,[114] they tend to be careful and conservative in approach. This tendency is even stronger in the ICJ because it does not have compulsory jurisdiction. Yet the demand for changed law is growing.

The smallness of the volume of work undertaken by the World Court is disappointing, not only for the lack of settlement of disputes peacefully, but also from the point of view of the development of international law. In the absence of a treaty, the ICJ remains the best means of objective determination of international law. Nevertheless, international lawyers should hold their view of the World Court in perspective. Judge Jennings has admonished:[115]

It is a besetting weakness of lawyers – and not only of international lawyers – to think of law, and even sometimes to attempt to define law, as if it consisted only of rules suitable to be applied by courts in adversary proceedings between two parties. This distorted view of the role of the law in a society is singularly inapt for international law which throughout its history has been employed much more as an instrument of diplomacy than of formal forensic confrontation. Naturally, courts and court-law are of great importance in international law; yet so also is that law which provides the frameworks, procedures and standards for international political decision; and it is certainly the further development of this latter kind of international law which presents the most urgent problem today.

OTHER MEANS OF PEACEFUL SETTLEMENT OF DISPUTES[116]

Adjudication is by no means the only procedure available for the application of international law and the peaceful settlement of international disputes. In fact, it is probably the least commonly applied process of conflict resolution in the international community.

---

[113] This reservation was omitted from the current declaration, reproduced above, in the light of the subsequent regulation of the subject by the U.N. Law of the Sea Convention, Art. 234, discussed *infra* in Chapter 11.

[114] For an assessment of the ICJ in this respect, see M. Lachs, "Some Reflections on the Contribution of the International Court of Justice to the Development of International Law" (1983), 10 *Syracuse J. Int. L. & Com.* 239.

[115] R.Y. Jennings, "General Course on Principles of International Law" (1967), 121 *Hague Recueil* 323, at 327–28.

[116] David Davies Memorial Institute of International Studies, *International Disputes: The Legal Aspects* (1972); H. Lauterpacht, *The Function of Law in the International Community* (1933); J.G. Merrills, *International Dispute Settlement* (1984); K.V. Raman, *International Dispute Settlement Through the United Nations* (1977).

States, nevertheless, are bound to solve their differences by peaceful means. The U.N. Charter Article 1(1)[117] declares the pacific settlement of disputes to be a purpose of the Organisation, in order to further the maintenance of international peace and security. Article 2(3) obliges states, members to settle their disputes by peaceful means. Chapter 6 of the U.N. Charter, on the Pacific Settlement of Disputes, elaborates these objectives and obligations. In particular, Article 33 provides a non-exclusive list of peaceful processes, including negotiation, inquiry, mediation, conciliation and arbitration. To these may be added the powers of the Security Council, by Article 34, to investigate any situation which might give rise to a dispute and, by Article 36, to recommend any appropriate method of adjustment of the differences between states, and the extension of the good offices of an intermediary, such as the Secretary General under Article 99.

International Law does not define an international dispute. The phrase clearly covers every situation arising amongst states and other international personalities which the parties care to treat as a dispute. In particular, disputes are not limited to legal differences but involve any combination of facts and policies. The choice of the means of resolution is up to the parties equally as much as the definition of the dispute, provided it is peaceful. By selecting adjudicative or arbitral means the parties treat the dispute as "justiciable", that is capable of solution by law. Typically the parties will at least initially give preeminence to the political elements of their dispute and will try to seek a settlement by diplomacy.

In many international disputes several methods of settlement are employed together or consecutively, or elements of them are integrated to meet the needs of the particular situation. Except for arbitration, which is a form of adjudication, it would be wrong to think that the peaceful means of dispute settlement are sharply differentiated and separately institutionalized procedures. Yet each method has a distinct characteristic which makes it worthy of separate consideration on its own merits. The materials that follow discuss each technique in turn, beginning with *inter partes* negotiation and proceeding through methods of third party intervention of increasingly authoritative character.

Negotiation[118]

Article 33 of the U.N. Charter does not state the various peaceful means of dispute settlement in any particular order of priority, but by far the most important method is direct negotiations between the parties in conflict. The reason is not far to seek. Negotiation offers each party complete control over its vital interests in the dispute at all stages along the way to resolution. But for a negotiated settlement to be achieved, each party must believe that the benefits to be gained from an agreement will be outweighed by the compromises it will have to make.

---

[117] See Appendix.
[118] The state of the art is summed up by G. Winham, "International Negotiation in an Age of Transition" (1979–80), 35 *International Journal* 1.

Forms of Negotiation
from J.G. Merrills, *International Dispute Settlement* (1984), at 6–9
(footnotes omitted)

Negotiations between states are usually conducted through "normal diplomatic channels," that is by the respective foreign offices, or by diplomatic representatives, who in the case of complex negotiations may lead delegations including representatives of several interested departments of the government concerned. As an alternative, if the subject matter is appropriate, negotiations may be carried out by what are termed the "competent authorities" of each party, that is by representatives of the particular ministry or department responsible for the matter in question – between trade departments in the case of a commercial agreement, for example, or defence ministries in negotiations concerning weapons' procurement. Where the competent authorities are subordinate bodies, they may be authorised to take negotiations as far as possible and to refer disagreements to a higher governmental level ... .

In the case of a recurrent problem or a situation requiring continuous supervision, states may decide to institutionalise negotiation by creating what is termed a mixed or joint commission. Thus neighbouring states commonly employ mixed commissions to deal with boundary delimitation, or other matters of common concern. The Soviet Union, for instance, has concluded treaties with a number of adjoining states, providing for frontier disputes and incidents to be referred to mixed commissions with power to decide minor disputes and to investigate other cases, before referring them for settlement through diplomatic channels.

Mixed commissions usually consist of an equal number of representatives of both parties and may be given either a broad brief of indefinite duration, or the task of dealing with a specific problem. An outstanding example of a commission of the first type is provided by the Canadian-United States International Joint Commission, which, since its creation in 1909, has dealt with a large number of issues including industrial development, air pollution and a variety of questions concerning boundary waters.

An illustration of the different functions that may be assigned to ad hoc commissions is to be found in the *Lake Lanoux* dispute. After being considered by the International Commission for the Pyrenees, a mixed commission established as long ago as 1875, the matter was referred to a Franco-Spanish Commission of Engineers, set up in 1949 to examine the technical aspects of the dispute. When the engineers' commission was unable to agree, France and Spain created a special mixed commission with the task of formulating proposals for the utilisation of Lake Lanoux and submitting them to the two governments for consideration. It was only when this commission was also unable to agree that the parties decided to refer the case to arbitration, though not before France had put forward (unsuccessfully) the idea of a fourth mixed commission, which would have had the function of supervising execution of the water diversion scheme and monitoring its day-to-day operation.

If negotiation through established machinery proves unproductive, "summit discussions" between heads of state or foreign ministers may be used in an attempt to break the deadlock. Though the value of such conspicuous means of negotiation should not be exaggerated, summit diplomacy may facilitate agreement by enabling official bureaucracies to be by-passed to some extent, while providing an incentive to agree in the form of enhanced prestige for the leaders concerned. It should be noted, however, that summit diplomacy is usually the culmination of a great deal of conventional negotiation and in some cases at least reflects nothing more than a desire to make political capital out of an agreement that is already assured.

NOTES

1) In Canadian practice[119] informal contacts with foreign governments may be made by senior officials of the federal government, as well as locally stationed diplomatic staff, on their own initiative and authority. Such contacts are likely to be preliminary to opening negotiations or to sound out opinion. Whether formal or informal, negotiations of any importance usually require ministerial, and even Cabinet, authorization. Even so, the actual negotiating is likely to be undertaken by a delegation of mostly middle-rank officials. A senior officer or a Minister will be the nominal leader but he may not be much involved until the final stages of agreement and signature are reached, unless the matter is of a high political character.

2) The Canada-United States International Joint Commission has responsibilities with respect to the waters which mark the international boundary between these two countries. Composed of three commissioners from each side, the Commission has a broad mandate which includes investigative and monitoring powers in some situations and quasi-judicial authority in others. The work of the commission has been a successful demonstration of bilateral means to reach peaceful accommodations over a shared resource.[120]

3) The world's press and domestic public opinion may nowadays have considerable impact on the course of intergovernmental negotiations. "The element of give and take which is usually an essential part of a successful negotiation is likely to be inhibited if every step is being monitored by interested pressure groups at home, while suspicion that the other side may simply be interested in eliciting a favourable audience reaction may lead serious proposals to be dismissed as mere propaganda."[121] The disarmament "talks" between the Super Powers are a case in point. These parties also engage in another practice dependant upon the modern media; their leaders send diplomatic messages to each other under the guise of public announcements and press conferences.

Good Offices, Mediation, Inquiry, and Conciliation

When the parties to an international dispute fail to settle their differences by negotiation between themselves, the introduction of a trusted stranger may help them. The intervention

---

[119] The conduct of negotiations by Canada in the largest multilateral conference to date – the Third U.N. Conference on the Law of the Sea – is analysed in A.L.C. de Mestral & L.H.J. Legault, "Multilateral Negotiation – Canada and the Law of the Sea Conference" (1979–80), 35 *Int. J.* 47.

[120] See M. Cohen, *The Regime of Boundary Waters – The Canadian-United States Experience* (1977); and R. Spencer et al., eds., *The International Joint Commission Seventy Years On* (1981).

[121] J.G. Merrills, *supra*, n. 116, at 13.

of a third party can occur in several ways, described as good offices, mediation, inquiry and conciliation. In essence, these processes are all aids to the resolution of a dispute by the parties themselves. The intervening third party does not decide the matter for them, he advises them. The differences between these processes are largely a matter of the degree of initiative taken by the intervenor to secure a settlement. While good offices connotes little more than a go-between who tries to induce the parties to negotiate, conciliation likely involves investigation of the dispute and presentation of a proposal for its solution. Mediation and inquiry lie in between. An inquiry may be made into the facts of the dispute; a mediator may assist the parties' negotiations.

Good Offices
from M. Lachs, (1980), 169 *Hague Recueil*, at 220–21 (footnotes omitted)

To begin with, the provision of good offices – what has been called "quiet diplomacy" – is an important function which may be entrusted to personalities with special qualifications on whom both parties agree. There have been many occasions where heads of States or governments have offered their good services and have been accepted, like the Chairman of the USSR Council of Ministers in the India-Pakistan dispute.[122] A particular role is reserved for the Secretary-General of the United Nations. He is the "chief administrative officer of the Organization." However, he may and should play a political role, which was foreseen very early when the United Nations was being created. He may be asked for or can offer his good offices in various forms and on different occasions and thus can play a very important role in the resolution of a dispute.

In quite a number of cases, the Secretary-General has in fact been able to assist in resolving disputes or has succeeded in arresting the deterioration of a situation by his actions conducted in time. As has been demonstrated in several concrete cases, it is especially his "quiet diplomacy" which may be fruitful in situations with a humanitarian background.

Speaking of the experience in this respect, U. Thant recalled:

Each Secretary-General must build as best he can on the Office as he inherited it. If he cannot hope to repeat all the successes of his predecessors, neither should he fear to try again where they failed.

Earlier U. Thant had pointed out:

The kind of problem involved is invariably delicate and difficult and usually involves the prestige and public position of the governments concerned. If a way out is to be found, it must, therefore, be through mutual confidence, mutual respect and absolute discretion. Any hint that an action of the Secretary-General might serve to score political points for one party or another, or, indeed, that credit might be claimed publicly on his behalf for this or that development, would

---

[122] Over Kashmir in 1965 (Ed.).

almost invariably and instantly render his efforts useless. Thus, it is often the case that while the Secretary-General is working privately with the parties in an attempt to resolve a delicate situation, he is criticized publicly for his inaction or even for lack of interest.

This is how the birth of the United Nations, apart from the machinery established and the principal organs provided for, has opened the way to an unofficial and quiet method for the settlement of disputes. These "good offices" may be extended to preventive action – by monitoring events; by establishing a "radar station," the Secretary-General could act in advance at a very early stage to prevent a political storm. This is of particular importance today when confrontation may so easily arise and, once a fact, can only with great difficulty be brought to an end.

NOTES

The Secretary-General is an international civil servant and the chief *administrative* officer of the United Nations. His position and power are defined by the Charter Articles 97–101 (See Appendix). Where in those articles is authority granted to him to intervene in disputes between member states? That successive Secretaries-General have intervened in international disputes, frequently to advantage, has not prevented questions being raised about their authority to do so by states that consider their actions an interference in sovereign or domestic affairs. The usual reply is that the Secretary-General is entitled under Article 99 "to bring to the attention of the Security Council any matter which in his opinion may threaten the maintenance of international peace and security" and, to do so, he has a right to take whatever steps he considers necessary to inform himself about a pending dispute.[123] Do you consider this implication is necessary to enable him to fulfill his functions? Is it a legitimate interpretation of Article 99? The Secretary-General may, of course, be invited by the parties or the Security Council to exercise his good officers, or to play any other role of assistance, in a dispute.

Mediation
from J.G. Merrills, *International Dispute Settlement* (1984),
at 20–21, 23, 30–32

Like good offices, mediation is essentially an adjunct of negotiation, but with the mediator as an active participant, authorised, and indeed expected, to advance his own proposals and to interpret, as well as to transmit, each party's proposals to the other. What distinguishes this kind of assistance from conciliation is that a mediator generally makes his proposals informally and on the basis of information supplied by the parties, rather than his own investigations, although in practice such distinctions tend to be blurred and in a

---

[123] V. Pechota, "The Quiet Approach: A Study of the Good Offices Exercised by the United Nations Secretary-General in the Cause of Peace," in K.V. Raman, *supra*, n. 116, at 585.

given case it may be difficult to draw the line between mediation and conciliation, or to say exactly when good offices ended and mediation began.

Mediation may be sought by the parties or offered spontaneously by outsiders. Once under way it provides the government in dispute with the possibility of a solution, but without any antecedent commitment to accept the mediator's suggestions. It therefore has the advantage of allowing them to retain control of the dispute, probably an essential requirement if negotiations are deadlocked on a matter of vital interest. On the other hand, if a face-saving compromise is what is needed, it may be politically easier to make the necessary concessions in the course of mediation than in direct negotiation. If a dispute concerns sensitive issues, the fact that the proceedings can be completely confidential is an advantage in any case. As with other means of dispute settlement, however, not every international dispute is suitable for mediation. The first requirement is a willing mediator. ...

Mediation may be performed by international organisations, by states or by individuals. For the United Nations and a number of regional organisations, the settlement of disputes is a basic institutional objective and as a result the Secretary-General and his regional counterparts are often engaged in providing good offices and mediation. Since it offers the opportunity to become involved in a dispute and to influence the outcome, the role of mediator also has attractions for states concerned to see a dispute resolved peacefully, or with an interest in a particular solution. Thus it is not unusual to find the course of an international dispute punctuated by offers of mediation from one or more outside parties. ...

Mediation cannot be forced on the parties to an international dispute, but only takes place if they consent. So unless they have taken the initiative and appointed a mediator already, their unwillingness to consider this form of assistance may prove a major stumbling block. This is because although a mediator's proposals are not binding, the very act of mediation has implications which may be unacceptable to either or both of the governments concerned. ...

Once mediation has begun, its prospects of success rest on the parties' willingness to make the necessary concessions. Though this can be encouraged by a skilful mediator in the ways described, the chances of a successful mediation often hinge on its timing.

In the Falklands crisis the aims of the parties were diametrically opposed. Argentina's objective was to rule the islands. Though Britain was not committed to retaining the Falklands indefinitely, it was prepared to relinquish sovereignty only on condition that the wishes of the inhabitants were respected, which in the circumstances made Argentine rule extremely unlikely. A mediated settlement therefore depended on whether either party was prepared to abandon its original aim and cut its losses. But mediation took place before the battles between the Argentine Air Force and the Royal Navy had indicated who had the military advantage. Thus mediation had to be tried at a time when both sides still had substantial hopes of a military solution and in those circumstances had little chance of success.

In the Kashmir and Rann of Kutch disputes, on the other hand, military action had already been tried and the offer of mediation could be timed to take advantage of the parties' search for some alternative. These disputes were therefore ripe for mediation. It is worth recalling, however, that despite this critical similarity, the effect of mediation in the two disputes was quite different. In the latter, ... mediation led eventually to a binding arbitration. In the Kashmir dispute, however, following the agreement on a cease-fire no progress was made in resolving the basic issue. When important interests are at stake, as in Kashmir, it will generally be much easier to negotiate a provisional solution than to achieve a permanent settlement. A cease-fire is better than nothing, of course, but like a temporary filling in a bad tooth may mean even more trouble in the future if steps are not taken to get to the root of the problem.

Sometimes, then, mediation may only be able to achieve a partial solution. Even that degree of progress will be impossible if the parties cling tenaciously to fundamentally incompatible positions – if, for instance, they are not prepared to acknowledge that a political solution is what is needed, rather than an endorsement of existing rights. In the Beagle Channel dispute Cardinal Samore's proposals would have been still-born if Chile had insisted on implementation of the Award with all its jurisdictional implications, just as mediation in the Falklands crisis would have been pointless had Britain refused to discuss the future status of the islands.

Thus mediation can only be as effective as the parties wish it to be and this is governed largely by their immediate circumstances. Though this is a major limitation on the usefulness of mediation, it is important to retain a sense of perspective. It would be quite wrong to think that a mediator is merely someone who lends his authority to an agreement that is already virtually made. On the contrary, by facilitating the parties' dialogue, providing them with information and suggestions, identifying and exploring their aims and canvassing a range of possible solutions, he can play a vital role in moving them towards agreement. Though success will often be incomplete and failure sometimes inevitable, the mediator's job is to do his best for the parties and trust that they will reciprocate.

Commissions of Inquiry

Investigation of the events giving rise to a dispute is a necessary part of all the processes of peaceful settlement. Commissions of inquiry, however, are institutional arrangements for the ascertainment of facts, separate and apart from efforts at settlement. They were introduced into international law by the Hague Conventions for the Pacific Settlement of International Disputes, 1899 and 1907. They are intended to provide a service of independent and objective fact-finding in the hope that clarification of the situation in dispute may help to dissolve contentious issues and to change favourably the attitudes and negotiating positions of the parties. The report of a commission is not binding or determinative, for the parties are free to decide what use and effect it shall have. Although the Hague Conventions created the process, a commission of inquiry has to be constituted on each occasion by agreement of the parties.

Commissions of inquiry under the Hague Conventions have not been frequent,[124] but the process of inquiry is a flexible addition to the battery of means to resolve international disputes and so it has been picked up by other organisations. For instance the International Court of Justice, under its Rules of Court Article 66, permits a fact-finding inquiry in

---

[124] For a discussion of them, see J.G. Merrills, *supra*, n. 116, c. 3.

the course of a case,[125] the I.C.A.O. Council ordered an investigation in the case of the *Destruction of Korean Airlines Flight 007*[126] and the new U.N. Convention on the Law of the Sea provides for the constitution of a special arbitral tribunal empowered to undertake inquiries.[127] The process of inquiry has also been varied and developed into other forms, the most significant of which is conciliation.

Conciliation[128]
from J.C. Merrills, *International Dispute Settlement* (1984) at 52, 60–64
(footnotes omitted)

Conciliation has been defined as:

a method for the settlement of international disputes of any nature according to which a Commission set up by the Parties either on a permanent basis or an *ad hoc* basis to deal with a dispute, proceeds to the impartial examination of the dispute and attempts to define the terms of a settlement susceptible of being accepted by them, or of affording the Parties, with a view to its settlement, such aid as they have requested.

The eclectic character of the method is at once apparent. If mediation is essentially an extension of negotiation, conciliation puts third party intervention on a formal legal footing and institutionalises it in a way comparable, but not identical, to inquiry or arbitration. For the fact-finding exercise that is the essence of inquiry may or may not be an important element in conciliation, while the search for terms "susceptible of being accepted" by the parties, but not binding on them, provides a sharp contrast with arbitration and a reminder of the link between conciliation and mediation. ...

What sort of process is conciliation? One view is that it is to be regarded as a kind of institutionalised negotiation. The task of the commission is to encourage and structure the parties' dialogue, while providing them with whatever assistance may be necessary to bring it to a successful conclusion. This approach, which proceeds from the premise that the resolution of disputes depends on securing the parties' agreement, finds an affinity between conciliation and mediation ... Another view is that conciliation is closer to inquiry or arbitration; that the commission's function is to provide information and advice as to the merits of the parties' positions and to suggest a settlement that corresponds to what they deserve, not what they claim. This approach ... reflects the historical link between conciliation and the procedure for enlarged inquiry contained in the Bryan treaties. ...

A conciliation commission has a duty to examine the nature and background of a dispute and so is usually equipped with wide powers of investigation. Unlike an inquiry,

---

[125] As in the *Corfu Channel Case*, [1949] I.C.J. Rep. 4, at 142, 152 and 258. See also W.F. Foster, "Fact Finding in the World Court" (1969), 7 *Can. Y.B. Int. L.* 150.

[126] See report of the incident *infra* in Chapter 6.

[127] (1982), 21 *Int. Leg. Mat.* 1261, Annex. VIII, Article 5.

[128] See J.P. Cot, *International Conciliation* (1972).

however, whose whole raison d'etre is to illuminate the dispute, a conciliation commission has as its objective the parties' conciliation. Its investigative powers are thus simply a means to an end. As a result, if it becomes apparent that the exposure of some matter might make conciliation more difficult, that line of investigation is unlikely to be pursued. In 1958 a Franco-Moroccan conciliation commission was set up to investigate the French authorities' diversion of an aircraft carrying Ben Bella and four other leaders of the Algerian revolt from Morocco to Tunis. The Commission was asked by Morocco to permit the questioning of all the passengers on the diverted plane, but refused to do so on the ground that "to have taken this evidence would, in the opinion of the Commission, have been likely to embitter Franco-Moroccan relations and thus defeat the purpose of the mission with which the Commission had been entrusted by the two governments." ...

[O]ne of the distinctive features of conciliation is that a commission's report takes the form of a set of proposals, not a decision. Thus even in cases where law has been a major consideration, the report is quite different from an arbitral award and not binding on the parties. This feature of conciliation has presented commissions with something of a dilemma. On the one hand they wish to make their proposals as persuasive as possible by supporting them with reasons; on the other they are unwilling to provide the parties with legal arguments or findings of fact that may be cited in subsequent litigation. The Belgo-Danish Commission adopted the curious expedient of accompanying a written statement of its conclusions with an oral explanation of its reasons. The Franco-Swiss and Italo-Swiss Commissions adopted the more satisfactory practice of providing a written account of both conclusions and reasons, subject to a restriction that "the opinion of the Commission on points of law may not be invoked by the parties before any tribunal, judicial or arbitral." A recent treaty of conciliation contains a provision to the same effect, indicating that the need for such precautions is well recognised.

Because the proposals of a conciliation commission can be either accepted or rejected, the usual practice is for the commission to give the parties a specified period of a few months in which to indicate their response. If its proposals are accepted the commission draws up a *proces-verbal* (agreement) recording the fact of conciliation and setting out the terms of the settlement. If the proposed terms are rejected, then conciliation has failed and the parties are under no further obligation.

NOTES

1) Although upwards of 200 treaties providing for conciliation have been concluded, less than 20 cases have been heard. The process has not fulfilled expectations. In theory conciliation serves a large variety of useful purposes. As Lauterpacht has enumerated them,[129] it brings the parties together; through a moratorium on their actions it prevents sudden breaches of the peace; it replaces rigid law with reasonable discourse about the controversy; it is marked by simplicity; it may have the advantages of the services of experts; and, as its findings are not binding in any case, it eases the conclusion of treaties

---

[129] *Supra*, n. 116, at 261.

on the pacific settlement of disputes. Conciliation is most useful in practice, Merrills suggests,[130] in disputes where legal issues are foremost but the parties want an equitable compromise. Such a combination of circumstances is not common.

2) Conciliation has been included in the dispute settlement procedures of a number of recent multilateral, law-making treaties, including the Vienna Convention on the Law of Treaties,[131] the International Covenant on Civil and Political Rights,[132] and the U.N. Convention on the Law of the Sea.[133] In addition, in 1981 the U.N. Commission on International Trade Law published a set of conciliation rules, including a model contract clause by which to invoke the rules. Belief in the possibilities of conciliation has demonstrably not abated, however, this confidence has yet to be honoured by practice under these conventions.

Arbitration[134]

In turning to arbitration the line is crossed from diplomatic methods of settling disputes to adjudication. The contrast is sharpened by the fact that an arbitral award is a binding decision. In choosing arbitration, the parties to a dispute invite others to resolve it for them.

Arbitration has a very long history. In modern times, its practice is usually traced to the series of arbitrations that arose from the Jay Treaty of 1794 between the United Kingdom and the United States. The popularity of arbitration as a means of composing international disputes in the nineteenth century culminated in the establishment of the Permanent Court of Arbitration through the Hague Conventions for the Pacific Settlement of International Disputes, 1899 and 1907. The effect of its creation was to institutionalize the process of arbitration. Each state, party to the Hague Conventions, appoints four persons to the panel of arbitrators. When two states, parties are in conflict and seek arbitration, they each select two arbitrators from the panel, only one of whom may be a national. The four arbitrators then choose an umpire.

The name "Permanent Court of Arbitration" may be misleading. As can be seen from the process, it is not a court in the sense that the World Court is, and it is not permanent. On each occasion the arbitral tribunal has to be constituted by the parties. Yet the idea of a stable panel of arbitrators paved the way for the creation of truly permanent organs of adjudication in the form of the World Court. The Permanent Court of Arbitration itself, though not the process of arbitration, has fallen into relative disuse. Its major use at present is to assist in the selection of the judges for the International Court of Justice.

---

[130] *Supra*, n. 116, at 66.

[131] (1969), 8 *Int. Leg. Mat.* 679, Art. 66 and Annex. See T.O. Elias, *The Modern Laws of Treaties* (1974), c. 13.

[132] (1967), 6 *Int. Leg. Mat.* 368, Art. 42.

[133] (1982), 21 *Int. Leg. Mat.* 1261, Art. 284 and Annex V.

[134] See K.S. Carlston, *The Process of International Arbitration* (1946); J.L. Simpson and H. Fox, *International Arbitration Law and Practice* (1959); and J.G. Wetter, *The International Arbitral Process: Public and Private* (1979), 5 volumes of materials and opinions.

The national groups of persons on the panel of arbitrators make the initial nominations of candidates for election as judges.[135]

In essence, arbitration is a form of adjudication which permits the parties to constitute and to operate their own court. Consequently, it has the attractions for states in disputes that they can select individuals as arbitrators in whom they have confidence and they can control the procedure that will be employed to resolve their conflict.

However, there are a great many details of procedure that must be taken care of in the *compromis d'arbitrage* or agreement for submission of a dispute to arbitration. Any omissions may mean the tribunal is not granted the necessary authority to complete the arbitration and the expectations of the parties, or one of them, is frustrated.

It must be appreciated that arbitration is only possible between states in dispute if, notwithstanding the depth of their differences over the substantive conflict, they genuinely desire a decision about it and are mutually trusting enough to negotiate an agreement about the procedure to obtain it. Unless the *compromis* is tightly drawn, it is easy for one side at a later stage, when feelings may be exacerbated or confidence in the process may have dissolved, to withdraw from or otherwise frustrate the arbitration.

These difficulties may be reduced in connection with disputes over matters which are the subject of a treaty between states if arbitral arrangements are written into their original agreement. It is obviously easier to establish a tribunal to decide possible future disputes, such as the interpretation of the treaty, at the time the parties are in full agreement. The most significant recent example is the elaborate machinery for dispute settlement which was so deliberately negotiated and included in the 1982 U.N. Convention on the Law of the Sea.[136] Arbitral arrangements are also frequently included in concession agreements and other contracts between governments and multinational corporations. The investing corporation cannot appear as a party to a case before the World Court, yet it may not be willing to subject its claims to the jurisdiction of the courts and the law of the state with whose government it is contracting. The obvious choice of an adjudicative process is arbitration. Recent instances, surrounding breach of petroleum concessions, are *Texaco v. Libya* and *LIAMCO v. Libya*.[137]

In the absence of any prior agreement to arbitrate, the parties must take care of all the details in their *compromis*. For the purpose of creating an *ad hoc* tribunal, the work of the International Law Commission may be helpful. Building on the experience of the Permanent Court of Arbitration, the General Act for the Pacific Settlement of International Disputes (1928)[138] and a host of bilateral treaties, the I.L.C. prepared a set of Model Rules on Arbitral Procedure.

---

[135] See *supra*, "The World Court."

[136] (1982), 21 *Int. Leg. Mat.* 1261, Arts. 279–99, Annex VII & VIII. See J.G. Merrills, *supra*, n. 116, c. 7. And see L.B. Sohn, "The Role of Arbitration in Recent International Multilateral Treaties" (1982–83), 23 *Va. J. Int. L.* 171.

[137] (1977), 53 I.L.R. 389; (1978), 17 *Int. Leg. Mat.* 1, reported *infra* in Chapter 9; and (1981), 20 *Int. Leg. Mat.* 1, respectively.

[138] 92 L.N.T.S. 343.

I.L.C. Model Rules on Arbitral Procedure, Art. 2
[1958] Y.B.I.L.C. 83

1. Unless there are earlier agreements which suffice for the purpose, for example in the undertaking to arbitrate itself, the parties having recourse to arbitration shall conclude a *compromis* which shall specify, as a minimum:

(a) The undertaking to arbitrate according to which the dispute is to be submitted to the arbitrators;

(b) The subject-matter of the dispute and, if possible, the points on which the parties are or are not agreed;

(c) The method of constituting the tribunal and the number of arbitrators;

2. In addition, the *compromis* shall include any other provisions deemed desirable by the parties, in particular:

(i) The rules of law and the principles to be applied by the tribunal, and the right, if any, conferred on it to decide *ex aequo et bono* as though it had legislative functions in the matter;

(ii) The power, if any, of the tribunal to make recommendations to the parties;

(iii) Such power as may be conferred on the tribunal to make its own rules of procedure;

(iv) The procedure to be followed by the tribunal; provided that, once constituted, the tribunal shall be free to override any provisions of the *compromis* which may prevent it from rendering its award;

(v) The number of members required for the constitution of a *quorum* for the conduct of the hearings;

(vi) The majority required for the award;

(vii) The time limit within which the award shall be rendered;

(viii) The right of the members of the tribunal to attach dissenting or individual opinions to the award, or any prohibition of such opinions;

(ix) The languages to be employed in the course of the proceedings;

(x) The manner in which the costs and disbursements shall be apportioned;

(xi) The services which the International Court of Justice may be asked to render.

NOTES

1) As their name suggests, these rules are not obligatory. They are a set of standards for the constitution and conduct of an arbitral tribunal which can be adopted by the disputing parties if they wish. They offer the opportunity to short-circuit some of the process of arranging the arbitration. They also serve as a reminder of what needs to be agreed. This list is not exhaustive but it does indicate the extensive range of matters that have to be attended to.

2) For commercial arbitrations involving transnational business disputes between multinational corporations and host governments several well known sets of rules are available. The parties may choose from procedures established, for instance, by the International

Chamber of Commerce,[139] the International Centre for Settlement of Investment Disputes,[140] or most recently by the U.N. Commission on International Trade Law (UNCITRAL). The Model Law on International Commercial Arbitration produced by UNCITRAL in 1985 has already been implemented by Canada[141] and several of the Provinces. The recent rapid growth of international commercial arbitration is also contributing to the development of a special body of transnational law made up eclectically from the rules of international law, common principles of national legal systems and the usages of international trade, and increasingly referred to as *lex mercatoria*.[142]

Trail Smelter Arbitration
(1931–41), 3 R.I.A.A. 1905, reported *infra* in Chapter 9

NOTES

1) The report of this affair includes the convention between Canada and the United States which constituted the arbitration. How completely does it fulfill the provisions of a *compromis* subsequently suggested by the I.L.C. Model Rules? Does it exceed them in any way?

2) Arbitration is regarded as a means of adjudication, that is a process of decision-making according to law. But along with control over the form and procedure of the tribunal, and the questions presented to it, the parties may also determine what law, national or international, shall be applied to their dispute. Indeed, they may also direct the tribunal to temper law with equitable considerations. In a matter wholly new to international law, the parties might go so far as to invite the tribunal to decide *ex aequo et bono*; in effect to legislate a solution for them. What laws or other criteria was the tribunal in the *Trail Smelter Arbitration* directed to apply? Why did the parties make this choice?

3) An arbitral award is final and binding on the parties. Nevertheless there may still be difficulties at the next stage of execution of the award. One side may assert the award is a nullity because the arbitrators exceeded their powers. The other side may complain that the award has not been complied with. Unfortunately, international law does not appear to provide any procedure to overcome these difficulties between states, should they arise. Resort to the International Court of Justice is not available, unless the parties expressly agree. This situation underscores the consensual basis of the arbitral process, and has to be resolved diplomatically.

---

[139] See W.L. Craig, W.W. Park, and J. Paulssen, *International Chamber of Commerce Arbitration* (1984), 2 binders.

[140] (1965), 575 U.N.T.S. 159. See A. Broches, "The Convention on the Settlement of Investment Disputes: Some Observations on Jurisdiction" (1966), 5 *Colum. J. Transnat. L.* 263.

[141] *Commercial Arbitration Act*, Stats. Can. 1986, c. 22.

[142] See, for instance, O. Lande, "The *Lex Mercatoria* in International Commercial Arbitration" (1985), 34 *Int. Comp. L.Q.* 747.

4) An award in a transnational commercial arbitration between a corporation and a government may be enforceable in a state where assets of the losing party can be found if the New York Convention on Recognition and Enforcement of Foreign Arbitral Awards,[143] or some similar bilateral treaty, can be brought into operation. Although Canada has recently ratified and implemented the New York Convention,[144] the prospects of enforcing awards against foreign governments are still surrounded with legal uncertainties.[145]

5) Since the awards of international arbitral tribunals are a subsidiary source for the determination of international law,[146] their publication is significant. Many have been collected and reprinted by the United Nations in a series of volumes entitled Reports of International Arbitral Awards (U.N.R.I.A.A.). Current awards of importance appear in International Legal Materials and the International Law Reports.

Agencies for Peaceful Settlement

The emphasis in this chapter has been upon the means of settling disputes, but the range of agencies by which these means may be effected should not be ignored. The various organs of the United Nations provide the greatest opportunity for, and preeminent example of, dispute settling machinery. In addition to the International Court of Justice, the General Assembly and the Security Council each have their own specific responsibilities for composing the peace.[147] The United Nations is so often involved in disputes between states because, in Pechota's estimation,[148] the Organization "seems to meet best the three essential conditions for a reasonably successful third-party intervention in the settlement." He notes that the United Nations has a standing which member states cannot ignore, offers methods and procedures known and generally agreeable to them, and disposes resources which can be turned to positive effect. In all it does, however, the United Nations is subject to the limitation that it shall not intervene in matters essentially within the domestic jurisdiction of any member state.[149]

The U.N. Charter Articles 52–54[150] also provide support for regional agencies which administer the means of pacific settlement of local disputes. There are many regional organizations which make extensive dispute settlement machinery available to member states.[151] Some obvious examples, which offer widely different procedures, are the European Economic Community, the Organization of African Unity, the Organization of American

---

[143] (1958), 330 U.N.T.S. 3. See A.J. van den Berg, *The New York Arbitration Convention of 1958* (1981); G. Gaja, *International Commercial Arbitration: New York Convention* (1985), 2 binders.

[144] *United Nations Foreign Arbitral Awards Convention Act*, Stats. Can. 1986, c. 21.

[145] See G.R. Delaume, "Arbitration with Governments: 'Domestic' v. 'International' Awards" (1983), 17 *Int. Lawyer* 687.

[146] I.C.J. Statute, Art. 38(1)(d), see Appendix.

[147] Discussed *supra* in Chapter 2.

[148] V. Pechota, "Complementary Structures of Third-Party Settlement of International Disputes," in K.V. Raman (ed.), *supra*, n. 116, at 153–54.

[149] Art. 2(7), see Appendix. Intervention is discussed *supra* in Chapter 2.

[150] See Appendix.

[151] For a good discussion of the range and role of regional organizations, see J.G. Merrills, *supra*, n. 116, c. 9.

States and the North Atlantic Treaty Organization. Furthermore, there are very many specialized agencies of the United Nations which provide organs for dispute settlement in their own fields. Some major ones, to which Canada is a party, include the International Civil Aviation Organization, the International Maritime Organization, and the General Agreement on Tariffs and Trade. Today there is an increasing number of institutions that have been created wholly for the purpose of promoting peaceful solutions to international disputes.[152] Thus the International Centre for Settlement of Investment Disputes conducts arbitrations of transnational business conflicts, and the European Court of Human Rights, the Inter-American Human Rights Court and the U.N. Petition System all determine human rights claims.[153]

The involvement of any of these non-adjudicative organizations in an international dispute does more than provide established machinery for its possible resolution. The presence of many interested states, members of the particular organization, in addition to the main disputants, can have a multilateralising effect that contributes to the diffusion of tension and thus increases the chances of settlement. In multilateral negotiations, for instance, the give and take necessary to reach a compromise is fractured between different pairs or groups of participants, so that a package deal may be struck that could never be reached bilaterally. The multilateral trade negotiations periodically conducted by the G.A.T.T. take advantage of this effect. The U.N. Convention on the Law of the Sea is another conspicuous example of a package deal. In other words, the multilateral setting of the organization or agency in which the conflict is handled, as well as the chosen means of settlement, may affect the outcome.

---

[152] From time to time interest is generated in the possibility of establishing bilateral standing machinery for third party settlement of the many problems which arise between Canada and the United States. See, for instance, the 1979 Report of a Joint Canadian Bar Association-American Bar Association Working Group, and E.B. Wang, "Adjudication of Canada-United States Disputes" (1981), 19 *Can. Y.B. Int. L.* 158. At press time, such a proposal was an item of confidential trade negotiations between the two countries.

[153] Discussed *infra* in Chapter 10.

CHAPTER FIVE

Inter-State Relations

INTRODUCTION

So long as international society is organised, as a matter of law, around the existence of states who exercise independent sovereign authority, there is a need for a mechanism of admission to that society of states. The concept of recognition fulfills this need. The criteria of statehood and of government, discussed in Chapter 2, have to be satisfied by any claimant to international legal personality, but their attainment is not by itself sufficient to grant entrance to the society of states. In the decentralised system of international law there is no single organ having collective authority to determine claims for admission by new states and new governments. The decision is left to the established governments of existing states to exercise their sovereign and independent judgment whether the claims of the new regime should be recognised. The result is a bilateral and reciprocal initiation of full international relations between the existing and the new regimes. The general recognition of the international legal personality of a state or government is only attained to the extent that such bilateral accords proliferate.

The process of recognition is important in international law because it opens the way to full inter-state relations. Both international and internal consequences flow from the act of recognition. From the point of view of a newly recognised regime, the most important effect is that it acquires all the rights at international law of a sovereign equal to other (recognising) states. This recognition may well be needed to bolster its recently gained authority. The rights that are acquired are both substantive and procedural. For instance, recognition of a new state typically results in the opening of diplomatic relations and the exchange of ambassadors.

Responsibilities, as well as rights, also accompany recognition. Indeed, recognition brings into play a whole body of international rules about the conduct of inter-state relations. It is this law which permits governments, through departments of external affairs, ambassadors, consuls, trade missions and other official representatives, freely to transact the daily business of diplomacy. There has long been universal appreciation of the mutual necessity of rules and procedures to facilitate these diplomatic contacts. Yet

every state, as a legally independent sovereign, has territorial authority to control the
entry, movement and activities of foreigners and foreign influences. Hence foreign state
representatives would risk the wrath of receiving governments every time they transmitted
displeasing communiques were there not also rules to protect the channels of diplomacy.
Thus much of the law of inter-state relations consists of rules that grant immunity from
the jurisdiction of the territorial sovereign to the foreign head of state, his government,
representatives and property.

This chapter explains the law of inter-state relations.[1] It begins in the first section with
a consideration of the process of recognition and continues with a discussion of its
consequences. Since by far the most important effects are in the accrual of certain state
immunities and diplomatic and consular immunities, these matters are taken up separately
in later sections of the chapter.

RECOGNITION[2]

The Practice of Recognition

Recognition has been described as: "The free act by which one or more States acknowledge the existence on a definite territory of a human society politically organized, independent of any other existing State, and capable of observing the obligations of international
law, and by which they manifest therefore their intention to consider it a member of the
international Community."[3] This description distinguishes two elements in an act of
recognition. It confirms first that the claimant to recognition must satisfy the legal criteria
for statehood. It goes on, secondly, to explain that the recognising state is publicly
expressing its decision to respect the claimant as an independent sovereign equal.

Recognition is not limited to states. It is also applied to new governments, to states
in a condition of belligerency, to organised and effective insurgents, and more loosely
to the territorial claims of states. The distinction between recognition of states and governments is most important. A recognised government cannot exist in the absence of a
recognised state. Typically, a new state will be recognised and at the same time the
regime which established it will be recognised as the government. In practice, changes
to states are not nearly so frequent as changes of governments. Most often the matter of
upper most concern is whether to recognise a new regime, which came to power by
revolutionary means, in an existing state. Unconstitutional changes of government,

---

[1] For consideration of the degree to which law and legal advisors influence inter-state relations, see L. Henkin,
How Nations Behave (2 ed., 1979); and R. St. J. Macdonald, "The Role of the Legal Adviser of Ministries
of Foreign Affairs" (1977), 156 *Hague Recueil* 376.

[2] See generally, H.M. Blix, "Contemporary Aspects of Recognition" (1970), 130 *Hague Recueil* 587; T.C.
Chen, *The International Law of Recognition* (1951); H. Lauterpacht, *Recognition in International Law* (1947);
D.P. O'Connell, *International Law* (2 ed., 1970), Vol. 1., cc. 5, 6; and from a Canadian viewpoint, see, E.
Binavince, "Canadian Practice in Matters of Recognition," in R. St. J. Macdonald, G. Morris and D.M.
Johnston, eds., *Canadian Perspectives on International Law and Organisation* (1974), at 153; L.C. Green,
International Law: A Canadian Perspective (1984), at 103.

[3] Resolution of Institut de Droit International, Brussels (1936), 30 *Am. J. Int. L. Supp.* 185.

alterations in the name, and even the limited movement of territorial boundaries do not upset the continuation of recognition of the state itself.

Though the description of recognition clearly acknowledges the power of existing states to recognise others, it does not explain whether this authority is a duty or a discretion. If a claimant fulfils the requirements of statehood, must other states respond with recognition; when may they react? These questions depend upon one's conceptual view of the effect of an act of recognition.

Theories of Recognition
from S. Williams and A.L.C. de Mestral, *An Introduction to International Law* (2 ed., 1987), at 80–81 (footnotes omitted)

There has been much legal argument on the actual effect of recognition. Recognition, it is true, implies not just an attestation that a state or government exists and has the qualifications to be recognized. This undoubtedly has been evidenced by the delays that can occur before recognition is extended even when a state or government is obviously in existence and effectively functioning. Once recognition has been extended the recognizing state has, in essence, agreed to the formalization of relations between itself and the recognized state or government.

The theories that have been advanced concerning actual effect centre around other, wider, implications of recognition. These theories are basically two in number. First, there is the constitutive theory. According to this theory, recognition has a constitutive effect. It is only through the act of recognition that international personality is conferred. It is recognition that creates the state and gives a new government legal personality and not the process by which they are factually formed. States and governments, according to this theory, are only established as subjects of international law by the will of the international community through recognition. Two striking difficulties arise. Is an unrecognized state bound by international law? What if a state is only recognized by some states and not by others.

Secondly, there is the declaratory theory or evidentiary theory. This theory adopts an opposing approach and in view of state practice may appear to be more in line with reality. It holds that statehood or governmental authority does exist prior to recognition. The recognition is only a formal acceptance of an already existing situation. Thus, it is the factual situation that produces the legal constitution of the entities and recognition does not have to be awaited for this purpose.

These two theories are directly in conflict. The first presents the picture of the unrecognized state in a sort of limbo. The second puts emphasis on the facts and belittles the effect of recognition. The difficulty lies in evaluating these two opposites. The correct position probably lies somewhere in between the two. The majority of opinion supports the declaratory theory. Practice points to it. Even when a state refuses to recognize a new state or government, it rarely contends that the new entity has no powers or obligations. The position has in fact been taken that rules of international law are binding upon unrecognized states or governments. The usual reference is made that recognition is being refused not on the grounds of lack of effective control or some such reason but on political grounds. For example the United States approach towards China until 1978 or the Arab world with respect to Israel. If the constitutive approach were to be used perhaps the government of the unrecognized state would not have to abide by any international rules *vis-à-vis* the non-recognizing state.

It has been suggested that there is a duty on states to recognize where the requisite factors are present. This approach, it is said, would lead the constitutive theory to be modernized. However, the arbitrariness of states' actions in this area does not support this duty. If such a duty were to exist, in what manner could it be enforced? Could a state demand recognition? At the present time each state must decide for itself whether or not to recognize another state or government.

In effect, the truth lies in both theories. Recognition is declaratory in that, for the most part, it is extended to entities that fulfill the factual qualifications; moreover it is constitutive, in that it enables states or governments to be brought out of a vacuum into the world of diplomacy and international relations as an equal.

NOTES

1) As can be seen from this extract, the constitutive theory places importance on the formal elements of recognition and thus tends to emphasize its legal characteristics. Those who agree with this approach may be expected to be more sympathetic to the view that a new state ought to be recognised by others as soon as it satisfies the minimum criteria.[4] Alternatively, the declaratory theory describes the fact that states often withhold recognition from a new state or government for ulterior political reasons precisely because recognition has such diplomatic as well as legal significance.[5]

2) The United Kingdom used to be one of the few states with a declared recognition policy in accordance with the constitutive theory. The U.K. government was of the opinion that recognition should not depend on whether it approved the regime in question.[6] The statement of policy rightly drew a distinction between recognition and diplomatic relations. Whether ambassadors are exchanged is an entirely discretionary matter. Though it is the normal occurrence upon recognition, there is nothing to prevent the recall of representatives and even the severance of diplomatic relations as a mark of disapproval of the existing government or a new regime. Thus there are many opportunities for the diplomatic display of political opinions other than the process of recognition.

3) The extent to which diplomacy and law are intermingled in decisions about recognition may be judged from the following examples of state practice.

Canadian Practice of Recognition
Reported in (1975), 13 *Can. Y.B. Int. L.* 354–55

[In a memorandum dated July 18, 1974, the Department of External Affairs wrote:] The purpose of this memorandum is to set out relevant legal principles on recognition.

---

[4] For instance, see H. Lauterpacht, *supra*, n. 2, at 61–63.
[5] For instance, see T.C. Chen, *supra*, n. 2, at 77–78.
[6] (1951) *U.K. Hansard*, H.C. vol. 485, Col. 2411.

Effective Control

Canadian practice in the recognition of new governments is to treat each situation on its own merits, with an appropriate politico-legal decision being taken in due course. This involves a decision as to whether an authority, claiming to be the government of a particular State, is in fact entitled to be regarded as representing that state on the international plane. On this connection *the essential question is whether the particular authority is regarded by Canada as able to exercise effective control, with a reasonable prospect of permanency, over the area which it claims to govern*. The support it enjoys from the population of that territory and evidence of its willingness to fulfil its international legal obligations are also usually taken into account. ...

Political Considerations

It should be noted that, while the act of recognition is legal in nature, the relevancy of political considerations is generally accepted in modern international practice. Thus *there exists scope for the exercise of a kind of, but perhaps not an arbitrary, discretion* in the determination as to whether the necessary conditions for recognition have been met. It is a policy decision to determine, on the merits and circumstances of each case, whether the legal conditions for recognition are fulfilled. On the other hand, the granting of recognition by the Canadian Government to another government is not viewed as signifying approval of the policies of that government, or for that matter, of the political philosophy of that government or of the manner in which it came into power.

Timing of Recognition

In general, after a change of government resulting from a coup d'etat, Canadian practice has been *to reserve our position for a period of time of sufficient length to permit reasoned determination of the extent of the authority of the new government and its likelihood of permanence*. In such situations, a decision on recognition may have to await the resolution of internal struggle. ...

A key factor with respect to the timing of recognition is that it ought not to be effected too early, inasmuch as this might in itself tend to constitute interference in the internal affairs of a sovereign state. In fact, so long as the "lawful government" has a reasonable prospect of reasserting its authority, recognition would constitute a violation of the non-intervention principle as set out in Article 2(7) of the United Nations Charter.

American Practice of Recognition[7]
Reported in (1977), 77 *U.S. Dept. of State Bulletin* 462

Diplomatic recognition of governments is a comparatively recent practice in the history of international relations. Traditionally some European governments used nonrecognition of revolutionary change to protect monarchies and to emphasize the unique legitimacy of dynastic heirs and their governments. France ignored this tradition by recognizing the

---

[7] L.T. Galloway, *Recognizing Foreign Governments: The Practice of the United States* (1978).

United States during our Revolutionary War. Later, when the revolutionary French Government took power in 1792, Thomas Jefferson, our first Secretary of State, instructed the U.S. envoy in Paris to deal with it because it had been formed by the will of the nation substantially declared.

Throughout most of the 19th century, the United States recognized stable governments without thereby attempting to confer approval. U.S. recognition policy grew more complex as various Administrations applied differing criteria for recognition and expressed differently the reasons for their decisions. For example, Secretary of State William Seward (1861–69) added as a criterion the government's ability to honor its international obligations; President Rutherford Hayes (1877–81) required a demonstration of popular support for the new government; and President Woodrow Wilson (1913–21) favored using recognition to spread democracy around the world by demanding free elections.

Other criteria have been applied since then. These include the degree of foreign involvement in the government as well as the government's political orientation, attitude toward foreign investment, and treatment of U.S. citizens, corporations, and government representatives.

One result of such complex recognition criteria was to create the impression among other nations that the United States approved of those governments it recognized and disapproved of those from which it withheld recognition. This appearance of approval, in turn, affected our decisions in ways that have not always advanced U.S. interests. In recent years, U.S. practice has been to deemphasize and avoid the use of recognition in cases of changes of governments and to concern ourselves with the question of whether we wish to have diplomatic relations with the new governments.

The Administration's policy is that establishment of relations does not involve approval or disapproval but merely demonstrates a willingness on our part to conduct our affairs with other governments directly. In today's interdependent world, effective contacts with other governments are of ever-increasing importance.

British Practice of Recognition[8]
(1980) *U.K. Hansard*, H.L. vol. 408, Cols. 1121–22

[The Foreign Secretary, Lord Carrington, stated in the House of Lords:]

...we have conducted a re-examination of British policy and practice concerning the recognition of Governments. This has included a comparison with the practice of our partners and allies. On the basis of this review we have decided that we shall no longer accord recognition to Governments. The British Government recognise States in accordance with common international doctrine.

Where an unconstitutional change of regime takes place in a recognised State, Gov-

---

[8] C.R. Symmons, "United Kingdom Abolition of the Doctrine of Recognition of Governments: A Rose by Another Name," [1981] *Pub L.* 249; and C. Warbrick, "The New British Policy on Recognition of Governments" (1981), 30 *Int. Comp. L.Q.* 568.

ernments of other States must necessarily consider what dealings, if any, they should have with the new regime, and whether and to what extent it qualifies to be treated as the Government of the State concerned. Many of our partners and allies take the position that they do not recognise Governments and that therefore no question of recognition arises in such cases. By contrast, the policy of successive British Governments has been that we should make and announce a decision formally recognising the new Government.

This practice has sometimes been misunderstood, and, despite explanations to the contrary, our recognition interpreted as implying approval. For example, in circumstances where there might be legitimate public concern about the violation of human rights by the new regime, or the manner in which it achieved power, it has not sufficed to say that an announcement of recognition is simply a neutral formality. We have therefore concluded that there are practical advantages in following the policy of many other countries in not according recognition to Governments. Like them, we shall continue to decide the nature of our dealings with regimes which come to power unconstitutionally in the light of our assessment of whether they are able of themselves to exercise effective control of the territory of the State concerned, and seem likely to continue to do so.

NOTES

1) The Canadian memorandum asserts that "the granting of recognition by the Canadian Government to another government is not viewed as signifying approval of the policies of that government. ..." How do you suppose the newly recognised government is likely to view Canadian recognition? Can the Canadian government overlook the likely response of the new regime in deciding whether to recognise it or not? On an earlier occasion the Secretary of State for External Affairs wrote:[9]

There is no obligation on Canada to recognize another state. Recognition can therefore be withheld, and has been withheld, in certain cases to indicate disapproval of policies especially repugnant to Canadians, such as those of the regime in Rhodesia.

2) The American and British statements eliminate the recognition of governments, but not of states. The recognition of a state remains a necessary precursor to having diplomatic relations with its government.

3) The elimination of the recognition of governments was first announced as long ago as 1930 by the then Foreign Minister of Mexico, Senor Estrada. As a result of the political use of recognition of the kind described in the American statement, Mexico felt its internal affairs had been unwarrantedly subjected to judgment by other states. Mexico therefore declared it would no longer make statements recognizing new governments, whether they came to power by constitutional or unconstitutional means. The Estrada Doctrine, as it

---

[9] Letter of January 25, 1972, reported in (1973), 11 *Can. Y.B. Int. L.* 307–8.

is sometimes known, is now followed more or less by a great number of countries.[10] The doctrine implies that recognition of governments is at worst harmful and at best unnecessary. Is this true?[11]

The British statement says "there are practical advantages" in not according recognition. Why is it beneficial to governments to avoid statements appearing to approve or disapprove of each other? The Pol Pot government in Kampuchea was notorious for its widespread violation of human rights. Sergeant Doe's coup in Liberia exacted a particularly brutal retaliation on the former government members. Britain had recognized these regimes before its change in recognition policy.

In the absence of recognition of governments, what significance is to be attached to maintaining or breaking diplomatic relations with a state? In a survey of 30 states, Nomura[12] discovered that the factors taken into account for decisions on recognition, where still accorded, or diplomatic relations are the same.

If two governments contest authority in the same state, as in Spain or Angola during civil war, what is a state that follows the Estrada doctrine to do?

4) Canada is now in a distinct minority amongst Western countries in continuing to pronounce about the recognition of governments. Would you advise the Canadian government to change its policy?

5) International law does not prescribe any particular form for an act of recognition of a state or a government. Recognition is a matter of the intent of the recognising government. As such, it may be accorded expressly by way of a diplomatic note, a personal message to the Head of State, or an exchange of communications between foreign ministries; it may even be made by a unilateral public statement, such as a declaration in Parliament. Recognition may also be implied by conduct, such as the opening of diplomatic relations or the signing of a bilateral treaty. But the intention to recognise must be clear and not ambiguous; thus a state that signs a multilateral treaty cannot be assumed without question to recognise all the other signatories, and certainly not when it enters a reservation to this effect.

6) The international community has not yet developed any form of collective recognition, at least not of governments. Common membership in an international organization does not necessarily signify unilateral recognition any more so than common participation in a multilateral treaty. Obviously, the smaller and more integrated the organisation is, the stronger is the implication of recognition amongst the membership. Warsaw Pact membership is an example. Yet even in an universal organisation, it may be argued that election to membership binds all the existing members. See, for example, U.N. Charter Article 4[13] which provides for admission of all "states" who satisfy certain criteria "in the judgment of the Organization." It is consequently very hard to argue that a member of the United Nations is not in fact a state, however there are members who do not

---

[10] L.T. Galloway, *supra*, n. 7, surveys the practice of many states, as well as tracing the history and evaluating the experience of the United States.

[11] See L.T. Galloway, *supra*, n. 7, at 148–51. Cp. M.J. Peterson, "Recognition of Governments Should Not Be Abolished" (1983), 77 *Am. J. Int. L.* 31.

[12] I. Nomura, "Recognition of Foreign Governments" (1982), 25 *Jap. Ann. Int. L.* 67.

[13] In the Appendix. And see the *Conditions of Admissions to the United Nations Case*, [1948] I.C.J. Rep. 57.

recognize each other as such. For instance, many of the Arab countries do not recognize the state of Israel. In these circumstances, what legal status does admission to the United Nations confer on members? Membership by states certainly does not imply anything about the recognition of their governments.

In regional organisations that are concerned about the external relations of their member states with non-members, there may be careful consideration given to recognition matters in order to achieve uniformity of action. Thus NATO members consulted over the non-recognition of the Kamal government in Afghanistan. The European Economic Community has the greatest collective authority, for it may develop a common European position on foreign policy matters. This power has been exercised in recognition questions, such as the decision not to recognise the Transkei as a separate state.

International Effects of Recognition

Under international law the effect of recognition is that the state or government which is recognised thereby acquires not only the respect of the recognising state for all the rights and privileges but also the duties associated with its new found authority. The principal measure of this status is admittance to the full range of international processes for the protection of a state's rights and duties. Thus the recognised state or government can then enter into diplomatic relations with other states by exchanging representatives and may conclude treaties with them. Non-recognition, with its consequent absence of diplomatic relations, may limit an unrecognised regime in pressing its rights, or other states in asserting its responsibilities, under international law. However, non-recognition does not necessarily affect the existence of such rights and duties.

Tinoco Arbitration
Great Britain v. Costa Rica
(1923), 1 R.I.A.A. 375

See the report of this case *supra* in Chapter 2.

NOTES

Though non-recognition of a government does not affect the rights and responsibilities of the state, their execution is hindered, even incapacitated. Thus treaties already in force will continue to bind the state but may be, in effect, inoperative during the period of an unrecognised government.[14] Conversely, foreigners travelling, investing or doing business in a country whose government is unrecognised do so with added risk since their national government has no direct diplomatic channels by which to protect them.

---

[14] See, for instance, the *Aaland Islands Case* (1920), L.N.O.J. Special Supp. (no. 3).

Internal Effects of Recognition

The newly recognised state or government may expect to have its sovereign authority respected in the recognising state by all organs of government. This respect is usually said to include a right:

   1) to sue in the courts of the recognising state;
   2) to take control of state property located in the recognising state;
   3) to have effect accorded to its legislative and executive acts of state; and
   4) to claim immunity from suit in the courts of the recognising state for itself, its property and its representatives.

These rights exist at international law so that the failure of the recognising government to accord them to the new authorities creates international responsibility. In Canada's case, this means that the courts, the police, the civil service, the legislatures and all the other parts of the federal and provincial governments are bound to respect these foreign states' rights. How effect is given to them is a matter of internal organisation by the recognising state. These materials discuss the Canadian arrangements, especially in judicial fora. Since state immunity is such a large and distinct topic it is treated separately in the next section.

Executive Certificates

Within the recognising state, the act of recognition by its government is a signal to all its other organs, including the courts, that they must now respect the international rights of the new foreign regime. Consequently, the first matter to consider is how the courts shall be informed about acts of recognition by the government.

In the case of diplomatic representatives accredited to Canada, when their credentials have been accepted by the Governor-in-Council their names are added to the diplomatic list published in the Royal Gazette. However, recognitions of the foreign regimes themselves are not formally published. The courts, therefore, have to ask the government whether it has granted recognition or not. This is typically done by addressing the Secretary of State for Foreign Affairs with a request for an Executive Certificate.

Re Chateau-Gai Wines Ltd. and A.-G. for Can.
[1970] Ex. C.R. 366, at 382–84

[In the course of a trade mark dispute over the use of the appellation champagne, the court had to consider the effect of the Canada-France Trade Agreement of 1933. One of the uncertainties was whether the signed treaty ever entered into force between the two countries.]

JACKETT, P.: ... In principle, as it seems to me, a question whether of fact or law or both, as to whether an international agreement between Canada and another country has come into force between Canada and another sovereign power so as to create international rights and obligations, must be determined, in case of doubt, in the same way as

(a) a question as to whether a person is a foreign sovereign power,

(b) a question as to what persons must be regarded as constituting the effective government of a foreign territory,

(c) a question as to whether a particular place must be regarded as being in Canada or as being under the authority of a foreign sovereign authority,

(d) a question as to whether Canada is at peace or at war with a foreign power, or

(e) a question as to whether a person in Canada is entitled to diplomatic privileges as being an ambassador of a foreign power or a member of the entourage of such an ambassador.

All such questions are questions within the realm of responsibility of the executive arm of government and, being questions on which the state should speak with one voice, they are questions with regard to which the courts should accept from the appropriate minister of the Crown a certificate as to Canada's position. In my opinion, this view of the law is well settled ... .

NOTES

1) The practice of seeking executive certificates is well settled indeed. President Jackett could cite cases going back to *Taylor v. Barclay*[15] in 1828. His enumeration of topics is an accurate statement of the matters on which the courts regularly request ministerial certificates. The courts decide for themselves a number of similar matters, such as the representative status of foreign government agencies and trading enterprises,[16] or the status of alleged foreign state property.[17] Are these not also "questions within the realm of responsibility of the executive arm of government"?

2) One of the cases relied upon by Jackett, P. was *The Arantzazu Mendi* which involved a request for a certificate concerning the status of the Nationalist Government of Spain during the Spanish Civil War. Lord Atkin remarked:[18]

I pause here to say that not only is this the correct procedure, but that it is the only procedure by which the Court can inform itself of the material fact whether the party sought to be impleaded or whose property is sought to be affected, is a foreign sovereign state.

Should Canadian courts follow Lord Atkin's dictum?[19] Why would the courts want to limit their sources of evidence of a "material fact"? For instance, what is the court to

---

[15] 2 Sim. 213; 57 E.R. 769.

[16] E.g., *Compania Mercantil Argentina v. U.S. Shipping Board* (1924), 93 Sol. J. 816 (C.A.); *Krajina v. Tass Agency*, [1949] 2 All E.R. 274 (C.A.); *Baccus S.R.L. v. Servicio National des Trigo*, [1957] 1 Q.B. 438 (C.A.).

[17] E.g., *Haile Selassie v. Cable and Wireless Ltd. (No. 2)*, [1939] Ch. 182 (C.A.), reported below.

[18] [1939] A.C. 256, at 264. See also the majority view in *Duff Development v. Kelantan*, [1924] A.C. 797 (H.L.), on which Lord Atkin relied.

[19] The issue is now affected by statute. See the *State Immunity Act*, S.C. 1982, c. 95, s. 13, reported *infra*, and the *Diplomatic and Consular Privileges and Immunities Act*, S.C. 1976–77, c. 31, s. 5, reported *infra*.

do if, because of the diplomatic delicacy of the situation, the government issues an insufficient or ambiguous certificate? See, for example, the certificate issued in *Luther v. Sagor*.[20] In *Duff Development v. Kelantan*, Lord Sumner said:[21]

...the Courts are bound ... to act on the best evidence and, if the question is whether some new State or some older State, whose sovereignty is not notorious, is a sovereign state or not, the best evidence is a statement, which the Crown condescends to permit the appropriate Secretary of State to give on its behalf.

3) The use of executive certificates is said to have a deeper purpose than merely being the means to inform the courts of the government's opinion. They fulfill that function, but the function itself is thought essential because, as Jackett P. said, "the State should speak with one voice." Lord Atkin stated this principle most clearly in *The Arantzazu Mendi*:[22]

Our State cannot speak with two voices on such a matter, the judiciary saying one thing, the executive another. Our Sovereign has to decide whom he will recognize as a fellow sovereign in the family of States; and the relations of the foreign State with ours in the matter of State immunities must flow from that decision alone.

Though the principle is frequently reiterated, the reasons for it have never been made plain by the courts. Do you consider the principle is necessary on account of the constitutional separation of powers between the executive government and the judiciary, or out of a fear of embarassing the government in the conduct of its foreign policy, or for any other reason? As a consequence of the principle the courts defer to the government and abnegate a part of their adjudicative function. Although the courts have never attempted to define the range of matters over which they will accept the decision of the government, they have included all the situations itemized by Jackett P. and also questions concerning the boundaries of a foreign state, the authority of foreign acts of state, the extent of national territory, and the protection of national sovereignty from foreign extra-territorial jurisdiction.[23]

4) Jackett P. said that executive certificates should be sought whether the question was "of fact or law or both," but Lord Atkin, in the quotation from *The Arantzazu Mendi* in point 2, spoke only of "material fact." Which opinion is correct? Harrison Moore coined the apt phrase "facts of state"[24] to cover all those matters which are decisions of policy for the government and thereafter become facts in the courts' determinations at law. Consider the situation faced by Jackett P.: what was the force and effect of a certain

---

[20] Reported after these notes. See A.B. Lyons, "Judicial Application of International Law and the 'Temporizing' Certificate of the Executive" (1952), 29 *Br. Y.B. Int. L.* 227.

[21] [1924] A.C. 797, at 824. This view was criticized by Lord Atkin in the *Arantzazu Mendi, supra*, n. 18.

[22] *Supra*, n. 18, at 264.

[23] For a critical view of the principle and its consequences, see H.M. Kindred, "Foreign Governments Before the Courts" (1980), 58 *Can. Bar Rev.* 602.

[24] In his *Act of State in English Law* (1906), at 33.

treaty? While it was undoubtedly right to ask the Secretary of State what had been done by Canada, does it necessarily follow that in law the intended result had been achieved? Whose job is it to interpret the effect of the treaty?

5) If the Canadian government was to abandon the practice of pronouncing on the recognition of foreign governments, should the courts continue to defer to the executive for guidance as to the status of future unconstitutional regimes? What purpose will executive certificates serve? What will become of the principle that the courts and the government should speak with one voice? Are the changes desirable?

Luther v. Sagor
[1921] 1 K.B. 456, rev'd. [1921] 3 K.B. 532 (C.A.)

[The plaintiff's saw mill and business was confiscated by decree of the Soviet Government following the Russian Revolution. Later, agents of the government sold some of the stock of plywood from the mill to the defendant company. When it imported the plywood into Britain, the plaintiff brought suit, claiming to be the true owner.]

ROCHE J.: ... it is clear that the defendants' claim to defeat the plaintiff's title depends in the first instance upon the decree ... being a valid legislative act which can be recognized as such in the Courts of this country.

Whether the decree in question is a valid legislative act which can be recognized as such by the Courts of this country must, in my judgment, depend upon whether the power from which it purports to emanate is what it apparently claims to be, a sovereign power, in this case the sovereign power of the Russian Federative Republic. The proper source of information as to a foreign power, its status and sovereignty, is the Sovereign of this country through the Government:

I therefore propose to deal with the case upon the information furnished by His Majesty's Secretary of State for Foreign Affairs. The attitude proper to be adopted by a Court of this country with regard to foreign governments or powers I understand to be as follows: (1.) If a foreign government is recognized by the Government of this country the Courts of this country may and must recognize the sovereignty of that foreign government and the validity of its acts: see *Republic of Peru v. Dreyfus* [38 Ch.D. 348.], and the cases there cited. (2.) If a foreign government, or its sovereignty, is not recognized by the Government of this country the Courts of this country either cannot, or at least need not, or ought not, to take notice of, or recognize such foreign government or its sovereignty. This negative proposition is, I think, also established and recognized by the judgment of Kay J. in *Republic of Peru v. Dreyfus* [38 Ch.D., pp. 357, 358, and 359.].

This being the law which must guide and direct my decision, I have to consider whether and in what sense the Government represented by M. Krassin in this matter is recognized by His Majesty's Government. The materials for a decision have been provided for me by the parties who have each by their solicitors asked for information from His Majesty's Secretary of State for Foreign Affairs.

[Roche J. first read the letter to the defendants, then the following letter to the plaintiffs.]

FOREIGN OFFICE,
27th November, 1920.

Gentlemen,

I am directed by Earl Curzon of Kedleston to acknowledge the receipt of your letter FT/A of November 19th, requesting certain information concerning the Russian Trade Delegation in this Country, and the Esthonian-Russian Peace Treaty. I am to inform you that for a certain limited purpose His Majesty's Government has regarded Monsieur Krassin as exempt from the process of the Courts, and also for the like limited purpose His Majesty's Government has assented to the claim that that which Monsieur Krassin represents in this Country is a State Government of Russia, but that beyond these propositions the Foreign Office has not gone, nor moreover do these expressions of opinion purport to decide difficult, and it may be very special questions of law upon which it may become necessary for the Courts to pronounce. I am to add that His Majesty's Government have never officially recognised the Soviet Government in any way.

It was said on behalf of the defendants that these communications were vague and ambiguous. I should rather say that they were guarded, but as clear as the indeterminate position of affairs in connection with the subject-matter of the communications enabled them to be; ... On these materials I am not satisfied that His Majesty's Government has recognized the Soviet Government as the Government of a Russian Federative Republic or of any sovereign state or power. I therefore am unable to recognize it, or to hold it has sovereignty, or is able by decree to deprive the plaintiff company of its property. Accordingly I decide this point against the defendants ... .

Judgment for plaintiffs.

On Appeal, BANKES L.J.: ... Upon the evidence which was before the learned judge I think that his decision was quite right.

In this Court the appellants asked leave to adduce further evidence, and as the respondents raised no objection, the evidence was given. It consisted of two letters from the Foreign Office dated respectively April 20 and 22, 1921. The first is in reply to a letter dated April 12, which the appellants' solicitors wrote to the Under Secretary of State for Foreign Affairs, asking for a "Certificate for production to the Court of Appeal that the Government of the Russian Socialist Federal Soviet Republic is recognized by His Majesty's Government as the de facto Government of Russia." To this request a reply was received dated April 20, 1921, in these terms: "I am directed by Earl Curzon of Kedleston to refer to your letter of April 12, asking for information as to the relations between His Majesty's Government and the Soviet Government of Russia. (2.) I am to inform you that His Majesty's Government recognize the Soviet Government as the de facto Government of Russia." The letter of April 22 is in reply to a request for information whether His Majesty's Government recognized the Provisional Government of Russia, and as to the period of its duration, and the extent of its jurisdiction. The answer contains (inter alia) the statement that the Provisional Government came into power on March 14, 1917, that it was recognized by His Majesty's Government as the then existing Government of Russia, and that the Constituent Assembly remained in session until December

13, 1917, when it was dispersed by the Soviet authorities. The statement contained in the letter of April 20 is accepted by the respondents' counsel as the proper and sufficient proof of the recognition of the Soviet Government as the de facto Government of Russia.

Under these circumstances the whole aspect of the case is changed, and it becomes necessary to consider matters which were not material in the Court below. The first is a question of law of very considerable importance – namely, what is the effect of the recognition by His Majesty's Government in April, 1921, of the Soviet Government as the de facto Government of Russia upon the past acts of that Government, and how far back, if at all, does that recognition extend. ...

On the first point counsel have been unable to refer the Court to any English authority. Attention has been called to three cases decided in the Supreme Court of the United States: *Williams v. Bruffy* [96 U.S. 176]; *Underhill v. Hernandez* [168 U.S. 250]; and *Oetjen v. Central Leather Co.* [246 U.S. 297]. In none of these cases is any distinction attempted to be drawn in argument between the effect of a recognition of a government as a de facto government and a recognition of a government as a government de jure, nor is any decision given upon that point; nor, except incidentally, is any mention made as to the effect of the recognition of a government upon its past acts. The mention occurs in two passages. ...

The second mention of the point occurs in the judgment of Fuller C.J. in *Underhill v. Hernandez* [168 U.S. 253]. He says, in speaking of civil wars: "If the party seeking to dislodge the existing government succeeds, and the independence of the government it has set up is recognized, then the acts of such government from the commencement of its existence are regarded as those of an independent nation." These are weighty expressions of opinion on a question of international law. Neither learned judge cites any authority for his proposition. Each appears to treat the matter as one resting on principle. On principle the views put forward by these learned judges appear to me to be sound. ...

An attempt was made by the respondents' counsel to draw a distinction between the effect of a recognition of a government as a de facto government and the effect of a recognition of a government as a government de jure, and to say that the latter form of recognition might relate back to acts of state of a date earlier than the date of recognition, whereas the former could not. Wheaton quoting from Mountague Bernard states the distinction between a de jure and a de facto government thus: "A de jure government is one which, in the opinion of the person using the phrase, ought to possess the powers of sovereignty, though at the time it may be deprived of them. A de facto government is one which is really in possession of them, although the possession may be wrongful or precarious." For some purposes no doubt a distinction can be drawn between the effect of the recognition by a sovereign state of the one form of government or of the other, but for the present purpose in my opinion no distinction can be drawn. The Government of this country having, to use the language just quoted, recognized the Soviet Government as the Government really in possession of the powers of sovereignty in Russia, the acts of that Government must be treated by the Courts of this country with all the respect due to the acts of a duly recognized foreign sovereign state.

SCRUTTON, L.J.: ... What the Court cannot do directly it cannot in my view do indirectly. If it could not question the title of the Government of Russia to goods brought by that Government to England, it cannot indirectly question it in the hands of a purchaser from that Government by denying that the Government could confer any good title to the property. This immunity follows from recognition as a sovereign state. Should there be any government which appropriates other people's property without compensation, the remedy appears to be to refuse to recognize it as a sovereign state. Then the Courts could investigate the title without infringing the comity of nations. But it is impossible to recognize a government and yet claim to exercise jurisdiction over its person or property against its will. Further, the Courts in questions whether a particular person or institution is a sovereign must be guided only by the statement of the sovereign on whose behalf they exercise jurisdiction. ...

In the present case we have from the Foreign Office a recognition of the Soviet Republic in 1921 as the de facto Government, and a statement that in 1917 the Soviet authorities expelled the previous Government recognized by His Majesty. It appears to me that this binds us to recognize the decree of 1918 by a department of the Soviet Republic, and the sale in 1920 by the Soviet Republic of property claimed by them to be theirs under that decree, as acts of a sovereign state the validity of which cannot be questioned by the Courts of this country.

[Warrington, L.J. delivered a concurring judgment.]

Appeal allowed.

NOTES

1) This case is the leading English authority[25] on the effects of recognition and non-recognition. It shows how sharply the courts draw the distinction between those effects even though their difference depends upon nothing more than the attitude of the government of the day at the time of the case. Do you find the results persuasive?

2) *Luther v. Sagor* is invoked in all the subsequent cases, some of which are reported here to elaborate individual effects of recognition.

Claims to State Property

A foreign state has a right to control and dispose of its own property as it wishes. But where there are two contending governments in the state, whether because of invasion or civil war, which has the better right to the state property? The issue was squarely presented in a series of cases arising out of the conquest of Ethiopia, or Abyssinia, by Italy in 1935.[26] Emperor Haile Selassie went into exile in London but he was still recognised by Great Britain as the legal sovereign of Ethiopia. At the same time the Italian authorities were recognised as exercising governmental power *de facto*. The English courts were faced with competing claims for state property both within and without

---

[25] See also *Princess Paley Olga v. Weisz*, [1929] 1 K.B. 718 (C.A.); and *Williams & Humbert Ltd. v. W & H Trade Marks (Jersey) Ltd.*, [1986] 1 All E.R. 129 (H.L.).

[26] As well as cases involving the Spanish civil war at approximately the same time. See *Banco de Bilbao v. Sancha and Rey*, [1938] 2 K.B. 176 (C.A.).

Ethiopia. Application of the principle in *Luther v. Sagor* that the recognised government had the right to state property provided no obvious remedy, since the British government had granted a degree of recognition to both claimants.

Haile Selassie v. Cable and Wireless Ltd. (No. 2)
[1939] Ch. 182, rev'd. 194 (C.A.)

[The property in issue in this case was a debt payable by the defendant company pursuant to its contract with the Director-General of Posts, Telegraphs and Telephones of Ethiopia for the transmission of wireless messages.]

BENNETT, J.: ... The question to be decided may I think be stated in these words. Does the fact that the Italian Government has been and is recognized by the British Government as the de facto government of Ethiopia vest in the Italian Government the right to sue for and obtain judgment in an English Court for a debt formerly due to and recoverable by the plaintiff as the sovereign authority of Ethiopia, the debt being due to the plaintiff as Emperor of Ethiopia and the British Government recognizing the plaintiff as the de jure Emperor of Ethiopia?

The defendants contended that the question was settled in their favour by authority.

...what has been decided in *Luther v. James Sagor & Co.* and the *Bank of Ethiopia v. National Bank of Egypt and Liguori* [[1937] Ch. 513] has reference exclusively to the acts of a de facto government and a de jure government, both recognized as such by His Majesty's Government and both claiming to have jurisdiction in the same area with reference to persons and property in that area.

The principle is that the Courts of this country will recognize and give effect to the acts of the former in relation to persons and property in the governed territory and will disregard and treat as a nullity the acts of the latter.

The present case is not concerned with the validity of acts in relation to persons or property in Ethiopia. It is concerned with the title to a chose in action – a debt, recoverable in England.

Having considered all the cases cited to me in argument, I have come to the conclusion that the point is not covered by English judicial authority.

I have to decide whether it is the law of England that the plaintiff, recognized by His Majesty's Government as the Emperor de jure of Ethiopia, has lost the right to recover the debt in a suit in this country, because the country in which he once ruled has been conquered by Italian arms and because His Majesty's Government recognizes that that country or the greater part of it is now ruled by the Italian Government.

It is unfortunate, I think, that the question has to be decided by a judge, for, in deciding it, it is impossible to avoid deciding on a claim made by a foreign sovereign state not a party to the proceedings. For this reason I shall say as little as possible.

My judgment is in favour of the plaintiff. ...

I ask myself why should the fact that the Italian army has conquered Ethiopia and that the Italian Government now rules Ethiopia divest the plaintiff of his right to sue.

The only reason can be, I suppose, that the money is not the plaintiff's own money, and that it is a sum which he is under some obligation to spend for the benefit of the people of Ethiopia – an obligation which he cannot now fulfil.

There is a clear answer to this suggestion. I think it undesirable that I should state it.

I hold that nothing has happened to divest the title formerly vested in him and that he is entitled to judgment for the sum agreed between the parties as the sum due from the defendants on January 1, 1936.

On Appeal, SIR WILFRED GREENE, M.R.: ... What has happened is this. As appears from a certificate signed by the direction of His Majesty's Principal Secretary of State for Foreign Affairs, dated November 30, 1938, His Majesty's Government no longer recognizes His Majesty Haile Selassie as de jure Emperor of Ethiopia; His Majesty's Government now recognizes His Majesty the King of Italy as de jure Emperor of Ethiopia; From that certificate two things emerge as the result of the recognition thereby evidenced. It is not disputed that in the Courts of this country His Majesty the King of Italy as Emperor of Abyssinia is entitled by succession to the public property of the State of Abyssinia, and the late Emperor of Abyssinia's title thereto is no longer recognized as existent. Further, it is not disputed that that right of succession is to be dated back at any rate to the date when the de facto recognition, recognition of the King of Italy as the de facto Sovereign of Abyssinia, took place. That was in December, 1936. Accordingly the appeal comes before us upon a footing quite different to that upon which the action stood when it was before Bennett J. We now have the position that in the eye of the law of this country the right to sue in respect of what was held by Bennett J. to be (and no dispute is raised with regard to it) part of the public State property, must be treated in the Courts of this country as having become vested in His Majesty the King of Italy as from a date, at the latest, in December, 1936, that is to say, before the date of the issue of the writ in this action. Now that being so, the title of the plaintiff to sue is necessarily displaced. When the matter was before Bennett J., the de jure recognition not having taken place, the question that he had to deal with was whether the effect of the de facto conquest of Abyssinia and the recognition de facto of the Italian Government's position in Abyssinia, operated to divest the plaintiff of his title to sue. Whether that decision was right or whether it was wrong is a question we are not called upon to answer, but what is admittedly the case is that if Bennett J. had had before him the state of affairs which we have before us, his decision would have been the other way.

[Scott and Clauson, L.JJ. concurred.]

Foreign Acts of State

The phrase ''act of state'' is not a term of art in international law. It is best known as a doctrine of American law but it is widely and variously used. It is employed here simply to refer to an official public act, whether legislative, executive or judicial, of a recognized foreign government.

A common predicament faces the legal system of every country. Since all states are sovereign equals, each state must respect the public acts of every other state it recognises. The problem is to determine how, and how far, to give effect to such acts of the foreign state in the recognizing state. As this problem is a matter for each national legal system to resolve, it is not surprising that different solutions have been found, and that they reflect the various arrangements for the separation of governmental powers to be found in different countries.

The American act of state doctrine has had a great influence well beyond the United States for several reasons. The United States courts were among the first to face the problem and so their judgments have provided a source of opinion for others. More recently, in the course of elaborating the doctrine to cope with the American division of constitutional authority over foreign affairs, the United States courts have exerted a certain international jurisdiction which has inevitably collided with the sovereign powers of foreign governments. In sum, the American act of state doctrine offers a rich comparative experience for other countries like Canada, as well as raising important questions about judicial responsibility internationally. In these materials some comparative sources are used, but the emphasis is placed upon the way Canadian courts[27] handle foreign acts of state.

Laane and Baltser v. The Estonian State Cargo & Passenger Steamship Line
[1949] S.C.R. 530

[The case concerned the distribution of the proceeds of a judicial sale of the S.S. Elize after her arrest in Saint John. Although registered in Estonia by her Estonian owners, the appellants Laane and Baltser, the Elize had left Estonia in July 1939 and had sailed exclusively between the United Kingdom and Canada until her arrest. During this time Estonia became a part of the U.S.S.R. and Canada recognised this change. By several decrees, the new Soviet government of the Estonian Republic purported to nationalize the Estonian shipping industry, including the appellants' business, and to fix compensation for expropriated ships at 25 per cent of their value. Shortly afterwards, the respondent state corporation was established to run the nationalized ships. The court was asked: "(1) Were the Decrees and Statutes herein recited effective in nationalizing the Steamship ELISE and transferring ownership to the plaintiff herein [the Estonian Steamship Line]? (2) Is the plaintiff entitled to maintain the action and receive the proceeds?"]

RINFRET, C.J.: ... The decrees relied on by it were declared illegal and unconstitutional by the English Court of Appeal in the *Talinna case*. It may be doubted whether their language was sufficient to vest the steamship *Elise* in the respondent. In the *Talinna case* it was held that they lacked the necessary wording to make them effective in that respect; and, further, that they were incomplete in the sense that the last stage to give them force of law had not been proceeded with. At the material time the *Elise* was in the Port of Saint John, Canada, a foreign country. She was then in possession of the appellants and the respondent never got possession of the ship, nor any control of her,

---

[27] See H.M. Kindred, "Acts of State and the Application of International Law in Canadian Courts" (1979), 10 *Rev. Droit Sherbrooke* 271.

before the ship was sold by the Marshal. The proceedings herein were instituted after the sale and were not directed against the ship herself, but against the proceeds of the sale, then deposited in a Canadian Admiralty Court.

Moreover, the decrees are of an evident confiscatory nature and, even if they purport to have extra-territorial effect, they cannot be recognized by a foreign country, under the well-established principles of international law. Quite independent of their illegality and unconstitutionality, they are not of such a character that they could be recognized in a British Court of Law.

For these reasons, the appeal should be maintained and the proceedings of the respondent dismissed. There should be an order that the proceeds of the sale of the *Elise* in Court should be paid out to Laane and Baltser.

RAND, J.: ... [T]here can be no doubt that once a private ship is voluntarily brought within a country's territory it is submitted to the laws of that country. The jurisdiction arising is primary and fundamental; but the particular law to be applied to determine legal relations in respect of the vessel is quite another matter. But, whether viewed as recognition of legal effects of foreign law or as affirmative enforcement of foreign law, that its application is through the act and authority of the territorial state follows from the language of Chief Justice Marshall in *Schooner Exchange v. M'Fadden* (1812), 7 Cranch 116, at 136:

All exceptions, therefore, to the full and complete power of a nation within its own territories, must be traced up to the consent of the nation itself. They can flow from no other legitimate source.

...the application [of foreign law] is by the territorial power and jurisdictionally with such modifications of a foreign rule as it pleases. It is what we should expect, therefore, that there are certain rules, more or less clearly defined, by which the enforcement in the domestic forum of a foreign law is refused.

It is now established that a common law jurisdiction will not enforce directly or indirectly the penal or the revenue laws of another state, to which Dicey in Rule 54, 5th Ed., adds, political law; and there is the general principle that no state will apply a law of another which offends against some fundamental morality or public policy.

The first question then is whether there is some such policy of New Brunswick with which the confirmation of the attempted acquisition of this vessel by Estonia would conflict. The taking of property for public purposes without compensation certainly clashes with our notions of the conditions which should attend the exercise of that power, and I should not view the proposed award of 25 per cent of the value as avoiding that conflict. The provincial law is invoked to effect the transfer of the appellant's property on those terms: and we must ask whether the considerations of international expediency so far transcend normal policy as to overcome the repugnance of our political conceptions toward such an act. I do not think they do.

The effect of the decrees bears elements also of analogy to the operation of a revenue law. A state imposes a tax as a small fraction of the property of its citizens, and it is taken for a public purpose. But whether the fraction is five or seventy-five per cent and even though limited to certain classes of property, coercion and public object are common to both cases. We refuse to aid a neighbour state in collecting the lesser exaction even though taxation is universally accepted as a proper state faculty; on what ground should we enforce the greater?

But there is what I think a still more important aspect in which the question is to be viewed. The acquisition of property here is not to be dissociated from the larger political policy of which it is in reality an incident. The matters before us evidence the fundamental change effected in the constitution of the Estonian state, of which that acquisition is only one, though an important, particular. What has been set up in a social organization in which the dominant position of the individual, as recognized in our polity, has been repudiated and in which the institution of private property, so far as that has to do with producing goods and services, has been abolished; and those functions, together with the existing means, taken over by the state. If at the time of the decrees every Estonian ship had been sunk, their principal purpose would still have been realized in vesting in the state, apart from ports and immoveable works in Estonia, the monopoly of carrying on shipping services.

What is asked of the foreign territorial law is, therefore, to aid in the execution of a fundamental political law of Estonia which serves no interest of the foreign state. The law of conflicts is concerned with the determination of rights in property and personal relations which are conceived as distinct from the law under which they arise; but, laws of the class in question are not migratory and are deemed to be operative only within their own territories. If the transfer of property by such a law of Estonia has been satisfied by the condition of territorial jurisdiction, the title will be recognized and enforced, as in England the similar decrees of Russia: *Luther v. Sagor*. ... But where that legislative basis is absent there is no warrant in international accommodation to call upon another state to exercise its sovereign power to supply the jurisdictional deficiency in completing such a political program: ... .

I would, therefore, allow the appeal and direct judgment in favour of the appellants with costs in both courts.

[Concurring opinions were delivered by Kerwin, J. (Estey, J. concurring) and Kellock, J.]

NOTES

1) In *Luther v. Sagor* Bankes and Scrutton L.JJ. said that the acts of a recognised government must be respected and may not be questioned by the courts.[28] In so saying they were repeating a principle founded in *Blad's Case*[29] in 1673 and *Duke of Brunswick v. King of Hanover*[30] in 1848 and already well established in United States courts. In 1897 in *Underhill v. Hernandez*, Fuller C.J. declared:[31]

---

[28] Reported *supra*, and stated even more forcefully by Warrington J., at 548.
[29] 3 Swan 602; 36 E.R. 991.
[30] 2 H.L. Cas. 1; 9 E.R. 993.
[31] 168 U.S. 250, at 252.

Every sovereign state is bound to respect the independence of every other sovereign state, and the courts of one country will not sit in judgment on the acts of the government of another done within its own territory. Redress of grievances, by reason of such acts must be obtained through the means open to be availed of by sovereign powers as between themselves.

See likewise, *Oetjen v. Central Leather Co.*[32] What fact distinguished *Laane and Baltser* from *Luther v. Sagor* and allowed the court to disregard the Estonian decree?

2) Did the Supreme Court in fact sit in judgment on the acts of the government of Estonia? Rand J. pointed out that although Estonian law governed the issue, it could only operate in a Canadian court through the authority of Canadian law. This is a principle of conflicts of law, not international law. By characterising the problem this way, Rand J. was able to apply well accepted controls of the forum state against unwanted intrusions of the foreign state. This degree of disrespect or disregard of the acts of a foreign state is acceptable in international law on account of its reciprocal character. Foreign states must have equal regard for Canadian sovereignty, particularly within its own territory and courts. The inclination is strong for Canadian courts to resolve act of state problems through conflicts of law.[33]

3) Suppose the Elize had been in an Estonian port and was beneficially owned by a Canadian company just prior to nationalization. How might the court then have decided the issue?

4) For a Canadian case in which the courts were prepared to sit in judgment of foreign laws without regard either to the presence or absence of recognition of the government, or to respect for foreign acts of state, see *Juelle v. Trudeau*.[34] The case was a classic example of title to moveable property, having been confiscated abroad, being refought within the Canadian jurisdiction. The plaintiffs alleged they were the true owners of seven horses bred from the stock of their stud farm in Cuba which was violently and illegally confiscated by Castro forces. The defendants pleaded that, having received an offer to sell the animals from a representative of the Cuban government, they purchased them in good faith from the registered owners in Cuba and had since peaceably possessed them and raced them in Canada. On the evidence, the trial court held the seizure contrary to Cuban law and of null effect upon the plaintiff's title. On appeal, the court regarded the confiscation as fully in compliance with Cuban law and hence effective to transfer ownership to the defendants' vendors. The cause for reversal was the sharply different reading of Cuban law between the two courts. The trial judge appears to have applied the pre-revolutionary law, while the justices of appeal referred to the decrees and constitutional amendments of Castro's government. Unfortunately at neither level did the court provide reasons for its particular assessment of Cuban controls on property.

5) Recognition principles in *Luther v. Sagor* and conflicts principles in *Laane and Baltser* led the courts away from their ordinary adjudicative function and the application

---

[32] (1918), 246 U.S. 297, at 303.
[33] See also *Brown, Gow, Wilson v. Beleggings-Societeit N.V.*, [1961] O.R. 815.
[34] (1968), 7 D.L.R. (3d) 82 (Q.S.C.); rev'd (1972), C.A. 870 (Que.).

of the usual Canadian sources of law. One of those sources is international law.[35] While it is undoubtedly correct that the courts of one country should not judge the acts of another by their own national laws, why should not they determine the validity of those acts by international law. Is a Canadian court obliged to give effect to an act of a foreign state which is contrary to international law? Consider the following experience of American and English courts.

Banco Nacional de Cuba v. Sabbatino[36]
(1964), 376 U.S. 398

[The Cuban government in effect confiscated and then resold for its own account to the same purchaser a cargo of sugar lying in a Cuban port. A Cuban state bank later brought this action in New York to recover the purchase price but its title to the sugar and its interest in the monies held in a U.S. bank were challenged by the original owner of the sugar, a corporation registered in Cuba but principally owned by American residents. It succeeded at trial and on appeal because the courts refused to apply the act of state doctrine in the face of a violation of international law, which they so found on the evidence that the Cuban acts were retaliatory, discriminatory and without adequate compensation.[36]

In reversing these decisions, the Supreme Court reasserted the force of the act of state doctrine even in the face of breaches of international law. It said of the doctrine:[37]]

...its continuing vitality depends on its capacity to reflect the proper distribution of functions between the judicial and political branches of the Government on matters bearing upon foreign affairs. It should be apparent that the greater the degree of codification or consensus concerning a particular area of international law, the more appropriate it is for the judiciary to render decisions regarding it, since the courts can then focus on the application of an agreed principle to circumstances of fact rather than on the sensitive task of establishing a principle not inconsistent with the national interest or with international justice. It is also evident that some aspects of international law touch more sharply on national nerves than do others; the less important the implications of an issue are for our foreign relations, the weaker the justification for exclusivity in the political branches.

[The actual decision in the case was a narrow one:[38]]

Therefore, rather than laying down or reaffirming an inflexible and all-encompassing rule in this case, we decide only that the Judicial Branch will not examine the validity of a taking of property within its own territory by a foreign sovereign government, extant

---

[35] *Supra*, Chapter 4, passim.

[36] See R. Falk, *The Role of Domestic Courts in the International Legal Order* (1964); Mooney, *Foreign Seizures: Sabbatino and the Act of State Doctrine* (1967), and a deluge of articles on this celebrated case.

[37] 427–28.

[38] 428.

and recognized by this country at the time of suit, ... even if the complaint alleges that the taking violates customary international law.

[And so the U.S. Supreme Court ordered the U.S. bank to pay money owed by a U.S. citizen over to a foreign government pursuant to a decree made in retaliation against the United States and in violation of international law.]

NOTES

1) Although the Supreme Court applied the act of state doctrine, it did not consider that international law required it to do so. Probably the more pertinent question is whether international law forbids a court from enforcing an illegal act of state. Instead, the Supreme Court acted in light of its position in the American legal system. In that context, clearly some balance has to be struck by the courts between upholding the constitutional division of national authority over foreign affairs and enforcing international law. Do you consider the criteria put forth by the U.S. Supreme Court are suitable for Canada? How should Canadian courts accommodate their deference to the government's recognition policy towards a foreign regime when a Canadian individual challenges the international legality of an act of expropriation of his property by that regime?

2) As a result of the flexible case by case approach to the act of state doctrine encouraged by *Sabbatino*, the U.S. Secretary of State has quite often intervened in subsequent cases by way of an *amicus* brief. The brief typically explains the government's foreign policy interests in the dispute and declares its view of the merits, including whether it regards the application of the act of state doctrine as desirable or not. Do you think a similar practice would be appropriate in Canada?

3) Such was the furor over *Sabbatino* that Congress quickly passed the "Hickenlooper Amendment" to the Foreign Assistance Act of 1961.[39] This reversed the particular decision in *Sabbatino* and thus rescued the possibility of an application of international law by the U.S. courts to foreign state acts of expropriation. There has since been a plentiful supply of cases about the scope of the Hickenlooper Amendment and the life of the American act of state doctrine outside of it.[40]

4) In Britain,[41] so great has been the influence of *Luther v. Sagor* on the courts that the House of Lords did not have the opportunity to consider whether it would "examine the validity" at international law of a foreign act of state until 1976. In 1953 in *The Rose*

---

[39] U.S.C. 22, §2370.

[40] And an equally plentiful supply of learned opinions. For a recent review of the progress of *Sabbatino* in the context of "restatement of the law," see M. Halberstrom, "Sabbatino Resurrected: The Act of State Doctrine in the Revised Restatement of U.S. Foreign Relations Law" (1985), 79 *Am. J. Int. L.* 68; and *Restatement (Revised) of Foreign Relations Law*, ss. 469, 470.

[41] See, D.L. Jones, "Act of Foreign State in English Law: The Ghost Goes East" (1981–82), 22 *Va. J. Int. L.* 433; H.M. Kindred, "Acts of State and the Application of International Law in English Courts" (1981), 19 *Can. Y.B. Int. L.* 271; and M. Singer, "The Act of State Doctrine of the United Kingdom: An Analysis, with Comparisons to United States Practice" (1981), 75 *Am. J. Int. L.* 283.

Mary,[42] a British court in Aden had held that Iranian legislative acts of nationalization were contrary to international law but the decision has been overshadowed by criticisms that the court applied erroneous views of international law.[43] When the House of Lords considered the matter in *Oppenheimer v. Cattermole*, Lord Cross, speaking for the majority, said:[44]

A judge should, of course, be very slow to refuse to give effect to the legislation of a foreign state in any sphere in which, according to accepted principles of international law, the foreign state has jurisdiction. He may well have an inadequate understanding of the circumstances in which the legislation was passed and his refusal to recognise it may be embarrassing to the branch of the executive which is concerned to maintain friendly relations between this country and the foreign country in question. But I think ... that it is part of the public policy of this country that our courts should give effect to clearly established rules of international law.

Lord Cross was concerned, like the U.S. Supreme Court in *Sabbatino*, to point out the need to balance the courts' responsibilities in the face of international law and the executive government's authority over foreign affairs by national law. But he established *prima facie* a centre of balance that was quite different from *Sabbatino*. What was it? Which approach would you consider more appropriate to a Canadian court faced with the same kind of issues, such as *Juelle v. Trudeau*.[45]

5) More recently in *Buttes Gas and Oil Co. v. Hammer and Occidental Petroleum Corp.* Lord Wilberforce spoke for the House of Lords, saying:[46]

It is one thing to assert that effect will not be given to a foreign municipal law or executive act if it is contrary to public policy, or to international law ... and quite another to claim that the courts may examine the validity, under international law, or some doctrine of public policy, of an act or acts operating in the area of transactions between states ... .

So I think that the essential question is whether ... there exists in English law a more general principle that the courts will not adjudicate on transactions of foreign sovereign states. Though I would prefer to avoid argument on terminology, it seems desirable to consider this principle, if existing, not as a variety of act of state but one for judicial restraint or abstention ... .

In my opinion there is, and for long has been, such a general principle, starting in English law, adopted and generalised in the law of the USA, which is effective and compelling in English courts. This principle is not one of discretion, but is inherent in the very nature of the judicial process.

Lord Wilberforce then traced the general principle from *Blad's Case* through *Underhill*,

---

[42] [1953] 1 W.L.R. 246. See also *In re Claim by Helbert Wagg & Co. Ltd..*, [1956] Ch. 323.
[43] K. Lipstein, [1956] *Camb. L.J.* 138, at 140; D.W. Greig, *International Law* (2 ed., 1976), at 62–63; and D.P. O'Connell, "A Critique of the Iranian Oil Litigation" (1955), 4 *Int. Comp. L.Q.* 267.
[44] [1976] A.C. 249, at 277–78. Cp. *Williams & Humbert Ltd. v. W & H Trade Marks (Jersey) Ltd.*, [1986] 1 All E.R. 129, at 138 (H.L.).
[45] Reported *supra* in Note 4 prior to the *Sabbatino* case.
[46] [1981] 3 All E.R. 616, at 628.

Oetjen, Luther v. Sagor and *Sabbatino* to the U.S. decisions in similar suits between the immediate litigants and concluded:[47]

Leaving aside all possibility of embarrassment in our foreign relations (which it can be said have not been drawn to the attention of the court by the executive), there are, to follow the Fifth Circuit Court of Appeals, no judicial or manageable standards by which to judge these issues, ...

Lord Wilberforce here asserted a general principle, wider than the act of state doctrine, that inter-state issues are not justiciable in the absence of judicial or manageable standards by which to judge them. Perhaps the issues in the case were unmanageable but it is difficult to appreciate why international law is not an adequate, not to say appropriate, standard of adjudication.

What do you gather is Lord Wilberforce's opinion of the status and scope of the act of state doctrine? Is it binding, or is it discretionary as in *Sabbatino*? To what extent is deference to the government's foreign policy an integral concern? Is intervention by the government to express its opinions intended to be encouraged?

6) Lord Wilberforce's views on acts of state are quite different from those of Lord Cross, who was not sitting in *Buttes*. Moreover, *Oppenheimer v. Cattermole* was not referred to in *Buttes*. Are the two viewpoints reconcilable? In what circumstances would an English court now sit in judgment of foreign law and public acts? Should a Canadian court follow suit?

Retroactivity of Recognition[48]

A special problem arises where the acts and events surrounding an action in the courts occurred before recognition was accorded. Are they to be ignored because the foreign state or government was then unrecognised, or should the grant of recognition be given retroactive effect?

Luther v. Sagor
Reported previously in this Section

NOTES

1) *Luther v. Sagor* is the leading English authority on this aspect of recognition as well. It decides not only that recognition is retroactive but that it extends back in time to validate all the public acts of the recognized government since it came to power. This decision raises two further questions. The first is a question of fact to determine in each case when a newly recognized government acquired power. In the case of a palace *coup d'etat*, the moment is usually clear. But in the event of a protracted civil war, it may be

---

[47] *Supra*, at 633.
[48] See D.P. O'Connell, *supra*, n. 2, at 185–92.

most uncertain. The courts usually ask the government to state in its executive certificate the date of inception of the regime, but even the government cannot always supply a firm reply.

2) The second problem is a question of law as to the effect of the acts of the previously recognised government committed after the inception of the new regime but before it is in turn recognised. There may be an interim period when the old and the new governments both have some effective power in the territory, or over the assets, of the state. How are the courts to handle a clash of authority between the acts of the then recognised government and the retroactively effective acts of the subsequently recognised government? Does the retroactive recognition of one regime and its actions impliedly invalidate retroactively the acts of the other?

Gdynia Amerika Linie Zeglugowe Spolka Akcyjna v. Boguslawski
[1953] A.C. 11, at 44–45 (H.L.)

[The Polish Government in Exile in London was recognised as the government of Poland by the British government throughout World War II. On June 28, 1945, a Communist Provisional Government was established with *de facto* control of Poland. At midnight on July 5–6, the British Government recognised the Provisional Government as the government of Poland in place of the Government in Exile. Meanwhile in anticipation of this event, on July 3 the Government in Exile had offered three months' severance pay to Polish seamen employed by the appellant, a government owned steamship line, if they wished to leave their employ rather than continue to serve under the Communist government. Boguslawski accepted the offer but the steamship company refused to pay. It claimed that recognition of the Communist government by the British government had retroactive effect and as a consequence the acts of the Government in Exile after June 28 were ineffective to create any duty to make the payments offered. In rejecting the argument, Lord Reid said:]

There is ample authority for the proposition that the recognition by the British Government of a new government of a foreign country has at least this effect. It enables and requires the courts of this country to regard as valid not only acts done by the new government after its recognition but also acts done by it before its recognition in so far as those acts related to matters under its control at the time when the acts were done. But there appears to be no English authority which goes beyond that. I do not accept the argument for the appellants that this necessarily or logically involves antedating for all purposes the withdrawal of the recognition of the old government. I do not see anything strange or even difficult in our saying that we still recognize that the old government was the Government of Poland up to midnight of July 5–6 but that we also now accept the validity of certain acts done by the new government before that time and while it was still unrecognized by us. ... we cannot recognize two different governments of the same country at the same time, and the British Government did not in fact recognize both the old and the new government at the same time. But I do not think that it is inconsistent with this principle to say that the recognition of the new government has certain retroactive effects, but that the recognition of the old government remains effective down to the date when it was in fact withdrawn.

NOTES

1) The crucial element in the decision that the recognition of two successive governments may overlap is the limitation of the authority of each of them to "acts related to matters under its control at the time when the acts were done." In *Boguslawski*'s case it was relatively easy to respect retroactively the acts of the new government committed in Poland since the time it had effective control there, yet to enforce the decrees of the old government in exile over extraterritorial affairs which the new authorities had not yet moved against. Greater difficulties will arise when both governments take action with respect to the same subject matter.

2) In *Civil Air Transport Inc. v. Central Air Transport Corp.*,[49] forty aircraft belonging to the Nationalist government of China were flown to Hong Kong shortly before the advancing Communist forces took full control of the mainland. The Nationalist government, having withdrawn to Taiwan, sold the aircraft but the individuals who flew them to Hong Kong seized control of them in the name of the new Communist government. Shortly afterwards the British government recognised the Communist authorities as the government of China in place of the Nationalist regime. The purchaser of the aircraft sued for their possession and succeeded because the Nationalist government was their owner and controller at the time of sale while their subsequent seizure was illegal under Hong Kong law. Viscount Simon stated on behalf of the Privy Council that "[p]rimarily, at any rate, retroactivity of recognition operates to validate acts of a de facto government which has subsequently become the new de jure government, and not to invalidate acts of the previous de jure government."[50] But he also observed:[51]

Subsequent recognition de jure of a new government as the result of a successful insurrection can in certain cases annul a sale of goods by a previous government. If the previous government sells goods which belong to it but are situated in territory effectively occupied at the time by insurgent forces acting on behalf of what is already a de facto new government, the sale may be valid if the insurgents are afterwards defeated and possession of the goods is regained by the old government. But if the old government never regains the goods and the de facto new government becomes recognized by H.M. Government as the de jure government, purchasers from the old government will not be held in her Majesty's courts to have a good title after that recognition.

Internal Consequences of Non-Recognition

The lack of recognition of a foreign regime by the government results in a failure by the courts to acknowledge that any legal consequences flow from legislative, executive or

---

[49] [1953] A.C. 70 (J.C.P.C.).
[50] *Supra*, at 93.
[51] *Supra*, at 93.

judicial actions in the foreign state. In *Carl-Zeiss-Stiftung v. Rayner & Keeler Ltd. (No. 2),*[52] in which the absence of recognition of East Germany was at stake, Lord Reid stated:

We must not only disregard all new laws and decrees made by the Democratic Republic or its Government, but we must also disregard all executive and judicial acts done by persons appointed by that Government because we must regard their appointments as invalid. The result of that would be far-reaching. Trade with the Eastern Zone of Germany is not discouraged. But the incorporation of every company in East Germany under any new law made by the Democratic Republic or by the official act of an official appointed by its Government would have to be regarded as a nullity, so that any such company could neither sue nor be sued in this country. And any civil marriage under any such new law, or owing its validity to the act of any such official, would also have to be treated as a nullity, so that we should have to regard the children as illegitimate. And the same would apply to divorces and all manner of judicial decisions, whether in family or commercial questions. And that would affect not only status of persons formerly domiciled in East Germany but property in this country the devolution of which depended on East German law.

Notwithstanding this devastating catalogue of disorder, the House of Lords in substance confirmed the principle established in *Luther v. Sagor.*[53] Thus, for instance, divorce decrees granted in Rhodesia during the unrecognised regime of Mr. Ian Smith after his unilateral declaration of independence have since been declared ineffective.[54] But perhaps the traditional approach is too unrealistic and increasingly irrelevant in the face of the growing practice of states not to pronounce on the recognition of new governments at all. It has certainly suffered attack at the hands of Lord Denning.

Hesperides Hotels Ltd. v. Aegean Turkish Holidays Ltd.
[1978] 1 Q.B. 205 (C.A.)

[In 1974 Turkish armed forces took control of the northern part of Cyprus, including two hotels at Kyrenia which were the subject of this case. When the Turkish Cypriot regime subsequently advertised the hotels for English visitors, the dispossessed Greek Cypriot owners sued its representative in England, together with the travel agency handling its business, for conspiracy to commit trespass. The British government stated in a certificate to the court that it did not recognise the Turkish Cypriot regime.]

LORD DENNING M.R.: ... Mr. Kemp submitted that, seeing that the "Turkish Federated State of Cyprus" was not recognised de jure or de facto by Her Majesty's Government, it followed that the courts of this country could not recognise or give effect

---

[52] [1967] 1 A.C. 853, at 907. Cp. the judgment of Lord Wilberforce, at 954, which left some opening for reconsideration.
[53] Reported *supra*.
[54] *Adams v. Adams*, [1970] 3 All E.R. 572.

to any of the acts or laws of this so-called state. They are all nullities in the eyes of English law, he said, and should be treated as such by the English courts. These courts could not, he said, even receive evidence of the acts and laws made by this so-called state.

[Lord Denning then noted a number of counsel's supporting authorities, including *Luther v. Sagor* and *Zeiss*, both reported previously. He continued:]

To those judicial statements, Mr. Kemp added most persuasively the book by the late Sir Hersch Lauterpacht *Recognition in International Law* (1948) and Chapter X on Recognition of Governments where he said at 145 et seq.

...no juridical existence can be attributed to an unrecognised government and ... no legal consequences of its purported factual existence can be admitted ... The correct and reasonable rule is that both the unrecognised government and its acts are a nullity. ...

That doctrine is said to be based on the need for the executive and the courts to speak with one voice. If the executive do not recognise the usurping government, nor should the courts: see *Government of the Republic of Spain v. S.S. Arantzazu Mendi (The Arantzazu Mendi)* [1939] A.C. 256, at 264, by Lord Atkin. But there are those who do not subscribe to that view. They say that there is no need for the executive and the judiciary to speak in unison. The executive is concerned with the *external* consequences of recognition, vis-à-vis other states. The courts are concerned with the *internal* consequences of it, vis-à-vis private individuals. So far as the courts are concerned, there are many who hold that the courts are entitled to look at the state of affairs actually existing in a territory, to see what is the law which is in fact effective and enforced in that territory, and to give such effect to it – in its impact on individuals – as justice and common sense require: provided always that there are no considerations of public policy against it. The most authoritive statement is that of Lord Wilberforce in *Carl Zeiss Stiftung v. Rayner & Keeler Ltd. (No. 2)* [1967] 1 A.C. 853, at 954, where he said:

...where private rights, or acts of everyday occurrence, or perfunctory acts of administration are concerned ... the courts may, in the interests of justice and common sense, where no consideration of public policy to the contrary has to prevail, give recognition to the actual facts or realities found to exist in the territory in question. ...

If it were necessary to make a choice between these conflicting doctrines, I would unhesitatingly hold that the courts of this country can recognise the laws or acts of a body which is in effective control of a territory even though it has not been recognised by Her Majesty's Government de jure or de facto: at any rate, in regard to the laws which regulate the day to day affairs of the people, such as their marriages, their divorces, their leases, their occupations, and so forth: and furthermore that the courts can receive evidence of the state of affairs so as to see whether the body is in effective control or not.

[Lord Denning then reviewed the evidence about the state of affairs in Cyprus and concluded:]

There is an effective administration in North Cyprus which has made laws governing the day to day lives of the people. According to these laws, the people who have occupied these hotels in Kyrenia are not trespassers. They are not occupying them unlawfully. They are occupying them by virtue of a lease granted to them under the laws or by virtue of requisitions made by the existing administration. If an action were brought in the courts of this northern part – alleging a trespass to land or to goods – it would be bound to fail. It follows inexorably that their conduct cannot be made the subject of a suit in England. Even if any of the present occupiers himself came to England and was sued here, the court would be bound to reject the claim. ...

Nor is the case made any better by being framed in conspiracy. If the acts in Kyrenia are not actionable here, nor is an agreement beforehand: see *Marrinan v. Vibart* [1963] 1 Q.B. 234; [1963] 1 Q.B. 528. As I said in *Ward v. Lewis* [1955] 1 W.L.R. 9, 11, it is often sought to get an added advantage by suing in conspiracy so as to overcome substantive rules of law. That is not permitted. The substantive law says that no action lies here for the trespass to the hotels or their contents in Kyrenia. The plaintiffs cannot overcome this rule or the substantive law by dressing it up as a conspiracy here to commit trespass there.

[Roskill and Scarman L.JJ. appended separate judgments concurring in the result.]

NOTES

1) In the *Zeiss*[55] case itself, the House of Lords managed to circumvent the lack of recognition of East Germany and its government by regarding its actions as within the subordinate powers delegated to it by the recognised governing authority, the Soviet Union. The English courts have strained to act upon reality rather than non-recognition on at least two other occasions.[56] The American courts have long made their own determinations about foreign regimes, unfettered by compulsory certificates denying recognition.[57]

2) If the Canadian government were to discontinue the practice of pronouncing on the recognition of foreign governments, what would be the effects on the traditional consequences of recognition and non-recognition before the court. Are they desirable?[58]

---

[55] *Supra*, n. 52. See D.W. Greig, "The Carl-Zeiss Case and the Position of an Unrecognised Government in English Law" (1967), 83 *L.Q. Rev.* 96.

[56] *Luigi Monta of Genoa v. Cechofracht Co. Ltd.*, [1956] 2 Q.B. 552; and *Re Al-Fin Corporation's Patent*, [1970] Ch. 160. They are discussed in H.M. Kindred, "Foreign Governments Before the Courts" (1980), 58 *Can. Bar. Rev.* 602; and J.G. Merrills, "Law, Politics and the Legislation of the Unrecognized Government" (1968–69), 3 *Ott. L. Rev.* 1.

[57] E.g., *Wulfsohn v. Russian Socialist Federated Soviet Republic* (1923), 234 N.Y. 372; 138 N.E. 24 (N.Y.C.A.); *Salimoff & Co. v. Standard Oil of New York* (1933), 262 N.Y. 220; 186 N.E. 679 (N.Y.C.A.); and *Upright v. Mercury Business Machines Co.* (1961), 23 N.Y.S. 2d 417. See S. Lubman, "The Unrecognized Government in American Courts: *Upright v. Mercury Business Machines*" (1962), 62 *Col. L.R.* 275. The practice has not been completely uniform. See *The Maret* (1944), 145 F. 2d 231 (C.A. 3d Circ.); and D.P. O'Connell, *supra* n. 2, at 172–80.

[58] See J.S. Davidson, "Beyond Recognition" (1981), 32 *N. Irl. Leg. Q.* 22.

STATE IMMUNITIES

Immunity Generally[59]

A recognised state is entitled by international law to immunity from the jurisdiction of the courts of other states. The basic reason behind the law is that, all states being sovereign equals, one cannot exercise authority over another. The old phrase "sovereign immunity" reflects the origin of the principle as a personal attribute of the foreign head of state. The sovereign head may use the courts to sue if he wishes, but he cannot be compelled to submit to their authority. He has this freedom as the personification of the state, and from him flows all the immunities allowed to officials, governmental agencies and state property nationally operating or held in his name.

The Schooner Exchange v. M'Faddon
(1812), 11 U.S. 116

[Two Americans claimed the Schooner Exchange belonged to them when she arrived in the port of Philadelphia. They alleged that two years previously the vessel had been seized at sea by French forces and wrongfully taken from them. The U.S. Attorney stated that a French public ship named the Balaou had been driven into Philadelphia by bad weather and, being owned by the Emperor of France, she ought to be released from the arrest of the claimants.]

MARSHALL C.J.: ... The jurisdiction of the nation within its own territory is necessarily exclusive and absolute. It is susceptible of no limitation not imposed by itself.

All exceptions, therefore, to the full and complete power of a nation within its own territories, must be traced up to the consent of the nation itself. They can flow from no other legitimate source ... .

The world being composed of distinct sovereignties, possessing equal rights and equal independence, whose mutual benefit is promoted by intercourse with each other, and by an interchange of those good offices which humanity dictates and its wants require, all sovereigns have consented to a relaxation in practice, in cases under certain peculiar circumstances, of that absolute and complete jurisdiction within their respective territories which sovereignty confers. ...

This full and absolute territorial jurisdiction being alike the attribute of every sovereign, and being incapable of conferring extra-territorial power, would not seem to contemplate foreign sovereigns nor their sovereign rights as its objects. One sovereign being in no

---

[59] See G.M. Badr, *State Immunity: An Analytical and Prognostic View* (1984); I. Sinclair, "The Law of Sovereign Immunity: Recent Developments" (1980), 167 *Hague Recueil* 133; S. Sucharitkul, "Immunities of Foreign States Before National Authorities" (1976), 149 *Hague Recueil* 87; the Australian Law Reform Commission, Report no. 24, *Foreign State Immunity* (1984); and International Law Commission, *Draft Articles on Jurisdictional Immunities of States*, U.N.G.A. Doc. A/41/10 (1986).

respect amenable to another; and being bound by obligations of the highest character not to degrade the dignity of his nation, by placing himself or its sovereign rights within the jurisdiction of another, can be supposed to enter a foreign territory only under an express license, or in the confidence that the immunities belonging to his independent sovereign station, though not expressly stipulated, are reserved by implication, and will be extended to him.

This perfect equality and absolute independence of sovereigns, and this common interest impelling them to mutual intercourse, and an interchange of good offices with each other, have given rise to a class of cases in which every sovereign is understood to wave the exercise of a part of that complete exclusive territorial jurisdiction, which has been stated to be the attribute of every nation.

1st. One of these is admitted to be the exemption of the person of the sovereign from arrest or detention within a foreign territory. ...

Why has the whole civilized world concurred in this construction? The answer cannot be mistaken. A foreign sovereign is not understood as intending to subject himself to a jurisdiction incompatible with his dignity, and the dignity of his nation, and it is to avoid this subjection that the license has been obtained. The character to whom it is given, and the object for which it is granted, equally require that it should be construed to impart full security to the person who has obtained it. This security, however, need not be expressed; it is implied from the circumstances of the case. ...

2d. A second case, standing on the same principles with the first, is the immunity which all civilized nations allow to foreign ministers. ...

3d. A third case in which a sovereign is understood to cede a portion of his territorial jurisidiction is, where he allows the troops of a foreign prince to pass through his dominions. ...

But the rule which is applicable to armies, does not appear to be equally applicable to ships of war entering the ports of a friendly power. The injury inseparable from the march of an army through an inhabited country, and the dangers often, indeed generally, attending it, do not ensue from admitting a ship of war, without special license, into a friendly port. ...

If there be no prohibition, the ports of a friendly nation are considered as open to the public ships of all powers with whom it is at peace, and they are supposed to enter such ports and to remain in them while allowed to remain, under the protection of the government of the place. ...

Are there reasons for denying the application of this principle to ships of war? ...

To the Court, it appears, that where, without treaty, the ports of a nation are open to the private and public ships of a friendly power, whose subjects have also liberty without special license, to enter the country for business or amusement, a clear distinction is to be drawn between the rights accorded to private individuals or private trading vessels, and those accorded to public armed ships which constitute a part of the military force of the nation.

The preceding reasoning, has maintained the propositions that all exemptions from territorial jurisdiction, must be derived from the consent of the sovereign of the territory; that this consent may be implied or expressed; and that when implied, its extent must be regulated by the nature of the case, and the views under which the parties requiring and conceding it must be supposed to act.

When private individuals of one nation spread themselves through another as business or caprice may direct, mingling indiscriminately with the inhabitants of that other, or when merchant vessels enter for the purposes of trade, it would be obviously inconvenient and dangerous to society, and would subject the laws to continual infraction, and the government to degradation, if such individuals or merchants did not owe temporary and local allegiance, and were not amenable to the jurisdiction of the country. Nor can the foreign sovereign have any motive for wishing such exemption. His subjects thus passing into foreign countries, are not employed by him, nor are they engaged in national pursuits. Consequently there are powerful motives for not exempting persons of this description from the jurisdiction of the country in which they are found, and no one motive for requiring it. The implied license, therefore, under which they enter can never be construed to grant such exemption.

But in all respects different is the situation of a public armed ship. She constitutes a part of the military force of her nation; acts under the immediate and direct command of the sovereign; is employed by him in national objects. He has many and powerful motives for preventing those objects from being defeated by the interference of a foreign state. Such interference cannot take place without affecting his power and his dignity. The implied license therefore under which such vessel enters a friendly port, may reasonably be construed, and it seems to the Court, ought to be construed, as containing an exemption from the jurisdiction of the sovereign, within whose territory she claims the rites of hospitality.

Upon these principles, by the unanimous consent of nations, a foreigner is amenable to the laws of the place; but certainly in practice, nations have not yet asserted their jurisdiction over the public armed ships of a foreign sovereign entering a port open for their reception. ...

[T]here is a manifest distinction between the private property of the person who happens to be a prince, and that military force which supports the sovereign power, and maintains the dignity and the independence of a nation. A prince, by acquiring private property in a foreign country, may possibly be considered as subjecting that property to the territorial jurisdiction; he may be considered as so far laying down the prince, and assuming the character of a private individual; but this he cannot be presumed to do with respect to any portion of that armed force, which upholds his crown, and the nation he is entrusted to govern. ...

It seems then to the Court, to be a principle of public law, that national ships of war, entering the port of a friendly power open for their reception, are to be considered as exempted by the consent of that power from its jurisdiction.

Without doubt, the sovereign of the place is capable of destroying this implication. He may claim and exercise jurisdiction either by employing force, or by subjecting such vessels to the ordinary tribunals. But until such power be exerted in a manner not to be misunderstood, the sovereign cannot be considered as having imparted to the ordinary tribunals a jurisdiction, which it would be a breach of faith to exercise. Those general statutory provisions therefore which are descriptive of the ordinary jurisdiction of the judicial tribunals, which give an individual whose property has been wrested from him, a right to claim that property in the courts of the country, in which it is found, ought not, in the opinion of this Court, to be so construed as to give them jurisdiction in a case, in which the sovereign power has impliedly consented to wave its jurisdiction.

The arguments in favor of this opinion which have been drawn from the general inability of the judicial power to enforce its decisions in cases of this description, from the consideration, that the sovereign power of the nation is alone competent to avenge wrongs committed by a sovereign, that the questions to which such wrongs give birth are rather questions of policy than of law, that they are for diplomatic, rather than legal discussion, are of great weight, and merit serious attention. ...

If the preceding reasoning be correct, the Exchange, being a public armed ship, in the service of a foreign sovereign, with whom the government of the United States is at peace, and having entered an American port open for her reception, on the terms on which ships of war are generally permitted to enter the ports of a friendly power, must be considered as having come into the American territory, under an implied promise, that while necessarily within it, and demeaning herself in a friendly manner, she should be exempt from the jurisdiction of the country. ...

NOTES

1) Chief Justice Marshall justified state immunity on the traditional grounds of sovereign equality and the dignity of states. There may also be functional reasons for the courts to refrain from deciding on foreign state matters. Consider the rationale for the act of state doctrine discussed in the previous section.

2) Sovereign equality of states is a reciprocal doctrine. If a foreign head of state cannot be expected to submit to the jurisdiction of the local courts, why should the local sovereign be expected to subjugate its jurisdiction to foreign authority? Did Marshall C.J. provide any answer? Is it more in keeping, nowadays, with the dignity of a foreign sovereign to submit to the rule of law than to claim to be above it?[60]

Scope of Immunity

The immunity of a foreign state is generally regarded as extending beyond the state itself and the head of state to:
— the government and all governmental organs,
— the leader of the government, the foreign minister and other ministers, officials and agents of the state with respect to their official acts,
— public corporations independently created but operating in effect as government organs, and
— state owned property.
Diplomatic, consular and other representatives abroad are excluded from this list because they are subject to separate privileges and immunities now fixed by multilateral treaty. These immunities are considered in the next section.

---

[60] Cf. Lord Denning's opinion in *Rahimtoola v. Nizam of Hyderabad*, [1958] A.C. 379, at 418 (H.L.).

Immunity is granted from all phases of judicial process. It is not limited to jurisdiction over the merits but is available against attachment before suit and against execution after judgment. For instance, submission by a state to the local jurisdiction in the merits of a case does not mean that its property may be subjected to execution to enforce a subsequent judgment against it. The property of the state is entitled to immunity from attachment and execution, unless the state submits further to the jurisdiction.

Even though a sovereign state may claim immunity in these kinds of situations, does it have a right to immunity on all such occasions? A positive answer was developed by the British courts and a doctrine of absolute immunity was laid down in *The Parlement Belge*.[61] This position was reiterated over and over on both sides of the Atlantic for many years. See, for instance, the clear statement of support for absolute immunity made by the Supreme Court of Canada in *Dessaulles v. Republic of Poland*.[62] But the growing interdependence of states and the increasing involvement of governments in commercial ventures in the twentieth century has forced many countries to the conclusion that the absolute theory is impractical and unreasonable. If a government department chooses to participate in the marketplace of a foreign state, why should it expect any different treatment or regulation than private trading parties? On this basis, a theory of restrictive immunity was founded and has flourished. Save for the Soviet Union and its allies,[63] the restrictive approach to state immunity is now almost universally practised as a matter of customary international law. The change has been quite rapid and recent. Not surprisingly many uncertainties remain, not least about the basic distinction between a sovereign act (*jure imperii*) which attracts immunity and a commercial act (*jure gestionis*) which no longer does so.

Although diplomatic immunity has long been the subject of treaty definition, first bilaterally and now multilaterally, state immunity is *par excellence* a matter of customary international law. Nevertheless in an effort to provide some order in times of changing practices, the states of Western Europe have adopted a Convention on State Immunity.[64] Its approach to the question of distinguishing between cases in which immunity is available and cases in which it is not is to include a list of particular situations where no immunity will be granted because the acts in question are acts *jure gestionis* or because the foreign state has consented to the court's jurisdiction. Britain signed this convention and implemented it by the *State Immunity Act 1978*.[65] Subsequent English cases, therefore, will likely be more determinative of the European Convention than of customary international law. However, shortly before the Convention came into force in Britain, the courts adopted the restrictive theory of immunity and so several cases from this period may still be of assistance in Canada. The United States has followed the restrictive theory since 1952. For reasons chiefly concerning the constitutional interrelation between the Department of

---

[61] (1880), L.R. 5 P.D. 197.
[62] [1944] 4 D.L.R. 1. And see the discussion of this history by Lord Denning in *Trendtex Trading Corp. Ltd. v. Central Bank of Nigeria*, [1977] 1 Q.B. 529 (C.A.), reported below.
[63] See C. Osakwe, ''A Soviet Perspective on Foreign Sovereign Immunity: Law and Practice'' (1982–83), 23 *Va. J. Int. L.* 13.
[64] Reprinted in (1972), 11 *Int. Leg. Mat.* 470.
[65] Stats. U.K. 1978, c. 33.

State and the American judiciary, the U.S. application of the restrictive theory has been clarified and confirmed by the *Foreign Sovereign Immunities Act of 1976*.[66]

Canada remained for some time in splendid isolation in the western world by continuing to apply the absolute theory of immunity. Notwithstanding a strong dissent by Laskin J. in *Congo v. Venne*,[67] the Supreme Court failed to take a firm position for change. This uncertainty at the top did not hinder several provincial courts from adopting a restrictive approach.[68] Towards the straightening out of these judicial dilemmas, Parliament has now passed the following *State Immunity Act*. It was desired by government officials in part because it had become impossible to explain simply to foreign states and their representatives what sovereign immunities they might expect to receive in Canada. Even so, such Parliamentary action is singularly remarkable for attempting to legislate customary international law. The source of this law is beyond Canada alone, yet the principle of supremacy of Parliament ensures that the courts will apply the international law crystallized in the *Act* even as the community of nation states change and develop it. The risk of such a development is increased by the fact that the International Law Commission already has under consideration a set of draft articles for a multilateral convention on state immunity.[69]

State Immunity Act[70]
S.C. 1982, c. 95.

Interpretation

2. In this Act, ''agency of a foreign state'' means any legal entity that is an organ of the foreign state but that is separate from the foreign state;

''commercial activity'' means any particular transaction, act or conduct or any regular course of conduct that by reason of its nature is of a commercial character;

''foreign state'' includes

(a) any sovereign or other head of the foreign state or of any political subdivision of the foreign state while acting as such in a public capacity,

---

[66] 28 U.S.C. ss. 1602-1611, reprinted in (1976), 15 *Int. Leg. Mat.* 1388.

[67] [1971] S.C.R. 997, reported below.

[68] See, for instance, *Zodiak International Products Inc. v. Polish People's Republic* (1977), 81 D.L.R. (3d) 656 (Que. C.A.); *Smith v. Canadian Javelin* (1976), 68 D.L.R. (3d) 428 (Ont. H.C.); J.L. Marasinghe, ''A Reassessment of Sovereign Immunity'' (1977), 9 *Ott. L.R.* 474; and H.M. Kindred, ''Foreign Governments Before the Courts'' (1980), 58 *Can. Bar R.* 602.

[69] *Supra*, n. 59. And see G. Triggs, ''An International Convention on Sovereign Immunity? Some Problems in Application of the Restrictive Theory'' (1982), 9 *Monash U.L.R.* 74.

[70] For commentary on the *Act*, see B.D. Coad, ''The Canadian State Immunity Act'' (1983), 14 *L. & Pol. Int. Bus.* 1197; H.L. Molot and M.L. Jewitt, ''The State Immunity Act of Canada'' (1982), 20 *Can. Y.B. Int. L.* 79; and D. Turp, ''Commentaire relatif a la Loi sur l'immunite des Etats etrangers devant les tribunaux'' (1983), 17 *Rev. Jur. Themis* 175.

(b) any government of the foreign state or of any political subdivision of the foreign
      state, including any of its departments, and any agency of the foreign state, and
(c) any political subdivision of the foreign state;
"political subdivision" means a province, state or other like political subdivision of
a foreign state that is a federal state.

State Immunity

3.(1) Except as provided by this Act, a foreign state is immune from the jurisdiction
of any court in Canada.

(2) In any proceedings before a court, the court shall give effect to the immunity
conferred on a foreign state by subsection (1) notwithstanding that the state has failed to
take any step in the proceedings.

4.(1) A foreign state is not immune from the jurisdiction of a court if the state waives
the immunity conferred by subsection 3(1) by submitting to the jurisdiction of the court
in accordance with subsection (2) or (4).

(2) In any proceedings before a court, a foreign state submits to the jurisdiction of
the court where it
  (a) explicitly submits to the jurisdiction of the court by written agreement or
        otherwise either before or after the proceedings commence;
  (b) initiates the proceedings in the court; or
  (c) intervenes or takes any step in the proceedings before the court.

(3) Paragraph (2)(c) does not apply to
  (a) any intervention or step taken by a foreign state in proceedings before a court
        for the purpose of claiming immunity from the jurisdiction of the court; or
  (b) any step taken by a foreign state in ignorance of facts entitling it to immunity
        if those facts could not reasonably have been ascertained before the step was
        taken and immunity is claimed as soon as reasonably practicable after they
        are ascertained.

(4) A foreign state that initiates proceedings in a court or that intervenes or takes any
step in proceedings before a court, other than an intervention or step to which paragraph
(2)(c) does not apply, submits to the jurisdiction of the court in respect of any third party
proceedings that arise, or counter-claim that arises, out of the subject-matter of the
proceedings initiated by the state or in which the state has so intervened or taken a step.

(5) Where, in any proceedings before a court, a foreign state submits to the jurisdiction
of the court in accordance with subsection (2) or (4), such submission is deemed to be
a submission by the state to the jurisdiction of such one or more courts by which those
proceedings may, in whole or in part, subsequently be considered on appeal or in the
exercise of supervisory jurisdiction.

5. A foreign state is not immune from the jurisdiction of a court in any proceedings
that relate to any commercial activity of the foreign state.

6. A foreign state is not immune from the jurisdiction of a court in any proceedings
that relate to
(a) any death or personal injury, or
(b) any damage to or loss of property that occurs in Canada.

7.(1) A foreign state is not immune from the jurisdiction of a court in any proceedings that relate to

(a) an action *in rem* against a ship owned or operated by the state, or

(b) an action *in personam* for enforcing a claim in connection with such a ship, if, at the time the claim arose or the proceedings were commenced, the ship was being used or was intended for use in a commercial activity.

(2) A foreign state is not immune from the jurisdiction of a court in any proceedings that relate to

(a) an action *in rem* against any cargo owned by the state if, at the time the claim arose or the proceedings were commenced, the cargo and the ship carrying the cargo were being used or were intended for use in a commercial activity; or

(b) an action *in personam* for enforcing a claim in connection with such cargo if, at the time the claim arose or the proceedings were commenced, the ship carrying the cargo was being used or was intended for use in a commercial activity.

(3) For the purpose of subsections (1) and (2), a ship or cargo owned by a foreign state includes any ship or cargo in the possession or control of the state and any ship or cargo in which the state claims an interest.

8. A foreign state is not immune from the jurisdiction of a court in any proceedings that relate to an interest of the state in property that arises by way of succession, gift or *bona vacantia*.

Procedure and Relief

9.(1) Service of an originating document on a foreign state, other than on an agency of the foreign state, may be made

(a) in any manner agreed on by the state;

(b) in accordance with any international Convention to which the state is a party; or

(c) in the manner provided in subsection (2).

(2) For the purposes of paragraph (1)(c), anyone wishing to serve an originating document on a foreign state may deliver a copy of the document, in person or by registered mail, to the Under-Secretary of State for External Affairs or a person designated by him for the purpose, who shall transmit it to the foreign state.

(3) Service of an originating document on an agency of a foreign state may be made

(a) in any manner agreed on by the agency;

(b) in accordance with any international Convention applicable to the agency; or

(c) in accordance with any applicable rules of court.

(4) Where service on an agency of a foreign state cannot be made under subsection (3), a court may, by order, direct how service is to be made.

(5) Where service of an originating document is made in the manner provided in subsection (2), service of the document shall be deemed to have been made on the day that the Under-Secretary of State for External Affairs or a person designated by him

pursuant to subsection (2) certifies to the relevant court that the copy of the document has been transmitted to the foreign state.

(6) Where, in any proceedings in a court, service of an originating document has been made on a foreign state in accordance with subsection (1), (3) or (4) and the state has failed to take, within the time limited therefor by the rules of the court or otherwise by law, the initial step required of a defendant or respondent in such proceedings in that court, no further step toward judgment may be taken in the proceedings except after the expiration of at least sixty days following the date of service of the originating document.

(7) Where judgment is signed against a foreign state in any proceedings in which the state has failed to take the initial step referred to in subsection (6), a certified copy of the judgment shall be served on the foreign state

(a) where service of the document that originated the proceedings was made on an agency of the foreign state, in such manner as is ordered by the court; or

(b) in any other case, in the manner specified in paragraph (1)(c) as though the judgment were an originating document.

(8) Where, by reason of subsection (7), a certified copy of a judgment is required to be served in the manner specified in paragraph (1)(c), subsections (2) and (5) apply with such modifications as the circumstances require.

(9) A foreign state may, within sixty days after service on it of a certified copy of a judgment pursuant to subsection (7), apply to have the judgment set aside.

10.(1) Subject to subsection (3), no relief by way of an injunction, specific performance or the recovery of land or other property may be granted against a foreign state unless the state consents in writing to such relief and, where the state so consents, the relief granted shall not be greater than that consented to by the state.

(2) Submission by a foreign state to the jurisdiction of a court is not consent for the purposes of subsection (1).

(3) This section does not apply to an agency of a foreign state.

11.(1) Subject to subsections (2) and (3), property of a foreign state that is located in Canada is immune from attachment and execution and, in the case of an action *in rem*, from arrest, detention, seizure and forfeiture except where

(a) the state has, either explicitly or by implication, waived its immunity from attachment, execution, arrest, detention, seizure or forfeiture, unless the foreign state has withdrawn the waiver of immunity in accordance with any term thereof that permits such withdrawal;

(b) the property is used or is intended for a commercial activity; or

(c) the execution relates to a judgment establishing rights in property that has been acquired by succession or gift or in immovable property located in Canada.

(2) Subject to subsection (3), property of an agency of a foreign state is not immune from attachment and execution and, in the case of an action *in rem*, from arrest, detention, seizure and forfeiture, for the purpose of satisfying a judgment of a court in any proceedings in respect of which the agency is not immune from the jurisdiction of the court by reason of any provision of this Act.

(3) Property of a foreign state

(a) that is used or is intended to be used in connection with a military activity, and

(b) that is military in nature or is under the control of a military authority or defence agency

is immune from attachment and execution and, in the case of an action *in rem*, from arrest, detention, seizure and forfeiture.

(4) Subject to subsection (5), property of a foreign central bank or monetary authority that is held for its own account and is not used or intended for a commercial activity is immune from attachment and execution.

(5) The immunity conferred on property of a foreign central bank or monetary authority by subsection (4) does not apply where the bank, authority or its parent foreign government has explicitly waived the immunity, unless the bank, authority or government has withdrawn the waiver of immunity in accordance with any term thereof that permits such withdrawal.

12.(1) No penalty or fine may be imposed by a court against a foreign state for any failure or refusal by the state to produce any document or other information in the course of proceedings before the court.

(2) Subsection (1) does not apply to an agency of a foreign state.

General

13.(1) A certificate issued by the Secretary of State for External Affairs, or on his behalf by a person authorized by him, with respect to any of the following questions, namely,

(a) whether a country is a foreign state for the purposes of this Act,

(b) whether a particular area or territory of a foreign state is a political subdivision of that state, or

(c) whether a person or persons are to be regarded as the head or government of a foreign state or of a political subdivision of the foreign state,

is admissible in evidence as conclusive proof of any matter stated in the certificate with respect to that question, without proof of the signature of the Secretary of State for External Affairs or other person or of that other person's authorization by the Secretary of State for External Affairs.

(2) A certificate issued by the Under-Secretary of State for External Affairs, or on his behalf by a person designated by him pursuant to subsection 9(2), with respect to service of an originating or other document on a foreign state in accordance with that subsection is admissible in evidence as conclusive proof of any matter stated in the certificate with respect to such service, without proof of the signature of the Under-Secretary of State for External Affairs or other person or of that other person's authorization by the Under-Secretary of State for External Affairs.

14. The Governor in Council may, on the recommendation of the Secretary of State for External Affairs, by order restrict any immunity or privileges under this Act in relation to a foreign state where, in the opinion of the Governor in Council, the immunity or privileges exceed those accorded by the law of that state.

15. Where, in any proceeding or other matter to which a provision of this Act and a provision of the *Visiting Forces Act* or the *Diplomatic and Consular Privileges and*

Immunities Act apply, there is a conflict between such provisions, the provision of this Act ceases to apply in such proceeding or other matter to the extent of the conflict.

16. Except to the extent required to give effect to this Act, nothing in this Act shall be construed or applied so as to negate or affect any rules of a court, including rules of a court relating to service of a document out of the jurisdiction of the court.

17. This Act does not apply to criminal proceedings or proceedings in the nature of criminal proceedings.

Legal Tests of Public or Commercial Acts

The adoption of the restrictive theory requires the courts to distinguish between acts *jure imperii* and *jure gestionis*. Their decisions have not been consistent for the reason that it is extremely difficult to draw a line between public and commercial activities. It is an ironic paradox that the restrictive approach has been introduced in an attempt to cope with government intervention in commercial affairs, when such involvement is itself a deliberate act of state policy.

The two seemingly most popular yet contending tests to distinguish commercial activities are to enquire into the purpose of the transaction (a public act has a public object), or to scrutinize the nature of the action (a commercial deal is a commercial act whoever transacts it). In truth, a precise distinction may be impossible.[71] The problem persists after the passage of the *State Immunity Act* because the statutory definition of "commercial activity" in section 2 is so broad. Too few occasions have so far arisen since the *Act* was passed for the courts to provide a definitive interpretation of this section, but some guidance may be obtained from prior case law and comparable legislation elsewhere.

U.K. State Immunity Act 1978
Stats. U.K. 1978, c. 33

1.(1) A State is immune from the jurisdiction of the courts of the United Kingdom except as provided in the following provisions of this Part of this Act. ...

3.(1) A State is not immune as respects proceedings relating to –

(a) a commercial transaction entered into by the State; or

(b) an obligation of the State which by virtue of a contract (whether a commercial transaction or not) falls to be performed wholly or partly in the United Kingdom.

(2) This section does not apply if the parties to the dispute are States or have otherwise agreed in writing; and subsection (1)(b) above does not apply if the contract (not being a commercial transaction) was made in the territory of the State concerned and the obligation in question is governed by its administrative law.

(3) In this section "commercial transaction" means

(a) any contract for the supply of goods or services;

(b) any loan or other transaction for the provision of finance and any guarantee or

---

[71] See the careful consideration of J. Crawford, "International Law and Foreign Sovereigns: Distinguishing Immune Transactions" (1983), 54 *Br. Y.B. Int. L.* 75.

indemnity in respect of any such transaction or of any other financial obligation; and

(c) any other transaction or activity (whether of a commercial, industrial, financial, professional or other similar character) into which a State enters or in which it engages otherwise than in the exercise of sovereign authority;

but neither paragraph of subsection (1) above applies to a contract of employment between a State and an individual.[72]

U.S. Foreign Sovereign Immunities Act of 1976[73]
28 U.S.C. 1602-1611; (1976) 15 *Int. Leg. Mat.* 1388

S. 1603 Definitions

For the purposes of this chapter ...

(d) A "commercial activity" means either a regular course of commercial conduct or a particular commercial transaction or act. The commercial character of an activity shall be determined by reference to the nature of the course of conduct or particular transaction or act, rather than by reference to its purpose.

(e) A "commercial activity carried on in the United States by a foreign state" means commercial activity carried on by such state and having substantial contact with the United States.

S. 1604 Immunity of a foreign state from jurisdiction

Subject to existing international agreements to which the United States is a party at the time of enactment of this Act a foreign state shall be immune from the jurisdiction of the courts of the United States and of the States except as provided in sections 1605 to 1607 of this chapter.

S. 1605 General exceptions to the jurisdictional immunity of a foreign state

(a) A foreign state shall not be immune from the jurisdiction of courts of the United States or of the States in any case ...

(2) in which the action is based upon a commercial activity carried on in the United States by the foreign state; or upon an act performed in the United States in connection with a commercial activity of the foreign state elsewhere; or upon an act outside the territory of the United States in connection with a commercial activity of the foreign state elsewhere and that act causes a direct effect in the United States.

---

[72] See C. Lewis, *State and Diplomatic Immunity* (2ed., 1985); F.A. Mann, "The State Immunity Act 1978" (1979), 50 *Br. Y.B. Int. L.* 43.

[73] See R.B. von Mehren, "The Foreign Sovereign Immunity Act of 1976" (1978), 17 *Colum. J. Transnat. L.* 33; and K.P. Simmons, "The Foreign Sovereign Immunity Act of 1976: Giving the Plaintiff his Day in Court" (1977/78), 46 *Ford L. Rev.* 543.

I.L.C. Draft Articles on Jurisdictional Immunities of States
As of 38th Session, 5 May — 11 July 1986, U.N.G.A. Doc. A/41/10

Article 11
COMMERCIAL CONTRACTS

1. If a State enters into a commercial contract with a foreign natural or juridical person and by virtue of the applicable rules of private international law, differences relating to the commercial contract fall within the jurisdiction of a court of another State, the State is considered to have consented to the exercise of that jurisdiction in a proceeding arising out of that commercial contract, and accordingly cannot invoke immunity from jurisdiction in that proceeding.

2. Paragraph 1 does not apply:
   (a)   in the case of a commercial contract concluded between States or on a government-to-government basis;
   (b)   if the parties to the commercial contract have otherwise expressly agreed.

Article 2
USE OF TERMS

1. For the purposes of the present articles: ...
   (b) ''commercial contract'' means:
    (i)   any commercial contract or transaction for the sale or purchase of goods or the supply of services,
    (ii) any contract for a loan or other transaction of a financial nature, including any obligation of guarantee in respect of any such loan or of indemnity in respect of any such transaction,
    (iii) any other contract or transaction, whether of a commercial, industrial, trading or professional nature, but not including a contract of employment of persons.

Article 3
INTERPRETATIVE PROVISIONS

...**2.** In determining whether a contract for the sale or purchase of goods or the supply of services is commercial, reference should be made primarily to the nature of the contract, but the purpose of the contract should also be taken into account if in the practice of that State that purpose is relevant to determining the non-commercial character of the contract.

Congo v. Venne
[1971] S.C.R. 997

[M. Venne, an architect, sued the Republic of the Congo for the cost of his professional services in preparing studies and sketches for a national pavilion which the Congo had proposed to build at Expo 67 but never did. The Congo claimed immunity from suit but this claim was rejected by the courts in Quebec.]

RITCHIE J. wrote for the majority: ... Mr. Justice Leduc, and consequently the Court of Appeal, adopted the view that the nature of the transaction here at issue was to be determined entirely on the basis that the respondent was a Montreal architect claiming against his employer and that the matter was therefore a purely private one. Considered from the point of view of the architect, it may well be that the contract was a purely commercial one, but, even if the theory of restrictive sovereign immunity were applicable, the question to be determined would not be whether the contractor was engaged in a private act of commerce, but whether or not the Government of the Congo, acting as a visiting sovereign State through its duly accredited diplomatic representatives, was engaged in the performance of a public sovereign act of State.

I think that it is of particular significance that the request for the respondent's services was made not only by the duly accredited diplomatic representatives of the Congo who were Commissioners General of the Exhibition, but also by the representative of the Department of Foreign Affairs of that country. ... This makes it plain to me that in preparing for the construction of its national pavilion, a Department of the Government of a foreign State, together with its duly accredited diplomatic representatives, were engaged in the performance of a public sovereign act of State on behalf of their country and that the employment of the respondent was a step taken in the performance of that sovereign act. It therefore follows in my view that the appellant could not be impleaded in the Courts of this country. ...

There is more than a suggestion in the reasons for judgment of the Court of Appeal that in determining whether the act of a foreign Sovereign is public or private, the burden of proof lies upon the Sovereign to show that the act was a public one if it is to be granted sovereign immunity. As I have indicated, there is no dispute as to the facts in the present case and, in my view, to the extent that it may have any bearing on the determination of this appeal, the question of whether the contract in question was purely private and commercial or whether it was a public act done on behalf of a sovereign State for State purposes, is one which should be decided on the record as a whole without placing the burden of rebutting any presumption on either party.

LASKIN J., (Hall J. concurring) in dissent: ... The one issue in this appeal is whether a claim of immunity, be it on an absolute basis or on a restrictive basis, must be conceded under the declinatory exception taken by the appellant. ...

I begin my consideration of the central point in this case by noting that we are not concerned here with any claims to property, tangible or intangible, by any foreign State or agency thereof. Nor are we concerned with the status of any corporate or other body alleged to be an organ of a foreign State. There is in the present case a formal admission by the respondent that the Democratic Republic of Congo is a sovereign State. This determines its status for the purposes of this case without the necessity of seeking a certificate from the Executive. No question is raised as to service of process, and hence only amenability to jurisdiction remains. ...

I refer now to Lord Denning's canvass of general principle in the *Rahimtoola*[74] case.

---

[74] *Rahimtoola v. Nizam of Hyderabad*, [1958] A.C. 379 (H.L.).

It will suffice to quote one passage, a summarizing one, which, to put it briefly, would substitute function for status as the determinant of immunity; it is in these words [at 422]:

...it seems to me that at the present time sovereign immunity should not depend on whether a foreign government is impleaded, directly or indirectly, but rather on the nature of the dispute. Not on whether "conflicting rights have to be decided," but on the nature of the conflict. Is it properly cognizable by our courts or not? If the dispute brings into question, for instance, the legislative or international transactions of a foreign government, or the policy of its executive, the court should grant immunity if asked to do so, because it does offend the dignity of a foreign sovereign to have the merits of such a dispute canvassed in the domestic courts of another country: but if the dispute concerns, for instance, the commercial transactions of a foreign government (whether carried on by its own departments or agencies or by setting up separate legal entities), and it arises properly within the territorial jurisdiction of our courts, there is no ground for granting immunity.

The considerations which, in my view, make it preferable to consider immunity from the standpoint of function rather than status do not rest simply on a rejection of the factors which had formerly been said to underlie it. Affirmatively, there is the simple matter of justice to a plaintiff; there is the reasonableness of recognizing equal accessibility to domestic Courts by those engaged in transnational activities, although one of the parties to a transaction may be a foreign State or an agency thereof; there is the promotion of international legal order by making certain disputes which involve a foreign State amenable to judicial processes, even though they be domestic; and, of course, the expansion of the range of activities and services in which the various States today are engaged has blurred the distinction between governmental and non-governmental functions or acts (or between so-called public and private domains of activity), so as to make it unjust to rely on status alone to determine immunity from the consequences of State action. ...

I note the general terms in which Lord Denning illustrated those classes of functions to which immunity should continue to attach. Another classification was proposed by the United States Court of Appeals for the Second Circuit in its reasons for judgment in the *Victory Transport* case;[75] ... it is as follows (at 360 of 336 F. 2d):

... we are disposed to deny a claim of sovereign immunity that has not been 'recognized and allowed' by the State Department unless it is plain that the activity in question falls within one of the categories of strictly political or public acts about which sovereigns have traditionally been quite sensitive. Such acts are generally limited to the following categories:

    (1)   internal administrative acts, such as expulsion of an alien.
    (2)   legislative acts, such as nationalization.
    (3)   acts concerning the armed forces.
    (4)   acts concerning diplomatic activity.
    (5)   public loans.

---

[75] *Victory Transport Inc. v. Comisaria General de Abastecimientos Y Transportes* (1964), 336 F. 2d 354; cert. den'd (1965), 381 U.S. 934.

We do not think that the restrictive theory adopted by the State Department requires sacrificing the interests of private litigants to international comity in other than these limited categories. ...

The need for distinctions "to render unto Caesar the things that are Caesar's" is obvious, and the two proposed classifications are useful aids. I resist the temptation in this case to add a classification of my own of activities in respect of which immunity should continue to attach; and the more so because the issue of initial jurisdiction raised by the declinatory exception, if it be taken to comprehend immunity on a restrictive basis, requires a conclusion only on whether the transaction in this case is so clearly within the claim of immunity as to make any further inquiry superfluous. For this purpose, I turn to the particular facts out of which the present litigation has arisen, so far as they can be gleaned from a rather sparse record and relevant legislation. ...

That record consists only of the declaration or claim, the declinatory exception, and two formal admissions to which reference has already been made. If the immunity claimed herein is to be tested on a restrictive basis, as I think it should be, there is, in my opinion, not enough in the record upon which a ready affirmation of immunity can be founded. The case must certainly proceed further for the claim to immunity to be determined.

Trendtex Trading Corp. Ltd. v. Central Bank of Nigeria
[1977] 1 Q.B. 529 (C.A.)

[The plaintiff sold cement which was destined for Nigeria to the use of the government of the day in its many building projects. The central Bank of Nigeria issued a letter of credit for the price of the cement. A very large number of similar contracts were also made. On becoming inundated with arriving shipments of cement, the succeeding Nigerian government had to take emergency action, which included ordering the Central Bank not to honour the letter of credit in this case. The plaintiff sued the Bank for payment.]

LORD DENNING M.R.: ... The Central Bank of Nigeria claim that they cannot be sued in this country on the letter of credit: because they are entitled to sovereign immunity. The plaintiff, Trendtex Trading Corporation, disputes this on the ground that this is an ordinary commercial transaction to which sovereign immunity does not apply. ...

The general picture
The doctrine of sovereign immunity is based on international law. It is one of the rules of international law that a sovereign state should not be impleaded in the courts of another sovereign state against its will. Like all rules of international law, this rule is said to arise out of the consensus of the civilised nations of the world. All nations agree upon it. So it is part of the law of nations.

To my mind this notion of a consensus is a fiction. The nations are not in the least agreed upon the doctrine of sovereign immunity. The courts of every country differ in their application of it. Some grant absolute immunity. Others grant limited immunity, with each defining the limits differently. There is no consensus whatever. Yet this does not mean that there is no rule of international law upon the subject. It only means that we differ as to what that rule is. Each country delimits for itself the bounds of sovereign immunity. Each creates for itself the exceptions from it. It is, I think, for the courts of this country to define the rule as best they can, seeking guidance from the decisions of the courts of other countries, from the jurists who have studied the problem, from treaties and conventions and, above all, defining the rule in terms which are consonant with justice rather than adverse to it. That is what the Privy Council did in *The Philippine Admiral* [1977] A.C. 373: see especially at 402–3; and we may properly do the same.

The two schools of thought

A fundamental question arises for decision. What is the place of international law in our English law? One school of thought holds to the doctrine of *incorporation*. It says that the rules of international law are incorporated into English law automatically and considered to be part of English law unless they are in conflict with an Act of Parliament. The other school of thought holds to the doctrine of *transformation*. It says that the rules of international law are not to be considered as part of English law except in so far as they have been already adopted and made part of our law by the decisions of the judges, or by Act of Parliament, or long established custom. The difference is vital when you are faced with a change in the rules of international law. Under the doctrine of incorporation, when the rules of international law change, our English law changes with them. But, under the doctrine of transformation, the English law does not change. It is bound by precedent. It is bound down to those rules of international law which have been accepted and adopted in the past. It cannot develop as international law develops.

(i) *The doctrine of incorporation.* The doctrine of incorporation goes back to 1737 in *Buvot v. Barbut* (1736) 3 Burr. 1481; 4 Burr. 2016; sub nom. *Barbuit's Case in Chancery* (1737) Forr. 280, in which Lord Talbot L.C. (who was highly esteemed) made a declaration which was taken down by young William Murray (who was of counsel in the case) and adopted by him in 1764 when he was Lord Mansfield C.J. in *Triquet v. Bath* (1764) 3 Burr. 1478:

Lord Talbot declared a clear opinion – "That the law of nations in its full extent was part of the law of England, ... that the law of nations was to be collected from the practice of different nations and the authority of writers." Accordingly, he argued and determined from such instances, and the authorities of Grotius, Barbeyrac, Binkershoek, Wiquefort, etc., there being no English writer of eminence on the subject.

That doctrine was accepted, not only by Lord Mansfield himself, but also by Sir William Blackstone, and other great names, too numerous to mention. In 1853 Lord Lyndhurst in the House of Lords, with the concurrence of all his colleagues there, declared that ... "the law of nations, according to the decision of our greatest judges, is part of the law of England": see Sir George Cornewall Lewis's book, *Lewis on Foreign Jurisdiction* (1859), at 66–67.

(ii) *The doctrine of transformation.* The doctrine of transformation only goes back to 1876 in the judgment of Cockburn C.J. in *Reg. v. Keyn* (1876), 2 Ex.D. 63, at 202–3:

For writers on international law, however valuable their labours may be in elucidating and ascertaining the principles and rules of law, cannot make the law. To be binding, the law must have received the assent of the nations who are to be bound by it. ...Nor, in my opinion, would the clearest proof of unanimous assent on the part of other nations be sufficient to authorise the tribunals of this country to apply, without an Act of Parliament, what would practically amount to a new law. In so doing, we should be unjustifiably usurping the province of the legislature.

To this I may add the saying of Lord Atkin in *Chung Chi Cheung v. The King*, [1939] A.C. 160, at 167–68:

So far, at any rate, as the courts of this country are concerned, international law has no validity save in so far as its principles are accepted and adopted by our own domestic law.

And I myself accepted this without question in *Reg. v. Secretary of State for the Home Department, Ex parte Thakrar*, [1974] Q.B. 684, at 701.

(iii) *Which is correct?* As between these two schools of thought, I now believe that the doctrine of incorporation is correct. Otherwise I do not see that our courts could ever recognise a change in the rules of international law. It is certain that international law does change. I would use of international law the words which Galileo used of the earth: "But it does move." International law does change: and the courts have applied the changes without the aid of any Act of Parliament. Thus, when the rules of international law were changed (by the force of public opinion) so as to condemn slavery, the English courts were justified in applying the modern rules of international law: see the "Statement of Opinion" by Sir R. Phillimore, Mr. M. Bernard and Sir H.S. Maine appended to the *Report of the Royal Commission on Fugitive Slaves* (1876), p. XXV, paras. 4 and 5. Again, the extent of territorial waters varies from time to time according to the rule of international law current at the time, and the courts will apply it accordingly: see *Reg. v. Kent Justices, Ex parte Lye*, [1967] 2 Q.B. 153, at 173, 189. The bounds of sovereign immunity have changed greatly in the last 30 years. The changes have been recognised in many countries, and the courts – of our country and of theirs – have given effect to them, without any legislation for the purpose, notably in the decision of the Privy Council in *The Philippine Admiral*, [1977] A.C. 373.

(iv) *Conclusion on this point.* Seeing that the rules of international law have changed – and do change – and that the courts have given effect to the changes without any Act of Parliament, it follows to my mind inexorably that the rules of international law, as existing from time to time, do form part of our English law. It follows, too, that a decision of this court – as to what was the ruling of international law 50 or 60 years ago – is not binding on this court today. International law knows no rule of stare decisis. If this court today is satisfied that the rule of international law on a subject has changed from what it was 50 or 60 years ago, it can give effect to that change – and apply the change in our English law – without waiting for the House of Lords to do it.

Has there been a change?

(i) *The doctrine of absolute immunity.* A century ago no sovereign state engaged in commercial activities. It kept to the traditional functions of a sovereign – to maintain law and order – to conduct foreign affairs – and to see to the defence of the country. It was in those days that England – with most other countries – adopted the rule of absolute immunity. It was adopted because it was considered to be the rule of international law at that time. In *The Parlement Belge* (1880), 5 P.D. 197, at 205, Brett L.J. said:

The exemption of the person of every sovereign from adverse suit is admitted to be a part of the law of nations ... [so also] of some property ... The universal agreement which has made these propositions part of the law of nations has been an implied agreement.

The rule was stated by Dicey in his work on *Conflict of Laws*, and repeated religiously by the judges thereafter. The classic restatement of it was made by Lord Atkin in *Compania Naviera Vascongado v. S.S. Cristina (The Cristina)*, [1938] A.C. 485, at 490:

The courts of a country will not implead a foreign sovereign, that is, they will not by their process make him against his will a party to legal proceedings whether the proceedings involve process against his person or seek to recover from him specific property or damages.

That doctrine was repeated by Viscount Simonds in *Rahimtoola v. Nizam of Hyderabad*, [1958] A.C. 379, at 394. He treated it as if it was a rule of English law, fixed and immutable, not to be departed from, even by the House of Lords itself.

(ii) *The doctrine of restrictive immunity.* In the last 50 years there has been a complete transformation in the functions of a sovereign state. Nearly every country now engages in commercial activities. It has its departments of state – or creates its own legal entities – which go into the market places of the world. They charter ships. They buy commodities. They issue letters of credit. This transformation has changed the rules of international law relating to sovereign immunity. Many countries have now departed from the rule of absolute immunity. So many have departed from it that it can no longer be considered a rule of international law. It has been replaced by a doctrine of restrictive immunity. This doctrine gives immunity to acts of a governmental nature, described in Latin as jure imperii, but no immunity to acts of a commercial nature, jure gestionis. In 1951 Sir Hersch Lauterpacht showed that, even at that date, many European countries had abandoned the doctrine of absolute immunity and adopted that of restrictive immunity – see his important article, "The Problem of Jurisdictional Immunities of Foreign States" in *The British Year Book of International Law, 1951*, vol. 28, at 220–272. Since that date there have been important conversions to the same view. Great impetus was given to it in 1952 in the famous "Tate letter" in the United States. Many countries have now adopted it. We have been given a valuable collection of recent decisions in which the courts of Belgium, Holland, the German Federal Republic, the United States of America and others have abandoned absolute immunity and granted only restrictive immunity. Most authoritative of all is the opinion of the Supreme Court of the United States in *Alfred Dunhill of London Inc. v. Republic of Cuba*. It was delivered on May 24, 1976, by White J. with the concurrence of the Chief Justice, Powell J. and Rehnquist J.:

Although it had other views in years gone by, in 1952, as evidenced by ... (the Tate letter) ... the United States abandoned the absolute theory of sovereign immunity and embraced the restrictive view under which immunity in our courts should be granted only with respect to causes of action arising out of a foreign state's public or governmental actions and not with respect to those arising out of its commercial or proprietary actions. This has been the official policy of our government since that time, as the attached letter of November 25, 1975, confirms ... "Such adjudications are consistent with international law on sovereign immunity."

To this I would add the European Convention on State Immunity (Basle, 1972), article 4, paragraph 1, which has been signed by most of the European countries.

[In the light of these changes, Lord Denning then adopted the restrictive approach to immunity.]

The application to this case

So I turn to see whether the transaction here was such as to attract sovereign immunity, or not. It was suggested that the original contracts for cement were made by the Ministry of Defence of Nigeria: and that the cement was for the building of barracks for the army. On this account it was said that the contracts of purchase were acts of a governmental nature, jure imperii, and not of a commercial nature, jure gestionis. They were like a contract of purchase of boots for the army. But I do not think this should affect the question of immunity. If a government department goes into the market places of the world and buys boots or cement – as a commercial transaction – that government department should be subject to all the rules of the market place. The seller is not concerned with the purpose to which the purchaser intends to put the goods.

There is another answer. Trendtex here are not suing on the contracts of purchase. They are claiming on the letter of credit which is an entirely separate contract. It was a straightforward commercial transaction. The letter of credit was issued in London through a London bank in the ordinary course of commercial dealings. It is completely within the territorial jurisdiction of our courts. I do not think it is open to the Government of Nigeria to claim sovereign immunity in respect of it. ...

Alter ego or organ of government

If we are still bound to apply the doctrine of absolute immunity, there is, even so, an important question arising upon it. The doctrine grants immunity to a foreign government or its department of state, or any body which can be regarded as an "alter ego or organ" of the government. But how are we to discover whether a body is an "alter ego or organ" of the government?

The cases on this subject are difficult to follow, even in this country: let alone those in other countries. And yet, we have to find what is the rule of international law for all of them. It is particularly difficult because different countries have different ways of arranging internal affairs. In some countries the government departments conduct all their business through their own offices – even ordinary commercial dealings – without setting up separate corporations or legal entities. In other countries they set up separate corporations or legal entities which are under the complete control of the department, but which enter into commercial transactions, buying and selling goods, owning and chartering ships, just like any ordinary trading concern. This difference in internal arrangements ought not to affect the availability of immunity in international law. A foreign department of state ought not to lose its immunity simply because it conducts some of its activities by means of a separate legal entity. It was so held by this court in *Baccus S.R.L. v. Servicio Nacional Del Trigo*, [1957] 1 Q.B. 438.

Another problem arises because of the internal laws of many countries which grant immunities and privileges to its own organisations. Some organisations can sue, or be sued, in their courts. Others cannot. In England we have had for centuries special immunities and privileges for "the Crown" – a phrase which has been held to cover many governmental departments and many emanations of government departments – but not nationalised commercial undertakings: see *Tamlin v. Hannaford*, [1950] 1 K.B. 18. The phrase "the Crown" is so elastic that under the Crown Proceedings Act 1947 the Treasury have issued a list of government departments covered by the Act. It includes even the Forestry Commission. It cannot be right that international law should grant or refuse absolute immunity, according to the immunities granted internally. I would put on one side, therefore, our cases about the privileges, prerogatives and exceptions of the "Crown."

It is often said that a certificate by the ambassador, saying whether or not an organisation is a department of state, is of much weight, though not decisive: see *Krajina v. Tass Agency*, [1949] 2 All E.R. 274. But even this is not to my mind satisfactory. What is the test which the ambassador is to apply? In the absence of any test, an ambassador may apply the test of control, asking himself: is the organisation under the control of a minister of state? On such a test, he might certify any nationalised undertaking to be a department of state. He might certify that a press agency or an agricultural corporation (which carried out ordinary commercial dealings) was a department of state, simply because it was under the complete control of the government.

I confess that I can think of no satisfactory test except that of looking to the functions and control of the organisation. I do not think that it should depend on the foreign law alone. I would look to all the evidence to see whether the organisation was under government control and exercised governmental functions. That is the way in which we looked at it in *Mellenger v. New Brunswick Development Corporation*, [1971] 1 W.L.R. 604, when I said, at 609:

The corporation ... has never pursued any ordinary trade or commerce. All that it has done is to promote the industrial development of the province in a way that a government department does.

With these considerations in mind, I turn to our problem.

Central Bank of Nigeria
At the hearing we were taken through the Act of 1958 under which the Central Bank of Nigeria was established, and of the amendments to it by later decrees. All the relevant provisions were closely examined: and we had the benefit of expert evidence on affidavit which was most helpful. The upshot of it all may be summarised as follows. (i) The Central Bank of Nigeria is a central bank modelled on the Bank of England. (ii) It has governmental functions in that it issues legal tender; it safeguards the international value of the currency; and it acts as banker and financial adviser to the government. (iii) Its affairs are under a great deal of government control in that the Federal Executive Council may overrule the board on monetary and banking policy and on internal administrative

policy. (iv) It acts as banker for other banks in Nigeria and abroad, and maintains accounts with other banks. It acts as banker for the states within the federation: but has few, if any, private customers.

In these circumstances I have found it difficult to decide whether or not the Central Bank of Nigeria should be considered in international law a department of the Federation of Nigeria, even though it is a separate legal entity. But, on the whole, I do not think it should be.

This conclusion would be enough to decide the case, but I find it so difficult that I prefer to rest my decision on the ground that there is no immunity in respect of commercial transactions, even for a government department.

[Stephenson and Shaw L.JJ. concurred in separate opinions.]

Iº Congreso del Partido[76]
[1983] 1 A.C. 244 (H.L.)

[In 1973 Cubazucar, a Cuban state trading enterprise, contracted to sell two shipments of sugar to Iansa, a Chilean company. One shipment was carried on the Playa Larga, which was a Cuban flag vessel, owned by Cuba, operated by Mambisa (another Cuban state enterprise) and chartered for the voyage to Chile by Cubazucar. The other shipment was loaded on the Marble Islands, which was foreign owned but chartered to Mambisa and sub-chartered to Cubazucar. While the Marble Islands was at sea and the Playa Larga was discharging at Valparaiso, Chile, a revolution occurred in that country resulting in the replacement of the socialist government of Allende with the right-wing government of Pinochet. The Cuban government strongly disapproved of the new Chilean government and so it directed Mambisa to order the Playa Larga to leave Chile and join the Marble Islands. Subsequently the Playa Larga returned to Cuba and Mambisa sold her remaining cargo of sugar. The Marble Islands was directed to Haiphong where her master sold her cargo to another Cuban state enterprise who donated it to the people of North Vietnam. While en route to Haiphong, the Marble Islands had been bought by the government of Cuba and re-registered in Cuba.

The Iº Congreso was a new trading vessel built in Britain for the government of Cuba and delivered to Mambisa. She was arrested by the plaintiffs, the Chilean buyers of the sugar, in an effort to recover the cargoes or their value. Cuba pleaded immunity successfully at first instance and before the Court of Appeal.]

In the House of Lords, LORD WILBERFORCE said:

The appellants contend that we have here (I take the case of *Playa Larga* for the present so as to avoid complication of statement) a commercial transaction, viz, a trading vessel, owned by the Republic of Cuba, carrying goods under normal commercial arrangements. Any claim arising out of this situation is, they assert, a claim of private law, and it is irrelevant that the purpose, for which the act giving rise to the claim was

---

[76] See H. Fox, ''State Immunity: The House of Lords' Decision in *Iº Congreso del Partido*'' (1982), 98 *L.Q.R.* 94.

committed, may have been of a political character (sc. briefly, to break off trading relations with a state, Chile, with which Cuba was not friendly). The appellants were able to cite a good deal of authority to support the proposition that it is the character of the relevant act that is decisive not its purpose ... .

In my opinion this argument, though in itself generally acceptable, burkes, or begs, the essential question which is "what is the relevant act?" It assumes that this is the initial entry into a commercial transaction and that this entry irrevocably confers upon later acts a commercial, or private law, character. Essentially it amounts to an assertion "once a trader always a trader." But this may be an over-simplification.

If a trader is always a trader, a state remains a state and is capable at any time of acts of sovereignty. The question arises, therefore, what is the position where the act upon which the claim is founded is quite outside the commercial, or private law, activity in which the state has engaged, and has the character of an act done jure imperii. The "restrictive" theory does not and could not deny capability of a state to resort to sovereign, or governmental action: it merely asserts that acts done within the trading or commercial activity are not immune. The inquiry still has to be made whether they were within or outside that activity. ...

The activities of states cannot always be compartmentalised into trading or governmental activities; and what is one to make of a case where a state has, and in the relevant circumstances, clearly displayed, both a commercial interest and a sovereign or governmental interest? To which is the critical action to be attributed? Such questions are the more difficult since they arise at an initial stage in the proceedings and, in all probability, upon affidavit evidence. ...

Under the "restrictive" theory the court has first to characterise the activity into which the defendant state has entered. Having done this, and (assumedly) found it to be of a commercial, or private law, character, it may take the view that contractual breaches, or torts, prima facie fall within the same sphere of activity. It should then be for the defendant state to make a case ... that the act complained of is outside that sphere, and within that of sovereign action. ...

[Having reviewed English, American, and German cases, Lord Wilberforce continued:]

The conclusion which emerges is that in considering, under the "restrictive" theory whether state immunity should be granted or not, the court must consider the whole context in which the claim against the state is made, with a view to deciding whether the relevant act(s) upon which the claim is based, should, in that context, be considered as fairly within an area of activity, trading or commercial, or otherwise of a private law character, in which the state has chosen to engage, or whether the relevant act(s) should be considered as having been done outside that area, and within the sphere of governmental or sovereign activity.

Whether the Republic of Cuba can claim immunity depends, if I am right as to the law, upon an examination of those acts in respect of which the claim is asserted. The appellants are certainly able to show, as a starting point, that this vessel was engaged in trade with the consent, if not with the active participation, of the Republic of Cuba. They were "doing business with a foreign government," to use the *Victory Transport*, 336 F. 2d 354, at 360 formulation. The question is whether the acts which gave rise to an alleged cause of action were done in the context of the trading relationship, or were done by the government of the Republic of Cuba acting wholly outside the trading relationship and in exercise of the power of the state. That this is not an easy question to answer is shown by the difference of judicial view, Robert Goff J. and Waller L.J. holding that Cuba's acts were governmental, Lord Denning M.R. that they were not. In my opinion it must be answered on a broad view of the facts as a whole and not upon narrow issues as to Cuba's possible contractual liability. I do not think that there is any doubt that the decision not to complete unloading at Valparaiso, or to discharge at Callao, was a political decision taken by the government of the Republic of Cuba for political and non-commercial reasons. I need not restate the history of events between September 11–20, 1973, which is very fully and clearly given by the learned judge. The change of government in Chile, and the events at Santiago in which the Cuban Embassy was involved, provoked a determination on the part of the government of Cuba to break off and discontinue trading relations with Chile. ...

Does this call for characterisation of the act of the Republic of Cuba in withdrawing *Playa Larga* and denying the cargo to its purchasers as done "jure imperii"? In my opinion it does not. Everything done by the Republic of Cuba in relation to *Playa Larga* could have been done, and, so far as evidence goes, was done, as owners of the ship: it had not exercised, and had no need to exercise, sovereign powers. It acted, as any owner of the ship would act, through Mambisa, the managing operators. It invoked no governmental authority. I have not overlooked Law No. 1256 which recited in vivid terms the (no doubt governmental) reaction of Cuba to the events in Chile – a law enacted on September 27, 1973, (and so subsequent to the decisive acts concerning the *Playa Larga*) though retrospective to September 11, 1973. But it seems to me clear that it was not this law – mainly a "freezing" or "blocking" enactment – which brought about, or had any effect upon action taken by *Playa Larga* prior to the ultimate sale of the cargo: that action was caused by instructions issued by the Cuban government as owner to Mambisa as operator of the vessel.

It may well be that those instructions would not have been issued, as they were, if the owner of *Playa Larga* had been anyone but a state: it is almost certainly the case that there was no commercial reason for the decision. But these consequences follow inevitably from the entry of states into the trading field. If immunity were to be granted the moment that any decision taken by the trading state were shown to be not commercially, but politically, inspired, the "restrictive" theory would almost cease to have any content and trading relations as to state-owned ships would become impossible. It is precisely to protect private traders against politically inspired breaches, or wrongs, that the restrictive theory allows states to be brought before a municipal court. It may be too stark to say of a state "once a trader always a trader": but, in order to withdraw its action from the sphere of acts done jure gestionis, a state must be able to point to some act clearly done jure imperii. Though, with much hesitation, I feel obliged to differ on this issue from the conclusion of the learned judge, I respectfully think that he well put this ultimate test, [1978] Q.B. 500, at 528:

...it is not just that the purpose or motive of the act is to serve the purposes of the state, but that the act is of its own character a governmental act, as opposed to an act which any private citizen can perform.

As to the *Playa Larga*, therefore, I find myself in agreement with Lord Denning M.R. and would allow the appeal. ...

[As to the Marble Islands:]

Lord Denning M.R. dealt with the case of *Marble Islands* briefly in these words [1980], 1 Lloyd's Rep. 23, at 31:

In the case of *Marble Islands* the origin of all that happened was a simple commercial transaction by which one of the state organisations of Cuba agreed to carry sugar to Chile and deliver it to the Chilean importers. The Cuban government induced its state organisation to repudiate that contract and ordered it to carry the sugar to North Vietnam.

However, the commercial transaction was not that of the Cuban state, but of an independent state organisation. The status of these organisations is familiar in our courts, and it has never been held that the relevant state is in law answerable for their actions. He continues, at 31:

The Cuban government then bought the vessel and, by its conduct, adopted the repudiation as its own. It continued the repudiative act and went on to carry the sugar to North Vietnam and handed it to the people there. The nature of the transaction was again the repudiation of a purely commercial obligation. Its purpose was two-fold – to show its hostility to Chile and to help the people of Vietnam. But the purpose does not matter. The act by its very nature was an act of repudiating a binding commercial obligation. Such an act does not give rise to sovereign immunity.

I regret that I cannot accompany this reasoning. Assuming that the actions of Mambisa amounted to a repudiation of contract, the action of the state – ex hypothesi, and in fact, not involved in any trading relationship – in ordering that repudiation cannot, with respect, amount to a repudiation by the state, or the distinction between jure imperii and jure gestionis would simply disappear. I cannot agree that there was ever any purely commercial obligation upon the Republic of Cuba or any binding commercial obligation: the republic never assumed any such obligation; it never entered the trading area; the cargo owners never entered into a commercial relation with it. I agree that the purpose, above, is not decisive but it may throw some light upon the nature of what was done. The acts of the Republic of Cuba were and remained in their nature purely governmental. The fact is, that if any wrong (contractually or delictually) was done as regards the cargo it was done by Mambisa. But in my opinion, in agreement with the learned judge, the acts complained of as regards the Republic of Cuba were acts jure imperii and so covered by immunity. I would dismiss the *Marble Islands* appeal ... .

[LORD DIPLOCK differed from Lord Wilberforce with respect to the Marble Islands. He said:] ...

The right asserted by the master to discharge and sell the perishable cargo in Haiphong is thus fairly and squarely based on private law (jus gestionis), the contractual terms contained in the bills of lading and the Commercial Code in force in Cuba. There is no suggestion that the cargo had been requisitioned by the Cuban government jure imperii nor is there any mention of the Law No. 1256 of September 27, 1973 ("the freezing law'') which froze all property and assets "located in Cuban territory" belonging to juridical persons such as Iansa in which the Chilean state owned an interest. ...

So all that was done in Haiphong in November to Iansa's sugar laden on *Marble Islands* was done upon the instructions of the Cuban government in purported reliance upon Mambisa's rights in private law (jus gestionis) and not upon any jus imperii of the Cuban state itself. It was only after the property in the sugar had been purportedly transferred to Alimport under the terms of the sale contract by delivery of the warehouse warrants that the sugar was then handed over by Alimport as a gift by the state of Cuba to the government of Vietnam. ...

So the legal position of the Cuban government after October 13, 1973, was that it had then acquired the ownership of a trading vessel *Marble Islands* then in mid-Pacific engaged in carrying cargo belonging to Iansa upon a voyage which the master claimed was authorised by a power to deviate contained in the bill of lading under which the cargo had been shipped. Mambisa from being demise charterer of *Marble Islands* had become managing operator of the vessel on behalf of the Cuban government, and legal possession of the cargo laden on her passed from Mambisa as former disponent owner to the Cuban government itself which in terms of English law became the "bailee" of Iansa's sugar. Thereafter, as the evidence discloses, everything that was done by the master was done on the express directions of the Cuban government; the Director and Senior Legal Adviser of the Ministry of Merchant Marine and Ports being sent to Haiphong in November to supervise what the master did there and the legal form and nature of the steps he took. ... The relevant transaction, viz. the discharge and sale of the cargo to Alimport at Haiphong was, as it seems to me, deliberately treated by the Cuban government as being effected under private [law] and not in the exercise of any sovereign powers.

For these reasons I for my part would allow the appeal in the case of the *Marble Islands* as well as in the case of the *Playa Larga*.

[The claim of immunity was disallowed in total. Lord Edmund Davies concurred with Lord Wilberforce in a separate opinion. Lords Keith and Bridge agreed with Lord Wilberforce as to the Playa Larga but with Lord Diplock as to the Marble Islands. Hence the appeal was allowed and Cuba's claim of immunity was wholly denied.]

NOTES

1) In deciding whether to deny a state immunity from suit because its activities were commercial, which judges in the previous cases applied a test of the purpose, and which a test of the nature, of the conduct under scrutiny?[77] Why? The Canadian and U.S. legislation directs the courts to consider only the nature of the act in question but it is not clear that this attempted distinction from the purpose of the act is a real one. The Australian Law Reform Commission has contended:[78]

---

[77] See also *Khan v. Fredson Travel* (1982), 133 D.L.R. (3d) 632 (Ont. H.C.).
[78] *Supra*, n. 59, at 28.

It is not possible to classify the nature of any human activity without reference to its purpose. The nature of an activity is not some abstract idea (certainly not for legal purposes), but rather the focussed, or relevant, or "central" purpose (according to some criterion). The classifications "governmental" and "commercial" are themselves purposive.

2) The difficulty of applying either test is compounded by the fact that the superficially simple dichotomy between public and commercial acts is probably inadequate. There is no international consensus on the limits of governmental involvement in trade and commerce. Some countries maintain relatively free market economies while others pursue distinctly interventionist economic policies. Yet other countries operate totally state-directed economic systems. Moreover, the term "commercial," as a single criterion for characterizing state acts that are not immune, is an overworked concept. As the Australian Law Reform Commission has also stated in connection with "commercial":[79]

It is too narrow in its coverage, since there are many relatively routine acts which are neither distinctive to states (i.e. "governmental") nor, in the absence of some special feature, commercial. And particular acts may be at the same time "commercial" and "governmental" (e.g. the letting of a contract for major public works), or they may have "commercial" and "governmental" elements inextricably mixed (e.g. an embassy car may be driving a diplomat to a meeting and the diplomat's spouse to a shopping centre). The problem of inextricably mixed activities is particularly acute in the area of execution of judgments against mixed funds. And finally, even when an act is itself apparently "governmental" (by whatever criteria) the *aspect* of the act which causes damage may have nothing in particular to do with its governmental character. For example, a car driving a diplomat to a meeting may simply be involved in an accident.

Was *Congo v. Venne* an instance where the foreign state's acts were "at the same time 'commercial' and 'governmental' "?[80] Was the *Congreso* case an example of "inextricably mixed" public and commerical acts by a government? The *State Immunity Act* defines "commercial activity" only in a most general way: see section 2. Do the more detailed definitions in the U.K. Act, section 3(3) and the I.L.C. Draft Arts. 2 and 3 provide any more help in determining what state conduct is commercial?

3) The overburdened category of "commercial activity" may be relieved by breaking down the circumstances in which immunity is denied into a number of discrete situations, each specifically defined and regulated. This has been done to a limited extent by the *State Immunity Act*: see sections 6, 7, and 8. A much longer list of acts and events for which a state has no immunity is set down in the U.K. Statute and the I.L.C. Draft Articles.

---

[79] Ibid., at 27.

[80] Cp. *Claim against the Empire of Iran* (1963), 45 I.L.R. 57 (Ger.); and *Planmount Ltd. v. Republic of Zaire*, [1981] 1 All E.R. 1110 (Q.B.), in both of which construction work on an ambassador's residence was treated as a commercial activity.

Immunity of State Organs and Property

Immunity of Governmental Organs

The immunities of foreign governmental organs are respected by the *State Immunity Act*, although they are subject to some special rules. However, before immunity may be claimed in a particular case, it has to be shown that the foreign defendant is a "political subdivision" or an "agency of a foreign state" within the meaning of section 2. Lacking an interpretative decision on this section, resort must be had to prior caselaw on the general question of qualifying status.

Baccus S.R.L. v. Servicio Nacional del Trigo
[1957] 1 Q.B. 438 (C.A.)

[The plaintiff sued for breach of a contract for the sale of rye. The defendant claimed it was entitled to immunity from suit because it was a department of the Spanish state even though it was organised in a corporate form.]

JENKINS L.J.: ... In my view of the evidence, it is reasonably plain that while the defendants undoubtedly were constituted a juristic personality with powers resembling those of a natural person, they were only accorded that status for the purposes for which they were formed; and the purposes for which they were formed were, briefly, the importing and exporting of grain for the Spanish Government in accordance with the directions of the Spanish Ministry of Agriculture and the policy from time to time laid down by the Spanish Government. Thus it seems to me that although their status was a corporate status, their functions were wholly those of a department of State. Are we then to hold that the State of Spain is deprived of sovereign immunity with respect to this activity of importing and exporting grain by reason of the fact that the defendants are a corporate body? In my view that would be plainly wrong. In these days the Government of a Sovereign State is not as a rule reposed in one personal sovereign: it is necessarily carried out through a complicated organization which ordinarily consists of many different ministries and departments. Where a particular ministry or department or instrument, call it what you will, is to be a corporate body or an unincorporated body seems to me to be purely a matter of governmental machinery. ...

In my view, it cannot be said that the operations of the defendants in this case are comparable to ordinary private trading operations. They are operations for which responsibility has been assumed by the State, and they are being carried out by the defendants under the supervision of the State in the shape of the Spanish Ministry of Agriculture, and I think such purposes as those can properly be classed as public purposes in this connexion.

SINGLETON L.J., dissenting: ... It is to be observed that in the present case, though there is evidence that Servicio Nacional del Trigo was a department of the Ministry of Agriculture of the State of Spain, there is also evidence, which is accepted on both sides, as far as I understand, that it was a juristic person or a legal entity under the laws of Spain. In that respect the case is different from the *Tass* case, and the point which here arises was there left open, ...

In the course of my judgment in the same case I said: "So far as I can see, there is no precedent for extending immunity to a corporate body carrying on business in this country, and I should wish for further argument before deciding that it could be so extended." ...

I regard a claim to extend sovereign immunity to a separate legal entity as an extension or as a claim to extend the doctrine. ...

I know of no case which goes as far as does the claim made by the defendants here. I cannot find that it has been almost universally recognized that if a government sets up a legal entity, something which may contract on its own behalf as a limited company does in this country, it can succeed in a claim for sovereign immunity in respect of the activities of that company or entity. The claim goes further than has been generally recognized, and, in the interests of good government, and in the interests of business relationship and business dealings throughout the world, I do not think that the claim ought to be allowed on the material before us.

[Parker L.J. wrote a separate judgment concurring with Jenkins L.J.]

NOTES

1) The reference to the *Tass* case is to *Krajina v. Tass Agency*.[81] There the plaintiff sought damages for libel by Tass, which was described as "the central information organ of the U.S.S.R." by the Soviet legislation establishing it. The court accepted the Soviet Ambassador's certification that Tass was a department of state and exercised the rights of a legal entity, and consequently held it was entitled to immunity. The readiness of the courts to accept the opinion of the interested ambassador is not nearly so great today. Consider the close and independent scrutiny that Lord Denning made of the Nigerian Central Bank in the *Trendtex* case reported previously.[82]

2) *Baccus* and *Tass* were both decided in times when immunity was absolute. *Baccus* is here reported to illustrate the antecedent question as to the governmental status of an independently constituted legal enterprise. Once the status to claim immunity is satisfied, there is still the question whether the character of its activities disqualify it from immunity. What do you consider would be the decision in *Baccus* and *Tass* today under the restrictive theory as imposed by the *State Immunity Act*?

3) Following are three cases affecting Canadian situations. The first one, *Mellenger v. New Brunswick Development Corp.*, has an added dimension that enquiry into the status of the defendant crown corporation had to be preceded by an investigation of the sovereign authority of the Province of New Brunswick. The second case, *Western Surety*

---

[81] [1949] 2 All E.R. 274 (C.A.).

[82] See also *Czarnikow v Rolimpex*, [1978] Q.B. 176 (C.A.): [1979] A.C. 351 (H.L.); and P.J. Kincaid, "Sovereign Immunity of Foreign State-Owned Corporations" (1976), 10 *Jo. World Tr. L.* 110.

Co. v. Elk Valley Logging Ltd., involved a similar issue about the sovereign character of Alberta for the purposes of inter-provincial immunity.[83] The court also decided that the *State Immunity Act* did not apply to Alberta because it refers to foreign states, meaning countries and provinces outside of Canada. See section 2.

Mellenger v. New Brunswick Development Corporation
[1971] 1 W.L.R. 604 (C.A.)

LORD DENNING M.R.: In this case Mr. Mellenger and Mr. Levin, both Canadian citizens, seek to sue the New Brunswick Development Corporation. They claim a sum of a quarter of a million pounds. They say that it is commission which has been earned by them for introducing an important commerical enterprise into New Brunswick. ...

[Counsel for the defendant] says that the New Brunswick Development Corporation is an arm of the Government of the Province of New Brunswick, and cannot be sued in this country. It is entitled to sovereign immunity. He produced two affidavits, one sworn by Mr. Paterson, the Agent-General in London of the Province of New Brunswick, the other by Mr. Hoyt, the solicitor for the corporation, who has come over from Canada. They produced the statute under which the corporation is established, which showed, they say, that it is an arm of the government.

...The British North America Act 1867 gave Canada a federal constitution. Under it the powers of government were divided between the dominion government and the provincial governments. Some of those powers were vested in the dominion government. The rest remained with the provincial governments. Each provincial government, within its own sphere, retained its independence and autonomy directly under the Crown. The Crown is sovereign in New Brunswick for provincial powers, just as it is sovereign in Canada for dominion powers: see *Liquidators of the Maritime Bank of Canada v. Receiver-General of New Brunswick*, [1892] A.C. 437. It follows that the Province of New Brunswick is a sovereign state in its own right, and entitled, if it so wishes, to claim sovereign immunity.

The next point is whether the New Brunswick Development Corporation can avail itself of the doctrine of sovereign immunity. If the corporation is part and parcel of the Government of New Brunswick – so much so as to be identified with it like a government department – it can clearly claim immunity. For this purpose we must turn to the statute which set it up. It was established by the New Brunswick Development Corporation Act of April 11, 1959. Section 1 says:

There is hereby constituted *on behalf of Her Majesty in right of New Brunswick* a body corporate under the name of The New Brunswick Development Corporation, ...

---

[83] Cp. *R. v. Eldorado Nuclear Ltd.* (1981), 121 D.L.R. (3d) 392 (Ont. Co. Ct.); aff'd (1981), 128 D.L.R. (3d) 82 (Ont. Div. Ct.), in which it was held that restricted sovereign immunity does not apply in the relations between the federal state of Canada and its component provinces.

Then follow sections which show the close connection of the corporation with the government. The Minister of Industry is an ex officio director. The other directors are appointed by the Lieutenant-Governor in Council. There is no issued capital. The corporation has no stocks or shares. Its principal power is (under section 3(1)(a)) to " ... assist, promote, encourage and advance the industrial development, prosperity and economic welfare of the province."

It is true that there is a later subsection [section 3(2)(a)] which gives the corporation power, subject to the approval of the Lieutenant-Governor in Council, to "carry on any business of an industrial, commercial or of any agricultural nature." But the evidence shows that the corporation has never exercised this later power. It has never pursued any ordinary trade or commerce. All that it has done is to promote the industrial development of the province in the way that a government department does, such as the Board of Trade in England. In the circumstances it seems to me that the corporation is really part and parcel of the Government of New Brunswick. The very words that it is constituted "on behalf of Her Majesty in right of New Brunswick" bring it within the words which were used [*per* Denning L.J.] in *Tamlin v. Hannaford*, [1950] 1 K.B. 18, at 25:

When Parliament intends that a new corporation should act on behalf of the Crown, it as a rule says so expressly, ...

On this ground alone, I would hold that the corporation is in the same position as a government department, and is entitled to plead sovereign immunity.

Apart, however, from the statute, the functions of the corporation, as carried out in practice, show that it is carrying out the policy of the Government of New Brunswick itself. It is its alter ego. If and in so far as the corporation played any part in this case, it was identified with the government. The evidence shows that the Premier of the province played a leading part. The corporation itself has never been legally involved in the transaction. It was not the owner of the land on which the factory is being built. The Airscrew Weyroc people bought it from some private owner. The corporation has made no contract with anyone about these transactions. But the Government of New Brunswick itself has done so. It agreed to guarantee a bond issue if required. There is no single point in which the corporation itself has been involved. It was just the alter ego of the government, and can claim sovereign immunity: see *Rahimtoola v. Nizam of Hyderabad*, [1958] A.C. 379, at 393, by Lord Simonds. ...

Seeing that the corporation is in the same position as a government department, it cannot be sued here. The Crown Proceedings Act 1947, does not authorise proceedings to be taken here against the Crown in respect of New Brunswick: see section 40(2)(b) of the Act. But I expect that New Brunswick has a statute similar to our 1947 statute, enabling the Crown to be sued there. This may enure, in the long run, to the benefit of the plaintiffs because they will be able to sue the corporation and the government there as defendants: and thus avoid any difficulty as to who is the proper defendant.

But this plea of sovereign immunity must, I think, succeed. The appeal should be allowed and the action dismissed.

[Phillimore L.J. concurred. Salmond L.J. concurred in a separate opinion.]

Western Surety Co. v. Elk Valley Logging Ltd. et al.
(1986), 31 B.L.R. 193 (B.C.S.C.)

[The plaintiff sued the sureties in British Columbia upon a performance bond it had provided on a construction project for the Province of Alberta within Alberta. One of the defendants joined the Province of Alberta to the action but it claimed sovereign immunity.]

CAMPBELL L.J.S.C.: ... The first question for consideration is whether Alberta is a sovereign state at least in the sense necessary to obtain immunity from these proceedings.

In an article in 47 C.B.R. 40 entitled "Interjurisdictional Immunity in Canadian Federalism " Professor Dale Gibson wrote at 59:

III. Interprovincial Immunity

To what extent may one Province bind the Crown of another Province by its laws? Suppose an employee of the British Columbia Government drives to Alberta in the course of his duties, and negligently injures someone in a collision while in Alberta. If the injured person sues the British Columbia Crown in British Columbia he will probably not succeed, since by British Columbia law the Crown is not liable in tort. If he sues in Alberta, where the Crown is liable in tort, he will probably meet a similar fate under existing law, *because of the principle that the courts will not entertain an action against a "foreign sovereign."* [Emphasis added.]

He states in the footnote:

It is arguable that the Crown in Right of another province is not a foreign sovereign, but I suspect that it would be so treated for this purpose. It is true, however, that one province has been held not to be a foreign state in the courts of another for the purpose of the rule that the courts of one state will not enforce the tax laws of another: *Weir v. Lohr* (1968), 65 D.L.R. (2d), 717 (Man. Q.B.), per Tritschler C.J., at 723: "In Manitoba the Province of Saskatchewan is not to be regarded as foreign State. Her Majesty in the Right of the Province of Saskatchewan is not a foreign Sovereign in Her Majesty's Court of Queen's Bench for Manitoba."

In any event, the provincial legislation imposing tort liability is usually so phrased to apply to the Crown of that province only. See s. 2(b) of the Manitoba Proceedings Against The Crown Act, R.S.M., 1954, c. 207.

The *Weir* case referred to in the footnote did not arise in the context of a sovereign immunity problem. The comments quoted from that case were obiter dicta and the learned judge went on to find in favour of the plaintiff on another basis.

I find more attraction in the comments of Lord Denning M.R. in *Mellenger v. N.B. Dev. Corp.*. ...

While that case can certainly be distinguished from this one on its facts, the logic in ... the judgments ... is most difficult to refute. I have no problem in holding that here Alberta is a sovereign state vis-à-vis the Province of British Columbia.

[The court next determined from the cases that "the restrictive theory [of immunity] is part of Canadian law at this time."]

Obviously it then must be decided whether Alberta was here engaged in a commercial activity in the sense described in the Canadian cases. What was the function of the transaction involving Alberta? The simple answer is highway building for the benefit of the public within its geographical boundaries. The defendant Hollowink says such was carried out in such a manner as to constitute commercial activity. It suggests the fact that the purpose of the contracts was to build a public highway is of no consequence. It says the character of the agreement is such that Alberta has stepped out of its protective shell of sovereignty and become a "person" for the purpose of this action, and that this is evidenced, inter alia, by its method of obtaining discontinuance of the suit brought in the Alberta Court. ...

When all the material here is examined, one cannot but conclude that the Department of Transport arm of Alberta was in the circumstances here under government control and exercising a government function within the Province of Alberta distinct from a commercial type function. The design, construction, alteration, repair and maintenance of highways are the responsibility of the department under the provisions of the Department of Transportation Act, R.S.A. 1980, c.D-30, and the Public Words Act, R.S.A. 1980, c.P-38. From those functions comes the involvement in this action through the third party proceedings. It cannot therefore, in my view, be said that the restrictive theory of sovereign immunity applies here and thus Alberta is entitled to claim sovereign immunity.

Ferranti-Packard Ltd. v. Cushman Rentals Ltd.
(1980), 30 O.R. (2d) 194; aff'd (1981), 31 O.R. (2d) 799 (O.C.A.)

REID J.: ... The issue before us is whether the doctrine of sovereign immunity applies so as to protect the New York State Thruway Authority from suit in this Court.

The learned Master (Davidson) held that the doctrine applied. He struck out the writ of summons that had been served on the Authority.

The background may be briefly stated. It is alleged that two electrical transformers manufactured by the plaintiff were being transported along a highway operated by the Authority. An accident occurred when the driver sought to pass under an overpass crossing the highway. The overpass was maintained as well by the Authority. One of the transformers came into contact with the overpass. Damage resulted. This action was commenced against the driver, the lessor of the truck carrying the transformers, and others, including the Authority. ...

Both counsel were satisfied to accept the doctrine of ... immunity as stated by Lord Denning M.R. in *Trendtex Trading Corp. v. Central Bank of Nigeria*, [1977] 1 Q.B. 529, at 559. Lord Denning said: "The doctrine grants immunity to a foreign government or its department of state, or any body which can be regarded as an alter ego or organ of the government." Lord Denning then asks the question: "But how are we to discover whether a body is an alter ego or organ of the government?" In the passage that follows those observations Lord Denning refers to different ways in which Governments conduct their business – in some cases dealing in commercial transactions directly with others and in other cases setting up "separate corporations or legal entities which are under the complete control of the department." The significance of this reference to "complete control'' is revealed in the following passage that occurs later in the same decision at 560:

I confess that I can think of no satisfactory test except that of looking to the functions and control of the organisation. I do not think that it should depend on the foreign law alone. I would look to all the evidence to see whether the organization was under government control and exercised governmental functions.

We have had the benefit of a thorough examination of the Statute of New York State that established the Authority, that is, the *New York State Thruway Authority Act* (the *Throughway Act*) and both counsel have gone through it with us to establish their cases ... .

The legislation reveals that the Authority is a body corporate and politic constituting a public corporation. It consists of three members who are appointed by the Governor with the consent of the Senate. Its responsibility is set out in detail in the legislation but it is basically to construct, maintain, and operate a throughway system in the State of New York.

Other provisions are to the effect that the Authority has power to sue and be sued (but only in the Court of Claims.) It has power to acquire real property, make contracts, fix and collect fees, rentals and charges for the use of the throughway "with an adequate margin of safety to produce sufficient revenue to meet the expense of maintenance and operation and to fulfil the terms of any agreement made with the holders of its notes or bonds ... ." I call particular attention to the latter provision for it suggests that the Authority is self-sufficient.

The Authority has power to borrow money and to issue negotiable notes and bonds and these bonds may be guaranteed by the State of New York. The legislation makes it plain that they are not automatically guaranteed but may be guaranteed at the choice of the Authority at the time of issue. It has express power to accept gifts or funds or property from the State of New York. It is provided, as well, that it may assume jurisdiction over State property and in those circumstances it must pay or become indebted to the State with respect to that property. It is expressly provided that judgments against it shall be paid out of moneys of the Authority. Money it derives from its operations or from any other source is paid to the comptroller of the State but specifically as agent of the Authority. It is provided that its money shall not be commingled with any other. The deposits may be secured by obligations of the State.

These are some of the provisions in the legislation called to our attention by the appellant seeking to establish that the Authority was not the alter ego of the State.

Similarly, Mr. Griffin called to our attention a number of provisions which he submitted indicated that there was so close a connection between the two that it could properly be held that the Authority was an *alter ego*. Among those provisions is one to the effect that officers and employees of the State shall not be deemed to have forfeited his office or employment by reason of his becoming a member of the Authority.

Furthermore, in respect of officers and employees, s. 355 provides that:

355(1) Officers and employees of state departments and agencies may be transferred to the authority ... without examination and without loss of any civil service status or rights.

Section 357 expresses the right I have already referred to in the Authority to assume jurisdiction over State property and that is submitted as an indication that the two are in effect interchangeable. Section 358(a) refers to "condemnation," which we understand to be expropriation; it provides that the Authority may acquire real property by condemnation and may acquire real property in the name of the State by deed.

Section 352 of the statute provides in express terms that: "...the Authority shall be regarded as performing a governmental function in carrying out its corporate purpose and in exercising the powers granted by this title". ...

We have considered all these provisions and our law in relation to them. There are cases in which the doctrine of sovereign immunity has been applied to governmental or State bodies so as to grant to those bodies the same immunity that was available to a sovereign State. One of those cases particularly drawn to our attention was *Mellenger et al. v. New Brunswick Development Corp.* ...

We think that is a very different situation from the one before us. There is a real separation in our opinion between the State of New York and the Authority. The Authority is set up to carry on what has all the earmarks of a commercial activity. There is no indication in the statute that it is not to be independent in establishing policy and carrying out its responsibility ... .

The provision in the statute declaring that it was "performing a governmental function" does not, therefore, imply that the Authority was a mere functionary of the State. The context of the statute is, in our opinion, wholly against that view.

An *alter ego* is another self, a reasonably exact counterpart. We think it is clear that that description does not fit the Authority in relation to the State.

Thus, we find ourselves in disagreement with the learned Master. The result is that the appeal must be allowed and the order of the Master will be set aside.

NOTES

1) In determining the status of a state-owned corporation or other separate legal entity, what can be gathered from these cases and *Trendtex*, reported above, as to the appropriate criteria? Consider how the courts looked to the enabling legislation, the organization of the enterprise, its functions, and the degree of political control.[84]

2) In *Ferranti-Packard* the Thruway Authority seems to have been disqualified because it was judged to have commercial functions and to be separate from the State of New York. What is commercial about operating a state's road system? Compare the *Western Surety* case. Why should the Thruway Authority's separate existence and independence of action matter so much? On that basis, even the courts might not be regarded as governmental organs.

---

[84] See also *Lorac Transport Ltd. v. The Ship "Atra"* (1984), 9 D.L.R. (4th) 129; *Bouchard v. J.L. Le Saux Ltée.* (1984), 45 O.R. (2d) 792 (Ont. Mast. Ch.); and *First National City Bank v. Banco Para el Comercio Exterior de Cuba* (1983), 462 U.S. 611; 103 S.Ct. 2591.

Immunity of State Property

The property of a foreign state is generally immune from attachment, judgment and execution under the *State Immunity Act*. See sections 10 and 11. However, immunity cannot be claimed for land, buildings, goods, chattels, money and other intangible assets unless they are "property of a foreign state." No guidance is provided by the *Act* as to the meaning in this statute of the very technical word "property," except in the cases of ships and cargo in section 7(3) and interests that arise "by way of succession, gift or *bona vacantia*" in section 8. Consequently, there must be doubt, where the foreign state's interest is less than ownership, whether the property, for which it claims immunity, has sufficient sovereign status to qualify for immunity. For instance:

1) Is a house, which is leased to a foreign government for use as a private residence by one of its representatives, the property of a foreign state?[85]

2) Are the Ottawa bank accounts of a foreign diplomatic mission open to attachment?[86]

There seems to be a further difficulty in these uncertain situations as to how any right to immunity shall be established, seeing that section 3 of the *Act* directs a court "to give effect to the immunity conferred on a foreign state ... notwithstanding that the state has failed to take any steps in the proceedings."

A particularly acute problem occurs when the plaintiff's claim is that his property has been wrongly taken or used by the foreign state defendant. Is the assertion of ownership of the property by the state sufficient to found its immunity and so to stay the action? The difficulty is that any investigation of the state's title to the property would appear to breach its right to immunity. Consider the situation in *The Schooner Exchange*, reported at the beginning of this section, and the following case.

Juan Ismael and Co. Inc. v. Government of Indonesia
[1955] A.C. 72 (J.C.P.C.)

[The plaintiff had previously chartered a ship to the Indonesian government, who still retained it after the charterparty was ended. The plaintiff claimed repossession but the government asserted that it had bought the vessel through an agent of the plaintiff's and claimed immunity for its property.]

EARL JOWITT: ... Where the foreign sovereign State is directly impleaded the writ will be set aside, but where the foreign sovereign State is not a party to the proceedings, but claims that it is interested in the property to which the action relates and is therefore indirectly impleaded, a difficult question arises as to how far the foreign sovereign government must go in establishing its right to the interest claimed. Plainly if the foreign government is required as a condition of obtaining immunity to prove its title to the property in question the immunity ceases to be of any practical effect. The difficulty was

---

[85] Cf. *Re Royal Bank of Canada and Corriveau and Cuba* (1980), 30 O.R. (2d) 653 (Ont. C.A.).

[86] Cp. *Alcom Ltd. v. Republic of Colombia*, [1984] 2 All E.R. 6 (H.L.), and see I.L.C. Draft Articles, *supra*, at n. 59, Arts. 21 and 23.

cogently expressed by Lord Radcliffe in the case of the *Dollfus Mieg*, [1952] A.C. 582, at 616 where he said: "A stay of proceedings on the ground of immunity has normally to be granted or refused at a stage in the action when interests are claimed but not established, and indeed to require him [i.e., the foreign sovereign] to establish his interest before the court (which may involve the court's denial of his claim) is to do the very thing which the general principle requires that our courts should not do."

In the case of *The Jupiter*, [1924] P. 236, where the writ was in rem against the ship, Scrutton L.J. based his judgment on the view that an assertion by a foreign sovereign that he claimed a right in property must be accepted by the court as conclusive without investigating whether the claim be good or bad. ... The view that a bare assertion by a foreign government of its claim is sufficient has the advantage of being logical, and simple in application, but it may lead to a very grave injustice if the claim asserted by the foreign government is in fact not maintainable, and the view of Scrutton L.J. has not found favour in subsequent cases. ...

In their Lordships' opinion a foreign government claiming that its interest in property will be affected by the judgment in an action to which it is not a party, is not bound as a condition of obtaining immunity to prove its title to the interest claimed, but it must produce evidence to satisfy the court that its claim is not merely illusory, nor founded on a title manifestly defective. The court must be satisfied that conflicting rights have to be decided in relation to the foreign government's claim. When the court reaches that point it must decline to decide the rights and must stay the action, but it ought not to stay the action before that point is reached.

[In the event the Privy Council found the Indonesian government's assertion "manifestly defective" and rejected the claim to immunity.]

NOTES

1) Is this the procedure anticipated by the *State Immunity Act* for dealing with claims of immunity for foreign state property?

2) Special rules are contained in section 7 of the *Act* regarding foreign state ships. Do they help to resolve the kind of dilemma that arose in the *Juan Ismael* case.[87]

3) While sections 10 and 11 of the *Act* protect the property of the foreign state, section 6 restricts its immunity where it is connected to the death, personal injury or loss of property of others. If a receiver, appointed by an American court, unlawfully seized property in Canada and an action in trespass is brought, can the United States claim immunity under customary international law?[88] Under the *State Immunity Act*?

Waiver of Immunity and Execution of Judgments

A foreign state may submit to the local jurisdiction and then it will be treated as having waived its immunity. See the *State Immunity Act* section 4. However, a submission purely for the purpose of claiming immunity will not amount to a waiver; section 4(3).

---

[87] See also the similar provisions in the *Federal Court Act*, R.S.C. 1970, (2nd Supp.), c.10, s. 43(7)(c).
[88] See *Carrato v. U.S.A.* (1982), 141 D.L.R. (3d) 456.

Formerly, a waiver was only effective if it was made in the face of the court.[89] In light of section 4(2)(a) however, it seems that a foreign state may waive its immunity before any proceedings are begun. Thus an appropriately worded jurisdiction clause in a contract with a foreign state should now suffice as a waiver of its immunity in any subsequent litigation about the agreement. Unfortunately, the statutory alteration of procedure in Canada is not as clear as in the U.K. *State Immunity Act 1978* which expressly declares that a state may submit to the jurisdiction "by a prior written agreement."[90]

Waiver of immunity to jurisdiction does not necessarily incur loss of immunity from specific judgments, (see section 10), or from attachment or execution of property (see section 11). A plaintiff seeking pre-judgment attachment for security may not be successful unless the foreign state owner makes a separate waiver of immunity; section 11(1)(a). A similar conclusion may be reached regarding attempts at post-judgment executions. Should there be immunity from execution or is the practice a hangover from the absolute theory?

In the pre-Act case of *Re Royal Bank of Canada and Corriveau and Cuba*,[91] Mr. Corriveau sought to enforce a default judgment against Cuba for breach of a lease of property as its chancellory. Shortly before the end of the lease Cuba allowed the water pipes in the building to freeze, causing extensive damage. Mr. Corriveau tried to execute his judgment for this damage against the funds in the Cuban account at the Royal Bank but Cuba objected. Cromarty J., after reviewing most of the principal authorities, remarked:[92]

International law appears to provide a protection against execution even if a judgment has been obtained. The *Diplomatic and Consular Privileges and Immunities Act*, by analogy, contemplates the present situation. Article 31, s. 2 in a paragraph separate from that which deals with immunity from the civil jurisdiction forbids execution. There is some support for this inference in the comment of Rand J. in *the City and County of St. John et al. v. Fraser-Brace Overseas Corp. et al*, [[1957] S.C.R. 263, at 268].

He went on to hold:[93]

The only record before me shows that the leased premises were for governmental use and that the moneys in the bank were in the "possession" of the foreign Sovereign State.

If the use of the leased premises was a public act by Cuba, as Cromarty J. seems to imply, perhaps there should not have been a judgment against Cuba at all. In any event, should immunity from execution depend upon the character of the original transaction or

---

[89] See *Mighell v. Sultan of Johore*, [1984] 1 Q.B. 149 (C.A.); *Duff Development Co. v. Government of Kelantan*, [1924] A.C. 797 (H.L.); and *Kahan v. Pakistan Federation*, [1951] 2 K.B. 1003 (C.A.).
[90] Stats. U.K. 1978, c. 33, s. 2(2).
[91] (1980), 30 O.R. (2d) 653 (Ont. C.A.).
[92] *Ibid.*, at 658.
[93] *Ibid.*, at 659.

upon the status of the property being seized? Consider this question in the light of the detailed provisions of the *State Immunity Act* sections 10 and 11.[94]

DIPLOMATIC IMMUNITIES

The rules and principles of diplomatic privileges and immunities are some of the oldest parts of international law. The present ones date from the beginnings of modern international law in the sixteenth century. The emergence of the nation state with the attendant development of communications, growth of trade and industry, and expansion of political alignments confronted heads of state with the need to maintain continuous official contact with each other. Thus the appointment of ambassadors and the maintenance of permanent legations early became commonplace.

The accreditation of diplomats necessitated some system to ensure the appropriate recognition of their status as foreign state representatives. Thus there developed an increasingly refined set of practices about diplomatic precedence, protocol, privilege and immunity. Supplemented by national laws, such as the English *Diplomatic Privileges Act, 1708*,[95] and numerous bilateral treaties, these practices had developed by this century into a large body of detailed rules of customary international law. This customary law has been codified since 1961 in the Vienna Convention on Diplomatic Relations, which was ratified by Canada in 1966 and subsequently implemented by the *Diplomatic and Consular Privileges and Immunities Act*.[96]

There are two principal theories put forward as bases for the privileges and immunities of diplomats. One is the so-called functional theory that diplomats ought to be at liberty to devote themselves fully to the service of their state. The second basis is that diplomats owe no allegiance to the receiving state and consequently are not subject to its laws. The former theory seems preferable as a description of the historical development of diplomatic relations and is affirmed by the Vienna Convention in its preamble as the purpose of the privileges and immunities.

This section concentrates on the law regarding diplomats,[97] although there are other bodies of rules respecting other state representatives and international persons. These include consuls, international organizations and their staff as well as the accredited representatives of the member states, judges of the International Court, special missions and visiting forces, all of which are mentioned briefly at the end of this section.

---

[94] And see J. Crawford, "Execution of Judgments and Foreign Sovereign Immunity" (1982), 75 *Am. J. Int. L.* 820; and the Australian Law Reform Commission, *supra*, n. 59, at 73–74.

[95] 7 Ann., c. 12.

[96] Stats. Can. 1976–77, c. 31, reported here after the Vienna Convention.

[97] See M. Hardy, *Modern Diplomatic Law* (1968); Ld. Gore-Booth, ed., *Satow's Guide to Diplomatic Practice* (5 ed., 1979); F. Przetacznik, *Protection of Officials of Foreign States according to International Law* (1983); B. Sen, *A Diplomat's Handbook of International Law and Practice*; and A. Dufour, "La protection des immunités diplomatique et consulaires au Canada" (1973), 11 *Can. Y.B. Int. L.* 123, and (1974), 12 *Can. Y.B. Int. L. 3*.

Vienna Convention on Diplomatic Relations
1966 Can. T.S. No. 29; 500 U.N.T.S. 95

The States Parties to the Present Convention,

Recalling that people of all nations from ancient times have recognized the status of diplomatic agents, ...

Realizing that the purpose of such privileges and immunities is not to benefit individuals but to ensure the efficient performance of the functions of diplomatic missions as representing states,

Affirming that the rules of customary international law should continue to govern questions not expressly regulated by the provisions of the present Convention,

Have agreed as follows:

Article 1

For the purpose of the present Convention, the following expressions shall have the meanings hereunder assigned to them:

(a) the "head of the mission" is the person charged by the sending state with the duty of acting in that capacity;

(b) the "members of the mission" are the head of the mission and the members of the staff of the mission;

(c) the "members of the staff of the mission" are the members of the diplomatic staff, of the administrative and technical staff and of the service staff of the mission;

(d) the "members of the diplomatic staff" are the members of the staff of the mission having diplomatic rank;

(e) a "diplomatic agent" is the head of the mission or a member of the diplomatic staff of the mission;

(f) the "members of the administrative and technical staff" are the members of the staff of the mission employed in the administrative and technical service of the mission;

(g) the "members of the service staff" are the members of the staff of the mission in the domestic service of the mission;

(h) a "private servant" is a person who is in the domestic service of a member of the mission and who is not an employee of the sending state;

(i) the "premises of the mission" are the buildings or parts of buildings and the land ancillary thereto, irrespective of ownership, used for the purposes of the mission including the residence of the head of the mission.

Article 2

The establishment of diplomatic relations between states, and of permanent diplomatic missions, takes place by mutual consent.

Article 3

1. The functions of a diplomatic mission consist *inter alia* in:

    (a) representing the sending state in the receiving state;

    (b) protecting in the receiving state the interests of the sending state and of its nationals, within the limits permitted by international law;

    (c) negotiating with the government of the receiving state;

    (d) ascertaining by all lawful means conditions and developments in the receiving state, and reporting thereon to the government of the sending state;

    (e) promoting friendly relations between the sending state and the receiving state, and developing their economic, cultural and scientific relations.

. . .

Article 9

1. The receiving State may at any time and without having to explain its decision, notify the sending State that the head of the mission or any member of the diplomatic staff of the mission is *persona non grata* or that any other member of the staff of the mission is not acceptable. In any such case, the sending State shall, as appropriate, either recall the person concerned or terminate his functions with the mission. A person may be declared *non grata* or not acceptable before arriving in the territory of the receiving State.

2. If the sending State refuses or fails within a reasonable period to carry out its obligations under paragraph 1 of this Article, the receiving State may refuse to recognize the person concerned as a member of the mission.

. . .

Article 22

1. The premises of the mission shall be inviolable. The agents of the receiving state may not enter them, except with the consent of the head of the mission.

2. The receiving state is under a special duty to take all appropriate steps to protect the premises of the mission against any intrusion or damage and to prevent any disturbance of the peace of the mission or impairment of its dignity.

3. The premises of the mission, their furnishings and other property thereon and the means of transport of the mission shall be immune from search, requisition, attachment or execution.

Article 23

1. The sending state and the head of the mission shall be exempt from all national, regional or municipal dues and taxes in respect of the premises of the mission, whether owned or leased, other than such as represent payment for specific services rendered. ...

Article 24

The archives and documents of the mission shall be inviolable at any time and wherever they may be.

Article 25

The receiving state shall accord full facilities for the performance of the functions of the mission.

Article 26

Subject to its laws and regulations concerning zones entry into which is prohibited or regulated for reasons of national security, the receiving state shall ensure to all members of the mission freedom of movement and travel in its territory.

Article 27

1. The receiving state shall permit and protect free communication on the part of the mission for all official purposes. In communicating with the government and the other missions and consulates of the sending state, wherever situated, the mission may employ all appropriate means, including diplomatic couriers and messages in code or cipher. However, the mission may install and use a wireless transmitter only with the consent of the receiving state.

2. The official correspondence of the mission shall be inviolable. Official correspondence means all correspondence relating to the mission and its functions.

3. The diplomatic bag shall not be opened or detained.

4. The packages constituting the diplomatic bag must bear visible external marks of their character and may contain only diplomatic documents or articles intended for official use.

5. The diplomatic courier, who shall be provided with an official document indicating his status and the number of packages constituting the diplomatic bag, shall be protected by the receiving state in the performance of his functions. He shall enjoy personal inviolability and shall not be liable to any form of arrest or detention.

· · ·

Article 29

The person of a diplomatic agent shall be inviolable. He shall not be liable to any form of arrest or detention. The receiving state shall treat him with due respect and shall take all appropriate steps to prevent any attack on his person, freedom or dignity.

Article 30

1. The private residence of a diplomatic agent shall enjoy the same inviolability and protection as the premises of the mission.

2. His papers, correspondence and, except as provided in paragraph 3 of Article 31, his property, shall likewise enjoy inviolability.

Article 31

1. A diplomatic agent shall enjoy immunity from the criminal jurisdiction of the receiving state. He shall also enjoy immunity from its civil and administrative jurisdiction, except in the case of:

    (a) a real action relating to private immovable property situated in the territory of the receiving state, unless he holds it on behalf of the sending state for the purposes of the mission;

    (b) an action relating to succession in which the diplomatic agent is involved as executor, administrator, heir or legatee as a private person and not on behalf of the sending state;

    (c) an action relating to any professional or commercial activity exercised by the diplomatic agent in the receiving state outside his official functions.

2. A diplomatic agent is not obliged to give evidence as a witness.

3. No measures of execution may be taken in respect of a diplomatic agent except in the cases coming under sub-paragraphs (a), (b) and (c) of paragraph 1 of this article, and provided that the measures concerned can be taken without infringing the inviolability of his person or of his residence.

4. The immunity of a diplomatic agent from the jurisdiction of the receiving state does not exempt him from the jurisdiction of the sending state.

Article 32

1. The immunity from jurisdiction of diplomatic agents and of persons enjoying immunity under Article 37 may be waived by the sending state.

2. Waiver must always be express.

3. The initiation of proceedings by a diplomatic agent or by a person enjoying immunity from jurisdiction under Article 37 shall preclude him from invoking immunity from jurisdiction in respect of any counter-claim directly connected with the principal claim.

4. Waiver of immunity from jurisdiction in respect of civil or administrative proceedings shall not be held to imply waiver of immunity in respect of the execution of the judgment, for which a separate waiver shall be necessary.

. . .

Article 34

A diplomatic agent shall be exempt from all dues and taxes, personal or real, national, regional or municipal, except [for sales taxes, property taxes on privately owned property, income taxes on private income within the receiving state, and a few other charges and fees.]

. . .

Article 36

1. The receiving state shall, in accordance with such laws and regulations as it may adopt, permit entry of and grant exemption from all customs duties, taxes, and related charges other than charges for storage, cartage and similar services, on:

    (a) articles for the official use of the mission;

(b) articles for the personal use of a diplomatic agent or members of his family forming part of his household, including articles intended for his establishment.

2. The personal baggage of a diplomatic agent shall be exempt from inspection, unless there are serious grounds for presuming that it contains articles not covered by the exemptions mentioned in paragraph 1 of this article, or articles the import or export of which is prohibited by the law or controlled by the quarantine regulations of the receiving state. Such inspection shall be conducted only in the presence of the diplomatic agent or of his authorized representative.

Article 37

1. The members of the family of a diplomatic agent forming part of his household shall, if they are not nationals of the receiving state, enjoy the privileges and immunities specified in Articles 29 to 36.

2. Members of the administrative and technical staff of the mission, together with members of their families forming part of their respective households, shall, if they are not nationals of or permanently resident in the receiving state, enjoy the privileges and immunities specified in Articles 29 to 35, except that the immunity from civil and administrative jurisdiction of the receiving state specified in paragraph 1 of Article 31 shall not extend to acts performed outside the course of their duties. They shall also enjoy the privileges specified in Article 36, paragraph 1, in respect of articles imported at the time of first installation.

3. Members of the service staff of the mission who are not nationals of or permanently resident in the receiving state shall enjoy immunity in respect of acts performed in the course of their duties, exemption from dues and taxes on the emoluments they receive by reason of their employment and the exemption contained in Article 33.

4. Private servants of members of the mission shall, if they are not nationals of or permanently resident in the receiving state, be exempt from dues and taxes on the emoluments they receive by reason of their employment. In other respects, they may enjoy privileges and immunities only to the extent admitted by the receiving state. However, the receiving state must exercise its jurisdiction over those persons in such a manner as not to interfere unduly with the performance of the functions of the mission.

Article 38

1. Except insofar as additional privileges and immunities may be granted by the receiving state, a diplomatic agent who is a national of or permanently resident in that state shall enjoy only immunity from jurisdiction and inviolability, in respect of official acts performed in the exercise of his functions.

2. Other members of the staff of the mission and private servants who are nationals of or permanently resident in the receiving state shall enjoy privileges and immunities only to the extent admitted by the receiving state. However, the receiving state must exercise its jurisdiction over those persons in such a manner as not to interfere unduly with the performance of the functions of the mission.

Article 39

1. Every person entitled to privileges and immunities shall enjoy them from the moment he enters the territory of the receiving state on proceeding to take up his post or, if already in its territory, from the moment when his appointment is notified to the Ministry for Foreign Affairs or such other ministry as may be agreed.

2. When the functions of a person enjoying privileges and immunities have come to an end, such privileges and immunities shall normally cease at the moment when he leaves the country, or on expiry of a reasonable period in which to do so, but shall subsist until that time, even in case of armed conflict. However, with respect to acts performed by such a person in the exercise of his functions as a member of the mission, immunity shall continue to subsist. ...

Article 40

[Protection for diplomats, their staff and families, and official communications when passing through the territory of a third state.]

Article 41

1. Without prejudice to their privileges and immunities, it is the duty of all persons enjoying such privileges and immunities to respect the laws and regulations of the receiving state. They also have a duty not to interfere in the internal affairs of that state.

2. All official business with the receiving state entrusted to the mission by the sending state shall be conducted with or through the Ministry for Foreign Affairs of the receiving state or such other ministry as may be agreed.

3. The premises of the mission must not be used in any manner incompatible with the functions of the mission as laid down in the present Convention or by other rules of general international law or by any special agreements in force between the sending and the receiving state.

· · ·

Article 43

The function of a diplomatic agent comes to an end, *inter alia*:
  (a) on notification by the sending state to the receiving state that the function of the diplomatic agent has come to an end;
  (b) on nomination by the receiving state to the sending state that, in accordance with paragraph 2 of Article 9, it refuses to recognize the diplomatic agent as a member of the mission.

Article 44

The receiving state must, even in case of armed conflict, grant facilities in order to enable persons enjoying privileges and immunities, other than nationals of the receiving state, and members of the families of such persons irrespective of their nationality, to leave at the earliest possible moment. It must, in particular, in case of need, place at their disposal the necessary means of transport for themselves and their property.

Diplomatic and Consular Privileges and Immunities Act
S.C. 1976-77, c. 31

2.(1) Subject to this section, Articles 1, 22 to 24 and 27 to 40 of the Vienna Convention on Diplomatic Relations, set out in Schedule I, ... have the force of law in Canada in respect of all countries (including Commonwealth countries), whether or not a party to the Conventions. ...

(4) If it appears to the Secretary of State for External Affairs that the privileges and immunities accorded to a Canadian diplomatic post or consular post in any country, or to persons connected with any such post, are less than those conferred by this Act on that country's diplomatic post or consular post, as the case may be, or on persons connected with any such post, he may by order withdraw from any or all of that country's posts or from any or all persons connected therewith such of the privileges and immunities so conferred as he deems proper.

(5) Where he deems it proper, the Secretary of State for External Affairs may by order restore any privilege or immunity withdrawn under subsection (4).

3. In the event of any inconsistency between this Act, the regulations, the orders made under section 2 or 4, or the provisions given the force of law by section 2, and any other law, this Act, the regulations, the orders and those provisions prevail to the extent of the inconsistency.

4. The Governor in Council may make such regulations and orders as are necessary for the purpose of giving effect to any of the provisions given the force of law by section 2.

5. If, in any action or proceeding, a question arises as to whether any person is entitled to a privilege or an immunity under this Act or any regulation or order, a certificate issued by or under the authority of the Secretary of State for External Affairs containing any statement of fact relevant to that question shall be received in evidence as conclusive proof of the fact so stated.

Diplomatic Asylum

The premises of a diplomatic mission are, by Article 22 of the Vienna Convention, both immune and inviolable. These terms overlap in some degree. Immunity mainly conveys freedom from legal process and duties, while inviolability chiefly suggests freedom from physical interference. The legal process, if allowed to run its course, could result in an order that would disturb the possession of the mission.

Although the premises of, and the personnel accredited to, the mission are secured from interference by the Convention, it makes no reference to the practice of granting asylum to others who enter there. Diplomatic asylum is contentious enough that it was purposefully avoided at the Vienna Conference. Its practice is most common in, but not limited to, Latin America where it is observed by treaties but is not part of customary international law. See the *Asylum Case* reported in Chapter 3.

If diplomatic asylum is not condoned by international law, nevertheless there is very little host states can do about it. If a foreign mission provides asylum to a political refugee, its immunity and inviolability prevents the host state from interfering. The wrath of the local government towards the individual in asylum is usually not so great as to risk endangering its foreign policy interests by intervening in the mission in breach of the law or by breaking diplomatic relations with the protecting state.

Legal Character and Duration of Immunity

Dickinson v. Del Solar
[1930] 1 K.B. 376

[Dickinson sued Del Solar in negligence for injuries suffered in a motor car accident. The third party, Del Solar's insurance company, asserted he had no legal liability because he was at the time First Secretary to the Peruvian Legation. But the Minister of the Legation forbad Del Solar from relying upon diplomatic immunity because the accident occurred when the car was being used for private purposes.]

LORD HEWART C.J.: ... Diplomatic agents are not, in virtue of their privileges as such, immune from legal liability for any wrongful acts. The accurate statement is that they are not liable to be sued in the English Courts unless they submit to the jurisdiction. Diplomatic privilege does not import immunity from legal liability, but only exemption from local jurisdiction. The privilege is the privilege of the Sovereign by whom the diplomatic agent is accredited, and it may be waived with the sanction of the Sovereign or of the official superior of the agent: ... In the present case the privilege was waived and jurisdiction was submitted to by the entry of appearance: ... and as Mr. Del Solar had so submitted to the jurisdiction it was no longer open to him to set up privilege. If privilege had been pleaded as a defence, the defence could, in the circumstances, have been struck out. Mr. Del Solar was bound to obey the direction of his Minister in the matter. In these circumstances ... the judgment clearly creates a legal liability against which the insurance company have agreed to indemnify him. ... I hold therefore that the third parties here are liable.

Ghosh v. D'Rozario
[1963] 1 Q.B. 106 (C.A.)

[Ghosh alleged that he had been slandered in 1956 by D'Rozario, who, at the time, was a staff member of the High Commission for India in the United Kingdom. In 1957 D'Rozario went to India but he returned to England as a private citizen in 1959, when he was served with a writ for the slander. In 1960 D'Rozario went back to India and returned once more to England as a diplomat at the High Commission. He then claimed immunity and sought a stay of the action.]

HOLROYD PEARCE L.J.: ... The real point in the case is whether, as a matter of principle, a defendant's diplomatic immunity which comes into existence after an action has been started, and while it is pending, necessitates a stay of those proceedings. It is conceded that had the defendant's diplomatic immunity existed when the writ was issued, the proceedings would not be maintainable. It is conceded further that the steps taken by the defendant earlier in the action when he had no diplomatic immunity cannot constitute any waiver or voluntary acceptance of jurisdiction by the defendant, for he had then no right of immunity which he could waive and, having been duly served, he was bound to submit to the jurisdiction. It is argued, however, that once this court has taken jurisdiction between the litigants, it will not relax its grasp even though facts occur thereafter which would create diplomatic immunity. ...

Diplomatic immunity is likely to create individual hardship. But this hardship must bow to a general overriding principle of comity between conflicting jurisdictions. An ambassador must live in a foreign land, and if he could be summoned before the tribunals of that foreign land, or coerced by its legal process, it would be an affront to his sovereign, and an interference with his work. For the same reasons it is necessary that the embassy staff as well as the ambassador should be immune. The immunity belongs to the State, and not to its representatives individually. There is no difference in principle between the ambassador and the humbler members of his staff providing that they are properly accredited, and on the necessary list. ...

But I prefer to decide the matter on a broader ground. It would be no less an affront and an interference to subject an ambassador to actions that were in existence before he acquired his diplomatic status and immunity than it would be to allow a writ to be served on him. Moreover, if a pre-existing action were allowed to proceed against an ambassador, it would create undesirable practical difficulties. The court could not order him or impose any sanction on his conduct. He could with impunity be a most unruly litigant. The mischief which the general rule is intended to avoid at the cost of some individual hardship would inevitably arise. In my judgment the general principles that confer diplomatic immunity against the initiation of proceedings confer an equal immunity against the continuation of pre-existing and hitherto properly constituted proceedings. I would, therefore, dismiss the appeal.

[Davies L.J. and Wilberforce J. concurred in separate opinions.]

NOTES

1) In the reverse situation, if a writ were to be issued against a defendant during his diplomatic posting and, rather than have it struck out as he might, if he were to allow the case to come on to trial after the end of his term of service, would the suit be upheld?[98]

2) If immunity is granted only from process and not from liability, it may be important to know when that immunity ends. Consider the situation that arose in Ottawa in 1983.[99] Palacios was the first secretary at the Nicaraguan embassy until early in July. He was charged later in the month with illegal possession of weapons and possession of cocaine for the purpose of trafficking. The Nicaraguan embassy stated that Palacios finished his official duties on July 12, nearly two weeks before he was charged, but he argued that

---

[98] See *Empson v. Smith*, [1966] 1 Q.B. 426 (C.A.); and *Shaw v. Shaw*, [1979] 3 All E.R. 1 (Fam. D.).
[99] See *Re Regina and Palacios* (1984), 45 O.R. (2d) 269 (Ont. C.A.), reported *supra* in Chapter 3.

his immunity continued until he left the country either for another post or for home. In fact Palacios went to the United States for a brief visit on July 16 and he was charged on his return to Canada. Was Palacios entitled to invoke immunity? See the Vienna Convention Article 39. Would it make any difference whether the alleged activities for which he was charged may have occurred before July 12 or afterwards?

Waiver of Diplomatic Immunity

The Vienna Convention declares that diplomatic immunity may be waived. See Article 32. Its provisions have clarified the rules about waiver. In particular, a waiver must be express and does not extend beyond immunity from suit unless a separate waiver of immunity from execution is also made. Where the Vienna Convention is not certain, customary law still applies. Thus, where Article 32(1) provides that diplomatic immunity "may be waived by the sending state" but says no more, the question who may act for the sending state has to be answered by resort to prior practice. In *R. v. Madan* it was said:[100]

...[I]t is clear that that waiver must be a waiver by a person with full knowledge of his rights and a waiver by or on behalf of the chief representative of the state in question. In other words, it is not the person entitled to a privilege who may waive it unless he does so as agent or on behalf of the representative of the country concerned; it must be the waiver of the representative of the state.

The immunity is the privilege of the state, not of the individual, and so members of the administrative and technical staff of the mission or of the service staff, or members of the family of a diplomatic agent entitled to diplomatic immunity cannot themselves waive their immunity: waiver, to be valid, can be done only by their superior, that is, the head of the mission. But it is not so clear as *Madan*'s case may suggest that the head of the mission can waive his own immunity. Schwarzenberger has argued that the head of the mission cannot do so because the right to immunity is enjoyed by the state, and is not granted to any diplomat in a personal capacity. He asserted that the immunity of the head of the mission can be waived only by or with the permission of his own government.[101]

Although the Convention allows for waiver of immunity, the practical question is whether foreign diplomats will waive their immunity, as they should, for ordinary matters of their personal lives not connected with or prejudicial to their official functions. Although the Vienna Conference adopted a resolution recommending that sending states should waive diplomatic immunity in civil actions with local citizens wherever the mission is unimpeded, the record in criminal matters shows an opposite tendency:[102]

---

[100] [1961] 1 All E.R. 588, at 591 (C.C.A.).

[101] G. Schwarzenberger and E.D. Brown, *A Manual of International Law* (6 ed., 1976), at 80.

[102] Reply by the Minister of External Affairs to a written question in the House of Commons, as reported in *The Globe & Mail*, September 17, 1983.

restrictive. Archives and documents belonging to the consulate are inviolable. As with diplomatic agents, consular officers must be treated with due respect and shall not be liable to arrest or detention pending trial except in the case of a grave crime and pursuant to a decision by the competent judicial authority. Canada has implemented this Convention in the same Act of 1977.[107] Section 2(3) of that Act stipulates that the reference in article 41(1) of the Vienna Convention on Consular Relations to a "grave crime" shall be construed in Canada as a reference to any offence created by an Act of Parliament for which an offender may be sentenced to imprisonment for five years or more.

Consular officers and employees enjoy a more limited immunity from jurisdiction than diplomats. In both criminal and civil matters immunity is restricted by article 43(1) to acts performed in the course of their consular functions. The provisions as to waiver are the same as in the earlier Convention.

Where diplomatic agents are assigned to the consular section of a mission they continue to enjoy the privileges and immunities recognized by the rules of international law on diplomatic relations.

C. Special Missions

Special missions or ad hoc missions are sent to certain countries for a specific and limited purpose. They supplement the diplomatic and consular missions in this regard. The use of such temporary missions has become more prevalent since the development of faster transportation.

As a result, no rules of customary international law can be said to have developed on this subject. Thus, the Convention of 1969 dealing with Special Missions[108] is not a codification of existing law and is not binding on non-parties. It is not certain yet whether the law will develop into customary rules by non-parties adhering to them. As of October 1986, this convention has not yet come into force.

The model for the Convention on Special Missions was the Vienna Convention on Diplomatic Relations of 1961. The only difference is that under article 8 the sending state must inform the host state of both the size and the composition of the mission. Article 17 provides that the mission must be located in a place agreed upon by the states concerned or be located in the Foreign Ministry of the host state. ...

D. Privileges and Immunities of the United Nations

Article 105 of the U.N. Charter provides in general terms that the United Nations should enjoy in the territory of each member state such privileges and immunities as are necessary for the fulfillment of its purposes. It further provides that the representatives of the member states at the United Nations and officials of the United Nations itself shall likewise enjoy the privileges and immunities that are necessary for the independent exercise of their functions.

---

[107] *Diplomatic and Consular Privileges and Immunities Act*, S.C. 1976–77, c. 31.
[108] U.N.G.A. Res. 2530 of December 8, 1969, reprinted in (1969), 8 *Int. Leg. Mat.* 73. Canada has not signed or ratified the Convention.

The General Assembly is authorized by article 105 of the Charter to make recommendations with a view to determining the details of these privileges and immunities, or to propose conventions for this purpose.

In relation to this authorization in 1946 the General Assembly of the United Nations adopted the Convention on the Privileges and Immunities of the United Nations.[109] Canada ratified this Convention on June 22, 1948, with a reservation relating to taxation. This convention provides, *inter alia*, for the following: immunity of United Nations property and assets from legal process unless such immunity is waived; inviolability of premises and archives and special privileges for its representatives including immunity from criminal jurisdiction.

A number of special agreements have also been concluded with those states in those territories the United Nations or one of its subsidiary organs meets or has its headquarters. For example, the agreement between the United States and the United Nations regarding the headquarters of the United Nations in New York.[110]

In 1947, the General Assembly adopted another Convention for the co-ordination of privileges and immunities of the specialized agencies with those of the United Nations itself.[111] Canada acceded to this Convention on the Privileges and Immunities of the Specialized Agencies on March 29, 1966. Again a reservation was made regarding taxes. The United Nations did not accept the Canadian instrument of accession deposited with the said reservation and Canada is not therefore listed among the parties to the Convention. The privileges and immunities are subject to waiver. In Canada the *Privileges and Immunities (N.A.T.O.) Act, 1970,*[112] and the *Privileges and Immunities (International Organizations) Act, 1970*[113] were passed to give effect to these provisions.

E. The International Court of Justice

Under the provisions of article 19 of the Statute of the Court, the judges of the International Court of Justice enjoy diplomatic privileges and immunities when acting in their official capacity.

F. Visiting Forces

Opinions have differed as to how far immunity should be extended to foreign visiting forces. United States practice generally favoured absolute immunity. Today it is not looked upon in such an exclusive manner. The remedy to avoid controversy from the

---

[109] Otherwise known as the General Convention (1949), 43 *Am. J. Int. L. Supp.* 1. This forms the Schedule to the *Privileges and Immunities (International Organizations) Act*, R.S.C. 1970, c. P-22.

[110] (1949), 43 *Am. J. Int. L. Supp.* 8. ...

[111] 33 U.N.T.S. 261, 290. Note that Canada has also signed a Headquarters Agreement with the International Civil Aviation Organization (I.C.A.O.), 1951 Can. T.S. No. 7. See also a Supplementary Exchange of Notes, 1971 Can. T.S. No. 17. See P. Dai, "The Headquarters Agreement between Canada and the International Civil Aviation Organization" (1964), 2 *Can. Y.B. Int. L.* 205. A Headquarters Agreement was also signed between Canada and the United Nations concerning the United Nations Audio-Visual Information Centre on Human Settlements, 1977 Can. T.S. No. 27.

[112] R.S.C. 1970, c. P-23.

[113] R.S.C. 1970, c. P-22.

United States viewpoint has been to conclude numerous special agreements with the host state. ...

The *Visiting Forces Act, 1970,*[114], applies today in respect of a state designated by the Governor in Council. Under s.5(1), the Canadian courts have jurisdiction in respect of acts or omissions constituting an offence against any Canadian laws committed by a member of a visiting force or a dependant, subject to s. 6(2). Sections 6(1) and 6(2) provide that the service authorities and service courts of a visiting force may exercise within Canada in relation to members of the force and their dependants criminal and disciplinary jurisdiction conferred upon them by the sending state, with respect to alleged offences concerning the property or security of the sending state, the person or property of another member of the visiting force or dependant, or an act done or an omission in the performance of official duty.

---

[114] R.S.C. 1970, c. V-6. Note that when Canadian forces are visiting other countries they are subject to Canadian criminal law and the local criminal law under sections 120 and 121 of the *National Defence Act*, R.S.C. 1970, c. N-4. Therefore, they are subject to the concurrent jurisdiction of Canadian service tribunals and the local courts. Immunity from the local jurisdiction in the absence of specific agreement would be based on customary international law. See Law Reform Commission Working Paper 37, *Extraterritorial Jurisdiction* (1984) 129. See also the North Atlantic Treaty Status of Forces Agreement, 1951, 1953 Can. T.S. No. 13, which is a multilateral treaty governing the exercise of jurisdiction between the sending and receiving states relating to visiting forces from a NATO state. For the jurisdictional immunities of United Nations forces see, e.g., the agreement between the United Nations and Cyprus, 1964, 492 U.N.T.S. 57.

CHAPTER SIX

State Jurisdiction Over Territory

INTRODUCTION

The terms "sovereignty" and "jurisdiction" are often used interchangeably in relation to the territory of a state. It is important to stress that "sovereignty" always implies jurisdiction, whereas the opposite is not the case. The term "jurisdiction"[1] is used to describe many different things, including the competence of a court ("civil" or "criminal" jurisdiction), the scope of authority of a particular state organ (jurisdiction over immigration) or of an organ of an international organization (jurisdiction of the U.N. Security Council), or the scope of authority of a state over its territory. In the last sense, "territorial jurisdiction" in international law means the competence of a state to prescribe and enforce rules of domestic law governing conduct within its territory (prescriptive and enforcement jurisdiction). The authority of a state to regulate conduct within its territory is supreme and is subject only to specific limitations set by customary international law or by treaty (for example, concerning diplomatic immunities described previously in Chapter 5, and certain basic human rights, considered later in Chapter 10).

In traditional international law the surface of the earth and the regions above and below may be subject to one of three possible regimes.[2] An area may be under the *sovereignty* of a state (e.g., the land territory of states); or it may be *res communis* (e.g., the high seas and outer space), shared by all nations and incapable of lawful appropriation by any

[1] See M. Akehurst, *A Modern Introduction to International Law* (4ed., 1982), at 102; I. Brownlie, *Principles of Public International Law* (3ed., 1979), at 298; J. Rousseau, *Droit international public* (1970-80), Vol. 3, at 134; J.G. Starke, *Introduction to International Law* (9 ed., 1984), at 193; S.A. Williams and J.-G. Castel, *Canadian Criminal Law, International and Transnational Aspects* (1981), at 3; *Restatement (Revised), Foreign Relations Law of the United States*, ss. 401-433.

[2] See J. Crawford, *The Creation of States in International Law* (1979); R. Jennings, *The Acquisition of Territory in International Law* (1963); M. Whiteman, 3 *Digest of International Law* 109-236 (3 ed., 1979); B. Larschan and B. Brennan, "The Common Heritage of Mankind Principle in International Law" (1983), 21 *Colum. J. Transnat. L.* 305; G. Schwarzenberger, "Title to Territory: Response to a Challenge" (1957), 51 *Am. J. Int. L.* 308.

state; or it may be *res nullius* (e.g., a piece of land unclaimed by any state), capable of lawful national appropriation. Apart from an unclaimed portion of Antarctica, there is no area of the planet earth which can today be characterized as *res nullius*. In recent years, beginning with the U.N.G.A. Seabed resolution of 1970,[3] a new legal category of territory has been added to the traditional ones – territory designated as the "Common Heritage of Mankind" (CHM) – which is governed by special rules. The areas subject to the regime of the CHM are the seabed, the ocean floor and the subsoil thereof, lying beyond the limits of national jurisdiction, as well as the moon and other celestial bodies. Although in some respects similar to the concept of *res communis*, the concept of the CHM, while still lacking precise definition, differs from the former. Thus according to B. Cheng, in peacetime, under the regime of *res communis*, "as long as a State respects the exclusive quasi- territorial jurisdiction of other States over their own ships, aircraft and spacecraft, general international law allows it to use the area or even to abuse it more or less as it wishes, including the appropriation of its natural resources. ..."[4] By contrast, the concept of the CHM, notes this author, incorporates "the idea that the management, exploitation and distribution of the natural resources of the area in question are matters to be decided by the international community ... and are not to be left to the initiative and discretion of individual States or their nationals". Although the subject of lengthy debates during the Third U.N. Conference on the Law of the Sea (1973-82), the CHM concept was for the first time incorporated in an international treaty in the 1979 Agreement Governing the Activities of States on the Moon and Other Celestial Bodies (Article 11).

Under the Montevideo Convention on the Rights and Duties of States (1933),[5] a "defined territory" is one of the indispensable attributes of statehood. The Convention is generally regarded as reflecting customary international law in the matter. The territory of each state, regardless of its size, is tri-dimensional; it consists of the surface (land and, if a coastal state, a portion of the sea), sub-surface (*usque ad inferos*) and a column of air to an as yet undetermined altitude coinciding with that state's land and sea boundaries. The territory of coastal states, in contrast with the territory of land-locked states, extends seawards to the outer limit of their territorial seas (maximum of 12 nautical miles) and to the continental shelf (200 nautical miles off shore, or even beyond for some states, such as Canada, possessing a greater continental margin). The territory of states endowed with so-called "historic bays" may also extend over a large maritime area, such as Hudson Bay in the case of Canada. Questions concerning a state's maritime domain are explored in Chapter 11 on the "Law of the Sea."

Possession of territory is so fundamental to statehood that a state would cease to exist if all of its territory were annexed to another state, and the act of annexation did not violate the U.N. Charter. However, in the exercise of its sovereignty, which includes full and exclusive authority over its territory, each state is free to transfer by agreement a part of that territory to another state (e.g., Russia's sale in 1867 of Alaska and France's

---

[3]G.A. Res. 2749, (XXV), 25 U.N. GAOR Supp. (No. 28) 24, reported in Chapter 11.
[4]"The Legal Regime of Airspace and Outer Space: The Boundary Problem, Functionalism versus Spatialism: The Major Premises" (1980), 5 *Annals Air & Space L.* 323, at 337. See also C. Joyner, "Legal Implications of the Concept of the Common Heritage of Mankind" (1986), 35 *Int. Comp. L.Q.* 190.
[5](1936), 165 *L.N.T.S.* 19; (1934), 28 *Am. J. Int. L. Supp.* 75; reported *supra* in Chapter 2.

sale in 1803 of Louisiana, both to the United States), or to form a territorial union with another state (e.g., the short-lived merger of Egypt and Syria in 1958 into the "United Arab Republic").

LAND TERRITORY

Acquisition of Territory

Traditional international law recognizes five different modalities for the acquisition of territory: occupation, cession, prescription, conquest and accretion. A state may acquire territory through *occupation* only if two conditions are satisfied: (1) the territory thus acquired must be *res nullius* (i.e., belonging to no other state or to the international community as a whole) and (2) the occupying state exercises effective control over such territory. The criteria for effective occupation vary from place to place and from time to time (see *Island of Palmas* arbitration following these comments).

Cession indicates the transfer of territory from one state to another by a treaty of cession. Thus in 1764, by the Treaty of Paris, France ceded Upper and Lower Canada to Britain and in 1898, by another Treaty of Paris, Spain ceded the Philippines to the United States. Similar to cession would be the acquisition of territory by a new state through the grant of independence by a former colonial power. Under international law, before the U.N. Charter, it was immaterial that a treaty of cession was imposed by force or a threat of force. However, following the adoption of the Charter and the Vienna Convention on the Law of Treaties, discussed in Chapter 3, a treaty of cession obtained through the unlawful use of force can no longer be regarded as valid. Thus, Article 2(4) of the Charter prohibits "the threat or use of force against the territorial integrity ... of any state" and Article 52 of the Vienna Convention declares any treaty "void if its conclusion has been procured by the threat or use of force in violation of the principles of international law embodied in the Charter of the United Nations."

A state which has peaceably occupied a certain territory with the knowledge of and without protest by the original sovereign (or claimant) may, after a period of time (probably measured in decades), acquire title to that territory through *prescription*.

Conquest denotes the acquisition of territority achieved through war and subsequent annexation of all or a part of the territory of the defeated enemy state. This mode of acquisition can no longer be reconciled with the principles of modern international law, for the same reasons as given above in regard to cession extracted by force.

Accretion – the least important among the modalities of acquisition – refers to the enlargement of a state's territory through natural forces, for example, through the change of course of a river or the recession of the sea. It should be pointed out that, in territorial disputes between states, more than one modality of acquisition will usually be invoked.

Island of Palmas Case
Netherlands v. United States
(1928), 2 R.I.A.A. 831

[Palmas (or Miangas) is a small isolated island situated about fifty miles south-east from the Island of Mindanao (the Philippines). The dispute had its origin in the visit to Palmas by U.S. General Leonard Wood, on Jan. 21, 1906. In the course of his visit the U.S. official discovered that the island was considered by the Netherlands to be a part of the Dutch East Indies. In the ensuing diplomatic controversy, the U.S. contended that the island of Palmas was included in the Philippine Archipelago ceded by Spain to the United States in 1898 by the Treaty of Paris. The Netherlands claimed sovereignty by virtue of its continuous and undisputed display of authority over the island during a long period of time. Eventually, the two countries agreed to submit their differences to arbitration.]

MAX HUBER, Arbitrator: ... In the first place the Arbitrator deems it necessary to make some general remarks on *sovereignty in its relation to territory*. ...

Sovereignty in the relation between States signifies independence. Independence in regard to a portion of the globe is the right to exercise therein, to the exclusion of any other State, the functions of a State. The development of the national organisation of States during the last few centuries and, as a corollary, the development of international law, have established this principle of the exclusive competence of the State in regard to its own territory in such a way as to make it the point of departure in settling most questions that concern international relations. The special cases of the composite State, of collective sovereignty, etc. do not fall to be considered here and do not, for that matter, throw any doubt upon the principle which has just been enunciated. Under this reservation it may be stated that territorial sovereignty belongs always to one, or in exceptional circumstances to several States, to the exclusion of all others. The fact that the functions of a State can be performed by any State within a given zone is, on the other hand, precisely the characteristic feature of the legal situation pertaining in those parts of the globe, which, like the high seas or lands without a master, cannot or do not yet form the territory of a State.

Territorial sovereignty is, in general, a situation recognised and delimited in space, either by so-called natural frontiers as recognised by international law or by outward signs of delimitation that are undisputed, or else by legal engagements entered into between interested neighbours, such as frontier conventions, or by acts of recognition of States within fixed boundaries. If a dispute arises as to the sovereignty over a portion of territory, it is customary to examine which of the States claiming sovereignty possesses a title – cession, conquest, occupation, etc. – superior to that which the other State might possibly bring forward against it. However, if the contestation is based on the fact that the other Party has actually displayed sovereignty, it cannot be sufficient to establish the title by which territorial sovereignty was validly acquired at a certain moment; it must also be shown that the territorial sovereignty has continued to exist and did exist at the moment which for the decision of the dispute must be considered as critical. This demonstration consists in the actual display of State activities, such as belongs only to the territorial sovereign.

Titles of acquisition of territorial sovereignty in present-day international law are either based on an act of effective apprehension, such as occupation or conquest, or, like cession, presuppose that the ceding and the cessionary Power or at least one of them, have the faculty of effectively disposing of the ceded territory. In the same way natural accretion can only be conceived of as an accretion to a portion of territory where there exists an actual sovereignty capable of extending to a spot which falls within its sphere of activity.

It seems therefore natural that an element which is essential for the constitution of sovereignty should not be lacking in its continuation. So true is this, that practice, as well as doctrine, recognizes – though under different legal formulae and with certain differences as to the conditions required – that the continuous and peaceful display of territorial sovereignty (peaceful in relation to other States) is as good as a title. The growing insistence with which international law, ever since the middle of the 18th century, has demanded that the occupation shall be effective would be inconceivable, if effectiveness were required only for the act of acquisition and not equally for the maintenance of the right. If the effectiveness has above all been insisted on in regard to occupation, this is because the question rarely arises in connection with territories in which there is already an established order of things. Just as before the rise of international law, boundaries of lands were necessarily determined by the fact that the power of a State was exercised within them, so too, under the reign of international law, the fact of peaceful and continuous display is still one of the most important considerations in establishing boundaries between States.

Territorial sovereignty, as has already been said, involves the exclusive right to display the activities of a State. This right has as corollary a duty: the obligation to protect within the territory the rights of other States, in particular their right to integrity and inviolability in peace and in war, together with the rights which each State may claim for its nationals in foreign territory. Without manifesting its territorial sovereignty in a manner corresponding to circumstances, the State cannot fulfil this duty. Territorial sovereignty cannot limit itself to its negative side, i.e. to excluding the activities of other States; for it serves to divide between nations the space upon which human activities are employed, in order to assure them at all points the minimum of protection of which international law is the guardian. ...

Manifestations of territorial sovereignty assume, it is true, different forms, according to conditions of time and place. Although continuous in principle, sovereignty cannot be exercised in fact at every moment on every point of a territory. The intermittence and discontinuity compatible with the maintenance of the right necessarily differ according as inhabited or uninhabited regions are involved, or regions enclosed within territories in which sovereignty is incontestably displayed or again regions accessible from, for instance, the high seas.

...The *title alleged by the United States of America* as constituting the immediate foundation of its claim is that of *cession*, brought about by the Treaty of Paris, which cession transferred all rights of sovereignty which Spain may have possessed in the region indicated in Article III of the said Treaty and therefore also those concerning the Island of Palmas (or Miangas).

It is evident that Spain could not transfer more rights than she herself possessed. ...

The essential point is therefore whether the Island of Palmas (or Miangas) at the moment of the conclusion and coming into force of the Treaty of Paris formed a part of the Spanish or Netherlands territory. The United States declares that Palmas (or Miangas) was Spanish territory and denies the existence of Dutch sovereignty; the Netherlands maintain the existence of their sovereignty and deny that of Spain. ...

In the last place there remains to be considered *title arising out of contiguity*. Although States have in certain circumstances maintained that islands relatively close to their shores belonged to them in virtue of their geographical situation, it is impossible to show the existence of a rule of positive international law to the effect that islands situated outside territorial waters should belong to a State from the mere fact that its territory forms the *terra firma* (nearest continent or island of considerable size). Not only would it seem that there are no precedents sufficiently frequent and sufficiently precise in their bearing to establish such a rule of international law, but the alleged principle itself is by its very nature so uncertain and contested that even Governments of the same State have on different occasions maintained contradictory opinions as to its soundness. The principle of contiguity, in regard to islands, may not be out of place when it is a question of allotting them to one State rather than another, either by agreement between the Parties, or by a decision not necessarily based on law; but as a rule establishing *ipso jure* the presumption of sovereignty in favour of a particular State, this principle would be in conflict with what has been said as to territorial sovereignty and as to the necessary relation between the right to exclude other States from a region and the duty to display therein the activities of a State. Nor is this principle of contiguity admissible as a legal method of deciding questions of territorial sovereignty; for it is wholly lacking in precision and would in its application lead to arbitrary results. This would be especially true in a case such as that of the island in question, which is not relatively close to one single continent, but forms part of a large archipelago in which strict delimitations between the different parts are not naturally obvious. ...

The conclusions to be derived from the above examination of the arguments of the Parties are the following:

The claim of the United States to sovereignty over the Island of Palmas (or Miangas) is derived from Spain by way of cession under the Treaty of Paris. The latter Treaty, though it comprises the island in dispute within the limits of cession, and in spite of the absence of any reserves or protest by the Netherlands as to these limits, has not created in favour of the United States any title of sovereignty such as was not already vested in Spain. The essential point is therefore to decide whether Spain had sovereignty over Palmas (or Miangas) at the time of the coming into force of the Treaty of Paris.

The United States base their claim on the titles of discovery, of recognition by treaty and of contiguity, i.e. titles relating to acts or circumstances leading to the acquisition of sovereignty; they have however not established the fact that sovereignty so acquired was effectively displayed at any time. The Netherlands on the contrary found their claim to sovereignty essentially on the title of the peaceful and continuous display of state authority over the island. Since this title would in international law prevail over a title of acquisition of sovereignty not followed by actual display of state authority, it is necessary to ascertain in the first place, whether the contention of the Netherlands is sufficiently established by evidence, and, if so, for what period of time. ...

The acts of indirect or direct display of Netherlands sovereignty at Palmas (or Miangas), especially in the 18th and early 19th centuries are not numerous, and there are considerable gaps in the evidence of continuous display. But apart from the consideration that the manifestations of sovereignty over a small and distant island, inhabited only by natives, cannot be expected to be frequent, it is not necessary that the display of sovereignty should go back to a very far distant period. It may suffice that such display existed in 1898, and had already existed as continuous and peaceful before that date long enough to enable any Power who might have considered herself as possessing sovereignty over the island, or having a claim to sovereignty, to have, according to local conditions, a reasonable possibility for ascertaining the existence of a state of things contrary to her real or alleged rights. ...

Since the moment when the Spaniards, in withdrawing from the Moluccas in 1666, made express reservations as to the maintenance of their sovereign rights, up to the contestation made by the United States in 1906, no contestation or other action whatever or protest against the exercise of territorial rights by the Netherlands over the Talautse (Sangi) Isles and their dependencies (Miangas included) has been recorded. The peaceful character of the display of Netherlands sovereignty for the entire period to which the evidence concerning acts of display relates (1700–1906) must be admitted.

There is moreover no evidence which would establish any act of display of sovereignty over the island by Spain or another Power, such as might counter-balance or annihilate the manifestations of Netherlands sovereignty. As to third Powers, the evidence submitted to the Tribunal does not disclose any trace of such action, at least from the middle of the 17th century onwards. These circumstances, together with the absence of any evidence of a conflict between Spanish and Netherlands authorities during more than two centuries as regards Palmas (or Miangas), are an indirect proof of the exclusive display of Netherlands sovereignty.

This being so, it remains to be considered first whether the display of state authority might not be legally defective and therefore unable to create a valid title of sovereignty, and secondly whether the United States may not put forward a better title to that of the Netherlands.

As to the conditions of acquisition of sovereignty by way of continuous and peaceful display of state authority (so-called prescription), some of which have been discussed in the United States Counter Memorandum, the following must be said:

The display has been open and public, that is to say that it was in conformity with usages as to exercise of sovereignty over colonial states. A clandestine exercise of state authority over an inhabited territory during a considerable length of time would seem to be impossible. An obligation for the Netherlands to notify to other Powers the establishment of suzerainty over the Sangi States or of the display of sovereignty in these territories did not exist. ...

The conditions of acquisition of sovereignty by the Netherlands are therefore to be considered as fulfilled. It remains now to be seen whether the United States as successors of Spain are in a position to bring forward an equivalent or stronger title. This is to be answered in the negative.

The title of discovery, if it had not been already disposed of by the Treaties of Münster and Utrecht would, under the most favourable and most extensive interpretation, exist only as an inchoate title, as a claim to establish sovereignty by effective occupation. An inchoate title however cannot prevail over a definite title founded on continuous and peaceful display of sovereignty.

The title of contiguity, understood as a basis of territorial sovereignty, has no foundation in international law.

The title of recognition by treaty does not apply, because even if the Sangi States, with the dependency of Miangas, are to be considered as "held and possessed" by Spain in 1648, the rights of Spain to be derived from the Treaty of Münster would have been superseded by those which were acquired by the Treaty of Utrecht. Now if there is evidence of a state of possession in 1714 concerning the island of Palmas (or Miangas), such evidence is exclusively in favour of the Netherlands. But even if the Treaty of Utrecht could not be taken into consideration, the acquiescence of Spain in the situation created after 1677 would deprive her and her successors of the possibility of still invoking conventional rights at the present time.

The Netherlands title of sovereignty, acquired by continuous and peaceful display of state authority during a long period of time going probably back beyond the year 1700, therefore holds good. ...

NOTES

1) In the *Clipperton Island* case[6] the Arbitrator, King Victor Emmanuel III of Italy stated:

It is beyond doubt that by immemorial usage having the force of law, besides the *animus occupandi*, the actual, and not the nominal, taking of possession is a necessary condition of occupation. This taking of possession consists of the act, or series of acts, by which the occupying state reduces to its possession the territory in question and takes steps to exercise exclusive authority there. Strictly speaking, and in ordinary cases, that only takes place when the state establishes in the territory itself an organization capable of making its laws respected. But this step is, properly speaking, but a means of procedure to the taking of possession, and, therefore, is not identical with the latter. There may also be cases where it is unnecessary to have recourse to this method. Thus, if a territory, by virtue of the fact that it was completely uninhabited, is, from the first moment when the occupying state makes its appearance there, at the absolute and undisputed disposition of that state, from that moment the taking of possession must be considered as accomplished, and the occupation is thereby completed.

2) As to acquisition of territory by cession, see *The St. Catherines Milling & Lumber Co. v. The Queen*, reported in the following Section.

Legal Status of Eastern Greenland Case
Denmark v. Norway
(1933), P.C.I.J. Rep., Ser.A/B, No. 53

[The dispute was triggered by Norway's proclamation of sovereignty over Eastern Greenland, an uncolonised part of the island. Denmark, which claimed sovereignty over the whole island, instituted proceedings against Norway in the Permanent Court of International Justice asking the Court to declare the Norwegian act invalid.]

---

[6] Mexico v. France (1931), 2 R.I.A.A. 1105.

THE COURT: ... The Danish submission ... that the Norwegian occupation of July 10, 1931, is invalid, is founded upon the contention that the area occupied was at the time of the occupation subject to Danish sovereignty; that the area is part of Greenland, and at the time of the occupation Danish sovereignty existed over all Greenland; consequently it could not be occupied by another Power.

In support of this contention, the Danish Government advances two propositions. The first is that the sovereignty which Denmark now enjoys over Greenland has existed for a long time, has been continuously and peacefully exercised, and, until the present dispute has not been contested by any Power. This proposition Denmark sets out to establish as a fact. The second proposition is that Norway has by treaty or otherwise herself recognized Danish sovereignty over Greenland as a whole and therefore cannot now dispute it.

The Norwegian submissions are that Denmark possessed no sovereignty over the area which Norway occupied on July 10, 1931, and that at the time of the occupation the area was *terra nullius*. Her contention is that the area lay outside the limits of the Danish colonies in Greenland and that Danish sovereignty extended no further than the limits of these colonies.

...On the Danish side it was maintained that the promise which in 1919 the Norwegian Minister for Foreign Affairs, speaking on behalf of his Government, gave to the diplomatic representative of the Danish Government ... debarred Norway from proceeding to any occupation of territory in Greenland, even if she had not by other acts recognized an existing Danish sovereignty there. ...

The two principal propositions advanced by the Danish Government will each be considered in turn. The first Danish argument is that the Norwegian occupation of part of the east coast of Greenland is invalid because Denmark has claimed and exercised sovereign rights over Greenland as a whole for a long time and has obtained thereby a valid title to sovereignty. The date at which such Danish sovereignty must have existed in order to render the Norwegian occupation invalid is the date at which the occupation took place, viz., July 10, 1931.

The Danish claim is not founded upon any particular act of occupation, but alleges – to use the phrase employed in the *Palmas Island* decision of the Permanent Court of Arbitration, April 4, 1928 – a title "founded on the peaceful and continuous display of State authority over the island." It is based upon the view that Denmark now enjoys all the rights which the King of Denmark and Norway enjoyed up till 1814. Both the existence and the extent of these rights must therefore be considered, as well as the Danish claim to sovereignty since that date.

It must be borne in mind, however, that as the critical date is July 10, 1931, it is not necessary that sovereignty over Greenland should have existed throughout the period during which the Danish Government maintains that it was in being. Even if the material submitted to the Court might be thought insufficient to establish the existence of that sovereignty during the earlier periods, this would not exclude a finding that it is sufficient to establish a valid title in the period immediately preceding the occupation. ...

Another circumstance which must be taken into account by any tribunal which has to adjudicate upon a claim to sovereignty over a particular territory, is the extent to which the sovereignty is also claimed by some other Power. In most of the cases involving claims to territorial sovereignty which have come before an international tribunal, there have been two competing claims to the sovereignty, and the tribunal has had to decide which of the two is the stronger. One of the peculiar features of the present case is that up to 1931 there was no claim by any Power other than Denmark to the sovereignty over Greenland. Indeed, up till 1921, no Power disputed the Danish claim to sovereignty.

It is impossible to read the records of the decisions in cases as to territorial sovereignty without observing that in many cases the tribunal has been satisfied with very little in the way of actual exercise of sovereign rights, provided that the other State could not make out a superior claim. This is particularly true in the case of claims to sovereignty over areas in thinly populated or unsettled countries. ...

It has been argued on behalf of Norway that after the disappearance of the two Nordic settlements, Norwegian sovereignty was lost and Greenland became a *terra nullius*. Conquest and voluntary abandonment are the grounds on which this view is put forward.

The word ''conquest'' is not an appropriate phrase, even if it was assumed that it was fighting with the Eskimos which led to the downfall of the settlements. Conquest only operates as a cause of loss of sovereignty when there is war between two States and by reason of the defeat of one of them sovereignty over territory passes from the loser to the victorious State. The principle does not apply in a case where a settlement has been established in a distant country and its inhabitants are massacred by the aboriginal population. Nor is the fact of ''conquest'' established. It is known now that the settlements must have disappeared at an early date, but at the time there seems to have been a belief that despite the loss of contact and the loss of knowledge of the whereabouts of the settlements one or both of them would again be discovered and found to contain the descendants of the early settlers.

As regards voluntary abandonment, there is nothing to show any definite renunciation on the part of the kings of Norway or Denmark. ...

In order to establish the contention that Denmark has exercised in fact sovereignty over all Greenland for a long time, Counsel for Denmark have laid stress on the long series of conventions – mostly commercial in character – which have been concluded by Denmark and in which, with the concurrence of the other contracting Party, a stipulation has been inserted to the effect that the convention shall not apply to Greenland.

...The importance of these treaties is that they show a willingness on the part of the States with which Denmark has contracted to admit her right to exclude Greenland. To some of these treaties, Norway has herself been a party.

...These treaties may also be regarded as demonstrating sufficiently Denmark's will and intention to exercise sovereignty over Greenland. There remains the question whether during this period ... she exercised authority in the uncolonized area sufficiently to give her a valid claim to sovereignty therein. In their arguments, Counsel for Denmark have relied chiefly on the concession granted in 1863 to Taylor of exclusive rights on the east coast for trading, mining, hunting, etc. The result of all the documents connected with the grant of the concession is to show that, on the one side, it was granted upon the footing that the King of Denmark was in a position to grant a valid monopoly on the east coast and that his sovereign rights entitled him to do so, and, on the other, that the concessionaires in England regarded the grant of a monopoly as essential to the success of their projects and had no doubts as to the validity of the rights conferred.

...The concessions granted for the erection of telegraph lines and the legislation fixing the limits of territorial waters in 1905 are also manifestations of the exercise of sovereign authority.

In view of the above facts, when taken in conjunction with the legislation she had enacted applicable to Greenland generally, the numerous treaties in which Denmark, with the concurrence of the other contracting party, provided for the non-application of the treaty to Greenland in general, and the absence of all claim to sovereignty over Greenland by any other Power, Denmark must be regarded as having displayed during this period of 1814 to 1915 her authority over the uncolonized part of the country to a degree sufficient to confer valid title to the sovereignty.

The applications which the Danish Government addressed to foreign governments between 1915 and 1921, seeking the recognition of Denmark's position in Greenland ... [must be dealt with] in some detail. The point at issue between the parties is whether Denmark was seeking a recognition of an existing title over all Greenland, as has been urged by her Counsel, or, as maintained by Counsel on behalf of Norway, whether she was trying to persuade the Powers to agree to an extension of her sovereignty to territory which did not as yet belong to her. ...

The Court has come to the conclusion that in judging the effect of these notes too much importance must not be attached to particular expressions here and there. The correspondence must be judged as a whole. One reason for this is that in some cases the notes were written by individual Danish diplomatic representatives, and, though no doubt they were based on the instructions these Ministers received, some variation must be expected and allowed for in the terms they used.

...Nevertheless, the conclusion which the Court has reached is that the view upheld by the Danish Government in the present case is right, and that the object which that Government was endeavouring to secure was an assurance from each of the foreign governments concerned that it accepted the Danish point of view that all Greenland was already subject to Danish sovereignty and was therefore content to see an extension of Denmark's activities to the uncolonized parts of Greenland. ...

The next government to be approached was the Norwegian. That Government had already manifested a desire to acquire Spitzbergen, and in April, 1919, the Danish Government had given the Norwegian Government to understand that, as there were no Danish interests in Spitzbergen which ran counter to those of Norway, Denmark would not oppose the Norwegian aspirations.

Early in July, 1919, the Danish Minister for Foreign Affairs learned ... that the Spitzbergen question was to come before a Committee of the Peace Conference.

Instructions were thereupon issued, on July 12, 1919, to the Danish Minister at Christiania to make to the Norwegian Minister for Foreign Affairs a communication to the effect that a Committee had just been constituted at the Peace Conference "for the purpose of considering the claims that may be put forward by different countries to Spitzbergen," and that the Danish Government would be prepared to renew before this Committee, the unofficial assurance already given to the Norwegian Government, according to which Denmark ... would raise no objection to Norway's claim. ... In making this statement to the Norwegian Minister for Foreign Affairs, the Danish Minister was to point out "that the Danish Government had been anxious for some years past to obtain the recognition by all the interested Powers of Denmark's sovereignty over the whole of Greenland and that it intended to place that question before the above-mentioned Committee"; that the Government of the United States of America had made a declaration that that Government would not oppose the extension of Danish political and economic interests over all Greenland; and further that the Danish Government counted on the Norwegian Government not making any difficulties with regard to such an extension.

When, on July 14, 1919, the Danish Minister saw the Norwegian Minister of Foreign Affairs, M. Ihlen, the latter merely replied "that the question would be considered." ... On July 22 following, the Minister for Foreign Affairs, after informing his colleagues of the Norwegian Cabinet, made a statement to the Danish Minister to the effect "that the Norwegian Government would not make any difficulties in the settlement of this question" (i.e., the question raised on July 14 by the Danish Government). These are the words recorded in the minute by M. Ihlen himself. According to the report made by the Danish Minister to his own Government, M. Ihlen's words were that "the plans of the Royal (Danish) Government respecting Danish sovereignty over the whole of Greenland ... would meet with no difficulty on the part of Norway."

...The memorandum addressed to the Norwegian Government ... repeats the Danish desire to obtain recognition by the Powers concerned of Danish sovereignty over the whole of that country. ... Mention is made of Spitzbergen and of how Denmark had said, in 1919, that she would not oppose the Norwegian claims there and that she reckoned on an extension of Danish sovereignty in Greenland not meeting with difficulties on the part of Norway. Reference is then made to the Ihlen declaration, and it is said that as this had only been verbal Denmark would now like to have a written confirmation of it. ...

The period subsequent to ... 1921 witnessed a considerable increase in the activity of the Danish Government on the eastern coast of Greenland. ...

These were all cases in which the Danish Government was exercising governmental functions in connection with the territory now under dispute.

The character of these Danish acts is not altered by the protests or reserves which, from time to time, were made by the Norwegian Government. ...

These acts, coupled with the activities of the Danish hunting expeditions which were supported by the Danish Government, the increase in the number of scientific expeditions engaged in mapping and exploring the country with the authorization and encouragement of the Government, even though the expeditions may have been organized by non-official institutions, the occasions on which the Godthaab, a vessel belonging to the State and placed at one time under the command of a naval officer, was sent to the East coast on inspection duty, the issue of permits by the Danish authorities, under regulations issued in 1930, to persons visiting the eastern coast of Greenland, show to a sufficient extent – even when separated from the history of the preceding periods – the two elements necessary to establish a valid title to sovereignty, namely; the intention and will to exercise such sovereignty and the manifestation of State activity.

It follows from the above that the Court is satisfied that Denmark has succeeded in establishing her contention that at the critical date, namely, July 10, 1931, she possessed a valid title to the sovereignty over all Greenland.

This finding constitutes by itself sufficient reason for holding that the occupation of

July 10, 1931, and any steps taken in this connection by the Norwegian Government, were illegal and invalid.

The Court will now consider the second Danish proposition that Norway had given certain undertakings which recognized Danish sovereignty over all Greenland. ...

This declaration by M. Ihlen has been relied on by Counsel for Denmark as a recognition of an existing Danish sovereignty in Greenland. The court is unable to accept this point of view. A careful examination of the words used and of the circumstances in which they were used, as well as of the subsequent developments, shows that M. Ihlen cannot have meant to be giving then and there a definitive recognition of Danish sovereignty over Greenland, and shows also that he cannot have been understood by the Danish Government at the time as having done so. ...

It is clear from the relevant Danish documents ... that the Danish attitude in the Spitzbergen question and the Norwegian attitude in the Greenland question were regarded in Denmark as interdependent, and this interdependence appears to be reflected also in M. Ihlen's minute of the interview. Even if this interdependence – which, in view of the affirmative reply of the Norwegian Government, in whose name the Minister for Foreign Affairs was speaking, would have created a bilateral engagement – is not held to have been established, it can hardly be denied that what Denmark was asking of Norway – ''not to make any difficulties in the settlement of the (Greenland) question'' – was equivalent to what she was indicating her readiness to concede in the Spitzbergen question – to refrain from opposing ''the wishes of Norway in regard to the settlement of this question.'' What Denmark desired to obtain from Norway was that the latter should do nothing to obstruct the Danish plans in regard to Greenland. The declaration which the Minister of Foreign Affairs gave on July 22, 1919, on behalf of the Norwegian Government, was definitely affirmative: ''I told the Danish Minister today that the Norwegian Government would not make any difficulty in the settlement of this question.''

The Court considers it beyond all dispute that a reply of this nature given by the Minister for Foreign Affairs on behalf of his Government in response to a request by the diplomatic representative of a foreign Power, in regard to a question falling within his province, is binding upon the country to which the Minister belongs.

...The Court is unable to regard the Ihlen declaration of July 22, 1919, otherwise than as unconditional and definitive.

...The Court is unable to read into the words of the Ihlen declaration ''in the settlement of this question'' – i.e., the Greenland question – a condition which would render the promise to refrain from making any difficulties inoperative should a settlement not be reached. The promise was unconditional and definitive. ...

It follows that, as a result of the undertaking involved in the Ihlen declaration of July 22, 1919, Norway is under an obligation to refrain from contesting Danish sovereignty over Greenland as a whole, and *a fortiori* to refrain from occupying a part of Greenland. ...

NOTES

1) Dissenting judgments were delivered by Judge Anzilotti and by Norwegian Judge Ad Hoc Vogt.

2) In *Minquiers and Ecrehos Case*[7] the International Court of Justice was called upon to determine whether France or the United Kingdom had sovereignty over a number of islets and rocks in the English Channel. By Special Agreement, the parties agreed to exclude the concept of *terra nullius* as a basis for resolving the competing claims. Both countries asserted in the course of the proceedings an ancient title to the disputed islets and rocks. On weighing the evidence submitted, the Court unanimously found for the United Kingdom. The decisive factor in the Court's decision was the more recent evidence of the exercise of "State functions" over the disputed territory by the United Kingdom.

3) The dispute between Thailand and Cambodia concerning the sovereignty over the Temple of Preah Vihear[8] was described by the International Court of Justice as follows: "Cambodia alleges a violation on the part of Thailand of Cambodia's territorial sovereignty over the region of the Temple of Preah Vihear and its precincts. Thailand replies by affirming that the area in question lies on the Thai side of the common frontier between the two countries and is under the sovereignty of Thailand." The Temple is an ancient sanctuary and, although partially in ruins, of great artistic and archeological interest. The Court examined the evidence presented by the parties in support of their claims and concluded that:

the most significant episode consisted of the visit paid to the Temple in 1930 by Prince Damrong, formerly Minister of the Interior, and at this time President of the Royal Institute of Siam, charged with duties in connection with the National Library and with archaeological monuments. The visit was part of an archaeological tour made by the Prince with the permission of the King of Siam, and it clearly had a quasi-official character. When the Prince arrived at Preah Vihear, he was officially received there by the French Resident for the adjoining Cambodian province, on behalf of the Resident Superior, with the French flag flying. The Prince could not possibly have failed to see the implications of a reception of this character. A clearer affirmation of title on the French Indo-Chinese side can scarcely be imagined. It demanded a reaction. Thailand did nothing. Furthermore, when Prince Damrong on his return to Bangkok sent the French Resident some photographs of the occasion, he used language which seems to admit that France, through her Resident, had acted as the host country.

The explanations regarding Prince Damrong's visit given on behalf of Thailand have not been found convincing by the Court. Looking at the incident as a whole, it appears to have amounted to a tacit recognition by Siam of the sovereignty of Cambodia (under French Protectorate) over Preah Vihear, through a failure to react in any way, on an occasion that called for a reaction in order to affirm or preserve title in the face of an obvious rival claim. What seems clear is that either Siam did not in fact believe she had any title – and this would be wholly consistent with her attitude all along, and thereafter, to the Annex I map and line – or else she decided not to assert it, which again means that she accepted the French claim, or accepted the frontier at Preah Vihear as it was drawn on the map. ...

---

[7] France v. United Kingdom, [1953] I.C.J. Rep. 47. See R. St. J. Macdonald, "The Minquiers and Ecrehos Case" (1954-55), 1 *McGill L.J.* 277.

[8] *Temple of Preah Vihear Case*, Cambodia v. Thailand, [1962] I.C.J. Rep. 6.

By a 9 to 3 vote the Court found that the Temple is situated in territory under the sovereignty of Cambodia (Kampuchea); and by 7 votes to 5 that Thailand was under an obligation to restore to Cambodia any archeological objects which had been removed from the Temple by the Thai authorities after the occupation of the Temple by Thailand in 1954.

Western Sahara Case
Adv. Op. [1975] I.C.J. Rep. 12.

[The facts and a different portion of this case are reported *supra* in Chapter 2. The Court was requested by the U.N. General Assembly to answer the following specific questions: I. Was Western Sahara at the time of colonization by Spain a territory belonging to no one (*terra nullius*)?; II. What were the legal ties between this territory and the Kingdom of Morocco and the Mauritanian entity?]

THE COURT: ...

77. In the view of the Court, for the purposes of the present Opinion, "the time of colonization by Spain" may be considered as the period beginning in 1884, when Spain proclaimed a protectorate over the Rio de Oro. ...

78. Although the Court has thus been asked to render an opinion solely upon the legal status and legal ties of Western Sahara as these existed at the period beginning in 1884, this does not mean that any information regarding its legal status or legal ties at other times is wholly without relevance for the purposes of this Opinion. It does, however, mean that such information has present relevance only in so far as it may throw light on the questions as to what were the legal status and the legal ties of Western Sahara at that period.

79. Turning to Question I, the Court observes that the request specifically locates the question in the context of "the time of colonization by Spain," and it therefore seems clear that the words "Was Western Sahara ... a territory belonging to no one (*terra nullius*)?" have to be interpreted by reference to the law in force at that period. The expression "*terra nullius*" was a legal term of art employed in connection with "occupation" as one of the accepted legal methods of acquiring sovereignty over territory. "Occupation" being legally an original means of peaceably acquiring sovereignty over territory otherwise than by cession or succession, it was a cardinal condition of a valid "occupation" that the territory should be *terra nullius* – a territory belonging to no-one – at the time of the act alleged to constitute the "occupation" (cf. Legal Status of Eastern Greenland, P.C.I.J., Series A/B, No. 53, at 44 f. and 63 f.). In the view of the Court, therefore, a determination that Western Sahara was a "*terra nullius*" at the time of colonization by Spain would be possible only if it were established that at that time the territory belonged to no-one in the sense that it was then open to acquisition through the legal process of "occupation."

80. Whatever differences of opinion there may have been among jurists, the State practice of the relevant period indicates that territories inhabited by tribes or peoples having a social and political organization were not regarded as *terrae nullius*. It shows that in the case of such territories the acquisition of sovereignty was not generally considered as effected unilaterally through "occupation" of *terra nullius* by original title but through agreements concluded with local rulers. On occasion, it is true, the word "occupation" was used in a non-technical sense denoting simply acquisition of sovereignty; but that did not signify that the acquisition of sovereignty through such agreements with authorities of the country was regarded as an "occupation" of a *"terra nullius"* in the proper sense of these terms. On the contrary, such agreements with local rulers, whether or not considered as an actual "cession" of the territory, were regarded as derivative roots of title, and not original titles obtained by occupation of *terrae nullius*.

81. In the present instance, the information furnished to the Court shows that at the time of colonization Western Sahara was inhabited by peoples which, if nomadic, were socially and politically organized in tribes and under chiefs competent to represent them. ...

84. Question II asks the Court to state "what were the legal ties between this territory" – that is, Western Sahara – "and the Kingdom of Morocco and the Mauritanian entity." The scope of this question depends upon the meaning to be attached to the expression "legal ties" in the context of the time of the colonization. ...

162. The materials and information presented to the Court show the existence, at the time of Spanish colonization, of legal ties of allegiance between the Sultan of Morocco and some of the tribes living in the territory of Western Sahara. They equally show the existence of rights, including some rights relating to the land, which constituted legal ties between the Mauritanian entity, as understood by the Court, and the territory of Western Sahara. On the other hand, the Court's conclusion is that the materials and information presented to it do not establish any tie of territorial sovereignty between the territory of Western Sahara and the Kingdom of Morocco or the Mauritanian entity. Thus the Court has not found legal ties of such a nature as might affect the application of resolution 1514 (XV) in the decolonization of Western Sahara and, in particular, of the principle of self-determination through the free and genuine expression of the will of the peoples of Territory. ...

NOTES

The Advisory Opinion of the Court[9] did not resolve the dispute about the status of Western Sahara. Following Spain's withdrawal from its former colony, Morocco and Mauritania partitioned the territory, ignoring the protests of Polisario (the local independence movement) which has been waging a guerrilla war ever since. In 1979 Mauritania renounced all claims to any part of Western Sahara and withdrew from the southern third of the territory in favor of Polisario.

---

[9] For comments on the history of the dispute and the Court's Opinion, see T. Franck, "The Stealing of the Sahara" (1976), 70 *Am. J. Int. L.* 694; M. Janis, "The International Court of Justice: Advisory Opinion on the Western Sahara" (1976), 17 *Harv. Int. L.J.* 609.

Boundary Disputes[10]

Throughout history, the boundaries of states have been the cause of countless armed conflicts and continue to be, though to a lesser extent, the source of international tension and controversy and, occasionally, of war. Since ancient times and up to the end of World War II, the boundaries of states would often be decided by war, resulting in the territorial expansion of the victor. In many cases boundaries thus drawn would subsequently be legitimized through treaties imposed by the victor upon the vanquished. In more recent times, states have been showing greater readiness to have their minor territorial disputes resolved through non-violent means, such as arbitration. A recent example is the long-festering dispute between Argentina and Chile concerning their maritime boundary in the region of the Beagle Channel which was resolved in 1984 through arbitration and papal intervention. Dissatisfied with the arbitral award of 1977, Argentina had refused to comply. Eventually, through the mediation of the Holy See, the dispute was terminated by the adoption of the Papal Proposal of December 12, 1980 and the subsequent signing on November 29, 1984 of the Treaty of Peace and Friendship between the two countries. The Treaty is largely based on the 1977 award.[11]

Major territorial disputes, however, continue unresolved, with virtually all states unwilling to submit to adjudication or arbitration. Examples of such major disputes abound and involve scores of countries: Argentina-United Kingdom (the Falklands); U.S.S.R.-China; Ethiopia-Somalia; South Africa-Namibia; Morocco (Western Sahara); Indonesia (Eastern Timor); Japan-U.S.S.R.; India-Pakistan (Kashmir); China-Taiwan; Israel-Syria (Golan Heights); Israel-Jordan (West Bank, Jerusalem); Iraq-Iran.

Territory of Canada

St. Catherines Milling and Lumber Co. v. The Queen
(1887), 13 S.C.R. 577, at 643

[The question before the Court was whether under the B.N.A. Act some 50,000 square miles of timberland in Ontario belonged to the Province of Ontario or the Dominion of Canada. The lands in question formed part of lands surrendered by an Indian tribe by a treaty to Canada. The excerpt which follows deals with the legal effects of the conquest of Canada by Great Britain and the subsequent cession by France by the Treaty of Paris, 1763.]

TASCHEREAU J.: ... There is no doubt of the correctness of the proposition laid down by the Supreme Court of Louisiana, in *Breaux v. Johns,* "that on the discovery of the American continent the principle was asserted or acknowledged by all European

---

[10] Various aspects of boundary disputes are extensively explored in S. Boggs, *International Boundaries* (1940); and M. Whiteman, *Digest of International Law* (1963), Vol. 2, at 1028 fwd., (1964) Vol. 3, at 1-871.
[11] See *Beagle Channel Arbitration* (1978), 17 *Int. Leg. Mat.* 632; and the Treaty of Friendship and related documents (1985), 24 *Int. Leg. Mat.* 3.

nations, that discovery followed by actual possession gave title to the soil to the Government by whose subjects, or by whose authority, it was made, not only against other European Governments but against the natives themselves. While the different nations of Europe respected the rights (I would say the claims) of the natives as occupants, they all asserted the ultimate dominion and title to the soil to be in the Sovereign." 4 La. An. 141.

That such was the case with the French Government in Canada, during its occupancy thereof, is an incontrovertible fact. The King was vested with the ownership of all the ungranted lands in the colony as part of the crown domain, and royal grant conveyed the full estate and entitled the grantee to possession. The contention, that the royal grants and charters merely asserted a title in the grantees against Europeans or white men, but that they were nothing but blank papers so far as the rights of the natives were concerned, was certainly not then thought of, either in France or in Canada. Neither in the commission or letters patent to the Marquis de la Roche in 1578 and 1598, nor in the charter to the Cent Associés in 1627, nor in the retrocession of the same in 1663, nor in the charter to the West Indies Company in 1664 nor in the retrocession of the same in 1674, by which proprietary Government in Canada came to an end, nor in the six hundred concessions of seigniories extending from the Atlantic to Lake Superior, made by these companies, or by the Kings themselves, nor in any grant of land whatever during the 225 years of the French domination, can be found even an allusion to, or a mention of, the Indian title.

On the contrary, in express terms, de la Roche was authorized to take possession of, and hold as his own property, all lands whatsoever that he might conquer from any one but the allies and confederates of the crown, and, likewise, the charter of the West Indies Company granted them the full ownership of all lands whatsoever, in Canada, which they would conquer, or from which they would drive away the Indians by force of arms. Such was the spirit of all the royal grants of the period. The King granted lands, seigniories, territories, with the understanding that if any of these lands, seigniories, or territories proved to be occupied by aborigines, on the grantees rested the onus to get rid of them, either by chasing them away by force, or by a more conciliatory policy, as they would think proper. In many instances, no doubt, the grantees, or the King himself, deemed it cheaper or wiser to buy them than to fight them, but that was never construed as a recognition of their right to any legal title whatsoever. The fee and the legal possession were in the King or his grantees.

Now when by the treaty of 1763, France ceded to Great Britain all her rights of sovereignty, property and possession over Canada, and its islands, lands, places and coasts, including, as admitted at the argument, the lands now in controversy, it is unquestionable that the full title to the territory ceded became vested in the new sovereign, and that he thereafter owned it in allodium as part of the crown domain, in as full and ample a manner as the King of France had previously owned it. That it should be otherwise for the lands now in dispute, I cannot see on what principle. To exclude from the full operation of the cession by France all the lands then occupied by the Indians, would be to declare that not an inch of land therby passed to the King of England, as, at that time, the whole of the unpatented lands of Canada were in their possession in as full and ample a manner as the 57,000 square miles of the territory in dispute can be said to be in possession of the 26,000 Indians who roam over it.

NOTES

1) The Treaty of Paris, 1763,[12] provided in article IV as follows:

His Most Christian Majesty renounces all pretensions which he has heretofore formed or might have formed to Nova Scotia or Acadia in all its parts, and guaranties the whole of it, and with all its dependencies, to the King of Great Britain: Moreover, his Most Christian Majesty cedes and guaranties to his said Britannick Majesty, in full right, Canada, with all its dependencies, as well as the island of Cape Breton and all the other islands and coasts in the gulph and river of St. Lawrence, and in general, every thing that depends on the said countries, lands, islands, and coasts, with the sovereignty, property, possession, and all rights acquired by treaty, or otherwise, which the Most Christian King and the Crown of France have had till now over the said countries, lands, islands, places, coasts, and their inhabitants, so that the Most Christian King cedes and makes over the whole to the said King, and to the Crown of Great Britain, and that in the most ample manner and form, without restriction, and without any liberty to depart from the said cession and guaranty under any pretence, or to disturb Great Britain in the possessions above mentioned. His Britannick Majesty, on his side, agrees to grant the liberty of the Catholick religion to the inhabitants of Canada: he will, in consequence, give the most precise and most effectual orders, that his new Roman Catholic subjects may profess the worship of their religion according to the rites of the Romish church, as far as the laws of Great Britain permit. His Britannick Majesty farther agrees, that the French inhabitants, or others who had been subjects of the Most Christian King in Canada, may retire with all safety and freedom wherever they shall think proper, and may sell their estates, provided it be to the subjects of his Britannick Majesty, and bring away their effects as well as their persons, without being restrained in their emigration, under any pretence whatsoever, except that of debts or of criminal prosecutions: The term limited for this emigration shall be fixed to the space of eighteen months, to be computed from the day of the exchange of the ratification of the present treaty.

2) The doctrine of state succession carries a right on the part of the successor state to the allegiance of those who were formerly subjects of the displaced power, unless they elect to leave the country immediately in order to avoid the consequences of such new allegiance. Questions of state succession, including change of nationality, are considered in Chapter 2.

---

[12] Sess. Paper No. 18, 6-7 Edw. VII, A. (1907).

Newfoundland[13]

The problems involved in the union of Newfoundland to Canada have had a long history. Delegates from Newfoundland participated in the conference at Quebec in 1864 when the broad outlines of Confederation were laid, but Newfoundland declined to enter union some five years later when the Confederation Party was defeated at the polls. The door, however, always remained open, section 146 of the British North America Act of 1867 providing for the entry at any time of Newfoundland, as well as of Prince Edward Island and British Columbia, on such terms and conditions as might mutually be agreed. Canadian policy throughout the years always was that the first move must come from Newfoundland. Following a financial collapse in 1894, overtures for union were made by Newfoundland, but negotiations broke down over financial terms, and no further formal moves towards union were made till 1947.

On March 20, 1947, the Governor of Newfoundland, on behalf of the Newfoundland National Convention, asked the Government of Canada whether it would receive a delegation to ascertain what fair and equitable basis might exist for the federal union of Newfoundland with Canada. The Canadian Government agreed and in June 1947 a delegation from the Convention came to Ottawa. Meetings with a Committee of the Cabinet continued till September. On October 29, 1947, the Prime Minister of Canada sent to the Governor of Newfoundland, for transmission to the National Convention, a statement of terms believed to constitute a fair and equitable basis of union, should the people of Newfoundland desire to enter into Confederation.

The statement of terms submitted by the Canadian Government was debated at length in the Newfoundland National Convention and during the campaigns for the two referenda which followed.

In the first referendum, held on June 3, 1948, three questions were before the people: continuation of commission of government, confederation, restoration of responsible government. In round numbers, the vote was about 22,000 for commission of government, about 64,000 for Confederation and about 69,400 for responsible government. In accordance with the conditions announced in advance, no proposed form of government having received a majority, a second referendum was required on the two leading forms.

In the second referendum, held on July 22, 1948, Confederation received a majority of about 7,000 votes and a majority of eighteen of the twenty-five electoral districts. In a statement issued on July 30, the Prime Minister of Canada said the result was "clear beyond all possibility of misunderstanding" and that the Government would be glad to receive with the least possible delay authorized representatives of Newfoundland "to negotiate the terms of union" on the basis of his letter of October 29, 1947 to the Governor of Newfoundland, and the document transmitted with it. A delegation was shortly thereafter appointed by the Governor of Newfoundland, and arrived in Ottawa on October 6, 1948, where negotiations were begun with a committee of the Cabinet.

---

[13] See (1949), 1 External Affairs, at 3-8, and Terms of Union of Newfoundland with Canada, *B.N.A. Act 1949*, 12-13 Geo.VI, c. 22, Schedule, R.S.C., 1952, Vol. VI at 6399 fwd. See also Report and Documents Relating to the Negotiations for the Union of Newfoundland with Canada (1949), Conference Series 1948, No. 2, Dept. of External Affairs, Ottawa.

On December 11, 1948, A Memorandum of Agreement was entered into between Canada and Newfoundland. The signature took place in the Senate Chamber in Ottawa. The terms of union were approved by the Canadian Parliament and the Newfoundland Commission of Government, and confirmed by the United Kingdom Parliament. Formal Union took place on March 31, 1949.

Frontiers of Canada[14]

Since Newfoundland joined the Union in 1949, all of Canada's land frontiers are with the United States of America. From Passamaquoddy Bay, bordered by New Brunswick and Maine, to the Straits of Juan de Fuca, bordered by British Columbia and Washington, the Canadian-United States boundary runs for 3,987 miles, over half of which (2,198 miles) is water boundary. The Alaska-Canada boundary of 1,540 miles runs from Portland Canal on the Pacific ocean to the Arctic Ocean near the mouth of the Mackenzie River. Difficulties have naturally arisen over boundaries between the two countries, but have always been settled by peaceful means in accord with the spirit of the Treaty of Ghent of December 24, 1814 that "there shall be a firm and universal peace between His Britannic Majesty and the United States."

Several maritime boundaries of Canada remain unsettled, e.g., in the Gulf of Maine, the Strait of Juan de Fuca, and in the area of Saint-Pierre-et-Miquelon archipelago. These matters are examined in Chapter 11 on the "Law of the Sea." Canada's Arctic frontiers are discussed below.

ARCTIC AND ANTARCTIC AREAS

The Arctic[15]

Features of the Arctic
from D. Pharand, "The Legal Status of the Arctic Regions"
(1979), 163 *Hague Recueil* 51

...[I]t should be specified that the criterion generally retained to define the Arctic is the tree line. It is an easy criterion to apply since it constitutes a visible natural boundary

---

[14] For a more detailed account of the treaties relevant to Canada's land frontiers, see J.-G. Castel, *International Law: Chiefly as Interpreted and Applied in Canada* (3ed., 1976), 217 fwd. See also P.E. Corbett, *The Settlement of Canadian-American Disputes* (1937); A. Poole, "The Boundaries of Canada" (1964), 42 *Can Bar Rev.* 100.

[15] See, D. Pharand, *The Law of the Sea of the Arctic* (1973); D. Pharand (with L. Legault), *The Northwest Passage: Arctic Straits* (1984); W. Westermeyer and K. Shusterich, eds., *United States Arctic Interests: The 1980s and 1990s* (1984); D. Pharand, "The legal régime of the Arctic: some outstanding issues" (1984), 39 *Int. J*, 742; D. Pharand, "L'Arctique et l'Antarctique: Patrimoine Commun de l'Humanité?" (1982), 7 *Annals Air & Space L*. 415.

and, in addition, it coincides roughly with the more scientific criterion, the 10° centigrade surface air isotherm for the warmest month of the year, July.

The Arctic and the Antarctic are often regarded in terms of their similarities. In fact, the Polar Regions have very little in common except for the climate and, even there, there is an appreciable difference since the Antarctic climate is considerably colder. A temperature of -105° Fahrenheit was recorded at the South Pole during the international geophysical year of 1957-1958, whereas it very seldom gets below -50° Fahrenheit in the Arctic. Whereas the Arctic consists of a deep ice-covered ocean surrounded by a continental belt, the Antarctic is an ice-covered continent surrounded by a vast maritime belt. As for the Poles themselves, the North Pole rests on 4,300 metres of water, covered by moving ice, whereas the South Pole rests on 3,300 metres of land covered by a solid ice cap, with an average thickness of 2,000 metres and possibly more than 4,500 metres in some places. ...

The Arctic Ocean and the peripheral seas are still of considerable importance to the super powers, particularly to Soviet naval strategy. Indeed, the Kola Peninsula on the Barents Sea is the home port of the northern fleet of the Soviet Union, which is the largest of its four fleets, within which we find all of the Soviet Delta-class submarines operating out of Murmansk.

On the American side of the Pole, the United States operate the Naval Arctic Research Laboratory at Point Barrow, Alaska, and although this is not a naval base for strategic submarines, it is well known that the United States has tested the feasibility of the Arctic Ocean for submarine navigation as early as 1957, with the *Nautilus*. The early warning systems established shortly after the Second World War were meant for bomber detection and are now somewhat obsolete by themselves, so they were supplemented by ballistic missile early warning systems. We find radar stations, as part of the system, in Alaska and Greenland, in particular. ...

In short, it may be said that the Arctic region is still of considerable strategic importance, being located between the super powers. And more particularly, the ice cover of the Arctic Ocean could be important to permit submarines armed with ballistic missiles to go undetected or, at least, to make detection much more difficult. ...

Aside from the remaining strategic importance of the Arctic Region, aspects of which we have just briefly alluded to, the economic importance is gaining considerable momentum in recent years because of the need to find new sources of energy supply, particularly oil and gas. These would appear to be quite plentiful in the Arctic continental shelf. In the Beaufort Sea, off the coast of Alaska, the recoverable reserves of the Prudhoe Bay oil and gas fields are estimated to be very considerable. On the Canadian side of the Beaufort Sea continental shelf, offshore drilling has been carried on for the last five years and, although no commercial oil discovery has yet been made, the expectations are still high that this will be done within the next couple of years. Although the other three Arctic powers have not been as active as the United States and Canada in investigating the continental shelf off their coast, they have all done some preliminary exploration. This is particularly so in the Barents Sea continental shelf where drilling operations are expected to begin within the next year or so. As for the Siberian continental shelf, which is the widest in the world, averaging some 400 miles wide, it represents a great potential for hydro-carbon deposits, but the Soviet Union does not appear to have begun exploration on a wide scale.

The Sector Theory
from I. Head, "Canadian Claims to Territorial Sovereignty in the
Arctic Regions"
(1963), 9 *McGill L.J.* 200 (footnotes omitted)

The practice of claiming sovereignty over a sector of the earth's surface, as measured by meridians of longitude, is not new. The first example is found in the Papal Bull *Inter Caetera* of Alexander VI, dated 4 May 1493, later replaced by the Treaty of Tordesillas concluded 7 June 1494 between Spain and Portugal. More recently, various States have circumscribed their claims to portions of Antarctica by meridians of longitude. And several states have subscribed at one time or another to the "sector theory."

The Arctic "sector theory" is rightly associated with Canada for it was first offered by a Canadian, and first debated in the Canadian Parliament. In the half century since the first appearance of the theory, many Canadian statesmen have taken great pains either to criticize it or praise it. Some have offered a disarming display of their open-minded attitude and have spoken on various occasions on both sides of the issue.

An Arctic sector is deceptively simple, and is compounded of only two ingredients: a base line or arc described along the Arctic Circle through territory unquestionably within the jurisdiction of a temperate zone state, and sides defined by meridians of longitude extending from the North Pole south to the most easterly and westerly points on the Arctic Circle pierced by the state. Under the theory, nations possessing territory extending into the Arctic regions have a rightful claim to all territory – be it land, water or ice – lying to their north. This claim springs from the geographical relationship of the claimant state to the claimed territory; the two areas must be contiguous along the Arctic Circle.

The Arctic sector theory was first publicly propounded by Pascal Poirier, a Canadian Senator, in 1907. Senator Poirier was at that time delivering a speech in the Senate, the upper house of Canada's bi-cameral Parliament in support of his own motion:

That it be resolved that the Senate is of the opinion that the time has come for Canada to make a formal declaration of possession of the lands and islands situated in the north of the Dominion, and extending to the north pole.

Poirier's resolution was abortive. His motion was neither seconded nor put to a vote. The draft resolution embodied in the motion was not accepted by the Senate, and never reached the floor of the House of Commons. Officially, Senator Poirier's Arctic sector theory was a one-man idea, but it rapidly attracted attention disproportionate to the importance attached to it by Poirer himself. ...

In 1938, Canada was evidently endorsing the sector theory. The Minister of Mines and Resources of the Liberal Government told the House of Commons that no foreign challenge to Canada's sovereignty in the Arctic could be successful. He referred to his understanding that international usage had established clearly certain principles upon which sovereignty could be claimed in remote areas of the Arctic which have never been

The Arctic

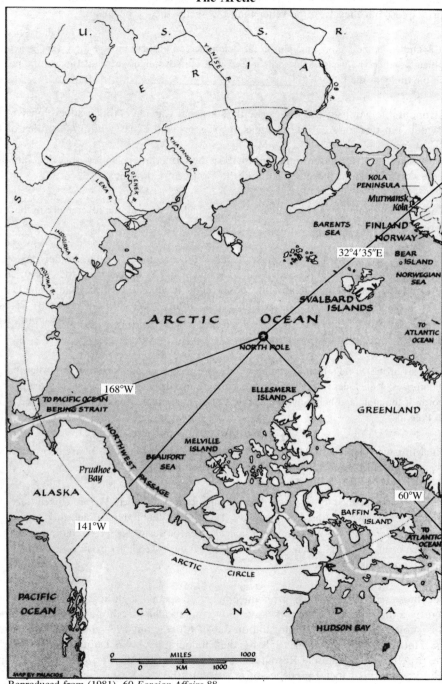

Reproduced from (1981), 60 *Foreign Affairs* 88.

visited by man, and that these principles were favourable to Canada. He did not enunciate the principles, but they were no other than the sector theory because:

What is known as the sector principle, in the determination of these areas is now very generally recognized, and on the basis of that principle *as well* our sovereignty extends right to the pole within the limits of the sector.

The Honourable Minister did not explicitly state that Canada claimed sovereignty to ice and water, but this may be inferred inasmuch as no land exists within 450 miles of the pole.

Prime Minister St. Laurent repeated in 1953 the Government's view that the Canadian boundary terminated at the pole. He told the House of Commons:

We must leave no doubt about our active occupation and exercise of our sovereignty in these lands right up to the pole.

The meaning of his words is not clear. Occupation precludes a claim under the sector theory, but how does a nation occupy the ice and water lying between the Arctic archipelago and the pole? Once again, the observer is invited to assume that Canada lays claim to ice and water as well as to land. That, at any rate, is what Lester B. Pearson wrote in 1946 when he was Canadian Ambassador to the United States. His words were unequivocal:

A large part of the world's total Arctic area is Canadian. One should know exactly what this part comprises. It includes not only Canada's northern mainland, but the islands and the frozen sea north of the mainland between the meridians of its east and west boundaries, extended to the North Pole.

The Minister of Northern Affairs and National Resources of the St. Laurent Government expressed contradictory views to the House of Commons in 1956:

We have never subscribed to the sector theory in application to the ice. We are content that our sovereignty exists over all the Arctic Islands. There is no doubt about it and there are no difficulties concerning it ... We have never upheld a general sector theory. To our mind the sea, be it frozen or in its natural liquid state, is the sea; and our sovereignty exists over the lands and over our territorial waters.

The most recent ministerial pronouncement, of special significance because it was voiced by a member of the Conservative Government and was the first policy statement on this subject made by an administration out of office from 1935 until 1957, was read to the House of Commons in 1958 by the Honourable Alvin Hamilton, Minister of Northern Affairs and National Resources. Mr. Hamilton was answering a question asked by Mr. Lesage, his Liberal predecessor in the portfolio:

Mr. Lesage – Are the waters of the Arctic ocean north of the Arctic archipelago up to the north pole, in the so-called Canadian sector, Canadian waters?

Hon. Alvin Hamilton – Mr. Speaker, the answer is that all the islands north of the mainland of Canada which comprise the Canadian Arctic archipelago are of course part of Canada. North of the limits of the archipelago, however, the position is complicated by unusual physical features. The Arctic ocean is covered for the most part of the year with polar pack ice having an average thickness of about eight feet. Leads of water do open up as a result of the pack ice being in continuous motion, but for practical purposes it might be said for the most part to be a permanently frozen sea. It will be seen, then, that the Arctic ocean north of the archipelago is not open water nor has it the stable qualities of land. Consequently the ordinary rules of international law may or may not have application. ...

Canada's claims to territorial sovereignty over the Arctic mainland and the islands of the archipelago within the Canadian "sector" have never been challenged by another state. The two nations most intimately concerned with this area are, coincidentally, the two most powerful and influential in the world – the United States and the Soviet Union. Between these two states lies Canada.

The U.S.S.R., having incorporated the sector theory as part of its national policy, would display inconsistency if it denied the Canadian claim. The Secretary of State for External Affairs of Canada reported to the House of Commons in 1959:

A search of departmental records has failed to disclose any dispute since 1900 between Canada and either the Union of Soviet Socialist Republics or the United States of America concerning the ownership of any portion of the Canadian Arctic.

The United States has neither disputed the claim nor made any of its own, its policy being one of reservation in both the Arctic and the Antarctic. It has not claimed on the basis of Peary's overland trip to the Pole in 1909 or Byrd's polar flight in 1926. Nor has it advanced a sector claim on the basis of the Alaskan penetration of the Arctic Circle. ...

NOTES

1) On July 10, 1963, in reply to a question as to the basis of Canadian claims to sovereignty over the islands in the Arctic Archipelago, Mr. Stewart, The Parliamentary Secretary to the Secretary of State for External Affairs, said:

Canadian sovereignty over these areas of the Arctic has been established mainly by continuous effective occupation since 1870, when Canada succeeded to the rights of Great Britain and began to provide for the administration of the Canadian Arctic. This sovereignty has remained undisturbed and – but for a dispute with Norway over the Sverdrup islands in 1930, which was subsequently settled in favour of Canada – has remained unchallenged.

His answer did not attempt to buttress the claim by reference to the sector theory or to any doctrine of contiguity.

2) On March 2, 1979, the following exchange between Erik Nielsen, M.P. for Yukon, and the Prime Minister took place in the House of Commons:[16]

Mr. Nielsen: A supplementary question, Mr. Speaker. Since Canada has always operated under the sector theory, the 141st meridian, therefore, would be the established boundary of Canada's territorial waters.

Can the Prime Minister assure us that the Canadian government is taking that stance; that it is insisting upon the application of the sector theory, and that the 141st meridian is the established rigid boundary of Canada's territorial waters in that area of the country?

Mr. Trudeau: Mr. Speaker, the sector theory is the one which gives us the broadest scope of sovereignty. It is, of course, the one we are pushing for and prefer, but it is not the one which is accepted in international law or by the United States.

It would be very nice to go up to the North Pole and say that part of the North Pole is ours, but it would be another thing to get the rest of the world to admit that claim. The hon. member knows the difficulties when there are competing claims by different countries. You have to resolve those claims by negotiation, as we have been successful in doing on the east coast and as we hope to be successful in doing elsewhere. Failing that, we will use the other means at our disposal under international law.

The Legal Status of the Arctic Regions
by D. Pharand (1979), 163 *Hague Recueil* 51

[While sovereignty over the land territory in the Arctic is no longer in dispute, potentially controversial issues remain unresolved. They include: the limits of the continental shelf of Arctic states; the scope of Canada's jurisdiction over the waters of its archipelago; and the nature of control Canada is entitled to exercise over the straits constituting the Northwest Passage. Professor Pharand surveys these and other issues:[17]]

There is no longer any question as to territorial sovereignty in the Arctic, but since jurisdiction on the continental shelf depends on territorial sovereignty, it is necessary to know exactly who owns what before attacking the problems relating to the continental shelf. ...There can be no doubt today that the Soviet Union has complete sovereignty over all of the islands north of its wide-ranging coast. ...

The continental shelf between Greenland and Ellesmere Island, of the Canadian Arctic archipelago, has already been established as far north as the Lincoln Sea, but there remains to be settled the shelf delimitation under the Lincoln Sea itself. The part of the continental shelf already delimited has been done on the basis of the equidistance principle, modified in certain sections by taking into account the special configuration of the coast and the

---

[16] H.C. *Debs.* (1979), Vol. IV, at 3758.
[17] See also D. Pharand, "The Legal Régime of the Arctic: Some Outstanding Issues" (1984), 39 *Int. J.* 742.

presence and size of islands in order to achieve an equitable result. It is reasonable to assume that the Parties will follow a similar approach to delimit the rest of the continental shelf in the Lincoln Sea.

Canada and the United States have not come to an agreement on the delimitation of their continental shelf in the Beaufort Sea between Alaska and the Yukon. Applying the equidistance principle, the delimitation line would be pulled over toward the Canadian side because of the slightly convex coast of Alaska and the concave coast of the Yukon. Furthermore, there is evidence that the concavity in question is continually being accentuated by a receding shoreline. It would thus appear that the special configuration of the coast would constitute a special circumstance and ought to justify a modification of the equidistance line.

In addition to the above, Canada has been using the 141st meridian of longitude as its western boundary for the exercise of different types of jurisdiction, in particular for the issuance of oil and gas exploration permits commencing in January 1965. It also used the 141st meridian, up to a distance of 100 nautical miles from the coast, in its Arctic Waters Pollution Prevention Act of 1970, to describe the waters over which it claimed pollution prevention jurisdiction. Then, in 1977, it used the 141st meridian again as the western boundary for its exclusive fishing zone in the Arctic up to 200 miles.

Legal Status of the Arctic Ocean

Except for the presence of ice floes on top of its waters, the Arctic Ocean is like any other ocean. The possibility of exercising the freedom of the seas, particularly the freedom of navigation, exists to a considerable degree already. Most of the other freedoms of the seas are also exercised, namely, the freedom of overflight, the freedom of fishing and the freedom of scientific research. The freedom to lay submarine cables and pipelines has not yet been exercised, but with the improved knowledge of the sea floor and of technology, that possibility certainly exists. In these circumstances, the waters of the Arctic Ocean must be considered as high seas, as in any other ocean.

The attitude of virtually all Arctic States has been in accord with the above conclusion. American submarines, icebreakers, aircraft and scientists on drifting ice stations, are all evidence that the United States considers the Arctic Ocean as high seas and open to all nations. As for the Soviet Union, it has been engaged in similar activities (especially marine scientific research) all over the Arctic Ocean for more than 25 years and, in spite of the opinion of some of its jurists to the contrary, it must be taken to subscribe to the freedom of the seas in the Arctic Ocean.

Canada has occasionally expressed doubt as to the status of the Arctic Ocean as high seas, particularly the Beaufort Sea, when discussing the status of the Northwest Passage. However, Canada's recent exploration of the Lomonosov Ridge by a group of scientists, installed on an ice floe floating across different sectors of the Arctic Ocean, would seem to indicate that it no longer believes, if it ever did, that the freedom of the seas is not applicable. ...

Legal Status of Ice Islands

Considering the extensive use being made of ice islands for marine scientific research, as well as a limited use for the exploration of the continental shelf, it would be preferable that they be submitted to some legal régime. This preference becomes apparent when ice islands, such as those of the Soviet Union, drift close to the coasts of other States. In such a case, the activities carried on aboard the ice island might understandably become of concern to the coastal State. More specifically, the latter might wish to verify the exact nature of the activities carried on, to ensure that its security and other national interests are not being affected.

The question of the legal status of ice islands is of comparatively recent origin, and no cutomary international law has yet developed through the practice of States. ...

Air Space over Arctic Lands and Islands

Since territorial sovereignty is now well established in the Arctic, the five Arctic States have complete and exclusive sovereignty over the air space above their respective territories. This includes sovereignty over Svalbard in favour of Norway, in spite of the limitations contained in the 1920 Treaty, since those limitations do not affect Norwegian sovereignty as such and, therefore, it extends to the air space above the archipelago. In other words, there is no more freedom of overflight over the Arctic territories and territorial waters than there is over territories situated anywhere else. ...

Air Space over the Arctic Ocean

It follows logically from what has been said already about the air space over the lands and islands, the shelf and the economic zone, that freedom of overflight exists all over the waters of the Arctic Ocean beyond the territorial sea. It was suggested by a few jurists, back in the 1930s, in particular by the Soviet writer, Lakhtine, that because of the presence of the ice cover, Arctic States should have complete sovereignty over their respective sectors, including the air space. With the advance in technology and knowledge of the precise physical character of the Arctic Ocean, this has not been suggested in recent years. And, indeed, the attitude of the various Arctic States has been to respect the freedom of overflight. This freedom has been respected, not only over the Arctic Ocean generally, but over the ice islands as well, even when they were occupied. For instance, American aircraft have flown over ice islands occupied by Soviet scientists and vice versa.

Air Space over the Northeast and Northwest Passages

Since those Passages are not used presently for international navigation, there would be no freedom of overflight where there is an overlap of territorial waters in those straits. In the Northeast Passage, this would apply to the Vilkitsky Straits, south of Severnaya Zemlya, linking the Kara and Laptev Seas. Those straits are approximately $22\frac{1}{2}$ and 11 miles wide. ... As for the Northwest Passage, there would be no freedom of overflight in Barrow Strait, where a small group of islands narrows the Passage to about 15 miles wide. ...

NOTES

1) In the aftermath of the controversial voyage of the U.S. Coast Guard icebreaker *Polar Sea* through the Canadian Arctic waters, in August 1985, Prime Minister Brian Mulroney unequivocally asserted Canada's sovereignty over the Northwest Passage: "There is no doubt that the Northwest Passage and that part of the world belongs to Canada. It is ours. We assert our sovereignty over it ... should there be a suggestion to the contrary by anyone, that would be an unfriendly act, and so construed by the government of Canada."[18] While the U.S. authorities informed the government of Canada that the voyage would be undertaken, they did not request Canadian permission.

2) Shortly thereafter, Joe Clark, Secretary of State for External Affairs, speaking in the House of Commons on September 10, 1985, announced a new policy of Canada for its Arctic waters. He said, *inter alia*:[19] "The voyage of the *Polar Sea* demonstrated that Canada, in the past, had not developed the means to ensure our sovereignty over time. ... I wish to declare to the House the policy of this government in respect of Canadian sovereignty in Arctic waters, ... Canada's sovereignty in the Arctic is indivisible. It embraces land, sea, and ice. It extends without interruption to the seaward-facing coasts of the Arctic islands. These islands are joined and not divided by the waters between them. They are bridged for most of the year by ice. From time immemorial Canada's Inuit people have used and occupied the ice as they have used and occupied the land. The policy of this government is to maintain the natural unity of the Canadian Arctic archipelago, and to preserve Canada's sovereignty over land, sea, and ice undiminished and undivided. That sovereignty has long been upheld by Canada. No previous government, however, has defined its precise limits or delineated Canada's internal waters and territorial sea in the Arctic. This government proposes to do so." The Minister for External Affairs announced a number of measures designed to implement the new policy, including (1) immediate adoption of an order-in-council establishing straight baselines around the Arctic archipelago, with effect from January 1, 1986 (see following map), and (2) enactment of a *Canadian Laws Offshore Application Act* designed to extend the application of federal and provincial laws to offshore areas around all the coasts of Canada to the full extent permitted under international law.[20]

3) Can Canada's claim to sovereignty over the Arctic waters be reconciled with the customary law of the sea; the 1958 Geneva High Seas Convention; the 1982 U.N. Convention on the Law of the Sea? Consider the materials on drawing baselines around Islands and Archipelagos contained in Chapter 11 on the "Law of the Sea."

---

[18] *The Gazette*, August 23, 1985, at Bl, col. 2.

[19] External Affairs Canada, Statements and Speeches, No. 85/7. See T.L. McDorman, "In the Wake of the 'Polar Sea': Canadian Jurisdiction and the Northwest Passage" (1986), 27 *Cahiers de Droit* 623.

[20] SOR85/872, made pursuant to the *Territorial Sea and Fishing Zones Act*, R.S.C. 1970, c.T-7, s.5(i), as amended by Stats. Can. 1969–70, c.68, s.3. The intended Act was introduced by Bill C-104 (1986) but was not passed before Parliament was prorogued. For an account of pollution prevention measures concerning Arctic waters, see discussion on "Protection of the Marine Environment" in Chapter 11.

The Canadian Arctic

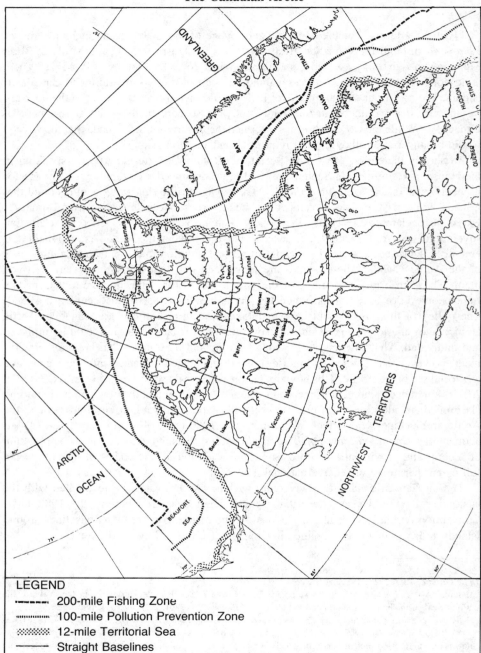

LEGEND
- ▬ ▬ ▬ 200-mile Fishing Zone
- ▪▪▪▪▪▪▪▪ 100-mile Pollution Prevention Zone
- ▨▨▨ 12-mile Territorial Sea
- ——— Straight Baselines

NOTE: All waters within the straight baselines are internal waters of Canada.

Reproduced from the Government of Canada.

Antarctica

The present legal regime of the vast, ice-covered continent of Antarctica is based on the Antarctic Treaty of Dec. 1, 1959.[21] From the original twelve signatories,[22] designated in the Treaty as Consultative Parties, the number of states parties had grown to 32 by 1985. Among these, Brazil, India, Poland, the Federal Republic of Germany, China and Uruguay have been accorded the privileged status of Consultative Parties, who are the only ones under the Treaty allowed to vote on policy matters. Seven of the original parties – Argentina, Australia, Chile, France, New Zealand, Norway and the United Kingdom – have territorial claims in Antarctica (see following map). Australia's claim is the largest, covering approximately two-fifths of the continent (2,300,000 sq. miles). The shape of the territorial claims is influenced by the so-called sector theory, once popular in the Arctic, with pie-shaped slices of sectors following longitudinal coordinates from the South Pole to a line near sixty degrees South latitude. The legal basis of the claims of the various state claimants differs: some rely on a combination of discovery, exploration and even "effective occupation," and others on the principles of contiguity and the sector theory. Belgium, Japan, South Africa, the Soviet Union and the United States – all Consultative Parties – have no territorial claims of their own and have consistently refused to recognize such claims advanced by other states. The claims of Argentina, Chile, and the United Kingdom overlap (in regard to Graham Land and neighbouring islands), while a relatively large sector of the continent remains unclaimed. In view of their pre-eminent role in the exploration of Antarctica, the position of the United States and the U.S.S.R. is bound to have a significant bearing on the future legal regime of the region.

The Antarctic Treaty is a unique legal document. By prohibiting all military activities in the region, it has made Antarctica the only fully demilitarized part of the earth and one where unrestricted on-site inspection is in force. It is also the only multilateral agreement which has effectively suspended, at least for thirty years, the final determination of the legal status of national claims to sovereignty over an entire continent. Despite the unsettled territorial claims, no significant conflict involving the contracting parties has occurred during the years since the signing of the Treaty. This could change, however, under pressure from developing countries, including some of the contracting parties, as the date for a review conference approaches (1991). A growing number of third world nations have been seeking in recent years to change the legal status of Antarctica by a new treaty which would make the whole continent a common heritage of mankind.[23]

---

[21] 402 U.N.T.S. 71, in force since 1961. See F. Auburn, *Antarctic Law and Politics* (1982); W. Bush, *Antarctica and International Law: A Collection of Inter-State and National Documents* (3 vols., 1982); S. Burton, "New Stresses on the Antarctic Treaty" (1979), 65 *Va. L. Rev.* 421; B.Boczek, "The Soviet Union and the Antarctic Regime" (1984), 78 *Am. J. Int. L.* 834; C. Joyner, "The Exclusive Economic Zone in Antarctica" (1981), 21 *Va. J. Int. L.* 691; E. Luard, "Who Owns the Antarctic?" (1984), 62 *Foreign Affairs* 1175; D. Pharand, "L'Arctique et l'Antarctique: Patrimoine Commun de l'Humanité?" (1982), 7 *Annals Air & Space L.* 415: K. Shusterich, "The Antarctic Treaty System: History, Substance, and Speculation" (1984), 39 *Int. J.* 800.

[22] The original signatories are Argentina, Australia, Belgium, Chile, France, Japan, New Zealand, Norway, South Africa, U.S.S.R., United Kingdom and United States.

[23] "The Question of Antarctica" was for the first time placed on the agenda of the U.N. General Assembly in 1983. A resolution then adopted by the Assembly called on the Secretary-General to undertake a "compre-

These efforts are primarily motivated by expectations of sharing in the living and mineral resources of the area.

The Antarctic Treaty
(1959), 402 U.N.T.S. 71

Article I

1. Antarctica shall be used for peaceful purposes only. There shall be prohibited, *inter alia*, any measures of a military nature, such as the establishment of military bases and fortifications, the carrying out of military maneuvers, as well as the testing of any type of weapons.

2. The present Treaty shall not prevent the use of military personnel or equipment for scientific research or for any other peaceful purpose.

Article IV

1. Nothing contained in the present Treaty shall be interpreted as:

  (a) a renunciation by any Contracting Party of previously asserted rights of or claims to territorial sovereignty in Antarctica;

  (b) a renunciation or diminution by any Contracting Party of any basis of claim to territorial sovereignty in Antarctica which it may have whether as a result of its activities or those of its nationals in Antarctica, or otherwise;

  (c) prejudicing the position of any Contracting Party as regards its recognition or non-recognition of any other State's right of or claim or basis of claim to territorial sovereignty in Antarctica.

2. No acts or activities taking place while the present Treaty is in force shall constitute a basis for asserting, supporting or denying a claim to territorial sovereignty in Antarctica or create any rights of sovereignty in Antarctica. No new claim, or enlargement of an existing claim, to territorial sovereignty in Antarctica shall be asserted while the present Treaty is in force.

Article V

1. Any nuclear explosions in Antarctica and the disposal there of radioactive waste material shall be prohibited.

2. In the event of the conclusion of international agreements concerning the use of

---

hensive, factual and objective'' study of the Antarctic Treaty system and member states were asked to submit their views on the matter. See Luard, *supra* n. 21, at 1183 fwd. In December 1985, a resolution adopted by the U.N. General Assembly called for ''international management and equitable sharing of the benefits'' of Antarctica's wealth. *N.Y. Times*, Dec. 4, 1985, at A11, col. 1. See also C. Joyner and P. Lipperman, ''Conflicting Jurisdiction in the Southern Ocean: The Case of an Antarctic Minerals Regime'' (1986), 27 *Va. J. Int. L.* 1.

Antarctica

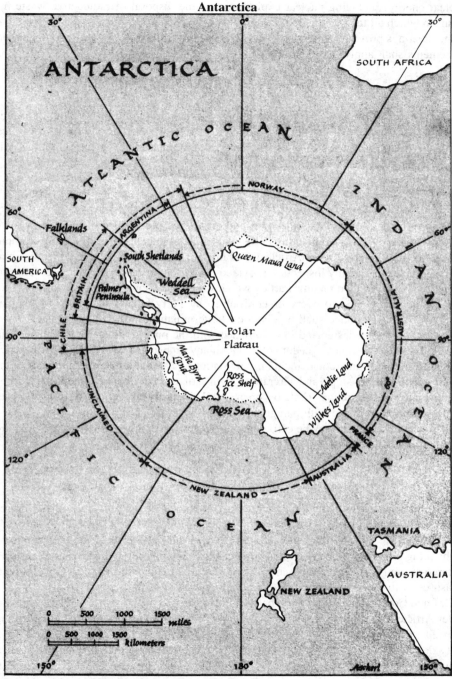

Reproduced from (1984), 62 *Foreign Affairs* 1176 (Part II).

nuclear energy, including nuclear explosions and the disposal of radioactive waste material, to which all the Contracting Parties whose representatives are entitled to participate in the meetings provided for under Article IX are parties, the rules established under such agreements shall apply in Antarctica.

Article VI

The provisions of the present Treaty shall apply to the area south of 60° South Latitude, including all ice shelves, but nothing in the present Treaty shall prejudice or in any way affect the rights, or the exercise of the rights of any State under international law with regard to the high seas within that area.

Article VII

1. In order to promote the objectives and ensure the observance of the provisions of the present Treaty, each Contracting Party whose representatives are entitled to participate in the meetings referred to in Article IX of the Treaty shall have the right to designate observers to carry out any inspection provided for by the present Article. Observers shall be nationals of the Contracting Parties which designate them. The names of observers shall be communicated to every other Contracting Party having the right to designate observers; and like notice shall be given of the termination of their appointment.

2. Each observer designated in accordance with the provisions of paragraph 1 of this Article shall have complete freedom of access at any time to any or all areas of Antarctica.

3. All areas of Antarctica, including all stations, installations and equipment within those areas, and all ships and aircraft at points of discharging or embarking cargoes or personnel in Antarctica, shall be open at all times to inspection by any observers designated in accordance with paragraph 1 of this Article.

4. Aerial observation may be carried out at any time over any or all areas of Antarctica by any of the Contracting Parties having the right to designate observers.

Article IX

1. Representatives of the Contracting Parties named in the preamble to the present Treaty shall meet at the City of Canberra within two months after the date of entry into force of the Treaty, and thereafter at suitable intervals, and places, for the purpose of exchanging information, consulting together on matters of common interest pertaining to Antarctica, and formulating and considering, and recommending to their Governments, measures in furtherance of the principles and objectives of the Treaty. ...

2. Each Contracting Party which has become a party to the present Treaty by accession under Article XIII shall be entitled to appoint representatives to participate in the meetings referred to in paragraph 1 of the present Article, during such time as that Contracting Party demonstrates its interest in Antarctica by conducting substantial scientific research activity there, such as the establishment of a scientific station or the despatch of a scientific expedition.

Article XII

1.(a) The present Treaty may be modified or amended at any time by unanimous agreement of the Contracting Parties whose representatives are entitled to participate in the meetings provided for under Article IX. Any such modification or amendment shall enter into force when the depositary Government has received notice from all such Contracting Parties that they have ratified it.

(b) Such modification or amendment shall thereafter enter into force as to any other Contracting Party when notice of ratification by it has been received by the depositary Government. Any such Contracting Party from which no notice of ratification is received within a period of two years from the date of entry into force of the modification or amendment in accordance with the provisions of subparagraph 1 (a) of this Article shall be deemed to have withdrawn from the present Treaty on the date of the expiration of such period.

2.(a) If after the expiration of thirty years from the date of entry into force of the present Treaty, any of the Contracting Parties whose representatives are entitled to participate in the meetings provided for under Article IX so requests by a communication addressed to the depositary Government, a Conference of all the Contracting Parties shall be held as soon as practicable to review the operation of the Treaty.

(b) Any modification or amendment to the present Treaty which is approved at such a Conference by a majority of the Contracting Parties there represented, including a majority of those whose representatives are entitled to participate in the meetings provided for under Article IX, shall be communicated by the depositary Government to all the Contracting Parties immediately after the termination of the Conference and shall enter into force in accordance with the provisions of paragraph 1 of the present Article.

NOTES

1) Subsequent to the conclusion of the Antarctic Treaty, two additional multilateral agreements regulating the activities within the region have been opened for signature – the Convention for the Conservation of Antarctic Seals (June 1, 1972)[24] and the Convention on the Conservation of Antarctic Marine Living Resources (May 20, 1980).[25] Negotiations for the establishment of a legal regime to govern the exploration and possible exploitation of mineral resources of Antarctica have been going on for quite some time.

2) Professor B. Boczek offers the following observation on the Soviet position in regard to the applicability of the sector theory to polar regions: "... the Arctic sector doctrine has not been openly and officially endorsed by the Soviet Union since to do so

---

[24] In force 1978. Reprinted in (1972), 11 *Int. Leg. Mat.* 251.
[25] In force 1982. Reprinted in (1980), 19 *Int. Leg. Mat.* 837.

would conflict with the Soviet position on the Antarctic, where the Soviets vigorously deny the validity of the doctrine as invoked by the claimant states.''[26]

3) Together with the Soviet Union, the principal polar country, Canada is not a party to the Antarctic Treaty. Is this position justified?

AIRSPACE AND OUTER SPACE

Airspace[27]

Chicago Convention on International Civil Aviation
(1944), 15 U.N.T.S. 295

PREAMBLE

Whereas the future development of international civil aviation can greatly help to create and preserve friendship and understanding among the nations and peoples of the world, yet its abuse can become a threat to the general security; and

Whereas it is desirable to avoid friction and to promote that cooperation between nations and peoples upon which the peace of the world depends;

Therefore, the undersigned governments having agreed on certain principles and arrangements in order that international civil aviation may be developed in a safe and orderly manner and that international air transport services may be established on the basis of equality of opportunity and operated soundly and economically;

Have accordingly concluded this Convention to that end.

Article 1

The contracting States recognize that every State has complete and exclusive sovereignty over the airspace above its territory.

Article 2

For the purpose of this Convention the territory of a State shall be deemed to be the land areas and territorial waters adjacent thereto under the sovereignty, suzerainty, protection or mandate of such State.

---

[26] *Supra*, n. 21, at 842.

[27] See T. Buergenthal, *Law-Making in the International Civil Aviation Organization* (1969); J.C. Cooper, *Explorations in Aerospace Law* (I. Vlasic, ed., 1968); D. Johnson, *Rights in Airspace* (1965); A. Lowenfeld, *Aviation Law – Cases and Materials* (2ed., 1981); E. McWhinney and M. Bradley, eds., *The Freedom of the Air* (1968); N. Mateesco-Matte, *Treatise on Air-Aeronautical Law* (1981); *Shawcross & Beaumont on Air Law* (4ed., P. Martin *et al.*, 1977); H. Wassenbergh and H. van Fenema, eds., *International Air Transport in the Eighties* (1981).

Article 3

(a) This Convention shall be applicable only to civil aircraft and shall not be applicable to state aircraft.

(b) Aircraft used in military, customs and police services shall be deemed to be state aircraft.

(c) No state aircraft of a contracting State shall fly over the territory of another State or land thereon without authorization by special agreement or otherwise, and in accordance with the terms thereof.

(d) The contracting States undertake, when issuing regulations for their state aircraft, that they will have due regard for the safety of navigation of civil aircraft.

Article 4

Each contracting State agrees not to use civil aviation for any purpose inconsistent with the aims of this Convention.

Chapter II
FLIGHT OVER TERRITORY OF CONTRACTING STATES

Article 5

Each contracting State agrees that all aircraft of the other contracting States, being aircraft not engaged in scheduled international air services shall have the right, subject to the observance of the terms of this Convention, to make flights into or in transit non-stop across its territory and to make stops for non-traffic purposes without the necessity of obtaining prior permission, and subject to the right of the State flown over to require landing. Each contracting State nevertheless reserves the right, for reasons of safety of flight, to require aircraft desiring to proceed over regions which are inaccessible or without adequate air navigation facilities to follow prescribed routes, or to obtain special permission for such flights.

Such aircraft, if engaged in the carriage of passengers, cargo, or mail for remuneration or hire on other than scheduled international air services, shall also, subject to the provisions of Article 7, have the privilege of taking on or discharging passengers, cargo, or mail, subject to the right of any State where such embarkation or discharge takes place to impose such regulations, conditions or limitations as it may consider desirable.

Article 6

No scheduled international air service may be operated over or into the territory of a contracting State, except with the special permission or other authorization of that State, and in accordance with the terms of such permission or authorization.

Article 8

No aircraft capable of being flown without a pilot shall be flown without a pilot over the territory of a contracting State without special authorization by that State and in accordance with the terms of such authorization. Each contracting State undertakes to insure that the flight of such aircraft without a pilot in regions open to civil aircraft shall be so controlled as to obviate danger to civil aircraft.

Article 9

(a) Each contracting State may, for reasons of military necessity or public safety, restrict or prohibit uniformly the aircraft of other States from flying over certain areas of its territory, provided that no distinction in this respect is made between the aircraft of the State whose territory is involved, engaged in international scheduled airline services, and the aircraft of the other contracting States likewise engaged. Such prohibited areas shall be of reasonable extent and location so as not to interfere unnecessarily with air navigation. Descriptions of such prohibited areas in the territory of a contracting State, as well as any subsequent alterations therein, shall be communicated as soon as possible to the other contracting States and to the International Civil Aviation Organization.

(b) Each contracting State reserves also the right, in exceptional circumstances or during a period of emergency, or in the interest of public safety, and with immediate effect, temporarily to restrict or prohibit flying over the whole or any part of its territory, on condition that such restriction or prohibition shall be applicable without distinction of nationality to aircraft of all other States.

(c) Each contracting State, under such regulations as it may prescribe, may require any aircraft entering the area contemplated in subparagraphs (a) or (b) above to effect a landing as soon as practicable thereafter at some designated airport within its territory.

Destruction of Korean Airlines Flight 007

The seriousness with which certain states view violations of their air sovereignty was illustrated by the incident involving the destruction of Korean Airlines flight 007 in September 1983. The following excerpts from the debates in the U.N. Security Council and the diplomatic notes addressed to the Soviet Union by the United States and Canada provide an illustration of the contradictory assertions regarding the circumstances of the incident (quite common to disputes involving aerial intrusions). The same excerpts also offer an indication of what states regard as the rules of international law governing the treatment of civilian aerial intruders.

Mrs. J. KIRKPATRICK (U.S. Ambassador to the United Nations):[28]
Most of the world outside the Soviet Union has heard by now of the Korean Air Lines flight 007 carrying 269 persons between New York and Seoul, which strayed off course into Soviet air space, was tracked by Soviet radar, was targeted by a Soviet SU-15, whose

---

[28] Security Council Doc. S/PV. 2471 (Sept. 6, 1983); reproduced in (1983), 22 *Int. Leg. Mat.* 1121.

pilot coolly, and after careful consideration, fired two air-launched missiles which destroyed the Korean airliner and apparently its 269 passengers and crew. ...

There are internationally agreed upon standards for intercepting unwelcome aircraft. Those internationally agreed upon standards call for serious efforts at identification, verification and warning and – if the case is serious – for intercepting the intruder and forcing it to land or to leave one's airspace. Sovereignty neither requires nor permits shooting down airliners in peacetime.

Recently the Soviets have implied that KAL 007 may have been mistaken for a United States aerial reconnaissance flight, but that is no more persuasive. The Korean Air Lines Boeing 747 was on a routine, scheduled flight. At the time it was shot down the United States reconnaissance plane referred to by the Soviets had been on the ground for more than one hour, more than 1,500 miles away. Moreover, the United States does not fly reconnaissance missions in Soviet airspace. We do regularly operate aircraft in international airspace to monitor Soviet compliance with SALT and other arms control agreements. The Soviet government knows what our usual flight patterns are and can readily identify these missions.

Mr. O. TROYANOVSKY (U.S.S.R. Ambassador to the United Nations):[29]

Today's statement by the representative of the United States is simply a further deliberate attempt to put the discussion on the wrong course. It is an attempt to avoid an answer to certain central questions. First, it is an irrefutable fact – and indeed, it has not been denied by American representatives – that the intruder plane had been in Soviet air space for some considerable time. It penetrated 500 kilometres inside Soviet territory. It ignored every attempt made by the Soviet ground services and air forces to identify it. It was unwilling to land at the nearest Soviet airfield. ...

Something further should be said about the general circumstances in which this gross violation of Soviet air space by the South Korean airliner occurred. Contrary to what has been suggested here by the representative of the United States, there have recently been deliberate violations of Soviet State borders by American planes. Such violations, committed with assumed impunity, have become more and more systematic: such violations occurred in 1982 on 22 February, 13 March and 4 and 7 May. There have been 12 similar violations so far this year – including one on 4 April by planes from the aircraft carriers *Midway* and *Enterprise*. In those instances the Soviet Union made official protests. There was, however no response from the United States. On the contrary, the activities of American reconnaissance planes near the air borders of the Soviet Union have increased: on 31 August of this year, on the eve of the South Korean plane's invasion of the air space of the Soviet Union, and in that same area, seven flights by American reconnaissance planes of the RC-135 type were recorded. On 31 August, from 1745 to 2049 hours, Moscow time, in an area directly contiguous to the point at which the South Korean plane entered Soviet air space and at a height of 8,000 metres, a reconnaissance plane of that type was observed carring out manoeuvres.

At the same time three United States warships appeared very close to Soviet waters. On 31 August at 2000 hours, 800 kilometres south-east of the town of Petropavlovsky-

---

[29] *Supra*, at 1125.

on-Kamchatka, a Soviet radar station discovered an unknown plane with radar characteristics similar to those of the RC-135 that was on course towards the Kamchatka
Peninsula also at the height of 8,000-9,000 metres. Subsequently the Soviet ground
stations tried to establish communication with it regarding the violation. However, the
aircraft did not reply and continued on the same course, going even deeper into the Soviet
air space. So as to identify the aircraft and give it assistance, air defence planes were
launched to meet it. There was no reaction by the intruder to their commands. It continued
on its flight with its navigational lights turned off, which was characteristic of flights by
American reconnaissance planes. The intruder flew over the Kamchatka territory and in
fact directly over the Soviet naval base and other military sites. When the intruder
aproached Sakhalin Island, another group of air defence planes was sent aloft to meet it
which once again tried to establish contact with it and to conduct it to the nearest Soviet
airport. However, the intruder not only continued on the same course without responding
to the warning manoeuvre carried out by the Soviet planes, but also changed its course
entering the airspace directly over the southern part of Sakhlin Island and flew over the
Soviet naval base while at the same time altering its altitude. It was only thereafter that
a warning shot was fired with tracers from the Soviet plane.

All these facts in aggregate suggest strongly that the course and nature of the flight
carried out by the South Korean airliner was not fortuitous, but rather a scenario that had
been prepared for this tragic event long before.

Mr. AMNEUS (Representative of Sweden to the United Nations):[30]

It is a well known fact that the Soviet Union has severe rules of its own for the
protection of the State boundary, enabling Soviet units to use force even against civilian
aircraft. Such rules and instructions are not in accordance with generally accepted norms
of international law relevant to civilian transportation.

All countries having air traffic to and from the Soviet Union have a right to demand
that Soviet authorities do not use force against their aircraft in cases of navigational faults.
All civilian aircraft must be treated in a manner that eliminates risks to the safety of the
aircraft and its passengers. Interception routines must be applied in such a strict way as
to eliminate any risk for mistake with regard to the identity of intercepted aircraft.

Mr. TROYANOVSKY (reading from the statement of the Soviet government):[31]

We will continue to act in keeping with our legislation, which is fully in accord with
international regulations. This wholly applies to the question of ensuring the security of
our borders.

It is the sovereign right of every State to protect its borders, in particular its air space.
This is one of the commonly recognized principles of international law on which relations
between States rest. So the U.S. President makes himself out as an ignoramus saying,
as he did in his address on September 5, that the Soviet Union guards its borders in what
it claims is its air space.

DIPLOMATIC NOTE submitted to the U.S.S.R. on September 8, 1983 by Canada's
Department of External Affairs (excerpt): [32]

---

[30] *Supra*, n. 28, at 1127.
[31] Security Council Doc. S/PV.2472 (Sept. 6, 1983), *supra*, n. 28, at 1128.
[32] Reproduced in (1983), 22 *Int. Leg. Mat.* 1190.

The Department is of the opinion that the actions of the Soviet military in destroying a civilian airliner constitute a flagrant breach of general principles of international law as well as of well-established rules and procedures of international civil aviation and cannot be justified on legal, moral or other grounds.

DIPLOMATIC NOTE submitted to the U.S.S.R. on September 16, 1983 by the U.S. Department of State (excerpt):[33]

The United States refers to the Soviet Union's action of September 1, 1983 in firing upon and destroying an unarmed civil airliner, Korean Air Lines Flight No. 007, in the vicinity of Sakhalin Island, thereby causing the deaths of 269 innocent persons. The United States considers this action as a flagrant and unjustifiable breach of applicable principles of international law and as a direct violation of internationally agreed procedures to be followed when an aircraft inadvertently intrudes on a state's territorial airspace. The United States submits that the Soviet Union's action was wrongful and gives rise to responsibility under international law to make reparation.

The United States Government therefore demands that the Soviet Union provide prompt, adequate, and effective compensation to the United States Government for the lives of United States nationals aboard Korean Air Lines Flight No. 007 and for any other compensable loss incurred by any United States national as a result of the Soviet Union's wrongful actions. The United States will advise the Soviet Union at a later date of the specific losses for which the United States considers the Soviet Union responsible under international law.

NOTES

1) The Chicago Convention does not explicitly prohibit the use of force against intruding civil aircraft. Neither the Convention nor customary law accords absolute immunity to civil aircraft entering foreign airspace without authorization.[34] A strong argument can be made, however, that the use of force against a civilian airliner is justified only in the most exceptional circumstances, when the vital security interests of the overflown

---

[33] *Supra*, at 1198. And see "Destruction of Korean Air Lines Boeing 747 Over Sea of Japan, 31 August 1983: Report of ICAO Fact-Finding Investigation" (1983), reproduced in part in (1984), 23 *Int. Leg. Mat.* 865. For a discussion of the legal issues involved in this incident, see B. Cheng "The Destruction of KAL Flight KE 007, and Article 3 Bis of the Chicago Convention," in J. van Gravesande and A. van der Veen Vonk, eds., *Air Worthy – Liber Amicorum Honouring Professor Dr. I.H. Ph. Diederiks-Verschoor* (1985), at 49; G. Guillaume, "La destruction, le 1er Septembre 1983, de l'avion des Korean Airlines (vol KE 007)" (1984), *Rev. Fr. D.A.* 215; F. Hassan, "The Shooting Down of Korean Airlines Flight 007 by the USSR and the Future of Air Safety for Passengers" (1984), 33 *Int. Comp. L. Q.* 712; P. Martin, "Destruction of Korean Air Lines Boeing 747 over Sea of Japan, 31 August 1983" (1984), 9 *Air L.* 138.

[34] For an overview of law and state practice, see W. Hughes, "Aerial Intrusions by Civil Airliners and the Use of Force" (1980), 45 *J. Air L. & Com.* 595; O. Lissitzyn, "The Treatment of Aerial Intruders in Recent Practice and International Law" (1953), 47 *Am. J. Int. L.* 559; and "Some Legal Implications of the U-2 and RB-47 Incidents" (1962), 56 *Am. J. Int. L.* 135; J. Sundberg, "Legitimate Responses to Aerial Intruders: The View from a Neutral State" (1985), 10 *Annals Air & Space L.* 251; Q. Wright, "Legal Aspects of the U-2 Incident" (1960), 54 *Am. J. Int. L.* 836.

state are at stake. This conclusion finds support in the virtually universal condemnation of the Soviet attack on the Korean airliner and, especially, in the resolution of the ICAO Council adopted on September 16, 1983 by a vote 26 in favor to 2 against, with 3 abstentions. In addition to "deeply deploring" the Soviet action, the Council asserted that "such use of armed force against international civil aviation is incompatible with the norms governing international behaviour and elementary considerations of humanity and with the rules, Standards and Recommended Practices enshrined in the Chicago Convention and its Annexes and invokes generally recognized legal consequences."[35]

2) States parties to the Chicago Convention are obliged to comply with the "Standards" adopted by ICAO and included in annexes to the Convention. However, in the event of impossibility of compliance, notification to the ICAO Council is mandatory under Article 38 of the Convention. "Recommended practices," also included in annexes, are non-obligatory; member states are merely expected to "endeavour to conform in accordance with the Convention." The "Standards" in force include the Rules of the Air appended to the Convention as Annex 2, which contain provisions relevant to the interception of civil aircraft. In 1986, the Council of ICAO adopted Amendment 27 to the Rules of the Air, of which the key provision reads in part:[36]

3.8.1 Interception of civil aircraft shall be governed by appropriate regulations and administrative directives issued by contracting States in compliance with the Convention on International Civil Aviation, and in particular Article 3(d) under which contracting States undertake, when issuing regulations for their State aircraft, to have due regard for the safety of navigation of civil aircraft.

Protocol to the Chicago Convention
(1984), 23 *Int. Leg. Mat.*705

[In the aftermath of the destruction by a Soviet fighter aircraft of Korean Airlines Flight 007, on September 1, 1983, the ICAO Assembly adopted unanimously on May 10, 1984 an amendment to the Chicago Convention – Article 3 bis – designed to prevent such incidents in the future. The amendment will enter into force when ratfied by 102 contracting states.]

Article 3 bis

(a) The contracting States recognize that every State must refrain from resorting to the use of weapons against civil aircraft in flight and that, in case of interception, the lives of persons on board and the safety of aircraft must not be endangered.

---

[35] Resolution of the Extraordinary Session of the Council – Appendix A, reprinted in (1983), 22 *Int. Leg. Mat.* 1150.

[36] Rules of the Air – Annex 2 to the Convention on International Civil Aviation (8 ed., July 1986). And see M. Milde, "Interception of Civil Aircraft vs. Misuse of Civil Aviation" (1986), 11 *Annals Air & Space L.* 105, for background information concerning this amendment.

This provision shall not be interpreted as modifying in any way the rights and obligations of States set forth in the Charter of the United Nations.

(b) The contracting States recognize that every State, in the exercise of its sovereignty, is entitled to require the landing at some designated airport of a civil aircraft flying above its territory without authority or if there are reasonable grounds to conclude that it is being used for any purpose inconsistent with the aims of this Convention; it may also give such aircraft any other instructions to put an end to such violations. For this purpose, the contracting States may resort to any appropriate means consistent with relevant rules of international law, including the relevant provisions of this Convention, specifically paragraph (a) of this Article. Each contracting State agrees to publish its regulations in force regarding the interception of civil aircraft.

(c) Every civil aircraft shall comply with an order given in conformity with paragraph (b) of this Article. To this end each contracting State shall establish all necessary provisons in its national laws or regulations to make such compliance mandatory for any civil aircraft registered in that State or operated by as person having his principal place of business or permanent residence in that State. Each contracting State shall make any violation of such applicable laws or regulations punishable by severe penalties and shall submit the case to its competent authorities in accordance with its laws or regulations.

(d) Each contracting State shall take appropriate measures to prohibit the deliberate use of any civil aircraft registered in that State or operated by an operator who has his principal place of business or permanent residence in that State for any purpose inconsistent with the aims of this Convention. This provision shall not affect paragraph (a) or derogate from paragraphs (b) and (c) of this Article.

NOTES

1) In the opinion of many observers, Article 3 bis poses a number of problems. For instance Professor B. Cheng asks: "Is Article 3 bis declaratory of general international law?"; "What is the meaning of the phrase 'to refrain'?"; "Is, under Article 3 bis, the duty not to endanger the safety of civil aircraft in flight and the lives of persons on board absolute?"[37]

2) Pursuant to the obligations regarding interception of civil aircraft imposed by Article 3 bis (b) and by the Rules of the Air reported above, ICAO has adopted the following "principles to be observed by States" in formulating and publishing the necessary regulations:[38]

1.1 To achieve the uniformity in regulations which is necessary for the safety of navigation

---

[37] B. Cheng, *supra*, n.33, at 59.
[38] Rules of the Air, Appendix B, *supra*, n. 36.

of civil aircraft due regard shall be had by Contracting States to the following principles when developing regulations and administrative directives:

    a)   interception of civil aircraft will be undertaken only as a last resort;

    b)   if undertaken, an interception will be limited to determining the identity of the aircraft, unless it is necessary to return the aircraft to its planned track, direct it beyond the boundaries of national airspace, guide it away from a prohibited, restricted or danger area or instruct it to effect a landing at a designated aerodrome;

    c)   practice interception of civil aircraft will not be undertaken;

    d)   navigational guidance and related information will be given to an intercepted aircraft by radiotelephony, whenever radio contact can be established; and

    e)   in the case where an intercepted civil aircraft is required to land in the territory overflown, the aerodrome designated for the landing is to be suitable for the safe landing of the aircraft type concerned.

1.2 Contracting States shall publish a standard method that has been established for the manoeuvering of aircraft intercepting a civil aircraft. Such method shall be designed to avoid any hazard for the intercepted aircraft.

Air Defence Identification Zones[39]

In December 1950, during the Korean war, the United States promulgated a set of rules establishing "Air Defense Identification Zones" (ADIZ) around its territory. The ADIZ rules were designed to control all air traffic in the airspace adjacent to the U.S. territory and extended hundreds of miles over the high seas. The declared purpose of the rules was to protect the United States against hostile aircraft. The rules required all aircraft intending to enter an ADIZ to file a flight plan with the appropriate U.S. aeronautical authority. In addition, the pilot in command of a foreign civil aircraft would not be admitted to the U.S. territory without making position reports when not less than one hour and not more than two hours average direct cruising distance from the United States. Five months later, Canada adopted similar regulations, under the title "Rules for the Security Control of Air Traffic" (CADIZ). Like their American counterpart, the Canadian rules "have been found necessary, in the interest of national security, to identify, locate and control aircraft operated within areas designated as Canadian Air Defence Identification Zones". (Purpose of the Rules, sec. 1.1). CADIZ rules also provide for the filing of flight plans by any aircraft prior to its penetration of the controlled airspace. "A violation of these rules will render the pilot of an aircraft liable to inflight interception by military interceptor aircraft" (CADIZ Rules, sec. 2.10.1). This practice of unilateral extension of jurisdiction by coastal states, initiated by the United States, was subsequently emulated by a number of other states, with virtually no protest. The tacit acquiescence

---

[39] J. Denaro, "States' Jurisdiction in Airspace under International Law" (1970), 36 J. *Air L. & Comm.* 688; I. Head, "ADIZ, International Law and Contiguous Airspace" (1964), 3 *Alta. L. Rev.* 182; J. Murchison, *The Contiguous Air Space Zone in International Law* (1955); Note, "Air Defense Identification Zones: Creeping Jurisdiction in the Airspace" (1978), 18 *Va. J. Int. L.* 485. See also M. Milde, "United Nations Convention on the Law of the Sea–Possible Implications for International Air Law" (1983), 8 *Annals Air & Space L.* 167.

accorded by the international community to a practice not in conformity with the freedom of the high seas is most likely due to three factors: (a) the slight inconvenience caused by the tolerant application of these rules in practice; (b) improved safety for all users of the airspace in question; and (c) improved security of coastal states through timely identification of aircraft in the vicinity of their territory. Although ADIZ rules remain in force to this day, they have never been formally authorized either through an official act of ICAO or through an international treaty such as the 1982 Convention on the Law of the Sea.

Military Aircraft in Foreign Airspace[40]

Military aircraft lawfully within the territory of a foreign state enjoy virtually the same immunity from local jurisdiction as do visiting warships. There might be a difference in the treatment accorded foreign aircraft and foreign warships when the entry is due to distress (i.e., without prior authorization by the receiving state). States might view with suspicion a foreign military aircraft penetrating their airspace by claiming distress. Simulated distress and fraudulent entry is much more likely to involve an aircraft than a warship.

States very strictly regulate the admission of foreign aircraft to their airspace. Unauthorized entry into the national airspace by a foreign military aircraft is often treated as being made with hostile intentions. Some states, as we have seen, assert the right to employ force not only against military aerial intruders but also against intruding civil aircraft.

Outer Space[41]

Unispace 82 Report
Second U.N. Conference on the Exploration and Peaceful Uses of Outer Space

The very first artificial satellites which gave birth to the Space Age were created as elements in a global scientific programme: the International Geophysical Year (IGY). The scientific results achieved by these devices, rudimentary as they were by today's standards, constituted the most important findings of the entire IGY. They discovered the enormous radiation belts, trapped by the Earth's magnetic field, which surround our planet, and they detected the never-ending stream of charged particles which emanate from our Sun, called the "solar wind." The solar wind interacts with the radiation belts

---

[40] See M. Peng, *Le Statut Juridique de l'Aéronef Militaire (1957)*, 75 fwd.

[41] See C.Christol, *The Modern International Law of Outer Space* (1982); J.Fawcett, *Outer Space–New Challenges to Law and Policy* (1984); N. Jasentuliyana and R. Lee, eds., *Manual on Space Law*, Vol. 1 (1979); M. Lachs, *The Law of Outer Space: An Experience in Contemporary Law-Making* (1972); M. McDougal, H. Lasswell and I. Vlasic, *Law and Public Order in Space* (1963); N. Matte, ed., *Space Activities and Emerging International Law* (1984); and P. Fauteux, "Canada's Participation in the Development of Space Law: How Well Does the Recent Past Bode for the Future?" in *Proceedings of the Conference on International Law: Critical Choices for Canada 1985-2000*, Queen's L.J. (1986) 415.

to affect terrestrial atmospheric phenomena from radio communications to the weather itself.

The promise of so auspicious a beginning has been more than fulfilled by the subsequent achievements in space science. Our spacecraft have catalogued the planets of our Solar System from Mercury to Saturn, along with most of the satellites of the gas giants Jupiter and Saturn. At this writing several of these spacecraft are en route to Uranus and Neptune, and even out of the Solar System altogether, still transmitting the scientific data being observed by their instruments. We have landed men and robot equipment on the Moon and have brought samples back to Earth for analysis. We have placed robot spacecraft on Mars and on Venus and have analysed these celestial neighbours to see what they can tell us about our own planet – how it evolved and what its future might be. We have studied the Earth's biosphere in great detail to learn more about the factors which affect our life in so many ways. We have explored the Sun and the stars with space-based telescopes and observatories, whose vantage point above the obscuring atmosphere has made possible most of the major findings in astronomy and astrophysics that were achieved during the past decade or two. ...

Of all the applications of space technology, satellite communications is the most widely used. First utilized for intercontinental communication, satellites are now used primarily for international communication. However, they are also being used by a growing number of countries for domestic communication. Satellites for international communication are operated by INTELSAT, EUTELSAT and INTERSPUTNIK. A global maritime communication system, INMARSAT, went into operation early in 1982. Some countries have their own operational domestic satellite communication systems (Canada, India, Indonesia, USA and USSR); many others have plans to set up such systems soon.

A communication satellite is simply a wholly self-contained electronic switchboard in orbit around the Earth. The vantage point offered by its orbit, high above the ground, is far superior to that of any mountaintop tower for line-of-sight access by distant transmitters or receivers. There is one particular orbit, 35,800 kilometres above the Earth's equator, in which a satellite travels at a speed which keeps pace exactly with the Earth's rotation. To an observer standing on the equator a satellite in this "geostationary orbit" therefore appears to remain fixed in the sky directly overhead. By the use of properly designed antennas and electronic communication equipment, such a satellite can be used to relay telephone, television, numerical data and facsimiles between any two points on Earth which can "see" the satellite. Since each satellite can be seen from over a third of the Earth's surface, such satellites can provide a complete global communications network, able to link any two "ground stations" with each other. ...

Meteorology has been a major field of space application. Various international programmes organized by the World Meteorological Organization (WMO) have met with considerable success, and observations from space are now an integral and important part of weather reporting and forecasting. Satellites are used for the dissemination of processed meteorological data to users all over the world and also for the collection of data from remote places. Cloud-cover pictures, atmospheric temperatures at different altitudes, sea surface temperatures, sea state, ice cover, precipitation and a wide variety of other data are collected by a number of meteorological satellites operated by several countries.

The present world-wide system, although owned and operated by several individual countries, is largely operational. It requires close cooperation between the satellite operators and the many nations of the world who use its data. The satellite meteorological system is especially important for developing countries, which do not have independent or alternative sources for much of this data and for whom weather forecasting is directly linked to national prosperity because of their dependence upon rain-fed agriculture. ...

"Remote sensing," in the context of space technology, involves observing the Earth and its atmosphere from orbit in various wavelengths of the electromagnetic spectrum (the colours of visible light are part of that spectrum).

Remote sensing has become an increasingly important application of space technology, even though there is as yet no formally "operational" system. Many countries – including some developing countries – use satellite remote sensing and analysis extensively. The US LANDSAT satellites have been the most widely used; other countries, including the USSR and India, also use their own remote sensing satellites. ...

A few countries have been using satellites for military applications, including communication, meteorology, navigation and surveillance. Some of these systems have been used for civilian purposes also (e.g., navigation) and surveillance satellites have provided the means of verifying arms limitation treaties. However, many countries are now concerned about the growing militarization of outer space and, in particular, the introduction of weapons systems into this otherwise peaceful environment. While the Outer Space Treaty of 1967 bars nuclear weapons or weapons of mass destruction from outer space, it does not directly ban deployment of other weapons. Discussions on maintaining outer space as a peaceful environment are, however, taking place in various fora of the United Nations. ...

United Nations interest in the peaceful uses of outer space was first expressed in October, 1957 shortly after the Soviet Union launched the first man-made satellite. The General Assembly urged States to give priority to reaching a disarmament agreement which would provide for the joint study of an inspection system designed to ensure that objects sent through outer space would be exclusively for peaceful and scientific purposes.

In 1959 the Assembly established the Committee on Peaceful Uses of Outer Space (COPUOS) to be the focal point of United Nations action in this field. The new Committee was requested to "review, as appropriate, the area of international co-operation and study practical and feasible means for giving effect to programmes in the peaceful uses of outer space which would appropriately be undertaken under United Nations auspices." Reflecting its interest in both the legal and technical aspects of outer space, the Committee has a Legal Subcommittee and a Scientific and Technical Subcommittee. ...

The work of COPUOS and its Legal Subcommittee has led to five international instruments dealing with the exploration and peaceful uses of outer space, liability for damage caused by space objects, registration of objects launched into outer space, return of astronauts and principles governing the use of the Moon and other celestial bodies. The Treaty on Principles Governing the Activities of States in the Exploration and Use of Outer Space Including the Moon and Other Celestial Bodies was opened for signature on 27 January, 1967 and came into force on 10 October, 1967. The Agreement on the Rescue of Astronauts, the Return of Astronauts and the Return of Objects Launched into Outer Space entered into force on 3 December, 1968.

The Convention on International Liability for Damage Caused by Space Objects came into force on 1 September, 1972. The Convention on the Registration of Objects Launched into Outer Space was opened for signature on 14 January, 1975 and came into force on 15 September, 1976. The Agreement Governing Activities of States on the Moon and other Celestial Bodies was opened for signature on 5 December, 1979.

Other legal work of COPUOS deals with such questions as the legal implications of remote sensing of the earth from space; principles to govern the use by States of artificial earth satellites for direct television broadcasting; and the definition and delimitation of outer space and outer space activities.

Outer Space Treaty
Treaty on Principles Governing the Activities of States in the Exploration and Use of Outer Space, including the Moon and Other Celestial Bodies
1967 Can. T.S. No. 19; 610 U.N.T.S. 205 (In force 1967)

Article I

The exploration and use of outer space, including the moon and other celestial bodies, shall be carried out for the benefit and in the interests of all countries, irrespective of their degree of economic or scientific development, and shall be the province of all mankind.

Outer space, including the moon and other celestial bodies, shall be free for exploration and use by all States without discrimination of any kind, on a basis of equality and in accordance with international law, and there shall be free access to all areas of celestial bodies.

There shall be freedom of scientific investigation in outer space, including the moon and other celestial bodies, and States shall facilitate and encourage international co-operation in such investigation.

Article II

Outer space, including the moon and other celestial bodies, is not subject to national appropriation by claim of sovereignty, by means of use or occupation, or by any other means.

Article III

States Parties to the Treaty shall carry on activities in the exploration and use of outer space, including the moon and other celestial bodies, in accordance with international law, including the Charter of the United Nations, in the interest of maintaining international peace and security and promoting international co-operation and understanding.

Article IV

States Parties to the Treaty undertake not to place in orbit around the earth any objects carrying nuclear weapons or any other kinds of weapons of mass destruction, install such weapons on celestial bodies, or station such weapons in outer space in any other manner.

The moon and other celestial bodies shall be used by all States Parties to the Treaty exclusively for peaceful purposes. The establishment of military bases, installations and fortifications, the testing of any type of weapons and the conduct of military manoeuvres on celestial bodies shall be forbidden. The use of military personnel for scientific research or for any other peaceful purposes shall not be prohibited. The use of any equipment or facility necessary for peaceful exploration of the moon and other celestial bodies shall also not be prohibited.

Article V

States Parties to the Treaty shall regard astronauts as envoys of mankind in outer space and shall render to them all possible assistance in the event of accident, distress, or emergency landing on the territory of another State Party or on the high seas. When astronauts make such a landing, they shall be safely and promptly returned to the State of registry of their space vehicle.

In carrying on activities in outer space and on celestial bodies, the astronauts of one State Party shall render all possible assistance to the astronauts of other States Parties.

States Parties to the Treaty shall immediately inform the other States Parties to the Treaty or the Secretary-General of the United Nations of any phenomena they discover in outer space, including the moon and other celestial bodies, which could constitute a danger to the life or health of astronauts.

Article VI

States Parties to the Treaty shall bear international responsibility for national activities in outer space, including the moon and other celestial bodies, whether such activities are carried on by governmental agencies or by non-governmental entities, and for assuring that national activities are carried out in conformity with the provisions set forth in the present Treaty. The activities of non-governmental entities in outer space, including the moon and other celestial bodies, shall require authorization and continuing supervision by the appropriate State Party to the Treaty. When activities are carried on in outer space, including the moon and other celestial bodies, by an international organization, responsibility for compliance with this Treaty shall be borne both by the international organization and by the States Parties to the Treaty participating in such organization.

Article VII

Each State Party to the Treaty that launches or procures the launching of an object into outer space, including the moon and other celestial bodies, and each State Party from whose territory or facility an object is launched, is internationally liable for damage to another State Party to the Treaty or to its natural or juridical persons by such object or its component parts on the Earth, in air space or in outer space, including the moon and other celestial bodies.

Article VIII

A State Party to the Treaty on whose registry an object launched into outer space is carried shall retain jurisdiction and control over such object, and over any personnel thereof, while in outer space or on a celestial body. Ownership of objects launched into outer space, including objects landed or constructed on a celestial body, and of their component parts, is not affected by their presence in outer space or on a celestial body or by their return to the Earth. Such objects or component parts found beyond the limits of the State Party to the Treaty on whose registry they are carried shall be returned to that State Party, which shall, upon request, furnish identifying data prior to their return.

Article XI

In order to promote international co-operation in the peaceful exploration and use of outer space, States Parties to the Treaty conducting activities in outer space, including the moon and other celestial bodies, agree to inform the Secretary-General of the United Nations as well as the public and the international scientific community, to the greatest extent feasible and practicable, of the nature, conduct, locations and results of such activites. On receiving the said information, the Secretary-General of the United Nations should be prepared to disseminate it immediately and effectively.

Moon Treaty[42]
Agreement Governing the Activities of States on the Moon and Other Celestial Bodies
U.N. Doc. A/34/664; (1979), 18 *Int. Leg. Mat.* 1434 (In force 1984)

[The most important provisions of the Moon Treaty and the only ones that materially expand the principles of the Outer Space Treaty deal with the legal regime of lunar resources. These provisions, incorporating the concept of the common heritage of mankind, are the main reason for the refusal of a number of countries to ratify the Treaty.]

Article 1

1. The provisions of this Agreement relating to the moon shall also apply to other celestial bodies within the solar system, other than the earth, except in so far as specific legal norms enter into force with respect to any of these celestial bodies.

2. For the purposes of this Agreement reference to the moon shall include orbits around or other trajectories to or around it.

Article 6

1. There shall be freedom of scientific investigation on the moon by all States Parties without discrimination of any kind, on the basis of equality and in accordance with international law.

2. In carrying out scientific investigations and in furtherance of the provisions of this Agreement, the States Parties shall have the right to collect on and remove from the moon samples of its mineral and other substances. Such samples shall remain at the

---

[42] See C. Christol, "The Moon Treaty Enters into Force" (1985), 79 *Am. J. Int. L.* 163; E. Galloway, "Agreement Governing the Activities of States on the Moon and Other Celestial Bodies" (1980), 5 *Annals Air & Space L.* 481.

disposal of those States Parties which caused them to be collected and may be used by them for scientific purposes. States Parties shall have regard to the desirability of making a portion of such samples available to other interested States Parties and the international scientific community for scientific investigation. States Parties may in the course of scientific investigations also use mineral and other substances of the moon in quantities appropriate for the support of their missions.

Article 11

1. The moon and its natural resources are the common heritage of mankind, which finds its expression in the provision of this Agreement, in particular in paragraph 5 of this article.

2. The moon is not subject to national appropriation by any claim of sovereignty, by means of use or occupation, or by any other means.

3. Neither the surface nor the subsurface of the moon, nor any part thereof or natural resources in place, shall become the property of any State, international intergovernmental or non-governmental organization, national organization or non-governmental entity or of any natural person. The placement of personnel, space vehicles, equipment, facilities, stations and installations on or below the surface of the moon, including structures connected with its surface or subsurface, shall not create a right of ownership over the surface or the subsurface of the moon or any areas thereof. The foregoing provisions are without prejudice to the international régime referred to in paragraph 5 of this article.

4. States Parties have the right to exploration and use of the moon without discrimination of any kind, on the basis of equality and in accordance with international law and the provisions of this Agreement.

5. States Parties to this Agreement hereby undertake to establish an international régime, including appropriate procedures, to govern the exploitation of the natural resources of the moon as such exploitation is about to become feasible. This provision shall be implemented in accordance with article 18 of this Agreement.

6. In order to facilitate the establishment of the international régime referred to in paragraph 5 of this article, States Parties shall inform the Secretary-General of the United Nations as well as the public and the international scientific community, to the greatest extent feasible and practicable, of any natural resources they may discover on the moon.

7. The main purposes of the international régime to be established shall include:

(a) The orderly and safe development of the natural resources of the moon;

(b) The rational management of those resources;

(c) The expansion of opportunities in the use of those resources;

(d) An equitable sharing by all States Parties in the benefits derived from those resources, whereby the interests and needs of the developing countries, as well as the efforts of those countries which have contributed either directly or indirectly to the exploration of the moon, shall be given special consideration.

8. All the activities with respect to the natural resources of the moon shall be carried out in a manner compatible with the purposes specified in paragraph 7 of this article and the provisions of article 6, paragraph 2, of this Agreement.

Convention on International Liability for Damage Caused by Space Objects[43]
1975 Can. T.S. No. 7; 961 U.N.T.S. 187 (In force 1972)

[Next to the Outer Space Treaty, the Space Liability Convention is the most important international agreement relating to space activities. It provides that a launching state is liable for damage caused on the surface of the earth or to aircraft in flight by objects it sent into space. The Convention is one of the rare multilateral treaties that provide for absolute liability of states for damages.]

Article I

For the purposes of this Convention:
  (a) The term "damage" means loss of life, personal injury or other impairment of health; or loss of or damage to property of States or of persons, natural or juridical, or property of international intergovernmental organizations;
  (b) The term "launching" includes attempted launching;
  (c) The term "launching State" means:
    (i) A State which launches or procures the launching of a space object;
    (ii) A State from whose territory or facility a space object is launched;
  (d) The term "space object" includes component parts of a space object as well as its launch vehicle and parts thereof.

Article II

A launching State shall be absolutely liable to pay compensation for damage caused by its space object on the surface of the earth or to aircraft in flight.

Article III

In the event of damage being caused elsewhere than on the surface of the earth to a space object of one launching State or to persons or property on board such a space object by a space object of another launching State, the latter shall be liable only if the damage is due to its fault or the fault of persons for whom it is responsible.

Article IV

1. In the event of damage being caused elsewhere than on the surface of the earth to a space object of one launching State or to persons or property on board such a space object by a space object of another launching State, and of damage thereby being caused to a third State or to its natural or juridical persons, the first two States shall be jointly and severally liable to the third State, to the extent indicated by the following:

---

[43] C. Christol, "International Liability for Damage Caused by Space Objects" (1980), 74 *Am. J. Int. L.* 346; W. Foster, "The Convention on International Liability for Damage Caused by Space Objects" (1972), 10 *Can. Y.B. Int. L.* 137; S. Gorove, "Liability in Space Law: An Overview" (1983), 8 *Annals Air & Space L.* 373.

(a) If the damage has been caused to the third State on the surface of the earth or to aircraft in flight, their liability to the third State shall be absolute;

(b) If the damage has been caused to a space object of the third State or to persons or property on board that space object elsewhere than on the surface of the earth, their liability to the third State shall be based on the fault of either of the first two States or on the fault of persons for whom either is responsible.

2. In all cases of joint and several liability referred to in paragraph 1 of this article, the burden of compensation for the damage shall be apportioned between the first two States in accordance with the extent to which they were at fault; if the extent of the fault of each of these States cannot be established, the burden of compensation shall be apportioned equally between them. Such apportionment shall be without prejudice to the right of the third State to seek the entire compensation due under this Convention from any or all of the launching States which are jointly and severally liable.

Article V

1. Whenever two or more States jointly launch a space object, they shall be jointly and severally liable for any damage caused.

2. A launching State which has paid compensation for damage shall have the right to present a claim for indemnification to other participants in the joint launching. The participants in a joint launching may conclude agreements regarding the apportioning among themselves of the financial obligation in respect of which they are jointly and severally liable. Such agreements shall be without prejudice to the right of a State sustaining damage to seek the entire compensation due under this Convention from any or all of the launching States which are jointly and severally liable.

3. A State from whose territory or facility a space object is launched shall be regarded as a participant in joint launching.

Article VI

1. Subject to the provisions of paragraph 2 of this article, exoneration from absolute liability shall be granted to the extent that a launching State establishes that the damage has resulted either wholly or partially from gross negligence or from an act or omission done with intent to cause damage on the part of a claimant State or of natural or juridical persons it represents.

2. No exoneration whatever shall be granted in cases where the damage has resulted from activities conducted by a launching State which are not in conformity with international law including, in particular, the Charter of the United Nations and the Treaty on Principles Governing the Activities of States in the Exploration and Use of Outer Space, including the Moon and Other Celestial Bodies.

Article VIII

1. A State which suffers damage, or whose natural or juridical persons suffer damage, may present to a launching State a claim for compensation for such damage.

2. If the State of nationality has not presented a claim, another State may, in respect of damage sustained in its territory by any natural or juridical person, present a claim to a launching State.

3. If neither the State of nationality nor the State in whose territory the damage was sustained has presented a claim or notified its intention of presenting a claim, another State may, in respect of damage sustained by its permanent residents, present a claim to a launching State.

Article XI

1. Presentation of a claim to a launching State for compensation for damage under this Convention shall not require the prior exhaustion of any local remedies which may be available to a claimant State or to natural or juridical persons it represents. ...

Article XII

The compensation which the launching State shall be liable to pay for damage under this Convention shall be determined in accordance with international law and the principles of justice and equity, in order to provide such reparation in respect of the damage as will restore the person, natural or juridical, State or international organization on whose behalf the claim is presented to the condition which would have existed if the damage had not occurred.

Article XIII

Unless the claimant State and the State from which compensation is due under this Convention agree on another form of compensation, the compensation shall be paid in the currency of the claimant State or, if that State so requests, in the currency of the State from which compensation is due.

Article XIV

If no settlement of a claim is arrived at through diplomatic negotiations as provided for in article IX, within one year from the date on which the claimant State notifies the launching State that it has submitted the documentation of its claim, the parties concerned shall establish a Claims Commission at the request of either party.

Article XV

1. The Claims Commission shall be composed of three members: one appointed by the claimant State, one appointed by the lauching State and the third member, the Chairman, to be chosen by both parties jointly. Each party shall make its appointment within two months of the request for the establishment of the Claims Commission. ...

Article XVIII

The Claims Commission shall decide the merits of the claim for compensation and determine the amount of compensation payable, if any.

Article XIX

1. The Claims Commission shall act in accordance with the provisions of article XII.

2. The decision of the Commission shall be final and binding if the parties have so agreed; otherwise the Commission shall render a final and recommendatory award, which the parties shall consider in good faith. The Commission shall state the reasons for its decision or award.

3. The Commission shall give its decision or award as promptly as possible and no later than one year from the date of its establishment, unless an extension of this period is found necessary by the Commission.

NOTES

1) The Space Liability Convention was invoked by the Canadian Government in its claim for compensation for damage caused by the disintegration of Soviet satellite *Cosmos 954* over northern Canada in 1978. The claim is discussed in the context of "State Responsibility" in Chapter 9.

2) In anticipation of the first manned landing on the Moon, on the initiative of the United States, in 1968 the Agreement on the Rescue of Astronauts, the Return of Astronauts and the Return of Objects launched into Outer Space was concluded.[44] The Agreement provides for procedures for aiding and repatriating astronauts in the event of accident or emergency landing. The parties also agreed to recover and return space objects which fall on their territory to the state of registry. However, the party on whose territory such space object is found may withhold its return until the launching state furnishes data identifying the object as belonging to it.

3) The feasibility of earth observation from space was demonstrated soon after the launching of the first artificial satellite. The potential usefulness of satellites for exploring the natural resources of the earth through remote sensing was highlighted by the launching of the U.S. Landsat spacecraft in 1972. The U.N. Outer Space Committee established a Working Group on remote sensing as early as 1971. Ever since, the legal, scientific and technical aspects of satellite remote sensing have been under intensive study by the Committee. The original intention to draft a treaty regulating the use of remote sensing from space had to be abandoned when, after years of debate, no agreement could be reached on an acceptable text. Instead, in 1986, the Committee agreed on fifteen principles to be submitted to the U.N. General Assembly in the form of a resolution.[45] The main stumbling block to agreement concerned the question of whether or not prior consent is required for a launching state to conduct remote sensing of the territory of another state and to dispose of information acquired to third parties. The agreed principles enunciate that the concept of freedom of outer space applies also to remote sensing activities conducted by satellite (Principle IV). However, such activities must not be carried out in a manner prejudicial to the rights and interests of states being observed (Principle IV). The latter must have access to the data concerning their territory without discrimination and at reasonable cost (Principle XII).

---

[44] 1975 Can. T.S. No. 6; 72 U.N.T.S. 119.

[45] See 41 U.N. GAOR, Supp. (No. 20); U.N. Doc. A/41/20 (1986), Report of the Committee on the Peaceful Uses of Outer Space, Annex II, reprinted in (1986), 25 *Int. Leg. Mat.* 1334.

Direct Broadcasting Satellites

The question of the legal regulation of international direct television broadcasting by satellites (DBS) was placed on the agenda of the U.N. Committee on the Peaceful Uses of Outer Space in 1969. After a decade of intensive negotiations, in which Canada played a leading role, the Committee remained unable to produce a draft treaty acceptable to all states. Differences concerning the sovereign rights of states to control the flow of information and the scope of regulations proved to be insurmountable. Thus, instead of a treaty, the majority opted for a U.N. General Assembly resolution containing the following set of principles.

Principles Governing the Use by States of Artificial Earth Satellites for International Direct Television Broadcasting[46]
U.N.G.A.Res. A/RES/37/92 (1983)

The General Assembly,...

Considering that several experiments of direct broadcasting satellite systems are operational in some countries and may be commercialized in the very near future,

   Taking into consideration that the operation of international direct broadcasting satellites will have significant international political, economic, social and cultural implications, ...

   Adopts the Principles Governing the Use by States of Artificial Earth Satellites for International Direct Television Broadcasting set forth in the annex to the present resolution.

ANNEX

A. *Purposes and objectives*

   1. Activities in the field of international direct television broadcasting by satellite should be carried out in a manner compatible with the sovereign rights of States, including the principle of non-intervention, as well as with the right of everyone to seek, receive and impart information and ideas as enshrined in the relevant United Nations instruments.

   2. Such activities should promote the free dissemination and mutual exchange of information and knowledge in cultural and scientific fields, assist in educational, social

---

[46] Reprinted in (1983), *Int. Leg. Mat.* 451. The resolution was adopted by a vote of 107 in favour, 13 against, with 13 abstentions. Virtually all Western States voted either against the resolution (e.g., U.K. U.S.) or abstained (e.g., Canada, France). Generally see N. Matte, *Aerospace Law – Telecommunications Satellites* (1982). On the role of the International Telecommunication Union in the regulation of the radio spectrum, see G. Codding and A. Rutkowski, *The International Telecommunication Union in a Changing World* (1982); D. Leive, *International Telecommunications and International Law: The Regulation of the Radio Spectrum* (1970).

and economic development, particularly in the developing countries, enhance the qualities of life of all peoples and provide recreation with due respect to the political and cultural integrity of States.

3. These activities should accordingly be carried out in a manner compatible with the development of mutual understanding and the strengthening of friendly relations and co-operation among all States and peoples in the interest of maintaining international peace and security.

B. *Applicability of international law*

4. Activities in the field of international direct television broadcasting by satellite should be conducted in accordance with international law, including the Charter of the United Nations, the Treaty on Principles Governing the Activities of States in the Exploration and Use of Outer Space, including the Moon and Other Celestial Bodies, of 27 January 1967, the relevant provisions of the International Telecommunication Convention and its Radio Regulations and of international instruments relating to friendly relations and co-operation among States and to human rights.

C. *Rights and benefits*

5. Every State has an equal right to conduct activities in the field of international direct television broadcasting by satellite and to authorize such activities by persons and entities under its jurisdiction. All States and peoples are entitled to and should enjoy the benefits from such activities. Access to the technology in this field should be available to all States without discrimination on terms mutually agreed by all concerned.

D. *International co-operation*

6. Activities in the field of international direct television broadcasting by satellite should be based upon and encourage international co-operation. Such co-operation should be the subject of appropriate arrangements. Special consideration should be given to the needs of the developing countries in the use of international direct television broadcasting by satellite for the purpose of accelerating their national development.

E. *Peaceful settlement of disputes*

7. Any international dispute that may arise from activities covered by these principles should be settled through established procedures for the peaceful settlement of disputes agreed upon by the parties to the dispute in accordance with the provisions of the Charter of the United Nations.

F. *State responsibility*

8. States should bear international responsibility for activities in the field of international direct television broadcasting by satellite carried out by them or under their jurisdiction and for the conformity of any such activities with the principles set forth in this document.

9. When international direct television broadcasting by satellite is carried out by an international intergovernmental organization, the responsibility referred to in paragraph 8 above should be borne by that organization and by the States participating in it.

G. Duty and right to consult

10. Any broadcasting or receiving State within an international direct television broadcasting satellite service established between them requested to do so by any other broadcasting or receiving State within the same service should promptly enter into consultations with the requesting State regarding its activities in the field of international direct television broadcasting by satellite, without prejudice to other consultations which these States may undertake with any other State on that subject.

H. Copyright and neighbouring rights

11. Without prejudice to the relevant provisions of international law, States should co-operate on a bilateral and multilateral basis for protection of copyright and neighbouring rights by means of appropriate agreemtents between the interested States or the competent legal entities acting under their jurisdiction. In such co-operation they should give special consideration to the interests of developing countries in the use of direct television broadcasting for the purpose of accelerating their national development.

I. Notification to the United Nations

12. In order to promote international co-operation in the peaceful exploration and use of outer space, States conducting or authorizing activities in the field of international direct television broadcasting by satellite should inform the Secretary-General of the United Nations, to the greatest extent possible, of the nature of such activities. On receiving this information, the Secretary-General should disseminate it immediately and effectively to the relevant specialized agencies, as well as to the public and the international scientific community.

J. Consultations and agreements between States

13. A State which intends to establish or authorize the establishment of an international direct television broadcasting satellite service shall without delay notify the proposed receiving State or States of such intention and shall promptly enter into consultation with any of those States which so requests.

14. An international direct television broadcasting satellite service shall only be established after the conditions set forth in paragraph 13 above have been met and on the basis of agreements and/or arrangements in conformity with the relevant instruments of the International Telecommunication Union and in accordance with these principles.

15. With respect to the unavoidable overspill of the radiation of the satellite signal, the relevant instruments of the International Telecommunication Union shall be exclusively applicable.

The Geostationary Satellite Orbit

The so-called geostationary orbit is located above the equator, 35,871 kilometres from the surface of the Earth. It is the ideal location for communication satellites; when placed in that orbit a satellite viewed from the Earth appears to be stationary, remaining at all times in the same position. It was early realized that the geostationary orbit is a limited natural resource that can accommodate only a limited number of communiction satellites. The location of the orbit and its rapid saturation with satellites belonging to a handful of developed nations has led several equatorial states to adopt in Bogota, Columbia on December 3, 1976 a declaration on the legal status of that part of outer space.[47] The Declaration proclaimed the segments of geostationary synchronous orbit coinciding with the boundaries of the subjacent states to be "part of the territory over which Equatorial states exercise their national sovereignty."

The question of the legal regime for the geostationary orbit has been on the agenda of the Legal Subcommittee of the U.N. Committee on the Peaceful Uses of Outer Space since 1978 (on the recommendation of the U.N.G.A. resolution 196(XXXII), of December 1977).[48] The International Communication Union, through its World Administrative Radio Conference, has also been actively seeking a solution to the problem. As of December 1986, no agreement was in sight because a substantial number of states, including most of the leading users of space telecommunications, maintain that geostationary orbits are inseparable from outer space and therefore are fully subject to the relevant provisions of the 1967 Outer Space Treaty. Whereas the Outer Space Treaty contains no specific rules with respect to such orbits, it does prohibit national appropriation by claim of sovereignty, by means of use or occupation, or by any other means. Thus, on both legal and practical grounds, major users of the orbit refuse to accept the view that by reason of their geographical position the equatorial countries should be considered as having special rights to segments of the geostationary orbit superjacent to their territories.

NOTES

1) The question of where the sovereign airspace ends and free outer space begins, also known as the question of the definition and delimitation of outer space, continues to defy all attempts at resolution. The question was originally raised at the time of the first satellite launching, in 1957, and for the last fifteen years has been regularly on the agenda of the U.N. Outer Space Committee.[49] Some states, led by the United States, insist that there is no need at this time to establish by treaty the boundary between sovereign airspace and free outer space. A definition or delimitation of outer space should be undertaken, these states argue, only when a practical need for one arises. The Soviet Union, supported by a number of other States, has proposed to draw the boundary at an altitude between 100 km and 110km above sea level. Included in the Soviet proposal is a provision allowing "innocent passage" through the airspace of one state of a space object of another state for the purpose of reaching orbit or returning to Earth. It is safe to predict that when eventually a consensus is reached, the upper boundary of sovereign airspace will not be higher than 100 km above sea level.

2) The next major area of international regulation of space activities may well be

---

[47] The full text of the Bogota Declaration is reprinted in N. Jasentuliyana and R. Lee, eds., *Manual on Space Law* Vol. 2 (1979), at 383.
[48] See J. Fawcett, *Outer Space – New Challenges to Law and Policy* (1984), at 51–79; R. Jakhu, "The Legal

related to permanently manned space stations. The Soviet Union has been operating for quite some time a modest space station – "Salyut"– and is currently building in orbit the much bigger "Mir," capable of housing up to 20 cosmonauts. The United States, in cooperation with the European Space Agency, Canada and Japan, is planning to launch in low Earth orbit an international space station by the mid-1990s. Among the foreseeable legal problems one can identify criminal and civil jurisdiction over events aboard such a multinational station and over visiting foreign spaceships, as well as compliance with multilateral space treaties.[50]

Nuclear Power Sources in Outer Space

Shortly after the accident of the Soviet *Cosmos 954*, on the initiative of Canada, the question of satellites with nuclear power sources (NPS) on board was placed on the agenda of the U.N. Outer Space Committee. Both the United States and the Soviet Union have been operating nuclear-powered spacecraft since the 1960's, and according to one estimate the number of such satellites in orbit by 1978 was "within the range of 25–100."[51] Whereas up to now, NPS aboard satellites have had rather small capacity due to weight limitations, with the building of bigger space structures, it is very likely that much more powerful, and therefore much more hazardous, NPS will be stationed in outer space, in the relative vicinity of the Earth. Satellites carrying NPS do not operate in a legal vacuum; they are subject to the provisions of the Space Liability Convention and the Outer Space Treaty. Nonetheless, in the aftermath of the *Cosmos 954* accident Canada, supported by a number of other countries, submitted to the Legal Sub-Committee of the U.N. Outer Space Committee a comprehensive survey of relevant rules of space law and concluded that there was an urgent need for supplementing that body of law with special rules concerning the use of NPS. Canada proposed that new principles be elaborated and eventually incorporated in an international treaty. *Inter alia*, these principles would make it mandatory for a state launching a space object with NPS aboard to inform states concerned in the event of malfunctioning of the object, and to promptly offer, if requested, assistance to the states threatened by the malfunctioning spacecraft. By December 1986, these two principles had been agreed upon in the U.N. Working Group charged with the drafting of principles relevant to the use of NPS in outer space.[52]

Status of the Geostationary Orbit" (1982), 7 *Annals Air & Space L.* 333; and "The Evolution of the ITU's Regulatory Regime Governing Space Radiocommunication Services and the Geostationary Satellite Orbit" (1983), 8 *Annals Air & Space L.* 381.

[49] See U.N. Doc. A/AC 105/370, Report of the Legal Sub-Committee on the Work of Its Twenty-Fifth Session (1986), at 10 and 31.

[50] See, e.g. Congress of the United States, Office of Technology Assessment, *Space Stations and the Law: Selected Legal Issues* (1986); H. DeSaussure, "The Impact of Manned Space Stations on the Law of Outer Space" (1984), 21 *San Diego L. Rev.* 985; N. Matte, "Space Stations: A Peaceful Use for Humanity?" (1985), 10 *Annals Air & Space L.* 417.

[51] N. Jasentuliyana, "A Perspective of the Use of Nuclear Power Sources in Outer Space" (1979), 4 *Annals Air & Space L.* 519.

[52] See U.N. Doc. A/AC.105/370, Report of the Legal Sub-Comm. on the Work of its Twenty-Fifth Session (1986), at 16.

CHAPTER SEVEN

Nationality

INDIVIDUALS

Nationality is the basic link between an individual and the state. An individual has the nationality of the state that confers it. Domestic law controls its acquisition and loss. However, there must be a genuine link between the state granting the nationality and the individual. In *Re Lynch* it was stated that:[1]

A man's nationality forms a continuing state of things and not a physical fact which occurs at a particular moment. A man's nationality is a continuing relationship between the sovereign State on the one hand and the citizen on the other. The fundamental basis of a man's nationality is his membership of an independent political community. This legal relationship involves rights and corresponding duties upon both – on the part of the citizen no less than on the part of the State.

The link of nationality is so important in international law because it is the basis of a state's jurisdiction over persons, both human and juridical, beyond its territory. Nationality is a two way relationship. Rights and obligations are implicit in a conferral of nationality by a state upon an individual. A state may formally espouse only the claims of its nationals in cases of injury done by another state; a state will be responsible for acts of its nationals undertaken on behalf of the state or, when done privately if the state has not been diligent in preventing the wrongful acts or in punishing them; states may only impose military service on their nationals unless an exemption has been granted by the national state of

---

[1] (1929–30), 5 *Ann. Dig.* 221, at 222 (U.S.-Mexico General Claims Commission). And see generally P. Weis, *Nationality and Statelessness in International Law* (2 ed., 1978); A.P. Mutharika, *The Right of Statelessness under International and National Law* (Looseleaf, 2 vols.); and S. Slosar, "La Citoyenneté canadienne et ses effets juridiques" (1979), 10 *Rev. de Droit U.* Sherbrooke 157.

the alien;[2] some states refuse to extradite their own nationals and correlatively have provisions in their penal law for criminal jurisdiction over the offence based on nationality.

The last fifty years has seen the emergence of rights on the part of the individual as well as obligations to the international community, as evidenced by individual criminal responsibility for war crimes, crimes against peace, crimes against humanity, genocide, *apartheid* and torture. The rights have been encapsulated in a hundred international human rights instruments. All these incidents of nationality are discussed in the subsequent chapters 8, 9 and 10 on Jurisdiction over Persons, State Responsibility and the Protection of Human Rights. This chapter explores the rules of nationality itself, starting with the need for a genuine link between state and individual.

Nottebohm Case
Liechtenstein v. Guatemala
[1955] I.C.J. Rep.4

[This case was submitted on December 17, 1951, by an application filed by Liechtenstein against Guatemala, claiming damages in respect of various war measures which Guatemala had taken against the person and property of Friedrich Nottebohm, who was born a German national but who was alleged to have become a citizen of Liechtenstein. Guatemala objected that Liechtenstein's claim was inadmissible: it thus put in issue the nationality of Nottebohm.]

THE COURT: ... In order to decide upon the admissibility of the Application, the Court must ascertain whether the nationality conferred on Nottebohm by Liechtenstein by means of a naturalization ... can be validly invoked as against Guatemala, whether it bestows upon Liechtenstein a sufficient title to the exercise of protection in respect of Nottebohm as against Guatemala and therefore entitles it to seise the Court of a claim relating to him. In this connection, Counsel for Liechtenstein said: "the essential question is whether Mr. Nottebohm, having acquired the nationality of Liechtenstein, that acquisition of nationality is one which must be recognized by other States". This formulation is accurate, subject to the twofold reservation that, in the first place, what is involved is not recognition for all purposes but merely for the purposes of the admissibility of the Application, and, secondly, that what is involved is not recognition by all States but only by Guatemala.

The Court does not propose to go beyond the limited scope of the question which it has to decide, namely whether the nationality conferred on Nottebohm can be relied upon as against Guatemala in justification of the proceedings instituted before the Court. It must decide this question on the basis of international law; to do so is consistent with the nature of the question and with the nature of the Court's own function. ...

Since no proof has been adduced that Guatemala has recognized the title to the exercise of protection relied upon by Liechtenstein as being derived from the naturalization which

---

[2] Some states have imposed this duty on permanent residents. See *Polites v. The Commonwealth* (1945), 70 C.L.R. 60 (Aust. H.C.).

it granted to Nottebohm, the Court must consider whether such an act of granting nationality by Liechtenstein directly entails an obligation on the part of Guatemala to recognize its effect, namely, Liechtenstein's right to exercise its protection. In other words, it must be determined whether that unilateral act by Liechtenstein is one which can be relied upon against Guatemala in regard to the exercise of protection. The Court will deal with this question without considering that of the validity of Nottebohm's naturalization according to the law of Liechtenstein.

It is for Liechtenstein, as it is for every sovereign State, to settle by its own legislation the rules relating to the acquisition of its nationality, and to confer that nationality by naturalization granted by its own organs in accordance with that legislation. It is not necessary to determine whether international law imposes any limitation on its freedom of decision in this domain. Furthermore, nationality has its most immediate, its most far-reaching and, for most people, its only effects within the legal system of the State conferring it. Nationality serves above all to determine that the person upon whom it is conferred enjoys the rights and is bound by the obligations which the law of the State in question grants to or imposes on its nationals. This is implied in the wider concept that nationality is within the domestic jurisdiction of the State.

But the issue which the Court must decide is not one which pertains to the legal system of Liechtenstein. It does not depend on the law or on the decision of Liechtenstein whether that State is entitled to exercise its protection, in the case under consideration. To exercise protection, to apply to the Court, is to place oneself on the plane of international law. It is international law which determines whether a State is entitled to exercise protection and to seise the Court.

The naturalization of Nottebohm was an act performed by Liechtenstein in the exercise of its domestic jurisdiction. The question to be decided is whether that act has the international effect here under consideration.

International practice provides many examples of acts performed by States in the exercise of domestic jurisdiction which do not necessarily or automatically have international effect, which are not necessarily and automatically binding on other States or which are binding on them only subject to certain conditions: this is the case, for instance, of a judgement given by the competent court of a State which it is sought to invoke in another State.

... In most cases arbitrators have not strictly speaking had to decide a conflict of nationality as between States, but rather to determine whether the nationality invoked by the applicant State was one which could be relied upon as against the respondent State, that is to say, whether it entitled the applicant State to exercise protection. International arbitrators, having before them allegations of nationality by the applicant State which were contested by the respondent State, have sought to ascertain whether nationality had been conferred by the applicant State in circumstances such as to give rise to an obligation on the part of the respondent State to recognize the effect of that nationality. In order to decide this question arbitrators have evolved certain principles for determining whether full international effect was to be attributed to the nationality invoked. The same issue is now before the Court: it must be resolved by applying the same principles.

... International arbitrators have decided in the same way numerous cases of dual nationality, where the question arose with regard to the exercise of protection. They have given their preference to the real and effective nationality, that which accorded with the facts, that based on stronger factual ties between the person concerned and one of the States whose nationality is involved. Different factors are taken into consideration, and their importance will vary from one case to the next: the habitual residence of the individual concerned is an important factor, but there are other factors such as the centre of his interests, his family ties, his participation in public life, attachment shown by him for a given country and inculcated in his children, etc.

Similarly, the courts of third States, when they have before them an individual whom two other States hold to be their national, seek to resolve the conflict by having recourse to international criteria and their prevailing tendency is to prefer the real and effective nationality.

The same tendency prevails in the writings of publicists and in practice. This notion is inherent in the provisions of Article 3, paragraph 2, of the Statute of the Court. National laws reflect this tendency when, *inter alia*, they make naturalization dependent on conditions indicating the existence of a link, which may vary in their purpose or in their nature but which are essentially concerned with this idea. The Liechtenstein Law of January 4th, 1934, is a good example.

The practice of certain States which refrain from exercising protection in favour of a naturalized person when the latter has in fact, by his prolonged absence, severed his links with what is no longer for him anything but his nominal country, manifests the view of these States that, in order to be capable of being invoked against another State, nationality must correspond with the factual situation. A similar view is manifested in the relevant provisions of the bilateral nationality treaties concluded between the United States of America and other States since 1868, such as those sometimes referred to as the Bancroft Treaties, and in the Pan-American Convention, signed at Rio de Janeiro on August 13th, 1906, on the status of naturalized citizens who resume residence in their country of origin.

The character thus recognized on the international level as pertaining to nationality is in no way inconsistent with the fact that international law leaves it to each State to lay down the rules governing the grant of its own nationality. The reason for this is that the diversity of demographic conditions has thus far made it impossible for any general agreement to be reached on the rules relating to nationality, although the latter by its very nature affects international relations. It has been considered that the best way of making such rules accord with the varying demographic conditions in different countries is to leave the fixing of such rules to the competence of each State. On the other hand, a State cannot claim that the rules it has thus laid down are entitled to recognition by another State unless it has acted in conformity with this general aim of making the legal bond of nationality accord with the individual's genuine connection with the State which assumes the defence of its citizens by means of protection as against other States. The requirement that such a concordance must exist is to be found in the studies carried on in the course of the last thirty years upon the initiative and under the auspices of the League of Nations and the United Nations. It explains the provision which the Conference for the Codification of International Law, held at The Hague in 1930, inserted in Article I of the Convention relating to the Conflict of Nationality Laws, laying down that the law enacted by a State for the purpose of determining who are its nationals "shall be recognized by other States in so far as it is consistent with ... international custom, and the principles of law generally recognized with regard to nationality." In the same spirit, Article 5 of the Convention refers to criteria of the individual's genuine connections for the purpose of resolving questions of dual nationality which arise in third States.

According to the practice of States, to arbitral and judicial decisions and to the opinions of writers, nationality is a legal bond having as its basis a social fact of attachment, a genuine connection of existence, interests and sentiments, together with the existence of reciprocal rights and duties. It may be said to constitute the juridical expression of the fact that the individual upon whom it is conferred, either directly by the law or as the result of an act of the authorities, is in fact more closely connected with the population of the State conferring nationality than with that of any other State. Conferred by a State, it only entitles that State to exercise protection vis-a-vis another State, if it constitutes a translation into juridical terms of the individual's connection with the State which has made him its national. ...

Since this is the character which nationality must present when it is invoked to furnish the State which has granted it with a title to the exercise of protection and to the institution of international judicial proceedings, the Court must ascertain whether the nationality granted to Nottebohm by means of naturalization is of this character or, in other words, whether the factual connection between Nottebohm and Liechtenstein in the period preceding, contemporaneous with and following his naturalization appears to be sufficiently close, so preponderant in relation to any connection which may have existed between him and any other State, that it is possible to regard the nationality conferred upon him as real and effective, as the exact juridical expression of a social fact of a connection which existed previously or came into existence thereafter.

Naturalization is not a matter to be taken lightly. To seek and to obtain it is not something that happens frequently in the life of a human being. It involves his breaking of a bond of allegiance and his establishment of a new bond of allegiance. It may have far-reaching consequences and involve profound changes in the destiny of the individual who obtains it. It concerns him personally, and to consider it only from the point of view of its repercussions with regard to his property would be to misunderstand its profound significance. In order to appraise its international effect, it is impossible to disregard the circumstances in which it was conferred, the serious character which attaches to it, the real and effective, and not merely the verbal preference of the individual seeking it for the country which grants it to him.

At the time of his naturalization does Nottebohm appear to have been more closely attached by his tradition, his establishment, his interests, his activities, his family ties, his intentions for the near future to Liechtenstein than to any other State? ...

The essential facts are as follows:

At the date when he applied for naturalization Nottebohm had been a German national from the time of his birth. He had always retained his connections with members of his family who had remained in Germany and he had always had business connections with that country. His country had been at war for more than a month, and there is nothing to indicate that the application for naturalization then made by Nottebohm was motivated by any desire to dissociate himself from the Government of his country.

He had been settled in Guatemala for 34 years. He had carried on his activities there. It was the main seat of his interests. He returned there shortly after his naturalization, and it remained the centre of his interests and of his business activities. He stayed there until his removal as a result of war measures in 1943. He subsequently attempted to return there, and he now complains of Guatemala's refusal to admit him. There, too, were several members of his family who sought to safeguard his interests.

In contrast, his actual connections with Liechtenstein were extremely tenuous. No settled abode, no prolonged residence in that country at the time of his application for naturalization: the application indicates that he was paying a visit there and confirms the transient character of this visit by its request that the naturalization proceedings should be initiated and concluded without delay. No intention of settling there was shown at that time or realized in the ensuing weeks, months or years – on the contrary, he returned to Guatemala very shortly after his naturalization and showed every intention of remaining there. If Nottebohm went to Liechtenstein in 1946, this was because of the refusal of Guatemala to admit him. No indication is given of the grounds warranting the waiver to the condition of residence, required by the 1934 Nationality Law, which waiver was implicitly granted to him. There is no allegation of any economic interests or of any activities exercised or to be exercised in Liechtenstein, and no manifestation of any intention whatsoever to transfer all or some of his interests and his business activities to Liechtenstein. It is unnecessary in this connection to attribute much importance to the promise to pay the taxes levied at the time of his naturalization. The only links to be discovered between the Principality and Nottebohm are the short sojourns already referred to and the presence in Vaduz of one of his brothers: but his brother's presence is referred to in his application for naturalization only as a reference to his good conduct. Furthermore, other members of his family have asserted Nottebohm's desire to spend his old age in Guatemala.

These facts clearly establish, on the one hand, the absence of any bond of attachment between Nottebohm and Liechtenstein and, on the the other hand, the existence of a long-standing and close connection between him and Guatemala, a link which his naturalization in no way weakened. That naturalization was not based on any real prior connection with Liechtenstein, nor did it in any way alter the manner of life of the person upon whom it was conferred in exceptional circumstances of speed and accommodation. In both respects, it was lacking in the genuineness requisite to an act of such importance, if it is to be entitled to be respected by a State in the position of Guatemala. It was granted without regard to the concept of nationality adopted in international relations.

Naturalization was asked for not so much for the purpose of obtaining a legal recognition of Nottebohm's membership in fact in the population of Liechtenstein, as it was to enable him to substitute for his status as a national of a belligerent State that of a national of a neutral State, with the sole aim of thus coming within the protection of Liechtenstein but not of becoming wedded to its traditions, its interests, its way of life or of assuming the obligations – other than fiscal obligations – and exercising the rights pertaining to the status thus acquired.

Guatemala is under no obligation to recognize a nationality granted in such circumstances. Liechtenstein consequently is not entitled to extend its protection to Nottebohm vis-à-vis Guatemala. ...

For these reasons,

The Court,

by eleven votes to three,

Holds that the claim submitted by the Government of the Principality of Liechtenstein is inadmissible.

NOTES

1) Is there a general principle of international law requiring a genuine link for the conferment of Nationality? Is "genuine" the same as "effective"?[3]

2) Why was it not relevant that Liechtenstein's law provided for loss of any prior nationality and Germany's law provided for loss of German nationality on acquisition of another nationality?

3) Could Liechtenstein have espoused a claim on behalf of Nottebohm against Germany? Could Guatemala have protected him against any state? If Nottebohm had in fact been born in Liechtenstein, and had become a permanent resident of Guatemala, could Liechtenstein have espoused a claim against Guatemala? Should Germany alone have been able to contest Nottebohm's naturalization? Note the importance in the eyes of the Court of the comparative ties of Nottebohm to Liechtenstein and Guatemala.[4]

Acquisition of Nationality
from S.A. Williams and A.L.C. de Mestral
An Introduction to International Law
(2ed., 1987), at 290, 292.

It is important to realize at the outset that although in referring to the status of an individual the terms citizen and national are used synonymously, in fact nationality is wider in scope. The term "citizen" refers to a person who is endowed with full political and civil rights in the state concerned. The term "national" although it includes a citizen also refers to a person who is not a citizen but yet has a right to the protection of the state and in turn owes allegiance to it. A national may be denied the rights of citizenship but will not lose the nationality itself on this basis. Thus, for example in *Kahane v. Parisi and the Austrian State*[5] it was held that although Jewish persons in Romania were denied the privileges of citizenship in many cases, they were still nationals of that state. ... Although it is up to the domestic law of each state to set down its own requirements, nevertheless the practice of states shows that most nationality laws have certain features in common.

---

[3] See I. Brownlie, *Principles of Public International Law* (3ed., 1979), at 396–98, 418.

[4] See Chapter 9 on "State Responsibility" for an analysis of the nationality of claims issue. See also the *Flegenheimer Claim* (1958), 25 I.L.R. 91 (Italian-United States Conciliation Committee); the *Canevaro* case (Italy v. Peru) (1912), 11 R.I.A.A. 397, translated in (1912), 6 *Am. J. Int. L.* 746, reported later in this section together with the *Hague Convention on Certain Questions Relating to the Conflict of Nationality Laws* (1930), 179 L.N.T.S. 89.

[5] (1929–30), 5 *Ann. Dig.* 213.

(a) Jus Soli and Jus Sanguinis

Nationality may be acquired by birth. This may result from birth in the territory of the state (*jus soli*) or from birth outside the territory of the state, but to parents who are nationals of the state (*jus sanguinis*). Some states have adopted one or the other of these principles. Others such as the United Kingdom and Canada have utilized both. ...

(b) Naturalization

This term is used in its widest sense to cover the acquistion of nationality after birth. Technically, it refers to an alien receiving a foreign nationality upon an application made by him. In general, nationality by naturalization may be acquired by one of several different methods: direct naturalization of a person under general naturalization laws, which in some countries is a judicial process, in others a legislative process and in still others an executive process; derivative naturalization, where for example a child who is minor becomes naturalized because of the naturalization of either or both his parents, where a spouse becomes naturalized through the other spouse's naturalization, or where an alien becomes naturalized through marriage to a citizen; adoption of an alien minor; group or collective naturalization, which occurs through the transfer of territory from one state to another, or where a state passes legislation with special reference to a certain class of persons and special legislation in individual cases.

Canadian Citizenship Act
S.C. 1974–75–76, c. 108, as am.

[Acquisition of Canadian citizenship by birth is regulated by section 3(1), as follows:]
Subject to this Act, a person is a citizen if
  (a) he was born in Canada after the coming into force of this Act;
  (b) he was born outside Canada after the coming into force of this Act and at the time of his birth one of his parents, other than a parent who adopted him, was a citizen;
[The Canadian Act is restrictive in its approach to the *jus soli* principle as illustrated by section 3(2), which provides:]
Paragraph 3(1)(a) does not apply to a person if, at the time of his birth, neither of his parents was a citizen or lawfully admitted to Canada for permanent residence and either of his parents was
  (a) a diplomatic or consular officer or other representative or employee in Canada of a foreign government;
  (b) an employee in the service of a person referred to in paragraph (a); or
  (c) an officer or employee in Canada of a specialized agency of the United Nations or an officer or employee in Canada of any other international organization to whom there is granted, by or under any Act of the Parliament of Canada, diplomatic privileges and immunities certified by the Secretary of State for External Affairs to be equivalent to those granted to a person or persons referred to in paragraph (a).
[Naturalization in Canada is governed by section 5 of the *Citizenship Act*, which provides in part:]

(1) The Minister shall grant citizenship to any person who, not being a citizen, makes application therefore and

  (a) is eighteen years of age or over;

  (b) has been lawfully admitted to Canada for permanent residence, ... and has, within the four years immediately preceding ... accumulated at least three years of residence in Canada; ...

  (c) has an adequate knowledge of one of the official languages of Canada;

  (d) has an adequate knowledge of Canada and of the responsibilities and privileges of citizenship; and

  (e) is not under a deportation order and is not the subject of a declaration by the Governor in Council made pursuant to section 17.

(2) The Minister shall grant citizenship

  (a) to any person, who not being a citizen, has been lawfully admitted to Canada for permanent residence and is the minor child of a citizen if an application for citizenship is made to the Minister by a person authorized by regulation to make the application on behalf of the minor child; ...

(3) The Minister may, in his discretion, waive on compassionate grounds,

  (a) in the case of any person, the requirements of paragraph (1)(c) or (d); and

  (b) in the case of any person under a disability, the requirement respecting age set forth in paragraph (1)(a), the requirement respecting length of residence in Canada set forth in paragraph (1)(b) or the requirement that the person take the oath of citizenship.

(4) In order to alleviate cases of special and unusual hardship or to reward services of an exceptional value to Canada, and notwithstanding any other provisions of this Act, the Governor in Council may, in his discretion, direct the Minister to grant citizenship to any person and, where such a direction is made, the Minister shall forthwith grant citizenship to the person named in the direction.

(5) A Canadian citizen, whether or not he is born in Canada, is entitled to all rights, powers and privileges and is subject to all obligations, duties and liabilities to which a person who is a citizen under paragraph 3(1)(a) is entitled or subject and has a like status to that of such persons.

Dual Nationality

By an application of the *jus sanguinis* and *jus soli* principles, coupled with naturalization an individual may have more than one nationality.

Hague Convention on Conflict of Nationality Laws
179 L.N.T.S. 89; 1930 Can. T.S. No.7.

Article 1

It is for each state to determine under its own law who are its nationals. This law shall be recognized by other States in so far as it is consistent with international conventions, international custom and the principles of law generally recognized with regard to nationality.

Article 2

Any question as to whether a person possesses the nationality of a particular State shall be determined in accordance with the laws of that State.

Article 3

Subject to the provisions of the present convention, a person having two or more nationalities may be regarded as its national by each of the States whose nationality he possesses.

Article 4

A State may not afford diplomatic protection to one of its nationals against a State whose nationality such person also possesses.

Article 5

Within a third State, a person having more than one nationality shall be treated as if he had only one. Without prejudice to the application of its law in matters of personal status and of any conventions in force, a third State shall, of the nationalities which any such person possesses, recognize exclusively in its territory either the nationality of the country in which he is habitually and principally resident, or the nationality of the country with which in the circumstances he appears to be most closely connected.

Article 6

Without prejudice to the liberty of a State to accord wider rights to renounce its nationality, a person possessing two nationalities acquired without any voluntary act on his part may renounce one of them with the authorization of the State whose nationality he desires to surrender.

This authorization may not be refused in the case of a person who has his habitual and permanent residence abroad, if the conditions laid down in the law of the State whose nationality he desires to surrender are satisfied.

Canevaro Case
Italy v. Peru
(1912), 11 R.I.A.A. 397; 6 *Am. J. Int. L.* 746
Permanent Court of Arbitration, The Hague

[This case concerned a claim made by Italy against Peru for a debt owed by that government to the Canevaro brothers. Concerning the status of Raphael Canevaro, the Court held that he was a Peruvian by birth and an Italian under article 4 of the Italian Civil Code, which assigned him that nationality because his father was Italian.]

THE COURT: ... And whereas, as a matter of fact, Raphael Canevaro has on several occasions acted as a Peruvian citizen, both by running as a candidate for the Senate, where none are admitted except Peruvian citizens and where he went to defend his election, and also especially by accepting the office of Consul General of the Netherlands, after soliciting the authorization of the Peruvian Government and the Peruvian Congress;

And whereas, under these circumstances, whatever Raphael Canevaro's status may be in Italy with respect to his nationality, the Government of Peru has a right to consider him as a Peruvian citizen and to deny his status as an Italian claimant;

And whereas, the claim of 1880 belongs at present to the three Canevaro brothers, two of whom are certainly Italians;

And one is justified in wondering whether this circumstance renders the law of 1889 inapplicable;

And whereas, the tribunal need not inquire what decision should be reached if the claim had belonged to Italians at the time the law was enacted which reduced to so large an extent the rights of the creditors of Peru, and whether the same sacrifices could be imposed on foreigners as on natives;

But at present it is solely a question of ascertaining whether the situation in which natives are placed, and which they have to accept, will be radically modified because foreigners are substituted for natives in one form or another; ...

NOTES

1) The Court held that Raphael Canevaro could not succeed against Peru. His two brothers who were solely Italians were successful in their claim.

2) Nationality laws may provide the individual with an option to retain or renounce nationality. Section 8 of the Canadian *Citizenship Act*[6] provides:

(1) A citizen may, upon application, renounce his citizenship if he

(a) is a citizen of a country other than Canada or, if his application is accepted, will become a citizen of a country other than Canada;

(b) is not the subject of a declaration by the Governor in Council made pursuant to section 18;

(c) is not under a disability; and

(d) does not reside in Canada.

(2) The Minister may, in his discretion, waive on compassionate grounds the requirements of paragraph (1)(c) or (d) with respect to any person who is not a minor.

(3) Where an application for renunciation is approved, the Minister shall issue a certificate of renunciation to the applicant and the applicant ceases to be a citizen after the expiration of the day on which the certificate is issued or such later day as the certificate may specify.

3) In reply to an enquiry about the possibility of a Canadian holding dual nationality

---

[6] Stats. Can. 1974–75–76, c. 108, as am.

becoming liable to foreign military service, the Department of External Affairs wrote in March 1968:[7]

... Many countries do not recognize the acquisition of another nationality by their citizens as affecting in any way the citizenship they already possess and are not prepared to relieve such persons of the responsibilities and obligations which devolve upon their citizens. Since this practice has the sanction of international law the authorities of the countries concerned are entitled in their territory to require all their citizens, whether dual nationals or otherwise, to comply with the stipulations of their laws, just as Canada insists that Canadian citizens who are also nationals of another country must be treated in Canada as having the same rights, privileges and responsibilities as all other Canadian citizens. It is considerations of this sort that have prompted us to issue a relevant caveat to Canadians with dual nationality in the pamphlet "Information for Canadians Travelling Overseas". ...

Statelessness

Statelessness can arise through a variety of circumstances: conflicts of nationality laws, changes of sovereignty over territory[8] or through denationalization by the state.

Stoeck v. Public Trustee
[1921] 2 Ch. 67

RUSSELL J.: The plaintiff sues the Public Trustee and the Attorney-General for a declaration that he was not on January 10, 1920 (the date when the Treaty of Peace with Germany came into force), and is not, a German national within the meaning of the Treaty of Peace Order, 1919, or the Treaty of Peace; and he also asks for other relief. The object of his action is to ascertain whether certain property in this country—namely, (i) a sum of 2722 pounds 11s. 6d.; (ii) a balance at the bank of 172 pounds 9s. 4d; and (iii) some furniture in store—are subject to the charge created by s. 1, sub-s. XVI, of the Treaty of Peace Order, and whether he can deal with such property without incurring the pains and penalties prescribed by sub-s. XVII of the same section. ...

The relevant personal history of the plaintiff is as follows: He was born in 1872 at Kreuznach in Rhenish Prussia. In October, 1895, he left Prussia and went to reside in Belgium. On June 26, 1896, he obtained his discharge from Prussian Nationality. He never subsequently applied for, or obtained the nationality of any German state. In November, 1896, he came to England, and made this country his permanent home. He was never naturalized here. In May, 1916, he was interned. In 1918 he was deported to Holland; thence he went to Germany and has resided there ever since. ...

The relevant question affecting the plaintiff is this: Is his property here property belonging to a German national and, therefore, property which is charged by the Treaty

---

[7] Quoted in J.G. Castel, *International Law* (3ed, 1976), at 464.
[8] See *supra*, Chapter 2, the discussion on "State Succession."

of Peace Order, and which he may not deal with except with the consent of the custodian or at the risk of fine and imprisonment? ...

The question for me to decide in this connection is whether the plaintiff on the evidence before me has satisfied me that he has lost his German nationality for all purposes. ...

This evidence satisfies me that the plaintiff has lost his German nationality for all purposes. It is not suggested that he has acquired any other nationality. If then such a condition is possible in law the plaintiff is a person of no nationality; he is a stateless person. Is such a condition possible in law? So far as international law is concerned, opinions appear to differ. ... After all the question of what State a person belongs to must ultimately be decided by the municipal law of the State to which he claims that he belongs; and, if no state exists according to the municipal law of which a given individual is its national, it is difficult to see to what State he can belong, how he can be other than a stateless person, or why an international lawyer or any one else should close his eyes to such a possibility.

How does the matter stand as regards German municipal law? It is clear on the evidence before me that German municipal law recognized the condition of a stateless person. ...

How does the matter stand in regard to English municipal law? ... The dearth of direct authority in English law upon this point is not to be wondered at. In truth the question of statelessness can have seldom arisen as an important or practical question. The division into subjects and aliens is clear and sufficient for the ordinary purposes of the common law; and the stateless person would be one of the aliens. But the present case has raised the question, and, upon consideration of the arguments addressed to me and the statutory enactments before referred to, I hold that the condition of a stateless person is not a condition unrecognized by the municipal law of this country.

There remains for consideration the contention that the words "German national" in the Treaty of Peace Order, and s. iv. of Part X of the Treaty of Peace, mean or include a German national according to English law. I confess I have difficulty in following this. Whether a person is a national of a country must be determined by the municipal law of that country. Upon this I think all text writers are agreed. It would be strange were it otherwise. How could the municipal law of England determine that a person *is* a national of Germany? It might determine that for the purposes of English municipal law a person shall be deemed to be a national of Germany, or shall be treated as if he were a national of Germany; but that would not constitute him a national of Germany, if he were not such according to the municipal law of Germany. In truth there is not and cannot be such an individual as a German national according to English law; and there could be no justification for interpreting or expanding the words "German national" in the manner suggested.

[A declaration for the plaintiff was granted.]

Problems of the Stateless Individual
from S.A. Williams and A.L.C. de Mestral
An Introduction to International Law
(2ed., 1987), at 289–90 (footnotes omitted)

The problem is a serious one, as persons without a nationality are under an extreme disability. Article 15 of the Universal Declaration of Human Rights, 1948 which was adopted by the General Assembly of the United Nations, lays down as a common standard to be achieved by states that "everyone has the right to a nationality."

The questions to be answered are how does such a condition arise and what can be done to prevent it? Answering the first is the simpler task. There are thousands of individuals who suffer this condition or whose nationality is a matter of dispute. At the present time, it is the prerogative of states to adopt their own nationality laws and there is no restriction on their liberty to adopt rules which may result in statelessness. For example, James Brown is born in state A of parents whose nationality is that of state B, while they are on holiday in state A. Under the law of state B, nationality is only given on the basis of birth on the territory of state B according to the *jus soli* principle. The law of state A provides that its nationality is only acquired at birth by individuals whose parents are nationals of state A. In this situation, James Brown would have neither the nationality of state A nor of state B. Statelessness may also result if nationality is taken away as a penalty or otherwise. Statelessness shows clearly that through the application of domestic laws in several states, a serious lacuna is left which threatens the application of the principles of international law.

What measures has the international community taken to reduce statelessness? Conventions have been signed that deal with the subject, but it must be remembered that the stumbling block to a solution is that it is the domestic law that deals with the subject at the state and individual levels. The 1948 Universal Declaration of Human Rights states that besides the fact that everyone should possess a nationality, no one should be arbitrarily deprived of nationality. This principle of possession is one that has been easily accepted by states but, as mentioned above, uniform practice has been hard to come by as each state has its own nationality laws which often can be at variance with those of another state. The United Nations Convention on the Reduction of Statelessness of 1961 ... achieved a limited measure of headway. It provides, *inter alia*, that persons who would otherwise be stateless should acquire the nationality of the state of birth.

The only way to prevent this disabling condition is to ensure that states take a flexible approach and do in fact allow for both the use of the *jus soli* and *jus sanguinis* theories, to oblige states not to adopt legislation that has the effect of denationalization, to encourage a liberal approach on the conferment of nationality on stateless persons and lastly to grant relief to such persons through international conventions which allow the use of identity or travel documents and to ensure the admission of such persons to states and employment within those states, thus leading to eventual nationalization.

Convention on the Status of Refugees[9]
(1954), 189 U.N.T.S. 137; 1969, Can. T.S. No. 6

Article 1

A. For the purposes of the present Convention, the term "refugee" shall apply to any person who: ...

---

[9] In force 1954. See also the Protocol Relating to the Status of Refugees (1967), 606 U.N.T.S. 267; 1969 Can.

(2) ...owing to well-founded fear of being persecuted for reasons of race, religion, nationality, membership of a particular social group or political opinion, is outside the country of his nationality and is unable or, owing to such fear, is unwilling to avail himself of the protection of that country; or who, not having a nationality and being outside the country of his former habitual residence as a result of such events, is unable or, owing to such fear, is unwilling to return to it.

Article 32

1. The Contracting States shall not expel a refugee lawfully in their territory save on grounds of national security or public order.

2. The expulsion of such a refugee shall be only in pursuance of a decision reached in accordance with due process of law. ...

3. The Contracting States shall allow such a refugee a reasonable period within which to seek legal admission into another country. ...

Article 33

1. No Contracting State shall expel or return ("refouler") a refugee in any manner whatsoever to the frontiers of territories where his life or freedom would be threatened on account of his race, religion, nationality, membership of a particular social group or political opinion. ...

NOTES

1) One solution open to some displaced individuals is to seek refugee status. The Refugee Convention does not confer upon refugees a right of entry to any state but, once admitted, they are guaranteed protection and other human rights intended to encourage their resettlement.

2) The definition of a refugee under the Convention is very restricted. It excludes millions of people who seek refuge, for instance, as a result of fleeing from national disasters or civil war. The most pressing need for these uprooted people is territorial asylum, but no right to asylum is yet assured by international law. The Universal Declaration of Human Rights states only that "Everyone has the right to seek and enjoy in other countries asylum from persecution" (Article 14). At the U.N. Conference on Territorial Asylum in 1977 member states failed to conclude a convention. Efforts to find

---

T.S. No. 29. (in force 1967). See generally A. Grahl-Madsen, *The Status of Refugees in International Law* (1972).

both temporary and long term solutions to the problems of refugees generally continue under the U.N. High Commissioner for Refugees.[10]

Marriage

At one time a woman automatically acquired her husband's nationality. Today, many states have abrogated this provision and the foreign woman will have a choice. It is a recognition in international law of gender equality.

Convention on the Nationality of Married Women
(1957), 309 U.N.T.S. 66; 1960 Can. T.S. No. 2.

Article 1

Each Contracting State agrees that neither the celebration nor the dissolution of a marriage between one of its nationals and an alien, nor the change of nationality by the husband during marriage, shall automatically affect the nationality of the wife.

Article 2

Each Contracting State agrees that neither the voluntary acquisition of the nationality of another State nor the renunciation of its nationality by one of its nationals shall prevent the retention of its nationality by the wife of such national.

Article 3

1. Each Contracting State agrees that the alien wife of one of its nationals may, at her request, acquire the nationality of her husband through specially privileged naturalization procedures; the grant of such nationality may be subject to such limitations as may be imposed in the interests of national security or public policy.

2. Each Contracting State agrees that the present Convention shall not be construed as affecting any legislation or judicial practice by which the alien wife of one of its nationals may, at her request, acquire her husband's nationality as a matter of right.

---

[10] See A. Grahl-Madsen, *Territorial Asylum* (1980); L.W. Holborn, *Refugees: A Problem of our Time, The Work of the United Nations High Commissioner for Refugees, 1951–1972* (2 vols., 1975); and J. Hucker, "Migration and Resettlement under International Law," in R.St.J. Macdonald, D.M. Johnston and G.L. Morris, eds., *The International Law and Policy of Human Welfare* (1978), at 327. Canadian practice is discussed in Government of Canada, Task Force on Immigration Practices and Procedures, *The Refugee Status Determination Process* (1981); and A. Gotlieb, "Canada and the Refugee Question in International Law" (1975), 13 *Can. Y.B. Int. L. 3*. But see now Government of Canada, *Refugee Determination in Canada* (the *Plaut Report*) (1985); and Bill C-55 (1987), *An Act to amend the Immigration Act, 1976*.

NOTES

Section 10(2) of the *Citizenship Act*[11] provides that:

(2) Notwithstanding any other provision of this Act, a woman who

(a) by virtue of any law of Canada in force at any time before the 1st day of January, 1947 had, by reason only of her marriage or the acquisition by her husband of a foreign nationality, ceased to be a British subject, and

(b) would have been a citizen had the former Act come into force immediately before her marriage or the acquisition by her husband of a foreign nationality,

acquires citizenship immediately upon the receipt by the Minister of a notice in writing by her that she elects to be a citizen.

Loss of Nationality

Nationality may be renounced. A child with two nationalities because of the dual principles of *jus soli* and *jus sanguinis* may be allowed to renounce one upon coming to majority. Section 7 of the *Citizenship Act*[12] provides:

Where a person who was born outside Canada after the coming into force of this Act is a citizen because at the time of his birth one of his parents was a citizen by virtue of paragraph 3(1)(b) or 3(1)(e), that person ceases to be a citizen upon attaining the age of twenty-eight years unless he

(a) makes application to retain his citizenship; and

(b) registers as a citizen and either resides in Canada for a period of at least one year immediately preceding the date of his application or establishes a substantial connection with Canada.

Some states do not allow a citizen to remain as such if he or she acquires a new nationality. This is not the case in Canada.

Denationalization may also occur by way of legislation. It may be used as a penalty for the commission of serious crimes such as treason, espionage or war crimes under international law. Section 9 of the *Citizenship Act*[13] provides as follows:

(1) Subject to section 17 but notwithstanding any other section of this Act, where the Governor in Council, upon a report from the Minister, is satisfied that any person has obtained, retained, renounced or resumed citizenship under this Act by false representation or fraud or by knowingly concealing material circumstances,

(a) the person ceases to be a citizen, or

(b) the renunciation of citizenship by the person shall be deemed to have had no effect, as of such date as, may be fixed by order of the Governor in Council with respect thereto.

---

[11] Stats. Can., 1974–75–76, c. 108, as am.

[12] See also section 8, reported *supra*, at n. 6.

[13] *Supra*, n. 9.

(2) A person shall be deemed to have obtained citizenship by false representation or fraud or by knowingly concealing material circumstances if

(a) he was lawfully admitted to Canada for permanent residence by false representation or fraud or by knowingly concealing material circumstances; and

(b) he subsequently obtained citizenship because he had been admitted to Canada for permanent residence.

Proof of Nationality

A duly authorized passport is only *prima facie* evidence of nationality.[14] States usually only issue passports to their nationals. However, such issuance does not create nationality. Eligibility in Canada depends upon whether the applicant is a Canadian citizen as defined in the *Citizenship Act*.

Canadian passports are issued by the Secretary of State for External Affairs in the exercise of the Royal Prerogative. There is no statute governing the issuance of Canadian passports and no person has a legal entitlement to one. In Canada the legal position is that the Secretary of State for External Affairs has discretionary power to issue or withhold a passport.

The Canadian government issues passports to Canadian citizens so they may possess evidence of their identity and national status when entering another country. Three types of passports are issued – ordinary, special and diplomatic. Any Canadian citizen may normally receive an ordinary passport. However, in certain instances, depending on the nature of their governmental or parliamentary duties and purposes of travel abroad, some Canadians are entitled to receive either a special or diplomatic passport.

Passports are rarely withheld except when the applicant is indebted to the Government for repatriation expenses. At the request of the police or judicial authorities, they may be withheld from a person who is charged with a serious criminal offence and is on bail while awaiting trial. In addition, it is sometimes necessary to withhold passport facilities for children under the age of sixteen years when there is a marital dispute involving custody and it appears that the parent applying for the passport does not have a clear legal right to take the child out of Canada.

Endorsements are placed in passports when the bearers have urgent reasons for travel and it has been decided to provide them with interim passport facilities even though they have not met all Departmental requirements: for example, they have not repaid the Department for financial assistance provided while they were abroad or they have failed to satisfy the Department that their last passports are non-recoverable. Also, when financial assistance is given to a Canadian citizen at a post abroad, unless he is issued an Emergency Passport for return to Canada, his ordinary passport is endorsed as being valid only for travel to Canada and countries en route.

---

[14] *Re Gur* (1971), 1 I.A.C. 384.

CORPORATIONS

Determining the nationality of corporations[15] is complicated by two features of their character. First, like individuals, they may have a variety of contacts with different countries. Thus a company, established and registered in one country, for tax purposes perhaps, may have its head office in another country and its main place of business in a third. Such a multinational enterprise is likely to have branch plants and offices in several other countries and to be owned by shareholders of many nationalities in constantly changing proportions as its shares are traded. How are these national connections significant in international law? Secondly, unlike individuals, corporations are juridical persons by virtue of national legislation. How should international law regard such entities of purely national origin and status? Furthermore, the company laws of different countries are not the same, in particular in the way they ascribe nationality. Thus the laws of one country may grant nationality to a corporation because it was created and registered there, while the legal system of another attaches nationality to the same corporation because its centre of business activities is within the jurisdiction. What cognizance should international law take of these differences in company laws? These difficult questions came before the World Court in the following case.

Barcelona Traction, Light and Power Co. Case[16]
Belgium v. Spain
[1970] I.C.J. Rep. 3

[The Barcelona Traction Co. had been formed under Canadian law. Its business involved the exploitation of hydroelectric facilities in Spain, where it had many operating subsidiaries. When the company was declared bankrupt in Spain, a very high percentage of its shares had been beneficially owned for more than twenty-five years by two large Belgian corporations. Belgium claimed compensation from Spain on account of the manner in which the Spanish authorities had permitted the bankruptcy of the company and the disposal of its assets. Spain raised several preliminary objections, in one of which it asserted that since the alleged injury was to the company, not the shareholders, Belgium had no standing to bring the claim. The Court ultimately dealt with this issue in its judgment on the merits.]

THE COURT: ...
33. When a state admits into its territory foreign investments or foreign nationals,

---

[15] See, generally, G.A. Ban Hecke, "Nationality of Companies Analysed" (1961), 8 *Ned. Tijdschrift Int. Recht* 223; R.E.L.V. Williams and M. Chrussachi, "The Nationality of Corporations" (1933), 49 *L.Q. Rev.* 334; Y. Hadari, "The Choice of National Law Applicable to the Multinational Enterprise and the Nationality of Such Enterprise," [1974] *Duke L.J.* 1; and T. Vogelaar, "Multinational Corporations and International Law" (1980), 27 *Ned. Tijdshrift Int. Recht* 69.

[16] See H.W. Briggs, "Barcelona Traction: The 'Jus Standi' of Belgium" (1971), 65 *Am. J. Int. L.* 327; R. Higgins, "Aspects of the Case Concerning the Barcelona Traction, Light and Power Company Ltd." (1970), 11 *Va. J. Int.* 327; and R.B. Lillich, "The Rigidity of Barcelona" (1971), 65 *Am. J. Int. L.* 522.

whether natural or juristic persons, it is bound to extend to them the protection of the law and assumes obligations concerning the treatment to be afforded them. ...

35. ...In order to bring a claim in respect of the breach of such an obligation, a State must first establish its right to do so, ... In the present case it is therefore essential to establish whether the losses allegedly suffered by Belgian shareholders in Barcelona Traction were the consequence of the violation of obligations of which they were the beneficiaries. In other words: has a right of Belgium been violated on account of its nationals' having suffered infringement of their rights as shareholders in a company not of Belgian nationality?

36. Thus it is the existence or absence of a right, belonging to Belgium and recognized as such by international law, which is decisive for the problem of Belgium's capacity. ...

38. In this field international law is called upon to recognize institutions of municipal law that have an important and extensive role in the international field. This does not necessarily imply drawing any analogy between its own institutions and those of municipal law, nor does it amount to making rules of international law dependent upon categories of municipal law. All it means is that international law has had to recognize the corporate entity as an institution created by States in a domain essentially within their domestic jurisdiction. This in turn requires that, whenever legal issues arise concerning the share-holders, as to which rights international law has not established its own rules, it has to refer to the relevant rules of municipal law. ...

41. Municipal law determines the legal situation not only of such limited liability companies but also of those persons who hold shares in them. ... The concept and structure of the company are founded on and determined by a firm distinction between the separate entity of the company and that of the shareholder, each with a distinct set of rights. The separation of property rights as between company and shareholder is an important man-ifestation of this distinction. So long as the company is in existence the shareholder has no right to the corporate assets.

44. Notwithstanding the separate corporate personality, a wrong done to the company frequently causes prejudice to its shareholders. But the mere fact that damage is sustained by both company and shareholder does not imply that both are entitled to claim com-pensation. ... Thus whenever a shareholder's interests are harmed by an act done to the company, it is to the latter that he must look to institute appropriate action; for although two separate entities may have suffered from the same wrong, it is only one entity whose rights have been infringed. ...

47. The situation is different if the act complained of is aimed at the direct rights of the shareholder as such. It is well known that there are rights which municipal law confers upon the latter distinct from those of the company, including the right to any declared dividend, the right to attend and vote at general meetings, the right to share in the residual assets of the company on liquidation. Whenever one of his direct rights is infringed, the shareholder has an independent right of action. ...

48. The Belgian Government claims that shareholders of Belgian nationality suffered damage in consequence of unlawful acts of the Spanish authorities and, in particular, that the Barcelona Traction shares, though they did not cease to exist, were emptied of all real economic content. It accordingly contends that the shareholders had an independent right to redress, notwithstanding the fact that the acts complained of were directed against the company as such. Thus the legal issue is reducible to the question of whether it is legitimate to identify an attack on company rights, resulting in damage to shareholders, with the violation of their direct rights. ...

50. In turning now to the international legal aspects of the case, the Court must, as already indicated, start from the fact that the present case essentially involves factors derived from municipal law – the distinction and the community between the company and the shareholder – which the Parties, however widely their interpretations may differ, each take as the point of departure of their reasoning. If the Court were to decide the case in disregard of the relevant institutions of municipal law it would, without justification, invite serious legal difficulties. It would lose touch with reality, for there are no corresponding institutions of international law to which the Court could resort. Thus the Court has, as indicated, not only to take cognizance of municipal law but also to refer to it. It is to rules generally accepted by municipal legal systems which recognize the limited company whose capital is represented by shares, and not to the municipal law of a particular State, that international law refers. In referring to such rules, the Court cannot modify, still less deform them.

51. On the international plane, the Belgian Government has advanced the proposition that it is inadmissible to deny the shareholders' national State a right of diplomatic protection merely on the ground that another State possesses a corresponding right in respect of the company itself. In strict logic and law this formulation of the Belgian claim to *jus standi* assumes the existence of the very right that requires demonstration. In fact the Belgian Government has repeatedly stressed that there exists no rule of international law which would deny the national State of the shareholders the right of diplomatic protection for the purpose of seeking redress pursuant to unlawful acts committed by another State against the company in which they hold shares. This, by emphasizing the absence of any express denial of the right, conversely implies the admission that there is no rule of international law which expressly confers such a right on the shareholders' national State.

52. International law may not, in some fields, provide specific rules in particular cases. In the concrete situation, the company against which allegedly unlawful acts were directed is expressly vested with a right, whereas no such right is specifically provided for the shareholder in respect of those acts. Thus the position of the company rests on a positive rule of both municipal and international law. As to the shareholder, while he has certain rights expressly provided for him by municipal law ... , appeal can, in the circumstances of the present case, only be made to the silence of international law. Such silence scarcely admits of interpretation in favour of the shareholder.

53. It is quite true, as was recalled in the course of oral argument in the present case, that concurrent claims are not excluded in the case of a person who, having entered the service of an international organization and retained his nationality, enjoys simultaneously the right to be protected by his national State and the right to be protected by the organization to which he belongs. This however is a case of one person in possession of two separate bases of protection, each of which is valid *(Reparation for Injuries Suffered in the Service of the United Nations,* Advisory Opinion, I.C.J. Reports 1949, at 185). There is no analogy between such a situation and that of foreign shareholders in a company which has been the victim of a violation of international law which has caused them damage. ...

55. The Court will now examine other grounds on which it is conceivable that the submission by the Belgian Government of a claim on behalf of shareholders in Barcelona Traction may be justified. ...

[The Court then took note of the municipal law practice of "lifting the veil" of incorporation in exceptional cases, and acknowledged that there may be special circumstances for doing likewise internationally in the interest of protecting shareholders.]

64. ... In this connection two particular situations must be studied: the case of the company having ceased to exist and the case of the company's national State lacking capacity to take action on its behalf.

65. As regards the first of these possibilities ... [t]here can, however, be no question but that Barcelona Traction has lost all its assets in Spain, and was placed in receivership in Canada, a receiver and manager having been appointed. It is common ground that from the economic viewpoint the company has been entirely paralyzed. ...

66. It cannot however, be contended that the corporate entity of the company has ceased to exist, or that it has lost its capacity to take corporate action. ... It has not become incapable in law of defending its own rights and the interests of the shareholders. In particular, a precarious financial situation cannot be equated with the demise of the corporate entity, which is the hypothesis under consideration: the company's status in law is alone relevant, and not its economic condition, nor even the possibility of its being "practically defunct" – a description on which argument has been based but which lacks all legal precision. Only in the event of the legal demise of the company are the shareholders deprived of the possibility of a remedy available through the company: it is only if they became deprived of all such possibility that an independent right of action for them and their government could arise.

67. In the present case, Barcelona Traction is in receivership in the country of incorporation. Far from implying the demise of the entity or of its rights, this much rather denotes that those rights are preserved for so long as no liquidation has ensued. Though in receivership, the company continues to exist. Moreover, it is a matter of public record that the company's shares were quoted on the stock-market at a recent date.

68. ... The Court is thus not confronted with the first hypothesis contemplated in paragraph 64, and need not pronounce upon it.

69. The Court will now turn to the second possibility, that of the lack of capacity of the company's national State to act on its behalf. The first question which must be asked here is whether Canada—the third apex of the triangular relationship—is, in law, the national State of Barcelona Traction.

70. In allocating corporate entities to States for purposes of diplomatic protection, international law is based, but only to a limited extent, on an analogy with the rules governing the nationality of individuals. The traditional rule attributes the right of diplomatic protection of a corporate entity to the State under the laws of which it is incorporated and in whose territory it has its registered office. These two criteria have been confirmed by long practice and by numerous international instruments. This notwithstanding, further or different links are at times said to be required in order that a right of diplomatic protection should exist.

Indeed, it has been the practice of some States to give a company incorporated under their law diplomatic protection solely when it has its seat (*siège social*) or management or centre of control in their territory, or when a majority or a substantial proportion of the shares has been owned by nationals of the State concerned. Only then, it has been held, does there exist between the corporation and the State in question a genuine connection of the kind familiar from other branches of international law. However, in the particular field of the diplomatic protection of corporate entities, no absolute test of the ''genuine connection'' has found general acceptance. Such tests as have been applied are of a relative nature, and sometimes links with one State have had to be weighed against those with another. In this connection reference has been made to the *Nottebohm* case ... . However, given both the legal and factual aspects of protection in the present case the Court is of the opinion that there can be no analogy with the issues raised or the decision given in that case.

71. In the present case, it is not disputed that the company was incorporated in Canada and has its registered office in that country. The incorporation of the company under the law of Canada was an act of free choice. Not only did the founders of the company seek its incorporation under Canadian law but it has remained under that law for a period of over 50 years. It has maintained in Canada its registered office, its accounts and its share registers. Board meetings were held there for many years; it has been listed in the records of the Canadian tax authorities. Thus a close and permanent connection has been established, fortified by the passage of over half a century. This connection is in no way weakened by the fact that the company engaged from the very outset in commercial activities outside Canada, for that was its declared object. Barcelona Traction's links with Canada are thus manifold.

72. Furthermore, the Canadian nationality of the company has received general recognition. Prior to the institution of proceedings before the Court, three other governments apart from that of Canada (those of the United Kingdom, the United States and Belgium) made representations concerning the treatment accorded to Barcelona Traction by the Spanish authorities. The United Kingdom Government intervened on behalf of bondholders and of shareholders. Several representations were also made by the United States Government, but not on behalf of the Barcelona Traction company as such.

73. Both Governments acted at certain stages in close co-operation with the Canadian Government. ...

74. As to the Belgian Government, its earlier action was also undertaken in close cooperation with the Canadian Government. The Belgian Government admitted the Canadian character of the company in the course of the present proceedings. It explicitly stated that Barcelona Traction was a company of neither Spanish nor Belgian nationality but a Canadian company incorporated in Canada. The Belgian Government has even conceded that it was not concerned with the injury suffered by Barcelona Traction itself, since that was Canada's affair. ...

76. In sum, the record shows that from 1948 onwards the Canadian Government made to the Spanish Government numerous representations which cannot be viewed otherwise than as the exercise of diplomatic protection in respect of the Barcelona Traction company. Therefore this was not a case where diplomatic protection was refused or remained in the sphere of fiction. It is also clear that over the whole period of its diplomatic activity the Canadian Government proceeded in full knowledge of the Belgian attitude and activity.

77. It is true that at a certain point the Canadian Government ceased to act on behalf of Barcelona Traction, for reasons which have not been fully revealed, though a statement made in a letter of 19 July 1955 by the Canadian Secretary of State for External Affairs suggests that it felt the matter should be settled by means of private negotiations. The Canadian Government has nonetheless retained its capacity to exercise diplomatic protection; no legal impediment has prevented it from doing so: no fact has arisen to render this protection impossible. It has discontinued its action of its own free will.

78. The Court would here observe that, within the limits prescribed by international law, a State may exercise diplomatic protection by whatever means and to whatever extent it thinks fit, for it is its own right that the State is asserting. Should the natural or legal persons on whose behalf it is acting consider that their rights are not adequately protected, they have no remedy in international law. All they can do is to resort to municipal law, if means are available, with a view to furthering their cause or obtaining redress. The municipal legislator may lay upon the State an obligation to protect its citizens abroad, and may also confer upon the national a right to demand the performance of that obligation, and clothe the right with corresponding sanctions. However, all these questions remain within the province of municipal law and do not affect the position internationally.

79. The State must be viewed as the sole judge to decide whether its protection will be granted, to what extent it is granted, and when it will cease. It remains in this respect a discretionary power the exercise of which may be determined by considerations of a political or other nature, unrelated to the particular case. Since the claim of the State is not identical with that of the individual or corporate person whose cause is espoused, the State enjoys complete freedom of action. Whatever the reasons for any change of attitude, the fact cannot in itself constitute a justification for the exercise of diplomatic protection by another government, unless there is some independent and otherwise valid ground for that. ...

81. The cessation by the Canadian Government of the diplomatic protection of Barcelona Traction cannot, then, be interpreted to mean that there is no remedy against the Spanish Government for the damage done by the allegedly unlawful acts of the Spanish authorities. ... Therefore there is no substance in the argument that for the Belgian Government to bring a claim before the Court represented the only possibility of obtaining redress for the damage suffered by Barcelona Traction and, through it, by its shareholders. ...

83. The Canadian Government's right of protection in respect of the Barcelona Traction company remains unaffected by the present proceedings. The Spanish Government has never challenged the Canadian nationality of the company, either in the diplomatic correspondence with the Canadian Government or before the Court. Moreover it has unreservedly recognized Canada as the national State of Barcelona Traction in both written pleadings and oral statements made in the course of the present proceedings. Consequently, the Court considers that the Spanish Government has not questioned Canada's right to protect the company. ...

88. It follows from what has already been stated above that, where it is a question of an unlawful act committed against a company representing foreign capital, the general rule of international law authorizes the national State of the company alone to make a claim.

89. Considering the important developments of the last half-century, the growth of foreign investments and the expansion of the international activities of corporations, in particular of holding companies, which are often multinational, and considering the way in which the economic interests of States have proliferated, it may at first sight appear surprising that the evolution of law has not gone further and that no generally accepted rules in the matter have crystallized on the international plane. Nevertheless, a more thorough examination of the facts shows that the law on the subject has been formed in a period characterized by an intense conflict of systems and interests. It is essentially bilateral relations which have been concerned, relations in which the rights of both the State exercising diplomatic protection and the State in respect of which protection is sought have had to be safeguarded. Here as elsewhere, a body of rules could only have developed with the consent of those concerned. The difficulties encountered have been reflected in the evolution of the law on the subject.

90. Thus, in the present state of the law, the protection of shareholders requires that recourse be had to treaty stipulations or special agreements directly concluded between the private investor and the State in which the investment is placed. States ever more frequently provide for such protection, in both bilateral and multilateral relations, either by means of special instruments or within the framework of wider economic arrangements. Indeed, whether in the form of multilateral or bilateral treaties between States, or in that of agreements between States and companies, there has since the second world war been considerable development in the protection of foreign investments. The instruments in question contain provisions as to jurisdiction and procedure in case of disputes concerning the treatment of investing companies by the States in which they invest capital. Sometimes companies are themselves vested with a direct right to defend their interests against States through prescribed procedures. No such instrument is in force between the Parties to the present case. ...

92. Since the general rule on the subject does not entitle the Belgian government to put forward a claim in this case, the question remains to be considered whether nonetheless, as the Belgian Government has contended during the proceedings, considerations of equity do not require that it be held to possess a right of protection ... a theory has been developed to the effect that the State of the shareholders has a right of diplomatic protection when the State whose responsibility is invoked is the national State of the company. Whatever the validity of this theory may be, it is certainly not applicable to the present case, since Spain is not the national State of Barcelona Traction.

93. On the other hand, the Court considers that, in the field of diplomatic protection as in all other fields of international law, it is necessary that the law be applied reasonably. It has been suggested that if in a given case it is not possible to apply the general rule that the right of diplomatic protection of a company belongs to its national State, considerations of equity might call for the possibility of protection of the shareholders in question by their own national State. This hypothesis does not correspond to the circumstances of the present case.

94. In view, however, of the discretionary nature of diplomatic protection, considerations of equity cannot require more than the possibility for some protector State to intervene, whether it be the national State of the company, by virtue of the general rule mentioned above, or, in a secondary capacity, the national State of the shareholders who claim protection. In this connection, account should also be taken of the practical effects of deducing from considerations of equity any broader right of protection for the national State of the shareholders. It must first of all be observed that it would be difficult on an equitable basis to make distinctions according to any quantitative test: it would seem that the owner of 1 per cent, and the owner of 90 per cent, of the share-capital should have the same possiblity of enjoying the benefit of diplomatic protection. The protector State may, of course, be disinclined to take up the case of the single small shareholder, but it could scarcely be denied the right to do so in the name of equitable considerations. In that field, protection by the national State of the shareholders can hardly be graduated according to the absolute or relative size of the shareholding involved. ...

96. The Court considers that the adoption of the theory of diplomatic protection of shareholders as such, by opening the door to competing diplomatic claims, could create an atmosphere of confusion and insecurity in international economic relations. The danger would be all the greater inasmuch as the shares of companies whose activity is international are widely scattered and frequently change hands. It might perhaps be claimed that, if the right of protection belonging to the national States of the shareholders were considered as only secondary to that of the national State of the company, there would be less danger of difficulties of the kind contemplated. However, the Court must state that the essence of a secondary right is that it only comes into existence at the time when the original right ceases to exist. As the right of protection vested in the national State of the company cannot be regarded as extinguished because it is not exercised, it is not possible to accept the proposition that in case of its non-exercise the national State of the shareholders have a right of protection secondary to that of the national State of the company. Furthermore, study of factual situations in which this theory might possibly be applied gives rise to the following observations.

97. The situations in which foreign shareholders in a company wish to have recourse to diplomatic protection by their own national State may vary. It may happen that the national State of the company simply refuses to grant it its diplomatic protection, or that it begins to exercise it (as in the present case) but does not pursue its action to the end. It may also happen that the national State of the company and the State which has committed a violation of international law with regard to the company arrive at a settlement of the matter, by agreeing on compensation for the company, but that the foreign share-holders find the compensation insufficient. Now, as a matter of principle, it would be difficult to draw a distinction between these three cases so far as the protection of foreign shareholders by their national State is concerned, since in each case they may have suffered real damage. Furthermore, the national State of the company is perfectly free to decide how far it is appropriate for it to protect the company, and is not bound to make public the reasons for its decision. To reconcile this discretionary power of the company's national State with a right of protection falling to the shareholders' national State would be particularly difficult when the former State has concluded, with the State which has contravened international law with regard to the company, an agreement granting the company compensation which the foreign shareholders find inadequate. If, after such a settlement, the national State of the foreign shareholders could in its turn put forward a claim based on the same facts, this would be likely to introduce into the negotiation of this kind of agreement a lack of security which would be contrary to the stability which it is the object of international law to establish in international relations.

98. It is quite true, as recalled in paragraph 53, that international law recognizes parallel rights of protection in the case of a person in the service of an international organization. Nor is the possibility excluded of concurrent claims being made on behalf of persons having dual nationality, although in that case lack of a genuine link with one of the two States may be set up against the exercise by that State of the right of protection. It must be observed, however, that in these two types of situation the number of possible protectors is necessarily very small, and their identity normally not difficult to determine. In this respect such cases of dual protection are markedly different from the claims to which recognition of a general right of protection of foreign shareholders by their various national States might give rise.

99. It should also be observed that the promoters of a company whose operations will be international must take into account the fact that States have, with regard to their nationals, a discretionary power to grant diplomatic protection or to refuse it. When establishing a company in a foreign country, its promoters are normally impelled by particular considerations; it is often a question of tax or other advantages offered by the host State. It does not seem to be in any way inequitable that the advantages thus obtained should be balanced by the risks arising from the fact that the protection of the company and hence of its shareholders is thus entrusted to a State other than the national State of the shareholders.

100. In the present case, it is clear from what has been said above that Barcelona Traction was never reduced to a position of impotence such that it could not have approached its national State, Canada, to ask for its diplomatic protection, and that, as far as appeared to the Court, there was nothing to prevent Canada from continuing to grant its diplomatic protection to Barcelona Traction if it had considered that it should do so.

101. For the above reasons, the Court is not of the opinion that, in the particular circumstances of the present case, *jus standi* is conferred in the Belgian government by considerations of equity. ...

103. Accordingly, the Court rejects the Belgian government's claim by fifteen votes to one, twelve votes of the majority being based on the reasons set out in the present judgment.

NOTES

1) In considering the nationality of a corporation, the Court said that the *Nottebohm* case, reported in the previous section, was not a suitable analogy. Why not? If a genuine link in the sense of that case is inappropriate, what is the rationale for ascribing a nationality to a company?

2) Although Belgium was refused standing in this case, the Court would have allowed the national state of the shareholders to bring a claim in certain circumstances. What are

they? The Canadian company was wound up in 1980. How might this event have affected any outstanding claims of the shareholders?

3) The majority judgment denied there had been any infringement of the direct rights of the shareholders. Do they have any independent economic interests in the corporation? If so, might the national state of the shareholders exercise its diplomatic protection over these interests?

4) The Barcelona Traction Co. was incorporated in 1911 in Canada by American principals because Canada could be used as a form of tax haven at that time. What lessons does the case hold for the use of tax havens in international tax planning? Consider paragraph 99.

5) Would it be contrary to international law for a foreign company to be put into bankruptcy in Canada? In such a case what jurisdiction would the Canadian court and the trustee in bankruptcy have over assets located outside of Canada?

6) Multinational enterprises are frequently organized as a holding company with several foreign subsidiaries each of which is separately established and registered. How do the principles of the *Barcelona Traction* case apply to such an enterprise? A decision that no country except the state of incorporation could ever act in international law in respect of damage to a corporation would obviously create grave difficulties. Consider the case of an expropriation by a state of the assets of a locally incorporated subsidiary of a foreign parent company, which is often a requirement for carrying on business in the jurisdiction. See paragraph 92.

SHIPS[17]

The term "nationality" when applied to a ship includes a legal link between that ship and a particular state. That link provides the legal basis for the rights and duties pertaining to the ship. Through the conferment of nationality, a ship acquires the right to navigate the world's oceans, to engage in fishing and maritime commerce and to enjoy the benefits deriving from treaties concluded by its state of nationality (also known as the "flag state" or the "state of registry"). Nationality, further, entitles the ship (as well as its crew and passengers) to the protection of the flag state at all times and in all places.

The nationality link also imposes burdens upon the ship. It remains subject to the laws and treaty commitments of the flag state for the duration of its operating life or until it lawfully changes its national character. In time of national emergency or war, it may be pressed into the service of the government of the flag state. It is moreover at all times subject to limitations on its right to carry on trade with other countries. For example, U.S. merchant ships are prohibited to enter the ports of Cuba, North Korea and Vietnam.

Because the high seas are not subject to the sovereignty of any one state, there is a

---

[17] See B. Boczek, *Flags of Convenience: An International Legal Study* (1962); M. McDougal, W. Burke and I. Vlasic, "The Maintenance of Public Order at Sea and the Nationality of Ships" (1960), 54 *Am. J. Int. L.* 25; H. Meyers, *The Nationality of Ships* (1967); M.R. Rienow, *The Test of the Nationality of a Merchant Vessel* (1937).

need to police them. This need has led through customary development to granting each state control and jurisdiction over ships lawfully flying its flag. Thus public order on the high seas, and indeed in all ocean spaces, came to be based on the institution of nationality of ships. The state of nationality is responsible in international law for the lawful conduct of its ships wherever they may be. The use of the high seas is granted only to ships which have the nationality of a state; conversely, on the high seas "stateless" ships or ships whose nationality is suspect may be stopped, boarded, inspected and even seized by warships of any nation.

International law has traditionally accorded states unlimited competence to confer their nationality on merchant ships by criteria of their own choice. The only restraint at customary international law was that once a nationality had been conferred by one state other states were precluded from ascribing their nationality to it at the same time. The 1958 Geneva Convention on the High Seas[18] Article 5 codified this principle and introduced a new requirement of a "genuine link" which "must exist between the State and the ship." This concept has since been confirmed in the U.N. Law of the Sea Convention Article 91 and its contents and application have now been elaborated in the U.N. Convention on Conditions for Registration of Ships. Neither of these treaties, which are reported below, are yet in force, but the Law of the Sea Convention on this point is generally regarded as expressing existing customary international law.

United Nations Convention on the Law of the Sea
U.N. Doc. A/CONF. 62/122 (1982), 21 *Int. Leg. Mat.* 1261

Article 90
RIGHT OF NAVIGATION

Every State, whether coastal or land-locked, has the right to sail ships flying its flag on the high seas.

Article 91
NATIONALITY OF SHIPS

1. Every State shall fix the conditions for the grant of its nationality to ships, for the registration of ships in its territory, and for the right to fly its flag. Ships have the nationality of the State whose flag they are entitled to fly. There must exist a genuine link between the State and the ship.

2. Every State shall issue to ships to which it has granted the right to fly its flag documents to that effect.

---

[18] 450 U.N.T.S. 82.

Article 92
STATUS OF SHIPS

1. Ships shall sail under the flag of one State only and, save in exceptional cases expressly provided for in international treaties or in this Convention, shall be subject to its exclusive jurisdiction on the high seas. A ship may not change its flag during a voyage or while in a port of call, save in the case of a real transfer of ownership or change of registry.

2. A ship which sails under the flags of two or more States, using them according to convenience, may not claim any of the nationalities in question with respect to any other State, and may be assimilated to a ship without nationality.

Article 93
SHIPS FLYING THE FLAG OF THE UNITED NATIONS, ITS SPECIALIZED AGENCIES AND THE INTERNATIONAL ATOMIC ENERGY AGENCY

The preceding articles do not prejudice the question of ships employed on the official service of the United Nations, its specialized agencies or the International Atomic Energy Agency, flying the flag of the organization.

Article 94
DUTIES OF THE FLAG STATE

1. Every State shall effectively exercise its jurisdiction and control in administrative, technical and social matters over ships flying its flag.

2. In particular every State shall:
   (a) maintain a register of ships containing the names and particulars of ships flying its flag, except those which are excluded from generally accepted international regulations on account of their small size; and
   (b) assume jurisdiction under its internal law over each ship flying its flag and its master, officers and crew in respect of administrative, technical and social matters concerning the ship.

3. Every State shall take such measures for ships flying its flag as are necessary to ensure safety at sea with regard, *inter alia*, to:
   (a) the construction, equipment and seaworthiness of ships;
   (b) the manning of ships, labour conditions and the training of crews, taking into account the applicable international instruments;
   (c) the use of signals, the maintenance of communications and the prevention of collisions.

4. Such measures shall include those necessary to ensure:
   (a) that each ship, before registration and thereafter at appropriate intervals, is surveyed by a qualified surveyor of ships, and has on board such charts, nautical publications and navigational equipment and instruments as are appropriate for the safe navigation of the ship;
   (b) that each ship is in the charge of a master and officers who possess appropriate qualifications, in particular in seamanship, navigation, communications and marine engineering, and that the crew is appropriate in qualification and numbers for the type, size, machinery and equipment of the ship;

  (c) that the master, officers and, to the extent appropriate, the crew are fully conversant with and required to observe the applicable international regulations concerning the safety of life at sea, the prevention of collisions, the prevention, reduction and control of marine pollution, and the maintenance of communications by radio.

  5. In taking the measures called for in paragraphs 3 and 4 each State is required to conform to generally accepted international regulations, procedures and practices and to take any steps which may be necessary to secure their observance.

  6. A State which has clear grounds to believe that proper jurisdiction and control with respect to a ship have not been exercised may report the facts to the flag State. Upon receiving such a report, the flag State shall investigate the matter and, if appropriate, take any action necessary to remedy the situation.

  7. Each State shall cause an inquiry to be held by or before a suitably qualified person or persons into every marine casualty or incident of navigation on the high seas involving a ship flying its flag and causing loss of life or serious injury to nationals of another State or serious damage to ships or installations of another State or to the marine environment. The flag State and the other State shall co-operate in the conduct of any inquiry held by that other State into any such marine casualty or incident of navigation.

Canada Shipping Act
R.S.C. 1970, c. S-9

  2. In this Act ...

"British ship" includes a Canadian ship; ...

"Canadian ship" means a ship registered in Canada either under this Act or under the *Merchant Shipping Acts* before the 1st day of August 1936; ...

  6. A ship shall be deemed not to be a British ship unless it is owned wholly by a person qualified to be an owner of a British ship, namely,

  (a) a British subject within the meaning of the *British Nationality Act, 1948*, as amended from time to time; or

  (b) a body corporate incorporated under the law of a Commonwealth country and having its principal place of business in that country.

  7.(1) Notwithstanding that an unregistered ship is owned wholly by persons qualified to be owners of British ships, that ship (unless it is exempted from registration or is not required to be registered by this Act or by the law of the port, whether in or out of Canada, to which it belongs) shall not be recognized in Canada, or for the purposes of this Act, as being entitled to the rights and privileges that heretofore have been or hereafter shall be accorded to British ships registered in any Commonwealth country.

  (2) Every British ship that is owned wholly by persons qualified to be owners of British ships and that is not registered out of Canada may be registered in Canada.

  (3) Every British ship that is so owned by persons so qualified a majority whereof, either in number or in extent of ownership, are residents of Canada, and every British ship that being so owned by persons so qualified, is, as to its management and use, principally controlled in Canada, shall, unless it is registered out of Canada, be registered in Canada.

(4) Any ship whatever may be detained until the master of the ship, if so required, produces the certificate of registry of the ship.

8. Ships not exceeding fifteen tons register tonnage employed solely in navigation on the lakes, rivers or coasts of Canada and pleasure yachts not exceeding twenty tons register tonnage wherever employed or operated are exempted from registry under this Act.

9.(1) The chief officer of customs at any port in Canada approved by the Governor in Council for the registry of ships shall be a registrar of British ships. ...

11. Every British ship shall before registry in Canada be surveyed by a surveyor of ships and its tonnage ascertained in accordance with the tonnage regulations of this Act, and the surveyor shall grant his certificate specifying the ship's tonnage and build, and such other particulars descriptive of the identity of the ship as may for the time being be required.

12.(1) Every British ship shall before registry in Canada be marked permanently and conspicuously ... [with its name, its official member, its register tonnage and its draught].

14. A person is not entitled to be registered as owner of a ship or of a share therein until he, or in the case of a corporation the person authorized by this Act to make declarations on behalf of the corporation, has made and signed a declaration of ownership, referring to the ship as described in the certificate of the surveyor, and containing ... [statements as to

(a) qualification to own a British ship,

(b) the time and place of building of the ship,

(c) the name of the master,

(d) the number of shares in the ship for which a part owner is entitled to be registered, and a declaration that no unqualified person has any legal interest in the ship.]

17.(1) As soon as the requirements of this Act preliminary to registry have been complied with, the registrar shall enter in the register book the following particulars respecting the ship:

(a) the name of the ship and the name of the port to which it belongs;

(b) the details comprised in the surveyor's certificate;

(c) the particulars respecting its origin stated in the declaration of ownership; and

(d) the name and description of its registered owner or owners, and if there are more owners than one, the proportions in which they are interested in the ship. ...

19. The port at which a British ship is registered for the time being shall be deemed its port of registry and the port to which it belongs. ...

23.(1) On completion of the registry of a ship, the registrar shall grant a certificate of registry comprising the particulars respecting the ship entered in the register book, with the name of the ship's master. ...

87.(1) If a person uses the National Flag of Canada and assumes the Canadian national character on board a ship owned in whole or in part by any persons not qualified to own a Canadian ship, for the purpose of making the ship appear to be a Canadian ship, the ship is subject to forfeiture under this Act, unless the assumption has been made for the purpose of escaping capture by an enemy or by a foreign ship of war in the exercise of some belligerent right. ...

88. If the master or owner of a Canadian ship does anything or permits anything to

Criminal Cases

from S.A. Williams and A.L.C. de Mestral *An Introduction to International Law* (2nd ed., 1987), at 125–26 (footnotes omitted).

...Traditionally, jurisdiction *in personam* or *in rem* refers to the power of the courts to enter judgments binding on particular persons or things. Although Canada may define the criminal character and consequences of conduct taking place entirely within Canada, this does not always mean the Canadian courts can enter judgment against a person found guilty of such conduct and sentence him if he is physically outside of Canada. In this situation even though the courts may have jurisdiction over the offence, they do not have jurisdiction over the person. Both are necessary. Correlatively, while Canadian authorities have the right to arrest a person while he is in Canada and although the Canadian courts would then have jurisdiction *in personam* over him, it does not follow that under international law Canada has the right to prosecute such a person under a Canadian statute when the unlawful acts were committed entirely abroad. This proposition is reinforced where the accused is an alien and the acts which were committed outside of Canada had no effects within Canada.

In this section we shall consider two questions: the reach of the legislative power of a state (jurisdiction over the crime) and the reach of the processes of its courts (jurisdiction over the person).

In international criminal law, judicial jurisdiction is subservient to legislative jurisdiction. The choice of law must precede the choice of court. Particular behaviour is only prohibited if there is some law that declares that it is. When a prosecution is initiated, this means that a law has already been chosen and the accused will be proceeded against pursuant to that law. This will determine which court has jurisdiction. For example, if the Criminal Code of Canada is applicable to the alleged offence, Canadian courts will have jurisdiction. If, on the other hand, the alleged offence is subject to some foreign law, Canadian courts will have no jurisdiction.

Domestic penal systems fix their own jurisdictional rules. Canadian law gives Canadian courts their rules of jurisdiction. Domestic systems do not take into account foreign laws. Canadian criminal courts are only interested in applying Canadian law. Thus, even though for example, Canadian rules of criminal law may be international by their object in that they may reach international activities, they are by their nature domestic rules.

...The practice of individual states with respect to the exercise of jurisdiction over persons, property, acts or events, is not uniform. This lack of uniformity has a historical and geographical origin. The Anglo-American tradition tends to follow the territorial principle of jurisdiction according to which a state may exercise jurisdiction over persons and property or acts occurring within its territory. This preference can be explained by the fact that the territories under Anglo-American control were dominated by sea-frontiers. Individuals could not move as quickly or easily between these states as they could between states with land boundaries. The Western European states take a much broader view of jurisdictional principles precisely because of the geographical lay out of a multiplicity of land or river frontiers. Movement between states has always been easier and to prevent fugitives from justice being able to escape trial, the nationality principle was established.

The Steamship Lotus
France v. Turkey
(1927), P.C.I.J. Ser. A, No. 10

[By a special agreement of October 12, 1926, the governments of France and Turkey submitted to the Permanent Court of International Justice the following questions:

1) Has Turkey, contrary to Article 15 of the Convention of Lausanne of July 24th, 1923, respecting conditions of residence and business and jurisdiction, acted in conflict with the principles of international law – and if so, what principles – by instituting following the collision which occurred on August 2nd, 1926, on the high seas between the French steamer *Lotus* and the Turkish steamer *Boz-Kourt* and upon the arrival of the French steamer at Constantinople – as well as against the captain of the Turkish steamship – joint criminal proceedings in pursuance of Turkish law against M. Demons, officer of the watch on board the *Lotus* at the time of the collision, in consequence of the loss of the *Boz-Kourt* having involved the death of eight Turkish sailors and passengers?

2) Should the reply be in the affirmative, what pecuniary reparation is due to M. Demons, provided, according to the principles of international law, reparation should be made in similar cases?]

THE COURT: ... On August 22, 1926, just before midnight, a collision occurred between the French mail steamer *Lotus*, proceeding to Constantinople, and the Turkish collier *Boz-Kourt*, between five and six nautical miles to the north of Cape Sigri (Mitylene). The *Boz-Kourt*, which was cut in two, sank, and eight Turkish nationals who were on board perished. After having done everything possible to succour the shipwrecked persons, of whom ten were able to be saved, the *Lotus* continued on its course to Constantinople, where it arrived on August 3rd.

At the time of the collision, the officer of the watch on board the *Lotus* was Monsieur Demons, a French citizen, lieutenant in the merchant service and first officer of the ship, whilst the movements of the *Boz-Kourt* were directed by its captain, Hassan Bey, who was one of those saved from the wreck. As early as August 3rd the Turkish police proceeded to hold an enquiry into the collision on board the *Lotus*; and on the following day, August 4th, the captain of the *Lotus* handed in his master's report at the French Consulate-General, transmitting a copy to the harbour master. On August 5th, Lieutenant Demons was requested by the Turkish authorities to go ashore to give evidence. The examination, the length of which incidentally resulted in delaying the departure of the *Lotus*, led to the placing under arrest of Lieutenant Demons – without previous notice being given to the French Consul General – and Hassan Bey, amongst others. This arrest, which has been characterized by the Turkish agent as arrest pending trial (*arrestation preventive*), was effected in order to ensure that the criminal prosecution instituted against the two officers, on a charge of manslaughter, by the Public Prosecutor of Stamboul, on the complaint of the families of the victims of the collision, should follow its normal course.

The case was first heard by the Criminal Court of Stamboul on August 28th. On that occasion, Lieutenant Demons submitted that the Turkish Courts had no jurisdiction; the Court, however, overruled his objection. When the proceedings were resumed on September 11th, Lieutenant Demons demanded his release on bail: this request was complied with on September 13th, the bail being fixed at 6,000 Turkish pounds. On September 15th, the Criminal Court delivered its judgment, the terms of which have not been communicated to the Court by the Parties. It is, however, common ground, that it sentenced Lieutenant Demons to eighty days' imprisonment and a fine of twenty-two pounds, Hassan Bey being sentenced to a slightly more severe penalty. ...

The prosecution was instituted in pursuance of Turkish legislation. The special agreement does not indicate what clause or clauses of that legislation apply. No document has been submitted to the Court indicating on what article of the Turkish Penal Code the prosecution was based; the French Government however declares that the Criminal Court claimed jurisdiction under Article 6 of the Turkish Penal Code, and far from denying this statement, Turkey, in the submissions of her countercase, contends that that article is in conformity with the principles of international law. It does not appear from the proceedings whether the prosecution was instituted solely on the basis of that article.

Article 6 of the Turkish Penal Code, Law No. 765 of March 1st, 1926 (Official Gazette No. 320 of March 13th, 1926), runs as follows:

[Translation:] Any foreigner who, apart from the cases contemplated by Article 4, commits an offence abroad to the prejudice of Turkey or of a Turkish subject, for which offence Turkish law prescribes a penalty involving loss of freedom for a minimum period of not less than one year, shall be punished in accordance with the Turkish Penal Code provided that he is arrested in Turkey. The penalty shall however be reduced by one third and instead of the death penalty, twenty years of penal servitude shall be awarded.

Nevertheless, in such cases, the prosecution will only be instituted at the request of the Minister of Justice or on the complaint of the injured Party.

If the offence committed injures another foreigner, the guilty person shall be punished at the request of the Minister of Justice, in accordance with the provisions set out in the first paragraph of this article, provided however that:

1) the article in question is one for which Turkish law prescribes a penalty involving loss of freedom for minimum period of three years;

2) there is no extradition treaty or that the extradition has not been accepted either by the government of the locality where the guilty person has committed the offence or by the government of his own country.

Even if the Court must hold that the Turkish authorities had seen fit to base the prosecution of Lieutenant Demons upon the above-mentioned Article 6, the question submitted to the Court is not whether that article is compatible with the principles of international law; it is more general. The Court is asked to state whether or not the principles of international law prevent Turkey from instituting criminal proceedings against Lieutenant Demons under Turkish law. ...

It is Article 15 of the Convention of Lausanne of July 24th, 1923, respecting conditions of residence and business and jurisdiction, which refers the contracting Parties to the principles of international law as regards the delimitation of their respective jurisdiction. This clause is as follows:

Subject to the provisions of Article 16, all questions of jurisdiction shall, as between Turkey and the other contracting Powers, be decided in accordance with the principles of international law.

... The Court, having to consider whether there are any rules of international law which may have been violated by the prosecution in pursuance of Turkish law of Lieutenant Demons, is confronted in the first place by a question of principle which, in the written and oral arguments of the two Parties, has proved to be a fundamental one. The French Government contends that the Turkish Courts, in order to have jurisdiction, should be able to point to some title to jurisdiction recognized by international law in favour of Turkey. On the other hand, the Turkish Government takes the view that Article 15 allows Turkey jurisdiction whenever such jurisdiction does not come into conflict with a principle of international law. ...

This way of stating the question is also dictated by the very nature and existing conditions of international law.

International law governs relations between independent States. The rules of law binding upon States therefore emanate from their own free will as expressed in conventions or by usages generally accepted as expressing principles of law and established in order to regulate the relations between these co-existing independent communities or with a view to the achievement of common aims. Restrictions upon the independence of States cannot therefore be presumed.

Now the first and foremost restriction imposed by international law upon a State is that – failing the existence of a permissive rule to the contrary – it may not exercise its power in any form in the territory of another State. In this sense jurisdiction is certainly territorial; it cannot be exercised by a State outside its territory except by virtue of a permissive rule derived from international custom or from a convention.

It does not, however, follow that international law prohibits a State from exercising jurisdiction in its own territory, in respect of any case which relates to acts which have taken place abroad, and in which it cannot rely on some permissive rule of international law. Such a view would only be tenable if international law contained a general prohibition to States to extend the application of their laws and the jurisdiction of their courts to persons, property and acts outside their territory, and if, as an exception to his general prohibition, it allowed States to do so in certain specific cases. But this is certainly not the case under international law as it stands at present. Far from laying down a general prohibition to the effect that States may not extend the application of their laws and the jurisdiction of their courts to persons, property and acts outside their territory, it leaves them in this respect a wide measure of discretion which is only limited in certain cases by prohibitive rules; as regards other cases, every State remains free to adopt the principles which it regards as best and most suitable. ...

In these circumstances, all that can be required of a State is that it should not overstep the limits which international law places upon its jurisdiction; within these limits, its title to exercise jurisdiction rests in its sovereignty.

It follows from the foregoing that the contention of the French Government to the effect that Turkey must in each case be able to cite a rule of international law authorizing her to exercise jurisdiction, is opposed to the generally accepted international law to which Article 15 of the Convention of Lausanne refers. Having regard to the terms of Article 15 and to the construction which the Court has just placed upon it, this contention would apply in regard to civil as well as to criminal cases, and would be applicable on conditions of absolute reciprocity as between Turkey and the other contracting Parties; in practice, it would therefore in many cases result in paralyzing the action of the courts, owing to the impossibility of citing a universally accepted rule on which to support the exercise of their jurisdiction.

Nevertheless, it has to be seen whether the foregoing considerations really apply as regards criminal jurisdiction, or whether this jurisdiction is governed by a different principle: this might be the outcome of the close connection which for a long time existed between the conception of supreme criminal jurisdiction and that of a State, and also by the especial importance of criminal jurisdiction from the point of view of the individual.

Though it is true that in all systems of law the principle of the territorial character of criminal law is fundamental, it is equally true that all or nearly all these systems of law extend their action to offences committed outside the territory of the State which adopts them, and they do so in ways which vary from State to State. The territoriality of criminal law, therefore, is not an absolute principle of international law and by no means coincides with territorial sovereignty.

This situation may be considered from two different standpoints corresponding to the points of view respectively taken up by the Parties. According to one of these standpoints, the principle of freedom, in virtue of which each State may regulate its legislation at its discretion, provided that in so doing it does not come in conflict with a restriction imposed by international law, would also apply as regarding law governing the scope of jurisdiction in criminal cases. According to the other standpoint, the exclusively territorial character of law relating to this domain constitutes a principle which, except as otherwise expressly provided, would *ipso facto*, prevent States from extending the criminal jurisdiction of their courts beyond their frontiers; the exceptions in question, which include for instance extraterritorial jurisdiction over nationals and over crimes directed against public safety, would therefore rest on special permissive rules forming part of international law.

Adopting, for the purposes of the argument, the standpoint of the latter of these two systems, it must be recognized that, in the absence of a treaty provision, its correctness depends upon whether there is a custom having the force of law establishing it. The same is true as regards the applicability of this system – assuming it to have been recognized as sound – in the particular case. It follows that, even from this point of view, before ascertaining whether there may be a rule of international law expressly allowing Turkey to prosecute a foreigner for an offence committed by him outside Turkey, it is necessary to begin by establishing both that the system is well-founded and that it is applicable in the particular case. Now, in order to establish the first of these points, one must, as has just been seen, prove the existence of a principle of international law restricting the discretion of States as regards criminal legislation.

Consequently, whichever of the two systems described above be adopted, the same result will be arrived at in this particular case: the necessity of ascertaining whether or not under international law there is a principle which would have prohibited Turkey, in the circumstances of the case before the Court, from prosecuting Lieutenant Demons. And moreover, on either hypothesis, this must be ascertained by examining precedents offering a close analogy to the case under consideration; for it is only from precedents of this nature that the existence of a general principle applicable to the particular case may appear. For if it were found, for example, that, according to the practice of states, the jurisdiction of the State whose flag was flown was not established by international law as exclusive with regard to collision cases on the high seas, it would not be necessary to ascertain whether there were a more general restriction; since, as regards that restriction – supposing that it existed – the fact that it had been established that there was no prohibition in respect of collision on the high seas would be tantamount to a special permissive rule.

The Court therefore must, in any event, ascertain whether or not there exists a rule of international law limiting the freedom of States to extend the criminal jurisdiction of their courts to a situation uniting the circumstances of the present case.

... The Court will now proceed to ascertain whether general international law, to which Article 15 of the Convention of Lausanne refers, contains a rule prohibiting Turkey from prosecuting Lieutenant Demons.

For this purpose, it will in the first place examine the value of the arguments advanced by the French Government, without however omitting to take into account other possible aspects of the problem, which might show the existence of a restrictive rule applicable in this case.

The arguments advanced by the French Government, other than those considered above, are, in substance, the three following:

1) International law does not allow a State to take proceedings with regard to offences committed by foreigners abroad, simply by reason of the nationality of the victim; and such is the situation in the present case because the offence must be regarded as having been committed on board the French vessel.

2) International law recognizes the exclusive jurisdiction of the State whose flag is flown as regards everything which occurs on board a ship on the high seas.

3) Lastly, this principle is especially applicable in a collision case.

As regards the first argument, the Court feels obliged in the first place to recall that its examination is strictly confined to the specific situation that its decision is asked for.

As has already been observed, the characteristic features of the situation of fact are as follows: there has been a collision on the high seas between two vessels flying different flags, on one of which was one of the persons alleged to be guilty of the offence, whilst the victims were on board the other.

This being so, the Court does not think it necessary to consider the contention that a State cannot punish offences committed abroad by a foreigner simply by reason of the nationality of the victim. For this contention only relates to the case where the nationality of the victim is the only criterion on which the criminal jurisdiction of the State is based. Even if that argument were correct generally speaking – and in regard to this the Court reserves its opinion – it could only be used in the present case if international law forbade Turkey to take into consideration the fact that the offence produced its effects on the Turkish vessel and consequently in a place assimilated to Turkish territory in which the application of Turkish criminal law cannot be challenged, even in regard to offences committed there by foreigners. But no such rule of international law exists. No argument has come to the knowledge of the Court from which it could be deduced that States recognize themselves to be under an obligation towards each other only to have regard to the place where the author of the offence happens to be at the time of the offence. On the contrary, it is certain that the courts of many countries, even of countries which have given their criminal legislation a strictly territorial character, interpret criminal law in the sense that offences, the authors of which at the moment of commission are in the territory of another State, are nevertheless to be regarded as having been committed in the national territory, if one of the constituent elements of the offence, and more especially its effects, have taken place there. French courts have, in regard to a variety of situations, given decisions sanctioning this way of interpreting the territorial principle. Again, the Court does not know of any cases in which governments have protested against the fact that the criminal law of some country contained a rule to this effect or that the courts of a country construed their criminal law in this sense. Consequently, once it is admitted that the effects of the offence were produced on the Turkish vessel, it becomes impossible to hold that there is a rule of international law which prohibits Turkey from prosecuting Lieutenant Demons because of the fact that the author of the offence was on board the French ship. ...

Nevertheless, even if the Court had to consider whether Article 6 of the Turkish Penal Code was compatible with international law, and if it held that the nationality of the victim did not in all circumstances constitute a sufficient basis for the exercise of criminal jurisdiction by the State of which the victim was a national, the Court would arrive at the same conclusion for the reasons just set out. For even were Article 6 to be held incompatible with the principles of international law, since the prosecution might have been based on another provision of Turkish law which would not have been contrary to any principle of international law, it follows that it would be impossible to deduce from the mere fact that Article 6 was not in conformity with those principles, that the prosecution itself was contrary to them. ...

The second argument put forward by the French Government is the principle that the State whose flag is flown has exclusive jurisdiction over everything which occurs on board a merchant ship on the high seas.

It is certainly true that – apart from certain special cases which are defined by inter-national law – vessels on the high seas are subject to no authority except that of the State whose flag they fly. In virtue of the principle of the freedom of the seas, that is to say, the absence of any territorial sovereignty upon the high seas, no State may exercise any kind of jurisdiction over foreign vessels upon them. Thus, if a war vessel, happening to be at the spot where a collision occurs between a vessel flying its flag and a foreign vessel, were to send on board the latter an officer to make investigations or to take evidence such an act would undoubtedly be contrary to international law.

But it by no means follows that a State can never in its own territory exercise jurisdiction over acts which have occurred on board a foreign ship on the high seas. A corollary of the principle of the freedom of the seas is that a ship on the high seas is assimilated to the territory of the State the flag of which it flies, for, just as in its own territory, that State exercises its authority upon it, and no other State may do so. All that can be said is that by virtue of the principle of the freedom of the seas, a ship is placed in the same position as national territory; but there is nothing to support the claim according to which the rights of the State under whose flag the vessel sails may go farther than the rights which it exercises within its territory properly so called. It follows that what occurs on board a vessel on the high seas must be regarded as if it occurred on the territory of the State whose flag the ship flies. If, therefore, a guilty act committed on the high seas produces its effects on a vessel flying another flag or in foreign territory, the same principles must be applied as if the territories of two different States were concerned, and the conclusion must therefore be drawn that there is no rule of international law prohibiting the State to which the ship on which the effects of the offence have taken place belongs, from regarding the offence as having been committed in its territory and prosecuting, accordingly, the delinquent.

This conclusion could only be overcome if it were shown that there was a rule of customary international law which, going further than the principle stated above, established the exclusive jurisdiction of the State whose flag was flown. ...

In the Court's opinion, the existence of such a rule has not been conclusively proved. ...

The Court therefore has arrived at the conclusion that the second argument put forward by the French Government does not, any more than the first, establish the existence of a rule of international law prohibiting Turkey from prosecuting Lieutenant Demons.

It only remains to examine the third argument advanced by the French Government and to ascertain whether a rule specially applying to collision cases has grown up, according to which criminal proceedings regarding such cases come exclusively within the jurisdiction of the State whose flag is flown. ...

So far as the Court is aware there are no decisions of international tribunals in this matter; but some decisions of municipal courts have been cited. Without pausing to consider the value to be attributed to the judgments of municipal courts in connection with the establishment of the existence of a rule of international law, it will suffice to observe that the decisions quoted sometimes support one view and sometimes the other.

...It will suffice to observe that, as municipal jurisprudence is thus divided, it is hardly possible to see in it an indication of the existence of the restrictive rule of international law which alone could serve as a basis for the contention of the French Government ... .

The conclusion at which the Court has therefore arrived is that there is no rule of international law in regard to collision cases to the effect that criminal proceedings are exclusively within the jurisdiction of the State whose flag is flown.

This conclusion moreover is easily explained if the manner in which the collision brings the jurisdiction of two different countries into play be considered.

The offence for which Lieutenant Demons appears to have been prosecuted was an act – of negligence or imprudence – having its origin on board the *Lotus*, whilst its effects made themselves felt on board the *Boz-Kourt*. These two elements are, legally, entirely inseparable, so much so that their separation renders the offence non-existent. Neither the exclusive jurisdiction of either State nor the limitations of the jurisdiction of each to the occurrences which took place on the respective ships would appear calculated to satisfy the requirements of justice and effectively to protect the interests of the two States. It is only natural that each should be able to exercise jurisdiction and to do so in respect of the incident as a whole. It is therefore a case of concurrent jurisdiction. ...

For these reasons, the Court, having heard both Parties, gives, by the President's casting vote – the votes being equally divided – judgment to the effect:

1) That, following the collision which occurred on August 2nd, 1926, on the high

seas between the French steamship *Lotus* and the Turkish steamship *Boz-Kourt*, and upon the arrival of the French ship at Stamboul, and in consequence of the loss of the *Boz-Kourt* having involved the death of eight Turkish nationals, Turkey, by instituting criminal proceedings in pursuance of Turkish law against Lieutenant Demons, officer of the watch on board the *Lotus* at the time of the collision, has not acted in conflict with the principles of international law, contrary to Article 15 of the Convention of Lausanne of July 24th, 1923, respecting conditions of residence and business and jurisdiction; ...

2) That, consequently, there is no occasion to give judgment on the question of the pecuniary reparation which might have been due to Lieutenant Demons if Turkey, by prosecuting him as above stated, had acted in a manner contrary to the principles of international law. ...

NOTES

1) As this case shows, there are few rigid limits on jurisdiction set down by customary international law. The practical limitation, however, is that no state will generally attempt to exercise jurisdiction over matters in which it has no substantial interest or connection.

2) The discrete ruling that in collisions at sea jurisdiction is not limited to the flag state has since been overtaken by the 1958 Geneva Convention on the High Seas Article 11, which is reiterated in the 1982 U.N. Convention on the Law of the Sea Article 97, discussed in the section on the ''High Seas'' in Chapter 11.

Bases of Jurisdiction

There are at least five bases upon which claims to jurisdiction over an offence[7] may be founded. International law does not place them in an hierarchical order. However, some are universally recognized while others are not. Nevertheless, on account of the fact that several bases may operate for the same criminal action, concurrent jurisdiction will result. For example, suppose an Italian crew member of a French merchant ship stabs a West German in the Canadian port of Halifax. Which of the States involved has jurisdiction over the stabbing offence? Does more than one? The role of international law here is to determine which domestic law or laws are to apply. Mann has aptly suggested:[8]

Jurisdiction ... is concerned with what has been described as one of the fundamental functions of public international law, *viz*, the function of regulating and delivering the respective competences of states, ''de conférer, de repartir et de réglementer les compétences.''

---

[7] Remember that jurisdiction over the offence (prescriptive jurisdiction) and over the person (enforcement jurisdiction) are both necessary in most states before a criminal prosecution may proceed. A state may have one and not the other. See Williams and Castel, *supra*, n. 3, at 7.

[8] F.A. Mann, *supra*, n. 3, at 15.

The five bases[9] that have been utilized by states are as follows:

Territorial Principle

The state in whose territory a crime was committed has jurisdiction over the offence. This is the primary working rule. Territory includes the land mass, internal waters and their beds, territorial sea and its subsoil and the air space above all of the former.[10] Territory has recently been extended to a 200-nautical mile exclusive economic zone and continental shelf for certain functional ends.[11]

It is a manifestation of state sovereignty that a state should have jurisdiction over all persons, citizens and aliens alike, and things within its territory.[12] Canada's position is basically a territorial one. Section 5(2) of the *Canadian Criminal Code* provides that:

Subject to this Act or any other Act of Parliament, no person shall be convicted or discharged under section 662.1 of an offence committed outside Canada.

In complicated situations there are four possible different applications of this principle. First, an act may be deemed to be committed in the place where it is commenced. This is the subjective or initiatory principle. Second, there is the objective or terminatory territorial principle that provides that the state where the act is consummated or where the last constituent element occurs or effects are felt takes jurisdiction over the offence. Third, the problem of what the term "committed" means was handled by Lord Diplock in *Treacy v. D.P.P.*[13] in a novel way. He promoted the theory that a state may take jurisdiction where any element of the offence takes place within its borders. This circumvents the difficulties and gaps that may result in choosing between the first two possibilities. Fourthly, a state may take jurisdiction over the offence where it has a legitimate interest in doing so. In *Libman v. The Queen*[14] the Supreme Court of Canada recently held that Canadian courts will take jurisdiction where a significant portion of the activities have taken place in Canada. It is this real and substantial link test that would appear the most appropriate and accord with conceptions of international comity.

Nationality Principle[15]

The nationality of the offender is accepted as a basis of jurisdiction and is utilized extensively by civil law countries. Common law countries, on the other hand, have been

---

[9] For an in-depth discussion see "Harvard Research Draft Convention on Jurisdiction with respect to Crime" (1935), 29 *Am. J. Int. L. Supp.* 439; S.A. Williams and J.-G. Castel, *supra*, n. 3, cc. 1–5; I. Brownlie, *supra*, n. 3, at 298–305; and C. Blakesley, *supra*, n. 3; *Restatement (Revised), Foreign Relations Law of the United States* ss. 401–404.

[10] See further Chapter 6 on "State Jurisdiction Over Territory."

[11] See Chapter 11 on the "Law of the Sea."

[12] See *Compania Naviera Vascongado v. Steamship Cristina*, [1938] A.C. 485, at 496, per Ld. MacMillan.

[13] [1971] A.C. 537 (H.L.).

[14] [1985] 2 S.C.R. 178.

[15] Acquisition and loss of nationality are discussed in Chapter 7.

reticent in their use of the nationality principle. States such as Canada only claim jurisdiction on this ground for a few serious crimes such as treason (s. 46(3) of the *Criminal
Code*), crimes against internationally protected persons (s. 6(1.2)(c) *Criminal Code*),
hostage-taking (s. 6(1.3) *Criminal Code*) and *inter alia* under *The Foreign Enlistment
Act, The Official Secrets Act* and *The Public Service Employment Act*.[16] They have not,
however, challenged its use by other states.

The nationality principle is the necessary corollary to the reluctance to extradite nationals which most civil law countries display. However, the nationality and territoriality
principles may create parallel concurrent jurisdiction over an offence and hence possible
double jeopardy. Therefore, the use of the nationality principle would be better confined
to serious offences.

Passive Personality (Nationality) Principle

By this principle a state may claim jurisdiction over crimes committed abroad, even by
aliens, against its nationals. Strong opposition has been expressed to the use of this
principle. It was contested by France in *The Steamship Lotus* but the Court reserved its
opinion as it was not the sole basis of Turkish jurisdiction. However, Judge Moore
expressed a dissenting opinion which included this condemnation:[17]

...the countries by which the claim [based upon the passive personality or nationality principle]
has been espoused are said to have adopted the "system of protection."

What, we may ask, is this system? In substance, it means that the citizen of one country,
when he visits another country, takes with him for his "protection" the law of his own country
and subjects those with whom he comes into contact to the operation of that law. In this way
the inhabitant of a great commercial city, in which foreigners congregate, may in the course of
an hour unconsciously fall under the operation of a number of foreign criminal codes. This is by
no means a fanciful supposition; it is merely an illustration of what is daily occurring, if the
"protective principle" is admissable. It is evident that this claim is at variance not only with the
principle of the exclusive jurisdiction of a state over its own territory, but also with the equally
well-settled principle that a person visiting a foreign country, far from radiating for his protection
the jurisdiction of his own country, falls under the dominion of the local law, and except so
far as his government may diplomatically intervene in case of a denial of justice, must look to
that law for his protection.

No one disputes the right of a state to subject its citizens abroad to the operations of its own
penal laws, if it sees fit to do so. This concerns simply the citizen and his own government,
and no other government can properly interfere. But the case is fundamentally different where a
country claims either that its penal laws apply to other countries and to what takes place
wholly within such countries, or, if it does not claim this, that it may punish foreigners for alleged
violations, even in their own country, of laws to which they were not subject. ...

The only examples of this principle in the *Canadian Criminal Code* are section 6(1.2)(d)(i)

---

[16] R.S.C. 1970, c. F-29; R.S.C. 1970, c. O-3 as amended; and R.S.C. 1970, c. P-32, as amended, respectively.
[17] (1927), P.C.I.J. Ser. A, No. 10, at 65. The judgment of the majority is reported *supra*.

and (ii) which gives jurisdiction to a Canadian court where acts or omissions take place abroad against persons who are internationally protected persons representing Canada, or members of their families, and section 6(1.4) which deals with hostage-taking.[18]

Protective Principle

Under this principle a state may exercise jurisdiction over acts committed abroad that are prejudicial to its security, territorial integrity and political independence. For example, the type of crimes covered could include espionage, treason and counterfeiting of currency, postage stamps, seals, passports or other public documents.

    Canada, the United Kingdom and the United States have not favoured this principle when unaccompanied by other factors tying the accused to the forum. They have intertwined the nationality principle, the detrimental "effects" approach and the protective principle.[19]

Universal Principle

Two possible interpretations of this principle have been put forward by states. First, that a state may exercise jurisdiction over all crimes, committed by anyone, wherever they occur. This is seldom if ever used.[20] The second is the more common. It utilizes the principle for serious crimes where the international nature of the offence justifies its universal repression. This is imperative in areas such as hostage-taking, hijacking and attacks on internationally protected persons where the states, to whom the other bases of jurisdiction are applicable, are unwilling to prosecute.

    Canada does not use this basis except in a limited fashion for piracy,[21] hijacking, attacks on civil aviation,[22] attacks on internationally protected persons[23] and hostage taking.[24] The key feature here is that a Canadian court will have jurisdiction over the offence if the offender is found to be present in Canada and he or she is not subjected to extradition.

---

[18] This section implements Canada's obligations under the 1973 Convention on the Prevention and Punishment of Crimes Against Internationally Protected Persons, U.N.G.A. Res. 3166 (XXVIII), reprinted in (1974), 13 *Int. Leg. Mat.* 41. Note also the 1979 Convention Against the Taking of Hostages, U.N. Doc. A/C.6/34/ L.23, reprinted in (1979), 18 *Int. Leg. Mat.* 1456.

[19] See the classic case of *Joyce v. D.P.P.*, [1946] A.C. 347 (H.L.), for analysis of what constitutes allegiance to the state. Also see *R. v. Casement*, [1917] 1 K.B. 98; and *R. v. Neuman* (1949), 3 S.A. 1238 (Sp. Crim. Ct. Transvaal).

[20] See the *Universal Jurisdiction* case (1958), 28 I.L.R. 341 (Austrian S.C.), and the *Hungarian Deserter* case (1959), 28 I.L.R. 343 (Austrian S.C.).

[21] Section 75(1) of the *Criminal Code*.

[22] Sections 6(1), 76(1), and 76(2) of the *Criminal Code*.

[23] Section 6(1.2) of the *Criminal Code*.

[24] Section 6(1.3) of the *Criminal Code*.

secondly on the protective and passive personality principles. As discussed earlier in this chapter, the protective principle is used to protect a state's vital interests. There must be a "linking point" between the crime and the state. The "linking point" in this case was that the crimes were committed against Jewish people, although at the time no state of Israel was in existence. The Court concluded that the connection between the State of Israel and the Jewish people needed no explanation. The defence had argued that the protective and passive personality principles could not operate here.

Excess of Jurisdiction

The exercise of jurisdiction which is prohibited or cannot be soundly based on any of the five principles previously considered may induce complaints from other states. The international responsibility that may befall a state which acts in excess of its jurisdiction is discussed in Chapter 9. The question here is how an excess of jurisdiction internationally will affect the authority of the state internally.

Unlawful Arrest in a Foreign State

If a fugitive from the criminal law of one state seeks refuge in another state, in order to be brought to trial he must be returned to the state that seeks to prosecute him. His presence may be secured lawfully by extradition,[36] or unlawfully by kidnapping in the refuge state or by enticement to enter the state of prosecution by fraud. The question that arises is whether an accused who has been obtained by extra-legal means can contest the jurisdiction of the court over him. Does the illegal act by law enforcement officers or other persons from the prosecuting state result in the court divesting itself of jurisdiction?[37] Or, is the kidnapping simply a violation of customary or conventional international law relating to the territorial sovereignty of the state of refuge that may be complained about by that state alone?

The usual stance in Canada, the United Kingdom and the United States has been that a fugitive should not succeed in escaping trial because he was illegally brought into the jurisdiction of the prosecuting state. The source of this practice can be found in the Roman law maxim, *mala captus bene detentus*, which means that the court once in possession of the accused has jurisdiction over him and all that is required is a fair trial.

Comment on Conviction after Unlawful Arrest
by S.A. Williams (1975), 53 *Can. Bar Rev.* 404 (footnotes omitted)

...One of the major problems raised by the present uncertain tendencies of the law concerning unlawful arrest is the question of policy. The interests of the individual offender are in juxtaposition with those of the state. Canadian as well as American courts have

---

[36] Discussed *infra*.

[37] See S.A. Williams and J.G. Castel, *Supra*, n. 3, at c. 7; and C. Cole, "Extradition Treaties Abound But Unlawful Seizures Continue," [1975] *Int. Persp.* (March/April) 40.

tended to promote the idea that illegality of some pre-trial events, although infringing the accused's rights, should not nullify his detention and excuse him from a crime he has committed. They have weighed the illegal arrest against the merits of the criminal charge. However, there is a conflicting theory as to the thought that criminals should be punished, and that is that a government should obey the law – even where criminals are concerned. Jurisdiction gained through illegal acts tend to reward brutality and lawlessness. Thus, one must consider whether it is in the social interest to excuse a criminal because the police or government agents used illegal means to bring him before the court.

...Government officials should not have a separate set of rules as regards their conduct. Respect for the authority of a government will seriously be affected if it fails itself to observe the law faithfully, and individual citizens feel that their liberty is at stake. A government should set an example to its people and if it is known to be breaking the law in order to secure criminal convictions what hope is there for society in general. The right to be protected from abduction into the jurisdiction of a state is a basic human right in a free society. The misplaced sense of justice on the part of governments or individual agents not to comply with legal machinery to bring offenders into the jurisdiction of the court must be condemned. The official who acts in an unlawful way may be criminally liable for kidnapping. He may also be liable civilly to the victim for trespass to the person. The criminal penalties are seldom used as there is no tendency on the part of states to prosecute their officers, and as regards the civil measures, there is little doubt that policemen are not affluent enough to warrant action against them personally unless their employers are made jointly liable. Thus, the most definite way by far of deterring the police from wilful lawlessness is to make it clear that criminals will not be tried who have been illegally secured.

United States v. Toscanino
(1974), 500 F. 2d 267 (U.S.C.A. 2d Cir.) (footnotes omitted)

[In this remarkable opinion the Court held that the requirement of due process, as understood in the United States, obliges a criminal court to divest itself of jurisdiction over an accused whose presence has been illegally obtained. The accused, Toscanino, appealing against his conviction of 20 years in prison and a $20,000.00 fine on a narcotics charge, countered that jurisdiction over him had been illegally acquired in that American agents had kidnapped him in Uruguay, used illegal electronic surveillance, tortured him and abducted him to the United States. He did not question the sufficiency of the actual evidence against him or any error in the conduct of the trial itself.]

MANSFIELD, Circuit Judge: ... On or about January 6, 1973 Francisco Toscanino was lured from his home in Montevideo, Uruguay by a telephone call. This call had been placed by or at the direction of Hugo Campos Hermedia. Hermedia was at that time and still is a member of the police in Montevideo, Uruguay. In this effort, however, and those that will follow in this offer, Hermedia was acting *ultra vires* in that he was the paid agent of the United States government. ...

The telephone call ruse succeeded in bringing Toscanino and his wife, seven months pregnant at the time, to an area near a deserted bowling alley in the City of Montevideo. Upon their arrival there Hermedia together with six associates abducted Toscanino. This was accomplished in full view of Toscanino's terrified wife by knocking him unconscious with a gun and throwing him into the rear seat of Hermedia's car. Thereupon Toscanino, bound and blindfolded, was driven to the Uruguayan-Brazilian border by a circuitous route. ...

At one point during the long trip to the Brazilian border discussion was had among Toscanino's captors as to changing the license plates of the abductor's car in order to avoid detection by the Uruguayan authorities. At another point the abductor's car was abruptly brought to a halt, and Toscanino was ordered to get out. He was brought to an apparently secluded place and told to lie perfectly still or he would be shot then and there. Although his blindfold prevented him from seeing, Toscanino could feel the barrel of the gun against his head and could hear the rumbling noises of what appeared to be an Uruguayan military convoy. A short time after the noise of the convoy had died away, Toscanino was placed in another vehicle and whisked to the border. There by pre-arrangement and again at the connivance of the United States government, the car was met by a group of Brazilians who took custody of the body of Francisco Toscanino.

At no time had there been any formal or informal request on the part of the United States of the government of Uruguay for the extradition of Francisco Toscanino nor was there any legal basis to justify this rank criminal enterprise. In fact, the Uruguayan government claims that it had no prior knowledge of the kidnapping nor did it consent thereto and had indeed condemned this kind of apprehension as alien to its laws.

Once in the custody of Brazilians, Toscanino was brought to Porto Alegre where he was held incommunicado for eleven hours. His requests to consult with counsel, the Italian Consulate, and his family were all denied. During this time he was denied all food and water.

Later that same day Toscanino was brought to Brasilia. ... For seventeen days Toscanino was incessantly tortured and interrogated. Throughout this entire period the United States government and the United States Attorney for the Eastern District of New York prosecuting this case was aware of the interrogation and did in fact receive reports as to its progress. Furthermore, during this period of torture and interrogation a member of the United States Department of Justice, Bureau of Narcotics and Dangerous Drugs was present at one or more intervals and actually participated in portions of the interrogation. ... [Toscanino's] captors denied him sleep and all forms of nourishment for days at a time. Nourishment was provided intravenously in a manner precisely equal to an amount necessary to keep him alive. Reminiscent of the horror stories told by our military men who returned from Korea and China, Toscanino was forced to walk up and down a hallway for seven or eight hours at a time. When he could no longer stand he was kicked and beaten but all in a manner contrived to punish without scarring. When he would not answer, his fingers were pinched with metal pliers. Alcohol was flushed into his eyes and nose and other fluids ... were forced up his anal passage. Incredibly, these agents of the United States government attached electrodes to Toscanino's earlobes, toes, and genitals. Jarring jolts of electricity were shot throughout his body, rendering him unconscious for indeterminate periods of time but again leaving no physical scars.

Finally on or about January 25, 1973 Toscanino was brought to Rio de Janeiro where he was drugged by Brazilian-American agents and placed on Pan American Airways Flight #202 destined for the waiting arms of the United States government. On or about January 26, 1973, he woke in the United States, was arrested on the aircraft, and was brought immediately to Thomas Puccio, Assistant United States Attorney.

At no time during the government's seizure of Toscanino did it ever attempt to accomplish its goal through any lawful channels whatever. From start to finish the government unlawfully, willingly and deliberately embarked upon a brazenly criminal scheme violating the laws of three separate countries.

The government prosecutor neither affirmed nor denied these allegations but claimed they were immaterial to the district court's power to proceed. ...

Toscanino's motion for an order vacating the verdict, dismissing the indictment and ordering his return to Uruguay was denied by the district court on November 2, 1973, without a hearing. Relying principally on the decisions of the Supreme Court in *Ker v. Illinois*, 119 U.S. 436, 7 S. Ct. 225, 30 L. Ed. 421 (1886), and *Frisbie v. Collins*, 342 U.S. 519, 72 S. Ct. 509, 96 L. Ed. 541 (1952), the court held that the manner in which Toscanino was brought into the territory of the United States was immaterial to the court's power to proceed, provided he was physically present at the time of trial.

[The Court proceeded to review the Supreme Court decisions in *Ker* and *Frisbie*.]

...While residing in Peru, Ker was indicted by an Illinois grand jury for larceny and embezzlement. At the request of the Governor of Illinois the President, invoking the current treaty of extradition between the United States and Peru, issued a warrant authorizing a Pinkerton agent to take custody of Ker from the authorities of Peru. The warrant, however, was never served, probably for the reason that by the time the agent arrived there armed forces of Chile, then at war with Peru, were in control of Lima. See Ker v. Illinois Revisited, 47 Am. J. Int'l L. 678 (1953). Instead Ker was forcibly abducted by the agent, placed aboard an American vessel and eventually taken to the United States, where he was tried and convicted in Illinois. The Supreme Court rejected Ker's argument that he was entitled by virtue of the treaty with Peru to a right of asylum there and held that the abduction of Ker did not violate the Due Process Clause of the Fourteenth Amendment (then less than 20 years old), which was construed as merely requiring that the party be regularly indicted and brought to trial "according to the forms and modes prescribed for such trials." The Court accordingly held that Ker might be tried by Illinois, regardless of the method by which it acquired control over him.

Sixty-six years later the Supreme Court again faced the question in *Frisbie v. Collins, supra*, in a slightly different context. There a Michigan state prisoner, petitioning for habeas corpus, alleged that he had been brought from Chicago, Illinois, to Michigan for trial only after he had been kidnapped, handcuffed and blackjacked in Chicago by Michigan police officers who had gone there to retrieve him. The prisoner claimed that his conviction in Michigan violated the Due Process Clause of the Fourteenth Amendment as well as the federal Kidnapping Act, 18 U.S.C. s. 1201, and was therefore a nullity. Rejecting the due process claim the Supreme Court explained:

This Court has never departed from the rule announced in *Ker v. Illinois*, 119 U.S. 436, 444, [7 S. Ct. 225, 229, 30 L. Ed. 421], that the power of a court to try a person for crime is not impaired by the fact that he had been brought within the court's jurisdiction by reason of a "forcible abduction." No persuasive reasons are now presented to justify overruling this line of cases. They rest on the sound basis that due process of law is satisfied when one present in court is convicted of crime after being fairly apprized of the charges against him and after a fair trial in accordance with constitutional procedural safeguards. 342 U.S. at 522.

Thus, under the so-called "Ker-Frisbie" rule, due process was limited to the guarantee of a constitutionally fair trial, regardless of the method by which jurisdiction was obtained over the defendant. Jurisdiction gained through an indisputably illegal act might still be exercised, even though the effect could be to reward police brutality and lawlessness in some cases.

[However, the Court was of the view that the Supreme Court had since expanded the concept of due process, extending it as regards obtaining evidence to the pre-trial conduct of law enforcement authorities.]

...Faced with a conflict between the two concepts of due process, the one being the restricted version found in *Ker-Frisbie* and the other the expanded and enlightened interpretation expressed in more recent decisions of the Supreme Court, we are persuaded that to the extent that the two are in conflict, the *Ker-Frisbie* version must yield. Accordingly we view due process as now requiring a court to divest itself of jurisdiction over the person of a defendant where it has been acquired as the result of the government's deliberate, unnecessary and unreasonable invasion of the accused's constitutional rights. This conclusion represents but an extension of the well-recognized power of federal courts in the civil context to decline to exercise jurisdiction over a defendant whose presence has been secured by force or fraud. See *In re Johnson*, 167 U.S. 120, 126, 17 S. Ct. 735, 42 L. Ed. 103 (1896), *Fitzgerald Construction Co. v. Fitzgerald*, 137 U.S. 98, 11 S. Ct. 36, 34 L.Ed. 608 (1890).

If the charges of government misconduct in kidnapping Toscanino and forcibly bringing him to the United States should be sustained, the foregoing principles would, as a matter of due process, entitle him to some relief. The allegations include corruption and bribery of a foreign official as well as kidnapping, accompanied by violence and brutality to the person. Deliberate misconduct on the part of United States agents, in violation not only of constitutional prohibitions but also of the federal Kidnapping Act, *supra*, and of two international treaties obligating the United States Government to respect the territorial sovereignty of Uruguay, is charged. See U.N. Charter, art. 2; O.A.S. Charter, art. 17.

...[N]ot only were several laws allegedly broken and crimes committed at the behest of government agents but the conduct was apparently unnecessary, as the extradition treaty between the United States and Uruguay, see 35 Stat. 2028, does not specifically exclude narcotics violations so that a representative of our government might have been able to conclude with Uruguay a special arrangement for Toscanino's extradition. *Cf. Fiocconi v. Attorney General of United States*, 339 F. Supp. 1242, 1244 (S.D.N.Y. 1972). ...

That international kidnappings such as the one alleged here violate the U.N. Charter was settled as a result of the Security Council debates following the illegal kidnapping in 1960 of Adolf Eichmann from Argentina by Israeli "volunteer groups." In response to a formal complaint filed by the U.N. representative from Argentina pursuant to article 35 of the U.N. Charter the Security Council, by eight votes to none (with two abstentions and one member – Argentina – not participating in the vote), adopted a resolution condemning the kidnapping and requesting "the Government of Israel to make appropriate reparation in accordance with the Charter of the United Nations and rules of international law ... " U.N. Doc. S/4349 (June 23, 1960), quoted in W. Friedmann, O. Lissitzyn & R. Pugh, International Law: Cases and Materials 497 (1969). The resolution merely recognized a long standing principle of international law that abductions by one state of persons located within the territory of another violate the territorial sovereignty of the second state and are redressable usually by the return of the person kidnapped. See The Vincenti Affair, 1 Hackworth 310 (1914); The Case of Blatt and Converse, 2 Hackworth 309 (1911).

Since the United States thus agreed not to seize persons residing within the territorial limits of Uruguay, appellant's allegations in this case are governed not by *Ker* but by the Supreme Court's later decision in *Cook v. United States*, 288 U.S. 102, 53 S. Ct. 305, 77 L. Ed. 641 (1933). In *Cook* officers of the United States Coast Guard boarded and seized a British vessel, the Mazel Tov, in violation of territorial limits fixed by a treaty then in force between the United States and Great Britain. The Supreme Court held that the government's subsequent libel for forfeiture of the vessel in the federal district court was properly dismissed, since under the treaty the forcible seizure was incapable of giving the district court power to adjudicate title to the vessel regardless of the vessel's physical presence within the court's jurisdiction.

[The case was remanded to the district court for an evidentiary hearing of Toscanino's allegations.]

NOTES

1) In later cases such as *U.S. v. Herrera*,[38] *U.S. ex rel Lujan v. Gengler*,[39] *U.S. v. Lira*,[40] and *Marschener v. U.S.*,[41] the Toscanino case has been distinguished and explained. It was distinguished in *Gengler* on the ground that although government agents do not have a carte blanche to bring defendants from abroad to the United States by the use of torture, brutality and similar outrageous conduct, not every violation of law by the government or irregularity in the circumstances of a defendant's arrival in the jurisdiction is sufficient to vitiate the proceedings in a criminal court. Here the conduct of the U.S. government agents was not outrageous and furthermore the offended state did not object to that conduct.

2) The Canadian cases of *R. v. Walton*[42] and *Re Hartnett and the Queen: Re Hudson and the Queen*[43] have applied the *mala captus bene detentus* maxim with slight concern

---

[38] 504 F. 2d 859 (U.S.C. A. 5th Circ., 1974).
[39] 510 F. 2d 62 (U.S.C. A. 2d Circ., 1975).
[40] 515 F. 2d 68 (U.S.C. A. 2d Circ., 1975).
[41] 470 F. Supp. 201 (U.S. Dist. Ct. D. Conn., 1979).
[42] (1905), 10 C.C.C. 269 (Ont. C.A.).
[43] (1973), 1 O.R. (2d) 206 (Ont. H.C.).

for the due process of law and the civil rights of the accused. Will the *Charter of Rights and Freedoms*[44] alter this position?[45]

3) Although the decision in Toscanino was welcomed by many, has it any real impact? Even without the back-tracking in the later cases, would it be exceedingly difficult for the accused to prove allegations of torture? Should evidence be produced, the threshold set appears to be intolerably high.

4) Unlawful enforcement in another state also formed the basis of the *Jaffe case*.[46] Mr. Jaffe was kidnapped in Toronto by two "bounty hunters" employed by a U.S. bail bonding agency. Then he was forcibly taken by them to Florida to answer outstanding criminal charges of fraud. Canada vigorously protested to the United States that the abduction was a violation of international law and Jaffe was eventually released.

HIJACKING AND OTHER TERRORIST ACTS[47]

Acts of international terrorism are of concern to the whole of the international community. However, the manner in which that community has sought to deal with the problem has not been in the form of a single comprehensive treaty. Rather, a piecemeal approach has been used. Several multilateral conventions have been adopted which deal with different types of terrorist acts such as hijacking and other attacks on civil aviation, attacks on diplomats and other internationally protected persons and the taking of hostages. This method of a convention-by-convention approach was the only one possible as some states would not agree to one convention dealing with all the aspects together.[48] The overriding wish is to join as many states parties as possible against each kind of terrorist activity and thus this piecemeal pattern of conventions has emerged.

In the following extracts from the various conventions two features will be apparent; first, the use of the different bases of jurisdiction over the offence, considered earlier in this Chapter, and secondly the concept of *aut dedere, aut judicare*, extradite or prosecute. It is encumbent on a state, which ratifies, to establish in its territory jurisdiction over the crime. Then, if an alleged offender is detained and he is not extradited to another state, he will be submitted to the local authorities for prosecution.

---

[44] 1982, as enacted by the *Canada Act 1982*, Stats. U.K. 1982, c. 11.

[45] Note that the *Canadian Bill of Rights*, R.S.C. 1970, App. III, did not. See *Re Hartnett, supra*, n. 43.

[46] See the fuller report of the case under "State Responsibility," *infra* in Chapter 9.

[47] See generally M.C. Bassiouni, ed., *International Terrorism and Political Crimes* (1975); A. Evans and J. Murphy, eds., *Legal Aspects of International Terrorism* (1978); R. Friedlander, *Terrorism* (1979–84) 4 vols; S.A. Williams and J.-G. Castel, *supra*, n. 3, at c.11.

[48] A comprehensive approach was taken in the 1937 Convention on the Prevention and Punishment of Terrorism, Hudson, *International Legislation*, Vol. 7, at 862; reprinted in S.A. Williams, *International Criminal Law Casebook* (1983), at 627. However, neither this convention nor a draft Convention dealing with the setting up of an international criminal court ever came into force.

Tokyo Convention on Offences Committed on Board Aircraft[49]
(1963), 704 U.N.T.S. 219; 1970 Can. T.S. No. 5

CHAPTER I
SCOPE OF THE CONVENTION
Article 1

1. This Convention shall apply in respect of:
(a) offences against penal law;
(b) acts which, whether or not they are offences, may or do jeopardize the safety of the aircraft or of persons or property therein or which jeopardize good order and discipline on board.

2. Except as provided in Chapter III, this Convention shall apply in respect of offences committed or acts done by a person on board any aircraft registered in a Contracting State, while that aircraft is in flight or on the surface of the high seas or of any other area outside the territory of any State.

3. For the purposes of this Convention, an aircraft is considered to be in flight from the moment when power is applied for the purpose of take-off until the moment when the landing run ends.

4. This Convention shall not apply to aircraft used in military, customs or police services.

Article 2

Without prejudice to the provisions of Article 4 and except when the safety of the aircraft or of persons or property on board so requires, no provision of this Convention shall be interpreted as authorizing or requiring any action in respect of offences against penal laws of a political nature or those based on racial or religious discrimination.

CHAPTER II
JURISDICTION
Article 3

1. The State of registration of the aircraft is competent to exercise jurisdiction over offences and acts committed on board.

---

[49] In force 1969. In 1986 there were 121 contracting parties. In Canada see ss. 2, 6, 75A and 432(d) of the *Criminal Code*. See E. McWhinney, ed., *Aerial Piracy and International Law* (1971); R.P. Boyle and R. Pulsifer, "The Tokyo Convention on Offences and Certain Other Acts Committed on Board Aircraft" (1964), 30 *J. Air L. Comm.* 305; G.F. FitzGerald, "The Development of International Rules Concerning Offences and Certain Other Acts Committed on Board Aircraft" (1963), 1 *Can. Y.B. Int. L.* 230; G.F. FitzGerald, "Offences and Certain Other Acts Committed on Board Aircraft: The Tokyo Convention of 1963" (1964), 2 *Can. Y. B. Int. L.* 191; J.J.L. Gutierrez, "Should the Tokyo Convention of 1963 be Ratified?" (1965), 31 *J. Air L. Comm.* 1; R.H. Mankiewicz, "Le droit pénal et l'aviation" (1957), 4 *McGill L.J.* 13; and (1963), 15 *Ext. Affairs* 415.

2. Each Contracting State shall take such measures as may be necessary to establish its jurisdiction as the State of registration over offences committed on board aircraft registered in such State.

3. This Convention does not exclude any criminal jurisdiction exercised in accordance with national law.

Article 4

A Contracting State which is not the State of registration may not interfere with an aircraft in flight in order to exercise its criminal jurisdiction over an offence committed on board except in the following cases:

(a) the offence has effect on the territory of such State;

(b) the offence has been committed by or against a national or permanent resident of such State;

(c) the offence is against the security of such State;

(d) the offence consists of a breach of any rules or regulations relating to the flight or manoeuvre of aircraft in force in such State;

(e) the exercise of jurisdiction is necessary to ensure the observance of any obligation of such State under a multilateral international agreement.

CHAPTER VI
OTHER PROVISIONS
Article 16

1. Offences committed on aircraft registered in a Contracting State shall be treated, for the purpose of extradition, as if they had been committed not only in the place in which they have occurred but also in the territory of the State of registration of the aircraft.

2. Without prejudice to the provisions of the preceding paragraph, nothing in this Convention shall be deemed to create an obligation to grant extradition.

Article 17

In taking any measures for investigation or arrest or otherwise exercising jurisdiction in connection with any offence committed on board an aircraft the Contracting States shall pay due regard to the safety and other interests of air navigation and shall so act as to avoid unnecessary delay of the aircraft, passengers, crew or cargo.

Hague Convention for the Suppression of the Unlawful Seizure of Aircraft[50]
1972 Can. T.S. No. 23; 22 U.S.T. 1641

Article 1

Any person who on board an aircraft in flight:

---

[50] 1970, in force 1977. In 1986 there were 126 contracting states. See the Canadian *Criminal Code*, ss. 6, 76.1,

(a) unlawfully, by force or threat thereof, or by any other form of intimidation, seizes, or exercises control of, that aircraft, or attempts to perform any such act, or

(b) is an accomplice of a person who performs or attempts to perform any such act commits an offence (hereinafter referred to as "the offence").

Article 2

Each Contracting State undertakes to make the offence punishable by severe penalties.

Article 3

1. For the purposes of this Convention, an aircraft is considered to be in flight at any time from the moment when all its external doors are closed following embarkation until the moment when any such door is opened for disembarkation. In the case of a forced landing, the flight shall be deemed to continue until the competent authorities take over the responsibility for the aircraft and for persons and property on board.

2. This Convention shall not apply to aircraft used in military, customs or police services.

3. This Convention shall apply only if the place of take-off or the place of actual landing of the aircraft on board which the offence is committed is situated outside the territory of the State of registration of that aircraft; it shall be immaterial whether the aircraft is engaged in an international or domestic flight.

4. In the cases mentioned in Article 5, this Convention shall not apply if the place of take-off and the place of actual landing of the aircraft on board which the offence is committed are situated within the territory of the same State where that State is one of those referred to in that Article.

5. Notwithstanding paragraphs 3 and 4 of this Article, Articles 6, 7, 8 and 10 shall apply whatever the place of take-off or the place of actual landing of the aircraft, if the offender or the alleged offender is found in the territory of a State other than the State of registration of that aircraft.

Article 4

1. Each Contracting State shall take such measures as may be necessary to establish its jurisdiction over the offence and any other act of violence against passengers or crew committed by the alleged offender in connection with the offence, in the following cases:

(a) when the offence is committed on board an aircraft registered in that State;

76.2, and 76.3. See also G.F. FitzGerald, "Towards Legal Suppression of Acts Against Civil Aviation" (1971), 585 *Int. Concil.* 51; and "Recent Proposals for Concerted Action Against States in Respect of Unlawful Interference with International Civil Aviation" (1974), 40 *J. Air L. and Comm.* 161; L.C. Green, "Piracy of Aircraft and the Law" (1972), 10 *Alta. L. Rev.* 72; R.T. Mankiewicz, "The 1970 Hague Convention" (1971), 37 *J. Air L. and Comm.* 195; N.M. Poulantzas, "The Anti-Hijack Convention of December 16th, 1970: An Article-by-Article Appraisal in the Light of Recent Developments" (1973), 2 *Anglo-American Rev.* 4; J.M. Sharp, "Canada and the Hijacking of Aircraft" (1973), 5 *Man. L.J.* 451.

(b) when the aircraft on board which the offence is committed lands in its territory with the alleged offender still on board;

(c) when the offence is committed on board an aircraft leased without crew to a lessee who has his principal place of business or, if the lessee has no such place of business, his permanent residence, in that State.

2. Each Contracting State shall likewise take such measures as may be necessary to establish its jurisdiction over the offence in the case where the alleged offender is present in its territory and it does not extradite him pursuant to Article 8 to any of the States mentioned in paragraph 1 of this Article.

3. This Convention does not exclude any criminal jurisdiction exercised in accordance with national law.

Article 6

1. Upon being satisfied that the circumstances so warrant, any contracting State in the territory of which the offender or alleged offender is present, shall take him into custody or take other measures to ensure his presence. The custody and other measures shall be as provided in the law of that State but may only be continued for such time as is necessary to enable any criminal or extradition proceedings to be instituted.

2. Such State shall immediately make a preliminary enquiry into the facts.

3. Any person in custody pursuant to paragraph 1 of this Article shall be assisted in communicating immediately with the nearest appropriate representative of the State of which he is a national.

4. When a State, pursuant to this Article, has taken a person into custody, it shall immediately notify the State of registration of the aircraft, the State mentioned in Article 4, paragraph 1(c), the State of nationality of the detained person and, if it considers it advisable, any other interested States of the fact that such person is in custody and of the circumstances which warrant his detention. The State which makes the preliminary enquiry contemplated in paragraph 2 of this Article shall promptly report its findings to the said States and shall indicate whether it intends to exercise jurisdiction.

Article 7

The Contracting State in the territory of which the alleged offender is found shall, if it does not extradite him, be obliged, without exception whatsoever and whether or not the offence was committed in its territory, to submit the case to its competent authorities for the purpose of prosecution. Those authorities shall take their decision in the same manner as in the case of any ordinary offence of a serious nature under the law of that State.

Article 8

1. The offence shall be deemed to be included as an extraditable offence in any extradition treaty existing between Contracting States. Contracting States undertake to include the offence as an extraditable offence in every extradition treaty to be concluded between them.

2. If a Contracting State which makes extradition conditional on the existence of a

treaty receives a request for extradition from another Contracting State with which it has no extradition treaty, it may at its option consider this Convention as the legal basis for extradition in respect of the offence. Extradition shall be subject to the other conditions provided by the law of the requested State.

3. Contracting States which do not make extradition conditional on the existence of a treaty shall recognize the offence as an extraditable offence between themselves subject to the conditions provided by the law of the requested State.

4. The offence shall be treated, for the purpose of extradition between Contracting States, as if it had been committed not only in the place in which it occurred but also in the territories of the States required to establish their jurisdiction in accordance with Article 4, paragraph 1.

Article 9

1. When any of the acts mentioned in Article 1(a) has occurred or is about to occur, Contracting States shall take all appropriate measures to restore control of the aircraft to its lawful commander or to preserve his control of the aircraft.

2. In the cases contemplated by the preceding paragraph, any Contracting State in which the aircraft or its passengers or crew are present shall facilitate the continuation of the journey of the passengers and crew as soon as practicable, and shall without delay return the aircraft and its cargo to the persons lawfully entitled to possession.

NOTES

1) The Tokyo Convention was the first in the civil aviation area with regard to terrorism. It is limited in its application. It deals primarily with the jurisdiction of the aircraft commander and jurisdiction over crimes committed on board aircraft. It does not define the offence of hijacking and it does not create an obligation to extradite.

2) The Hague Convention seeks to fill the gaps left by the Tokyo Convention. It provides for the "offence" and the means for prosecution. Note in particular the bases of jurisdiction in Article 4. Does Article 4(2) provide for a type of universal jurisdiction? Is Article 4(1)(c) the passive personality principle?

3) The Convention deals with extradition in Article 8. What is its effect? Can extradition be refused on account of the political offence exception to extradition? If so, is there an obligation to prosecute? See Article 7. Note Article 4(2)(ii) of the Extradition Treaty between Canada and the United States[51] which provides that the political offence exception shall not apply to the unlawful seizure of control of an aircraft or any other form of intimidation on board aircraft.

4) Refer to the materials on the Entebbe Raid in Chapter 2. What obligations did Uganda owe to the other states involved in light of the fact that it, like Israel and France, was a party to the Hague Convention?

---

[51] 1976 Can. T.S. No. 3.

5) The Montreal Convention for the Suppression of Unlawful Acts Against the Safety of Civil Aviation, 1971[52] completes the scheme. It deals with acts of violence against aircraft in flight and in service as defined in that Convention; acts against air navigation facilities or their operation; and communication of false information that endangers the safety of an aircraft in flight. Like the Hague Convention it provides for wide bases of jurisdiction over the offence and the concept of *aut dedere, aut judicare*.

6) Note additionally the bilateral approach of the Canada-Cuba Agreement of 1973, renewed in 1979.[53] However, in this agreement extradition may be refused for political reasons and there is no *aut dedere, aut judicare* concept.

7) On July 17th, 1978, at the Bonn Economic Summit meeting, a declaration was made to stop air traffic to safe-haven states:

The Heads of State and Government, concerned about terrorism and the taking of hostages, declare that their Governments will intensify their joint efforts to combat international terrorism. To this end, in cases where a country refuses extradition or prosecution of those who have hijacked an aircraft and/or do not return such aircraft, the Heads of State and Government are jointly resolved that their Governments shall take immediate action to cease all flights to that country. At the same time, their Governments will initiate action to halt all incoming flights from that country or from any country by the airlines of the country concerned.

They urge other Governments to join them in this commitment.

This declaration is an important political commitment but is it a binding international agreement? Does it evince the kind of intent to be legally bound that is required of a treaty?[54]

8) There have been similar provisions as to jurisdiction, extradition and prosecution in the Convention on the Protection and Punishment of Crimes Against Internationally Protected Persons, including Diplomatic Agents, 1973[55] and in the International Convention Against the Taking of Hostages, 1979.[56]

The additional feature of the 1979 Hostages Convention is that it provides for jurisdiction over the offence by the state that is the target of the hostage taking.[57] Reference must also be made to the "anti-Entebbe" provision[58] which recognizes that nothing in the Convention shall justify the violation of the territorial integrity or political independence of a state in contravention of the Charter of the United Nations.

---

[52] 1973 Can. T.S. No. 6; 24 U.S.T. 564. As of 1986 there were 127 contracting States.

[53] 1973 Can. T.S. No. 11. See also the European Convention on the Suppression of Terrorism, 1977 E.T.S. No. 97.

[54] On the essential elements of a treaty, see the materials *supra* in Chapter 3.

[55] In force 1977, 1035 U.N.T.S. 167; (1974), 13 *Int. Leg. Mat.* 41.

[56] (1979), 18 *Int. Leg. Mat.* 1456, not yet in force.

[57] See Art. 5(1)(c).

[58] See Art. 14.

EXTRADITION[59]

Introduction
from S.A. Williams and J.-G. Castel,
Canadian Criminal Law, International and Transnational Aspects
(1981), at 337–40 (some footnotes omitted)

Extradition can be defined as the giving up of a person by a state in whose territory he or she is present, at the request of another state in whose jurisdiction that person is accused of having committed or has been convicted of a crime. International law has developed this procedure as a means whereby fugitives from justice are extradited and tried or punished in the requesting state for the crimes they have committed against its laws.

In theory, extradition can be carried out on the basis of reciprocity or under a treaty. There is in fact no duty to extradite where there is no treaty. Canada, as a matter of practice, does not grant extradition in the absence of a treaty,[60] although she may pass laws providing for extradition and provisions to that effect in the absence of a treaty are to be found in Part II of the *Extradition Act*.[61] This was done for the first time in 1974 with the Federal Republic of Germany and it was the only occasion since the beginning of the Second World War that Canada had an extradition arrangement with that country. However, the Act only applied, with respect to offences committed after the date of proclamation. On July 11th, 1977 Canada signed a new extradition treaty with the Federal Republic of Germany.[62] Part II of the Act was also extended to Brazil, effective from September 14th, 1979.[63] Canada has 43 extradition treaties with other states, including France, Greece, Hungary, Israel, Mexico, Nicaragua, Switzerland, Tonga, and the United States of America.

Most of Canada's extradition treaties were in fact concluded by Great Britain and pre-date 1925. Several of these are still in force together with any subsequent amendments made to them. One of the most famous was the Webster-Ashburton Treaty of 1842 concluded between the United States and Great Britain. It provided not only for the settlement of boundaries between British possessions in North America and the United States but also the suppression of the African slave trade, and the return of criminals in certain cases. This treaty continued in operation until recently, with amendments by supplementary Conventions.[64]

---

[59] S. Bedi, *Extradition in International Law and Practice* (1966); G.V. LaForest, *Extradition To and From Canada* (2 ed., 1977); I. Shearer, *Extradition in International Law* (1971).

[60] See *Re Insull* (1933), 60 C.C.C. 254, at 257 (Ont. S.C.), where the court stated that "extradition is purely a creature of the treaty and the statute." See also *State of Utah v. Peters* (1936), 66 C.C.C. 75; [1936] 4 D.L.R. 509 (Alta D.C.). Note, however, removal pursuant to the *Immigration Act*, S.C. 1976–77, c. 52, as am., as a substitute for extradition.

[61] R.S.C. 1970, c. E-21.

[62] In force September 30th, 1979, 1979 Can. T.S. No. 18.

[63] *Canada Gazette*, Part 1, October 1979, at 6480.

[64] 1952 Can. T.S. No. 12. See Arts. X and XI.

A new treaty came into force between Canada and the United States on March 22nd, 1976.[65] It will probably serve as a model for all future Canadian extradition treaties. It can be looked upon as heralding a second generation of Canadian extradition treaties. The old arrangements between the two states have been expressly terminated and replaced by the new treaty which revises and updates the previously in force list of extraditable crimes. Most notably, certainly from the viewpoint of public international law and international criminal law, it is provided that hijacking and offences against internationally protected persons, such as visiting heads of state, foreign ministers and diplomats, are extraditable between the two states and extradition cannot be refused on the ground that these offences were of a political nature.

The reason behind the development of such arrangements is state sovereignty. States were, and even today are, unwilling to concede advantages to other states unless the concessions proceed on the basis of reciprocity. The treaties create mutual obligations to return accused or convicted persons.

I. DOMESTIC LEGISLATION

…The purpose behind the Canadian *Extradition Act* [reprinted hereafter] is to ensure that the domestic law conforms with Canada's external obligations. As extradition is a part of the criminal law, it falls within section 91(27) of the *British North America Act* *[Constitution Act, 1867]* and a federal statute must give effect to the relevant treaties. The Act provides that it is to be read so as to provide for the execution of the treaties and it would appear from the wording that should there be an inconsistency, the treaty will prevail over the Act. The Act covers all extradition treaties with foreign states. It is important to note that if a crime is listed in a treaty between Canada and another state and is not listed in the Act, it is still extraditable.

As the matter of granting extradition is one of concern to the state to which a request is made, the regulation of the procedures is left to the domestic law of that state. Thus, there can often occur conflicts or divergences between the approaches taken by various states, notably concerning the extradition of nationals, the evidence required of the guilt of the accused by the requested state, and the powers of the judiciary or executive in the matter.

II. REASONS BEHIND EXTRADITION

In addition to protecting the sovereignty of states, extradition is used to prevent a person escaping justice. It involves a common fight against crime. Certain considerations have helped to produce the present generally accepted rules concerning extradition.

First, a state in whose territory an accused person has sought refuge frequently cannot prosecute him, usually, because it lacks jurisdiction over the offence. Thus, extradition utilizes the maxim *aut dedere aut judicare* (extradite or prosecute). Second, it is often more practicable for the state where the offence has been committed to try the offender not only for evidentiary reasons but also because that state is in fact most interested in the offence. Third, if extradition did not take place and states had no regard for one

---

[65] 1976 Can. T.S. No. 3; 27 U.S.T. 983.

another's laws, crime would be encouraged. Criminals, especially in an era of fast and easy international transportation would flee to the nearest safe haven.

Extradition Act
R.S.C. 1970, c. E-21

INTERPRETATION

2. In this Act

"conviction" or "convicted" does not include the case of a condemnation under foreign law by reason of contumacy; but "accused person" includes a person so condemned;

"extradition arrangement" or "arrangement" means a treaty, convention or arrangement that extends to Canada made by Her Majesty with a foreign state for the surrender of fugitive criminals;

"extradition crime" may mean any crime that, if committed in Canada, or within Canadian jurisdiction, would be one of the crimes described in Schedule I; and, in the application of this Act to the case of any extradition arrangement, "extradition crime" means any crime described in such arrangement, whether or not it is comprised in that Schedule;

"foreign state" includes every colony, dependency and constituent part of the foreign state; and every vessel of a foreign state is deemed to be within the jurisdiction of and to be part of the state;

"fugitive" or "fugitive criminal" means a person being or suspected of being in Canada, who is accused or convicted of an extradition crime committed within the jurisdiction of a foreign state;

"judge" includes any person authorized to act judicially in extradition matters;

"warrant", in the case of a foreign state, includes any judicial document authorizing the arrest of a person accused or convicted of crime. R.S., c. 322, s. 2.

PART I
EXTRADITION UNDER TREATY
Application of Part

3. In the case of any foreign state with which there is an extradition arrangement, this Part applies during the continuance of such arrangement; but no provision of this Part that is inconsistent with any of the terms of the arrangement has effect to contravene the arrangement; and this Part shall be so read and construed as to provide for the execution of the arrangement. R.S., c. 322, s. 3. ...

Extradition from Canada

10.(1) Whenever this Part applies a judge may issue his warrant for the apprehension of a fugitive on a foreign warrant of arrest, or an information or complaint laid before him, and on such evidence or after such proceedings as in his opinion would, subject to this Part, justify the issue of his warrant if the crime of which the fugitive is accused, or of which he is alleged to have been convicted, had been committed in Canada.

(2) The judge shall forthwith send a report of the fact of the issue of the warrant, together with certified copies of the evidence and foreign warrant, information or complaint, to the Minister of Justice, R.S., c. 322, s. 10. ...

12. Every fugitive criminal of a foreign state, to which this Part applies, is liable to be apprehended, committed and surrendered in the manner provided in this Part, whether the crime or conviction, in respect of which the surrender is sought, was committed or took place before or after the date of the arrangement, or before or after the time when this Part is made to apply to such state, and whether there is or is not any criminal jurisdiction in any court of Her Majesty's Realms and Territories over the fugitive in respect of the crime. R.S., c. 322, s. 12.

13. The fugitive shall be brought before a judge, who shall, subject to this Part, hear the case, in the same manner, as nearly as may be, as if the fugitive was brought before a justice of the peace, charged with an indictable offence committed in Canada. R.S., c. 322, s. 13.

14. The judge shall receive upon oath, or affirmation, if affirmation is allowed by law, the evidence of any witness tendered to show the truth of the charge or the fact of the conviction. R.S., c. 322, s. 14.

15. The judge shall receive, in like manner, any evidence tendered to show that the crime of which the fugitive is accused or alleged to have been convicted is an offence of a political character, or is, for any other reason, not an extradition crime, or that the proceedings are being taken with a view to prosecute or punish him for an offence of a political character. R.S., c. 322, s. 15.

16. Depositions or statements taken in a foreign state on oath, or on affirmation, where affirmation is allowed by the law of the state, and copies of such depositions or statements and foreign certificates of, or judicial documents stating the fact of conviction may, if duly authenticated, be received in evidence in proceedings under this Part. R.S., c. 322, s. 16. ...

18.(1) The judge shall issue his warrant for the committal of the fugitive to the nearest convenient prison, there to remain until surrendered to the foreign state, or discharged according to law,

    (a) in the case of a fugitive alleged to have been convicted of an extradition crime, if such evidence is produced as would, according to the law of Canada, subject to this Part, prove that he was so convicted, and

    (b) in the case of a fugitive accused of an extradition crime, if such evidence is produced as would, according to the law of Canada, subject to this Part, justify his committal for trial, if the crime had been committed in Canada.

(2) If such evidence is not produced, the judge shall order him to be discharged. R.S., c. 322, s. 18.

19. Where the judge commits a fugitive to prison, he shall, on such committal,

    (a) inform him that he will not be surrendered until after the expiration of fifteen days, and that he has a right to apply for a writ of *habeas corpus*, and

    (b) transmit to the Minister of Justice a certificate of the committal, with a copy of all the evidence taken before him not already so transmitted, and such report upon the case as he thinks fit. R.S., c. 322, s. 19.

20.(1) A requisition for the surrender of a fugitive criminal of a foreign state who is, or is suspected to be, in Canada, may be made to the Minister of Justice

(a) by any person recognized by him as a consular officer of that state resident at Ottawa, or

(b) by any minister of that state communicating with the Minister of Justice through the diplomatic representative of Her Majesty in that state.

(2) If neither of these modes is convenient, then the requisition shall be made in such other mode as is settled by arrangement. R.S., c. 322, s. 20.

21. No fugitive is liable to surrender under this Part if it appears

(a) that the offence in respect of which proceedings are taken under this Act is one of a political character, or

(b) that such proceedings are being taken with a view to prosecute or punish him for an offence of a political character. R.S. c. 322, s. 21.

22. Where the Minister of Justice at any time determines

(a) that the offence in respect of which proceedings are being taken under this Part is one of a political character,

(b) that the proceedings are, in fact, being taken with a view to try or punish the fugitive for an offence of a political character, or

(c) that the foreign state does not intend to make a requisition for surrender,

he may refuse to make an order for surrender, and may, by order under his hand and seal, cancel any order made by him, or any warrant issued by a judge under this Part, and order the fugitive to be discharged out of custody on any committal made under this Part; and the fugitive shall be discharged accordingly. R.S., c. 322, s. 22.

23. A fugitive shall not be surrendered until after the expiration of fifteen days from the date of his committal for surrender, or, if a writ of *habeas corpus* is issued, until after the decision of the court remanding him. R.S. c. 322, s. 23.

24. A fugitive who has been accused of an offence within Canadian jurisdiction, not being the offence for which his surrender is asked, or who is undergoing sentence under a conviction in Canada, shall not be surrendered until after he has been discharged, whether by acquittal or by expiration of his sentence, or otherwise. R.S., c. 322, s. 24.

25. Subject to this Part, the Minister of Justice upon the requisition of the foreign state, may, under his hand and seal, order a fugitive who has been committed for surrender to be surrendered to the person or persons who are, in his opinion, duly authorized to receive him in the name and on behalf of the foreign state, and he shall be so surrendered accordingly. R.S., c. 322, s. 25. ...

Extradition from a Foreign State

30.(1) A requisition for the surrender of a fugitive criminal from Canada, who is or is suspected to be in any foreign state with which there is an extradition arrangement, may be made by the Minister of Justice.

(a) to a consular officer of that state resident at Ottawa, or

(b) to the Minister of Justice or any other minister of that state, through the diplomatic representative of Her Majesty in that state.

(2) If neither of these modes is convenient, the requisition shall be made in such other mode as is settled by arrangement. R.S., c. 322, s. 30. ...

33. Where any person accused or convicted of an extradition crime is surrendered by a foreign state, in pursuance of any extradition arrangement, he is not, until after he has been restored or has had an opportunity of returning to the foreign state within the meaning of the arrangement, subject, in contravention of any of the terms of the arrangement, to a prosecution or punishment in Canada for any other offence committed prior to his surrender, for which he should not, under the arrangement, be prosecuted. R.S., c. 322, s. 33.

List of Crimes

34. The list of crimes in Schedule I shall be construed according to the law existing in Canada at the date of the alleged crime, whether by common law or by statute made before or after the 28th day of April, 1877, and as including only such crimes, of the descriptions comprised in the list, as are, under that law, indictable offences. R.S., c. 322, s. 34.

PART II
EXTRADITION IRRESPECTIVE OF TREATY

35.(1) This part does not come into force, with respect to fugitive offenders from any foreign state, until it has been declared by proclamation of the Governor General to be in force and effect as regards such foreign state, from and after a day to be named in the proclamation.

36. This Part applies to any crime, mentioned in Schedule III, that is committed after the coming into force of this Part as regards any foreign state to which this Part has by proclamation been declared to apply. R.S., c. 322, s. 36.

37.(1) Where no extradition arrangement exists between Her Majesty and a foreign state, or where an extradition arrangement, extending to Canada, exists between Her Majesty and a foreign state, but does not include the crimes mentioned in Schedule III, it is nevertheless lawful for the Minister of Justice to issue his warrant for the surrender to such foreign state of any fugitive offender from that foreign state charged with or convicted of any of the crimes mentioned in Schedule III.

(2) The arrest, committal, detention, surrender and conveyance out of Canada of a fugitive offender referred to in subsection (1) is governed by Part I, and all the provisions of that Part apply to all steps and proceedings in relation to such arrest, committal, detention, surrender and conveyance out of Canada in the same manner and to the same extent as they would apply if the said crimes were included and specified in an extradition arrangement between Her Majesty and the foreign state, extending to Canada. R.S., c. 322, s. 37. ...

39. The list of crimes in Schedule III shall be construed according to the law existing in Canada at the date of the commission of the alleged crime, whether by common law or by statute, and as including only such crimes, of the description comprised in the list, as are, under that law, indictable offences. R.S., c. 322, s. 39.

40. No warrant shall issue under this Part for the extradition of any person to any state or country in which by the law in force in such state or country such person may be tried after such extradition for any other offence than that for which he has been extradited, unless an assurance has first been given by the executive authority of the state or country that the person whose extradition has been claimed will not be tried for any other offence than that in respect of which the extradition has been claimed. R.S., c. 322, s. 40.

SCHEDULE I
LIST OF CRIMES

1. Murder, or attempt or conspiracy to murder;
2. Manslaughter;
3. Counterfeiting or altering money, and uttering counterfeit or altered money;
4. Forgery, counterfeiting or altering, or uttering what is forged, counterfeited or altered;
5. Larceny or theft;
6. Embezzlement;
7. Obtaining money or goods, or valuable securities, by false pretenses;
8. Crimes against bankruptcy or insolvency law;
9. Fraud by a bailee, banker, agent, factor, trustee, or by a director or member or officer of any company, which fraud is made criminal by any Act for the time being in force;
10. Rape;
11. Abduction;
12. Child stealing;
13. Kidnapping;
14. False imprisonment;
15. Burglary, housebreaking or shop-breaking;
16. Arson;
17. Robbery;
18. Threats, by letter or otherwise, with intent to extort;
19. Perjury or subornation of perjury;
20. Piracy by municipal law or law of nations, committed on board of or against a vessel of a foreign state;
21. Criminal scuttling or destroying a vessel of a foreign state at sea, whether on the high seas or on the Great Lakes of North America, or attempting or conspiring to do so;
23. Assault on board a vessel of a foreign state at sea, whether on the high seas or on the Great Lakes of North America, with intent to destroy life or to do grievous bodily harm;
24. Revolt, or conspiracy to revolt, by two or more persons on board a vessel of a

foreign state at sea, whether on the high seas or on the Great Lakes of North America, against the authority of the master;

24. Any offence under

(a) sections 52, 58, 59, 77 to 79, 143 to 147, 149, 156, 174, 343 to 349, 351 to 354, subsection 355(1), sections 356, 358, 359, 363 and paragraph 423(1)(a) of the *Criminal Code*;

(b) Part VI of the *Criminal Code* except sections 240 and 254 to 281;

(c) Part VII of the *Criminal Code*, except subsection 299(2) and sections 323 and 331;

(d) Part IX of the *Criminal Code*, except sections 394, 396, 397 and 402 to 405;

(e) Part X of the *Criminal Code*, except section 412;

that is not included in any foregoing portion of this Schedule.

25. Any offence that is, in the case of the principal offender, included in any foregoing portion of this Schedule, and for which the fugitive criminal, though not the principal, is liable to be tried or punished as if he were the principal. R.S., c. 322, First Sch.; 1953–54, c. 51, s. 751.

[Schedule III, referred to in s. 36 is similar to Schedule I, except that it does not include the offences listed in 8, 14, 18, 19 and 24.]

Federal Republic of Germany v. Rauca
(1983), 41 O.R. (2d) 225 (Ont. C.A.)

[Helmut Rauca, a naturalized Canadian citizen and a former member of the Gestapo was charged in the Federal Republic of Germany with the murder of approximately 11,500 people between August, 1941, and December, 1943. The Federal Republic of Germany made a request to Canada pursuant to the Extradition Treaty of 1979[66] for his return to Germany for prosecution.

The case caused a number of fascinating issues:

1) Did extradition infringe the rights of a Canadian citizen under section 6(1) of *The Charter of Rights and Freedoms* to remain in Canada?

2) Was extradition allowable because of the overriding provisions of section 1 of *The Charter* providing that the rights guaranteed were subject to "such reasonable limits prescribed by law as can be demonstrably justified in a free and democratic society"?

3) Was there an extraditable crime?

4) Did the Federal Republic of Germany have jurisdiction over the offence?

5) Was there a *prima facie* case against Rauca?

Evans C.J.H.C. conducted the extradition hearing. He concluded that Rauca should be committed for surrender. Rauca applied for a writ of *habeas corpus* but this application was dismissed on November 4th, 1982. An appeal was launched to the Court of Appeal of Ontario.

---

[66] 1979 Can. T.S. No. 18. And see Government of Canada, *Report of the Commission of Inquiry on War Criminals* (Deschênes Commission) (1986).

The following extracts are restricted to the question of jurisdiction over the offence.]

THE COURT: ... *The facts concerning the territory of the Requesting State*

The offences are alleged to have occurred in Lithuania. Prior to World War I, Lithuania was part of the Russian Empire. After that war, it became a separate sovereign State with Kaunas as its capital. In the early stages of World War II, Lithuania was occupied by the Soviet Union. With the onset of hostilities between Germany and the Soviet Union on June 22, 1941, the German army invaded Lithuania, and by the end of June, the German forces were in complete control of the country. They retained control until August, 1944.

In March, 1933, the Reichstag delegated the authority to enact laws to the government of the Reich, without the participation of the Reichstag. This authorization remained in effect until 1945. During that period, Germany was governed by Adolf Hitler, as Führer.

By a decree of the Fuhrer dated July 17, 1941, the three Baltic States – Latvia, Lithuania and Estonia – together with part of Byelorussia were created a Reich Commissariat under the name "Ostland." Heinrich Lohse was appointed Reich Commissioner for the new territory and provision was made for dividing the Reich Commissariat into general districts with a general commissioner in charge. Lohse divided the new territory into four districts, one of which was Lithuania with Adrian Von Renteln as general commissioner. Under the general commissioner, there were district and city commissariats, and below them local administrations. The decree of July 17, 1941, turned over the civil administration of the territory to the Reich Minister for the Occupied Eastern Territories, and by a further decree of the Fuhrer of the same date, Alfred Rosenberg was appointed to that position.

By ordinance of August 4, 1941, Alfred Rosenberg, as Reich Minister for the Occupied Eastern Territories, ordered and decreed that at the headquarters of each Reich Commissioner, there was to be a German superior court, and at the headquarters of each general commissioner, a German court. The German courts were given jurisdiction in all criminal matters in so far as they were not assigned for jurisdiction to another court for trial (Peter Botte deposed that such an assignment was never effected for cases involving a German national as principal or victim). By a further ordinance of the same date, Rosenberg decreed that German courts and other German agencies were to apply, when trying punishable offences, the Penal Code and the Rules of Criminal Procedure of the Reich, unless otherwise decreed.

Dr. Hilberg testified that during the time that the German civil administration was in operation in Ostland, there was no other government in power in Lithuania. There was an indigenous Lithuanian administration, but it had to take its orders from the German authorities; it had no capability of acting on its own. ...

Murder is a criminal offence in both Canada and the Requesting State. There is a treaty between Canada and the Requesting State concerning extradition, signed at Ottawa, July 11, 1977, and in force as of September 30, 1979. Murder is the first crime listed in the schedule to the treaty.

In his deposition of July 22, 1982, Peter Botte stated that murder was a crime in the German Reich at the time of the commission of the alleged offences and was punishable with death. It is now, according to Botte, punishable in the Requesting State with life imprisonment, and there is no statute of limitations. In his deposition of July 22nd, Botte made the following statement concerning the appellant's liability to prosecution during the National-Socialist regime for the killing of Jews:

The crimes which for political, racist or anti-religious reasons were either ordered or tolerated by the National-Socialist leadership, particularly as regards the extermination of the Jewish population in those areas where the latter was dominant, could not be prosecuted under criminal law at that time because the "Führer will" ("Führerwille") of the "Führer" and chancellor of the Reich, Adolf Hitler, who according to the legal situation at the time was held to be equal to the law, was opposed to such prosecution.

However, the killing of Jews was still murder under the German Criminal Code and, as Botte points out in his deposition of July 22nd, the courts of the Requesting State have always affirmed their jurisdiction over the prosecution of criminal offences committed during the National-Socialist regime.

In his deposition of July 22nd, Botte dealt with the relationship of the German Reich to the Requesting State. According to Botte, the Requesting State is identical with the German Reich and "therefore has the authority to prosecute criminal offences which had been subject to prosecution under the criminal law of the German Reich prior to May 8, 1945." Under what is known as the "Basic Law" (a statute of the Requesting State dated May 23, 1949), as interpreted by the West German Federal Constitutional Court, the German Reich survived the collapse of 1945 and continues to exist. A new West German State was not created with the establishment of the Federal Republic of Germany, but instead a part of Germany was reorganized. The Requesting State is not the "legal successor" to the German Reich, but is identical with the German Reich, even though territorially it is not identical with the Reich. ...

Jurisdiction of the Federal Republic of Germany

This issue concerns the meaning and effect of art. 1(1) of the treaty between Canada and the Requesting State. That article provides:

(1) The Contracting Parties undertake, subject to the provisions and conditions prescribed in this treaty, to extradite to each other any person found within the territory of the requested state who is subject to prosecution by a competent authority of the requesting state for, or convicted by such an authority of, an offence committed within the territory of the requesting state and who is claimed by that authority for the purpose of prosecution or for the purpose of carrying out a sentence.

The appellant's second main ground of attack on the warrant of committal is that, if the offences were committed as alleged, they were not committed within the territory of the Requesting State.

After considering the evidence, Evans C.J.H.C. held: ...

Germany was in *de facto* occupation of Lithuania in 1941. It was part of the territory of

Germany through conquest. The fact that it was forced at a later date to relinquish possession does not alter the fact that at the relevant time, it was German territory.

The appellant submits "that a *de facto* imposition of authority through military occupation and the force of arms is an insufficient basis for a nation to subsequently claim that at the time of the offences the occupied country was within its legal 'territory.' "

The courts in other places have considered the meaning and effect to be given to similar provisions in such treaties and have held that *de facto* jurisdiction is sufficient to found a request for extradition and that *de jure* jurisdiction is not necessary. ...

[The Court reviewed the caselaw and concluded:]

The principles underlying those decisions on this issue are applicable here. In recognizing that the requesting party had jurisdiction under the treaty to seek extradition of this fugitive from Canada, Canada does not recognize the Government of Germany of those days or that it was sovereign where those offences are said to have taken place. When determining the meaning of the word "territory" as used by the parties to the treaty, one may consider their circumstances and relationship. As a country committed to the destruction of the wartime Government of Germany and the liberation of the countries occupied by it, Canada, like its allies, was also determined to bring to justice those German personnel who were parties to atrocities and war crimes committed in the occupied countries. On the other hand, the Republic of Germany has recognized that it has an obligation to punish German personnel who committed such crimes and that it is a proper place (although perhaps not the only one) for the trial of men and women charged with such offences for a German national is by the German law punishable there for such crimes wherever committed.

The evidence establishes that the place where the alleged offences took place was occupied and under the *de facto* control of Germany. In our opinion, "territory" as used in the treaty under consideration includes those areas occupied and under the de facto control of Germany during the Second World War. We therefore are of the view that Evans C.J.H.C. was right in holding that the Requesting State had jurisdiction to seek extradition of the fugitive. The appeal on this ground also fails.

NOTES

1) Helmut Rauca was returned to the Federal Republic of Germany where he died in jail before his trial. His case posed an important question about jurisdiction over the offence: must the requesting state still be in control of the territory where the crime was committed? The answer since *Rauca* is no.

2) Could Rauca have excused himself by claiming that what he did was the subject of superior orders? Could an argument be made that the atrocities committed were sanctioned by Hitler and therefore law?

3) The surrender of fugitives to and from Commonwealth countries is called rendition and is governed by the *Fugitive Offenders Act*.[67] Under this legislation there is no list of

---

[67] R.S.C. 1970, c. F-32. See P. O'Higgins, "Extradition Within the Commonwealth" (1960), 9 *Int. Comp. L.Q.* 486.

extraditable offences, no provisions on double criminality or specialty, and no exemptions for political offenders. Why should there be differences such as these between Commonwealth rendition and non-Commonwealth extradition? The Law Reform Commission in Working Paper 37[68] stated:

> While we cannot, in the course of this general study on jurisdiction, do more than scratch the surface of the large and complex subjects of extradition and rendition, we have seen enough to convince us of the need to modernize our statutes concerning these subjects. However, before that can be done, the federal Government will have to seek answers to questions such as: Should "political offence" be defined in legislation? Does Canada need two Acts? Would not one suffice? Is there any longer a need to differentiate between "extradition" and "rendition?" Should depositions from other countries admitted in evidence at extradition hearings in Canada be subject to the hearsay rule or be subject to their deponents being cross-examined?

The Political Offence Exception[69]

Most extradition treaties deny the extradition of political offenders. This exception is well recognized as a means to preserve political asylum, but its operation is fraught with controversy. As previously noted, the aim of the anti-terrorism conventions is to prevent a fugitive escaping justice on account of a refusal to extradite him by providing for his prosecution. However, in the absence of such an obligation and certainly in the many areas not covered by these conventions, the political offence exception will still operate and the fugitive will go unprosecuted.

The term political offence covers two concepts. First, there are the pure political offences such as treason and espionage which are directed at the state and are clearly non-extraditable. They are not even listed as extraditable offences. Secondly, there is the relative political offence which is an ordinary crime that is so closely connected with political acts or events that it takes on a political colour. It is up to the requested state (either its courts or its executive depending on its legal system) to decide whether or not such an action is political. This is a domestic matter, for there is no international definition. In Canada, the exception is preserved by sections 21 and 22 of the Extradition Act, reprinted above. The following cases display the difficulties of its application.

Re State of Wisconsin and Armstrong
(1973), 32 D.L.R. (3d) 265 (F.C.A.)
(Leave to appeal to S.C.C. denied)

[The United States requested the extradition of Karleton Armstrong from Canada for first degree murder and arson. The alleged offences occurred in the course of the bombing of

---

[68] *Supra*, n. 3, at 137.
[69] See M.C. Bassiouni, *Terrorism and Political Crimes* (1975); "Ideologically Motivated Offenses and the Political Offenses Exception in Extradition – A Proposed Juridical Standard for an Unruly Problem" (1969–70), 19 *De Paul L. Rev.* 217; J.-G. Castel and M. Edwardh, "Political Offences: Extradition and Deportation – Recent Canadian Developments" (1975), 13 *Osgoode H.L.J.* 89; A. Evans, "Reflections Upon the Political Offence in International Practice" (1963), 57 *Am. J. Int. L.* 1; M.D. Szabo, "Political Crimes: A Historical Perspective" (1972), 2 *Denver J. Int. L. and Pol.* 7. As to political offences within Canada, see P. MacKinnon, "Conspiracy and Sedition as Canadian Political Crimes" (1977), 23 *McGill L.J.* 622.

the University of Wisconsin, Army Math Research Centre and other campus buildings during a period of strong public sentiment against the war in Vietnam.]

THURLOW, J.: ... In the course of hearing argument on the issue the Court raised the further question whether the learned Judge had jurisdiction to determine the political character or otherwise of the alleged offences or to discharge the applicant if he should be of the opinion that the political character of the offences was established. On this point counsel for the applicant took the position that the extradition Judge had such jurisdiction. Counsel for the State of Wisconsin supported the view that the Judge did not have such jurisdiction but expressed his preference for a determination by this Court upholding the learned Judge's conclusion on the merits.

Article II

[of the Canada – United States Extradition Treaty]

A fugitive criminal shall not be surrendered, if the offence in respect of which his surrender is demanded be one of a political character, or if he proves that the requisition for his surrender has in fact been made with a view to try or punish him for an offence of a political character.

No person surrendered by either of the High Contracting Parties to the other shall be triable or tried, or be punished for any political crime or offence, or for any act connected therewith, committed previously to his extradition.

If any question shall arise as to whether a case comes within the provisions of this Article, the decision of the authorities of the Government in whose jurisdiction the fugitive shall be at the time shall be final.

Article III

No person surrendered by or to either of the High Contracting Parties shall be triable or be tried for any crime or offence committed prior to his extradition, other than the offence for which he was surrendered, until he shall have had an opportunity of returning to the country from which he was surrendered.

It would seem from the second paragraph of the foregoing that the political character of the offence might conceivably be raised as a defence at the trial in the demanding State even though it would not be available if the State acquired jurisdiction other than through extradition from Canada. But whether it would constitute a defence at trial or not it does not appear to me that anything in the language of the treaty requires or authorizes an extradition Judge to determine the question. What he is to consider is the evidence of criminality and its sufficiency to sustain the charge and if the evidence is sufficient for that purpose he is to commit.

The statute itself, in s. 9, authorizes all the designated Judges to "act judicially in extradition matters under this Part" and for that purpose confers on them "all the powers and jurisdiction of any judge or magistrate of the province" but goes on to provide that this shall not be construed as conferring jurisdiction in *habeas corpus* matters. What the

Judge is to do in exercise of his authority under the *Extradition Act* is specifically set out in ss. 13, 14, 15, 18 and 19. ...

It will be observed that while the extradition Judge is required by s. 15 to receive evidence tendered to show the political character of the offence, etc., nowhere in these provisions is he empowered to decide that question. Moreover, having regard to the definition in s. 2 and to the extradition arrangement between Canada and the United States the expression "extradition crime" in these sections must be treated in this case as meaning "any crime described in such arrangement" and when ss. 13, 14, 15, 18, and 19 are read with this definition in mind it does not appear to me that the extradition Judge is authorized to decide that the offence is of a political character or that it is for that reason not an extradition crime or to discharge the fugitive for such a reason ... .

This conclusion is sufficient in my view to dispose of the whole issue on this application with respect to the political character of the offences. ...

[Cameron, D.J. concurred with Thurlow, J.]

SWEET, D.J.: ... It is fundamental that the general, basic purpose of extradition and the enabling legislation is simply to provide co-operatively a means whereby a fugitive from one jurisdiction apprehended in another may be returned for trial in the jurisdiction whence he fled. It is a phase of co-operation between two States relative to the administration of the criminal law in each. However, to preserve the availability of political asylum in proper cases, Parliament included in the Act ss. 21 and 22.

It follows that a submission that the offence charged has political character must carefully be examined. The motivation of the fugitive, of which more is said below, is important but much more is required than a mere assertion by the fugitive that he was politically motivated.

Furthermore, I do not think that the person accused can unilaterally cause the offence to be political. Viscount Radcliffe said in *Schtraks*,[70] " ... if the central government stands apart and is concerned only to enforce the criminal law ... I see no reason why fugitives should be protected by this country from its jurisdiction on the ground that they are political offenders."

Neither do I think that a person, sympathetic with the aims of a significant number of persons in a movement to endeavour to bring about a change in governmental policy by legal means and who, himself, commits a crime with the avowed purpose of achieving those aims because he thinks legal means are ineffective, can create a haven for himself in this nation so as to avoid punishment for those crimes.

The actions of the offender should, if anything, be even more closely scrutinized and they would bear even more severe testing before being categorized as political within the meaning of s. 21 when, as here, there is violence directed, not against responsible functionaries or property of the government desired to be overthrown or whose policy it is desired to change, but against the person or property of a third party.

Furthermore, and in any event, as I see it, if it is not established on the extradition proceedings that the fugitive is guilty of the offence charged the question of "political

---

[70] Ed: *Schtraks v. Government of Israel*, [1964] A.C. 556.

character'' could not be determined at that hearing even if the tribunal did have jurisdiction in the premises. Here the fugitive did not admit guilt nor has guilt been otherwise established.

I am in agreement that the evidence produced by the State of Wisconsin before the extradition Judge is sufficient to indicate that degree of probability to justify committal for trial if the crimes had been committed in Canada. However, that is not a finding of guilt.

In submitting that the offences charged are of a political character, it seems to me that the highest at which the applicant can put his position is to say: "I do not admit the offences but if I did commit them they are of a political character," or "they are of a political character whoever committed them."

The character of the offence is relevant but the character of the offence may vary with the individual. Murder and arson are not political *per se* though it would seem from the jurisprudence that under some circumstances they might have a "political character." Although not the only factor motivation has significance in the determination as to whether an offence has political character. It would seem to me that a tribunal could not reasonably be expected to reach a conclusion on motivation of the perpetrator, whoever he might be, without even knowing who the perpetrator was or what moved him.

On some occasions the surrounding circumstances might make it seem that an occurrence or incident has political character. Nevertheless the motivation of a person, present and apparently associating himself with the incident and others politically moved, who then and there commits a crime, could be without any connection with the political aims of the others. The motivation of that person could, for example, be nothing more than to satisfy a personal grudge.

Though the incident and circumstances have relevance it is not the incident nor the circumstances which are charged. It is the individual who is charged. It is the individual the foreign State seeks to have extradited. It is the individual who is before the extradition tribunal.

Motivation is of the mind. It precedes and is a causative factor of the deed. Surrounding facts and circumstances may tend to affirm or discredit a declaration as to motive. Still in a sane person only he can actually be aware of his motive – only he knows why he did the act unless, of course, he tells the truth about it to someone else. How, then, can an accused person be heard to indicate the motive inducing an act unless he admits doing it?

It is my opinion that the matter of "political character" could not arise for decision by the extradition tribunal in this case and could not there be a defence against extradition even if that tribunal had jurisdiction to deal with it.

I understand that applicant's counsel submits there exists in the United States of America a significant public opinion against the policy of the Government of the United States in connection with the war in Vietnam and an expressed desire on the part of many there that that Government bring that war to an end. As I understand it, it is also the position of counsel for the applicant that the applicant was part of that movement and that, as a result, all of the charges against him are associated with that movement and have, thereby, a political character.

Also, as I understand Mr. Ruby's position on behalf of the applicant, expressed during his argument, it is that if there is a significant movement to bring about a change in governmental policy and if, with the intention of furthering the aims of that movement, an individual commits a crime, the offence is one of a political character within the meaning of s. 21 even though all others in the movement attempt to achieve their aims only by peaceful, legal means. It is a position with which I do not agree.

If it could be said there is acceptable evidence here that the applicant or the offences in respect of which he stands indicted, are a part of what might be described as that anti-Vietnam war movement, it would, at most, be tenuous. There are what counsel for the applicant refers to as the "communiqués." I do not consider them impressive to show the connection. There is no hard evidence as to whence they came. If their content is written by the bomber, as I understand is Mr. Ruby's theory, and if the bomber is the applicant, surely they would be self-serving. I do not think that the affidavits filed on behalf of the applicant are persuasive to show connection between the bomber and the arsonist, whoever he may be, and that movement.

Further, if it could be said that there is sufficient evidence to show an association between the bomber and the arsonist and that movement, I do not consider that that in itself is sufficient for the applicant to shelter under s. 21 of the *Extradition Act*.

There is evidence that in the general area where the bombing and arson occurred there was activity in that movement which went beyond verbal protest and included some violence. However, the evidence does not establish that that violence reached the stage of bombing and arson unless the incidents in respect of which the applicant is accused could be included. I do not think the evidence establishes that bombing and arson were generally accepted activities in the anti-Vietnam war movement in the area.

There was no significant evidence offered that the applicant or, for that matter, anyone involved in the anti-Vietnam war movement was being prosecuted in the United States for his beliefs or for the aims of the movement or for his attempts to accomplish those aims by peaceful means. There is no evidence that those who shared the views of the persons who made up the movement were not permitted to speak freely, to voice their views, to protest or peaceably to demonstrate. There is no evidence that those persons, or any witness who felt that the applicant should not be extradited, needed political asylum.

It was argued that the bombing was considered by some people of prominence to be a political act. The "evidence" so-called of this, was publication in newspapers. Even if one could assume that those persons were quoted properly and that they made such statements and held such views they would be only personal views. It is not they who decide whether the offences were of a political character within the meaning of the *Extradition Act* of Canada.

Although the conduct of the war in Vietnam is the responsibility of the Government of the United States of America, the buildings bombed and burned were not the property of that Government, but appear to be the property of the State of Wisconsin. They were some of the buildings comprising the facilities of the University of Wisconsin, a place of learning.

It is my opinion that the offences in respect of which the extradition proceedings were taken were not of a political character within the meaning of s. 21 of the *Extradition Act*.

In any event the evidence is such as to justify a conclusion that, to use the words of Viscount Radcliffe in *Schtraks*, "the central government stands apart and is concerned only to enforce the criminal law" alleged to have been violated.

I turn now to the matter as to jurisdiction of the extradition tribunal to decide upon the presence or absence of "political character" in determining whether a warrant of committal should issue. It is my opinion that it does not have such jurisdiction ...

In my opinion the matter of political asylum is left by the *Extradition Act* solely within executive discretion.

I would dismiss the application.

Re Commonwealth of Puerto Rico and Hernandez
[1973] 1 O.R. 60; 30 D.L.R. (3d) 260;
aff'd. (No. 2), (1974), 42 D.L.R. (3d) 541 (F.C.A.)

HONEYWELL, Co. Ct. J.: ... This is an application by the Commonwealth of Puerto Rico and by the Government of the United States of America under the *Extradition Act*, R.S.C. 1970, c. E-21, for the extradition of Humberto Pagan Hernandez, who was charged in Puerto Rico for the crime of murder and who has been found in Canada. It is not disputed that the accused in the prisoner's box is the person so charged.

Murder is a crime under the Puerto Rican Penal Code and also under s. 212 of the *Criminal Code* of Canada. It is an extradition offence under Sch. III to the *Extradition Act*, and this Act applies to citizens of the United States of America by reason of the Ashburton Treaty of 1842, and subsequent extradition conventions.

The basic issues which were to be dealt with on this hearing are the following:

1. Was a murder actually committed?

2. Was the accused the person who committed the murder?

3. Was the crime an offence of a political character or are the proceedings being taken with a view to prosecute or punish him for an offence of a political character?

I am not trying the accused or determining whether he is or is not guilty of the offence charged. Under s. 13 of the Act I am holding a hearing similar to a preliminary hearing which a Justice would hold where an accused is charged with an indictable offence in Canada. My duty is to determine whether the prosecution has adduced sufficient evidence to put the accused on his trial. ...

The circumstances out of which the charge arose are as follows:

On March 11, 1971, a confrontation arose between the students at the University of Puerto Rico and cadets in the R.O.T.C. course, as a result of which the chancellor called in the police to restore order. A large number of the students were involved, estimates ranging as high as 3,000 and they were attempting to attack the R.O.T.C. cadets and the R.O.T.C. building.

The Commandante of the Police, Mercado Vega, was shot and killed at about 12:45 p.m. while on duty in the university grounds. At the time he was shot, Mercado was at or about a spot marked on a plan, filed as an exhibit, which plan was prepared by a qualified engineer. The spot which the engineer indicated on the plan was that which had been pointed out to him on the ground by a witness, Atilamo. This spot is 140.55 ft.

directly south of a monument which is also shown on the plan. The evidence was that Mercado was facing in a generally easterly direction toward the students' centre, and was in the process of turning when the bullet struck him in what I might describe as the left armpit.

There is evidence that at that time a person was observed firing a revolver from the side of the monument in the direction of Mercado, but there were no other persons in that general vicinity. There were many students in and in front of the student centre. Two spent bullets were found in or about the girls' gymnasium further south but in a direct line with Mercado and the monument. The expert evidence is that all three bullets were fired from the same gun. I will go no further into the evidence on this issue as I am satisfied that there is sufficient evidence adduced that Mercado was killed deliberately and intentionally by some person shooting at him from the monument and that this constitutes murder, both under the Puerto Rican Penal Code and the Canadian *Criminal Code*.

The next question is whether the accused is the person who was at the monument and who fired the bullet which killed Mercado.

The only evidence tendered to establish this was the direct evidence of Lieutenant Atilamo who saw the assailant at the monument and who later identified Pagan as being that person.

[The Court reviewed this evidence and concluded:]

... On the total evidence of identity given by Atilamo, I am satisfied that there is not probable cause to believe Pagan guilty of the crime charged against him, and he should not be extradited but should be discharged.

By s. 21 of the *Extradition Act*, it is provided that no fugitive is liable to surrender if it appears that the offence is one of a political character or that the proceedings are taken with a view to prosecute or punish him for an offence of a political character. In view of the findings I have made above that there is insufficient evidence which would justify the committal of the accused for trial and the consequent decision to discharge him from custody, it should not be necessary for me to consider whether or not the charge against the accused is one of a political character. Counsel have, however, asked me to make a finding in this regard in view of the lengthy evidence that was tendered by the parties and in view of the thorough argument submitted by counsel on this question, I am prepared to do so, ...

The question, "What is an offence of a political character?" is very difficult to answer. The crime of murder is normally a non-political offence, but it may be found to be a political offence in the light of the circumstances existing when it is committed. My reading of the cases referred to me and the lengthy comments of the Judges in the Courts concerned leave me with the conviction that the very wide variety of circumstances that can exist which might give rise to an allegation of "political character" would make it impossible to attempt to be specific as to its meaning.

In *Schtraks v. Government of Israel et al.*, [1962] 3 All E.R. 529, at 538, Viscount Radcliffe said:

What, then, is an offence of political character? The courts, I am afraid, have been asking this question at intervals ever since it was first posed judicially in 1890 in *Re Castioni*, [1891]

1 Q.B. 149, and no definition has yet emerged or by now is ever likely to. Indeed, it has come to be regarded as something of an advantage that there is no definition.

Generally speaking, the courts' reluctance to offer a definition has been due, I think, to the realization that it has been virtually impossible to find one that does not cover too wide a range.

In *Re Castioni* (1890), 60 L.J. 22., Denman, J., used the following words which have since been quoted in other cases [at 27]

I think that in order to bring the case within the words of the Act, and to avoid extradition for such an act as an act of murder, which is one of the extradition offences, it must be *at least* shown that the act which is done is being done in furtherance of, and as sort of overt act in the course of and with the intention of assisting in a political matter, such as a political rising consequent upon a *great* dispute between two parties in the State as to which is to have the government in its hands – that it must be something of that sort before it can be brought within the meaning of the words used in the Act.

I have italicized the words "at least" and "great" as they have sometimes been overlooked.

Defence counsel submitted that I cannot look narrowly at the actual events on the campus on March 11th to determine the question but must look at the whole political situation in Puerto Rico and its past history in order to place the events of March 11th in their proper perspective. In my view, the question in issue should be determined by looking primarily at the events of the day and the actual circumstances of the murder. The general political climate of Puerto Rico at the time is of secondary interest. It is important only if it is a predominant factor in the circumstances of the murder. It is not relevant that the act subsequently became a major political issue if it was not of a predominantly political character at the time when it occurred: *Schtraks v. Government of Israel, supra.*

In my opinion, the murder of Colonel Mercado was not an offence of a political character. What took place on March 11th, was, in essence, a one-sided "on campus" confrontation between students of the University of Puerto Rico and the cadets of the Officers Training Corps. Its object was not to overthrow the government but rather to force the university authorities to divorce the R.O.T.C. from the campus. This antagonism between students and cadets had existed for some years and it was the practice of students to harass the cadets at every opportunity. It was not a unique situation as there was similar opposition to the R.O.T.C. in other universities in the United States but, in Puerto Rico, the existence of independence groups on the campus increased the hostility. Whether the R.O.T.C. remained on campus or not was a matter for the university authorities.

The state police were called to restore order by the chancellor about noon and, on their arrival, the students became more violent and there was some gun-fire. A number of the police and of the students were killed or wounded. One cannot deny that political considerations were involved in the antagonism toward the cadets, but I cannot feel persuaded that this could be considered a political rising against the government or that the murder of Colonel Mercado could be considered an act in furtherance of a political rising.

The actual shooting of Mercado was deliberate and intentional and in the circumstances was without apparent justification as the killer was not himself in any danger and Mercado was not using his weapon. It would appear that the simple object of the killer was to kill a policeman because he was a policeman, even though he was only doing his duty to try and maintain law and order.

The wording used in s. 21(b) of the *Extradition Act* "that such proceedings are being taken with a view to prosecute or punish him for an offence of a political character", is not clear. If the offence referred to is intended to mean the same offence in respect to which proceedings are being taken under the *Extradition Act*, then the subsection would appear to have little meaning. I have found that the offence of murder in this case was not an offence of a political character, and the crime of murder is its own justification for taking the proceedings. If the offence referred to in the subsection is a different offence than the offence of murder, as charged, then it would be in contravention of the extradition conventions with the United States of America under which he can only be tried for the actual offence for which he was extradited. It is not to be assumed that a foreign state would act contrary to its international agreements. If, on the other hand, the subsection means that although he will be tried for the offence for which he is being extradited, this is only a pretence and in fact he will be judged and punished by reason of a political offence or offences. In this case, I would reject that possibility. The evidence persuades me that an accused would be entitled to and would get a fair trial on any charge. The penalty for first degree murder is life imprisonment and there is, in any case, no room for further punishment by reason of a fugitive's political offences. The offence for which extradition is asked is so serious that the suggestion of ulterior motive can be rejected.

Accused discharged.

NOTES

1) If the extradition judge does not have authority to determine the political character of the acts charged, who does? Review the *Extradition Act* ss. 21 and 22.

2) On the question of mutual assistance in criminal matters, see the treaty signed by Canada and the United States in 1985 and reported at the end of the next section. The parties agree to provide mutual legal assistance in all matters relating to the investigation, prosecution and suppression of offences as defined by the treaty.

3) Once the fugitive has been committed for surrender, he must be informed by the extradition judge that surrender will not take place for 15 days and that he may apply for a writ of *habeas corpus*. Under section 19 of the *Extradition Act* the extradition judge should then transmit to the Minister of Justice the certificate of committal, evidence not already transmitted and any report he may have.[71] The only review possible is by way of this writ. Since *Minister of Indian Affairs and Northern Development v. Ranville*[72] it

---

[71] See Williams and Castel, *supra*, n. 3, at 398–402.
[72] [1982] 2 S.C.R. 518.

is clear that there is no longer a right of review of the extradition judge's decision open to the fugitive, or the requesting state, under section 28 of the *Federal Court Act*.[73]

When hearing the application for *habeas corpus* the judge is not an appeal court on questions of fact. He may, however, determine the sufficiency of the evidence and decide whether the offence is extradictable.

EXTRATERRITORIAL ASSERTIONS OF JURISDICTION

Introduction[74]

Few topics have generated more disagreement and controversy between states, and jurists, than the extraterritorial application of national laws. Defining what is meant by the phrase, "extraterritorial application of national laws," gives rise to problems in itself: here it is taken to mean the asserted rights of a state to impose its laws on conduct engaged in by persons who are not its residents or nationals and which occurs outside of its territory. In short it covers the assertions of jurisdiction over the activities of foreigners abroad.[75]

Two trends may be noted in this context. The first is a growing recognition of the increasing interdependence of states. As a result of modern technology, particulary in the area of communications, many events which formerly would not have taken place in more than one jurisdiction now may take place in several and may have therefore a transnational nature. This is true of activities governed both by civil and criminal law. Many governments have recognized that they need to extend their jurisdiction beyond traditional territorial notions in order to ensure that their publics, or indeed, perhaps even the interests of a foreign public, are protected against injurious acts which occur beyond their borders and thus also within the jurisdictions of another state. The resulting problem is a conflict of concurrent jurisdiction over transnational events. Sorting out which law or policy should govern these events sometimes requires balancing the competing claims of two states having possibly different policy objectives, each of which may be basing its jurisdictional claim on different contacts with the event ("liens de reattachement"). Solutions are likely to depend on which forum and whose rules determine the threshold issues of what factors will justify the assertion of jurisdiction.

The second trend is a hardening of attitudes towards assertions of jurisdiction extra-territorially. Certain countries have extended their jurisdiction beyond the limits which others are willing to accept as being reasonable in international law. There have thus been strong reactions to the "excessive" jurisdictional claims by certain states. As oc-

---

[73] R.S.C. 1970, c. 10 (2nd Supp.). For a detailed account of procedures that existed before *Ranville*, see S.M. Morrison, "Extradition from Canada: Rights of the Fugitive Following Committal for Surrender" (1977), 19 *Crim. L. Q.* 366.

[74] Generally see M. Akehurst, "Jurisdiction in International Law" (1972-73), 46 *Br. Y.B. Int. L.* 145; D.W. Bowett, "Jurisdiction: Changing Patterns of Authority over Activities and Resources," in R. St. J. Macdonald and D.M. Johnston, *The Structure and Process of International Law* (1983), at 555; A.V. Lowe, "The Problem of Extraterritorial Jurisdiction: Economic Sovereignty and the Search for a Solution" (1985), 34 *Int. Comp. L. Q.* 725; H.G. Maier, "Extraterritorial Jurisdiction at a Crossroads: an Intersection Between Public and Private International Law" (1982), 76 *Am. J. Int. L.* 280; *Restatement (Revised), Foreign Relations Law of the United States*, ss. 401–403.

[75] The leading international case concerning the limits which International Law imposes on the exercise of state jurisdiction is *The Steamship Lotus*, (1927), P.C.I.J. Ser. A, No. 10, reported *supra*.

casion suits, however, the objectors may themselves be culprits of their own objections.

Examples of Canadian law applying extraterritorially are infrequent. Canadian criminal law, which traditionally, as set out in section 5(2) of the *Code*, is not to be interpreted as applying outside of Canada, now applies to a variety of events beyond our borders. Under the pressure of recent events, Canada has been required to extend its jurisdiction in such matters as aircraft hijacking, for the protection of our diplomats abroad and in the event of hostage taking, as discussed in Section 2 above. As early as the *Arctic Waters Pollution Protection Act* of 1970, Canada had indicated its willingness to extend the application of Canadian laws beyond its borders where special national needs required it.

Reaction to the perceived exorbitant assertion of jurisdiction usually occurs where a foreign state applies its laws, not only to events which have their primary links with it, but also to other events of limited connection, that in other respects are perfectly licit under their local law. Similarly, objection is likely to be raised when a state tries to impose its legal process, not only on its own nationals while abroad, but also on foreigners who may be associated with them in lawful ways according to the law of their own countries. The range of these irritants has greatly increased in recent years. Initially American anti-trust laws were the sole cause for alarm but lately extraterritorial jurisdiction has also been asserted in other subject areas, such as export controls, taxation, securities, asset controls, corrupt practices, bankruptcy and insolvency. The exercise of procedural authority extraterritorially also occurs. Attempts have been made against completely foreign companies to subject them to jurisdiction and courts have ordered the subpoena of witnesses and the production of documents located abroad.

The international legal issues involved in questions of extraterritoriality are complex, particularly as the right to exercise jurisdiction may vary depending on whether one is concerned with the jurisdiction to legislate, to adjudicate or to enforce. The exercise of jurisdiction in each of these three areas depends upon a different basis, a factor highlighted in instances such as the Iranian assets controls enacted by the United States. Indeed different subject areas, whether civil or criminal, raise different problems and may have to be approached from individual perspectives. This section provides examples of different assertions of, and reactions to, extraterritorial authority with a view to discovering the degree to which international law imposes limits on state jurisdiction.

Examples and Reactions

U.S. Export Controls[76]
(1982), 21 *Int. Leg. Mat.* 853

[The *Export Administration Act* of 1979[77] gives to the President the power to control exports from the United States in support of various foreign policy goals including

---

[76] See H. Moyer & L. Mabry, "Export Controls as Instruments of Foreign Policy: The History, Legal Issues and Policy Lessons of Three Recent Cases" (1983), 15 *L. & Pol. Int. Bus.* 1; P. Merciai," The Euro-Siberian Gas Pipeline Dispute – A Compelling Case for the Adoption of Jurisdictional Codes of Conduct" (1984), 8 *Maryland J. Int. L. & Trade* 1.

[77] P.L. 96–72, as amended by P.L. 99–64 of July 12, 1985; 50 U.S.C. App. ss. 2401–2420; (1979), 18 *Int. Leg. Mat.* 1508, and (1982), 21 *Int. Leg. Mat.* 164.

strategic, human rights, regional stability, anti-terriorism and other considerations. Because of the definition of who is an American national, these controls may be extended to foreign subsidiaries of United States corporations thus on occasion interfering with the ability of such corporations to conform to the foreign or domestic policy requirements of the governments of the place of their incorporation. In addition, the regulations have been extended to include technology acquired from U.S. sources, even where the acquirers of such technology are not United States nationals.

Set out below as examples of the scope and purpose of these controls are two recent communications by the Department of Commerce's International Trade Administration concerning Amendments to the Export Administration Regulations.]

Department of Commerce
International Trade Administration
15 CFR Parts 379, 385, and 399
Controls on Exports of Petroleum Transmission and Refining Equipment to the U.S.S.R.
Summary: Under current regulations, a validated export license is required for foreign policy purposes for the export to the U.S.S.R. (including Estonia, Latvia, and Lithuania) of specified oil and gas exploration and production equipment, and technical data related to oil and gas exploration and production. This rule imposes new foreign policy controls on exports to the U.S.S.R. (including Estonia, Latvia, and Lithuania) of commodities for transmission (including transportation) and refinement of petroleum or natural gas and technical data related to oil and gas transmission or refinement. These controls also apply to Afghanistan.

Regulatory Changes
At the direction of the President and pursuant to section 6 of the Export Administration Act of 1979, the Department of Commerce is expanding the existing oil and gas controls applicable to the U.S.S.R. to include commodities and technical data for transmission (including transportation) or refinement of petroleum or natural gas for energy usage, excluding petrochemical feedstocks. This action is in response to the Soviet Union's heavy and direct responsibility for the repression in Poland. Presently, under 15 CFR 385.2(c) the Department of Commerce controls exports of specified oil and gas exploration and production equipment, technical data (other than GTDR) related to oil and gas exploration and production, and other commodities that require a validated export license for shipment to the Soviet Union and that are intended for use in oil or gas exploration or production. This rule expands the existing controls by applying the controls to the areas of refinement for energy usage and transmission. The commodities and technical data covered by this rule are also subject to the rule, effective December 30, 1981, which suspended the processing of all licensing for export to the U.S.S.R.

Further, the regulations affecting exports of technical data to other destinations are revised. Most types of technical data that are not generally available to the public presently may be exported under General License GTDR to all destinations except Cuba, North Korea, Vietnam, Cambodia, the U.S.S.R., East European communist countries, Laos, and the People's Republic of China. For technical data related to oil and gas exploration and production, use of General License GTDR is conditioned on the exporter receiving written assurance from the importer that neither the data nor the direct product thereof is intended to be shipped, directly or indirectly, to the U.S.S.R. This rule imposes on the export of technical data related to the transmission and refining of petroleum or natural gas, the condition that General License GTDR not be used unless the exporter has received written assurance from the importer that neither the technical data nor the direct product thereof is intended to be shipped, directly or indirectly to the U.S.S.R.

Pursuant to section 6 of the Export Administration Act of 1979 and following consultation with the Department of State, it has been determined that this rule is necessary to further significantly the foreign policy of the United States. Appropriate persons in industry and the Congress have been consulted, and the criteria set forth in section 6(b) of the Act have been considered.

Pursuant to section 4(c), it has been determined that, notwithstanding foreign availability, failure to take this action would be detrimental to the foreign policy of the United States.

Pursuant to section 6(d), it has been determined that there are no feasible alternative means of achieving the purpose of this action. As provided in section 6(g) efforts are being made to obtain cooperation of countries that produce comparable items.

Department of Commerce
International Trade Administration
15 CFR Parts 376, 379 and 385
Amendment of Oil and Gas Controls to the U.S.S.R.
Summary: At the direction of the President, export controls on oil and gas goods and technology to the U.S.S.R. are amended to include exports of non-U.S. origin goods and technical data by U.S. owned or controlled companies wherever organized or doing business, as well as certain foreign produced products of U.S. technical data not previously subject to controls. The regulations are also revised to state that certain policy guidance is inapplicable to exports to the U.S.S.R. and Poland.

Regulatory Changes
At the direction of the President and pursuant to section 6 of the Export Administration Act of 1979, as amended, the Department of Commerce is amending the existing oil and gas controls applicable to the U.S.S.R. Current controls restrict exports and reexports of U.S. origin oil and gas goods and technical data. This rule expands these controls to restrict exports to the U.S.S.R. of non-U.S. origin goods or technical data by U.S. owned or controlled foreign firms. The current controls also restrict the export of foreign produced products of U.S. technical data if the export of the data from the United States was subject to the receipt of a written assurance from the foreign importer against the transfer of the data or its products to proscribed destinations.

This rule amends controls on foreign produced products of U.S. technical data to include products of U.S. data in cases where the right to the use of the data abroad is subject to a licensing agreement with persons subject to the jurisdiction of the U.S. or requires the payment of royalties or other compensation to any such persons or in cases where the recipient of the technical data has agreed to abide by U.S. export control regulations.

As stated by the President, the objective of the United States in imposing sanctions has been and continues to be to advance reconciliation in Poland. There has been no movement by the U.S.S.R. toward this objective.

Pursuant to section 6 of the Export Administration Act of 1979 and at the direction of the President, it has been determined that the expansion of oil and gas controls is necessary to further significantly the foreign policy of the United States. As required by section 6(g), attempts to obtain cooperation of countries that produce comparable items have been made, but have been unsuccessful.

Pursuant to section 4(c), it has been determined that, notwithstanding availability of some of these goods and data from foreign sources, failure to take this action would be detrimental to the foreign policy of the United States. It also has been determined under section 6(d) that there are no feasible alternative means of achieving the purpose of this action.

Appropriate persons in industry and the Congress have been consulted, and the criteria set forth in section 6(b) of the Act have been considered.

These regulations also explain that the policy guidance contained in s. 385.2 of the Export Administration Regulations concerning exports to Country Groups Q.W. and Y. does not apply to the U.S.S.R. or Poland. A General Order issued on December 30, 1981 (15 CFR 390.8) suspended the processing of validated licenses and other authorizations for export to the U.S.S.R. Furthermore, because the situation in Poland creates the unacceptable risk of diversion to unauthorized end-uses and/or end-users, export licenses and other authorizations for export licenses and other authorizations for export of national security or nuclear non-proliferation controlled items destined for Poland will not be issued.

European Communities' Comments on U.S. Export Controls[78]
(1982), 21 *Int. Leg. Mat.* 891

I. *Introduction*

1. On June 22, 1982, the Department of Commerce at the direction of President Reagan and pursuant to Section 6 of the Export Administration Act amended Sections 376.12, 379.8 and 385.2 of the Export Administration Regulations. These amendments amounted to an expansion of the existing U.S. controls on the export and re-export of goods and technical data relating to oil and gas exploration, exploitation, transmission and refinement.

---

[78] These E.C. observations depend, to some extent, on the nationality of corporations, considered *supra* in Chapter 7. And see A.V. Lowe, "Public International Law and the Conflict of Laws: The European Response to the U.S. Export Administration Regulations" (1984), *Int. Comp. L.Q.* 515.

The European Community believes that the U.S. regulations as amended contain sweeping extensions of U.S. jurisdiction which are unlawful under international law. Moreover, the new Regulations and the way in which they affect contracts in the course of performance seems to run counter to criteria of the Export Aministration Act and also to certain principles of U.S. public law. ...

II. *The Amendments Under International Law*

A. Generally accepted bases of jurisdiction in international law

4. The U.S. measures as they apply in the present case are unacceptable under international law because of their extra-territorial aspects. They seek to regulate companies not of U.S. nationality in respect of their conduct outside the United States and particularly the handling of property and technical data of these companies not within the United States.

They seek to impose on non-U.S. companies the restriction of U.S. law by threatening them with discriminatory sanctions in the field of trade which are inconsistent with the normal commercial practice established between the U.S. and the E.C.

In this way the Amendments of June 22, 1982, run counter to the two generally accepted bases of jurisdiction in international law: the territoriality and the nationality principles.[79]

5. The *territoriality principle* (i.e. the notion that a state should restrict its rule-making in principle to persons and goods within its territory and that an organization like the European Community should restrict the applicability of its rules to the territory to which the Treaty setting it up applies) is a fundamental notion of international law, in particular insofar as it concerns the regulation of the social and economic activity in a state. The principle that each state – and *mutatis mutandis* the Community insofar as powers have been transferred to it – has the right freely to organize and develop its social and economic system has been confirmed many times in international fora. The American measures clearly infringe the principle of territoriality, since they purport to regulate the activities of companies in the E.C. not under the territorial competence of the U.S.

6. The *nationality principle* (i.e. the prescription of rules for nationals, wherever they are) cannot serve as a basis for the extension of U.S. jurisdiction resulting from the Amendments, i.e. (i) over companies incorporated in E.C. Member States on the basis of some corporate link (parent-subsidiary) or personal link (e.g. shareholding) to the U.S.; (ii) over companies incorporated in E.C. Member States, either because they have a tie to a U.S.-incorporated company, subsidiary or other "U.S. controlled" company through a licensing agreement, royalty payments, or payment of other compensation, or because they have bought certain goods originating in the U.S.

7. *ad* (*i*) The Amendments in two places purport to subject to U.S. jurisdiction companies, wherever organized or doing business, which are subsidiaries of U.S. companies or under the control of U.S. citizens, U.S. residents or even persons actually within the U.S. This implies that the United States is seeking to impose its corporate nationality on companies of which the great majority are incorporated and have their registered office elsewhere, notably in E.C. Member States.

---

[79] See, Restatement (2nd) of the Foreign Relations Law of the U.S. (1972), paras. 17 and 30, respectively.

Such action is not in conformity with recognized principles of international law. In the *Barcelona Traction* case, the International Court of Justice declared that two traditional criteria for determining the nationality of companies; i.e. the place of incorporation and the place of the registered office of the company concerned, had been "confirmed by long practice and by numerous international instruments." The Court also scrutinized other tests of corporate nationality, but concluded that these had not found general acceptance. The Court consequently placed primary emphasis on the traditional place of incorporation and the registered office in deciding the case in point.[80] This decision was taken within the framework of the doctrine of diplomatic protection, but reflects a general principle of international law.

8. *ad* (*ii*) The notion inherent in the subjection to U.S. jurisdiction of companies with no tie to the U.S. whatsoever, except for a technological link to a U.S. company, or through possession of U.S. origin goods, can only be that this technology or such goods should somehow be considered as unalterably "American" (even though many of the patents involved are registered in the Member States of the European Community). This seems the only possible explanation for the U.S. Regulations given the fact that national security is not at stake here. ...

Goods and technology do not have any nationality and there are no known rules under international law for using goods or technology situated abroad as a basis of establishing jurisdiction over the persons controlling them. Several Court cases confirm the U.S. jurisdiction does not follow U.S. origin goods once they have been discharged in the territory of another country.[81]

9. The Amendments of 22 June, 1982, therefore, cannot be justified under the nationality principle, because they ignore the two traditional criteria for determining the nationality of companies reconfirmed by the International Court of justice and because they purport to give some notion of "nationality" to goods and technologies so as to establish jurisdiction over persons handling them.

The purported direct extension of U.S. jurisdiction to non-U.S. incorporated companies not using U.S. origin technology or components is *a fortiori* objectionable to the E.C., because neither of these (in themselves invalid) justifications could apply.

10. The last mentioned case exemplifies to what extent the wholesale infringement of the nationality principle exacerbates the infringement of the territoriality principle. Thus even E.C. incorporated companies in the example mentioned above according to the Amendments would have to ask special written permission not of the E.C., but of the U.S. authorities in order to obtain permission to export goods produced in the E.C. and based on E.C. technology from the territory to which the E.C. Treaties apply to the U.S.S.R. The practical impact of the Amendments to the Export Administration Regulations is that E.C. companies are pressed into service to carry out U.S. trade policy towards the U.S.S.R., even though these companies are incorporated and have their

---

[80] [1970] I.C.J. Rep. 3, at 43.
[81] *American President Lines v. China Mutual Trading Co.*, [1953] A.M.C. 1510, at 1526 (Hong Kong Sup. Ct.); and *Moens v. Ahlers North German Lloyd* (1966), 30 R.W. 360 (Tribunal of Commerce, Antwerp).

registered office within the Community which has its own trade policy towards the U.S.S.R.

The public policy ("ordre public") of the European Community and of its Member States is thus purportedly replaced by U.S. public policy which European companies are forced to carry out within the E.C. if they are not to lose export privileges in the U.S. or to face other sanctions. This is an unacceptable interference in the affairs of the European Community.

11. Furthermore, it is reprehensible that present U.S. Regulations encourage non-U.S. companies to submit "voluntarily" to this kind of mobilization for U.S. purposes.

Compagnie Européenne des Pétroles S.A. v. Sensor Nederland B.V.
(1983), 22 *Int. Leg. Mat.* 66 (Distr. Ct., The Hague)

[The plaintiff C.E.P., a French company "domiciled in Paris," made a contract with Sensor, a Netherlands company "domiciled at the Hague," for the delivery of materials to be used in the construction of a Soviet pipeline. Upon an order of the U.S. President embargoing the delivery of materials, Sensor claimed that, as a subsidiary of an American company, it was relieved from complying with its contract. The U.S. Export Administration Regulations in question applied to any "partnership, association, corporation or other organization, wherever organized or doing business, that is owned or controlled by ... citizens or residents or corporations incorporated in the United States."]

THE COURT: ... 7.2 Under point 4 above it has been found that the contract between C.E.P. and Sensor is governed by Netherlands law. To what extent, therefore, is it necessary to take into account a measure under U.S. law that operates in restraint of trade?

In answering that question, the first consideration must be that that measure extends to the transaction between C.E.P. and Sensor simply and solely via the jurisdiction rule of section (2)(iv). The object of that rule is manifestly to endow the measure with effects vis-a-vis corporations located outside the United States which conclude contracts outside the United States with non-American corporations.

That is the situation that arises in the present case. What particularly merits attention is the fact that, under international law as commonly interpreted, Sensor Netherland B.V. has Netherlands nationality, having been organized in the Netherlands under Netherlands law and both its registered office and its real centre of administration being located within the Netherlands. In accordance with this interpretation, the Treaty of Friendship, Commerce and Navigation between the Kingdom of the Netherlands and the United States of America of March 27, 1956, provides in Article XXIII, third paragraph:

Companies constituted under the applicable laws and regulations within the territories of either Party shall be deemed companies thereof and shall have their juridical status recognized within the territories of the other Party.

7.3 The circumstances that the trade embargo imposed by the American authorities has been endowed with extra-territorial effects as hereinbefore described raises the question as to whether the jurisdiction rule that brings about such effects is compatible with international law.

The starting-point for answering such questions is the universally accepted rule of international law that in general it is not permissible for a State to exercise jurisdiction over acts performed outside its borders. Exceptions to this rule are, however, possible, for instance under the so-called "nationality principle" or the "protection principle" (the "universality principle" can be disregarded here).

The American jurisdiction rule would not appear to be justified by the nationality principle in so far as that rule brings within its scope companies of other than U.S. nationality.

The position would be different if, in the first place, the criterion "owned or controlled by persons specified in paragraphs (i), (ii), or (iii) of this section" were intended to be a yardstick for the (U.S.) nationality of the corporation – which is possible – and, moreover, if that criterion were accepted in international law side by side with the criterion hereinbefore referred to under 7.2; but in general, according to the views held outside the United States, this has to be regarded as in itself dubious, and in the relations between the United States and the Netherlands it is out of the question, having regard to the treaty provision hereinbefore cited under 7.2. The consequence of this is that the nationality principle offers insufficient basis for the jurisdiction rule here at issue.

Under the protection principle, it is permissible for a State to exercise jurisdiction over acts – wheresoever and by whomsoever performed – that jeopardize the security or credit worthiness of that State or other State interests. Such other State interests do not include the foreign policy interest that the U.S. measure seeks to protect. The protection principle cannot therefore be invoked in support of the validity of the jurisdiction rule here at issue.

It is also of importance to examine whether the acts of exportation covered by the American embargo, in so far as they are performed outside the United States, have direct and illicit effects within the territory of the United States. If that is the case, then those acts can be regarded as having been performed within the United States and on that ground brought within the jurisdiction of the United States under generally accepted rules of international law.

It cannot, however, be seen how the export to Russia of goods not originating in the United States by a non-American exporter could have any direct and illicit effect within the United States. Via this route too, therefore, the jurisdiction rule cannot be brought into compatibility with international law.

The foregoing does not entail that, measured by international law standards, the jurisdiction rule has to be denied all effects.

It is not unacceptable, for instance, that its effects should extend to American citizens who, wishing to evade the American embargo, to that end set up a non-American corporation outside the United States.

There is, however, no evidence to suggest that this has occurred in the present case.

If the jurisdiction rule nevertheless has the object of bringing a case such as that here at issue within the scope of the American measure, that rule must to that extent be deemed to be incompatible.

Under these circumstances the jurisdiction rule cannot have the consequence that the Netherlands courts will take the American embargo into account.

The foregoing does not in any way impair the jurisdiction rule of paragraphs (i), (ii) and (iii) of section (2).

Under the rules of Netherlands private international law, even where Netherlands law has to be applied to an international contract, as in the present case, the Netherlands courts are nevertheless, under certain circumstances, bound to accord priority over Netherlands law to the application of mandatory provisions of foreign law.

Among the circumstances under which the Netherlands courts are required to accord such priority is the situation in which the contract meets the condition of showing a sufficient nexus with the foreign country concerned.

That condition is not fulfilled in the present case ... .

It follows from the foregoing that Sensor's reliance on the American embargo fails and that the claim, against which no defence other than that hereinbefore discussed has been adduced, must be allowed, Sensor being ordered to pay costs.

NOTES

To what extent does the Court's view of the appropriateness of the foreign legislation determine its willingness to give it extraterritorial effect? In *Laane and Baltser v. The Estonian State Cargo and Passenger Steamship Line*[82], Rand J., in rejecting the application of Estonian legislation as confiscatory stated, "what is asked of the foreign territorial law is, therefore, to aid in the execution of a fundamental political law of Estonia which serves no interest of the foreign state".

Anti-Trust Actions[83]

Anti-trust legislation poses particularly acute problems when applied to activities beyond the borders of the state exercising jurisdiction. Implicit in such legislation are states' concepts concerning the relative advantages or disadvantages of minimizing competition, decentralizing economic decision-making, fixing prices, allocating national human and other resources to achieve certain national goals, and other economic policies which are designed to respond to that state's levels of economic development. Such policies are a reflection of basic political notions which undergird a state's economic structure. The application of such policies to activities carried on in other states risks interfering with their pursuit of similar goals within their own territory.

---

[82] [1949] S.C.R. 530, reported *supra* in Chapter 5. See also *British Nylon Spinners Ltd. v. Imperial Chemical Industries Ltd.*, [1952] 2 All E.R. 780 (C.A.); *Fruehauf Corp. v. Massardy*, [1965] J.C.P.II 14, 274 bis; G. Craig, "Application of the Trading with the Enemy Act to Foreign Corporations Owned by Americans: Reflections on *Fruehauf v. Massardy*" (1970), 83 *Harv. L. Rev.* 579.

[83] J. Atwood & K. Brewster, *Anti-trust and American Business Abroad* (2 ed., 1981); J.G. Castel, "The Extraterritorial Effects of Anti-trust Laws" (1983), 179 *Hague Recueil* 21.

United States v. Aluminum Co. of America
(1945), 148 F.2d 416 (U.S.C.A. 2d Circ.)

[Sixty-three American and foreign companies were accused of violating the *Sherman Act* section 1, which renders illegal every contract or conspiracy in restraint of interstate or foreign trade or commerce of the United States. Part of the case concerned evidence that the foreign defendants had made an arrangement in 1931 and again in 1936 in Switzerland by which they had agreed to fix world prices and to share markets in aluminum. The trial court dismissed the complaint and the United States appealed.]

LEARNED HAND D.J.: ... Did either the agreement of 1931 or that of 1936 violate s. 1 of the Act? The answer does not depend upon whether we shall recognize as a source of liability a liability imposed by another state. On the contrary we are concerned only with whether Congress chose to attach liability to the conduct outside the United States of persons not in allegiance to it. That being so, the only question open is whether Congress intended to impose the liability, and whether our own Constitution permitted it to do so: as a court of the United States, we cannot look beyond our own law. Nevertheless, it is quite true that we are not to read general words, such as those in this Act, without regard to the limitations customarily observed by nations upon the exercise of their powers; limitations which generally correspond to those fixed by the "Conflict of Laws." We should not impute to Congress an intent to punish all whom its courts can catch, for conduct which has no consequences within the United States . ... On the other hand, it is settled law ... that any state may impose liabilities, even upon persons not within its allegiance, for conduct outside its borders that has consequences within its borders which the state reprehends; and these liabilities other states will ordinarily recognize. ... It may be argued that this Act extends further. Two situations are possible. There may be agreements made beyond our borders not intended to affect imports, which do affect them, or which affect exports. Almost any limitation of the supply of goods in Europe, for example, or in South America, may have repercussions in the United States if there is trade between the two. Yet when one considers the international complications likely to arise from an effort in this country to treat such agreements as unlawful, it is safe to assume that Congress certainly did not intend the Act to cover them. Such agreements may on the other hand intend to include imports into the United States, and yet it may appear that they have had no effect upon them. That situation might be thought to fall within the doctrine that intent may be a substitute for performance in the case of a contract made within the United States; or it might be thought to fall within the doctrine that a statute should not be interpreted to cover acts abroad which have no consequence here. We shall not choose between these alternatives; but for argument we shall assume that the Act does not cover agreements, even though intended to affect imports or exports, unless its performance is shown actually to have had some effect upon them. ...

Both agreements would clearly have been unlawful, had they been made within the United States; and it follows from what we have just said that both were unlawful, though made abroad, if they were intended to affect imports and did affect them. [The Court concluded that the *Sherman Act* had been violated and issued an injunction to restrain the foreign defendants from entering any similar cartel to restrict aluminum imports into the United States.]

Timberlane Lumber Co. v. Bank of America
(1976), 549 F.2d 597 (U.S.C.A. 9th Circ.) (references omitted)

[The plaintiffs claimed that the defendant bank had conspired with others in Honduras and in the United States to prevent the plaintiff's Honduran subsidiary from milling lumber in Honduras and exporting it to the United States. Timberlane had sought to go into business in Honduras by acquiring some of the assets of an insolvent Honduran company, which was a debtor of the defendant bank, but it was disrupted by its competitors who conspired by a series of questionable dealings and court orders backed by troops to cripple the milling operation and to cause the false arrest of the manager. Timberlane alleged that this harassment directly and substantially affected the foreign commerce of the United States, but the District Court dismissed the action. Timberlane appealed.]

CHOY, Circuit Judge: ... That American law covers some conduct beyond this nation's borders does not mean that it embraces all, however. Extraterritorial application is understandably a matter of concern for the other countries involved. Those nations have sometimes resented and protested, as excessive intrusions into their own spheres, broad assertions of authority by American courts. ... Our courts have recognized this concern and have, at times, responded to it, even if not always enough to satisfy all foreign critics. ...In any event, it is evident that at some point the interests of the United States are too weak and the foreign harmony incentive for restraint too strong to justify an extraterritorial assertion of jurisdiction.

What that point is or how it is determined is not defined by international law. ... Nor does the Sherman Act limit itself. In the domestic field the Sherman Act extends to the full reach of the commerce power. ... To define it somewhat more modestly in the foreign commerce area courts have generally, and logically, fallen back on a narrower construction of congressional intent, such as expressed in Judge Learned Hand's oft-cited opinion in *Alcoa* ... .

Despite its description as "settled law," *Alcoa's* assertion has been roundly disputed by many foreign commentators as being in conflict with international law, comity, and good judgment. Nonetheless, American courts have firmly concluded that there is some extraterritorial jurisdiction under the Sherman Act.

Even among American courts and commentators, however, there is no consensus on how far the jurisdiction should extend. The district court here concluded that a "direct and substantial effect" on United States foreign commerce was a prerequisite, without stating whether other factors were relevant or considered. ... Other courts have used different expressions, however. ...

The effects test by itself is incomplete because it fails to consider other nations' interests. Nor does it expressly take into account the full nature of the relationship between the actors and this country. Whether the alleged offender is an American citizen, for instance, may make a big difference; applying American laws to American citizens raises fewer problems than application to foreigners. ...

American courts have, in fact, often displayed a regard for comity and the prerogatives of other nations and considered their interests as well as other parts of the factual circumstances, even when professing to apply an effects test. To some degree, the requirement for a ''substantial'' effect may silently incorporate these additional considerations, with ''substantial'' as a flexible standard that varies with other factors. The intent requirement suggested by *Alcoa* ... is one example of an attempt to broaden the court's perspective, as is drawing a distinction between American citizens and non-citizens. ...

A tripartite analysis seems to be indicated. As acknowledged above, the anti-trust laws require in the first instance that there be some effect – actual or intended – on American foreign commerce before the federal courts may legitimately exercise subject matter jurisdiction under those statutes. Second, a greater showing of burden or restraint may be necessary to demonstrate that the effect is sufficiently large to present a cognizable injury to the plaintiffs and, therefore, a civil violation of the anti-trust laws. ... Third, there is the additional question which is unique to the international setting of whether the interests of, and links to, the United States – including the magnitude of the effect on American foreign commerce – are sufficiently strong, vis-a-vis those of other nations, to justify an assertion of extraterritorial authority.

It is this final issue which is both obscured by undue reliance on the ''substantiality'' test and complicated to resolve. An effect on United States commerce, although necessary to the exercise of jurisdiction under the anti-trust laws, is alone not a sufficient basis on which to determine whether American authority should be asserted in a given case as a matter of international comity and fairness. ...

What we prefer is an evaluation and balancing of the relevant considerations in each case – in the words of Kingman Brewster, a ''jurisdictional rule of reason''. ...

The elements to be weighed include the degree of conflict with foreign law or policy, the nationality or allegiance of the parties and the locations or principal places of business of corporations, the extent to which enforcement by either state can be expected to achieve compliance, the relative significance of effects on the United States as compared with those elsewhere, the extent to which there is explicit purpose to harm or affect American commerce, the foreseeability of such effect, and the relative importance to the violations charged of conduct within the United States as compared with conduct abroad. A court evaluating these factors should identify the potential degree of conflict if American authority is asserted. A difference in law or policy is one likely sore spot, though one which may not always be present. Nationality is another; though foreign governments may have some concern for the treatment of American citizens and business residing there, they primarily care about their own nationals. Having assessed the conflict, the court should then determine whether in the face of it the contacts and interests of the United States are sufficient to support the exercise of extraterritorial jurisdiction.

We conclude, then, that the problem should be approached in three parts: Does the alleged restraint affect, or was it intended to affect, the foreign commerce of the United States? Is it of such a type and magnitude so as to be cognizable as a violation of the Sherman Act? As a matter of international comity and fairness, should the extraterritorial jurisdiction of the United States be asserted to cover it? The district court's judgment found only that the restraint involved in the instant suit did not produce a direct and substantial effect on American foreign commerce. That holding does not satisfy any of these inquiries.

[The case was remanded to allow the proper inquiries to be made.]

NOTES

1) The thrust of this court's view of comity has been followed in some other cases, for example *Mannington Mills Inc. v. Congoleum* Corp.[84] Much of its reasoning has been followed in the recent revision of the *Restatement of Foreign Relations Law of the United States*, ss. 403 & 415, which sets out a series of criteria to which courts should refer in order to determine the relative merits of U.S. claims to jurisdiction over those of other states. Unfortunately this "interest balancing" test has not been followed by all U.S. jurisdictions.[85] In a recent decision in the *Timberlane* case the Court rejected the necessity of showing a "direct and substantial effect" on the foreign commerce of the United States in order for the anti-trust laws to be applied to conduct abroad.[86]

2) This aggressive extension of jurisdiction seems particularly offensive to some observers in light of the U.S. *Foreign Trade Anti-Trust Improvements Act of 1982*[87] which specifically exempts from the application of the anti-trust laws domestic United States arrangements which have as their purpose the furthering of exports from the United States and which do not have a substantial and reasonably forseeable effect on domestic commerce. The U.S. thus renders legal local conduct by Americans which, if engaged in by foreigners in their own country, would be illegal under American law.

3) German merger law has been applied to the merger of corporations in other countries and the German statute specifically applies to all restraints on competition which have an effect in Germany, "even when they are caused outside of the territorial scope of the statute." The German courts, in applying this statute, are conscious of the limits which international law imposes on the exercise of jurisdiction and consider the sovereign interests of other states involved.[88]

4) The European Commission has also applied the competition rules of the E.E.C. in an extraterritorial fashion,[89] although its authority to do so was contested before the European Court of Justice in the following case. Note the Court's approach to the jurisdiction question: did it apply the effects doctrine?

---

[84] (1979), 595 F. 1287 (U.S. C.A. 3d Circ.), and note, W. Wenberg, "Mannington Mills, Inc. v. Congoleum Corp.: A Further Step Toward a Complete Subject Matter Jurisdiction Test" (1980), 2 *Northwest J. Int. L. & B.* 241.

[85] See *Laker Airways v. Sabena* (1984), 731 F. 909, at 948–53 (U.S. C.A. D.C. Circ.); *Zenith Radio Corp. v. Matsushita Electric* (1980), 494 F. Supp. 1161 (E.D. Pa.).

[86] See Note (1985), 79 *Am. J. Int. L.* 735.

[87] (1982) 96 Stat. 1246; 15 U.S.C. 61, 45a. See J. Kirman, "U.S. Exporters Showing Increased Interest in Anti-trust Protection Legislation" (1983), 3 *West's Int. L. Bull.* 12. Cp. *Combines Investigation Act*, R.S.C. 1970, c.23, s. 32(4), as amended.

[88] D. Gerber, "The Extraterritorial Application of the German Antitrust Laws" (1983), 77 *Am. J. Int. L.* 756.

[89] See B. Barak, *The Application of the Competition Rules (Anti-trust Law) of the European Community* (1981).

**Europemballage Corporation and Continental Can Company Inc.
v. E.C. Commission**
[1973] C.M.L. Rep. 199

[In 1969 Continental Can Co. Inc. of New York acquired an 85.8% holding in a German firm. In 1970 it incorporated a Delaware subsidiary, Europemballage Corporation, which opened an office in Europe and also acquired a 90% interest in a Dutch company at about the same time. The European Commission instituted proceedings against the two American companies under Article 86 of the Treaty of Rome which prohibits the abuse of a dominant position within the Common Market that affects trade between the Member States. The Commission found a violation of Article 86 and ordered that a scheme of divestiture be presented to it. The two corporations attacked the decision of the Commission before the European Court of Justice alleging, *inter alia*, that the Commission lacked jurisdiction, given that the two corporations were not European nationals.

The Advocate General, Herr Karl Roemer, was of the view that Article 86 applied to the two companies' activities in Europe and that the Commission had subject matter and *in personam* jurisdiction both based upon the "effects doctrine" as set out in the *Alcoa* case and because the two companies were effectively carrying on business in Europe through their controlled subsidiaries.]

THE COURT: ... The applicant companies maintain that according to the general principles of public international law, as an undertaking with a seat outside the Community, Continental Can is not subject to the jurisdiction of the Commission or the Court of Justice; that the Commission therefore had no power to issue the challenged decision against Continental Can or to address to it the demand contained in Article 2 of the decision; and that furthermore the unlawful conduct in respect of which the Commission took proceedings was not directly attributable to Continental Can but to Europemballage.

The applicant companies cannot deny that Europemballage, set up on 20 February 1970 by Continental Can, is a subsidiary company of Continental Can. The fact that the subsidiary has its own legal personality cannot rule out the possibility that its conduct may be imputed to its parent company. This is particularly the case where the subsidiary does not determine its market behaviour autonomously but mainly follows the instructions of the parent company.

It is established that Continental Can caused Europemballage to make an offer to buy to the Thomassen & Drijver-Verblifa shareholders in Holland and provided the necessary funds for this purpose. On 8 April 1970 Europemballage bought the Thomassen & Drijver-Verblifa shares and bonds offered to it on that date. Therefore this transaction on the basis of which the Commission adopted the decision in question must be attributed not only to Europemballage but also and mainly to Continental Can. Community law is applicable to such an acquisition which affects the market conditions within the Community. The fact that Continental Can does not have a seat in the territory of one of the member-States does not suffice to remove it from the jurisdiction of Community law.

The plea of lack of jurisdiction must therefore be rejected.

Canadian Practice

The Interpretation Act.[90] Section 8(3) states:

Every Act of the Parliament of Canada now in force enacted prior to the 11th day of December 1931 that in terms or by necessary or reasonable implication was intended, as to the whole or any part thereof, to have extraterritorial operation, shall be construed as if at the date of its enactment the Parliament of Canada then had full power to make laws having extraterritorial operations as provided by the *Statute of Westminster, 1931.*

The provisions of the *Combines Investigation Act*[91] against combines and other market controlling and price fixing arrangements would presumably apply to conduct outside Canada designed to affect markets inside Canada and which would be an offence if committed in Canada,[92] although there have been cases of conduct outside Canada with effects on Canada which were considered beyond the scope of the Act.[93] It also contains several sections directed against certain conduct of individuals abroad:

31.7 Where, on application by the Director, and after affording every person against whom an order is sought a reasonable opportunity to be heard, the Commission finds that a supplier outside Canada has refused to supply a product or otherwise discriminated in the supply of a product to a person in Canada (the "first" person) at the instance of and by reason of the exertion of buying power outside Canada by another person, the Commission may order any person in Canada (the "second" person) by whom or on whose behalf or for whose benefit the buying power was exerted

(a) to sell any such product of the supplier that the second person has obtained or obtains to the first person at the laid-down cost in Canada to the second person of such product and on the same terms and conditions as the second person obtained or obtains from the supplier; or

(b) not to deal or to cease to deal, in Canada, in such product of the supplier.

32.1(1) Any company, wherever incorporated, that carries on business in Canada and that implements, in whole or in part in Canada, a directive, instruction, intimation of policy or other communication to the company or any person from a person in a country other than Canada who is in a position to direct or influence the policies of the company, which communication is for the purpose of giving effect to a conspiracy, combination, agreement or arrangement entered into outside Canada that, if entered into in Canada, would have been in violation of section 32, is, whether or not any director or officer of the company in Canada has knowledge of the

---

[90] R.S.C. 1970, c. I-23, as amended.

[91] R.S.C. 1970, c. C-23, as amended by R.S.C. 1970, (2nd supp.) c.10; S.C. 1974–75–76, c.76; 1976–77, c.28; 1985, c.19.

[92] *R. v. Campbell* (1965) 46 D.L.R. (2d) 83 (Ont. C.A.), aff'd (1966), 58 D.L.R. (2d) 673 (S.C.C.), where an overt act was done in Canada in furtherance of an agreement entered into in the United States.

[93] See Canada, Royal Commission on Farm Machinery, *Special Report on Prices of Tractors and Combines in Canada and Other Countries* (1969) (price fixing of farm machinery in the U.K. which related to prices in Canada); Restrictive Trade Practices Commission, *Report on Trade Practices in Phospherous Products and Sodium Chlorate Industries* (1966); "The Japanese Drum Case," reported in R. Roberts, *Anti-combines and Anti-trust* (1980), at 328.

conspiracy, combination, agreement or arrangement, guilty of an indictable offence and is liable on convinction to a fine in the discretion of the court.

The *Foreign Investment Review Act*[94], now the *Investment Canada Act*[95] has been applied to mergers of foreign corporations when the control over a Canadian business enterprise is thereby affected.[96]

Production of Documents Located Abroad

Problems often arise when courts, or other authorities, seek to obtain evidence located abroad, in order to enforce their laws (of whatever kind). Thus in *U.S. v. First National City Bank*,[97] a case involving the production of documents in the United States, in violation of German banking secrecy laws, the court held:

The important interest of the United States in the enforcement of the subpoena warrants little discussion. The federal Grand Jury before which Citibank was summoned is conducting a criminal investigation of alleged violations of the antitrust laws. These laws have long been considered cornerstones of this nation's economic policies, have been vigorously enforced and the subject of frequent interpretation by our Supreme Court. We would have great reluctance, therefore, to countenance any device that would place relevant information beyond the reach of this duly impaneled Grand Jury or impede or delay its proceedings.

Without access to relevant business records located abroad, a major commercial crime case or an antitrust suit may be severely crippled. But, naturally such cases have often led to diplomatic protests by the foreign countries involved. The Canadian government has appeared in some cases before the American Courts to protest this form of jurisdiction.

United States v. Bank of Nova Scotia
(1984), 740 F. 2d 817 (C.A. 11th Circ.)

[In the course of a narcotics investigation, a court in Florida ordered production of banking records held by the bank in its Grand Cayman Islands branch. Furnishing these documents would, under the banking secrecy laws of that jurisdiction, have subjected the bank to criminal liability and jeopardized its banking license to carry on business there. There existed a "Gentleman's Agreement" between the U.S. and the Grand Cayman Islands providing procedures whereby such records could be obtained. In spite of this the court ordered the bank to furnish the records directly and upon its failure to comply fined it $25,000 per day (totalling $1,825,000). On appeal from this fine to the U.S. Supreme

---

[94] Stats. Can. 1973–74, c. 46, as amended, repealed by Stats. Can. 1985, c. 20
[95] Stats. Can. 1985, c. 20.
[96] *Dow Jones & Co. Inc. v. A. -G. of Canada* (1981), 122 D.L.R. (3d) 731 (F.C.A.); *A. -G. of Canada v. Fallbridge Holdings Ltd.* (1986), 31 B.L.R. 57 (F.C.A.)
[97] (1968), 396 F. 2d 897 (U.S.C.A. 2d Circ.).

Court *certiorari* was denied. The Canadian government stated in its brief filed with the Supreme Court:]

International law, starting from the basic notions of sovereignty and the sovereign equality of states, accords primacy to regulations of states – whether by statute, order of a court, or otherwise – taken within their own territory. See, e.g., *Banco Nacional de Cuba v. Sabbatino*, 376 U.S. 398, 428 (1964). That general principle applies in this situation as well, where two states issued directly conflicting commands.

Whether the issue involved here was doing an act, (i.e., disclosing the information requested) or refraining from doing an act, (i.e., preserving the confidential character of the banking records in question), the U.S. command to the Bank was to be carried out in the Cayman Islands. The statement of the Court of Appeals that "the Cayman Grand Court purported to control conduct in the United States" ... is clearly mistaken. The records and the information sought by the grand jury were located in the Cayman Islands, and the Grand Court sought to control conduct *only* in the Cayman Islands.

An analogous situation might occur, for example, if the government of a Middle Eastern state in which the Bank of Nova Scotia maintains an office issued an order requiring the Bank to disclose information concerning the alleged business relations between a customer of its Miami office and Israel. For the Miami office to supply that information would violate the foreign political boycott provisions of the Export Administration Act of 1979, 50 U.S.C. App. s. 24(7) (a)(1)(D) (1982), and would place the Bank in a situation of irreconcilable commands. It would surely be the position of the United States, including the Department of Commerce and any U.S. court that might hear the issue, that disclosure or nondisclosure of the information was an activity centered in the United States. The United States would surely protest, as would Canada, if the Middle Eastern state imposed sanctions on the Bank of Nova Scotia for obeying U.S. law in the United States.

U.S. law has modified the rule according preference to the territorial state by requiring persons before the court to make good faith efforts to secure release or waiver from statutory prohibitions. See, e.g., *Restatement (Revised) of Foreign Relations Law*, s. 420(2). But the Restatement clearly limits contempt sanctions to parties, and until this case and *United States v. Bank of Nova Scotia*, 691 F.2D 1384 (11th Cir. 1982), cert. denied, 103 S.Ct. 3086 (1983) (*"Bank of Nova Scotia I"*), no court in the United States had imposed contempt on non party custodians, where the information sought was at all relevant times located outside the United States, and the U.S. attorney made no effort to justify the U.S. government's need for the disclosure (other than asserting the institutional importance of all grand juries), and in particular failed to demonstrate that alternative intergovernmental avenues to obtain the evidence were exhausted. ...

No prior U.S. case is known in which an American court has ordered any person before it, let alone a non-party, noninvestigatory target, to act in defiance of the order of a foreign court. Yet that is just what the District Court did in the present case in its order of October 20, 1983, as upheld by the Court of Appeals.

The significance of the order of the Cayman court in the present case is threefold. First, it distinguishes this case from *Bank of Nova Scotia 1*, supra, and *United States v. Field*, 532 F.2d 404 (5th Cir.), cert. denied, 429 U.S. 940 (1976), in which no foreign court order was involved. Second, it distinguishes this case from other cases in which the plea that disclosure would violate the law of a foreign state was in doubt, either because the law itself was not clear, see, e.g., *United States v. First National City Bank*, 396 F.2d 897, 903–05 (2d Cir. 1968), or because it depended on the interest of the foreign state in the matter at issue and that interest was not clear. See, e.g., *United States v. Vetco*, 691 F.2d 1281, 1289 (9th Cir.), cert. denied, 454 U.S. 1098 (1981). In the present case, there could be no question at the time of the District Court's order on October 20, 1983, that the Cayman law applied, and that it prohibited the Bank's compliance with the subpoena.

Third, the judgment of the Grand Court of Cayman of May 31, 1983 met all the requirements for recognition and respect by the District Court. See, e.g., *Somportex Ltd. v. Philadelphia Chewing Gum Corp.*, 453 F.2d 435 (3d Cir. 1971), cert. denied, 405 U.S. 1017 (1972); *Restatement (Revised)*, supra, ss. 491–92 (Tent. Draft No. 4, 1983). No justification has been presented by the United States for declining to recognize this judgment. The May 31 judgment of the Cayman court was fully effective and binding on October 20, 1983, but was not even mentioned in the Order of that date issued by the District Court. There was no respect for foreign judgments, and no consideration of comity. The fact that a respected District Court could so disregard fundamental principles of relations among states and courts to the point of not even considering them shows the need for guidelines, and accordingly the need for review by this Court. ...

It is evident that the subpoena at issue here failed to meet the standards of section 1783 in several respects. The prosecution avoided initial screening by the court, as well as the territorial limits of the statute and Rules, by acting as if what was involved was a routine subpoena to a local bank. The theory apparently was that physical power over a single office and a few employees of the Bank in Miami gave the grand jury authority to require production of records from anywhere the Bank had an office – in this case some 1,200 offices in 52 countries on 6 continents. Some 45 foreign banks have representation in Miami; several hundred have representation in New York and other major American financial centers. It seems improbable that the U.S. Congress contemplated threats and sanctions against U.S. offices of foreign banks as a way around the restraints it placed on subpoenas issued under the authority of the United States, and no such intent should be imputed. See *Commodity Futures Trading Commission v. Nahas*, 738 F.2d 487 (D.C. Cir. 1984); *Federal Trade Commission v. Compagnie de Saint-Gobain-Pont-a-Mousson*, 636 F.2d 1300 (D.C. Cir. 1980).[98]

NOTES

1) If Canada has been unable to stop the documentary demands and fines of U.S. courts against its nationals in their territorial jurisdiction, it has been able and willing to prevent access to requested documents within its own jurisdiction. Both the legislatures

---

[98] See Comment, (1981), 75 *Am. J. Int. L.* 369; and J.G. Castel, "Compelling Disclosure by a Non-Party Litigant in Violation of Foreign Bank Secrecy Laws: Recent Developments in Canada-United States Relations" (1985), 23 *Can. Y.B. Int. L.* 261.

and the courts have been called in aid of this objective. The first such statute was the 1947 *Business Records Protection Act* of Ontario.[99] It simply prohibited the discovery of documents of Canadian companies in foreign litigation. There has since been enacted the Quebec *Business Concerns Records Act*,[100] and the Canada *Foreign Extraterritorial Measures Act*,[101] to be discussed later. A thorough analysis of the U.S. courts' response to blocking statutes as a justification for failure to comply with an order for production of documents is made in *Graco Inc. v. Kremlin Inc.*[102]

2) A particularly galling feature of American demands for documentary evidence is that they may be made not only to support criminal prosecutions brought by the U.S. government but also to aid private parties in civil litigation. Private antitrust suits for treble damages are a unique possibility under U.S. law. While Canada may exercise diplomatic pressures to discourage the U.S. government from pursuing an antitrust prosecution, it is powerless to influence private litigation that runs counter to Canadian economic and foreign policies. This was exactly the Canadian predicament in the uranium cartel dispute, which produced such a strong blocking reaction:[103]

Uranium Cartel Litigation
Gulf Oil Corp. v. Gulf Canada Ltd.
[1980] 2 S.C.R. 39

[Westinghouse Electric Corporation had long term, fixed price contracts to supply uranium within the United States. As a result of unforeseen large increases in the world price of uranium, Westinghouse became faced with colossal losses and law suits for breach of these contracts. In response, Westinghouse began its own antitrust actions against the international cartel of uranium producers who, it alleged, had conspired to fix the world price. The cartel had been formed in 1972 amongst governments and mining corporations in Canada, Australia, the United Kingdom, France and South Africa as a means to protect their uranium industries after the loss of the important American market as a result of an U.S. embargo on imports imposed to protect U.S. domestic producers. Gulf Oil Corporation, of the United States, and Gulf Canada Ltd., its Canadian subsidiary, were two of the defendants in the suit brought by Westinghouse in Chicago. In pre-trial proceedings, demands for the discovery of certain documents held by Gulf Canada Ltd. in Canada were made but refused. A hearing was held for the purpose of issuing letters rogatory to

---

[99] R.S.O. 1980, c. 56.

[100] R.S.Q. 1977, c. D-12.

[101] Stats. Can. 1984, c. 49, reproduced *infra*.

[102] (1984) 101 F.D.R. 503 (N.D. Ill., E.D.).

[103] Documentary requests in the form of letters rogatory were also blocked in Ontario, *Re Westinghouse Electric Corp. and Duquesne Light Co.* (1977), 16 O.R. (2d) 273 (Ont. H.C.), and in England, *Rio Tinto Zinc Corp. v. Westinghouse Electric Corp.*, [1978] 2 W.L.R. 81 (H.L.), where Lord Wilberforce based his rejection on the possible prejudice to the sovereignty of the United Kingdom. See also R.T. Rankin, ''The Supreme Court of Canada and the International Uranium Cartel: Gulf Oil and Canadian Sovereignty'' (1981), 2 *Sup. Ct. L. Rev.* 410.

the judicial authorities in Canada to enforce the disclosure of the documents.[104] In the course of judgment, District Judge Marshall encapsulated the international conflict:

> Several defendants ... rely on broad notions of "international comity" for the proposition that we should balance the vital national interests of the United States and the foreign countries to determine which interests predominate ... . The competing interests here display irreconcilable conflict on precisely the same plane of national policy. Westinghouse seeks to enforce this nation's antitrust laws against an alleged international marketing arrangement among uranium-producers, and to that end has sought documents located in foreign countries where those producers conduct their business. In specific response to this and other related litigation in the American courts, three foreign governments have enacted nondisclosure legislation which is aimed at nullifying the impact of American antitrust legislation by prohibiting access to those same documents. It is simply impossible to judicially "balance" these totally contradictory and mutually negating actions.

In issuing the letters rogatory, Marshall D.J. observed:

> The order will serve to declare Westinghouse's right to the discovery it seeks, thereby framing the competing interests of the United States and the foreign governments on a plane where the potential moderation of the exercise of their conflicting enforcement jurisdictions can be meaningfully considered.

Gulf Oil Corp. then sought enforcement of the letters rogatory by the Supreme Court of Canada.]

LASKIN C.J.C.: ... In both the Chicago and California actions, orders were made for the production of documents in Canada in the possession or under the control of Gulf Minerals and Gulf Canada. It was the position of Gulf Oil and Gulf Minerals that the documents were relevant to issues in the respective actions and were necessary to establish their defence to the claims made in the two actions. Because of the *Uranium Information Security Regulations* (to which I will refer later) the Canadian subsidiaires were unwilling to violate the prohibition against disclosure prescribed by the *Regulations* or to risk the penalties prescribed for breach. Were it not for the *Regulations*, they were quite prepared to make disclosure and thus to assist their parent company in the two actions.

Gulf Oil thereupon applied for the letters rogatory which it now seeks to have enforced by this Court. ...

I should point out that the letters rogatory were sought by Gulf Oil in order to avoid sanctions orders which might result in default judgments or a denial of the right to raise defences to which the Canadian documents would be relevant. ...

I come now to consider the *Uranium Information Security Regulations* [Can. Consol. Regs. 1979, c. 366, passed pursuant to the *Atomic Energy Control Act*, R.S.C. 1970, c. A-19, s. 9]. ...

---

[104] *In re Uranium Antitrust Litigation* (1979), 480 F. Supp. 1138 (N.D. Ill., E.D.). See also *In re Westinghouse Electric Uranium Contracts Litigation* (1977), 563 F. 2d 992 (U.S. C.A. 10th Circ.).

In the substituted regulations, a definition of "foreign tribunal" was introduced as s. 2 and it defined the term to include any court or grand jury and any person authorized or permitted under foreign law to take or receive evidence whether on behalf of a court or grand jury or otherwise. Section 3 was in these words:

3. No person who has in his possession or under his control any note, document or other written or printed material in any way related to conversations, discussions or meetings that took place between January 1, 1972 and December 31, 1975 involving that person or any other person in relation to the exporting from Canada or marketing for use outside Canada of uranium or its derivatives or compounds shall

   (a) release any such note, document or material or disclose or communicate the contents thereof to any person, foreign government or branch or agency thereof or to any foreign tribunal unless

     (i) he is required to do so by or under a law of Canada, or

     (ii) he does so with the consent of the Minister of Energy, Mines and Resources; or

   (b) fail to guard against or take reasonable care to prevent the unauthorized release of any such note, document or material or the disclosure or communication of the contents thereof. ...

If they were validly enacted, the application to enforce the letters rogatory must fail because (1) the Minister of Energy, Mines and Resources has, despite various submissions to him, refused consent to disclosure and, (2) in my opinion, this is not a case where an order for disclosure should be made, assuming that such an order would come within the exception for disclosure under the words "by or under a law of Canada". ...

The participation of the government of Canada in the cartel arrangement was made known to the public, and it seems to me that the resistance to disclosure was not so much a matter of the maintenance of secrecy as it was of an assertion of Canadian sovereignty to resist the extraterritorial application of United States antitrust laws.

The government of Canada was on record in the Chicago action by an *amicus* brief presented to Judge Marshall that it regarded its sovereign position to be put in question by the attempt to secure disclosure of the information now sought under the letters rogatory. I quote here a small portion of the brief.

Canada considered it contrary to her sovereign prerogatives for foreign tribunals to question the propriety or legality of the actions of Canadian uranium producers that were taken outside the United States and were required by Canadian law or taken in implementation of Canadian government policy. Accordingly, when it became clear that documents located in Canada bearing on the international uranium marketing arrangement might be removed to the United States in response to proceedings there, the Canadian government promulgated the Regulations to serve a vital national interest, particularly the preservation of Canada's past and future sovereign authority to secure compliance with its own laws and policies respecting a vital Canadian natural resource in the face of assertions of jurisdiction by non-Canadian tribunals. These Regulations were not procured by members of the uranium industry, and they were not adopted to protect the commercial interests of those companies.

...it is the policy rather than the regulations that, in this case, is a factor in the Court's exercise of its discretion.

Robins J, in the *Westinghouse* case [supra, n. 103] took account of the policy in refusing to enforce certain letters rogatory and did so, as I read his reasons, even apart from Crown privilege which was asserted before him and apart from the regulations. Thus, he said (at 290 of 16 O.R. 2d):

> The enforcement of letters rogatory is always a matter within the discretionary power of the Court. Their enforcement is based upon international comity or courtesy proceeding from the law of nations. Inherent in the idea of international comity is a mutuality of purpose and of power. As a matter of principle Courts of justice of different countries are in aid of justice under a mutual obligation consistent with their own jurisdiction to assist each other in obtaining testimony upon which the rights of a cause may depend; so generally are individuals under a duty to give their testimony to Courts of justice in all inquires where it may be material. Courts in Canada recognize, and have often said, that, in the interests of comity, judicial assistance should whenever possible be given at the request of Courts of other countries: see, for example, *National Telefilm Associates Inc. v. United Artists' Corp. et al.* (1958), 14 D.L.R. (2d) 343, generally, Castel, *Canadian Conflict of Laws* (1975), at 691 *et seq.* It is also fundamental that comity will not be exercised in violation of the public policy of the state to which the appeal is made or at the expense of injustice to its citizens; and comity leaves to the Court whose power is invoked the determination of the legality, propriety or rightfulness of its exercise. ...

Counsel for Gulf Oil submitted that public policy or public interest immunity should not be attached to trading or commercial activities of the government; that it should not be recognized in respect of communications between persons who are not government employees or Ministers of the Crown or between government employees of Ministers and other persons; that, in any event, the public interest relied upon was not adequately described and that it was not shown how the public interest would be damaged by disclosure of the documents requested under the letters rogatory.

The last point may be answered shortly. It is not for a Court, when called upon to consider whether it should enforce letters rogatory, to take issue with the government's determination of public policy or to measure its impact. It may be that different considerations will operate where a Canadian court is concerned with Canadian litigation arising out of issues turning on Canadian law. Nor do I think that there is any doubt in this application by Gulf Oil as to what is the public policy which the government of Canada asserts. Again, there may be room for closer examination, and even assessment, where in Canadian litigation Crown privilege is asserted and the Court may be disposed to examine the documents for which the privilege is claimed. I do not agree that any such assessment or examination is invariably required to enable a Court to consider whether, in its discretion, it should enforce letters rogatory calling for the production of the documents for purposes of proceedings before a foreign tribunal.

Gulf Oil relied on *Burmah Oil Co. Ltd. v. Bank of England* (Attorney-General intervening) ([1979] 3 All E.R. 700) in support of the first two points in the above-mentioned submission. ...

I do not find anything in the *Burmah Oil* case, and, in particular, in the reasons of

Lord Edmund-Davies relied on by counsel for Gulf Oil, to support his contention that public policy considerations should not be recognized in respect of trading or commercial activities of the government. I can understand that the matter may be one of degree. However, where the government is party to the arrangements out of which the documents, whose disclosure is sought, emerge, and it has promoted the arrangements as a facet of its energy policy in which the marketing of uranium is a central feature, I fail to see how public policy can be ignored in the interests of comity towards a foreign court, as if the policy was essentially a reflection of private considerations without any public, governmental interest. Again, the voluminous documents (said to cover 25,000 pages) are not simply private documents drawn up as a result of discussions and negotiations in which the government of Canada played no part but, concededly, reflect an input by representatives of the government.

Foreign Extraterritorial Measures Act
S.C. 1984, c. 49

3.(1) Where, in the opinion of the Attorney General of Canada, a foreign tribunal has exercised, is exercising or is proposing or likely to exercise jurisdiction or powers of a kind or in a manner that has adversely affected or is likely to adversely affect significant Canadian interests in relation to international trade or commerce involving a business carried on in whole or in part in Canada or that otherwise has infringed or is likely to infringe Canadian sovereignty, he may by order prohibit or restrict

(a) the production before or the disclosure or identification to, or for the purposes of, a foreign tribunal of records that, at any time while the order is in force, are in Canada or are in the possession or under the control of a Canadian citizen or a person resident in Canada;

(b) the doing of any act in Canada, in relation to records that at any time while the order is in force are in Canada or are in the possession or under the control of a Canadian citizen or a person resident in Canada, that will, or is likely to, result in the records, or information as to the contents of the records or from which the records might be identified, being produced before or disclosed or identified to, or for the purposes of, a foreign tribunal; and

(c) the giving by a person, at a time when he is a Canadian citizen or a resident of Canada, of information before, or for the purposes of, a foreign tribunal in relation to, or in relation to the contents or identification of, records that, at any time while the order is in force, are or were in Canada or under the control of a Canadian citizen or a person resident in Canada.

(2) Where production before or disclosure or identification to, or for the purposes of a foreign tribunal of a record and the giving by a person of information before, or for the purposes of, a foreign tribunal in relation to, or in relation to the contents or identification of, a record is prohibited or restricted by an order under subsection (1), a tribunal in Canada shall not, for the purposes of proceedings before the foregin tribunal,

(a) where the order is in the nature of a prohibition, receive the record or information; or

(b) where the order is in the nature of a restriction, receive the record or information if, as a result of so doing, the order may be contravened.

(3) An order under this section may

(a) be directed to a particular person or to a class of persons;

(b) relate to a particular foreign tribunal or to a class of foreign tribunals; and

(c) relate to a particular record or to a class of records.

Seizure of Records

4. Where, on an application by or on behalf of the Attorney General of Canada, a superior court is satisfied that an order under section 3 may not be complied with in relation to some or all of the records in Canada to which it relates, the court may issue a warrant authorizing a person named therein or a peace officer to seize those records and to deliver them to the court or a person designated by the court for safekeeping while the order under section 3 remains in force, on such terms as to access to the records or return of all or any of the records, as are fixed by the court having regard to the object to which the order under section 3 is directed.

Measures of a Foreign State or Foreign Tribunal

5.(1) Where, in the opinion of the Attorney General of Canada, a foreign state or a foreign tribunal has taken or is proposing or is likely to take measures affecting international trade or commerce of a kind or in a manner that has adversely affected or is likely to adversely affect significant Canadian interests in relation to international trade or commerce involving business carried on in whole or in part in Canada, or that otherwise has infringed or is likely to infringe Canadian sovereignty, the Attorney General of Canada may, with the concurrence of the Secretary of State for External Affairs, by order

(a) require any person in Canada to give notice to him of any such measures, or of any directives, instructions, intimations of policy or other communications relating to such measures from a person who is in a position to direct or influence the policies of the person in Canada; or

(b) prohibit any person in Canada from complying with such measures, or with any directives, instructions, intimations of policy or other communications relating to such measures from a person who is in a position to direct or influence the policies of the person in Canada.

(2) For the purpose of subsection (1), measures taken or to be taken by a foreign state or foreign tribunal include laws, judgments and rulings made or to be made by the foreign state or foreign tribunal and directives, instructions, intimations of policy and other communications issued by or to be issued by the foreign state or foreign tribunal.

Orders of the Attorney General

8.(1) Where a foreign tribunal has, whether before or after the coming into force of this Act, given a judgment in proceedings instituted under an anti-trust law and, in the opinion of the Attorney General of Canada the recognition or enforcement of the judgment in Canada has adversely affected or is likely to adversely affect significant Canadian interests in relation to international trade or commerce involving a business carried on in whole or in part in Canada or otherwise has infringed or is likely to infringe Canadian sovereignty, he may

(a) in the case of any judgment, by order declare that the judgment shall not be recognized or enforceable in any manner in Canada; or

(b) in the case of a judgment for a specified amount of money, by order declare that, for the purposes of the recognition and enforcement of the judgment in Canada, the amount of the judgment shall be deemed to be reduced to such amount as is specified in the order.

(2) Every order made by the Attorney General of Canada under subsection (1) shall be published in the Canada Gazette and each such order comes into force on the later of the day it is so published and a day specified in the order as the day on which it is to come into force.

(3) While an order made by the Attorney General of Canada under subsection (1) is in force,

(a) in the case of an order under paragraph (1)(a), the judgment to which it relates shall not be recognized and is not enforceable in Canada; and

(b) in the case of an order under paragraph (1)(b), the judgment to which it relates may, if enforceable apart from this Act, be recognized and enforced in Canada as if the amount specified in the order were substituted for the amount of the judgment, and not otherwise.

(4) In any proceedings in Canada to recognize or enforce a judgment given by a foreign tribunal in proceedings instituted under an anti-trust law, or to enforce a concurrent or subsequent judgment for contribution or indemnity related to such a judgment, no inference shall be drawn from the fact that the Attorney General of Canada has not made an order under Subsection (1) in respect of the judgment.

Recovery of Damages

9.(1) Where a judgment in respect of which an order has been made under section 8 has been given against a party who is a Canadian citizen or a resident of Canada, a corporation incorporated by or under a law of Canada or a province or a person carrying on business in Canada, that party may, in Canada, sue for and recover from a person in whose favour the judgment is given

(a) in the case of an order under paragraph (8)(1)(a), any amount obtained from that party by that person under the judgment; and

(b) in the case of an order under paragraph (8)(1)(b), any amount obtained from that party by that person under the judgment that is in excess of the amount to which the judgment is deemed to be reduced.

(2) A court that renders judgment in favour of a party pursuant to subsection (1) may, in addition to any other means of enforcing judgment available to the court, order the seizure and sale of shares of any corporation incorporated by or under a law of Canada or a province in which the person against whom the judgment is rendered has a direct or indirect beneficial interest, whether the share certificates are located inside or outside Canada.

NOTES

1) In the *Gulf Oil* case, was the Supreme Court's response to the letters rogatory the one that Judge Marshall should have expected? Did it show "moderation of the exercise of ... conflicting enforcement jurisdiction"? Indeed, did Judge Marshall show any? In what forum did he hope such moderation would be "meaningfully considered"?

2) Both courts referred to international comity. What scope is there for the operation of this worthwhile principle in this kind of case?

3) Would a process of judicial balancing of conflicting national interests be a better approach to these kinds of jurisdictional disputes? What would such a process do to national state sovereignty and equality?

4) Before issuing the letters rogatory, the U.S. court made a serious effort to review the contending interests, but the Supreme Court, as the case report shows, deferred its own judgment to the viewpoint of the Canadian government. Why is this an appropriate stance for a court of law? What is the proper role of the Supreme Court in cases touching on foreign policy?

5) The *Foreign Extraterritorial Measures Act*[105] was passed in reaction to the greatly increased extraterritorial assertions of jurisdiction. These assertions have not been limited to orders for the discovery of documents but have included other procedural demands, such as subpoenas to foreign witnesses and the enforcement of punitive damage awards abroad. The response of the Act is correspondingly wide ranging and severe. The legislation contains three elements: a gag component, empowering the Attorney-General to prohibit the removal of records from Canada, or the compliance with orders within Canada, to satisfy a foreign court process (sections 3, 4 & 5); a blocking element, enabling the Attorney-General to prohibit the enforcement within Canada of a foreign antitrust judgment (section 8); and a claw-back provision, whereby "excessive" damages obtained in a foreign jurisdiction, (such as the possibility of triple damages in an American antitrust case), may be sued for and recovered in Canada (section 9). Section 7 backs up these tough provisions by making it an indictable offence to contravene a gag order under section 3 or 5. Is there any problem with the constitutional validity of sections 8 and 9 of this Act? Does the claw-back provision represent a proportional response to foreign judgments or is it a form of extraterritorial jurisdiction in itself?

6) Measure may only be taken under the Act when the foreign state order adversely affects significant Canadian interests in international trade or infringes Canadian sovereignty. These two criteria are quite different grounds for action. The infringement of sovereignty is a public matter touching high state policy and foreign relations, such as can be seen in the *Gulf Oil* case. The test of adverse effects on Canadian trade also covers government policy, in this case towards the economy, but it would additionally seem to permit action where an individual trader or corporation is likely to be injured. The powers given to the Attorney-General certainly allow him to make general, or specific and personal, gag and blocking orders.

---

[105] See W. Graham, "The Foreign Extraterritorial Measures Act" (1986), 11 *Can. Bus. L.J.* 410.

7) The *Combines Investigation Act*[106] also contains provisions to counter extra-territorial assertions of jurisdiction. Section 31.5 gives to the Restrictive Trade Practices Commission power to prohibit the implementation in Canada of foreign laws, policy decisions, judgments, decrees, orders or other process which would adversely affect competition in Canada, Canadian foreign trade, or a Canadian Trade or industry.[107]

8) Some seventeen states have adopted legislation similar to the *Foreign Extra-territorial Measures Act*. The *Protection of Trading Interests Act* of the United Kingdom[108] clearly served as a model for the Canadian statute. Australia has enacted legislation to restrict the enforcement of foreign judgments,[109] and France has passed a law to the same effect as well as to control the removal of records and information.[110]

International Accords

The conflicts over jurisdiction have persuaded states to reach out for international accords. If the riddle of extraterritorial jurisdiction cannot be resolved, then perhaps the conflicts can be prevented by intergovernmental cooperation.

OECD Recommendation on Notification, Exchange of Information and Coordination of Action
(1979) c (70) 154

1(a) when a Member country undertakes under its restrictive business practices laws an investigation or proceeding involving important interests of another Member country or countries, it should notify such Member country or countries in a manner and at a time deemed appropriate, if possible in advance and in any event at a time that would facilitate comments or consultations; such advance notification would enable the pro-ceeding Member country, while retaining full freedom of ultimate decision, to take account of such views as the other Member country may find it feasible to take under its own laws to deal with the restrictive business practices;

   (b)   where two or more Member countries proceed against a restrictive business practice in international trade, they should endeavour to coordinate their action insofar as appropriate and practicable;

2 through consultations or otherwise, the Member countries should cooperate in developing or applying mutually satisfactory and beneficial measures for dealing with restrictive business practices as their legitimate interests permit them to disclose; and should allow,

---

[106] R.S.C. 1970, c. C-23, as amended.
[107] See R. Roberts, *Anti-Combines and Antitrust* (1980), at 328 fwd.
[108] Stats. U.K. 1980, c. 11; see A.V. Lowe, "Blocking Extraterritorial Jurisdiction: The British Protection of Trading Interests Act, 1980" (1981), 75 *Am. J. Int. L.* 257.
[109] See the *Foreign Antitrust Judgments (Restriction of Enforcement) Act 1979*, reprinted in (1979), 18 *Int. Leg. Mat.* 869.
[110] See the *Law Relating to the Communication of Economic, Commercial, Industrial, Financial or Technical Documents or Information to Foreign National or Legal Persons*, Law No. 80-538 [1980] J.O. 1799; B. Herzog, "The 1980 French Law on Documents and Information" (1981), 75 *Am. J. Int. L.* 382.

subject to appropriate safeguards, including those relating to confidentiality, the disclosure of information to the competent authorities of Member, countries by the other parties concerned, whether accomplished unilaterally or in the context of bilateral or multilateral understandings, unless such cooperation or disclosure would be contrary to significant national interests.

Canada-United States
Memorandum of Understanding on Anti-trust Laws[111]
(1984), 23 *Int. Leg. Mat.* 275

2. *Notification in General*
   (1) The Parties will notify each other whenever they become aware that their anti-trust investigations or proceedings, or actions relating to anti-trust investigations or proceedings of the other Party, involve national interests of the other or require the seeking of information located in the territory of the other. ...
4. *Consultation*
   Either Party may request consultations when it believes that an anti-trust investigation, proceeding (including for the purposes of this paragraph a private suit pursuant to the anti-trust laws of either Party), business review, advisory opinion or compliance procedure, or action relating to an anti-trust investigation or proceeding, is likely to affect its significant national interests or require the seeking of information from its territory. Such requests will be made and honoured promptly.
6. *Consideration of the Other Party's Significant Interest*
   Each Party will give careful consideration to the significant national interests of the other at all stages of an anti-trust investigation, inquiry or prosecution. The significant national interests of a Party may be general or specific in nature depending on the activity in question and may vary in significance according to the importance of the goals of the relevant government policies and the extent to which achievement of those goals may be impaired by acceding to the expressed interests of the other Party. While a significant national interest may exist even in the absence of any governmental connection with the activity in question, it is recognized that such interests would normally be reflected in antecedent laws, decisions or statements of policy by the competent authorities.
7. *Elimination or Minimization of Conflicts*
   (1) Each Party will normally refrain from initiating or continuing particular elements of any investigative or enforcement procedures, to the extent they affect a national interest or require the seeking of information from the territory of the other Party, until either (i) a reasonable period has elapsed after notification without receipt of a response requesting consultations, or (ii) it has in good faith provided the other Party with an opportunity for requested consultations and has given serious consideration to any information and views provided in the course of the consultations. Where, because of an exceptional circum-

---

[111] See B. Campbell, "The Canada-United States Antitrust Notification and Consultative Procedure, A Study in Bilateral Conflict Resolution" (1978), 56 *Can. Bar Rev.* 459.

stance, immediate action must be taken, an opportunity for consultation will be provided as soon as feasible thereafter.

(2) The Party which believes its significant national interests are likely to be affected by the proposed actions of the other Party will, consistent with paragraph 10 below and its national laws and interests, explain in sufficient detail its significant national interests and its role, if any, in the activity in question to enable the other Party to give serious consideration to them.

(3) The good faith consideration that is to be accorded to the national interest of the other Party during consultations may lead to the avoidance or minimization of a conflict of national interests. If each Party asserts that its own national interest is predominant and it is unable to defer to the expressed national interest of the other, they will nonetheless seek to reduce, by accommodation and compromise, the scope and intensity of the conflict and its effects.

Canada-United States
Treaty on Mutual Legal Assistance in Criminal Matters
(1985), 24 *Int. Leg. Mat.* 1092

Article II
SCOPE OF APPLICATION

1. The Parties shall provide, in accordance with the provisions of this Treaty, mutual legal assistance in all matters relating to the investigation, prosecution and suppression of offences.

2. Assistance shall include:
(a) examining objects and sites;
(b) exchanging information and objects;
(c) locating or identifying persons;
(d) serving documents;
(e) taking the evidence of persons;
(f) providing documents and records;
(g) transferring persons in custody;
(h) executing requests for searches and seizures.

3. Assistance shall be provided without regard to whether the conduct under investigation or prosecution in the Requesting State constitutes an offence or may be prosecuted by the Requested State.

4. This Treaty is intended solely for mutual legal assistance between the Parties. The provisions of this Treaty shall not give rise to a right on the part of a private party to obtain, suppress or exclude any evidence or to impede the execution of a request.

Article III
OTHER ASSISTANCE

1. The Parties, including their competent authorities, may provide assistance pursuant to other agreements, arrangements or practices.

2. The Central Authorities may agree, in exceptional circumstances, to provide assistance pursuant to this Treaty in respect of illegal acts that do not.constitute an offence within the definition of offence in Article I.

Article IV
OBLIGATION TO REGQUET ASSISTANCE

1. A Party seeking to obtain documents, records or other articles known to be located in the territory of the other Party shall request assistance pursuant to the provisions of this Treaty, except as otherwise agreed pursuant to Article III(1).

2. Where denial of a request or delay in its execution may jeopardize successful completion of an investigation or prosecution, the Parties shall promptly consult, at the instance of either Party, to consider alternative means of assistance.

3. Unless the Parties otherwise agree, the consultations shall be considered terminated 30 days after they have been requested, and the Parties' obligations under this Article shall then be deemed to have been fulfilled.

Article V
LIMITATIONS ON COMPLIANCE

1. The Requested State may deny assistance to the extent that
   (a) the request is not made in conformity with the provisions of this Treaty; or
   (b) execution of the request is contrary to its public interest, as determined by its Central Authority.

2. The Requested State may postpone assistance if execution of the request would interfere with an ongoing investigation or prosecution in the Requested State.

3. Before denying or postponing assistance pursuant to this Article, the Requested State, through its Central Authority,
   (a) shall promptly inform the Requesting State of the reason for considering denial or postponement; and
   (b) shall consult with the Requesting State to determine whether assistance may be given subject to such terms and conditions as the Requested State deems necessary.

4. If the Requesting State accepts assistance subject to the terms and conditions referred to in paragraph 3(b), it shall comply with said terms and conditions.

NOTES

1) These international instruments move away from the contest of jurisdictions.[112] What alternative avenues of dispute avoidance do they offer? Are they likely to succeed? For instance, would they have been of assistance in the uranium cartel litigation?

---

[112] For their implementation, see Bill C-58 (1987), *Mutual Legal Assistance in Criminal Matters Act*. See also the UNCTAD Set of Multilaterally Agreed Equitable Principles and Rules for the Control of Restrictive Business Practices, U.N.G.A. Res. 63 (XXV), 35 U.N. GAOR, Supp. (No. 48) 123; (1980), 19 *Int. Leg. Mat.* 813.

2) Other U.S. bilateral agreements specifically directed towards antitrust actions contain more formal provisions than those in the Canada-U.S. Memorandum of Understanding. The United States-Federal Republic of Germany agreement of 1976[113] concentrates on cooperation and assistance between national antitrust authorities and provides for the exchange of information in activities having a substantial effect in the domestic or international trade of either party. The U.S.-Australia agreement of 1982[114] emphasizes the avoidance of conflicts rather than mutual assistance as its origins are found in the strained relations between the two states produced by antitrust actions (both civil and criminal) in the United States involving Australian defendants.

---

[113] (1976), 15 *Int. Leg. Mat.* 1982.

[114] (1982), 21 *Int. Leg. Mat.* 702; See S.D. Ramsey, "The United States-Australian Antitrust Cooperation Agreement: A Step in the Right Direction" (1983), 24 *Va. J. Int. L.* 127.

CHAPTER NINE

State Responsibility

This chapter deals with the responsibility of a state for its internationally wrongful acts or omissions. For instance, a state may be held responsible for a breach of treaty, for the injury it causes to the territory or property of another state or to its diplomatic representatives or to the person or property of aliens within its territory. The international responsibility of a state imposes an obligation to make reparation.

Historically, the general theory of state responsibility originated from the principle that a state is responsible under international law for injury caused to an alien by conduct attributable to the state. Today, however, state responsibility is no longer limited to responsibility for injury to the person or property of aliens. It arises from the breach by a state of any international obligation. Thus, state responsibility is closely connected with the rights and duties of states, the permanent sovereignty of states over their natural resources and the principles of international law applicable to friendly relations and co-operation among states.[1]

---

[1] In general, see C.F. Amerasinghe, *State Responsibility for Injuries to Aliens* (1967); F.G. Dawson and I.L.Head, *International Law, National Tribunals and the Rights of Aliens* (1971); F.V. Garcia-Amador, "State Responsibility – Some New Problems" (1958), 94 *Hague Recueil* 369; R.B. Lillich, *International Claims: Their Adjudication by International Commissions* (1962); R.B. Lillich and G.A. Christenson, *International Claims: Their Preparation and Presentation* (1962); R.B. Lillich, ed., *International Law of State Responsibility for Injuries to Aliens* (1983); C.H.P. Law, *The Local Remedies Rule in International Law* (1961); M.M. Whiteman, *Damages in International Law* (3 vols., 1937 and 1943).

GENERAL THEORY OF RESPONSIBILITY

General Principles

International Law Commission, Draft Articles on State Responsibility
[1979] Y.B.I.L.C. II, 91; (1979), 18 *Int. Leg. Mat.* 1568.

Article 1
RESPONSIBILITY OF A STATE FOR ITS INTERNATIONALLY WRONGFUL ACTS

Every internationally wrongful act of a State entails the international responsibility of that State.

Article 2
POSSIBILITY THAT EVERY STATE MAY BE HELD TO HAVE COMMITTED AN
INTERNATIONALLY WRONGFUL ACT

Every State is subject to the possibility of being held to have committed an internationally wrongful act entailing its international responsibility.

Article 3
ELEMENTS OF AN INTERNATIONALLY WRONGFUL ACT OF A STATE

There is an internationally wrongful act of a State when:
  (a) conduct consisting of an action or omission is attributable to the State under international law; and
  (b) that conduct constitutes a breach of an international obligation of the State.

Article 4
CHARACTERIZATION OF AN ACT OF A STATE AS INTERNATIONALLY WRONGFUL

An act of a State may only be characterized as internationally wrongful by international law. Such characterization cannot be affected by the characterization of the same act as lawful by internal law.

Article 19
INTERNATIONAL CRIMES AND INTERNATIONAL DELICTS

1. An act of a State which constitutes a breach of an international obligation is an internationally wrongful act, regardless of the subject-matter of the obligation breached.

2. An internationally wrongful act which results from the breach by a State of an international obligation so essential for the protection of fundamental interests of the international community that its breach is recognized as a crime by that community as a whole, constitutes an international crime.

3. Subject to paragraph 2, and on the basis of the rules of international law in force, an international crime may result, *inter alia*, from:

    (a) a serious breach of an international obligation of essential importance for maintenance of international peace and security, such as that prohibiting aggression;

    (b) a serious breach of an international obligation of essential importance for safeguarding the right of self-determination of peoples, such as that prohibiting the establishment or maintenance by force of colonial domination;

    (c) a serious breach on a widespread scale of an international obligation of essential importance for safeguarding the human being, such as those prohibiting slavery, genocide, *apartheid*;

    (d) a serious breach of an international obligation of essential importance for the safeguarding and preservation of the human environment, such as those prohibiting massive pollution of the atmosphere or of the seas.

4. Any internationally wrongful act which is not an international crime in accordance with paragraph 2, constitutes an international delict.

NOTES

On the question whether a state may be criminally liable, the International Law Commission had this to say:[2]

It seems undeniable that today's unanimous and prompt condemnation of any direct attack on international peace and security is paralleled by almost universal disapproval on the part of States towards certain other activities. Contemporary international law has reached the point of condemning outright the practice of certain States in forcibly keeping other peoples under colonial domination or forcibly imposing internal régimes based on discrimination and the most absolute racial segregation, in imperilling human life and dignity in other ways, or in so acting as gravely to endanger the preservation and conservation of the human environment. The international community as a whole, and not merely one or other of its members, now considers that such acts violate principles formally embodied in the Charter and, even outside the scope of the Charter, principles which are now so deeply rooted in the conscience of mankind that they have become particularly essential rules of general international law. There are enough manifestations of the views of States to warrant the conclusion that in the general opinion, some of these acts genuinely constitute "international crimes," that is to say, international wrongs which are more serious than others and which as such, should entail more severe legal consequences ... in adopting the designation, "international crime," the Commission intends only to refer to "crimes" of the State, to acts attributable to the State as such. Once again it wishes to sound a warning against any confusion between the expression "international crime" as used in this article and similar expressions, such as "crime under international law," "war crime," "crime against peace," "crime against humanity," etc., which are used in a number of conventions and international instruments to designate certain heinous individual crimes, for which those instruments require

---

[2] [1976] Y.B.I.L.C. II, at 109, 119.

States to punish the guilty persons adequately, in accordance with the rules of their internal law. Once again, the Commission takes this opportunity of stressing that the attribution to the State of an internationally wrongful act characterized as an "international crime" is quite different from the incrimination of certain individuals-organs for actions connected with the commission of an "international crime" of the State, and that the obligation to punish such individual actions does not constitute the form of international responsibility specially applicable to a State committing an "international crime" or, in any case, the sole form of this responsibility.

Illustrations

This section contains examples of different types of incidents creating direct or indirect state responsibility. Direct responsibility is incurred by a state whenever it commits any unlawful act immediately towards another state. Examples are the invasion of foreign territory, the seizure or destruction of foreign ships or aircraft, and the breach of a treaty. Responsibility also arises when either the harm suffered by the claimant state is indirect or the liability of the respondent state is indirect. An example of the former is the failure of the respondent state to remedy an injury it has caused to a national of the claimant state. An instance of the latter is the neglect of the respondent state to take adequate measures for the prevention of harm to the claimant state by private individuals. In reading the following illustrative cases, consider how each might be classified.

Seizure or Destruction of Private Property

The Jessie, Thomas F. Bayard, and Pescawha
American and British Claims Arbitration (1926),
Neilsen's Report 479; 6 R.I.A.A. 57

THE TRIBUNAL (Fromageot, Fitzpatrick, Anderson): It is admitted that the *Jessie*, the *Thomas F. Bayard*, and the *Pescawha*, all of them British schooners, cleared at Port Victoria, B.C., for sealing and sea otter hunting and were in June, 1909, actually engaged in hunting sea otters in the North Pacific Ocean; that on June 23, 1909, while on the high seas near the north end of Cherikof Islands, they were boarded by an officer from the United States Revenue Cutter Bear who, having searched them for seal skins and found none, had the firearms found on board placed under seal, entered his search in the ship's log, and ordered that the seals should not be broken while the vessels remained north of 35° north latitude, and east of 180° west longitude.

The United States Government admits in its Answer to the British Memorial that there was no agreement in force during the year 1909 specifically authorizing American officers to seal up the arms and ammunition on board British sealing vessels, and that the action of the Commander of the Bear in causing the arms of the Jessie, the Thomas F. Bayard, and the Pescawha to be sealed was unauthorized by the Government of the United States.

The United States Government, however, denies any liability in these cases, first, because the boarding officer acted in the *bona fide* belief that he had authority so to act, and second, because there is no evidence on the claims except the declaration of the interested parties, and because these claims are patently of an exaggerated and fraudulent nature.

I. *As to the liability*: It is a fundamental principle of international maritime law that, except by special convention or in time of war, interference by a cruiser with a foreign vessel pursuing a lawful avocation on the high seas is unwarranted and illegal, and constitutes a violation of the sovereignty of the country whose flag the vessel flies.

It is not contested that at the date and place of interference by the United States naval authorities there was no agreement authorizing those authorities to interfere as they did with the British schooners, and, therefore, a legal liability on the United States Government was created by the acts of its officers now complained of.

It is unquestionable that the United States naval authorities acted *bona fide*, but though their *bona fides* might be invoked by the officers in explanation of their conduct to their own Government, its effect is merely to show that their conduct constituted an error in judgment, and any government is responsible to other governments for errors in judgment of its officials purporting to act within the scope of their duties and vested with power to enforce their demands.

The alleged insufficiency of proof as to the damage and the alleged exaggeration and fraudulent character of the claims, do not affect the question of the liability itself. They refer only to its consequences, that is to say, the determination of damages and indemnity. ...

NOTES

1) This case is often cited in support of the view that the presence of intention or negligence on the part of the actor is not a condition precedent of state responsibility which arises from the commission of the prohibited act alone. Actually it is not definitely settled whether state responsibility is objective or subjective.[3]

2) In the *I'm Alone*[4] case the Commissioners to whom the dispute was submitted were of the opinion that the sinking by the United States Revenue of a vessel of Canadian registry engaged in rum-running in the United States, was an unlawful act as it was not justified by any provision of the 1924 Convention which governed the case.

3) Note that a state is under a general obligation to prevent the use of its territory by persons or groups planning to commit hostile acts against a foreign state.[5] The responsibility of the state in such a case is measured by the degree of the "due diligence" which it shows in carrying out its general obligation in the particular circumstances. Thus a state must show due diligence in preventing the organization within its jurisdiction of military expeditions intended to effect an attack upon the territory of a friendly state.

---

[3] See, for instance, *Home Missionary Society Claim* (U.S. v. Great Britain) (1920), 6 R.I.A.A. 42; *Caire Claim* (France v. Mexico) (1929), 5 R.I.A.A. 516; *Corfu Channel Case (Merits)* (U.K. v. Albania), [1949] I.C.J. Rep. 4, reported in Chapter 11; and *Cosmos 954 Claim*, reported later in this Section.
[4] Canada v. U.S. (1935), 3 R.I.A.A. 1609; (1935), 29 *Am. J. Int. L.* 326, reported in Chapter 11.
[5] See the "Declaration on Principles of International Law" and the notes thereto, in Chapter 2.

Transboundary Intrusions

A state is responsible for acts or omissions taking place within its territory that have the effect of polluting the territory of another state including its territorial waters and its air.

Trail Smelter Arbitration
United States v. Canada
(1931-1941), 3 R.I.A.A. 1905

[In 1896, a smelter was started near the locality of Trail, B.C. In 1906, the Consolidated Mining and Smelting Company of Canada, Limited, acquired and operated the smelter. From 1925, at least, to 1937, damage occurred in the state of Washington resulting from the sulphur dioxide emitted from the smelter.

The first attempt to resolve the problems growing out of the operation of the smelter by means of an investigation by the International Joint Commission proved unacceptable so in 1935 Canada and the United States negotiated a specific agreement for arbitration.]

Convention for Settlement of Difficulties Arising
from Operation of Smelter at Trail, B.C.

The President of the United States of America, and His Majesty the King of Great Britain, Ireland and the British dominions beyond the Seas, Emperor of India, in respect of the Dominion of Canada,

Considering that the Government of the United States has complained to the Government of Canada that fumes discharged from the smelter of the Consolidated Mining and Smelting Company at Trail, British Columbia, have been causing damage in the State of Washington, and

Considering further that the International Joint Commission, established pursuant to the Boundary Waters Treaty of 1909, investigated problems arising from the operation of the smelter at Trail and rendered a report and recommendations thereon, dated February 28, 1931, and

Recognizing the desirability and necessity of effecting a permanent settlement, ... have agreed upon the following Articles:

Article 1

The Government of Canada will cause to be paid to the Secretary of State of the United States, to be deposited in the United States Treasury, within three months after ratification of this Convention have been exchanged, the sum of three hundred and fifty thousand dollars, United States currency, in payment of all damage which occurred in the United States, prior to the first day of January, 1932, as a result of the operation of the Trail Smelter.

Article II

The Governments of the United States and of Canada, hereinafter referred to as "the Governments," mutually agree to constitute a tribunal hereinafter referred to as "the Tribunal," for the purpose of deciding the questions referred to it under the provisions of Article III. The Tribunal shall consist of a chairman and two national members.

The Chairman shall be a jurist of repute who is neither a British subject nor a citizen of the United States. He shall be chosen by the Governments, or, in the event of failure to reach agreement within nine months after the exchange of ratifications of this convention, by the President of the Permanent Administrative Council of the Permanent Court of Arbitration at The Hague described in Article 49 of the Convention for the Pacific Settlement of International Disputes concluded at The Hague on October 18, 1907.

The two national members shall be jurists of repute, who have not been associated directly or indirectly, in the present controversy. One member shall be chosen by each of the Governments.

The Governments may each designate a scientist to assist the Tribunal.

Article III

The Tribunal shall finally decide the questions, hereinafter referred to as "the Questions," set forth hereunder, namely:

1) Whether damage caused by the Trail Smelter in the State of Washington has occurred since the first day of January, 1932, and, if so, what indemnity should be paid therefor?

2) In the event of the answer to the first part of the preceding Question being in the affirmative, whether the Trail Smelter should be required to refrain from causing damage in the State of Washington in the future and, if so, to what extent?

3) In the light of the answer to the preceding Question, what measures or régime, if any, should be adopted or maintained by the Trail Smelter?

4) What indemnity or compensation, if any, should be paid on account of any decision or decisions rendered by the Tribunal pursuant to the next two preceding Questions?

Article IV

The Tribunal shall apply the law and practice followed in dealing with cognate questions in the United States of America as well as international law and practice, and shall give consideration to the desire of the high contracting parties to reach a solution just to all parties concerned.

Article X

The Tribunal, in determining the first question and in deciding upon the indemnity, if any, which should be paid in respect to the years 1932 and 1933, shall give due regard to the results of investigations and inquiries made in subsequent years.

Investigators, whether appointed by or on behalf of the Governments, either jointly or severally, or the Tribunal, shall be permitted at all reasonable times to enter and view and carry on investigations upon any of the properties upon which damage is claimed to have occurred or to be occurring, and their reports may, either jointly or severally, be submitted to and received by the Tribunal for the purpose of enabling the Tribunal to decide upon any of the Questions.

Article XI

The Tribunal shall report to the Governments its final decisions, together with the reasons on which they are based, as soon as it has reached its conclusions in respect to the Questions, and within a period of three months after the conclusion of proceedings. Proceedings shall be deemed to have been concluded when the Agents of the two Governments jointly inform the Tribunal that they have nothing additional to present. Such period may be extended by agreement of the two Governments.

Upon receiving such report, the Governments may make arrangements for the disposition of claims for indemnity for damage, if any, which may occur subsequently to the period of time covered by such report.

Interim Decision

[On April 16, 1938, the Tribunal reported its "final decision" on Question No. 1, as well as its temporary decisions on Questions No. 2 and No. 3, and provided for a temporary régime thereunder. Concerning Question No. 1, in the statement presented by the Agent for the Government of the United States, claims for damages of $1,849,156.16 with interest of $250,855.01 – total $2,100,011.17 – were presented, divided into seven categories, in respect of (a) cleared land and improvements, (b) of uncleared land and improvements; (c) live stock; (d) property in the town of Northport; (e) wrong done the United States in violation of sovereignty, measured by cost of investigation from January 1, 1932, to June 30, 1936; (f) interest on $350,000 accepted in satisfaction of damage to January 1, 1932, but not paid on that date; (g) business enterprises. The area claimed to be damaged contained "more than 140,000 acres," including the town of Northport. The Tribunal disallowed the claims of the United States with reference to items (c),(d),(e),(f) and (g) but allowed them, in part, with respect to the remaining items (a) and (b). It gave the following reasons:]

THE TRIBUNAL: ... (7) The United States in its Statement presents two further items of damages claimed by it, as follows: (Item e) which the United States terms "damages in respect of the wrong done the United States in violation of sovereignty"; and (Item f) which the United States terms, "damages in respect of interest on $350,000 eventually accepted in satisfaction of damage to January 1, 1932, but not paid until November 2, 1935."

With respect to (Item e), the Tribunal finds it unnecessary to decide whether the facts proven did or did not constitute an infringement or violation of sovereignty of the United States under international law independently of the Convention, for the following reason:

By the Convention, the high contracting parties have submitted to this Tribunal the questions of the existence of damage caused by the Trail Smelter in the State of Washington, and of the indemnity to be paid therefor, and the Dominion of Canada has assumed under Article XII, such undertakings as will ensure due compliance with the decision of this Tribunal. The Tribunal finds that the only question to be decided on this point is the interpretation of the Convention itself. The United States in its Statement itemizes under the claim of damage for "violation of sovereignty" only money expended "for the investigation undertaken by the United States Government of the problems created in the United States by the operation of the Smelter at Trail." The Tribunal is of opinion that it was not within the intention of the parties, as expressed in the words "damage caused by the Trail Smelter" in Article III of the Convention, to include such moneys expended. This interpretation is confirmed by a consideration of the proceedings and of the diplomatic correspondence leading up to the making of the Convention. Since the United States has not specified any other damage based on an alleged violation of its sovereignty, the Tribunal does not feel that it is incumbent upon it to decide, whether, in law and in fact, indemnity for such damage could have been awarded if specifically alleged. Certainly, the present controversy does not involve any such type of facts as the persons appointed under the Convention of January 23, 1934, between the United States of America and the Dominion of Canada felt to justify them in awarding to Canada damages for violation of sovereignty in the *I'm Alone* award of January 5, 1935. And in other cases of international arbitration cited by the United States, damages awarded for expenses were awarded, not as compensation for violation of national sovereignty, but as compensation for expenses incurred by individual claimants in prosecuting their claims for wrongful acts by the offending Government.

In his oral argument, the Agent for the United States, Mr. Sherley, claimed repayment of the aforesaid expenses of investigations on a further and separate ground, *viz.*, as an incident to damages, saying: "Costs and interest are incident to the damage, the proof of the damage which occurs through a given act complained of," and again: "The point is this, that it goes as an incident to the award of damage." The Tribunal is unable to accept this view. While in cases involving merely the question of damage to individual claimants, it may be appropriate for an international tribunal to award costs and expenses as an incident to other damages proven, the Tribunal is of opinion that such costs and expenses should not be allowed in a case of arbitration and final settlement of a long pending controversy between two independent Governments, such as this case, where each Government has incurred expenses and where it is to the mutual advantage of the two Governments that a just conclusion and permanent disposition of an international controversy should be reached.

[In conclusion, the Tribunal answered Question No. 1 as follows:]

Damage caused by the Trail Smelter in the State of Washington has occurred since the first day of January, 1932, and up to October 1, 1937, and the indemnity to be paid therefor is seventy-eight thousand dollars ($78,000), and is to be complete and final indemnity and compensation for all damage which occurred between such dates. Interest at the rate of six per centum per year will be allowed on the above sum of seventy-eight thousand dollars ($78,000) from the date of the filing of this report and decision until date of payment. This decision is not subject to alteration or modification by the Tribunal hereafter. The fact of existence of damage, if any, occurring after October 1, 1937, and the indemnity to be paid therefor, if any, the Tribunal will determine in its final decision.

[Answering Questions No. 2 and No. 3, the Tribunal decided that, until a final decision should be made, the Trail Smelter should be subject to a temporary régime and a trial period was established to a date not later than October 1, 1940, in order to enable the Tribunal to establish a permanent régime based on a "more adequate and intensive study," since the Tribunal felt that the information that had been placed before it did not enable it to determine at that time with sufficient certainty upon a permanent régime.]

Final Decision

[Reported by the Tribunal on March 11, 1941.]

THE TRIBUNAL: ... As between the two countries involved, each has an equal interest that if a nuisance is proved, the indemnity to damaged parties for proven damage shall be just and adequate and each has also an equal interest that unproven or unwarranted claims shall not be allowed. For, while the United States' interests may now be claimed to be injured by the operations of a Canadian corporation, it is equally possible that at some time in the future Canadian interests might be claimed to be injured by an American corporation. As has well been said: "It would not be to the advantage of the two countries concerned that industrial effort should be prevented by exaggerating the interests of the agricultural community. Equally, it would not be to the advantage of the two countries that the agricultural community should be oppressed to advance the interest of industry."

Considerations like the above are reflected in the provisions of the Convention in Article IV, that "the desire of the high contracting parties" is "to reach a solution just to all parties concerned." And the phraseology of the questions submitted to the Tribunal clearly evinces a desire and an intention that, to some extent, in making its answers to the questions, the Tribunal should endeavour to adjust the conflicting interests by some "just solution" which would allow the continuance of the operation of the Trail Smelter but under such restrictions and limitations as would, as far as foreseeable, prevent damage in the United States, and as would enable indemnity to be obtained, if in spite of such restrictions and limitations, damage should occur in the future in the United States. ...

The second question under Article III of the Convention is as follows:

In the event of the answer to the first part of the preceding question being in the affirmative, whether the Trail Smelter should be required to refrain from causing damage in the State of Washington in the future and, if so, to what extent?

Damage has occurred since January 1, 1932, as fully set forth in the previous decision. To that extent, the first part of the preceding question has thus been answered in the affirmative.

As has been said above, the report of the International Joint Commission ... contained a definition of the word "damage" excluding "occasional damage that may be caused by SO_2 fumes being carried across the international boundary in air pockets or by reason of unusual atmospheric conditions," as far, at least, as the duty of the Smelter to reduce the presence of that gas in the air was concerned.

The correspondence between the two Governments during the interval between that report and the conclusion of the Convention shows that the problem thus raised was what parties had primarily in mind in drafting Question No. 2. Whilst Canada wished for the adoption of the report, the United States stated that it could not acquiesce in the proposal to limit consideration of damage to damage as defined in the report (letter of the Minister of the United States of America at Ottawa to the Secretary of State for External Affairs of the Dominion of Canada, January 30, 1934). The view was expressed that "so long as fumigations occur in the State of Washington with such frequency, duration and intensity as to cause injury," the conditions afforded "grounds of complaint on the part of the United States, regardless of the remedial works ... and regardless of the effect of those works" (same letter).

The first problem which arises is whether the question should be answered on the basis of the law followed in the United States or on the basis of international law. The Tribunal, however, finds that this problem need not be solved here as the law followed in the United States in dealing with the quasi-sovereign rights of the States of the Union, in the matter of air pollution, whilst more definite, is in conformity with the general rules of international law.

Particularly in reaching its conclusions as regards this question as well as the next, the Tribunal has given consideration to the desire of the high contracting parties "to reach a solution just to all parties concerned."

As Professor Eagleton puts in (*Responsibility of States in International Law*, 1928, at 80): "A State owes at all times a duty to protect other States against injurious acts by individuals from within its jurisdiction." A great number of such general pronouncements by leading authorities concerning the duty of a State to respect other States and their territory have been presented to the Tribunal. These and many others have been carefully examined. International decisions, in various matters, from the *Alabama* case onward, and also earlier ones, are based on the same general principle, and, indeed, this principle, as such, has not been questioned by Canada. But the real difficulty often arises rather when it comes to determine what, *pro subjecta materie*, is deemed to constitute an injurious act.

A case concerning, as the present one does, territorial relations, decided by the Federal Court of Switzerland between the Cantons of Soleure and Argovia, may serve to illustrate the relativity of the rule. Soleure brought a suit against her sister State to enjoin use of a shooting establishment which endangered her territory. The court, in granting the injunction, said: "This right (sovereignty) excludes ... not only the usurpation and exercise of sovereign rights (of another State) ... but also an actual encroachment which might prejudice the natural use of the territory and the free movement of its inhabitants." As a result of the decision, Argovia made plans for the improvement of the existing installations. These, however, were considered as insufficient protection by Soleure. The Canton of Argovia then moved the Federal Court to decree that the shooting be again permitted after completion of the projected improvements. This motion was granted. "The demand of the Government of Soleure," said the Court, "that all endangerment be absolutely abolished apparently goes too far." The Court found that all risk whatever had not been eliminated, as the region was flat and absolutely safe shooting ranges were only found in the mountain valleys; that there was a federal duty for the communes to provide facilities for military target practice and that "no more precautions may be demanded for shooting ranges near the boundaries of two Cantons than are required for shooting ranges in the interior of a Canton." (R.O.26, I, at 450, 451; R.O.41, I, at 137; see D. Schindler, "The Administration of Justice in the Swiss Federal Court in Inter-cantonal Disputes" (1921), 15 *Am. J. Int. L.* 172–74.)

No case of air pollution dealt with by an international tribunal has been brought to the attention of the Tribunal nor does the Tribunal know of any such case. The nearest analogy is that of water pollution. But, here also, no decision of an international tribunal has been cited or has been found.

There are, however, as regards both air pollution and water pollution, certain decisions of the Supreme Court of the United States which may legitimately be taken as a guide in this field of international law, for it is reasonable to follow by analogy, in international cases, precedents established by that Court in dealing with controversies between States of the Union or with other controversies concerning the quasi-sovereign rights of such States, where no contrary rule prevails in international law and no reason for rejecting such precedents can be adduced from the limitations of sovereignty inherent in the Constitution of the United States. ...

Great progress in the control of fumes has been made by science in the last few years and this progress should be taken into account.

The Tribunal, therefore, finds that the above decisions, taken as a whole, constitute an adequate basis for its conclusions, namely, that, under the principles of international law, as well as of the law of the United States, no State has the right to use or permit the use of its territory in such a manner as to cause injury by fumes in or to the territory of another or the properties or persons therein, when the case is of serious consequence and the injury is established by clear and convincing evidence.

The decisions of the Supreme Court of the United States which are the basis of these conclusions are decisions in equity and a solution inspired by them, together with the régime hereinafter prescribed, will, in the opinion of the Tribunal, be "just to all parties concerned," as long, at least, as the present conditions in the Columbia River Valley continue to prevail.

Considering the circumstances of the case, the Tribunal holds that the Dominion of Canada is responsible in international law for the conduct of the Trail Smelter. Apart from the undertakings in the Convention, it is, therefore, the duty of the Government of the Dominion of Canada to see to it that this conduct should be in conformity with the obligation of the Dominion under international law as herein determined.

The Tribunal, therefore, answers Question No. 2 as follows: (2) So long as the present conditions in the Columbia River Valley prevail, the Trail Smelter shall be required to refrain from causing any damage through fumes in the State of Washington; the damage herein referred to and its extent being such as would be recoverable under the decisions of the courts of the United States in suits between private individuals. The indemnity for such damage should be fixed in such manner as the Governments, acting under Article XI of the Convention, should agree upon.

NOTES

1) Further to the case, a supplementary agreement to the Convention established a tribunal to decide questions of indemnity and the future regime arising from the operation of the smelter at Trail, British Columbia.[6]

2) Consider the language of the judgment of the International Court of Justice in the *Corfu Channel Case*, reported in Chapter 11, that every state has an "obligation not to allow knowingly its territory to be used for acts contrary to the rights of other States."[7] Is the difference of language of legal significance? Can these precepts be applied to the problem of acid rain?[8]

In the case of *Military Activities In and Against Nicaragua*[9] the Court made it clear that, in addition to the obvious violation of one state's sovereignty when another lays mines within its territorial waters, if a state lays mines in any waters in which foreign vessels have rights of access or passage and fails to provide any warning or notification, it is also in breach of international law.

3) The explosion of a Soviet nuclear reactor at Chernobyl in the spring of 1986 and the consequent pollution of several countries raised the question of Soviet international responsibility. Do the principles in the previous cases provide any assistance on this question? On September 26, 1986, this nuclear accident led to the signature by fifty states, including Canada, of the Convention on Early Notification of a Nuclear Accident and the Convention on Assistance in the Case of Nuclear Accident or Radiological Emergency.

Cosmos 954 Claim
Canada v. U.S.S.R.
(1979), 18 *Int. Leg. Mat* 899

[On September 18, 1977, the Soviet Union placed in orbit a satellite identified as Cosmos 954, and, as required, officially informed the Secretary General of the United Nations of this fact. The satellite carried on board a nuclear reactor working on uranium enriched with isotope of uranium 235. On January 24, 1978, the satellite entered the earth's atmosphere intruding into Canadian air space at about 11:53 a.m. G.M.T. to the north of the Queen Charlotte Islands on the west coast of Canada. On re-entry and disintegration, debris from the satellite were deposited on Canadian territory, including portions of the

---

[6] Exchange of Notes at Washington, 17 November 1949 and 24 January 1950; 3 U.S.T. 539; T.I.A.S. 2412; 151 U.N.T.S. 171. For comments on the case, see A.K. Kuhn, "The Trail Smelter Arbitration" (1941), 35 *Am. J. Int. L.* 665, and J.E. Read, "The Trail Smelter Dispute" (1963), 1 *Can. Y.B. Int. L.* 213. Compare the *Lake Lanoux Case* (Spain v. France) (1957), 12 R.I.A.A. 281, and the *Nuclear Tests Cases* (Australia and New Zealand v. France), [1974] I.C.J. Rep. 253 and 457.

[7] U.K. v. Albania, [1949] I.C.J. Rep. 4, at 22.

[8] Consult I.H. van Lier, *Acid Rain and International Law* (1981), and P. Ballantyne, "International Liability for Acid Rain" (1983), 41 *U.T. Fac. L. Rev.* 63.

[9] [1986] I.C.J. Rep. 14, at 111–12, 128–29.

Northwest Territories, Alberta and Saskatchewan. Immediately, the Canadian Armed Forces and the Atomic Energy Control Board of Canada undertook operations directed at locating, recovering, removing and testing the debris and cleaning up the affected areas. The operations took place in two phases: Phase I from January 24, 1978 to April 20, 1978 and Phase II from April 21, 1978 to October 15, 1978. The total cost incurred by the various Canadian Departments and agencies involved in Phases I and II of the operations was around fourteen million dollars, six million of which Canada claimed from the Soviet Union.

Canada's Statement of Claim was based jointly and separately on: (a) the relevant international agreements and in particular the 1972 Convention on International Liability for Damage Caused by Space Objects[10] to which both Canada and the Union of Soviet Socialist Republics are parties, and (b) general principles of international law. The statement of claim asserted:]

On behalf of CANADA: ...
(a) International Agreements
15. Under Article II of the Convention on International Liability for Damage caused by Space Objects, hereinafter also referred to as the Convention, "A launching State shall be absolutely liable to pay compensation for damage caused by its space object on the surface of the earth. ..." The Union of Soviet Socialist Republics, as the launching State of the Cosmos 954 satellite, has an absolute liability to pay compensation to Canada for the damage caused by this satellite. The deposit of hazardous radioactive debris from the satellite throughout a large area of Canadian territory, and the presence of that debris in the environment rendering part of Canada's territory unfit for use, constituted "damage to property" within the meaning of the Convention.

16. The intrusion into Canadian air space of a satellite carrying on board a nuclear reactor and the break-up of the satellite over Canadian territory created a clear and immediate apprehension of damage, including nuclear damage, to persons and property in Canada. The Government of the Union of Soviet Socialist Republics failed to give the Government of Canada prior notification of the imminent re-entry of the nuclear powered satellite and failed to provide timely and complete answers to the Canadian questions of January 24, 1978 concerning the satellite. It thus failed to minimize the deleterious results of the intrusion of the satellite into Canadian air space.

17. Under general principles of international law, Canada had a duty to take the necessary measures to prevent and reduce the harmful consequences of the damage and thereby to mitigate damages. Thus, with respect to the debris, it was necessary for Canada to undertake without delay operations of search, recovery, removal, testing and clean-up. These operations were also carried out in order to comply with the requirements of the domestic law of Canada. Moreover, Article VI of the Convention imposes on the claimant State a duty to observe reasonable standards of care with respect to damage caused by a space object.

18. The operations described in paragraph 8 above [clean-up] would not have been necessary and would not have been undertaken had it not been for the damage caused

---

[10] 1975 Can. T.S. No. 7; 961 U.N.T.S. 187, reported *supra* in Chapter 6.

by the hazardous radioactive debris from the Cosmos 954 satellite on Canadian territory and the reasonable apprehension of further damage in view of the nature of nuclear contamination. As a result of these operations, the areas affected have been restored, to the extent possible, to the condition which would have existed if the intrusion of the satellite and the deposit of the debris had not occurred. The Departments and Agencies of the Government of Canada involved in these operations incurred, as a result, considerable expense, particularly with regard to the procurement and use of services and equipment, the transportation of personnel and equipment and the establishment and operation of the necessary infrastructure. The costs included by Canada in this claim were incurred solely as a consequence of the intrusion of the satellite into Canadian air space and the deposit on Canadian territory of hazardous radioactive debris from the satellite.

19. In respect of compensation for damage caused by space objects, the Convention provides for " ... such reparation in respect of the damage as will restore ... [the claimant] to the condition which would have existed if the damage had not occurred" (Article XII). In accordance with its Preamble, the Convention seeks to ensure " ... the prompt payment ... [under its terms] of a full and equitable measure of compensation to victims of such damage" (Fourth preambular paragraph). Canada's claim includes only those costs which were incurred in order to restore Canada to the condition which would have existed if the damage inflicted by the Cosmos 954 satellite had not occurred. The Convention also provides that "The compensation which the launching State shall be liable to pay for damage under this Convention shall be determined in accordance with international law and the principles of justice and equity ... " (Article XII). In calculating the compensation claimed, Canada has applied the relevant criteria established by general principles of international law and has limited the costs included in its claim to those costs that are reasonable, proximately caused by the intrusion of the satellite and deposit of debris and capable of being calculated with a reasonable degree of certainty.

20. The liability of the Union of Soviet Socialist Republics for damage caused by the satellite is also founded in Article VII of the Treaty on Principles Governing the Activities of States in the Exploration and Use of Outer Space, including the Moon and Other Celestial Bodies, done in 1967, and to which both Canada and the Union of Soviet Socialist Republics are parties. This liability places an obligation on the Union of Soviet Socialist Republics to compensate Canada in accordance with international law for the consequences of the intrusion of the satellite into Canadian air space and the deposit on Canadian territory of hazardous radioactive debris from the satellite.

(b) General Principles of International Law

21. The intrusion of the Cosmos 954 satellite into Canada's air space and the deposit on Canadian territory of hazardous radioactive debris from the satellite constitutes a violation of Canada's sovereignty. This violation is established by the mere fact of the trespass of the satellite, the harmful consequences of this intrusion, being the damage caused to Canada by the presence of hazardous radioactive debris and the interference with the sovereign right of Canada to determine the acts that will be performed on its territory. International precedents recognize that a violation of sovereignty gives rise to an obligation to pay compensation.

22. The standard of absolute liability for space activities, in particular activities in-

of the state of Florida. Jaffe, accused of fraudulent land dealings in Florida, had jumped bail and returned to Canada. When the Florida court issued a bench warrant for his arrest, the bail bondsmen kidnapped Jaffe at his home in Toronto and took him against his will back to Florida, where he was tried on twenty eight counts of fraud and for his failure to appear to the charges. Jaffe was convicted and sentenced to thirty five years in jail and a fine of $152,250.00

It was alleged that the judge in Florida had provided the bail bonding agency with an incentive for the abduction as he had ordered the forfeiture of the bond which it had put up for Jaffe. The Canadian government protested to the United States government about the abduction. The Canadian Embassy in Washington presented six diplomatic notes, which objected to the breach of United States treaty obligations and the violation of Canadian sovereignty. Since at the time of Jaffe's abduction the rendition of fugitives from justice between the United States and Canada was governed by the Treaty on Extradition of December 3, 1971,[16] the action taken by the bail bondsmen at the instigation of Florida constituted a flagrant violation of that treaty, which was ignored. This international wrongful act entailed the responsibility of the United States towards Canada.

After many different initiatives had been taken, Jaffe succeeded in his appeal against the convictions for fraud and in November 1983 he was released from his Florida jail and allowed to return to Canada. Since then perjury charges have been laid against Jaffe in Florida, though it remains to be seen whether his extradition will be sought for these charges. In 1986 the two bail bondsmen were extradited to, and prosecuted in, Canada for kidnapping Jaffe.

NOTES

1) In what way did the kidnapping of Mr. Jaffe constitute a violation of Canadian sovereignty?

2) Why was the United States responsible for the wrongful acts of private individuals such as these bail bondsmen?[17]

Imputability

General Principles

International Law Commission: Draft Articles on State Responsibility
[1979] Y.B.I.L.C. II, 91; (1979), 18 *Int. Leg. Mat.* 1568.

THE ACT OF THE STATE UNDER INTERNATIONAL LAW

---

[16] 1976 Can. T.S. No. 3; 27 U.S.T. 983.
[17] See the discussion on "Imputability" in the next Section.

Article 5
ATTRIBUTION TO THE STATE OF THE CONDUCT OF ITS ORGANS

For the purposes of the present articles, conduct of any State organ having that status under the internal law of that State shall be considered as an act of the State concerned under international law, provided that organ was acting in that capacity in the case in question.

Article 6
IRRELEVANCE OF THE POSITION OF THE ORGAN IN THE ORGANIZATION OF THE STATE

The conduct of an organ of the State shall be considered as an act of that State under international law, whether that organ belongs to the constituent, legislative, executive, judicial or other power, whether its functions are of an international or an internal character and whether it holds a superior or a subordinate position in the organization of the State.

Article 7
ATTRIBUTION TO THE STATE OF THE CONDUCT OF OTHER ENTITIES EMPOWERED TO EXERCISE ELEMENTS OF THE GOVERNMENTAL AUTHORITY

1. The conduct of an organ of a territorial governmental entity within a State shall also be considered as an act of that State under international law, provided that organ was acting in that capacity in the case in question.

2. The conduct of an organ of an entity which is not a part of the formal structure of the State or of a territorial governmental entity, but which is empowered by the internal law of that State to exercise elements of the governmental authority, shall also be considered as an act of the State under international law, provided that organ was acting in that capacity in the case in question.

Article 8
ATTRIBUTION TO THE STATE OF THE CONDUCT OF PERSONS ACTING IN FACT ON BEHALF OF THE STATE

The conduct of a person or group of persons shall also be considered as an act of the State under international law if:

   (a) it is established that such person or group of persons was in fact acting on behalf of that State; or

   (b) such person or group of persons was in fact exercising elements of the governmental authority in the absence of the official authorities and in circumstances which justified the exercise of those elements of authority.

Article 9
ATTRIBUTION TO THE STATE OF THE CONDUCT OF ORGANS PLACED AT ITS DISPOSAL BY ANOTHER STATE OR BY AN INTERNATIONAL ORGANIZATION

The conduct of an organ which has been placed at the disposal of a State by another State or by an international organization shall be considered as an act of the former State

NOTES

under international law, if that organ was acting in the exercise of elements of the governmental authority of the State at whose disposal it has been placed.

1) In the *Jaffe* case, in the previous section, the attribution of the internationally wrongful acts or omissions to the United States was based on its liability for the acts and omissions of the officials of the State of Florida.[18] Similarly, in the Polish Art Treasures affair, also in the last section, the federal government was responsible for the action of the provincial authorities.

2) The case of the *U.S. Diplomatic and Consular Staff in Tehran*[19] shows the different ways a state may be attributed with responsibility for the unlawful acts of private citizens. The International Court of Justice held that responsibility for the seizure of the American embassy and hostages was not directly imputable to the state of Iran in the absence of evidence that the actions of the "militants" in occupying the premises were taken on the orders of government officials. As to the seizure, therefore, Iran could only be responsible indirectly for failure to take appropriate steps to ensure the security of the embassy and its staff. However, when Ayatollah Khomeini and other members of the government, instead of taking measures to protect the embassy from further molestation, approved its continued occupation, the "militants" became, in legal effect, agents of Iran for whose persisting acts the state itself was directly responsible. Compare I.L.C. Draft Articles 8, above, and 11, below.

3) The *Military Activities In and Against Nicaragua* case is a further illustration of these principles. The International Court held the United States was directly imputed with responsibility for a number of attacks on Nicaragua which had been planned and directed by U.S. agents.[20] However, the evidence available was insufficient to attribute to the United States the acts committed by the *Contras* in the course of their operations within Nicaragua. The Court said:[21]

For this conduct to give rise to legal responsibility of the United States, it would in principle have to be proved that that State had effective control of the military or paramilitary operations in the course of which the alleged violations were committed.

4) The principle that a federal state is responsible internationally for the acts of its provincial or state authorities, arose also between Canada and the United States in the *Cutting* case,[22] which involved the international responsibility of the Canadian government for the refusal of the province of Quebec to comply with a judgment of a Quebec court.

---

[18] See also *Eichmann* case (1961–62), 36 I.L.R. 5 and S. Williams and J.-G. Castel, *Canadian Criminal Law, International and Transnational Aspects* (1981), at 144–48.

[19] [1980] I.C.J. Rep. 3, reported *supra*, in Chapter 5. See paras. 56–62, 69–74, 79, 90–91, 95.

[20] [1986] I.C.J. Rep. 14, at 48–51.

[21] *Supra*, at 65.

[22] [1930] 2 D.L.R. 297 (Que. S.C.).

The Superior Court of Quebec had held that two hundred and seventy-five shares of stock of the Bank of Montreal, which were registered under the by-laws of that Bank in New York, were not subject to succession duties of $13,000 imposed by the province of Quebec and paid under protest by the executor of the estate of a United States citizen. The court also held that the executor was entitled to reimbursement of the sum with interest from the date of payment. The Quebec authorities repaid the duty but refused to pay the interest, and the Department of State protested to the Canadian government. In a note of October 11, 1938, the Canadian government stated that it was not prepared to admit liability for the province of Quebec in respect of the claim. To avoid any suggestion that it was responsible for denial of justice, it stated that it was ready to have the question of liability and the circumstances of the case determined by international arbitration. Subsequently, however, the Canadian government decided that the cost of arbitration rendered proceedings inadvisable and a cheque for the interest was transmitted to the United States under a note of July 8, 1941, from the Department of External Affairs.

Acts Ultra Vires

International Law Commission: Draft Articles on State Responsibility
[1979] Y.B.I.L.C. II, 91; (1979), 18 *Int. Leg. Mat.* 1568

Article 10
ATTRIBUTION TO THE STATE OF CONDUCT OF ORGANS ACTING OUTSIDE THEIR COMPETENCE OR CONTRARY TO INSTRUCTIONS CONCERNING THEIR ACTIVITY

The conduct of an organ of a State, of a territorial governmental entity or of an entity empowered to exercise elements of the governmental authority, such organ having acted in that capacity, shall be considered as an act of the State under international law even if, in the particular case, the organ exceeded its competence according to internal law or contravened instructions concerning its activity.

NOTES

The International Law Commission commented:[23]

In the opinion of the Commission there is no need to reopen the discussion on the basic criterion which has been affirmed in diplomatic practice and in the decisions of international tribunals in this century, *i.e.* the criterion of the attribution to the State, as a subject of international law, of the acts and omissions of its organs which have acted in that capacity, even when they have contravened the provisions of municipal law concerning their activity. This criterion is based on the need for clarity and security in international relations which seems to be the dominant theme in modern international life. In international law, the State must recognize that it acts whenever

---

[23] [1975] Y.B.I.L.C. II, 67.

persons or groups of persons whom it has instructed to act in its name in a given area of activity appear to be acting effectively in its name. Even when in so doing those persons or groups exceed the formal limits of their competence according to municipal law or contravene the provisions of that law or of administrative ordinances or internal instructions issued by their superiors, they are nevertheless acting, even though improperly, within the scope of the discharge of their functions. The State cannot take refuge behind the notion that, according to the provisions of its legal system, those actions or omissions ought not to have occurred or ought to have taken a different form. They have nevertheless occurred and the State is therefore obliged to assume responsibility for them and to bear the consequences provided for in international law.

T.H. Youmans Claim
United States v. Mexico
General Claims Commission (1926), 4 R.I.A.A. 110

THE COMMISSION (van Vollenhoven, Nielsen, MacGregor): **1.** Claim for damages in the amount of $50,000.00 is made in this case by the United States of America against the United Mexican States in behalf of Thomas H. Youmans, the son of Henry Youmans, an American citizen, who, together with two other Americans, John A. Connelly and George Arnold, was killed at the hands of a mob on March 14, 1880, at Angangueo, State of Michoacán, Mexico. The occurrences giving rise to the claim as stated in the Memorial are substantially as follows:

2. At the time when the killing took place Connelly and Youmans were employed by Justin Arnold and Clinton Stephens, American citizens, who were engaged under a contract with a British corporation in driving a tunnel, known as the San Hilario Tunnel, in the town of Angangueo, a place having a population of approximately 7,000 people. The work was being done by Mexican laborers resident in the town under the supervision of the Americans. On the day when these men were killed Connelly, who was Managing Engineer in the construction of the tunnel at Angangueo, had a controversy with a laborer, Cayentano Medina by name, over a trifling sum of about twelve cents which the laborer insisted was due to him as wages. Connelly, considering the conduct of the laborer to be offensive, ejected the latter from the house in which Connelly lived and to which Medina had come to discuss the matter. Subsequently Medina, who was joined by several companions, began to throw stones at Connelly while the latter was sitting in front of his house and approached the American with a drawn machete. Connelly, with a view to frightening his assailant, fired shots into the air from a revolver. The American having withdrawn into the house, Medina attempted to enter, and his companions followed. Connelly thereupon fired at Medina with a shotgun and wounded him in the legs. Soon the house was surrounded by a threatening mob, which increased until it numbered about a thousand people. Connelly, Youmans, and Arnold, realizing the seriousness of their situation, prepared to defend themselves against the mob. Connelly's employer, Clinton Stephens, on hearing shots, went to the house and learned from Connelly what had happened. Upon Stephen's advice Connelly undertook to surrender himself to the local authorities, but was driven back into the house by the mob. The attack against Connelly when he endeavored to surrender to police authorities was led by Pedro Mondragón, a person styled the *Jefe de Manzana*, with whom Connelly had been on friendly terms. Stephens, followed by a part of the mob, proceeded to the *Casa Municipal* and requested the Mayor, Don Justo Lopez, to endeavor to protect the American in the house. The Mayor promptly went to the house, but was unable to quiet the mob. He then returned to his office and ordered José Maria Mora, *Jefe de la Tropa de la Seguridad Publica*, who held the rank of Lieutenant in the forces of the State of Michoacán, to proceed with troops to quell the riot and put an end to the attack upon the Americans. The troops, on arriving at the scene of the riot, instead of dispersing the mob, opened fire on the house, as a consequence of which Arnold was killed. The mob renewed the attack, and while the Americans defended themselves as best they could, several members of the mob approached the house from the rear, where there were no windows, and set fire to the roof. Connelly and Youmans were forced to leave, and as they did so they were killed by the troops and members of the mob. Their bodies were dragged through the streets and left under a pile of stones by the side of the road so mutilated as scarcely to be recognizable. At night they were buried by employees of the Mining Company in its cemetery at Trojes. ...

11. The claim made by the United States is predicated on the failure of the Mexican Government to exercise due diligence to protect the father of the claimant from the fury of the mob at whose hands he was killed. ...In connection with the contention with respect to the failure of the authorities to protect Youmans from the acts of the mob, particular emphasis is laid on the participation of soldiers which is asserted to be in itself a ground of liability. In behalf of the respondent Government it is contended that ... even if it were assumed that the soldiers were guilty of such participation, the Mexican Government should not be held responsible for the wrongful acts of ten soldiers and one officer of the State of Michoacán, who, after having been ordered by the highest official in the locality to protect American citizens, instead of carrying out orders given them acted in violation of them in consequence of which the Americans were killed. ...

13. With respect to the question of responsibility for the acts of soldiers there are citations in the Mexican Government's brief of extracts from a discussion of a subcommittee of the League of Nations Committee of Experts for the Progressive Codification of International Law. The passage quoted, which deals with the responsibility of a State for illegal acts of officials resulting in damages to foreigners, begins with a statement relative to the acts of an official accomplished "outside the scope of his competency, that is to say, if he has exceeded his powers." An illegal act of this kind, it is stated in the quotation, is one that can not be imputed to the State. Apart from the question whether the acts of officials referred to in this discussion have any relation to the rule of international law with regard to responsibility for acts of soldiers, it seems clear that the passage to which particular attention is called in the Mexican Government's brief is concerned solely with the question of the authority of an officer as defined by domestic law to act for his Government with reference to some particular subject. Clearly it is not intended by the rule asserted to say that no wrongful act of an official acting in the discharge of duties entrusted to him can impose responsibility on a Government under international law because any such wrongful act must be considered to be "outside the scope of his competency." If this were the meaning intended by the rule it would follow that no wrongful acts committed by an official could be considered as acts for which his Government could be held liable. We do not consider that any of these passages from the discussion of the subcommittee quoted in the Mexican brief are at variance with the view which we take that the action of the troops in participating in the murder at Angangueo imposed a direct responsibility on the Government of Mexico.

14. Citation is also made in the Mexican brief to an opinion rendered by Umpire Lieber in which effect is evidently given to the well-recognized rule of international law that a Government is not responsible for malicious acts of soldiers committed in their private capacity. Awards have repeatedly been rendered for wrongful acts of soldiers acting under the command of an officer. ... Certain cases coming before the international tribunals may have revealed some uncertainty whether the acts of soldiers should properly be regarded as private acts for which there was no liability on the State, or acts for which the State should be held responsible. But we do not consider that the participation of the soldiers in the murder at Angangueo can be regarded as acts of soldiers committed in their private capacity when it is clear that at the time of the commission of these acts the men were on duty under the immediate supervision and in the presence of a commanding officer. Soldiers inflicting personal injuries or committing wanton destruction or looting always act in disobedience of some rules laid down by superior authority. There could be no liability whatever for such misdeeds if the view were taken that any acts committed by soldiers in contravention of instructions must always be considered as personal acts. ...

17. The Commission therefore decides that the Government of the United Mexican States must pay to the Government of the United States of America the sum of $20,000.00 (twenty thousand dollars) without interest on behalf of Thomas H. Youmans.

Acts of Private Citizens and Rebels

International Law Commission: Draft Articles on State Responsibility
[1979] Y.B.I.L.C. II, 91; (1979), 18 *Int. Leg. Mat.* 1568

Article 11
CONDUCT OF PERSONS NOT ACTING ON BEHALF OF THE STATE

1. The conduct of a person or a group of persons not acting on behalf of the State shall not be considered as an act of the State under international law.

2. Paragraph 1 is without prejudice to the attribution to the State of any other conduct which is related to that of the persons or groups of persons referred to in that paragraph and which is to be considered as an act of the State by virtue of articles 5 to 10.

Article 14
CONDUCT OF ORGANS OF AN INSURRECTIONAL MOVEMENT

1. The conduct of an organ of an insurrectional movement, which is established in the territory of a State or in any other territory under its administration, shall be considered as an act of that State under international law.

2. Paragraph 1 is without prejudice to the attribution to a State of any other conduct which is related to that of the organ of the insurrectional movement and which is to be considered as an act of that State by virtue of articles 5 to 10.

3. Similarly, paragraph 1 is without prejudice to the attribution of the conduct of the organ of the insurrectional movement to that movement in any case in which such attribution may be made under international law.

Article 15
ATTRIBUTION TO THE STATE OF THE ACT OF AN INSURRECTIONAL MOVEMENT WHICH BECOMES THE NEW GOVERNMENT OF A STATE OR WHICH RESULTS IN THE FORMATION OF A NEW STATE

1. The act of an insurrectional movement which becomes the new government of a State shall be considered as an act of that State. However, such attribution shall be without prejudice to the attribution to that State of conduct which would have been previously considered as an act of the State by virtue of articles 5 to 10.

RESPONSIBILITY FOR INJURIES TO ALIENS

Over the last two hundred years, international law has developed standards and procedures to protect the life, liberty, and economic security of nationals of one state who visit, live or conduct business activities in another state. As Hackworth stated:[24]

> The admission of aliens into a State immediately calls into existence certain correlative rights and duties. The alien has a right to the protection of the local law. He owes a duty to observe that law and assumes a relationship toward the State of his residence sometimes referred to as "temporary allegiance."
>
> The State has the right to expect that the alien shall observe its laws and that his conduct shall not be incompatible with the good order of the State and of the community in which he resides or sojourns. It has the obligation to give him that degree of protection for his person and property which he and his State have the right to expect under local law, under international law, and under treaties and conventions between his State and the State of residence. Failure of the alien or of the State to observe these requirements may give rise to responsibility in varying degrees, the alien being amenable to the local law or subject to expulsion from the State, or both, and the State being responsible to the alien or to the State of which he is a national.
>
> We are here concerned primarily with responsibility of the State. State responsibility may arise directly or indirectly. It does not arise merely because an alien has been injured or has suffered loss within the State's territory. If the alien has suffered an injury at the hands of a private person his remedy usually is against that person, and State responsibility does not arise in the absence of a dereliction of duty on the part of the State itself in connection with the injury, as for example by failure to afford a remedy, or to apply an existing remedy. When local remedies are available

---

[24] *Digest of International Law* (1943), vol. 5, at 471–72.

the alien is ordinarily not entitled to the interposition of his government until he has exhausted those remedies and has been denied justice. This presupposes the existence in the State of orderly judicial and administrative processes. In theory an unredressed injury to an alien constitutes an injury to his State, giving rise to international responsibility.

International Minimum Standard or National Treatment?

Neer Claim
United States v. Mexico
General Claims Commission (1926), 4 R.I.A.A. 60, at 61–2.

VAN VOLLENHOVEN, Presiding Commissioner: Without attempting to announce a precise formula, it is in the opinion of the Commission possible ... to hold (first) that the propriety of governmental acts should be put to the test of international standards, and (second) that the treatment of an alien, in order to constitute an international delinquency, should amount to an outrage, to bad faith, to wilful neglect of duty, or to an insufficiency of governmental action so far short of international standards that every reasonable and impartial man would readily recognize its insufficiency. Whether the insufficiency proceeds from deficient execution of an intelligent law or from the fact that the laws of the country do not empower the authorities to measure up to international standards is immaterial.

NOTES

1) In the *Cadenhead* case[25] the Arbitration Tribunal said:

It has not been shown that there was a denial of justice, or that there were any special circumstances or grounds of exception to the generally recognized rule of international law that a foreigner within the United States is subject to its public law, and has no greater rights than nationals of that country.

2) The standard of conduct which a state is expected to pursue in its dealings with aliens has been the subject of considerable controversy. The Latin American states, against which large number of international claims have been presented, have often maintained that no violation of international law is committed as long as there is no discrimination against the alien. It is thus a perfect defense to a claim, to assert that nationals of the respondent state are treated in the same fashion as was the alien. However, to date international tribunals have generally taken the view that, although a state must as a

---

[25] U.K. v. U.S. (1920), *Nielsen's Report* 506; 6 R.I.A.A. 40. See also the *B.E. Chattin Claim, infra* in the next Section.

minimum not discriminate against aliens, its conduct must ultimately be judged by international standards, and that a state may not be heard in its defense to allege that its nationals are treated in exactly the same way as aliens. It may be said in defense of the position of the Latin American states that it may be justifiable to apply local standards to a natural or juristic person maintaining a permanent residence in a given state; the individual or corporation must be considered to have assumed the risks associated with residence in that state. Thus, if state A in time of war requisitions the property of a corporation of state B permanently established in state A, compensation should be limited to the same amount which nationals of state A are receiving, especially if property is being requisitioned by state B on the same basis as by state A. However, if means of transportation owned by an alien and temporarily within the jurisdiction of a state are requisitioned by that state in time of war in the exercise of its right of angary, full compensation according to international law ought to be paid for the property so taken.

When we turn from the protection of property to the protection of the person and of the fundamental rights and freedoms of individuals, it is difficult to maintain that an alien should have no protection under international law because all nationals of the state concerned are subjected to the same injustices.

Today, developing states in Africa and Asia as well as socialist states have joined Latin American states in their rejection of the existence of an international minimum standard of treatment which must be accorded to aliens. However, this diversity of opinion should be understood in the wider context of the growth of universal human rights of individuals, whether nationals or aliens.[26]

3) It must be pointed out that the national treatment standard or the international minimum standard only applies to certain areas of activity by aliens. In other areas, it is perfectly legitimate under customary international law for states to treat aliens as such in their discretion and to limit their activities, for instance, by preventing them from holding a public office. The mere fact that the law and procedure of the state in which the alien resides differ from those of the country of which he is a national does not of itself afford justification for complaint.

Mistreatment of Aliens

Admission and Expulsion

Attorney General for Canada v. Cain
[1906] A.C. 542, at 546 (J.C.P.C.)

THE PRIVY COUNCIL:
One of the rights possessed by the supreme power in every State is the right to refuse to permit an alien to enter that State, to annex what conditions it pleases to the permission to enter it, and to expel or deport from the State, at pleasure, even a friendly alien,

---

[26] See Chapter 10 on "Protection of Human Rights."

especially if it considers his presence in the State opposed to its peace, order, and good government, or to its social or material interests.

NOTES

1) Does the *Canadian Charter of Rights* affect this statement of the law? Consider sections 6 and 7:[27]

6.(2) Every ... person who has the status of a permanent resident of Canada has the right
(a) to move to and take up residence in any province; and
(b) to pursue the gaining of a livelihood in any province.
7. Everyone has the right to life, liberty and security of the person and the right not to be deprived thereof except in accordance with the principles of fundamental justice.

2) In *Re Janoczka*,[28] it was stated:

The right of expulsion of a foreign citizen whose presence is found to be objectionable does not seem to be conditional on the acquiescence of the country of the foreign citizenship but apparently international comity requires that communication take place. Such communication takes the form of a passport application. At all events the practice to that effect does exist and must be recognized.

Detention and Physical Injury

Quintanilla Claim
United States v. Mexico
General Claims Commission (1926), 4 R.I.A.A. 101, at 102–3

VAN VOLLENHOVEN, Presiding Commissioner:
1. This claim is presented by the United Mexican States against the United States in behalf of F. Quintanilla and M.I. Perez de Quintanilla, Mexican nationals, father and mother of Alejo Quintanilla, a young man, who was killed on or about July 16, 1922, not far from Edinburg, Hidalgo County, Texas, U.S.A. On July 15, 1922, about 5 p.m., said Alejo Quintanilla in a lonely spot had lassoed a girl of fourteen years, Agnes Casey, who was on horseback, and thrown her from the horse; she screamed, and the young Mexican fled. She told the occurrence to her father, Tom Casey with whom Quintanilla had been employed some time before; the father the next morning went to lodge his complaint with the authorities, first to Edinburg (the County seat), where he did not find the sheriff, and then to Donna, where he found the deputy sheriff, one Sam A. Bernard. According to the record, this deputy sheriff with three other men, whose names are not

---

[27] And see *Singh et al. v. Minister of Employment and Immigration*, [1985] 1 S.C.R. 177.
[28] [1933] 1 D.L.R. 123, at 128 (Man. C.A.).

mentioned, went to Quintanilla's house, took him from it, and the deputy sheriff with one Walter Weaver placed him in a motor car and drove with him, first to Casey's house, where they put on a new tire, and then in the direction of Edinburg to take him to the county jail. On July 18, 1922, about noon, Quintanilla's corpse was found near the side of this road, some three miles from Edinburg, traces showing that he had been taken there in a motor car. Bernard and Weaver were accused by the Mexican Consul at Hidalgo, Texas, and were accordingly arrested, but released on bail; Bernard's appointment as a deputy sheriff was cancelled by his sheriff on July 22, 1922. The public prosecutor made investigations and submitted the case to the Grand Jury, but the Grand Jury deferred it from 1922 to 1923, from 1923 to 1924, and never took action upon it. ...

2. It appears from the record that Quintanilla was taken into custody on July 16, 1922, by a deputy sheriff of the State of Texas, to put him at the disposal of the judicial officers; it is left uncertain whether this official was provided with any authorization to take Quintanilla from his house and arrest him. The United States Government never reported what this deputy sheriff did with Quintanilla after he had taken him under custody. The young man apparently never reached the county jail. The deputy sheriff may have changed his mind and set him at liberty, and after that Quintanilla may have been murdered by an unknown person. An enemy of Quintanilla may have come up and taken him from the car. The companion of the deputy sheriff, who was not an official, may have killed Quintanilla; or the two custodians may have acted in self-defence. The United States Government has been silent on all of this. The only thing the record clearly shows is that Quintanilla was taken into custody by a State official, and that he never was delivered to any jail. The first question before this Commission, therefore, is whether under international law these circumstances present a case for which a Government must be held liable.

3. The Commission does not hesitate to answer in the affirmative. The most notable parallel in international law relates to war prisoners, hostages, and interned members of a belligerent army and navy. ... The case before this Commission is analogous. A foreigner is taken into custody by a state official. It would go too far to hold that the Government is liable for everything which may befall him. But it has to account for him. The Government can be held liable if it is proven that it has treated him cruelly, harshly, unlawfully; so much the more it is liable if it can say only that it took him into custody – either in jail or in some other place and form – and that it ignores what happened to him.

4. The question then arises whether this duty to account for a man in Governmental custody is modified by the fact that the custodian himself is accused of having killed his prisoner and, as an accused, can not be made to testify against himself. The two things clearly are separate. If the Government is obligated to state what happened to the man in its custody, its officials are bound to inform their Governments. It might be that the custodians themselves perish in a calamity together with the men in their custody, and therefore can not furnish any information. But if they are alive, and are silent, the Government has to bear the consequences. The Commission holds, therefore, that under international law ... the respondent Government is liable for the damages originating in this act of a State official and resulting in injustice.

Noyes Claim
United States v. Panama
General Claims Arbitration (1933), 6 R.I.A.A. 308, at 309–11

THE COMMISSION (Van Heeckeren, Root, Alfaro): ...

In this case a claim is made against the Republic of Panama by the United States of America on behalf of Walter A. Noyes, who was born, and has ever remained, an American citizen. The sum of $1,683 is claimed as an indemnity for the personal injuries and property losses sustained by Mr. Noyes through the attacks made upon him on June 19, 1927, in, and in the neighborhood of, the village of Juan Díaz, situated not far from Panama City. The claim is based upon an alleged failure to provide to the claimant adequate police protection, to exercise due diligence in the maintenance of order and to take adequate measures to apprehend and punish the aggressors. ...

The village of Juan Díaz has only a small population, but on June 19, 1927, several hundreds of adherents of the party then in control of the Government had gathered there for a meeting. The police on the spot had not been increased for the occasion; it consisted of the usual three policemen stationed there. In the course of the day the authorities in Panama City learned that the crowd in Juan Díaz had become unruly under the influence of liquor. The chief of the police, General Pretelt, thereupon drove thither with reinforcements. ...

At about 3.00 p.m. the claimant passed through the village in his automobile, on his return to Panama City from a trip to the Tapia River bridge. In the center of the village a crowd blocked the road and Mr. Noyes stopped and sounded his horn, whereupon the crowd slowly opened. Whilst he was progressing very slowly through it, he had to stop again, because somebody lurched against the car and fell upon the running-board. Thereupon members of the crowd smashed the windows of the car and attacked Mr. Noyes, who was stabbed in the wrist and hurt by fragments of glass. A police officer who had been giving orders that gangway should be made for the automobile, but who had not before been able to reach the car, then sprang upon the running-board and remained there, protecting the claimant and urging him to get away as quickly as possible. He remained with Mr. Noyes, until the latter had got clear of the crowd. At some distance from Juan Díaz the claimant was further attacked by members of the same crowd, who pursued him in a bus and who forced him to drive his car off the road and into a ditch. He was then rescued by General Pretelt who, having come from the opposite direction, had, after reaching the plaza of the village, returned upon his way in order to protect Mr. Noyes against his pursuers.

The facts related above show that in both instances the police most actively protected the claimant against his assailants and that in the second instance the protection was due to the fact that the authorities sent reinforcements from Panama City upon learning that the conditions in Juan Díaz rendered assistance necessary. The contention of the American Agent however is, that the Panamanian Government incurred a liability under international law, because its officials had not taken the precaution of increasing for that day the police force at Juan Díaz, although they knew some time in advance that the meeting would assemble there.

The mere fact that an alien has suffered at the hands of private persons an aggression, which could have been averted by the presence of a sufficient police force on the spot, does not make a government liable for damages under international law. There must be shown special circumstances from which the responsibility of the authorities arises: either their behavior in connection with the particular occurrence, or a general failure to comply with their duty to maintain order, to prevent crimes or to prosecute and punish criminals.

There were no such circumstances in the present case. Accordingly a lack of protection has not been established. ...

The claim is disallowed.

Maladministration of Justice

B.E. Chattin Claim
United States v. Mexico
General Claims Commission (1927), 4 R.I.A.A. 282, at 283–299.

VAN VOLLENHOVEN, Presiding Commissioner:

1. This claim is made by the United States of America against the United Mexican States on behalf of B.E. Chattin, an American national. Chattin, who since 1908 was an employee (at first freight conductor, thereafter passenger conductor) of the Ferrocarril Sud-Pacífico de México (Southern Pacific Railroad Company of Mexico) and who in the Summer of 1910 performed his duties in the State of Sinaloa, was on July 9, 1910, arrested at Mazatlan, Sinaloa, on a charge of embezzlement; was tried there in January, 1911, convicted on February 6, 1911, and sentenced to two years' imprisonment; but was released from the jail at Mazatlán in May or June, 1911, as a consequence of disturbances caused by the Madero revolution. He then returned to the United States. It is alleged that the arrest, the trial and the sentence were illegal, that the treatment in jail was inhuman, and that Chattin was damaged to the extent of $50,000.00 which amount Mexico should pay. ...

3. The circumstances of Chattin's arrest, trial and sentence were as follows. In the year 1910 there had arisen a serious apprehension on the part of several railroad companies operating in Mexico as to whether the full proceeds of passenger fares were accounted for to these companies. The Southern Pacific Railroad Company of Mexico applied on June 15, 1910, to the Governor of the State of Sinaloa, in his capacity as chief of police of the State, co-operating with the federal police, in order to have investigations made of the existence and extent of said defrauding of their lines within the territory of his State. On or about July 8, 1910, one Cenobio Ramirez, a Mexican employee (brakeman) of the said railroad, was arrested at Mazatlán on a charge of fraudulent sale of railroad tickets of the said company, and in his appearance before the District Court in that town he accused the conductor Chattin – who since May 9, 1910, had charge of trains operating between Mazatlán and Acaponeta, Nayarit – as the principal in the crime with which he, Ramirez, was charged; whereupon Chattin also was arrested by the Mazatlán police, on

July 9 (not 10), 1910. On August 3 (not 13), 1910, his case was consolidated not only with that of Ramirez, but also with that of three more American railway conductors (Haley, Englehart and Parrish) and of four more Mexicans. After many months of preparation and a trial at Mazatlán, during both of which Chattin, it is alleged, lacked proper information, legal assistance, assistance of an interpreter and confrontation with the witnesses, he was convicted on February 6, 1911, by the said District Court of Mazatlán as stated above. The case was carried on appeal to the Third Circuit Court at Mexico City, which court on July 3, 1911, affirmed the sentence. In the meantime (May or June, 1911) Chattin had been released by the population of Mazatlán which threw open the doors of the jail in the time elapsing between the departure of the representatives of the Díaz régime and the arrival of the Madero forces. ...

5. It has been alleged, in the first place, that Chattin, contrary to the Mexican Constitution of 1857, was arrested merely on an oral order. The Court's decision rendered February 6, 1911, stated that the court record contained "the order dated July 9, which is the written order based on the reasons for the detention of Chattin"; and among the court proceedings there are to be found (a) a decree ordering Chattin's arrest, dated July 9, 1910, and (b) a decree for Chattin's "formal imprisonment," dated July 9, 1910, as well. Even if the first decree had been issued some hours after Chattin's arrest, for which there is no proof except the statement by the police prefect that Chattin was placed in a certain jail on the Judge's "oral order," the irregularity would have been inconsequential to Chattin. The Third Circuit Court at Mexico City, when called upon to examine the second decree given on July 9, 1910, held on October 27, 1910, that it had been regular but for the omission of the crime imputed (which was known to Chattin from the examination to which he was previously submitted on July 9, 1910), and therefore the Court affirmed it after having amended it by inserting the name of Chattin's alleged crime. The United States has alleged that, since the sentence rendered on February 6, 1911, held that "the confession of the latter" (Ramirez) "does not constitute in itself a proof against the other" (Chattin), the Court confessed that Chattin's arrest had been illegal. No such inference can be made from the words cited, though the thought might have been expressed more clearly: a statement, insufficient as evidence for a conviction, can under Mexican law (as under the laws of many other countries) furnish a wholly sufficient basis for an arrest and formal imprisonment.

6. Before taking up the allegations relative to irregular court proceedings against Chattin and to his having been convicted on insufficient evidence, it seems proper to establish that the present case is of a type different from most other cases so far examined by this Commission in which defective administration of justice was alleged.

7. In the Kennedy Case (U.S.-Mexico, General Claims Commission, Opinion of Commissioners, 1927, at 289) and nineteen more cases before this commission it was contended that, a citizen of either country having been wrongfully damaged either by a private individual or by an executive official, the judicial authorities had failed to take proper steps against the person or persons who caused the loss or damage. A governmental liability proceeding from such a source is usually called "indirect liability," though, considered in connection with the alleged delinquency of the government itself, it is quite as direct as its liability for any other act of its officials. The liability of the government may be called remote or secondary only when compared with the liability of the person who committed the wrongful act (for instance, the murder) for that very act. Such cases of *indirect governmental liability* because of lack of proper action by the judiciary are analogous to cases in which a government might be held responsible for denial of justice in connection with nonexecution of private contracts, or in which it might become liable to victims of private or other delinquencies because of lack of protection by its executive or legislative authorities.

8. Distinct from this so-called indirect government liability is the *direct responsibility* incurred on account of acts of the government itself, or its officials, unconnected with any previous wrongful act of a citizen. If such governmental acts are acts of executive authorities, either in the form of breach of government contracts made with private foreigners, or in the form of other delinquencies of public authorities, they are at once recognized as acts involving direct liability; for instance, collisions caused by public vessels, reckless shooting by officials, unwarranted arrest by officials, mistreatment in jail by officials, etc. As soon, however, as mistreatment of foreigners *by the courts* is alleged to the effect that damage sustained is caused by the *judiciary* itself, a confusion arises from the fact that authors often lend the term "denial of justice" as well to these cases of the second category, which are different in character from a "denial of justice" of the first category. So also did the tribunal in the *Yuille, Shortridge & Company* case (under the British memorandum of March 8, 1861, accepted by Portugal; De Lapradelle et Politis, II, at 103), so Umpire Thornton sometimes did in the 1868 Commission (Moore, 3140, 3141, 3143; *Burn, Pratt* and *Ada* cases). It would seem preferable not to use the expression in this manner. The very name "denial of justice" *(dénégation de justice, déni de justice)* would seem inappropriate here, since the basis of claims in these cases does not lie in the fact that the courts refuse or deny redress for an injustice sustained by a foreigner because of an act of someone else, but lies in the fact that the courts themselves did injustice. In the British and American claims arbitration Arbitrator Pound one day put it tersely in saying that there must be "an injustice antecedent to the denial, and then the denial after it" (Nielsen's Report, 258, 261).

9. How confusing it must be to use the term "denial of justice" for both categories of governmental acts, is shown by a simple deduction. If "denial of justice" covers not only governmental acts implying so-called indirect liability, but also acts of direct liability, and if, on the other hand, "denial of justice" is applied to acts of executive and legislative authorities as well as to acts of judicial authorities – as is often being done – there would exist no international wrong which would not be covered by the phrase "denial of justice," and the expression would lose its value as a technical distinction.

10. The practical importance of a consistent cleavage between these two categories of governmental acts lies in the following. In cases of direct responsibility, insufficiency of governmental action entailing liability is not limited to flagrant cases such as cases of bad faith or wilful neglect of duty. So, at least, it is for the non-judicial branches of government. Acts of the *judiciary*, either entailing direct responsibility or indirect liability (the latter called denial of justice, proper), are not considered insufficient unless the wrong committed amounts to an outrage, bad faith, wilful neglect of duty, or insufficiency of action apparent to any unbiased man. Acts of the executive and legislative branches, on the contrary, share this lot only then, when they engender a so-called *indirect* liability in connection with acts of others; and the very reason why this type of acts often is covered by the same term "denial of justice" in its broader sense may be partly in this, that to such acts or inactivities of the executive and legislative branches engendering *indirect* liability, the rule applies that a government cannot be held responsible for them unless the wrong done amounts to an outrage, to bad faith, to wilful neglect of duty, or to an insufficiency of governmental action so far short of international standard that every reasonable and impartial man would readily recognize its insufficiency. With reference to *direct* liability for acts of the executive it is different. In the *Mermaid* case (under the Convention of March 4, 1868, between Great Britain and Spain) the Commissioners held that even an act of mere clumsiness on the part of a gunboat – a cannon shot fired at a ship in an awkward way – when resulting in injustice renders the government to whom that public vessel belongs liable (De Lapradelle et Politis, II, 496; compare Moore, 5016). In the *Union Bridge Company* case the British American arbitral tribunal decided that an act of an executive officer may constitute an international tort for which his country is liable, even though he acts under an erroneous impression and without wrongful intentions (Nielsen's Report, at 380). ...

11. When, therefore, the American Agency in its brief mentions with great emphasis the existence of a "denial of justice" in the *Chattin* case, it should be realized that the term is used in its improper sense which sometimes is confusing. It is true that *both* categories of government responsibility – the direct one and the so-called indirect one – should be brought to the test of international standards in order to determine whether an international wrong exists, and that for *both* categories convincing evidence is necessary to fasten liability. It is moreover true that, as far as acts of the *judiciary* are involved, the view applies to *both* categories that "it is a matter of the greatest political and international delicacy for one country to disacknowledge the judicial decision of a court of another country" (*Garrison's* case; Moore, 3129), and to *both* categories the rule applies that state responsibility is limited to judicial acts showing outrage, bad faith, wilful neglect of duty, or manifestly insufficient governmental action. But the distinction becomes of importance whenever acts of the *other* branches of government are concerned; then the limitation of liability (as it exists for *all* judicial acts) does not apply to the category of direct responsibility, but only to the category of so-called indirect or derivative responsibility for acts of the executive and legislative branches, for instance on the ground of lack of protection against acts of individuals.

12. The next allegation on the American side is that Chattin's trial was held in an illegal manner. The contentions are: (a) that the Governor of the State, for political reasons, used his influence to have this accused and three of his fellow conductors convicted; (b) that the proceedings against the four conductors were consolidated without reason; (c) that the proceedings were unduly delayed; (d) that an exorbitant amount of bail was required; (e) that the accused was not duly informed of the accusations; (f) that the accused lacked the aid of counsel; (g) that the accused lacked the aid of an interpreter; (h) that there were no oaths required of the witnesses; (i) that there was no such a thing as a confrontation between the witnesses and the accused; and (j) that the hearings in open court which led to sentences of from two years' to two years and eight months' imprisonment lasted only some five minutes. It was also contended that the claimant had been forced to march under guard through the streets of Mazatlán; but the Commission in paragraph 3 of its opinion in the *Faulkner* case (Docket No. 47) rendered November

2, 1926, has already held that such treatment is incidental to the treatment of detention and suspicion, and cannot in itself furnish a separate basis for a complaint. ...

15. For undue delay of the proceedings (allegation c), there is convincing evidence in more than one respect. The formal proceedings began on July 9, 1910. Chattin was not heard in court until more than one hundred days thereafter. The stubs and perhaps other pieces of evidence against Chattin were presented to the Court on August 3, 1910; Chattin however, was not allowed to testify regarding them until October 28, 1910.

Between the end of July, and October 8, 1910, the Judge merely waited. The date of an alleged railroad ticket delinquency of Chattin's (June 29, 1910) was given by a witness on October 21, 1910; but investigation of Chattin's collection report of that day was not ordered until November 11, 1910, and he was not heard regarding it until November 16, nor confronted with the only two witnesses (Delgado and Sarabia) until November 17, 1910. The witnesses named by Ramirez in July were not summoned until after November 22, 1910, at the request of the Prosecuting Attorney, with the result that, on the one hand, several of them – including the important witness Manuel Virgen – had gone, and that, on the other hand, the proceedings had to be extended from November 18, to December 13. On September 3, 1910, trial had been denied Parrish, and on November 5, it was denied Chattin, Haley and Englehart; though no testimony against them was ever taken after October 21 (Chattin), and though the absence of the evidence ordered on November 11 and after November 22 and due exclusively to the Judge's *laches*. Unreliability of Ramirez's confession had been suggested by Chattin's lawyer on August 16, 1910; but it apparently was only after a similar suggestion of Camou on October 6, 1910, that the Judge discovered that the confession of Ramirez did not "constitute in itself a proof against" Chattin. New evidence against Chattin was sought for. It is worthy of note that one of the two new witnesses, Estebán Delgado, who was summoned on October 12, 1910, had already been before the police prefect on July 8, 1910, in connection with Ramirez's alleged crime. If the necessity of new evidence was not seriously felt before October, 1910, this means that the Judge either had not in time considered the sufficiency of Ramirez's confession as proof against Chattin, or had allowed himself an unreasonable length of time to gather new evidence. The explanation cannot be found in the consolidation of Chattin's case with those of his three fellow conductors, as there is no trace of any judicial effort to gather new testimony against these men after July, 1910. Another remarkable proof of the measure of speed which the Judge deemed due to a man deprived of his liberty, is in that, whereas Chattin appealed from the decree of his formal imprisonment on July 11, 1910 – an appeal which would seem to be of rather an urgent character – "the corresponding copy for the appeal" was not remitted to the appellate Court until September 12, 1910; this Court did not render judgment until October 27, 1910; and though its decision was forwarded to Mazatlán on October 31, 1910, its receipt was not established until November 12, 1910. ...

22. The whole of the proceedings discloses a most astonishing lack of seriousness on the part of the Court. ... There is no trace of an effort to find one Manuel Virgen, who, according to the investigations of July 21, 1910, might have been mixed in Chattin's dealings, nor to examine one Carl or Carrol Collins, a dismissed clerk of the railroad company concerned, who was repeatedly mentioned as forging tickets and passes and as having been discharged for that very reason. One of the Mexican brakemen, Batriz, stated on August 8, 1910, in court that "it is true that the American conductors have among themselves schemes to defraud in that manner the company, the deponent not knowing it for sure"; but again no steps were taken to have this statement verified or this brakeman confronted with the accused Americans. No disclosures were made as to one pass, one "half-pass" and eight perforated tickets shown to Chattin on October 28, 1910, as pieces of evidence; the record states that they were the same documents as presented to Ramirez on July 9, 1910, but does not attempt to explain why their number in July was eight (seven tickets and one pass) and in October was ten. No investigation was made as to why Delgado and Sarabia felt quite certain that June 29 was the date of their trip, a date upon the correctness of which the weight of their testimony wholly depended. No search of the houses of these conductors is mentioned. Nothing is revealed as to a search of their persons on the days of their arrest; when the lawyer of the other conductors, Haley and Englehart, insisted upon such an inquiry, a letter was sent to the Judge at Culiacán, but was allowed to remain unanswered. Neither during the investigations nor during the hearings in open court was any such thing as an oral examination or cross-examination of any importance attempted. It seems highly improbable that the accused have been given a real opportunity during the hearings in open court, freely to speak for themselves. It is not for the Commission to endeavor to reach from the record any conviction as to the innocence or guilt of Chattin and his colleagues; but even in case they were guilty, the Commission would render a bad service to the Government of Mexico if it failed to place the stamp of its disapproval and even indignation on a criminal procedure so far below international standards of civilization as the present one. If the wholesome rule of international law as to respect for the judiciary of another country – referred to in paragraph 11 above – shall stand, it would seem of the utmost necessity that appellate tribunals when, in exceptional cases, discovering proceedings of this type should take against them the strongest measures possible under constitution and laws, in order to safeguard their country's reputation. ...

24. In Mexican law, as in that of other countries, an accused cannot be convicted unless the Judge is convinced of his guilt and has acquired this view from legal evidence. An international tribunal never can replace the important first element, that of the Judge's being convinced of the accused's guilt; it can only in extreme cases, and then with great reserve, look into the second element, the legality and sufficiency of the evidence.

25. It has been alleged that among the grounds for Chattin's punishment was the fact that he had had conversations with Ramirez who had confessed to his own guilt. This allegation is erroneous; the conversations between two men only were cited to deny Chattin's contention made on July 13, 1910, that he had only seen Ramirez around the city at some time, without knowing where or when, and his contention made on July 9, 1910, to the effect that he did not remember Ramirez's name. It has been alleged that the testimony of Delgado and Sarabia merely applied to the anonymous passenger conductor on a certain train; but the record clearly states that the description given by these witnesses of the conductor's features coincided with Chattin's appearance, and that both formally recognized Chattin at their confrontation on November 17, 1910. Mention has been made, on the other hand, of a docket of evidence gathered by the railway company itself against some of its conductors; though it is not certain that the Court has been influenced by this evidence in considering the felony proven, it can scarcely have failed to work its influence on the penalty imposed.

26. From the record there is no convincing evidence that the proof against Chattin, scanty and weak though it may have been, was not such as to warrant a conviction. Under the article deemed applicable the medium penalty fixed by law was imposed, and deduction made of the seven months Chattin had passed in detention from July 1910, till February, 1911. It is difficult to understand the sentence unless it be assumed that the Court, for some reason or other, wished to punish him severely. The most acceptable explanation of this supposed desire would seem to be the urgent appeals made by the American chief manager of the railroad company concerned, the views expressed by him and contained in the record, and the dangerous collection of anonymous accusations which were not only inserted in the court record at the very last moment, but which were even quoted in the decision of February 6, 1911, as evidence to prove "illegal acts of the nature which forms the basis of this investigation." The allegation that the Court in this matter was biased against American citizens would seem to be contradicted by the fact that, together with the four Americans, five Mexicans were indicted as well, four of whom had been caught and have subsequently been convicted – that one of these Mexicans was punished as severely as the Americans were – and that the lower penalties imposed on the three others are explained by motives which, even if not shared, would seem reasonable. The fact that the Prosecuting Attorney who did not share the Judge's views applied merely for "insignificant penalties" – as the first decision establishes – shows, on the one hand, that he disagreed with the Court's wish to punish severely and with its interpretation of the Penal Code, but shows on the other hand that he also considered the evidence against Chattin a sufficient basis for his conviction. If Chattin's guilt was sufficiently proven, the small amount of the embezzlement (four pesos) need not in itself have prevented the Court from imposing a severe penalty. ...

29. Bringing the proceedings of Mexican authorities against Chattin to the test of international standards (paragraph 11), there can be no doubt of their being highly insufficient. Inquiring whether there is convincing evidence of these unjust proceedings (paragraph 11), the answer must be in the affirmative. Since this is a case of alleged responsibility of Mexico for injustice committed by its judiciary, it is necessary to inquire whether the treatment of Chattin amounts even to an outrage, to bad faith, to wilful neglect of duty, or to an insufficiency of governmental action recognizable by every unbiased man (paragraph 11); and the answer here again can only be in the affirmative.

30. An illegal arrest of Chattin is not proven. Irregularity of court proceedings is proven with reference to absence of proper investigations, insufficiency of confrontations, withholding from the accused the opportunity to know all of the charges brought against him, undue delay of the proceedings, making the hearings in open court a mere formality, and a continued absence of seriousness on the part of the Court. Insufficiency of the evidence against Chattin is not convincingly proven; intentional severity of the punishment is proven, without its being shown that the explanation is to be found in unfairmindedness of the Judge. Mistreatment in prison is not proven. Taking into consideration, on the one hand, that this is a case of direct governmental responsibility, and, on the other hand, that Chattin, because of his escape, has stayed in jail for eleven months instead of for two years, it would seem proper to allow in behalf of this claimant damages in the sum of $5,000.00, without interest. ...

The Commission decides that the Government of the United Mexican States is obligated to pay to the Government of the United States of America, on behalf of B.E. Chattin, $5,000.00 (five thousand dollars), without interest.

[Separate opinions of Nielsen and MacGregor, Commissioners, omitted.]

NOTES

1) Hackworth, in his *Digest of International Law*, described denials of justice thus:[29]

In a broad sense denial of justice may result from acts or omissions of authorities of any one or more of the three branches of government, *i.e.*, the executive, legislative, or judicial. There is a wide variance in the use of the term as is illustrated by the fact that some employ it to cover any delinquency on the part of an organ of the government resulting in injury to an alien, while others in employing the term restrict it to denial of access to judicial remedies. It is more frequently employed in connection with acts or omissions of the judicial branch, as distinguished from other branches of the government, since, generally speaking, exhaustion of available judicial remedies is a prerequisite to a valid complaint that the alien has been denied justice. Denial of justice may consist either of denial of access to the courts or of injustice at their hand. It may not be predicated solely on the fact that the decision of the court might have been different or that reasonable men might differ as to its correctness. Nations are considered to be equal, and with but few exceptions judgments of their courts of last resort are considered to be and are accepted as just and proper. There is, therefore, a strong presumption in favor of their correctness, and a complainant who bases his grievance upon an alleged denial of justice by the courts assumes the obligation of establishing by clear evidence that the presumption does not apply to his case. As a general proposition if the decision appears to have been unjust and is shown to have been influenced by improper motives; if corruption of the court is shown to have existed; or if there was prejudice or discrimination against the alien because of his nationality or against aliens generally; or if there was unconscionable delay by the court or other grave irregularities resulting in serious injustice; the foundation is laid for diplomatic representation or for international adjudication.

2) According to the report of a Sub-Committee of the League of Nations Committee of Experts for the Progressive Codification of International Law,[30] "Denial of Justice consists in refusing to allow foreigners easy access to the courts to defend those rights which the national law accords them. A refusal of the competent judge to exercise jurisdiction also constitutes a denial of justice."

---

[29] Vol. 5, at 526–27. See also A.H. Feller, *The Mexican Claims Commissions 1923–1934: A Study in the Law and Procedure of International Tribunals* (1935).

[30] (1926), 20 *Am. J. Int. L. Sp. Supp.* 177, at 202.

3) In the *Neer case*[31] Commissioner Nielsen thought it "useful and proper to apply the term denial of justice in a broader sense than that of a designation solely of a wrongful act on the part of the judicial branch of the government. I consider that a denial of justice may, broadly speaking, be properly regarded as the general ground of diplomatic intervention." A wider view is also expressed in the Harvard Draft Convention on the Responsibility of States for Damage Done in Their Territory to the Person or Property of Foreigners:[32]

Article 9

...Denial of justice exists when there is a denial, unwarranted delay or obstruction of access to courts, gross deficiency in the administration of judicial or remedial process, failure to provide those guarantees which are generally considered indispensable to the proper administration of justice, or a manifestly unjust judgment. An error of a national court which does not produce manifest injustice is not a denial of justice.

Misappropriation of Alien Property

Expropriation

There are few if any issues in international law today on which opinion seems to be so divided as the limitations on a state's power to expropriate the property of aliens. There is of course authority, in international judicial and arbitral decisions, in the expressions of national governments and among commentators for the view that a taking is improper under international law if it is not for a public purpose, is discriminatory, or is without provision for prompt, adequate and effective compensation. However, Communist countries, although they have in fact provided a degree of compensation after diplomatic efforts, commonly recognize no obligation on the part of the taking country. Certain representatives of the newly independent and underdeveloped countries have questioned whether rules of state responsibility toward aliens can bind nations that have not consented to them and it is argued that the traditionally articulated standards governing expropriation of property reflect "imperialist" interests and are inappropriate to the circumstances of emergent states.

The disagreement as to relevant international law standards reflects an even more basic divergence between the national interests of capital importing and capital exporting nations and between the social ideologies of those countries that favor state control of a considerable portion of the means of production and those that adhere to a free enterprise system. It is difficult to imagine the courts of this country embarking on adjudication in an area which touches more sensitively the practical and ideological goals of the various members of the community of nations.

---

[31] U.S. v. Mexico (1926), 4 R.I.A.A. 60, at 64.
[32] (1929), 23 *Am. J. Int. L. Sp. Supp.* 131, at 134.

So stated Mr. Justice Harlan in *Banco Nacional de Cuba v. Sabbatino*.[33]

In the 19th century the responsibility of a State for expropriation (or nationalization, which is merely a species of expropriation) was regarded as a clear basis for an international claim. At the present time the widening control by States over the national economy and over almost every aspect of private enterprise, and the measures of nationalization of different industries adopted by so many States make it difficult if not impossible to treat as contrary to international law an expropriation of foreign property based on grounds of public utility, security or the national interest in accordance with a declared policy applied without discrimination to the citizens of the expropriating State and to aliens alike.

However, if the expropriation measure is in violation of a treaty or of a special arrangement between the government and aliens, or of a recognized principle of international law, the measure then becomes *per se* a wrongful act which involves state responsibility. The expropriation measure itself is the wrongful act, rather than the non-performance of obligations arising out of the expropriation, such as the failure to compensate.

Today, it appears that the right of a state to expropriate foreign property for a public purpose related to its internal needs, is recognized by customary international law. However, expropriation measures that are arbitrary or discriminatory or which are motivated by considerations of a political nature unrelated to the internal well being of the taking state are illegal and invalid. What amounts to expropriation and whether compensation must be paid in accordance with international law are questions that are not yet settled. The traditional answers espoused by the United States, now reformulated in the revised *Restatement* of U.S. law, may be contrasted with the various U.N. documents on the same issues.

Restatement (Revised), Foreign Relations Law of the United States
(1987)

§712. Economic Injury to Nationals of Other States

A state is responsible under international law for injury resulting from:

1) a taking by the state of the property of a national of another state that is (a) not for a public purpose, or (b) discriminatory, or (c) not accompanied by provision for just compensation; for compensation to be just under this Subsection, it must, in the absence of exceptional circumstances, be in an amount equivalent to the value of the property taken, be paid at the time of taking, or within a reasonable time thereafter with interest from the date of taking, and be in a form economically usable by the foreign national;

2) a repudiation or breach by the state of a contract with a national of another state

(a) where the repudiation or breach is (i) discriminatory; or (ii) motivated by non-commercial considerations and compensatory damages are not paid; or

(b) where the foreign national is not given an adequate forum to determine his claim of breach or is not compensated for any breach determined to have occurred;

---

[33] (1964), 84 S.Ct. 923, at 940–1; 376 U.S. 398, at 428–50.

3) other arbitrary or discriminatory acts or omissions by the state that impair property or other economic interests of a national of another state.

NOTES

1) President Reagan has reiterated that:[34] ''Under international law no U.S. investment should be expropriated unless the taking (a) is done for a public purpose; (b) is accomplished under due process of law; (c) is non-discriminatory; (d) does not violate any previous contractual arrangements between the national or company concerned and the government making the expropriation; (e) is accompanied by prompt, adequate and effective compensation.''

2) In Canada, several aspects of the National Energy Program, especially the Crown share or back-in provision which gives the Canadian Crown the right to take retroactively a twenty-five percent share of existing exploration and production interests, may violate international law since the *Canada Oil and Gas Act*[35] provides no compensation to foreign investors deprived of that share.[36]

Resolution on Permanent Sovereignty over Natural Resources
U.N.G.A. Resolution 1803 (XVII), 17 U.N. GAOR,
Supp. (No. 17) 15; U.N. Doc. A/S217 (1962)

The General Assembly, ...
Declares that:
  1. The right of peoples and nations to permanent sovereignty over their natural wealth and resources must be exercised in the interest of their national development and of the well-being of the people of the State concerned. ...
  3. In cases where authorization is granted, the capital imported and the earnings on that capital shall be governed by the terms thereof, by the national legislation in force, and by international law. The profits derived must be shared in the proportions freely agreed upon, in each case, between the investors and the recipient State, due care being taken to ensure that there is no impairment, for any reason, of that State's sovereignty over its natural wealth and resources.
  4. Nationalization, expropriation or requisitioning shall be based on grounds or reasons of public utility, security or the national interest which are recognized as overriding purely individual or private interests, both domestic and foreign. In such cases the owner shall

---

[34] Office of the White House Press Secretary, Statement by the President on International Investment Policy (1983).

[35] S.C. 1981, c. 81, s. 27.

[36] Ss. 61(2), 36(3), but see ss. 29 and 41. See E. Mendes, ''The Canadian National Energy Program: An Example of Assertion of Economic Sovereignty or Creeping Expropriation in International Law'' (1981), 14 *Vanderbilt J. Trans. L.* 475; C. Olmstead *et al.*, ''Expropriation in the Energy Industry: Canada's Crown Share Provision as a Violation of International Law'' (1984), 29 *McGill L. J.* 439.

be paid appropriate compensation, in accordance with the rules in force in the State taking such measures in the exercise of its sovereignty and in accordance with international law. In any case where the question of compensation gives rise to a controversy, the national jurisdiction of the State taking such measures shall be exhausted. However, upon agreement by sovereign States and other parties concerned, settlement of the dispute should be made through arbitration or international adjudication. ...

8. Foreign investment agreements freely entered into by or between sovereign States shall be observed in good faith; States and international organizations shall strictly and conscientiously respect the sovereignty of peoples and nations over their natural wealth and resources in accordance with the Charter and the principles set forth in the present resolution.

NOTES

The Resolution was adopted by 87 votes to 2 (France, South Africa) with twelve abstentions (Soviet Union and a number of socialist countries). As to whether the Resolution reflects the state of customary international law, see *Texaco v. Libya* reported below, especially para. 87.

Charter of Economic Rights and Duties of States
U.N.G.A. Resolution 3281 (XXIX), Dec. 12, 1974, 29 U.N. GAOR,
Supp. (No. 31) 50; U.N. Doc. A/9631 (1974), reported in full in Chapter 12

Article 2

1. Every State has and shall freely exercise full permanent sovereignty, including possession, use and disposal, over all its wealth, natural resources and economic activities.

2. Each State has the right:

(a) To regulate and exercise authority over foreign investment within its national jurisdiction in accordance with its laws and regulations and in conformity with its national objectives and priorities. No State shall be compelled to grant preferential treatment to foreign investment;

(b) To regulate and supervise the activities of transnational corporations within its national jurisdiction and take measures to ensure that such activities comply with its laws, rules and regulations and conform with its economic and social policies. Transnational corporations shall not intervene in the internal affairs of a host State. Every State should, with full regard for its sovereign rights, co-operate with other States in the exercise of the right set forth in this subparagraph;

(c) To nationalize, expropriate or transfer ownership of foreign property in which case appropriate compensation should be paid by the State adopting such measures, taking into account its relevant laws and regulations and all circumstances that the State considers pertinent. In any case where the question of compensation gives rise to a controversy, it shall be settled under the domestic law of the nationalizing State and by its tribunals, unless it is freely and mutually agreed by all States concerned that other peaceful means be sought on the basis of the sovereign equality of States and in accordance with the principle of free choice of means.

Article 16

1. It is the right and duty of all States, individually and collectively, to eliminate colonialism, *apartheid*, racial discrimination, neo-colonialism and all forms of foreign aggression, occupation and domination, and the economic and social consequences thereof, as a prerequisite for development. States which practise such coercive policies are economically responsible to the countries, territories and peoples affected for the restitution and full compensation for the exploitation and depletion of, and damages to, the natural and all other resources of those countries, territories and peoples. It is the duty of all States to extend assistance to them.

2. No State has the right to promote or encourage investments that may constitute an obstacle to the liberation of a territory occupied by force.

NOTES

1) The Charter was adopted by 120 votes to 6 with 10 abstentions. Negative votes were cast by Belgium, Denmark, the Federal Republic of Germany, Luxembourg, the United Kingdom and the United States. Abstaining were Austria, Canada, France, Ireland, Israel, Italy, Japan, the Netherlands, Norway and Spain.

2) The Canadian position was explained in a statement made in the Second Committee of the 29th Session of the U.N. General Assembly by the Canadian Representative on Dec. 6, 1974:[37]

My delegation does not deny the right of a state to nationalize foreign property but it does maintain that this right is conditional upon the payment of compensation. The question of what amount of compensation is just or equitable will naturally depend upon the particular circumstances of each individual case, but my delegation is unable to accept a text which seeks to establish the principle that a state may nationalize or expropriate foreign property without compensation, in effect to confiscate such property. This, in the view of my delegation, is the effect of paragraph 2(c) of Article 2.

I wish to refer now, Mr. Chairman, to an issue which constitutes one of the most important obstacles to my Delegation's support of the Charter as a whole, namely the absence of any reference in Article 2 to the applicability of international law to the treatment of foreign investment. There is, of course, a very relevant distinction between the body of law to be applied in the event of a

---

[37] Press Release No.43

dispute and the tribunal which is to apply that law. It is clear that, in the absence of a relevant acceptance of the compulsory jurisdiction of the International Court of Justice (in the case of disputes between states) or some other agreement between the parties respecting disputes settlement, jurisdiction in respect of a dispute rests with the appropriate tribunal of the host state.

This does not, however, alter the fact that the host state's measures must be carried out in conformity with its international legal obligations. There is, of course, disagreement among states over whether such obligations arise only from treaties or from principles of customary international law as well.

3) As to whether Article 2(2)(c) reflects the state of customary international law or constitutes only an emergent principle, see *Texaco v. Libya* reported below. Since the Charter is a resolution of the General Assembly, it can have legal force only if, and so far as it declares or restates existing principles or rules of international law.

4) Note that Article 2(2)(c) adopts the term "appropriate" compensation from resolution 1803 (XVII).

5) What is meant by the phrase that "compensation should be paid ... taking into account ... all circumstances that the state considers pertinent"? Does it mean that national treatment need not be offered to foreign investors?

6) Should the following circumstances be taken into consideration in order to reduce or eliminate the compensation to be paid: the nature of the circumstances in which the foreign investment was made, the real enrichment of the expropriating state, excessive profits, unpaid taxes, questionable financial practices, environmental damage and employee benefits?

7) What is the relevance of Article 16 to the interpretation of Article 2(2)(c)?

Measure of Compensation
from I.L.C. Working Paper (XIV)/ SCI/Wp1 (1962)

[In this working paper submitted to the International Law Commission in 1962, Professor Jimenez de Arechaga examined the general rules of international law which, in the absence of specific treaties, govern the international obligations imposed on a State as a consequence of measures of nationalization affecting the property owned by foreign States, foreign individuals, or foreign companies.]

The claim for adequate, prompt and effective compensation

One position on the question under consideration is that general international law requires the State which has taken measures of nationalization affecting properties owned by foreigners, to accompany such measures by adequate, prompt and effective compensation. Such was, for instance, the position firmly maintained by the United States, in the diplomatic discussions which took place with Mexico, concerning the measures of nationalization of land and oil properties adopted by the latter country.

The main criticism levelled against this requirement of prompt and adequate compensation is that, although it may be applicable to individual expropriations, it would make it impossible to adopt basic reforms or to take nationalization measures on a wide scale and of a general and impersonal character. The Government of Mexico stated in its reply to the United States that "the transformation of a country, that is to say, the future of the nation, could not be halted by the impossibility of paying immediately the value of the properties belonging to a small number of foreigners who seek only a lucrative end." (Note from Eduardo Hay, Foreign Minister of Mexico, dated 3 August 1938, International Conciliation, No. 346, at 527.)

In some academic circles in the United States, an alternative has been proposed to the requirement of prompt compensation. The 1961 Harvard Research Draft Convention on the responsibility of States for damages caused to the person or property of foreigners, proposes, according to the traditional view in that country, that compensation must be prompt, adequate and effective. However, the draft admits that if property is taken by a State in furtherance of a general programme of economic and social reform, the just compensation *may be paid over a reasonable period of years*, in the form of bonds bearing a reasonable rate of interest. [(1961), 55 *Am. J. Int. L.* 545.] (For the rule referred to in the text and the corresponding comment, see 553–63.)

The practice of States confirms that in the case of nationalizations, the payment of deferred compensations has been offered and accepted even by countries affiliated to the traditional doctrine under consideration. ...

The thesis of the equality between nationals and foreigners

In the above referred diplomatic controversy between the United States and Mexico, the latter took the view that because of the complete equality between foreigners and nationals, the former could not claim compensation when it was not paid to the affected nationals.

"The foreigner who voluntarily moves to a country which is not his own, in search of a personal benefit, accepts in advance, together with the advantages which he is going to enjoy, the risks to which he may find himself exposed. It would be unjust that he should aspire to a privileged position safe from any risk, but availing himself, on the other hand, of the effort of the nationals which must be to the benefit of the collectivity." (Communication referred to in Note from Eduardo Hay, at 529–30.) ...

It has been observed in support of this view that in most cases the foreign capital invested in an under-developed country while it is exposed to greater risks, also obtains higher profits.

According to this doctrine, when an expropriation or nationalization measure affects adversely the rights of foreign subjects, those foreigners would possess no specific claim to compensation, other than that which may be recognized to nationals, such as the ordinary remedies conferred by municipal law before national tribunals. The responsibility of the State would only exist when there has been discrimination against the foreigners as such, because of xenophobic feelings or similar reasons. ...

The United States jurist Borchard made an argument against the theory of the community of fortune, pointing out that the equality of treatment of foreigners and nationals would be justified if they possessed exactly the same rights, but in fact foreigners are as a rule deprived of political rights, and as such they cannot influence the measures adopted by the Government, while nationals have such means of exerting influence over their Governments. ...

According to the doctrine of complete equality of treatment, the foreign subjects may be totally deprived of protection if the municipal law denies any right of compensation to nationals. Now, the question under consideration is to know whether there is an international law obligation to compensate for the taking of foreign-owned property. If such an obligation exists, it is obvious that it cannot be disregarded by the unilateral act of a State which under its municipal law denies compensation to its nationals. ...

The doctrine of equality of nationals and foreigners has not been followed in the recent practice of States. Even those States which have gone further in their nationalization policies, to the extent of denying a right to full compensation to the affected nationals, have discriminated in favour of foreign owned property, and their own nationalization laws admit the possibility of a greater protection for this foreign property.

The thesis that no compensation is due and its practical application

The Government of Mexico, in the above referred diplomatic controversy with the United States also held that "there is in international law no rule universally accepted in theory nor carried out in practice, which makes obligatory the payment of immediate compensation, nor even of deferred compensation, for expropriations of a general and impersonal character like those which Mexico has carried out for the purpose of redistribution of the land." (Note from Eduardo Hay, at 527).

A similar position had been taken by the Soviet Union at the Genoa Conference, where their representatives stated that the USSR "cannot be forced to assume any responsibility toward foreign powers and their nationals ... for the nationalization of private property." (Reply of the USSR delegation to memorandum of 2 May 1922, Saxon Mills, The Genoa Conference, at 409.)

In a recent book on the subject of nationalizations, by Konst. Katzarov, this position is justified on the ground that "integral nationalization leads in fact to the reparation of an injustice, and to the restitution in favour of the collectivity of what belongs to it, and therefore, it is not to be expected that the former owners should be indemnified." (Théorie de la Nationalisation (1960), at 421.)

However, this author, when examining the laws and practice followed on this matter by several Communist States points out that "many recent laws relating to nationalization show a tendency to look for a compromise ... in the sense that they reserve the possibility of granting a freshly negotiated indemnity. In acting in such a way, the conflicts which arise between the conception of the nationalizing State and the conceptions of the States interested in such a measure and affected by it, have been taken into account. ...This has an importance of principle in connection with the legitimation of the nationalization in International Law and indicates the desire felt by the nationalizing States of not coming in conflict against the international "ordre public." It is on this juridical basis that all the international agreements concerning the settlement of indemnities have been concluded. In all these cases, the indemnity has been determined independently of the level of indemnities of municipal law, and it is habitually a higher one. The negotiation, in those international agreements, of a superior compensation is not – or does not represent only – an economic or political compromise, but it is founded on the concrete provisions of the laws establishing the nationalization." (Katzarov, *op. cit.,* at 438.)

This writer adds: "those special provisions in the laws try precisely to make it possible to discuss the amount of the indemnities in the framework of international relations, in order to adapt the nationalization to the international 'ordre public': the legislator seems to have understood that it could not participate in an international discussion invoking as the only argument, its sovereign estimation of the indemnity and the denial of judicial control.'' (*Op. cit.*, at 452.)

Finally, this writer states that: ''The possibility of solving the questions arising from nationalizations, lies in the conclusion of an agreement between the nationalizing State and the States whose subjects are affected by the nationalization. From here it results that the procedure relating to this settlement is transformed into a State to State question. In the majority of cases it is in this way that have been settled after the second world war the relations established by the nationalizations with foreign subjects. A State may always claim that the rules of international law are observed with respect to its subjects, and, in particular, that the right to an appropriate indemnization be recognized in case of nationalization. The evolution of international life leads to more and more frequent use of the negotiation between States of a global compensation, and the hope is often expressed that this procedure should be improved.'' (*Op. cit.*, at 453, 455, 456).

The global compensation agreements

After the second world war it has become a widespread practice to settle the international questions arising from nationalization measures in global compensation agreements, the so-called ''lump-sum'' agreements, of which there had also been some examples in the past. (See Whiteman, Damages in International Law, vol. III, at 2063 and Christensen in (1961), 55 *Am. J. of Int. L.* 617–18.)

Through these agreements, the State which has adopted nationalization measures pays a global amount as compensation to the State of nationality of the affected owners of nationalized property. In order to determine the amount of compensation, account is taken, totally or partially, of the different individual claims arising on the same grounds, i.e., on the nationalization measures, although such claims are presented jointly by the claimant State. This State, as a ''*quid-pro-quo*'' of the compensation received, declares in its own name and in that of its nationals, that all claims which arise from such nationalization measures, become extinguished or cancelled.

These agreements do not provide in all cases for full or even adequate compensation and often they only represent a percentage of the existing claims. (See Christensen, *op. cit.*, at 622, and Foighel, *op. cit.*, at 117, Asian-African Legal Consultative Committee, Report of the fourth session, at 142–43.) Very often such ''en bloc'' agreements allow for the indemnization being paid over a number of years. (The agreement between Poland and the United States provided for the payment of 40 millions of U.S. dollars in 20 annual instalments from 1961. Rode, in (1961), 55 *Am. J. of Int. L.* 455.) Finally, consideration may be taken of the financial capacity of the indemnifying State: for that purpose, they may be accompanied by the granting of credits or by commercial agreements designed to make it possible for the indemnifying State to meet the agreed payments.

On its part, the State receiving the global compensation may or may not distribute it among the affected individuals or companies ''*pro-rata*'' of the values received. In the first case, it is necessary for the damaged parties to submit their individual claims for consideration to organs set up under the municipal law of the State of their nationality. ...

All the above referred ''en bloc'' compensation-agreements, taken together, constitute a recognition by the various legal systems of the civilized world that the State which nationalizes foreign-owned property has, under general international law, a duty to compensate the State of nationality of those foreign owners. The amount and opportunity of such compensation cannot, however, be established on the basis of those treaties, constituting as they do in the majority of cases, *transactional settlements*.

This duty to compensate has been recognized and executed by the States involved in these questions, whatever may have been the position initially adopted with respect to the existence or inexistence of such a legal obligation.

The social and economic basis of this legal duty is obvious and it explains the different treatment given in practice to nationals and to foreigners. The mutual interest in the reestablishment of normal currents of international trade is a strong incentive for States to reach compensatory agreements, as soon as the friction originated by the adoption of the measures is overcome and the positions of principle publicly taken by the Foreign Offices have been forgotten.

Capital exporting countries have an obvious interest in favouring a rule of law which protects, at least to a certain extent, their own interests and those of their nationals abroad. And with regard to under-developed countries, although a first reaction might be to deny such an obligation, a more intelligent consideration of their long-range interests soon convinces them of the convenience to recognize and support such a rule, because there is a very strong possibility that, in its absence, the foreign investments which these countries need for their economic development, would not be made, at least at the same volume and rate of interest.

For such reasons, the rule that the nationalization of foreign owned property implies a duty to compensate operates in the well-understood self-interest of all states.

NOTES

1) Granted that compensation must be paid, is it to be adequate, prompt, and effective? The traditional legal basis for the claim that in the case of expropriation, adequate, prompt, and effective compensation should be paid to foreign owners is the principle of respect for acquired rights in general and for private property rights in particular. This principle no longer corresponds to present realities, since an important group of States deny the right of ownership of the means of production to individuals and private corporations. It is thus necessary to take into account the existence of different economic systems not in order to deny an obligation to compensate, which as pointed out previously continues to be valid, but to arrive at a legal foundation for such an obligation. Such legal foundations could be the principle of unjust enrichment.[38]

Some individuals, in this case aliens in a community, in consequence of no fault on their part, are being asked to make a sacrifice of their private property for the general welfare of the community, while other members of this community are not asked to make corresponding sacrifices. The compensation paid to the owners of the property taken

---

[38] See A.A. Fatouros, "Legal Security for International Investment," in W.G. Friedmann and R.C. Pugh eds., *Legal Aspects of Foreign Investment* (1959) 699, at 723.

represents precisely the corresponding contribution made by the rest of the community in order to equalize the financial incidence of the taking of individual property. The community has been enriched by the sacrifice of the individuals concerned and must compensate them for their impoverishment which was not shared by everyone. Thus what constitutes "fair," "just," or "adequate" compensation in any given case depends upon one's assessment of the actual benefit which has accrued to the community at large from the property taken, and the extent to which the rest of the community should share the sacrifice thus made by the former owners. Of course the compensation paid should not exceed the actual impoverishment of the former owners.

In the *Lena Goldfields Arbitrations*[39] compensation was given to prevent the unjust enrichment of the expropriating state.

2) It seems reasonable to support the view that a foreign creditor should agree to accept payment of compensation in instalments where he has a justified expectation of payments being adequate and effective. "Prompt" compensation does not necessarily mean payment in advance, but does imply payment within a reasonable period of time after the taking. In this connection the paying capacity of the debtor government should be taken into consideration as well as its enrichment. The amount of compensation should be reasonable and equitable, measured by the enrichment of the state, and effective in the sense that the compensation should be paid in a beneficial form which is of real economic value to the former owner. It is not the currency in which payment is effectuated that is decisive but rather its proper use. It is improper that compensation which has been promptly paid should be immediately frozen by foreign exchange laws precluding the removal of the compensation from the state granting it.

3) The standards of valuation to be used in order to establish the amount of compensation payable are quite numerous and at the present time there is no consensus as to which is the most appropriate. Some of these standards are: fair market value,[40] book value,[41] capitalization of expected benefits,[42] equitable restitution,[43] and forced sale value. Less than full value has been accepted in lump sum settlements with East European countries and in lowered book value settlements on an individual basis on behalf of the oil companies in the Middle East area.

Breach of Contract

Texaco v. Libya
(1977), 53 I.L.R. 389; 17 *Int. Leg. Mat.* 1

[By a series of decrees in 1973 and 1974 the Libyan government nationalized the rights and property of the two plaintiff oil companies, Texaco and California Asiatic, in Libya.

---

[39] (1929–30), 5 Ann. Dig. 3.

[40] See for instance, s. 24(2) of *Expropriation Act*, R.S.C. 1970, c. 16, 1st Supp., as am.

[41] J.S. McCosker, "Book Values in Nationalization Settlements," in R.B. Lillich, *The Valuation of Nationalized Property in International Law* (1973), vol. 2, at 36.

[42] D.R. Weigel and B.H. Weston, "Valuation upon the Deprivation of Foreign Enterprise: A Policy-Oriented Approach to the Problem of Compensation under International Law," in R.B. Lillich, *supra*, n.41, vol. 1, at 3.

[43] D.A. Lapres, "Principles of Compensation for Nationalized Property" (1977), 26 *Int. Comp. L.Q.* 97.

The companies claimed this action breached their Deeds of Concession from the government and they sought arbitration, as was their right under those deeds. Libya opposed the appointment of an arbitrator, claiming its acts of nationalization were not subject to arbitration because they were acts of sovereignty, and it took no further part in the case. A major task in the arbitration was to determine the governing law. Clause 28 of the Deeds of Concession expressed a choice of applicable law:

This concession shall be governed by and interpreted in accordance with the principles of the Law of Libya common to the principles of international law and in the absence of such common principles then by and in accordance with the general principles of law, including such of those principles as may have been applied by international tribunals.

In his interpretation of this clause, Professor Rene Dupuy, the sole arbitrator, considered the process and consequences of what he called the "internationalization" of concession agreements.]

AWARD OF THE ARBITRATOR: ...

40. ... the internationalization of contracts entered into between States and foreign private persons can result in various ways which it is now time to examine.

41. ... At the outset, it is accepted that the reference made by the contract, in the clause concerning the governing law, to the general principles of law leads to this result. These general principles, being those which are mentioned in Article 38 of the Statute of the International Court of Justice, are one of the sources of international law: they may appear alone in the clause or jointly with a national law, particularly with the law of the contracting State.

In the present dispute, general principles of law have a subsidiary role in the governing law clause and apply in the case of lack of conformity between the principles of Libyan law and the principles of international law: but precisely the expression "principles of international law" is of much wider scope than "general principles of law," because the latter contribute with other elements (international custom and practice which is accepted by the law of nations) to constitute what is called the "principles of international law." To take the same terms used by the Permanent Court of International Justice in its judgment in the *"Lotus"* case ([1927] P.C.I.J., No. 10, Ser. A, at 16): the meaning of the "words 'principles of international law', as ordinarily used, can only mean international law as it is applied between all nations belonging to the community of States." Now, these principles of international law must, in the present case, be the standard for the application of Libyan law since it is only if Libyan law is in conformity with international law that it should be applied. Therefore, the reference which is made mainly to the principles of international law and, secondarily, to the general principles of law must have as a consequence the application of international law to the legal relations between the parties. ...

42. International arbitration case law confirms that the reference to the general principles of law is always regarded to be a sufficient criterion for the internationalization of a contract. ...

It should be noted that the invocation of the general principles of law does not occur only when the municipal law of the contracting state is not suited to petroleum problems. ... It is also justified by the need for the private contracting party to be protected against unilateral and abrupt modifications of the legislation in the contracting State: it plays, therefore, an important role in the contractual equilibrium intended by the parties. ...

44. ... Another process for the internationalization of a contract consists in inserting a clause providing that possible differences which may arise in respect of the interpretation and the performance of the contract shall be submitted to arbitration.

Such a clause has a twofold consequence:

– on the one hand ... the institution of arbitration shall be that established by international law.

– on the other hand, as regards the law applicable to the merits of the dispute itself, the inclusion of an arbitration clause leads to a reference to the rules of international law.

Even if one considers that the choice of international arbitration proceedings cannot by itself lead to the exclusive application of international law, it is one of the elements which makes it possible to detect a certain internationalization of the contract. The *Sapphire International Petroleum Ltd.* award is quite explicit: "If no positive implication can be made from the arbitral clause, it is possible to find there a negative intention, namely to reject the exclusive application of Iranian law" (35 *Int'l L.R.* 136 (1963), at 172): this is what led the arbitrator in that case, in the absence of any explicit reference to the law applicable, not to apply automatically Iranian law, thus dismissing any presumption in its favor. It is therefore unquestionable that the reference to international arbitration is sufficient to internationalize a contract, in other words, to situate it within a specific legal order – the order of the international law of contracts.

45. ... A third element of the internationalization of the contracts in dispute results from the fact that it takes on a dimension of a new category of agreements between States and private persons: economic development agreements. ...

Several elements characterize these agreements: in the first place, their subject matter is particularly broad: they are not concerned only with an isolated purchase or performance, but tend to bring to developing countries investments and technical assistance, particularly in the field of research and exploitation of mineral resources, or in the construction of factories on a turnkey basis. Thus, they assume a real importance in the development of the country where they are performed: it will suffice to mention here the importance of the obligations assumed in the case under consideration by the concession holders in the field of road and port infrastructures and the training on the spot of qualified personnel. The party contracting with the State was thus associated with the realization of the economic and social progress of the host country.

In the second place, the long duration of these contracts implies close cooperation between the State and the contracting party and requires permanent installations as well as the acceptance of extensive responsibilities by the investor.

Finally, because of the purpose of the cooperation in which the contracting party must participate with the State and the magnitude of the investments to which it agreed, the contractual nature of this type of agreement is reinforced: the emphasis on the contractual nature of the legal relation between the host State and the investor is intended to bring about an equilibrium between the goal of the general interest sought by such relation and the profitability which is necessary for the pursuit of the task entrusted to the private enterprise. The effect is also to ensure to the private contracting party a certain stability which is justified by the considerable investments which it makes in the country concerned. The investor must in particular be protected against legislative uncertainties, that is to say the risks of the municipal law of the host country being modified, or against any government measures which would lead to an abrogation or rescission of the contract. Hence, the insertion, as in the present case, of so-called stabilization clauses: these clauses tend to remove all or part of the agreement from the internal law and to provide for its correlative submission to *sui generis* rules as stated in the *Aramco* award, or to a system which is properly an international law system. From this latter point of view, the following considerations should be noted, which were mentioned in the *Sapphire* award, and which stress the interest of the internationalization of the contract:

Such a solution seems particularly suitable for giving the guarantees of protection which are indispensable for foreign companies, since these companies undergo very considerable risks in bringing financial and technical aid to countries in the process of development. It is in the interest of both parties to such agreements that any disputes between them should be settled according to the general principles universally recognized and should not be subject to the particular rules of national laws. ... (35 *Int'l L.R.* 136 (1963), at 175-76.)

C. *Meaning and scope of the internationalization of the contracts in dispute*
46. The Tribunal must specify the meaning and the exact scope of internationalization of a contractual relationship so as to avoid any misunderstanding: indeed to say that international law governs contractual relations between a State and a foreign private party neither means that the latter is assimilated to a State nor that the contract entered into with it is assimilated to a treaty.

This distinction is worth making, because the situation of individuals, and more generally private persons, in respect of international law, has recently been the subject matter of important doctrinal debates on the occasion of which excessive positions sometimes may have been stated. Thus, for some:

The rules of economic international law concern not only States but directly the individuals; because economic and social progress has as its objective to assure its direct application to those concerned. The result is that individuals are directly the subjects of economic or social international law. (P. Vellas, 1 *Droit International Economique et Social* (1965), at 30.)

47. This Tribunal will abstain from going that far: it shall only consider as established today the concept that legal international capacity is not solely attributable to a State and that international law encompasses subjects of a diversified nature. If States, the original subjects of the international legal order, enjoy all the capacities offered by the latter, other subjects enjoy only limited capacities which are assigned to specific purposes. The proposition which has just been stated is in conformity with the statement by the International Court of Justice in its *Advisory Opinion on Reparations of 11 April 1949* under which "the subjects of law, in any legal system, are not necessarily identical in their nature or in the extent of their rights and their nature depends on the needs of the community" ([1949] I.C.J. 174, at 178). In other words, stating that a contract between a State and a private person falls within the international legal order means that for the purposes of interpretation and performance of the contract, it should be recognized that a private contracting party has specific international capacities. But, unlike a State, the private person has only a limited capacity and his quality as a subject of international law does enable him only to invoke, in the field of international law, the rights which he derives from the contract. ...

50. The Tribunal must in this respect make two observations in order to clarify the scope of the internationalization of the contracts in dispute:

– in the first place, the national law (that is: the principles of Libyan law) can be raised to the level of the international legal order: in other words, the national law is incorporated into the international legal order as a body of substantive law ("règles matérielles"), by reason of its normative content which becomes a set of rules to be applied by the International Tribunal. The grounds of its applicability does not result from the automatic operation of the sovereignty of the contracting State, but from the common will of the parties: the national law of the contracting State is therefore regarded as *lex contractus* by incorporation. This is what Professor Weil expressed in the following terms ("Les Clauses de Stabilisation ou d'Intangibilité Insérées dans les Accords de Développement Economique," in Mélanges Offerts à Charles Rousseau 301 (1975), at 319-20):

... Municipal law does not therefore apply in itself but as a law of renvoi. The presence in the contract of a provision referring to the municipal law of the host State does not therefore necessarily mean that internationalization must be ruled out: if such internationalization results from the other characteristics of the contract – and this is the case with most economic development agreements – the contract will nonetheless be internationalized, and national law will therefore be applicable as a law of renvoi on the basis of the choice of the parties as authorized by the international law applicable in the field of contracts. ...

– in the second place, the municipal law of the contracting State itself includes principles of international law: every municipal law is a vehicle for the general principles of law as provided for under Article 38 of the Statute of the International Court of Justice. Under this generic name of general principles of law, reference is made in fact to certain principles common to the legal systems of the various States of the world. They constitute a source of international law which originates in the various municipal laws: therefore, the application of municipal law does not exclude the application of the general principles of law which themselves are part and parcel of the principles of international law.

51. Applying the principles stated above, the Arbitral Tribunal will refer:

(1) On the one hand, as regards the principles of Libyan law: regardless of the source of Libyan law taken into consideration, whether we refer to the Sharia, the Sacred Law of Islam (a special reference should be made to Surah 5 of the Koran which begins with the verse: "O ye believers, perform your contracts!") or to the Libyan Civil Code which includes on this point two basic articles illustrating the value which Libyan law attaches to the principle of the respect of the word given:

–Article 147, under which "The contract makes the law of the parties. It can be revoked or altered only by mutual consent of the parties or for reasons provided by the law";

– Article 148, under which "A contract must be performed in accordance with its contents and in compliance with the requirements of good faith," one is led to the same conclusion, that is: that Libyan law recognizes and sanctions the principle of the binding force of contracts.

(2) On the other hand, as regards the principles of international law: from this second point of view, it is unquestionable, as written by Professor Jessup in concluding his opinion (at 71) that the maxim " 'pacta sunt servanda' is a general principle of law; it is an essential foundation of international law."

No international jurisdiction whatsoever has ever had the least doubt as to the existence, in international law, of the rule *pacta sunt servanda*: it has been affirmed vigorously both in the *Aramco* award in 1958 and in the *Sapphire* award in 1963. One can read, indeed, in the *Sapphire* award, that "it is a fundamental principle of law, which is constantly being proclaimed by international Courts, that contractual undertakings must be respected. The rule 'pacta sunt servanda' is the basis of every contractual relationship" (35 Int'l L.R. 136 (1963), at 181). This Tribunal cannot but reaffirm this in its turn by stating that the maxim *pacta sunt servanda* should be viewed as a fundamental principle of international law.

52. The conformity, on this essential point, of the principles of Libyan law with the principles of international law relieves the Tribunal from discussing the matter further – in particular from going to the second part provided for subsidiarily in Clause 28 of the Deeds of Concession – and enables it to conclude that the Deeds of Concession in dispute have a binding force.

SECTION II: Did the Libyan Government, in adopting the nationalization measures of 1973 and 1974, breach its obligations under the contracts?

53. The Tribunal must now rule on the point whether, in adopting nationalization measures in 1973 and 1974, the defendant Government has, or has not, breached its obligations arising from the contracts it executed. For this purpose, this Tribunal should examine the various reasons which could be envisaged in order to justify the defendant Government's behavior and which, if established, would constitute reasons for freeing or exonerating it from the obligation which it had assumed and from its related responsibilities.

Three types of reasons could be put forward in order to justify, or attempt to justify, the behavior of the defendant Government: ...

– the second reason could be based on the concept of sovereignty and on the very nature of measures of nationalization;

– the third reason, lastly, could be deduced from the present status of international law, and in particular from certain resolutions concerning natural resources and wealth as adopted, in the last few years, by the United Nations. ...

B. *The concept of sovereignty and the nature of measures of nationalization*

58. Prior to any consideration concerning nationalizations, it is necessary to rule in respect of an objection raised by the defendant: in the Memorandum addressed to the President of the International Court of Justice on 26 July 1974, the Libyan Government contended in effect that the plaintiff companies could not invoke the procedure provided for in Clause 28 of the Deeds of Concession on the ground that nationalization terminated not only the agreement which linked them to the Libyan State, but also their legal status. This Tribunal cannot regard nationalization measures as having such a radical effect.

Although they concern the total assets of the companies located within the territory of the State which nationalizes, such nationalizations cannot purport to destroy the existence of these companies as legal entities.

It should be observed, at the outset, that such a claim can only have the value of a *petitio principii*, since it tends to nullify the clauses of the contract relating to the settlement of disputes, clauses which this Tribunal has concluded survived any denunciation or abrogation of contractual links by reason of the inherent juridical nature of such provisions and taking account of the case law in the matter. Furthermore, it is a well-known rule that nationalizations do not, in principle, produce any extra-territorial effect and that they cannot, in any case, impair or affect the existence of companies as legal entities which do not have the nationality of the nationalizing State.

59. This being so, the right of a State to nationalize is unquestionable today. It results from international customary law, established as the result of general practices considered by the international community as being the law. The exercise of the national sovereignty to nationalize is regarded as the expression of the State's territorial sovereignty. Territorial sovereignty confers upon the State an exclusive competence to organize as it wishes the economic structures of its territory and to introduce therein any reforms which may seem to be desirable to it. It is an essential prerogative of sovereignty for the constitutionally authorized authorities of the State to choose and build freely an economic and social system. International law recognizes that a State has this prerogative just as it has the prerogative to determine freely its political regime and its constitutional institutions. The exclusive nature of such a right is in fact confirmed by the fact that in practice a decision to nationalize very often is made by the organ which is regarded as the supreme level in the internal hierarchy of State institutions. ...

61. Even though, for a State, the decision of nationalizing is an expression of its sovereignty, which this Tribunal fully recognizes, does not the exercise of the right to nationalize know some limits in the international order? In particular, does the act of sovereignty which constitutes the nationalization authorize a State to disregard its international commitments assumed by it within the framework of its sovereignty?

It is clear from an international point of view that it is not possible to criticize a nationalization measure concerning nationals of the State concerned, or any measure affecting aliens in respect of whom the State concerned has made no particular commitment to guarantee and maintain their position. On the assumption that the nationalizing State has concluded with a foreign company a contract which stems from the municipal law of that State and is completely governed by that law the resolution of the new situation created by nationalization will be subject to the legal and administrative provisions then in force.

62. But the case is totally different where the State has concluded with a foreign contracting party an internationalized agreement, either because the contract has been subjected to the municipal law of the host country, viewed as a mere law of reference, applicable as of the effective date of the contract, and "stabilized" on that same date by specific clauses, or because it has been placed directly under the aegis of international law. Under these two assumptions, the State has placed itself within the international legal order in order to guarantee vis-à-vis its foreign contracting party a certain legal and economic status over a certain period of time. In consideration for this commitment, the partner is under an obligation to make a certain amount of investments in the country concerned and to explore and exploit at its own risks the petroleum resources which have been conceded to it.

Thus, the decision of a State to take nationalizing measures constitutes the exercise of an internal legal jurisdiction but carries international consequences when such measures affect international legal relationships in which the nationalizing State is involved. ...

68. Lastly, and without prejudice to anything which may be said later as to the legal value of the Resolutions of the General Assembly of the United Nations, it should be noted that dismissing the objections made by certain delegations, this body has stated in Resolution 1803, dated 14 December 1962, on the permanent sovereignty over natural resources, that "[f]oreign investment agreements freely entered into by, or betweeen, sovereign States shall be observed in good faith. ..." Thus, this text places on the same footing agreements entered into between States and agreements concluded by a State and foreign private enterprises.

The result is that a State cannot invoke its sovereignty to disregard commitments freely undertaken through the exercise of this same sovereignty and cannot, through measures belonging to its internal order, make null and void the rights of the contracting party which has performed its various obligations under the contract.

This impossibility of nullifying, in the name of the sovereignty of the State, a bilateral agreement to which the State could only commit itself within the framework of its own sovereignty, is recognized by legal writers: ...

69. Such is the present state of international positive law. The fact that various nationalization measures in disregard of previously concluded agreements have been accepted in fact by those who were affected, either private companies or by the States of which they were nationals, cannot be interpreted as recognition by international practice of such a rule; the amicable settlements which have taken place having been inspired basically by considerations of expediency and not of legality. Nothing prohibits the parties involved in a nationalization, that is the parties which promulgated the measures as well as those affected, from negotiating a new agreement leading to a new legal status.

70. It is therefore necessary to examine in the light of these principles whether the nationalization measures decreed by the Libyan Government with respect to the plaintiffs disregard any specific commitment undertaken by that Government, a commitment which should have been sufficient to protect the plaintiffs from such a decision.

The Deeds of Concession entered into by the parties do not include any provision by which the Libyan Government limited its recourse to nationalization. However, Clause 16 of the Deeds of Concession contains a stabilization clause with respect to the rights of the concession holder. As consideration for the economic risks to which the foreign contracting parties were subjected, the Libyan State granted them a concession of a minimum duration of 50 years and, more specifically, containing a non-aggravation clause, Clause 16, which provided:

The Government of Libya will take all steps necessary to ensure that the company enjoys all the rights conferred by this concession. The contractual rights expressly created by this concession shall not be altered except by mutual consent of the parties.

Another paragraph was added to this provision under the Royal Decree of December 1961 and became an integral part of the contract on the basis of the Agreement of 1963. It provides:

This Concession shall throughout the period of its validity be construed in accordance with the Petroleum Law and the Regulations in force on the date of execution of the agreement of amendment by which this paragraph (2) was incorporated into the concession agreement. Any amendment to or repeal of such Regulations shall not affect the contractual rights of the Company without its consent.

71. Such a provision, the effect of which is to stabilize the position of the contracting party, does not, in principle, impair the sovereignty of the Libyan State. Not only has the Libyan State freely undertaken commitments but also the fact that this clause stabilizes the petroleum legislation and regulations as of the date of the execution of the agreement does not affect in principle the legislative and regulatory sovereignty of Libya. Libya reserves all its prerogatives to issue laws and regulations in the field of petroleum activities in respect of national or foreign persons with which it has not undertaken such a commitment. Clause 16 only makes such acts invalid as far as contracting parties are concerned – with respect to whom this commitment has been undertaken – during the period of applicability of the Deeds of Concession. Any changes which may result from the adoption of new laws and regulations must, to affect the contracting parties, be agreed to by them. This is so not because the sovereignty of Libya would be reduced, but simply by reason of the fact that Libya has, through an exercise of its sovereignty, undertaken commitments under an international agreement, which, for its duration, is the law common to the parties.

Thus, the recognition by international law of the right to nationalize is not sufficient ground to empower a State to disregard its commitments, because the same law also recognizes the power of a State to commit itself internationally, especially by accepting the inclusion of stabilization clauses in a contract entered into with a foreign private party. ...

73. Thus, in respect of the international law of contracts, a nationalization cannot prevail over an internationalized contract, containing stabilization clauses, entered into between a State and a foreign private company. The situation could be different only if one were to conclude that the exercise by a State of its right to nationalize places that State on a level outside of and superior to the contract and also to the international legal order itself, and constitutes an ''act of government'' (''acte de gouvernement'') which is beyond the scope of any judicial redress or any criticism. ...

C. *The present state of international law and the resolutions concerning natural resources and wealth adopted by the United Nations*

80. This Tribunal has stated that it intends to rule on the basis of positive law, but now it is necessary to determine precisely the content of positive law and to ascertain the place which resolutions by the General Assembly of the United Nations could occupy therein.

In its Preliminary Award of 27 November 1973, this Tribunal postponed the examination of the objection raised by the Libyan Government in its Memorandum of 26 July 1974 according to which:

Nationalization is an act related to the sovereignty of the State. This fact has been recognized by the consecutive Resolutions of the United Nations on the sovereignty of States over their natural resources, the last being Resolution No. 3171 of the United Nations General Assembly adopted on December 13, 1973, as well as paragraph (4/E) of Resolution No. 3201 (S. VI) adopted on 1 May, 1974. The said Resolutions confirm that every State maintains complete right to exercise full sovereignty over its natural resources and recognize Nationalization as being a legitimate and internationally recognized method to ensure the sovereignty of the State upon such resources. Nationalization, being related to the sovereignty of the State, is not subject to foreign jurisdiction. Provisions of the International Law do not permit a dispute with a State to be referred to any Jurisdiction other than its national Jurisdiction. In affirmance of this principle, Resolutions of the General Assembly provide that any dispute related to Nationalization or its consequences should be settled in accordance with provisions of domestic law of the State.

81. At the stage of the Preliminary Award, it was premature to go into these arguments, since they were related to the merits of the case. Now, this Tribunal must examine the relevancy and the scope of these arguments to the instant case.

The practice of the United Nations, referred to in the Libyan Government's Memorandum, does not contradict in any way the status of international law as indicated above. This Tribunal wishes first to recall the relevant passages for this case of Resolution 1803 (XVII) entitled "Permanent Sovereignty over Natural Resources," as adopted by the General Assembly on 14 December 1962: (see *supra*) ...

82. The Memorandum of the Libyan Government which has just been quoted relies, however, on more recent Resolutions of the General Assembly (3171 and 3201 (S-VI), in particular) which, according to this Government would as a practical matter rule out any recourse to international law and would confer an exclusive and unlimited competence upon the legislation and courts of the host country.

Although not quoted in the Libyan Memorandum, since subsequent to the date of 26 July 1974, Resolution 3281 (XXIX), proclaimed under the title "Charter of Economic Rights and Duties of the States" and adopted by the General Assembly on 12 December 1974, should also be mentioned with the two Resolutions in support of the contention made by the Libyan Government. Two portions of such Resolutions are of particular interest in the present case:

–Resolution 3201 (S-VI) adopted by the General Assembly on 1 May 1974 under the title "Declaration on the Establishment of a New International Economic Order," Article 4, paragraph (e):

Full permanent sovereignty of every State over its natural resources and all economic activities. In order to safeguard these resources, each State is entitled to exercise effective control over them and their exploitation with means suitable to its own situation, including the right to nationalization or transfer of ownership to its nationals, this right being an expression of the full permanent sovereignty of the State. No State may be subjected to economic, political or any other type of coercion to prevent the free and full exercise of this inalienable right.

– Article 2 of Resolution 3281 (XXIX) [reproduced *supra*] ...

Substantial differences thus exist between Resolution 1803 (XVII) and the subsequent Resolutions as regards the role of international law in the exercise of permanent sovereignty over natural resources. This aspect of the matter is directly related to the instant case under consideration; this Tribunal is obligated to consider the legal validity of the above-mentioned Resolutions and the possible existence of a custom resulting therefrom.

83. The general question of the legal validity of the Resolutions of the United Nations has been widely discussed by the writers. This Tribunal will recall first that, under Article 10 of the U.N. Charter, the General Assembly only issues "recommendations," which have long appeared to be texts having no binding force and carrying no obligations for the Member States.

Refusal to recognize any legal validity of United Nations Resolutions must, however, be qualified according to the various texts enacted by the United Nations. These are very different and have varying legal value, but it is impossible to deny that the United Nations' activities have had a significant influence on the content of contemporary international law. In appraising the legal validity of the above-mentioned Resolutions, this Tribunal will take account of the criteria usually taken into consideration, i.e., the examination of voting conditions and the analysis of the provisions concerned.

84. (1) With respect to the first point, Resolution 1803 (XVII) of 14 December 1962 was passed by the General Assembly by 87 votes to 2, with 12 abstentions. It is particularly important to note that the majority voted for this text, including many States of the Third World, but also several Western developed countries with market economies, including the most important one, the United States. The principles stated in this Resolution were therefore assented to by a great many States representing not only all geographical areas but also all economic systems.

From this point of view, this Tribunal notes that the affirmative vote of several developed countries with a market economy was made possible in particular by the inclusion in the Resolution of two references to international law, and one passage relating to the importance of international cooperation for economic development. According to the representative of Tunisia:

...the result of the debate on this question was that the balance of the original draft resolution was improved – a balance between, on the one hand, the unequivocal affirmation of the inalienable right of States to exercise sovereignty over their natural resources and, on the other hand, the reconciliation or adaptation of this sovereignty to international law, equity and the principles of international cooperation. (17 U.N. GAOR 1122, U.N. Doc. A/PV. 1193 (1962).)

The reference to international law, in particular in the field of nationalization, was therefore an essential factor in the support given by several Western countries to Resolution 1803 (XVII).

85. On the contrary, it appears to this Tribunal that the conditions under which Resolutions 3171 (XXVII), 3201 (S-VI) and 3281 (XXIX) (Charter of the Economic Rights and Duties of States) were notably different:

– Resolution 3171 (XXVII) was adopted by a recorded vote of 108 votes to 1, with 16 abstentions, but this Tribunal notes that a separate vote was requested with respect to the paragraph in the operative part mentioned in the Libyan Government's Memorandum whereby the General Assembly stated that the application of the principle according to which nationalizations effected by States as the expression of their sovereignty implied that it is within the right of each State to determine the amount of possible compensation and the means of their payment, and that any dispute which might arise should be settled in conformity with the national law of each State instituting measures of this kind. As a consequence of a roll-call, this paragraph was adopted by 86 votes to 11 (Federal Republic of Germany, Belgium, Spain, United States, France, Israel, Italy, Japan, The Netherlands, Portugal, United Kingdom), with 23 abstentions (South Africa, Australia, Austria, Barbados, Canada, Ivory Coast, Denmark, Finland, Ghana, Greece, Haiti, India, Indonesia, Ireland, Luxembourg, Malawi, Malaysia, Nepal, Nicaragua, Norway, New Zealand, Philippines, Rwanda, Singapore, Sri Lanka, Sweden, Thailand, Turkey).

This specific paragraph concerning nationalizations, disregarding the role of international law, not only was not consented to by the most important Western countries, but caused a number of the developing countries to abstain.

– Resolution 3201 (S-VI) was adopted without a vote by the General Assembly, but the statements made by 38 delegates showed clearly and explicitly what was the position of each main group of countries. The Tribunal should therefore note that the most important Western countries were opposed to abandoning the compromise solution contained in Resolution 1803 (XVII).

– The conditions under which Resolution 3281 (XXIX), proclaiming the Charter of Economic Rights and Duties of States, was adopted also show unambiguously that there was no general consensus of the States with respect to the most important provisions and in particular those concerning nationalization. Having been the subject matter of a roll-call vote, the Charter was adopted by 118 votes to 6, with 10 abstentions.

The analysis of votes on specific sections of the Charter is most significant insofar as the present case is concerned. From this point of view, paragraph 2 (c) of Article 2 of the Charter, which limits consideration of the characteristics of compensation to the State and does not refer to international law, was voted by 104 to 16, with 6 abstentions, all of the industrialized countries with market economies having abstained or having voted against it.

86. Taking into account the various circumstances of the votes with respect to these Resolutions, this Tribunal must specify the legal scope of the provisions of each of these Resolutions for the instant case.

A first general indication of the intent of the drafters of the Charter of Economic Rights and Duties of States is afforded by the discussions which took place within the Working Group concerning the mandatory force of the future text. As early as the first session of the Working Group, differences of opinion as to the nature of the Charter envisaged gave rise to a very clear division between developed and developing countries. Thus, representatives of Iraq, Sri Lanka, Egypt, Kenya, Morocco, Nigeria, Zaire, Brazil, Chile, Guatemala, Jamaica, Mexico, Peru and Rumania held the view that the draft Charter should be a legal instrument of a binding nature and not merely a declaration of intention.

On the contrary, representatives of developed countries, such as Australia, France, Federal Republic of Germany, Italy, Japan, United Kingdom and United States expressed doubt that it was advisable, possible or even realistic to make the rights and duties set forth in a draft Charter binding upon States (Report of the Working Party on its 1st Session, U.N. Doc. TD/B/AC. 12/1 (1973), at 6).

The form of resolution adopted did not provide for the binding application of the text to those to which it applied, but the problem of the legal validity to be attached to the Charter is not thereby solved. In fact, while it is now possible to recognize that resolutions of the United Nations have a certain legal value, this legal value differs considerably, depending on the type of resolution and the conditions attached to its adoption and its provisions. Even under the assumption that they are resolutions of a declaratory nature, which is the case of the Charter of Economic Rights and Duties of States, the legal value is variable. Ambassador Castañeda, who was Chairman of the Working Group entrusted with the task of preparing this Charter, admitted that "it is extremely difficult to determine with certainty the legal force of declaratory resolutions," that it is "impossible to lay down a general rule in this respect," and that "the legal value of the declaratory resolutions therefore includes an immense gamut of nuances" ("La Valeur Juridique des Résolutions des Nations Unies," 129 R.C.A.D.I. 204 (1970), at 319-20).

As this Tribunal has already indicated, the legal value of the resolutions which are relevant to the present case can be determined on the basis of circumstances under which they were adopted and by analysis of the principles which they state:

– With respect to the first point, the absence of any binding force of the resolutions of the General Assembly of the United Nations implies that such resolutions must be accepted by the members of the United Nations in order to be legally binding. In this respect, the Tribunal notes that only Resolution 1803 (XVII) of 14 December 1962 was supported by a majority of Member States representing all of the various groups. By contrast, the other Resolutions mentioned above, and in particular those referred to in the Libyan Memorandum, were supported by a majority of States but not by any of the developed countries with market economies which carry on the largest part of international trade.

87. (2) With respect to the second point, to wit the appraisal of the legal value on the basis of the principles stated, it appears essential to this Tribunal to distinguish between those provisions stating the existence of a right on which the generality of the States has expressed agreement and those provisions introducing new principles which were rejected by certain representative groups of States and having nothing more than a *de lege ferenda* value only in the eyes of the States which have adopted them: as far as the others are concerned, the rejection of these same principles implies that they consider them as being *contra legem*. With respect to the former, which proclaim rules recognized by the community of nations, they do not create a custom but confirm one by formulating it and specifying its scope, thereby making it possible to determine whether or not one is confronted with a legal rule. As has been noted by Ambassador Castañeda, "[such resolutions] do not create the law: they have a declaratory nature of noting what does exist" (129 R.C.A.D.I. 204 (1970), at 315).

On the basis of the circumstances of adoption mentioned above and by expressing an *opinio juris communis*, Resolution 1803 (XVII) seems to this Tribunal to reflect the state of customary law existing in this field. Indeed, on the occasion of the vote on a resolution finding the existence of a customary rule, the States concerned clearly express their views. The consensus by a majority of States belonging to the various representative groups indicates without the slightest doubt universal recognition of the rules therein incorporated, *i.e.*, with respect to nationalization and compensation the use of the rules in force in the nationalizing State, but all this in conformity with international law.

88. While Resolution 1803 (XVII) appears to a large extent as the expression of a real general will, this is not at all the case with respect to the other Resolutions mentioned above, which has been demonstrated previously by analysis of the circumstances of adoption. In particular, as regards the Charter of Economic Rights and Duties of States, several factors contribute to denying legal value to those provisions of the document which are of interest in the instant case.

– In the first place, Article 2 of this Charter must be analyzed as a political rather than as a legal declaration concerned with the ideological strategy of development and, as such, supported only by non-industrialized States.

– In the second place, this Tribunal notes that in the draft submitted by the Group of 77 to the Second Commission (U.N. Doc. A/C. 2/L.1386 (1974), at 2), the General Assembly was invited to adopt the Charter "as a first measure of codification and progressive development" within the field of the international law of development. However, because of the opposition of several States, this description was deleted from the text submitted to the vote of the Assembly. This important modification led Professor Virally to declare:

It is therefore clear that the Charter is not a first step to codification and progressive development of international law, within the meaning of Article 13, para. 1 (a) of the Charter of the United Nations, that is to say an instrument purporting to formulate in writing the rules of customary law and intended to better adjust its content to the requirements of international relations. The persisting difference of opinions in respect to some of its articles prevented reaching this goal and it is healthy that people have become aware of this. ("La Charte des Droits et Devoirs Economiques des Etats. Notes de Lecture," 20 A.F.D.I. 57 (1974), at 59.)

The absence of any connection between the procedure of compensation and international law and the subjection of this procedure solely to municipal law cannot be regarded by this Tribunal except as a *de lege ferenda* formulation, which even appears *contra legem* in the eyes of many developed countries. Similarly, several developing countries, although having voted favorably on the Charter of Economic Rights and Duties of States as a whole, in explaining their votes regretted the absence of any reference to international law.

89. Such an attitude is further reinforced by an examination of the general practice of relations between States with respect to investments. This practice is in conformity, not with the provisions of Article 2 (c) of the above-mentioned Charter conferring exclusive jurisdiction on domestic legislation and courts, but with the exception stated at the end of this paragraph. Thus a great many investment agreements entered into between industrial States or their nationals, on the one hand, and developing countries, on the other, state, in an objective way, the standards of compensation and further provide, in case of dispute regarding the level of such compensation, the possibility of resorting to an international tribunal. In this respect, it is particularly significant in the eyes of this Tribunal that no fewer than 65 States, as of 31 October 1974, had ratified the Convention on the

Settlement of Investment Disputes between States and Nationals of other States, dated March 18, 1965.

90. The argument of the Libyan Government, based on the relevant resolutions enacted by the General Assembly of the United Nations, that any dispute relating to nationalization or its consequences should be decided in conformity with the provisions of the municipal law of the nationalizing State and only in its courts, is also negated by a complete analysis of the whole text of the Charter of Economic Rights and Duties of States.

From this point of view, even though Article 2 of the Charter does not explicitly refer to international law, this Tribunal concludes that the provisions referred to in this Article do not escape all norms of international law. Article 33, paragraph 2, of this Resolution states as follows: "2. In their interpretation and application, the provisions of the present Charter are interrelated and each provision should be construed in the context of the other provisions." Now, among the fundamental elements of international economic relations quoted in the Charter, principle (j) is headed as follows: "Fulfillment in good faith of international obligations."

Analyzing the scope of these various provisions, Ambassador Castañeda, who chaired the Working Group charged with drawing up the Charter of Economic Rights and Duties of States, formally stated that the principle of performance in good faith of international obligations laid down in Chapter I(j) of the Charter applies to all matters governed by it, including, in particular, matters referred to in Article 2. Following his analysis, this particularly competent and eminent scholar concluded as follows:

The Charter accepts that international law may operate as a factor limiting the freedom of the State should foreign interests be affected, even though Article 2 does not state this explicitly. This stems legally from the provisions included in other Articles of the Charter which should be interpreted and applied jointly with those of Article 2. ("La Charte des Droits et Devoirs Economiques des Etats. Note sur son Processus d'Elaboration." 20 A.F.D.I. 31 (1974), at 54.)

91. Therefore, one should note that the principle of good faith, which had already been mentioned in Resolution 1803 (XVII), has an important place even in Resolution 3281 (XXIX) called "The Charter of Economic Rights and Duties of States." One should conclude that a sovereign State which nationalizes cannot disregard the commitments undertaken by the contracting State: to decide otherwise would in fact recognize that all contractual commitments undertaken by a State have been undertaken under a purely permissive condition on its part and are therefore lacking of any legal force and any binding effect. From the point of view of its advisability, such a solution would gravely harm the credibility of States since it would mean that contracts signed by them did not bind them: it would introduce in such contracts a fundamental imbalance because in these contracts only one party – the party contracting with the State – would be bound. In law, such an outcome would go directly against the most elementary principle of good faith and for this reason it cannot be accepted.

SECTION III: Is the Libyan Government required to perform and give full effect to the Deeds of Concession?

92. It being admitted, as has previously been established, that the defendant Government, by adopting the nationalization measures promulgated in 1973 and 1974, has failed

3) It is clear that agreements between two sovereign states with respect to economic matters are international agreements governed by public international law. Contracts between nationals and corporations of the host state and foreign private investors, are private contracts governed by the law determined by the conflict of laws rules of either the host or foreign state. What is not clear is whether economic development contracts or concessions giving the right to exploit natural resources or to establish manufacturing industries between sovereign states and foreign private investors are international agreements or private contracts governed by public international law, the private law of the host or foreign state or general principles of law recognized by civilized nations. Can a state contract away its sovereignty, that is, its power to take unilateral action in the future? Has a private investor rights and duties under international law? It would seem that the basic question does not relate to sovereignty but to the nature of the obligation arising under the contract or concession. When a sovereign state contracts with an alien, it undertakes well-defined obligations, one of which is to respect the terms of the contract. Thus, if the contract is abrogated in the future by the host state, there is a breach of this obligation. Once it is determined that the contract has been broken according to the relevant applicable law, it is easy to link the breach with a violation of international law.

4) The sanctity of the state's contractual obligation could be based on the concepts of acquired or vested rights (the property rights acquired or vested under the law of the host state cannot be destroyed without compensation and are entitled to international protection), unjustified enrichment (the state unjustifiably enriched at the expense of the injured foreign investor is bound to make a just reparation), estoppel (the host state having enticed the foreign investor to act to his detriment cannot deny him recovery), abuse of rights (the host state cannot use its sovereign rights arbitrarily to the detriment of the foreign investor), or *pacta sunt servanda* (the host state is under a general obligation to observe and respect its contracts). These concepts are general principles of law recognized by civilized nations which are also sources of international law, as discussed in Chapter 3.

5) Economic development contracts or concessions may be legally abrogated or modified by virtue of the doctrine *rebus sic stantibus* (vital change of circumstances)[48], the passage of legislation for the protection of a *bona fide* public interest (health, safety, etc.), an express clause in the contract conferring that power on the host state in accordance with stipulated conditions, or as punishment for an offence against the criminal law of the host state (smuggling, tax evasion, breach of currency laws) provided these offences are recognized by international law or the practice of states, and the punishment is reasonable according to civilized standards and proportional to the offence committed.

Investment Protection Arrangements

As a result of the great rush of nationalizations in newly independent states during the previous two decades, most capital supplying states now provide some form of government

---

[48] Explained *supra* in Chapter 3.

sponsored insurance for the foreign investment of their nationals as a protection against expropriation. In outline, the Canadian arrangements are as follows.

Canadian Export Development Corporation[49]

Any person, partnership, corporation, government agency or other legal entity carrying on business or other activities in Canada planning a new investment in a foreign country can apply to the Export Development Corporation (EDC) for foreign investment insurance against certain defined political risks. The investment can be made directly in a foreign enterprise or indirectly through a related company based in Canada, the host country or even a third country. The Foreign Investment Insurance Service offers contracts of insurance covering the following three categories of political risks:

  (i) Inconvertibility
 (ii) Expropriation
(iii) War, Revolution and Insurrection.

The investor can apply for a contract covering any or all, or any combination of these three risks.

Insurance is available only for new investments. This limitation arises from a basic statutory purpose of the programme which is to facilitate the movement of Canadian goods and services abroad and, in addition, to utilize Canadian capital and skills in a manner which contributes to the economic and social progress of Canada as well as the host countries. However, a new investment can include a significant expansion, modernization or development of an existing enterprise. Additionally, investments in oil and mineral exploration and development are eligible for insurance coverage.

Investments which are clearly ineligible for insurance coverage include loans to foreign governments, portfolio investments, investments solely in land, short-term investments and investments which do not result in immediate or future benefits to Canada.

The investment must be of some economic advantage to Canada such as promoting the sale of capital goods and services abroad, the development and preservation of foreign markets, the earnings of foreign exchange or the securing of sources of raw materials not available in Canada. To be eligible under the program, new investments must also be of economic advantage to the host country and meet with host government approval.

Canada has also entered into bilateral agreements in respect of investments insured by EDC. These agreements specifically state that suitable arrangements are in effect through which EDC, if the need arises, would be subrogated to an insured investor's property and rights existing in the host country as protected by an EDC guarantee. Here is an example.

Canada-Indonesia Foreign Investment Insurance Agreement
1973 Can. T.S. No. 32

1. In the event of payment by the Export Development Corporation, as the agency of the Government of Canada for investment insurance purposes, under a contract of

---

[49] See Export Development Corporation Act, R.S.C. 1970, c. E-18, as am., s. 34. For a fuller consideration, see J.-G. Castel, A.L.C. de Mestral and W.C. Graham, *International Business Transactions and Economic Relations* (1986), at 371.

insurance with Canadian private investors operating in the territory of the Republic of Indonesia for any loss or damage sustained in connection with such Canadian investments, for which a document of admission has been issued by the Government of the Republic of Indonesia, by reason of:

(a) any action by the Government of the Republic of Indonesia, that prohibits or restricts transfer of any money to which a Canadian investor is entitled pursuant to the prevailing laws and regulations of the Republic of Indonesia;

(b) nationalization/revocation of ownership rights of Canadian investors, restrictions of the rights of control and/or management of the investments concerned by the Government of the Republic of Indonesia or its agency thereof;

(c) war, riot, insurrection, revolution or rebellion in the territory of the Republic of Indonesia, notwithstanding the right of the Republic of Indonesia to limit its liability in such circumstances and responsibilities thereof are accepted by the Government of the Repulic of Indonesia;

the said Corporation, hereinafter called the "INSURING AGENCY", shall be authorized by the Government of the Republic of Indonesia to exercise the rights having been lawfully devolved on it, or having been assigned to it by the predecessor in title.

2. To the extent that the laws and regulations of the Republic of Indonesia partially or wholly invalidate the acquisition of any interest in any property within its national territory by the Insuring Agency, the Government of the Republic of Indonesia shall permit the Canadian investor and the Insuring Agency to make appropriate arrangements pursuant to which such interests are transferred to an entity permitted to own such interests under the laws and regulations of the Republic of Indonesia.

3. The Insuring Agency shall assert no greater rights than those of the transferring Canadian investor under the laws and regulations of the Republic of Indonesia with respect to any interest transferred or succeeded to as contemplated in paragraph 1 of this Agreement.

The Government of Canada does, however, reserve its right to assert a claim in its sovereign capacity in the event of denial of justice or other question of state responsibility as defined in international law.

4. Should the said Insuring Agency acquire, under investment insurance contracts, amounts and credits in the lawful currency of the Republic of Indonesia, the Government hereof shall accord to those funds treatment no different than that which it would accord if such funds were to remain with the Canadian investor, and such funds shall be freely available to the Government of Canada to meet its expenditures in the national territory of the Republic of Indonesia.

5. This Agreement shall apply only with respect to insured Canadian private capital investments in projects or activities approved in writing by a document of admission issued by the Government of the Republic of Indonesia pursuant to the Foreign Capital Investment Law of 1967 (Law No. 1 of 1967) as amended by Law No. 11 of 1970.

6.(a) Disputes concerning the interpretation or implementation and application of provisions of this Agreement or any claim arising out of investments insured in accordance with this Agreement, against either of the two Governments, which in the opinion of the other presents a question of public international law shall be settled, insofar as possible, by means of diplomatic channels between the two Governments;

(b) If such disputes cannot be resolved within a period of three months following the request for such negotiations, the question shall be submitted, at the request of either Government, to an ad hoc tribunal for settlement in accordance with applicable principles and rules of public international law; only the respective Governments may request arbitral procedure and participate in it;

(c) The arbitral tribunal shall be composed of three members, and shall be established as follows: each Government shall appoint one arbitrator and these two arbitrators shall nominate a third arbitrator as chairman who shall be a national of a third state;

(d) If either Government has not appointed its arbitrator and has not followed the invitation of the other Government to make such an appointment within two months, the arbitrator shall be appointed upon the request of that Government by the President of the International Court of Justice;

(e) If the two arbitrators are unable to reach an agreement on the choice of the third arbitrator within two months after their appointment, the latter shall be appointed upon the request of either Government by the President of the International Court of Justice;

(f) If, in the cases specified under points (d) and (e) of this paragraph the President of the International Court of Justice is prevented from carrying out the said function or if he is a national of either Government, the appointment shall be made by the Vice-President, and if the latter is prevented from carrying out the said function or if he is a national of either Government, the appointment shall be made by the next senior Judge of the Court who is not a national of either Government;

(g) Unless the two Governments decide otherwise the arbitral tribunal shall determine its own procedure;

(h) The tribunal shall reach its decision by a majority of votes and such decision shall be final and binding on both Governments;

(i) Each of the Governments shall pay the expense of its member and its representation in the proceedings before the arbitral tribunal; expenses of the chairman and other costs shall be paid in equal parts by the two Governments. The arbitral tribunal may adopt other regulations concerning costs.

7.(a) If either Government considers it desirable to modify the provisions of this Agreement, this procedure may be carried out through a request for consultations and/or by correspondence and shall begin not later than 60 days from the date of the request;

(b) The modifications of the Agreement agreed between the two Governments shall enter into force upon their confirmation on the date which shall be mutually agreed upon by an Exchange of Notes.

In the event of termination, the provisions of this Agreement shall continue to apply, in respect of insurance contracts concluded between the Government of Canada and Canadian investors operating in the territory of the Republic of Indonesia while the Agreement was in force, for the duration of such contracts; provided that in no case shall the Agreement continue to apply to those contracts for a period longer than fifteen (15) years from the date of termination of this Agreement.

NOTES

1) Do you think that an insurance program stimulates the flow of new investment funds to the capital importing states that would not otherwise be made?[50]

2) What advantage do you perceive from the point of view of Canada and the host state to the bilateral approach of providing legal security for international investments as compared with other alternatives? Does the agreement with Indonesia deal with the determination of the substantive rights and duties of the parties?

3) The Convention on the Settlement of Investment Disputes between States and Nationals of other States,[51] to which Canada is not yet a party due to constitutional difficulties over its implementation, provides facilities for submission to conciliation or arbitration of investment disputes between contracting states and nationals of other contracting states (Arts. 1-2). The facilities are provided by the International Centre for Settlement of Investment Disputes which has its seat at the principal offices of the World Bank. The Centre maintains a Panel of Conciliators and a Panel of Arbitrators from which the parties to a dispute may choose the members of the Conciliation Commission or the Arbitral Tribunal to which their dispute is to be submitted (Arts. 2-15, 28-31 and 36-40).

The jurisdiction of the Centre with regard to the settlement of disputes is founded on the *written consent* of the parties, which must be given for every case and extends to all "legal disputes arising out of an investment" between a contracting state or any constituent sub-division or agency of a contracting state and a national of another contracting state (whether a natural or juridical person) (Art. 25(1)). Thus, the mere fact that a state becomes a party to the Convention will not impose obligations on it as regards the settlement of disputes, since it remains free to accept or reject the conciliation or arbitration organized by the Centre. Moreover, at any time, any contracting state "may ... notify the Centre of the Class or Classes of disputes which it would or would not consider submitting to the jurisdiction of the Centre" (Art. 25(4)). Both the Conciliation Commission (Art. 32(1)) and the Arbitral Tribunal (Art. 41(1)) are the judges of their own competence.

The Convention provides in Art. 42(1) that the Arbitral Tribunal shall decide a dispute in accordance with rules of law as may be agreed by the parties and that, in "the absence of such agreement, the Tribunal shall apply the law of the Contracting State party to the dispute (including its rules on the conflict of laws) and such rules of international law as may be applicable." The arbitral award must state the reasons on which it is based and is invalid if it fails to do so (Art. 52(1)(e)).

An award rendered under the Convention is binding on the parties, and is not subject to any appeal or to any other remedy except those provided for in the Convention (Art. 53). The remedies provided for are revision (Art. 51) and annulment (Art. 52) of the award. In addition, either party may request the Arbitral Tribunal to interpret its award (Art. 53). Contracting states are bound to recognize and enforce an award as if it were

---

[50] In general, see T. Meron, *Investment Insurance in International Law* (1976).
[51] (1965), 575 U.N.T.S. 159.

a final judgment of a national court, subject only to a foreign state's customary rights to immunity from execution (Arts. 54-55).

The Convention also contains provisions on the status, immunities and privileges of the Centre, conciliators, arbitrators and certain other persons, including officials or employees of the Secretariat (Art. 18-24). It also provides for the financing of the Centre by contracting states (Art. 17). Further, and this is important from the point of view of implementation by Canada, it is stipulated that each contracting state must take such legislative or other measures as may be necessary for making the provisions of the Convention effective in its territory (Art. 69).

4) Would it be advisable to restrict investment to countries that are signatories to the Convention on the Settlement of Investment Disputes or in the case of Canada, countries which have entered into special agreements with respect to foreign investment? Such agreements vary in the way they treat investments. They may provide for national treatment or most favoured treatment; they may refer to a general international law standard or they may contain specific clauses dealing with such incidents as establishment, acquisition and disposition of property, non-discrimination in taxation, exchange control, property protection, access to court and settlement of disputes.

PROCEDURAL ENFORCEMENT OF CLAIMS

Espousal and Nationality of Claims

Mavrommatis Palestine Concessions Case
Greece v. U.K.
(1924), P.C.I.J., Ser. A, No. 2, at 12

[The Greek Government brought an action against the British Government for the alleged refusal of the Palestine authorities under British mandate to recognize the rights acquired by Mr. Mavrommatis, a Greek national, under contracts which he had entered with the Ottoman Empire, the predecessor sovereign in Palestine.]

THE COURT: ... In the case of the Mavrommatis concessions it is true that the dispute was at first between a private person and a State – i.e. between M. Mavrommatis and Great Britain. Subsequently, the Greek Government took up the case. The dispute then entered upon a new phase; it entered the domain of international law, and became a dispute between two States.

...It is an elementary principle of international law that a State is entitled to protect its subjects, when injured by acts contrary to international law committed by another State, from whom they have been unable to obtain satisfaction through the ordinary channels. By taking up the case of one of its subjects and by resorting to diplomatic action or international judicial proceedings on his behalf, a State is in reality asserting its own rights – its right to ensure, in the person of its subjects, respect for the rules of international law.

The question, therefore, whether the present dispute originates in an injury to a private interest, which in point of fact is the case in many international disputes, is irrelevant from this standpoint. Once a State has taken up a case on behalf of one of its subjects before an international tribunal, in the eyes of the latter the State is sole claimant.

NOTES

In the *Reparations case* the International Court of Justice stated:[52]

Competence to bring an international claim is, for those possessing it, the capacity to resort to the customary methods recognized by international law for the establishment, the presentation and the settlement of claims. Among these methods may be mentioned protest, request for an enquiry, negotiation, and request for submission to an arbitral tribunal or to the Court in so far as this may be authorized by the Statute.

This capacity certainly belongs to the State; a State can bring an international claim against another State. Such a claim takes the form of a claim between two political entities, equal in law, similar in form, and both the direct subjects of international law. It is dealt with by means of negotiation, and cannot, in the present state of the law as to international jurisdiction, be submitted to a tribunal, except with the consent of the States concerned.

Panevezys-Saldutiskis Railway Case
Estonia v. Lithuania
(1939), P.C.I.J., Ser. A/B, No. 76, at 16.

THE COURT: ... In taking up the case of one of its nationals, by resorting to diplomatic action or international judicial proceedings on his behalf, a State is in reality asserting its own right, the right to ensure in the person of its nationals respect for the rules of international law. This right is necessarily limited to intervention on behalf of its own nationals because, in the absence of a special agreement, it is the bond of nationality between the State and the individual which alone confers upon the State the right of diplomatic protection, and it is as a part of the function of diplomatic protection that the right to take up a claim and to ensure respect for the rules of international law must be envisaged. Where the injury was done to the national of some other State, no claim to which such injury may give rise falls within the scope of the diplomatic protection which a State is entitled to afford nor can it give rise to a claim which that State is entitled to espouse.

NOTES

1) In the *I'm Alone* case[53] Canada had claimed damages against the United States as the result of the destruction by an American Coast Guard vessel of the I'm Alone, a

---

[52] [1949] I.C.J. Rep. 174, at 177-78; reported *supra* in Chapter 2.
[53] (1935), 3 R.I.A.A. 1609; reported *infra* in Chapter 11.

vessel under Canadian registry and flying the Canadian flag, engaged in smuggling liquor into the United States. The Commissioners designated by the United States and Canada to pass upon the claim declined to recommend the payment of indemnity for the destruction of the vessel since it was found to be beneficially owned by citizens of the United States and under their direction and control.

2) International law requires that for a claim to be sustainable the claimant must be a national of the state which is presenting the claim both at the time when the injury occurred and continuously thereafter up to the date of formal presentation of the claim. In practice however it is sufficient to prove nationality at the date of injury and of presentation of the claim.[54]

3) As to who is a national see Chapter 7, on "Nationality." In some cases a state may present a claim on behalf of permanent residents or even aliens whose rights have been violated. See Chapter 10 on the "Protection of Human Rights."

Exhaustion of Local Remedies and Waiver of Claims

Ambatielos Arbitration
Greece v. United Kingdom
(1956), 12 R.I.A.A. 83; 23 I.L.R. 306

[Greece espoused the claims of its national, Mr. Ambatielos, arising out of his contract with the U.K. government for the purchase of certain ships. In rejecting the claims, the Commission applied the international rule that requires prior exhaustion of local remedies.]

THE COMMISSION: ...,
The rule thus invoked by the United Kingdom Government is well established in international law. Nor is its existence contested by the Greek Government. It means that the State against which an international action is brought for injuries suffered by private individuals has the right to resist such an action if the persons alleged to have been injured have not first exhausted all the remedies available to them under the municipal law of that State. The defendant State has the right to demand that full advantage shall have been taken of all local remedies before the matters in dispute are taken on the international level by the State of which the persons alleged to have been injured are nationals.

In order to contend successfully that international proceedings are inadmissible, the defendant State must prove the existence, in its system of internal law, of remedies which have not been used. The views expressed by writers and in judicial precedents, however, coincide in that the existence of remedies which are obviously ineffective is held not to be sufficient to justify the application of the rule. Remedies which could not rectify the situation cannot be relied upon by the defendant State as precluding an international action.

The Greek Government contends that in the present case the remedies which English

---

[54] See "International Claims" (1957), 9 *External Affairs* 326; (1966), 18 *External Affairs* 11, and E.B. Wang, "Nationality of Claims and Diplomatic Intervention" (1965), 43 *Can. Bar Rev.* 136.

law offered to Mr. Ambatielos were ineffective and that, accordingly, the rule is not applicable.

The ineffectiveness of local remedies may result clearly from the municipal law itself. That is the case, for example, when a Court of Appeal is not competent to reconsider the judgment given by a Court of first instance on matters of fact, and when, failing such reconsideration, no redress can be obtained. ...

Furthermore, however, it is generally considered that the ineffectiveness of available remedies, without being legally certain, may also result from circumstances which do not permit any hope of redress to be placed in the use of those remedies. But in a case of that kind it is essential that such remedies, if they had been resorted to, would have proved to be *obviously futile*. ...

If the rule of exhaustion of local remedies is relied upon against the action of the claimant State, what is the test to be applied by an international tribunal for the purpose of determining the applicability of the rule?

As the arbitrator ruled in the *Finnish Vessels* Case[55] of 9th May, 1934, the only possible test is to assume the truth of the facts on which the claimant State bases its claim. ...

In the Ambatielos Case, failure to use certain means of appeal is ... relied upon by the United Kingdom Government, but reliance is also placed on the failure of Mr. Ambatielos to adduce before Mr. Justice Hill evidence which it is now said would have been essential to establish his claims. There is no doubt that the exhaustion of local remedies requires the use of the means of procedure which are essential to redress the situation complained of by the person who is alleged to have been injured. ...

The rule requires that "local remedies" shall have been exhausted before an international action can be brought. These "local remedies" include not only reference to the courts and tribunals, but also the use of the procedural facilities which municipal law makes available to litigants before such courts and tribunals. It is the whole system of legal protection, as provided by municipal law, which must have been put to the test before a State, as the protector of its nationals, can prosecute the claim on the international plane. ...

It is clear, however, that [this view] ... cannot be strained too far. Taken literally, it would imply that the fact of having neglected to make use of some means of procedure – even one which is not important to the defence of the action – would suffice to allow a defendant State to claim that local remedies have not been exhausted, and that, therefore, an international action cannot be brought. This would confer on the rule of the prior exhaustion of local remedies a scope which is unacceptable.

In the view of the Commission the non-utilisation of certain means of procedure can be accepted as constituting a gap in the exhaustion of local remedies only if the use of these means of procedure were essential to establish the claimant's case before the municipal courts. ...

As regards Claim A [for compensation for breach of contract], the questions of the non-exhaustion of local remedies thus raised are:

---

[55] *Finland v. Great Britain* (1934), 3 R.I.A.A. 1479.

(1) In the 1922 proceedings Mr. Ambatielos failed to call (as he could have done) the witnesses who, as he now says, were essential to establish his case. ...

It is not possible for the Commission to decide on the evidence before it the question whether the case would have been decided in favour of Mr. Ambatielos if Major Laing had been heard as a witness. The Commission has not heard the witnesses called before Mr. Justice Hill and cannot solely on the documentary evidence put before the Commission form an opinion whether the testimony of Major Laing would have been successful in establishing the claim of Mr. Ambatielos before Mr. Justice Hill. The Commission cannot put itself in the position of Mr. Justice Hill in this respect.

The test as regards the question whether the testimony of Major Laing was essential must therefore be what the claimant Government in this respect has contended, viz. that the testimony of Major Laing would have had the effect of establishing the claim put forward by Mr. Ambatielos before Mr. Justice Hill.

Under English Law Mr. Ambatielos was not precluded from calling Major Laing as a witness.

In so far as concerns Claim A, the failure of Mr. Ambatielos to call Major Laing as a witness at the hearing before Mr. Justice Hill must therefore be held to amount to non-exhaustion of the local remedy available to him in the proceedings before Mr. Justice Hill.

It may be that the decision of Mr. Ambatielos not to call Major Laing as a witness, with the result that he did not exhaust local remedies, was dictated by reasons of expediency – quite understandable in themselves – in putting his case before Mr. Justice Hill. This, however, is not the question to be determined. The Commission is not concerned with the question as to whether he was right or wrong in acting as he did. He took his decision at his own risk.

(2) The second question as to non-exhaustion raised by the United Kingdom Government is the failure of Mr. Ambatielos to make use of or exhaust his appellate rights. ...

The refusal of the Court of Appeal to give leave to adduce the evidence of Major Laing did not, of course, in itself prevent this general appeal from being proceeded with.

The Greek Government argues by way of explanation that to proceed with the general appeal once the decision of the Court of Appeal not to admit the Laing evidence had been given would have been futile because the Laing evidence was essential to enable the Court to arrive at a decision favourable to Mr. Ambatielos.

The reason why Mr. Ambatielos was not allowed to call Major Laing in the Court of Appeal was, in the words of Lord Justice Scrutton, that "One of the principal rules which this Court adopts is that it will not give leave to adduce further evidence which might have been adduced with reasonable care at the trial of the action."

Accordingly, the failure of Mr. Ambatielos to exhaust the local remedy before Hill J. by not calling Major Laing as a witness, is the reason why it was futile for him to prosecute his appeal.

It would be wrong to hold that a party who, by failing to exhaust his opportunities in the Court of first instance, has caused an appeal to become futile should be allowed to rely on this fact in order to rid himself of the rule of exhaustion of local remedies.

It may be added that Mr. Ambatielos did not submit to the Court of Appeal any argument suggesting, or any evidence to show, that any illegal or improper manoeuvres by his opponents had prevented him from calling Major Laing or producing any documents.

...In so far as concerns the appeal to the House of Lords, it is of course unlikely that the Court would have differed from the decision of the Court of Appeal, refusing to allow Major Laing to be called as a witness in the latter Court. If it is held that such an appeal would *not* have been obviously futile, the failure of Mr. Ambatielos to appeal to the House of Lords must be regarded as a failure to exhaust local remedies. If, on the other hand, it is held that an appeal to the House of Lords *would* have been obviously futile, Mr. Ambatielos must likewise be held to have lost his hope of a successful appeal, by reason of his failure to call Major Laing.

NOTES

1) The rule regarding exhaustion of local remedies is inapplicable to a case of direct injury caused by one state to another. Local remedies need not be exhausted when the violation was caused by an act of a state for which that state denies responsibility, as in the case of shooting down a foreign commercial aircraft such as occurred in the *Destruction of Korean Airlines Flight 007*, reported previously in Chapter 6.

2) As the Commission in *Ambatielos* also noted, failure to exhaust local remedies will not constitute a bar to a claim if it can be clearly established that in the circumstances of the case an appeal to a higher national tribunal would have had no effect.

3) A state may waive the requirement of exhaustion of local remedies, allowing claims against it to be brought by another state directly to an international tribunal. For example, Article V of the convention establishing the Mexican-United States General Claims Commission,[56] provided that no claim should be "disallowed or rejected by the Commission by the application of the general principle of international law that the legal remedies must be exhausted as a condition precedent to the validity or allowance of any claim."

Calvo Clause

An alien who has been injured by a state in a manner wrongful under international law can always waive or settle his claim prior to diplomatic intervention by the state of which he is a national provided the waiver or settlement is not made under duress.[57]

Some states in order to avoid foreign diplomatic intervention require aliens to waive in advance such intervention and to submit all their disputes to the local law and courts exclusively. This is called the Calvo clause after its advocate, an Argentinian jurist named Carlos Calvo.

---

[56] (1923), 9 Bevans 935, at 938.
[57] See the *Tattler Claim* (U.S. v. Great Britain) (1920), 6 R.I.A.A. 48.

North American Dredging Company Claim
(1926), 4 R.I.A.A. 26.

[Article 18 of an agreement between the North American Dredging Company and the Government of Mexico provided that:

The contractor and all persons who, as employees or in any other capacity, may be engaged in the execution of the work under this contract either directly or indirectly, shall be considered as Mexicans in all matters, within the Republic of Mexico, concerning the execution of such work and the fulfilment of this contract. They shall not claim, nor shall they have, with regard to the interests and the business connected with this contract, any other rights or means to enforce the same than those granted by the laws of the Republic to Mexicans, nor shall they enjoy any other rights than those established in favor of Mexicans. They are consequently deprived of any rights as aliens, and under no conditions shall the intervention of foreign diplomatic agents be permitted, in any matter related to this contract.

The United States on behalf of the company claimed damages for breach of the contract by the government of Mexico. The Commission sustained the Mexican motion to dismiss the claim on the ground that a contract containing a Calvo clause precluded its consideration by an international commission.]

THE COMMISSION: ...

14. Reading this article [article 18 quoted above] as a whole, it is evident that its purpose was to bind the claimant to be governed by the laws of Mexico and to use the remedies existing under such laws. ... But this provision did not, and could not, deprive the claimant of his American citizenship and all that that implies. It did not take from him his undoubted right to apply to his own Government for protection if his resort to the Mexican tribunals or other authorities available to him resulted in a denial or delay of justice as that term is used in international law. In such a case the claimant's complaint would be not that his contract was violated but that he had been denied justice. The basis of his appeal would be not a construction of his contract, save perchance in an incidental way, but rather an internationally illegal act.

15. What, therefore, are the rights which claimant waived and those which he did not waive in subscribing to article 18 of the contract? (a) He waived his right to conduct himself as if no competent authorities existed in Mexico; as if he were engaged in fulfilling a contract in an inferior country subject to a system of capitulations; and as if the only real remedies available to him in the fulfillment, construction, and enforcement of this contract were international remedies. All these he waived and had a right to waive. (b) He did not waive any right which he possessed as an American citizen as to any matter not connected with the fulfillment, execution, or enforcement of this contract as such. (c) He did not waive his undoubted right as an American citizen to apply to his Government for protection against the violation of international law (internationally illegal acts) whether growing out of this contract or out of other situations. (d) He did not and could not affect the right of his Government to extend to him its protection in general or to extend to him its protection against breaches of international law. But he did frankly and unreservedly

agree that in consideration of the Government of Mexico awarding him this contract, he did not need and would not invoke or accept the assistance of his Government with respect to the fulfillment and interpretation of his contract and the execution of his work thereunder. ...

18. If it were necessary to demonstrate how legitimate are the fears of certain nations with respect to abuses of the right of protection and how seriously the sovereignty of those nations within their own boundaries would be impaired if some extreme conceptions of this right were recognized and enforced, the present case would furnish an illuminating example. The claimant, after having solemnly promised in writing that it would not ignore the local laws, remedies, and authorities, behaved from the very beginning as if article 18 of its contract had no existence in fact. It used the article to procure the contract, but this was the extent of its use. It has never sought any redress by application to the local authorities and remedies which article 18 liberally granted it and which, according to Mexican law, are available to it, even against the Government, without restrictions, both in matter of civil and of public law. ...

20. Under article 18 of the contract ... the present claimant is precluded from presenting to its Government any claim relative to the interpretation or fulfillment of this contract. If it had a claim for denial of justice, for delay of justice or gross injustice, or for any other violation of international law committed by Mexico to its damage, it might have presented such a claim to its Government, which in turn could have espoused it and presented it here. Although the claim as presented falls within the first clause of Article I of the Treaty, describing claims coming within this Commission's jurisdiction, it is not a claim that may be rightfully presented by the claimant to its Government for espousal and hence is not cognizable here[58]. ...

Canadian Practice

Canadian Espousal of Claims
based on J.-G. Castel, *Legal Services Provided by the Department of External Affairs with Respect to International Judicial Co-operation and Other Matters*, Department of External Affairs, (1987)

The Government of Canada may, in conformity with generally accepted principles of customary international law, only espouse claims in respect of loss of human life, property, rights, interests or debts of Canadians where the individuals concerned were Canadian citizens at the time of loss, confiscation, expropriation or nationalization. Further, the claim must have belonged to Canadian citizens at all times since they arose and the claimants must be Canadian citizens at the time these claims are presented.

The Government of Canada will normally not espouse a claim of a Canadian against a foreign state until all local legal remedies (i.e., the remedies available to him up to and including the court of final appeal in the foreign state) have been exhausted without satisfaction. However, if in exhausting these local legal remedies the claimant has met

---

[58] See also *Restatement (Revised) Foreign Relations Law of the United States* (1987), s.713, comment g. "'Calvo' laws and clauses."

with prejudice or obstruction constituting a denial of justice, there may be grounds on which the Government of Canada could intervene on his behalf to secure redress.

In cases of special merit where the claimant does not fulfil the conditions set out above, the Government of Canada may consider using its "good offices" and direct an inquiry to foreign authorities but it will not formally espouse such a claim.

As regards claims by companies, the Government of Canada, pursuant to customary international law as interpreted in the *Barcelona Traction* case,[59] may espouse claims in respect of property nationalized or otherwise taken abroad only where the claims belong to a company incorporated under the laws of Canada or of any province of Canada and where the company was so incorporated on the date on which the claim arose.

There is a further requirement in Canadian practice, and that is that company claims will normally only be espoused by the Government of Canada where there is a "substantial" Canadian interest in the company. Whether such a "substantial" Canadian interest exists so as to justify Canadian diplomatic intervention will depend, *inter alia*, on factors such as where it carries on its business, whether it has active trading interests in Canada, and the extent to which the company is beneficially owned in Canada.

Where Canadian citizens have an interest, as shareholders or otherwise, in a foreign company and where the state under the laws of which that company was incorporated and of which it is thus a national causes economic loss to the company, the Government of Canada may intervene to protect the interests of such citizens. Canadian citizens who are shareholders in a foreign company which suffered loss at the hands of a foreign government are thus eligible for espousal of their claims by the Government of Canada. Such claims, moreover, may be included in claims negotiations leading to lump-sum settlement agreements.

There are, nevertheless, questions of public policy in such cases and it is usually necessary, therefore, to consider each case on its merits. The Government of Canada may also intervene on behalf of a Canadian shareholder of a foreign company incorporated in a foreign state if that company is injured by the acts of a third state. In such a case, the intervention may be made in concert with the government of the state in which the company was incorporated.

Procedure

When a Canadian citizen brings to the attention of the Department of External Affairs a *prima facie* valid claim against a foreign state in respect of which he has exhausted all local legal remedies without success, the Department may decide to intervene formally through the exercise of good offices or espousal of the claim in accordance with established principles of international law. The decision as to which course of action is to be followed depends in large part on the facts of the individual case. When a state has undertaken a policy of general nationalization and, as a result, the property of a large number of Canadian citizens has been affected, it has been customary first to obtain an agreement in principle with the state concerned to negotiate a general settlement of Canadian claims.

---

[59] [1970] I.C.J. Rep. 3, reported *supra* in Chapter 7.

Such preliminary agreements are then publicized and interested persons are invited to file completed claims questionnaires with the Department of External Affairs. Following a period of assessment and preparation, those claims considered to be valid are made known to the other state and negotiations begin for a lump-sum settlement.

If such a settlement is reached, regulations respecting the distribution of the proceeds of the settlement are passed by Order-in-Council and the claims are subsequently formally referred to the Foreign Claims Commission (established in 1970) for a Report and Recommendation as to the amount to be awarded in respect of each claim of which it has notice. While the question of whether the claimant is eligible to participate in a claims settlement between Canada and a foreign state is subject to a report and recommendation of the Foreign Claims Commission, ministerial approval is required in order for an award to be made. Advancement of the claim during negotiations and its acceptance as being *prima facie* valid by the other side, create no rights to a share of the settlement for individual claimants. Such a right is created only by Ministerial approval of a Foreign Claims Commission Report and Recommendation on a particular claim.

While Canadian claims settlement agreements in the form of lump-sum settlements will reflect in a general way, the number and value of claims submitted by Canadian citizens to the Canadian Government, such settlements are not regarded as the total sum of a series of individually-accepted claims.

Exercise of Good Offices

The Canadian Government, at its discretion, may in certain circumstances support and make diplomatic representations on behalf of a claim which is of uncertain validity, on the merits or on grounds of international law. For example, the Government may consider a request for assistance in respect to the claim of a new Canadian who was not a Canadian citizen at the time of the events giving rise to the claim. Under the rule of continuous nationality, the Government cannot formally espouse this claim (unless it rests on provisions of a specific treaty) but it may instruct the Canadian Embassy or Consulate in the foreign locality concerned to lend assistance short of espousal where such action is considered to be useful and appropriate.

Such informal assistance, where an effort is made to facilitate a settlement without the Government thereby becoming a party to the dispute, is often referred to as an exercise of "good offices." It may take many forms, including, for example, enquiries as to the present status of the dispute, as to the procedure which the claimant should follow to press his own claim under local laws, or it may be in the form of a request for reconsideration or review of a decision of an agency of the foreign government. An intervention as an exercise of good offices may, at the discretion of the Government, and depending upon the circumstances of the case, be made at a high level and may be accompanied by strong representations. As a pratical matter, the distinction between formal espousal and an exercise of good offices may be somewhat blurred. It must be recognized, however, that in many cases the possibility of effective assistance by the Government of Canada in cases which do not meet the international requirements for espousal, will be severely circumscribed. Where, for example, a number of claims valid under international law are outstanding against, or under negotiation with the foreign government, support by Canada for other claims, without regard to traditional rules of eligibility, may prejudice efforts made to obtain satisfaction of the valid claims. In such a case, an informal exercise of good offices on behalf of a claimant may not only be futile but counter-productive. Accordingly, in the exercise of its sovereign discretion in presenting international claims, the Government of Canada will be closely guided by accepted principles of international law and practice.

Canada-France Treaty on Compensation for Nationalized Gas Works
1951 Can. T.S. No. 2

The Canadian Government and the French Government, having regard to the effects of the French laws and decrees relating to the nationalization of gas and electricity undertakings on the rights of Canadian holders of shares and interests in nationalized undertakings and also of direct Canadian owners of nationalized gas and electricity installations, have agreed as follows:

1. The French Government undertakes to accord to Canadian nationals who are holders of shares and interests in nationalized undertakings and also to direct owners of nationalized gas and electricity installations who apply therefor the terms of compensation defined in the Terms of Settlement annexed hereto.

2. The French Government shall accord to the Canadian Government most-favoured-nation treatment in respect of the compensation of such holders and owners of Canadian nationality.

If the French Government, in particular, accords to another Government for the benefit of its nationals compensation with respect to similar shares and interests in the form of payments in French francs of larger sums or compensation bearing a higher rate of interest or discharged by a smaller number of annual payments or enjoying special transfer facilities, the Canadian Government shall be entitled to claim on behalf of its nationals the substitution to the terms of the present Agreement the corresponding terms of compensation granted to the nationals of that other Government.

Such substitution would apply in respect of Canadian credits which had not been redeemed at the date of the option.

If the option is exercised it shall apply to all Canadian holders and owners and not merely to some of them.

3. The Canadian Government undertakes, provided that the French Government carries out the obligations assumed by it under this Agreement and the Terms of Settlement annexed thereto, not to recognize, nor to refer to any international tribunal, nor to support by diplomatic action, any claims which may be made by Canadian physical or juridical persons on the basis of Law No. 46-628 of April 8, 1946, and the laws and decrees relating thereto.

4. Any dispute arising from the interpretation or the application of this Agreement which cannot be settled by direct negotiation between the two governments shall be submitted to arbitration.

In that event each of the Contracting Governments shall appoint an arbitrator.

If, within a period of two months from the date on which the case has been referred to the two arbitrators, the latter have not agreed upon a solution, the two Governments shall by mutual agreement appoint a third arbitrator. Failing agreement on such appointment within a further period of one month, the President of the International Court of Justice shall be requested to appoint such an arbitrator.

The decision of the arbitrators shall be final and binding for both parties. It shall be given within a period of not more than six months from the date of appointment of the third arbitrator.

5. This Agreement shall enter into force on the date of its signature. Done in duplicate at Paris on January 26, 1951.

TERMS OF SETTLEMENT ACCORDED BY THE FRENCH GOVERNMENT

for Compensation to Canadian Claimants Affected by Law No. 46-628 of April 8, 1946. Relating to the Nationalization of Gas and Electricity and by the Laws and Decrees Relating Thereto

PART I – DECLARATION OF ACCEPTANCE

Article 1. The provisions of the present Terms of Settlement shall apply to Canadian physical or juridical persons who are entitled to compensation under the Law of April 8, 1946, and the Laws and Decrees relating thereto and who file before May 31, 1951, a declaration accepting the present Terms of Settlement with the authority in Canada designated by the Canadian Government with the agreement of the French Government. After that date compensation in respect of nationalization shall be governed solely by the provisions of the French laws and decrees.

Canadian nationals making such a declaration shall provide the authority in Canada or any person designated by it with evidence that the rights to which they lay claim belonged on January 1st, 1946, and since then without interruption to Canadian physical or juridical persons in accordance with the rules set forth in the Annex hereto establishing the means of giving effect to the present Terms of Settlement.

The provisions of the present Terms of Settlement shall also apply to Canadian physical or juridical persons producing evidence:

1. that after January 1st, 1946, they have exercised rights to subscribe securities as of right or rights of allotment relating to interests which belonged to them before that date;

2. that in the case of securities acquired between January 1st, 1946, and April 8, 1946, the ownership of such securities was not French at any time during that period;

3. that the title to the securities was conveyed to them owing to death having occurred during the period mentioned in the sub-paragraph 2 above.

The French Government excludes from the application of the present Agreement:

(a) Canadian juridical persons more than 25% of whose capital is held by enemy interests.

(b) Canadian juridical persons in which the rights to more than 50% of the capital belong to French interests.

PART IV – PROVISIONS CONCERNING
REINVESTMENT OF AMOUNTS RECEIVED AS COMPENSATION

Article 11. The capital value of the compensation, including the redemption premium, must be used or reinvested only in France. In order to facilitate the reinvestment of these funds in France they shall be transferred to an approved bank to the credit of accounts opened in the name of Canadian nationals concerned. These accounts shall be called "Canadian Reinvestment Accounts".

PART VI – DEFINITIONS

Article 14. In the present Terms of Settlement and the annexes thereto, the expressions
   2. "France" shall mean the metropolitan territory of France and the other territories of the Franc monetary area (including the C.E.A. area).
   3. "Canadian persons" shall mean:
   (a) physical persons who at the date on which they make the declaration provided for in Article 1 of this Agreement are citizens of Canada;
   (b) juridical persons incorporated or constituted under the laws in force in Canada.

ANNEX III

Under these Rules and Regulations, the interests belonging to enemy nationals are considered as enemy interests.
   I. *The enemy countries are:*
   Germany within its boundaries as of December 31, 1937.
   Japan within its boundaries as of December 8, 1941 (exclusively of territories occupied by its military forces).
   II. *Enemy nationals:*
Those citizens of one of the two above-mentioned countries, who are residing either in enemy territory or in a neutral country, or in allied territory, except when, in the latter case, their property has not been placed under custody or has been released from custody, are considered as enemy nationals.
   III. *Change in nationality:*
German nationals who have acquired another nationality after September 1, 1939, are considered as enemy nationals unless they have acquired the nationality of an allied country before January 1, 1946, or have been granted permanent residence in that country.
   IV. *Special cases:*
Stateless persons of German origin may not be considered as German nationals if the German Government had deprived them of this status before September 1, 1939.

Canada-U.K.-U.S.S.R. Treaty on Compensation for Nickel Mines
(1944) Can. T.S. No. 29

[In 1944 a protocol was signed in Moscow concerning the compensation to be paid by the government of the U.S.S.R. for the transfer to Soviet ownership of the nickel mines in the Petsamo district. This district was ceded by Finland to the Soviet Union under the Armistice Agreement on September 29, 1944. The nickel concession was owned by the International Nickel Company of Canada through its subsidiary, The Mond Nickel Company of the United Kingdom. The text of the protocol follows:]

On the occasion of the signing of the Armistice Agreement with the Government of Finland, the Government of Canada, the Government of the Union of Soviet Socialist Republics and the Government of the United Kingdom of Great Britain and Northern Ireland are agreed that:

In connection with the return by Finland to the Soviet Union of the former Soviet territory of the oblast of Petsamo (Pechenga) and the consequent transfer to ownership of the Soviet Union of nickel mines (including all property and installations appertaining thereto) operated in the said territory for the benefit of the Mond Nickel Company and the International Nickel Company of Canada, the Soviet Government will pay to the Government of Canada during the course of six years from the date of the signing of the present Protocol in equal instalments, the sum of 20 million United States dollars as full and final compensation of the above mentioned companies. For the purpose of this payment United States dollars will be reckoned at the value of 35 dollars to one ounce of gold.

NOTES

1) The Soviet Union did not keep to the schedule for payment but eventually the full sum, partly in U.S. dollars and partly in sterling equivalent, was handed over and accepted. Orders-in-Council were passed to authorize payment by Canada to the International Nickel Company, representing itself and the Mond Nickel Company, of all sums received by the Canadian Government from the Soviet Government pursuant to the protocol.[60]

2) Canada has signed a number of lump-sum compensation agreements, as, for instance, with Bulgaria in 1966, Hungary in 1970, Poland and Romania in 1971 and Czechoslovakia in 1973. For example, articles I and II of the Agreement with Poland[61] provide as follows:

Article I

The Government of Poland shall pay to the Government of Canada the sum of $1,225,000 (one million two hundred and twenty-five thousand) Canadian dollars in full and final settlement of Canadian claims arising before the date of the coming into force of this Agreement against the Government of Poland and Polish natural and juridical persons in respect of:

    (1)   property, rights or other interests nationalized or otherwise taken by the application of Polish legislation or administrative decisions;

---

[60] P.C. 2551, April 12, 1945; P.C. 4602, November 12, 1947; P.C. 1771, November 19, 1953.
[61] 1971 Can. T.S. No. 39. See also Foreign Claims (Poland), Settlement Regulations SOR/72-395, as am. by SOR/75-62.

(2) debts owed by enterprises nationalized, or otherwise taken by the application of Polish legislation or administrative decisions.

Article II

For the purpose of this Agreement "Canadian claims" shall mean:

(1) claims of natural persons who were Canadian citizens on the date of the coming into force of this Agreement and who were or whose legal predecessors were Canadian citizens on the date of the coming into force of the legislation or of the other similar measures referred to in Article I or on the date on which the relevant measures were first applied to their property, rights or interests;

(2) claims of juridical persons which on the date of the coming into force of this Agreement were incorporated or constituted pursuant to the laws of Canada and who were, or whose legal predecessors were Canadian natural or juridical persons on the date of the coming into force of the legislation or of the other similar measures referred to in Article I or on the date on which the relevant measures were first applied to the property, rights or interests.

REPARATION

A state that has violated an international obligation is required to terminate the wrongful act[62] and in appropriate cases to make reparation. What is loosely known as reparation may take two forms: reparation properly so called, or satisfaction. Reparation in its strict sense may in turn consist of either restitution pure and simple, or damages; or it may consist partly of restitution and partly of damages. The purpose of reparation is simply to restore pre-existing conditions or to compensate for material injury.

Satisfaction is a term primarily applied to compensation for the moral or non-material consequences of an act for which a state is internationally responsible. Some of the common forms satisfaction may take include apology or amends of a diplomatic character. In some cases a pecuniary compensation is paid not as reparation for a material wrong, but as an additional apology for the wrongful act committed.

State responsibility can be expressed not only in the form of restitution or of financial reparation, but also in the form of sanctions, particularly when the state violated the rights of other states rather than those of individuals. Thus the responsibility of a state in international law is broader than civil responsibility under municipal law. A violation which is an international crime should support a claim for punitive damages.

The Lusitania Cases
United States v. Germany
Mixed Claims Commission (1923) 7 R.I.A.A. 32

[The Lusitania, a British liner, was torpedoed without warning by a German U-boat off the coast of Ireland on May 7, 1915 during the period of American neutrality. The German Government assumed liability for the losses sustained by American nationals, of whom 128 had died.]

PARKER, Umpire: ... The Commission finds that Germany is financially obligated to pay to the United States all losses suffered by American nationals, stated in terms of dollars, where the claims therefor have continued in American ownership, which losses have resulted from death or from personal injury or from loss of, or damage to, property, sustained in the sinking of the *Lusitania*. ...

In this decision rules applicable to the measure of damages in *death cases* will be considered. In formulating such rules and determining the weight to be given to decisions ... [on] this subject, it is important to bear in mind the basis of recovery in death cases in the jurisdictions announcing such decisions.

At common law there existed no cause of action for damages caused by the death of a human being. [British, United States and German legislation, all recognise a] right to maintain such actions. ...

The statutes enacted in common-law jurisdictions conferring a cause of action in death cases where none before existed have frequently limited by restrictive terms the rules for measuring damages in such cases. The tendency, however, of both statutes and decisions is to give such elasticity to those restrictive rules as to enable courts and juries in applying them to the facts of each particular case to award full and fair compensation for the injury suffered and the loss sustained. ...

In most of the jurisdictions where the civil law is administered and where the right of action for injuries resulting in death has long existed independent of any code of statute containing restrictions on rules for measuring damages, the courts have not been hampered in so formulating such rules and adapting them to the facts of each case as to give complete compensation for the loss sustained.

It is a general rule of both civil and the common law that every invasion of private rights imports an injury and that for every such injury the law gives a remedy. ... That remedy must be commensurate with the injury received ... and is measured by pecuniary standards. ...

In death cases the right of action is for the loss sustained by the *claimants*, not by the estate. The basis of damage is not the physical or mental suffering of the deceased or his loss or the loss to his estate, but the losses resulting to claimants from his death. The inquiry then is: What amount will compensate claimants for such losses?

Bearing in mind that we are not concerned with any problem involving the punishment of a wrongdoer, but only with the naked question of fixing the amount which will compensate for the wrong done, our formula expressed in general terms for reaching that end is: Estimate the amounts (a) which the decedent, had he not been killed, would probably have contributed to the claimant, add thereto (b) the pecuniary value to such claimant of the deceased's personal services in claimant's care, education, or supervision, and also add (c) reasonable compensation for such mental suffering or shock, if any, caused by the violent severing of family ties, as claimant may actually have sustained by reason of such death. The sum of those estimates, reduced to its present cash value, will generally represent the loss sustained by claimant.

In making such estimates there will be considered ... [*inter alia*] the age, sex, health, condition and station in life, occupation, ... mental and physical capacity, ... earning capacity and customary earnings of the deceased and the uses made of such earnings by him: [his] probable duration of life ... but for the fatal injury ... ; the reasonable probability that the earning capacity ... would either have increased or decreased; the age, sex, health, condition and station in life, and probable life expectancy of each of the claimants; ... neither the physical pain nor the mental anguish which the *deceased* may have suffered will be considered as elements of damage; the amount of insurance on the life of the deceased collected by his estate or by the claimants will not be taken into account in computing the damages which claimants may be entitled to recover; no exemplary, punitive, or vindictive damages can be assessed. ...

That one injured is, under the rules of international law, entitled to be compensated for an injury inflicted, resulting in mental suffering, injury to his feelings, humiliation, shame, degradation, loss of social position or injury to his credit or to his reputation, there can be no doubt, and such compensation should be commensurate to the injury. Such damages are very real, and the mere fact that they are difficult to measure or estimate by money standards makes them none the less real and affords no reason why the injured person should not be compensated therefor as compensatory damages, but not as a penalty. ...

The industry of counsel has failed to point us to any money award by an international arbitral tribunal where exemplary, punitive, or vindictive damages have been assessed against one sovereign nation in favour of another presenting a claim on behalf of its nationals. ... A sufficient reason why such damages cannot be awarded by *this* Commission is that it is without the power to make such awards under the terms of its charter – the Treaty of Berlin. It will be borne in mind that this is a "Treaty between the United States and Germany Restoring Friendly Relations" – a Treaty of Peace. Its terms negative the concept of the imposition of a penalty by the United States against Germany, save that the undertaking by Germany to make reparation to the United States and its nationals as stipulated in the Treaty may partake of the nature of a penalty. Part VII of the Treaty of Versailles ... deals with "Penalties." It is significant that these provisions were *not* incorporated in the Treaty of Berlin.

In negotiating the Treaty of Peace, the United States and Germany were, of course, dealing directly with each other. Had there been any intention on the part of the United States to exact a penalty either as a punishment or as an example and a deterrent, such intention would have been clearly expressed in the Treaty itself; and, had it taken the form of a money payment, would have been claimed by the Government of the United States on its own behalf and not on behalf of its nationals. As to such nationals, care was taken to provide for full and adequate "indemnities," "reparations," and "satisfaction" of their claims for losses, damages, or injuries suffered by them. ... For the enormous cost to the Government of the United States in prosecuting the war no claim is made against Germany. ... In view of this frank recognition by the Government of the United States of Germany's inability to make to it full and complete reparation for all of the consequences of the war, how can it be contended that there should be read into the Treaty an obligation on the part of Germany to pay penalties to the Government of the United States for the use and benefit of a small group of American nationals for whose full and complete compensation for losses sustained adequate provision has been made?

The United States is in effect making one demand against Germany on some 12,500 counts. That demand is for compensation and reparation for certain losses sustained by the United States and its nationals. While in determining the amount which Germany is to pay each claim must be considered separately, no one of them can be disposed of as an isolated claim or suit, but must be considered in relation to all others presented in this one demand. In all of the claims the parties are the same. They must all be determined and disposed of under the same Treaty and by the same tribunal. If it were possible to read into the Treaty a provision authorising this Commission to assess a penalty against Germany as a punishment or as an example or deterrrent, what warrant is there for allocating such penalty or any part of it to any particular claim, and how should it be distributed? ...

If it were competent for this Commission to impose such a penalty, what penalty stated in terms of dollars would suffice as a deterrent? And if this Commission should arrogate to itself the authority to impose in the form of damages a penalty which would effectively serve as a deterrent, wherein lie the boundaries of its powers? It is not hampered with any constitutional limitation save those found in the Treaty; and if the power to impose a penalty exists under the Treaty may not the Commission exercise that power in a way to affect the future political relations of the two Governments? The mere statement of the question is its answer. Putting the inquiry only serves to illustrate how repugnant to the fundamental principles of international law is the idea that this Commission should treat as justiciable the question as to what penalty should be assessed against Germany as a punishment for the alleged wrongdoing. It is our opinion that as between sovereign nations the question of the right and power to impose penalties, unlimited in amount, is political rather than legal in its nature, and therefore not a subject within the jurisdiction of this Commission.

The Treaty is our charter. We cannot look beyond its express provisions or its clear implications in assessing damages in any particular claim. We hold that its clear and unambiguous language does not authorise the imposition of penalties. Hence the fundamental maxim, "It is not allowable to interpret that which has no need of interpretation," applies. But all of the rules governing the interpretation of treaties would lead to the same result. ... Some of these are: The Treaty is based upon the resolution of the Congress of the United States, accepted and adopted by Germany. The language, being that of the United States and framed for its benefit, will be strictly construed against it. Treaty provisions must be so construed as to best conform to accepted principles of international law rather than in derogation of them. Penal clauses in treaties are odious and must be construed most strongly against those asserting them.

The Treaty is one between two sovereign nations – a Treaty of Peace. There is no place in it for any vindictive or punitive provisions. Germany must make compensation and reparation for all losses falling within its terms sustained by American nationals.

That compensation must be full, adequate, and complete. To this extent Germany will be held accountable. But this Commission is without power to impose penalties for the use and benefit of private claimants when the Government of the United States has exacted none.

This decision ... shall be determinative of all cases growing out of the sinking of the steamship *Lusitania*. ...

Chorzow Factory (Indemnity) Case
(1928), P.C.I.J., Ser. A, No. 17

[In its judgment No. 7 concerning *German Interests in Polish Upper Silesia*, 1926,[63] the Permanent Court of International Justice held that the attitude adopted by the Polish Government towards the Oberschlesische Stickstoffwerke A.-G. and the Bayerische Stickstoffwerke A.-G. in taking possession of the nitrate factory at Chorzow was incompatible with the provisions of the Geneva Convention 1922,[64] between Germany and Poland, concerning Upper Silesia. The German Government now sought to recover an indemnity from Poland in respect of the damage suffered by these companies.

The Court, by nine votes to three, ruled that Poland owed reparation to Germany in respect of damage suffered by the two companies and reserved the amount of compensation due until after an expert inquiry had been held.]

THE COURT: ... It is a principle of international law that the reparation of a wrong may consist in an indemnity corresponding to the damage which the nationals of the injured State have suffered as a result of the act which is contrary to international law. This is even the most usual form of reparation. ... The reparation due by one State to another does not however change its character by reason of the fact that it takes the form of an indemnity for the calculation of which the damage suffered by a private person is taken as the measure. The rules of law governing the reparation are the rules of international law in force between the two States concerned, and not the law governing relations between the State which has committed a wrongful act and the individual who has suffered damage. Rights or interests of an individual, the violation of which rights causes damage, are always in a different plane to rights belonging to a State, which rights may also be infringed by the same act. The damage suffered by an individual is never therefore identical in kind with that which will be suffered by a State; it can only afford a convenient scale for the calculation of the reparation due to the State. ... The Court observes that it is a principle of international law, and even a general conception of law, that any breach of an engagement involves an obligation to make reparation. ... [I]n estimating the damage caused by an unlawful act, only the value of property, rights and interests which have been affected and the owner of which is the person on whose behalf compensation is claimed, or the damage done to whom is to serve as a means of gauging the reparation claimed, must be taken into account. This principle, which is accepted in the jurisprudence

---

[63] (1926), P.C.I.J., Ser. A. No. 7.
[64] 16 Martens, Nouveau recueil général (3 sér), at 645.

of arbitral tribunals, has the effect, on the one hand, of excluding from the damage to be estimated, injury resulting for third parties from the unlawful act and, on the other hand, of not excluding from the damage the amount of debts and other obligations for which the injured party is responsible. The damage suffered by the Oberschlesische in respect of the Chorzow undertaking is therefore equivalent to the total value – but to that total only – of the property, rights and interests of this Company in that undertaking, without deducting liabilities. ...

The action of Poland which the Court has judged to be contrary to the [1922] Geneva Convention [on Upper Silesia] is not an expropriation – to render which lawful only the payment of fair compensation would have been wanting; it is a seizure of property, rights and interests which could not be expropriated even against compensation, save under the exceptional conditions fixed by Article 7 of the said Convention. As the Court has expressly declared in Judgment No. 8, reparation is in this case the consequence not of the application of Articles 6 to 22 of the Geneva Convention, but of acts contrary to those Articles.

It follows that the compensation due to the German Government is not necessarily limited to the value of the undertaking at the moment of dispossession, plus interest to the day of payment. This limitation would only be admissible if the Polish Government had had the right to expropriate, and if its wrongful act consisted merely in not having paid to the two Companies the just price of what was expropriated; in the present case, such a limitation might result in placing Germany and the interests protected by the Geneva Convention, on behalf of which interests the German Government is acting, in a situation more unfavourable than that in which Germany and these interests would have been if Poland had respected the said Convention. Such a consequence would not only be unjust, but also and above all incompatible with the aim of Article 6 and the following articles of the Convention – that is to say, the prohibition, in principle, of the liquidation of the property, rights and interests of German nationals and of companies controlled by German nationals in Upper Silesia – since it would be tantamount to rendering lawful liquidation and unlawful dispossession indistinguishable in so far as their financial results are concerned.

The essential principle contained in the actual notion of an illegal act – a principle which seems to be established by international practice and in particular by the decisions of arbitral tribunals – is that reparation must, as far as possible, wipe out all the consequences of the illegal act and reestablish the situation which would, in all probability, have existed if that act had not been committed. Restitution in kind, or, if this is not possible, payment of a sum corresponding to the value which a restitution in kind would bear; the award, if need be, of damages for loss sustained which would not be covered by restitution in kind or payment in place of it – such are the principles which should serve to determine the amount of compensation due for an act contrary to international law.

This conclusion particularly applies as regards the Geneva Convention, the object of which is to provide for the maintenance of economic life in Upper Silesia on the basis of respect for the *status quo*. The dispossession of an industrial undertaking – the expropriation of which is prohibited by the Geneva Convention – then involves the obligation to restore the undertaking and, if this be not possible, to pay its value at the time of the indemnification, which value is designed to take the place of restitution which has become impossible. To this obligation, in virtue of the general principles of international law, must be added that of compensating loss sustained as the result of the seizure. The impossibility, on which the Parties are agreed, of restoring the Chorzow factory could therefore have no other effect but that of substituting payment of the value of the undertaking for restitution; it would not be in conformity either with the principles of law or with the wish of the Parties to infer from that agreement that the question of compensation must henceforth be dealt with as though an expropriation properly so called was involved. ...

Faced with the task of determining what sum must be awarded to the German Government in order to enable it to place the dispossessed Companies as far as possible in the economic situation in which they would probably have been if the seizure had not taken place, the Court considers that it cannot be satisfied with the data for assessment supplied by the Parties. ...

And finally as regards the sum agreed on at one moment by the two Governments during the negotiations which followed Judgment No. 7 – which sum, moreover, neither Party thought fit to rely on during the present proceedings – it may again be pointed out that the Court cannot take into account declarations, admissions or proposals which the Parties may have made during direct negotiations between themselves, when such negotiations have not led to a complete agreement. ...Possible but contingent and indeterminate damage ... in accordance with the jurisprudence of arbitral tribunals, cannot be taken into account. ...

It may be admitted, as the Court has said in Judgment No. 8, that jurisdiction as to the reparation due for the violation of an international convention involves jurisdiction as to the forms and methods of reparation. If the reparation consists in the payment of a sum of money, the Court may therefore determine the method of such payment. For this reason it may well determine to whom the payment shall be made, in what place and at what moment; in a lump sum or maybe by instalments; where payment shall be made; who shall bear the costs, etc. It is then a question of applying to a particular case the general rules regarding payment, and the Court's jurisdiction arises quite naturally out of its jurisdiction to award monetary compensations.

But this principle would be quite unjustifiably extended if it were taken as meaning that the Court might have cognizance of any question whatever of international law, even quite foreign to the convention under consideration, for the sole reason that the manner in which such question is decided may have an influence on the effectiveness of the reparation asked for. Such an argument seems hardly reconcilable with the fundamental principles of the Court's jurisdiction which is limited to cases specially provided for in treaties and conventions in force.

NOTES

1) In the *Cayuga Indians Claim*[65] the tribunal said:

By the third prayer of the Memorial, Great Britain seeks a declaration that the Canadian Cayugas

---

[65] Great Britain v. United States (1926), *Nielsen's Report* 307, at 330-31, 6 R.I.A.A. 173, at 189-90.

are entitled to the annuity for the future. Great Britain ... is not entitled to such a declaration. Nor have we jurisdiction to make a declaration that the Canadian Cayugas are entitled to share in the annuity for the future. Our powers are limited to a money award, and we must consider how we may frame a money award so as to give effect by that means to the substantive rights of the parties and reach a just result. Accordingly we think the award should contain two elements: (1) An amount equal to a just share in the payment of the annuity from 1849; (2) a capital sum which at five per cent interest will yield half of the amount of the annuity for the future. If by means of an award the United States is held to pay these sums, we think that Government will have been required to perform the covenant in Article IX of the Treaty of Ghent so far as specific performance may be achieved through a money award. The Canadian Cayugas are in a legal condition of pupilage. A sum in the hands of their *quasi* guardian sufficient to pay their share of the annuities for the future will fully protect them and give them what they are entitled to under the Treaty of Ghent.

In explanation of the way in which we have arrived at the amount of the award, we may say that as to the second element, we have taken a sum sufficient to yield an income equal to half of the annuity because the evidence is too uncertain and controversial and the relative numbers [of Cayugas in Canada] fluctuate too much to permit of an exact proportion. Hence, in the absence of any clear mathematical basis of distribution, we proceed upon the maxim that equality is equity. In view of all the evidence we are satisfied that it is not New York nor the United States that will suffer by reason of any margin of error. As to the first element, as it is palpable that in any possible reckoning the Canadian Cayugas have always been numerically much more than half the tribe, we feel that we should be quite justified in awarding sixty per cent of the payments after 1849. But out of abundant caution and in view of the fact that New York actually paid out the whole amount each year under claim of right, we fix the whole amount, including both the elements above set forth, at one hundred thousand dollars.

See also the *Corfu Channel* case (Assessment of Compensation),[66] where the Court considered "the true measure of compensation in the present case to be the replacement cost of the Saumarez [British war vessel] at the time of its loss."

2) As to restitution in kind, see the *Temple of Preah Vihear Case*, discussed in Chapter 6.[67] By contrast, the *I'm Alone Case*[68] reported in Chapter 11 is an example of material satisfaction. The Commissioners recommended the payment by the United States of $25,000 as material amends in respect of the wrong committed by that country in sinking the Canadian vessel. They also recommended that the United States apologize to the Canadian Government.

Self Help

A state, victim of a violation of an international obligation by another state, may resort to limited measures of self-help that would be unlawful were they not in response to the

[66] [1949] I.C.J. Rep. 244, at 249.
[67] (Cambodia v. Thailand) (1962) I.C.J. Rep. 6, at 36-37. See also *Texaco v. Libya* (1977), 53 I.L.R. 389; (1978) 17 *Int. Leg. Mat.* 1, reported *supra*, *Martini Case*, Italy v. Venezuela (1930), 2 R.I.A.A. 975, but cp. *Libyan American Oil Co. v. Libya* (1981), 20 *Int. Leg. Mat.* 1, at 122-25.
[68] (1935), 3 R.I.A.A. 1609, 29 *Am. J. Int. L.* 326.

violation. Such measures must be necessary[69] to terminate the violation, prevent further violation or remedy such violation provided they are not out of proportion to the violation and the injury suffered. So, for example, in the case of the *Destruction of Korean Airlines Flight 007*, reported in Chapter 6, the Canadian response (temporary revocation of landing rights) was related to the violation. Particular measures of self-help are sometimes specified in international agreements. For instance, the General Agreement on Tariffs and Trade (G.A.T.T.) Article XXIII sets out specific steps which a contracting party may take in the event of nullification or impairment by others of its rights under the agreement.

NOTES

1) Is self-help a form of retorsion or reprisal and therefore illegal? What are the permissible limits of self-help: see U.N. Charter Articles 2(4) and 51 in the Appendix and the previous discussion on "Self Defence" in Chapter 2.[70]

2) In the *Corfu Channel Case*, reported in Chapter 11, was the action of the British Navy permissible self-help?[71] What of the blocking of Iranian official assets in response to the seizure of U.S. diplomatic and consular personnel as hostages?[72] Was the bombing of Libyan airports and other military installations by the United States in April 1986 a legitimate form of self-help for a Libyan inspired terrorist attack on U.S. military personnel?

---

[69] See *The Caroline* (1837), 2 Moore 409; and R.Y. Jennings "The *Caroline* and McLeod Cases" (1938), 32 *Am. J. Int. L.* 82.

[70] For a good analysis, see also *Restatement (Revised), Foreign Relations Law of the United States*, § 905 on "Unilateral Remedies" and the Comment and Reporters' Notes thereto.

[71] See [1949] I.C.J. Rep. 4, at 35.

[72] See *U.S. Diplomatic and Consular Staff in Tehran Case*, [1980] I.C.J. Rep. 3, at 17-18, 28-29.

CHAPTER TEN

Protection of Human Rights

INTRODUCTION[1]

The term "human rights" refers to a multi-faceted, evolving group of concepts whose roots frequently extend beyond the traditional boundaries of law into virtually every element of society. History and political science reveal that some of the primary sources of many present-day civil and political rights stem from the privileges shared by the select group of "citizens" of Greek city states. Religious dogma has contributed to the development of human rights (*e.g.*, certain elements of racial equality and non-discrimination) and trends in philosophy provide yet another major source (*e.g.*, much of the rationale for the constitutional enshrinement of rights set out in the American *Declaration of Independence* and *Bill of Rights* and, similarly, the justification for the French Revolution and the basis of its *Declaration des droits de l'homme et du citoyen*). Undoubtedly, as well, economic pressure plays a major role in their evolution and, in certain instances, may well provide the most reasonable explanation for why a state – particularly one with a refined and stable political and legal system such as Canada – will readily confer one class of human rights on a particular group of persons (*e.g.*, to enjoy just and favourable conditions of work[2]) and yet refuse to grant another to a different group (*e.g.*, freedom from sex-based discrimination, which may still be denied, in certain cases, both to Indian women who have married non-Indians and the offspring of such unions[3]).

---

[1] See H. Hannum, *Guide to International Human Rights Practice* (1984); International Commission of Jurists, *The Rule of Law & Human Rights: Principles & Definitions* (1966); H. Lauterpacht, *International Law & Human Rights* (1950; reprinted, 1968); R. Lillich and F. Newman (eds.), *International Human Rights: Problems of Law & Policy* (1979); M. McDougal, *et al.*, *Human Rights & World Public Order* (1980); P. Sieghart, *The International Law of Human Rights* (1983); L. Sohn and T. Buergenthal (eds.), *International Protection of Human Rights* (1973; 2nd ed. in preparation); K. Vasak, *The International Dimensions of Human Rights* (1982).

[2] Canada's attempt to adhere to four early international labour conventions resulted in the notorious constitutional division of powers case: see the *Labour Conventions* case *supra*, in Chapter 3.

[3] See the *Lovelace Case*, reported *infra*.

As human rights are a product of the combined cultural, economic, legal, political, social and religious backgrounds of a people, it is not surprising to discover that they exist in one form or another in every nation, nor to observe that particular aspects of them are unique to each individual society. The close ties between human rights and the social and cultural milieux with which they are associated create difficulties when attempting to compare the rights of one jurisdiction with those of another. In turn, this poses a challenge to assertions that the concepts embodied by the term human rights can be universal. Indeed, the differing ideologies and other factors that separate the world into its well-known East/West and North/South political schisms are also frequent causes for similar divisions on human rights issues.[4] In addition, the concepts are so much a result of the intermingling of the complex elements within individual societies, that neighbouring countries whose respective populations share common backgrounds oftentimes develop antagonistic views about the relative importance, and method of assuring the protection, of human rights. For example, our neighbour, the United States of America, chose armed rebellion to reject British authority in favour of a new system of government based upon a written constitution setting out specific inalienable rights of the individual. Canada, on the other hand, embarked upon a different road to independence and – at least until the adoption of the *Charter of Rights and Freedoms* – accepted the older, antithetical system of English rule by parliamentary sovereignty.

Even if particular cultural similarities, economic factors, legal institutions, political theories and religious beliefs are threads common to the fabric of specific groups of nations, it is unlikely that they are combined, in precisely the same warp and woof, in any two states nor, more importantly, that all of them are shared universally. International law and relations, however, are common to all states. More significantly, every nation, no matter how new or small or undeveloped, exerts at least some influence on these legal and political systems. Because the international law of human rights is a construct of these systems, it reflects universal norms or, at least, the closest thing to them that presently exists. International human rights law, therefore, may well prove to be the role model upon which individual national standards should be measured and determined.

UNIVERSAL STANDARDS

Development of Universal Standards

Like its evolution in municipal jurisdictions, the development of human rights regimes in international fora is the result of the influence of a number of complex factors. However, as it is generally agreed that the watershed of this relatively modern branch of international law is the United Nations Charter, the study is simplified by the resulting historical division: the period leading up to 24 October 1945 (when the *UN Charter* had been ratified by 29 states, thus bringing the United Nations into formal existence), and the one extending to, and including, the present day.

---

[4] See *infra*, the "Consideration of State Reports by the Human Rights Committee," for some examples of both the differing ideologies about, and varying capacities to meet, international human rights commitments.

Before the U.N. Charter

The period before the Charter is generally considered to be merely developmental in nature because individual human rights concerns arose on a piecemeal basis and appeared to lack a central focus. For example, there were laws governing diplomatic immunity and the rights of aliens, and the International Labour Organization (ILO) – a body which dates back to 1919 – had established a number of conventions dealing with labour-related human rights matters.[5] In addition, treaties abolishing the slave trade and regulating the conduct of war existed, and minority rights conventions (resulting from the redrafting of state boundary lines in Europe following World War I) had been in force. Even though such instruments applied and certain human rights issues were a concern of the ill-fated League of Nations, their effect was not considerable because of the overpowering view of the absolutism of state sovereignty. Even more so than now, this period was reflective of the traditional view that individuals are, at most, objects and not subjects of international law. They are objects in that the vast majority of human rights conventions circumscribed their conduct. Moreover, international law imposed punishment, or liability, upon individuals found to be in violation. However, it seldom granted them sufficient recognition to initiate any form of action on their own behalf for violations which detrimentally affected them. It is in this sense that individuals were not usually regarded as subjects of the international legal system – a privilege reserved almost exclusively for states and, to a lesser extent, international organizations.

Even though the restricted view of the individual's degree of personality at international law continues to be the rule, significant changes have occurred since the entry into force of the UN Charter. Taking as their model the earlier minority rights treaties,[6] some recent conventions dealing with a broader scope of human rights concepts provide individuals with the right to lodge complaints which can result in inquiries into the conduct of, or actions by international bodies against, states that have caused them injury and which have agreed to permit them to enjoy that enhanced degree of recognition as entities at international law.

Provisions of the U.N. Charter[7]

Read the UN Charter, Preamble, Arts. 1, 8, 13, 55, 56, 57, 62, 63, 73, 74, 76, and 88 (reproduced in the Appendix).

NOTES

The atrocities – particularly those which occurred in Europe – during the Second World War gave rise to a general belief that states should be made to adhere to minimal norms

---

[5] *Supra*, n. 2. See also International Labour Organization, *International Labour Conventions & Recommendations: 1919–1981* (1982).

[6] See L.C. Green, "Protection of Minorities in the League of Nations & the United Nations," in A. Gotlieb, ed., *Human Rights, Federalism & Minorities* (1970), at 180.

[7] See L. Goodrich, *et al.*, *Charter of the United Nations: Comments & Documentary* (3d ed., 1969); A. Petrenko, "The Human Rights Provisions of the United Nations Charter" (1978), 9 *Man. L.J.* 53.

in the treatment of their own citizens. The desire to make human rights a vital, functioning aspect of international law led to the inclusion of provisions in the UN Charter referring to them. Generally speaking, the present-day international law of human rights stems from these references. While the inclusion of human rights in the *Charter* was a relatively easy task, the delimitation of state sovereignty needed to ensure firm enforcement procedures to guarantee them was a much more difficult chore. To date, that has not been completed because the concept of enforcement powers to support international human rights commitments has never received a considerable degree of *de facto* acceptance.[8] The allies forced the defeated axis nations to include human rights provisions and guarantees to abide by the rules of international law in the post-war revisions of their respective national constitutions. In addition, a number of countries (including, most recently, Canada) have added human rights provisions akin to those in the UN Charter to their constitutions. Otherwise, there is little to show that states have accepted that the human rights provisions of the UN Charter should infringe upon their sovereignty enough to condone the type of compulsory adherence to international human rights norms which should be the subject of a direct enforcement mechanism.[9] Nevertheless, the legal, moral and political validity of international human rights standards is sufficiently recognized by most states – even those with the worst record of human rights violations – to warrant a justification for their breaches. States usually account for their violations by referring to "problems" (most often threats to the regime in power) existing within their territories which prohibit them from acting in a more acceptable manner. Chile has provided a good example of what appears to have become a common rationalization for excessive human rights violations.[10] Contrast this with one that may be even more insidious, namely that of Iran, which justifies its many breaches of human rights commitments on the ground of religious dictates.[11]

Universal Declaration of Human Rights[12]

[The concern for human rights which was manifest by the general references to them in the UN Charter continued once the United Nations became functional. The organization

---

[8] The term "enforcement" does not adequately describe the kind of mechanisms that are normally chosen to ensure compliance with treaties, particularly ones dealing with human rights. "Implementation" is the more accurate term because the intent is usually not to force adherence upon unwilling states but to encourage and assist in the development of an atmosphere that fosters respect for, and compliance with, minimum standards. See T. Buergenthal and others, "UN Human Rights Covenants Become Law: So What?" (1976), 70 *Proc. Am. Soc. Int. L.* 97; J. Humphrey, "The Implementation of International Human Rights Law" (1978), 24 *N.Y.L. School L. Rev.* 31.

[9] See R. Falk, *Human Rights & State Sovereignty* (1981). At the domestic level, Canadian courts have rejected the contention that the UN Charter's provisions are binding on Canada. See *Re Drummond Wren*, [1945] O.R. 778 (H.C.), and *Re Noble and Wolf*, [1948] O.R. 579, aff'd by the Ont. C.A. and rev'd. on other grounds by the Supreme Court of Canada, [1951] S.C.R. 64.

[10] *Infra*, n. 29, *Consideration of State Reports by the Human Rights Committee* – Chile.

[11] *Infra*, n. 31, *Consideration of State Reports by the Human Rights Committee* – Iran.

[12] U.N.G.A. Res. 217 (III), 3 U.N. GAOR Supp. (No. 13) 71, U.N. Doc. A/810 (1948). See R. Cassin,

established a Commission on Human Rights early in 1946, whose first act was to prepare a Declaration of Human Rights. It was adopted without dissenting vote (48 in favour, 8 abstentions, 2 nations absent) by the U.N. General Assembly at its Paris session on 10 December 1948. Of all the international human rights instruments, the Declaration can claim to be the one that is most truly universal. Although it is only a General Assembly resolution, that document has been the basis of not only the majority of international and regional human rights treaties which followed, but also the foundation for other types of instruments such as declarations of intent (*e.g.*, the Helsinki Final Acts, 1975[13]) and human rights guarantees in many recent domestic constitutions.]

Now, therefore, the General Assembly

Proclaims this Universal Declaration of Human Rights as a common standard of achievement for all peoples and all nations, to the end that every individual and every organ of society, keeping this Declaration constantly in mind, shall strive by teaching and education to promote respect for these rights and freedoms and by progressive measures, national and international, to secure their universal and effective recognition and observance both among the peoples of Member States themselves and among the peoples of territories under their jurisdiction.

Article 1

All human beings are born free and equal in dignity and rights. They are endowed with reason and conscience and should act towards one another in a spirit of brotherhood.

Article 2

Everyone is entitled to all the rights and freedoms set forth in this Declaration without distinction of any kind, such as race, colour, sex, language, religion, political or other opinion, national or social origin, property, birth or other status.

Furthermore, no distinction shall be made on the basis of political, jurisdictional or

---

"Looking Back on the Universal Declaration of 1948" (1968), 15 *Rev. Contemp. L.* 13; J. Humphrey, "The Universal Declaration of Human Rights" (1949), 27 *Can. Bar. Rev.* 203; B.G. Ramcharan, *Human Rights: Thirty Years After the Universal Declaration* (1979).

[13] From 1973–1975 interested nations met a number of times for a continuing Conference on Security & Co-operation in Europe. They hoped to improve international relations, particularly between the East and West, in order to promote peaceful harmony in Europe. The result was a document signed by 35 states which "is not eligible for registration under Article 102 of the Charter of the United Nations" and, therefore, cannot be binding on states. The so-called "Final Acts" received a great deal of publicity, and because of it, that document has become far more important in the eyes of many laymen than most binding treaties. This has generated arguments supporting the view that the Final Acts have become more binding on states than was the original intention. See Russell, "The Helsinki Declaration: Brobdingnag or Lilliput?" (1976), 70 *Am. J. Int. L.* 242; S. Williams and A. de Mestral, *An Introduction to International Law* (2d ed., 1987), at 319.

international status of the country or territory to which a person belongs, whether it be independent, trust, non-self-governing or under any other limitation of sovereignty.

Article 3

Everyone has the right to life, liberty and security of person.

Article 4

No one shall be held in slavery or servitude; slavery and the slave trade shall be prohibited in all their forms.

Article 5

No one shall be subjected to torture or to cruel, inhuman or degrading treatment or punishment.

Article 6

Everyone has the right to recognition everywhere as a person before the law.

Article 7

All are equal before the law and are entitled without any discrimination to equal protection of the law. All are entitled to equal protection against any discrimination in violation of this Declaration and against any incitement to such discrimination.

Article 8

Everyone has the right to an effective remedy by the competent national tribunals for acts violating the fundamental rights granted him by the constitution or by law.

Article 9

No one shall be subjected to arbitrary arrest, detention or exile.

Article 10

Everyone is entitled in full equality to a fair and public hearing by an independent and impartial tribunal, in the determination of his rights and obligations and of any criminal charge against him.

Article 11

1. Everyone charged with a penal offence has the right to be presumed innocent until proved guilty according to law in a public trial at which he has had all the guarantees necessary for his defence.

2. No one shall be held guilty of any penal offence on account of any act or omission which did not constitute a penal offence, under national or international law, at the time when it was committed. Nor shall a heavier penalty be imposed than the one that was applicable at the time the penal offence was committed.

Article 12

No one shall be subjected to arbitrary interference with his privacy, family, home or correspondence, nor to attacks upon his honour and reputation. Everyone has the right to the protection of the law against such interference or attacks.

Article 13

1. Everyone has the right to freedom of movement and residence within the borders of each State.

2. Everyone has the right to leave any country, including his own, and to return to his country.

Article 14

1. Everyone has the right to seek and to enjoy in other countries asylum from persecution.

2. This right may not be invoked in the case of persecutions genuinely arising from non-political crimes or from acts contrary to the purposes and principles of the United Nations.

Article 15

1. Everyone has the right to a nationality.

2. No one shall be arbitrarily deprived of his nationality nor denied the right to change his nationality.

Article 16

1. Men and women of full age, without any limitation due to race, nationality or religion, have the right to marry and to found a family. They are entitled to equal rights as to marriage, during marriage and at its dissolution.

2. Marriage shall be entered into only with the free and full consent of the intending spouses.

3. The family is the natural and fundamental group unit of society and is entitled to protection by society and the State.

Article 17

1. Everyone has the right to own property alone as well as in association with others.

2. No one shall be arbitrarily deprived of his property.

Article 18

Everyone has the right to freedom of thought, conscience and religion; this right includes freedom to change his religion or belief, and freedom, either alone or in community with others and in public or private, to manifest his religion or belief in teaching, practice, worship and observance.

Article 19

Everyone has the right to freedom of opinion and expression; this right includes freedom to hold opinions without interference and to seek, receive and impart information and ideas through any media and regardless of frontiers.

Article 20

1. Everyone has the right to freedom of peaceful assembly and association.

2. No one may be compelled to belong to an association.

Article 21

1. Everyone has the right to take part in the government of his country, directly or through freely chosen representatives.

2. Everyone has the right of equal access to public service in his country.

3. The will of the people shall be the basis of the authority of the government; this will shall be expressed in periodic and genuine elections which shall be by universal and equal suffrage and shall be held by secret vote or by equivalent free voting procedures.

Article 22

Everyone, as a member of society has the right to social security and is entitled to realization, through national effort and international cooperation and in accordance with the organization and resources of each State, of the economic, social and cultural rights indispensable for his dignity and the free development of his personality.

Article 23

1. Everyone has the right to work, to free choice of employment, to just and favourable conditions of work and to protection against unemployment.

2. Everyone, without any discrimination, has the right to equal pay for equal work.

3. Everyone who works has the right to just and favourable remuneration ensuring for himself and his family an existence worthy of human dignity, and supplemented, if necessary, by other means of social protection.

4. Everyone has the right to form and to join trade unions for the protection of his interest.

Article 24

1. Everyone has the right to rest and leisure, including reasonable limitation of working hours and periodic holidays with pay.

Article 25

1. Everyone has the right to standard of living adequate for the health and well-being of himself and of his family, including food, clothing, housing and medical care and necessary social services, and the right to security in the event of unemployment, sickness, disability, widowhood, old age or other lack of livelihood in circumstances beyond his control.

2. Motherhood and childhood are entitled to special care and assistance. All children, whether born in or out of wedlock, shall enjoy the same social protection.

Article 26

1. Everyone has the right to education. Education shall be free, at least in the elementary and fundamental stages. Elementary education shall be compulsory. Technical and professional education shall be made generally available and higher education shall be equally accessible to all on the basis of merit.

2. Education shall be directed to the full development of the human personality and to the strengthening of respect for human rights and fundamental freedoms. It shall promote understanding, tolerance and friendship among all nations, racial or religious groups, and shall further the activities of the United Nations for the maintenance of peace.

3. Parents have a prior right to choose the kind of education that shall be given to their children.

Article 27

1. Everyone has the right freely to participate in the cultural life of the community, to enjoy the arts and to share in scientific advancement and its benefits.

2. Everyone has the right to the protection of the moral and material interests resulting from any scientific, literary or artistic production of which he is the author.

Article 28

Everyone is entitled to a social and international order in which the rights and freedoms set forth in this Declaration can be fully realized.

Article 29

1. Everyone has duties to the community in which alone the free and full development of his personality is possible.

2. In the exercise of his rights and freedoms everyone shall be subject only to such limitations as are determined by law solely for the purpose of securing due recognition and respect for the rights and freedoms of others and of meeting the just requirements of morality, public order and the general welfare in a democratic society.

3. These rights and freedoms may in no case be exercised contrary to the purposes and principles of the United Nations.

Article 30

Nothing in this Declaration may be interpreted as implying for any State, group or person any right to engage in any activity or to perform any act aimed at the destruction of any of the rights and freedoms set forth herein.

NOTES

The juridical status of the Universal Declaration has been a long-standing source of controversy.[14] Some have argued that it cannot give rise to binding obligations at international law, while others hold that the constant reference to, and incorporation of, it and the adherence to its principles by a large number of states over the past decades have elevated it to the status of *jus cogens*. A middle view regards the Universal Declaration as binding upon Member States of the UN because: (1) they have expressly accepted its obligations under the UN Charter, Arts. 55 and 56; (2) it now constitutes a legitimate interpretation of Art. 55(c) of the UN Charter; and (3) the Proclamation of Teheran[15] (adopted by the representatives of 84 states which met in Iran from 22 April to 13 May 1968 for a UN International Conference on Human Rights "to review the progress made in the twenty years since the adoption of the [Declaration] and to formulate a programme for the future") have made it so.

Major U.N. Covenants on Human Rights[16]

Once the Universal Declaration had been accepted by the UN General Assembly, the Commission on Human Rights began working on a treaty which was intended to elaborate the rights and impose binding obligations upon states choosing to ratify it. This proved to be a far more difficult task than drafting a mere UN General Assembly resolution, and both the Commission and the Third Committee of the General Assembly struggled from 1948–1966 to obtain an acceptable result. Above and beyond the major question of how the treaty provisions would be enforced or implemented, the Commission encountered a number of problems, one of which was the division of opinion concerning what rights it should contain. The West stressed the importance of civil and political rights, while the East and some Third World representatives argued for the inclusion of economic, social and cultural rights. Another division arose between some states advocating the inclusion of provisions allowing individuals to petition when governments had violated their human rights and others arguing that the very nature of international law precludes all entities but sovereign states and international organizations from possessing that degree of personality. These fundamental divisions of opinion resulted in two separate treaties;

---

[14] See Sieghart, *supra*, n. 1, at 53–54.

[15] U.N. Doc. A/CONF.32/41 (1968). Like the Helsinki Final Acts, *supra*, n. 13, the authority of this "solemn declaration" as a legally binding commitment is subject to debate.

[16] A large number of states of every political persuasion are parties to the two human rights treaties referred to in this section (*infra*, n. 17 and n. 18). One state notable for its absence as a party is the U.S.A., which has not ratified any general human rights treaty.

the International Covenant of Economic, Social and Cultural Rights[17] (CESCR) and the International Covenant on Civil and Political Rights[18] (CCPR). Additionally, the right of individual petition was included in neither treaty, but drafted as an Optional Protocol[19] to the CCPR (there was no protocol for the CESCR because the rights with which it deals are too subjective to permit individuals to complain).

After nearly twenty years' delay, the General Assembly approved the treaties. However, it took a further decade before they were ratified by enough states to come into force (the CESCR on 3 January 1976 and the CCPR on 23 March 1976).

International Covenant on Economic, Social and Cultural Rights[20]

The substantive rights of the Covenant deal with work, trade unions, social security, the family, standards of living, health, education, culture and the benefits of scientific progress.

This Covenant shares some similarities with the *CCPR*, immediately following, in that it contains general provisions making its specific rights applicable "without discrimination of any kind such as race, colour, language, religion, political or other opinion, national or social origin, property, birth or other status" (Art. 2.1). In addition, Art. 3 of both Covenants dictate that states ensure "the equal right of men and women to the enjoyment of all" the rights set out in them respectively. Interestingly, Art. 1 of both Covenants is the same – word for word – and refers to two new rights: self-determination of all peoples to "freely determine their political status and freely pursue their economic, social and cultural development"; and to "freely dispose of their natural wealth and resources."[21]

While civil and political rights require that a state merely adopt a passive role (*e.g.*, it needs do little other than refrain from treating individuals in certain ways), an obligation to ensure economic, social and cultural rights demands that a state take upon itself active obligations. Although courts and other investigatory bodies can usually establish fairly objective tests to determine whether there is compliance with the former set of rights, it is difficult, if not impossible, to do so with the latter ones, primarily because they are so closely tied to the economic situation and political ideologies of individual nations. As a result, most economic, social and cultural rights are looked upon as goals which states must strive to achieve rather than obligations that must presently be met. It is not surprising, then, to discover that the implementation provisions are virtually non-existent

---

[17] Signed 1966, Annex to G.A. Res. 2200A, 21 U.N. GAOR, Supp. (No. 16) 49, U.N. Doc. A/6316, (1966). As of 1 January 1984, there were 80 ratifications. It came in force for Canada on 19 August 1976.

[18] Signed 1966, Annex to G.A. Res. 2200A, 21 U.N. GAOR, Supp. (No. 16) 52, U.N. Doc. A/6316, (1966). As of 1 January 1984, there were 77 ratifications. It came in force for Canada on 19 August 1976.

[19] Signed 1966. Annex to G.A. Res. 2200A, 21 U.N. GAOR, Supp. (No. 16) 59, U.N. Doc. A/6316 (1966). As of 1 January 1984, there were 31 ratifications. It came in force for Canada on 19 August 1976.

[20] See R.St.J. Macdonald *et al.*, eds., *The International Law and Policy of Human Welfare* (1978); Vierdag, "The Legal Nature of the Rights Granted by the International Covenant on Economic, Social and Cultural Rights" (1978), 9 *Neth. Y.B. Int. L.* 69. As with civil and political rights, the Western European nations have demonstrated their concern for this type of right in advance of the U.N. See the *European Social Charter*, signed 1961; in force 1965 with 13 ratifications as of 1 January 1984; Council of Europe, European Treaty Series, no. 35.

[21] Should these rights be in both treaties? See *A.D. Case*, *infra*, at n. 42.

in the CESCR. The treaty requires states to submit reports "on the measures which they have adopted and the progress made in achieving the observance of" those rights (Art. 16.1). The reports which, technically, are considered by the UN Economic and Social Council, are examined and can be referred to appropriate UN specialized agencies for the purpose of formulating plans to assist states in deciding what measures – either domestic or international – might be advisable "to contribute to the effective progressive implementation of the Covenant" (Art. 22). The implementation procedures,[22] at least for the foreseeable future, demonstrate that the purpose of this treaty is not so much to provide a mechanism to safeguard rights as it is to foster and develop a climate to promote them within states, particularly in developing nations that lack financial and technical competence.

International Covenant on Civil and Political Rights[23]

Article 2

1. Each State Party to the present Covenant undertakes to respect and to ensure to all individuals within its territory and subject to its jurisdiction the rights recognized in the present Covenant, without distinction of any kind, such as race, colour, sex, language, religion, political or other opinion, national, or social origin, property, birth or other status.

2. Where not already provided for by existing legislative or other measures, each State Party to the present Covenant undertakes to take the necessary steps, in accordance with its constitutional processes and with the provisions of the present Covenant, to adopt such legislative or other measures as may be necessary to give effect to the rights recognized in the present Covenant.

3. Each State Party to the present Covenant undertakes:

(a) To ensure that any person whose rights or freedoms as herein recognized are violated shall have an effective remedy, notwithstanding that the violation has been committed by persons acting in an official capacity;

(b) To ensure that any person claiming such a remedy shall have his right thereto determined by competent judicial, administrative or legislative authorities, or by any other competent authority provided for by the legal system of the State, and to develop the possibilities of judicial remedy;

(c) To ensure that the competent authorities shall enforce such remedies when granted.

---

[22] See Alston, "The United Nations' Specialized Agencies & Implementation of the International Covenant on Economic, Social & Cultural Rights" (1979), 18 *Colum. J. Transnat. L.* 79; B.G. Ramcharan, "Implementation of the International Covenant on Economic, Social and Cultural Rights" (1976), 23 *Neth. Int. L. Rev.* 151.

[23] See L. Henkin, ed., *The International Bill of Rights: The Covenant on Civil & Political Rights* (1981); Lippman, "Human Rights Revisited: The Protection of Human Rights Under the International Covenant on Civil & Political Rights" (1980), 10 *Cal. W. Int. L.J.* 450; O. Schacter, "The Obligation of the Parties to Give Effect to the Covenant on Civil & Political Rights" (1979), 73 *Am. J. Int. L.* 462.

Article 3

The States Parties to the present Covenant undertake to ensure the equal right of men and women to the enjoyment of all civil and political rights set forth in the present Covenant.

Article 4

1. In time of public emergency which threatens the life of the nation and the existence of which is officially proclaimed, the States Parties to the present Covenant may take measures derogating from their obligations under the present Covenant to the extent strictly required by the exigencies of the situation, provided that such measures are not inconsistent with their other obligations under international law and do not involve discrimination solely on the ground of race, colour, sex, language, religion or social origin.

2. No derogation from articles 6, 7, 8 (paragraphs 1 and 2), 11, 15, 16 and 18 may be made under this provision.

3. Any State Party to the present Covenant availing itself of the right of derogation shall immediately inform the other States Parties to the present Covenant, through the intermediary of the Secretary-General of the United Nations, of the provisions from which it has derogated and of the reasons by which it was actuated. A further communication shall be made, through the same intermediary, on the date on which it terminates such derogation.

Article 5

1. Nothing in the present Covenant may be interpreted as implying for any State, group or person any right to engage in any activity or perform any act aimed at the destruction of any of the rights and freedoms recognized herein or at their limitation to a greater extent than is provided for in the present Covenant.

2. There shall be no restriction upon or derogation from any of the fundamental human rights recognized or existing in any State Party to the present Covenant pursuant to law, conventions, regulations or custom on the pretext that the present Covenant does not recognize such rights or that it recognizes them to a lesser extent.

Article 6

1. Every human being has the inherent right to life. This right shall be protected by law. No one shall be arbitrarily deprived of his life.

2. In countries which have not abolished the death penalty, sentence of death may be imposed only for the most serious crimes in accordance with the law in force at the time of the commission of the crime and not contrary to the provisions of the present Covenant and to the Convention on the Prevention and Punishment of the Crime of Genocide. This penalty can only be carried out pursuant to a final judgment rendered by a competent in any way from any obligation assumed under the provisions of the Convention on the Prevention and Punishment of the Crime of Genocide.

4. Anyone sentenced to death shall have the right to seek pardon or commutation of the sentence. Amnesty, pardon or commutation of the sentence of death may be granted in all cases.

5. Sentence of death shall not be imposed for crimes committed by persons below eighteen years of age and shall not be carried out on pregnant women.

6. Nothing in this article shall be invoked to delay or to prevent the abolition of capital punishment by any State Party to the present Covenant.

Article 7

No one shall be subjected to torture or to cruel, inhuman or degrading treatment or punishment. In particular, no one shall be subjected without his free consent to medical or scientific experimentation.

Article 8

1. No one shall be held in slavery; slavery and the slave-trade in all their forms shall be prohibited.

2. No one shall be held in servitude.

3. (a) No one shall be required to perform forced or compulsory labour;

     (b) Paragraph 3(a) shall not be held to preclude, in countries where imprisonment with hard labour may be imposed as a punishment for a crime, the performance of hard labour in pursuance of a sentence to such punishment by a competent court;

     (c) For the purpose of this paragraph the term "forced or compulsory labour" shall not include:

         (i) Any work or service, not referred to in subparagraph (b), normally required of a person who is under detention in consequence of a lawful order of a court, or of a person during conditional release from such detention;

         (ii) Any service of a military character and, in countries where conscientious objection is recognized, any national service required by law of conscientious objectors;

         (iii) Any service exacted in cases of emergency or calamity threatening the life or well-being of the community;

         (iv) Any work or service which forms part of normal civil obligations.

Article 9

1. Everyone has the right to liberty and security of person. No one shall be subjected to arbitrary arrest or detention. No one shall be deprived of his liberty except on such grounds and in accordance with such procedure as are established by law.

2. Anyone who is arrested shall be informed, at the time of arrest, of the reasons for his arrest and shall be promptly informed of any charges against him.

3. Anyone arrested or detained on a criminal charge shall be brought promptly before a judge or other officer authorized by law or exercise judicial power and shall be entitled to trial within a reasonable time or to release. It shall not be the general rule that persons awaiting trial shall be detained in custody, but release may be subject to guarantees to appear for trial, at any other stage of the judicial proceedings, and, should occasion arise, for execution of the judgment.

4. Anyone who is deprived of his liberty by arrest or detention shall be entitled to take proceedings before a court, in order that that court may decide without delay on the lawfulness of his detention and order his release if the detention is not lawful.

5. Anyone who has been the victim of unlawful arrest or detention shall have an enforceable right to compensation.

Article 10

1. All persons deprived of their liberty shall be treated with humanity and with respect for the inherent dignity of the human person.

2. (a) Accused persons shall, save in exceptional circumstances, be segregated from convicted persons and shall be subject to separate treatment appropriate to their status as unconvicted persons;

(b) Accused juvenile persons shall be separated from adults and brought as speedily as possible for adjudication.

3. The penitentiary system shall comprise treatment of prisoners the essential aim of which shall be their reformation and social rehabilitation. Juvenile offenders shall be segregated from adults and be accorded treatment appropriate to their age and legal status.

Article 11

No one shall be imprisoned merely on the ground of inability to fulfil a contractual obligation.

Article 12

1. Everyone lawfully within the territory of a State shall, within that territory, have the right to liberty of movement and freedom to choose his residence.

2. Everyone shall be free to leave any country, including his own.

3. The above-mentioned rights shall not be subject to any restrictions except those which are provided by law, are necessary to protect national security, public order (*ordre public*), public health or morals or the rights and freedoms of others, and are consistent with the other rights recognized in the present Covenant.

4. No one shall be arbitrarily deprived of the right to enter his own country.

Article 13

An alien lawfully in the territory of a State Party to the present Covenant may be expelled therefrom only in pursuance of a decision reached in accordance with law and shall, except where compelling reasons of national security otherwise require, be allowed to submit the reasons against his expulsion and to have his case reviewed by, and be represented for the purpose before, the competent authority or a person or persons especially designated by the competent authority.

Article 14

1. All persons shall be equal before the courts and tribunals. In the determination of any criminal charge against him, or of his rights and obligations in a suit of law, everyone shall be entitled to a fair and public hearing of a competent, independent and impartial tribunal established by law. The Press and the public may be excluded from all or part of a trial for reasons of morals, public order (*ordre public*) or national security in a democratic society, or when the interest of the private lives of the parties so requires, or the extent strictly necessary in the opinion of the court in special circumstances where publicity would prejudice the interests of justice; but any judgment tendered in a criminal case or in a suit at law shall be made public except where the interest of juvenile persons otherwise requires or the proceedings concern matrimonial disputes or the guardianship of children.

2. Everyone charged with a criminal offence shall have the right to be presumed innocent until proved guilty according to law.

3. In the determination of any criminal charge against him, everyone shall be entitled to the following minimum guarantees, in full equality:

(a) To be informed promptly and in detail in a language which he understands of the nature and cause of the charge against him;

(b) To have adequate time and facilities for the preparation of his defence and to communicate with counsel of his own choosing;

(c) To be tried without undue delay;

(d) To be tried in his presence, and to defend himself in person or through legal assistance of his own choosing; to be informed, if he does not have legal assistance, of this right; and to have legal assistance assigned to him, in any case where the interests of justice so require, and without payment by him in any such case if he does not have sufficient means to pay for it;

(e) To examine, or have examined, the witnesses against him and to obtain the attendance and examination of witnesses on his behalf under the same conditions as witnesses against him;

(f) To have the free assistance of an interpreter if he cannot understand or speak the language used in court;

(g) Not to be compelled to testify against himself or to confess guilt.

4. In the case of juvenile persons, the procedure shall be such as will take account of their age and the desirability of promoting their rehabilitation.

5. Everyone convicted of a crime shall have the right to his conviction and sentence being reviewed by a higher tribunal according to law.

6. When a person has by a final decision been convicted of a criminal offence and when subsequently his conviction has been reversed or he has been pardoned on the ground that a new or newly discovered fact shows conclusively that there has been a miscarriage of justice, the person who has suffered punishment as a result of such

Art. 4.3 to cover the public emergency within the meaning of Art. 4.1 to excuse it from compliance with Arts. 9, 10.2, 10.3, 12.1, 14, 17, 19.2, 21 or 22.[27]]

199. With reference to article 12 of the Covenant and to the reservations made thereto by the United Kingdom, information was requested on any exceptions to the rights inscribed in that article in addition to those included in the reservations, and on whether there was any possibility of appeal against the application of the "immigration controls" in respect of persons who did not have the right of abode in the United Kingdom. Concern was expressed by some members in respect of some inhabitants of ex-dependent territories who still held British passports but did not seem to have absolute right to entry into the United Kingdom. The reservation to that effect was thought to be so sweeping that there was some doubt as to whether it might not be extended, as far as immigration was concerned, to the prohibition of discrimination as set out in articles 2 and 26 of the Covenant. Information was requested on the extent to which the Covenant's provisions concerning the prohibition of racial discrimination were complied with in the framework of the United Kingdom immigration policy. ...

219. In relation to the "immigration controls" practised in the United Kingdom in respect of some inhabitants of ex-dependent territories who still held British passports, the representative gave a historical background to the status of such persons and to the rules governing their entry into the United Kingdom. He stated that article 12, paragraph 4, of the Covenant dealt with arbitrary acts and that the control in force was not arbitrary but governed by statute. To prevent misunderstanding, however, his country had, on ratifying the Covenant, entered a reservation on that article. ...

224. Replying to questions under articles 3, 23 and 24 of the Covenant, he pointed out that a woman who had married a British subject could acquire the nationality of her husband on application, but that men who had married women of British nationality could acquire British nationality only by registration or naturalization. On the other hand, the mother, unlike the father, could not transmit her nationality to her children, that approach being motivated by a concern to avoid too many cases of dual nationality.

Sweden[28]

70. With regard to the statement made in the report to the effect that it had not been found necessary to lay down provisions equivalent to those of the Covenant in an independent Swedish statute because existing domestic law was in full accord with the obligations to be assumed by Sweden under the Covenant, some members asked whether it was possible for an individual to directly invoke the provisions of the Covenant before a court or administrative tribunal, or to call for the annulment of a law which ran counter to the Covenant. One member observed that the report, like others describing mainly constitutional and legal provisions, was incomplete as regards the actual situation af-

---

[27] *Supra*, n. 25, at 36.
[28] *Supra*, n. 25, at 12–14.

fecting, in the terms of article 40 of the Covenant, the progress made in the enjoyment of rights.

71. Information was sought on the manner in which the proclaimed equality between men and women was implemented, with particular reference to the rights of men and women regarding the devolution of property, succession and legal representation.

72. With regard to article 4 of the Covenant, it was noted that the report contained no information on what legal measures could be taken during a period of emergency. The representative of Sweden was asked how a public emergency could be declared, what the extent of the control exercised by Parliament was or whether such control was exclusively an executive prerogative. Some members requested clarification on the reference in the report to the limitation on certain rights and freedoms permitted in the Constitution in order to satisfy "a purpose which is acceptable in a democratic society" and on the authorities which were entitled to impose such limitations. ...

84. The representative of Sweden commented on the observations and questions summarized in the preceding paragraphs. He stated that the courts and the administrative authorities had the right to examine the constitutionality of laws and regulations. As regards article 3 of the Covenant, he stated that there were no legislative provisions relating to the principle of equality of the sexes and that a Government Commission was drafting a bill on the question. With reference to article 4 of the Covenant, he stated that no provision was made for the suspension of the Constitution in a public emergency and that in such a situation no law contrary to chapter 2 of the Swedish Constitution, which guarantees certain freedoms and rights, could be enacted.

Chile[29]

73. All members agreed that the report of the Government of Chile did not give any account of the problems affecting civil and political rights to which the *Ad Hoc* Working Group of the Commission on Human Rights and resolutions of the United Nations have repeatedly referred. Some members also drew attention to the fact that the report had been submitted by an authority which owed its very existence to the elimination of the political rights of the Chilean people although the Government had attempted to create the impression that legal continuity had been maintained with the Chilean Constitution of 1925. Other members stated that the report failed to meet the requirements of article 40, paragraph 2, of the Covenant since it merely provided an idealized and abstract picture of the legal framework which should ensure the protection of civil and political rights in Chile and that the description itself contained contradictions in reasoning and ambiguous

---

[29] *Report of the Human Rights Committee*, 34 U.N. GAOR Supp. (No. 40) 18 U.N. Doc. A/34/40 (1979). As Chile's report was deemed to be unsatisfactory, the Committee requested that it compile a supplementary one containing more detail and responding to specific queries raised by its first report. While Chile appeared a second time to speak to its response to that demand, the Committee Chairman prefaced the meeting by complaining that the state had ignored the requests of the Committee and that its supplementary report, therefore, was also below standard. See *Report of the Human Rights Committee*, 39 U.N. GAOR Supp. (No. 40) 78, U.N. Doc. A/39/40 (1984).

legal formulations and made no reference to the practical enforcement of the legal norms for the protection of fundamental rights. They considered that the report which had been submitted ignored the true situation in the country and did not make for proper examination of that situation. Consequently it was necessary to ask the Government of Chile to submit a further report in which an analysis would be made of the manner in which each Covenant right is in practice implemented, the rights which have been derogated from, the justification for and the extent of the derogation. ...

74. Some members referred to certain concepts which were regarded as justifying restrictions on human rights in Chile, such as those of ''national security'' and ''latent subversion,'' and pointed out that the Covenant did not authorize any derogation from its obligations on the grounds of ''latent subversion''. They inquired whether the concept of ''national security'' was defined in terms of the stability of the régime or the stability of the State and whether it was invoked when the government feared for its stability or when its interests had been threatened. They also asked how the term ''latent subversion'' should, in the view of the Government of Chile, be defined since, in those countries of Latin America where illiteracy, poverty and disease were rife, there could be said to exist a state of latent subversion that would last as long as social and political rights had not been substantially implemented.

Union of Soviet Socialist Republics[30]

432. The representative of the USSR commented on the observations and questions summarized in the preceding paragraphs. He stressed that all basic provisions of the Covenant had been incorporated in the Constitution and thus had become constitutional rights. Citizens of the USSR could invoke the provisions of the Covenant before State authorities and courts if they so wished. In the further development process of the Soviet legislation, the provisions of the Covenant would continue to be taken into consideration. As regards the interrelation between individual and collective rights of Soviet citizens, it was covered by the constitutional clause according to which the law of life was the concern of all for the good of everyone and the concern of everyone for the good of all. ...

445. Commenting on questions under article 19 of the Covenant, he stated that a citizen of the USSR could express any opinion in newspapers and journals, the number of which exceeded 10,000. The law of life in the Soviet Union was the unity of society, State, people and individuals, and there was no contradiction to the Covenant in the fact that laws were issued by the will of the people, reflected their interests, served their purposes and contributed to the development of the people's Soviet State. Article 46 of the Constitution stated that citizens of the USSR had the right to enjoy cultural benefits, and cultural exchanges with other countries showed that there was freedom in the field of cultural and artistic activities. ...

447. With regard to article 22 of the Covenant, he pointed out that there was no social

---

[30] *Supra*, n. 25, at 72–75.

basis for a multi-party system in the USSR. The Communist Party of the USSR, which was the leading and guiding force of Soviet society, did not issue any laws; it determined the general perspectives of the development of society and functioned within the framework of the Soviet Constitution. There was no need for the Soviet people to create "free alternative trade unions" because all Soviet trade unions were free.

Iran[31]

301. Members of the Committee welcomed the fact that the Iranian Government had submitted its report and expressed appreciation for the additional information provided by the representative of the reporting State concerning the revolutionary process which laid the foundation of a new society which had started in that country. While understanding the difficulties of an internal and an external nature that Iran had to face during its revolutionary process which might have affected the preparation of a report, members of the Committee regretted that the report under consideration was narrower in scope than article 40 of the Covenant envisaged, that it did not follow the general guidelines for the submission of reports established by the Committee, that the information provided had been limited to a description of laws and regulations and that no mention had been made of other measures to implement the various provisions of the Covenant as indicated in its article 2, paragraph 2, nor of remedies available to those who believed that their rights under the Covenant had been violated. Noting that every revolution had its own laws, members of the Committee needed more detailed information on the revolutionary process itself in order to ascertain how far it affected the human rights situation in the country and what its effects were in relation to the Covenant. Members of the Committee noted with satisfaction the intention of the Iranian Government to submit shortly a more comprehensive report which would strengthen the dialogue that had just started between the Committee and that Government and wished to know when exactly the new report would be submitted. ...

324. With reference to article 2 of the Covenant, [the Iranian representative] stressed that the criteria for determining the validity of any law would be the values given by God and transmitted to earth, that since human traits were considered to be in harmony with revealed values, values derived from human civilization and from reason were held to be close to Islamic values, and that whenever divine law conflicted with man-made law, divine law would prevail. He explained that the Koran contained guidance on a comprehensive range of matters involving morals, historical analysis, a criminal code and precepts regarding the distribution of wealth, teachings on community growth and spiritual values, and when a nation recognized and accepted the principles of Islam, as the basis for its existence, Islamic precepts would be followed in resolving problems. However, in Shi'ite canon law the basic requirements governing the continuity of community life could be viewed in historical terms, and the divine laws could be interpreted and implemented accordingly. Unfortunately, the conspiracies that had occurred in Iran

---

[31] *Report of the Human Rights Committee*, 37 U.N. GAOR Supp. (No. 40) 66–72, U.N. Doc. A/37/40 (1982).

since the revolution had prevented the Government from having sufficient time to develop new laws along those lines. Nevertheless, an attempt was being made to establish, at an early date, the three separate powers of the judiciary, the executive and the legislative in conformity with Islamic law. After the legislative power had been established, the relative conformity of each law with Islamic precepts would be determined.

Guinea[32]

[Consideration of the report submitted by Guinea had been postponed on 4 sessions reserved for it because state representatives failed to appear. After repeated warnings, the Committee examined the report in the absence of a state delegation and found it to be unacceptable.]

155. After consideration of the report, the Committee learned that on 4 November 1983 three representatives of the Government of Guinea had visited the Human Rights Liaison Office in New York and had conveyed the firm wish of their Government to fulfil its reporting obligations under the Covenant in future and had blamed lack of co-ordination for the Government's failure to respond to the various requests sent to it. They also indicated the need for specialized training in human rights matters for officials in charge of the preparation of the report. The Committee took note of this visit expressing appreciation at Guinea's reaction, though unofficial, to its consideration of the report.

156. In conclusion, members of the Committee decided to request a new report from the Government of Guinea not later than 30 September 1984, which should be prepared in accordance with the Committee's general guidelines as to the form and content of States reports under article 40 and most particularly should keep in view the questions and comments made by members of the Committee during the consideration of the first report. ...

160. At its twenty-second session, the Committee decided to authorize one of its members, Mr. Ndiaye, to make himself available for consultations with the Government of Guinea with a view to ascertaining the ways in which the Government could be assisted in fulfilling its reporting obligations under the Convenant.

NOTES

1) Guidelines concerning the form and contents of reports are documented in Annex IV of the *Report of the Human Rights Committee* (1977) and in Annexes IV and VI of its 1981 *Report*. They are required to be in two parts. The first is a description of the general legal framework within which civil and political rights are protected in the reporting state. This part should contain a statement about what rights are protected, when derogations can occur, how the provisions of the CCPR can be invoked before, and

---

[32] *Report of the Human Rights Committee* (1984) *supra*, n. 29, at 32.

directly enforced by, domestic tribunals, what authorities have jurisdiction respecting human rights, what remedies individuals might have and what measures have been taken to ensure the domestic implementation of the provisions of the CCPR. The second part is more detailed, and requires that states outline, in relation to the provisions of each substantive Article in the CCPR, all legislative and other measures in force in regard to each right, any restrictions or limitations of a *de jure, de facto* or temporary nature affecting the enjoyment of such rights, and any other factors or difficulties affecting the enjoyment of them.

2) Do these sections from state reports, read in conjunction with the CCPR, suggest that truly universal human rights norms exist, or are in the process of becoming established? Why (or why not)?

3) Is there a "sliding scale" of human rights norms which the Human Rights Committee applies to accommodate the differing levels of capabilities of states (*e.g.*, the United Kingdom on the one hand, and Guinea on the other)? What arguments might be made in support or denial of such an approach to human rights?

4) Are any of the reasons given by states for reneging on their international human rights commitments legitimate?

5) Would these state reports be helpful in evaluating the Canadian domestic human rights situation (*e.g.*, contrast the Canadian constitutional provisions for suspending human rights with those outlined by Sweden in the oral comments on its report, and justify both)?

United Nations Petition System[33]

There are two major procedures which the United Nations provides for individuals to lodge complaints against states for human rights violations. They differ from one another quite radically. One is open to virtually anyone who is able to send a communication. That opportunity is provided by Resolution 1503 of the Economic and Social Council[34]. It permits individual complaints to be received, and allows the Human Rights Commission (or its Subcommission on the Prevention of Discrimination and Protection of Minorities) to catalogue and coordinate them. This procedure does not provide for the consideration of particular claims. Instead, its purpose is to legitimate a compilation of violations by individual states. When sufficient numbers of valid claims have been registered against any state or states, the documentation assists the United Nations in determining whether there is reliable evidence to demonstrate the existence of persistent breaches of human rights by any sovereign that are tantamount to "gross violations." While the procedure is, of and by itself, of little significance, it may prove useful, in the long run, in encouraging states to accept and adhere to basic human rights norms.

---

[33] For information on the petition system for human rights treaties, see Ton Zuidjuick, "The Right to Petition the United Nations Because of Violations of Human Rights" (1981), 59 *Can. Bar. Rev.* 103; and M. Tardu, *Human Rights: The International Petition System* (1979).

[34] See D.L. Shelton, "Individual Complaint Machinery Under the United Nations 1503 Procedure and the Optional Protocol to the International Convention on Civil and Political Rights," in Hannum, *supra*, n. 1, at 59.

The second procedure can have a more immediate impact. Its application is somewhat restricted in that it is available only to individuals situate in states that are parties to both the CCPR and its companion, the Optional Protocol to that treaty.

Optional Protocol to the CCPR[35]

Article 2

Subject to the provisions of article 1, individuals who claim that any of their rights enumerated in the Covenant have been violated and who have exhausted all available domestic remedies may submit a written communication to the Committee for consideration.

Article 3

The Committee shall consider inadmissible any communication under the present Protocol which is anonymous, or which it considers to be an abuse of the right of submission of such communications or to be incompatible with the provisions of the Covenant.

Article 4

1. Subject to the provisions of article 3, the Committee shall bring any communications submitted to it under the present Protocol to the attention of the State Party to the present Protocol alleged to be violating any provision of the Covenant.

2. Within six months, the receiving State shall submit to the Committee written explanations or statements clarifying the matter and the remedy, if any, that may have been taken by that State.

Article 5

1. The Committee shall consider communications received under the present Protocol in the light of all written information made available to it by the individual and by the State Party concerned.

2. The Committee shall not consider any communication from an individual unless it has ascertained that:

    (a) The same matter is not being examined under another procedure of international investigation or settlement;

    (b) The individual has exhausted all available domestic remedies. This shall not be the rule where the application of the remedies is unreasonably prolonged.

3. The Committee shall hold closed meetings when examining communications under the present Protocol.

---

[35] Signed 19 December 1966. Annex to G.A. Res. 2200A, 21 U.N. GAOR, Supp. (No. 16) 59, U.N. Doc. A/6316 (1966).

4. The Committee shall forward its views to the State Party concerned and to the individual. ...

Article 7

Pending the achievement of the objectives of resolution 1514 (XV) adopted by the General Assembly of the United Nations on 14 December 1960 concerning the Declaration on the Granting of Independence to Colonial Countries and Peoples, the provisions of the present Protocol shall in no way limit the right of petition granted to these peoples by the Charter of the United Nations and other international conventions and instruments under the United Nations and its specialized agencies.

Article 8

1. The present Protocol is open for signature by any State which has signed the Covenant.

2. The present Protocol is subject to ratification by any State which has ratified or acceded to the Covenant. Instruments of ratification shall be deposited with the Secretary-General of the United Nations.

3. The present Protocol shall be open to accession by any State which has ratified or acceded to the Covenant.

4. Accession shall be effected by the deposit of an instrument of accession with the Secretary-General of the United Nations.

5. The Secretary-General of the United Nations shall inform all States which have signed the present Protocol or acceded to it of the deposit of each instrument of ratification or accession. ...

Article 10

The provisions of the present Protocol shall extend to all parts of federal States without any limitations or exceptions.

NOTES

1) As of 1 January 1984, 31 states had ratified the Optional Protocol (approximately 40% of the states parties to the CCPR). Some nations (*e.g.*, the U.S.S.R.) would not ratify it because they firmly believe that individuals should have no standing at international law, while others (*e.g.*, the Federal Republic of Germany, France, Spain and the United Kingdom) see no reason to do so, ostensibly because they are parties to other human rights treaties such as the European Convention[36] which permit individual petitions. (The latter rationale has not prevented countries like Denmark, Iceland, Italy, Luxem-

---

[36] Reported in the next section.

bourg, the Netherlands, Norway, Portugal, or Sweden from becoming parties to the Optional Protocol.)

2) Although the recognition accorded to the individual by this instrument[37] seems, at first glance, to be impressive, the implementation provisions of the Covenant are not altered by it. A state must be committed to ensuring that its laws accord with its international undertakings. If it is not, this procedural instrument is of no practical value and it will only help to make "official" or "documented" lists of the human rights violations of particular states more lengthy. Contrast, for example, the situation in Uruguay, (with violations stemming from at least 35 cases against it), where virtually nothing has been done by its government, with Mauritius and Finland, each of which acted quickly to correct the one outstanding breach each had committed.

3) As with the procedures governing state reports under the CCPR, credit must go to the Human Rights Committee for establishing ones that facilitate individual complaints and get to the crux of most issues raised by them. In essence, all communications in any case addressed to the Committee are sent to the other party for reply. Further, the onus is usually placed upon the state to provide the necessary information and explanations giving rise to a complaint, although its "author" is permitted to add to, or refute, what the state has produced or stated. Complaints are processed through two possible stages dealing with admissibility and merits respectively. All proceedings must be in written form in accordance with guidelines established by the Committee.[38]

Weismann Case
R.7/31[39]

[This case is typical of the great majority determined by the Human Rights Committee in that it was against Uruguay and deals with the human rights breaches resulting from a suspension of rights by the military junta (which came into power shortly after Uruguay had ratified the Optional Protocol), allegedly "on a strictly temporary basis, because of the grave situation menacing the life of the country."[40]

Both a husband and his wife were arrested in February 1976 and kept incommunicado for many months. During their second year of imprisonment, a military judge convicted the husband of "subversive association" because of his political views and sentenced him to 3 years, less the time already spent in custody. His spouse, convicted of "assisting

---

[37] The relationship between the CCPR and the Optional Protocol is discussed *supra* at the beginning of the last section.

[38] By the time the Committee was preparing its 1984 Report (*supra*, n. 29, at 110) it had acquired sufficient experience and information to publish a substantial description of procedural guidelines governing communications under the Optional Protocol (*ibid.*, at 110–18) and a precis of its findings on many substantive issues set out in the Covenant (*ibid.*, at 118–28). This is a valuable reference document for anyone interested in the Committee's "case work" and, undoubtedly, will be expanded and amended in future Reports.

[39] *Report of the Human Rights Committee*, 35 U.N. GAOR Supp. (No. 40) 111 U.N. Doc. A/35/40 (1980).

[40] Introduction by the Uruguayan representative of the state report presented to the Human Rights Committee. See *Report of the Human Rights Committee*, *supra*, n. 31, at 58.

a subversive association,'' had her sentence suspended because of the time already spent in gaol. Neither person was permitted to engage legal counsel, and they were held for at least 6 months after their respective prison terms had expired. In this case, the Committee considered that there were violations of Arts. 7, 10(1), 9(3) and (4), 14(1) and (3), 15(1), 19(2) and 25 of the CCPR after finding the state had not established a valid defense under Arts. 4 and 19(3) of the CCPR or Art. 5(2)(b) of the Optional Protocol.

This case exemplifies how the Committee has overcome the problem of establishing evidence. Once it deems that a complaint is admissible, the onus of proof shifts to the state to deny the accusations against it or to provide a justifiable reason for its actions that accord with the Committee's interpretation of the Covenant. The Committee said:]

With regard to the exhaustion of domestic remedies, the Committee notes that the submissions and explanations of the Government still do not show in any way that in the particular circumstances of the two individuals concerned at the time of the events complained of, there were remedies available which they should have pursued. The Committee has been informed by the Government in another case (R.2/9) that the remedy of *habeas corpus* is not applicable to persons arrested under prompt security measures. Moreover, Beatriz Weismann and Alcides Lanza have explained that they had no effective contact with lawyers to advise them of their rights or to assist them in exercising them. ...

The Human Rights Committee has considered whether acts and treatment, which are *prima facie* not in conformity with the Covenant, could for any reasons be justified under the Covenant in the circumstances. The Government has referred to provisions of Uruguayan law, in particular the Prompt Security Measures. However, the Covenant (art. 4) does not allow national measures derogating from any of its provisions except in strictly defined circumstances, and the Government has not made any submissions of fact or law to justify such derogation. Moreover, some of the facts referred to above raise issues under provisions from which the Covenant does not allow any derogation under any circumstances.

Motta Case
R. 2/11[41]

[The majority of cases dealt with by the Committee do not seem to raise considerable evidentiary problems, possibly because major violators wish to avoid the intensified examination of their activities which will result if they concoct facts that others would refute. As a result, the Committee appears to have little difficulty in reaching conclusions on the facts. Its summary of the present case, in which Uruguay was found to be in violation of Arts. 7, 10 (1) and 9 (3) and (4), is a fairly common one:]

The Committee therefore decided to base its views on the following facts which have either been essentially confirmed by the State party or are uncontested except for denials of a general character offering no particular information or explanation: Alberto Grille

---

[41] *Supra*, n. 39, at 132.

Motta was arrested on 7 February 1976. About one month later, he was brought before a military judge without having any opportunity to consult a lawyer beforehand and after having been held completely *incommunicado* with the outside world. On 17 May 1976 he was ordered to be tried on charges of subversive association and attempting to undermine the morale of the armed forces under articles 60 (V) and 58 (3) respectively of the Military Penal Code. The remedy of *habeas corpus* was not available to him. He was arrested, charged and committed for trial on the grounds of his political views, associations and activities.

A.D. Case
R.78/1980[42]

The communication was sent by the Grand Captain of the Mikmaq tribal society, who has asserted that Canada is in violation of Art. 1 of the CCPR, which guarantees the right to self-determination. The author rejected outright the applicability of Art. 27 and stated that the objective of the communication was ''that the traditional Government of the Mikmaq tribal society be recognized as such and that the Mikmaq nation be recognized as a State'' (its territory would include Nova Scotia, Prince Edward Island and parts of Newfoundland, New Brunswick and the Gaspé Peninsula of Quebec).

Canada objected to the admissibility of the communication on the ground that Art. 1 ''cannot affect the territorial integrity of a State, a principle asserted in United Nations declarations such as the 'Declaration on the Granting of Independence to Colonial Peoples' (General Assembly Resolution 1514 (XV) of 14 December 1960), the 'Declaration on Principles of International Law Concerning Friendly Relations and Co-operation among States in accordance with the Charter of the United Nations' (General Assembly Resolution 2625 (XXV) of 24 October 1970).'' It further objected that Art. 1(1) of the Covenant is a collective right and therefore does not fulfil the requirements of Arts. 1 and 2 of the Optional Protocol, that the remedy of statehood goes beyond the competence of the Committee, and that the author had not established that he is duly authorized to act on behalf of the Mikmaq nation.

The author replied that the argument about territorial integrity was invalid in this case because the complaint centered on the fact that the land in question never lawfully became a part of Canada, and that the right of self-determination was an individual as well as a collective right, citing a UN study on the Right to Self-Determination, UN Doc. E/CN.4/Sub.2/405/Rev. 1 (1980) prepared by the Special Rapporteur of the Sub-Commission on Prevention of Discrimination and Protection of Minorities. The author also stated that, if the Committee felt incompetent to handle the complaint, it should refer the case to the

---

[42] *Report of the Human Rights Committee* (1984), *supra*, n. 29, at 200. During its first few years, communications dismissed on the grounds of inadmissibility were not reported in its annual report. Later, the Committee decided there was merit in publishing them, but it chose to do so by referring only to the initials of the complainants.

UN Economic and Social Council for an advisory opinion on the issue from the International Court of Justice.

After several questions were raised concerning the *bona fides* of the author to act for the Mikmaq peoples, the Committee determined that the case was inadmissible on the grounds that "the author has not proven that he is authorized to act as a representative on behalf of the Mikmaq tribal society" nor that "he is personally a victim of a violation of any rights contained in the Covenant."[43]

Aumeeruddy-Cziffra Case
R. 9/35[44]

[Amendments by the state to its Immigration and Deportation Acts made the rights to residency and citizenship of male foreigners who married female Mauritians subject to arbitrary review. Previously, automatic citizenship was granted to foreigners who married Mauritian citizens regardless of any sex-based distinctions. The government explained that the legislative amendments changing two domestic acts, which led to the complaint by 20 Mauritian women, "were passed following certain events in connection with which some foreigners (spouses of Mauritian women) were suspected of subversive activities." The Committee found that only some of the petitioners had been detrimentally affected by the new laws, while others (whose cases were not considered as a result) were only potentially affected.]

The Committee takes the view that the common residence of husband and wife has to be considered as the normal behaviour of a family. Hence, and as the State party has admitted, the exclusion of a person from a country where close members of his family are living can amount to an interference within the meaning of article 17. In principle, article 17 (1) applies also when one of the spouses is an alien. Whether the existence and application of immigration laws affecting the residence of a family member is compatible with the Covenant depends on whether such interference is either "arbitrary or unlawful" as stated in article 17 (1), or conflicts in any other way with the State party's obligations under the Covenant.

Since, however, this situation results from the legislation itself, there can be no question of regarding this interference as "unlawful" within the meaning of article 17 (1) in the present cases. It remains to be considered whether it is "arbitrary" or conflicts in any other way with the Covenant.

The protection owed to individuals in this respect is subject to the principle of equal

---

[43] Ruling out the case on the Committee's grounds for inadmissibility might only have put off an inevitable one on the merits of self-determination, because there is no reason to suspect that a future application of the same nature by Indians in Canada will not substantiate an authority to act. Further, the case raises the spectre of land claims settlements between Canada and its aboriginal people. The availability of the Committee to hear such claims – even if they are to be declared inadmissible – may encourage the state to act more quickly at the domestic level in order to avoid a possible censure by the Committee on a matter that could prove to be an issue of considerable importance to the entire nation.

[44] *Report of the Human Rights Committee*, 36 U.N. GAOR Supp. (No. 40) 134, U.N. Doc. A/36/40 (1981).

treatment of the sexes which follows from several provisions of the Covenant. It is an obligation of the State parties under article 2 (1) generally to respect and ensure the rights of the Covenant "without distinction of any kind, such as ... (i.a.) sex," and more particularly under article 3 "to ensure the equal right of men and women to the enjoyment" of all these rights, as well as under article 26 to provide "without any discrimination" for "the equal protection of the law."

The authors who are married to foreign nationals are suffering from the adverse consequences of the statutes discussed above only because they are women. The precarious residence status of their husbands, affecting their family life as described, results from the 1977 laws which do not apply the same measures of control to foreign wives. In this connexion the Committee has noted that under section 16 of the Constitution of Mauritius sex is not one of the grounds on which discrimination is prohibited. ...

The Committee considers that it is also unnecessary to say whether the existing discrimination should be called an "arbitrary" interference with the family within the meaning of article 17. Whether or not the particular interference could as such be justified if it were applied without discrimination does not matter here. Whenever restrictions are placed on a right guaranteed by the Covenant, this has to be done without discrimination on the ground of sex. Whether the restriction in itself would be in breach of that right regarded in isolation, is not decisive in this respect. It is the enjoyment of the rights which must be secured without discrimination. Here it is sufficient, therefore, to note that in the present position an adverse distinction based on sex is made, affecting the alleged victims in their enjoyment of one of their rights. No sufficient justification for this difference has been given. The Committee must then find that there is a violation of articles 2 (1) and 3 of the Covenant, in conjunction with article 17 (1).

At the same time each of the couples concerned constitutes also a "family" within the meaning of article 23 (1) of the Covenant, in one case at least – that of Mrs. Aumeeruddy-Cziffra – also with a child. They are therefore as such "entitled to protection by society and the State" as required by that article, which does not further describe that protection. The Committee is of the opinion that the legal protection or measures a society or a State can afford to the family may vary from country to country and depend on different social, economic, political and cultural conditions and traditions.

Again, however, the principle of equal treatment of the sexes applies by virtue of articles 2 (1), 3 and 26, of which the latter is also relevant because it refers particularly to the "equal protection of the law." Where the Covenant requires a substantial protection as in article 23, it follows from those provisions that such protection must be equal, that is to say not discriminatory, for example on the basis of sex.

It follows that also in this line of argument the Covenant must lead to the result that the protection of a family cannot vary with the sex of the one or the other spouse. Though it might be justified for Mauritius to restrict the access of aliens to their territory and to expel them therefrom for security reasons, the Committee is of the view that the legislation which only subjects foreign spouses of Mauritian women to those restrictions, but not foreign spouses of Mauritian men, is discriminatory with respect to Mauritian women and cannot be justified by security requirements.

The Committee therefore finds that there is also a violation of articles 2 (1), 3 and 26 of the Covenant in conjunction with the right of the three married co-authors under article 23 (1).[45]

Maroufidou Case
R.13/58[46]

[This case involved a Greek national living in Sweden who became involved with a person caught preparing to commit a terrorist act in the country. As the complainant's part in the crime was minor (she had attempted to conceal evidence), the Swedish government chose to deport her in accordance with the appropriate legislation in lieu of conducting a prosecution. During the course of the complaint, the author made several changes in her case presentation, probably in an attempt to account for each new piece of incriminating evidence which the state submitted in response to the Committee's invitations to explain the situation. Eventually, the author changed her plea from a claim of innocence to one based upon a technical interpretation of the domestic law. She argued that Sweden was in breach of Art. 13 of the CCPR because it failed to expel her ''in pursuance of a decision reached in accordance with law.'' As a result, the Committee had to determine how it would respond to a challenge to carry out what would be, in essence, a review of the Swedish interpretation of its own domestic law.]

The Committee takes the view that the interpretation of domestic law is essentially a matter for the courts and authorities of the State party concerned. It is not within the powers or functions of the Committee to evaluate whether the competent authorities of the State party in question have interpreted and applied the domestic law correctly in the case before it under the Optional Protocol, unless it is established that they have not interpreted and applied it in good faith or that it is evident that there has been an abuse of power.

In the light of all written information made available to it by the individual and the explanations and observations of the State party concerned, the Committee is satisfied that in reaching the decision to expel Anna Maroufidou the Swedish authorities did interpret and apply the relevant provisions of Swedish law in good faith and in a reasonable manner and consequently that the decision was made ''in accordance with law'' as required by article 13 of the Covenant.

Lovelace Case
R.6/24[47]

[The petitioner was an Indian woman who married a non-Indian, thereby losing her status pursuant to s. 12(1)(b) of *Indian Act*.[48] When her marriage broke up, she returned to her

---

[45] By way of a Note dated 15 June 1983, Mauritius informed the Committee that, pursuant to its findings in this case, ''the two impugned Acts have now been amended ... so as to remove the discriminatory effects of those laws on grounds of sex'' (*Report of the Human Rights Committee*, [1984] supra, n. 29, at 254).

[46] *Supra*, n. 44, at 160.

[47] *Supra*, n. 44, at 166.

[48] R.S.C. 1970, c. I-6 until its amendment in 1985. See also *Attorney General for Canada v. Lavell* and *Isaac*

friends and family on the Tobique Indian Reserve in New Brunswick. Attempts were made to force her to leave, on the ground that she lacked Indian status. She complained to the Human Rights Committee, arguing that the *Indian Act* violated the CCPR because it discriminated on the basis of sex (Indian men do not lose status if they marry non-Indian women).

After a number of delays and communications between the parties and the Committee, during which the state attempted to justify the law on the ground that the Indian leadership was not in favour of removing that form of discrimination from the legislation and that, in accordance with Art. 27 of the CCPR, s. 12(1)(b) was intended to protect minorities, the Committee found that Canada was in violation of its commitments. With the exception of one member who claimed, in a separate opinion, that the state was discriminatory, the Committee refrained from making a finding based on sex-based discrimination – primarily because the petitioner lost her Indian status before the Covenant came into force for Canada. Instead, it turned to the state's major legal argument for justification of the law to establish the ground for the violation by it. The Committee determined:]

The rights under article 27 of the Covenant had to be secured to "persons belonging" to the minority. At present Sandra Lovelace does not qualify as an Indian under Canadian legislation. However, the Indian Act deals primarily with a number of privileges which, as stated above, do not as such come within the scope of the Covenant. Protection under the Indian Act and protection under article 27 of the Covenant therefore have to be distinguished. Persons who are born and brought up on a reserve, who have kept ties with their community and wish to maintain these ties must normally be considered as belonging to that minority within the meaning of the Covenant. Since Sandra Lovelace is ethnically a Maliseet Indian and has only been absent from her home reserve for a few years during the existence of her marriage, she is, in the opinion of the Committee, entitled to be regarded as "belonging" to this minority and to claim the benefits of article 27 of the Covenant. The question whether these benefits have been denied to her, depends on how far they extend.

The right to live on a reserve is not as such guaranteed by article 27 of the Covenant. Moreover, the Indian Act does not interfere directly with the functions which are expressly mentioned in that article. However, in the opinion of the Committee the right of Sandra Lovelace to access to her native culture and language "in community with the other members" of her group, has in fact been, and continues to be interfered with, because there is no place outside the Tobique Reserve where such a community exists. On the other hand, not every interference can be regarded as a denial of rights within the meaning of article 27. Restrictions on the right to residence, by way of national legislation, cannot be ruled out under article 27 of the Covenant. This also follows from the restrictions to article 12 (1) of the Covenant set out in article 12 (3). The Committee recognizes the need to define the category of persons entitled to live on a reserve, for such purposes as those explained by the Government regarding protection of its resources and preservation

---

et al. v. Bedard, [1974] S.C.R. 1349, which dismissed a lower court decision holding that s. 12(1)(b) contravened the equality provisions of the *Bill of Rights*, S.C. 1960, c. 44.

of the identity of its people. However, the obligations which the Government has since undertaken under the Covenant must also be taken into account.

In this respect, the Committee is of the view that statutory restrictions affecting the right to residence on a reserve of a person belonging to the minority concerned, must have both a reasonable and objective justification and be consistent with the other provisions of the Covenant, read as a whole. Article 27 must be construed and applied in the light of the other provisions mentioned above, such as articles 12, 17 and 23 in so far as they may be relevant to the particular case, and also the provisions against discrimination, such as articles 2, 3 and 26, as the case may be. It is not necessary, however, to determine in any general manner which restrictions may be justified under the Covenant, in particular as a result of marriage, because the circumstances are special in the present case.

The case of Sandra Lovelace should be considered in the light of the fact that her marriage to a non-Indian has broken up. It is natural that in such a situation she wishes to return to the environment in which she was born, particularly as after the dissolution of her marriage her main cultural attachment again was to the Maliseet band. Whatever may be the merits of the Indian Act in other respects, it does not seem to the Committee that to deny Sandra Lovelace the right to reside on the reserve is reasonable, or necessary to preserve the identity of the tribe. The Committee therefore concludes that to prevent her recognition as belonging to the band is an unjustifiable denial of her rights under article 27 of the Covenant, read in the context of the other provisions referred to.

In view of this finding, the Committee does not consider it necessary to examine whether the same facts also show separate breaches of the other rights invoked. The specific rights most directly applicable to her situation are those under article 27 of the Covenant. The rights to choose one's residence (article 12), and the rights aimed at protecting family life and children (articles 17, 23 and 24) are only indirectly at stake in the present case. The facts of the case do not seem to require further examination under those articles. The Committee's finding of a lack of a reasonable justification for the interference with Sandra Lovelace's rights under article 27 of the Covenant also makes it unnecessary, as suggested above (paragraph 12), to examine the general provisions against discrimination (articles 2, 3 and 26) in the context of the present case, and in particular to determine their bearing upon inequalities predating the coming into force of the Covenant for Canada.

NOTES

1) In a lengthy Note dated 6 June 1983, Canada declared that it was endeavouring to eliminate the discrimination giving rise to this case by amending the *Indian Act*. After considerable delay and debate, the Federal Government amended the *Indian Act* in 1985.[49]

---

[49] *Report of the Human Rights Committee* (1984), *supra*, n. 29, at 250. In that communication, Canada also noted that an application by at least one other Indian woman was before the Committee. Apparently, the Committee has agreed to hold off consideration of any "Indian women" complaints until the effects of the equality provisions of Canada's *Charter of Rights and Freedoms* and the amendments to the *Indian Act* in S.C. 1985, c. 27, can be determined.

The equality provisions of the *Canadian Charter of Rights and Freedoms* which had just come into force provided the main reason for so doing. Canada's outstanding international human rights violation was of secondary importance. The amendments help to eliminate sex-based discrimination against female Indians by abolishing s.12(1)(b) of the *Act* and by reinstating Indian status to women who had involuntarily lost it. It does not, however, give their children automatic band membership rights (they are held in abeyance while the child is a dependent of the mother, and could later be decided by local band councils). Thus, some discrimination remains. It lies in the uncertainty created by the status of the children of women who return to the reserve or who have acquired rights by marriage. Some women fear returning to, or remaining on, a reserve because, while its band has to permit the women to raise their children there, it might later establish membership criteria designed to force their offspring, on the attainment of adulthood, from the community into an alien culture.

2) Some male Indian leaders have said that they will challenge the applicability of the equality provisions of the *Charter of Rights and Freedoms* to the government of reserves. They rely on Part II of the *Constitution Act, 1982* (s. 35), which recognizes and affirms the "rights of the aboriginal peoples of Canada," and s. 25 of its *Charter* (Part I), which guarantees that "certain rights and freedoms" set out in the *Charter* "shall not be construed so as to abrogate or derogate from any aboriginal, treaty or other rights or freedoms that pertain to the aboriginal peoples of Canada. ..." They claim that the Constitution protects the right to preserve their culture which may, at times, include the right to maintain a social structure of which sex-based discrimination is a part.

3) The *Charter* provisions of the Constitution may, in effect, provide the state with an irrefutable challenge to the admissibility of communications submitted pursuant to the Optional Protocol. As it presently stands, most Canadian human rights issues have yet to be decided by a court of final instance because *Charter* arguments now apply to them. As a result, Canada could argue (at least for the next few years) that the Human Rights Committee must refuse to consider almost all communications because domestic remedies have not been exhausted. While the enforcement mechanisms of a state's legal system are far superior to those of international tribunals (thereby making a *Charter* argument a better vehicle than the Committee for ensuring adherence to human rights standards) a few politically sensitive issues affecting groups who have little influence in government (*e.g.*, prisoners' rights, discrimination against Indian women), may well receive a more objective hearing in an international forum.

Hartikainen Case
R. 9/40[50]

[The author, a school teacher in Finland, complained about a prohibition on the freedom of religion and belief, because children who did not receive formal religious instruction were required to enroll in a compulsory replacement course (a history of religions and

---

[50] *Supra*, n. 44, at 147.

ethics) taught at the schools. While the state, in reviewing its legislation to determine whether its laws complied with the Covenant felt this to be an inoffensive provision, the author complained otherwise, arguing that there was a Christian bias to the curriculum and material of that course. The case generated a good deal of correspondence, in which both parties responded to the information and arguments presented by the other. The Committee noted, with some surprise, that there had been no objection to the admissibility of the case because it was not clear how the author "can actually be said to be generally affected, as some parents or guardians under Art. 1 of the Optional Protocol" (a condition for the admissibility of communications). The Committee felt, however, that there was no reason to dwell on the concept of a "victim" in the case, because of its findings on the merits.]

The Committee does not consider that the requirement of the relevant provisions of Finnish legislation that instruction in the study of the history of religions and ethics should be given instead of religious instruction to students in schools whose parents or legal guardians object to religious instruction is in itself incompatible with article 18 (4), if such alternative course of instruction is given in a neutral and objective way and respects the convictions of parents and guardians who do not believe in any religion. In any event, paragraph 6 of the School System Act expressly permits any parents or guardians who do not wish their children to be given either religious instruction or instruction in the study of the history of religions and ethics to obtain exemption therefrom by arranging for them to receive comparable instruction outside of school.

The State party admits that difficulties have arisen in regard to the existing teaching plan to give effect to these provisions, (which teaching plan does appear, in part at least, to be religious in character), but the Committee believes that appropriate action is being taken to resolve the difficulties and it sees no reason to conclude that this cannot be accomplished, compatibly with the requirements of article 18 (4) of the Covenant, within the framework of the existing laws.[51]

Hertzberg Case
R.14/61[52]

[This complaint resulted from various forms of media censorship by the state broadcasting system of programmes dealing with homosexuality (*e.g.*, a radio programme discussion about discrimination against homosexuals in the work place resulted in criminal charges; a radio programme which included a review of a book and an interview with a homosexual about life as one in Finland was censored). The communication stated that the censorship

---

[51] On 20 June 1983, the Finnish Government notified the Committee that it had amended its legislation concerning ethics and history of religions course and that its National Board of Education had made provision to monitor the instruction of those courses and draw up a teachers' guide to the instruction of it (*Report of the Human Rights Committee* (1984), *supra*, n. 29, at 255).

[52] *Supra*, n. 31, at 161.

was permitted because the authorities had deliberately adopted a wide interpretation of the relevant provisions of the *Finnish Penal Code*:

> If someone publicly engages in an act violating sexual morality, thereby giving offense, he shall be sentenced for publicly violating sexual morality to imprisonment for at most six months or to a fine.
>
> Anyone who publicly encourages indecent behaviour between persons of the same sex shall be sentenced for encouragement to indecent behaviour between members of the same sex as decreed in subsection 1.

The state defended its stand by arguing that the communication should be ruled inadmissible because its authors were attempting to distort the concept of freedom of speech set out in Art. 19 of the CCPR. It held that, if their view was accepted, it would severely restrict the right of owners of a means of communication from determining what material they wished to publish or broadcast. When the Committee ruled the communication to be admissible, the state argued that its reason for prohibiting the programmes in question was to ''reflect the prevailing moral conceptions in Finland as interpreted by the Parliament and by large groups of the population.'' It claimed that the law did not hinder the presentation of factual information on homosexuality, that there been no convictions resulting from the charges brought under the relevant provisions of its *Penal Code*, that any restriction on freedom of expression that might exist in the case is justified by Art. 19(3) of the CCPR, and that the decisions of the Finnish Broadcasting Company were not censorship decisions, but constituted ones based on ''general considerations of programme policy in accordance with the internal rules of the company.''

After discounting some of the complaints in the communication because they did not disclose whether an individual had suffered ''an actual violation'' (the Committee does not believe its mandate permits it to ''review in the abstract whether national legislation contravenes the Coyenant''), the Committee accepted that the rights, under Art. 19(2) of the CCPR, of some of the authors had been restricted. However, it found that as ''morals differ widely'' and as ''there is no universally applicable standard,'' consequently, ''a certain margin of discretion must be accorded to the responsible national authorities.'' The report states:]

The Committee finds that it cannot question the decision of the responsible organs of the Finnish Broadcasting Corporation that radio and TV are not the appropriate forums to discuss issues related to homosexuality, as far as a programme could be judged as encouraging homosexual behaviour. According to article 19 (3), the exercise of the rights provided for in article 19 (2) carries with it special duties and responsibilities for those organs. As far as radio and TV programmes are concerned, the audience cannot be controlled. In particular, harmful effects on minors cannot be excluded.

Accordingly, the Human Rights Committee is of the view that there has been no violation of the rights of the authors of the communication under article 19 (2) of the Covenant.

[The individual opinion of Mr. Torkel Opsahl, who agreed with his Committee's conclusions but wished to "clarify certain points" is a valuable addition to the views of the majority:]

This conclusion prejudges neither the right to be different and live accordingly, protected by article 17 of the Covenant, nor the right to have general freedom of expression in this respect, protected by article 19. Under article 19 (2) and subject to article 19 (3), everyone must in principle have the right to impart information and ideas – positive or negative – about homosexuality and discuss any problem relating to it freely, through any media of his choice and on his own responsibility.

Moreover, in my view the conception and contents of "public morals" referred to in article 19 (3) are relative and changing. State-imposed restrictions on freedom of expression must allow for this fact and should not be applied so as to perpetuate prejudice or promote intolerance. It is of special importance to protect freedom of expression as regards minority views, including those that offend, shock or disturb the majority. Therefore, even if such laws as paragraph 9 (2) of chapter 20 of the Finnish Penal Code may reflect prevailing moral conceptions, this is in itself not sufficient to justify it under article 19 (3). It must also be shown that the application of the restriction is "necessary."

However, as the Committee has noted, this law has not been directly applied to any of the alleged victims. The question remains whether they have been more indirectly affected by it in a way which can be said to interfere with their freedom of expression, and if so, whether the grounds were justifiable.

It is clear that nobody – and in particular no State – has any duty under the Covenant to promote publicity for information and ideas of all kinds. Access to media operated by others is always and necessarily more limited than the general freedom of expression. It follows that such access may be controlled on grounds which do not have to be justified under article 19 (3).

It is true that self-imposed restrictions on publishing, or the internal programme policy of the media, may threaten the spirit of freedom of expression. Nevertheless, it is a matter of common sense that such decisions either entirely escape control by the Committee or must be accepted to a larger extent than externally imposed restrictions such as enforcement of criminal law or official censorship, neither of which took place in the present case. Not even media controlled by the State can under the Covenant be under an obligation to publish all that may be published. It is not possible to apply the criteria of article 19 (3) to self-imposed restrictions. Quite apart from the "public morals" issue, one cannot require that they shall be only such as are "provided by law and are necessary" for the particular purpose. Therefore I prefer not to express any opinion on the possible reasons for the decisions complained of in the present case.

The role of mass media in public debate depends on the relationship between journalists and their superiors who decide what to publish. I agree with the authors of the communication that the freedom of journalists is important, but the issues arising here can only partly be examined under article 19 of the Covenant.

[The following members of the Committee associated themselves with the individual opinion submitted by Mr. Opsahl: Mr. Rajsoomer Lallah, Mr. Walter Surma Tarnopolsky.]

Pinkney Case
R.7/27[53]

[The petitioner, a self-described black American political activist, was convicted of extortion and sentenced to 5 years in jail while visiting Canada. His appeal against the conviction was dismissed by the B.C. Court of Appeal and a deportation order was to be effected on his release.

The petitioner raised numerous complaints before the Committee, of which only two were deemed to have any merit; that his mail was subject to excessive censorship; and that his appeal had been delayed for an unreasonable period of time (34 months) as a result of "various administrative mishaps in the Official Reporter's Office."

On the issue of censorship of correspondence, the state was almost found to be in violation of the Covenant. Only a paucity of facts prevented it from being so (although the potential existed for an abuse, no evidence could show there was any). Fortunately as well, the rules concerning freedom of correspondence for prisoners had been revised just after this complaint so that powers of censorship were spelled out more precisely. In the Committee's view:]

32. Although these rules were only enacted subsequent to Mr. Pinkney's departure from the Lower Mainland Regional Correction Centre, in practice they were being applied when he was detained in that institution. This means that privileged correspondence, defined in section 1 of the regulations as meaning 'correspondence addressed by an inmate to a Member of Parliament, Members of the Legislative Assembly, barrister or solicitor, commissioner of corrections, regional director of corrections, chaplain, or the director of inspection and standards', were not examined or subject to any control or censorship. As for non-privileged correspondence, it was only subject to censorship if it contained matter that threatened the management, operation, discipline or security of the correctional centre. At the time when Mr. Pinkney was detained therein, the procedure governing prisoners' correspondence did not allow for a general restriction on the right to communicate with government officials. Mr. Pinkney was not denied this right. To seek to restrict his communication with various government officials while at the same time allowing his access to his lawyers would seem a futile gesture since through his lawyers, he could put his case to the various government officials whom he was allegedly prevented from contacting.

[In addition, Canada was found to be in violation of Art. 14(3)(c) and (5) of the CCPR because of the delay in producing the transcripts of the trial for the appeal:]

22. As regards the next aspect, however, the Committee, having considered all the information relating to the delay of two and a half years in the production of the transcripts of the trial for the purposes of the appeal, considers that the authorities of British Columbia must be considered objectively responsible. Even in the particular circumstances this delay appears excessive and might have been prejudicial to the effectiveness of the right to appeal. At the same time, however, the Committee has to take note of the position of

---

[53] *Supra*, n. 31, at 101.

the Government that the Supreme Court of Canada would have been competent to examine these complaints. This remedy, nevertheless, does not seem likely to have been effective for the purpose of avoiding delay. The Committee observes on this point that the right under Article 14 (3) (c) to be tried without undue delay should be applied in conjunction with the right under Article 14 (5) to review by a higher tribunal, and that consequently there was in this case a violation of both of these provisions taken together.

MacIsaac Case
R.55/1979[54]

[The Report of the Committee states:]

On 26 November 1968, the author was sentenced to a term of eight years imprisonment on counts of armed robbery. On 21 March 1972, after serving *circa* three years and four months, the author was released on parole from a federal penitentiary in Campbellford, Ontario. On 27 June 1975, he was convicted of a criminal offence while still being on parole and, on 25 July 1975, he was sentenced to a term of 14 months imprisonment. Pursuant to the conviction, by operation of the Parole Act 1970, the time which the author had spent on parole from 21 March 1972 to 27 June 1975 (three years, three months and six days) was automatically forfeited and he was required to re-serve that time. The author was again released on 7 May 1979, to serve the remaining part of his sentence under mandatory supervision.

On 15 October 1977, the Criminal Law Amendment Act 1977 was proclaimed in force. The new law, *inter alia*, repealed certain provisions of the Parole Act 1970 and, in effect, abolished automatic forfeiture of time spent on parole (forfeiture of parole) upon subsequent conviction for an indictable offence committed while still on parole. The Criminal Law Amendment Act 1977 now stipulates that only the sanction of revocation of parole is presently applicable to persons on parole, which sanction is invoked at the discretion of the National Parole Board rather than automatically by law upon conviction of an indictable offence. Section 31 (2) (a) of the Criminal Law Amendment Act 1977 provides further that, upon revocation of parole, any time that a person had spent on parole after the coming into force of this provision, that is after 15 October 1977, is credited against his/her sentence. Consequently, a person presently in the position in which the author found himself on 27 June 1975 would not necessarily attract any sanction concerning revocation of parole and, even if such a sanction were to be invoked, would not be required to re-serve the period of time spent on parole after 15 October 1977.

The author claims that, by specifying that section 31 (2) (a) of the Criminal Law Amendment Act 1977 shall not be retroactive, the Government of Canada has contravened

---

[54] *Report of the Human Rights Committee*, 38 U.N. GAOR Supp. (No. 40) 111, U.N. Doc. A/38/40 (1983). This case is the same as an earlier complaint against Canada – the *Van Duzen Case*, R.12/50, *supra*, n. 31, at 150. It was declared admissible but later dismissed (after considerable argument had been submitted by both sides and considered by the Committee) on the ground that the author had been set free earlier than he had expected and, therefore, was no longer actually suffering from any alleged violation.

article 15 (1) of the Covenant. He submits that section 31 (2) (a), in providing that time spent on parole after 15 October 1977 is not to be re-served in prison upon revocation of that parole, constitutes a lighter penalty within the meaning of article 15 of the Covenant. He further submits that, contrary to article 2 (2) of the Covenant, the Government of Canada has failed to enact legislation to give effect to article 15.

The author submits that in the present state of the law in Canada, any recourse to domestic courts, for the purpose of obtaining the remedy he seeks, would be futile. He therefore endeavoured to seek relief by applying, on 5 September 1978, for the Royal Prerogative of Mercy. This recourse was unsuccessful and the author claims that the rejection by the Government of Canada of the application for an executive remedy, that is to say the exercise of the Royal Prerogative of Mercy, constitutes a violation of article 2 (3) (a) of the Covenant.

In the absence of more precise submissions from the author in the present case, the Committee has attempted to examine in what way, if any, the position of the alleged victim was affected by the situation of which he basically complains. It notes that the system for dealing with recidivists was changed by the 1977 Act, to make it more flexible. The Act as amended provides, instead of the automatic forfeiture of parole, for a system of revocation at the discretion of the National Parole Board and sentencing for the recidivist offence at the discretion of the judge. However, the recidivist cannot be made to re-serve the full time spent on parole. Apparently, the author's claim in the present case is that he would have been released earlier on the hypothesis that the new provisions had been applied to him retroactively. The Committee notes that it is not clear how this should have been done. However, here a comparison with the system existing before 1977 is necessary. Under the old system, the judge exercised his discretion in deciding the length of a penalty to be imposed. In the case of Mr. MacIsaac, whose second sentence was rendered in 1975, the recidivist offence carried a possible sentence of up to 14 years. While noting that Mr. MacIsaac's criminal record was "serious" and explicitly mentioning the fact that Mr. MacIsaac's parole had been forfeited, the judge in 1975 sentenced him to 14 months. The Committee notes that one cannot focus only on the favourable aspects of a hypothetical situation and fail to take into account that the imposition of the 14-month sentence on Mr. MacIsaac for a recidivist offence was explicitly linked with the forfeiture of parole. In Canadian law there is no single fixed penalty for a recidivist offence. The law allows a scale of penalties for such offences and full judicial discretion to set the term of imprisonment (e.g. up to 14 years for the offence of breaking and entering and theft as in Mr. MacIsaac's case). It follows that Mr. MacIsaac has not established the hypothesis that if parole had not been forfeited, the judge would have imposed the same sentence of 14 months and that he would therefore have been actually released prior to May of 1979. The Committee is not in a position to know, nor is it called upon to speculate, how the fact that his earlier parole was forfeited may have influenced the penalty meted out for the offence committee while on parole. The burden of proving that in 1977 he has been denied an advantage under the new law and that he is therefore a "victim" lies with the author. It is not the Committee's function to make a hypothetical assessment of what would have happened if the new Act had been applicable to him.

The Canadian Criminal Law Amendment Act 1977 in this light, and as explained by the State party, only entails a modification in the system of dealing with recidivist cases and leaves the question as to whether the total effect in the individual case will be a "lighter penalty" to the judge who sentences the recidivist offender. The new law does not necessarily result automatically, for those to whom it is applied, in a lighter penalty compared to that under the earlier legislation. The judge entrusted with sentencing the recidivist – now as before – is bound to take into account the facts of every case, including, of course, the revocation or forfeiture of parole, and exercise his discretion in sentencing within the prescribed scale of statutory minimum and maximum penalties.

These considerations lead to the conclusion that it cannot be established that in fact or law the alleged victim was denied the benefit of a "lighter" penalty to which he would have been entitled under the Covenant.

For these reasons the Human Rights Committee, acting under article 5 (4) of the Optional Protocol to the International Covenant on Civil and Political Rights is of the view that the facts of the present case do not disclose any violation of article 15 (1) of the Covenant.

NOTES

1) Does the growing body of "case law" arising from the individual complaints establish a set of universal human rights norms? Why (or why not)?

2) Does the jurisprudence arising from the observations made by the Human Rights Committee in response to the individual complaints determine law that applies to *all* states parties to the CCPR, even though less than 1/2 of them have ratified the Optional Protocol?

3) Using the sections of the cases cited above, compare the Canadian responses to its international human rights violations with those of other states (*e.g.*, Uruguay, Mauritius and Finland). Is the Canadian record acceptable?

4) Is it possible to devise a method of determining which nations have good, bad or indifferent records of human rights? Consider whether such a method can be devised to accommodate states that:

    a)   are not a party to any general human rights convention (*e.g.*, the U.S.A.);

    b)   are a party to general human rights conventions (*e.g.*, Guinea and the U.S.S.R.); and

    c)   are a party to both general human rights conventions and a treaty granting the right of individual petition for alleged violations (*e.g.*, Canada and Uruguay).

Is there any value in making such comparisons? How should the human rights record of countries be determined and measured against international norms?

Specific UN Conventions on Human Rights[55]

A number of the human rights that existed before the UN Charter continued after World War II and live on in treaty form today.[56] In addition, the interest generated by particular

---

[55] See Hannum; Sieghart; and Vasak, supra n. 1.
[56] See *supra*, of the "Development of Universal Standards."

human rights issues gave rise to a number of conventions.[57] Some of the treaties were intended to be open for universal ratification while others are the product of regional organizations. Although many of them elaborate certain rights set out in the so-called "International Bill of Rights" (the Universal Declaration, CESCR and CCPR), a number deal with tangential areas of concern.

While the implementation procedures associated with most of the specific conventions accord with what has become the international norm (the lack of direct enforcement strength[58]), their total product (usually a vast bulk of information compiled in the form of state reports submitted pursuant to individual treaty commitments) has created an impressive body of fact, opinion and viewpoints. Although it necessitates considerable research, a particular human rights issue can be investigated by examining different conventions referring to it and the many and varied responses generated by states pursuant to their commitments under them. This type of study can provide a useful background to examine the meaning and applicability of particular rights in any specific case.

Like many nations, Canada is a party to a number of human rights conventions, almost all of which rely primarily upon reporting procedures by states as the central part of their monitoring activity to ensure compliance with the obligations set out in them (the Optional Protocol to the CCPR, naturally, provides an exception to that rule for Canada). The human rights treaties to which Canada is a party are listed below:[59]

– CESCR; CCPR and the Declaration regarding Art. 41 (competence of the Human Rights Committee to receive communications from one state against another); Optional Protocol to the CCPR.

– Convention on the Prevention and Punishment of the Crime of Genocide, signed 1948; in force 1951; 78 U.N.T.S. 277 (19/8/76).

– Slavery Convention, signed 1926 (6/8/28), as amended by the Protocol of 7 December 1953; in force 1955; 212 U.N.T.S. 17 and 182 U.N.T.S. 51 (17/12/55).

– Supplementary Convention on the Abolition of Slavery, the Slave Trade and Institutions and Practices Similar to Slavery, signed 1956; in force 1957; 266 U.N.T.S. 266 (10/1/63).

– ILO Convention (No. 105) Concerning the Abolition of Forced Labour, signed 1957; in force 1959; 320 U.N.T.S. 291 (4/7/60).

– Convention Relating to the Status of Refugees, signed 1951; in force 1954; 189 U.N.T.S. 150 (2/9/69).

– Protocol Relating to the Status of Refugees, signed 1967; in force 1967; 606 U.N.T.S. 267 (4/6/69).

– Convention on the Reduction of Statelessness, signed 1961; in force 1975; U.N. Doc. A/CONF.9/15 (15/10/78).

---

[57] See J.-B. Marie, "International Instruments Relating to Human Rights: Classification and Chart Showing Ratifications as of 1 January 1984" (1983), 4 *H.R.L.J.* 503. This article is the basis from which relevant treaty dates, parties, etc., cited in this chapter have been determined.

[58] Supra, n. 8.

[59] *Supra*, n. 57. The date of entry into force for Canada is set out in brackets following the citation of each treaty.

− ILO Convention (No. 87) Concerning Freedom of Association and Protection of the Right to Organize, signed 1948; in force 1950; 68 U.N.T.S. 17 (23/3/73).
− Convention on the Political Rights of Women, signed 1953; in force 1954; 193 U.N.T.S. 135 (30/1/57).
− Convention on the Nationality of Married Women, signed 1957; in force 1958; 309 U.N.T.S. 65 (21/10/59).
− Geneva Convention for the Amelioration of the Condition of the Wounded and Sick in Armed Forces in the Field, signed 1949; in force 1950; 75 U.N.T.S. 31.
− Geneva Convention for the Amelioration of the Wounded, Sick and Shipwrecked Members of the Armed Forces at Sea, signed 1949; in force 1950; 75 U.N.T.S. 85.
− Geneva Convention Relative to the Treatment of Prisoners of War, signed 1949; in force 1950; 75 U.N.T.S. 135.
− Geneva Convention Relative to the Protection of Civilian Persons in Time of War, signed 1949; in force 1950; 75 U.N.T.S. 287.
− International Covenant on the Elimination of All Forms of Racial Discrimination, signed 1965; in force 1969; 660 U.N.T.S. 195 (13/11/70) [*N.B.*: A Declaration regarding Art. 14, which grants competence of the Committee on the Elimination of All Forms of Discrimination to receive communications from individuals entered into force on 3 December 1982. As of 1 January 1984, 10 declarations had been made. Canada was not one of the declarants.]
− Convention on the Elimination of All Forms of Discrimination Against Women, signed 1979; in force 1981; G.A. Res. 34/180, 34 U.N. GAOR, Supp. (No. 46) 193, U.N. Doc. A/34/46 (1979) (10/1/82).
− ILO Convention (No. 100) Concerning Equal Remuneration for Men and Women Workers for Work of Equal Value, signed 1951; in force 1953; 165 U.N.T.S. 303 (16/11/73).
− ILO Convention (No. 111) Concerning Discrimination in Respect of Employment and Occupation, signed 1958; in force 1960; 362 U.N.T.S. 31 (26/11/65).
− ILO Convention (No. 122) Concerning Employment Policy, in force for Canada on 16/9/57.
− Convention on the Prevention of Crimes Against Internationally-Protected Persons, in force for Canada on 4/8/76.
− Constitution of the International Refugee Organization, in force for Canada on 20/8/48.
− Agreement Relating to Refugee Seamen, in force for Canada on 28/8/69.
− Protocol Relating to Refugee Seamen, in force for Canada, 10/2/75.

The Bureau of Legal Affairs of the Canadian Department of External Affairs reported that, on 23 August 1985, Canada signed the Convention Against Torture and Other Cruel, Inhuman or Degrading Treatment or Punishment and that, "Discussions are continuing with the provinces and territories with a view to considering legislative changes that may be necessary to enable Canada to fully implement the Convention and subsequently to ratify it."[60]

---

[60] Bureau of Legal Affairs, Department of External Affairs, *Some Examples of Current Issues of International Law of Particular Importance to Canada*, October 1986, at 2.

Reporting Obligations Under Major U.N. International Human Rights Instruments

	International Convention on the Elimination of All Forms of Racial Discrimination (CERD)	International Covenant on Economic, Social and Cultural Rights (ICESCR)	International Covenant on Civil and Political Rights (ICCPR)	International Convention on the Suppression and Punishment of the Crime of Apartheid	Convention on the Elimination of All Forms of Discrimination against Women (CEDAW)
Entry into force	4 January 1969	3 January 1976	23 March 1976	18 July 1976	3 September 1981
Number of States parties as at 1 September 1984	124	83	80	79	60
Supervisory body	Committee on the Elimination of Racial Discrimination	Sessional Working Group of Governmental Experts	Human Rights Committee	Group of Three	Committee on the Elimination of Discrimination against Women
Established by	Convention	Economic and Social Council Decision 1982/83	Covenant	Convention	Convention
Composition	18 experts	15 governmental experts	18 experts	3 members of Commission on Human Rights who are representatives of States Parties	23 experts
Canadian Members	Ronald St. J. Macdonald (1972-1976)	None	Walter Tarnopolsky (1977-1983) Gisele Côté-Harper (1983-1984)	Canada not party	Marie Caron (1982-1988)
Duration of term	4 years	3 years	4 years	1 year	4 years
Type of reports States parties undertake to submit	on the legislative, judicial, administrative and other measures which they have adopted and which give effect to the provisions of the Convention	on the measures they have adopted and the progress made in achieving the rights recognized in the Covenant	on the measures they have adopted which give effect to the rights recognized in the Covenant and on the progress made in the enjoyment of those rights	on the legislative, judicial, administrative or other measures that they have adopted and that give effect to the provisions of the Convention	on the legislative, judicial, administrative or other measures which they have adopted to give effect to the Convention and on the progress made
Periodicity of reporting after entry into force — Initial	1 year	6 year cycle (but in three biennial stages for specific groups of articles)	1 year	2 years	1 year
Thereafter	2 years		5 years	2 years	4 years
Periodicity established by	Convention (art. 9)	Economic and Social Council resolution 1988 (LX)	Committee (Rules of Procedure)	Convention	Convention (art. 18)
Annual report of Supervisory Body goes to	General Assembly	Economic and Social Council	General Assembly through the Economic and Social Council	Commission on Human Rights	General Assembly through the Economic and Social Council
Canadian Reports, U.N. Document No. and Date Submitted	1st report CERD/C/R. 25/Add. 5 Sept. 1971 (Feb. 1972). 2nd report CERD/C/R. 53/Add. 6 Feb. 1974 (Apr. 1974) 3rd report CERD/C/R. 78/Add. 6 Feb. 1976 (Aug. 1976) 4th report CERD/C/52 Dec. 1978 (Apr. 1979) 5th report CERD/C/50/Add. 6,7 Oct. 1980 (April 1981) 6th report CERD/C/76/Add. 6,7 Dec. 1982 (July 1983) 7th report overdue 8th report Feb. 1986 (March	Art. 6-9 E/1978/8/Add. 32 April 1981 (April 1982) Art. 10-12 E/1980/6/Add. 32 March 1983 (Apr. 1984) Art. 13-15 E/1986/49 (April 1986)	First Report CCPR/C/1 Add. 43 March 1979 (March 1980) Supplementary Report CCPR/C/1/Add. 62 Sept. 1983 (Oct. 1984)	N/A	First Report CEDAW/C/5/Add. 16 June 1983 (January 1985)

The preceding chart[61] shows the human rights treaties to which Canada belongs and for which reporting obligations exist. Canadians who have held positions associated with those conventions are included also. In addition, note that Professor John Humphrey (McGill) was the first Director of the UN Division of Human Rights and author of the first draft of the Universal Declaration, while Professor R.St.J. Macdonald is now a judge on the European Court of Human Rights, appointed by the state of Lichtenstein.

REGIONAL STANDARDS

The complexities associated with developing a global accord on issues very close to the cultural, economic, legal, political and social fabric of nations should be considerably lessened if it were done at a more intimate, regional level. So far as human rights are concerned, this theory has worked effectively in just one area of the world – Western Europe – even though there is in force an American Convention on Human Rights[62] and there exists an African Charter on Human Rights and Peoples' Rights.[63] The difficulty plaguing most regions is the same as that encumbering the UN at a global level; the states represent a cultural, economic and social melange of such diversity that agreement on fundamental issues has not yet proved possible. The American Convention, for example, is a product of the Organization of American States, with which Canada has some status for certain purposes, but of which it is not a member. Although it has the potential to become a substantial instrument, the American Convention has not yet done so, probably because of the great differences between the states in the region (*e.g.*, the USA and Cuba, which have not ratified it, and Nicaragua and El Salvador, which have). The African Charter of the Organization of African Unity is not yet in force, largely because it is a relatively new instrument, but also because of the divisiveness between states in the region.

Protection of Human Rights in Europe

While the UN floundered in disagreement over what ultimately became the CESCR, the CCPR, and its Optional Protocol, the Council of Europe had drafted, and opened for ratification, a treaty based upon the Universal Declaration. In addition, the European Convention for the Protection of Rights and Fundamental Freedoms[64] entered into force

---

[61] Provided by Mrs. C. Swords, Department of External Affairs.

[62] Signed 1969; in force 1978 with 17 ratifications as of 1 January 1984; OAS Treaty Series No. 36.

[63] Signed 1981; not in force with 10 ratifications as of 1 January 1984; OAU Doc. CAB/LEG/67/3/Rev. 5.

[64] Hereinafter called the European Convention. Signed 1950; in force 1953 with 21 ratifications as of 1 January 1984; Council of Europe, European Treaty Series, No. 5. See Hannum; McDougal *et al*; Sieghart; Sohn and Buergenthal; and Vasak, *supra*, n. 1. Also see F. Castberg, *The European Convention on Human Rights* (1974); A.Z. Drzemczewski, *European Human Rights Convention in Domestic Law* (1983); J.E.S. Fawcett, *The Application of The European Convention on Human Rights* (1969); F.G. Jacobs, *The European Convention on Human Rights* (1975); L. Mikaelsen, *European Protection of Human Rights* (1980); H. Petzold, *The European Convention on Human Rights: Cases & Materials* (5 ed., 1984); A.H. Robertson, *Human Rights in Europe* (2 ed., 1977.).

more than 12 years before the texts of the major UN Conventions had been agreed upon. Throughout the intervening years, six Protocols to that treaty have been opened for ratification (two of which have added to the rights set out in the Convention) and the European Social Charter,[65] dealing with economic, social and cultural rights, has entered into force.

The European Convention has proved to be the most successful of all the international human rights instruments, largely because the original member states of the Council of Europe shared similar cultural backgrounds and limited the rights contained in the original treaty to those which most Western European nations, still recalling the horrors of World War II, were anxious to guarantee for future generations. Additionally, the common human rights goals which unified those nations encouraged them to include in the treaty the potential for enhanced powers of implementation. The European Convention was followed in 1955 by the entry into force of the right of individual petition (Art. 25 of the treaty, which individual states must voluntarily declare to be in force). This, in turn, was followed by the entry into force on 8 September 1958 of the jurisdiction of the European Court of Human Rights (Art. 46 – another section of the treaty to which each state must voluntarily declare itself to be bound).

The success of the European Convention is unprecedented. The only problem with it is that many individuals do not understand what rights it grants. As a result, even today, a large number of communications from individual complainants received by the European Commission of Human Rights must be declared inadmissible because the gist of them bear no relation to the rights which the Convention was drafted to protect. The following excerpt from the Introduction of a recent "Stock-taking" report[66] from the Commission demonstrates the notoriety and work generated by the treaty:

Of the individual communications received in the course of 1985, for which 2,831 provisional files were opened by the Secretariat, 596 were registered as applications within the meaning of Article 25, i.e. approximately 21%. Amongst the 582 applications decided upon in 1985, 512 were declared inadmissible or struck off the list, either *de plano* or after communication to the respondent Government, i.e. approximately 88%, and 70 were declared admissible, i.e. 12%.

During the same period, the Commission gave notice of 115 individual applications to the respondent Government, adopted 51 Reports on the merits (Article 31), 10 Reports on friendly settlements, including one inter-State case (Article 30), and one Report for the information of the Committee of Ministers after having struck the case off its list (Rule 54 of the Rules of Procedure).

The total number of applications pending before the Commission on 31 December 1984 was 820, while on 31 December 1985 it was 930.

---

[65] *Supra*, n. 20.
[66] European Commission of Human Rights, *Stock-taking on the European Convention on Human Rights: A Periodic Note on the Concrete Results Achieved Under the Convention*, Supplement 1985 (Strasbourg, 1986) ix.

European Convention for the Protection of Rights and Fundamental Freedoms
(1950) Eur. T.S. No. 5; Council Eur. Doc. H(79) 4(1979)

Article 2

1. Everyone's right to life shall be protected by law. No one shall be deprived of his life intentionally save in the execution of a sentence of a court following his conviction of a crime for which this penalty is provided by law.

2. Deprivation of life shall not be regarded as inflicted in contravention of this Article when it results from the use of force which is no more than absolutely necessary:

(a) in defence of any person from unlawful violence;

(b) in order to effect a lawful arrest or to prevent the escape of a person lawfully detained;

(c) in action lawfully taken for the purpose of quelling a riot or insurrection.

Article 3

No one shall be subjected to torture or to inhuman or degrading treatment or punishment.

Article 4

1. No one shall be held in slavery or servitude.

2. No one shall be required to perform forced or compulsory labour.

3. For the purpose of this Article the term – forced or compulsory labour – shall not include:

(a) any work required to be done in the ordinary course of detention imposed according to the provisions of Article 5 of this Convention or during conditional release from such detention;

(b) any service of a military character or, in case of conscientious objectors in countries where they are recognised, service exacted instead of compulsory military service;

(c) any service exacted in case of an emergency or calamity threatening the life or well-being of the community;

(d) any work or service which forms part of normal civic obligations.

Article 5

1. Everyone has the right to liberty and security of person. No one shall be deprived of his liberty save in the following cases and in accordance with a procedure prescribed by law:

(a) the lawful detention of a person after conviction by a competent court;

(b) the lawful arrest or detention of a person for non-compliance with the lawful order of a court or in order to secure the fulfilment of any obligation prescribed by law;

(c) the lawful arrest or detention of a person effected for the purpose of bringing him before the competent legal authority on reasonable suspicion of having committed an offence or when it is reasonably considered necessary to prevent his committing an offence or fleeing after having done so;

(d) the detention of a minor by lawful order for the purpose of educational supervision or his lawful detention for the purpose of bringing him before the competent legal authority;

(e) the lawful detention of persons for the prevention of the spreading of infectious diseases, of persons of unsound mind, alcoholics or drug addicts or vagrants;

(f) the lawful arrest or detention of a person to prevent his effecting an unauthorised entry into the country or of a person against whom action is being taken with a view to deportation or extradition.

2. Everyone who is arrested shall be informed promptly, in a language which he understands, of the reasons for his arrest and of any charge against him.

3. Everyone arrested or detained in accordance with the provisions of paragraph 1(c) of this Article shall be brought promptly before a judge or other officer authorised by law to exercise judicial power and shall be entitled to trial within a reasonable time or to release pending trial. Release may be conditioned by guarantees to appear for trial.

4. Everyone who is deprived of his liberty by arrest or detention shall be entitled to take proceedings by which the lawfulness of his detention shall be decided speedily by a court and his release ordered if the detention is not lawful.

5. Everyone who has been the victim of arrest or detention in contravention of the provisions of this Article shall have an enforceable right to compensation.

Article 6

1. In the determination of his civil rights and obligations or of any criminal charge against him, everyone is entitled to a fair and public hearing within a reasonable time by an independent and impartial tribunal established by law. Judgment shall be pronounced publicly but the press and public may be excluded from all or part of the trial in the interests of morals, public order or national security in a democratic society, where the interests of juveniles or the protection of the private life of the parties so require, or to the extent strictly necessary in the opinion of the court in special circumstances where publicity would prejudice the interests of justice.

2. Everyone charged with a criminal offence shall be presumed innocent until proved guilty according to law.

3. Everyone charged with a criminal offence has the following minimum rights:

(a) to be informed promptly, in a language which he understands and in detail, of the nature and cause of the accusation against him;

(b) to have adequate time and facilities for the preparation of his defence;

(c) to defend himself in person or through legal assisance of his own choosing or, if he has not sufficient means to pay for legal assistance, to be given it free when the interests of justice so require;

(d) to examine or have examined witnesses against him and to obtain the attendance and examination of witnesses on his behalf under the same conditions as witnesses against him;

(e) to have the free assistance of an interpreter if he cannot understand or speak the language used in court.

Article 7

1. No one shall be held guilty of any criminal offence on account of any act or omission which did not constitute a criminal offence under national or international law at the time when it was committed. Nor shall a heavier penalty be imposed than the one that was applicable at the time the criminal offence was committed.

2. This Article shall not prejudice the trial and punishment of any person for any act or omission which, at the time when it was committed, was criminal according to the general principles of law recognised by civilised nations.

Article 8

1. Everyone has the right to respect for his private and family life, his home and his correspondence.

2. There shall be no interference by a public authority with the exercise of this right except such as is in accordance with the law and is necessary in a democratic society in the interests of national security, public safety or the economic well-being of the country, for the prevention of disorder or crime, for the protection of health or morals, or for the protection of the rights and freedoms of others.

Article 9

1. Everyone has the right to freedom of thought, conscience and religion; this right includes freedom to change his religion or belief and freedom, either alone or in community with others and in public or private, to manifest his religion or belief, in worship, teaching, practice and observance.

2. Freedom to manifest one's religion or beliefs shall be subject only to such limitations as are prescribed by law and are necessary in a democratic society in the interests of public safety, for the protection of public order, health or morals, or for the protection of the rights and freedoms of others.

Article 10

1. Everyone has the right to freedom of expression. This right shall include freedom to hold opinions and to receive and impart information and ideas without interference by public authority and regardless of frontiers. This Article shall not prevent States from requiring the licensing of broadcasting, television or cinema enterprises.

2. The exercise of these freedoms, since it carries with it duties and responsibilities, may be subject to such formalities, conditions, restrictions or penalties as are prescribed by law and are necessary in a democratic society, in the interests of national security, territorial integrity or public safety, for the prevention of disorder or crime, for the protection of health or morals, for the protection of the reputation or rights of others, for preventing the disclosure of information received in confidence, or of maintaining the authority and impartiality of the judiciary.

Article 11

1. Everyone has the right to freedom of peaceful assembly and to freedom of association with others, including the right to form and to join trade unions for the protection of his interests.

2. No restrictions shall be placed on the exercise of these rights other than such as are prescribed by law and are necessary in a democratic society in the interests of national security or public safety, for the prevention of disorder or crime, for the protection of health or morals or for the protection of the rights and freedoms of others. This Article shall not prevent the imposition of lawful restrictions on the exercise of these rights by members of the armed forces, of the police or of the administration of the State.

Article 12

Men and women of marriageable age have the right to marry and to found a family, according to the national laws governing the exercise of this right.

Article 13

Everyone whose rights and freedoms as set forth in this Convention are violated shall have an effective remedy before a national authority notwithstanding that the violation has been committed by persons acting in an official capacity.

Article 14

The enjoyment of the rights and freedoms set forth in this Convention shall be secured without discrimination on any ground such as sex, race, colour, language, religion, political or other opinion, national or social origin, association with a national minority, property, birth or other status.

Article 15

1. In time of war or other public emergency threatening the life of the nation any High Contracting Party may take measures derogating from its obligations under this Convention to the extent strictly required by the exigencies of the situation, provided that such measures are not inconsistent with its other obligations under international law.

2. No derogation from Article 2, except in respect of deaths resulting from lawful acts of war, or from Articles 3, 4 (para. 1) and 7 shall be made under this provision.

3. Any High Contracting Party availing itself of this right of derogation shall keep the Secretary-General of the Council of Europe fully informed of the measures which it has taken and the reasons therefor. It shall also inform the Secretary-General of the Council of Europe when such measures have ceased to operate and the provisions of the Convention are again fully executed.

Article 16

Nothing in Articles 10, 11 and 14 shall be regarded as preventing the High Contracting Parties from imposing restrictions on the political activity of aliens.

Article 17

Nothing in this Convention may be interpreted as implying for any State, group or person any right to engage in any activity or perform any act aimed at the destruction of any of the rights and freedoms set forth herein or at their limitation to a greater extent than is provided for in the Convention.

Article 18

The restrictions permitted under this Convention to the said rights and freedoms shall not be applied for any purpose other than those for which they have been prescribed.

First Protocol to the European Convention, 1952
Council Eur. Doc. H(79) 4(1979)

Article I

Every natural or legal person is entitled to the peaceful enjoyment of his possessions. No one shall be deprived of his possessions except in the public interest and subject to the conditions provided for by law and by the general principles of international law.

The preceding provisions shall not, however, in any way impair the right of a State to enforce such laws as it deems necessary to control the use of property in accordance with the general interest or to secure the payment of taxes or other contributions or penalties.

Article II

No person shall be denied the right to education. In the exercise of any functions which it assumes in relation to education and to teaching, the State shall respect the right of parents to ensure such education and teaching in conformity with their own religious and philosophical convictions.

Article III

The High Contracting Parties undertake to hold free elections at reasonable intervals by secret ballot, under conditions which will ensure the free expression of the opinion of the people in the choice of the legislature.

Fourth Protocol to the European Convention, 1963
Council Eur. Doc. H(79) 4(1979)

Article 1

No one shall be deprived of his liberty merely on the ground of inability to fulfil a contractual obligation.

Article 2

1. Everyone lawfully within the territory of a state shall, within that territory, have the right to liberty of movement and freedom to choose his residence.

2. Everyone shall be free to leave any country, including his own.

3. No restrictions shall be placed on the exercise of these rights other than such as are in accordance with law and are necessary in a democratic society in the interests of national security or public safety, for the maintenance of *ordre public*, for the prevention of crime, for the protection of health or morals, or for the protection of the rights and freedoms of others.

4. The rights set forth in paragraph 1 may also be subject, in particular areas, to restrictions imposed in accordance with law and justified by the public interest in a democratic society.

Article 3

1. No one shall be expelled, by means either of an individual or of a collective measure, from the territory of the State of which he is a national.

2. No one shall be deprived of the right to enter the territory of the State of which he is a national.

Article 4

Collective expulsion of aliens is prohibited.

European Petition System

The *European Convention* refers to three bodies that are charged with protecting the human rights of individuals: the Committee of Ministers of the Council of Europe (Committee), the European Commission of Human Rights (Commission) and the European Court of Human Rights (Court). The Committee is a political body of the Council of Europe while the Commission and the Court are creatures of the European Convention.

The members of the Commission are elected by the Committee from names submitted by the national delegations in the Parliamentary Assembly of the Parliament of Europe of states parties to the treaty. (Article 21.1). There are an equal number of Commissioners as there are states parties to the treaty and no two Commissioners can be nationals of the same state (Article 20). Commissioners are bound to act independently of their respective countries of origin (Article 23), hold office for 6 years and may be re-elected (Article 22). The members of the Court are elected in a manner similar to Commissioners (Article 39) from candidates "of high moral character [who] must either possess the qualifications required for appointment to high judicial office or be juriconsultants of recognized competence" (Article 39). The number of judges is "equal to that of the Members of the Council of Europe" and no two can be nationals of the same state (Article 38). Judges hold office for a 9-year period but may be re-elected (Article 40).

The greater part of the work load resulting from the rights and obligations created by the Convention falls upon the Commission. The Commission, like many of the domestic human rights ones in the various jurisdictions of Canada, has a threefold function. Its first responsibility is to receive and cull all complaints about alleged breaches of the Convention. They may be in the form of references from other state parties (Article 24) or by way of petitions from individuals, groups of individuals or non-governmental organizations claiming to be victims of human rights violations, provided that the State against whom a petition is made has accepted the right of individual petition (Article 25).

The Convention provides that the Commission must determine the admissibility of the individual petitions sent to it. (References by State parties are handled somewhat differently). For example, it must reject any petition alleging a violation of rights not protected by the Convention (Article 25.1), domestic remedies must have been exhausted by the petitioner, who must also have made a timely application (Article 26), and anonymous petitions, those previously dealt with by the Commission or which are before other human rights tribunals, and those which are "incompatible with the provisions of the ... Convention, manifestly ill-founded or an abuse of the right of petition" must be rejected (Article 27). The determination of the admissibility of a complaint can involve a lengthy investigation and is governed by a set procedure evolved through practice.

Once a complaint is deemed to be acceptable, the major function of the Commission begins. It must investigate the alleged breach to ascertain the facts and, like the various Canadian human rights commissions, attempt to effect a settlement between parties if necessary (Article 29). Should a reconciliation occur, the members of the Commission must unanimously agree to it, after which the Commission must file a report about the matter to the Committee and the state or states concerned (Article 30).

If there is no solution, the Commission must submit a report containing an outline of the facts of the case and its opinion as to whether they disclose a breach (Article 31.1). It can also make proposals (Article 31.3) in the report, which must be sent to the Committee and the affected state or states (Article 31.2). Eventually, all reports of the Commission, both settlements and opinions, are published.[67]

Once the Commission has submitted its report, or opinion, to the Committee of Ministers, the case may be determined either by the Committee or by the Court. The Court can become seized of the matter provided that the state or states involved are subject to its compulsory jurisdiction or have consented to it. Article 48 stipulates that the only entities empowered to refer a case to the Court are the Commission itself or any state involved in it (one whose national is a victim of the alleged violation, the state which referred the case to the Commission, or the state that was the target of the complaint).[68] An individual complainant has no standing to bring an issue before the Court. Proceedings before the Court (all of which are published[69]) are of an adversarial nature

---

[67] See *The European Commission on Human Rights: Decisions & Reports*; and the *Yearbooks of the European Convention on Human Rights*.

[68] Article 1 of the Second Protocol gives the Committee of Ministers the right to request "advisory opinions on legal questions concerning the interpretation of the Convention" and its Protocols. However, that Article limits the type of opinions by prohibiting requests concerned with "any question relating to the content or scope of the rights or freedoms defined in Section 1 of the Convention and [its] Protocols, or with any other question which the Commission, the Court or the Committee ... might have to consider in consequence of any such proceedings as could be instituted in accordance with the Convention."

[69] See *Yearbook of the European Convention on Human Rights*; *Series A: Judgments & Decisions*; and *Series B: Pleadings, Oral Arguments & Documents*.

and are analogous to those of a trial court. The Commission acts as an impartial, objective party before the Court.

The Committee, by a two-thirds majority vote, must decide the case if it is not referred to the Court "within a period of three months from the date of transmission of the Report to the Committee ... " (Article 32).[70]

Two sample judgments of the Court follow. Note the difference in views between the finding of the Court and its outline of the Commission's report in the first of these cases.

Case of Abdulaziz, Cabales, and Balkandali[71]

The applicants, two of whom were not British citizens, were permanently settled in the U.K. Their respective husbands, who were not British citizens, were prohibited from remaining in, or journeying to, the country to join them. The applicants alleged that they were the victims of sexual and racial discrimination. Because of the inability to reach a friendly settlement, the Commission prepared a report to establish the facts and state an opinion about whether the Government breached its obligations under the Convention.

The Commission found that changes in the state's Immigration Rules (in force on 1 March 1980) were intended to curtail "primary immigration" (*e.g.*, someone likely to become the head of a household and take employment). "Secondary immigration" (*e.g.*, wives and children of those lawfully in the country) were not affected. The rules were part of an immigration policy designed to help alleviate domestic social and unemployment problems to which the great increase in immigration in the 1950s and early 1960s was believed to have contributed. Subsequent changes in the *British Nationality Act 1981* and Immigration Rules did not assist the women in their appeals to the British authorities.

The applicants argued that the U.K. was in breach of Art. 8[72] and Art. 8 in conjunction with Arts. 14, 3 and 13.

The Commission expressed the opinion that:[73]

...there had been a violation of Article 14, in conjunction with Article 8, on the ground of sexual discrimination (unanimously);

...there had been no violation of the same Articles on the ground of racial discrimination (nine votes to three);

...the original application of the 1980 Rules in the case of Mrs. Balkandali constituted discrimination

---

[70] See *Yearbook of the European Convention on Human Rights; Collection of Resolutions of the Committee of Ministers: 1959–1983* (1984); and H. Miehsler and H. Petzold, *European Convention on Human Rights: Texts & Documents*, Vol. 1 (1980), Vol. 2 (1982).

[71] Council of Europe, *Case of Abdulaziz, Cabales, & Balkandali* (15/1983/71/107–109), Judgment of the European Court of Human Rights, 28 May 1985.

[72] Part of their argument referred to the UN Human Rights Committee's views in the *Aumeeruddy-Cziffra Case*, *supra*, at n. 44.

[73] *Supra*, n. 71, at 22. See also, Council of Europe, Application Nos. 9214/80, 9473/81 & 9474/81, *Report of the Commission*, adopted 12 May 1983.

on the ground of birth, contrary to Article 14 in conjunction with Article 8 (eleven votes with one abstention);

...the absence of effective domestic remedies for the applicants' claims under Articles 3, 8 and 14 constituted a violation of Article 13 (eleven votes to one);

...it was not necessary to pursue a further examination of the matter in the light of Articles 3 and 8.

The case was referred to the Court for determination. Its judgment on the applicability of Article 8 alone turned on whether the state had failed to respect the family life of the applicants. The Court concluded that, while Article 8 might impose positive obligations on a state to ensure an effective "respect" for family life, there was no evidence to demonstrate failure on the part of the State so to do. It said:

...as far as those positive obligations are concerned, the notion of "respect" is not clear-cut: having regard to the diversity of the practices followed and the situations obtaining in the Contracting States, the notion's requirements will vary considerably from case to case. Accordingly, [each State enjoys] a wide margin of appreciation in determining the steps to be taken to ensure compliance with the Convention with due regard to the needs and resources of the community and of individuals ... [The] extent of a State's obligation to admit to its territory relatives of settled immigrants will vary according to the particular circumstances of the person involved.[74]

The Court noted that none of the applicants had left a family behind when they emigrated to the U.K. Instead, they had first established themselves there and afterwards married foreigners, whom they knew would have difficulty obtaining immigrant status. Moreover, the Court noted that, as the applicants had not proven the existence of any barriers "to establishing family life in their own or their respective spouse's home countries or that there were special reasons why that could not be expected of them."[75]

The Court, also made findings on alleged violations of Article 14 taken together with Article 8. These included allegations of discrimination on the grounds of race, birth (in the case of Mrs. Balkandali) and sex. On the first, the Court held that its examination of the evidence revealed no discrimination on the basis of race, notwithstanding a conclusion by a minority of the Commission that, in practice, the effect of the State's immigration rules was to so discriminate. On the second issue, the Court disagreed with the majority of the Commission by holding that there could be discrimination by birth in certain immigration matters when a country chose to discriminate in favour of persons born in, or having a parent born within, its territory. Because those individuals might have close ties with the country the Court said there was justification to avoid the hardship resulting to those of them who married foreigners and would otherwise have to move abroad. While the Court accepted that Mrs. Balkandali had established close links to the U.K. by virtue of prolonged settlement in the country, it held that there was no violation on those grounds because "there are in general persuasive social reasons for giving special

---

[74] *Supra*, n. 71, at 27.
[75] Ibid.

treatment to those whose link with a foreign country stems from birth within it. The difference of treatment must therefore be regarded as having had an objective and reasonable justification and, in particular, its results have not been shown to transgress the principle of proportionality.''[76]

In addressing the issue of sex based discrimination, the U.K. based its main arguments on a dual need: the protection of the domestic labour market (the defence being that, as men were more likely to enter the market than women, it restricted the entry of male spouses and not female ones); and the maintenance of effective immigration control and social order by easing the strain caused by large immigrations and to benefit both settled immigrants and the indigenous population. The court held that, while the needs were legitimate, the method (discrimination on the basis of sex) of achieving them was supported neither on the facts of the cases nor on the State's work force statistics. It held that, equality of the sexes being a major goal of the member states of the Council of Europe, ''very weighty reasons would have to be advanced before a difference of treatment on the ground of sex could be regarded as compatible with the Convention.''[77]

Even though the Court found a violation grounded on sex based discrimination, it dismissed an alleged violation of Article 3 because there was evidence of neither ''contempt or lack of respect for the personality of the applicants'' nor any intent to ''humiliate or debase'' the applicants.[78]

Finally, the Court found that the U.K. was in violation of Article 13. This occurred because there was discrimination on the ground of sex, the European Convention had not been incorporated into the domestic laws of the country, and, as a result, there could be no ''effective remedy'' for the applicants.

Handyside Against United Kingdom[79]

[Mr. Handyside owned a publishing firm specializing in leftist political literature. He published a text, *The Little Red Schoolbook*, which was an English translation of a Danish book published and freely available in at least 11 Western European countries. Advertised as a reference work for school children, its contents presented factual aspects of educational and sexual activities from the bias of a left-wing, counter-culture viewpoint.

As a result of a number of complaints from the public, the authorities seized all copies of the book and successfully prosecuted Handyside under the British *Obscene Publications Act* for possessing ''obscene books ... for publication for gain''. The finding of the magistrate's court was affirmed on appeal by the Inner London Quarter Sessions court, in spite of contradictory expert evidence on whether the book was, in fact, obscene.

The operative section of the statute defined ''obscene'' as an article whose effect is:

---

[76] *Supra*, n. 71, at 35.
[77] Ibid., at 31.
[78] Ibid.
[79] (1976), Eur. Court H.R., Ser. A, No. 24.

such as to tend to deprave and corrupt persons who are likely, having regard to all relevant circumstances, to read, see or hear the matter contained or embroidered in it.

The British courts held that Mr. Handyside was guilty under the *Act* because the book "was intended for children passing through a highly critical stage of their development" and that it represented a one-sided opinion "of an extreme kind, unrelieved by any indication that there were alternative views. Further, they found the book to possess a "tendency to deprave and corrupt" because it negated "the sense of some responsibility to the community as well as oneself" by, *e.g.*, condoning illegal activities such as the use of marijuana, and sexual intercourse by minors. Finally, the courts rejected the statutory defence that, notwithstanding its obscene content, the book was "for the public good on the ground that it is in the interests of science, literature, art or learning, or of other objects of general concern" because the beneficial aspects of its content were negated by the setting and context in which they were situated.

The complainant argued that a number of breaches of the Convention had been made by the U.K., and both the Commission and the Court disagreed (with dissenting views expressed) on each of them. For the purposes of brevity, only the view of the majority of the Court on the issue of freedom of expression will be examined. That aspect of the case dealt with the right of the state to limit the freedom (Art. 10.2) and the extent to which it took measures to do so. The Court examined the case in the light of the following facts and allegations:

1) other states parties to the Convention did not find the publication to be offensive and a global (or, at least, a regional) standard should be applicable; and

2) the publishers of pornographic material freely available in the U.K. had not been prosecuted, thereby indicating that the complainant was chosen for prosecution by the state for his political views rather than other, *bona fide* reasons.]

THE EUROPEAN COURT: ...

The Court points out that the machinery of protection established by the Convention is subsidiary to the national systems safeguarding human rights (judgment of 23 July 1968 on the merits of the "Belgian Linguistic" case, Series A No. 6, at 35, § 10 *in fine*). The Convention leaves to each Contracting State, in the first place, the task of securing the rights and freedoms it enshrines. The institutions created by it make their own contribution to this task but they become involved only through contentious proceedings and once all domestic remedies have been exhausted (Article 26).

These observations apply, notably, to Article 10 § 2. In particular, it is not possible to find in the domestic law of the various Contracting States a uniform European conception of morals. The view taken by their respective laws of the requirements of morals varies from time to time and from place to place, especially in our era which is characterised by a rapid and far-reaching evolution of opinions on the subject. By reason of their direct and continuous contact with the vital forces of their countries, States authorities are in principle in a better position than the international judge to give an opinion on the exact content of these requirements as well as on the "necessity" of a "restriction" or "penalty" intended to meet them. The Court notes at this juncture that, whilst the adjective "necessary," within the meaning of Article 10 § 2, is not synonymous with "indispensable'' (cf., in Articles 2 § 2 and 6 § 1, the words "absolutely necessary" and "strictly necessary" and, in Article 15 § 1, the phrase "to the extent strictly required by the exigencies of the situation"), neither has it the flexibility of such expressions as "admissible," "ordinary" (cf. Article 4 § 3), "useful" (cf. the French text of the first paragraph of Article 1 of Protocol No. 1), "reasonable" (cf. Articles 5 § 3 and 6 § 1) or "desirable." Nevertheless, it is for the national authorities to make the initial assessment of the reality of the pressing social need implied by the notion of "necessity" in this context.

Consequently, Article 10 § 2 leaves to the Contracting States a margin of appreciation. This margin is given both to the domestic legislator ("prescribed by law") and to the bodies, judicial amongst others, that are called upon to interpret and apply the laws in force ... .

Nevertheless, Article 10 § 2 does not give the Contracting States an unlimited power of appreciation. The Court, which, with the Commission, is responsible for ensuring the observance of those States' engagements (Article 19), is empowered to give the final ruling on whether a "restriction" or "penalty" is reconcilable with freedom of expression as protected by Article 10. The domestic margin of appreciation thus goes hand in hand with a European supervision. Such supervision concerns both the aim of the measure challenged and its "necessity"; it covers not only the basic legislation but also the decision applying it, even one given by an independent court. In this respect, the Court refers to Article 50 of the Convention ("decision or ... measure taken by a legal authority or any other authority") as well as to its own case-law (Engel and others judgment of 8 June 1976, Series A no. 22. at 41–42, § 100).

The Court's supervisory functions oblige it to pay the utmost attention to the principles characterising a "democratic society." Freedom of expression constitutes one of the essential foundations of such a society, one of the basic conditions for its progress and for the development of every man. Subject to paragraph 2 of Article 10, it is applicable not only to "information" or "ideas" that are favourably received or regarded as inoffensive or as a matter of indifference, but also to those that offend, shock or disturb the State or any sector of the population. Such are the demands of that pluralism, tolerance and broadmindedness without which there is no "democratic society." This means, amongst other things, that every "formality," "condition," "restriction" or "penalty" imposed in this sphere must be proportionate to the legitimate aim pursued.

From another standpoint, whoever exercises his freedom of expression undertakes "duties and responsibilities" the scope of which depends on his situation and the technical means he uses. The Court cannot overlook such a person's "duties" and "responsibilities" when it enquires, as in this case, whether "restrictions" or "penalties" were conducive to the "protection of morals" which made them "necessary" in a "democratic society."

It follows from this that it is in no way the Court's task to take the place of the competent national courts but rather to review under Article 10 the decisions they delivered in the exercise of their power of appreciation.

However, the Court's supervision would generally prove illusory if it did no more than examine these decisions in isolation: it must view them in the light of the case as a whole, including the publication in question and the arguments and evidence adduced by the applicant in the domestic legal system and then at the international level. The Court must decide, on the basis of the different data available to it, whether the reasons given by the national authorities to justify the actual measures of ''interference'' they take are relevant and sufficient under Article 10 § 2 ... .

Following the method set out above, the Court scrutinized under Article 10 § 2 the individual decisions complained of, in particular, the judgment of the Inner London Quarter Sessions.

For its part the Court finds that the anti-authoritarian aspects of the Schoolbook as such were not held in the judgment of 29 October 1971 to fall foul of the 1959/1964 Acts. Those aspects were taken into account only insofar as the appeal court considered that, by undermining the moderating influence of parents, teachers, the Churches and youth organisations, they aggravated the tendency to ''deprave and corrupt'' which in its opinion resulted from other parts of the work. It should be added that the revised edition was allowed to circulate freely by the British authorities despite the fact that the anti-authoritarian passages again appeared there in full and even, in some cases, in stronger terms (paragraph 35 above). As the Government noted, this is hard to reconcile with the theory of a political intrigue.

The Court thus allows that the fundamental aim of the judgment of 29 October 1971, applying the 1959/1964 Acts, was the protection of the morals of the young, a legitimate purpose under Article 10 § 2. Consequently the seizures effected on 31 March and 1 April 1971, pending the outcome of the proceedings that were about to open, also had this aim.

It remains to examine the ''necessity'' of the measures in dispute, beginning with the said seizures. ...

If the applicant is right, their object should have been at the most one or a few copies of the book to be used as exhibits in the criminal proceedings. The Court does not share this view since the police had good reasons for trying to lay their hands on all the stock as a temporary means of protecting the young against a danger to morals on whose existence it was for the trial court to decide. The legislation of many Contracting States provides for a seizure analogous to that envisaged by section 3 of the English 1959/1964 Acts. ...

The treatment meted out to the Schoolbook and it publisher in 1971 was, according to the applicant and the minority of the Commission, all the less ''necessary'' in that a host of publications dedicated to hard core pornography and devoid of intellectual or artistic merit allegedly profit by an extreme degree of tolerance in the United Kingdom. They are exposed to the gaze of passers-by and especially of young people and are said generally to enjoy complete impunity, the rare criminal prosecutions launched against them proving, it was asserted, more often than not abortive due to the great liberalism shown by juries. The same was claimed to apply to sex shops and much public entertainment.

The Government countered this by the remark, supported by figures, that the Director of Public Prosecutions does not remain inactive nor does the police, despite the scanty manpower resources of the squad specialising in this field. Moreover, they claim that, in addition to proceedings properly so called, seizures were frequently made at the relevant time under the ''disclaimer/caution procedure'' (paragraph 26 above).

In principle it is not the Court's function to compare different decisions taken, even in apparently similar circumstances, by prosecuting authorities and courts; and it must, just like the respondent Government, respect the independence of the courts. Furthermore and above all, the Court is not faced with really analogous situations: as the Government pointed out, the documents in the file do not show that the publications and entertainment in question were aimed, to the same extent as the Schoolbook (paragraph 52 above), at children and adolescents having ready access thereto.

The applicant and the minority of the Commission laid stress on the further point that, in addition to the original Danish edition, translations of the "Little Book" appeared and circulated freely in the majority of the member States of the Council of Europe.

Here again, the national margin of appreciation and the optional nature of the "restrictions" and "penalties" referred to in Article 10 § 2 prevent the Court from accepting the argument. The Contracting States have each fashioned their approach in the light of the situation obtaining in their respective territories; they have had regard, *inter alia*, to the different views prevailing there about the demands of the protection of morals in a democratic society. The fact that most of them decided to allow the work to be distributed does not mean that the contrary decision of the Inner London Quarter Sessions was a breach of Article 10. Besides, some of the editions published outside the United Kingdom do not include the passages, or at least not all the passages, cited in the judgment of 19 October 1971 as striking examples of a tendency to "deprave and corrupt."

NOTES

Compare the jurisprudence arising from the European Convention to that arising from the *CCPR*. Consider whether they complement or contradict one another and whether both, together, might give rise to a global body of international human rights law or merely separate bodies of jurisprudence, each of which might only be regionally applicable.

Influence on Canadian Law[80]

The rule at international law is clear: a state cannot rely upon its domestic law or constitution to avoid its international legal obligations. In Canada's domestic legal fora

---

[80] See A.F. Bayefsky, "The Impact of the European Convention on Human Rights in the United Kingdom: Implications for Canada" (1981), 13 *Ottawa L. Rev.* 507; J. Claydon, "The Application of International Human Rights Law by Canadian Courts" (1981), 30 *Buffalo L. Rev.* 727; J. Claydon, "International Human Rights Law and the Interpretation of the Canadian Charter of Rights and Freedoms" (1982), 4 *Sup. Ct. L. Rev.* 287; M. Cohen, "Towards a Paradigm of Theory and Practice: The Canadian Charter of Rights and Freedoms – International Law Influences and Reactions," in J. Makarczyk, ed., *Essays in International Law in Honour of Manfred Lachs* (1984), at 65; M. Cohen and A. Bayefsky, "The Canadian Charter of Rights and Freedoms and Public International Law" (1983), 61 *Can. Bar Rev.* 265; E.P. Mendes, "Interpreting the Canadian Charter of Rights and Freedoms: Applying International and European Jurisprudence on the Law and Practice of Fundamental Rights" (1982), 20 *Alta. L. Rev.* 383; W.S. Tarnopolsky, "A Comparison Between the Canadian Charter of Rights and Freedoms and the International Covenant on Civil and Political Rights" (1982–3), 8 *Queen's L.J.* 211; and W.S. Tarnopolsky, "The New Canadian Charter of Rights and Freedoms as Compared and Contrasted With the American Bill of Rights" (1983), 5 *H.R. Quart.* 227.

however, the rule is not so well defined.[81] It is complicated by our Constitution, which permits the Federal Executive to ratify treaties without prior resort to any democratically elected body such as Parliament and sets out the division of powers in a way that frequently requires provincial implementation of international obligations entered into by a Federal representative. The matter is further complicated in Canada by its courts' view of how treaties and legislation are related, and by the complex and, perhaps, unresolved question about whether there is a difference between the way in which customary international law and treaty law can become a part of the body of the Canadian domestic law. Additionally, those difficulties have not been helped by a practising bar and bench that could be better versed in public international law.

While the attitude of our courts is difficult to gauge, it is noteworthy to see that, more and more frequently, advocates appearing before them are placing a greater reliance upon Canada's international legal obligations. This may be particularly true in cases dealing with human rights issues. For example, in a freedom of association case, *Re Alberta Provincial Employees and the Crown*,[82] the court referred to at least a dozen international human rights instruments which Canada has ratified and others to which Canada is not a party. They included the CESCR and a number of International Labour Organisation conventions. In a second case on freedom of association,[83] the court referred to two other documents emanating from the ILO.

In *Federal Republic of Germany v. Rauca*,[84] a case involving the extradition of an alleged war criminal, the court considered the CCPR and the European Convention, some of its Protocols and Explanatory Reports on the Protocols so far as they related to the issues in the case.

Bhindi v. B.C. Projectionists, Loc. 348 of Int. Alliance of Motion Pictures Machine Operators of U.S. and Can.[85] provides an interesting glimpse of the possible use that Canadian courts can make of international human rights materials when considering the interpretation and application of the *Charter of Rights and Freedoms*. There, the court considered the applicability of jurisprudence of the European Court of Human Rights dealing with the issue of compulsory trade union membership. Although the court ruled that the European case to which counsel had referred it was not applicable to the situation, the court also held that it would, when appropriate, consider the rationale in the decisions of the European Court of Human Rights even though Canada is not a party to the European Convention. Some other examples of the consideration Canadian courts have given to international human rights jurisprudence include *R. v. King, R. v. Morgentaler, Smoling & Scott*, and *R. v. Videoflicks et al.*[86] These examples are, by no means, the only ones to have done so, but are used here merely to illustrate the potential use to which inter-

---

[81] See *supra*, Chapter 4.

[82] (1980), 120 D.L.R. (3d) 590 (Alta. Q.B.).

[83] *Re Service Employees' International Union, Local 204 and Broadway Manor Nursing Home* (1983), 44 O.R. (2d) 392 (Div.Ct.).

[84] (1983), 41 O.R. (2d) 225 (C.A.).

[85] (1985), 63 B.C.L.R. 352 (B.C.S.C.).

[86] [1984] 4 W.W.R. 531 (Alta Q.B.); (1984), 12 D.L.R. (4th) 502 (Ont. H.C.); and (1984), 5 O.A.C. 1 (C.A.), respectively.

national human rights law may be put in the domestic legal system. Indeed, these examples show that Canadian courts are not easily swayed (nor should they be) by the work done at the international level. Rather, they demonstrate that international human rights law can act as a touchstone or guide in the development of domestic human rights law.

The potential of the relationship between the international law of human rights and Canadian domestic law – particularly the developing law of the *Charter of Rights and Freedoms* – is of interest. For example, international human rights law can act as a universal norm – minimum standard – by which the courts can define, and measure adherence to, human rights in Canada. This will help the courts to avoid the deplorable state of confusion and contradiction that its case law dealing with the *Bill of Rights*[87] created. Further, it will permit the courts to avoid the shortsightedness that too much reliance upon domestic law can breed.[88]

An awareness of the international law of human rights can help Canadian courts to curtail the undesirable jurisprudential influence of foreign states. This is particularly important now that a written, constitutional protection of human rights exists. The *Canadian Charter of Rights and Freedoms* has extracted the Canadian constitutional and legal system from the old British concept of absolute parliamentary sovereignty and directed it toward the American one. While the political process has promulgated this change of direction, the courts must be careful not to over-react. They must, for example, both refrain from adopting a blind adherence to British law and avoid an unpremeditated jump too readily on the bandwagon of American jurisprudence.

Paradoxically, one must temper the warning against blindly following a path set by the domestic human rights laws of foreign countries by considering that, in certain circumstances, they may have adopted international human rights law in a manner worthy of consideration by Canadian courts. A landmark decision by the Federal Court of Appeal in the U.S.A. provides an example of note. When examining the case that follows, recall the numerous international human rights treaties to which Canada is a party and consider whether the commitment to human rights is such that Canadian courts, if called upon to do so, could improve the law in Canada by making a similar finding. Should the Canadian domestic legal system admit the crystalization of customary international legal norms of human rights?

Filartiga v. Pena-Irala
(1980), 630 F. 2d 876 (U.S.C.A. 2d Circ.)

[The plaintiffs, Paraguayan citizens, who had applied for political asylum in the United States in 1978, brought an action against the defendant, the former head of police of

---

[87] *E.g.*, see *Robertson & Rosetanni v. The Queen*, [1963] S.C.R. 651, *R. v. Drybones*, [1970] S.C.R. 282, and *A.-G. for Canada v. Lavell*, [1974] S.C.R. 1349. The majority judgment in the last two cases was based upon the dissenting judgment of the prior case.

[88] *E.g.*, the Supreme Court of Canada decision in the *Lavell* case, *ibid.*, contain a number of individual judgments, some of which can be read to interpret the phrase "equality before the law" to mean that the Federal Government was permitted to define any number of individuals as a specific group, which it could then treat in any manner it saw fit, regardless of how fair it was, provided that it treated everyone within that group in the same way.

Asuncion who was in the United States as a visitor. The cause of action was based on
the allegation that the defendant had tortured the plaintiffs' son and brother because of
one plaintiff's political opposition to the Paraguayan regime. The action was said to arise
under "wrongful death statutes; the United Nations Charter; the Universal Declaration
on Human Rights; the United Nations Declaration against Torture; the American Declaration of the Rights and Duties of Man; and other pertinent declarations, documents
and practices constituting the customary law of human rights and the law of Nations."
Jurisdiction was based upon the United States Judiciary Act of 1789[89] which gives jurisdiction to the Federal District Court in "all causes where an alien sues for a tort ... in
violation of the law of nations." The trial court held that it did not have jurisdiction.
The plaintiffs appealed.]

KAUFMAN C.J.: ... Since appellants do not contend that their action arises directly
under a treaty of the United States, a threshold question on the jurisdictional issue is
whether the conduct alleged violates the law of nations. In light of the universal condemnation of torture in numerous international agreements, and the renunciation of torture
as an instrument of official policy by virtually all of the nations of the world (in principle
if not in practice), we find that an act of torture committed by a state official against one
held in detention violates established norms of the international law of human rights, and
hence the law of nations. ...

The United Nations Charter makes it clear that in this modern age a state's treatment
of its own citizens is a matter of international concern. ...

While this broad mandate has been held not to be wholly self-executing, this ... observation
alone does not end our inquiry. For although there is no universal agreement as to the
precise extent of the "human rights and fundamental freedoms" guaranteed to all by the
Charter, there is at present no dissent from the view that the guaranties include, at a bare
minimum, the right to be free from torture. This prohibition has become part of customary
international law, as evidenced and defined by the Universal Declaration of Human Rights,
which states, in the plainest of terms, "no one shall be subjected to torture." The General
Assembly has declared that the Charter precepts embodied in this *Universal Declaration*
"constitute basic principles of international law.".

These U.N. declarations are significant because they specify with great precision the
obligations of member nations under the Charter. Since their adoption, "[m]embers can
no longer contend that they do not know what human rights they promised in the Charter
to promote". ...Moreover, a U.N. Declaration is according to one authoritative definition,
"a formal and solemn instrument, suitable for rare occasions when principles of great
and lasting importance are being enunciated". ...Accordingly, it has been observed that
the Universal Declaration of Human Rights "no longer fits into the dichotomy of 'binding
treaty' against non-binding pronouncement,' but is rather an authoritative statement of
the international community." ...Thus, a Declaration creates an expectation of adherence,
and "insofar as the expectation is gradually justified by State practice, a declaration may
by custom become recognized as laying down rules binding upon the States." Indeed,

---

[89] 28 U.S.C. s. 1350.

several commentators have concluded that the Universal Declaration has become, *in toto*, a part of binding, customary international law. ...

Turning to the act of torture, we have little difficulty discerning its universal renunciation in the modern usage and practice of nations. The international consensus surrounding torture has found expression in numerous international treaties and accords ... International Covenant on Civil and Political Rights, European Convention for the Protection of Human Rights and Fundamental Freedoms; the substance of these international agreements is reflected in modern municipal – i.e. national-law as well. Although torture was once a routine concomitant of criminal interrogations in many nations, during the modern and hopefully more enlightened era it has been universally renounced. According to one survey, torture is prohibited, expressly or implicitly, by the constitution of over fifty-five nations, including both the United States and Paraguay. Our State Department reports a general recognition of this principle:

> There now exists an international consensus that recognizes basic human rights and obligations owed by all governments to their citizens. ... There is no doubt that these rights are often violated; but virtually all governments acknowledge their validity. ...

Having examined the sources from which customary international law is derived – the usage of nations, judicial opinions and the works of jurists – we conclude that official torture is now prohibited by the law of nations. The prohibition is clear and unambiguous, and admits of no distinction between treatment of aliens and citizens. Accordingly, we must conclude that the dictum in *Dreyfus v. von Finck*, supra, 534 F.2d, at 31, to the effect that "violations of international law do not occur when the aggrieved parties are nationals of the acting state," is clearly out of tune with the current usage and practice of international law. The treaties and accords cited above, as well as the express foreign policy of our own government, all make it clear that international law confers fundamental rights upon all people vis-a-vis their own governments. While the ultimate scope of those rights will be a subject for continuing refinement and elaboration, we hold that the right to be free from torture is now among them.

[The Court then examined the other issues raised in the case and concluded that it did have jurisdiction.]

CHAPTER ELEVEN

Law of the Sea

INTRODUCTION[1]

The law of the sea is one of the most ancient and complex branches of international law. Despite its antiquity, it is also one of the most dynamic and changing areas of the law. The international community has a very considerable stake in ensuring stability and certainty in the law of the sea but new uses of the sea and new technologies, in this century as in the past, have put pressure on old rules, and have forced change. What is most remarkable about the law of the sea is that, given the high degree of common use, a clear rule of some sort has always emerged within a relatively short period of time.

Customary law has long been and continues to be a central element of the law of the sea. Virtually all modern rules of the law of the sea are grounded in custom. However, major efforts have been made to codify the law during the course of the twentieth century. The first efforts related to the status of certain international straits; they were followed by drafts proposed by the League of Nations in 1930.[2] After lengthy preparatory work by the International Law Commission, the First United Nations Conference on the Law of the Sea, convened at Geneva in 1958, adopted four comprehensive conventions: The Convention on the Territorial Sea and the Contiguous Zone; the Convention on the High Seas; the Convention on Fishing and Conservation of the Living Resources of the High

---

[1] See I. Brownlie, *Principles of Public International Law* (3 ed., 1979), at 183-257; R.R. Churchill and A.V. Lowe, *The Law of the Sea* (1983); C.J. Colombos, *The International Law of the Sea* (6 ed., 1967); M.H. Nordquist, "United Nations Convention on the Law of the Sea 1982, A Commentary," Vols. 1 (1985-); D.P. O'Connell, *The Law of the Sea*, 2 vols. (1982-84); and C. Rousseau, *Droit International Public*, Vol. IV (1980), at 269-601. See also B. Johnson and M.W. Zacher, eds., *Canadian Foreign Policy and the Law of the Sea* (1977); and D.M. Johnston, *Canada and the New International Law of the Sea* (1985). Extensive documentation is available in *New Directions in the Law of the Sea*, 10 vols. (1973-81), kept up to date by a New Series, 2 vols., looseleaf; and S. Oda, *The International Law of the Ocean Development*, 2 vols., looseleaf (1977-).

[2] See C. Rousseau, *Droit International Public*, Vol. IV (1980), at 405-22 and 364-66.

Seas; and the Convention on the Continental Shelf.[3] All four conventions entered into force and were ratified by a considerable number of states. Many which did not ratify considered that the conventions on the territorial sea, high seas and continental shelf codified important areas of the law, and thus in practice followed them relatively closely. Canada was in this position although it eventually ratified the Convention on the Continental Shelf. The four Geneva Conventions represented a considerable achievement but they fell short of universal acceptance and as the *North Sea Continental Shelf Cases*[4] showed, not all the provisions of these law-making conventions codified or achieved the status of customary international law. The Convention on Fishing on the High Seas met the greatest resistance as it appeared to many coastal states to restrict their jurisdiction to the advantage of distant water states. In practice, for Canada, fisheries were governed by bilateral arrangements with the U.S.A. such as the Halibut Treaty[5], the Frazer River Salmon Fisheries Treaty[6], general reciprocal fisheries treaties[7] or regional arrangements such as the International Convention on Northwest Atlantic Fisheries.[8]

Within a decade of the adoption of the 1958 Geneva Conventions it became clear that the process of change was continuing. Some old law was crumbling, as in the area of fisheries, and complex new problems were emerging with respect to the exploitation of polymetallic nodules to be found on large areas of the deep ocean floor. In December 1967 the spectre of the extension of continental shelf claims out into the middle of the ocean was raised at the United Nations. As a result an *ad hoc* Committee was established to explore the issues. One year later the "Seabed Committee" was established with 36 members and was given a mandate to identify the issues and prepare the agenda of a new conference on the law of the sea. The Third United Nations Conference on the Law of the Sea held its first session in December 1973 and its final eleventh session in December 1982. The U.N. Convention on the Law of the Sea[9] which emerged from that conference is the most ambitious effort at codification and progressive development of international law ever attempted by the U.N. It is comprised of 17 parts, 320 articles and 9 annexes. The Convention covers all the traditional law of the sea: (with the partial exception of military uses) including territorial sea, high seas, rights of navigation, international straits, and the continental shelf. It also contains extensive additions to the law on new topics (the common heritage of mankind beyond national jurisdiction, archipelagic states, the exclusive economic zone, protection of the marine environment and marine scientific research) or new law on traditional topics (innocent passage, transit passage through straits, fisheries, delimitation of the continental shelf). There are also extensive passages on compulsory dispute settlement. The Convention is the most comprehensive document

---

[3] 516 U.N.T.S. 205; 450 U.N.T.S. 82; 559 U.N.T.S. 285; 499 U.N.T.S. 311, 1970 Can. T.S. No. 4, respectively.

[4] [1969] I.C.J. Rep. 3, reported in Chapter 3.

[5] 1931 Can. T.S. No. 2.

[6] 1937 Can. T.S. No. 10; now replaced by the Pacific Salmon Treaty, done Janurary 28, 1985.

[7] 1970 Can. T.S. No. 11; 1972 No. 13; 1973 No. 16, No. 23; 1974 No. 14; 1976 No. 32; 1977 No. 23.

[8] 1950 Can. T.S. No. 10; 1967 No. 17; 1969 No. 34.

[9] *U.N. Conference on the Law of the Sea, Official Records*, Vol. I-XVII, (1973-1984). The Convention appears in Vol. XVII, at 151-221, and is reprinted in (1982), 21 *Int.Leg.Mat.* 1261.

to be produced on the law of the sea. Since the hopes of early and broad ratification have been dashed by the United States, it has become of great importance to determine (1) which articles of the Convention codify customary international law or general principles of international law; (2) which articles have obtained the status of new customary international law by virtue of recent state practice; (3) which articles will only enter into force for states when and as they ratify the Convention and (4) which elements of the law of the sea are not covered by the Convention at all.

At the present time, state practice and the other indicia of customary international law continue to be an important source of law. For an interim period many states continue to be governed by the 1958 Geneva conventions. As of November 1986, 32 states had ratified the 1982 United Nations Convention on the Law of the Sea.[10] A further important source of law is the host of more specialized conventions, (many drawn up under the aegis of the International Maritime Organization, in the U.N. Environment Program and other U.N. agencies), dealing with navigation, environmental protection, passage through straits, continental shelf and economic zone delimitation. Judicial and arbitral decisions have also played an important part in developing the law of the sea in the past four decades.

MARINE ZONES

Territorial Sea[11]

Definition and Delimitation

United Nations Convention on the Law of the Sea
U.N. Doc. A/CONF. 62/122 (1982), 21 *Int. Leg. Mat.* 1261

Article 2
LEGAL STATUS OF THE TERRITORIAL SEA, OF THE AIR SPACE OVER THE TERRITORIAL
SEA AND OF ITS BED AND SUBSOIL

1. The sovereignty of a coastal State extends, beyond its land territory and internal waters and, in the case of an archipelagic State, its archipelagic waters, to an adjacent belt of sea, described as the territorial sea.

2. This sovereignty extends to the air space over the territorial sea as well as to its bed and subsoil.

---

[10] At that time the Convention had been signed by 159 states. U.N. *Law of the Sea Bulletin*, No. 8 (November 1986), at 6. Pursuant to Art. 308, the Convention will come into force 12 months after it has been ratified by 60 states.

[11] See P.C. Jessup, *The Law of Territorial Waters and Maritime Jurisdiction* (1927); D.P. O'Connell, *supra*, n.1, at cc.3-10, 17, 23 and 24; and J.-Y. Morin, "Les eaux territoriales du Canada au regard du droit international" (1963), 1 *Can.Y.B.Int.L.* 82.

3. The sovereignty over the territorial sea is exercised subject to this Convention and to other rules of international law.

Article 3
BREADTH OF THE TERRITORIAL SEA

Every State has the right to establish the breadth of its territorial sea up to a limit not exceeding 12 nautical miles, measured from baselines determined in accordance with this Convention.

Article 4
OUTER LIMIT OF THE TERRITORIAL SEA

The outer limit of the territorial sea is the line every point of which is at a distance from the nearest point of the baseline equal to the breadth of the territorial sea.

Article 5
NORMAL BASELINE

Except where otherwise provided in this Convention, the normal baseline for measuring the breadth of the territorial sea is the low-water line along the coast as marked on large-scale charts officially recognized by the coastal State.

Article 7
STRAIGHT BASELINES

1. In localities where the coastline is deeply indented and cut into, or if there is a fringe of islands along the coast in its immediate vicinity, the method of straight baselines joining appropriate points may be employed in drawing the baseline from which the breadth of the territorial sea is measured.

2. Where because of the presence of a delta and other natural conditions the coastline is highly unstable, the appropriate points may be selected along the furthest seaward extent of the low-water line and, notwithstanding subsequent regression of the low-water line, the straight baselines shall remain effective until changed by the coastal State in accordance with this Convention.

3. The drawing of straight baselines must not depart to any appreciable extent from the general direction of the coast, and the sea areas lying within the lines must be sufficiently closely linked to the land domain to be subject to the régime of internal waters.

4. Straight baselines shall not be drawn to and from low-tide elevations, unless light-houses or similar installations which are permanently above sea level have been built on them or except in instances where the drawing of baselines to and from such elevations has received general international recognition.

5. Where the method of straight baselines is applicable under paragraph 1, account may be taken, in determining particular baselines, of economic interests peculiar to the region concerned, the reality and the importance of which are clearly evidenced by long usage.

6. The system of straight baselines may not be applied by a State in such a manner as to cut off the territorial sea of another State from the high seas or an exclusive economic zone.

Article 8
INTERNAL WATERS

1. Except as provided in Part IV, waters on the landward side of the baseline of the territorial sea form part of the internal waters of the State.

2. Where the establishment of a straight baseline in accordance with the method set forth in article 7 has the effect of enclosing as internal waters areas which had not previously been considered as such, a right of innocent passage as provided in this Convention shall exist in those waters.

Article 9
MOUTHS OF RIVERS

If a river flows directly into the sea, the baseline shall be a straight line across the mouth of the river between points on the low-water line of its banks.

Article 10
BAYS

1. This article relates only to bays the coasts of which belong to a single State.

2. For the purposes of this Convention, a bay is a well-marked indentation whose penetration is in such proportion to the width of its mouth as to contain land-locked waters and constitute more than a mere curvature of the coast. An indentation shall not, however, be regarded as a bay unless its area is as large as, or larger than, that of the semi-circle whose diameter is a line drawn across the mouth of that indentation.

3. For the purpose of measurement, the area of an indentation is that lying between the low-water mark around the shore of the indentation and a line joining the low-water marks of its natural entrance points. Where, because of the presence of islands, an indentation has more than one mouth, the semi-circle shall be drawn on a line as long as the sum total of the lengths of the lines across the different mouths. Islands within an indentation shall be included as if they were part of the water area of the indentation.

4. If the distance between the low-water marks of the natural entrance points of a bay does not exceed 24 nautical miles, a closing line may be drawn between these two low-water marks, and the waters enclosed thereby shall be considered as internal waters.

5. Where the distance between the low-water marks of the natural entrance points of a bay exceeds 24 nautical miles, a straight baseline of 24 nautical miles shall be drawn within the bay in such a manner as to enclose the maximum area of water that is possible with a line of that length.

6. The foregoing provisions do not apply to so-called "historic" bays, or in any case where the system of straight baselines provided for in article 7 is applied.

Diagram of the Construction of Baselines

A Indentation is larger than a semi-circle whose diameter is two closing lines, and is therefore a bay. Thus bay closing lines (which total less than 24 miles) are baselines.

B Straight baseline on indented coast fringed with islands.

C Indentation is smaller than area of semi-circle drawn on closing line. Therefore this is not a bay.

D An island generating its own territorial sea.

E Baseline is a line drawn across the mouth of the river that flows directly into the sea.

F Harbour works forming part of the baseline.

G Low tide elevations. One is less than 12 miles from the coast and therefore forms the baseline. The other is more than 12 miles and therefore does not affect the construction of the baseline.

On the rest of the coast the baseline is the low-water mark.

——— Outer limit of the 12 mile territorial sea

miles

0   12

From Churchill and Lowe, *supra*, n.1, at 39.

NOTES

1) The concept of the territorial sea has not changed from 1958 to 1982. However, archipelagic states (to be discussed shortly) are now permitted to claim territorial waters status within the archipelago.

2) The 1982 Convention has finally resolved the vexed question of the outer limit of the territorial sea. Subject to acceptance of the new regime of passage through straits (discussed later), this limit is fixed at 12 nautical miles. As of November 1986, 120 states claimed 12 miles or less; 20 states claimed between 20 – 200 miles.[12] Does this mean that the states of Latin America and Africa claiming "territorial"or "patrimonial" seas of up to 200 miles must immediately drop their claims?

3) The articles of the 1982 Convention otherwise closely follow the 1958 Geneva Convention on the Territorial Sea and the Contiguous Zone. Article 7(2) was added at the behest of Bangladesh for reasons of local geography. These articles are grounded in customary law as evidenced by state practice and the following decision of the World Court. In the light of this judgment, for what purposes may a state have recourse to the system of straight baselines? How long may a baseline be in order to respect Article 7? Article 10(4) refers to 24 miles but the practice of states, including Canada, involves baselines of between 30 – 50 miles and even longer in certain remote parts of the world.

Anglo-Norwegian Fisheries Case
United Kingdom v. Norway
[1951] I.C.J. Rep. 116

[A dispute arose as to the legality of Norway's action in enclosing the coastal archipelago fringing its territory with straight baselines marking the inner limit of its territorial sea. Foreign vessels, including those of the United Kingdom, were excluded from these waters. It was claimed by Norway that coastal communities were highly dependent on fishing in the waters of the *skjaergaard*. Several baselines were over 30 miles long, one measured 44 miles.]

THE COURT: ... The Court has no difficulty in finding that, for the purpose of measuring the breadth of the territorial sea, it is the low-water mark as opposed to the high-water mark, or the mean between two tides, which has generally been adopted in the practice of States. This criterion is the most favourable to the coastal State and clearly shows the character of territorial waters as appurtenant to the land territory. The Court notes that the Parties agree as to this criterion, but that they differ as to its application.

The Parties also agree that in the case of a low-tide elevation (drying rock) the outer

---

[12] U.N. *Law of the Sea Bulletin*, No.8 (November 1986), at 28.

edge at low water of this low-tide elevation may be taken into account as a base-point for calculating the breadth of the territorial sea. ...

The Court finds itself obliged to decide whether the relevant low-water mark is that of the mainland or of the "skjaergaard." Since the mainland is bordered in its western sector by the "skjaergaard" which constitutes a whole with the mainland, it is the outer line of the "skjaergaard," which must be taken into account in delimiting the belt of Norwegian territorial waters. This solution is dictated by geographic realities.

Three methods have been contemplated to effect the application of the low-water mark rule. The simplest would appear to be the method of the tracé parallèle, which consists of drawing the outer limit of the belt of territorial waters by following the coast in all its sinuosities. This method may be applied without difficulty to an ordinary coast, which is not too broken. Where a coast is deeply indented and cut into, as is that of Eastern Finnmark, or where it is bordered by an archipelago such as the "skjaergaard" along the western sector of the coast here in question, the base-line becomes independent of the low-water mark, and can only be determined by means of a geometric construction. In such circumstances the line of the low-water mark can no longer be put forward as a rule requiring the coast line to be followed in all its sinuosities. Nor can one characterize as exceptions to the rule the very many derogations which would be necessitated by such a rugged coast; the rule would disappear under the exceptions. Such a coast, viewed as a whole, calls for the application of a different method; that is, the method of base-lines which, within reasonable limits, may depart from the physical line of the coast. ...

The Court now comes to the question of the length of the base-lines drawn across the waters lying between the various formations of the "skjaergaard." Basing itself on the analogy with the alleged general rule of ten miles relating to bays, the United Kingdom Government still maintains on this point that the length of straight lines must not exceed ten miles.

In this connection, the practice of States does not justify the formulation of any general rule of law. The attempts that have been made to subject groups of islands or coastal archipelagoes to conditions analogous to the limitations concerning bays (distance between the islands not exceeding twice the breadth of the territorial waters, or ten or twelve sea miles), have not got beyond the stage of proposals.

Furthermore, apart from any question of limiting the lines to ten miles, it may be that several lines can be envisaged. In such cases the coastal State would seem to be in the best position to appraise the local conditions dictating the selection.

Consequently, the Court is unable to share the view of the United Kingdom Government, that "Norway, in the matter of base-lines, now claims recognition of an exceptional system." As will be shown later, all that the Court can see therein is the application of general international law to a specific case. ...

It does not at all follow that, in the absence of rules having the technically precise character alleged by the United Kingdom Government, the delimitation undertaken by the Norwegian Government in 1935 is not subject to certain principles which make it possible to judge as to its validity under international law. The delimitation of sea areas has always an international aspect; it cannot be dependent merely upon the will of the coastal State as expressed in its municipal law. Although it is true that the act of delimitation is necessarily a unilateral act, because only the coastal State is competent to undertake it, the validity of the delimitation with regard to other States depends upon international law.

In this connection, certain basic considerations inherent in the nature of the territorial sea, bring to light certain criteria which, though not entirely precise, can provide courts with an adequate basis for their decisions, which can be adapted to the diverse facts in question.

Among these considerations, some reference must be made to the close dependence of the territorial sea upon the land domain. It is the land which confers upon the coastal State a right to the waters off its coasts. It follows that while such a State must be allowed the latitude necessary in order to be able to adapt its delimitation to practical needs and local requirements, the drawing of base-lines must not depart to any appreciable extent from the general direction of the coast.

Another fundamental consideration, of particular importance in this case, is the more or less close relationship existing between certain sea areas and the land formations which divide or surround them. The real question raised in the choice of base-lines is in effect whether certain sea areas lying within these lines are sufficiently closely linked to the land domain to be subject to the regime of internal waters. This idea, which is at the basis of the determination of the rules relating to bays, should be liberally applied in the case of a coast, the geographical configuration of which is as unusual as that of Norway.

Finally, there is one consideration not to be overlooked, the scope of which extends beyond purely geographical factors: that of certain economic interests peculiar to a region, the reality and importance of which are clearly evidenced by a long usage.

Norway puts forward the 1935 Decree as the application of a traditional system of delimitation, a system which she claims to be in complete conformity with international law. The Norwegian Government has referred in this connection to an historic title, the meaning of which was made clear by Counsel for Norway at the sitting on October 12th, 1951: "The Norwegian Government does not rely upon history to justify exceptional rights, to claim areas of sea which the general law would deny; it invokes history, together with other factors, to justify the way in which it applies the general law." This conception of an historic title is in consonance with the Norwegian Government's understanding of general rules of international law. In its view, these rules of international law take into account the diversity of facts and, therefore, concede that the drawing of base-lines must be adapted to the special conditions obtaining in different regions. In its view, the system of delimitation applied in 1935, a system characterized by the use of straight lines, does not therefore infringe the general law: it is an adaptation rendered necessary by local condition.

Canada, Territorial Sea and Fishing Zones Act
R.S.C. 1970, c.T-7, as am. by R.S.C. 1970 (1st Supp.) c.45

3.(1) Subject to any exceptions under section 5, the territorial sea of Canada comprises those areas of the sea having, as their inner limits, the baselines described in section 5 and, as their outer limits, lines measured seaward and equidistant from such base-lines so that each point of the outer limit line of the territorial sea is distant twelve nautical miles from the nearest point of the baseline.

(2) The internal waters of Canada include any areas of the sea that are on the landward side of the baselines of the territorial sea of Canada. ...

5.(1) The Governor in Council may, by order, issue one or more lists of geographical coordinates of points from which baselines may be determined and may, as he deems necessary, amend such lists.

(2) In respect of any area for which geographical coordinates of points have been listed in a list issued pursuant to subsection (1) and subject to any exceptions in the list for the use of the low water line along the coast between given points and the use of the low water lines of low tide elevations situated wholly or partly at a distance not exceeding the breadth of the territorial sea from the coast, baselines are straight lines joining the consecutive geographical coordinates of points so listed. ...

(5) For the purposes of this section, low tide elevations are naturally formed areas of land that are surrounded by and above water at low tide but submerged at high tide.

NOTES

1) Canada has exercised jurisdiction over the territorial sea on its east and west coasts out to 12 nautical miles since the Act was amended in 1970. The baselines for measuring the territorial sea were originally set in 1967. See the following maps.[13] To what degree is the enabling Act consistent with the provisions of the Law of the Sea Convention? With customary international law as evidenced in the *Anglo-Norwegian Fisheries Case?*

2) As section 3(2) of the Act states, all the areas of the sea to landward of the baselines are internal waters of Canada and thus are as fully part of its sovereign territory as the land mass. For certain regulatory purposes connected to shipping and customs, Canada makes a further subdivision of its internal waters with respect to the Great Lakes and their means of access from the oceans via the St. Lawrence River. Thus within the regime of internal waters the *Canada Shipping Act*[14] distinguishes the "inland waters of Canada," meaning:

... all the rivers, lakes and other navigable fresh waters within Canada, and includes the St. Lawrence River as far seaward as a straight line drawn
  (a)   from Cap des Rosiers to West Point Anticosti Island, and
  (b)   from Anticosti Island to the north shore of the St. Lawrence River along the meridian of longitude sixty-three degrees west.

---

[13] Based on C.R.C. cc. 1547, 1550. See L. Herman, "Proof of Offshore Territorial Claims in Canada" (1982), 7 *Dal.L.Jo*. 3. Canadian jurisdiction over Arctic waters, including a map of baselines, is considered *supra*, Chapter 6.

[14] R.S.C. 1970, c. S-9, s.2. A similar definition is contained in the *Customs Act*, R.S.C. 1970, c. C-40, s.2(1), as am. by Stats.Can. 1974-75-76, c. 5, s.1.

Map of Canadian Baselines, East Coast
Derived from (1982-83), 7 *Dal.L.Jo.* 32, 33, and 35

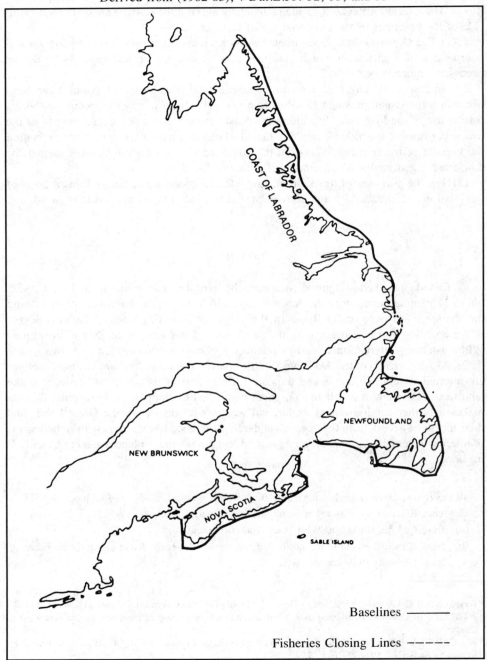

COAST OF LABRADOR

NEWFOUNDLAND

NEW BRUNSWICK

NOVA SCOTIA

SABLE ISLAND

Baselines ————

Fisheries Closing Lines – – – – –

Map of Canadian Baselines, West Coast
Derived from (1982-83), 7 *Dal.L.Jo.* 34 and 36

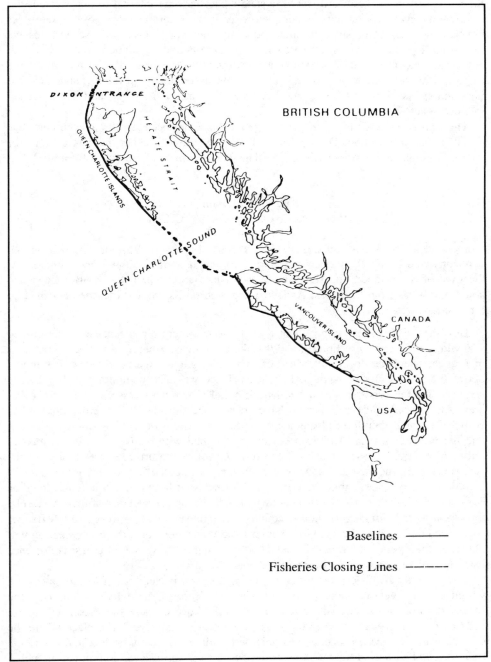

Baselines ———

Fisheries Closing Lines ------

Jurisdiction in Internal Waters

Since the sea on the landward side of a state's baselines are internal to that state, it has sovereignty over those waters as completely as over its land territory. But a state does not have to exercise its authority and frequently does not choose to do so with respect to visiting merchant vessels, at least when its interests and population are not affected. A typical incident would be a disturbance amongst the crew aboard a foreign ship while in port. The port state might take no action on the assumption that the flag state also has jurisdiction, as discussed in Chapter 7 on the Nationality of Ships, and has a greater interest to act.

The next two cases show how in practice a balance has been struck between port state and flag state jurisdiction. Does it appear from these cases whether the deference of the local·sovereign to the jurisdiction of the flag state is a matter of law or of comity?

R. v. Anderson
(1868), 11 Cox Crim. C. 198 (C.C.A.)

[Anderson, an American seaman aboard a British ship out of Yarmouth, Nova Scotia, was convicted by an English court for the manslaughter of a fellow crew member. At the time of the offence, the ship was in the river Garonne half way to Bordeaux and about 300 yards from the shore. Anderson appealed on the ground that the court had no jurisdiction over him.]

BOVILL, C.J.: There is no doubt that the place where the offence was committed was within the territory of France, and that the prisoner was therefore subject to the laws of France, which the local authorities of that realm might have enforced if so minded; but at the same time, in point of law, the offence was also committed within British territory, for the prisoner was a seaman on board a merchant vessel, which, as to her crew and master, must be taken to have been at the time under the protection of the British flag, and, therefore, also amenable to the provisions of the British law. It is true that the prisoner was an American citizen, but he had with his own consent embarked on board a British vessel as one of the crew. Although the prisoner was subject to the American jurisprudence as an American citizen, and to the law of France as having committed an offence within the territory of France, yet he must also be considered as subject to the jurisdiction of British law, which extends to the protection of British vessels, though in ports belonging to another country. ... it appears that, with regard to offences committed on board of foreign vessels within the French territory, the French nation will not assert their police law unless invoked by the master of the vessel, or unless the offence leads to a disturbance of the peace of the port. ...

If the offence had been committed on the high seas it is clear that it would have been within the jurisdiction of the Admiralty, and the Central Criminal Court has now the same extent of jurisdiction. Does it make any difference because the vessel was in the river Garonne half-way between the sea and the head of the river? The place where the offence was committed was in a navigable part of the river below bridge, and where the tide ebbs and flows, and great ships do lie and hover. An offence committed at such a place, according to the authorities, is within the Admiralty jurisdiction, and it is the same as if the offence had been committed on the high seas. On the whole I come to the conclusion that the prisoner was amenable to the British law, and that the conviction was right.

[Channel B., Byles, Blackburn and Lush JJ. added concurring opinions.]

Wildenhus' Case
(1887), 120 U.S.1

[Wildenhus, a Belgian national, killed a fellow Belgian crew member on board a Belgian ship while it was docked in the port of Jersey City, New Jersey. Wildenhus was detained by American police but the Belgian consul applied for a writ of *habeas corpus* to take control of him, alleging that U.S. authorities lacked jurisdiction at international law and citing a consular treaty between the United States and Belgium which provided: "The respective ... consuls ... shall have exclusive charge of the internal order of the merchant vessels of their nation, and shall alone take cognizance of all differences which may arise, either at sea or in port, between the captains, officers and crews, ... the local authorities shall not interfere except when the disorder that has arisen is of such a nature as to disturb tranquillity and public order on shore, or in the port, or when a person of the country or not belonging to the crew shall be concerned therein."]

WAITE C.J.: ... It is part of the law of civilized nations that when a merchant vessel of one country enters the ports of another for the purposes of trade, it subjects itself to the law of the place to which it goes, unless by treaty or otherwise the two countries have come to some different understanding or agreement. ... As the owner has voluntarily taken his vessel for his own private purposes to a place within the dominion of a government other than his own, and from which he seeks protection during his stay, he owes that government such allegiance for the time being as is due for the protection to which he becomes entitled.

From experience, however, it was found long ago that it would be beneficial to commerce if the local government would abstain from interfering with the internal discipline of the ship and the general regulation of the rights and duties of the officers and crew towards the vessel or among themselves. And so by comity it came to be generally understood among civilized nations that all matters of discipline and all things done on board which affected only the vessel or those belonging to her, and did not involve the peace or dignity of the country, or the tranquillity of the port, should be left by the local government to be dealt with by the authorities of the nation to which the vessel belonged as the laws of that nation or the interests of its commerce should require. But if crimes are committed on board of a character to disturb the peace and tranquillity of the country to which the vessel has been brought, the offenders have never by comity or usage been entitled to any exemption from the operation of the local laws for their punishment, if the local tribunals see fit to assert their authority. Such being the general public law on this subject, treaties and conventions have been entered into by nations having commercial intercourse, the purpose of which was to settle and define the rights and duties of the contracting parties with respect to each other in these particulars, and thus prevent the inconvenience that might arise from attempts to exercise conflicting jurisdiction. ...

The treaty is part of the supreme law of the United States, and has the same force and effect in New Jersey that it is entitled to elsewhere. If it gives the Consul of Belgium exclusive jurisdiction over the offense which it is alleged has been committed within the territory of New Jersey, we see no reason why he may not enforce his rights under the Treaty by writ of *habeas corpus* in any proper court of the United States. This being the case, the only important question left for our determination is whether the thing which has been done – the disorder that has arisen – on board this vessel is of a nature to disturb the public peace, or, as some writers term it, the "public repose" of the people who look to the State of New Jersey for their protection. If the thing done – "the disorder," as it is called in the Treaty – is of a character to affect those on shore or in the port when it becomes known, the fact that only those on the ship saw it when it was done, is a matter of no moment. Those who are not on the vessel pay no special attention to the mere disputes or quarrels of the seamen while on board, whether they occur under deck or above. Neither do they as a rule care for anything done on board which relates only to the discipline of the ship, or to the preservation of order and authority. Not so, however, with crimes which from their gravity awaken a public interest as soon as they become known, and especially those of a character which every civilized nation considers itself bound to provide a severe punishment for when committed within its own jurisdiction. In such cases inquiry is certain to be instituted at once to ascertain how or why the thing was done, and the popular excitement rises or falls as the news spreads and the facts become known. It is not alone the publicity of the act, or the noise and clamor which attends it, that fixes the nature of the crime, but the act itself. If that is of a character to awaken public interest when it becomes known, it is a "disorder" the nature of which is to affect the community at large, and consequently to invoke the power of the local government whose peoples have been disturbed by what was done. The very nature of such an act is to disturb the quiet of a peaceful community, and to create, in the language of the Treaty, a "disorder" which will "disturb tranquillity and public order on shore on in the port." The principle which governs the whole matter is this: Disorders which disturb only the peace of the ship or those on board are to be dealt with exclusively by the sovereignty of the home of the ship, but those which disturb the public peace may be suppressed, and, if need be, the offenders punished by the proper authorities of the local jurisdiction. It may not be easy at all times to determine to which of the two jurisdictions a particular act of disorder belongs. Much will undoubtedly depend on the attending circumstances of the particular case, but all must concede that felonious homicide is a subject for the local jurisdiction, and that if the proper authorities are proceeding with the case in a regular way the consul has no right to interfere to prevent it. That, according to the petition for the *habeas corpus*, is this case.

Canada Shipping Act
R.S.C. 1970, c. S-9

683.(1) Notwithstanding anything in the *Criminal Code* or any other Act where any person, being a British subject domiciled in Canada, is charged with having committed any offence on board any Canadian ship on the high seas or in any port or harbour in a Commonwealth country other than Canada or in any foreign port or harbour or on board any British ship registered out of Canada or any foreign ship to which he does not belong, or, not being such a British subject, is charged with having committed any offence on board any Canadian ship on the high seas, and that person is found within Canada, any court that would have had cognizance of the offence if it had been committed within the limits of its ordinary jurisdiction has jurisdiction to try the offence as if it had been so committed. ...

684. All offences against property or person committed in or at any place either ashore or afloat out of a Commonwealth country by any master, seaman, or apprentice who at the time when the offence is committed is, or within three months previously has been, employed in any Canadian ship, shall be deemed to be offences of the same nature respectively, and are liable to the same punishments respectively, and are inquired of, heard, tried, determined and adjudged in the same manner and by the same courts and in the same places as if those offences had been committed within Canada.

NOTES

1) These sections from the *Canada Shipping Act* express the jurisdiction that Canada asserts as the flag state in a foreign port and elsewhere. Are they fully consistent with international law? Consider the ''Bases of Jurisdiction'' of a state described in Chapter 8.

2) Another well recognised exception to the jurisdiction of the port state is the immunity granted to a ship that enters one of its harbours in distress. The plea of entry in distress is often raised by those who stand accused of smuggling, previously for rum running and nowadays for drug trading. In these circumstances the courts have admitted the right to immunity but have applied it strictly. The right of distress is recognized in the *Customs Act*[15] and was expressed in *Cashin v. The King*[16] to be a rule of customary international law to the effect that:

> a ship, compelled through stress of weather, duress or other unavoidable cause to put into a foreign port, is ... exempt from liability to the penalties and forfeitures which, had she entered the port voluntarily, she would have incurred.

The right of distress is not solely a matter of sheltering from harsh weather but may arise from the urgent need to make repairs or to cope with a mutiny, or any other cause of genuine necessity. But there must be a real and irresistible distress; a little bad weather

---

[15] R.S.C. 1970, c. C-40, s. 173.
[16] [1935] 4 D.L.R. 547, at 551-52 (Ex.C.). However, the court excluded exemption from Canadian revenue laws in apparent contradiction with the principle it had just stated.

or difficulties that are self-induced will not suffice to support a plea for immunity from the jurisdiction.[17]

Islands and Archipelagos[18]

United Nations Convention on the Law of the Sea

Article 121
RÉGIME OF ISLANDS

1. An island is a naturally formed area of land, surrounded by water, which is above water at high tide.

2. Except as provided for in paragraph 3, the territorial sea, the contiguous zone, the exclusive economic zone and the continental shelf of an island are determined in accordance with the provisions of this Convention applicable to other land territory.

3. Rocks which cannot sustain human habitation or economic life of their own shall have no exclusive economic zone or continental shelf.

Article 46
USE OF TERMS

For the purposes of this Convention:
  (a) "archipelagic State" means a State constituted wholly by one or more archipelagos and may include other islands;
  (b) "archipelago" means a group of islands, including parts of islands, interconnecting waters and other natural features which are so closely interrelated that such islands, waters and other natural features form an intrinsic geographical, economic and political entity, or which historically have been regarded as such.

Article 47
ARCHIPELAGIC BASELINES

1. An archipelagic State may draw straight archipelagic baselines joining the outermost points of the outermost islands and drying reefs of the archipelago provided that within such baselines are included the main islands and an area in which the ratio of the area of the water to the area of the land, including atolls, is between 1 to 1 and 9 to 1.

2. The length of such baselines shall not exceed 100 nautical miles, except that up to

---

[17] *The Queen City v. The King*, [1931] S.C.R. 387; *R. v. Flahaut*, [1935] 2 D.L.R. 685 (N.B.C.A.); *R. v. Salvador* (1981), 45 N.S.R.(2d) 192 (N.S.C.A.).

[18] See D.P. O'Connell, *supra.*, n.1, at 236; P.E.J. Rodgers, *Midocean Archipelagos and International Law* (1981); and L.L. Herman, "The Modern Concept of the Off-Lying Archipelago in International Law" (1935), 23 *Can.Y.B.Int.L.* 172.

3 per cent of the total number of baselines enclosing any archipelago may exceed that length, up to a maximum length of 125 nautical miles.

3. The drawing of such baselines shall not depart to any appreciable extent from the general configuration of the archipelago.

4. Such baselines shall not be drawn to and from low-tide elevations, unless lighthouses or similar installations which are permanently above sea level have been built on them or where a low-tide elevation is situated wholly or partly at a distance not exceeding the breadth of the territorial sea from the nearest island. ...

Article 48
MEASUREMENT OF THE BREADTH OF THE TERRITORIAL SEA, THE CONTIGUOUS ZONE, THE EXCLUSIVE ECONOMIC ZONE AND THE CONTINENTAL SHELF

The breadth of the territorial sea, the contiguous zone, the exclusive economic zone and the continental shelf shall be measured from archipelagic baselines drawn in accordance with article 47.

Article 49
LEGAL STATUS OF ARCHIPELAGIC WATERS, OF THE AIR SPACE OVER ARCHIPELAGIC WATERS AND OF THEIR BED AND SUBSOIL

1. The sovereignty of an archipelagic State extends to the waters enclosed by the archipelagic baselines drawn in accordance with article 47, described as archipelagic waters, regardless of their depth or distance from the coast.

2. This sovereignty extends to the air space over the archipelagic waters, as well as to their bed and subsoil, and the resources contained therein.

3. This sovereignty is exercised subject to this Part.

4. The régime of archipelagic sea lanes passage established in this Part shall not in other respects affect the status of the archipelagic waters, including the sea lanes, or the exercise by the archipelagic State of its sovereignty over such waters and their air space, bed and subsoil, and the resources contained therein.

NOTES

1) The rule on islands repeats Article 10(1) of the 1958 Geneva Convention on the Territorial Sea and the Contiguous Zone. Article 121(3) is an innovation designed to restrict abusive claims to exclusive economic zones on the basis of claims to reefs and low tide elevations.

2) Is Canada justified in claiming an exclusive fishing zone and continental shelf 200 miles beyond Sable Island—a small sand bar situated at some 125 miles from Nova Scotia and inhabited only by birds, wild ponies and a few government biologists?

3) The sovereignty over archipelagic waters recognized in Article 49 is subject to the right of innocent passage (Article 52). By Article 53, the archipelagic state may designate sea lanes and air routes through its waters, but in doing so it must include all the passage routes normally used for international navigation and overflight.

4) Does Canada have any interest in claiming the status of an archipelagic state? Does it have any right to? Canada's Arctic archipelago ratio of water to land is 1:0.9; that is some 5 times more favourable than the water:land ratio of Indonesia, which promulgated archipelagic baselines as long ago as 1957. Can any state claim the status of an archipelagic state before entry into force of the 1982 Convention? Canada announced a set of baselines in the Arctic with effect in 1986: see the discussion of Canada's claims in the Arctic contained in Chapter 6.

Innocent Passage Through the Territorial Sea

United Nations Convention on the Law of the Sea

Article 17
RIGHT OF INNOCENT PASSAGE

Subject to this Convention, ships of all States whether coastal or land-locked, enjoy the right of innocent passage through the territorial sea.

Article 18
MEANING OF PASSAGE

1. Passage means navigation through the territorial sea for the purpose of:
(a) traversing that sea without entering internal waters or calling at a roadstead or port facility outside internal waters; or
(b) proceeding to or from internal waters or a call at such roadstead or port facility.
2. Passage shall be continuous and expeditious. However, passage includes stopping and anchoring, but only in so far as the same are incidental to ordinary navigation or are rendered necessary by *force majeure* or distress or for the purpose of rendering assistance to persons, ships or aircraft in danger or distress.

Article 19
MEANING OF INNOCENT PASSAGE

1. Passage is innocent so long as it is not prejudicial to the peace, good order or security of the coastal State. Such passage shall take place in conformity with this Convention and with other rules of international law.
2. Passage of a foreign ship shall be considered to be prejudicial to the peace, good order or security of the coastal State if in the territorial sea it engages in any of the following activities:
(a) any threat or use of force against the sovereignty, territorial integrity or political independence of the coastal State, or in any other manner in violation of the principles of international law embodied in the Charter of the United Nations:
(b) any exercise or practice with weapons of any kind:

(c) any act aimed at collecting information to the prejudice of the defence or security of the coastal State:

(d) any act of propaganda aimed at affecting the defence or security of the coastal State:

(e) the launching, landing or taking on board of any aircraft:

(f) the launching, landing or taking on board of any military device:

(g) the loading or unloading of any commodity, currency or person contrary to the customs, fiscal, immigration or sanitary laws and regulations of the coastal State:

(h) any act of wilful and serious pollution contrary to this Convention:

(i) any fishing activities:

(j) the carrying out of research or survey activities:

(k) any act aimed at interfering with any systems of communication or any other facilities or installations of the coastal State:

(l) any other activity not having a direct bearing on passage.

Article 21
LAWS AND REGULATIONS OF THE COASTAL STATE RELATING TO INNOCENT PASSAGE

1. The coastal State may adopt laws and regulations, in conformity with the provisions of this Convention and other rules of international law, relating to innocent passage through the territorial sea, in respect of all or any of the following:

(a) the safety of navigation and the regulation of maritime traffic:

(b) the protection of navigational aids and facilities and other facilities or installations:

(c) the protection of cables and pipelines:

(d) the conservation of the living resources of the sea:

(e) the prevention of infringement of the fisheries laws and regulations of the coastal State:

(f) the preservation of the environment of the coastal State and the prevention, reduction and control of pollution thereof:

(g) marine scientific research and hydrographic surveys:

(h) the prevention of infringement of the customs, fiscal, immigration or sanitary laws and regulations of the coastal State.

2. Such laws and regulations shall not apply to the design, construction, manning or equipment of foreign ships unless they are giving effect to generally accepted international rules or standards.

3. The coastal State shall give due publicity to all such laws and regulations.

4. Foreign ships exercising the right of innocent passage through the territorial sea shall comply with all such laws and regulations and all generally accepted international regulations relating to the prevention of collisions at sea.

Article 23
FOREIGN NUCLEAR-POWERED SHIPS AND SHIPS CARRYING NUCLEAR OR OTHER INHERENTLY DANGEROUS OR NOXIOUS SUBSTANCES

Foreign nuclear-powered ships and ships carrying nuclear or other inherently dangerous or noxious substances shall, when exercising the right of innocent passage through the territorial sea, carry documents and observe special precautionary measures established for such ships by international agreements.

Article 24
DUTIES OF THE COASTAL STATE

1. The coastal State shall not hamper the innocent passage of foreign ships through the territorial sea except in accordance with this Convention. In particular, in the application of this Convention or of any laws or regulations adopted in conformity with this Convention, the coastal State shall not:

    (a) impose requirements on foreign ships which have the practical effect of denying or impairing the right of innocent passage; or

    (b) discriminate in form or in fact against the ships of any State or against ships carrying cargoes to, from or on behalf of any State.

2. The coastal State shall give appropriate publicity to any danger to navigation, of which it has knowledge, within its territorial sea.

NOTES

1) The right of foreign vessels, including military vessels, to pass through the territorial sea is fundamental to international commerce and navigation. Many major shipping routes pass close to the shoreline or through narrow international straits. Customary international law[19] and the 1958 Geneva Convention defined innocent passage very much as is found above in articles 17, 18 and 19(1). A general balance was struck between sovereignty and the right of navigation. With the extension of claims beyond 3 miles and the proliferation of laws on pollution from ships after 1969, the maritime powers became alarmed at the possible erosion of the right of innocent passage and so, at the Third U.N. Conference, they insisted upon a much more precise definition of the right.

2) Are articles 19(2), 21, 23 and 24 now binding upon coastal states or are they free to impose other laws upon passing ships which pollute their territorial sea? What is meant by "generally accepted international rules and standards"? Who declares their existence?[20]

Civil and Criminal Jurisdiction and Immunities

United Nations Convention on the Law of the Sea

Article 27
CRIMINAL JURISDICTION ON BOARD A FOREIGN SHIP

1. The criminal jursidiction of the coastal State should not be exercised on board a foreign ship passing through the territorial sea to arrest any person or conduct any

---

[19] See the *Corfu Channel Case*, [1949] I.C.J. Rep. 4, reported *infra*, in the section on "International Straits."
[20] See R.M. McGonigle and M. Zacher, *Politics, Pollution and International Law* (1979); G. Timagenis, *International Control of Marine Pollution* (1980).

investigation in connection with any crime committed on board the ship during its passage, save only in the following cases:

    (a) if the consequences of the crime extend to the coastal State:

    (b) if the crime is of a kind to disturb the peace of the country or the good order of the territorial sea:

    (c) if the assistance of the local authorities has been requested by the master of the ship or by a diplomatic agent or consular officer of the flag State: or

    (d) if such measures are necessary for the suppression of illicit traffic in narcotic drugs or psychotropic substances.

2. The above provisions do not affect the right of the coastal State to take any steps authorized by its laws for the purpose of an arrest or investigation on board a foreign ship passing through the territorial sea after leaving internal waters.

3. In the cases provided for in paragraphs 1 and 2, the coastal State shall, if the master so requests, notify a diplomatic agent or consular officer of the flag State before taking any steps, and shall facilitate contact between such agent or officer and the ship's crew. In cases of emergency this notification may be communicated while the measures are being taken.

4. In considering whether or in what manner an arrest should be made, the local authorities shall have due regard to the interests of navigation.

5. Except as provided in Part XII or with respect to violations of laws and regulations adopted in accordance with Part V, the coastal State may not take any steps on board a foreign ship passing through the territorial sea to arrest any person or to conduct any investigation in connection with any crime committed before the ship entered the territorial sea, if the ship, proceeding from a foreign port, is only passing through the territorial sea without entering internal waters.

Article 28
CIVIL JURISDICTION IN RELATION TO FOREIGN SHIPS

1. The coastal State should not stop or divert a foreign ship passing through the territorial sea for the purpose of exercising civil jurisdiction in relation to a person on board the ship.

2. The coastal State may not levy execution against or arrest the ship for the purpose of any civil proceedings, save only in respect of obligations or liabilities assumed or incurred by the ship itself in the course or for the purpose of its voyage through the waters of the coastal State.

3. Paragraph 2 is without prejudice to the right of the coastal State, in accordance with its laws, to levy execution against or to arrest, for the purpose of any civil proceedings, a foreign ship lying in the territorial sea, or passing through the territorial sea after leaving internal waters.

Article 29
DEFINITION OF WARSHIPS

For the purposes of this Convention, ''warship'' means a ship belonging to the armed forces of a State bearing the external marks distinguishing such ships of its nationality, under the command of an officer duly commissioned by the government of the State and whose name appears in the appropriate service list or its equivalent, and manned by a crew which is under regular armed forces discipline.

Article 30
NON-COMPLIANCE BY WARSHIPS WITH THE LAWS AND REGULATIONS OF THE COASTAL STATE

If any warship does not comply with the laws and regulations of the coastal State concerning passage through the territorial sea and disregards any request for compliance therewith which is made to it, the coastal State may require it to leave the territorial sea immediately.

Article 31
RESPONSIBILITY OF THE FLAG STATE FOR DAMAGE CAUSED BY A WARSHIP OR OTHER GOVERNMENT SHIP OPERATED FOR NON-COMMERCIAL PURPOSES

The flag State shall bear international resonsibility for any loss or damage to the coastal State resulting from the non-compliance by a warship or other government ship operated for non-commercial purposes with the laws and regulations of the coastal State concerning passage through the territorial sea or with the provisions of this Convention or other rules of international law.

Article 32
IMMUNITIES OF WARSHIPS AND OTHER GOVERNMENT SHIPS OPERATED FOR NON-COMMERCIAL PURPOSES

With such exceptions as are contained in subsection A and in articles 30 and 31, nothing in this Convention affects the immunities of warships and other government ships operated for non-commercial purposes.

Article 33
CONTIGUOUS ZONE

1. In a zone contiguous to its territorial sea, described as the contiguous zone, the coastal State may exercise the control necessary to:
  (a) prevent infringement of its customs, fiscal, immigration or sanitary laws and regulations within its territory or territorial sea;
  (b) punish infringement of the above laws and regulations committed within its territory or territorial seas.

2. The contiguous zone may not extend beyond 24 nautical miles from the baselines from which the breadth of the territorial sea is measured.

NOTES

1) These articles follow the 1958 Geneva Convention on the Territorial Sea and the Contiguous Zone. The application of these articles has grown more complex with the

emergence of claims to enforce coastal state pollution laws; they must be read together with the articles in Part XII on Protection of the Marine Environment, which are considered later in this chapter.

2) These articles also reflect the general rules of state immunity of military vessels and government vessels used for non-commercial purposes. Article 31 is an addition to the similar provisions of the 1958 Geneva Convention on the Territorial Sea and Contiguous Zone; arguably it adds nothing to customary law. It must be noted that the Third United Nations Conference on the Law of the Sea rejected attempts to deny the right of innocent passage to military vessels.

3) Are coastguard, icebreaking and police vessels covered by Articles 29-32? What is the relationship of Articles 29-32 to Articles 27 and 28? What degree of immunity do these vessels enjoy in internal waters and ports?[21]

4) The limited purpose of the contiguous zone, mentioned in Article 33, is to allow a state to protect its coastal waters from the effects of certain activities beyond its territorial sea. Smuggling is an example and the Hovering Acts were early assertions of this jurisdiction.[22] Article 33 grants a state exactly the same powers as it has under the Geneva Convention on the Territorial Sea and thus perpetuates some ambiguity about the authority to police the contiguous zone. If, by subsection 1(b), a state may "punish" infringements in its territorial sea, what by subsection 1(a) may it do to "prevent" violations in its contiguous zone? The Article also extends the width of the contiguous zone to 12 miles beyond the 12 mile limit of the territorial sea. The contiguous zone therefore geographically overlaps with the exclusive economic zone considered subsequently.

Exercise of Jurisdiction by Canada

A number of specific laws protect the internal waters and territorial sea of Canada or govern conduct on board ships which are fishing, surveying or exercising the right of innocent passage.[23] But the general body of Canadian law, apart from the *Criminal Code*, does not apply to these coastal areas or activities. "The basic rule of public law governing the application of Canadian law to the offshore is that no law, whether statute or common law, extends beyond the low water-mark unless specifically extended by Parliament or a Provincial Legislature."[24] Furthermore, a province, generally speaking, has no authority to apply its laws extraterritorially.

---

[21] In Canada, see the *State Immunity Act*, Stats. Can. 1982, c. 5 especially s.3, 7(1), 11(3), reported *supra*, in Chapter 5. See also *Federal Court Act*, R.S.C. 1970, (2nd supp.), c. 10, s.43(7)(c).

[22] For example, see *Croft v. Dunphy*, [1933] A.C. 156(P.C.); *Cashin v. The King*, [1935] Ex. C.R. 103, 4 D.L.R. 547; and J. Brierly, "The Doctrine of the Contiguous Zone and the Dicta in *Croft v. Dunphy*" (1933), 14 *Br.Y.B.Int.L.* 155. See now the *Customs Act* R.S.C. 1970, c. C-40, ss.2(1), 141, which assert Canadian customs jurisdiction over vessels hovering in "Canadian customs waters," i.e., in a belt of sea "that is adjacent to and extends nine marine miles beyond" the territorial sea of Canada.

[23] The principal Canadian statutes are the *Canada Shipping Act*, Part XX, R.S.C. 1970, c. S-9; the *Coastal Fisheries Protection Act*, R.S.C. 1970, c. C-21; the *Customs Act*, R.S.C. 1970, c. C-40, as am.; the *Fisheries Act*, R.S.C. 1970, c. F-14, as am.; and the *Territorial Sea and Fishing Zones Act*, R.S.C. 1970, c. T-7, as am. R.S.C. 1970 (1st supp.), c. 45. See also the *Customs and Excise Offshore Application Act*, Stats. Can. 1984, c. 17.

[24] A.L.C. de Mestral, " The Law Applicable to the Canadian East-Coast Offshore" (1983), 21 *Alta. L.R.* 63, at 64.

The *Criminal Code* section 433 provides:

(1) Where an offence is committed by a person, whether or not he is a Canadian citizen, on the territorial sea of Canada or on internal waters between the territorial sea and the coast of Canada, whether or not it was committed on board or by means of a Canadian ship, the offence is within the competence and shall be tried by the court having jurisdiction in respect of similar offences in the territorial division nearest to the place where the offence was committed, and shall be tried in the same manner as if the offence had been committed within that territorial division.

(2) No proceedings for an offence to which subsection (1) applies other than an offence for which the accused is punishable on summary conviction shall, where the accused is not a Canadian citizen, be instituted without the consent of the Attorney General of Canada.

This section cannot resolve many jurisdictional uncertainties in the offshore areas, such as the authority of the police or the law applicable to oil rigs and other installations on the continental shelf beyond the territorial sea. In 1986, the government introduced Bill C-104, the *Canadian Laws Offshore Application Act*, which would have provided for the application of all federal and provincial laws in the coastal areas of Canada to the fullest extent permitted under international law. It would also have made a complementary increase in the ambit of the *Criminal Code*. However, the Bill did not pass before Parliament was prorogued.

Historic Waters of Canada

Like many countries, Canada has claims that certain bodies of water which might otherwise be classified as high seas (or exclusive economic zone today), are more properly classified as internal waters. These historic claims are usually developed over long periods of time and are grounded in special reasons of geography, security or economic necessity. They all imply a closer relationship between waters and the surrounding land than is generally the case, thus justifying the argument that the waters form an integral part of the land and must be subject to the complete sovereignty of the coastal state. The possible existence of historic waters is acknowledged in the U.N. Law of the Sea Convention Article 10 (6), reported in the preceding subsection on the "Territorial Sea." However, the criteria for the proof of a claim of historic waters are not defined there but rest on customary international law. The strength of Canada's claims varies from one area to another; they raise problems of regional attachment and, with respect to the Arctic, form part of the Canadian mystique of Canada as a northern power. It would be unwise to underestimate Canadian attachment to these claims or the seriousness of the international problems that they raise for other states, in particular the U.S.A.[25]

The following commentary does not purport to give an exhaustive picture of Canadian

---

[25] For an early review of the issues, see "Historic Bays," memorandum of the Secretariat of the United Nations, *U.N. Conference on the Law of the Sea, Official Records*, Vol. 1 (1958), at 1. See also L. Bouchez, *The Regime of Bays in International Law* (1964), at 199-302; D.P. O'Connell, *supra*, n.1, at 417-38; and M.P. Strohl, *The International Law of Bays* (1963), at 231-367.

claims but simply to highlight some important ones. Many of these claims have been asserted by members of the Canadian Government in the course of Parliamentary debates. Thus concerning Hudson Bay, in 1957 the Minister of Northern Affairs and Natural Resources asserted:[26]

The waters of Hudson Bay are Canadian waters by historic title in accordance with the universally accepted international law doctrine applying to historic bays. Canada regards as inland waters all the waters west of a line drawn across the entrance to Hudson Strait from Button Island to Hatton Head on Resolution Island.

As to the Bay of Fundy, in 1962 Prime Minister Diefenbaker said:[27]

The Bay of Fundy has always been considered, since the earliest days, first by Great Britain and thereafter by successive Canadian governments, as Canadian territorial waters. As far back as 1763 it was described in official documents as being comprised within the boundaries of what is now Canada. There are strong geographic and economic considerations for this.

Regarding the Gulf of St. Lawrence, prime Minister St-Laurent in 1949 stated:[28]

We intend to contend and hope to be able to get acquiescence in the contention that the water west of Newfoundland constituting the Gulf of St. Lawrence shall become an inland sea. We hope that with Newfoundland as a part of Canadian territory, the Gulf of St. Lawrence west of Newfoundland will all become territorial waters of Canada, whereas before there would be only the usual off-shore portion that would thus become part of the territorial waters. Of course that is a matter which is not governed by statutes; it is the comity of nations. It is our intention to assert that position and it is our hope that it will be recognized as a valid contention.

The Bureau of Legal Affairs of the Department of External Affairs has also written[29] that Canada has similar historic claims to the waters of Dixon Entrance, Hecate Strait and Queen Charlotte Sound on the British Columbia coast. These bodies of water together with the Bay of Fundy and the Gulf of St. Lawrence have since been declared exclusive Canadian fishing zones under the *Territorial Sea and Fishing Zones Act*. However, their delimitation by ''fisheries closing lines'' is not the same as enclosure within Canadian sovereignty by baselines, which so far have not been drawn.[30] The extent of Canada's

---

[26] H.C. *Debs.* 1169 (14 November 1957). See V.K. Johnston, ''Canada's Title to Hudson Bay and Hudson Strait'' (1934), 15 *Br.Y.B.Int.L.*1.

[27] H.C. *Debs.* 1650 (15 November 1962). See G.V. LaForest, ''Canadian Inland Waters of the Atlantic Provinces and the Bay of Fundy Incident'' (1963), 1 *Can.Y.B.Int.L.* 149.

[28] H.C. *Debs.* 368 (8 February 1949). See F. Rigaldies, ''Le statut du golfe du Saint-Laurent en droit international public'' (1985), 23 *Can.Y.B.Int.L.* 80.

[29] Letter dated 17 December 1973, reprinted in (1974), 12 *Can.Y.B.Int.L.* 279. And see C. Bourne and D. McRae, ''Maritime Jurisdiction in the Dixon Entrance: The Alaska Boundary Re-examined'' (1976), 14 *Can.Y.B.Int.L.* 175.

[30] See maps and references concerning Canadian baselines in the previous Section on ''Territorial Sea.''

sovereignty in Arctic waters and their recent enclosure is discussed in Chapter 6 on "The Arctic."

The courts have also had occasion to consider some of Canada's claims to historic waters, typically in the context of determining the extent of territorial jurisdiction offshore. In *Direct U.S. Cable Co. v. Anglo-American Telegraph Co.*[31] a dispute arose between competing telegraphic companies about the laying of transatlantic cables through Conception Bay. The Privy Council decided that Newfoundland legislation governed the rights of the companies inasmuch as the waters of Conception Bay formed part of Newfoundland. In *Mowat v. McFee*[32] a fisherman objected to the seizure of his boat and nets by a fisheries officer for salmon fishing in the Bay of Chaleurs in violation of *The Fisheries Act*. The Supreme Court, in rejecting his writ for trespass, held *The Fisheries Act* applied to the full extent of the Bay of Chaleurs since the whole of its waters were within the Dominion of Canada.

The decisions of the courts have not often discussed the concept of historic waters at international law. Their judgments have frequently been based on the English common law principle that the limit of territorial authority was the low-water mark along the coast, even though international law would respect a greater assertion of sovereignty. In the application of this principle the courts have admitted a number of modifications. They have recognized that the territorial limit could be extended seawards, so far as permitted in international law, by the express declaration of a competent legislature. The two previous cases exemplify this process. The courts have also accepted as part of sovereign territory any area of the sea that is *inter fauces terrae* (literally, within the jaws of the land). Thus bays and estuaries between jutting headlands might be treated as part of the country or province into which they project. On occasion, owing to their geographical interrelation to the surrounding land, these portions of the sea have alternatively been called inland waters.

The *Reference Re Ownership of the Bed of the Strait of Georgia*[33] was a case involving inland waters in this sense. The Supreme Court was asked to determine whether the seabed covered by the waters between mainland British Columbia and Vancouver Island was the property of Canada or of British Columbia. The Court held in favour of the Province on the basis of the territorial description of the colonies of Vancouver Island and British Columbia when they were united and the wording of the British Statute forming the new colony. It made its interpretation of those documents in part by assimilating the sea in the Georgia Strait to waters *inter fauces terrae*.

The concept of historic waters would appear to be an additional ground to claim territorial jurisdiction beyond the low-water mark, but it has not often been treated by the courts as a separate basis for their decisions. Perhaps the reason is that those areas of the sea that might be claimed historically are likely the same ones that are so intimately connected to the land as to be inland waters. This seems to have been the situation in the following case. In any event, the judgments discussed all of these ideas.

---

[31] (1877), 2 App. Cas. 394.
[32] (1880), 5 S.C.R. 66.
[33] (1984) 1 S.C.R. 388. See G. Marston, "The Strait of Georgia Reference" (1985), 23 *Can.Y.B.Int.L.* 34.

Re Dominion Coal Co. and County of Cape Breton
(1963), 40 D.L.R. (2d) 593 (N.S.S.C.)

[This case involved the power of the municipality of the County of Cape Breton, Nova Scotia, to assess for taxes the submarine properties belonging to two coal mining companies located below the low-water mark. The Court was agreed that if the properties were beyond the territorial limits of the municipality they were not assessable, but it was not unanimous in determining those limits. In particular, the judges were unable to agree about the status of Spanish Bay. Isley C.J.'s judgment represents the majority opinion that Spanish Bay was outside the municipality because it could not be regarded as inland waters. Two judges also considered whether Spanish Bay might qualify as historic waters.]

ISLEY C.J.: ... Is Spanish Bay, so-called, the waters of which cover the submarine areas in question, and the outer boundary of which is an imaginary line drawn from Point Aconi to Low Point, within the limits of Cape Breton County? The answer to this question, in my opinion, must be in the negative if Spanish Bay as so defined is not an "interior or national water." (This phrase is taken from *Colombos on International Law of the Sea*, 4th ed., 74) In *The Queen v. Keyn* (1876), 2 Ex.D. 63, Cockburn C.J., at 162, said:

By the old common law of England, every offence was triable in the county only in which it had been committed, as from that county alone the "pais," as it was termed — in other words, the jurors by whom the fact was to be ascertained — could come. But only so much of the land of the outer coast as was uncovered by the sea was held to be within the body of the adjoining county. If an offence was committed in a bay, gulf, or estuary, *inter fauces terrae*, the common law could deal with it, because the parts of the sea so circumstanced were held to be within the body of the adjacent county or counties; but, along the coast, on the external sea, the jurisdiction of the common law extended no further than to low-water mark.

And at 198:

For, if the sea thus becomes part of the territory, as though it were actually *inter fauces terrae*, it seems to follow that it must become annexed to the main land, and so become part of the adjoining county.

... I do not think that Spanish Bay is an interior or national water or *inter fauces terrae* within the meaning of that term as used in so many cases. I think that the outside limit of a county at common law is low-water mark (not high-water mark) and that this is clear from the opinions of numerous Judges who expressed opinions in *The Queen v. Keyn* ... [His Lordship referred to *Direct United States Cable Co. v. Anglo-American Telegraph Co.* (1877), 2 App. Cas. 394 and noted that:] In the present case there is no evidence of any usage indicating that Spanish Bay has ever been treated as part of Cape Breton County.

In *The Fagernes*, [1927] P. 311 ... It was decided that the part of Bristol Channel in question was not within the realm, but mainly, if not wholly, because the Attorney-

General, in answer to a question by the Court, said that the Crown did not claim that particular part of the Bristol Channel as being within the territorial jurisdiction of the King. ...

In my opinion, the fact that the Crown in the right of Nova Scotia owns the coal under the marine belt (assuming, but not deciding, this to be the case) has no bearing on the question whether the marine belt is part of the county. Nor, in my view, does the marking of an area on charts, old or new, as Spanish Bay, indicate that it is an interior or national water.

I may add that according to my measurements on the Canadian Hydrographic Service chart put in evidence, the length of the imaginary line from Point Aconi to Low Point is not about 2.5 times the greatest distance from any point on the seashore to the imaginary line but about 3.2 times (2.9 divided into 9.2). No instance has been brought to my attention of a so-called bay having such a configuration having been regarded as a territorial water, let alone an interior water.

MACDONALD J.: ... The second contention of the Municipality is ... that regardless of its configuration (or depth of penetration or width of mouth) Spanish Bay, within the line of headlands, is a historic bay which forms part of the territory of Nova Scotia (1) because of the continued exercise of dominion over it by the British Crown, acquiesced in by other nations; or (2) because it has by competent statute been declared to be part of the territory subject to the Legislature of Nova Scotia.

In *The Fagernes*, [1926] P. 185, at 189, it is pointed out that both grounds were relied on to bring Conception Bay within the Colony of Newfoundland and the jurisdiction of its Legislature (*Direct United States Cable Co. v. Anglo-American Telegraph Co.* (1877), 2 App. Cas. 394); and the latter ground to bring the Bay of Chaleur within the Province of New Brunswick (*Mowat v. McFee* (1880), 5 S.C.R. 66).

This doctrine calls for the incorporation of the bay within the land territory of the Province by a species of prescription or by direct legislative enactment; it is not enough that the water be historic in the sense of ancient.

Leaving prescription aside as being completely unproved, the first question is whether there is any Imperial enactment incorporating Spanish Bay within the realm; and no such enactment has been adduced. The second question must be whether the Government of Canada has designated the bay as a territorial or national waterway of Canada, under powers in that behalf vested in it by various statutes of Canada, or whether the Legislature of Nova Scotia has purported to incorporate the bay within the limits of its subordinate creature, the Municipality; and no substantial evidence to support either conclusion has been adduced. Upon the contrary, the relevant boundary of the Municipality as defined under provincial law excludes the idea that the waters of the bay are, to any extent, within the Municipality. The Assessment Act does not purport to delegate powers of taxation in respect of property situate under the bay or beyond that boundary; and, indeed, could not do so validly if, as seems probable, such property is beyond the limits of the Province itself.

Accordingly, with great respect for any contrary opinion, I must hold that this contention fails. ...

CURRIE J. dissenting: ... In the text books and the case law the waters adjacent to a state's territory are generally described as (a) the open sea, (b) territorial, (c) interior or inland. Also to be found is another category called historic bays. ...

(c) (2) Spanish Bay is in my opinion an inland water. It is not a mere curvature of the coast; it is a well-marked indentation. Unfortunately there was no oral evidence of scientific witnesses given on this point, and this Court is therefore denied the help that might have been given by competent marine surveyors and hydrographers. However, I think an examination of the map, No. 4367 (on exhibit), published by the Canadian Hydrographic Service, 1937, and 1944-46, establishes that Spanish Bay has those characteristics which readily mark a water as a bay, and in this instance is an inland water. Such an examination should not overlook nor dismiss the two heavily marked indentations of the two large estuaries created by the estuary of the Little Bras d'Or entrance to the Bras d'Or lakes to the north of Spanish Bay and the large estuary that is the great harbour of Sydney and Sydney River to the south of Spanish Bay. I can find no authority in the many cases I have read which holds or even suggests that in the determination of what is a bay such estuaries with their obvious deep and wide indentation should be excluded from consideration. I can find no authority which says that merely because the estuary of Sydney Harbour is in fact a harbour, that therefore it should not receive its proper designation as a well-marked indentation in Spanish Bay. I think that even without Little Bras d'Or and Sydney Harbour, it can be said that Spanish Bay is a well-marked indentation. The inclusion of these estuaries puts the matter beyond doubt. The territorial waters are capable of being measured from a baseline drawn from the headland of Point Aconi to the headland of Low Point. Therefore the waters called Spanish Bay and the land enclosed therein, that is to say, the landward enclosure formed by these headlands, a distance of $9^{1}/_{4}$ miles, are not territorial waters, but are inland waters. ...

Later in this decision I shall attempt to show that not only does Spanish Bay and the subsoil beneath belong to an unlimited extent to the coastal state which is sovereign of the surface, but also that for the purposes of this appeal these waters are *intra fauces terrae* and at common law form part of the country which they adjoin.

(c) (3) Spanish Bay is a historic inland water. Indeed, a strong argument can be made that all bays and inlets in Nova Scotia are historic bays. Brierly, *The Law of Nations*, at 172, states that historic bays are those over which the coastal state has publicly claimed and exercised jurisdiction and this jurisdiction has been accepted by other states. It is said in the *North Atlantic Coast Fisheries Arbitration* case, reproduced in Briggs, *The Law of Nations*, at 284, and Green, *International Law Through the Cases*, and cited with approval in *The "Fagernes,"* [1927] P. 311, at 325:

The interpretation must take into account all the individual circumstances which, for any of the different bays, are to be appreciated; the relation of its width to the length of penetration inland; the possibility and the necessity of its being defended by the State in whose territory it is indented; the special value which it has for the industry of the inhabitants of its shores; the distance which it is secluded from the highways of nations on the open sea and other circumstances not possible to enumerate ... . [See also *Capital City Canning & Packing Co. v Anglo-British Columbia Packing Co.* (1905), 11 B.C.R. 333, at 339.]

There can be no doubt that the coastal authority has unquestioned possession of the headlands of Spanish Bay, that the geological character of the bay intimately affects the affairs of the territorial Sovereign, that the interests of national integrity, of industry and commerce, with the large steel plant at Sydney, the coal mines of Cape Breton, etc., are concerned with control of this bay; that all such factors, and many more, enable it to be said that Spanish Bay has been publicly claimed and that its jurisdiction has been accepted by other states and that it falls within the term "effective occupation" in *The "Fagernes."*

In connection with this matter of a historic bay, a further consideration may be advanced. Before Confederation each of the Maritime Provinces enacted and enforced statutes called "hovering" Acts, with the intention that the baseline of territorial waters should be drawn from the headlands of bays and that they empowered customs and excise officers to board any ship in any port or bay in the Province or hovering within three miles of the coasts and bays. One of these enacted by the Province of Nova Scotia, confirmed by Order in Council of Great Britain, was 1836, 6 Wm. IV, c. 8. ...

To hold, as I think it can be, that Spanish Bay is a historic bay, and that for a long time there has been "effective occupation" of the bay, within the comments in *The "Fagernes,"* would, I submit, avoid the application here of the doubtful criterion of "a well marked indentation," where reliance must rest upon a mere visual examination of one or two maps, unsupported by the assistance that would be given by a visual examination of the area or the evidence of competent surveyors and hydrographers. If it can be held, as I think it should be, that Spanish Bay is a bay by virtue of its physical nature, or by virtue of its historic aspects, or by virtue of the principle of "effective occupation," then the rule will apply that to ascertain the baseline, the points of land stretching farthest to sea, that is Point Aconi and Low Point, need only be considered, and that the waters enclosed by such baseline would be inland waters and *intra fauces terrae*.

NOTES

1. From a reading of this case, what are the criteria for the proof of a claim of historic waters?[34]

2. For an important decision of the U.S. Supreme Court concerning the alleged historic waters of the State of Alaska see *U.S.* v. *Alaska*, where the Court took a conservative view of Alaska's claim in applying a test of "continuous and exclusive assertions of dominion."[35]

---

[34] See G.V. LaForest, "The Delimitation of National Territory: Re Dominion Coal Company and County of Cape Breton" (1964), 2 *Can.Y.B.Int.L.* 233.
[35] (1975) 422 U.S. 184, S. Ct. 2240.

International Straits[36]

United Nations Convention on the Law of the Sea

Article 37
SCOPE OF THIS SECTION

This section applies to straits which are used for international navigation between one part of the high seas or an exclusive economic zone and another part of the high seas or an exclusive economic zone.

Article 38
RIGHT OF TRANSIT PASSAGE

1. In straits referred to in article 37, all ships and aircraft enjoy the right of transit passage, which shall not be impeded; except that, if the strait is formed by an island of a State bordering the strait and its mainland, transit passage shall not apply if there exists seaward of the island a route through the high seas or through an exclusive economic zone of similar convenience with respect to navigational and hydrographical characteristics.

2. Transit passage means the exercise in accordance with this Part of the freedom of navigation and overflight solely for the purpose of continuous and expeditious transit of the strait between one part of the high seas or an exclusive economic zone and another part of the high seas or an exclusive economic zone. However, the requirement of continuous and expeditious transit does not preclude passage through the strait for the purpose of entering, leaving or returning from a State bordering the strait, subject to the conditions of entry to that State.

3. Any activity which is not an exercise of the right of transit passage through a strait remains subject to the other applicable provisions of this Convention.

Article 45
INNOCENT PASSAGE

1. The régime of innocent passage, in accordance with Part II, section 3, shall apply in straits used for international navigation:
  (a) excluded from the application of the régime of transit passage under article 38, paragraph 1; or
  (b) between a part of the high seas or an exclusive economic zone and the territorial sea of a foreign State.

2. There shall be no suspension of innocent passage through such straits.

---

[36] See E. Brüel, *International Straits*, 2 vols. (1947); R. Lapidoth, *Les détroits en droit international* (1972); and D.P. O'Connell, *supra*, n.1, at 299-337.

NOTES

1) Prior to 1982 the law governing navigation through international straits rested upon customary international law and a number of bilateral or regional conventions dealing with particular straits, such as the Montreux Convention 1936 on passage through the Dardannelles[37] as well as the 1958 Geneva Convention on the Territorial Sea and Contiguous Zone, article 16(4) which prohibited the suspension of innocent passage of foreign ships "through straits which are used for international navigation." The extension of the territorial sea from 3 to 12 miles has the effect of enclosing many major straits. As part of the negotiations at the Third U.N. Conference on the Law of the Sea the maritime powers called for the establishment of a new right of "transit passage" through straits. This right is a guarantee of transit, not simply of innocent passage. It applies to civil and military vessels and constitutes a considerable strengthening of the right of navigation.

2) Is the right of transit passage binding upon coastal straits states? If so, on what basis? What straits are subject to the right of transit passage? Does the North West passage meet the definition of a "strait used for international navigation?" The government of Canada has always maintained the contrary. See Article 234 reported later in the section on "Protection of the Marine Environment" and Chapter 6 on the Arctic. Consider the following case.

Corfu Channel Case (Merits)
United Kingdom v. Albania
[1949] I.C.J. Rep. 4

[Two, out of a squadron of four, British warships were heavily damaged by mines during transit of the Corfu Channel within the territorial sea of Albania. Subsequently, other British warships mineswept the Channel. By agreement, the parties submitted the following two questions to the Court:

(1) Is Albania responsible under international law for the explosions which occurred on
      October 22, 1946, in Albanian waters and for the damage and loss of human life which
      resulted from them and is there any duty to pay compensation?
(2) Has the United Kingdom under international law violated the sovereignty of the Albanian
      People's Republic by reason of the acts of the Royal Navy in Albanian waters on
      October 22 and on November 12 and 13, 1946, and is there any duty to give satisfaction?]

THE COURT: ... The two ships were mined in Albanian territorial waters in a previously swept and check-swept channel just at the place where a newly laid minefield consisting of moored contact German GY mines was discovered three weeks later. The damage sustained by the ships was inconsistent with damage which could have been caused by floating mines, magnetic ground mines, magnetic moored mines, or German GR mines, but its nature and extent were such as would be caused by mines of the type

---

[37] 173 L.N.T.S. 213.

In addition to the passage of the United Kingdom warships on October 22nd, 1946, the second question in the Special Agreement relates to the acts of the Royal Navy in Albanian waters on November 12th and 13th, 1946. This is the minesweeping operation called ''Operation Retail'' by the Parties during the proceedings. ...

The United Kindom Government does not dispute that ''Operation Retail'' was carried out against the clearly expressed wish of the Albanian Government. It recognizes that the operation had not the consent of the international mine clearance organizations, that it could not be justified as the exercise of a right of innocent passage, and lastly that, in principle, international law does not allow a State to assemble a large number of warships in the territorial waters of another State and to carry out minesweeping in those waters. The United Kingdom Government states that the operation was one of extreme urgency, and that it considered itself entitled to carry it out without anybody's consent.

... the explosions of October 22nd, 1946, in a channel declared safe for navigation, and one which the United Kingdom Government, more than any other government, had reason to consider safe, raised quite a different problem from that of a routine sweep carried out under the orders of the mine clearance organizations. These explosions were suspicious; they raised a question of responsibility.

Accordingly, this was the ground on which the United Kingdom Government chose to establish its main line of defence. According to that Government, the *corpora delicti* must be secured as quickly as possible, for fear they should be taken away, without leaving traces, by the authors of the minelaying or by the Albanian authorities. This justification took two distinct forms in the United Kingdom Government's arguments. It was presented first as a new and special application of the theory of intervention, by means of which the State intervening would secure possession of evidence in the territory of another State, in order to submit it to an international tribunal and thus facilitate its task.

The Court cannot accept such a line of defence. The Court can only regard the alleged right of intervention as the manifestation of a policy of force, such as has, in the past, given rise to most serious abuses and such as cannot, whatever be the present defects in international organization, find a place in international law. Intervention is perhaps still less admissible in the particular form it would take here; for, from the nature of things, it would be reserved for the powerful States, and might easily lead to perverting the administration of international justice itself.

The United Kingdom Agent, in his speech in reply, has further classified ''Operation Retail'' among methods of self-protection or self-help. The Court cannot accept this defence either. Between independent States, respect for territorial sovereignty is an essential foundation of international relations. The Court recognizes that the Albanian Government's complete failure to carry out its duties after the explosions, and the dilatory nature of its diplomatic notes, are extenuating circumstances for the action of the United Kingdom Government. But to ensure respect for international law, of which it is the organ, the Court must declare that the action of the British Navy constituted a violation of Albanian sovereignty.

This declaration is in accordance with the request made by Albania through her Counsel, and is in itself appropriate satisfaction.

Exclusive Economic Zone[38]

United Nations Convention on the Law of the Sea

Article 55
SPECIFIC LEGAL RÉGIME OF THE EXCLUSIVE ECONOMIC ZONE

The exclusive economic zone is an area beyond and adjacent to the territorial sea, subject to the specific legal régime established in this Part, under which the rights and jurisdiction of the coastal State and the rights and freedoms of other States are governed by the relevant provisions of this Convention.

Article 56
RIGHTS, JURISDICTION AND DUTIES OF THE COASTAL STATE IN THE
EXCLUSIVE ECONOMIC ZONE

1. In the exclusive economic zone, the coastal State has:
(a) sovereign rights for the purpose of exploring and exploiting, conserving and managing the natural resources, whether living or non-living, of the waters superjacent to the sea-bed and of the sea-bed and its subsoil, and with regard to other activities for the economic exploitation and exploration of the zone, such as the production of energy from the water, currents and winds;
(b) jurisdiction as provided for in the relevant provisions of this Convention with regard to:
    (i)   the establishment and use of artificial islands, installations and structures;
    (ii) marine scientific research;
    (iii) the protection and preservation of the marine environment;
(c) other rights and duties provided for in this Convention.
2. In exercising its rights and performing its duties under this Convention in the exclusive economic zone, the coastal State shall have due regard to the rights and duties of other States and shall act in a manner compatible with the provisions of this Convention.
3. The rights set out in this article with respect to the sea-bed and subsoil shall be exercised in accordance with Part VI.[39]

Article 57
BREADTH OF THE EXCLUSIVE ECONOMIC ZONE

The exclusive economic zone shall not extend beyond 200 nautical miles from the baselines from which the breadth of the territorial sea is measured.

---

[38] See W.C. Extavour, *The Exclusive Economic Zone* (1979).
[39] Part VI deals with the continental shelf, which is considered in the next section.

Article 58

RIGHTS AND DUTIES OF OTHER STATES IN THE EXCLUSIVE ECONOMIC ZONE

1. In the exclusive economic zone, all States, whether coastal or land-locked, enjoy, subject to the relevant provisions of this Convention, the freedoms referred to in article 87 of navigation and overflight and of the laying of submarine cables and pipelines, and other internationally lawful uses of the sea related to these freedoms, such as those associated with the operation of ships, aircraft and submarine cables and pipelines, and compatible with the other provisions of this Convention.

2. Articles 88 to 115 and other pertinent rules of international law apply to the exclusive economic zone in so far as they are not incompatible with this Part.

3. In exercising their rights and performing their duties under this Convention in the exclusive economic zone, States shall have due regard to the rights and duties of the coastal State and shall comply with the laws and regulations adopted by the coastal State in accordance with the provisions of this Convention and other rules of international law in so far as they are not incompatible with this Part.

Article 59

BASIS FOR THE RESOLUTION OF CONFLICTS REGARDING THE ATTRIBUTION OF RIGHTS AND JURISDICTION IN THE EXCLUSIVE ECONOMIC ZONE

In cases where this Convention does not attribute rights or jurisdiction to the coastal State or to other States within the exclusive economic zone, and a conflict arises between the interests of the coastal State and any other State or States, the conflict should be resolved on the basis of equity and in the light of all the relevant circumstances, taking into account the respective importance of the interests involved to the parties as well as to the international community as a whole.

Article 60

ARTIFICIAL ISLANDS, INSTALLATIONS AND STRUCTURES IN THE EXCLUSIVE ECONOMIC ZONE

1. In the exclusive economic zone, the coastal State shall have the exclusive right to construct and to authorize and regulate the construction, operation and use of:
(a) artificial islands;
(b) installations and structures for the purposes provided for in article 56 and other economic purposes;
(c) installations and structures which may interfere with the exercise of the rights of the coastal State in the zone.

2. The coastal State shall have exclusive jurisdiction over such artificial islands, installations and structures, including jurisdiction with regard to customs, fiscal, health, safety and immigration laws and regulations.

NOTES

1) The scope of a state's rights under Article 56(1)(a) with respect to fishing are elaborated by Articles 61-67, which may be read in the later section on "Fisheries."

Together with Part XI dealing with the seabed beyond national jurisdiction, the provisions on the exclusive economic zone constitute the principal innovations of the 1982 Convention. These articles are remarkable in many respects, not least in respect of the speed with which they appear to have become rules of international law by virtue of state practice. Almost as soon as agreement was expected to be reached at the Third U.N. Conference on the Law of the Sea in 1975, 200 mile fishing zones were proclaimed by such influential states as U.S.A., Canada, the European Economic Community members, U.S.S.R. and Japan. At the same time a number of states proclaimed full-fledged exclusive economic zones; Mexico and France were among the first. As of November 1986, 20 states, including Canada, had proclaimed a 200 mile exclusive fishing zone and 69 states, including U.S.A., U.S.S.R. and U.K. had proclaimed exclusive economic zones.[40]

2) One of the principal problems in negotiating the exclusive economic zone was the definition of the nature of the zone. This was not simply a matter of abstract theory since a decision to retain the status of high seas would have left questions of high seas freedoms unchanged. On the other hand, a decision to equate the zone with the territorial sea would have raised the spectre of restrictions on freedom of navigation. The ultimate resolution clearly creates a regime of law which is *sui generis*, while Article 58(2) expressly preserves all high seas freedoms which are not incompatible with the rights enjoyed by coastal states in the zone. But how should a conflict of uses of the zone be resolved, in favour of the coastal state's sovereign rights or the other states' high seas freedoms? Does the coastal state have authority to police the zone? Consider Article 59.

3) At this time coastal states clearly may claim an exclusive economic zone, but they must do so expressly since the rights do not arise by mere operation of the law as with the continental shelf. Note that in Article 57 the zone may extend for 200 nautical miles from a state's baselines, not from the outer frontier of its territorial sea.

4) What is the distinction to be made between "sovereign rights" and "jurisdiction"? Are non-parties and non-signatories to the 1982 Convention required to respect exclusive economic zone claims by coastal states? Is there an argument that states may claim a 200 mile fishing zone but not yet an exclusive economic zone?

The answer to some of these questions will emerge only from state practice and authoritative interpretation of the 1982 Convention. A conservative view of international law and the development of customary law by multilateral conference diplomacy would lead to the conclusion that much of the text is not yet law. There is a contrary view based upon the lengthy and difficult negotiations over some ten years and the fact of very broad approval of the text as expressed by 149 signatures of the Final Act, and 159 signatures of the Convention.

5) The exclusive economic zone encompasses all the waters over which Canada has historic claims to full sovereignty. At the U.N. Conference, Canada argued successfully for a new, more functional law of the sea which lays less stress on sovereignty: should Canada now abandon its historic claims? How good are Canada's claims, set out in the earlier section on "Historic Waters" in face of the U.N. Convention?

---

[40] U.N. *Law of the Sea Bulletin* No. 8 (November 1986), at 25-28.

Continental Shelf [41]

The Truman Proclamation
(September 28, 1945), 10 Fed.Reg. 12303

Whereas the Government of the United States of America, aware of the long range world-wide need for new sources of petroleum and other minerals, holds the view that efforts to discover and make available new supplies of these resources should be encouraged; and ...

Whereas recognized jurisdiction over these resources is required in the interest of their conservation and prudent utilization when and as development is undertaken; and

Whereas it is the view of the Government of the United States that the exercise of jurisdiction over the natural resources of the subsoil and sea bed of the continental shelf by the contiguous nation is reasonable and just, since the effectiveness of measures to utilize or conserve these resources would be contingent upon cooperation and protection from the shore, since the continental shelf may be regarded as an extension of the land mass of the coastal nation and thus naturally appurtenant to it, since these resources frequently form a seaward extension of a pool or deposit lying within the territory, and since self-protection compels the coastal nation to keep close watch over activities off its shores which are of the nature necessary for utilization of these resources:

Now therefore, I, Harry S. Truman, President of the United States of America, do hereby proclaim the following policy of the United States of America with respect to the natural resources of the subsoil and sea bed of the continental shelf.

Having concern for the urgency of conserving and prudently utilizing its natural resources, the Government of the United States regards the natural resources of the subsoil and sea bed of the continental shelf beneath the high seas but contiguous to the coasts of the United States as appertaining to the United States, subject to its jurisdiction and control. In cases where the continental shelf extends to the shores of another state, or is shared with an adjacent state, the boundary shall be determined by the United States and the state concerned in accordance with equitable principles. The character as high seas of the waters above the continental shelf and the right to their free and unimpeded navigation are in no way thus affected.

Geneva Convention on the Continental Shelf
(1958), 499 U.N.T.S. 311

Article 1

For the purpose of these articles, the term "continental shelf" is used as referring (a) to the seabed and subsoil of the submarine areas adjacent to the coast but outside the

---

[41] See R.D. Eckert, *The Enclosure of Ocean Resources* (1979); and M.L. Jewett, "The Evolution of the Legal Regime of the Continental Shelf" (1984), 22 *Can.Y.B.Int.L.* 153, and (1985), 23 *Can.Y.B.Int.L.* 201.

areas of the territorial sea, to a depth of 200 metres or, beyond that limit, to where the depth of the superjacent waters admits of the exploitation of the natural resources of the said areas; (b) to the seabed and subsoil of similar submarine areas adjacent to the coasts of islands.

United Nations Convention on the Law of the Sea

Article 76
DEFINITION OF THE CONTINENTAL SHELF

1. The continental shelf of a coastal State comprises the sea-bed and subsoil of the submarine areas that extend beyond its territorial sea throughout the natural prolongation of its land territory to the outer edge of the continental margin or to a distance of 200 nautical miles from the baselines from which the breadth of the territorial sea is measured where the outer edge of the continental margin does not extend up to that distance.

2. The continental shelf of a coastal State shall not extend beyond the limits provided for in paragraphs 4 to 6.

3. The continental margin comprises the submerged prolongation of the land mass of the coastal State and consists of the sea-bed and subsoil of the shelf, the slope and the rise. It does not include the deep ocean floor with its oceanic ridges or the subsoil thereof.

4.(a) For the purposes of this Convention the coastal State shall establish the outer edge of the continental margin wherever the margin extends beyond 200 nautical miles from the baselines from which the breadth of the territorial sea is measured, by either:

(i) a line delineated in accordance with paragraph 7 by reference to the outermost fixed points at each of which the thickness of sedimentary rocks is at least 1 per cent of the shortest distance from such point to the foot of the continental slope; or

(ii) a line delineated in accordance with paragraph 7 by reference to fixed points not more than 60 nautical miles from the foot of the continental slope.

(b) In the absence of evidence to the contrary, the foot of the continetnal slope shall be determined as the point of maximum change in the gradient at its base.

5. The fixed points comprising the line of the outer limits of the continental shelf on the sea-bed, drawn in accordance with paragraph 4(a) (i) and (ii), either shall not exceed 350 nautical miles from the baselines from which the breadth of the territorial sea is measured or shall not exceed 100 nautical miles from the 2,500-metre isobath, which is a line connecting the depth of 2,500 metres.

6. Notwithstanding the provisions of paragraph 5, on submarine ridges, the outer limit of the continental shelf shall not exceed 350 nautical miles from the baselines from which the breadth of the territorial sea is measured. This paragraph does not apply to submarine elevations that are natural components of the continental margin, such as its plateaux, rises, caps, banks and spurs.

7. The coastal State shall delineate the outer limits of its continental shelf, where that shelf extends beyond 200 nautical miles from the baselines from which the breadth of the territorial sea is measured, by straight lines not exceeding 60 nautical miles in length, connecting fixed points, defined by co-ordinates of latitude and longitude.

8. Information on the limits of the continental shelf beyond 200 nautical miles from the baselines from which the breadth of the territorial sea is measured shall be submitted by the coastal State to the Commission on the Limits of the Continental Shelf set up under Annex II on the basis of equitable geographical representation. The Commission shall make recommendations to coastal States on mattters related to the establishment of the outer limits of their continental shelf. The limits of the shelf established by a coastal State on the basis of these recommendations shall be final and binding.

9. The coastal State shall deposit with the Secretary-General of the United Nations charts and relevant information, including geodetic data, permanently describing the outer limits of its continental shelf. The Secretary-General shall give due publicity thereto.

10. The provisions of this article are without prejudice to the question of delimitation of the continental shelf between States with opposite or adjacent coasts.

Article 77
RIGHTS OF THE COASTAL STATE OVER THE CONTINENTAL SHELF

1. The coastal State exercises over the continental shelf sovereign rights for the purpose of exploring it and exploiting its natural resources.

2. The rights referred to in paragraph 1 are exclusive in the sense that if the coastal State does not explore the continental shelf or exploit its natural resources, no one may undertake these activities without the express consent of the coastal State.

3. The rights of the coastal State over the continental shelf do not depend on occupation, effective or notional, or on any express proclamation.

4. The natural resources referred to in this Part consist of the mineral and other non-living resources of the sea-bed and subsoil together with living organisms belonging to sedentary species, that is to say, organisms which, at the harvestable stage, either are immobile on or under the sea-bed or are unable to move except in constant physical contact with the sea-bed or the subsoil.

Article 82
PAYMENTS AND CONTRIBUTIONS WITH RESPECT TO THE EXPLOITATION OF THE CONTINENTAL SHELF BEYOND 200 NAUTICAL MILES

1. The coastal State shall make payments or contributions in kind in respect of the exploitation of the non-living resources of the continental shelf beyond 200 nautical miles from the baselines from which the breadth of the territorial sea is measured.

2. The payments and contributions shall be made annually with respect to all production at a site after the first five years of production at that site. For the sixth year, the rate of payment or contribution shall be 1 per cent of the value or volume of production at the site. The rate shall increase by 1 per cent for each subsequent year until the twelfth year and shall remain at 7 per cent thereafter. Production does not include resources used in connection with exploitation.

3. A developing State which is a net importer of a mineral resource produced from

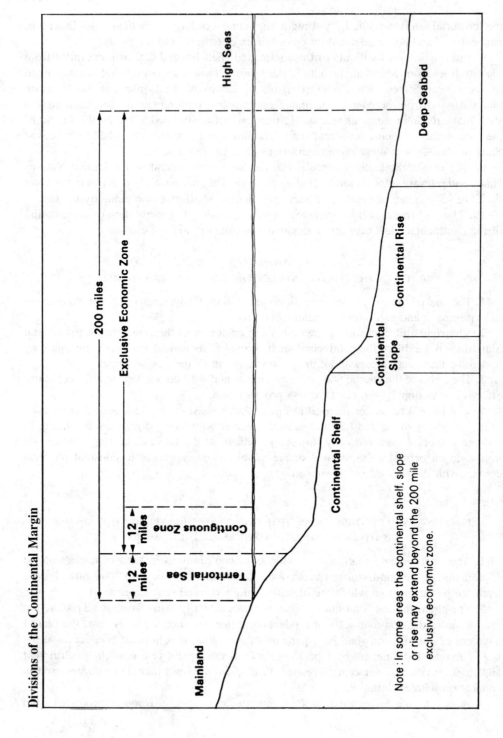

Divisions of the Continental Margin

Mainland

Territorial Sea

Contiguous Zone

Exclusive Economic Zone

High Seas

12 miles

12 miles

200 miles

Continental Shelf

Continental Slope

Continental Rise

Deep Seabed

Note: In some areas the continental shelf, slope or rise may extend beyond the 200 mile exclusive economic zone.

its continental shelf is exempt from making such payments or contributions in respect of that mineral resource.

4. The payments or contributions shall be made through the Authority, which shall distribute them to States Parties to this Convention, on the basis of equitable sharing criteria, taking into account the interests and needs of developing States, particularly the least developed and the land-locked among them.

Re Newfoundland Continental Shelf
[1984] 1 S.C.R. 86

[The Court was asked: "In respect of the mineral and other natural resources of the seabed and subsoil of the continental shelf" in an area offshore Newfoundland beyond the territorial sea, "has Canada or Newfoundland:
1) the right to explore and exploit the said mineral and other natural resources, and
2) legislative jurisdiction to make laws in relation to the exploration and exploitation of the said mineral and other natural resources?"]

THE COURT: ...
The Nature of Continental Shelf Rights
The reference speaks of the *right to explore and exploit* mineral and other natural resources. The precise language is taken from international law. Article 2 of the 1958 Geneva Convention on the Continental Shelf, signed in 1958, in force in 1964 upon receiving the requisite number of ratifications, and ratified by Canada in 1970, reads as follows:

Article 2

1. The coastal State exercises over the continental shelf sovereign rights for the purpose of exploring it and exploiting its natural resources.

2. The rights referred to in paragraph 1 of this article are exclusive in the sense that if the coastal State does not explore the continental shelf or exploit its natural resources, no one may undertake these activities, or make a claim to the continental shelf, without the express consent of the coastal State.

3. The rights of the coastal State over the continental shelf do not depend on occupation, effective or notional, or on any express proclamation.

4. The natural resources referred to in these articles consist of the mineral and other non-living resources of the sea-bed and subsoil together with living organisms belonging to sedentary species, that is to say, organisms which, at the harvestable stage, either are immobile on or under the sea-bed or are unable to move except in constant physical contact with the sea-bed or the subsoil.

Both Canada and Newfoundland claim the rights of the coastal State recognized by international law. Neither purports to claim anything more or anything different. Neither Canada nor Newfoundland made any claims to the continental shelf prior to the codification of the regime in the 1958 Geneva Convention. The rights claimed are those accorded by operation of international law.

There has developed in international law a carefully constructed regime respecting the continental shelf. International law was forced to take note of the continental shelf when, in the middle of this century, the technology was developed to exploit offshore resources. A consensus developed that the exploitation should be under the control of the coastal State. The 1958 Geneva Convention was drafted so as to do no more than was necessary to achieve this result. Thus the Convention does not grant "sovereignty" over the continental shelf but rather "sovereign rights to explore and exploit."

These limited rights co-exist with the rights of other nations to make use of the seabed for submarine cables and pipelines (Article 4) and do not affect the status of the superjacent waters or airspace (Article 3). They stand in marked contrast to the full sovereignty (saving only other nations' rights of innocent passage) which international law accords to coastal States over their territorial sea.

In the *North Sea Continental Shelf* cases, I.C.J. Reports 1969, at 3, the International Court of Justice, at 29, referred to the notion of appurtenance:

> ... the right of the coastal State to its continental shelf areas is based on its sovereignty over the land domain, of which the shelf area is the natural prolongation into and under the sea.

Continental shelf rights arise as an extension of the coastal State's sovereignty, but it is an extension in the form of something less than full sovereignty. The Court referred to the "title" in the continental shelf (at 31) and said the shelf may be "deemed" to be part of the coastal State's territory in a certain sense (at 31). But in the ordinary meaning of the term, the continental shelf is not part of a coastal State's territory. The coastal State cannot "own" the continental shelf as it can "own" its land territory. The regulation by international law of the uses to which the continental shelf may be put is simply too extensive to consider the shelf to be part of the State's territory. International law concedes dominion to the State in its land territory, subject to certain definite restrictions. By contrast, in the continental shelf the limited rights that international law accords are the sum total of the coastal State's rights. ...

At international law, then, the continental shelf off Newfoundland is outside the territory of the nation state of Canada. Since, as a matter of municipal law, neither Canada nor Newfoundland purports to claim anything more than international law recognizes, we are here concerned with an area outside the boundaries of either Newfoundland or Canada. In other words, we are concerned with extraterritorial rights.

Much of the argument in the present case is based on the assumption that continental shelf rights are proprietary. We do not think continental shelf rights are proprietary in the ordinary sense. In the words of the 1958 Geneva Convention, they are "sovereign rights" and they appertain to the coastal State as an extension of rights beyond where its ordinary sovereignty is exercised. In pith and substance they are an extraterritorial manifestation of, and an incident of, the external sovereignty of a coastal State. ...

The State of International Law in 1949

Up to now we have been making assumptions about international law most favourable to Newfoundland's position ... We turn now to examine these assumptions and to consider the international law question.

In the late 1940's there was some discussion between the Commission of Government of Newfoundland and the United Kingdom government about the possibility of a claim to the continental shelf being made "by or on behalf of Newfoundland," but no such claim was ever made. Accordingly, in order for Newfoundland to have acquired continental shelf rights under international law prior to its joining Canada in 1949, it must be shown that by that date international law had reached the stage not only of recognizing as valid State claims to the continental shelf, but also that States that had made no such claim were accorded the rights in question *ipso jure*, that is to say, by operation of law. There is no question that the current position at international law is that no such claim is necessary. Paragraph 3 of Article 2 of the 1958 Geneva Convention states this expressly:

The rights of the coastal State over the continental shelf do not depend on occupation, effective or notional, or on any express proclamation.

The question is whether international law had sufficiently crystallized to make this the law in 1949. ...

[The Court considered the sources of international law posited in its Statute Article 38(1) but quickly dismissed treaties and general principles as inapplicable in this case.]

The critical issue then is whether the sovereign right, arising *ipso jure*, to explore and exploit in the continental shelf was a matter of customary international law by 1949.

The positive law on the continental shelf had its inception in State claims. The first was in 1942, concerning the Gulf of Paria between Venezuela and Trinidad. A treaty concluded between Venezuela and the United Kingdom contained a mutual agreement to recognize each other's claims to sovereignty over designated submarine areas in this Gulf. The United Kingdom followed up on the Treaty by passing an order in council, dated August 6, 1942 declaring that the submarine areas:

shall be annexed to and form part of His Majesty's dominions and shall be attached to the colony of Trinidad and Tobago for administrative purposes, and the said submarine areas are annexed and attached accordingly.

The British proceeded upon the theory that the seabed beyond territorial waters was *res nullius* – the property of nobody – and could therefore be appropriated only by occupation. This is quite different from the manner in which international law ultimately developed.

More in keeping with the current international law approach to the continental shelf was the claim of the United States by the *Truman Proclamation*, dated September 28, 1945 ... .

In the *North Sea Continental cases*, [[1969] I.C.J. Rep. 3, reported *supra.*, Chapter

3] ... the International Court of Justice confirmed that the *Truman Proclamation* was the starting point of the positive law on the subject.

Prior to Newfoundland's entry into Confederation, seven Latin American States (Mexico, Argentina, Panama, Nicaragua, Chile, Peru, and Costa Rica) issued decrees in respect of the continental shelf, all of which used language broader than that of the *Truman Proclamation*. All claimed at least sovereignty over the continental shelf; most treated it as territorial. A majority claimed not only the continental shelf, but also the superjacent waters. Some States claimed the geographic shelf to a limited depth; others claimed to a limit of 200 miles from the coast, whatever the depth.

To complete the picture prior to Newfoundland's entry into Canada, reference must be made to the United Kingdom's extension, by order in council, of the territorial boundaries of two additional colonies: Jamaica and the Bahamas, both on November 26, 1948.

Within six months of Newfoundland's joining Confederation there were claims by 13 additional States, mostly from the Persian Gulf. Most of the Persian Gulf declarations were drafted by the British authorities because the States concerned were then British protectorates. Even with the inclusion of these 13 additional claims the numbers were not large and the terms of the claims were far from uniform.

In 1950 the International Law Commission began its work on the continental shelf. There were several comments among the members which indicated they perceived they were engaged in the progressive development of international law rather than the codification of existing law. In 1950 the special *rapporteur*, J.P.A. François, in his first memorandum to the Commission, expressed the view that continental shelf rights were not yet part of international law:

[TRANSLATION] Does international law recognize a rule that control and jurisdiction, or even sovereignty, over the seabed and subsoil of the continental shelf, and the superjacent waters, beyond the territorial limit, belong to the riparian state?

The *Rapporteur* does not feel that an affirmative answer can be given to this question at this time. The number of proclamations claiming special rights continues to increase, it is true, but is still limited. Most states have not so far claimed such rights, and they have not expressly recognized the validity of such claims. In certain cases, where rights of sovereignty have been claimed, formal protests have been made. In cases involving rights of control and jurisdiction, doubts subsist as to the scope of such claims: are they much less extensive than sovereignty itself? ...

In this situation the *Rapporteur* feels the conclusion should be avoided that international law at present recognizes as a rule of customary law that either sovereignty or control and jurisdiction over the continental shelf belong to the riparian state, *ipso facto* or simply as the result of a notional occupation. ...

Confirmation of these views is to be found in the 1952 decision of Lord Asquith in the *Abu Dhabi Arbitration* (1952), 1 *International and Comparative Law Quarterly* 247, much relied upon by the Attorney General of Canada. The arbitration concerned the construction of a 1939 contract. One of the issues was whether concessions had been granted in the submarine areas beyond the territorial sea of Abu Dhabi. Lord Asquith said at 253-56:

> Directed, as I apprehend I am, to apply a simple and broad jurisprudence to the construction of this contract, it seems to me that it would be a most artificial refinement to read back into the contract the implications of a doctrine not mooted till seven years later, and, if the view which I am about to express is sound, not even today admitted to the canon of international law ...

[His Lordship raised many questions about the doctrine of the Continental Shelf and concluded:]

> Neither the practice of nations nor the pronouncements of learned jurists give any certain or consistent answer to many – perhaps most – of these questions. I am of opinion that there are in this field so many ragged ends and unfilled blanks, so much that is merely tentative and exploratory, that in no form can the doctrine claim as yet to have been assumed hitherto the hard lineaments or the definitive status of an established rule of international law.

The Attorney General of Newfoundland for his part relies on the contrary opinion expressed by Professor H. Lauterpacht (incidentally, the losing counsel in the *Abu Dhabi Arbitration*) in "Sovereignty over Submarine Areas," [1950] *British Yearbook of International Law* 376. Writing in 1950, Lauterpacht said, at 376-77 and 394:

> ...the doctrine and the practice of the continental shelf ... has now, in any case, become part of international law by unequivocal positive acts of some states, including the leading maritime Powers, and general acquiescence on the part of others. ...

> Moreover, assuming that we are confronted here with the creation of new international law by custom, what matters is not so much the number of states participating in its creation and the length of the period within which that change takes place, as the relative importance, in any particular sphere, of states inaugurating the change. In a matter closely related to the principle of the freedom of the seas the conduct of the two principal maritime Powers – such as Great Britain and the United States – is of special importance. With regard to the continental shelf and submarine areas generally these two states inaugurated the development and their initiative was treated as authoritative almost as a matter of course from the outset. This was so in particular having regard to the traditional attachment of these states to the principle of the freedom of the seas and the customary limit of the territorial waters.

On the general issue of the existence of continental shelf rights, Lauterpacht seems, in the context of the entire article, to have succeeded only in demonstrating that this doctrine *ought* to be accepted into international law. In any event, however, on the crucial issue of whether rights in the continental shelf arise *ipso jure* Lauterpacht provides little support for Newfoundland's position; indeed he leans to the view that a proclamation was necessary (at 418-19):

> A proclamation is a means by which a title, claimed or acquired, is announced. It is not a *source*

of a title or a means of acquiring it. *That does not mean that it is meaningless or unnecessary.* When the Rulers of various Skeikdoms in the Persian Gulf were advised in 1949 by the British authorities that the issue of a proclamation is a pre-requisite of their effective assertion of rights over the adjacent submarine areas, the advice was given in deference to an obvious proposition of order and orderliness which requires that a person – or a state – asserting a claim, however inherently valid, must make his claim known by a formal pronouncement or notification. *This is so especially if the subject of the claim in question is novel in character, undefined in extent, and likely to require determination in relation to similar claims by other persons or states.* Accordingly, the issue of the proclamations of the continental shelf in no way militates against the view that they were of declaratory character in relation to what was considered to be a title claimed or acquired by or belonging to the state by reference to a legal basis other than occupation. (Emphasis added.)

We think Lauterpacht's comments give rise to a further point. During the embryonic stage of the development of a rule of international law it is difficult to say that rights arise *ipso jure* when it is not yet settled what those rights are. In 1949, in the absence of any proclamation by Newfoundland, one would have been hard pressed to state with any precision what rights were consistent with State practice to that date. We think this point is reinforced by the fact that in the documents relating to the consideration given to making a claim by or on behalf of Newfoundland, there was no hint that anyone thought Newfoundland rights in the continental shelf already existed.

We conclude that international law had not sufficiently developed by 1949 to confer, *ipso jure,* the right of the coastal State to explore and exploit the continental shelf. We think that in 1949 State practice was neither sufficiently widespread to constitute a general practice nor sufficiently consistent to constitute settled law. Furthermore, several of the early State claims exceeded that which international law subsequently recognized in the 1958 Geneva Convention. International law on the continental shelf developed relatively quickly, but it had not attained concrete form by 1949.

The Attorney General of Newfoundland argues, in the alternative, that even if continental shelf rights were not part of customary international law in 1949, the subsequent developments had retroactive effect. The following passage of the *North Sea Continental Shelf* cases, *supra*, at 22, is cited in support of that proposition:

Delimitation in an equitable manner is one thing, but not the same thing as awarding a just and equitable share of a previously undelimited area, even though in a number of cases the results may be comparable, or even identical.

...the doctrine of the just and equitable share appears to be wholly at variance with what the Court entertains no doubt is the most fundamental of all the rules of law relating to the continental shelf, enshrined in Article 2 of the 1958 Geneva Convention, though quite independent of it, – namely that the rights of the coastal State in respect of the area of continental shelf that constitutes a natural prolongation of its land territory into and under the sea *exist ipso facto and ab initio,* by virtue of its sovereignty over the land, and an extension of it in an exercise of sovereign rights for the purpose of exploring the seabed and exploiting its natural resources.

In short, there is here an inherent right. In order to exercise it, no special legal process has to be gone through, nor have any special legal acts to be performed. Its existence can be declared (and many States have done this) but does not need to be constituted. Furthermore, the right does not depend on its being exercised. To echo the language of the Geneva Convention, it is "exclusive" in the sense that if the coastal State does not choose to explore or exploit the areas of shelf appertaining to it, that is its own affair, but no one else may do so without its express consent. (Emphasis added.)

The Court of Appeal in the *Newfoundland Reference,* [(1983), 145 D.L.R. (3rd) 9] ... decided the international law point in Newfoundland's favour, on the basis of this retroactivity argument. The Court said, at 39:

The phrase "*ipso facto and ab initio*" used by the court [the International Court of Justice], may be interpreted as meaning that the rights in international law extended back in geological time, as suggested by D.P. O'Connell, or to when sovereignty over the land mass was first established and recognized, or to when the submarine areas in question became exploitable as a result of modern developments of science and technology, or, more specifically, to when these areas became the object of active interest of States. In our opinion, the last is the most logical and is in accord with British practice at the time.

There was no issue of retroactivity in the *North Sea Continental Shelf* cases. We do not think the terms "*ipso facto*" and "*ab initio*" were meant to suggest retroactivity. The point of this passage was simply to counter the German argument that the Court was dealing with the delineation of new areas. The Newfoundland Court of Appeal listed possible starting dates for the "*ab initio*" reference, but left out one – the time at which international law recognized continental shelf rights. We think that is what the "*ab initio*" refers to. As noted earlier, the discussions in the International Law Commission considered that the doctrine of continental shelf rights arising *ipso jure* enunciated new law. The development of customary or conventional international law is, by definition, the development of new law. There is no concept in international law of discovering law that always was. In our view, continental shelf rights have no retroactive application to a time before they were recognized by international law.

Even if there were a retroactive element to continental shelf rights, we do not, in any event, see how this would help Newfoundland's case. The Newfoundland argument amounts to this: In 1949 there were no continental shelf rights recognized at international law so that Newfoundland had no such rights when it joined Canada. Subsequently, however, international law did recognize these rights with retroactive effect. Even if international law as to the continental shelf were to have retroactive effect, we think the benefit would accrue to the entity within Canada currently competent to acquire continental shelf rights and that entity is not Newfoundland but Canada. We agree with the following passage of Gibbs J., dissenting on other grounds, in *New South Wales v. Commonwealth of Australia* (1975), 135 C.L.R. 337, at 416:

To say that the rights of coastal states in respect of the continental shelf existed from the beginning of time may or may not be correct as a matter of legal theory. In fact, however, the rights now recognized represent the response of international law to modern developments of science and technology, which permit the seabed to be exploited in a way which it was quite impossible for governments or lawyers of earlier centuries to foresee. In this matter the arguments of history are stronger than those of logic. In truth, when the Act was passed, the States had not asserted and did not have the rights to the continental shelf which the convention now accords to coastal states. Those rights, if theoretically inherent in the sovereignty of coastal states, were in fact the result of the operation of a new legal principle. When those rights were recognized by the international law the Commonwealth was the international person entitled to assert them, and it did so. The assertion by the Commonwealth of those rights in no way interfered with any existing right of any State.

We therefore conclude that Newfoundland could not, upon its entry into Confederation, have held rights to explore and exploit in the continental shelf by virtue of international law, because international law then conferred no such rights. Nor was it in any position to acquire such rights subsequent to Confederation.

Legislative Jurisdiction

The conclusion that Canada has the right to explore and exploit in the continental shelf leads easily to the conclusion that Canada has legislative jurisdiction. There is nothing in s. 92 of the *Constitution Act, 1867* which could confer legislative jurisdiction upon Newfoundland in respect of such rights held by Canada. Legislative jurisdiction falls to Canada under the peace, order, and good government power in its residual capacity.

NOTES

1) The Supreme Court also decided against Newfoundland on constitutional grounds. It stated:[42]

Assuming, *arguendo*, that a right to explore and exploit the continental shelf was recognized by international law in 1949, we conclude that on Union it would have had to devolve as an incident of external sovereignty, whether from the Crown in right of Newfoundland or, as we think, from the Crown in right of the United Kingdom, to the only entity within Canada possessing external sovereignty—the Crown in right of Canada. Even if – contrary to our opinion—Newfoundland did have the external sovereignty necessary to acquire continental shelf rights prior to joining Canada, the effect of the Terms of Union would be that Canada, not Newfoundland would have the right to explore and exploit the continental shelf.

By these conclusions, the Supreme Court dismissed Newfoundland's primary argument that its historical and constitutional position distinguished its case from the Court's previous decision in *Re Ownership of Offshore Mineral Rights of British Columbia*[43] which also favoured Canada. In that case, the Court additionally decided that jurisdiction over the seabed of the territorial sea belonged to Canada as well. The Court followed the old

---

[42] [1984] 1 S.C.R. 86, at 116.
[43] [1967] S.C.R. 792.

in article 33, the pursuit may only be undertaken if there has been a violation of the rights for the protection of which the zone was established.

2. The right of hot pursuit shall apply *mutatis mutandis* to violations in the exclusive economic zone or on the continental shelf, including safety zones around continental shelf installations, of the laws and regulations of the coastal State applicable in accordance with this Convention to the exclusive economic zone or the continental shelf, including such safety zones.

3. The right of hot pursuit ceases as soon as the ship pursued enters the territorial sea of its own State or of a third State.

4. Hot pursuit is not deemed to have begun unless the pusuing ship has satisfied itself by such practicable means as may be available that the ship pursued or one of its boats or other craft working as a team and using the ship pursued as a mother ship is within the limits of the territorial sea, or, as the case may be, within the contiguous zone or the exclusive economic zone or above the continental shelf. The pursuit may only be commenced after a visual or auditory signal to stop has been given at a distance which enables it to be seen or heard by the foreign ship.

5. The right of hot pursuit may be exercised only by warships or military aircraft, or other ships or aircraft clearly marked and identifiable as being on government service and authorized to that effect.

6. Where hot pursuit is effected by an aircraft:

(a) the provisions of paragraphs 1 to 4 shall apply *mutatis mutandis*;

(b) the aircraft giving the order to stop must itself actively pursue the ship until a ship or another aircraft of the coastal State, summoned by the aircraft, arrives to take over the pursuit, unless the aircraft is itself able to arrest the ship. It does not suffice to justify an arrest outside the territorial sea that the ship was merely sighted by the aircraft as an offender or suspected offender, if it was not both ordered to stop and pursued by the aircraft itself or other aircraft or ships which continue the pursuit without interruption.

7. The release of a ship arrested within the jurisdiction of a State and escorted to a port of that State for the purposes of an inquiry before the competent authorities may not be claimed solely on the ground that the ship, in the course of its voyage, was escorted across a portion of the exclusive economic zone or the high seas, if the circumstances rendered this necessary.

8. Where a ship has been stopped or arrested outside the territorial sea in circumstances which do not justify the exercise of the right of hot pursuit, it shall be compensated for any loss or damage that may have been thereby sustained.

The I'm Alone[49]
Canada v. United States
(1935), 3 R.I.A.A. 1609; 29 *Am.J.Int.L*. 327

[On March 22, 1929 the *I'm Alone* a rum-runner of Canadian registry was sunk on the high seas some 200 miles from the coast by the U.S. Revenue cutter the *Dexter* after a

---

[49] See W.C. Dennis, "The Sinking of The I'm Alone" (1929), 23 *Am.J.Int.L*. 351; G.G. Fitzmaurice, "The

lengthy pursuit. Pursuit began, according to the U.S. government $10^1/_2$ miles from the coast (thus within the 12 mile customs zone) and $14^1/_2$ miles according to the government of Canada. In any event, pursuit began outside the 3 mile territorial sea. The *I'm Alone* was originally sighted and followed by the *Wolcott,* also a U.S. revenue vessel.

On these facts the Arbitral Commissioners held that there was a right of hot pursuit and that pursuit had been continuous. However, the Commissioners also held that the intentional sinking of a foreign registered vessel violated both the treaty in force between the U.S.A. and Canada (U.K.) and public international law.]

THE COMMISSIONERS (Willis van Devanter and Lyman P. Duff:) ... Only questions numbered One and Three and the answers given thereto are now material. These are stated in the interim report as follows:

The question numbered one is in the following terms:

The first question is whether the Commissioners may inquire into the beneficial or ultimate ownership of the I'm Alone or of the shares of the corporation that owned the ship. If the Commissioners are authorized to make this inquiry, a further question arises as to the effect of indirect ownership and control by citizens of the United States upon the Claim; viz., whether it would be an answer to the Claim under the Convention, or whether it would go to mitigation of damages, or whether it would merely be a circumstance that should actuate the claimant Government in refraining from pressing the claim, in whole or in part.

The answer given to this question is as follows:

The Commissioners think they may inquire into the beneficial or ultimate ownership of the I'm Alone and of the shares of the corporation owning the ship; as well as into the management and control of the ship and the venture in which it was engaged; and that this may be done as a basis for considering the recommendations which they shall make. But the Commissioners reserve for further consideration the extent to which, if at all, the facts of such ownership, management and control may affect particular branches or phases of the claim presented.

The question numbered three is in the following terms:

The third question is based upon the assumption that the United States Government had the right of hot pursuit in the circumstances and was entitled to exercise the rights under Article 2 of the Convention at the time when the Dexter joined the Wolcott in the pursuit of the I'm Alone. It is also based upon the assumption that the averments set forth in paragraph eight of the Answer are true. The question is whether in the circumstances, the Government of the United States was legally justified in sinking the I'm Alone.

The answer given to this question is as follows:

On the assumptions stated in the question, the United States might, consistently with the Convention, use necessary and reasonable force for the purpose of affecting the objects of boarding, searching, seizing and bringing into port the suspected vessel; and if sinking should occur incidentally, as a result of the exercise of necessary and reasonable force

---

Case of The I'm Alone'' (1936), 17 *Br.Y.B.Int.L.* 82; and N.A.M. MacKenzie, Comment (1929), 7 *Can.Bar Rev.* 407.

for such purpose, the pursuing vessel might be entirely blameless. But the Commissioners think that, ... the admittedly intentional sinking of the suspected vessel was not justified by anything in the Convention.

The preliminary questions having been answered, the Commissioners made the following recommendations as to the future conduct of the case:

First: that the agents be instructed by their respective Governments to prepare and submit to the Commissioners separate statements setting forth in detail the contentions of their respective Governments as to the ultimate beneficial interests in the vessel and in the cargo, together with specifications of the documents and witnesses relied upon to substantiate their respective contentions:

Second: that the agents be similarly instructed to submit to the Commissioners either a joint statement or separate statements (in either case specifically itemized) of the sums which should be payable by the United States in case the Commissioners finally determine that compensation is payable by that Government.

Statements were submitted to the Commissioners pursuant to these recommendations; and, on December 28, 1934, the Commissioners convened for the purpose of hearing further evidence and oral argument touching the matters in dispute; and the hearing was concluded on January 3, 1935. The Commissioners now present their joint final report.

It will be recalled that the I'm Alone was sunk on the 22nd day of March, 1929, on the high seas, in the Gulf of Mexico, by the United States revenue cutter Dexter. By their interim report the Commissioners found that the sinking of the vessel was not justified by anything in the Convention. The Commissioners now add that it could not be justified by any principle of international law.

The vessel was a British ship of Canadian registry; after her construction she was employed for several years in rum running, the cargo being destined for illegal introduction into, and sale in the United States. In December, 1928, and during the early months of 1929, down to the sinking of the vessel on the 22nd day of March, of that year, she was engaged in carrying liquor from Belize, in British Honduras to an agreed point or points in the Gulf of Mexico, in convenient proximity to the coast of Louisiana, where the liquor was taken from her in smaller craft, smuggled into the United States, and sold there.

We find as a fact that, from September, 1928, down to the date when she was sunk, the I'm Alone, although a British ship of Canadian registry, was *de facto* owned, controlled, and at the critical times, managed, and her movements directed and her cargo dealt with and disposed of, by a group of persons acting in concert who were entirely, or nearly so, citizens of the United States, and who employed her for the purposes mentioned. The possibility that one of the group may not have been of United States nationality we regard as of no importance in the circumstances of this case.

The Commissioners consider that, in view of the facts, no compensation ought to be paid in respect of the loss of the ship or the cargo.

The act of sinking the ship, however, by officers of the United States Coast Guard, was, as we have already indicated, an unlawful act; and the Commissioners consider that the United States ought formally to acknowledge its illegality, and to apologize to His Majesty's Canadian Government therefor; and, further, that as a material amend in respect of the wrong the United States should pay the sum of $25,000 to His Majesty's Canadian Government; and they recommend accordingly.

The Commissioners have had under consideration the compensation which ought to be paid by the United States to His Majesty's Canadian Government for the benefit of the captain and members of the crew, none of whom was a party to the illegal conspiracy to smuggle liquor into the United States and sell the same there. The Commissioners recommend that compensation be paid as follows:

For the captain, John Thomas Randell, the sum of	$ 7,906.00
For John Williams, deceased, to be paid to his proper representatives	1,250.50
For Jens Jansen	1,098.00
For James Barrett	1,032.00
For William Wordsworth, deceased, to be paid to his proper representatives	907.00
For Eddie Young	999.50
For Chesley Hobbs	1,323.50
For Edward Fouchard	965.00
For Amanda Mainguy, as compensation in respect of the death of Leon Mainguy, for the benefit of herself and the and the children of Leon Mainguy (Henriette Mainguy, Jeanne Mainguy and John Mainguy) the sum of	10,185.00

NOTES

1) The articles of the 1982 Convention on the High Seas are a codification of customary international law and are virtually identical to those of the 1958 Geneva Convention on the High Seas. They represent the central core of the international law of the sea including such fundamental concepts as freedom of navigation, flag state jurisdiction and the prohibition of piracy. One change to be noted is that allowing hot pursuit to begin in the exclusive economic zone.

2) The authority of the flag state over its ships on the high seas involves both rights and duties of government. The duties in respect of marine pollution are further expanded in Part XII of the 1982 Convention dealing with the Protection and Preservation of the Marine Environment. (See *infra*.) By virtue of these rules the flag state exercises exclusive jurisdiction over persons and cargo as well as the design, crew, maintenance and navigation of the vessel. The nationality and flag of a vessel are governed by Articles 90-94, reported and discussed in Chapter 7. It is to be noted that article 97, by giving the flag state exclusive jurisdiction over an accident reverses the controversial decision of the World Court in the case of the *Steamship Lotus* (France v. Turkey), reported in Chapter 8.

3) The exclusivity of flag state jurisdiction is restricted with respect to ships engaged in piracy, slavery and drug smuggling. To a lesser degree it is also limited within the territorial sea and the E.E.Z. by Part XII of the 1982 Convention. However, despite great pressure from coastal states, including Canada, except in very special areas (see *infra*

"Protection of Marine Environment"), the primacy of the flag state in civil and criminal matters has been maintained and is still absolute with respect to military vessels. Thus, interference with a foreign ship on the high seas is closely circumscribed even when an international crime such as piracy is suspected. (See Article 110.) But exclusive flag state authority may always be relinquished by treaty, such as the Canada-United States Convention for the Preservation of the Halibut Fishery of the Northern Pacific Ocean and Bering Sea,[50] which permits fishery officers of both states to seize vessels of either country for fishing in contravention of the Convention.

4) Although pirates were driven from the shores of North America and Europe long ago, they are still a commonplace hazard to shipping around the coasts of West Africa, Indonesia and some other parts of Asia. Piracy[51] is the classic example of an offence of universal jurisdiction, that is every state may arrest and prosecute pirates apprehended on the high seas regardless of their nationality.[52] Piracy *jure gentium* is strictly defined in the Convention but individual states, who are of necessity the enforcers of the law against pirates, are not inhibited by this definition from prescribing the crime and its penalties in different terms in their national legislation. In Canada, for instance, the *Criminal Code* section 75 makes it an offence, punishable by imprisonment for life, to do "any act that, by the law of nations, is piracy." Then section 76 adds an offence, carrying fourteen years incarceration, against "piratical acts," which include stealing a Canadian ship or its cargo, causing a mutiny or counseling others to do so. However, to the extent that national prescriptions of piracy exceed international law, jurisdiction to enforce them cannot be based on the universality principle.

5) As the case of *The I'm Alone* shows, the rules in the Convention surrounding the right of hot pursuit[53] are not a complete code. Supplementation by customary international law is necessary. Yet the Convention does set some specific limits to the right. By reading together paragraphs 1, 2 and 4 of Article 111, it is clear that hot pursuit may only begin if the escaping ship has failed to stop after it has been given a visual or auditory signal, which it could reasonably have received, while it was in a marine zone of the coastal state. A radio signal is not sufficient to found the right of pursuit, even though nowadays the offending vessel is likely to carry radar equipment by which it may identify its pursuers and head for the high seas long before they can come within sight or hailing distance. It is also clear that a foreign ship may only be pursued for a violation of the laws applicable in the particular marine zone in which it was signalled to stop.

Since no statute has been passed in Canada to implement these treaty rules,[54] Canadian courts have applied the right of hot pursuit as a matter of customary international law. In doing so they have allowed a liberal right of pursuit, which at times is difficult to regard as compatible with international law. For instance, in the recent case of *R. v. Sunila and Soleyman*,[55] the arrested foreign ship had been followed continuously by a

---

[50] 1953 Can.T.S. No. 41.

[51] See B.H. Dubner, *The Law of International Sea Piracy* (1980).

[52] See the discussion of "Bases of Jurisdiction," *supra*, Chapter 8.

[53] See, generally, N.M. Poulantzas, *The Right of Hot Pursuit in International Law* (1969).

[54] Passing reference is made to pursuit in the *Customs Act*, R.S.C. 1970, c. C-40, s. 141(12).

[55] (1986), 71 N.S.R. (2d) 300 (N.S.C.A.), purportedly applying *The Ship North v. The King* (1906), 37 S.C.R. 385. See also *Fudge v. The King*, [1940] Ex.C.R. 187.

Canadian destroyer ever since its rendezvous with a shore boat inside the territorial sea to transfer its illicit cargo of drugs, but it was many miles onto the high seas before it was ever ordered to heave to. Though the court was well aware of the rules in the 1958 Geneva Convention, which in this respect are repeated verbatim in the 1982 U.N. Convention, and even regarded them, rightly, as a codification of customary laws, it held that to expect the pursuing destroyer to have signalled the fleeing ship before coming within range to prevent its escape would have been unreasonable and that the arrest was properly conducted.[56] The court also made a generous interpretation of the combination of vessels used by the drug smugglers when it declared, without discussion, that the foreign ship was a mother ship of the Canadian shore boat, even though they and their crews had different nationalities and shared no personal connections.[57]

6) What are the potential conflicts between the freedom of navigation and coastal state rights in the exclusive economic zone?

DELIMITATION PROBLEMS

The problem of delimitation of the continental shelf is as old as the concept itself. With the emergence of the exclusive economic zone, delimitation has become one of the major diplomatic and legal problems of the decade. The Truman Proclamation of 1945 speaks of delimitation "in accordance with equitable principles." The International Law Commission developed a proposal which laid considerable stress upon equidistance. It was enshrined in Article 6 of the 1958 Geneva Convention on the Continental Shelf but it met with almost equal favour and disfavour according to the geographic situation of states. As the decision in the *North Sea Continental Shelf* cases indicated, the contents of Article 6 did not become a rule of customary international law binding upon non-parties to the convention. This judgment did much to reinforce the importance of equity as the basis of delimitation, but subsequent decisions, insofar as they are capable of a principled interpretation, tend to show that equidistance and equity are not as far apart as might be thought and that in any case a host of factors (social, economic, geographic, geologic, geomorphologic, historical proportionality or general direction of the coast) are applicable to the determination of each boundary.

When the opportunity came to set down principles for delimitation at the Third United Nations Conference on the Law of the Sea, the states opposed to the equidistance rule were able to show conclusively that it could not be the basis of consensus, even though an equally large number of states, including Canada, supported retention of the contents of Article 6 in the new convention. The results of a protracted and often bitter negotiation were the two parallel Articles 74 and 83 on delimitation of the EEZ and the continental shelf respectively.

With the emergence of 200 mile fishing zones or the full EEZ it became largely

---

[56] Cp. *Gillam v. U.S.* (1928), 27 F. (2d) 296 (U.S.C.A., 4th Circ.).

[57] See *The Henry L. Marshall* (1922), 286 F. 260. Cp. *The Tenyu Maru* (1910), 4 Alaska R. 136; and *The Marjorie E. Bachman* (1925), 4 F. (2d) 405 (Dist.Ct.Mass.).

theoretical to envisage delimitation of the continental shelf alone or separate fishing and continental shelf boundaries. The first major delimitation dispute subsequent to 1982, the Gulf of Maine case between Canada and the U.S.A., involved resolution of a "single maritime boundary" rather than separate shelf and fishing zone disputes. The range of relevant factors in these circumstances is clearly greater but it is difficult to identify them all or to assess their respective weight.

The Truman Proclamation
Reported *supra*, in the Section on the "Continental Shelf."

Geneva Convention on the Continental Shelf
(1958), 499 U.N.T.S. 311

Article 6

1. Where the same continental shelf is adjacent to the territories of two or more States whose coasts are opposite each other, the boundary of the continental shelf appertaining to such States shall be determined by agreement between them. In the absence of agreement, and unless another boundary line is justified by special circumstances, the boundary is the median line, every point of which is equidistant from the nearest points of the baselines from which the breadth of the territorial sea of each State is measured.

2. Where the same continental shelf is adjacent to the territories of two adjacent States, the boundary of the continental shelf shall be determined by agreement between them. In the absence of agreement, and unless another boundary line is justified by special circumstances, the boundary shall be determined by application of the principle of equidistance from the nearest points of the baselines from which the breadth of the territorial sea of each State is measured.

3. In delimiting the boundaries of the continental shelf, any lines which are drawn in accordance with the principles set out in paragraphs 1 and 2 of this article should be defined with reference to charts and geographical features as they exist at a particular date, and reference should be made to fixed permanent identifiable points on the land.

United Nations Convention on the Law of the Sea
Article 74/83

1. The delimitation of the exclusive economic zone/continental shelf between States with opposite or adjacent coasts shall be effected by agreement on the basis of international law, as referred to in Article 38 of the Statute of the International Court of Justice, in order to achieve an equitable solution.

2. If no agreement can be reached within a reasonable period of time, the States concerned shall resort to the procedures provided for in Part XV. [Settlement of Disputes]

3. Pending agreement as provided for in paragraph 1, the States concerned, in a spirit of understanding and co-operation, shall make every effort to enter into provisional arrangements of a practical nature and, during this transitional period, not to jeopardize or hamper the reaching of the final agreement. Such arrangements shall be without prejudice to the final delimitation.

4. Where there is an agreement in force between the States concerned, questions relating to the delimitation of the exclusive economic zone/continental shelf shall be determined in accordance with the provisions of that agreement.

North Sea Continental Shelf Cases
Federal Republic of Germany v. Denmark and v. Netherlands
[1969] I.C.J. Rep. 3, reported in Chapter 3

English Channel Arbitration[58]
France v. United Kingdom
(1979), 18 *Int. Leg. Mat.* 397

[This arbitration involved the delimitation of the continental shelves of France and the United Kingdom in the Channel and the adjacent Atlantic Ocean. It was rendered difficult by the presence of the British Channel Islands close to France and the Scilly Isles off the south west tip of England, as well as the changing characterization of the seabed as between opposite coastlines in the Channel but adjacent coasts in the Atlantic. The dispute fell to be decided under the Geneva Convention Article 6.]

THE COURT OF ARBITRATION: ...

70. The Court does not overlook that under Article 6 the equidistance principle ultimately possesses an obligatory force which it does not have in the same measure under the rules of customay law; for Article 6 makes the application of the equidistance principle a matter of treaty obligation for Parties to the Convention. But the combined character of the equidistance-special circumstances rule means that the obligation to apply the equidistance principle is always one qualified by the condition "unless another boundary line is justified by special circumstances." ... In short, the role of the "special circumstances" condition in Article 6 is to ensure an equitable delimitation; and the combined "equidistance-special circumstances rule," in effect, gives particular expression to a general norm that, failing agreement, the boundary between States abutting on the same continental shelf is to be determined on equitable principles. In addition, Article 6 neither defines "special circumstances" nor lays down the criterion by which it is to be assessed whether any given circumstances justify a boundary line other than the equidistance line. Consequently, even under Article 6 the question whether the use of the equidistance principle or some other method is appropriate for achieving an equitable delimitation is

---

[58] See D.M. McRae, "Delimitation of the Continental Shelf between the United Kingdom and France: The Channel Arbitration" (1977), 15 *Can.Y.B.Int.L.* 173.

very much a matter of appreciation in the light of the geographical and other circumstances. In other words, even under Article 6 it is the geographical and other circumstances of any given case which indicate and justify the use of the equidistance method as the means of achieving an equitable solution rather than the inherent quality of the method as a legal norm of delimitation. ...

103. In the English channel, leaving aside the particular situation resulting from the Channel Islands being located off the French coast, the geographical and the legal frame of reference for determining the course of the boundary of the continental shelf is patently that of a delimitation between "opposite" States. ... the Parties themselves are in accord on this point; and, the Channel Islands region apart, they are also agreed that within the English Channel the boundary should, in principle, be the median line. The Court has already indicated that this is also its own opinion. The effects of irregularities in the coastline of each State are, broadly, offset by the effects of irregularities in the coastline of the other, and a median line boundary will thus result in a generally equitable delimitation as between the Parties. ...

[The Court then rejected the U.K. submission that the presence of a geographical feature known as the Hurd Deep justified a different boundary.]

108. In any event, having regard to the essential continuity of the continental shelf in the Channel and the Atlantic region, there does not seem to be any legal ground for discarding the equidistance or any other method of delimiting the boundary in favour simply of such a feature as the Hurd Deep-Hurd Deep Fault Zone. Should the equidistance line not appear to the Court to constitute the appropriate boundary in any area, it will be because some geographical feature amounts to a "special circumstances" justifying another boundary under Article 6 or, by rendering the equidistance line inequitable, calls under customary law for the use of some other method. It follows that any alternative boundary would have either to be one justified by the "special circumstances" or one apt to correct the inequity caused by the particular geographical feature. But the axis of the Hurd Deep-Hurd Deep Fault Zone is placed where it is simply as a fact of nature, and there is no intrinsic reason why a boundary along that axis should be the boundary which is justified by the special circumstance under Article 6 or which, under customary law, is needed to remedy the particular inequity. ...

145. The next task of the Court is to determine the boundary (or boundaries) in the Channel Islands region, ...

146. In this region the Parties remain agreed that the geographical and legal framework for determining the boundary is one of States the coast of which are opposite each other; and that, in consequence, the boundary should, in principle, be the median line. They are, however, in sharp disagreement as to the role which should be allowed to the coasts of the Channel Islands as coasts of the United Kingdom "opposite" to those of France. The French Republic maintains that in this part of the Channel, the relevant "opposite" coasts are those of mainlands of France and the United Kingdom; and that the Channel Islands should be treated as a separate territory located within the continental shelf of the French mainland. The United Kingdom, on the other hand, insists that in this part of the English Channel the Channel Islands themselves constitute the relevant "opposite" coast of the United Kingdom for the purpose of delimiting the median line. As a result, the boundaries advocated by the Parties in this region bear almost no relation to each other, except in the narrow waters to the east and south of the Channel Islands where the delimitation of the boundary falls outside the Court's competence. ...

191. The continental shelf of the Channel Islands and of the mainlands of France and of the United Kingdom, in law, appertains to each of them as being the natural prolongation of its land territory under the sea. The physical continuity of the continental shelf of the English Channel means that geographically it may be said to be a natural prolongation of each one of the territories which abut upon it. The question for the Court to decide, however, is what areas of continental shelf are to be considered as *legally* the natural prolongation of the Channel Islands rather than of the mainland of France. In international law, as the United Kingdom emphasized in the pleadings, the concept of the continental shelf is a juridical concept which connotes the natural prolongation under the sea not of a continent or geographical land mass but of the land territory of each State. And the very fact that in international law the continental shelf is a juridical concept means that its scope and the conditions for its application are not determined exclusively by the physical facts of geography but also by legal rules. Moreover, it is clear both from the insertion of the "special circumstances" provision in Article 6 and from the emphasis on "equitable principles" in customary law that the force of the cardinal principle of "natural prolongation of territory" is not absolute, but may be subject to qualification in particular situations.

192. Accordingly, in the opinion of the Court, the principle of natural prolongation of territory cannot be said to require that the continental shelf to the north and north-west of the Channel Islands should be considered as automatically and necessarily appurtenant to them rather than to the French Republic. The United Kingdom itself ... does not contest that in the application of the equidistance-special circumstances rule there may be some difference in the treatment of islands by reason of their geographical situations, size and importance. Nor, in particular, does it contest the possibility of pleading special circumstances justifying a boundary other than the median line where islets or small islands belonging to one country are nearer to the coast of an opposite country. Yet, if the force of the principle of natural prolongation of territory were absolute, a small island would block the natural prolongation of the territory of the nearby mainland in the same way, if not always to the same extent, as a larger island. The question of the appurtenance to the Channel Islands of the areas of continental shelf extending to their north and north-west is not therefore resolved merely by referring to the principle of natural prolongation of territory.

193. At the same time, the theory advanced by Counsel for the French Republic to reconcile its claim to those areas with the principle of natural prolongation of territory is altogether unconvincing. This explanation ... that the natural prolongation of France's mainland in some way turns around the Channel Island, simply states the result which would follow from the Court's acceptance of the French Republic's claim; it does nothing to reconcile that claim with the right of the Channel Islands also to the application of the principle of the natural prolongation of their territories under the sea. Similarly, the general geological argument advanced by the French Republic that the Channel Islands region, including the Channel Islands themselves, form part of the armorican structure of the French mainland does nothing to resolve the problem. It, in effect, begs the question by simply passing over the fact that the Channel Islands themselves have their own individual existence and are under the sovereignty of the United Kingdom, not the French Republic.

194. The true position, in the opinion of the Court, is that the principle of natural prolongation of territory is neither to be set aside nor treated as absolute in a case where islands belonging to one State are situated on continental shelf which would otherwise constitute a natural prolongation of the territory of another State. The application of that principle in such a case, as in other cases concerning the delimitation of the continental shelf, has to be appreciated in the light of all the relevant geographical and other circumstances. When the question is whether areas of continental shelf, which geologically may be considered a natural prolongation of the territories of two States, appertain to one State rather than to the other, the legal rules constituting the juridical concept of the continental shelf take over and determine the question. Consequently, in these cases the effect to be given to the principle of natural prolongation of the coastal State's land territory is always dependent not only on the particular geographical and other circumstances but also on any relevant considerations of law and equity.

195. The legal rules to be applied in the Channel Islands region, the Court has held, are those of customary international law, rather than of Article 6 of the Convention. Under customary law, the method adopted for delimiting the boundary must, while applying the principle of natural prolongation of territory, also ensure that the resulting delimitation of the boundary accords with equitable principles. In other words, the question is whether the Channel Islands should be given the full benefit of the application of the principle of natural prolongation in the areas to their north and north-west or whether their situation close to the mainland of France requires, on equitable grounds, some modification of the application of the principle in those areas. In the opinion of the Court, the doctrine of the equality of States which, *inter alia*, the French Republic invokes as justifying a curtailment of the continental shelf attributable to the Channel Islands, cannot be considered as constituting such an equitable ground. The doctrine of the equality of States, applied generally to the delimitation of the continental shelf, would have vast implications for the division of the continental shelf among the States of the world, implications which have been rejected by a majority of States and which would involve, on a huge scale, that refashioning of geography repudiated in the *North Sea Continental Shelf* cases. Any ground of equity, the Court considers, is rather to be looked for in the particular circumstances of the present case and in the particular equality of the two States in their geographical relation to the continental shelf of the Channel.

196. In paragraph 131, the Court has already drawn attention to the approximate equality of the mainland coastlines of the Parties on either side of the English Channel, and to the resulting equality of their geographical relation to the continental shelf of the Channel, if the Channel Islands themselves are left out of account. The presence of these British islands close to the French coast, if they are given full effect in delimiting the continental shelf, will manifestly result in a substantial diminution of the area of continental shelf which would otherwise accrue to the French Republic. This fact by itself appears to the Court to be, *prima facie*, a circumstance creative of inequity and calling for a method of delimitation that in some measure redresses the inequity. If this conclusion is tested by applying the equidistance-special circumstances rule of Article 6, instead of the rules of customary law, it appears to the Court that the presence of the Channel

Islands close to the French coast must be considered, *prima facie*, as constituting a "special circumstance" justifying a delimitation other than the median line proposed by the United Kingdom.

197. The Court refers to the presence of the Channel Islands close to the French coast as constituting a circumstance creative of inequity, and a "special circumstance" within the meaning of Article 6, merely *prima facie*, because a delimitation, to be "equitable" or "justified," must be so in relation to both Parties and in the light of all the relevant circumstances. The United Kingdom, moreover, maintains that the specific features of the Channel Islands region militate positively in favour of the delimitation it proposes. It invokes the particular character of the Channel Islands as not rocks or islets but populous islands of certain political and economic importance; it emphasizes the close ties between the islands and the United Kingdom and the latter's responsibility for their defence and security; and it invokes these as calling for the continental shelf of the islands to be linked to that of the United Kingdom. Above all, it stresses that at best it is only in the open waters of the English Channel to their west and north that they have any possibility of an appreciable area of continental shelf. In the light of all these considerations, it submits that to divide this area to the west and north of the islands between the Channel Islands and the French Republic by the median line which it proposes does not involve any "disproportion or exaggeration."

198. The Court accepts the equitable considerations invoked by the United Kingdom as carrying a certain weight; and, in its view, they invalidate the proposal of the French Republic restricting the Channel Islands to a six-mile enclave around the islands, consisting of a three-mile zone of continental shelf added to their three-mile zone of territorial sea. They do not, however, appear to the court sufficient to justify the disproportion or remove the imbalance in the delimitation of the continental shelf as between the United Kingdom and the French Republic which adoption of the United Kingdom's proposal would involve. The Court therefore concludes that the specific features of the Channel Islands region call for an intermediate solution that effects a more appropriate and a more equitable balance between the respective claims and interests of the Parties.

199. The Court considers that the primary element in the present problem is the fact that the Channel Islands region forms part of the English Channel, throughout the whole length of which the Parties face each other as opposite States having almost equal coastlines. The problem of the Channel Islands apart, the continental shelf boundary in the Channel indicated by both customary law and Article 6, as the Court has previously stated, is a median line running from end to end of the Channel. The existence of the Channel Islands close to the French coast, if permitted to divert the course of that mid-Channel median line, effects a radical distortion of the boundary creative of inequity. The case is quite different from that of small islands on the right side of or close to the median line, and it is also quite different from the case where numerous islands stretch out one after another long distances from the mainland. The precedents of semi-enclaves, arising out of such cases, which are invoked by the United Kingdom, do not, therefore, seem to the Court to be in point. The Channel Islands are not only "on the wrong side" of the mid-Channel median line but wholly detached geographically from the United Kingdom.

200. The case of St. Pierre et Miquelon, although it clearly presents some analogies with the present case, also differs from it in important respects. First, that case is not one of islands situated in a channel between the coasts of opposite States, so that no question arises there of a delimitation between States, whose coastlines are in an approximately equal relation to the continental shelf to be delimited. Secondly, there being nothing to the east of St. Pierre et Miquelon except the open waters of the Atlantic Ocean, there is more scope for redressing inequities than in the narrow waters of the English Channel. Even so, it appears from the *Relevé des Conclusions* that a delimitation according no more than a 12-mile zone of territorial sea to St. Pierre et Miquelon has been agreed between the French Republic and Canada. True, it also appears that this agreement includes a reservation of certain special privileges for St. Pierre et Miquelon; but for these special privileges there is a counterpart in the considerable extent of continental shelf left to Canada in the Atlantic to seawards of the islands.

201. In the actual circumstances of the Channel Islands region, where the extent of the continental shelf is comparatively modest and the scope for adjusting the equities correspondingly small, the Court considers that the situation demands a twofold solution. First, in order to maintain the appropriate balance between the two States in relation to the continental shelf as riparian States of the Channel with approximately equal coastlines, the Court decides that the primary boundary between them shall be a median line, ... In the light of the Court's previous decisions regarding the course of the boundary in the English Channel, this means that throughout the whole length of the Channel comprised within the arbitration area the primary boundary of the continental shelf will be a mid-Channel median line. In delimiting its course in the Channel Islands region, ... the Channel Islands themselves are to be disregarded, since their continental shelf must be the subject of a second and separate delimitation.

202. The second part of the solution is to delimit a second boundary establishing, *vis-à-vis* the Channel Islands, the southern limit of the continental shelf held by the Court to be appurtenant to the French Republic in this region to the south of the mid-Channel median line. This second boundary must not, in the opinion of the Court, be so drawn as to allow the continental shelf of the French Republic to encroach upon the established 12-mile fishery zone of the Channel Islands. The Court therefore further decides that this boundary shall be drawn at a distance of 12 nautical miles from the established baselines of the territorial sea of the Channel Islands. The effect will be to accord to the French Republic a substantial band of continental shelf in mid-Channel which is continuous with its continental shelf to the east and west of the Channel Islands region; and at the same time to leave to the Channel Islands, to their north and to their west, a zone of seabed and subsoil extending 12 nautical miles from the baselines of the two Bailiwicks. The result, so far as the Channel Islands are concerned, is to enclose them in an enclave formed, to their north and west, by the boundary of the 12-mile zone just described by the Court and, to their east, south and south-west by the boundary between them and the coasts of Normandy and Brittany, the exact course of which it is outside the competence of the Court to specify.

[With regard to the Atlantic region to the west of the Channel, the Court generally applied the equidistance principle as between adjacent states, but made a partial exception on account of the Scilly Isles.]

248. The Court considers that the method of delimitation which it adopts for the

Atlantic region must be one that has relation to the coasts of the Parties actually abutting on the continental shelf of that region. Essentially, these are the coasts of Finistère and Ushant on the French side and the coasts of Cornwall and the Scilly Isles on the United Kingdom side. The island of Ushant not only forms part, geologically, of the land mass of France but lies no more than ten nautical miles from the French coast within the territorial sea of the French mainland. Indeed, the island forms one of the links in the system of straight baselines along the French coast established by the French Republic in 1964. The Scilly Isles likewise form part of the land mass of the United Kingdom and, although some 21 miles distant from the mainland, they are unquestionably islands offshore of the United Kingdom which, both geographically and politically, form part of its territory. In fact, the existing 12-mile fishery zones of the mainland and of the Scilly Isles merge into one and, if the United Kingdom exercises the right which it claims to establish a 12-mile territorial sea, the same will be the case with their territorial sea. Both Ushant and the Scilly Isles are, moreover, islands of a certain size and populated; and, in the view of the Court, they both constitute natural geographical facts of the Atlantic region which cannot be disregarded in delimiting the continental shelf boundary without "refashioning geography." The problem therefore is, without disregarding Ushant and the Scillies, to find a method of remedying in an appropriate measure the distorting effect on the course of the boundary of the more westerly position of the Scillies and the disproportion which it produces in the areas of continental shelf accuring to the French Republic and the United Kingdom.

249. The court notes that in a large proportion of the delimitations known to it, where a particular geographical feature has influenced the course of a continental shelf boundary, the method of delimitation adopted has been some modification or variant of the equidistance principle rather than its total rejection. In the present instance, the problem also arises precisely from the distorting effect of a geographical feature in circumstances in which the line equidistant from the coasts of the two States would otherwise constitute the appropriate boundary. Consequently, it seems to the Court to be in accord not only with the legal rules governing the continental shelf but also with State practice to seek the solution in a method modifying or varying the equidistance method rather than to have recourse to a wholly different criterion of delimitation. The appropriate method, in the opinion of the Court, is to take account of the Scilly Isles as part of the coastline of the United Kingdom but to give them less than their full effect in applying the equidistance method. Just as it is not the function of equity in the delimitation of the continental shelf completely to refashion geography, so it is also not the function of equity to create a situation of complete equity where nature and geography have established an inequity. Equity does not, therefore, call for coasts, the relation of which to the continental shelf is not equal, to be treated as having completely equal effects. What equity calls for is an appropriate abatement of the disproportionate effects of a considerable projection on to the Atlantic continental shelf of a somewhat attenuated portion of the coast of the United Kingdom. ...

251. A number of examples are to be found in State practice of delimitations in which only partial effect has been given to offshore islands situated outside the territorial sea of the mainland. The method adopted has varied in response to the varying geographical and other circumstances of the particular cases; but in one instance, at least, the method employed was to give half, instead of full, effect to the offshore island in delimiting the equidistance line. The method of giving half effect consists in delimiting the line equidistant between the two coasts, first, without the use of the offshore island as a base-point and, secondly, with its use as a base-point; a boundary giving half-effect to the island is then the line drawn mid-way between those two equidistance lines. This method appears to the Court to be an appropriate and practical method of abating the disproportion and inequity which otherwise results from giving full effect to the Scilly Isles as a base-point for determining the course of the boundary.

Saint-Pierre and Miquelon

The differences between Canada and France over the delimitation of the continental shelf of Saint-Pierre and Miquelon may be much influenced by the award in the *English Channel Arbitration* insofar as it deals with the rights of islands. These two French islands are located less than 9.5 nautical miles west and southwest of Newfoundland's Burin Peninsula. Negotiations[59] between Canada and France on the delimitation of the continental shelf off Newfoundland began in 1967. In 1978, after the two countries had extended their fishing zones to 200 nautical miles, the negotiations were expanded to include fisheries jurisdiction as well.

The French position since 1978 has been that Saint-Pierre and Miquelon are entitled, in principle, to a full 200-mile exclusive economic zone, and that the maritime boundary with Canada is to be determined on the basis of equidistance measured from the nearest points on the coasts of the two islands and of Newfoundland and Nova Scotia. This would result in a total maritime zone for Saint Pierre and Miquelon of approximately 13,500 square nautical miles. Canada's position has been that France is entitled in law to no more than a 12-mile territorial sea. The boundary negotiations have been complicated by the fact that any agreement regarding an EEZ for Saint-Pierre and Miquelon could have a significant impact on Canadian fisheries allocations to France and because of the possibility of exploiting hydrocarbons in portions of the disputed area.

Since January 1984 there has been agreement that, in order to maintain a favourable atmosphere for the boundary negotiations, both countries would exercise mutual restraint and would forego the boarding and inspection of the other's vessels in the disputed area. Nevertheless, there have been difficulties in their relations arising from Canadian concern that France has been overfishing the resources of the area. These differences led to an arbitration in 1986 over the interpretation of the Canada-France Agreement on Mutual Fishing Relations, which has governed their reciprocal fishing rights since 1972. See the Agreement and the note on the *La Bretagne* arbitration in the next Section on ''Fisheries.''

After twenty years of fruitless negotiations both countries seem to have accepted that agreement is unattainable, for in January 1987 they concluded a treaty by which the question of a maritime boundary will be submitted to third party adjudication. Current negotiations are concerned with the form of the tribunal and the questions that will be put to it. Separate negotiations are also proceeding concurrently over interim fish quotas

---

[59] As described in a memorandum of the Department of External Affairs on *Current Issues of International Law of Particular Importance to Canada* (October 1986), at 12.

for France through 1991, by which time a boundary decision is expected to have been attained.

Should Saint-Pierre and Miquelon be awarded no more continental shelf than the Channel Islands? Or can it be argued that their geography gives them a right to claim an extensive continental shelf far out to sea on the basis of equidistance? In light of the history of negotiations, it seems unlikely that delimitation of the continental shelf will occur without reference to the superjacent waters. How might a single maritime boundary be constructed? See the following case on the *Gulf of Maine* for guidance.

Gulf of Maine Case[60]
Canada v. United States
[1984] I.C.J. Rep. 246; 23 *Int. Leg. Mat.* 1197

[Canada and the United States went to the International Court in 1981 when it became clear that the two governments were unable to effect a joint fisheries management regime in the Gulf of Maine after their respective extensions of 200 mile fishing zones in 1976 and 1977. The only solution was to undertake national regulation on each side of a maritime boundary. This case is of special interest as it was the first involving a request to the Court to determine a "single maritime boundary" involving both shelf and fisheries jurisdiction.]

THE CHAMBER OF THE COURT: ...

79. ... The time has ... come to begin consideration of the problem of ascertaining the rules of law, in the international legal order, which govern the matter at issue in the present case. In the Chamber's opinion, the association of the terms "rules" and "principles" is no more than the use of a dual expression to convey one and the same idea, since in this context "principles" clearly means principles of law, that is, it also includes rules of international law in whose case the use of the term "principles" may be justified because of their more general and more fundamental character. ...

81. In a matter of this kind, international law—and in this respect the Chamber has logically to refer primarily to customary international law—can of its nature only provide a few basic legal principles, which lay down guidelines to be followed with a view to an essential objective. It cannot also be expected to specify the equitable criteria to be applied or the practical, often technical, methods to be used for attaining that objective—which remain simply criteria and methods even where they are also, in a different sense, called "principles." Although the practice is still rather sparse, owing to the relative newness of the question, it too is there to demonstrate that each specific case is, in the final analysis, different from all the others, that it is monotypic and that, more often than not, the most appropriate criteria, and the method or combination of methods most likely to yield a result consonant with what the law indicates, can only be determined in relation to each particular case and its specific characteristics. This precludes the possibility of

---

[60] L.H. Legault and D.M. McRae, "The Gulf of Maine Case" (1984), 22 *Can.Y.B.Int.L.* 267

those conditions arising which are necessary for the formation of principles and rules of customary law giving specific provisions for subjects like those just mentioned. ...

[The Chamber then reviewed briefly the Geneva Convention on the Continental Shelf Article 6 and its own jurisprudence on delimitation.]

94. Turning ... to the proceedings of the Third United Nations Conference on the Law of the Sea and the final result of that Conference, the Chamber notes in the first place that the Convention adopted at the end of the Conference has not yet come into force and that a number of States do not appear inclined to ratify it. This, however, in no way detracts from the consensus reached on large portions of the instrument and, above all, cannot invalidate the observation that certain provisions of the Convention, concerning the continental shelf and the exclusive economic zone, which may, in fact, be relevant to the present case, were adopted without any objections. The United States, in particular, in 1983, that is to say after the Special Agreement had come into force, proclaimed an economic zone on the basis of Part V of the 1982 Convention. This proclamation was accompanied by a statement by the President to the effect that in that respect the Convention generally confirmed existing rules of international law. Canada, which has not at present made a similar proclamation, has for its part also recognized the legal significance of the nature and purpose of the new 200-mile regime. This concordance of views is worthy of note, even though the present Judgment is not directed to the delimitation of the exclusive economic zone as such. In the Chamber's opinion, these provisions, even if in some respects they bear the mark of the compromise surrounding their adoption, may nevertheless be regarded as consonant at present with general international law on the question.

95. In this connection, attention should be drawn to the identical definition, in Article 74, paragraph 1, and Article 83, paragraph 1, relating respectively to the exclusive economic zone and to the continental shelf, of the rule of international law respecting delimitation. That identical definition is as follows:

The delimitation of [the exclusive economic zone] [the continental shelf] between States with opposite or adjacent coasts shall be effected by agreement on the basis of international law, as referred to in Article 38 of the Statute of the International Court of Justice, in order to achieve an equitable solution.

It is thus limited to expressing the need for settlement of the problem by agreement and recalling the obligation to achieve an equitable solution. Although the text is singularly concise it serves to open the door to continuation of the development effected in this field by international case law.

96. It should be noted that the symmetry of the two texts, relating to the delimitation of the continental shelf and of the exclusive economic zone, is most interesting in a case like the present one, where a single boundary line is to be drawn both for the sea-bed and for the superjacent fishery zone, which is included in the exclusive economic zone concept. The identity of the language which is employed, even though limited of course to the determination of the relevant principles and rules of international law, is particularly significant.

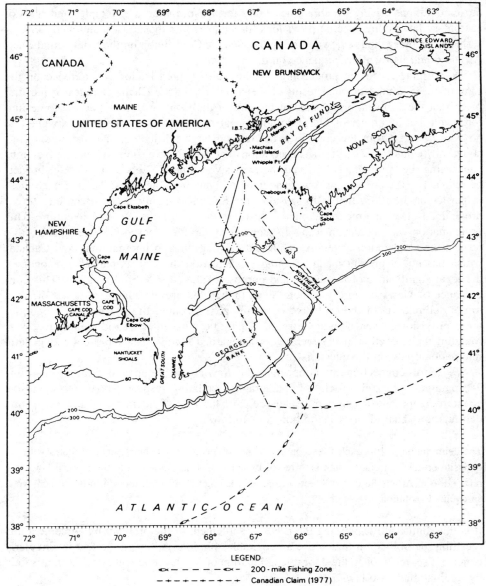

LEGEND

⊶– – – – – –⊶   200 - mile Fishing Zone
–·–+–+–+–+–+   Canadian Claim (1977)
–··—··—··—··—   United States Claim (1977)
–·—··—·—··—·—   Canadian Claim (1979)
– – – – – – –   United States Claim (1982)
————————   Boundary Drawn by the Chamber

Source: (1984), 22 *Can.Y.B.Int.L.* 277

97. The Chamber has now to assess the respective positions of the Parties in the present dispute in the light of the findings that have so far been made.

98. While stressing that, unfortunately, the points on which they disagreed were more numerous than those on which they agreed, the Parties were at pains to state, when considering the ''rules and principles of international law'' which, they held, should govern maritime delimitations, that they were at one in believing in the existence of a ''fundamental norm'' of international law. According to them, this norm must apply to any delimitation and, *a fortiori*, to the drawing of a single maritime boundary like that sought in the Gulf of Maine area.

99. According to Canada's definition, the ''fundamental norm'' in question requires that this course be

determined according to the applicable law, in conformity with equitable principles, having regard to all relevant circumstances, in order to achieve an equitable result.

According to the United States definition, which recalls those in the Court's Judgments of 1969 and 1982,

the delimitation of a single maritime boundary requires the application of equitable principles, taking account of all circumstances prevailing in the area concerned, in order to achieve an equitable solution.

While the difference apparent at first sight due to the absence in the United States definition of the words ''according to the applicable law'' is not negligible, the oral arguments have shown that it is in fact unimportant, since the United States stated explicitly that it too believed that delimitation should be effected on the basis of the applicable principles and rules of international law.

100. The common conclusion of the Parties as to the ''fundamental norm'' governing, in their opinion, the question of maritime delimitations seems, therefore, to be closely related to the conclusion reached by analysis of international case law and also, in the end, to that arrived at by the Third Conference on the Law of the Sea. ...

[The Chamber then examined each party's contentions as to specific rules of law within the ''fundamental norm,'' but rejected all of them. Canada argued that title to a shelf or zone is conferred on a state by reason of its adjacency to the coast but the Chamber held that adjacency is only a necessary physical condition and not a legal principle. The United States hypothesized a system of primary and secondary coastlines which the Chamber stigmatized as unacceptable both in geography and in law.]

110. Each Party's reasoning is in fact based on a false premise. The error lies precisely in searching general international law for, as it were, a set of rules which are not there. This observation applies particularly to certain ''principles'' advanced by the Parties as constituting well-established rules of law, e.g., the idea advocated by Canada that a single maritime boundary should ensure the preservation of existing fishing patterns which are vital to the coastal communities in the area concerned, or the idea advocated by the United States that such a boundary should make it possible to ensure the optimum conservation and management of living resources and at the same time reduce the potential for future disputes between the Parties. One could add to these the ideas of "non-encroachment" upon the coasts of another State or of "no cutting-off" of the seaward projection of the coasts of another State, and others which the Parties put forward in turn, which may in given circumstances constitute equitable criteria, provided, however, that no attempt is made to raise them to the status of established rules endorsed by customary international law.

111. A body of detailed rules is not to be looked for in customary international law which in fact comprises a limited set of norms for ensuring the co-existence and vital co-operation of the members of the international community, together with a set of customary rules whose presence in the *opinio juris* of States can be tested by induction based on the analysis of a sufficiently extensive and convincing practice, and not by deduction from preconceived ideas. It is therefore unrewarding, especially in a new and still unconsolidated field like that involving the quite recent extension of the claims of States to areas which were until yesterday zones of the high seas, to look to general international law to provide a ready-made set of rules that can be used for solving any delimitation problems that arise. A more useful course is to seek a better formulation of the fundamental norm, on which the Parties were fortunate enough to be agreed, and whose existence in the legal convictions not only of the Parties to the present dispute, but of all States, is apparent from an examination of the realities of international legal relations.

112. The Chamber therefore wishes to conclude this review of the rules of international law on the question to which the dispute between Canada and the United States relates by attempting a more complete and, in its opinion, more precise reformulation of the "fundamental norm" already mentioned. For this purpose it will, *inter alia*, draw also upon the definition of the "actual rules of law ... which govern the delimitation of adjacent continental shelves—that is to say, rules binding upon States for all delimitations" which was given by the Court in its 1969 Judgment in the *North Sea Continental Shelf* cases (*I.C.J. Reports 1969*, at 46-47, para. 85). What general international law prescribes in every maritime delimitation between neighbouring States could therefore be defined as follows:

(1) No maritime delimitation between States with opposite or adjacent coasts may be effected unilaterally by one of those States. Such delimitation must be sought and effected by means of an agreement, following negotiations conducted in good faith and with the genuine intention of achieving a positive result. Where, however, such agreement cannot be achieved, delimitation should be effected by recourse to a third party possessing the necessary competence.

(2) In either case, delimitation is to be effected by the application of equitable criteria and by the use of practical methods capable of ensuring, with regard to the geographic configuration of the area and other relevant circumstances, an equitable result. ...

113. ... The Chamber must now proceed to consider these equitable criteria and the practical methods which are in principle applicable in the actual delimitation process. ...

115. The starting point for this analysis may once again be an examination of the 1958 Convention on the Continental Shelf, more specifically of the second sentence of each of paragraphs 1 and 2 of Article 6 which, as we have seen, do not, like the first sentence, enunciate a principle or rule of international law, but contemplate, *inter alia*, the use of a particular practical method for the actual implementation of the delimitation process. As already stated, this method employs a single technique for continental shelf delimitation, but in the form of a median line in maritime areas between opposite coasts, and a lateral equidistance line where the coasts of the two States are adjacent. This method is inspired by and derives from a particular equitable criterion: namely, that the equitable solution, at least prima facie, is an equal division of the areas of overlap of the continental shelves of the two litigant States. The applicability of this method is, however, subject to the condition that there are no special circumstances in the case which would make that criterion inequitable, by showing such division to be unreasonable and so entailing recourse to a different method or methods or, at the very least, appropriate correction of the effect produced by the application of the first method.

116. In the light of these explanations the question therefore arises whether the fact (already noted by the Chamber) that the 1958 Convention on the Continental Shelf is in force between the Parties does or does not make it obligatory to use, for the delimitation requested in the present case, the method specified in Article 6 of that Convention and, by implication, the application of the criterion on which it is based.

117. No doubts have been expressed on either side as to the fact that both Parties regard themselves as bound by the Convention to which they have both acceded.

118. The Chamber therefore takes the view that if a question as to the delimitation of the continental shelf only had arisen between the two States, there would be no doubt as to the mandatory application of the method prescribed in Article 6 of the Convention, always subject, of course, to the condition that recourse is to be had to another method or combination of methods where special circumstances so require.

119. The purpose of the present proceedings is not, however, to obtain a delimitation of the continental shelf alone, as it might have been if they had taken place prior to the adoption by the two Parties of an exclusive fishery zone and the consequent emergence of the idea of delimitation by a single line. Their purpose is—and both Parties have abundantly emphasized the fact—to draw a single delimitation line for both the continental shelf and the superjacent fishery zone. It is doubtful whether a treaty obligation which is in terms confined to the delimitation of the continental shelf can be extended, in a manner that would manifestly go beyond the limits imposed by the strict criteria governing the interpretation of treaty instruments, to a field which is evidently much greater, unquestionably heterogeneous, and accordingly fundamentally different. Apart from this formal, but important, consideration, there is the more substantive point that such an interpretation would, in the final analysis, make the maritime water mass overlying the continental shelf a mere accessory of that shelf. Such a result would be just as unacceptable as the converse result produced by simply extending to the continental shelf the application of a method of delimitation adopted for the "water column" only and its fish resources.

120. In this connection, the Chamber would also observe that it is not possible to employ, in refutation of the foregoing, the argument that the method contemplated by Article 6 of the Convention on the Continental Shelf is also provided for, in similar terms, in Article 12 and Article 24, paragraph 3, of the Convention of the same date on the Territorial Sea and the Contiguous Zone. The situation of the territorial sea and the contiguous zone, conceived as subject to the sovereignty of the coastal State, or subject to the exercise of customs controls and similar measures, intended to prevent violations of its territorial sovereignty, cannot be treated as an analogy. There is nothing here which is comparable with the reservation of the exclusive rights of exploitation of resources of a maritime area extending to 200 miles; there is therefore nothing which could justify the idea of an extension thereto of criteria and delimitation methods expressly contemplated for the narrow strip of sea defined for a quite different purpose. ...

157. There has been no systematic definition of the equitable criteria that may be taken into consideration for an international maritime delimitation, and this would in any event be difficult *a priori*, because of their highly variable adaptability to different concrete situations. Codification efforts have left this field untouched. Such criteria have however been mentioned in the arguments advanced by the parties in cases concerning the determination of continental shelf boundaries, and in the judicial or arbitral decisions in those cases. There is, for example, the criterion expressed by the classic formula that the land dominates the sea; the criterion advocating, in cases where no special circumstances require correction thereof, the equal division of the areas of overlap of the maritime and submarine zones appertaining to the respective coasts of neighbouring States; the criterion that, whenever possible, the seaward extension of a State's coast should not encroach upon areas that are too close to the coast of another State; the criterion of preventing, as far as possible, any cut-off of the seaward projection of the coast or of part of the coast of either of the States concerned; and the criterion whereby, in certain circumstances, the appropriate consequences may be drawn from any inequalities in the extent of the coasts of two States into the same area of delimitation.

158. With regard to these and other possible criteria, the Chamber does not think it would be useful to undertake a more or less complete enumeration in the abstract of the criteria that are theoretically conceivable, or an evaluation, also in the abstract, of their greater or lesser degree of equitableness. As the Chamber has emphasized a number of times, their equitableness or otherwise can only be assessed in relation to the circumstances of each case, and for one and the same criterion it is quite possible to arrive at different, or even opposite, conclusions in different cases. The essential fact to bear in mind is, as the Chamber has stressed, that the criteria in question are not themselves rules of law and therefore mandatory in the different situations, but "equitable," or even "reasonable," criteria, and that what international law requires is that recourse be had in each case to the criterion, or the balance of different criteria, appearing to be most appropriate to the concrete situation.

159. Unlike the equitable criteria by which the delimitation must be guided, the practical methods that can be used for effecting the material delimitation have of course been the subject of certain *a priori* analyses. In this connection, mention may be made of the observations in the Court's Judgment in the *North Sea Continental Shelf* cases regarding the work done on the subject by the International Law Commission and its request for advice from a Committee of Experts (*I.C.J. Reports 1969*, at 35, para. 53). During the course of that work mention was made of the use, according to circumstances, of the method of the lateral equidistance line or the median line, the method which was finally adopted by the Commission (and later by the 1958 Convention) as applicable, provided always that special circumstances do not justify the use of another method. But, as the Court also recalled, mention was then made concurrently of other possible methods: that of drawing a line perpendicular to a coast, or to the general direction of a coast; that of drawing a boundary prolonging an existing division of territorial waters, or the direction of the final segment of a land boundary, or the overall direction of such boundary. This list was moreover by no means exhaustive. These different methods, and others, have been used in turn in different delimitations effected by direct agreement between neighbouring States; in this connection statistical considerations afford no indication either of the greater or lesser degree of appropriateness of any particular method, or of any trend in favour thereof discernible in international customary law.

163. The Chamber considers, therefore, that there are not two kinds of methods, those which are intrinsically appropriate, on the one hand, and those which are inappropriate or less appropriate, on the other. The greater or lesser appropriateness of one method or another can only be assessed with reference to the actual situations in which they are used, and the assessment made in one situation may be entirely reversed in another. Nor is there any method of which it can be said that it must receive priority, a method with whose application every delimitation operation could begin, albeit subject to its effects being subsequently corrected or it being even discarded in favour of another, if those effects turned out to be clearly unsatisfactory in relation to the case. In each specific instance the circumstances may make a particular method seem the most appropriate at the outset, but there must always be a possibility of abandoning it in favour of another if subsequently this proved justified. Above all there must be willingness to adopt a combination of different methods whenever that seems to be called for by differences in the circumstances that may be relevant in the different phases of the operation and with reference to different segments of the line. ...

191. ... In this final phase of the decision-making process, the Chamber must therefore arrive at the concrete determination of the delimitation line that it is required to draw (a) while basing itself for the purpose on the criteria which it finds most likely to prove equitable in relation to the relevant circumstances of the case and (b) while making use, in order to apply these criteria to the case, of the practical method or combination of methods which it deems the most appropriate; all this with the final aim in view of reaching an equitable result in the above circumstances. ...

195. To return to the immediate concerns of the Chamber, it is, accordingly, towards an application to the present case of criteria more especially derived from geography that it feels bound to turn. What is here understood by geography is of course mainly the geography of coasts, which has primarily a physical aspect, to which may be added, in the second place, a political aspect. Within this framework, it is inevitable that the Chamber's basic choice should favour a criterion long held to be as equitable as it is simple, namely that in principle, while having regard to the special circumstances of the case, one should aim at an equal division of areas where the maritime projections of the coasts of the States between which delimitation is to be effected converge and overlap.

196. Nevertheless, it is not always the case that the choice of this basic criterion appears truly equitable when it, and it alone, is exclusively applied to a particular situation. The multiplicity and diversity of geographical situations frequently call for this criterion to be adjusted or flexibly applied to make it genuinely equitable, not in the abstract, but in relation to the varying requirements of a reality that takes many shapes and forms. To mention only the situation involved in the present proceedings, it is a fact that the Parties, and one of them in particular, with the aid of comparisons with situations considered in previous cases, persistently emphasized the importance they attached to one concrete aspect or another of the geographical situation in the present case. The Chamber cannot but recognize, to a certain extent, that the concerns thus expressed were not wholly unfounded. It does not here intend to enter into detailed considerations, for it will be sufficient to note in general at this stage that, in the present case, the situation arising out of the physical and political geography of the delimitation area does not present ideal conditions for the full, exclusive application of the criterion specified at the end of the previous paragraph. Some corrections must be made to certain effects of its application that might be unreasonable, so that the concurrent use of auxiliary criteria may appear indispensable. Having regard to the special characteristics of the area, the auxiliary criterion which the Chamber has particularly in mind is that whereby a fair measure of weight should be given to a by no means negligible difference within the delimitation area between the lengths of the respective coastlines of the countries concerned. It also has in mind the likewise auxiliary criterion whereby it is held equitable partially to correct any effect of applying the basic criterion that would result in cutting off one coastline, or part of it, from its appropriate projection across the maritime expanses to be divided, or then again the criterion – it too being of an auxiliary nature – involving the necessity of granting some effect, however limited, to the presence of a geographical feature such as an island or group of small islands lying off a coast, when strict application of the basic criterion might entail giving them full effect or, alternatively, no effect. ...

198. The equitable nature of the criteria adopted in the light of the circumstances of the case will emerge the more convincingly – one might almost say tangibly – after the transition from the preliminary phase of choosing equitable criteria to the next phase, in which these criteria are to be reflected in the drawing of a particular delimitation line with the aid of appropriate practical methods.

199. As regards these practical methods, it can be said at the outset that, given the equitable criteria which the Chamber feels bound to apply in the case referred to it for judgment, the choice to be made is predetermined. Methods must be chosen which are instruments suitable for giving effect to those criteria and not other criteria of a fundamentally different kind. Just as the criteria to which they must give effect are basically founded upon geography, the practical methods in question can likewise only be methods appropriate for use against a background of geography. Moreover, like the underlying criteria, the methods employed to give them effect must, in this particular case, be just as suitable for the delimitation of the sea-bed and its subsoil as for the delimitation of the superjacent waters and their fishery resources. In the outcome, therefore, only geometrical methods will serve. ...

201. In this connection, the Chamber would emphasize the necessity of not allowing oneself to be too easily swayed by the perfection which is apparent *a priori*, from the viewpoint of equally dividing a disputed area, in a line drawn in strict compliance with the canons of geometry, i.e., line so constructed that each point in it is equidistant from the most salient points on the respective coastlines of the parties concerned. In an apposite passage of the 1969 Judgment on the *North Sea Continental Shelf* cases (*I.C.J. Reports 1969,* at 36, para. 57), the Court showed how, in determining the course of a delimitation line intended to "effect an equal division of the particular area involved" between two coasts, no account need be taken of the presence of "islets, rocks and minor coastal projections, the disproportionally distorting effect of which can be eliminated by other means.'' In pursuance of this remark, the Chamber likewise would point out the potential disadvantages inherent in any method which takes tiny islands, uninhabited rocks or low-tide elevations, sometimes lying at a considerable distance from terra firma, as basepoint for the drawing of a line intended to effect an equal division of a given area. If any of these geographical features possess some degree of importance, there is nothing to prevent their subsequently being assigned whatever limited corrective effect may equitably be ascribed to them, but that is an altogether different operation from making a series of such minor features the very basis for the determination of the dividing line, or from transforming them into a succession of basepoints for the geometrical construction of the entire line. It is very doubtful whether a line so constructed could, in many concrete situations, constitute a line genuinely giving effect to the criterion of equal division of the area in question, especially when it is not only a terrestrial area beneath the sea which has to be divided but also a maritime expanse in the proper sense of the term, since in the latter case the result may be even more debatable.

202. Furthermore, a line which, on account of the refinements in the technical method used to determine its course, follows a complicated or even a zigzag path, made up of a succession of segments on different bearings, might, if need be, seem acceptable as a boundary dividing the sea-bed alone, i.e., a boundary to be observed in the exploration and exploitation of the resources located in given areas of the subsoil. But there would seem to be far less justification for adopting such a line as a limit appropriate to maritime fishery zones, i.e., areas whose exploitable resources are not, for the most part, resources attached to the soil. Exploitation of the sea's fishery resources calls for the existence of clear boundaries of a constant course, that do not compel those engaging in such activity to keep checking their position in relation to the complicated path of the line to be respected. ...

205. Regarding the choice and use of methods, one general observation must be made. The delimitation line to be drawn in a given area will depend upon the coastal config-uration. But the configuration of the Gulf of Maine coastline, on which the delimitation to be effected between the maritime and submarine zones of the two countries depends throughout its length, is such as to exclude any possibility of the boundary's being formed by a basically unidirectional line, either over the whole distance between the point of departure and the terminal triangle or even over the sector between the point of departure and the closing line of the Gulf.

206. ... the Chamber considers that it will here be apposite, by way of reminder, to repeat its observation that it is only in the northeastern sector of the Gulf that the prevailing relationship of the coasts of the United States and Canada is that of lateral adjacency as between part of the coast of Maine and part of the Nova Scotian coast. In the sector closest to the closing line, the prevailing relationship is, on the contrary, one of oppo-siteness as between the facing stretches of the Nova Scotian and Massachusetts coasts. Accordingly, in the first sector, geography itself demands that, whatever the practical method selected, the boundary should be a lateral delimitation line. In the second, it is once again geography which prescribes that the delimitation line should rather be a median line (whether strict or corrected remains to be determined) for delimitation as between opposite coasts, and it is moreover geography yet again which requires that this line,

given the almost perfect parallelism of the two facing coasts involved, should also follow
a direction practically parallel to theirs. ...

230. The fundamental rule of general international law governing maritime delimitations, the rule which provided the Chamber with its starting-point for the reasoning so
far followed, requires that the delimitation line be established while applying equitable
criteria to that operation, with a view to reaching an equitable result. It is precisely by
the adoption of a basic criterion whose equitable character is generally admitted and has
been sanctioned by the authority of the Court, and by also resorting, where necessity
arose, to auxiliary criteria which are also equitable, and, finally, by putting those criteria
into practice through the methods judged most appropriate to that end, that the Chamber
has succeeded in drawing the delimitation line requested of it by the Parties. Its last
remaining task before formulating its final decision will be to ascertain whether the result
thus arrived at may be considered as intrinsically equitable, in the light of all the circumstances which may be taken into account for the purposes of that decision.

231. In fact, such verification is not absolutely necessary where the first two segments
of the line are concerned. Within the Gulf, i.e., landward of its closing line, it would
scarcely be possible to assess the equitable character of the delimitation there carried out
on the basis of any other than the dominant parameters provided by the physical and
political geography of the area. And it is precisely those parameters which served the
Chamber as a guide in determining the parts of the line which are to take effect in this
portion of the delimitation area. Moreover, attention may be drawn to the fact that the
Parties did not make any special reference to the fishing resources of this portion of the
delimitation area when pointing out the general importance of those resources for their
economies; neither did the Parties refer to any explorations carried out in this sector with
a view to the discovery and exploitation of petroleum resources.

232. The question may take on a different complexion, however, in regard to the
third segment of the line, whose effect will be felt in that part of the delimitation area
which lies outside and far from the shores of the Gulf and which, not so long ago, was
part of the high seas. For present purposes, it must be borne in mind that this final segment
of the line is the one of greatest interest to the Parties, on account of the presence of
Georges Bank. This Bank is the real subject of the dispute between the United States
and Canada in the present case, the principal stake in the proceedings, from the viewpoint
of the potential resources of the subsoil and also, in particular, that of fisheries that are
of major economic importance. Some enquiry whether, in addition to the factors provided
by the geography of the Gulf itself, there are no others that should be taken into account,
is therefore an understandable step. It might well appear that other circumstances ought
properly to be taken into consideration in assessing the equitable character of the result
produced by this portion of the delimitation line, which is destined to divide the riches
of the waters and shelf of this Bank between the two neighbouring countries. These other
circumstances may be summed up by what the Parties have presented as the data provided
by human and economic geography, and they are thus circumstances which, though in
the Chamber's opinion ineligible for consideration as criteria to be applied in the delimitation process itself, may ... be relevant to assessment of the equitable character of a
delimitation first established on the basis of criteria borrowed from physical and political
geography.

233. In the eyes of the United States, the main consideration here is the historical presence of man in the disputed areas. It believes the decisive factor here to be the activities pursued by the United States and its nationals since the country's independence and even before, activities which they claim to have been alone in pursuing over the greater part of that long period. This reasoning is simple and somewhat akin to the invocation of historic rights, though that expression has not been used. This continuous human presence took the form especially of fishing, and of the conservation and management of fisheries, but it also included other maritime activities concerning navigational assistance, rescue, research, defence, etc. All these activities, said greatly to exceed in duration and scale the more recent and limited activities of Canada and its nationals, must, according to the United States, be regarded as a major relevant circumstance for the purpose of reaching an equitable solution to the delimitation problem.

234. On the other hand it was Canada which, in the course of the proceedings, laid the greater emphasis on what it considered to be the decisive importance of socio-economic aspects. However, it was not a question, in its view, of invoking any historic rights such as might compete with those rights on which the United States was in effect relying. The only period which in Canada's eyes should be regarded as relevant was the recent one leading up to, or even continuing beyond, the time when both States finally decided to go ahead with the institution of exclusive fishery zones. Canada was of the view that attention should be especially concentrated on two aspects: the distribution of fish stocks in the various parts of the area, and the fishing practices respectively established and followed by the two Parties. As already noted in Section IV, paragraph 110, it sought to erect into an equitable principle of determining force for the purposes of delimitation, the idea that any single maritime boundary should ensure the maintenance of the existing fishing patterns that are in its view vital to the coastal communities of the region in question. In other words, the Chamber, in carrying out the delimitation, should aim to avoid in any way harming the economic and social development of the centres of population in Nova Scotia, bearing in mind that that development had been possible thanks to the contribution made by the product of the Canadian fisheries established on the Georges Bank, especially in the last 15 years.

235. The Chamber cannot adopt these positions of the Parties. Concerning that of the United States, it can only confirm its decision not to ascribe any decisive weight, for the purposes of the delimitation it is charged to carry out, to the antiquity or continuity of fishing activities carried on in the past within that part of the delimitation area which lies outside the closing line of the Gulf. Until very recently, as the Chamber has recalled, these expanses were part of the high seas and as such freely open to the fishermen not only of the United States and Canada but also of other countries, and they were indeed fished by very many nationals of the latter. The Chamber of course readily allows that, during that period of free competition, the United States, as the coastal State, may have been able at certain places and times – no matter for how long – to achieve an actual predominance for its fisheries. But after the coastal States had set up exclusive 200-mile fishery zones, the situation radically altered. Third States and their nationals found themselves deprived of any right of access to the sea areas within those zones and of any position of advantage they might have been able to achieve within them. As for the United States, any mere factual predominance which it had been able to secure in the area was transformed into a situation of legal monopoly to the extent that the localities in question became legally part of its own exclusive fishery zone. Conversely, to the extent that they had become part of the exclusive fishery zone of the neighbouring State, no reliance could any longer be placed on that predominance. Clearly, whatever preferential situation the United States may previously have enjoyed, this cannot constitute in itself a valid ground for its now claiming the incorporation into its own exclusive fishery zone of any area which, in law, has become part of Canada's.

236. In any case, the purpose of the delimitation cannot conceivably be held to lie in the maintenance of such a position, or even of its restoration in the event of its having weakened in the course of time. To a certain extent, moreover, the same considerations hold good as regards the position of Canada, even if it appears undeniable that, from some aspects, the development of this country's fisheries is more notably a phenomenon of the present day and has been having an obvious socio-economic impact on the communities inhabiting certain counties of Nova Scotia. But the fact remains that Canada, like the United States, has preferred the policy of reserving for itself an ''exclusive'' fishery zone to that of free-for-all competition in the exploitation of an open sea. To take such a step may give rise to drawbacks alongside the unquestionable advantages. However, there is no reason to consider *de jure* that the delimitation which the Chamber has now to carry out within the areas of overlapping apparent as between the respective exclusive fishery zones must result in each Party's enjoying an access to the regional fishing resources which will be equal to the access it previously enjoyed *de facto*. Neither is there any reason why the delimitation should provide a Party in certain places with a compensation equivalent to what it loses elsewhere.

237. It is, therefore, in the Chamber's view, evident that the respective scale of activities connected with fishing – or navigation, defence or, for that matter, petroleum exploration and exploitation – cannot be taken into account as a relevant circumstance or, if the term is preferred, as an equitable criterion to be applied in determining the delimitation line. What the Chamber would regard as a legitimate scruple lies rather in concern lest the overall result, even though achieved through the application of equitable criteria and the use of appropriate methods for giving them concrete effect, should unexpectedly be revealed as radically inequitable, that is to say, as likely to entail catastrophic repercussions for the livelihood and economic well-being of the population of the countries concerned.

238. Fortunately, there is no reason to fear that any such danger will arise in the present case on account of the Chamber's choice of delimitation line or, more especially, the course of its third and final segment. This crosses the waters covering Georges Bank at such a distance from that feature's extremity in the direction of the Northeast Channel as to leave on the Canadian side the greater part of the ''Northern Edge and Peak'' of the Bank, where the greatest concentrations of the sedentary species – in particular scallop – exploited by Canadian fishermen are to be found. In fact, according to the information furnished by Canada, in the period 1972-1976, i.e., prior to the two neighbouring countries' institution of their exclusive fishery zones, Canadian fishermen were responsible for the major part of scallop landings; the Canadian catches were taken mainly from the ''Northern Edge and Peak'' of Georges Bank, while those of the United States came mainly from the vicinity of the Great South Channel. Thus Canada may still be sure of very nearly all the major locations of its catches; and it will be remembered that it is precisely the product of these fisheries that Canada regards as important for the economy of Nova Scotia and its ports. Conversely, the localities in which the same sedentary species have been traditionally fished by the United States, which are clustered mainly in the vicinity of the Great South Channel, will lie entirely on the United States side of the dividing line. As regards lobster-fishing, the Canadian fisheries are mainly concentrated in Corsair Canyon, on the northeastern side of the line, whereas those of the United States are concentrated rather on its southwestern side. In the case of other fisheries, more particularly those concerning free-swimming fish, the calculation is not so simple, and is necessarily less precise. By and large, however, an examination of the statistics, which are sometimes difficult to compare, leads the Chamber to the conclusion that nothing less than a decision which would have assigned the whole of Georges Bank to one of the Parties might possibly have entailed serious economic repercussions for the other.

239. As regards the other major aspect to be viewed from the same angle, it may be pointed out that the delimitation line drawn by the Chamber so divides the main areas in which the subsoil is being explored for its mineral resources as to leave on either side broad expanses in which prospecting has been undertaken in the past and may be resumed to the extent desired by the Parties.

240. Moreover the Chamber considers that there is no need to overestimate any difficulties that may arise from the division of Georges Bank, with the resources of its waters and subsoil, resulting from the delimitation line which it has drawn in accordance with law and with the equitable criteria whose application is called for by the law itself. It is unable to discern any inevitable source of insurmountable disputes in the fact that its decision has not endorsed the single management of this Bank's fisheries, and the assignment to one country of the task of conserving them, which the United States would have preferred to see instituted. Nor can it imagine that incidents due to navigational errors or possible infringements occurring after the establishment of the delimitation line could not be settled directly and adequately. Canada and the United States have to their credit too long a tradition of friendly and fruitful co-operation in maritime matters, as in so many other domains, for there to be any need to fear an interruption of that co-operation, which clearly now becomes all the more necessary, not only in the field of fisheries but also in that of hydrocarbon resources. By once more joining in a common endeavour, the Parties will surely be able to surmount any difficulties and take the right steps to ensure the positive development of their activities in the important domains concerned.

241. In short, the Chamber sees in the above findings confirmation of its conviction that in the present case there are absolutely no conditions of an exceptional kind which might justify any correction of the delimitation line it has drawn. The Chamber may therefore confidently conclude that the delimitation effected in compliance with the governing principles and rules of law, applying equitable criteria and appropriate methods accordingly, has produced an equitable overall result.

Maritime Boundaries of Canada[61]

In addition to the disputed boundary with France surrounding Saint-Pierre and Miquelon, Canada also shares marine frontiers with Greenland and, in several areas in addition to the Gulf of Maine, with the United States. The Greenland boundary has been resolved by an agreement with Denmark[62] which draws an adjusted median line through the continental shelf between the two countries. With regard to the maritime boundaries between Canada and the United States, the Department of External Affairs has written:[63]

While the judgment, in October 1984, of a Chamber of the International Court of Justice (ICJ) fixed a single maritime boundary between Canada and the United States in a large portion of the Gulf of Maine area, several maritime boundaries remain unsettled between the two countries.

Gulf of Maine—Landward and Seaward Extensions

Under the terms of the agreement submitting the Gulf of Maine maritime boundary dispute to a Chamber of the ICJ, the Chamber was to fix the single maritime boundary seaward from a point 39 nautical miles from the terminus of the land boundary. The reason for not having the Chamber rule on the maritime boundary landward from this point related largely to the dispute over Machias Seal Island, which is claimed by both countries. The eventual seaward extension of the continental shelf dividing line will also have to be agreed in due course.

Strait of Juan de Fuca

The international boundary inside the Strait was fixed in the last century and is not the subject of dispute.

There is no agreement between Canada and the United States regarding the extension of the maritime boundary seaward of the Strait. The United States' position has been to espouse equidistance, using a line drawn by reference to coastal sinuosities.

Dixon Entrance

Inside the Entrance, the Canadian position is that the "A-B Line," established by the 1903 Alaska Boundary Tribunal, is the international boundary with respect to both land and sea. The Americans, who earlier claimed a three-mile territorial sea and a nine-mile contiguous fishing zone in the area, now maintain that the maritime boundary should follow a median line, more or less equally dividing the waters inside the Entrance between Canada and the United States.

There is no agreement between Canada and the United States regarding the extension of the maritime boundary seaward of the Dixon Entrance. The United States' position has been to espouse equidistance.

---

[61] See K. Beauchamp, M. Crommelin, and A.R. Thompson, "Jurisdictional Problems in Canada's Offshore" (1973), 11 *Alta.L.R.* 431.

[62] 1974 Can.T.S. No. 9.

[63] From a memorandum of the Bureau of Legal Affairs on *Current Issues of International Law of Particular Importance to Canada* (October 1986), at 16.

Beaufort Sea

The USA claims a maritime boundary based on equidistance from the termination of the land boundary on the 141st meridian. The Canadian position, based on our interpretation of the language of Article III of the 1825 Russian-British Convention of St. Petersburg, is that the maritime boundary should follow the 141st meridian — in effect, a direct seaward extension of the land boundary.

No negotiations with the United States to resolve any of these boundary issues have taken place since the Gulf of Maine case.

NOTES

Is it possible to list all the potentially relevant factors for the purposes of boundary delimitation? How is the lawyer to determine priority of factors? What is the difference between continental shelf and single maritime boundary delimitation? Have the decisions developed a coherent set of legal rules?[64]

RESOURCE MANAGEMENT AND ENVIRONMENTAL PROTECTION

Fisheries[65]

Few areas of the law of the sea reveal better the processes of development of international law than the law of fisheries during the last three decades. Originally the rule was simply one of freedom to fish beyond three miles. This rule was altered somewhat by the 1958 Geneva Convention on Fishing on the High Seas which recognized the ''special interest'' of the coastal state and allowed it to impose temporary conservation measures beyond the territorial sea subject to reaching an agreement with interested states within 12 months. This regime did not protect the interests of coastal states. Iceland was the first to react. An extended exclusive fisheries jurisdiction was proclaimed, thus beginning a series of ''cod wars.''[66] Norway and Canada also found the regime unworkable.

Canada worked closely with the other signatories of the International Convention for

---

[64] See *Continental Shelf (Tunisia v. Libya)*, [1982] I.C.J.Rep. 82; *Continental Shelf (Libya v. Malta)*, [1985] I.C.J.Rep. 13; and *Delimitation of the Maritime Boundary (Guinea v. Guinea-Bissau)* (1986), 25 *Int.Leg.Mat.* 251. And see S.P. Jagota, *Maritime Boundary* (1985); D.M. Johnston, *The Theory and History of Ocean Boundary-Making* (1987); D.M. Johnston and P.M. Saunders, *Ocean Boundary Making: Regional Issues and Development* (1987). On the application of equity, see C. de Visscher, *De l'equité dans le reglement arbitral ou judiciaire des litiges de droit international public* (1972). See also A.L.W. Munkman, ''Adjudication and Adjustment – International Judicial Decision and the Settlement of Territorial and Boundary Disputes'' (1972-73), 46 *Br.Y.B.Int.L.* 1, at 100.

[65] P. Finkle, *Fisheries Management in the Northwest Atlantic: Canadian Perspectives* (1974); D.M. Johnston, *The International Law of Fisheries* (1965); G. Knight, ed., *The Future of International Fisheries Management* (1975); G. Knight, *Managing the Sea's Living Resources* (1977); and A.W. Koers, *International Regulation of Marine Fisheries* (1973).

[66] See, e.g., the *Fisheries Jurisdiction Case* (United Kingdom v. Iceland) *Interim Measures*, [1972] I.C.J.Rep. 12; *Merits*, [1974] I.C.J.Rep. 3.

the Northwest Atlantic Fisheries (ICNAF) first negotiated in 1949.[67] This organization recognized Canada's interest but only as one more member state and did not necessarily give priority to Canada as a coastal state. In 1970 Canada extended its territorial sea from 3 to 12 nautical miles and closed the Bay of Fundy, the Gulf of St. Lawrence and the Queen Charlotte Sound to foreign fishing.[68] The exclusion of foreign fishermen was rendered uncontroversial by the prior negotiation of phase-out agreements with those states which had traditionally fished these waters.[69] These agreements proved to be only temporary way stations to a larger objective. During the mid-1970's Canada sought and achieved recognition of its priority interests in ICNAF.

At the same time, Canada was promoting the concept of exclusive fisheries jurisdiction within a 200 mile exclusive economic zone at the Third U.N. Law of the Sea Conference. Agreement on the broad outlines of exclusive fisheries jurisdiction seems to have been reached during the course of 1974-75. Mexico was the first major state to adopt a 200 mile exclusive economic zone in 1975. The United States followed for fisheries in 1976, and on January 1, 1977, Canada extended its fisheries jurisdiction to 200 miles. The multilateral groundwork had been laid.

The regional groundwork was assured by denunciation of the ICNAF and signature of a new regional arrangement, governing scientific research and fisheries beyond 200 miles, the Convention on Future Multilateral Cooperation in the Northwest Atlantic Fisheries (NAFO).[70] Bilateral problems were avoided by signing a second series of phasing-out agreements based on the fisheries articles of the emerging draft text of the U.N. Convention. The first and most significant was the Canada-Norway Agreement[71] on their mutual fisheries relations, which proved to be the general model for a series of subsequent agreements with other countries,[72] and the first of a series of abortive reciprocal arrangements with the United States.[73] The essence of these agreements was to permit foreign fishing subject to Canadian law, and subject to there being fish surplus to Canadian harvesting capacity. These agreements, together with denunciation of ICNAF, reversed any direct threat of challenge and reinforced Canada's assertion that a 200 mile fishing zone was justified by customary international law as evidenced by the negotiating texts at the Law of the Sea Conference.[74]

---

[67] 157 U.N.T.S. 157; 1950 Can.T.S. No. 10, as am.

[68] See the discussion and maps surrounding the report of the *Territorial Sea and Fishing Zones Act, supra,* in the Section on the "Territorial Sea," as well as the materials herein. See also A.E. Gotlieb, "The Canadian Contribution to the Concept of a Fishing Zone in International Law" (1964), 2 *Can.Y.B.Int.L.* 55; and J.-Y. Morin, "Les zone de peche de Terre-Neuve et du Labrador a la lumière de l'evolution du droit international" (1968), 6 *Can.Y.B.Int.L.* 91.

[69] E.g., U.S.A., 1970 Can.T.S. No. 11, as am.; Norway, 1971 Can.T.S. No. 27; U.S.S.R., 1971 Can.T.S. No. 9; and Denmark, France, Portugal, Spain, and U.K., all unpublished.

[70] 1979 Can.T.S. No. 11.

[71] 1976 Can.T.S. No. 4, reported hereafter.

[72] Poland, 1976 Can.T.S. No. 5; U.S.S.R., 1976 No. 6; Spain, 1976 Can.T.S. No. 7; Portugal, 1977 Can.T.S. No. 2; Cuba, 1977 Can.T.S. No. 17; Bulgaria, 1977 Can.T.S. No. 28; German Democratic Republic, 1977 Can.T.S. No. 30; Romania, 1978 Can.T.S. No. 2; Japan 1978 Can.T.S. No. 8.

[73] 1973 Can.T.S. No. 23.

[74] See A.L.C. de Mestral, "Accord entre le Canada et la Norvège sur leur relations en matière de pêche" (1976), 14 *Can.Y.B.Int.L.* 270.

Lasting agreement with the United States proved impossible. A new agreement[75] survived only a brief period in the face of opposition in the U.S. Senate and by 1978 a special negotiator in boundary questions was appointed to seek agreement on a fishing regime and boundaries on all or any of the four Canada-U.S. maritime frontiers. A treaty dealing with reciprocal fisheries and boundary dispute resolution was signed in 1979, but it was never ratified by the U.S. Senate. Subsequently the Gulf of Maine boundary dispute was submitted to a Chamber of the World Court.[76] Only careful diplomacy avoided fish wars on the East and West Coasts. Even after the Court decision in 1984, the only agreement which Canada and the United States have reached is the long-awaited and important Treaty Concerning Pacific Salmon.[77]

At the Third U.N. Conference on the Law of the Sea Canada was particularly concerned to gain protection of salmon originating in Canadian waters. In this respect Canada and the other interested states were successful despite their minority status. By virtue of Article 66 a broad prohibition against fishing for anadromous species on the high seas was established. This article does not resolve the problem of salmon interception in the U.S. or Greenland/Denmark economic zones, and therefore separate agreements have been necessary.

Geneva Convention on Fishing and Conservation of the Living Resources of the High Seas
(1958), 559 U.N.T.S 285

Article 1

1. All States have the right for their nationals to engage in fishing on the high seas, subject (a) to their treaty obligations, (b) to the interests and rights of coastal States as provided for in this Convention, (c) to the provisions contained in the following Articles concerning conservation of the living resources of the high seas.

2. All States have the duty to adopt, or to co-operate with other States in adopting, such measures for their respective nationals as may be necessary for the conservation of the living resources of the high seas. ...

Article 6

1. A coastal State has a special interest in the maintenance of the productivity of the living resources in any area of the high seas adjacent to its territorial sea.

2. A coastal State is entitled to take part on an equal footing in any system of research and regulation for purposes of conservation of the living resources of the high seas in that area, even though its nationals do not carry on fishing there.

3. A State whose nationals are engaged in fishing in any area of the high seas adjacent

---

[75] 1977 Can.T.S. No. 23.
[76] [1984] I.C.J. Rep. 246, reported in the last section.
[77] Done at Ottawa January 25, 1985; in force March 18, 1985.

to the territorial sea of a State shall, at the request of that coastal State, enter into negotiations with a view to prescribing by agreement the measures necessary for the conservation of the living resources of the high seas in that area. ...

United Nations Convention on the Law of the Sea

[First read Articles 55-59 reproduced *supra* in the Section on the "Exclusive Economic Zone."]

Article 61
CONSERVATION OF THE LIVING RESOURCES

1. The coastal State shall determine the allowable catch of the living resources in its exclusive economic zone.

2. The coastal State, taking into account the best scientific evidence available to it, shall ensure through proper conservation and management measures that the maintenance of the living resources in the exclusive economic zone is not endangered by over-exploitation. As appropriate, the coastal State and competent international organizations, whether subregional, regional or global, shall co-operate to this end.

3. Such measures shall also be designed to maintain or restore populations of harvested species at levels which can produce the maximum sustainable yield, as qualified by relevant environmental and economic factors, including the economic needs of coastal fishing communities and the special requirements of developing States, and taking into account fishing patterns, the interdependence of stocks and any generally recommended international minimum standards, whether subregional, regional or global.

4. In taking such measures the coastal State shall take into consideration the effects on species associated with or dependent upon harvested species with a view to maintaining or restoring populations of such associated or dependent species above levels at which their reproduction may become seriously threatened.

5. Available scientific information, catch and fishing effort statistics, and other data relevant to the conservation of fish stocks shall be contributed and exchanged on a regular basis through competent international organizations, whether subregional, regional or global, where appropriate and with participation by all States concerned, including States whose nationals are allowed to fish in the exclusive economic zone.

Article 62
UTILIZATION OF THE LIVING RESOURCES

1. The coastal State shall promote the objective of optimum utilization of the living resources in the exclusive economic zone without prejudice to article 61.

2. The coastal State shall determine its capacity to harvest the living resources of the exclusive economic zone. Where the coastal State does not have the capacity to harvest the entire allowable catch, it shall, through agreements or other arrangements and pursuant to the terms, conditions, laws and regulations referred to in paragraph 4, give other States access to the surplus of the allowable catch, having particular regard to the provisions of articles 69 and 70, especially in relation to the developing States mentioned therein.

3. In giving access to other States to its exclusive economic zone under this article, the coastal State shall take into account all relevant factors, including, *inter alia*, the significance of the living resources of the area to the economy of the coastal State concerned and its other national interests, the provisions of articles 69 and 70, the requirements of developing States in the subregion or region in harvesting part of the surplus and the need to minimize economic dislocation in States whose nationals have habitually fished in the zone or which have made substantial efforts in research and identification of stocks.

4. Nationals of other States fishing in the exclusive economic zone shall comply with the conservation measures and with the other terms and conditions established in the laws and regulations of the coastal State. These laws and regulations shall be consistent with this Convention and may relate, *inter alia*, to the following:

(a) licensing of fishermen, fishing vessels and equipment, including payment of fees and other forms of remuneration, which, in the case of developing coastal States, may consist of adequate compensation in the field of financing, equipment and technology relating to the fishing industry;

(b) determining the species which may be caught, and fixing quotas of catch, whether in relation to particular stocks or groups of stocks or catch per vessel over a period of time or to the catch by nationals of any State during a specified period;

(c) regulating seasons and areas of fishing, the types, sizes and amount of gear, and the types, sizes and number of fishing vessels that may be used;

(d) fixing the age and size of fish and other species that may be caught;

(e) specifying information required of fishing vessels, including catch and effort statistics and vessel position reports;

(f) requiring, under the authorization and control of the coastal State, the conduct of specified fisheries research programmes and regulating the conduct of such research, including the sampling of catches, disposition of samples and reporting of associated scientific data;

(g) the placing of observers or trainees on board such vessels by the coastal State;

(h) the landing of all or any part of the catch by such vessels in the ports of the coastal State;

(i) terms and conditions relating to joint ventures or other co-operative arrangements;

(j) requirements for the training of personnel and the transfer of fisheries technology, including enhancement of the coastal State's capability of undertaking fisheries research;

(k) enforcement procedures.

5. Coastal States shall give due notice of conservation and management laws and regulations.

Article 63

STOCKS OCCURRING WITHIN THE EXCLUSIVE ECONOMIC ZONES OF TWO OR MORE
COASTAL STATES OR BOTH WITHIN THE EXCLUSIVE ECONOMIC ZONE AND IN AN
AREA BEYOND AND ADJACENT TO IT

1. Where the same stock or stocks of associated species occur within the exclusive economic zones of two or more coastal States, these States shall seek, either directly or through appropriate subregional or regional organizations, to agree upon the measures necessary to co-ordinate and ensure the conservation and development of such stocks without prejudice to the other provisions of this Part.

2. Where the same stock or stocks of associated species occur both within the exclusive economic zone and in an area beyond and adjacent to the zone, the coastal State and the States fishing for such stocks in the adjacent area shall seek, either directly or through appropriate subregional or regional organizations, to agree upon the measures necessary for the conservation of these stocks in the adjacent area.

Article 64
HIGHLY MIGRATORY SPECIES

1. The coastal State and other States whose nationals fish in the region for the highly migratory species listed in Annex I shall co-operate directly or through appropriate international organizations with a view to ensuring conservation and promoting the objective of optimum utilization of such species throughout the region, both within and beyond the exclusive economic zone. In regions for which no appropriate international organization exists, the coastal State and other States whose nationals harvest these species in the region shall co-operate to establish such an organization and participate in its work.

2. The provisions of paragraph 1 apply in addition to the other provisions of this Part. ...

Article 66
ANADROMOUS STOCKS

1. States in whose rivers anadromous stocks originate shall have the primary interest in and responsibility for such stocks.

2. The State of origin of anadromous stocks shall ensure their conservation by the establishment of appropriate regulatory measures for fishing in all waters landward of the outer limits of its exclusive economic zone and for fishing provided for in paragraph 3(b). The State of origin may, after consultations with the other States referred to in paragraphs 3 and 4 fishing these stocks, establish total allowable catches for stocks originating in its rivers.

3. (a) Fisheries for anadromous stocks shall be conducted only in waters landward of the outer limits of exclusive economic zones, except in cases where this provision would result in economic dislocation for a State other than the State of origin. With respect to such fishing beyond the outer limits of the exclusive economic zone, States concerned shall maintain consultations with a view to achieving agreement on terms and conditions of such fishing giving due regard to the conservation requirements and the needs of the State of origin in respect of these stocks.

(b) The State of origin shall co-operate in minimizing economic dislocation in such other States fishing these stocks, taking into account the normal catch and the mode of operations of such States, and all the areas in which such fishing has occurred.

(c) States referred to in subparagraph (b), participating by agreement with the State of origin in measures to renew anadromous stocks, particularly by expenditures for that purpose, shall be given special consideration by the State of origin in the harvesting of stocks originating in its rivers.

(d) Enforcement of regulations regarding anadromous stocks beyond the exclusive economic zone shall be by agreement between the State of origin and the other States concerned.

4. In cases where anadromous stocks migrate into or through the waters landward of the outer limits of the exclusive economic zone of a State other than the State of origin, such State shall co-operate with the State of origin with regard to the conservation and management of such stocks.

5. The State of origin of anadromous stocks and other States fishing these stocks shall make arrangements for the implementation of the provisions of this article, where appropriate, through regional organizations.

Article 67
CATADROMOUS SPECIES

1. A coastal State in whose waters catadromous species spend the greater part of their life cycle shall have responsibility for the management of these species and shall ensure the ingress and egress of migrating fish.

2. Harvesting of catadromous species shall be conducted only in waters landward of the outer limits of exclusive economic zones. When conducted in exclusive economic zones, harvesting shall be subject to this article and the other provisions of this Convention concerning fishing in these zones.

3. In cases where catadromous fish migrate through the exclusive economic zone of another State, whether as juvenile or maturing fish, the management, including harvesting, of such fish shall be regulated by agreement between the State mentioned in paragraph 1 and the other State concerned. Such agreement shall ensure the rational management of the species and take into account the responsibilities of the State mentioned in paragraph 1 for the maintenance of these species.

Canada-Norway Agreement on Mutual Fisheries Relations
1976 Can. T.S. No. 4

Article I

The Government of Canada and the Government of Norway undertake to ensure close co-operation between the two countries in matters pertaining to the conservation and utilization of the living resources of the sea. They shall take appropriate measures to facilitate such co-operation and shall continue to consult and co-operate in international negotiations and organizations with a view to achieving common fisheries objectives.

Article II

1. The Government of Canada undertakes, upon the extension of the area under Canadian fisheries jurisdiction, to permit Norwegian vessels to fish within this area, beyond the present limits of the Canadian territorial sea and fishing zones off the Atlantic coast, for allotments, as appropriate, of parts of total allowable catches surplus to Canadian harvesting capacity, in accordance with the provisions of paragraphs 2 and 3 of this Article.

2. In the exercise of its sovereign rights in respect of living resources in the area referred to in paragraph 1, the Government of Canada shall determine annually, subject to adjustment when necessary to meet unforeseen circumstances:

(a) the total allowable catch for individual stocks or complexes of stocks, taking into account the interdependence of stocks, internationally accepted criteria, and all other relevant factors;

(b) the Canadian harvesting capacity in respect of such stocks; and

(c) after appropriate consultations, allotments, as appropriate, for Norwegian vessels of parts of surpluses of stocks or complexes of stocks.

3. To fish for allotments pursuant to the provisions of paragraphs 1 and 2, Norwegian vessels shall obtain licences from the competent authorities of the Government of Canada. They shall comply with the conservation measures and other terms and conditions established by the Government of Canada and shall be subject to the laws and regulations of Canada in respect of fisheries.

4. The Government of Norway undertakes to co-operate with the Government of Canada, as appropriate in light of the development of fisheries relations between the two countries pursuant to the provisions of this Article, in scientific research for purposes of conservation and management of the living resources of the area under Canadian fisheries jurisdiction off the Atlantic coast.

Article III

The Government of Canada and the Government of Norway recognize that the states in whose rivers anadromous stocks originate have the primary interest in and responsibility for such stocks and agree that fishing for anadromous species should not be conducted in areas beyond the limits of national fisheries jurisdiction. They will continue to work together for the establishment of permanent multilateral arrangements reflecting this position.

Article IV

The Government of Canada and the Government of Norway undertake to co-operate directly or through appropriate international organizations to ensure proper management and conservation of the living resources of the high seas beyond the limits of national fisheries jurisdiction, including areas of the high seas beyond and immediately adjacent to the areas under their respective fisheries jurisdiction, taking into account their interests in such resources.

Article V

The Government of Norway shall take measures to ensure that Norwegian fishing vessels operate in compliance with the provisions of this Agreement.

Map of Fishing Zones 1, 2, and 4

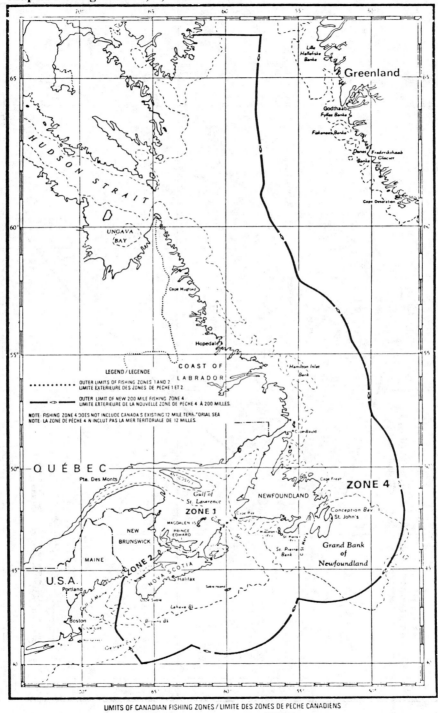

LIMITS OF CANADIAN FISHING ZONES / LIMITE DES ZONES DE PÈCHE CANADIENS

(EAST COAST)   (CÔTE EST)

Map of Fishing Zones 3 and 5

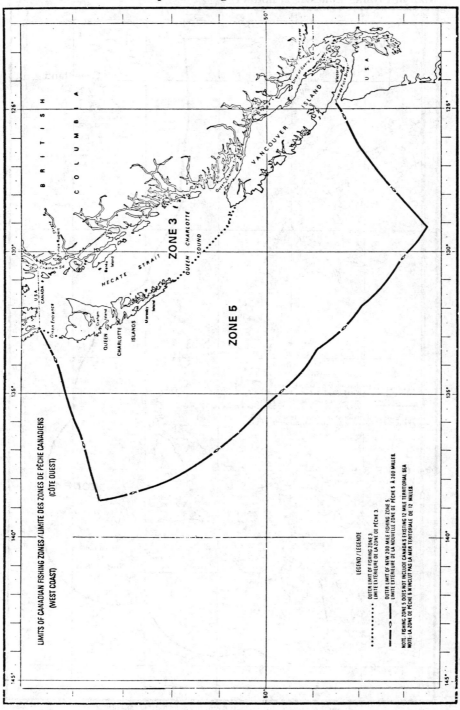

Canadian Fishing Zones

Pursuant to the powers in the *Territorial Sea and Fishing Zones Act*,[78] the Canadian government declared exclusive Canadian fishing zones by stages. In 1970, it established three zones by promulgating fisheries closing lines for the Gulf of St. Lawrence, the Bay of Fundy and Queen Charlotte Sound. Then in 1977 it created two more zones, one each in the Atlantic and the Pacific, extending 200 nautical miles beyond the previous closing lines and the straight baselines around the coast. See the preceding maps.[79] Upon creation of the offshore zones the existing *Fisheries Act* and *Coastal Fisheries Protection Act*[80] applied automatically throughout their full extent and provided the basis for the making of elaborate new regulations.[81]

Gulf of Maine Case
Canada v. United States
[1984] I.C.J. Rep. 246; 23 *Int.Leg.Mat.* 1197

Read Paragraph 94 of the judgment reported in the last section.

NOTES

1) The announcement of overlapping exclusive fishing zones by Canada and the United States gave impetus to the Gulf of Maine dispute. How was it that the Court in rendering its judgment in the case did not raise the issue of the legality of unilaterally declared 200 mile zones more fully? Was this simply because neither party before the Court objected? Is the freedom of fishing within 200 miles of shore now completely extinct as a right of states?

2) Does Canada have an internationally enforceable obligation to share the fish of its 200 mile zone which are surplus to Canadian harvesting capacity? Can a foreign state, such as Norway, declare that Canada has a surplus? Should highly migratory fish be regulated by coastal states alone? Can Canada be sure that no state has a right to catch salmon originating in Canadian waters on the high seas?

Canada-France Agreement on Mutual Fishing Relations
March 27, 1972 (unpublished)

Article 1

The Government of France renounces the privileges established to its advantage in fishery matters by the Convention signed at London, on April 8, 1904, between the United

---

[78] R.S.C. 1970, c. T-7, s.4, as am. R.S.C. 1970 (1st.supp.), c.45.

[79] Prepared by the Canadian Hydrographic Service and based on C.R.C. 1978, cc. 1547 and 1548, as am. SOR/79-107 and SOR/85-229. See also the Arctic fishing zone declared by C.R.C. 1978, c. 1549, and illustrated on a "Map of the Canadian Arctic," *supra*, Chapter 6.

[80] *Supra*, n. 23.

[81] *Inter alia*, the *Coastal Fisheries Protection Regulations*, C.R.C. 1978, c. 413, as am.

Kingdom and France. The present agreement supersedes all previous treaty provisions relating to fishing by French nationals off the Atlantic coast of Canada.

Article 2

In return, the Canadian Government undertakes in the event of a modification to the juridical regime relating to the waters situated beyond the present limits of the territorial sea and fishing zones of Canada on the Atlantic coast, to recognize the right of French nationals to fish in these waters subject to possible measures for the conservation of resources, including the establishment of quotas. The French Government undertakes for its part to grant reciprocity to Canadian nationals off the coast of Saint-Pierre and Miquelon.

Article 3

Fishing vessels registered in metropolitan France may continue to fish from January 15 to May 15 each year, up to May 15, 1986, on an equal footing with Canadian vessels, in the Canadian fishing zone within the Gulf of St. Lawrence, east of the meridian of longitude 61 degrees 30 mins west, subject to the provisions of Articles 5 and 6.

Article 4

In view of the special situation of Saint-Pierre and Miquelon and as an arrangement between neighbours:

(a) French coastal fishing boats registered in Saint-Pierre and Miquelon may continue to fish in the areas where they have traditionally fished along the coasts of Newfoundland, and Newfoundland coastal fishing boats shall enjoy the same right along the coasts of Saint-Pierre and Miquelon;

(b) A minimum of ten French trawlers registered in Saint-Pierre and Miquelon, of a maximum length of 50 metres, may continue to fish along the coasts of Newfoundland, of Nova Scotia (with the exception of the Bay of Fundy), and in the Canadian fishing zone within the Gulf of St. Lawrence, on an equal footing with Canadian trawlers; Canadian trawlers registered in the ports on the Atlantic coast of Canada may continue to fish along the coasts of Saint-Pierre and Miquelon on an equal footing with French trawlers.

Article 5

French fishing vessels covered by the provision of Article 3 must not direct their fishing effort to the taking of species other than those which they have traditionally exploited in the five-year period immediately preceding this agreement, nor shall they substantially increase the level of such effort.

Article 6

1. Canadian fishery regulations shall be applied without discrimination in fact or in law to the French fishing vessels covered by Articles 3 and 4, including regulations concerning the dimensions of vessels authorized to fish less than 12 miles from the Atlantic coast of Canada.

2. French fishery regulations shall be applied under the same conditions to the Canadian fishing vessels covered by Article 4.

3. Before promulgating new regulations applicable to these vessels, the authorities of each of the parties shall give three months prior notice to the authorities of the other party.

Article 7

The French patrol vessel which usually accompanies the French fishing fleet may continue to exercise its functions of assistance in the Gulf of St. Lawrence.

Article 8

The line defined in the annex to the present agreement determines, in the area between Newfoundland and the islands of Saint-Pierre and Miquelon, the limit of the territorial waters of Canada and of the zones submitted to the fishery jurisdiction of France.

Article 9

No provision of the present agreement shall be interpreted as prejudicing the views and future claims of either party concerning internal waters, territorial waters or jurisdiction with respect to fisheries or the resources of the continental shelf, or the bilateral or multilateral agreements to which either government is a party.

Article 10

1. The contracting parties shall establish a Commission to consider all disputes concerning the application of this agreement.

2. The Commission shall consist of one national expert nominated by each of the parties for ten years. In addition, the two Governments shall designate by mutual agreement a third expert who shall not be a national of either party.

3. If, in connection with any dispute referred to the Commission by either of the contracting parties, the Commission has not within one month reached a decision acceptable to the contracting parties, reference shall be made to the third expert. The Commission shall then sit as an arbitral tribunal under the chairmanship of the third expert.

4. Decisions of the Commission sitting as an arbitral tribunal shall be taken by a majority, and shall be binding on the contracting parties.

La Bretagne

The treaty with France was the last of the first series of "phasing-out" agreements signed by Canada between 1970-72. It is different from the others because of the location of the French islands of Saint-Pierre and Miquelon within what is now the 200 mile fishing zone of Canada. Thus Article 2 recognizes the right of French nationals to fish in Canadian waters along the Atlantic coast. Article 3 has excluded fishing vessels from metropolitan France from fishing in the Gulf of St. Lawrence since May 15, 1986 but Articles 4 and 6 allow ten boats registered in Saint-Pierre and Miquelon to fish there as well as along the Atlantic coast, subject to Canadian fishery regulations.

The scope of these provisions became the subject of arbitration between Canada and France in 1986[82] as a result of Canadian fears about French overfishing. When Canada proclaimed its 200 mile fishing zone, France also claimed a similar zone in a large area offshore Saint-Pierre and Miquelon. Since the two countries have overlapping jurisdictional claims, neither can restrict the activities of the other in the disputed areas. As the 1986 deadline for the exclusion of metropolitan French vessels from the Gulf of St. Lawrence approached, France increased its fishing activities in the disputed area and for the first time added factory freezer trawlers, of maximum size for entry into the Gulf, to the registry of Saint-Pierre and Miquelon. Matters came to a head when applications were made to Canadian authorities in 1985 for licences for three vessels out of Saint-Pierre, La Bretagne and two other similar 50 metre factory trawlers with fish filleting capacity, to operate both within and without the Gulf of St. Lawrence. The amended licence eventually granted by Canada carried a limitation:

In accordance with the current Canadian prohibition against the filleting of traditional groundfish species at sea by Canadian vessels, the La Bretagne is permitted to process groundfish species in the Gulf of St. Lawrence to the headed, gutted form only.

The French government objected to this proviso as a limitation of their nationals' rights in violation of the treaty. The two states failed to settle their differences by negotiation but did agree to arbitration over the application of the treaty, particularly Articles 4 and 6, in this situation. Canada contended that the treaty "sanctions the right for trawlers registered in Saint-Pierre and Miquelon to fish in the Canadian fishing zone within the Gulf of St. Lawrence, on an equal footing with Canadian vessels in compliance, without discrimination in fact or in law, with Canadian fishery regulations which prohibit filleting in the Gulf." France asserted with respect to Article 4(b) "that its sole object is the right to fish exercised by the French trawlers registered in Saint-Pierre and Miquelon and that, as filleting the fish taken is not to fish, Canada may not use the regulatory power which derives from Article 6 ... for purposes other than the protection of the fishery resources of its exclusive fishing zone."[83]

The majority of the Tribunal, P. de Visscher (Belg., Chairman) and J.-P. Queneudec (Fr.), D. Pharand (Can.) dissenting, in effect preferred the French interpretation of the treaty. There was no disagreement that Canada, consistent with the U.N. Law of the Sea Convention Articles 56, 61 and 62, could exercise sovereign rights in respect of its exclusive fisheries zone subject only to its special agreement with France. However, the majority considered that the French trawlers' rights in Article 4(b) to enjoy fishing "on an equal footing" with Canadian vessels grants them a right of access to exploit the

---

[82] *Dispute Concerning Filleting within the Gulf of St. Lawrence,* Arbitral Award of July 17, 1986.
[83] Award para. 24.

resource on the same basis as Canadian trawlers but does not subject them in all respects to the national treatment given to Canadians. In particular, the "Canadian Regulations" referred to in Article 6, whatever they may mean for Canadians, do not extend in the context of the Canada – France treaty as of 1972, or the parties' subsequent practice, or the U.N. Convention, beyond those laws which fix the conditions solely for fish-catching activities. Since Canada cannot prohibit fish-processing aboard French vessels the majority had only to hold that a freezer trawler is a kind of trawler within Article 4(b) to enjoin the Canadian prevention of their operation in the Gulf of St. Lawrence.

As a result of this award, Canada is unable to regulate the manner of handling the fish caught by St. Pierre boats in the Gulf of St. Lawrence but it retains a measure of control over the volume of fish taken by reason of the allocation of quotas to France. By virtue of Article 2, French nationals have a right to fish in Canadian waters, but Canada equally has a right to conserve the fish stocks by quotas. Negotiations are proceeding to establish these quotas through 1991, by which time a decision delimiting the maritime boundary between Canada and the French territories should have been made. See the note on St. Pierre and Miquelon in the last section on "Boundary Delimitation." After that, reconsideration of the 1972 treaty with France will likely be necessary.

Protection of the Marine Environment[84]

United Nations Convention on the Law of the Sea

Article 192
GENERAL OBLIGATION

States have the obligation to protect and preserve the marine environment.

Article 193
SOVEREIGN RIGHT OF STATES TO EXPLOIT THEIR NATURAL RESOURCES

States have the sovereign right to exploit their natural resources pursuant to their environmental policies and in accordance with their duty to protect and preserve the marine environment.

Article 194
MEASURES TO PREVENT, REDUCE AND CONTROL POLLUTION OF THE MARINE ENVIRONMENT

1. States shall take, individually or jointly as appropriate, all measures consistent with this Convention that are necessary to prevent, reduce and control pollution of the marine

---

[84] See J. Barros and D.M. Johnston, *The International Law of Pollution* (1974); D.M. Johnston, ed., *The Environmental Law of the Sea* (1981); J.W. Kindt, *Marine Pollution and the Law of the Sea*, 4 vols. (1986); J. Schneider, *World Public Order of the Environment* (1979); and A. Timagenis, *International Control of Marine Pollution* (1980).

environment from any source, using for this purpose the best practicable means at their disposal and in accordance with their capabilities, and they shall endeavour to harmonize their policies in this connection.

2. States shall take all measures necessary to ensure that activities under their jurisdiction or control are so conducted as not to cause damage by pollution to other States and their environment, and that pollution arising from incidents or activities under their jurisdiction or control does not spread beyond the areas where they exercise sovereign rights in accordance with this Convention.

3. The measures taken pursuant to this Part shall deal with all sources of pollution of the marine environment. These measures shall include, *inter alia,* those designed to minimize to the fullest possible extent:

(a) the release of toxic, harmful or noxious substances, especially those which are persistent, from land-based sources, from or through the atmosphere or by dumping;

(b) pollution from vessels, in particular measures for preventing accidents and dealing with emergencies, ensuring the safety of operations at sea, preventing intentional and unintentional discharges, and regulating the design, construction equipment, operation and manning of vessels;

(c) pollution from installations and devices used in exploration or exploitation of the natural resources of the sea-bed and subsoil, in particular measures for preventing accidents and dealing with emergencies, ensuring the safety of operations at sea, and regulating the design, construction, equipment, operation and manning of such installations or devices;

(d) pollution from other installations and devices operating in the marine environment, in particular measures for preventing accidents and dealing with emergencies, ensuring the safety of operations at sea, and regulating the design, construction, equipment, operation and manning of such installations or devices.

4. In taking measures to prevent, reduce or control pollution of the marine environment, States shall refrain from unjustifiable interference with activities carried out by other States in the exercise of their rights and in pursuance of their duties in conformity with this Convention.

5. The measures taken in accordance with this Part shall include those necessary to protect and preserve rare or fragile ecosystems as well as the habitat of depleted, threatened or endangered species and other forms of marine life.

Article 211
POLLUTION FROM VESSELS

1. States, acting through the competent international organization or general diplomatic conference, shall establish international rules and standards to prevent, reduce and control pollution of the marine environment from vessels and promote the adoption, in the same manner, wherever appropriate, of routing systems designed to minimize the threat of accidents which might cause pollution of the marine environment including the coastline, and pollution damage to the related interests of coastal States. Such rules and standards shall, in the same manner, be re-examined from time to time as necessary.

2. States shall adopt laws and regulations for the prevention, reduction and control of pollution of the marine environment from vessels flying their flag or of their registry. Such laws and regulations shall at least have the same effect as that of generally accepted international rules and standards established through the competent international organization or general diplomatic conference.

3. States which establish particular requirements for the prevention, reduction and control of pollution of the marine environment as a condition for the entry of foreign vessels into their ports or internal waters or for a call at their off-shore terminals shall give due publicity to such requirements and shall communicate them to the competent international organization. Whenever such requirements are established in identical form by two or more coastal States in an endeavour to harmonize policy, the communication shall indicate which States are participating in such co-operative arrangements. Every State shall require the master of a vessel flying its flag or of its registry, when navigating within the territorial sea of a State participating in such co-operative arrangements, to furnish, upon the request of that State, information as to whether it is proceeding to a State of the same region participating in such co-operative arrangements and, if so, to indicate whether it complies with the port entry requirements of that State. This article is without prejudice to the continued exercise by a vessel of its right of innocent passage or to the application of article 25, paragraph 2.

4. Coastal States may, in the exercise of their sovereignty within their territorial sea, adopt laws and regulations for the prevention, reduction and control of marine pollution from foreign vessels, including vessels exercising the right of innocent passage. Such laws and regulations shall, in accordance with Part II, section 3, not hamper innocent passage of foreign vessels.

5. Coastal States, for the purpose of enforcement as provided for in section 6, may in respect of their exclusive economic zones adopt laws and regulations for the prevention, reduction and control of pollution from vessels conforming to and giving effect to generally accepted international rules and standards established through the competent international organization or general diplomatic conference. ...

Article 234
ICE-COVERED AREAS

Coastal States have the right to adopt and enforce non-discriminatory laws and regulations for the prevention, reduction and control of marine pollution from vessels in ice-covered areas within the limits of the exclusive economic zone, where particularly severe climatic conditions and the presence of ice covering such areas for most of the year create obstructions or exceptional hazards to navigation, and pollution of the marine environment could cause major harm to or irreversible disturbance of the ecological balance. Such laws and regulations shall have due regard to navigation and the protection and preservation of the marine environment based on the best available scientific evidence.

NOTES

1) Part XII of the Convention, consisting of Articles 192-237, establishes a general framework for global and regional cooperation in the prevention of pollution of the sea.

It expects states to monitor the marine environment, and to assess and publish the potential impacts of marine activities under their jurisdiction. It requires states to adopt laws against pollution from land based and seabed activities, by dumping and through the atmosphere, as well as from ships. It obliges states to enforce these laws and applicable international standards, subject to certain safeguards regarding, for instance, investigation of foreign ships and rights of passage, and subject to the immunity of warships. It holds states responsible for the fulfillment of these obligations both by their own acts and by others within their jurisdiction.

In addition to setting out the general scope of the duties on all states to protect the marine environment, the Convention also sets a balance for their execution by coastal and flag states, who do not share the same interests in prescribing and enforcing pollution standards. To some extent, it moderates national jurisdiction to prescribe pollution laws by reference to "generally accepted international rules." As to enforcement power, it is shared three ways among flag, coastal and port states, whose authority is consequently to be found not only in Part XII but also in the articles on particular marine zones elsewhere in the Convention. See, for example, the previous materials on rights in the "Territorial Sea" and in the "Exclusive Economic Zone." Part XII grants primacy to flag state enforcement in areas beyond the territorial sea where valid but overlapping jurisdiction may arise. In particular, Article 228 obliges the coastal state to suspend proceedings against a foreign ship if the flag state also prosecutes it, but this limit on the coastal state's jurisdiction is suspended when it has suffered major damage or the flag state has repeatedly disregarded its enforcement duties.

2) This part of the 1982 Convention is almost entirely new law when compared to the four 1958 Geneva Conventions. However, since 1958 a host of specialized conventions on ship safety, ship construction, pollution from ships, and pollution of the seas from land based sources have been adopted under the aegis of the International Maritime Organization, the U.N. Environment Programme, the United Nations itself, and on a regional and bilateral basis.[85] The impulsion for the development of these conventions developed at the 1972 Stockholm Conference on the Human Environment where the need for marine environmental protection was stressed. It can thus be argued that there is a solid groundwork of principles and treaty law which are in part codified by the 1982 Convention. The duty to preserve and protect the marine environment, the extension of coastal state jurisdiction within a 200 mile zone, and tighter flag state obligations are all in this category. However, the issues are not free of controversy and it is certainly open to states to argue that Part XII cannot be invoked against them until they ratify the Convention.

3) Of particular interest to Canada is Article 234 which gives coastal states extensive discretionary powers, which normally would be denied to them by the Convention, in ice-covered areas. Canada was one of the prime movers of this Article and the Canadian delegation worked hard to obtain the consent of the U.S.A. and the U.S.S.R. in particular, as well as broad support within the conference. What is the legal status of Article 234?

---

[85] See the references in n. 84 and the documents in S. Oda, *supra*, n. 1, at Part XI.

4) In 1970, Canada enacted the *Arctic Waters Pollution Prevention Act,*[86] which gave the federal government wide powers to regulate shipping within 100 nautical miles of land in the Arctic. The provisions of the Act apply to "arctic waters" which are described as frozen or liquid waters "adjacent to the mainland and islands of the Canadian Arctic within the area enclosed by the sixtieth parallel of north latitude, the one hundred and forty-first meridian of longitude and a line measured seaward from the nearest Canadian land a distance of 100 nautical miles."[87] The Act prescribes offences and penalties for pollution of arctic waters by the deposit of waste, which is comprehensively defined to cover any substance that would degrade the waters to an extent detrimental to their use by man or by wildlife and plants that are useful to man. Offending conduct may also result in civil responsibility for pollution damage on an absolute liability basis. The Act provides regulatory powers regarding (1) the financial responsibility of anyone engaging in activities in the arctic waters or the seabed under them, (2) the creation of shipping safety control zones, (3) the prescription of minimum standards for ships, including hull and fuel tank construction, navigational aids, safety equipment, pilotage and icebreaker escorts, and (4) the destruction or removal of ships in distress which are causing pollution by depositing waste. The provisions of the Act and the regulations are enforced by Pollution Prevention Officers who have wide powers, including authority to seize a ship anywhere in the arctic waters or the territorial sea of Canada on reasonable suspicion of having committed an offence. When the Arctic Act was passed, Canada was subjected to strong international protest, especially from the United States. Is the Act legitimated by Article 234 of the U.N. Convention? Is Canada now prohibited from enforcing pollution standards which are more severe than those prescribed by "generally accepted international rules and standards" against foreign ships in other areas of the sea? Consider Article 211.

DEEP SEABED[88]

Until recent years the status of the seabed beyond national jurisdiction was only a problem of theoretical interest. One could maintain that it constituted *res nullius* or *res communis,*[89] and there appeared to be little doubt that the freedoms of the high seas included the

---

[86] R.S.C. 1970 (1st Supp.), c. 2, and C.R.C. 1978, cc. 353-356, as am. See J.A. Beesley, "The Canadian Approach to International Environmental Law" (1973), 11 *Can.Y.B.Int.L.* 3; R.B. Bilder, "The Canadian Arctic Waters Pollution Prevention Act: New Stresses on the Law of the Sea" (1970-71), 69 *Mich.L.R.*I; L. Henkin, "Arctic Anti-Pollution: Does Canada Make or Break International Laws?" (1971), 65 *Am.J.Int.L.* 131; and R. St.J. Macdonald, G.L. Morris and D.M. Johnston, "The Canadian Initiative to Establish a Maritime Zone for Environmental Protection" (1971), 21 *U.T.L.J.* 247. See also that part of Chapter 6 on "Jurisdiction in the Arctic."

[87] *Supra*, s. 3(1). An exception is made where the coasts of Canada and Greenland are opposed at less than 100 miles, when a line of equidistance is used instead.

[88] R.P. Anand, *The Legal Regime of the Sea-Bed and the Developing Countries* (1975); R.C. Ogley, *Internationalizing the Seabed* (1984); G. Pontecorvo, ed., *The New Order of the Oceans* (1986); and A.M. Post, *Deep Sea Mining and the Law of the Sea* (1983).

[89] See the "Introduction" to Chapter 6, *supra*, for an explanation of these terms.

freedom to take living and non-living resources from the seabed, insofar as this was a practical possibility. By the late 1960's interest was focussed upon the extraction of magnesium, lead, zinc, nickel and copper from the polymetallic nodules to be found on many parts of the ocean floor. Experiments began and feasibility studies were done as to possible industrial exploitation. Several large international consortia were formed to investigate the prospects. To date, technical and economic factors have inhibited exploitation and commercial development does not seem likely until the next century. However, as a result of fears of extended national continental shelf claims and suggestions that revenue could be generated from these resources to assist the Third World, intense interest was focused on the Third U.N. Conference on the Law of the Sea. U.N. Resolutions were adopted declaring these resources to be the common heritage of mankind and calling upon all states to refrain from exploitation pending establishment of an international regime. This regime was created on paper in 1982 by Part XI of the U.N. Convention on the Law of the Sea. Unfortunately, the United States, objecting to provisions on quantity controls, licensing and mandatory transfer of technology, made these objections the reason for refusing to sign the Convention and succeeded in establishing an alternative regime of mutual recognition of claims with some of the potential producers.[90] The issue is now stalemated, with the United States and its allies on one side and the vast majority of states of the world on the other. One side maintains arguments based upon freedom of the high seas, the other arguing that the world community has unequivocally made new law.

Seabed Declaration
Declaration of principles governing the sea-bed and the ocean floor, and subsoil thereof, beyond the limits of national jurisdiction.
U.N.G.A. Res. 2749 (XXV), 25 U.N.GAOR Supp. (No. 28) 24; U.N. Doc. A/8028 (1970)

The General Assembly solemnly declares that: ...
   1. The sea-bed and ocean floor, and the subsoil thereof, beyond the limits of national jurisdiction (hereinafter referred to as the area), as well as the resources of the area, are the common heritage of mankind.
   2. The area shall not be subject to appropriation by any means by States or persons, natural or juridical, and no State shall claim or exercise sovereignty or sovereign rights over any part thereof.
   3. No State or person, natural or juridical, shall claim, exercise or acquire rights with respect to the area or its resources incompatible with the international regime to be established and the principles of this Declaration.
   4. All activities regarding the exploration and exploitation of the resources of the area and other related activities shall be governed by the international regime to be established. ...

---

[90] In addition to the United States, amongst its treaty partners neither the Federal Republic of Germany nor the United Kingdom have signed the Convention.

7. The exploration of the area and the exploitation of its resources shall be carried out for the benefit of mankind as a whole. ...

9. On the basis of the principles of this Declaration, an international regime applying to the area and its resources and including appropriate international machinery to give effect to its provisions shall be established by an international treaty of a universal character, generally agreed upon. The regime shall, *inter alia,* provide for the orderly and safe development and rational management of the area and its resources and for expanding opportunities in the use thereof and ensure the equitable sharing by States in the benefits derived therefrom, taking into particular consideration the interests and needs of the developing countries, whether land-locked or coastal. ...

13. Nothing herein shall affect:

(a) The legal status of the waters superjacent to the area or that of the air space above those waters;

(b) The rights of coastal States with respect to measures to prevent, mitigate or eliminate grave and imminent danger to their coastline or related interests from pollution or threat thereof resulting from, or from other hazardous occurrences caused by, any activities in the area, subject to the international regime to be established.

14. Every State shall have the responsibility to ensure that activities in the area, including those relating to its resources, whether undertaken by governmental agencies, or non-governmental entities or persons under its jurisdiction, or acting on its behalf, shall be carried out in conformity with the international regime to be established. The same responsibility applies to international organizations and their members for activities undertaken by such organizations or on their behalf. Damage caused by such activities shall entail liability.

Moratorium Resolution
U.N.G.A. Res. 2574, 24 U.N.GAOR Supp. (No. 30) 11 (1969)

The General Assembly ...

Declares that, pending the establishment of the aforementioned international regime:

(a) States and persons, physical or juridical, are bound to refrain from all activities of exploitation of the resources of the area of the sea-bed and ocean floor, and the subsoil thereof, beyond the limits of national jurisdiction;

(b) No claim to any part of that area or its resources shall be recognized.

NOTES

1) The 1970 Seabed Declaration was adopted without dissenting vote. The resolution calling for a moratorium was adopted in 1969 with a large measure of support (62 votes), but a number of states interested in seabed mining voted against (28) or abstained (28).

Pending entry into force of the U.N. Law of the Sea Convention, as envisaged by the Seabed Declaration Article 9, what is the legal force of these resolutions?[91]

2) What does it mean to say the seabed and its resources are "the common heritage of mankind"? Compare the principles of the Seabed Declaration with the use of a similar phrase in the Moon Treaty, reproduced in that part of Chapter 6 on "Outer Space." Note what the Seabed Resolution does not declare, in particular how the benefits of the common heritage shall be acquired and distributed.

Claim of Exclusive Mining Rights by Deepsea Ventures Inc.
(1975), 14 *Int. Leg. Mat.* 51

The Honorable Henry A. Kissinger   November 4, 1974
Secretary of State ...
My dear Mr. Secretary:

Deepsea Ventures, Inc., a Delaware corporation having its principal place of business in the County of Gloucester, The Commonwealth of Virginia, U.S.A., respectfully makes of record, by filing with your office this *Notice of Discovery and Claim of Exclusive Mining Rights and Request for Diplomatic Protection and Protection of Investment, by Deepsea Ventures, Inc.* (hereinafter "Claim"), as authorized by its Board of Directors by resolution dated 30 October 1974, ...

Deepsea Ventures, Inc., (hereinafter "Deepsea"), hereby gives public notice that it has discovered and taken possession of, and is now engaged in developing and evaluating, as the first stages of mining, a deposit of seabed manganese nodules (hereinafter "Deposit"). The Deposit, ... is encompassed by ... lines drawn ... [in the Pacific Ocean roughly 1900 nautical miles south west of Los Angeles].

These lines include approximately 60,000 square kilometers for purposes of development and evaluation of the Deposit encompassed therein, which area will be reduced by Deepsea to 30,000 square kilometers upon expiration of a term of 15 years (absent force majeure) from the date of this notice or upon commencement (absent force majeure) of commercial production from the Deposit, whichever event occurs first. The Deposit lies on the abyssal ocean floor, in water depths ranging between 2300 to 5000 meters and is more than 1000 kilometers from the nearest island, and more than 1300 kilometers seaward of the outer edge of the nearest continental margin. It is beyond the limits of seabed jurisdiction presently claimed by any State. The overlying waters are, of course, high seas.

The general area of the Deposit was identified in August of 1964 by the predecessor in interest of Deepsea, and the Deposit was discovered by Deepsea on August 31, 1969.

Further exploration, evaluation, engineering development and processing research have been carried out to enable the recovery of the specific manganese nodules of the Deposit and the production of products and byproducts therefrom. ...

Deepsea respectfully requests the diplomatic protection of the United States Govern-

---

[91] Consider the discussion on "Law-Making Through International Organizations" *supra*, Chapter 3.

ment with respect to the exclusive mining rights described and asserted in the foregoing Claim, and any other rights which may hereafter accrue to Deepsea as a result of its activities at the site of the Deposit, and similar protection of the integrity of its investments heretofore made and now being undertaken, and to be undertaken in the future.

This request is made prior to any known interference with the rights now being asserted, and prior to any known impairment of Deepsea's investment. It is intended to give the Department immediate notice of Deepsea's Claim for the purpose of facilitating the protection of Deepsea's rights and investments should this be required as a consequence of any future actions of the United States Government or other States, persons, or organizations. ...

Respectfully,
Deepsea Ventures, Inc.

Canadian Response to Deepsea Ventures Inc.'s Claim
(1975), 14 *Int. Leg. Mat.* 67-68

It is the policy of the Canadian Government to seek, through the Development of International Law, in appropriate fora, the establishment of a legal regime to govern the exploration and exploitation of the resources of the deep seabed beyond the limits of national jurisdiction. Indeed, this is the task that is now being pursued by the Third United Nations Law of the Sea Conference, to which Canada attaches the greatest importance. Canada subscribed at an early stage in the work of the United Nations in this respect to the concept that the exploitation of these resources should be carried out for the benefit of mankind as a whole.

The Canadian Government, therefore, does not accept the assertion by Deepsea Ventures Inc. that it has exclusive mining rights or some priority in time over that portion of the international seabed area as described in the notice to the Secretary of State, or that it has acquired any rights to that area or the resources thereof through its activities.

The Canadian Government reserves its position concerning the legal rights of States and their nationals with respect to the area of the seabed beyond the limits of national jurisdiction, pending the outcome of the Third United Nations Law of the Sea Conference.

NOTES

1) The claim of Deepsea Ventures, a private company, has no status in international law as such. However, to the extent that it is supported by the Government of the United States, this claim, when contrasted with the Canadian response reflects two very different views of international law and of the international law-making process. The United States view would allow any government to do as it wishes unless it agrees to be limited or becomes bound by a rule of customary international law, which is not easy in the face of steadfast opposition by a major power. The second view allows greater possibility for the development of customary law and pays much more respect to the expression of majoritarian views as expressed by the General Assembly of the United Nations.

2) In 1980 the U.S. Congress passed the *Deep Seabed Hard Mineral Resources Act*.[92] This legislation was designed to provide suitable domestic authorization and international protection for American corporations wishing to engage in deepsea mining. Congress stated that exploration and commercial exploitation of the mineral resources of the deep seabed are freedoms of the high seas which are restrained only to the extent of reasonable regard for the exercise by other states of these or other freedoms recognised at international law. Therefore, Congress established an interim legal regime for deepsea mining "until such time as a Law of the Sea Treaty enters into force with respect to the United States." In creating this interim regime, the United States limited the exercise of its authority to persons and vessels engaged in deepsea mining who are subject to its jurisdiction, and did not assert sovereignty or exclusive rights to the seabed or its resources as such. Canada has refused to adopt similar legislation, although several states of Europe and Japan have done so.[93]

United Nations Convention on the Law of the Sea

Article 1
USE OF TERMS AND SCOPE

1. For the purposes of this Convention:
(1) "Area" means the sea-bed and ocean floor and subsoil thereof, beyond the limits of national jurisdiction;
(2) "Authority" means the International Sea-Bed Authority;
(3) "activities in the Area" means all activities of exploration for, and exploitation of, the resources of the Area;

Article 136
COMMON HERITAGE OF MANKIND

The Area and its resources are the common heritage of mankind.

Article 137
LEGAL STATUS OF THE AREA AND ITS RESOURCES

1. No State shall claim or exercise sovereignty or sovereign rights over any part of the Area or its resources, nor shall any State or natural or juridical person appropriate any part thereof. No such claim or exercise of sovereignty or soverign rights nor such appropriation shall be recognized.
2. All rights in the resources of the Area are vested in mankind as a whole, on whose

---

[92] 30 U.S.C. ss. 1401-1403, 1411-1428, 1441-1444, 1461-1471, reprinted in (1980), 19 *Int.Leg.Mat.* 1003.
[93] E.g., U.K. *Deep Sea Mining (Temporary Provisions) Act*, 1981, c. 53. See also the legislation of France (1982), 21 *Int.Leg.Mat.* 808; Federal Republic of Germany (1981), 20 *Int.Leg.Mat.* 393; Japan (1983), 22 *Int.Leg.Mat.* 102; and Italy (1985), 24 *Int.Leg.Mat.* 983.

behalf the Authority shall act. These resources are not subject to alienation. The minerals recovered from the Area, however, may only be alienated in accordance with this Part and the rules, regulations and procedures of the Authority.

3. No State or natural or juridical person shall claim, acquire or exercise rights with respect to the minerals recovered from the Area except in accordance with this Part. Otherwise, no such claim, acquisition or exercise of such rights shall be recognized.

Article 140
BENEFIT OF MANKIND

1. Activities in the Area shall, as specifically provided for in this Part, be carried out for the benefit of mankind as a whole, irrespective of the geographical location of States, whether coastal or land-locked, and taking into particular consideration the interests and needs of developing States and of peoples who have not attained full independence or other self-governing status recognized by the United Nations in accordance with General Assembly resolution 1514 (XV) and other relevant General Assembly resolutions.

2. The Authority shall provide for the equitable sharing of financial and other economic benefits derived from activities in the Area through any appropriate mechanism, on a non-discriminatory basis, in accordance with article 160, paragraph 2(f)(i).

Article 141
USE OF THE AREA EXCLUSIVELY FOR PEACEFUL PURPOSES

The Area shall be open to use exclusively for peaceful purposes by all States, whether coastal or land-locked, without discrimination and without prejudice to the other provisions of this Part.

Article 150
POLICIES RELATING TO ACTIVITIES IN THE AREA

Activities in the Area shall, as specifically provided for in this Part, be carried out in such a manner as to foster healthy development of the world economy and balanced growth of international trade, and to promote international co-operation for the over-all development of all countries, especially developing States, and with a view to ensuring:

(a) the development of the resources of the Area;

(b) orderly, safe and rational management of the resources of the Area, including the efficient conduct of activities in the Area and, in accordance with sound principles of conservation, the avoidance of unnecessary waste;

(c) the expansion of opportunities for participation in such activities consistent in particular with articles 144 and 148;

(d) participation in revenues by the Authority and the transfer of technology to the Enterprise and developing States as provided for in this Convention;

(e) increased availability of the minerals derived from the Area as needed in conjunction with minerals derived from other sources, to ensure supplies to consumers of such minerals;

(f) the promotion of just and stable prices remunerative to producers and fair to consumers for minerals derived both from the Area and from other sources, and the promotion of long-term equilibrium between supply and demand;

(g) the enhancement of opportunities for all States Parties, irrespective of their social and economic systems or geographical location, to participate in the development of the resources of the Area and the prevention of monopolization of activities in the Area;

(h) the protection of developing countries from adverse effects on their economies or on their export earnings resulting from a reduction in the price of an affected mineral, or in the volume of exports of that mineral, to the extent that such reduction is caused by activities in the Area, as provided in article 151;

(i) the development of the common heritage for the benefit of mankind as a whole; and

(j) conditions of access to markets for the imports of minerals produced from the resources of the Area and for imports of commodities produced from such minerals shall not be more favourable than the most favourable applied to imports from other sources.

Article 152
EXERCISE OF POWERS AND FUNCTIONS BY THE AUTHORITY

1. The Authority shall avoid discrimination in the exercise of its powers and functions, including the granting of opportunities for activities in the Area.

2. Nevertheless, special consideration for developing States, including particular consideration for the land-locked and geographically disadvantaged among them, specifically provided for in this Part shall be permitted.

Article 153
SYSTEM OF EXPLORATION AND EXPLOITATION

1. Activities in the Area shall be organized, carried out and controlled by the Authority on behalf of mankind as a whole in accordance with this article as well as other relevant provisions of this Part and the relevant Annexes, and the rules, regulations and procedures of the Authority.

2. Activities in the Area shall be carried out as prescribed in paragraph 3:

(a) by the Enterprise, and

(b) in association with the Authority by States Parties, or state enterprises or natural or juridical persons which possess the nationality of States Parties or are effectively controlled by them or their nationals, when sponsored by such States, or any group of the foregoing which meets the requirements provided in this Part and in Annex III.

3. Activities in the Area shall be carried out in accordance with a formal written plan of work drawn up in accordance with Annex III and approved by the Council after review by the Legal and Technical Commission. In the case of activities in the Area carried out as authorized by the Authority by the entities specified in paragraph 2(b), the plan of work shall, in accordance with Annex III, article 3, be in the form of a contract. Such contracts may provide for joint arrangements in accordance with Annex III, article 11.

4. The Authority shall exercise such control over activities in the Area as is necessary for the purpose of securing compliance with the relevant provisions of this Part and the Annexes relating thereto, and the rules, regulations and procedures of the Authority, and the plans of work approved in accordance with paragraph 3. States Parties shall assist the Authority by taking all measures necessary to ensure such compliance in accordance with article 139.

5. The Authority shall have the right to take at any time any measures provided for under this Part to ensure compliance with its provisions and the exercise of the functions of control and regulation assigned to it thereunder or under any contract. The Authority shall have the right to inspect all installations in the Area used in connection with activities in the Area.

6. A contract under paragraph 3 shall provide for security of tenure. Accordingly, the contract shall not be revised, suspended or terminated except in accordance with Annex III, articles 18 and 19.

NOTES

1) Articles 156-191 establish a new body known as the International Sea-Bed Authority[94] to administer Part XI of the Convention on the Area. All states parties to the Convention are automatically equal members of the Authority, which has its headquarters in Jamaica. The Authority is to be comprised of the Assembly, the Council, the Secretariat and the Enterprise. The Assembly will be the general policy organ, made up of all members of the Authority who will decide matters of substance by two-thirds majority vote. The Council will be the executive body, which will work through two sub-organs, the Economic Planning Commission and the Legal and Technical Commission. The Council will be composed of thirty-six members elected by the Assembly in a carefully structured process so as to fairly reflect the diversity of states' interests. The members will take decisions of substance by two-thirds or three-quarters majorities, depending on the specific subject matter. The Enterprise will be the operative arm of the Authority for the exploration and exploitation of the resources of the Area. By Annex IV to the Convention, it is created as a nearly autonomous body with limited liability, subject only to the general policies of the Assembly and the directives of the Council. It will have its own Governing Board, Director-General and staff and is intended to become financially self-supporting. In many respects the Enterprise will resemble a public corporation that operates on commercial principles and is answerable in the first instance to the Council. The Sea-Bed Authority as a whole is created an international legal person with responsibilities, privileges and immunities for itself, its staff, and the representatives of its member states comparable to any other intergovernmental organization.

2) There has been wide acceptance of the idea that the resources of the seabed are ''the common heritage of mankind'' in the sense that they are not subject to the sovereignty or sovereign rights of any state or person. The problem for the U.N. Law of the Sea

---

[94] See R. Ogley, *supra* n. 88, at 194.

Conference was to negotiate an agreement for the exploitation of seabed minerals which was consistent with this idea and satisfied all countries.[95] Generally speaking, developed and developing countries were deeply divided on this issue. The developing countries wanted to see the Area wholly controlled by the Sea-Bed Authority and its resources extracted by the Enterprise. Developed states desired a system of national or private corporate undertakings which at most would be licensed and regulated by the international Authority. The compromise that was finally arranged is substantially set out in Articles 150, 152 and 153. In particular, Article 153(2) partially meets the wishes of both developing and developed countries through a system of "parallel access" by the Enterprise and by private parties. The distribution of access will be made by the Authority according to the principles and policies contained in Articles 150 and 152. What guiding economic and social policies do they express? Do they provide a consistent set of principles that will support the rational management of seabed resources?

Part of the compromise arrangement is a system of periodic reviews of the international regime every five years and a general Review Conference after fifteen years to consider amendments to the Convention (Articles 154 and 155). These Articles helped to cement the compromise by making it less immutable. In particular, the developing countries want to limit the period in which private parties may have access to the Area to the start-up years of the Authority. Nevertheless, the arrangements of Part XI as a whole are still not acceptable to the United States, which has pressed ahead with its own plans for seabed mining by means of the following "Provisional Understanding" with several of its major trading partners in the developed world.

Provisional Understanding Regarding Deep Seabed Mining
Between Belgium, France, Federal Republic of Germany, Italy, Japan,
Netherlands, United Kingdom and United States
(1984), 23 *Int. Leg. Mat.* 1354

1.(1) No Party shall issue an authorization in respect of an application, or seek registration, for an area included:

    (a) within an area which is covered in another application filed in conformity with the agreements for voluntary conflict resolution reached on 18 May 1983 and 15 December 1983 and being still under consideration by another Party;

    (b) within an area claimed in any other application which has been filed in conformity with national law and this Agreement,

        (i) prior to the signature of this Agreement, or

        (ii) earlier than the application or request for registration in question, and which is still under consideration by another Party; or

    (c) within an authorization granted by another Party in conformity with this Agreement.

    (2) No Party shall itself engage in deep seabed operations in an area for which, in accordance with this paragraph, it shall not issue an authorization or seek registration.

------

[95] See R. Ogley, *supra.* 88, at 134.

2. The Parties shall, as far as possible, process applications without delay. To this end, each Party shall, with reasonable dispatch, make an initial examination of each application to determine whether it complies with requirements for minimum content of applications under its national law, and thereafter determine the applicant's eligibility for the issuance of an authorization.

3. Each Party shall immediately notify the other Parties of each application for an authorization which it accepts, including applications already received, and of each amendment to such an application. Each Party shall also immediately notify the other Parties after it has taken action subsequently with respect to an application or any action with respect to an authorization.

4. No Party shall authorize, or itself engage in, exploitation of the hard mineral resources of the deep seabed before 1 January 1988.

5.(1) The Parties shall consult together:

(a) prior to the issuance of any authorization or before themselves engaging in deep seabed operations or seeking registration for an area;

(b) with regard to any arrangements between one or more Parties and another State or States for the avoidance of overlapping in deep seabed operations;

(c) with regard to relevant legal provisions and any modification thereof; and

(d) generally with a view to coordinating and reviewing the implementation of this Agreement.

(2) The relevant Parties shall consult together in the event that two or more applications are filed simultaneously.

6.(1) To the extent permissible under national law, a Party shall maintain the confidentiality of the coordinates of application areas and other proprietary or confidential commercial information received in confidence from any other Party in pursuance of cooperation in regard to deep seabed operations. In particular:

(a) the confidentiality of the coordinates of application areas shall be maintained until any overlap involving such an area is resolved and the relevant authorization is issued; and

(b) the confidentiality of other proprietary or confidential commercial information shall be maintained in accordance with national law as long as such information retains its character as such.

(2) Denunciation or other action by a Party pursuant to paragraph 14 of this Agreement shall not affect the Parties' obligations under this paragraph.

NOTES

1) Is the United States correct in contending that until the U.N. Convention is in force and has been ratified by the United States, its longstanding freedom of the high seas cannot be abridged by the rest of the international community? Is it justifiable for a state to negotiate the Convention as a package and then to reject one major element? What position should Canada now take?

2) In the light of the national legislation and exploratory investments already committed by a number of countries, the final session of the U.N. Conference also had to make

arrangements for provisional entry into force of the regime of exploitation of the resources of the Area and for the maintenance of rights acquired under the provisional regime. Out of regard for what came to be known as Preparatory Investment Protection, the Conference established a Preparatory Commission which has since held several meetings with a view to setting up the provisional regime. The reluctance of the United States to participate, adverse market factors and unresolved technical difficulties have slowed this process.[96]

---

[96] See R. Ogley, *supra.* n. 88, at 224; and M.A. Dubs, "Minerals of the Deep Sea, Myth and Reality," in G. Pontecorvo, *supra.*, n. 88, at 85.

CHAPTER TWELVE

From Sovereignty to Common Interest

INTERNATIONAL LAW OF COOPERATION?

International law is not a static system. Perceptive commentators observe that it is undergoing far-reaching structural change. That much is agreed. But the nature of the transformation and the attainment of a new world order is a matter of some doubt and much personal interpretation.[1] In this, the final Chapter, it is appropriate to take stock of the present condition of international law, as exposed in the previous Chapters, and to look for the indications of change.

The international legal system is founded on the sovereignty of states. Much of the history of international law[2] is the story of the legal consecration of the nation state as the prototypical unit of organization of community life and the slow evolution of its rights and responsibilities as an independent, procedural equal amongst other like sovereign authorities. The fundamental significance of the concept of sovereignty was held up to view by the Permanent Court in *The Steamship Lotus*[3] when it maintained that a state could not be restrained in the exercise of its freedom of action except if there existed a rule of law to curb it. The substance of international law as developed in its classical era consisted of a relatively few prohibitory rules about a limited range of state conduct. The scope of the rules was generally to control, and, to a lesser extent, to correct, acts by one state that interfered with the rights and independence of another. Otherwise, international law abstained from impeding a state's freedom of action with respect to its population, its territory and its resources or in exploring and exploiting other parts of the world not subject to the sovereignty of any state. In short, classical international law was a minimal system for the coexistence of sovereign states.

---

[1] See, e.g., the collections of opinions in R. Falk, F. Kratochwil and S.H. Mendlovitz eds., *International Law: A Contemporary Perspective* (1985); R.St.J. Macdonald, D.M. Johnston, G.L. Morris eds., *The International Law and Policy of Human Welfare* (1978); and R.St.J. Macdonald and D.M. Johnston eds., *The Structure and Process of International Law* (1983).

[2] Refer to Chapter 1.

[3] (1927), P.C.I.J. Ser. A., No. 10, reported *supra* in Chapter 8.

But as this system evolved, other principles that deny the exclusiveness of states' rights have also been developing. These principles reflect the economic, military and political realities of this century, which is marked by interdependence of states, community of human interests, and unity of the global physical environment. Recognition of these realities has found expression in modern international law and their influence is a distinctive feature of the United Nations' era.

The new rules that promote, for instance, economic development and human welfare, are the opposite of the earlier prohibitions rooted in sovereignty. Communal objectives of this kind demand positive acts of cooperation and therefore depend upon a substructure of affirmative rules of organization and obligation. The growth in contemporary international law of such new concepts and principles has been aptly described by Wolfgang Friedmann as an inchoate law of cooperation (see the extract of his views reproduced below). The purpose of the concluding Chapter is to explore this idea and to seek the evidence of the extent to which ''this new dimension of international law ... affects some of the most firmly established concepts concerning both the universality and the reality of international law.'' In brief, this Chapter invites consideration whether sovereignty is giving way to cooperation, even to joint action in the common interest.

The Changing Structure of International Law
by W. Friedman (1964), at 60–66 (footnotes omitted)

The changing structure of contemporary international relations is reflected in more diversified patterns of modern international law. Just as modern international relations are no longer essentially a matter of diplomatic interstate relations, but affect groups and individuals and reach into many domains of social and economic life, so modern international law moves on different levels.

They can briefly be characterised as follows:

The International Law of Coexistence

First, there is the traditional sphere of diplomatic interstate relations, represented by the classical system of international law. These rules aim at the peaceful coexistence of all states regardless of their social and economic structure.

The principal object of these rules of coexistence is the regulation of the conditions of mutual diplomatic intercourse and, in particular, of the rules of mutual respect for national sovereignty. The substance of these rules is found in the classic texts on international law: the rules regulating membership of the family of nations, including the recognition of new states and governments; the rules governing the limits of national territories and of territorial jurisdiction; the jurisdictional and diplomatic immunities of foreign sovereigns; the principles of responsibility incurred by a state for injury done to the lives or properties of the subjects of another state; the adjustment of the rights of belligerent states and neutral states in the rules of war and neutrality, and the formal implementation of these principles by custom, treaty or adjudication.

In the original Marxist conception, which regarded the state as an instrument of capitalist domination to be replaced by international and world-wide class divisions, this system of international law would have lost all significance. In the actuality of the present world, where Communist régimes have adopted and indeed sanctified the traditional aspects of state sovereignty, it retains its universal validity. ...

International Law of Co-operation: Universal Concerns

To this traditional sphere of diplomatic existence and the corresponding rules of international law, modern needs and developments have added many new areas expressing the need for positive co-operation which has to be implemented by international treaties and in many cases permanent international organisations. This move of international society, from an essentially negative code of rules of abstention to positive rules of co-operation, however fragmentary in the present state of world politics, is an evolution of immense significance for the principles and structure of international law. ... this new dimension of international law deeply affects some of the most firmly established concepts concerning both the universality and the reality of international law. It affects both the meaning and the significance of sanction in international legal relations. The extension in the range of universal human concerns calling for international regulation is a response to the profound changes in the physical and social structure of international society. ...

International Law of Co-operation: Regional Groupings

To the extent, however, that international law expands from what is essentially a set of rules of abstention, to organised international co-operation, it becomes more sensitive to the divergencies of internal systems, as expressed in their political ideology, their legal structure and their economic organisation. The building of "co-operative" international law proceeds today on different levels of universality, depending on the extent of the common interests and values that bind the participants. Certain types of the new international law are developing today on the universal level, because they reflect universal interests of mankind. Others, depending on a more closely knit community of values and purposes, proceed on a more restrictive level of international organisation, mostly of a regional pattern (notably in the West European Communities). The borderline between the two groups is not an absolute one, and it will obviously shift in accordance with changing political configurations. It represents nevertheless a fairly definite and important division in the processes of international legal development.

The basic reason for the simultaneous development of international legal organisation and new substantive principles of international law derives from the fact that law must reflect and respond to such need and that at this time only some concerns of mankind are felt to be of sufficiently strong universal urgency to make some measure of universal legal organisation possible. But at the same time certain groupings of nations, more closely bound to each other by common values, common interests, common fears and stronger affinities in their social and legal structure, are proceeding to develop common legal organisations and a corresponding evolution of their substantive laws in fields where mankind as a whole is still too disunited or too disparate to attempt legal organisation and integration. ...

The New Dimensions of International Law

The recognition that the structure of international society has undergone some basic changes, and that, correspondingly, international law is now developing on several levels, one continuing the traditional international law of diplomatic coexistence, and the other two implementing the quest for both universal and regional international co-operation and organisation must lead to a far-reaching reorientation in our conceptions of the science and study of contemporary international law. ...

The shift in the structure of international law has been vividly formulated by Wilfred Jenks:[4]

... [T]he emphasis of the law is increasingly shifting from the formal structure of the relationship between States and the delimitation of their jurisdiction to the development of substantive rules on matters of common concern vital to the growth of an international community and to the individual well-being of the citizens of its member States. We shall also find that as the result of this change of emphasis the subject-matter of the law increasingly includes cross-frontier relationships of individuals, organisations and corporate bodies which call for appropriate legal regulation on an international basis. ...

NOTES

In these passages, Friedmann and Jenks indicate that the development of the law of cooperation has many facets. It is time to explore them. First, reproduced below is an opinion that draws attention to two new precepts for regulating the physical resources of the world. Then there appear the United Nations' resolutions calling forth the establishment of a new international economic order. Afterwards it will be appropriate to review the other materials in this volume for further indications of the legal expression of common interests. Finally, the legal sources on recent endeavours to found international regimes in two current areas of global concern will be taken up for discussion. Environment and disarmament have been selected for scrutiny because they are quintessentially common interests of our time. While one concerns the physical surroundings and the other reflects the human condition, both challenge the international legal system to invent new concepts and new processes of cooperation for the survival of the world.

State Sovereignty and the Effective Management of a Shared Universal Resource
by D.J. Fleming et al. (1985), 10 *Annals Air & Space L.* 327, at 327–32
(footnotes omitted)

Sovereignty, which denotes the legal personality of a state in modern day public international law, is a concept rooted in the late sixteenth century. Its origin is affiliated with

---

[4] W. Jenks, *The Common Law of Mankind* (1958), at 17.

the *de jure* recognition of the territorial state, and relates to the centralized power (most frequently, at that time, an absolute monarch) of the entity within the country that exercised total lawmaking and law-enforcing powers over its territory. ...

Unfortunately, as the power of the early sovereign nations increased (seemingly in correlation with a declining influence of the Roman empire and the papacy) the Machiavellian view of the state as a totally self-sufficient, nonmoral entity escalated to prominence. It displaced the belief that sovereignty was merely "the residuum of power ... within the confines laid down by international law" and provided a justification for states to extend (so far as their individual brute force permitted) their spheres of control (hence, sovereignty) beyond their original respective boundaries into the territories of weaker neighbours. The lack of justification for such actions – other than to extend the range of one's power – threatened the basis of any form of international legal order, including the very one which granted legitimacy to the sovereignty of states. The resulting decline of accountability for the acts of sovereigns led to chaos among nations, primarily because it precluded any of them from ever relying upon the good faith of its neighbours – particularly the ones that demonstrated signs of health and vigour. This lack of predictability, especially as it related to the traditional patterns and rules of co-existence (a major purpose of early public international law concerned matters of war and peace between states), generated a change in sentiment favouring the return of some form of binding international legal order which, in making nations accountable for their actions, confirmed the validity of affiliating state sovereignty more closely to the *de jure* territorial boundaries of nations. However, as the arguments in support of a return to international legal order were then only moral precepts, the extent to which international law could bind states – and, therefore, the definition of the scope of sovereign power – was imprecise.

At present, the definition of sovereignty is no more precise than before, but there has been a confirmation of the moral precepts that once provided the justification for an adherence to international law. It has, in fact, reinforced and, to a large extent, displaced them in favour of a far more tangible and, therefore, convincing factor: the self-interest of states, be it economic, political, social or a combination thereof. Technological developments in the fields of transportation and communications have made it more convenient and, hence, beneficial for nations to develop mutual reliances than to seek to overrun one another. In turn, this has provided them with good reason to establish viable and continuing relations – something that requires states to submit to an external, regulatory body of rules (public international law) to ensure the continuance of a reasonable measure of predictability in inter-state relationships. The transformation of international law from a preoccupation with coexistence to one based upon co-operation has heralded a return to the respect for international legal order ... .

The pre-eminence of the legal personality of the territorial state reflects a major division of the physical resources of the globe into those which are, and those which are not, under the control of a state. The resources which are not the subject of any national jurisdiction are now most usually referred to as the "common heritage of mankind" – a term generated by a communication of 17 August 1967 sent to the U.N. Secretary-General by Ambassador Pardo of Malta. It focused upon specific geographical areas of the world and proposed a "Declaration and Treaty Concerning the Reservation Exclusively for Peaceful Purposes of the Seabed and of the Ocean Floor," which sought to limit the potential extension of state sovereignty over them. Ambassador Pardo proposed that those areas be reserved for the collective benefit of the global community, deeming them to be the common heritage of mankind. The treatment that states must accord to any area so designated remains that which was contained in the declaration. It encompasses four aspects:

1)   such areas are not subject to appropriation by states;
2)   all states must share in the management of them;
3)   there must be an active sharing of the benefits reaped from the exploitation of their resources; and
4)   the areas must be dedicated exclusively to peaceful purposes.

Ambassador Pardo's reference to the common heritage of mankind was predicated upon the recognition that, being territorially-based resources, they could easily become the subject of state acquisition and, hence, fall within the sovereign authority of individual nations. Additionally, the treatment to be accorded to them (e.g., that individual states must limit their jurisdictional claims over the areas) reflects that aspect of their nature.

The concept identified as the common heritage of mankind achieved instant notoriety and acceptance, largely because of the rising influence in international fora of the developing world. Like other nations, that group realized that both the value of those resources had increased and the technology to exploit them had developed. Further, it did not wish to be deprived of the resource potential of unclaimed portions of the globe which the industrialized nations possessed the expertise to exploit. ...

In addition to the common heritage of mankind, there exists a different category of resources which are not territorially based and which may not have been recognized as sufficiently unique to warrant separate classification. They are best described as "shared universal resources". The term "shared" is used because the resources to which it refers are subject to independent, simultaneous and potentially conflicting use by sources operating within the sovereign jurisdiction of different states. Additionally, they are "universal" in nature because they bear no relation to any territorial foundation. One such resource is the electromagnetic spectrum, a portion of which – the radio frequency spectrum (RFS) – has been the subject of international control and regulation since 1906, merely ten years after the issuance of the first patent to exploit its potential.

Like all international resources, the RFS is unique in many ways. However, its most salient characteristic from the point of view of use and regulation is the non-territorial aspect of its nature. From its earliest commercial function as a modality to correspond with ships at sea, nations have recognized that the most important and valuable aspect of the RFS is its utilisation as a medium to communicate, without the need of any physical connection, to – or with – large numbers spread throughout a broad area. As the region to which the ability to transfer messages is dictated by laws of physics that are unrelated to the territorial delimitations of states, the spectrum resource has never been, nor can ever become, subject to their sovereign authority. Indeed, the most significant attribute of the RFS is that *there is neither a threat to, nor an infringement upon, state sovereignty by any international regulatory regime that nations might establish to govern it.* The pattern established by the regulations governing spectrum management which have, over time, proven to be the most successful validates this premise. Further, the history of international control of the RFS provides considerable evidence to show that the community of nations has not yet fully realized the irrelevance of claims to the spectrum resource that are based upon sovereignty. This is the case even though countries appreciate the necessity of international co-operation for the exploitation of the spectrum. Indeed, the concept of *nécessité fait loi* is, perhaps, more applicable to the control of radiocommunications than any other regulated international legal regime.

International Telecommunications

The International Telecommunication Union (ITU), one of the oldest functioning international institutions) manages virtually every form of international telecommunication, including those which employ the radio frequency spectrum as their medium of transmission. It does so by scheduling conferences at which member states establish and modify the international regulations that dictate the technical aspects of the various forms of international telecommunication. Adherence to those regulations ensures that transmissions are not garbled by interference, that receiving and transmitting devices in every jurisdiction are compatible with one another and that states respect the right of international telecommunication.[5]

In recent years, the conflicting demands of different groups of countries have made it increasingly difficult for the ITU to provide international regulations that can meet the approval of the community of nations. This is the result of a conflict of interests between states, which developed because of a growing reliance upon communications, an expansion (caused by progress in both telecommunications and computer technology) of the various services that communications can provide, and an ever widening gap between the technologically advanced and the less developed states. The former seek to modify international regulations to permit the implementation of costly, advanced telecommunication facilities (*e.g.* a global maritime distress and safety system, high definition television transmissions, passenger telephone services on airplanes, national and international cellular telephone systems, enhanced computer data transfer systems). The less developed states oppose these moves because they lack even the most basic telecommunication facilities (*e.g.* comprehensive, national telephone systems). Further, they argue that they cannot afford to implement the technological changes that the more advanced states are demanding, and that their economic development is now hindered by an inability to compete in the world marketplace, which is controlled by those who have access to the various telecommunication systems offering effective, rapid "information transfer" facilities.[6]

The division between the technologically advanced and the less developed states is primarily a "North-South" one. The states in the developing world believe that changes to accommodate further technological breakthroughs are depriving them of their rights

---

[5] See generally G.A. Codding Jr., *The International Telecommunication Union: An Experiment in International Cooperation* (1952); J. Evanson, "Aspects of International Law Relating to Modern Radio Communications" (1965), 115 *Hague Recueil* 477; G.A. Codding Jr. and A.M. Rutkowski, *The International Telecommunication Union in a Changing World* (1982).

[6] See generally *North-South: A Programme for Survival* (the *Brandt Report*), Report of the Independent Commission on International Development Issues (1980); *Many Voices, One World: Communication and Society Today and Tomorrow* (the *McBride Report*) (1980); and *The Missing Link*, report of the Independent Commission for World Wide Telecommunications Development (1984).

to exploit international telecommunication resources like the radio frequency spectrum. Moreover, they claim that changing international regulations to meet the demands of the technologically advanced states will deprive them of the less expensive, dated forms of telecommunication upon which they must still rely (*e.g.* short-wave radio communication, which is little used in the western world, but is the major form of communication in most other areas). Additionally, the less developed states complain that proposed changes to enhance newer forms of telecommunication which they hope to utilize (*e.g.* satellite systems) are making those facilities even more costly and, therefore, impossible to afford.

As a result, the less developed states, which constitute a large majority of the ITU, (as they do the United Nations), are demanding that, before they will vote in favour of certain changes to international telecommunication regulations, the technologically advanced states must agree to subsidize the telecommunication developments of countries that cannot afford basic systems or newer, more advanced ones. In effect, the lesser developed nations are demanding a "right to technology". The justification for their demands is based upon their view of the right that all members of the international community have to exploit a shared universal resource. This, they interpret, as being a right to an equal or, at least minimal, share of the product (*e.g.* telecommunication systems) of the resource.

NOTES

1) Consider the difference between what the general principles of international law governing world resources might be when the traditional notion of state "sovereignty" applies and, alternatively, under the developing one of "common interest."

2) List the various resources or areas of the globe that might best be governed by a "common interest" approach and provide a justification for so doing in each case. Moreover, categorize each item listed as falling under the descriptive rubric of either "common heritage of mankind" or "shared universal resource."

3) Are different legal principles applicable to the international governance of those "common interest" resources and areas you have categorized as being "common heritage" and those which you have listed under the title "shared universal resource"? What are the general legal principles that should govern each category?

4) Recall the present difficulties in which the so-called "debtor nations" currently find themselves and the potential impact of those difficulties on the private and public financial institutions of the "lender nations." Is there a world economic order that the international community might now consider to be a "common interest", and if so, what legal principles should apply to its governance? Keep this in mind when considering the resolutions on a New International Economic Order reported after these notes.

5) Are the various elements of the environment (*e.g.* the air, international lakes, rivers and water tables, the oceans, sections of the deep seabed) "resources" or "areas" of the globe? What international legal principles should apply to govern any portion of the environment that is shared by states? Consider this again during examination of the next Section of this Chapter dealing with environmental issues.

6) Are the destructive forces that a state is able to concoct (*e.g.* nuclear weapons,

Article 11

All States should co-operate to strengthen and continuously improve the efficiency of international organizations in implementing measures to stimulate the general economic progress of all countries, particularly of developing countries, and therefore should co-operate to adapt them, when appropriate, to the changing needs of international economic co-operation.

Article 12

1. States have the right, in agreement with the parties concerned, to participate in subregional, regional and interregional co-operation in the pursuit of their economic and social development. All States engaged in such co-operation have the duty to ensure that the policies of those groupings to which they belong correspond to the provisions of the present Charter and are outward-looking, consistent with their international obligations and with the needs of international economic co-operation, and have full regard for the legitimate interests of third countries, especially developing countries.

2. In the case of groupings to which the States concerned have transferred or may transfer certain competences as regards matters that come within the scope of the present Charter, its provisions shall also apply to those groupings, in regard to such matters, consistent with the responsibilities of such States as members of such groupings. Those States shall co-operate in the observance by the groupings of the provisions of this Charter.

Article 13

1. Every State has the right to benefit from the advances and developments in science and technology for the acceleration of its economic and social development.

2. All States should promote international scientific and technological co-operation and the transfer of technology, with proper regard for all legitimate interests including, *inter alia*, the rights and duties of holders, suppliers and recipients of technology. In particular, all States should facilitate the access of developing countries to the achievements of modern science and technology, the transfer of technology and the creation of indigenous technology for the benefit of the developing countries in forms and in accordance with procedures which are suited to their economies and their needs.

3. Accordingly, developed countries should co-operate with the developing countries in the establishment, strengthening and development of their scientific and technological infrastructures and their scientific research and technological activities so as to help to expand and transform the economies of developing countries.

4. All States should co-operate in research with a view to evolving further internationally accepted guidelines or regulations for the transfer of technology, taking fully into account the interests of developing countries.

Article 14

Every State has the duty to co-operate in promoting a steady and increasing expansion and liberalization of world trade and an improvement in the welfare and living standards of all peoples, in particular those of developing countries. Accordingly, all States should co-operate, *inter alia*, towards the progressive dismantling of obstacles to trade and the improvement of the international framework for the conduct of world trade and, to these ends, co-ordinated efforts shall be made to solve in an equitable way the trade problems of all countries, taking into account the specific trade problems of the developing countries. In this connexion, States shall take measures aimed at securing additional benefits for the international trade of developing countries so as to achieve a substantial increase in their foreign exchange earnings, the diversification of their exports, the acceleration of the rate of growth of their trade, taking into account their development needs, an improvement in the possibilities for these countries to participate in the expansion of world trade and a balance more favourable to developing countries in the sharing of the advantages resulting from this expansion, through, in the largest possible measure, a substantial improvement in the conditions of access for the products of interest to the developing countries and, wherever appropriate, measures designed to attain stable, equitable and remunerative prices for primary products.

Article 15

All States have the duty to promote the achievement of general and complete disarmament under effective international control and to utilize the resources released by effective disarmament measures for the economic and social development of countries, allocating a substantial portion of such resources as additional means for the development needs of developing countries.

Article 16

1. It is the right and duty of all States, individually and collectively, to eliminate colonialism, *apartheid*, racial discrimination, neo-colonialism and all forms of foreign aggression, occupation and domination, and the economic and social consequences thereof, as a prerequisite for development. States which practise such coercive policies are economically responsible to the countries, territories and peoples affected for the restitution and full compensation for the exploitation and depletion of, and damages to, the natural and all other resources of those countries, territories and peoples. It is the duty of all States to extend assistance to them.

2. No State has the right to promote or encourage investments that may constitute an obstacle to the liberation of a territory occupied by force.

Article 17

International co-operation for development is the shared goal and common duty of all States. Every State should co-operate with the efforts of developing countries to accelerate their economic and social development by providing favourable external conditions and by extending active assistance to them, consistent with their development needs and objectives, with strict respect for the sovereign equality of States and free of any conditions derogating from their sovereignty.

Article 18

Developed countries should extend, improve and enlarge the system of generalized non-reciprocal and non-discriminatory tariff preferences to the developing countries consistent with the relevant agreed conclusions and relevant decisions as adopted on this subject, in the framework of the competent international organizations. Developed countries should also give serious consideration to the adoption of other differential measures, in areas where this is feasible and appropriate and in ways which will provide special and more favourable treatment, in order to meet the trade and development needs of the developing countries. In the conduct of international economic relations the developed countries should endeavour to avoid measures having a negative effect on the development of the national economies of the developing countries, as promoted by generalized tariff preferences and other generally agreed differential measures in their favour.

Article 19

With a view to accelerating the economic growth of developing countries and bridging the economic gap between developed and developing countries, developed countries should grant generalized preferential, non-reciprocal and non-discriminatory treatment to developing countries in those fields of international economic co-operation where it may be feasible.

Article 20

Developing countries should, in their efforts to increase their over-all trade, give due attention to the possibility of expanding their trade with socialist countries, by granting to these countries conditions for trade not inferior to those granted normally to the developed market economy countries.

Article 21

Developing countries should endeavour to promote the expansion of their mutual trade and to this end may, in accordance with the existing and evolving provisions and procedures of international agreements where applicable, grant trade preferences to other developing countries without being obliged to extend such preferences to developed countries, provided these arrangements do not constitute an impediment to general trade liberalization and expansion.

Article 22

1. All States should respond to the generally recognized or mutually agreed development needs and objectives of developing countries by promoting increased net flows of real resources to the developing countries from all sources, taking into account any obligations and commitments undertaken by the States concerned, in order to reinforce the efforts of developing countries to accelerate their economic and social development.

2. In this context, consistent with the aims and objectives mentioned above and taking into account any obligations and commitments undertaken in this regard, it should be their endeavour to increase the net amount of financial flows from official sources to developing countries and to improve the terms and conditions thereof.

3. The flow of development assistance resources should include economic and technical assistance.

Article 23

To enhance the effective mobilization of their own resources, the developing countries should strengthen their economic co-operation and expand their mutual trade so as to accelerate their economic and social development. All countries, especially developed countries, individually as well as through the competent international organizations of which they are members, should provide appropriate and effective support and co-operation.

Article 24

All States have the duty to conduct their mutual economic relations in a manner which takes into account the interests of other countries. In particular, all States should avoid prejudicing the interests of developing countries.

Article 25

In furtherance of world economic development, the international community, especially its developed members, shall pay special attention to the particular needs and problems of the least developed among the developing countries, of land-locked developing countries and also island developing countries, with a view to helping them to overcome their particular difficulties and thus contribute to their economic and social development.

Article 26

All States have the duty to coexist in tolerance and live together in peace, irrespective of differences in political, economic, social and cultural systems, and to facilitate trade between States having different economic and social systems. International trade should be conducted without prejudice to generalized non-discriminatory and non-reciprocal preferences in favour of developing countries, on the basis of mutual advantage, equitable benefits and the exchange of most-favoured-nation treatment.

Article 27

1. Every State has the right to enjoy fully the benefits of world invisible trade and to engage in the expansion of such trade.

2. World invisible trade, based on efficiency and mutual and equitable benefit, furthering the expansion of the world economy, is the common goal of all States. The role of developing countries in world invisible trade should be enhanced and strengthened consistent with the above objectives, particular attention being paid to the special needs of developing countries.

3. All States should co-operate with developing countries in their endeavours to increase their capacity to earn foreign exchange from invisible transactions, in accordance with the potential and needs of each developing country and consistent with the objectives mentioned above.

Article 28

All States have the duty to co-operate in achieving adjustments in the prices of exports of developing countries in relation to prices of their imports so as to promote just and equitable terms of trade for them, in a manner which is remunerative for producers and equitable for producers and consumers.

CHAPTER III. COMMON RESPONSIBILITIES TOWARDS THE INTERNATIONAL COMMUNITY

Article 29

The sea-bed and ocean floor and the subsoil thereof, beyond the limits of national jurisdiction, as well as the resources of the area, are the common heritage of mankind. On the basis of the principles adopted by the General Assembly in resolution 2749 (XXV) of 17 December 1970, all States shall ensure that the exploration of the area and exploitation of its resources are carried out exclusively for peaceful purposes and that the benefits derived therefrom are shared equitably by all States, taking into account the particular interests and needs of developing countries; an international régime applying to the area and its resources and including appropriate international machinery to give effect to its provisions shall be established by an international treaty of a universal character, generally agreed upon.

Article 30

The protection, preservation and enhancement of the environment for the present and future generations is the responsibility of all States. All States shall endeavour to establish their own environmental and developmental policies in conformity with such responsibility. The environmental policies of all States should enhance and not adversely affect the present and future development potential of developing countries. All States have the responsibility to ensure that activities within their jurisdiction or control do not cause damage to the environment of other States or of areas beyond the limits of national jurisdiction. All States should co-operate in evolving international norms and regulations in the field of the environment.

Article 31

All States have the duty to contribute to the balanced expansion of the world economy, taking duly into account the close inter-relationship between the well-being of the developed countries and the growth and development of the developing countries, and the fact that the prosperity of the international community as a whole depends upon the prosperity of its constituent parts.

Article 32

No State may use or encourage the use of economic, political or any other type of measures to coerce another State in order to obtain from it the subordination of the exercise of its sovereign rights. ...

NOTES

1) Do the provisions of the Declaration and the Charter of Economic Rights and Duties of States[8] provide a consistent set of principles for a new international economic order? What are to be its dimensions?[9]

2) How would the new order differ from the old order? Review the purposes and principles of the U.N. Charter, especially Articles 1, 2, 55, 56 and 74 (reproduced in the Appendix), in light of their elaborative interpretation by the General Assembly in its Declaration on Principles of International Law Concerning Friendly Relations (reproduced in Chapter 2). What changes have to be made to these basic principles of international law in order to realize the NIEO?[10]

3) It is interesting to contrast the two concepts of permanent sovereignty over national resources, and common heritage of mankind in the resources beyond the limits of national jurisdiction. The common heritage principle already has relevance not only to the deep seabed, but also to the moon and outer space generally, and, eventually perhaps, to Antarctica. Refer to the Section entitled "Deep Seabed" in Chapter 11 on "Law of the Sea" and to the Sections concerning "Antarctica" and "Outer Space" in Chapter 6 on "State Jurisdiction over Territory."[11] Are the emerging principles of common heritage the same for different areas of application?[12]

4) In the previous extract, Professor Fleming and his colleagues make an important distinction between the territorial basis of common heritage and the shared universal

---

[8] The Charter was adopted by 120 votes to 6 with 10 abstentions. Largely due to the differences over Art. 2, the vote split along the division between western states and developing countries.

[9] See generally M. Bedjaoui, *Towards a New International Economic Order* (1979); J.N. Bhagwati ed., *The New International Economic Order: The North-South Debate* (1977); K. Hossain ed., *Legal Aspects of the New International Economic Order* (1980); E. Laszlo et al., *The Objectives of the New International Economic Order* (1979); O. de Rivero B., *New Economic Order and International Development Law* (1980); and M. Wigdor, "Canada and the New International Economic Order: Some Legal Implications" (1982), 20 *Can.Y.B. Int.L.* 161. *Cf.* O. Schachter, *Sharing the World's Resources* (1977).

[10] See I. Bernier, "Souveraineté et Interdependance dans le nouvel ordre économique international" and E.-U. Petersmann, "The New International Economic Order: Principles, Politics and International Law" in R.St.J. Macdonald et al., *Human Welfare, supra* n. 1, at 425 and 449, respectively.

[11] And see C. Joyner, "Legal Implications of the Concept of the Common Heritage of Mankind" (1986), 35 *Int.Comp.L.Q.* 190; B. Larschan and B.C. Brennan, "The Common Heritage of Mankind Principle in International Law" (1982–83), 21 *Col.J.Trans.Nat.L.* 305; and A. Pardo and C.Q. Christol, "The Common Interest: Tension Between the Whole and the Parts", in R.St.J. Macdonald et al., *Structure and Process, supra* n. 1, at 643.

[12] Compare the common heritage in great works of art and other cultural property in general. See S.A. Williams, *The International and National Protection of Movable Cultural Property, A Comparative Study* (1978), 52 fwd.

resource of the radio frequency spectrum which has no territorial foundation. Sovereign appropriation of the spectrum is impossible; hence a cooperative regime governing its use is the only means to exploit it. Is this approach relevant to the geostationary satellite orbit? Refer to the Section on "Outer Space" in Chapter 6 on "State Jurisdiction over Territory." Are there other resources of the world that might usefully be viewed from this perspective?

5) A quite different aspect of the law of cooperation is presented in the work of international organizations.[13] Their existence is a recognition of the need for intergovernmental cooperation to achieve ends that independent states cannot accomplish for themselves individually. The provisions of universal postal service, the international protection of copyright, the preservation of uniform standards for shipping, the promotion of world health and the funding of international development are all examples of cooperative responses to human needs. It is noticeable that the development of the international organizations created to serve humanity has involved a chronological enlargement in the scope of activities and methods of delivery. Early organizations like the Universal Postal Union and the Berne Union (now expanded into the World Intellectual Property Organization) were formed to provide a specific service amongst separate nation states on a reciprocal basis. More recently created bodies like the World Health Organization and the United Nations Development Programme, have far broader and more fundamental objectives which require collective and affirmative action to change the human condition. In all of these organizations there is still a central role for nation states, for they are the organizational units which wield political authority and thus remain, for the time being, the only means to organize the necessary collective action. The difficulties that can beset a common cause of humanity that depends for its authorization upon the political will of legally sovereign and equal states is only too apparent in the highly publicized disagreements within the United Nations itself. Part of the paradox is that often some of the voices calling for structural change in international society, such as the developing countries, are at the same time jealously conservative adherents of state sovereignty. Nevertheless, the work of the United Nations and its specialized agencies in the economic and social fields is a considerable record of collective accomplishments in the common interest in only a few recent years.

6) Organizations, especially international but also non-governmental ones, also present some inchoate alternatives to the authority of the nation state. While replacement of the state is not in prospect, the addition of these new though limited subjects of international law has begun to distribute the authority of the international legal system into collective hands. Refer to the Section on "International Organizations" in Chapter 2 on "International Legal Persons." International organizations have also become the principle means of law-making in the international legal system, through the process of multilateral treaties, and may therefore hold the key to transformation of the substantive rules of international law. The vehicle of a multilateral law-making treaty may be used to different ends. Thus

---

[13] See generally C. Archer, *International Organizations* (1983); A.L. Bennett, *International Organizations* (3ed. 1984); D.W. Bowett, *The Law of International Institutions* (4ed. 1982); R. Jütte and A. Grosse-Jütte, *The Future of International Organization* (1981); F.L. Kirgis Jr., *International Organizations in Their Legal Setting* (1977); E. Luard, *International Agencies: The Emerging Framework of Interdependence* (1977); and H.G. Schermers, *International Institutional Law* (2ed. 1980).

the Vienna Convention on Diplomatic Relations is essentially a statement of uniform rules for the conduct of business between states in a condition of coexistence. Though essential to intergovernmental relations, it is but a codification of traditional procedures. Refer to the Section on "Diplomatic Immunities" in Chapter 5 on "Inter-State Relations." By contrast, the Third United Nations Conference on the Law of the Sea, by far the longest, largest and most comprehensive multilateral treaty-making endeavour ever undertaken, produced a convention which, while it extended national state jurisdiction in coastal areas, created a whole new communal regime for the deep seabed. Refer to Chapter 11 on "Law of the Sea."

7) A further dimension to the growing respect for the common interest is provided by the changing status of individuals in international law. Once without rights, individuals now have a limited but real personality at international law and a burgeoning body of human rights. Formerly only aliens were protected under very general and disputed minimum standards of treatment and then, not in their own right, but only as objects of international law. Refer to the Section on "Responsibility for Injuries to Aliens" in Chapter 9 on "State Responsibility." Now human rights attach to everyone without regard to nationality and are, in principle, opposable to any signatory state. Weak though the enforcement procedures may still be, the territorial jurisdiction of the sovereign state over its population has been decisively breached in favour of the universal interest in respect for human life. Refer to Chapter 10 on "Protection of Human Rights."

8) A number of other examples of the law of cooperation can be reviewed in the pages of this book. Among them may be mentioned collective measures to maintain international peace and security which may be taken under Chapter VII of the U.N. Charter. The innovation of these powers has been extremely important in relations between states. The ability to invoke U.N. Peace Keeping forces has permitted a community response to threats to international peace, and their deployment has impressed a solution in favour of the common interest in peace over belligerent states in many parts of the world. Refer to the Section on "Non-Intervention" in Chapter 2 on "International Legal Persons." A further significant example of common interest is the conservation of resources, illustrated here by the international law of fisheries. First the Geneva Convention and now the U.N. Convention on the Law of the Sea establish principles for the conservation of fish stocks and the allocation of harvest shares. States are bound to manage the fisheries within their jurisdiction in order to achieve optimal utilization for the common good. Refer to the Section on "Resource Management and Environmental Protection" in Chapter 11 on "Law of the Sea."

9) On the bilateral level, the peaceful relations across the long frontier between Canada and the United States has encouraged a variety of cooperative arrangements.[14] The accident of political geography which has resulted in the sharing of extensive boundary waters has persuaded the two states to establish special joint machinery, known as the International Joint Commission. See the discussion in the next Section on "Protection of the Environment." Many agreements have been made on mutual assistance in coastal navigation and a long standing Convention for the Protection of Migratory Birds[15] also exists. More recently a series of understandings on cooperation in the enforcement of competition

---

[14] See W.R. Willoughby, *The Joint Organizations of Canada and the United States* (1979).
[15] (1916), U.S.T.S. 628, 12 Bevans 375.

policy have been made. These agreements call for early notification and consultation in anti-trust actions and mutual assistance in criminal law matters which have transborder effects. Refer to the Section on "Extraterritorial Assertions of Jurisdiction" in Chapter 8 on "State Jurisdiction over Persons." The treaty on cooperative development of the waters of the Columbia River is another recognition of mutual interest.[16] The current problem of acid rain is an example of a situation in need of a cooperative solution.[17] The most recent bilateral achievement is the Pacific Salmon Treaty.[18] This agreement imposes shared responsibility and benefit in the salmon that inhabit the rivers and sea along the North Pacific coast. It calls for joint management of both the conservation and the exploitation of salmon. Contrast the situation on the Atlantic coast, where the common interest in joint management of the fisheries in the Gulf of Maine has so far failed to gain ascendancy over independent activities on either side of a man-made maritime boundary[19] that artificially dissects the unity of the living resources of the area.

10) These examples of the law of cooperation in action occur in all fields of international law to some degree. There are many more instances. Can you suggest some? What is their cumulative impact on international law? The next two sections may be regarded as case studies of this question.

PROTECTION OF THE ENVIRONMENT

General Principles[20]

Transboundary Pollution
from S.A. Williams, "Public International Law Governing Transboundary Pollution," [1984] *Int.Bus.Lawyer* 243 (footnotes omitted)

Over the last decade there has been clearly evidenced an increasing domestic concern for the protection of the human environment. The amounts of pollutants that are transported

---

[16] 542 U.N.T.S. 224; 1964 Can.T.S. No. 2; 15 U.S.T. 1555. See N.A. Swainson, *Conflict over the Columbia* (1979); R.W. Johnson, "The Columbia Basin," in A.H. Garretson, R.D. Hayton and C.J. Olmstead, *The Law of International Drainage Basins* (1967), at 167; and A.E. Utton, "The Columbia River Treaty and Protocol" (1966), 1 *Land Water L.R.* 181.

[17] See D.M. Johnston and P. Finkle, "Acid Precipitation in North America: The Case for Transboundary Cooperation" (1981), 4 *Vanderbilt J.Trans.L.* 787.

[18] Done at Ottawa, January 28, 1985.

[19] See the *Gulf of Maine Case*, [1984] I.C.J.Rep. 246, reported *supra* in Chapter 11.

[20] See J. Barros and D.M. Johnston, *The International Law of Pollution* (1974); O.P. Dwivedi ed., *Protecting the Environment* (1974); W.P. Gormley, *Human Rights and Environment: The Need for International Co-operation* (1976); J.L. Hargrove ed., *Law, Institutions and Global Environment* (1972); J. Schneider, *World Public Order of the Environment* (1979); A.L. Springer, *The International Law of Pollution* (1983); L.A. Teclaff and A.E. Utton eds., *International Environmental Law* (1974); J.A. Beesley, "The Canadian Approach to International Environmental Law" (1973), 11 *Can.Y.B.Int.L.* 3; D.M. Johnston, "International Environmental Law: Recent Developments and Canadian Contributions" in R.St.J. Macdonald, G.L. Morris, D.M.

across borders, or the threatened risk of such happening has raised this concern to one of international importance.

The crisis is clear. The solution less so ... . The crisis is both complicated and far reaching in all its compound ramifications for today and for the future of mankind. It is an absolute necessity to envisage transboundary pollution in a broad environmental context. It is submitted that transboundary pollution problems can only be treated comprehensively when the broader environmental concerns have been identified and come to grips with. The problem of transboundary pollution is multifaceted and each facet, whether it be concerned with air or water pollution cannot be dealt with in a vacuum. All types of pollution hazards are fatal dangers to the planetary ecosystem. That ecosystem is complex and interrelated. Any solutions to the problems posed by such dangers must likewise be interrelated.

... [The term transboundary pollution is] used to encompass environmental pollution from many sources. The connecting factor is that the phrase is used to denote "pollution" that emanates from the territory of one state and causes injury, actual or prospective in another state. It is clear that pollution does not respect international boundaries. Hazardous air pollution may be produced in one state and cause damage within the borders of another state. Environmental pollution may be caused by chemicals such as sulphur dioxide (SO_2) and nitrogen oxide (NO_x) being put into the air in state X and along with other products being vented upwards, especially by tall stacks, undergoing complex chemical reactions high in the atmosphere and then circulating with the air masses, with the end result that after perhaps travelling hundreds or even thousands of miles, acid precipitation falls in state Y. Smoke and fumes may be blown from one state to another. Hazardous liquid and solid wastes may be discharged on to the land and into inland waters causing damage to health and property in another state. This may be of particular danger where two states share a common drainage basin. Oil pollution and effluent waste disposal may cause damage to the maritime environment offshore. Other methods of possible injury could include: thermal pollution; radiation of the atmosphere; nuclear emissions into the atmosphere; disturbance of the oxygen-carbon dioxide balance and the nitrogen cycle and by the use of pesticides, defoliants and other chemicals harmful to people and to the environment that surrounds them.

The protection of the environment on both the domestic and the international levels would at first blush appear to be a relatively recent preoccupation of governments and international bodies. However, in the space of some ten years or so it can be said to have [come to] occupy today an important place in international law. The subject in legal terms is a novel one. Therefore, the law is still very much in the process of development. It will be seen that there are glaring lacunae in the law and that the fundamental principles that underlie the law are not easy to discern. Any analysis of international environmental

Johnston, *Canadian Perspective on International Law and Organization* (1974), at 555; A. Kiss, "The International Protection of the Environment" in R.St.J. Macdonald and D.M. Johnston eds., *The Structure and Process of International Law* (1983), at 1069; S.A. Williams, "Public International Law Governing Transboundary Pollution," [1984] *Int.Bus.Lawyer* 243; and Symposium on "The International Legal Aspects of Pollution" (1971), 21 *U.T.L.J.* 173. A rich collection of documents is available in B. Rüster and B. Simma *The Protection of the Human Environment* (30 Vols. 1975–82).

law of necessity has to begin with existing rules of public international law. It is the fundamental rules of state sovereignty, territorial integrity, state responsibility and principles of maritime jurisdiction that provide the basic framework within which international environmental law has developed.

NOTES

1) The extent to which the traditional rules of international law provide a framework for dealing with environmental problems may be investigated in the context of three aspects; (1) the existence of obligations to prevent pollution, (2) the conditions upon which responsibility may be incurred by a state, and (3) the liability that flows from breach of an obligation for which a state can be held responsible.[21] The existence of a duty to protect the environment depends upon the extent of state sovereignty. Consider the materials on the "Rights and Duties of States" in Chapter 2 previously discussed.[22] May a state claim on the basis of territorial sovereignty that it can allow hazardous activities to take place on its territory and that other states have no right to interfere? What can a state that is injured by such activities argue with respect to its territorial sovereignty?

2) For an analysis of the factors necessary for a claim by one state against another look to Chapter 9 on "State Responsibility." Can the principles, which to a large extent have developed around injuries suffered by aliens abroad, be extended to cover situations involving environmental pollution? For instance, the principles of imputability may help to determine whether a state may be held responsible for polluting activities. Can a state plead a rule or the lack of a rule in its own law as a defence to a claim made against it?[23] When pollution occurs, does state responsibility arise when no action is taken to prosecute the perpetrators or access to the courts by the victims is denied or obstructed? To find a state liable it is necessary to prove its default. What do international principles of strict and fault liability suggest as the applicable standard of default in the event of pollution?[24]

3) In addition to the uncertainty involved in extrapolating traditional principles of international law, environmental claims raise a host of new issues which those principles do not address. For example, regarding states' obligations for pollution, it is necessary to define the nature of pollution, to establish the kind and degree of environmental degradation that is unacceptable, and to agree upon contamination levels as well as emission standards. The extent of states' duties to prevent pollution must also be developed. In this regard, the scope of obligations to monitor the environment, to exchange information and data, to warn of pollution risks, to notify and consult before engaging in hazardous activities, and in general to cooperate with other states all need elaboration.

---

[21] See I. Van Lier, *Acid Rain and International Law* (1981), at 95–134.

[22] And see G. Handl, "Territorial Sovereignty and the Problem of Transnational Pollution" (1975), 69 *Am.J.Int.L.* 50.

[23] See *Free Zones Case* (1932), P.C.I.J. Ser.A/B, No. 46, at 167.

[24] See L.F.E. Goldie, "Liability for Damage and the Progressive Development of International Law" (1965), 14 *Int.Comp.L.Q.* 1189; and A. Kiss, *supra*, n. 20, at 1071.

With respect to the responsibility and liability of states, it is essential to conclude arrangements regarding, *inter alia*, local procedures for claims, abatement programmes, insurance against pollution risks, mitigation of damage, quantification of compensation, and remedial measures to restore the environment. To raise these issues is to demonstrate that traditional approaches to state responsibility are not likely to generate the kinds of regulation required. Preservation of the common environment demands new perspectives. They will involve community of action and affirmative obligations for environmental protection. The materials in the rest of this Section selectively illustrate these developments, first as a matter of general principles and then in the context of international rivers and lakes.

Stockholm Declaration on the Human Environment
U.N. Doc. A/CONF. 48/14 (1972), 11 *Int.Leg.Mat.* 1416

The United Nations Conference on the Human Environment, Having met at Stockholm from 5 to 16 June 1972, and *Having considered* the need for a common outlook and for common principles to inspire and guide the peoples of the world in the preservation and enhancement of the human environment, ...

STATES THE COMMON CONVICTION THAT ...

Principle 6

The discharge of toxic substances or of other substances and the release of heat, in such quantities or concentrations as to exceed the capacity of the environment to render them harmless, must be halted in order to ensure that serious or irreversible damage is not inflicted upon ecosystems. The just struggle of the peoples of all countries against pollution should be supported.

Principle 21

States have, in accordance with the Charter of the United Nations and the principles of international law, the sovereign right to exploit their own resources pursuant to their own environmental policies, and the responsibility to ensure that activities within their jurisdiction or control do not cause damage to the environment of other States or of areas beyond the limits of national jurisdiction.

Principle 22

States shall co-operate to develop further the international law regarding liability and compensation for the victims of pollution and other environmental damage caused by activities within the jurisdiction or control of such States to areas beyond their jurisdiction.

Principle 23

Without prejudice to such criteria as may be agreed upon by the international community, or to standards which will have to be determined nationally, it will be essential in all cases to consider the systems of values prevailing in each country, and the extent of the applicability of standards which are valid for the most advanced countries but which may be inappropriate and of unwarranted social cost for the developing countries.

Principle 24

International matters concerning the protection and improvement of the environment should be handled in a co-operative spirit by all countries, big or small, on an equal footing. Co-operation through multilateral or bilateral arrangements or other appropriate means is essential to prevent, reduce or eliminate adverse environmental effects resulting from activities conducted in all spheres, in such a way that due account is taken of the sovereignty and interests of all States.

NOTES

1) This declaration was adopted by acclamation at the United Nations Conference on the Human Environment. Present at the Conference were 113 states. The Soviet bloc states did not attend because the German Democratic Republic was not asked to participate. The Declaration represents a basic charter laying down the foundation for the future development of international environmental law. Some scholars have expressed the view that it reflects existing rules of customary international law. Its principles are reflected in Article 30 of the Charter of the Economic Rights and Duties of States[25] and incorporated 1982 Law of the Sea Treaty. It was argued by Australia and New Zealand in the Nuclear Tests Cases[26] that the Declaration reflects the attitude of the international community.

2) The Stockholm Declaration was accompanied by 109 recommendations. In December, 1972, the U.N. General Assembly endorsed the recommendations and created a new agency, the United Nations Environment Programme (UNEP) to carry them out. A voluntary fund was established to finance UNEP's work which has included projects in pollution monitoring and control, conservation, environmental aspects of development and events like the 1976 Vancouver Conference on Human Settlements.

---

[25] U.N.G.A. Res. 3281 (XXIX), December 12, 1974, 29 U.N.GAOR, Supp. (No. 31) 50, U.N. Doc. A/9631 (1974), reported in the previous Section.

[26] [1974] I.C.J. Rep. 253 and 457.

Trail Smelter Arbitration
United States v. Canada
(1931–41), 3 R.I.A.A. 1905, reported in Chapter 9

Corfu Channel Case (Merits)
United Kingdom v. Albania
[1949] I.C.J. Rep. 4, reported in Chapter 11

Lake Lanoux Arbitration
France v. Spain
(1957), 12 R.I.A.A. 281; 24 *Int.L.R.* 101

[France proposed to use Lake Lanoux for hydroelectric purposes but Spain objected that the scheme would interfere with the flow of boundary waters contrary to a treaty of 1866 between the two states. The Tribunal first found in favour of France that its development scheme would not breach the treaty, and in so doing it made an important statement of principle about possible liability for pollution. The Tribunal went on to consider what conduct was expected of France towards Spain in the realization of its scheme. In particular, Spain argued that the proposed scheme required the prior agreement of both states.]

THE TRIBUNAL: ...
One might have attacked this conclusion [that the French plans were not in breach of the treaty] in several different ways.
It could have been argued that the works would bring about an ultimate pollution of the waters of the Carol or that the returned waters would have a chemical composition or a temperature or some other characteristic which could injure Spanish interests. Spain could then have claimed that her rights had been impaired in violation of the Additional Act. Neither in the dossier nor in the pleadings in this case is there any trace of such an allegation.
[As to the Spanish contention that its agreement with the French scheme was necessary, the Tribunal said:]
... To admit that jurisdiction in a certain field can no longer be exercised except on the condition of, or by way of, an agreement between two States, is to place an essential restriction on the sovereignty of a State, and such restriction could only be admitted if there were clear and convincing evidence. Without doubt, international practice does reveal some special cases in which this hypothesis has become reality; thus, sometimes two States exercise conjointly jurisdiction over certain territories (joint ownership, *co-imperium*, or *condominium*); likewise, in certain international arrangements, the representatives of States exercise conjointly a certain jurisdiction in the name of those States or in the name of organizations. But these cases are exceptional, and international judicial decisions are slow to recognize their existence, especially when they impair the territorial sovereignty of a State, as would be the case in the present matter.
In effect, in order to appreciate in its essence the necessity for prior agreement, one must envisage the hypothesis in which the interested States cannot reach agreement. In

such case, it must be admitted that the State which is normally competent has lost its right to act alone as a result of the unconditional and arbitrary opposition of another State. This amounts to admitting a ''right of assent,'' a ''right of veto,'' which at the discretion of one State paralyses the exercise of the territorial jurisdiction of another.

That is why international practice prefers to resort to less extreme solutions by confining itself to obliging the States to seek, by preliminary negotiations, terms for an agreement, without subordinating the exercise of their competences to the conclusion of such an agreement. Thus, one speaks, although often inaccurately, of the "obligation of negotiating an agreement." In reality, the engagements thus undertaken by States take very diverse forms and have a scope which varies according to the manner in which they are defined and according to the procedures intended for their execution; but the reality of the obligations thus undertaken is incontestable and sanctions can be applied in the event, for example, of an unjustified breaking off of the discussions, abnormal delays, disregard of the agreed procedures, systematic refusals to take into consideration adverse proposals or interests, and, more generally, in cases of violation of the rules of good faith.

... States are today perfectly conscious of the importance of the conflicting interests brought into play by the industrial use of international rivers, and of the necessity to reconcile them by mutual concessions. The only way to arrive at such compromises of interests is to conclude agreements on an increasingly comprehensive basis. International practice reflects the conviction that States ought to strive to conclude such agreements: there would thus appear to be an obligation to accept in good faith all communications and contracts which could, by a broad comparison of interests and by reciprocal good will, provide States with the best conditions for concluding agreements. This point will be referred to again later on, when enquiring what obligations rest on France and Spain in connection with the contracts and the communications preceding the putting in hand of a scheme such as that relating to Lake Lanoux.

But international practice does not so far permit more than the following conclusion: the rule that States may utilize the hydraulic power of international watercourses only on condition of a *prior* agreement between the interested States cannot be established as a custom, even less as a general principle of law. ...

The ... question is to determine the method by which these interests can be safeguarded. If that method necessarily involves communications, it cannot be confined to purely formal requirements, such as taking note of complaints, protests or representations made by the downstream State. The Tribunal is of the opinion that, according to the rules of good faith, the upstream State is under the obligation to take into consideration the various interests involved, to seek to give them every satisfaction compatible with the pursuit of its own interests, and to show that in this regard it is genuinely concerned to reconcile the interests of the other riparian State with its own. ...

As a matter of form, the upstream State has, procedurally, a right of initiative; it is not obliged to associate the downstream State in the elaboration of its schemes. If, in the course of discussions, the downstream State submits schemes to it, the upstream State must examine them, but it has the right to give preference to the solution contained in its own scheme provided that it takes into consideration in a reasonable manner the interests of the downstream State.

... In the case of Lake Lanoux, France has maintained to the end the solution which consists in diverting the waters of the Carol to the Ariège with full restitution. By making this choice France is only making use of a right; the development works of Lake Lanoux are on French territory, the financing of and responsibility for the enterprise fall upon France, and France alone is the judge of works of public utility which are to be executed on her own territory, save for the provisions of Articles 9 and 10 of the Additional Act, which, however, the French scheme does not infringe.

On her side, Spain cannot invoke a right to insist on a development of Lake Lanoux based on the needs of Spanish agriculture. In effect, if France were to renounce all of the works envisaged on her territory, Spain could not demand that other works in conformity with her wishes should be carried out. Therefore, she can only urge her interests in order to obtain, within the framework of the scheme decided upon by France, terms which reasonably safeguard them.

It remains to be established whether this requirement has been fulfilled.

When one examines the question of whether France, either in the course of the dealings or in her proposals, has taken Spanish interests into sufficient consideration, it must be stressed how closely linked together are the obligation to take into consideration, in the course of negotiations, adverse interests and the obligation to give a reasonable place to these interests in the solution finally adopted. A State which has conducted negotiations with understanding and good faith ... is not relieved from giving a reasonable place to adverse interests in the solution it adopts simply because the conversations have been interrupted, even though owing to the intransigence of its partner. Conversely, in determining the manner in which a scheme has taken into consideration the interests involved, the way in which negotiations have developed, the total number of the interests which have been presented, the price which each Party was ready to pay to have those interests safeguarded, are all essential factors in establishing ... the merits of that scheme.

[The Tribunal held that, although the parties had failed to reach agreement, France had sufficiently involved Spain in the preparation of its development scheme.]

NOTES

1) The award in the *Trail Smelter Arbitration* has been considered as the *locus classicus* of international environmental law.[27] However, as Professor Williams has observed:[28]

... [I]t should be noted that what the Tribunal said as to liability can be considered as *obiter dicta*, on account of the fact that Canada had admitted liability for damage suffered in the United States resulting from sulphur dioxide emissions from the Cominco smelter at Trail, British Columbia. The Tribunal's function was only to assess the nature and extent of the compensation to be paid by Canada. Also, the principle of international law stated by the Tribunal can be questioned as it would be difficult to say that in 1931–41 there was sufficient state practice and

---

[27] G. Handl, *supra* n. 22, at 60.
[28] S.A. Williams, *supra* n. 20.

opinio juris. The Tribunal referred also to the law of the United States.[29] Reference to domestic legal systems and decisions by national tribunals is valid as a subsidiary source of international law. Nevertheless, the bold principle it was propounding should have found support in more than a few United States municipal air pollution cases, as well as to analogies with water pollution. These criticisms aside, it is clear the holding of the Tribunal has today become an integral part of international environmental law and can be said to have widespread acceptance by states.

2) Although the *Corfu Channel Case* did not concern environmental pollution, some of the International Court's statements, in particular its pronouncement that every state has an "obligation not to allow knowingly its territory to be used for acts contrary to the rights of other States," can be interpreted as an affirmation of a state's responsibility to take precautions against the exportation of pollution that might reasonably be prevented and to pay compensation for the damage caused when it does occur.[30]

3) As evidence of customary international law prior to the Stockholm Declaration, these three cases provide an inadequate basis for dealing with pollution problems. To what extent do they support the view that the principles of the Stockholm Declaration reflect existing international law? In what ways does the Declaration surpass them?

4) In addition to customary law, certain general principles of law are acknowledged as the basis of obligations towards the environment.[31] One such fundamental principle is the maxim "*Sic utere tuo, ut non alienum laedas*," meaning "Use your own property so as not to injure that of another." Can this principle be discerned in the previous cases? Sometimes the maxim is treated as equivalent to the general principle of good neighbourliness, which certainly underlies interstate relations and finds specific recognition in the U.N. Charter Article 74 (reproduced in the Appendix).

5) There are no general global conventions dealing with air pollution, the planetary ecosystem, environmental quality or with water pollution in international rivers, lakes or common drainage basins. Some general conventions exist on other subjects yet have as one of their goals the protection of the environment. For example, the 1963 Limited Nuclear Test Ban Treaty[32] bans nuclear weapons tests in the atmosphere, outer space, and under water. Only underground testing is allowed, provided it does not permit radioactive debris to escape into the atmosphere.

6) The U.N. General Assembly recently has been taking steps to promote cooperation in safeguarding the balance and quality of nature.[33] By a resolution in 1982, the United Nations adopted the World Charter for Nature.[34] Professor Williams has commented:[35]

This Charter reinforces the concept of conservation of all areas of the earth and special protection

---

[29] It was directed to apply United States law by the compromise.

[30] See J. Barros and D.M. Johnston, *supra* n. 20, at 69.

[31] See I. van Lier, *supra* n. 21, at 100.

[32] 480 U.N.T.S. 43, reported in the next Section.

[33] See U.N.G.A. Res.35/7 (November 5, 1980) and annexed Draft World Charter for Nature, reprinted in (1981), 20 *Int.Leg.Mat.* 462.

[34] U.N.G.A. Res.37/7 (November 9, 1982), reprinted in (1983), 22 *Int.Leg.Mat.* 455.

[35] S.A. Williams, *supra* n. 20, at 248.

to unique areas and samples of the different ecosystems and habitats of rare and endangered species. It stresses that discharge of pollutants into natural systems should be avoided,[36] but where this is not possible, such pollutants shall be treated at source. This would appear in the context of transboundary pollution to posit the view that states must ensure that activities located within their jurisdictions do not damage natural systems within their own territory, within other states or in areas beyond national jurisdiction.[37] This resolution reinforces the duty on states to strive for the objectives and requirements set out in the Charter on Nature. In the mind of this writer the Charter and the resolution are policy goals for the future. They may have the cumulative effect with the other documents and cases of germinating at some stage a rule of customary international law.

Undoubtedly, they carry forward the spirit of the Stockholm Declaration.

7) Alongside these global approaches, efforts to substantiate legal standards and co-operative action against pollution have also been made on a regional basis and according to the feature of the environment that needs protecting. Some of these efforts ante-date the Stockholm Declaration. Some have achieved considerable detail and sophistication. Two examples of the features of the environment which have received specific attention are the oceans, and international rivers and lakes. The latter will be developed later in the context of experience with the Great Lakes. The example chosen to illustrate regional developments is the OECD Principles concerning Transfrontier Pollution, which follow these notes.

8) Regarding the oceans, great concern about their degradation has now found expression in Part XII of the U.N. Convention on the Law of the Sea, which deals with protection and preservation of the marine environment. See the previous discussion of this subject in Chapter 11. In addition to the umbrella provisions of that convention there is a substantial record of other multilateral agreements on specific aspects or areas of pollution of the sea. The list includes:
- International Convention for the Prevention of Pollution of the Sea by Oil, 1954;[38]
- International Convention relating to Intervention on the High Seas in Cases of Oil Pollution Casualties, 1969;[39]
- International Convention on Civil Liability for Oil Pollution Damage, 1969;[40]
- International Convention on the Establishment of an International Fund for Compensation for Oil Pollution Damage, 1971;[41]
- Oslo Convention for the Prevention of Marine Pollution by Dumping from Ships and Aircraft, 1972;[42]

---

[36] *Supra*, n. 34, Article 12.
[37] *Supra*, n. 34, Article 21(b).
[38] 327 U.N.T.S. 3; 1958 Can.T.S. No. 31.
[39] (1970), 9 *Int.Leg.Mat.* 25.
[40] (1970), 9 *Int.Leg.Mat.* 45.
[41] (1972), 11 *Int.Leg.Mat.* 284. This treaty supplements the Civil Liability Convention, 1969. Compensation may also be available from two oil tanker owners' pollution funds bearing the acronyms TOVALOP and CRISTAL; see (1969), 8 *Int.Leg.Mat.* 497 and (1971), 10 *Int.Leg.Mat.* 137, respectively. See E. Gold, *Handbook on Marine Pollution* (1985).
[42] (1972), 11 *Int.Leg.Mat.* 262. Applies to the North Sea and part of the Atlantic only.

- London Convention on the Prevention of Marine Pollution by Dumping of Wastes and Other Matter, 1972;[43]
- International Convention for the Prevention of Pollution from Ships, 1973, and its Protocol of 1978;[44]
- Paris Convention for the Prevention of Pollution from Land-Based Sources, 1974;[45]
- Barcelona Convention for the Protection of the Mediterranean Sea Against Pollution, 1976;[46]
- London Convention on Civil Liability for Oil Pollution Damage Resulting from Exploration and Exploitation of Seabed Minerals and Resources, 1976;[47]
- Abidjan Convention for Cooperation in the Protection and Development of the Marine and Coastal Environment of the West and Central African Region, 1981;[48]
- Cartagena Convention for the Protection and Development of the Marine Environment of the Wider Caribbean Region, 1983;[49] and
- Convention for the Protection of the Natural Resources and Environment of the South Pacific Region, 1986.[50]

OECD Principles Concerning Transfrontier Pollution
Council Recommendation C(74) 224; (1975), 14 *Int.Leg.Mat.* 242

The Council, ...

Considering that the protection and improvement of the environment are common objectives of Member countries;

Considering that the common interests of countries concerned by transfrontier pollution should induce them to co-operate more closely in a spirit of international solidarity and to initiate concerted action for preventing and controlling transfrontier pollution;

Having regard to the Recommendations of the United Nations Conference on the Human Environment held in Stockholm in June 1972 and in particular those Principles of the Declaration on the Human Environment which are relevant to transfrontier pollution;

On the proposal of the Environment Committee;

I. RECOMMENDS that, without prejudice to future developments in international law and international co-operation in relation to transfrontier pollution, Member countries should be guided in their environmental policy by the principles concerning transfrontier pollution contained in this Recommendation and its Annex, which is an integral part of this Recommendation. ...

---

[43] (1972), 11 *Int.Leg.Mat.* 1291.
[44] (1973), 12 *Int.Leg.Mat.* 1319, and (1978), 17 *Int.Leg.Mat.* 546.
[45] (1975), 13 *Int.Leg.Mat.* 352.
[46] (1976), 15 *Int.Leg.Mat.* 290.
[47] (1977), 16 *Int.Leg.Mat.* 1451.
[48] (1981), 20 *Int.Leg.Mat.* 746.
[49] (1983), 22 *Int.Leg.Mat.* 227.
[50] (1987), 26 *Int.Leg.Mat.* 38.

ANNEX

SOME PRINCIPLES CONCERNING TRANSFRONTIER POLLUTION

Title A

INTRODUCTION

This Annex sets forth some principles designed to facilitate the development of harmonized environmental policies with a view to solving transfrontier pollution problems. Their implementation should be based on a fair balance of rights and obligations among countries concerned by transfrontier pollution.

These principles should subsequently be supplemented and developed in the light of work undertaken by the OECD or other appropriate international organisations.

For the purpose of these principles, pollution means the introduction by man, directly or indirectly, of substances or energy into the environment resulting in deleterious effects of such a nature as to endanger human health, harm living resources and ecosystems, and impair or interfere with amenities and other legitimate uses of the environment.

Unless otherwise specified, these principles deal with pollution originating in one country and having effects within other countries.

Title B

INTERNATIONAL SOLIDARITY

1. Countries should define a concerted long-term policy for the protection and improvement of the environment in zones liable to be affected by transfrontier pollution.

Without prejudice to their rights and obligations under international law and in accordance with their responsibility under Principle 21 of the Stockholm Declaration, countries should seek, as far as possible, an equitable balance of their rights and obligations as regards the zones concerned by transfrontier pollution.

In implementing this concerted policy, countries should among other things:

a) take account of:
   - levels of existing pollution and the present quality of the environment concerned;
   - the nature and quantities of pollutants;
   - the assimilative capacity of the environment, as established by mutual agreement by the countries concerned, taking into account the particular characteristics and use of the affected zone;
   - activities at the source of pollution and activities and uses sensitive to such pollution;
   - the situation, prospective use and development of the zones concerned from a socio-economic standpoint;

b) define:
   - environmental quality objectives and corresponding protective measures;

c) promote:
   - guidelines for a land-use planning policy consistent with the requirements both of environmental protection and socio-economic development;

d) draw up and maintain up to date:

     i) lists of particularly dangerous substances regarding which efforts should be made to eliminate polluting discharges, if necessary by stages, and

    ii) lists of substances regarding which polluting discharges should be subject to very strict control. ...

3. Countries should endeavour to prevent any increase in transfrontier pollution, including that stemming from new or additional substances and activities, and to reduce, and as far as possible eliminate any transfrontier pollution existing between them within time limits to be specified.

Title C

PRINCIPLE OF NON-DISCRIMINATION

4. Countries should initially base their action on the principle of non-discrimination, whereby:

a) polluters causing transfrontier pollution should be subject to legal or statutory provisions no less severe than those which would apply for any equivalent pollution occurring within their country, under comparable conditions and in comparable zones, taking into account, when appropriate, the special nature and environmental needs of the zone affected;

b) in particular, without prejudice to quality objectives or standards applying to transfrontier pollution mutually agreed upon by the countries concerned, the levels of transfrontier pollution entering into the zones liable to be affected by such pollution should not exceed those considered acceptable under comparable conditions and in comparable zones inside the country in which it originates, taking into account, when appropriate, the special state of the environment in the affected country;

c) any country whenever it applies the Polluter-Pays Principle should apply it to all polluters within this country without making any difference according to whether pollution affects this country or another country;

d) persons affected by transfrontier pollution should be granted no less favourable treatment than persons affected by a similar pollution in the country from which such transfrontier pollution originates.

Title D

PRINCIPLE OF EQUAL RIGHT OF HEARING

5. Countries should make every effort to introduce, where not already in existence, a system affording equal right of hearing, according to which:

a) whenever a project, a new activity or a course of conduct may create a significant risk of transfrontier pollution and is investigated by public authorities, those who may be affected by such pollution should have the same rights of standing in judicial or administrative proceedings in the country where it originates as those of that country;

b) whenever transfrontier pollution gives rise to damage in a country, those who are affected by such pollution should have the same rights of standing in judicial or administrative proceedings in the country where such pollution originates as those of that country, and they should be extended procedural rights equivalent to the rights extended to those of that country.

6. Prior to the initiation in a country of works or undertakings which might create a significant risk of transfrontier pollution, this country should provide early information to other countries which are or may be affected. It should provide these countries with relevant information and data, the transmission of which is not prohibited by legislative provisions or prescriptions or applicable international conventions, and should invite their comments.

7. Countries should enter into consultation on an existing or foreseeable transfrontier pollution problem at the request of a country which is or may be directly affected and should diligently pursue such consultations on this particular problem over a reasonable period of time.

8. Countries should refrain from carrying out projects or activities which might create a significant risk of transfrontier pollution without first informing the countries which are or may be affected and, except in cases of extreme urgency, providing a reasonable amount of time in the light of circumstances for diligent consultation. Such consultations held in the best spirit of co-operation and good neighbourliness should not enable a country to unreasonably delay or to impede the activities or projects on which consultations are taking place.

Title F
WARNING SYSTEMS AND INCIDENTS

9. Countries should promptly warn other potentially affected countries of any situation which may cause any sudden increase in the level of pollution in areas outside the country of origin of pollution, and take all appropriate steps to reduce the effects of any such sudden increase.

10. Countries should assist each other, wherever necessary, in order to prevent incidents which may result in transfrontier pollution, and to minimise, and if possible eliminate, the effects of such incidents, and should develop contingency plans to this end.

Title G
EXCHANGE OF SCIENTIFIC INFORMATION, MONITORING MEASURES AND RESEARCH

11. Countries concerned should exchange all relevant scientific information and data on transfrontier pollution, when not prohibited by legislative provisions or prescriptions or by applicable international conventions. They should develop and adopt pollution measurement methods providing results which are compatible.

12. They should, when appropriate, co-operate in scientific and technical research programmes inter alia for identifying the origin and pathways of transfrontier pollution, any damage caused and the best methods of pollution prevention and control, and should share all information and data thus obtained.

They should, where necessary, consider setting up jointly, in zones affected by transfrontier pollution, a permanent monitoring system or network for assessing the levels of pollution and the effectiveness of measures taken by them to reduce pollution. ...

Title J
INTERNATIONAL AGREEMENTS

15. Countries should endeavour to conclude, where necessary, bilateral or multilateral agreements for the abatement of transfrontier pollution in accordance with the above principles, ...

NOTES

1) These Principles of the OECD[51] begin to spell out the mutual obligations called forth by the Stockholm Declaration. They also echo the earlier cases, for instance the Principle of Information and Consultation is reminiscent of the *Lake Lanoux Arbitration*. Has the OECD set down a complete and sufficient set of principles? What do they contribute to the issues of state responsibility and liability for polluting activities?

2) In North America, in response to Principle 22 of the Stockholm Declaration, Canadian and American Bar Associations, the Uniform Law Conference of Canada and the National Conference of Commissioners on Uniform State Laws have recommended procedures by which victims of transboundary pollution can be compensated through litigation. This work has culminated in the consideration by a number of Canadian provinces and American states, situated along the international border, of legislation that gives out of jurisdiction victims standing to sue in the courts of the jurisdiction in which the polluter is situated. Up to the present the law has been that actions for trespass, nuisance or negligence must be made in the courts with jurisdiction over the injured land.[52] Ontario is the only jurisdiction in the Great Lakes area to have enacted a reciprocal access statute; see the *Transboundary Pollution Reciprocal Access Act, 1986*.[53] Manitoba and Prince Edward Island have passed similar statutes.[54] Missouri, Montana, Colorado and New Jersey have also passed like legislation and a number of other provinces and states are considering doing so. Because of the reciprocal nature of this procedure, a victim can only have access to the other jurisdiction's courts if the legislatures of both the victim and the alleged polluter have adopted such legislation.

---

[51] See S.C. McCaffrey, "The OECD Principles Concerning Transfrontier Pollution: Commentary" (1975), 1 *Env.Pol.& Law* 2.

[52] See *British South Africa Co. v. Companhia de Moçambique*, [1893] A.C. 602 (H.L.); and *Hesperides Hotels Ltd. v. Aegean Turkish Holidays Ltd.*, [1978] 1 Q.B. 205 (C.A.); rev'd. in pt. [1979] A.C. 508 (H.L.), reported *supra* in Chapter 5. See J.-G. Castel, *Canadian Conflicts of Law* (2ed. 1976), at 405-9.

[53] S.O. 1986, c. 10.

[54] *The Transboundary Pollution Reciprocal Access Act*, S.M. 1985–86, c. 11; and *Transboundary Pollution (Reciprocal Access) Act*, S.P.E.I. 1985, c. 43, respectively.

International Rivers and Lakes[55]

The fact that many major rivers and lakes, or more generally freshwater drainage basins, in all parts of the world traverse national frontiers is a complicating reality that riparian states have to live with. No matter whether the relationship is one of upstream-downstream or opposing riparian neighbours, the waters of an international river basin are a shared resource. Conditions for the shared use of the waters are consequently essential. But the process of apportioning access is made more complex by the variety, and sometimes conflicts, of uses which co-basin states may claim. Thus navigation, hydroelectric power, irrigation, fishing, human consumption, recreation, waste disposal and many other uses, may all have to be accommodated in an international regime.

Principles on cooperative use and management of international rivers and lakes have not been long developed. Local institutions and rules were sufficient to regulate the use, chiefly for navigation, of the principal rivers of Europe, such as the Danube, the Oder, the Rhine and the Rhone, at least until the twentieth century. Greater demands on international rivers, especially to divert them for hydroelectric purposes and thus to disturb those traditional uses dependent on their seasonal flow, spurred the development of legal theories as to rights of access. To begin with, states made assertions of exclusive rights to the waters of international rivers. An upstream state might claim unlimited territorial sovereignty over the river (The Harmon Doctrine) while a downstream state might assert a riparian right to the unfettered natural flow, or prior use, and thus appropriation, of the waters.[56] But none of these approaches responds to the needs of more than a few of the co-basin states and consequently they did not survive.

The principles of shared use and responsibility which have now met with general approval owe much of their development to the work of the International Law Association. This non-governmental organization of international lawyers has made a point of codifying many areas of the law. The set of rules on international rivers which were adopted at its Helsinki Conference in 1966 are regularly referred to even though they emanate from an unofficial source.

Helsinki Rules on the Uses of the Waters of International Rivers
International Law Association, 52nd Conference, August 1966

Article IV

Each basin State is entitled, within its territory, to a reasonable and equitable share in the beneficial use of the water of an international drainage basin.

---

[55] See generally F.J. Berber, *Rivers in International Law* (1959); D.A. Caponera, *The Law of International Water Resources* (1980); A.H. Garretson et al. eds., *The Law of International Drainage Basins* (1967); J.G. Lammers, *Pollution of International Watercourses* (1984); L.A. Teclaff, *The River Basin in History and Law* (1967); and *Water Law in Historical Perspective* (1985); and R. Zacklin and L. Calfisch, *The Legal Regime of International Rivers and Lakes* (1981); C.B. Bourne, "Canada and the Law of International Drainage Basins," in R.St.J. Macdonald, G.L. Morris, D.M. Johnston eds., *Canadian Perspectives on International Law and Organization* (1974) 468; and S.A. Williams, "Public International Law and Water Quantity Management in a Common Drainage Basin: The Great Lakes" (1986), 18 *Case W.Res.J.Int.L.* 155.

[56] See C.B. Bourne, "International Law and Pollution of International Rivers and Lakes" (1971), 6 *U.B.C.L.R.* 115; and S.A. Williams, *supra* n. 55, at 168–73.

Comment:

(a) GENERAL

This Article reflects the key principle of international law in this area that every basin State in an international drainage basin has the right to the reasonable use of the waters of the drainage basin. It rejects the unlimited sovereignty position, exemplified by the "Harmon Doctrine," which has been cited as supporting the proposition that a State has the unqualified right to utilize and dispose of the waters of an international river flowing through its territory; such a position imports its logical corollary, that a State has no right to demand continued flow from co-basin States.

The Harmon Doctrine has never had a wide following among States and has been rejected by virtually all States which have had occasion to speak out on the point. ...

This Article recognizes that each basin State has rights equal in kind and correlative with those of each co-basin State. Of course, equal and correlative rights of use among the co-basin States does not mean that each such State will receive an identical share in the uses of the waters. Those will depend upon the weighing of factors considered in Article V of this Chapter.

A use of a basin State must take into consideration the economic and social needs of its co-basin States for use of the waters, and *vice-versa*. This consideration may result in one co-basin State receiving the right to use water in quantitatively greater amounts than its neighbors in the basin. The idea of equitable sharing is to provide the maximum benefit to each basin State from the uses of the waters with the minimum detriment to each.

(b) BENEFICIAL USE

To be worthy of protection a use must be "beneficial," that is to say, it must be economically or socially valuable, as opposed, for example, to a diversion of waters by one State merely for the purpose of harrassing another.

A "beneficial use" need not be *the* most productive use to which the water may be put, nor need it utilize the most efficient methods known in order to avoid waste and insure maximum utilization. As to the former, to provide otherwise would dislocate numerous productive and, indeed, essential portions of national economies; the latter, while a patently imperfect solution, reflects the financial limitations of many States; in its application, the present rule is not designed to foster waste but to hold States to a duty of efficiency which is commensurate with their financial resources. Of course, the ability of a State to obtain international financing will be considered in this context. Thus, State A, an economically advanced and prosperous State which utilizes the inundation method of irrigation, might be required to develop a more efficient and less wasteful system forthwith, while State B, an underdeveloped State using the same method, might be permitted additional time to obtain the means to make the required improvements.

Article V

1) What is a reasonable and equitable share within the meaning of Article IV is to be determined in the light of all the relevant factors in each particular case.

2) Relevant factors which are to be considered include, but are not limited to:

    (a) the geography of the basin, including in particular the extent of the drainage area in the territory of each basin State;

    (b) the hydrology of the basin, including in particular the contribution of water by each basin State;

    (c) the climate affecting the basin;

    (d) the past utilization of the waters of the basin, including in particular existing utilization;

    (e) the economic and social needs of each basin State;

    (f) the population dependent on the waters of the basin in each basin State;

    (g) the comparative costs of alternative means of satisfying the economic and social needs of each basin State;

    (h) the availability of other resources;

    (i) the avoidance of unnecessary waste in the utilization of waters of the basin;

    (j) the practicability of compensation to one or more of the co-basin States as a means of adjusting conflicts among uses; and

    (k) the degree to which the needs of a basin State may be satisfied, without causing substantial injury to a co-basin State.

3) The weight to be given to each factor is to be determined by its importance in comparison with that of other relevant factors. In determining what is a reasonable and equitable share, all relevant factors are to be considered together and a conclusion reached on the basis of the whole.

Comment:

GENERAL

This Article provides the express, but flexible guidelines essential to insuring the protection of the "equal right" of all basin States to share the waters. Under the rules set forth "all the relevant factors" must be considered. An exhaustive list of factors cannot readily be compiled, for there would likely be others applicable to particular cases.

This Article states some of the factors to be considered in determining what is a reasonable and equitable share.

Stated somewhat more generally, the factor-analysis approach seeks primarily to determine whether (i) the various uses are compatible; (ii) any of the uses is essential to human life, (iii) the uses are socially and economically valuable, (iv) other resources are available, (v) any of the uses is "existing" within the meaning of Article VIII, (vi) it is feasible to modify competing uses in order to accommodate all to some degree, (vii) financial contributions by one or more of the interested basin States for the construction of works could result in the accommodation of competing uses, (viii) the burden could be adjusted by the payment of compensation to one or more of the co-basin States, and (ix) overall efficiency of water utilization could be improved in order to increase the amount of available water.

In short, no factor has a fixed weight nor will all factors be relevant in all cases. Each factor is given such weight as it merits relative to all the other factors. And no factor occupies a position of preeminence per se with respect to any other factor. Further, to be relevant, a factor must aid in the determination or satisfaction of the social and economic needs of the co-basin states.

Article VI

A use or category of uses is not entitled to any inherent preference over any other use or category of uses.

Comment:

PREFERENTIAL USE

Historically, navigation was preferred over other uses of water, irrespective of the later needs of the particular drainage basin involved. In the past twenty-five years, however, the technological revolution and population explosion, which have led to the rapid growth of nonnavigational uses have resulted in the loss of the former pre-eminence accorded navigational uses. Today, neither navigation nor any other use enjoys such a preference. A drainage basin must be examined on an individual basis and a determination made as to which uses are most important in that basin or, in appropriate cases, in portions of the basin.

It has been said that domestic use has succeeded navigation as a preferential use. However, substantial authority supporting the proposition has not been found. Moreover, no artificial preference is necessary, and, indeed, the granting of such a preference would be inconsistent with a principle of equitable utilization which relies on an inductive process of determination. Granting domestic use an artificial preference can foster the very injustice in the uses of the waters of the basin which its proponents fear will arise by its absence. The purpose in insuring domestic uses a preference is to make certain that these uses – the basis of all life – are assured a first charge on the waters. ...

Article IX

As used in this Chapter, the term "water pollution" refers to any detrimental change resulting from human conduct in the natural composition, content, or quality of the waters of an international drainage basin. ...

Article X

1. Consistent with the principle of equitable utilization of the waters of an international drainage basin, a State
  (a) must prevent any new form of water pollution or any increase in the degree of existing water pollution in an international drainage basin which would cause substantial injury in the territory of a co-basin State, and
  (b) should take all reasonable measures to abate existing water pollution in an international drainage basin to such an extent that no substantial damage is caused in the territory of a co-basin State.
2. The Rule stated in paragraph 1 of this Article applies to water pollution originating
  (a) within the territory of the State, or
  (b) outside the territory of the State, if it is caused by the State's conduct. ...

Article XI

1. In the case of a violation of the rule stated in paragraph 1 (a) of Article X of this Chapter, the State responsible shall be required to cease the wrongful conduct and compensate the injured co-basin State for the injury that has been caused to it.

2. In a case falling under the rule stated in paragraph 1 (b) of Article X, if a State fails to take reasonable measures, it shall be required promptly to enter into negotiations with the injured State with a view toward reaching a settlement equitable under the circumstances. ...

Montreal Rules on Water Pollution in an International Drainage Basin
International Law Association, 60th Conference, August 1982

Article 1

Consistent with the Helsinki Rules on the equitable utilization of the waters on an international drainage basin, states shall ensure that activities conducted within their territory or under their control conform with the principles set forth in these Articles concerning water pollution in an international drainage basin. In particular, states shall:
   a)   prevent new or increased water pollution that would cause substantial injury in the territory of another state;
   b)   take all reasonable measures to abate existing water pollution to such an extent that no substantial injury is caused in the territory of another state; and
   c)   attempt to further reduce any such water pollution to the lowest level that is practicable and reasonable under the circumstances.

Article 2

Notwithstanding the provision of Article 1, states shall not discharge or permit the discharge of substances generally considered to be highly dangerous into the waters of an international drainage basin.

Article 3

In order to give effect to Articles 1 and 2 above, states shall enact all necessary laws and regulations and adopt efficient and adequate administrative measures and judicial procedures for the enforcement of these laws and regulations.

Article 4

In order to give effect to the provisions of these Articles, states shall cooperate with the other states concerned.

Article 5

Basin states shall:
   (a)   inform the other states concerned regularly of all relevant and reasonably available data, both qualitative and quantitative, on the pollution of waters of the basin, its causes, its nature, the damage resulting from it, and the preventive procedures;
   (b)   notify the other states concerned in due time of any activities envisaged in their

own territories that may involve a significant threat of, or increase in, water pollution in the territories of those other states; and

(c) promptly inform states that might be affected, of any sudden change of circumstances that may cause or increase water pollution in the territories of those other states.

Article 6

Basin states shall consult one another on actual or potential problems of water pollution in the drainage basin so as to reach, by methods of their own choice, a solution consistent with their rights and duties under international law. This consultation, however, shall not unreasonably delay the implementation of plans that are the subject of the consultation.

Article 7

In order to ensure an effective system of prevention and abatement of water pollution of an international drainage basin, basin states should set up appropriate international administrative machinery for the entire basin. In any event, they should:

(a) coordinate or pool their scientific and technical research programmes to combat water pollution;

(b) establish harmonized, coordinated, or unified networks for permanent observation and pollution control; and

(c) establish jointly water quality objectives and standards for the whole or part of the basin.

Article 8

States should provide remedies for persons who are or may be adversely affected by water pollution in an international drainage basin. In particular, states should, on a non-discriminatory basis, grant these persons access to the judicial and administrative agencies of the state in whose territory the pollution originates, and should provide, by agreement or otherwise, for such matters as the jurisdiction of courts, the applicable law, and the enforcement of judgments.

Article 9

In the case of a breach of a state's international obligations relating to water pollution in an international drainage basin, that state shall cease the wrongful conduct and shall pay compensation for the injury resulting therefrom.

Article 10

When it is contended that the conduct of a state is not in accordance with its obligations under these Articles, that state shall promptly enter into negotiations with the complaining state with a view of reaching a solution that is equitable under the circumstances.

NOTES

1) The principle of "equitable utilization" stated in Articles IV and V of the Helsinki Rules is a recognition of common interest *par excellence*.[57] Most of the rest of the articles supplement this principle. Growing international concern about pollution led to inclusion of the three specific Articles IX–XI. What do they add to pre-existing customary international law? How do they extend the principle of equitable utilization? Notice how wide is the definition of pollution in Article IX compared to the *later* Principle 6 of the Stockholm Declaration, reproduced above.

2) Does the right to an equitable share in the use of the waters of a common river include an equal right to pollute them? For instance, might riparian states determine the load of a particular pollutant which the river could assimilate and then apportion the amount between them? Note that Article IX refers only to a "detrimental change" of water quality and Article X imposes liability only for pollution that creates "substantial injury" to a co-basin state.[58]

3) The Montreal Rules are an elaboration of the Helsinki Rules in the area of pollution. In what ways do they amend or add to Articles IX–XI? Are they a codification or a development of current customary law?

4) The International Law Commission has also taken up the subject of the "Law of Non-Navigational Uses of International Watercourses." It has been proceeding to formulate a draft convention on the subject: the progress may be followed in the annual reports to the U.N. General Assembly to be found in Part 2 of the *Yearbooks* of the I.L.C. since it began the work in 1974.[59]

Canada-United States Great Lakes Water Quality Agreement[60]
(1978) Can.T.S. No. 20; 30 U.S.T. 1383; TIAS 9257

[By 1970 The Great Lakes System had become seriously polluted. The pollution had many sources, including industrial processes, urban usages and shipping wastes. The poor condition of the lake waters was revealed convincingly in a study and report by the International Joint Commission (IJC). This body was set up in 1909 by the Boundary

---

[57] See J. Lipper, "Equitable Utilization" in A.H. Garretson et al., *supra*, n. 55, at 15.

[58] See C.B. Bourne, *supra*, n. 56, at 123.

[59] See also Institut de Droit International, Athens Resolution on the Pollution of Rivers and Lakes and International Law, 1979 (1980), 58 *Annuaire*, Part 2, at 104, 196. The various sets of rules are compared by C.B. Bourne, "International Law on Shared Fresh Water Resources," in *Proceedings of the Conference on International Law: Critical Choices for Canada 1985–2000* (1986), *Queen's L.J.* 342. As to pollution of transboundary ground water see L.A. Teclaff and A.E. Utton, *International Groundwater Law* (1981).

[60] See F.E. Moseley, *The United States-Canadian Great Lakes Pollution Agreement: A Study in International Water Pollution Control* (1978); D.C. Piper, *The International Law of the Great Lakes* (1967); R.B. Bilder, "Controlling Great Lakes Pollution: A Study in United States-Canadian Environmental Cooperation" (1971–72), 70 *Mich.L.R.* 469; C.B. Bourne, *supra* n. 56; H.L. Dickstein, "International Lake and River Pollution Control: Questions of Method" (1973), 12 *Colum.J.Trans.L.* 487; and H. Landis, "Legal Controls of Pollution in the Great Lakes Basin" (1970), 48 *Can.Bar.Rev.* 66.

Waters Treaty[61] between the United States and Great Britain, on behalf of Canada, for the purpose of aiding in the settlement and prevention of disputes over the use of the boundary waters. The IJC was given a number of powers, variously of an investigative, administrative and adjudicative character, which it might in some situations exercise on its own authority and in others upon reference or request of either or both states.[62] The 1909 Treaty also declared that the boundary waters "shall not be polluted on either side to the injury of health or property on the other,"[63] though it did not express a mandate regarding pollution to the IJC. In the course of more than seventy years, the IJC has helped to resolve a variety of transboundary difficulties, most frequently to do with navigation and water diversion projects, along many parts of the common frontier. But none of its efforts has had such an impact as its report on the polluted condition of Lake Erie, Lake Ontario and the international section of the St. Lawrence River, which led swiftly to this Agreement. The original arrangements of 1972, which were directed only to the boundary waters within the Great Lakes System, has now been superseded by the Agreement of 1978, as follows:]

> *The Government of the United States of America and the Government of Canada,*
> *Having* in 1972 entered into an Agreement on Great Lakes Water Quality;
> *Reaffirming* their determination to restore and enhance water quality in the Great Lakes System;
> *Continuing* to be concerned about the impairment of water quality on each side of the boundary to an extent that is causing injury to health and property on the other side, as described by the International Joint Commission;
> *Reaffirming* their intent to prevent further pollution of the Great Lakes Basin Ecosystem owing to continuing population growth, resource development and increasing use of water;
> *Reaffirming* in a spirit of friendship and cooperation the rights and obligations of both countries under the Boundary Waters Treaty, signed on January 11, 1909, and in particular their obligation not to pollute boundary waters;
> *Continuing* to recognize the rights of each country in the use of its Great Lakes waters;
> *Having decided* that the Great Lakes Water Quality Agreement of April 15, 1972 and subsequent reports of the International Joint Commission provide a sound basis for new and more effective cooperative actions to restore and enhance water quality in the Great Lakes Basin Ecosystem;
> *Recognizing* that restoration and enhancement of the boundary waters can not be achieved independently of other parts of the Great Lakes Basin Ecosystem with which these waters interact;
> *Concluding* that the best means to preserve the aquatic ecosystem and achieve improved water quality throughout the Great Lakes System is by adopting common objectives,

[61] U.S.T.S. 548; 1910 Br.T.S. 23.
[62] See L.M. Bloomfield and G.F. Fitzgerald, *Boundary Waters Problems of Canada and the United States* (1958); M. Cohen, *The Regime of Boundary Waters – The Canadian-United States Experience* (1977); R. Spencer et al. eds., *The International Joint Commission Seventy Years On* (1981); and F.J.E. Jordan, "The International Joint Commission and Canada-United States Boundary Relations," in R.St.J. Macdonald et al., *supra* n. 55, at 522.
[63] *Supra* n. 61, Article IV.

developing and implementing cooperative programs and other measures, and assigning special responsibilities and functions to the International Joint Commission;

Have agreed as follows:

Article I

DEFINITIONS

As used in this Agreement:

    (a) "Agreement" means the present Agreement as distinguished from the Great Lakes Water Quality Agreement of April 15, 1972;

    (b) "Annex" means any of the Annexes to this Agreement, each of which is attached to and forms an integral part of this Agreement;

    (c) "Boundary waters of the Great Lakes System" or "boundary waters" means boundary waters, as defined in the Boundary Waters Treaty, that are within the Great Lakes System;

    (d) "Boundary Waters Treaty" means the Treaty between the United States and Great Britain Relating to Boundary Waters, and Questions Arising Between the United States and Canada, signed at Washington on January 11, 1909;

    (e) "Compatible regulations" means regulations no less restrictive than the agreed principles set out in this Agreement;

    (f) "General Objectives" are broad descriptions of water quality conditions consistent with the protection of the beneficial uses and the level of environmental quality which the Parties desire to secure and which will provide overall water management guidance;

    (g) "Great Lakes Basin Ecosystem" means the interacting components of air, land, water and living organisms, including man, within the drainage basin of the St. Lawrence River at or upstream from the point at which this river becomes the international boundary between Canada and the United States;

    (h) "Great Lakes System" means all of the streams, rivers, lakes and other bodies of water that are within the drainage basin on the St. Lawrence River at or upstream from the point at which this river becomes the international boundary between Canada and the United States;

    (i) "Harmful quantity" means any quantity of a substance that if discharged into receiving water would be inconsistent with the achievement of the General and Specific Objectives;

    (j) "Hazardous polluting substance" means any element or compound identified by the Parties which, if discharged in any quantity into or upon receiving waters or adjoining shorelines, would present an imminent and substantial danger to public health or welfare; for this purpose, "public health or welfare" encompasses all factors affecting the health and welfare of man including but not limited to human health, and the conservation and protection of flora and fauna, public and private property, shorelines and beaches;

    (k) "International Joint Commission" or "Commission" means the International Joint Commission established by the Boundary Waters Treaty;

(l) ''Monitoring'' means a scientifically designed system of continuing standardized measurements and observations and the evaluation thereof;

(m) ''Objectives'' means the General Objectives adopted pursuant to Article III and the Specific Objectives adopted pursuant to Article IV of this Agreement;

(n) ''Parties'' means the Government of Canada and the Government of the United States of America;

(o) ''Phosphorus'' means the element phosphorus present as a constituent of various organic and inorganic complexes and compounds;

(p) ''Research'' means development, demonstration and other research activities but does not include monitoring and surveillance of water or air quality;

(q) ''Science Advisory Board'' means the Great Lakes Science Advisory Board of the International Joint Commission established pursuant to Article VIII of this Agreement;

(r) ''Specific Objectives'' means the concentration or quantity of a substance or level of effect that the Parties agree, after investigation, to recognize as a maximum or minimum desired limit for a defined body of water or portion thereof, taking into account the beneficial uses or level of environmental quality which the Parties desire to secure and protect;

(s) ''State and Provincial Governments'' means the Governments of the States of Illinois, Indiana, Michigan, Minnesota, New York, Ohio, Wisconsin, and the Commonwealth of Pennsylvania, and the Government of the Province of Ontario;

(t) ''Surveillance'' means specific observations and measurements relative to control or management;

(u) ''Terms of Reference'' means the Terms of Reference for the Joint Institutions and the Great Lakes Regional Office established pursuant to this Agreement, which are attached to and form an integral part of this Agreement;

(v) ''Toxic substance'' means a substance which can cause death, disease, behavioural abnormalities, cancer, genetic mutations, physiological or reproductive malfunctions or physical deformities in any organism or its offspring, or which can become poisonous after concentration in the food chain or in combination with other substances;

(w) ''Tributary waters of the Great Lakes System'' or ''tributary waters'' means all the waters within the Great Lakes System that are not boundary waters;

(x) ''Water Quality Board'' means the Great Lakes Water Quality Board of the International Joint Commission established pursuant to Article VIII of this Agreement.

Article II

PURPOSE

The purpose of the Parties is to restore and maintain the chemical, physical, and biological integrity of the waters of the Great Lakes Basin Ecosystem. In order to achieve this purpose, the Parties agree to make a maximum effort to develop programs, practices and technology necessary for a better understanding of the Great Lakes Basin Ecosystem and to eliminate or reduce to the maximum extent practicable the discharge of pollutants into the Great Lakes System.

Consistent with the provisions of this Agreement, it is the policy of the Parties that:

(a) The discharge of toxic substances in toxic amounts be prohibited and the discharge of any or all persistent toxic substances be virtually eliminated;

(b) Financial assistance to construct publicly owned waste treatment works be provided by a combination of local, state, provincial, and federal participation; and

(c) Coordinated planning processes and best management practices be developed and implemented by the respective jurisdictions to ensure adequate control of all sources of pollutants.

Article III
GENERAL OBJECTIVES

The Parties adopt the following General Objectives for the Great Lakes System. These waters should be:

(a) Free from substances that directly or indirectly enter the waters as a result of human activity and that will settle to form putrescent or otherwise objectionable sludge deposits, or that will adversely affect aquatic life or waterfowl;

(b) Free from floating materials such as debris, oil, scum, and other immiscible substances resulting from human activities in amounts that are unsightly or deleterious;

(c) Free from materials and heat directly or indirectly entering the water as a result of human activity that alone, or in combination with other materials, will produce colour, odour, taste, or other conditions in such a degree as to interfere with beneficial uses;

(d) Free from materials and heat directly or indirectly entering the water as a result of human activity that alone, or in combination with other materials, will produce conditions that are toxic or harmful to human, animal, or aquatic life; and

(e) Free from nutrients directly or indirectly entering the waters as a result of human activity in amounts that create growths of aquatic life that interfere with beneficial uses.

Article IV
SPECIFIC OBJECTIVES

1. The Parties adopt the Specific Objectives for the boundary waters of the Great Lakes System as set forth in Annex 1, subject to the following:

(a) The Specific Objectives adopted pursuant to this Article represent the minimum levels of water quality desired in the boundary waters of the Great Lakes System and are not intended to preclude the establishment of more stringent requirements.

(b) The determination of the achievement of Specific Objectives shall be based on statistically valid sampling data.

(c) Notwithstanding the adoption of Specific Objectives, all reasonable and practicable measures shall be taken to maintain or improve the existing water quality in those areas of the boundary waters of the Great Lakes System where such water quality is better than that prescribed by the Specific Objectives, and in those areas having outstanding natural resource value.

(m) *Surveillance and Monitoring*. Implementation of a coordinated surveillance and monitoring program in the Great Lakes System, in accordance with Annex 11, to assess compliance with pollution control requirements and achievement of the Objectives, to provide information for measuring local and whole lake response to control measures, and to identify emerging problems.

2. The Parties shall develop and implement such additional programs as they jointly decide are necessary and desirable to fulfil the purpose of this Agreement and to meet the General and Specific Objectives.

Article VII
POWERS, RESPONSIBILITIES AND FUNCTIONS OF THE
INTERNATIONAL JOINT COMMISSION

1. The International Joint Commission shall assist in the implementation of this Agreement. Accordingly, the Commission is hereby given, by a Reference pursuant to Article IX of the Boundary Waters Treaty, the following responsibilities:

(a) Collation, analysis and dissemination of data and information supplied by the Parties and State and Provincial Governments relating to the quality of the boundary waters of the Great Lakes System and to pollution that enters the boundary waters from tributary waters and other sources;

(b) Collection, analysis and dissemination of data and information concerning the General and Specific Objectives and the operation and effectiveness of the programs and other measures established pursuant to this Agreement;

(c) Tendering of advice and recommendations to the Parties and to the State and Provincial Governments on problems of and matters related to the quality of the boundary waters of the Great Lakes System including specific recommendations concerning the General and Specific Objectives, legislation, standards and other regulatory requirements, programs and other measures, and intergovernmental agreements relating to the quality of these waters;

(d) Tendering of advice and recommendations to the Parties in connection with matters covered under the Annexes to this Agreement;

(e) Provision of assistance in the coordination of the joint activities envisaged by this Agreement;

(f) Provision of assistance in and advice on matters related to research in the Great Lakes Basin Ecosystem, including identification of objectives for research activities, tendering of advice and recommendations concerning research to the Parties and to the State and Provincial Governments, and dissemination of information concerning research to interested persons and agencies;

(g) Investigations of such subjects related to the Great Lakes Basin Ecosystem as the Parties may from time to time refer to it.

2. In the discharge of its responsibilities under this Reference, the Commission may exercise all of the powers conferred upon it by the Boundary Waters Treaty and by any legislation passed pursuant thereto including the power to conduct public hearings and to compel the testimony of witnesses and the production of documents.

3. The Commission shall make a full report to the Parties and to the State and Provincial

Governments no less frequently than biennially concerning progress toward the achievement of the General and Specific Objectives including, as appropriate, matters related to Annexes to this Agreement. This report shall include an assessment of the effectiveness of the programs and other measures undertaken pursuant to this Agreement, and advice and recommendations. In alternate years the Commission may submit a summary report. The Commission may at any time make special reports to the Parties, to the State and Provincial Governments and to the public concerning any problem of water quality in the Great Lakes System.

4. The Commission may in its discretion publish any report, statement or other document prepared by it in the discharge of its functions under this Reference.

5. The Commission shall have authority to verify independently the data and other information submitted by the Parties and by the State and Provincial Governments through such tests or other means as appear appropriate to it, consistent with the Boundary Waters Treaty and with applicable legislation.

6. The Commission shall carry out its responsibilities under this Reference utilizing principally the services of the Water Quality Board and the Science Advisory Board established under Article VIII of this Agreement. The Commission shall also ensure liaison and coordination between the institutions established under this Agreement and other institutions which may address concerns relevant to the Great Lakes Basin Ecosystem, including both those within its purview, such as those Boards related to Great Lakes levels and air pollution matters, and other international bodies, as appropriate.

Article VIII
JOINT INSTITUTIONS AND REGIONAL OFFICE

1. To assist the International Joint Commission in the exercise of the powers and responsibilities assigned to it under this Agreement, there shall be two Boards:

(a) A Great Lakes Water Quality Board which shall be the principal advisor to the Commission. The Board shall be composed of an equal number of members from Canada and the United States, including representatives from the Parties and each of the State and Provincial Governments; and

(b) A Great Lakes Science Advisory Board which shall provide advice on research to the Commission and to the Water Quality Board. The Board shall further provide advice on scientific matters referred to it by the Commission, or by the Water Quality Board in consultation with the Commission. The Science Advisory Board shall consist of managers of Great Lakes research programs and recognized experts on Great Lakes water quality problems and related fields.

2. The members of the Water Quality Board and the Science Advisory Board shall be appointed by the Commission after consultation with the appropriate government or governments concerned. The functions of the Boards shall be as specified in the Terms of Reference appended to this Agreement.

3. To provide administrative support and technical assistance to the two Boards, and to provide a public information service for the programs, including public hearings, undertaken by the International Joint Commission and by the Boards, there shall be a Great Lakes Regional Office of the International Joint Commission. Specific duties and organization of the Office shall be as specified in the Terms of Reference appended to this Agreement.

4. The Commission shall submit an annual budget of anticipated expenses to be incurred in carrying out its responsibilities under this Agreement to the Parties for approval. Each Party shall seek funds to pay one-half of the annual budget so approved, but neither Party shall be under an obligation to pay a larger amount than the other toward this budget.

Article IX
SUBMISSION AND EXCHANGE OF INFORMATION

1. The International Joint Commission shall be given at its request any data or other information relating to water quality in the Great Lakes System in accordance with procedures established by the Commission.

2. The Commission shall make available to the Parties and to the State and Provincial Governments upon request all data or other information furnished to it in accordance with this Article.

3. Each Party shall make available to the other at its request any data or other information in its control relating to water quality in the Great Lakes System.

4. Notwithstanding any other provision of this Agreement, the Commission shall not release without the consent of the owner any information identified as proprietary information under the law of the place where such information has been acquired.

Article X
CONSULTATION AND REVIEW

1. Following the receipt of each report submitted to the Parties by the International Joint Commission in accordance with paragraph 3 of Article VII of this Agreement, the Parties shall consult on the recommendations contained in such report and shall consider such action as may be appropriate, including:

    (a) The modification of existing Objectives and the adoption of new Objectives;

    (b) The modification or improvement of programs and joint measures; and

    (c) The amendment of this Agreement or any Annex thereto.

Additional consultations may be held at the request of either Party on any matter arising out of the implementation of this Agreement.

2. When a Party becomes aware of a special pollution problem that is of joint concern and requires an immediate response, it shall notify and consult the other Party forthwith about appropriate remedial action.

3. The Parties shall conduct a comprehensive review of the operation and effectiveness of this Agreement following the third biennial report of the Commission required under Article VII of this Agreement.

Article XI
IMPLEMENTATION

1. The obligations undertaken in this Agreement shall be subject to the appropriation of funds in accordance with the constitutional procedures of the Parties.

2. The Parties commit themselves to seek:

(a) The appropriation of the funds required to implement this Agreement, including the funds needed to develop and implement the programs and other measures provided for in Article VI of this Agreement, and the funds required by the International Joint Commission to carry out its responsibilities effectively;

(b) The enactment of any additional legislation that may be necessary in order to implement the programs and other measures provided for in Article VI of this Agreement; and

(c) The cooperation of the State and Provincial Governments in all matters relating to this Agreement. ...

NOTES

1) Contrast the general nature of the Helsinki Rules with the specific standards and concrete arrangements of the Great Lakes Agreement. The degree of detail in the latter shows that to move beyond basic principles to the actual protection of the environment is a very complex matter. In what ways does the Great Lakes Agreement give substance to the obligation not to pollute expressed in general terms in the Boundary Waters Treaty of 1909?

2) In the Great Lakes Agreement, many water quality objectives are stated. They each require affirmative action. Who is obliged actually to control and abate pollution of the Great Lakes?

3) What are the particular duties of the two contracting states (federal governments)? Because the Great Lakes are shared boundary waters, their quality can only be preserved if both sides fulfill their affirmative and continuous obligations. If one side should fail to take pollution control measures actively enough, what could be done about it?

4) Though the objectives of the Agreement are mutually beneficial, to what extent are they to be attained by joint efforts as opposed to complementary but individual actions? In the areas of individual responsibility, do the parties have to implement the pollution standards in the same way? Does it matter if they don't? Moseley has reflected on the following steps to cooperative solutions of transfrontier pollution problems:[64]

(1) clear designation of the area of pollution boundary;

(2) assessment of the cause of pollution;

(3) development and promulgation of environmental quality criteria;

(4) assessment of pollution control technology;

(5) establishment of environmental quality standards; and

(6) development and implementation of abatement and control strategies.

The first four of these actions can best be taken jointly, as well as supporting activities such as research on the effects of pollution, on the development of pollution control technology, and in carrying out the comprehensive monitoring and surveillance necessary to measure the progress

---

[64] F.E. Moseley, *supra* n. 60, at 205–7, citing an unpublished paper by W.H. Mansfield III.

and success of abatement efforts. In the lower Great Lakes, steps one and two enumerated above were undertaken jointly by the United States and Canada, and to a partial extent steps three and five were also joint activities. Steps four and six have primarily been accomplished separately. To the extent possible, therefore, the process of problem definition and the seeking of remedies ought to be undertaken jointly. Joint endeavors in the first two steps of problem definition may well be a condition for success, while steps three and four dealing with the context in which remedies will have to be sought are less essential as joint activities but still very important. The last two steps will probably be reserved for separate action given the present emphasis upon state sovereignty. However if water quality objectives are sought instead or prior to standards, such objectives may be, as in the Canadian-United States Agreement, an essential part of the package.

5) By Article VII, the International Joint Commission is given a role to "assist in the implementation of this Agreement." In fact the IJC is loaded with many responsibilities, but what authority does it have to carry them through to effective action against pollution? Should it have other powers? Does it have the means for effective water quality management of the Great Lakes?

6) Both states have made serious efforts to implement the Agreement effectively. National enabling legislation[65] has provided administrative bodies, pollution programmes and procedures, and a flow of funds to build preventive systems. Despite the complexity of the problems and difficulties, particularly on the American side, in achieving clean-up levels by target dates, by 1978 it was possible to conclude that "the evidence of movement and progress toward managing the flow of water pollutants in the Great Lakes System appears convincing."[66]

7) The Great Lakes States and Ontario and Quebec signed the Great Lakes Charter in 1985[67] to provide for consultation and long-term cooperative management of the Great Lakes ecosystem. Does this agreement have the force of an international treaty? Can it be used as a means of obtaining federal support in both countries for water quality and quantity issues?

8) The use and consumption of the waters of the Great Lakes is equally as much a transboundary management problem as the protection of their quality. Can the Great Lakes Provinces or States unilaterally, or as a group, prevent or regulate diversions out of or into the common drainage basin? This appears to be another situation in which the IJC has a role to play.[68]

COLLECTIVE DISARMAMENT

Although the U.N. Charter does not call for immediate disarmament, it does envisage a system of international security that would ensure "the least diversion for armaments of

---

[65] *Canada Water Act*, R.S.C. 1970 (1st Supp.), c. 5; Ontario *Water Resources Act*, R.S.O. 1980, c. 361; U.S. *Federal Water Pollution Control Act Amendments of 1972*, 33 U.S.C., ss. 1251–1376.

[66] F.E. Moseley, *supra*, n. 60, at 198.

[67] Great Lakes Governors Task Force on Water Diversion and Great Lakes Institutions, *Final Report and Recommendations – A Report to the Governors and Premiers of the Great Lakes States and Provinces* (1985).

[68] See the Boundary Waters Treaty, *supra* n. 61; and S.A. Williams, *supra* n. 55.

the world's human and economic resources'' (Article 26). From the beginning of the United Nations, disarmament, particularly nuclear disarmament, has been the major and a continuing preoccupation of the world organization.[69] The very first resolution adopted by the General Assembly on (January 24, 1946) called for the ''elimination from national armaments of atomic weapons and of all other major weapons adaptable to mass destruction.'' That resolution, as well as many that followed, failed to prevent what eventually came to be known as the nuclear arms race. Owing to Great Power disagreements, more than forty years since the first use of an atomic weapon at Hiroshima there has been virtually no progress towards nuclear disarmament. However, during that period some twenty multilateral and bilateral arms regulation agreements have been concluded, including the 1963 Limited Nuclear Test Ban Treaty, the 1967 Treaty of Tlatelolco (creating a nuclear-free zone in Latin America), the Outer Space Treaty of 1967, the 1968 Treaty on the Non-Proliferation of Nuclear Weapons, and the 1972 U.S.-U.S.S.R. bilateral treaty limiting the acquisition of anti-ballistic missile systems (the ABM Treaty).

Post-war disarmament negotiations have been held in various fora, with varying numbers of participating states. The United Nations continues to provide the principal forum for multilateral negotiations, although some of the most important arms limitation agreements have been concluded through bilateral (e.g., the ABM Treaty) and trilateral negotiations (e.g. the Limited Test Ban Treaty). Currently, the principal world-wide negotiating body for arms control is the Conference on Disarmament (CD), created in 1978. The CD is composed of five nuclear-weapon states and 35 other states representing all regions of the world. Although formally not a U.N. body, the CD reports annually to the U.N. General Assembly and is guided in its work by relevant General Assembly resolutions. Since its establishment, the CD has dealt with issues such as a ban on chemical and radiological weapons, arms control in outer space and nuclear arms control. As of January 1987, it has been unable to achieve agreement on any of the topics on its agenda.

The U.N. General Assembly has held two special sessions devoted entirely to disarmament – the first took place in 1978 and the second in 1982. The 1978 session adopted a comprehensive text – ''*Final Document*'' – which included a declaration on disarmament and a programme of action. Adopted by consensus, the *Final Document* provides a framework for disarmament efforts in the years ahead. In stark contrast to the first special session, the second session ended in failure without any agreement on a substantive document by the participating states. Nevertheless, the *Final Document* of the 1978 U.N. Special Session, as the following excerpts show, continues to serve the aims of collective disarmament.

---

[69] For a complete record of disarmament proceedings in the United Nations since 1945 see United Nations, *The United Nations and Disarmament 1945–1970* (1970), and the annual publication of *The United Nations Disarmament Yearbook*. A. Myrdal, *The Game of Disarmament* (rev. ed. 1982) provides an excellent insight into the arms control negotiations by an experienced Swedish participant. The role of law in earlier arms control negotiations (up to 1963) is explored in A. Gotlieb, *Disarmament and International Law* (1965). For critical analysis of the state of arms control negotiations after the U.N. Second Special Session on disarmament see I. Vlasic, ''Raison d'Etat v. Raison de l'Humanité – The United Nations SSOD II and Beyond'' (1983), 28 *McGill L.J.* 455. A review of Canadian government involvement in disarmament negotiations is provided by Ambassador J.A. Beesley, ''1984 and Beyond: Canadian Policy on Arms Control and Disarmament'' (1983), 28 *McGill L.J.* 783.

Final Document of the 1978 U.N. Special Session on Disarmament
U.N. Doc. A/RES/S-10/2 (1978), 17 *Int. Leg. Mat.* 1016

11. Mankind today is confronted with an unprecedented threat of self-extinction arising from the massive and competitive accumulation of the most destructive weapons ever produced. Existing arsenals of nuclear weapons alone are more than sufficient to destroy all life on earth. Failure of efforts to halt and reverse the arms race, in particular the nuclear arms race, increases the danger of the proliferation of nuclear weapons. Yet the arms race continues. Military budgets are constantly growing, with enormous consumption of human and material resources. The increase in weapons, especially nuclear weapons, far from helping to strengthen international security, on the contrary weakens it. The vast stockpiles and tremendous build-up of arms and armed forces and the competition for qualitative refinement of weapons of all kinds, to which scientific resources and technological advances are diverted, pose incalculable threats to peace. This situation both reflects and aggravates international tensions, sharpens conflicts in various regions of the world, hinders the process of détente, exacerbates the differences between opposing military alliances, jeopardizes the security of all States, heightens the sense of insecurity among all States, including the non-nuclear-weapon States, and increases the threat of nuclear war.

12. The arms race, particularly in its nuclear aspect, runs counter to efforts to achieve further relaxation of international tension, to establish international relations based on peaceful coexistence and trust between all States, and to develop broad international cooperation and understanding. The arms race impedes the realization of the purposes, and is incompatible with the principles, of the Charter of the United Nations, especially respect for sovereignty, refraining from the threat or use of force against the territorial integrity or political independence of any State, the peaceful settlement of disputes and non-intervention and non-interference in the internal affairs of States. It also adversely affects the right of peoples freely to determine their systems of social and economic development, and hinders the struggle for self-determination and the elimination of colonial rule, racial or foreign domination or occupation. Indeed, the massive accumulation of armaments and the acquisition of armaments technology by racist régimes, as well as their possible acquisition of nuclear weapons, present a challenging and increasingly dangerous obstacle to a world community faced with the urgent need to disarm. It is, therefore, essential for purposes of disarmament to prevent any further acquisition of arms or arms technology by such régimes, especially through strict adherence by all States to relevant decisions of the Security Council. ...

14. Since the process of disarmament affects the vital security interests of all States, they must all be actively concerned with and contribute to the measures of disarmament and arms limitation, which have an essential part to play in maintaining and strengthening international security. Therefore the role and responsibility of the United Nations in the sphere of disarmament, in accordance with its Charter, must be strengthened. ...

16. In a world of finite resources there is a close relationship between expenditure on armaments and economic and social development. Military expenditures are reaching ever higher levels, the highest percentage of which can be attributed to the nuclear-weapon States and most of their allies, with prospects of further expansion and the danger of further increases in the expenditures of other countries. The hundreds of billions of dollars spent annually on the manufacture or improvement of weapons are in sombre and dramatic contrast to the want and poverty in which two thirds of the world's population live. This colossal waste of resources is even more serious in that it diverts to military purposes not only material but also technical and human resources which are urgently needed for development in all countries, particularly in the developing countries. Thus, the economic and social consequences of the arms race are so detrimental that its continuation is obviously incompatible with the implementation of the new international economic order based on justice, equity and co-operation. Consequently, resources released as a result of the implementation of disarmament measures should be used in a manner which will help to promote the well-being of all peoples and to improve the economic conditions of the developing countries.

17. Disarmament has thus become an imperative and most urgent task facing the international community. No real progress has been made so far in the crucial field of reduction of armaments. However, certain positive changes in international relations in some areas of the world provide some encouragement. Agreements have been reached that have been important in limiting certain weapons or eliminating them altogether, as in the case of the Convention on the Prohibition of the Development, Production and Stockpiling of Bacteriological (Biological) and Toxin Weapons and on Their Destruction and excluding particular areas from the arms race. The fact remains that these agreements relate only to measures of limited restraint while the arms race continues. These partial measures have done little to bring the world closer to the goal of general and complete disarmament. For more than a decade there have been no negotiations leading to a treaty on general and complete disarmament. The pressing need now is to translate into practical terms the provisions of this Final Document and to proceed along the road of binding and effective international agreements in the field of disarmament.

18. Removing the threat of a world war – a nuclear war – is the most acute and urgent task of the present day. Mankind is confronted with a choice: we must halt the arms race and proceed to disarmament or face annihilation.

19. The ultimate objective of the efforts of States in the disarmament process is general and complete disarmament under effective international control. The principal goals of disarmament are to ensure the survival of mankind and to eliminate the danger of war, in particular nuclear war, to ensure that war is no longer an instrument for settling international disputes and that the use and the threat of force are eliminated from international life, as provided for in the Charter of the United Nations. Progress towards this objective requires the conclusion and implementation of agreements on the cessation of the arms race and on genuine measures of disarmament, taking into account the need of States to protect their security.

20. Among such measures, effective measures of nuclear disarmament and the prevention of nuclear war have the highest priority. To this end, it is imperative to remove the threat of nuclear weapons, to halt and reverse the nuclear arms race until the total elimination of nuclear weapons and their delivery systems has been achieved, and to prevent the proliferation of nuclear weapons. At the same time, other measures designed to prevent the outbreak of nuclear war and to lessen the danger of the threat or use of nuclear weapons should be taken.

to respond to a massive conventional attack in a "battlefield" situation, would be inconsistent with the law. Since, by their very nature these flexible nuclear weapons and strategies are designed for deliberate escalation of hostilities for purposes of inflicting unacceptable harm on the adversary, they are in direct conflict with the prohibition against disproportionate response (Rule 6). Furthermore, the use of "battlefield" nuclear weapons is likely to take place in close proximity to innocent civilian populations, and the radiological effects would almost certainly extend to the territory of neutrals. Such destruction would make it impossible for a "victorious" occupant to carry out its legal obligations towards any surviving inhabitants of the occupied territory. Most important, however, is the fact that military and political experts are in unanimous agreement in skepticism about the prospects of controlling even the most limited "battlefield" or "tactical" nuclear war once the firebreak has been crossed. With the possibility of victory frustrated by the certainty of escalation to general nuclear war, here again there would be no military purpose for using nuclear weapons in the first place.

Based on this analysis, we conclude that in any of the contexts envisaged by current policies, the use of nuclear weapons would be illegal. We must, therefore, unequivocally condemn nuclear warfare.

Limited Nuclear Test Ban Treaty
480 U.N.T.S. 43; (1963), 2 *Int. Leg. Mat.* 889

The Governments of the United States of America, the United Kingdom of Great Britain and Northern Ireland, and the Union of Soviet Socialist Republics, hereinafter referred to as the "Original Parties",

Proclaiming as their principal aim the speediest possible achievement of an agreement on general and complete disarmament under strict international control in accordance with the objectives of the United Nations which would put an end to the armaments race and eliminate the incentive to the production and testing of all kinds of weapons, including nuclear weapons,

Seeking to achieve the discontinuance of all test explosions of nuclear weapons for all time, determined to continue negotiations to this end, and desiring to put an end to the contamination of man's environment by radioactive substances,

Have agreed as follows:

Article I

1. Each of the Parties to this Treaty undertakes to prohibit, to prevent, and not to carry out any nuclear weapon test explosion, or any other nuclear explosion, at any place under its jurisdiction or control:

  (a) in the atmosphere; beyond its limits, including outer space; or under water, including territorial waters or high seas; or

  (b) in any other environment if such explosion causes radioactive debris to be present outside the territorial limits of the State under whose jurisdiction or control such explosion is conducted. It is understood in this connection that the provisions of this subparagraph are without prejudice to the conclusion of a treaty resulting in the permanent banning of all nuclear test explosions, including all such explosions underground, the conclusion of which, as the Parties have stated in the Preamble to this Treaty, they seek to achieve.

2. Each of the Parties to this Treaty undertakes furthermore to refrain from causing, encouraging, or in any way participating in, the carrying out of any nuclear weapon test explosion, or any other nuclear explosion, anywhere which would take place in any of the environments described, or have the effect referred to, in paragraph 1 of this Article.

Article II

1. Any Party may propose amendments to this Treaty. The text of any proposed amendment shall be submitted to the Depositary Governments which shall circulate it to all Parties to this Treaty. Thereafter, if requested to do so by one-third or more of the Parties, the Depositary Governments shall convene a conference, to which they shall invite all the Parties, to consider such amendment.

2. Any amendment to this Treaty must be approved by a majority of the votes of all the Parties to this Treaty, including the votes of all of the Original Parties. The amendment shall enter into force for all Parties upon the deposit of instruments of ratification by a majority of all the Parties, including the instruments of ratification of all of the Original Parties.

Article III

1. This Treaty shall be open to all States for signature. Any State which does not sign this Treaty before its entry into force in accordance with paragraph 3 of this Article may accede to it at any time.

2. This Treaty shall be subject to ratification by signatory States. Instruments of ratification and instruments of accession shall be deposited with the Governments of the Original Parties – the United States of America, the United Kingdom of Great Britain and Northern Ireland, and the Union of Soviet Socialist Republics – which are hereby designated the Depositary Governments.

3. This Treaty shall enter into force after its ratification by all the Original Parties and the deposit of their instruments of ratification.

4. For States whose instruments of ratification or accession are deposited subsequent to the entry into force of this Treaty, it shall enter into force on the date of the deposit of their instruments of ratification or accession.

5. The Depositary Governments shall promptly inform all signatory and acceding States of the date of each signature, the date of deposit of each instrument of ratification of and accession to this Treaty, the date of its entry into force, and the date of receipt of any requests for conferences or other notices.

6. This Treaty shall be registered by the Depositary Governments pursuant to Article 102 of the Charter of the United Nations.

Article IV

This Treaty shall be of unlimited duration.

Each Party shall in exercising its national sovereignty have the right to withdraw from the Treaty if it decides that extraordinary events, related to the subject matter of this Treaty, have jeopardized the supreme interests of its country. It shall give notice of such withdrawal to all other Parties to the Treaty three months in advance.

Treaty on the Non-Proliferation of Nuclear Weapons
729 U.N.T.S. 161; (1968), 7 *Int. Leg. Mat.* 811

The States concluding this Treaty, hereinafter referred to as the "Parties to the Treaty,"

Considering the devastation that would be visited upon all mankind by a nuclear war and the consequent need to make every effort to avert the danger of such a war and to take measures to safeguard the security of peoples,

Believing that the proliferation of nuclear weapons would seriously enhance the danger of nuclear war,

In conformity with resolutions of the United Nations General Assembly calling for the conclusion of an agreement on the prevention of wider dissemination of nuclear weapons, ...

Declaring their intention to achieve at the earliest possible date the cessation of the nuclear arms race and to undertake effective measures in the direction of nuclear disarmament,

Urging the co-operation of all States in the attainment of this objective,

Recalling the determination expressed by the Parties to the 1963 Treaty banning nuclear weapons tests in the atmosphere, in outer space and under water in its Preamble to seek to achieve the discontinuance of all test explosions of nuclear weapons for all time and to continue negotiations to this end,

Desiring to further the easing of international tension and the strengthening of trust between States in order to facilitate the cessation of the manufacture of nuclear weapons, the liquidation of all their existing stockpiles, and the elimination from national arsenals of nuclear weapons and the means of their delivery pursuant to a Treaty on general and complete disarmament under strict and effective international control, ...

Have agreed as follows:

Article I

Each nuclear-weapon State Party to the Treaty undertakes not to transfer to any recipient whatsoever nuclear weapons or other nuclear explosive devices or control over such weapons or explosive devices directly, or indirectly; and not in any way to assist, encourage, or induce any non-nuclear-weapon State to manufacture or otherwise acquire nuclear weapons or other nuclear explosive devices, or control over such weapons or explosive devices.

Article II

Each non-nuclear-weapon State Party to the Treaty undertakes not to receive the transfer from any transferor whatsoever of nuclear weapons or other nuclear explosive devices or of control over such weapons or explosive devices directly, or indirectly; not to manufacture or otherwise acquire nuclear weapons or other nuclear explosive devices;

and not to seek or receive any assistance in the manufacture of nuclear weapons or other nuclear explosive devices.

Article III

1. Each non-nuclear-weapon State Party to the Treaty undertakes to accept safeguards, as set forth in an agreement to be negotiated and concluded with the International Atomic Energy Agency in accordance with the Statute of the International Atomic Energy Agency and the Agency's safeguards system, for the exclusive purpose of verification of the fulfilment of its obligations assumed under this Treaty with a view to preventing diversion of nuclear energy from peaceful uses to nuclear weapons or other nuclear explosive devices. Procedures for the safeguards required by this Article shall be followed with respect to source or special fissionable material whether it is being produced, processed or used in any principal nuclear facility or is outside any such facility. The safeguards required by this Article shall be applied on all source or special fissionable material in all peaceful nuclear activities within the territory of such State, under its jurisdiction, or carried out under its control anywhere.
2. Each State Party to the Treaty undertakes not to provide: *(a)* source or special fissionable material, or *(b)* equipment or material especially designed or prepared for the processing, use or production of special fissionable material, to any non-nuclear-weapon State for peaceful purposes, unless the source or special fissionable material shall be subject to the safeguards required by this Article. ...

Article VI

Each of the Parties to the Treaty undertakes to pursue negotiations in good faith on effective measures relating to cessation of the nuclear arms race at an early date and to nuclear disarmament, and on a treaty on general and complete disarmament under strict and effective international control.

Article VII

Nothing in this Treaty affects the right of any group of States to conclude regional treaties in order to assure the total absence of nuclear weapons in their respective territories.

Article VIII

... **3.** Five years after the entry into force of this Treaty, a conference of Parties to the Treaty shall be held in Geneva, Switzerland, in order to review the operation of this Treaty with a view to assuring that the purposes of the Preamble and the provisions of the Treaty are being realised. At intervals of five years thereafter, a majority of the Parties to the Treaty may obtain, by submitting a proposal to this effect to the Depositary Governments, the convening of further conferences with the same objective of reviewing the operation of the Treaty.

Treaty of Tlatelolco for the Prohibition of Nuclear Weapons in Latin America

634 U.N.T.S. 281; (1967), 6 *Int. Leg. Mat.* 521

PREAMBLE

In the name of their peoples and faithfully interpreting their desires and aspirations, the Governments of the States which sign the Treaty for the Prohibition of Nuclear Weapons in Latin America,

Desiring to contribute, so far as lies in their power, towards ending the armaments race, especially in the field of nuclear weapons, and towards strengthening a world at peace, based on the sovereign equality of States, mutual respect and good neighbourliness,

Recalling that the United Nations General Assembly, in its Resolution 808 (IX), adopted unanimously as one of the three points of a coordinated programme of disarmament "the total prohibition of the use and manufacture of nuclear weapons and weapons of mass destruction of every type",

Recalling that militarily denuclearized zones are not an end in themselves but rather a means for achieving general and complete disarmament at a later stage, ...

Convinced:

That the incalculable destructive power of nuclear weapons has made it imperative that the legal prohibition of war should be strictly observed in practice if the survival of civilization and of mankind itself is to be assured,

That nuclear weapons, whose terrible effects are suffered, indiscriminately and inexorably, by military forces and civilian population alike, constitute, through the persistence of the radioactivity they release, an attack on the integrity of the human species and ultimately may even render the whole earth uninhabitable,

That general and complete disarmament under effective international control is a vital matter which all the peoples of the world equally demand,

That the proliferation of nuclear weapons, which seems inevitable unless States, in the exercise of their sovereign rights, impose restrictions on themselves in order to prevent it, would make any agreement on disarmament enormously difficult and would increase the danger of the outbreak of a nuclear conflagration,

That the establishment of military denuclearized zones is closely linked with the maintenance of peace and security in the respective regions, ...

Have agreed as follows:

OBLIGATIONS
Article 1

1. The Contracting Parties hereby undertake to use exclusively for peaceful purposes the nuclear material and facilities which are under their jurisdiction, and to prohibit and prevent in their respective territories:

    (a) The testing, use, manufacture, production or acquisition by any means whatsoever of any nuclear weapons, by the Parties themselves, directly or indirectly, on behalf of anyone else or in any other way, and

(b) The receipt, storage, installation, deployment and any form of possession of any nuclear weapons, directly or indirectly, by the Parties themselves, by anyone on their behalf or in any other way.

2. The Contracting Parties also undertake to refrain from engaging in, encouraging or authorizing, directly or indirectly, or in any way participating in the testing, use, manufacture, production, possession or control of any nuclear weapon. ...

DEFINITION OF TERRITORY
Article 3

For the purposes of this Treaty, the term "territory" shall include the territorial sea, air space and any other space over which the State exercises sovereignty in accordance with its own legislation. ...

DEFINITION OF NUCLEAR WEAPONS
Article 5

For the purposes of this Treaty, a nuclear weapon is any device which is capable of releasing nuclear energy in an uncontrolled manner and which has a group of characteristics that are appropriate for use for warlike purposes. An instrument that may be used for the transport or propulsion of the device is not included in this definition if it is separable from the device and not an indivisible part thereof.

Seabed Arms Control Treaty
23 U.S.T. 701; (1971), 10 *Int. Leg. Mat.* 146

Article I

1. The States Parties to this Treaty undertake not to emplant or emplace on the seabed and the ocean floor and in the subsoil thereof beyond the outer limit of a sea-bed zone, as defined in article II, any nuclear weapons or any other types of weapons of mass destruction as well as structures, launching installations or any other facilities specifically designed for storing, testing or using such weapons.

2. The undertakings of paragaraph 1 of this article shall also apply to the sea-bed zone referred to in the same paragraph, except that within such sea-bed zone, they shall not apply either to the coastal State or to the sea-bed beneath its territorial waters.

3. The States Parties to this Treaty undertake not to assist, encourage or induce any State to carry out activities referred to in paragraph 1 of this article and not to participate in any other way in such actions.

Article II

For the purpose of this Treaty, the outer limit of the sea-bed zone referred to in article I shall be coterminous with the twelve-mile outer limit of the zone referred to in part II of the Convention on the Territorial Sea and the Contiguous Zone, signed at Geneva on 29 April 1958, and shall be measured in accordance with the provisions of part I, section II, of that Convention and in accordance with international law.

Article III

1. In order to promote the objectives of and ensure compliance with the provisions of this Treaty, each State Party to the Treaty shall have the right to verify through observation the activities of other States Parties to the Treaty on the sea-bed and the ocean floor and in the subsoil thereof beyond the zone referred to in article I, provided that observation does not interfere with such activities.

Geneva Gas Protocol
(1925), 94 L.N.T.S. 65; (1975), 14 *Int. Leg. Mat.* 49

The Undersigned Plenipotentiaries, in the name of their respective Governments:

Whereas the use in war of asphyxiating, poisonous or other gases, and of all analogous liquids, materials or devices, has been justly condemned by the general opinion of the civilized world; and

Whereas the prohibition of such use has been declared in Treaties to which the majority of Powers of the world are Parties; and

To the end that this prohibition shall be universally accepted as a part of International Law, binding alike the conscience and the practice of nations;

Declare:

That the High Contracting Parties, so far as they are not already Parties to Treaties prohibiting such use, accept this prohibition, agree to extend this prohibition to the use of bacteriological methods of warfare and agree to be bound as between themselves according to the terms of this declaration.

The High Contracting Parties will exert every effort to induce other States to accede to the present Protocol. Such accession will be notified to the Government of the French Republic, and by the latter to all signatory and acceding Powers, and will take effect on the date of the notification by the Government of the French Republic.

Biological Weapons Convention
26 U.S.T. 583; (1972), 11 *Int. Leg. Mat.* 310

The States Parties to this Convention,

Determined to act with a view to achieving effective progress towards general and complete disarmament, including the prohibition and elimination of all types of weapons of mass destruction, and convinced that the prohibition of the development, production and stockpiling of chemical and bacteriological (biological) weapons and their elimination, through effective measures, will facilitate the achievement of general and complete disarmament under strict and effective international control,

Recognizing the important significance of the Protocol for the Prohibition of the Use in War of Asphyxiating, Poisonous or Other Gases, and of Bacteriological Methods of Warfare, signed at Geneva on June 17, 1925, and conscious also of the contribution which the said Protocol has already made, and continues to make, to mitigating the horrors of war,

Reaffirming their adherence to the principles and objectives of that Protocol and calling upon all States to comply strictly with them,

Recalling that the General Assembly of the United Nations has repeatedly condemned all actions contrary to the principles and objectives of the Geneva Protocol of June 17, 1925,

Desiring to contribute to the strengthening of confidence between peoples and the general improvement of the international atmosphere,

Desiring also to contribute to the realization of the purposes and principles of the Charter of the United Nations,

Convinced of the importance and urgency of eliminating from the arsenals of States, through effective measures, such dangerous weapons of mass destruction as those using chemical or bacteriological (biological) agents,

Recognizing that an agreement on the prohibition of bacteriological (biological) and toxin weapons represents a first possible step towards the achievement of agreement on effective measures also for the prohibition of the development, production and stockpiling of chemical weapons, and determined to continue negotiations to that end,

Determined, for the sake of all mankind, to exclude completely the possibility of bacteriological (biological) agents and toxins being used as weapons,

Convinced that such use would be repugnant to the conscience of mankind and that no effort should be spared to minimize this risk,

Have agreed as follows:

Article I

Each State Party to this Convention undertakes never in any circumstances to develop, produce, stockpile or otherwise acquire or retain:

1. Microbial or other biological agents, or toxins whatever their origin or method of production, of types and in quantities that have no justification for prophylactic, protective or other peaceful purposes;

2. Weapons, equipment or means of delivery designed to use such agents or toxins for hostile purposes or in armed conflict.

Article II

Each State Party to this Convention undertakes to destroy, or to divert to peaceful purposes, as soon as possible but not later than nine months after the entry into force of the Convention, all agents, toxins, weapons, equipment and means of delivery specified in article I of the Convention, which are in its possession or under its jurisdiction or control. In implementing the provisions of this article all necessary safety precautions shall be observed to protect populations and the environment.

Article III

Each State Party to this Convention undertakes not to transfer to any recipient whatsoever, directly or indirectly, and not in any way to assist, encourage, or induce any State, group of States or international organizations to manufacture or otherwise acquire any of the agents, toxins, weapons, equipment or means of delivery specified in article I of the Convention.

Article IV

Each State Party to this Convention shall, in accordance with its constitutional processes, take any necessary measures to prohibit and prevent the development, production, stockpiling, acquisition or retention of the agents, toxins, weapons, equipment and means of delivery specified in article I of the Convention, within the territory of such State, under its jurisdiction or under its control anywhere.

Article V

The States Parties to this Convention undertake to consult one another and to cooperate in solving any problems which may arise in relation to the objective of, or in the application of the provisions of, the Convention. Consultation and cooperation pursuant to this article may also be undertaken through appropriate international procedures within the framework of the United Nations and in accordance with its Charter.

Article VI

1. Any State Party to this Convention which finds that any other State Party is acting in breach of obligations deriving from the provisions of the Convention may lodge a complaint with the Security Council of the United Nations. Such a complaint should include all possible evidence confirming its validity, as well as a request for its consideration by the Security Council.

2. Each State Party to this Convention undertakes to cooperate in carrying out any investigation which the Security Council may initiate, in accordance with the provisions of the Charter of the United Nations, on the basis of the complaint received by the Council. The Security Council shall inform the States Parties to the Convention of the results of the investigation.

Article VII

Each State Party to this Convention undertakes to provide or support assistance, in accordance with the United Nations Charter, to any Party to the Convention which so requests, if the Security Council decides that such Party has been exposed to danger as a result of violation of the Convention.

Article VIII

Nothing in this Convention shall be interpreted as in any way limiting or detracting from the obligations assumed by any State under the Protocol for the Prohibition of the Use in War of Asphyxiating, Poisonous or Other Gases, and of Bacteriological Methods of Warfare, signed at Geneva on June 17, 1925.

Article IX

Each State Party to this Convention affirms the recognized objective of effective prohibition of chemical weapons and, to this end, undertakes to continue negotiations in good faith with a view to reaching early agreement on effective measures for the prohibition of their development, production and stockpiling and for their destruction, and on appropriate measures concerning equipment and means of delivery specifically designed for the production or use of chemical agents for weapons purposes.

Article XII

Five years after the entry into force of this Convention, or earlier if it is requested by a majority of Parties to the Convention by submitting a proposal to this effect to the Depositary Governments, a conference of States Parties to the Convention shall be held at Geneva, Switzerland, to review the operation of the Convention, with a view to assuring that the purposes of the preamble and the provisions of the Convention, including the provisions concerning negotiations on chemical weapons, are being realized. Such review shall take into account any new scientific and technological developments relevant to the Convention.

NOTES

1) This is the only arms control treaty concluded since 1945 that obligates the contracting parties actually to eliminate (''destroy'') an entire category of weapons from their arsenals and to do it within a relatively short period of time. Recent spectacular advances in bio-technology and the interest shown by the military in genetic engineering have led some observers to wonder whether the Convention unequivocally applies also to this novel activity. Although Article I (1) seems to be all encompassing, nonetheless, an amendment to the Convention explicitly prohibiting the use of bio-technology for military (weapons) purposes might be desirable.

2) Negotiations on banning chemical weapons have been under way since 1970. Their objective is to expand the 1925 Geneva Protocol that prohibits the use of chemical weapons in warfare but allows the contracting parties to possess them for deterrent purposes.

3) Canada is a party to this and all the previous treaties except the Treaty of Tlatelolco.

Environmental Modification Convention
31 U.S.T. 333; (1977), 16 *Int. Leg. Mat.* 88

Article I

1. Each State Party to this Convention undertakes not to engage in military or any other hostile use of environmental modification techniques having widespread, long-lasting or severe effects as the means of destruction, damage or injury to any other State Party.

2. Each State Party to this Convention undertakes not to assist, encourage or induce any State, group of States or international organization to engage in activities contrary to the provisions of paragraph 1 of this article.

Article II

As used in article I, the term "environmental modification techniques" refers to any technique for changing – through the deliberate manipulation of natural processes – the dynamics, composition or structure of the earth, including its biota, lithosphere, hydrosphere and atmosphere, or of outer space.

Article III

1. The provisions of this Convention shall not hinder the use of environmental modification techniques for peaceful purposes and shall be without prejudice to the generally recognized principles and applicable rules of international law concerning such use.

Limitations on Military Uses of Outer Space[76]

Attempts to limit the growing militarization of outer space have not been successful. It is estimated that at least 75 percent of all satellite launchings to date have been exclusively or partly for military purposes. The Outer Space Treaty of 1967, reproduced in Chapter 6, is the basic legal instrument regulating activities of states in the domain of space. The Treaty contains only one article explicitly referring to the military uses of space: see Article IV. This Article prohibits the placing of nuclear weapons and other kinds of weapons of mass destruction in earth orbit and on celestial bodies. The Moon Agreement, also reproduced in Chapter 6, in essence reiterates the prohibitions of the Outer Space Treaty as they relate to celestial bodies: see Article III.

The 1963 Limited Test Ban Treaty, reproduced here, was the first multilateral agreement to include provisions relating to weapons in outer space. This Treaty prohibits "any nuclear weapon test explosion, or any other nuclear explosion" in, *inter alia*, outer space: see Article I(1).

A serious weakness of the Outer Space Treaty and the ABM Treaty (which follows) is that neither explicitly prohibits anti-satellite weapons (ASATs). One could argue, however, that ASATs cannot be reconciled with the over-all aims of the Outer Space Treaty and especially with the obligation contained in Article I to the effect that "the

---

[76] See B. Jasani ed., *Outer Space – A New Dimension of the Arms Race* (1982); N. Jasentuliyana ed., *Maintaining Outer Space for Peaceful Uses* (1984); B. Cheng, "The Legal Status of Outer Space and Relevant Issues: Delimitation of Outer Space and Definition of Peaceful Use" (1983), 11 *J. Space L.* 89; N. Jasentuliyana, "Arms Control in Outer Space: A Review of Recent United Nations Discussions" (1984), 9 *Annals Air & Space L.* 329; M. Russell, "Military Activities in Outer Space: Soviet Legal Views" (1984), 24 *Harv. Int. L.J.* 153; and I. Vlasic, "Disarmament Decade, Outer Space and International Law" (1981), 26 *McGill L.J.* 135.

use of outer space ... shall be carried out for the benefit and in the interest of all countries. ...''

Anti-Ballistic Missile Treaty
23 U.S.T. 3435; TIAS No. 7503; (1972), 11 *Int. Leg. Mat.* 784

The United States of America and the Union of Soviet Socialist Republics, hereinafter referred to as the Parties,

Proceeding from the premise that nuclear war would have devastating consequences for all mankind,

Considering that effective measures to limit anti-ballistic missile systems would be a substantial factor in curbing the race in strategic offensive arms and would lead to a decrease in the risk of outbreak of war involving nuclear weapons,

Proceeding from the premise that the limitation of anti-ballistic missile systems, as well as certain agreed measures with respect to the limitation of strategic offensive arms, would contribute to the creation of more favorable conditions for further negotiations on limiting strategic arms,

Mindful of their obligations under Article VI of the Treaty on the Non-Proliferation of Nuclear Weapons,

Declaring their intention to achieve at the earliest possible date the cessation of the nuclear arms race and to take effective measures toward reductions in strategic arms, nuclear disarmament, and general and complete disarmament,

Desiring to contribute to the relaxation of international tension and the strengthening of trust between States,

Have agreed as follows:

Article I

1. Each Party undertakes to limit anti-ballistic missile (ABM) systems and to adopt other measures in accordance with the provisions of this Treaty.

2. Each Party undertakes not to deploy ABM systems for a defense of the territory of its country and not to provide a base for such a defense, and not to deploy ABM systems for defense of an individual region except as provided for in Article III of this Treaty.

Article II

1. For the purpose of this Treaty an ABM system is a system to counter strategic ballistic missiles or their elements in flight trajectory, currently consisting of:

  (a) ABM interceptor missiles, which are interceptor missiles constructed and deployed for an ABM role, or of a type tested in an ABM mode;

  (b) ABM launchers, which are launchers constructed and deployed for launching ABM interceptor missiles; and

  (c) ABM radars, which are radars constructed and deployed for an ABM role, or of a type tested in an ABM mode.

2. The ABM system components listed in paragraph 1 of this Article include those which are:
  (a) operational;
  (b) under construction;
  (c) undergoing testing;
  (d) undergoing overhaul, repair or conversion; or
  (e) mothballed.

Article III

Each Party undertakes not to deploy ABM systems or their components except that:
  (a) within one ABM system deployment area having a radius of one hundred and fifty kilometers and centered on the Party's national capital, a Party may deploy: (1) no more than one hundred ABM launchers and no more than one hundred ABM interceptor missiles at launch sites, and (2) ABM radars within no more than six ABM radar complexes, the area of each complex being circular and having a diameter of no more than three kilometers; and
  (b) within one ABM system deployment area having a radius of one hundred and fifty kilometers and containing ICBM silo launchers, a Party may deploy: (1) no more than one hundred ABM launchers and no more than one hundred ABM interceptor missiles at launch sites, (2) two large phased-array ABM radars comparable in potential to corresponding ABM radars operational or under construction on the date of signature of the Treaty in an ABM system deployment area containing ICBM silo launchers, and (3) no more than eighteen ABM radars each having a potential less than the potential of the smaller of the above-mentioned two large phased-array ABM radars.

Article IV

The limitations provided for in Article III shall not apply to ABM systems or their components used for development or testing, and located within current or additionally agreed test ranges. Each Party may have no more than a total of fifteen ABM launchers at test ranges.

Article V

1. Each Party undertakes not to develop, test, or deploy ABM systems or components which are sea-based, air-based, space-based, or mobile land-based.

2. Each Party undertakes not to develop, test, or deploy ABM launchers for launching more than one ABM interceptor missile at a time from each launcher, nor to modify deployed launchers to provide them with such a capability, nor to develop, test, or deploy automatic or semi-automatic or other similar systems for rapid reload of ABM launchers.

Article VI

To enhance assurance of the effectiveness of the limitations on ABM systems and their components provided by this Treaty, each Party undertakes:

   (a) not to give missiles, launchers, or radars, other than ABM interceptor missiles, ABM launchers, or ABM radars, capabilities to counter strategic ballistic missiles or their elements in flight trajectory, and not to test them in an ABM mode; and

   (b) not to deploy in the future radars for early warning of strategic ballistic missile attack except at locations along the periphery of its national territory and oriented outward.

Article VII

Subject to the provisions of this Treaty, modernization and replacement of ABM systems or their components may be carried out.

Article VIII

ABM systems or their components in excess of the numbers or outside the areas specified in this Treaty, as well as ABM systems or their components prohibited by this Treaty, shall be destroyed or dismantled under agreed procedures within the shortest possible agreed period of time.

Article IX

To assure the viability and effectiveness of this Treaty, each Party undertakes not to transfer to other States, and not to deploy outside its national territory, ABM systems or their components limited by this Treaty.

Article X

Each Party undertakes not to assume any international obligations which would conflict with this Treaty.

Article XI

The Parties undertake to continue active negotiations for limitations on strategic offensive arms.

Article XII

1. For the purpose of providing assurance of compliance with the provisions of this Treaty, each Party shall use national technical means of verification at its disposal in a manner consistent with generally recognized principles of international law.

2. Each Party undertakes not to interfere with the national technical means of verification of the other Party operating in accordance with paragraph 1 of this Article.

3. Each Party undertakes not to use deliberate concealment measures which impede verification by national technical means of compliance with the provisions of this Treaty. This obligation shall not require changes in current construction, assembly, conversion, or overhaul practices.

Article XIII

1. To promote the objectives and implementation of the provisions of this Treaty, the Parties shall establish promptly a Standing Consultative Commission, within the framework of which they will:

  (a) consider questions concerning compliance with the obligations assumed and related situations which may be considered ambiguous;

  (b) provide on a voluntary basis such information as either Party considers necessary to assure confidence in compliance with the obligations assumed;

  (c) consider questions involving unintended interference with national technical means of verification;

  (d) consider possible changes in the strategic situation which have a bearing on the provisions of this Treaty;

  (e) agree upon procedures and dates for destruction or dismantling of ABM systems or their components in cases provided for by the provisions of this Treaty;

  (f) consider, as appropriate, possible proposals for further increasing the viability of this Treaty, including proposals for amendments in accordance with the provisions of this Treaty;

  (g) consider, as appropriate, proposals for further measures aimed at limiting strategic arms.

2. The Parties through consultation shall establish, and may amend as appropriate, Regulations for the Standing Consultative Commission governing procedures, composition and other relevant matters.

Article XIV

1. Each Party may propose amendments to this Treaty. Agreed amendments shall enter into force in accordance with the procedures governing the entry into force of this Treaty.

2. Five years after entry into force of this Treaty, and at five-year intervals thereafter, the Parties shall together conduct a review of this Treaty.

Article XV

1. This Treaty shall be of unlimited duration.

2. Each Party shall, in exercising its national sovereignty, have the right to withdraw from this Treaty if it decides that extraordinary events related to the subject matter of this Treaty have jeopardized its supreme interests. It shall give notice of its decision to the other Party six months prior to withdrawal from the Treaty. Such notice shall include a statement of the extraordinary events the notifying Party regards as having jeopardized its supreme interests.

NOTES

1) On July 3, 1974, the United States and the Soviet Union signed a Protocol to the ABM Treaty.[77] The Protocol limits each party to one ABM site. The Soviet Union chose

---

[77] 27 U.S.T. 1645; TIAS No. 8276; (1974); 13 *Int. Leg. Mat.* 904. In force May 24, 1976.

to maintain its ABM defence of Moscow and the United States opted to keep ABM defence of its inter-continental ballistic missile emplacements near Grand Forks, N. Dakota. The U.S. ABM system at Grand Forks has been on an inactive status since 1976. Following its entry into force, the Protocol became an integral part of the 1972 Treaty. The key articles of the Protocol provide:

Article I

1. Each Party shall be limited at any one time to a single area out of the two provided in Article III of the Treaty for deployment of anti-ballistic missile (ABM) systems or their components and accordingly shall not exercise its right to deploy an ABM system or its components in the second of the two ABM system deployment areas permitted by Article III of the Treaty, except as an exchange of one permitted area for the other in accordance with Article II of this Protocol.

2. Accordingly, except as permitted by Article II of this Protocol: the United States of America shall not deploy an ABM system or its components in the area centered on its capital, as permitted by Article III(a) of the Treaty, and the Soviet Union shall not deploy an ABM system or its components in the deployment area of intercontinental ballistic missile (ICBM) silo launchers permitted by Article III(b) of the Treaty.

Article II

1. Each Party shall have the right to dismantle or destroy its ABM system and the components thereof in the area where they are presently deployed and to deploy an ABM system or its components in the alternative area permitted by Article III of the Treaty, provided that prior to initiation of construction, notification is given in accord with the procedure agreed to by the Standing Consultative Commission, during the year beginning October 3, 1977, and ending October 2, 1978, or during any year which commences at five year intervals thereafter, those being the years for periodic review of the Treaty, as provided in Article XIV of the Treaty. This right may be exercised only once.

2) Does the ABM Treaty permit research on new ballistic missile defence technologies, such as the "Strategic Defence Initiative" (SDI) inaugurated by the United States in March 1983? Is the distinction between "research" and "development" clearly drawn in that Treaty?[78]

---

[78] For an official account of the reasons for the SDI research programme, its ultimate objectives and its legality, see "The President's Strategic Defense Initiative," *Dept. of State Bull.* 65 (March 1985). See also A.H. Chayes, "Testing and Development of 'Exotic' Systems Under the ABM Treaty: The Great Reinterpretation Caper" (1986), 99 *Harv. L. Rev.* 1956; S. Drell, P. Farley and D. Holloway, "Preserving the ABM Treaty: A Critique of the Reagan Strategic Defense Initiative" (1984), 9 *Int. Security* 51; P. Meredith, "The Legality of a High-Technology Missile Defense System: The ABM and Outer Space Treaties" (1984), 78 *Am. J. Int. L.* 418; M. Smith, "Legal Implications of a Space-Based Ballistic Missile Defense" (1985), 15 *Calif. West. Int. L. J.* 52; and A. Sofaer, "The ABM Treaty and the Strategic Defense Initiative" (1986), 99 *Harv. L. Rev.* 1972.

Operation Dismantle v. The Queen
[1985] 1 S.C.R. 441; (1985), 18 D.L.R. (4th) 481

The judgment of Dickson, Estey, McIntyre, Chouinard and Lamer JJ. was delivered by
DICKSON J. – This case arises out of the appellants' challenge under s. 7 of the
Canadian Charter of Rights and Freedoms to the decision of the federal cabinet to permit
the testing of the cruise missile by the United States of America in Canadian territory.
The issue that must be addressed is whether the appellants' statement of claim should be
struck out, before trial, as disclosing no reasonable cause of action. In their statement of
claim, the appellants seek: (i) a declaration that the decision to permit the testing of the
cruise missile is unconstitutional; (ii) injunctive relief to prohibit the testing; and (iii)
damages. Cattanach J. of the Federal Court, Trial Division, refused the respondents'
motion to strike. The Federal Court of Appeal unanimously allowed the respondents'
appeal, struck out the statement of claim and dismissed the appellants' action. ...

In my opinion, if the appellants are to be entitled to proceed to trial, their statement
of claim must disclose facts, which, if taken as true, would show that the action of the
Canadian government could cause an infringement of their rights under s. 7 of the *Charter*.
I have concluded that the causal link between the actions of the Canadian government,
and the alleged violation of appellants' rights under the *Charter* is simply too uncertain,
speculative and hypothetical to sustain a cause of action. Thus, although decisions of the
federal cabinet are reviewable by the courts under the *Charter*, and the government bears
a general duty to act in accordance with the *Charter's* dictates, no duty is imposed on
the Canadian government by s. 7 of the *Charter* to refrain from permitting the testing of
the cruise missile.

I

The Appellants' Statement of Claim

The relevant portion of the appellants' statement of claim is found in paragraph 7
thereof. The deprivation of s. 7 *Charter* rights alleged by the appellants and the facts
they advance to support this deprivation are described as follows:

7. The plaintiffs state and the fact is that the testing of the cruise missile in Canada is a violation
of the collective rights of the Plaintiffs and their members and all Canadians, specifically their
right to security of the person and life in that:

   (a) the size and eventual dispersion of the air-launched cruise missile is such that the missile
cannot be detected by surveillance satellites, thus making verification of the extent of
this nuclear weapons system impossible;

   (b) with the impossibility of verification, the future of nuclear weapons' control and limitation
agreements is completely undermined as any such agreements become practically
unenforceable;

   (c) the testing of the air-launched cruise missiles would result in an increased American
military presence and interest in Canada which would result in making Canada more likely
to be the target of a nuclear attack;

   (d) as the cruise missile cannot be detected until approximately eight minutes before it reaches
its target, a ''Launch on Warning'' system would be necessary in order to respond to

the cruise missile thereby eliminating effective human discretion and increasing the likelihood of either a pre-emptive strike or an accidental firing, or both;

(e)   the cruise missile is a military weapon, the development of which will have the effect of a needless and dangerous escalation of the nuclear arms race, thus endangering the security and lives of all people.

Section 7 of the *Charter* provides in English:

7. Everyone has the right to life, liberty and security of the person and the right not to be deprived thereof except in accordance with the principles of fundamental justice.

... to succeed at trial, the appellants would have to demonstrate, *inter alia*, that the testing of the cruise missile would cause an increase in the risk of nuclear war. It is precisely this link between the cabinet decision to permit the testing of the cruise and the increased risk of nuclear war which, in my opinion, they cannot establish. It will not be necessary therefore to address the issue of whether the deprivations of life and security of the person advanced by the appellants could constitute violations of s. 7.

The statement of claim speaks of weapons control agreements being "practically unenforceable," Canada being "more likely to be the target of a nuclear attack," "increasing the likelihood of either a pre-emptive strike or an accidental firing, or both," and "escalation of the nuclear arms race." All of these eventualities, culminating in the increased risk of nuclear war, are alleged to flow from the Canadian government's single act of allowing the United States to test the cruise missile in Canada.

Since the foreign policy decisions of independent and sovereign nations are not capable of prediction, on the basis of evidence, to any degree of certainty approaching probability, the nature of such reactions can only be a matter of speculation; the causal link between the decision of the Canadian government to permit the testing of the cruise and the results that the appellants allege could never be proven.

An analysis of the specific allegations of the statement of claim reveals that they are all contingent upon the possible reactions of the nuclear powers to the testing of the cruise missile in Canada. The gist of paragraphs (a) and (b) of the statement of claim is that verification of the cruise missile system is impossible because the missile cannot be detected by surveillance satellites, and that, therefore, arms control agreements will be unenforceable. This is based on two major assumptions as to how foreign powers will react to the development of the cruise missile: first, that they will not develop new types of surveillance satellites or new methods of verification, and second, that foreign powers will not establish new modes of co-operation for dealing with the problem of enforcement. With respect to the latter of these points, it is just as plausible that lack of verification would have the effect of enhancing enforceability than of undermining it, since an inability on the part of nuclear powers to verify systems like the cruise could precipitate a system of enforcement based on co-operation rather than surveillance.

As for paragraph (c), even if it were the case that the testing of the air-launched cruise missile would result in an increased American military presence and interest in Canada, to say that this would make Canada more likely to be the target of a nuclear attack is to assume certain reactions of hostile foreign powers to such an increased American presence. It also makes an assumption about the degree to which Canada is already a possible target of nuclear attack. Given the impossibility of determining how an independent sovereign nation might react, it can only be a matter of hypothesis whether an increased American presence would make Canada more vulnerable to nuclear attack. It would not be possible to prove it one way or the other.

Paragraph (d) assumes that foreign states will not develop their technology in such a way as to meet the requirements of effective detection of the cruise and that there will therefore be an increased likelihood of pre-emptive strike or an accidental firing, or both. Again, this assumption concerns how foreign powers are likely to act in response to the development of the cruise. It would be just as plausible to argue that foreign states would improve their technology with respect to detection of missiles, thereby decreasing the likelihood of accidental firing or pre-emptive strike.

Finally, paragraph (e) asserts that the development of the cruise will lead to an escalation of the nuclear arms race. This again involves speculation based on assumptions as to how foreign powers will react. One could equally argue that the cruise would be the precipitating factor in compelling the nuclear powers to negotiate agreements that would lead to a de-escalation of the nuclear arms race.

One final assumption, common to all the paragraphs except (c), is that the result of testing of the cruise missile in Canada will be its development by the United States. In all of these paragraphs, the alleged harm flows from the production and eventual deployment of the cruise missile. The effect that the testing will have on the development and deployment of the cruise can only be a matter of speculation. It is possible that as a result of the tests, the Americans would decide *not* to develop and deploy the cruise since the very reason for the testing is to establish whether the missile is a viable weapons system. Similarly, it is possible that the Americans would develop the cruise missile even if testing were not permitted by the Canadians.

In the final analysis, exactly what the Americans will decide to do about development and deployment of the cruise missile, whether tested in Canada or not, is a decision that they, as an independent and sovereign nation, will make for themselves. Even with the assistance of qualified experts, a court could only speculate on how the American government may make this decision, and how important a factor the results of the testing of the cruise in Canada will be in that decision.

What can be concluded from this analysis of the statement of claim is that all of its allegations, including the ultimate assertion of an increased likelihood of nuclear war, are premised on assumptions and hypotheses about how independent and sovereign nations, operating in an international arena of radical uncertainty, and continually changing circumstances, will react to the Canadian government's decision to permit the testing of the cruise missile. ...

In the present case, the speculative nature of the allegation that the decision to test the cruise missile will lead to an increased threat of nuclear war makes it manifest that no duty is imposed on the Canadian government to refrain from permitting the testing. The government's action simply could not be proven to cause the alleged violation of s. 7 of the *Charter* and, thus, no duty can arise.

The approach which I have taken is not based on the concept of justiciability. I agree in substance with Madame Justice Wilson's discussion of justiciability and her conclusion that the doctrine is founded upon a concern with the appropriate role of the courts as the forum for the resolution of different types of disputes. I have no doubt that disputes of a political or foreign policy nature may be properly cognizable by the courts. My concerns in the present case focus on the impossibility of the Court finding, on the basis of evidence, the connection, alleged by the appellants, between the duty of the government to act in accordance with the *Charter of Rights and Freedoms* and the violation of their rights under s. 7. As stated above, I do not believe the alleged violation – namely, the increased threat of nuclear war – could ever be sufficiently linked as a factual matter to the acknowledged duty of the government to respect s. 7 of the *Charter*. ...

WILSON J.: This litigation was sparked by the decision of the Canadian government to permit the United States to test the cruise missile in Canada. It raises issues of great difficulty and considerable importance to all of us.

The appellants are a group of organizations and unions claiming to have a collective membership of more than 1.5 million Canadians. ...

Each of the five judges who sat on the appeal to the Federal Court of Appeal delivered separate reasons for allowing the appeal. Four of the five (Pratte, Le Dain, Marceau and Hugessen JJ.) held that a breach of s. 7 of the *Charter* must involve a failure to comply with the principles of fundamental justice and the appellants had not alleged any such failure.

Three of the justices (Pratte, Marceau and Hugessen JJ.) were of the opinion that the facts as alleged did not constitute a violation of the right to life, liberty and security of the person as guaranteed by s. 7. Pratte and Hugessen JJ. thought that any breach of s. 7 would only occur as the result of actions by foreign powers who were not bound by the *Charter*. Pratte J. went further and stated that the only "liberty and security of the person" that was protected by s. 7 was security against arbitrary arrest or detention. Marceau J. felt that s. 7 could never have "any higher mission than that of protecting the life and the freedom of movement of the citizens against arbitrary action and despotism by people in power."

Two of the justices (Ryan and Le Dain JJ.) would have allowed the appeal on the fundamental ground that the issue was inherently non-justiciable and therefore incapable of adjudication by a court. Ryan J. thought that the question whether national security was impaired, and hence whether the plaintiffs' own personal security had been affected, was not triable because it was not susceptible of proof. Le Dain J. took the central issue to be the effect of testing cruise missiles on the risk of nuclear conflict, a matter which he asserted to be non-justiciable as involving factors either inaccessible to a court or incapable of being evaluated by it. The other three judges did not directly address this point. ...

None of the five judges was prepared to say that the cabinet's decision to test the cruise missile was unreviewable because it involved a "political question." Pratte and Marceau JJ. expressly rejected this argument, Le Dain and Hugessen JJ. did not consider it necessary to deal with it, and Ryan J. did not mention it. ...

The question before us is not whether the government's defence policy is sound but whether or not it violates the appellants' rights under s. 7 of the *Charter of Rights and Freedoms*. This is a totally different question. I do not think there can be any doubt that this is a question for the courts. Indeed, s. 24(1) of the *Charter*, also part of the Constitution, makes it clear that the adjudication of that question is the responsibility of "a court of competent jurisdiction." While the court is entitled to grant such remedy as it "considers appropriate and just in the circumstances," I do not think it is open to it to relinquish its jurisdiction either on the basis that the issue is inherently non-justiciable or that it raises a so-called "political question": ...

In my view, several of the allegations contained in the statement of claim are statements of intangible fact. Some of them invite inferences; others anticipate probable consequences. They may be susceptible to proof by inference from real facts or by expert testimony or "through the application of common sense principles": see *Leyland Shipping Co. v. Norwich Union Fire Insurance Society*, [1918] A.C. 350, at 363, *per* Lord Dunedin. We may entertain serious doubts that the plaintiffs will be able to prove them by any of these means. It is not, however, the function of the Court at this stage to prejudge that question. I agree with Cattanach J. that the statement of claim contains sufficient allegations to raise a justiciable issue. ...

If the appellants are relying on s. 52(1) of the *Constitution Act, 1982* as the source of their right to a declaration of unconstitutionality, which it would appear from their factum that they are, it is noted that that provision is directed to "laws" which are inconsistent with the provisions of the Constitution.

Counsel for the appellants submitted in oral argument that they should not be prejudiced in the relief sought by the absence of any law authorizing, ratifying or implementing the agreement between Canada and the United States since legislation, they submitted, should have been passed. The government should not therefore be allowed to immunize itself against judicial review under s. 52 of the *Constitution Act, 1982* by its own omission to do that which it ought to have done. ...

Although little, if any, argument has been addressed in this case to the question whether the government's decision to permit testing of the cruise missile in Canada falls within the meaning of the word "law" as used in s. 52 of the *Constitution Act, 1982*, I am prepared to assume, without deciding, that it does. I am also prepared to assume that the appellants could establish their standing to bring an action under s. 52. The question remains, however, whether the appellants' claim raises a serious question of constitutional inconsistency. This in turn depends on the answer to the question whether the government's decision violates the appellants' rights under s. 7. If it does not, there is no inconsistency with the provisions of the Constitution. ...

The concept of "right" as used in the *Charter* must also, I believe, recognize and take account of the political reality of the modern state. Action by the state or, conversely, inaction by the state will frequently have the effect of decreasing or increasing the risk to the lives or security of its citizens. It may be argued, for example, that the failure of government to limit significantly the speed of traffic on the highways threatens our right to life and security in that it increases the risk of highway accidents. Such conduct, however, would not, in my view, fall within the scope of the right protected by s. 7 of the *Charter*.

In the same way, the concept of "right" as used in the *Charter* must take account of the fact that the self-contained political community which comprises the state is faced with at least the possibility, if not the reality, of external threats to both its collective well-being and to the individual well-being of its citizens. In order to protect the community against such threats it may well be necessary for the state to take steps which incidentally increase the risk to the lives or personal security of some or all of the state's citizens. Such steps, it seems to me, cannot have been contemplated by the draftsman of the *Charter* as giving rise to violations of s. 7. As John Rawls states in *A Theory of Justice* (1971), at 213:

The government's right to maintain public order and security is ... a right which the government must have if it is to carry out its duty of impartially supporting the conditions necessary for everyone's pursuit of his interests and living up to his obligations as he understands them. ...

I agree with Le Dain J. that the essence of the appellants' case is the claim that permitting the cruise missile to be tested in Canada will increase the risk of nuclear war. But even accepting this allegation of fact as true, which as I have already said I think we must do on a motion to strike, it is my opinion for the reasons given above that this state of affairs could not constitute a breach of s. 7. Moreover, I do not see how one can distinguish in a principled way between this particular risk and any other danger to which the government's action *vis-à-vis* other states might incidentally subject its citizens. A declaration of war, for example, almost certainly increases the risk to most citizens of death or injury. Acceptance of the appellants' submissions, it seems to me, would mean that any such declaration would also have to be regarded as a violation of s. 7. I cannot think that that could be a proper interpretation of the *Charter*.

This is not to say that every governmental action that is purportedly taken in furtherance of national defence would be beyond the reach of s. 7. If, for example, testing the cruise missile posed a direct threat to some specific segment of the populace – as, for example, if it were being tested with live warheads – I think that might well raise different considerations. A court might find that that constituted a violation of s. 7 and it might then be up to the government to try to establish that testing the cruise with live warheads was justified under s. 1 of the *Charter*. Section 1, in my opinion, is the uniquely Canadian mechanism through which the courts are to determine the justiciability of particular issues that come before it. It embodies through its reference to a free and democratic society the essential features of our constitution including the separation of powers, responsible government and the rule of law. It obviates the need for a "political questions" doctrine and permits the Court to deal with what might be termed "prudential" considerations in a principled way without renouncing its constitutional and mandated responsibility for judicial review. It is not, however, called into operation here since the facts alleged in the statement of claim, even if they could be shown to be true, could not in my opinion constitute a violation of s. 7. ...

Appeal dismissed with costs.

NOTES

This case is extremely important for the conclusion by a unanimous Court that government decisions are subject to judicial review under the *Canadian Charter of Rights and Free-*

doms.[79] As a result, for some purposes Canadian government decisions regarding armaments policy may be questioned in the courts as well as in Parliament. But what are to be the criteria for their adjudication? Dickson C.J. struck out the action because the causal connection between the government's decision to permit testing of the cruise missile and the alleged breach of the *Charter* section 7, in his judgment, was not capable of proof. Why was it appropriate to strike out the action before the plaintiffs had a chance to go to trial and to make their proof? For the purposes of the motion to strike, Wilson J. was prepared to admit the plaintiffs' allegation that the government's decision would increase the risk of nuclear war, but found no resulting breach of section 7. Does Wilson J. convincingly interpret the scope of section 7? Does international law binding on Canada provide any guidance to the Court?

---

[79] See H.N. Janisch, Annotation (1985), 12 *Admin. L.R.* 18. Compare the U.S. situation where a similar attempt to have nuclear weapons judicially declared unconstitutional failed to overcome the "political questions" doctrine, by which American courts decline to adjudicate issues of government policy; see *Greenham Women Against Cruise Missiles v. Reagan* (1985), 755 F. 2nd 34 (U.S.C.A. 2nd Circ.).

Appendix

CHARTER OF THE UNITED NATIONS
As Signed 1945 and Amended 1965, 1968 and 1973

WE THE PEOPLES OF THE UNITED NATIONS DETERMINED to save succeeding generations from the scourge of war, which twice in our life-time has brought untold sorrow to mankind, and

to reaffirm faith in fundamental human rights, in the dignity and worth of the human person, in the equal rights of men and women and of nations large and small, and

to establish conditions under which justice and respect for the obligations arising from treaties and other sources of international law can be maintained, and

to promote social progress and better standards of life in larger freedom,

AND FOR THESE ENDS to practice tolerance and live together in peace with one another as good neighbours, and

to unite our strength to maintain international peace and security, and

to ensure, by the acceptance of principles and the institution of methods, that armed force shall not be used, save in the common interest, and

to employ international machinery for the promotion of the economic and social advancement of all peoples,

HAVE RESOLVED TO COMBINE OUR EFFORTS TO ACCOMPLISH THESE AIMS Accordingly, our respective Governments, through representatives assembled in the city of San Francisco, who have exhibited their full powers found to be in good and due form, have agreed to the present Charter of the United Nations and do hereby establish an international organization to be known as the United Nations.

CHAPTER I

PURPOSES AND PRINCIPLES

Article 1

The Purposes of the United Nations are:

1. To maintain international peace and security, and to that end: to take effective collective measures for the prevention and removal of threats to the peace, and for the suppression of acts of aggression or other breaches of the peace, and to bring about by peaceful means, and in conformity with the principles of justice and international law, adjustment or settlement of international disputes or situations which might lead to a breach of the peace;

2. To develop friendly relations among nations based on respect for the principle of equal rights and self-determination of peoples, and to take other appropriate measures to strengthen universal peace;

3. To achieve international co-operation in solving international problems of an economic, social, cultural, or humanitarian character, and in promoting and encouraging respect for human rights and for fundamental freedoms for all without distinction as to race, sex, language, or religion; and

4. To be a centre for harmonizing the actions of nations in the attainment of these common ends.

Article 2

The Organization and its Members, in pursuit of the Purposes stated in Article 1, shall act in accordance with the following Principles.

1. The Organization is based on the principle of the sovereign equality of all its Members.

2. All Members, in order to ensure to all of them the rights and benefits resulting from membership, shall fulfil in good faith the obligations assumed by them in accordance with the present Charter.

3. All Members shall settle their international disputes by peaceful means in such a manner that international peace and security, and justice, are not endangered.

4. All Members shall refrain in their international relations from the threat or use of force against the territorial integrity or political independence of any state, or in any other manner inconsistent with the Purposes of the United Nations.

5. All Members shall give the United Nations every assistance in any action it takes in accordance with the present Charter, and shall refrain from giving assistance to any state against which the United Nations is taking preventive or enforcement action.

6. The Organization shall ensure that states which are not Members of the United Nations act in accordance with these Principles so far as may be necessary for the maintenance of international peace and security.

7. Nothing contained in the present Charter shall authorize the United Nations to intervene in matters which are essentially within the domestic jurisdiction of any state or shall require the Members to submit such matters to settlement under the present Charter;

but this principle shall not prejudice the application of enforcement measures under Chapter VII.

CHAPTER II

MEMBERSHIP

Article 3

The original Members of the United Nations shall be the states which, having participated in the United Nations Conference on International Organization at San Francisco, or having previously signed the Declaration by United Nations of 1 January 1942, sign the present Charter and ratify it in accordance with Article 110.

Article 4

1. Membership in the United Nations is open to all other peace-loving states which accept the obligations contained in the present Charter and, in the judgment of the Organization, are able and willing to carry out these obligations.

2. The admission of any such state to membership in the United Nations will be effected by a decision of the General Assembly upon the recommendation of the Security Council.

Article 5

A Member of the United Nations against which preventive or enforcement action has been taken by the Security Council may be suspended from the exercise of the rights and privileges of membership by the General Assembly upon the recommendation of the Security Council. The exercise of these rights and privileges may be restored by the Security Council.

Article 6

A Member of the United Nations which has persistently violated the Principles contained in the present Charter may be expelled from the Organization by the General Assembly upon the recommendation of the Security Council.

CHAPTER III

ORGANS

Article 7

1. There are established as the principal organs of the United Nations: a General Assembly, a Security Council, an Economic and Social Council, a Trusteeship Council, an International Court of Justice, and a Secretariat.

2. Such subsidiary organs as may be found necessary may be established in accordance with the present Charter.

Article 8

The United Nations shall place no restrictions on the eligibility of men and women to participate in any capacity and under conditions of equality in its principal and subsidiary organs.

CHAPTER IV

THE GENERAL ASSEMBLY

Composition

Article 9

1. The General Assembly shall consist of all the Members of the United Nations.
2. Each Member shall have not more than five representatives in the General Assembly.

Functions and powers

Article 10

The General Assembly may discuss any questions or any matters within the scope of the present Charter or relating to the powers and functions of any organs provided for in the present Charter, and, except as provided in Article 12, may make recommendations to the Members of the United Nations or to the Security Council or to both on any such questions or matters.

Article 11

1. The General Assembly may consider the general principles of co-operation in the maintenance of international peace and security, including the principles governing disarmament and the regulation of armaments, and may make recommendations with regard to such principles to the Members or to the Security Council or to both.

2. The General Assembly may discuss any questions relating to the maintenance of international peace and security brought before it by any Member of the United Nations, or by the Security Council, or by a state which is not a Member of the United Nations in accordance with Article 35, paragraph 2, and, except as provided in Article 12, may make recommendations with regard to any such questions to the state or states concerned or to the Security Council or to both. Any such question on which action is necessary shall be referred to the Security Council by the General Assembly either before or after discussion.

(3) The General Assembly may call the attention of the Security Council to situations which are likely to endanger international peace and security.

(4) The powers of the General Assembly set forth in this Article shall not limit the general scope of Article 10.

Article 12

1. While the Security Council is exercising in respect of any dispute or situation the functions assigned to it in the present Charter, the General Assembly shall not make any

recommendation with regard to that dispute or situation unless the Security Council so requests.

2. The Secretary-General, with the consent of the Security Council, shall notify the General Assembly at each session of any matters relative to the maintenance of international peace and security which are being dealt with by the Security Council and shall similarly notify the General Assembly, or the Members of the United Nations if the General Assembly is not in session, immediately the Security Council ceases to deal with such matters.

Article 13

1. The General Assembly shall initiate studies and make recommendations for the purpose of:
    (a) promoting international co-operation in the political field and encouraging the progressive development of international law and its codification;
    (b) promoting international co-operation in the economic, social, cultural, educational, and health fields, and assisting in the realization of human rights and fundamental freedoms for all without distinction as to race, sex, language or religion.

2. The further responsibilities, functions and powers of the General Assembly with respect to matters mentioned in paragraph (1)(b) above are set forth in Chapters IX and X.

Article 14

Subject to the provisions of Article 12, the General Assembly may recommend measures for the peaceful adjustment of any situation, regardless of origin, which it deems likely to impair the general welfare or friendly relations among nations, including situations resulting from a violation of the provisions of the present Charter setting forth the Purposes and Principles of the United Nations.

Article 15

1. The General Assembly shall receive and consider annual and special reports from the Security Council; these reports shall include an account of the measures that the Security Council has decided upon or taken to maintain international peace and security.

2. The General Assembly shall receive and consider reports from the other organs of the United Nations.

Article 16

The General Assembly shall perform such functions with respect to the international trusteeship system as are assigned to it under Chapters XII and XIII, including the approval of the trusteeship agreements for areas not designated as strategic.

Article 17

1. The General Assembly shall consider and approve the budget of the Organization.

2. The expenses of the Organization shall be borne by the Members as apportioned by the General Assembly.

3. The General Assembly shall consider and approve any financial and budgetary arrangements with specialized agencies referred to in Article 57 and shall examine the administrative budgets of such specialized agencies with a view to making recommendations to the agencies concerned.

Voting

Article 18

1. Each member of the General Assembly shall have one vote.

2. Decisions of the General Assembly on important questions shall be made by two thirds majority of the members present and voting. These questions shall include: recommendations with respect to the maintenance of international peace and security, the election of the non-permanent members of the Security Council, the election of the members of the Economic and Social Council, the election of members of the Trusteeship Council in accordance with paragraph 1(c) of Article 86, the admission of new Members to the United Nations, the suspension of the rights and privileges of membership, the expulsion of Members, questions relating to the operation of the trusteeship system, and budgetary questions.

3. Decisions on other questions, including the determination of additional categories of questions to be decided by a two-thirds majority, shall be made by a majority of the members present and voting.

Article 19

A Member of the United Nations which is in arrears in the payment of its financial contributions to the Organization shall have no vote in the General Assembly if the amount of its arrears equals or exceeds the amount of the contributions due from it for the preceding two full years. The General Assembly may, nevertheless, permit such a Member to vote if it is satisfied that the failure to pay is due to conditions beyond the control of the Member.

Procedure

Article 20

The General Assembly shall meet in regular annual sessions and in such special sessions as occasion may require. Special sessions shall be convoked by the Secretary-General at the request of the Security Council or of a majority of the Members of the United Nations.

Article 21

The General Assembly shall adopt its own rules of procedure. It shall elect its President for each session.

Article 22

The General Assembly may establish such subsidiary organs as it deems necessary for the performance of its functions.

CHAPTER V

THE SECURITY COUNCIL

Composition

Article 23

1. The Security Council shall consist of fifteen Members of the United Nations. The Republic of China, France, the Union of Soviet Socialist Republics, the United Kingdom of Great Britain and Northern Ireland, and the United States of America shall be permanent members of the Security Council. The General Assembly shall elect ten other Members of the United Nations to be non-permanent members of the Security Council, due regard being specially paid, in the first instance to the contribution of Members of the United Nations to the maintenance of international peace and security and to the other purposes of the Organization, and also to equitable geographical distribution.

2. The non-permanent members of the Security Council shall be elected for a term of two years. In the first election of the non-permanent members after the increase of the membership of the Security Council from eleven to fifteen, two of the four additional members shall be chosen for a term of one year. A retiring member shall not be eligible for immediate re-election.

3. Each member of the Security Council shall have one representative.

Functions and Powers

Article 24

1. In order to ensure prompt and effective action by the United Nations, its Members confer on the Security Council primary responsibility for the maintenance of international peace and security, and agree that in carrying out its duties under this responsibility the Security Council acts on their behalf.

2. In discharging these duties the Security Council shall act in accordance with the Purposes and Principles of the United Nations. The specific powers granted to the Security Council for the discharge of these duties are laid down in Chapters VI, VII, VIII , and XII.

3. The Security Council shall submit annual and, when necessary, special reports to the General Assembly for its consideration.

Article 25

The Members of the United Nations agree to accept and carry out the decisions of the Security Council in accordance with the present Charter.

Article 26

In order to promote the establishment and maintenance of international peace and security with the least diversion for armaments of the world's human and economic resources, the Security Council shall be responsible for formulating, with the assistance of the Military Staff Committee referred to in Article 47, plans to be submitted to the Members of the United Nations for the establishment of a system for the regulation of armaments.

Voting

Article 27

1. Each member of the Security Council shall have one vote.

2. Decisions of the Security Council on procedural matters shall be made by an affirmative vote of nine members.

3. Decisions of the Security Council on all other matters shall be made by an affirmative vote of nine members including the concurring votes of the permanent members; provided that, in decisions under Chapter VI, and under paragraph 3 of Article 52, a party to a dispute shall abstain from voting.

Procedure

Article 28

1. The Security Council shall be so organized as to be able to function continuously. Each member of the Security Council shall for this purpose be represented at all times at the seat of the Organization.

2. The Security Council shall hold periodic meetings at which each of its members may, if it so desires, be represented by a member of the government or by some other specially designated representative.

3. The Security Council may hold meetings at such places other than the seat of the Organization as in its judgment will best facilitate its work.

Article 29

The Security Council may establish such subsidiary organs as it deems necessary for the performance of its functions.

Article 30

The Security Council shall adopt its own rules of procedure, including the method of selecting its President.

Article 31

Any Member of the United Nations which is not a member of the Security Council may participate, without vote, in the discussion of any question brought before the Security Council whenever the latter considers that the interests of that Member are specially affected.

Article 32

Any Member of the United Nations which is not a member of the Security Council or any state which is not a Member of the United Nations, if it is a party to a dispute under consideration by the Security Council, shall be invited to participate, without vote, in the discussion relating to the dispute. The Security Council shall lay down such conditions as it deems just for the participation of a state which is not a Member of the United Nations.

CHAPTER VI

PACIFIC SETTLEMENT OF DISPUTES

Article 33

1. The parties to any dispute, the continuance of which is likely to endanger the maintenance of international peace and security, shall, first of all, seek a solution by negotiation, enquiry, mediation, conciliation, arbitration, judicial settlement, resort to regional agencies or arrangements, or other peaceful means of their own choice.

2. The Security Council shall, when it deems necessary, call upon the parties to settle their dispute by such means.

Article 34

The Security Council may investigate any dispute, or any situation which might lead to international friction or give rise to a dispute, in order to determine whether the continuance of the dispute or situation is likely to endanger the maintenance of international peace and security.

Article 35

1. Any Member of the United Nations may bring any dispute, or any situation of the nature referred to in Article 34, to the attention of the Security Council or of the General Assembly.

2. A state which is not a Member of the United Nations may bring to the attention of the Security Council or of the General Assembly any dispute to which it is a party if it accepts in advance, for the purposes of the dispute, the obligations of pacific settlement provided in the present Charter.

3. The proceedings of the General Assembly in respect of matters brought to its attention under this Article will be subject to the provisions of Articles 11 and 12.

Article 36

1. The Security Council may, at any stage of a dispute of the nature referred to in Article 33 or of a situation of like nature, recommend appropriate procedures or methods of adjustment.

2. The Security Council should take into consideration any procedures for the settlement of the dispute which have already been adopted by the parties.

3. In making recommendations under this Article the Security Council should also take into consideration that legal disputes should as a general rule be referred by the parties to the International Court of Justice in accordance with the provisions of the Statute of the Court.

Article 37

1. Should the parties to a dispute of the nature referred to in Article 33 fail to settle it by the means indicated in that Article, they shall refer it to the Security Council.

2. If the Security Council deems that the continuance of the dispute is in fact likely to endanger the maintenance of international peace and security, it shall decide whether

to take action under Article 36 or to recommend such terms of settlement as it may consider appropriate.

Article 38

Without prejudice to the provisions of Articles 33 to 37, the Security Council may, if all the parties to any dispute so request, make recommendations to the parties with a view to a pacific settlement of the dispute.

CHAPTER VII

ACTION WITH RESPECT TO THREATS TO THE PEACE, BREACHES OF THE PEACE, AND ACTS OF AGGRESSION

Article 39

The Security Council shall determine the existence of any threat to the peace, breach of the peace, or act of aggression and shall make recommendations, or decide what measures shall be taken in accordance with Articles 41 and 42, to maintain or restore international peace and security.

Article 40

In order to prevent an aggravation of the situation, the Security Council may, before making the recommendations or deciding upon the measures provided for in Article 39, call upon the parties concerned to comply with such provisional measures as it deems necessary or desirable. Such provisional measures shall be without prejudice to the rights, claims, or position of the parties concerned. The Security Council shall duly take account of failure to comply with such provisional measures.

Article 41

The Security Council may decide what measures not involving the use of armed force are to be employed to give effect to its decisions, and it may call upon the Members of the United Nations to apply such measures. These may include complete or partial interruption of economic relations and of rail, sea, air, postal, telegraphic, radio, and other means of communication, and the severance of diplomatic relations.

Article 42

Should the Security Council consider that measures provided for in Article 41 would be inadequate or have proved to be inadequate, it may take such action by air, sea, or land forces as may be necessary to maintain or restore international peace and security. Such action may include demonstrations, blockade, and other operations by air, sea, or land forces of Members of the United Nations.

Article 43

1. All Members of the United Nations, in order to contribute to the maintenance of international peace and security, undertake to make available to the Security Council, on its call and in accordance with a special agreement or agreements, armed forces, assist-

ance, and facilities, including rights of passage, necessary for the purpose of maintaining international peace and security.

2. Such agreement or agreements shall govern the numbers and types of forces, their degree of readiness and general location, and the nature of the facilities and assistance to be provided.

3. The agreement or agreements shall be negotiated as soon as possible on the initiative of the Security Council. They shall be concluded between the Security Council and Members or between the Security Council and groups of Members and shall be subject to ratification by the signatory states in accordance with their respective constitutional processes.

Article 44

When the Security Council has decided to use force it shall, before calling upon a Member not represented on it to provide armed forces in fulfilment of the obligations assumed under Article 43, invite that Member, if the Member so desires, to participate in the decisions of the Security Council concerning the employment of contingents of that Member's armed forces.

Article 45

In order to enable the United Nations to take urgent military measures, Members shall hold immediately available national air-force contingents for combined international enforcement action. The strength and degree of readiness of these contingents and plans for their combined action shall be determined, within the limits laid down in the special agreement or agreements referred to in Article 43, by the Security Council with the assistance of the Military Staff Committee.

Article 46

Plans for the application of armed force shall be made by the Security Council with the assistance of the Military Staff Committee.

Article 47

1. There shall be established a Military Staff Committee to advise and assist the Security Council on all questions relating to the Security Council's military requirements for the maintenance of international peace and security, the employment and command of forces placed at its disposal, the regulation of armaments, and possible disarmament.

2. The Military Staff Committee shall consist of the Chiefs of Staff of the permanent members of the Security Council or their representatives. Any Member of the United Nations not permanently represented on the Committee shall be invited by the Committee to be associated with it when the efficient discharge of the Committee's responsibilities requires the participation of that Member in its work.

3. The Military Staff Committee shall be responsible under the Security Council for the strategic direction of any armed forces placed at the disposal of the Security Council. Questions relating to the command of such forces shall be worked out subsequently.

4. The Military Staff Committee, with the authorization of the Security Council and after consultation with appropriate regional agencies, may establish regional subcommittees.

Article 48

1. The action required to carry out the decisions of the Security Council for the maintenance of international peace and security shall be taken by all the Members of the United Nations or by some of them, as the Security Council may determine.

2. Such decisions shall be carried out by the Members of the United Nations directly and through their action in the appropriate international agencies of which they are members.

Article 49

The Members of the United Nations shall join in affording mutual assistance in carrying out the measures decided upon by the Security Council.

Article 50

If preventive or enforcement measures against any state are taken by the Security Council, any other state, whether a Member of the United Nations or not, which finds itself confronted with special economic problems arising from the carrying out of those measures shall have the right to consult the Security Council with regard to a solution of those problems.

Article 51

Nothing in the present Charter shall impair the inherent right of individual or collective self-defence if an armed attack occurs against a Member of the United Nations, until the Security Council has taken measures necessary to maintain international peace and security. Measures taken by Members in the exercise of this right of self-defence shall be immediately reported to the Security Council and shall not in any way affect the authority and responsibility of the Security Council under the present Charter to take at any time such action as it deems necessary in order to maintain or restore international peace and security.

CHAPTER VIII

REGIONAL ARRANGEMENTS

Article 52

1. Nothing in the present Charter precludes the existence of regional arrangements or agencies for dealing with such matters relating to the maintenance of international peace and security as are appropriate for regional action, provided that such arrangements or agencies and their activities are consistent with the Purposes and Principles of the United Nations.

2. The Members of the United Nations entering into such arrangements or constituting such agencies shall make every effort to achieve pacific settlement of local disputes through such regional arrangements or by such regional agencies before referring them to the Security Council.

3. The Security Council shall encourage the development of pacific settlement of local

disputes through such regional arrangements or by such regional agencies either on the initiative of the states concerned or by reference from the Security Council.

4. This Article in no way impairs the application of Articles 34 and 35.

Article 53

1. The Security Council shall, where appropriate, utilize such regional arrangements or agencies for enforcement action under its authority. But no enforcement action shall be taken under regional arrangements or by regional agencies without the authorization of the Security Council, with the exception of measures against any enemy state, as defined in paragraph 2 of this Article, provided for pursuant to Article 107 or in regional arrangements directed against renewal of aggressive policy on the part of any such state, until such time as the Organization may, on request of the Governments concerned, be charged with the responsibility for preventing further aggression by such a state.

2. The term enemy state as used in paragraph 1 of this Article applies to any state which during the Second World War has been an enemy of any signatory of the present Charter.

Article 54

The Security Council shall at all times be kept fully informed of activities undertaken or in contemplation under regional arrangements or by regional agencies for the maintenance of international peace and security.

CHAPTER IX

INTERNATIONAL ECONOMIC AND SOCIAL CO-OPERATION

Article 55

With a view to the creation of conditions of stability and well-being which are necessary for peaceful and friendly relations among nations based on respect for the principle of equal rights and self-determination of peoples, the United Nations shall promote:

    (a) higher standards of living, full employment, and conditions of economic and social progress and development;

    (b) solutions of international economic, social, health, and related problems; and international cultural and educational co-operation; and

    (c) universal respect for, and observance of, human rights and fundamental freedoms for all without distinction as to race, sex, language, or religion.

Article 56

All Members pledge themselves to take joint and separate action in co-operation with the Organization for the achievement of the purposes set forth in Article 55.

Article 57

1. The various specialized agencies, established by intergovernmental agreement and having wide international responsibilities, as defined in their basic instruments, in eco-

nomic, social, cultural, educational, health, and related fields, shall be brought into relationship with the United Nations in accordance with the provisions of Article 63.

2. Such agencies thus brought into relationship with the United Nations are hereinafter referred to as specialized agencies.

Article 58

The Organization shall make recommendations for the co-ordination of the policies and activities of the specialized agencies.

Article 59

The Organization shall, where appropriate, initiate negotiations among the states concerned for the creation of any new specialized agencies required for the accomplishment of the purposes set forth in Article 55.

Article 60

Responsibility for the discharge of the functions of the Organization set forth in this Chapter shall be vested in the General Assembly and, under the authority of the General Assembly, in the Economic and Social Council, which shall have for this purpose the powers set forth in Chapter X.

CHAPTER X

THE ECONOMIC AND SOCIAL COUNCIL

Composition

Article 61

1. The Economic and Social Council shall consist of fifty-four Members of the United Nations elected by the General Assembly.

2. Subject to the provisions of paragraph 3, eighteen members of the Economic and Social Council shall be elected each year for a term of three years. A retiring member shall be eligible for immediate re-election.

3. At the first election after the increase in the membership of the Economic and Social Council from twenty-seven to fifty-four members, in addition to the members elected in place of the nine members whose term of office expires at the end of that year, twenty-seven additional members shall be elected. Of these twenty-seven additional members, the term of office of nine members so elected shall expire at the end of one year, and of nine other members at the end of two years, in accordance with arrangements made by the General Assembly.

4. Each member of the Economic and Social Council shall have one representative.

Functions and Powers

Article 62

1. The Economic and Social Council may make or initiate studies and reports with respect to international economic, social, cultural, educational, health, and related matters

and may make recommendations with respect to any such matters to the General Assembly, to the Members of the United Nations, and to the specialized agencies concerned.

2. It may make recommendations for the purpose of promoting respect for, and observance of, human rights and fundamental freedoms for all.

3. It may prepare draft conventions for submission to the General Assembly, with respect to matters falling within its competence.

4. It may call, in accordance with the rules prescribed by the United Nations, international conferences on matters falling within its competence.

Article 63

1. The Economic and Social Council may enter into agreements with any of the agencies referred to in Article 57, defining the terms on which the agency concerned shall be brought into relationship with the United Nations. Such agreements shall be subject to approval by the General Assembly.

2. It may co-ordinate the activities of the specialized agencies through consultation with and recommendations to such agencies and through recommendations to the General Assembly and to the Members of the United Nations.

Article 64

1. The Economic and Social Council may take appropriate steps to obtain regular reports from the specialized agencies. It may make arrangements with the Members of the United Nations and with the specialized agencies to obtain reports on the steps taken to give effect to its own recommendations and to recommendations on matters falling within its competence made by the General Assembly.

2. It may communicate its observations on these reports to the General Assembly.

Article 65

The Economic and Social Council may furnish information to the Security Council and shall assist the Security Council upon its request.

Article 66

1. The Economic and Social Council shall perform such functions as fall within its competence in connexion with the carrying out of the recommendations of the General Assembly.

2. It may, with the approval of the General Assembly, perform services at the request of Members of the United Nations and at the request of specialized agencies.

3. It shall perform such other functions as are specified elsewhere in the present Charter or as may be assigned to it by the General Assembly.

Voting

Article 67

1. Each member of the Economic and Social Council shall have one vote.

2. Decisions of the Economic and Social Council shall be made by a majority of the members present and voting.

Procedure

Article 68

The Economic and Social Council shall set up commissions in economic and social fields and for the promotion of human rights, and such other commissions as may be required for the performance of its functions.

Article 69

The Economic and Social Council shall invite any Member of the United Nations to participate, without vote, in its deliberations on any matter of particular concern to that Member.

Article 70

The Economic and Social Council may make arrangements for representatives of the specialized agencies to participate, without vote, in its deliberations and in those of the commissions established by it, and for its representatives to participate in the deliberations of the specialized agencies.

Article 71

The Economic and Social Council may make suitable arrangements for consultation with non-governmental organizations which are concerned with matters within its competence. Such arrangements may be made with international organizations and, where appropriate, with national organizations after consultation with the Member of the United Nations concerned.

Article 72

1. The Economic and Social Council shall adopt its own rules of procedure, including the method of selecting its President.

2. The Economic and Social Council shall meet as required in accordance with its rules, which shall include provision for the convening of meetings on the request of a majority of its members.

CHAPTER XI

DECLARATION REGARDING NON-SELF-GOVERNING TERRITORIES

Article 73

Members of the United Nations which have or assume responsibilities for the administration of territories whose peoples have not yet attained a full measure of self-government recognize the principle that the interests of the inhabitants of these territories are paramount, and accept as a sacred trust the obligation to promote to the utmost, within the system of international peace and security established by the present Charter, the well-being of the inhabitants of these territories, and, to this end:

(a) to ensure, with due respect for the culture of the peoples concerned, their political, economic, social, and educational advancement, their just treatment, and their protection against abuses;

(b) to develop self-government, to take due account of the political aspirations of the peoples, and to assist them in the progressive development of their free political institutions, according to the particular circumstances of each territory and its peoples and their varying stages of advancement;

(c) to further international peace and security;

(d) to promote constructive measures of development, to encourage research, and to co-operate with one another and, when and where appropriate, with specialized international bodies with a view to the practical achievement of the social, economic, and scientific purposes set forth in this Article; and

(e) to transmit regularly to the Secretary-General for information purposes, subject to such limitation as security and constitutional considerations may require, statistical and other information of a technical nature relating to economic, social, and educational conditions in the territories for which they are respectively responsible other than those territories to which Chapters XII and XIII apply.

Article 74

Members of the United Nations also agree that their policy in respect of the territories to which this Chapter applies, no less than in respect of their metropolitan areas, must be based on the general principle of good neighbourliness, due account being taken of the interests and well-being of the rest of the world, in social, economic, and commercial matters.

CHAPTER XII

INTERNATIONAL TRUSTEESHIP SYSTEM

Article 75

The United Nations shall establish under its authority an international trusteeship system for the administration and supervision of such territories as may be placed thereunder by subsequent individual agreements. These territories are hereinafter referred to as trust territories.

Article 76

The basic objectives of the trusteeship system, in accordance with the Purposes of the United Nations laid down in Article 1 of the present Charter, shall be:

(a) to further international peace and security;

(b) to promote the political, economic, social, and educational advancement of the inhabitants of the trust territories, and their progressive development towards self-government or independence as may be appropriate to the particular circumstances of each territory and its peoples and the freely expressed wishes of the peoples concerned, and as may be provided by the terms of each trusteeship agreement;

(c) to encourage respect for human rights and for fundamental freedoms for all
     without distinction as to race, sex, language, or religion, and to encourage
     recognition of the interdependence of the peoples of the world; and
(d) to ensure equal treatment in social, economic, and commercial matters for all
     Members of the United Nations and their nationals, and also equal treatment
     for the latter in the administration of justice, without prejudice to the attainment
     of the foregoing objectives and subject to the provisions of Article 80.

Article 77

1. The trusteeship system shall apply to such territories in the following categories as
may be placed thereunder by means of trusteeship agreements:
(a) territories now held under mandate
(b) territories which may be detached from enemy states as a result of the Second
     World War; and
(c) territories voluntarily placed under the system by states responsible for their
     administration.
2. It will be a matter for subsequent agreement as to which territories in the foregoing
categories will be brought under the trusteeship system and upon what terms.

Article 78

The trusteeship system shall not apply to territories which have become Members of the
United Nations, relationship among which shall be based on respect for the principle of
sovereign equality.

Article 79

The terms of trusteeship for each territory to be placed under the trusteeship system,
including any alteration or amendment, shall be agreed upon by the states directly concerned, including the mandatory power in the case of territories held under mandate by
a Member of the United Nations, and shall be approved as provided for in Articles 83
and 85.

Article 80

1. Except as may be agreed upon in individual trusteeship agreements, made under
Articles 77, 79, and 81, placing each territory under the trusteeship system, and until
such agreements have been concluded, nothing in this Chapter shall be construed in or
of itself to alter in any manner the rights whatsoever of any states or any peoples or the
terms of existing international instruments to which Members of the United Nations may
respectively be parties.
2. Paragraph 1 of this Article shall not be interpreted as giving grounds for delay or
postponement of the negotiation and conclusion of agreements for placing mandated and
other territories under the trusteeship system as provided for in Article 77.

Article 81

The trusteeship agreement shall in each case include the terms under which the trust
territory will be administered and designate the authority which will exercise the admin-